ESSENTIALS OF
SOCIOLOGY

W. W. Norton & Company, Inc.
New York • London

ESSENTIALS OF
SOCIOLOGY

Anthony Giddens

LONDON SCHOOL OF ECONOMICS

Mitchell Duneier

CITY UNIVERSITY OF NEW YORK
GRADUATE CENTER

PRINCETON UNIVERSITY

Richard P. Appelbaum

UNIVERSITY OF CALIFORNIA,
SANTA BARBARA

W. W. Norton & Company has been independent since its founding in 1923, when William Warder Norton and Mary D. Herter Norton first published lectures delivered at the People's Institute, the adult education division of New York City's Cooper Union. The Nortons soon expanded their program beyond the Institute, publishing books by celebrated academics from America and abroad. By mid-century, the two major pillars of Norton's publishing program—trade books and college texts—were firmly established. In the 1950s, the Norton family transferred control of the company to its employees, and today—with a staff of four hundred and a comparable number of trade, college, and professional titles published each year—W. W. Norton & Company stands as the largest and oldest publishing house owned wholly by its employees.

Copyright © 2006 by Anthony Giddens, Mitchell Duneier, and Richard P. Appelbaum

Editor: Karl Bakeman
Project Editor: Dexter Gasque
Assistant Managing Editor, College: Lory Frenkel
Editorial Assistants: Sarah Solomon, Rebecca Arata
Photo Research: Stephanie Romeo
Production Manager: JoAnn Simony
Composition by GGS Book Services
Manufacturing by VonHoffmann, Jefferson City
Book design by Rubina Yeh

Library of Congress Cataloging-in-Publication Data

Giddens, Anthony.
    Essentials of sociology / Anthony Giddens, Mitchell Duneier, Richard P. Appelbaum.
      p. cm.
    Includes bibliographical references and index.
    ISBN 0-393-92774-1 (pbk.)
    1. Sociolgy.   I. Duneier, Mitchell.   II. Appelbaum, Richard P.   III. Title.

HM585.G52 2005
301—dc22

                        2005048244

W. W. Norton & Company, Inc., 500 Fifth Avenue, New York, N.Y. 10110
    www.wwnorton.com

W. W. Norton & Company Ltd., Castle House, 75/76 Wells Street, London W1T 3QT

2 3 4 5 6 7 8 9 0

CONTENTS

Chapter 4: Social Interaction and Everyday Life 85

Chapter 5: Groups, Networks, and Organizations 103

Chapter 6: Conformity, Deviance, and Crime 131

Chapter 10: Ethnicity and Race 253

Chapter 11: Families and Intimate Relationships 283

Chapter 12: Education and Religion 309

Chapter 13: Politics and Economic Life 341

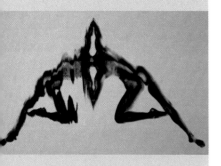

Chapter 14: Health, Illness, Sexuality, and Aging 379

his book was written in the belief that sociology has a key role to play in modern intellectual culture and a central place within the social sciences. Our aim has been to write a book that combines some originality with an analysis of the basic issues that interest sociologists today. In some places, we attempt to bring the reader into a subject through the use of ethnographies written for this book. The book does not try to introduce overly sophisticated notions; nevertheless, ideas and findings drawn from the cutting edge of the discipline are incorporated throughout. We hope it is not a partisan treatment; we endeavored to cover the major perspectives in sociology and the major findings of contemporary American research in an evenhanded, although not indiscriminate, way.

About the Essentials Edition

The *Essentials of Sociology* is based on the Fifth Edition of our best-selling text, *Introduction to Sociology*. We created the Essentials edition for instructors and students who are looking for a briefer book that could fit into a compressed academic schedule. We have reduced the length of the book by roughly one-third, and we reduced the number of chapters from 20 to 16. We made the abridgements by cutting topics to focus the chapters on the core ideas of sociology, while still retaining the themes that have made the text a successful teaching tool.

Major Themes

The book is constructed around a number of basic themes, each of which helps to give the work a distinctive character. The newest theme is *public sociology*, reflected in a series of boxes inspired by the 2004 annual meeting of the American Sociological Association. At this meeting, Michael Burawoy's pathbreaking presidential address called for the discipline to draw on the insights and methods of sociology to involve ordinary people in studying and solving the social problems that afflict them. The book features thirteen boxes that profile sociologists engaged in public sociology in diverse arenas: for example, Boston sociology professor Diane Vaughan's influential research on the *Challenger* shuttle disaster, which helped shape subsequent governmental investigations; a report on the working conditions of the University of California-Berkeley's service staff by three Berkeley grad students, which garnered wide spread publicity; and an essay by Brandeis professor David Cunningham about his annual social movements course, in which he takes students around the country to visit different communities and participate in various social and political movements. It is our hope that the Public Sociology boxes will inspire students to draw on their sociological imaginations to become more publicly involved and will provide some useful ideas for instructors who wish to generate class projects that directly engage students in the real world. In his speech, Burawoy also emphasized that public sociology cannot exist without a professional sociology that develops a body of theoretical knowledge and empirical findings. The central task of the book is to explain what the discipline of sociology has to offer along these lines.

A second theme of the book is that of the *world in change*. Sociology was born of the transformations that wrenched the industrializing social order of the West away from the ways of life characteristic of earlier societies. The world that was created by these changes is the primary object of concern of sociological analysis. The pace of social change has continued to accelerate, and it is possible that we stand on the threshold of transitions as significant as those that occurred in the late eighteenth and nineteenth centuries. Sociology has prime responsibility for charting the transformations of the past and for grasping the major lines of development taking place today.

Another fundamental theme of the book is the *globalizing of social life*. For far too long, sociology has been dominated by the view that societies can be studied as independent entities. But even in the past, societies never really existed in isolation. In current times, we can see a clear acceleration in processes of global integration. This is obvious, for example, in the expansion of international trade across the world. The emphasis on globalization also connects closely with the weight given to the interdependence of the industrialized and developing worlds today.

The book also focuses on the importance of *comparative* study. Sociology cannot be taught solely by understanding the institutions of any one particular society. While we have slanted the discussion toward the United States, we have also balanced it with a rich variety of materials drawn from other cultures. These include research carried out in other Western countries, as well as Russia and the Eastern European societies, which are currently undergoing substantial changes. The book also includes much more material on developing countries than has been usual in introductory texts. In addition, we strongly emphasize the relationship between sociology and anthropology, whose concerns overlap comprehensively. Given the close connections that now mesh societies across the world with one another, and the virtual disappearance of traditional social systems, sociology and anthropology have increasingly become indistinguishable.

A fifth theme is the necessity of taking a *historical approach* to sociology. This involves more than just filling in the historical context within which events occur. One of the most important developments in sociology over the past few years has been an increasing emphasis on historical analysis. This should be understood not solely as applying a sociological outlook to the past, but as a way of contributing to our understanding of institutions in the present. Recent work in historical sociology is discussed throughout the text and provides a framework for the interpretations offered in the chapters.

Throughout the text, particular attention is given to *issues of gender*. The study of gender is ordinarily regarded as a specific field within sociology as a whole—and this volume contains a chapter that specifically explores thinking and research on the subject (Chapter 9). However, questions about gender relations are so fundamental to sociological analysis that they cannot simply be considered a subdivision. Thus, many chapters contain sections concerned with issues of gender.

A seventh theme is the *micro and macro link*. At many points in the book, we show that interaction in micro-level contexts affects larger social processes and that such macro-level processes influence our day-to-day lives. We emphasize that one can better understand a social situation by analyzing it at both the micro and macro levels.

The final major theme is the relation between the *social* and the *personal*. Sociological thinking is a vital help to self-understanding, which in turn can be focused back on an improved understanding of the social world. Studying sociology should be a liberating experience: The field enlarges our sympathies and imagination, opens up new perspectives on the sources of our own behavior, and creates an awareness of cultural settings different from our own. Insofar as sociological ideas challenge dogma, teach appreciation of cultural variety, and allow us insight into the working of social institutions, the practice of sociology enhances the possibilities of human freedom.

All of the chapters in the book have been updated and revised to reflect the most recent available data. Additionally, four chapters have received special attention: Chapter 6 (*Conformity, Deviance, and Crime*) has significant new material on the increasing trend to use the criminal justice system to regulate poverty in the United States. Since the 1970s, the U.S. penal system has grown continuously to the point where today nearly two million people are in prison or jail. We examine the effect of incarceration on the future life chances of inmates and on inequality trends in the United States. Increasingly, we recognize that penal institutions are also stratification institutions. Chapter 10 (*Ethnicity and Race*) works toward new definitions of race and ethnicity that take account of the need to transcend simple folk understandings. In particular, we no longer accept at face value the clear-cut distinction between race and ethnicity, which has been forcefully challenged by many scholars in recent years. The chapter also includes new research on mixed race identity, which is included to illustrate clearly the complexities associated with definitions of race and ethnicity. Chapter 12 (*Education and Religion*) features an examination of religious nationalism and violence that draws on recent research to argue that under certain conditions, ordinary conflicts can be recast as "cosmic wars" that must be won at all costs. The chapter shows that religious violence is found today among all major religious groups—Muslims, Sikhs, Jews, Hindus, Christians, and even Buddhists. Chapter 13 (*Politics and Economic Life*) has significant new material on politics and voting to reflect recent trends (through the 2004 election) in party identification and voter turnout, including an examination of some possible reasons for voter apathy. There is also an expanded discussion of interest groups, Political Action Committees, and campaign finance reform.

Organization

There is very little abstract discussion of basic sociological concepts at the beginning of this book. Instead, concepts are explained when they are introduced in the relevant chapters, and we have sought throughout to illustrate them by means of concrete examples. While these are usually taken from sociological research, we have also used material from other sources (such as newspaper articles). We have tried to keep the writing style as simple and direct as possible, while endeavoring to make the book lively and full of surprises.

The chapters follow a sequence designed to help achieve a progressive mastery of the different fields of sociology, but we have taken care to ensure that the book can be used flexibly and is easy to adapt to the needs of individual courses. Chapters can be deleted or studied in a different order without much loss. Each has been written as a fairly autonomous unit, with cross-referencing to other chapters at relevant points.

Study Aids

The pedagogy in the Essentials edition is identical to the popular material in the Fifth Edition of *Introduction to Sociology*. Designed to facilitate critical thinking and reinforce important concepts, each chapter begins with a chapter organizer, which highlights the learning objectives of each section and allows students to preview that chapter's discussion. *Essentials of Sociology* includes an in-text study guide that includes keyword and concept-review questions and data exercises linking material in the text to real-world data on the Web.

Another helpful aid is the use of a global icon to indicate examples of the changing world or the globalization process, or comparisons of U.S. society with other societies. Social change, the globalization of social life, and comparative analysis are all important themes of this text. The icon will help alert readers to discussions of these themes.

Further Research: Reading and Libraries

Libraries contain abundant sources of information that can be used to follow up or expand on issues discussed here. References are given throughout the text and are listed fully in the bibliography at the end. We have also included a short appendix that provides a guide to library resources and how to use them.

Acknowledgments

During the writing of this book, many individuals offered comments and advice on particular chapters, and, in some cases, large parts of the text. They helped us see issues in a different light, clarified some difficult points, and allowed us to take advantage of their specialist knowledge in their respective fields. We are deeply indebted to them.

Anthony Troy Adams, Eastern Michigan University
Angelo A. Alonzo, Ohio State University
Michael Blain, Boise State University
Deirdre Boden, Washington University, St. Louis
Richard J. Bord, Pennsylvania State University
Gerard A. Brandmeyer, University of South Florida
Phil Brown, Brown University
Annette Burfoot, Queen's University
Lee Clarke, Rutgers University, New Brunswick
Stephen E. Cornell, University of California, San Diego
Steven P. Dandaneau, University of Dayton
Lynn Davidman, University of Pittsburgh
Judith F. Dunn, Pennsylvania State University
Mark Eckel, McHenry County College
John V. A. Ehle, Jr., Northern Virginia Community College
Eliot Freidson, New York University
J. William Gibson, California State University, Long Beach
Richard H. Hall, University at Albany, SUNY
John Hartman, University at Buffalo, SUNY
Rick Helmes-Hayes, University of Waterloo

Wanda Kaluza, Camden County College
Paul Kingston, University of Virginia
Janet Koenigsamen, West Virginia University
Cora B. Marrett, University of Wisconsin
Garth Massey, University of Wyoming
Greg Matoesian, Fontbonne College
William H. McBroom, University of Montana
Katherine McClelland, Franklin and Marshall College
Greg McLauchlan, University of Oregon
Angela O'Rand, Duke University
Celia J. Orona, San Jose State University
Thomas Petee, Auburn University
Jennifer L. Pierce, University of Minnesota
Brian Powell, Indiana University
Allan Pred, University of California, Berkeley
Tomi-Ann Roberts, Colorado College
Roland Robertson, University of Pittsburgh
Martin Sanchez-Jankowski, University of California, Berkeley
Jack Sattel, Normandale Community College
Andrew Scull, University of California, San Diego
David R. Segal, University of Maryland, College Park
Peter Singelmann, University of Missouri, Kansas City
Craig St. John, University of Oklahoma
Judith Stepan-Norris, University of California, Irvine
Joel C. Tate, Germanna Community College
France Winddance Twine, University of California, Santa Barbara
Christopher K. Vanderpool, Michigan State University
Henry A. Walker, Cornell University
Chaim I. Waxman, Rutgers University, New Brunswick
Timothy P. Wickham-Crowley, Georgetown University
Paul Root Wolpe, University of Pennsylvania
Dennis H. Wrong, New York University
Irving M. Zeitlin, University of Toronto

We would like to thank the numerous readers of the text who have written with comments, criticisms, and suggestions for improvements. We have adopted many of their recommendations in this edition.

We have many others to thank as well. We are especially grateful to Barbara Gerr, who did a marvelous job of copyediting the book, and offered numerous suggestions for alterations and improvements that have contributed in important ways to the final form of the volume. We are also extremely grateful to project editor Dexter Gasque, assistant managing editor Lory Frenkel, production manager JoAnn Simony, and editorial assistant Sarah Solomon for managing the myriad details involved in producing this book.

We are also grateful to our editors at Norton, Steve Dunn, Melea Seward, and Karl Bakeman, who have made many direct contributions to the various chapters, and have ensured that we have made reference to the very latest research. Particular thanks are due also to Deborah Carr of Rutgers University and Neil Gross of Harvard University, two of the most outstanding young sociologists in the United States. Both had a tremendous influence on many chapters in the book. We would also like to register our thanks to a number of graduate students whose contributions have proved invaluable: Alair MacLean, Sharmila Rudrappa,

Susan Munkres, Blackhawk Hancock, Ann Meier, Katherina Zippel, Paul LePore, Wendy Carter, Josh Rossol, and David Yamane. Joe Conti, UCSB graduate student in sociology, proved to be a tireless and creative researcher, ferreting out the most recent data on every conceivable topic. He also provided his considerable expertise on the World Trade Organization for the discussion in Chapter 16. Denise Shanks, our electronic media editor, deserves special thanks for creating the elegant new Web site to accompany the book. Finally, Neil Hoos and Stephanie Romeo showed unusual flair and originality in the selections made for illustrating the book.

ESSENTIALS OF
SOCIOLOGY

Developing a Sociological Perspective

Learn what sociology covers as a field and how everyday topics like love and romance are shaped by social and historical forces.

Recognize that sociology is more than just acquiring knowledge; it also involves developing a sociological imagination. Learn that studying sociology leads us to see that we construct society through our actions and are constructed by it. Understand that two of the most important components of the sociological imagination are developing a global perspective and understanding social change.

The Development of Sociological Thinking

Learn how sociology originated and how it developed. Think about the theoretical issues that frame the study of sociology. Be able to name some of the leading social theorists and the concepts they contributed to the study of sociology. Learn the different theoretical approaches modern sociologists bring to the field.

Sociological Questions

Be able to name the different types of questions sociologists try to answer in their research—factual, theoretical, comparative, and developmental.

The Research Process

Learn the steps of the research process, and be able to complete the process yourself.

Research Methods

Familiarize yourself with all the different methods available to sociological research, and know the advantages and disadvantages of each.

Research in the Real World: Methods, Problems, and Pitfalls

See how research methods were combined in a real study, and recognize the problems the researcher faced.

CHAPTER ONE

SOCIOLOGY: THEORY AND METHOD

from the tragic terrorist attacks on the World Trade Center and the Pentagon to the mass murder at Columbine High School in Littleton, Colorado, the world today is intensely worrying, yet full of the most extraordinary promise for the future. It is a world awash with change, marked by deep conflicts, tensions, and social divisions, as well as by the destructive onslaught of modern technology on the natural environment. Yet we have possibilities of controlling our destiny and shaping our lives for the better that would have been unimaginable to earlier generations.

How did this world come about? Why are our conditions of life so different from those of our parents and grandparents? What directions will change take in the future? These questions are the prime concern of sociology, a field of study that consequently has a fundamental role to play in modern intellectual life.

Sociology is the scientific study of human social life, groups, and societies. It is a dazzling and compelling enterprise, as its subject matter is our own behavior as social beings. The scope of sociological study is extremely wide, ranging from the analysis of passing encounters between individuals on the sidewalk to the investigation of global social processes such as the rise of Islamic fundamentalism. A brief example will provide an initial taste of the nature and objectives of sociology.

Have you ever been in love? Almost certainly you have. Most people who are in their teens or older know what being in love is like. Love and romance provide, for many of us, some of the

3

most intense feelings we ever experience. Why do people fall in love? The answer at first sight seems obvious. Love expresses a mutual physical and personal attachment two individuals feel for one another. These days, we might be skeptical of the idea that love is "forever," but falling in love, we tend to think, is an experience arising from universal human emotions. It seems natural for a couple who fall in love to want personal and sexual fulfillment in their relationship, perhaps in the form of marriage.

Yet this situation, which seems so self-evident to us today, is in fact very unusual. Falling in love is *not* an experience most people across the world have—and where it does happen, it is rarely thought of as having any connection to marriage. Only in modern times have love and sexuality come to be seen as closely connected. In the Middle Ages and for centuries afterward, men and women married mainly in order to keep property in the hands of family or to raise children to work the family farm. Romantic love first made its appearance in courtly circles as a characteristic of extramarital sexual adventures indulged in by members of the aristocracy. Until about two centuries ago, it was wholly confined to such circles and kept specifically separate from marriage. Relations between husband and wife among aristocratic groups were often cool and distant—certainly compared to our expectations of marriage today. Among both rich and poor, the decision of whom to marry was made by family and kin, not by the individuals concerned, who had little or no say in the matter.

This remains true in many non-Western countries today. In Afghanistan under the rule of the Taliban, where Islam underwent a major revival and became the basis of an important political movement, men were prohibited from speaking to women they were not related or married to, and marriages were arranged by parents. If a girl and boy were seen by authorities to be speaking with one another, they would be whipped so severely that one or both of them could be left seriously injured, if not dead. The ruling Taliban government saw romantic love as deeply offensive, so much so that one of its first acts as a new power in 1996 was to outlaw music and films. Like many in the non-Western world, the ruling Taliban believed Afghanistan was being inundated by Hollywood movies and American rock music and videos, filled as they are with sexual images. Osama bin Laden launched his terrorist attacks against the United States from Afghanistan, and the rhetoric of his followers has partly been aimed at criticizing such kinds of Western influences.

Neither romantic love, then, nor its association with marriage can be understood as natural features of human life. Rather, it has been shaped by broad social and historical influences. These are the influences sociologists study.

Most of us see the world in terms of the familiar features of our own lives. Sociology demonstrates the need to take a much broader view of why we are as we are, and why we act as we do. It teaches us that what we regard as inevitable, good, or true may not be such, and that the "natural" in our life is strongly influenced by historical and social forces. Understanding the subtle yet complex and profound ways in which our individual lives reflect the contexts of our social experience is basic to the sociological outlook.

Developing a Sociological Perspective

In the aftermath of the attack by suicide terrorists on the World Trade Center and the Pentagon on September 11, 2001, many Americans asked themselves how such an event could have occurred and why anyone would want to carry it out. You undoubtedly encountered many explanations for this event in the mass media, and some of the inescapable ones were sociological. The war that America and its allies have had to fight has not been merely against the country of Afghanistan, whose former Taliban government supported the terrorists. The war is also against groups, networks, and organizations that stretch around the world. A key sociological question has to do with how human beings coordinate their activities in groups, networks, and organizations. In order to understand how the World Trade Center and Pentagon attacks were possible, many analysts have focused on understanding the kinds of coordinated activity that culminated in the attack of September 11. Over time, they came to see that events on September 11 did not occur through the efforts of a loose network or group, but were carried out by a single hierarchical organization whose leaders planned the attack, coordinated all the activities, and received financial support from Osama bin Laden.

One of the things we have seen in discussions of the September 11 attacks is that our lives are connected to other societies that extend around the world. The people who worked in the World Trade Center did not imagine that their lives had very much to do with events being coordinated in Afghanistan. They also might not have imagined that their lives would come to an end due to large-scale global processes that have drawn different societies into interrelation with one another. The world in which we live today makes us much more *interdependent* with others, even those thousands of miles away, than people have ever been previously.

Likewise, in the aftermath of the 1999 mass murder at Columbine High School in Littleton, Colorado, many Americans asked themselves how and why two high school students could murder thirteen of their classmates and teachers and then take their own lives. One explanation focused on the social cliques at Columbine High, which divided into "jocks," "preps," "geeks," "goths," and other groups. It was well known that the two murderers, part of a group called the "Trenchcoat Mafia," were teased and embarrassed by their classmates, especially the "jocks." It was also reported that the two teens were obsessed with the video game *Doom,* in which each player tries to make the most kills. Many saw this as the embodiment of American culture's glorification of violence. The police also investigated how the two killers procured the guns and bombs used in the massacre. Many commentators denounced the easy availability of these weapons in American society. Others saw the tragedy as a symbol of the emptiness of suburban life, where young people have few public places to go and socialize with others.

While explanations like these focus on the social causes of violence in the United States, sociology can provide an even deeper understanding of events such as mass murder. Sociology shows us the need to look beyond the surface of people's actions and study the social context in order to understand what happened. Sociology can also teach us to try to identify general patterns of behavior in particular individuals and to be systematic in explaining the social influences on these behavioral patterns (Berger, 1963). A sociologist must look at a wide array of evidence before accepting any single explanation. Thus, a sociologist studying the Columbine High killings might study other mass murders and look to see if there was a pattern in the group characteristics—such as social class, race, gender, age, or cultural background—of the murderers and victims. This might lead a sociologist to ask why mass

In an image from airport surveillance tape, two men identified by authorities as suspected hijackers Mohammed Atta (*right*) and Abdulaziz Alomari (*center*) pass through airport security on September 11, 2001, at Portland International Jetport in Maine. The two men took a commuter flight to Boston before boarding American Airlines Flight 11, which was one of four jetliners hijacked on September 11, and one of two that were crashed into New York's World Trade Center.

murders like the one at Columbine High seem to be mostly the doing of young, middle-class, white men and then explain why this is the case (Patterson, 1999). In other words, a sociologist would not simply ask, "What led these two students at Columbine High to commit mass murder?" but also, "What social factors explain why mass murders have occurred in the United States?"

Another question sociologists ask is, "What holds society together?" When you think of it, the very existence of an orderly society is remarkable. Take as an example the use of anthrax to kill innocent citizens in the United States. Isn't it amazing how rarely such terrorism has been attempted in the United States? The existence of order in the country is something we have long taken for granted. When you think of it, though, living is partly an act of faith that order will be maintained from minute to minute in skyscrapers and on sidewalks and everywhere in between. It is the faith that incidents such as the bioterrorism of sending anthrax through the mail, or the September 11 attacks, or the acts of the Trenchcoat Mafia will be few. But though we must take this order for granted in order to live our lives, sociologists seek to understand how such order comes about. For the sociologist who wants to know how society is possible in the first place, the interesting question is not merely why someone sends anthrax through the mail or why someone shoots up a high school. It is, more important, why such acts happen so infrequently. Why are so many willing to work together to maintain the social order? And isn't it unsettling that in a society where so many work to maintain this order, just nineteen hijackers or two high school students are capable of doing so much harm?

Learning to think sociologically—looking, in other words, at the broader view—means cultivating the imagination. As sociologists, we need to imagine, for example, what the experience of sex and marriage is like for people—the majority of humankind until recently—to whom ideals of romantic love appear alien or even absurd. Or we need to image what life was like for the victims and the murderers in the 2001 terrorist attacks and at Columbine High. Studying sociology *cannot* be just a routine process of acquiring knowledge. A sociologist is someone who is able to break free from the immediacy of personal circumstances and put things in a wider context. Her work depends on what the American sociologist C. Wright Mills, in a famous phrase, called the **sociological imagination** (Mills, 1959).

The sociological imagination requires us, above all, to *"think ourselves away" from the familiar routines of our daily lives in order to look at them anew.* Consider the simple act of drinking a cup of coffee. What could we find to say, from a sociological point of view, about such an apparently uninteresting piece of behavior? An enormous amount. We could point out first of all that coffee is not just a refreshment. It possesses *symbolic value* as

Three businessmen relax and chat over coffee (left). A group of workers on a hashish plantation smoke hash during a break (right). In both instances, the socially acceptable consumption of a drug serves as an occasion to socialize.

part of our day-to-day social activities (see the accompanying "Globalization and Everyday Life"). Often the ritual associated with coffee drinking is much more important than the act of consuming the drink itself. Two people who arrange to meet for coffee are probably more interested in getting together and chatting than in what they actually drink. Drinking and eating in all societies, in fact, provide occasions for social interaction and the enactment of rituals—and these offer a rich subject matter for sociological study.

Second, coffee is a *drug* containing caffeine, which has a stimulating effect on the brain. Coffee addicts are not regarded by most people in Western culture as drug users. Like alcohol, coffee is a socially acceptable drug, whereas marijuana, for instance, is not. Yet there are societies that tolerate the consumption of marijuana or even cocaine but frown on both coffee and alcohol. Sociologists are interested in why these contrasts exist.

Third, an individual who drinks a cup of coffee is caught up in a complicated set of *social and economic relationships* stretching across the world. The production, transport, and distribution of coffee require continuous transactions between people thousands of miles away from the coffee drinker. Studying such global transactions is an important task of sociology, since many aspects of our lives are now affected by worldwide social influences and communications.

Finally, the act of sipping a cup of coffee presumes a whole process of *past social and economic development*. Along with other now-familiar items of Western diets—like tea, bananas, potatoes, and white sugar—coffee only began to be widely consumed in the late 1800s. Although the drink originated in the Middle East, its mass consumption dates from the period of Western colonial expansion about a century and a half ago. Virtually all the coffee we drink in the Western countries today comes from areas (South America and Africa) that were colonized by Europeans; it is in no sense a "natural" part of the Western diet.

Studying Sociology

As individuals, we all know a great deal about ourselves and about the societies in which we live. We tend to think we have a good understanding of why we act as we do, without needing sociologists to tell us! And to some degree this is true. Yet there are definite boundaries to such self-knowledge, and it is one of the main tasks of sociology to show us what these are.

The sociological imagination allows us to see that many events that seem to concern only the individual actually reflect larger social issues. Try applying this sort of outlook to your own life. Consider, for instance, why you are turning the pages of this book at all—why you have decided to study sociology. You might be a reluctant sociology student, taking the course only to fulfill a requirement. Or you might be enthusiastic to find out more about the subject. Whatever your motivations, you are likely to have a good deal in common, without necessarily knowing it, with others studying sociology. Your private decision reflects your position in the wider society.

Do the following characteristics apply to you? Are you young? White? From a professional or white-collar background? Have you done, or do you still do, some part-time work to boost your income? Do you want to find a good job when you leave school but are not especially dedicated to studying? Do you not really know what sociology is but think it has something to do with how people behave in groups? More than three quarters of you will answer yes to all these questions. College students are not typical of the population as a whole but tend to be drawn from more privileged backgrounds. And their attitudes usually reflect those held by friends and acquaintances.

*"How would you like me to answer that question?
As a member of my ethnic group, educational class,
income group, or religious category?"*

The social backgrounds from which we come have a great deal to do with what kinds of decisions we think appropriate.

But suppose you answered "no" to one or more of these questions. You might come from a minority-group background or one of poverty. You may be someone in midlife or older. If so, however, further conclusions probably follow. You will likely have had to struggle to get where you are; you might have had to overcome hostile reactions from friends and others when you told them you were intending to go to college; or you might be combining school with full-time parenthood and/or work.

Although we are all influenced by the social contexts in which we find ourselves, none of us is simply *determined* in his or her behavior by those contexts. We possess, and create, our own individuality. It is the business of sociology to investigate the connections between *what society makes of us and what we make of ourselves.* Our activities both structure—give shape to—the social world around us and at the same time are structured *by* that social world.

The concept of **social structure** is an important one in sociology. It refers to the fact that the social contexts of our lives do not just consist of random assortments of events or actions; they are structured, or *patterned,* in distinct ways. There are regularities in the ways we behave and in the relationships we have with one another. But social structure is not like a physical structure, such as a building, which exists independently of human actions. Human societies are always in the process of **structuration.**

They are reconstructed at every moment by the very "building blocks" that compose them—human beings like you and me.

As an example, consider again the case of coffee. A cup of coffee does not automatically arrive in your hands. You choose, for example, to go to a particular café, whether to drink your coffee black or light, and so forth. As you make these decisions, along with millions of other people, you shape the market for coffee and affect the lives of coffee producers living perhaps thousands of miles away on the other side of the world.

Developing a Global Perspective

As we just saw in our discussions of the terrorist attacks and of the sociological dimensions of drinking a cup of coffee, all our local actions—the ways in which we relate to one another in face-to-face contexts—form part of larger social settings that extend around the globe. These connections between the *local* and the *global* are quite new in human history. They have accelerated over the past thirty or forty years as a result of the dramatic advances in communications, information technology, and transportation. The development of jet planes, large, speedy container ships, and other means of fast travel has meant that people and goods can be continuously transported across the world. And our worldwide system of satellite communication, established only some thirty years ago, has made it possible for people to get in touch with each other instantaneously.

American society is influenced every moment of the day by **globalization,** the growth of world interdependence, a social phenomenon that will be discussed throughout this book. Globalization should not be thought of simply as the development of worldwide networks—social and economic systems that are remote from our individual concerns. It is a local phenomenon, too. For example, only a few years ago, when they dined out, most Americans were faced with a limited choice. In many U.S. towns and cities today, a single street might feature Italian, Chinese, Japanese, Thai, French, and other types of restaurants next door to each other. In turn, the dietary decisions we make are consequential for food producers who might live on the other side of the world. Another everyday aspect of globalization can be found in your closet and drawers. If you take a look at the labels of your clothes and see the many various countries in which they were manufactured, then you are experiencing globalization firsthand.

Do college students today have a global perspective? By at least one measure, the answer is yes. Furthermore, their activist values suggest that many students also possess a sociological imagination. According to an annual survey of more than 281,064 first-year college students, a record 47.5 percent of all students who entered U.S. colleges in 2001 reported that

The Sociology of Coffee

The world drinks about 2.25 billion cups [of coffee] per day—the United States alone drinks one fifth of this. Coffee drinking is a cultural fixture that says as much about us as it does about the bean itself. Basically a habit forming stimulant, coffee is nonetheless associated with relaxation and sociability. In a society that combines buzzing overstimulation with soul-aching meaninglessness, coffee and its associated rituals are, for many of us, the lubricants that make it possible to go on.

Perhaps for this reason coffee occupies a distinctive niche in our cultural landscape. Along with alcohol, it is the only beverage to engender public houses devoted to its consumption. . . . Uniquely, though, coffee is welcome in almost any situation, from the car to the boardroom, from the breakfast table to the public park, alone or in company of any kind. Since its adoption as a beverage, coffee has been offered as an antipode to alcohol—more so even than abstinence, perhaps in recognition of a human need for joyfully mood-altering substances and the convivial social interactions that go along with them.

Only a handful of consumer goods has fueled the passions of the public as much as coffee. . . . [C]offee has inspired impassioned struggles on the battlefields of economics, human rights, politics, and religion, since its use first spread. Coffee

they had "participated in organized demonstrations" concerned with social, political, and economic issues during the previous year. This was the highest percentage since the UCLA survey began asking the question in 1966 (Sax, L. J., Lindholm, J. A., Astin, A. W., Korn, W. S., and Mahoney, K. M., 2001). This upsurge in activist values suggests that many entering college students possess a sociological imagination: They recognize that their private lives are shaped by larger social forces. The demonstrations these students participated in were concerned with a wide range of issues, including the growing power of global institutions such as the World Trade Organization and the World Bank, the production of clothing in overseas sweatshops, global warming, environmental destruction, and the right of workers to be paid a living wage (Meatto, 2000). Concern with these issues reflects an awareness that globalization has a direct effect on our daily, private lives.

Developing a global perspective has great importance for sociology. A global perspective not only allows us to become more aware of the ways that we are connected to people in other societies; it also makes us more aware of the many problems the world faces at the beginning of the twenty-first century. The global perspective opens our eyes to the fact that our interdependence with other societies means that our actions have consequences for others and that the world's problems have consequences for us.

Understanding Social Change

The changes in human ways of life in the last two hundred years, such as globalization, have been far-reaching. We have become accustomed, for example, to the fact that most of the may be a drink for sharing, but as a commodity it invites protectionism, oppression, and destruction. Its steamy past implicates the otherwise noble bean in early colonialism, various revolutions, the emergence of the bourgeoisie, international development, technological hubris, crushing global debt, and more. These forces, in turn, have shaped the way coffee has been incorporated into our culture and economy. Colonialism, for example, served as the primary reason for and vehicle of coffee's expansion throughout the globe; colonial powers dictated where coffee went and where it did not and established trading relationships that continue to this day.

The story of coffee also reveals how (and why) we interact with a plethora of other commodities, legal or not. Surprising similarities exist, for example, between coffee's early history and the current controversy over marijuana. Today's national debate over the merits of marijuana, although young by comparison, is the modern version of the strife surrounding coffee in other ages. The social acceptability of each has been affected by religious and political opinion, conflicting health claims, institutionalized cultural norms, and the monied interests of government and private industry. The evolution of coffee's social acceptability highlights the delicate dance of interests and "truths" that governs the ways in which we structure our societies.

Coffee is consumed with great fervor in rich countries such as the United States yet is grown with few exceptions in the poorest parts of the globe. In fact, it is the second most valuable item of legal international trade (after petroleum), and the largest food import of the United States by value. It is the principal source of foreign exchange for dozens of countries around

the world. The coffee in your cup is an immediate, tangible connection with the rural poor in some of the most destitute parts of the planet. It is a physical link across space and cultures from one end of the human experience to the other.

The coffee trading system that has evolved to bring all this about is an intricate knot of economics, politics, and sheer power—a bizarre arena trod . . . by some of the world's largest transnational corporations, by enormous governments, and by vast trading cartels. The trip coffee takes from the crop to your cup turns out not to be so straightforward after all, but rather a turbulent and unpredictable ride through the waves and eddies of international commodity dynamics, where the product itself becomes secondary to the wash of money and power.

SOURCE: Gregory Dicum and Nina Luttinger, *The Coffee Book: Anatomy of an Industry from Crop to the Last Drop* (New York: The New Press, 1999), pp. ix–xi. Used with permission.

population does not work on the land and lives in towns and cities rather than in small rural communities. But this was *never* the case until the middle of the nineteenth century. For virtually all of human history, the vast majority of people had to produce their own food and shelter and lived in tiny groups or in small village communities. Even at the height of the most developed traditional civilizations—such as ancient Rome or traditional China—less than 10 percent of the population lived in urban areas; everyone else was engaged in food production in a rural setting. Today, in most of the industrialized societies, these proportions have become almost completely reversed. Quite often, more than 90 percent of the people live in urban areas, and only 2 to 3 percent of the population work in agricultural production.

It is not only the environment surrounding our lives that has changed; these transformations have radically altered, and continue to alter, the most personal and intimate side of our daily existence. To extend a previous example, the spread of ideals of romantic love was strongly conditioned by the transition from a rural to an urban, industrialized society. As people moved into urban areas and began to work in industrial production, marriage was no longer prompted mainly by economic motives—by the need to control the inheritance of land and to work the land as a family unit. "Arranged" marriages—fixed through the negotiations of parents and relatives—became less and less common. Individuals increasingly began to initiate marriage relationships on the basis of emotional attraction and in order to seek personal fulfillment. The idea of "falling in love" as a basis for contracting a marriage tie was formed in this context.

Sociology had its beginnings in the attempts of thinkers to understand the initial impact of these transformations that accompanied industrialization in the West. Our world today is radically different from that of former ages; it is the task of sociology to help us understand this world and what future it is likely to hold for us.

The Development of Sociological Thinking

Trying to understand something as complex as the impact of industrialization on society raises the importance of theory to sociology. Factual research shows *how* things occur. Yet sociology does not just consist of collecting facts, however important and interesting they may be. We also want to know *why* things happen, and in order to do so we have to learn to construct explanatory theories. For instance we know that industrialization has had a major influence on the emergence of modern societies. But what are the origins and preconditions of industrialization? Why do we find differences between societies in their industrialization processes? Why is industrialization associated with changes in ways of criminal punishment, or in family and marriage systems? To respond to such questions, we have to develop theoretical thinking.

Theories and Theoretical Approaches

Theories involve constructing abstract interpretations that can be used to explain a wide variety of situations. Of course, factual research and theories can never completely be separated. We can only develop valid theoretical approaches if we are able to test them out by means of factual research. We need theories to help us make sense of facts. Contrary to popular assertion, facts do not speak for themselves. Many sociologists work primarily on factual research, but unless they are guided by some knowledge of theory, their work is unlikely to explain the complexity of modern societies. This is true even of research carried out with strictly practical objectives.

Without a **theoretical approach**, we would not know what to look for in beginning a study or in interpreting the results of research. However, the illumination of factual evidence is not the only reason for the prime position of theory in sociology. Theoretical thinking must respond to general problems posed by the study of human social life, including issues that are philosophical in nature. Deciding to what extent sociology should be modeled on the natural sciences are questions that do not yield easy solutions. They have been handled in different ways in the various theoretical approaches that have sprung up in the discipline.

Early Theorists

We human beings have always been curious about the sources of our own behavior, but for thousands of years our attempts to understand ourselves relied on ways of thinking passed down from generation to generation, often expressed in religious terms. Although writers from earlier periods provided insights into human behavior and society, the systematic study of society is a relatively recent development whose beginnings date back to the late 1700s and early 1800s. The background to the origins of sociology was the series of sweeping changes ushered in by the French Revolution of 1789 and the emergence of the Industrial Revolution in Europe. The shattering of traditional ways of life wrought by these changes resulted in the attempts of thinkers to develop a new understanding of both the social and natural worlds.

A key development was the use of science instead of religion to understand the world. The types of questions these nineteenth-century thinkers sought to answer—What is human nature? Why is society structured like it is? How and why do societies change?—are the same questions sociologists try to answer today.

AUGUSTE COMTE

There were many contributors to early sociological thinking. Particular prominence, however, is usually given to the French author Auguste Comte (1798–1857), if only because he invented the word *sociology*. Comte originally used the term *social physics,* but some of his intellectual rivals at the time were also

Auguste Comte (1798–1857).

making use of that term. Comte wanted to distinguish his own views from theirs, so he introduced *sociology* to describe the subject he wished to establish.

Comte believed that this new field could produce a knowledge of society based on scientific evidence. He regarded sociology as the last science to be developed—following physics, chemistry, and biology—but as the most significant and complex of all the sciences. Sociology, he believed, should contribute to the welfare of humanity by using science to understand and therefore predict and control human behavior. In the later part of his career, Comte drew up ambitious plans for the reconstruction of French society in particular and for human societies in general, based on scientific knowledge.

ÉMILE DURKHEIM

The works of another French writer, Émile Durkheim (1858–1917), have had a much more lasting impact on modern sociology than those of Comte. Although he drew on aspects of Comte's work, Durkheim thought that many of his predecessor's ideas were too speculative and vague and that Comte had not successfully carried out his program—to establish sociology on a scientific basis. To become scientific, according to Durkheim, sociology must study **social facts,** aspects of social life that shape our actions as individuals, such as the state of the economy or the influence of religion. Durkheim believed that we must study social life with the same objectivity as scientists study the natural world. His famous first principle of sociology was "Study social facts as *things!*" By this he meant that social life can be analyzed as rigorously as objects or events in nature.

Like a biologist studying the human body, Durkheim saw society as a set of independent parts, each of which could be studied separately. A body consists of various specialized parts, each of which contributes to sustaining the continuing

Émile Durkheim (1858–1917).

life of the organism. These necessarily work in harmony with one another; if they do not, the life of the organism is under threat. So it is, according to Durkheim, with society. For a society to have a continuing existence over time, its specialized institutions (such as the political system, the religion, the family, and the educational system) must work in harmony with each other and function as an integrated whole. Durkheim referred to this social cohesion as **"organic solidarity."** He argued that the continuation of a society thus depends on cooperation, which in turn presumes a general consensus, or agreement, among its members over basic values and customs.

Another major theme pursued by Durkheim, and by many others since, is that the societies of which we are members exert **social constraint** over our actions. Durkheim argued that society has primacy over the individual person. Society is far more than the sum of individual acts; when we analyze social structures, we are studying characteristics that have a "firmness" or "solidity" comparable to those of structures in the physical world. Social structure, according to Durkheim, constrains our activities in a parallel way, setting limits on what we can do as individuals. It is "external" to us, just as the walls of the room are.

One of Durkheim's most famous studies was concerned with the analysis of suicide (Durkheim, 1966; orig. 1897). Suicide seems to be a purely personal act, the outcome of extreme personal unhappiness. Durkheim showed, however, that social factors exert a fundamental influence on suicidal behavior—**anomie,** a feeling of aimlessness or despair provoked by modern social life being one of these influences. Suicide rates show regular patterns from year to year, he argued, and these patterns must be explained sociologically. Many objections can be raised against Durkheim's study, but it remains a classic work whose relevance to sociology today is by no means exhausted. According to Durkheim, processes of change in the modern world are so rapid and intense that they give rise to major social difficulties, which he linked to anomie. Traditional moral controls and standards, which used to be supplied by religion, are largely broken down by modern social development, and this leaves many individuals in modern societies feeling that their daily lives lack meaning.

KARL MARX

The ideas of Karl Marx (1818–1883) contrast sharply with those of Comte and Durkheim, but like them, he sought to explain the changes in society that took place over the time of the industrial revolution. When he was a young man, Marx's political activities brought him into conflict with the German authorities; after a brief stay in France, he settled permanently in exile

Karl Marx
(1818–1883).

in Britain. Marx's viewpoint was founded on what he called the **materialist conception of history.** According to this view, it is not the ideas or values human beings hold that are the main sources of social change, as Durkheim claimed. Rather, social change is prompted primarily by economic influences. The conflicts between classes—the rich versus the poor—provide the motivation for historical development. In Marx's words, "All human history thus far is the history of class struggles."

Though he wrote about various phases of history, Marx concentrated on change in modern times. For him, the most important changes were bound up with the development of capitalism. **Capitalism** is a system of production that contrasts radically with previous economic systems in history, involving as it does the production of goods and services sold to a wide range of consumers. Those who own capital, or factories, machines, and large sums of money, form a ruling class. The mass of the population make up a class of wage workers, or a working class, who do not own the means of their livelihood but must find employment provided by the owners of capital. Capitalism is thus a class system in which conflict between classes is a commonplace occurrence because it is in the interests of the ruling class to exploit the working class and in the interests of the workers to seek to overcome that exploitation.

According to Marx, in the future capitalism will be supplanted by a society in which there are no classes—no divisions between rich and poor. He didn't mean by this that all inequalities between individuals will disappear. Rather, societies will no longer be split into a small class that monopolizes economic and political power and the large mass of people who benefit little from the wealth their work creates. The economic system will come under communal ownership, and a more equal society than we know at present will be established.

Marx's work had a far-reaching effect on the twentieth-century world. Until recently, before the fall of Soviet communism, more than a third of the earth's population lived in societies whose governments claimed to derive their inspiration from Marx's ideas. In addition, many sociologists have been influenced by Marx's ideas about class divisions.

MAX WEBER

Like Marx, Max Weber (pronounced "Vaber," 1864–1920) cannot be labeled simply a sociologist; his interests and concerns ranged across many areas. Born in Germany, where he spent most of his academic career, Weber was an individual of wide learning. Like other thinkers of his time, Weber sought to understand social change. He was influenced by Marx but was also strongly critical of some of Marx's major views. He rejected the materialist conception of history and saw class conflict as less significant than did Marx. In Weber's view, economic factors are important, but ideas and values have just as much impact on social change.

Some of Weber's most influential writings were concerned with comparing the leading religious systems in China and India with those of the West; Weber concluded that certain aspects of Christian beliefs strongly influenced the rise of capitalism. He argued that the capitalist outlook of Western societies did not emerge, as Marx supposed, only from economic changes. In Weber's view, cultural ideas and values help shape society and affect our individual actions.

One of the most persistent concerns of Weber's work was the study of bureaucracy. A **bureaucracy** is a large organization that is divided into jobs based on specific functions and staffed by officials ranked according to a hierarchy. Industrial firms, government organizations, hospitals, and schools are all examples of bureaucracies. Weber believed the advance of bureaucracy to be an inevitable feature of our era. Bureaucracy makes it possible for these large organizations to run efficiently, but at the same time it poses problems for effective democratic participation in modern societies. Bureaucracy

Max Weber
(1864–1920).

TABLE 1.1

Interpreting Modern Development

DURKHEIM
1. The main dynamic of modern development is the **division of labor** as a basis for social cohesion and **organic solidarity.**
2. Durkheim believed that sociology must study **social facts** as things, just as science would analyze the natural world. His study of suicide led him to stress the important influence of social factors, qualities of a society external to the individual, on a person's actions. Durkheim argued that society exerts **social constraint** over our actions.

MARX
1. The main dynamic of modern development is the expansion of **capitalism.** Rather than being cohesive, society is divided by class differences.
2. Marx believed that we must study the divisions within a society that are derived from the economic inequalities of capitalism.

WEBER
1. The main dynamic of modern development is the **rationalization** of social and economic life.
2. Weber focused on why Western societies developed so differently from other societies. He also emphasized the importance of cultural ideas and values on social change.

involves the rule of experts, whose decisions are made without much consultation with those whose lives are affected by them.

Weber's contributions range over many other areas, including the study of the development of cities, systems of law, types of economy, and the nature of classes. He also produced a range of writings concerned with the overall character of sociology itself. According to Weber, humans are thinking, reasoning beings; we attach meaning and significance to most of what we do, and any discipline that deals with human behavior must acknowledge this.

Neglected Founders

Although Comte, Durkheim, Marx, and Weber are, without doubt, foundational figures in sociology, other important thinkers from the same period made contributions that must also be taken into account. Very few women or members of racial minorities were given the opportunity to become professional sociologists during the "classical" period of the late nineteenth and early twentieth centuries. In addition, the few that were given the opportunity to do sociological research of lasting importance have frequently been neglected by the field. These individuals deserve the attention of sociologists today.

HARRIET MARTINEAU

Harriet Martineau (1802–1876) was born and educated in England. She was the author of over fifty books, as well as numerous essays. Martineau is now credited with introducing sociology to England through her translation of Comte's founding treatise of the field, *Positive Philosophy* (Rossi, 1973). In addition, Martineau conducted a firsthand systematic study of American society during her extensive travels throughout the United States in the 1830s, which is the subject of her book

Harriet Martineau
(1802–1876).

Society in America. Martineau is significant to sociologists today for several reasons. First, she argued that when one studies a society, one must focus on all its aspects, including key political, religious, and social institutions. Second, she insisted that an analysis of a society must include an understanding of women's lives. Third, she was the first to turn a sociological eye on previously ignored issues, including marriage, children, domestic and religious life, and race relations. As she once wrote, "The nursery, the boudoir, and the kitchen are all excellent schools in which to learn the morals and manners of a people" (Martineau, 1962). Finally, she argued that sociologists should do more than just observe, they should also act in ways to benefit a society. As a result, Martineau was an active proponent of both women's rights and the emancipation of slaves.

W. E. B. DU BOIS

W. E. B. Du Bois (1868–1963) was the first African American to earn a doctorate at Harvard University. Du Bois's contributions to sociology were many. Perhaps most important is the concept of "double consciousness," which is a way of talking about identity through the lens of the particular experiences of African Americans. He argued that American society let African Americans see themselves only through the eyes of others: "It is a particular sensation, this double consciousness, this sense of always looking at one's soul by the tape of a world that looks on in amused contempt and pity. One ever feels his two-ness—an American, a Negro, two souls, two thoughts, two unreconciled strivings, two warring ideals in one dark body, whose dogged strength alone keeps it from being torn asunder" (Du Bois, 1903). Du Bois made a persuasive claim that one's sense of self and one's identity are greatly influenced by historical experiences and social circumstances—in the case of African Americans, the impact of slavery, and following

W. E. B. Du Bois (1868–1963).

emancipation, segregation and prejudice. Throughout his career, Du Bois focused on race relations in the United States; as he said in an often repeated quote, "the problem of the twentieth century is the problem of the color line." His influence on sociology today is evidenced by continued interest in the questions that he raised, particularly his concern that sociology must explain "the contact of diverse races of men." Du Bois was also the first social researcher to trace the problems faced by African Americans to their social and economic underpinnings, a connection that most sociologists now widely accept. Finally, Du Bois became known for connecting social analysis to social reform. He was one of the founding members of the National Association for the Advancement of Colored People (NAACP) and a long-time advocate for the collective struggle of African Americans. Later in his life, Du Bois became disenchanted by the lack of progress in American race relations and moved to the African nation of Ghana, where he died in 1963.

Modern Theoretical Approaches

While the origins of sociology were mainly European, in this century the subject has become firmly established worldwide, and some of the most important developments have taken place in the United States. The following sections explore these developments.

SYMBOLIC INTERACTIONISM

The work of George Herbert Mead (1863–1931), a philosopher teaching at the University of Chicago, had an important influence on the development of sociological thought, in particular through a perspective called **symbolic interactionism.** Mead placed particular importance on the study of *language* in analyzing the social world. According to him, language allows us to become self-conscious beings—aware of our own individuality. The key element in this process is the **symbol,** something that *stands for* something else. For example, the word *tree* is a symbol by means of which we represent the object tree. Once we have mastered such a concept, Mead argued, we can think of a tree even if none is visible; we have learned to think of the object symbolically. Symbolic thought frees us from being limited in our experience to what we actually see, hear, or feel.

Unlike animals, according to Mead, human beings live in a richly symbolic universe. This applies even to our very sense of self. Each of us is a self-conscious being because we learn to look at ourselves as if from the outside—we see ourselves as others see us. When a child begins to use "I" to refer to that object (herself) whom others call "you," she is exhibiting the beginnings of self-consciousness.

Virtually all interactions between individuals, symbolic interactionists say, involve an exchange of symbols. When we interact with others, we constantly look for clues to what type of behavior is appropriate in the context and how to interpret what others are up to. Symbolic interactionism directs our attention to the detail of interpersonal interaction and how that detail is used to make sense of what others say and do. For instance, suppose two people are out on a date for the first time. Each is likely to spend a good part of the evening sizing the other up and assessing how the relationship is likely to develop, if at all. Neither wishes to be seen doing this too openly, although each recognizes that it is going on. Both individuals are careful about their own behavior, being anxious to present themselves in a favorable light; but, knowing this, both are likely to be looking for aspects of the other's behavior that would reveal his or her true opinions. A complex and subtle process of symbolic interpretation shapes the interaction between the two.

FUNCTIONALISM

Symbolic interactionism is open to the criticism that it concentrates too much on things that are small in scope. Symbolic interactionists have found difficulty in dealing with larger-scale structures and processes—the very thing that a rival tradition of thought, **functionalism,** tends to emphasize. Functionalist thinking in sociology was originally pioneered by Comte, who saw it as closely bound up with his overall view of the field.

To study the *function* of a social activity is to analyze the contribution that that activity makes to the continuation of the society as a whole. The best way to understand this idea is by analogy to the human body, a comparison Comte, Durkheim, and other functionalist authors made. To study an organ such as the heart, we need to show how it relates to other parts of the body. When we learn how the heart pumps blood around the body, we then understand that the heart plays a vital role in the continuation of the life of the organism. Similarly, analyzing the function of some aspect of society, such as religion, means showing the part it plays in the continued existence and health of a society. Functionalism emphasizes the importance of *moral consensus* in maintaining order and stability in society. Moral consensus exists when most people in a society share the same values. Functionalists regard order and balance as the normal state of society—this social equilibrium is grounded in the existence of a moral consensus among the members of society. According to Durkheim, for instance, religion reaffirms people's adherence to core social values, thereby contributing to the maintenance of social cohesion.

Functionalism became prominent in sociology through the writings of Talcott Parsons and Robert K. Merton, each of whom saw functionalist analysis as providing the key to the development of sociological theory and research. Merton's version of functionalism has been particularly influential.

Merton distinguished between manifest and latent functions. **Manifest functions** are those known to, and intended by, the participants in a specific type of social activity. **Latent functions** are consequences of that activity of which participants are unaware. To illustrate this distinction, Merton used the example of a rain dance performed by the Hopi Tribe of Arizona and New Mexico. The Hopi believe that the ceremony will bring the rain they need for their crops (manifest function). This is why they organize and participate in it. But using Durkheim's theory of religion, Merton argued that the rain dance also has the effect of promoting the cohesion of the Hopi society (latent function). A major part of sociological explanation, according to Merton, consists in uncovering the latent functions of social activities and institutions.

For a long while, functionalist thought was probably the leading theoretical tradition in sociology, particularly in the United States. In recent years, its popularity has declined as its limitations have become apparent. While this was not true of Merton, many functionalist thinkers (Talcott Parsons is an example) unduly stressed factors leading to social cohesion at the expense of those producing division and conflict. In addition, it has seemed to many critics that functional analysis attributes to societies qualities they do not have. Functionalists often wrote as though societies have "needs" and "purposes," even though these concepts make sense only when applied to individual human beings. Figure 1.1 shows how functionalism relates to other theoretical approaches in sociology.

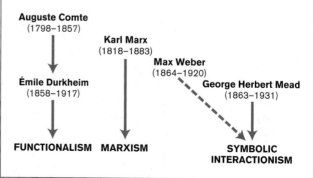

FIGURE 1.1

Theoretical Approaches in Sociology

The unbroken lines indicate direct influence, the dotted line an indirect connection. Mead is not indebted to Weber, but Weber's views—stressing the meaningful, purposive nature of human action—have affinities with the themes of symbolic interactionism.

Auguste Comte (1798–1857)

Karl Marx (1818–1883)

Max Weber (1864–1920)

Émile Durkheim (1858–1917)

George Herbert Mead (1863–1931)

FUNCTIONALISM   **MARXISM**   **SYMBOLIC INTERACTIONISM**

MARXISM AND CLASS CONFLICT

Functionalism and symbolic interactionism are not the only modern theoretical traditions of importance in sociology. A further influential approach is **Marxism.** Marxists, of course, all trace their views back in some way to the writings of Karl Marx. But numerous interpretations of Marx's major ideas are possible, and there are today schools of Marxist thought that take very different theoretical positions.

In all of its versions, Marxism differs from non-Marxist traditions of sociology in that its authors see it as a combination of sociological analysis and political reform. Marxism is supposed to generate a program of radical political change. Moreover, Marxists lay more emphasis on conflict, class divisions, power, and ideology than many non-Marxist sociologists, especially most of those influenced by functionalism. The concept of **power**—and a closely associated notion, that of **ideology**—are of great importance to Marxist sociologists and to sociology in general. By *power* is meant the capability of individuals or groups to make their own concerns or interests count, even when others resist. Power sometimes involves the direct use of force but is almost always accompanied by the development of ideas (ideologies), which are used to *justify* the actions of the powerful. Power, ideology, and conflict are always closely connected. Many conflicts are *about* power, because of the rewards it can bring. Those who hold most power may depend mainly on the influence of ideology to retain their dominance but are usually able also to use force if necessary.

FEMINISM AND FEMINIST THEORY

Feminist theory is one of the most prominent areas of contemporary sociology. This is a notable development, since issues of gender are scarcely central in the work of the major figures who established the discipline. Sociologists did not add the study of women and gender inequality to their concerns without a pitched battle. The success of feminism's entry into sociology required a fundamental shift in the discipline's approach.

Many feminist theorists brought their experiences in the women's movement of the 1960s and 1970s to their work as sociologists. Like Marxism, feminism makes a link between sociological theory and political reform. Many feminist sociologists have been advocates for political and social action to remedy the inequalities between women and men in both the public and private spheres.

Feminist sociologists argue that women's lives and experiences are central to the study of society. Sociology, like most academic disciplines, has presumed a male point of view. Driven by a concern with women's subordination in American society, feminist sociologists highlight gender relations and gender inequality as important determinants of social life in terms of both social interaction and social institutions such as the family, the workplace, and the educational system. Feminist theory emphasizes that gendered patterns and gendered inequalities are not natural, but socially constructed.

Today, feminist sociology is characterized by a focus on the intersection of gender, race, and class. A feminist approach to the study of inequality has influenced new fields of study, like men's studies, sexuality studies, and gay and lesbian studies.

RATIONAL CHOICE THEORY

The sociologist Max Weber had a very interesting way of dividing up the actions of human beings. He thought that all behavior could be divided into four categories: (1) behavior that is oriented toward higher values, such as politics; (2) behavior that is oriented toward habit, such as walking to school on a path you have taken before; (3) behavior that is oriented toward affect (emotions), such as falling in love; and (4) behavior that is oriented toward self-interest, such as making money. Behavior that falls into the last of these categories is often called "instrumental" or "rational action." In recent years, many sociologists have come to follow an approach that focuses on the last of these categories. This has led numerous scholars to ask under what conditions the behavior of human beings can be said to be rational responses to opportunities and constraints.

The **rational choice approach** to human behavior posits that if you could have only a single variable to explain society, self-interest would be the best one to work with. A person who believes in this approach might even try to use it to explain things that seem irrational. One popular rational choice theory sees decisions to marry as maximizing self-interest in a marriage market. This theory has been used to explain why marriage has declined the most in poor African American communities where rates of employment have been low. The explanation is that it is not in the self-interest of women to marry men who cannot support them (Wilson, 1987). Such an explanation goes against other, competing explanations suggesting that poor African Americans don't marry because they don't share mainstream values. The rational choice argument is that this decline in marriage has little to do with values and much to do with self-interest under existing conditions. According to this theory, if employment rates for black men changed, so too would the number of "eligible" men and the desire of women to marry them.

Rational choice theorists tend to believe that there are few irrational mysteries in life. Although a rational choice approach is often quite useful, there are some aspects of life that it would have trouble explaining. Consider, for example, an angry driver who tries to teach a lesson to other offending drivers by, for instance, tailgating a tailgater. Self-interest does not make this action sensible. Even if the lesson is well learned, the "teacher" is unlikely to reap personally the benefits of the student's progress (Katz, 1999).

POSTMODERN THEORY

Advocates of the idea of **postmodernism** claim that the classic social thinkers took their inspiration from the idea that history has a shape—it "goes somewhere" and leads to progress—and that now this notion has collapsed. There are no longer any "grand narratives," or metanarratives—overall conceptions of history or society—that make any sense (Lyotard, 1985). Not only is there no general notion of progress that can be defended, there is no such thing as history. The postmodern world is not destined, as Marx hoped, to be a socialist one. Instead, it is one dominated by the new media, which "take us out" of our past. Postmodern society is highly pluralistic and diverse. In countless films, videos, TV programs, and Web sites, images circulate around the world. We come into contact with many ideas and values, but these have little connection with the history of the areas in which we live, or indeed with our own personal histories. Everything seems constantly in flux.

One of the important theorists of postmodernity is the French author Jean Baudrillard, who believes that the electronic media have destroyed our relationship to our past and created a chaotic, empty world. Baudrillard was strongly influenced by Marxism in his early years. However, he argues, the spread of electronic communication and the mass media have reversed the Marxist theorem that economic forces shape society. Instead, social life is influenced above all by signs and images.

New York's Times Square serves as the backdrop for live television programs such as MTV's *TRL* and ESPN's *SportsCenter*. Covered with advertisements and constantly in flux, it epitomizes Baudrillard's theories of postmodern society.

In a media-dominated age, Baudrillard says, meaning is created by the flow of images, as in TV programs. Much of our world has become a sort of make-believe universe in which we are responding to media images rather than to real persons or places. Thus, when Diana, Princess of Wales, died in 1997, there was an enormous outpouring of grief, not only in Britain but all over the world. Yet were people mourning a real person? Baudrillard would say not. Diana existed for most people only through the media. Her death was more like an event in a soap opera than a real event in the way in which people experienced it. Baudrillard speaks of "the dissolution of life into TV."

Theoretical Thinking in Sociology

So far in this chapter we have been concerned with theoretical approaches, which refer to broad, overall orientations to the subject matter of sociology. However, we can draw a distinction between theoretical approaches and theories. Theories are more narrowly focused and represent attempts to explain particular social conditions or types of event. They are usually formed as part of the process of research and in turn suggest problems to which research investigations should be devoted. An example would be Durkheim's theory of suicide, referred to earlier in this chapter.

Innumerable theories have been developed in the many different areas of research in which sociologists work. Sometimes theories are very precisely set out and are even occasionally expressed in mathematical form—although this is more common in other social sciences (especially economics) than in sociology.

Some theories are also much more encompassing than others. Opinions vary about whether it is desirable or useful for sociologists to concern themselves with very wide-ranging theoretical endeavors. Robert K. Merton (1957), for example, argues forcefully that sociologists should concentrate their attention on what he calls *theories of the middle range*. Rather than attempting to create grand theoretical schemes (in the manner of Marx, for instance), we should be concerned with developing more modest theories.

Middle-range theories are specific enough to be tested directly by empirical research, yet sufficiently general to cover a range of different phenomena. A case in point is the theory of *relative deprivation*. This theory holds that how people evaluate their circumstances depends on whom they compare themselves to. Thus, feelings of deprivation do not conform directly to the level of material poverty individuals experience. A family living in a small home in a poor area, where everyone is in more or less similar circumstances, is likely to feel less deprived than a family living in a similar house in a neighborhood where the majority of the other homes are much larger and the other people more affluent.

It is indeed true that the more wide ranging and ambitious a theory is, the more difficult it is to test empirically. Yet there seems no obvious reason why theoretical thinking in sociology should be confined to the "middle range."

Assessing theories, and especially theoretical approaches, in sociology is a challenging and formidable task. Theoretical debates are by definition more abstract than controversies of a more empirical kind. The fact that there is not a single theoretical approach that dominates the whole of sociology might seem to be a sign of weakness in the subject. But this is not the case at all: The jostling of rival theoretical approaches and theories is an expression of the vitality of the sociological enterprise. In studying human beings—ourselves—theoretical variety rescues us from dogma. Human behavior is complicated and many sided, and it is very unlikely that a single theoretical perspective could cover all of its aspects. Diversity in theoretical thinking provides a rich source of ideas that can be drawn on in research and stimulates the imaginative capacities so essential to progress in sociological work.

Levels of Analysis: Microsociology and Macrosociology

One important distinction between the different theoretical perspectives we have discussed in this chapter involves the level of analysis each is directed at. The study of everyday behavior in situations of face-to-face interaction is usually called **microsociology. Macrosociology** is the analysis of large-scale social systems, like the political system or the economic order. It also includes the analysis of long-term processes of change, such as the development of industrialism. At first glance, it might seem as though micro analysis and macro analysis are distinct from one another. In fact, the two are closely connected (Knorr-Cetina and Cicourel, 1981; Giddens, 1984).

Macro analysis is essential if we are to understand the institutional background of daily life. The ways in which people live their everyday lives are greatly affected by the broader institutional framework, as is obvious when the daily cycle of activities of a culture such as that of the medieval period is compared with life in an industrialized urban environment. In modern societies, as has been pointed out, we are constantly in contact with strangers. This contact may be indirect and impersonal. However, no matter how many indirect or electronic relations we enter into today, even in the most complex societies, the presence of other people remains crucial. While we

may choose just to send an acquaintance an e-mail message on the Internet, we can also choose to fly thousands of miles to spend the weekend with a friend.

Micro studies are in turn necessary for illuminating broad institutional patterns. Face-to-face interaction is clearly the main basis of all forms of social organization, no matter how large scale. Suppose we are studying a business corporation. We could understand much about its activities simply by looking at face-to-face behavior. We could analyze, for example, the interaction of directors in the boardroom, people working in the various offices, or the workers on the factory floor. We would not build up a picture of the whole corporation in this way, since some of its business is transacted through printed materials, letters, the telephone, and computers. Yet we could certainly contribute significantly to understanding how the organization works.

In later chapters, we will see further examples of how interaction in micro contexts affects larger social processes, and how macro systems in turn influence more confined settings of social life.

Sociological Questions

Durkheim, Marx, and the other founders of sociology thought of it as a science. But can we really study human social life in a scientific way? To answer this question, we must first understand what the word means. What is science?

Science is the use of *systematic methods of empirical investigation, the analysis of data, theoretical thinking, and the logical assessment of arguments* to develop a body of knowledge about a particular subject matter. Sociology is a scientific endeavor, according to this definition. It involves systematic methods of empirical investigation, the analysis of data, and the assessment of theories in the light of evidence and logical argument.

It is the business of sociological research in general to go beyond surface-level understandings of ordinary life. Good research should help us understand our social lives in a new way. It should take us by surprise, in the questions that it asks and in the findings it comes up with. The issues that concern sociologists, in both their theorizing and their research, are often similar to those that worry other people. But the results of such research frequently run counter to our commonsense beliefs.

What are the circumstances in which racial or sexual minorities live? How can mass starvation exist in a world that is far wealthier than it has ever been before? What effects will the increasing use of the Internet have on our lives? Is the family beginning to disintegrate as an institution? Sociologists try to provide answers to these and many other questions. Their findings are by no means conclusive. Nevertheless, it is always the aim of sociological theorizing and research to break away from the speculative manner in which the ordinary person usually considers such questions. Good sociological work tries to make the questions as precise as possible and seeks to gather factual evidence before coming to conclusions. To achieve these aims, we must know the most useful **research methods** to apply in a given study and how to best analyze the results.

Some of the questions that sociologists ask in their research studies are largely **factual,** or empirical, **questions.** Factual information about one society, of course, will not always tell us whether we are dealing with an unusual case or a general set of influences. Sociologists often want to ask **comparative questions,** relating one social context within a society to another or contrasting examples drawn from different societies. There are significant differences, for example, between the social and legal systems of the United States and Canada. A typical comparative question might be: How much do patterns of criminal behavior and law enforcement vary between the two countries?

In sociology, we need not only to look at existing societies in relation to one another but also to compare their present and past. The questions sociologists ask in this case are **developmental questions.** To understand the nature of the modern world, we have to look at previous forms of society and also study the main direction that processes of change have taken. Thus, we can investigate, for example, how the first prisons originated and what they are like today.

Factual—or what sociologists usually prefer to call **empirical—investigations** concern how things occur. Yet sociology does not consist of just collecting facts, however important and interesting they may be. We always need to interpret what facts mean, and to do so we must learn to pose **theoretical questions.** Many sociologists work primarily on empirical questions, but unless they are guided in research by some knowledge of theory their work is unlikely to be illuminating (see Table 1.2).

At the same time, sociologists strive not to attain theoretical knowledge for its own sake. A standard view is that although values should not be permitted to bias conclusions, social research should be relevant to real-world concerns. In this chapter, we look further into such issues by asking whether it is possible to produce objective knowledge. First, we examine the stages involved in sociological research. We then compare the most widely used research methods as we consider some actual investigations. As we shall see, there are often significant differences between the way research should ideally be carried out and real-world studies.

The Research Process

Let us first look at the stages normally involved in research work. The research process takes in a number of distinct steps, leading from when the investigation is begun to the time its findings are published or made available in written form.

TABLE 1.2

A Sociologist's Line of Questioning

Factual question	What happened?	During the 1980s, there was an increase in the proportion of women in their thirties bearing children for the first time.
Comparative question	Did this happen everywhere?	Was this a global phenomenon, or did it occur just in the United States, or only in a certain region of the United States?
Developmental question	Has this happened over time?	What have been the patterns of childbearing over time?
Theoretical question	What underlies this phenomenon?	Why are more women now waiting until their thirties to bear children? What factors would we look at to explain this change?

Defining the Research Problem

All research starts from a research problem. This is sometimes an area of factual ignorance: We may simply wish to improve our knowledge about certain institutions, social processes, or cultures. A researcher might set out to answer such questions as: What proportion of the population holds strong religious beliefs? Are people today really disaffected with "big government"? How far does the economic position of women lag behind that of men?

The best sociological research, however, begins with problems that are also puzzles. A puzzle is not just a lack of information, but a *gap in our understanding*. Much of the skill in producing worthwhile sociological research consists in correctly identifying puzzles.

Rather than simply answering the question "What is going on here?" puzzle-solving research tries to contribute to our understanding of *why* events happen as they do. Thus, we might ask: Why are patterns of religious belief changing? What accounts for the decline in the proportions of the population voting in presidential elections in recent years? Why are women poorly represented in high-status jobs?

No piece of research stands alone. Research problems come up as part of ongoing work; one research project may easily lead to another because it raises issues the researcher had not previously considered. A sociologist may discover puzzles by reading the work of other researchers in books and professional journals or by being aware of specific trends in society. For example, over recent years, an increasing number of programs seek to treat the mentally ill while they continue to live in the community rather than confining them in asylums. Sociologists might be prompted to ask: What has given rise to this shift in attitude toward the mentally ill? What are the likely consequences both for the patients themselves and for the rest of the community?

Reviewing the Evidence

Once the problem is identified, the next step taken in the research process is usually to review the available evidence in the field; it might be that previous research has already satisfactorily clarified the problem. If not, the sociologist will need to sift through whatever related research does exist to see how useful it is for his purpose. Have previous researchers spotted the same puzzle? How have they tried to resolve it? What aspects of the problem has their research left unanalyzed? Drawing upon others' ideas helps the sociologist to clarify the issues that might be raised and the methods that might be used in the research.

Making the Problem Precise

A third stage involves working out a clear formulation of the research problem. If relevant literature already exists, the researcher might return from the library with a good notion of how to approach the problem. Hunches about the nature of the

In looking at this painting by Brueghel, we can observe the number of people, what each is doing, the style of the buildings, or the colors the painter chose. But without the title, *Netherlandish Proverbs*, these facts tell us nothing about the picture's meaning. In the same way, sociologists need theory as a context for their observations.

problem can sometimes be turned into definite **hypotheses**—educated guesses about what is going on—at this stage. If the research is to be effective, a hypothesis must be formulated in such a way that the factual material gathered will provide evidence either supporting or disproving it.

Working Out a Design

The researcher must then decide just *how* the research materials are to be collected. A range of different research methods exists, and which one the researcher chooses depends on the overall objectives of the study as well as the aspects of behavior to be analyzed. For some purposes, a survey (in which questionnaires are normally used) might be suitable. In other circumstances, interviews or an observational study might be appropriate. We shall learn more about various research methods later.

Carrying Out the Research

At the point of actually proceeding with the research, unforeseen practical difficulties can easily crop up. It might prove impossible to contact some of those to whom questionnaires are to be sent or those whom the researcher wishes to interview. A business firm or government agency may be unwilling to let the researcher carry out the work planned. Difficulties such as these could potentially bias the result of the study and give her a false interpretation. For example, if the researcher is studying how business corporations have complied with affirmative action programs for women, then companies that have not complied might not want to be studied. The findings could be biased as a result.

Interpreting the Results

Once the material has been gathered to be analyzed, the researcher's troubles are not over—they may be just beginning! Working out the implications of the data collected and relating these back to the research problem are rarely easy. Although it may be possible to reach a clear answer to the initial questions, many investigations are in the end less than fully conclusive.

Reporting the Findings

The research report, usually published as a journal article or book, provides an account of the nature of the research and seeks to justify whatever conclusions are drawn. This is a final stage only in terms of the individual research project. Most reports indicate questions that remain unanswered and suggest further research that might profitably be done in the future. All individual research investigations are part of the continuing process of research taking place within the sociological community.

Reality Intrudes!

The preceding sequence of steps is a simplified version of what happens in actual research projects (see Figure 1.2). In real sociological research, these stages rarely succeed each other so neatly, and there is almost always a certain amount of sheer muddling through. The difference is a bit like that between the

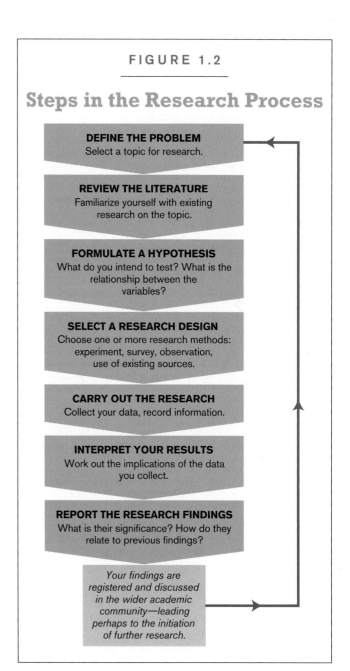

FIGURE 1.2

Steps in the Research Process

DEFINE THE PROBLEM
Select a topic for research.

REVIEW THE LITERATURE
Familiarize yourself with existing research on the topic.

FORMULATE A HYPOTHESIS
What do you intend to test? What is the relationship between the variables?

SELECT A RESEARCH DESIGN
Choose one or more research methods: experiment, survey, observation, use of existing sources.

CARRY OUT THE RESEARCH
Collect your data, record information.

INTERPRET YOUR RESULTS
Work out the implications of the data you collect.

REPORT THE RESEARCH FINDINGS
What is their significance? How do they relate to previous findings?

Your findings are registered and discussed in the wider academic community—leading perhaps to the initiation of further research.

recipes outlined in a cookbook and the actual process of preparing a meal. Experienced cooks often don't work from recipes at all, yet they might cook better than those who do. Following fixed schemes can be unduly restricting; much outstanding sociological research could not in fact be fitted rigidly into this sequence, although most of the steps would be there.

Research Methods

Let's now look at the various research methods sociologists commonly employ in their work (see Table 1.3).

Ethnography

An investigator using **ethnography** (or firsthand studies of people, using **participant observation** or interviewing) hangs out or works or lives with a group, organization, or community and perhaps takes a direct part in its activities. An ethnographer cannot usually just be present in the place she studies, but must explain and justify her presence to its members. She must gain the cooperation of the community and sustain it over a period of time, if any worthwhile results are to be achieved.

For a long while, it was usual for research based on participant observation to exclude any account of the hazards or problems that had to be overcome, but more recently the published reminiscences and diaries of field workers have been more open about them. Frequently, field workers must cope with feelings of loneliness—it isn't easy to fit into a social context or community where you don't really belong. The researcher may be constantly frustrated because the members of the group refuse to talk frankly about themselves; direct queries may be welcomed in some contexts but meet with a chilly silence in others. Some types of fieldwork may even be physically dangerous; for instance, a researcher studying a delinquent gang might be seen as a police informer or might become unwittingly embroiled in conflicts with rival gangs.

TABLE 1.3

Three of the Main Methods Used in Sociological Research

RESEARCH METHOD	STRENGTHS	LIMITATIONS
Ethnography	Usually generates richer and more in-depth information than other methods.	Can only be used to study relatively small groups or communities.
	Ethnography can provide a broader understanding of social processes.	Findings might only apply to groups or communities studied; not easy to generalize on the basis of a single fieldwork study.
Surveys	Make possible the efficient collection of data on large numbers of individuals.	Material gathered may be superficial; if questionnaire is highly standardized, important differences between respondents' viewpoints may be glossed over.
	Allow for precise comparisons to be made between the answers of respondents.	Responses may be what people profess to believe rather than what they actually believe.
Experiments	Influence of specific variables can be controlled by the investigator.	Many aspects of social life cannot be brought into the laboratory.
	Are usually easier for subsequent researchers to repeat.	Responses of those studied may be affected by their experimental situation.

In traditional works of ethnography, accounts were presented without very much information about the observer. This was because it was believed that an ethnographer could present objective pictures of the things they studied. More recently, ethnographers have increasingly tended to talk about themselves and the nature of their connection to the people under study. Sometimes, for example, it might be a matter of trying to consider how one's race, class, or gender affected the work, or how the power differences between observer and observed distorted the dialogue between them.

ADVANTAGES AND LIMITATIONS OF FIELDWORK

Where it is successful, ethnography provides information on the behavior of people in groups, organizations, and communities, and also how those people understand their own behavior. Once we see how things look from inside a given group, we are likely to develop a better understanding not only of that group, but of social processes that transcend the situation under study.

But fieldwork also has major limitations. Only fairly small groups or communities can be studied. And much depends on the skill of the researcher in gaining the confidence of the individuals involved; without this skill, the research is unlikely to get off the ground at all. The reverse is also possible. A researcher could begin to identify so closely with the group that she becomes too much of an "insider" and loses the perspective of an outside observer. Or a researcher may interpret the situation she is studying and reach conclusions that are more about her own effects on the situation than she or her readers ever realize.

Surveys

Interpreting field studies usually involves problems of generalization. Since only a small number of people are under study, we cannot be sure that what is found in one context will apply in other situations as well, or even that two different researchers would come to the same conclusions when studying the same group. This is usually less of a problem in survey research. In a **survey,** questionnaires are either sent or administered directly in interviews to a selected group of people—sometimes as many as several thousand. This group of people is referred to by sociologists as a **population.** Fieldwork is best suited for in-depth studies of small slices of social life; survey research tends to produce information that is less detailed but that can usually be applied over a broad area.

STANDARDIZED AND OPEN-ENDED QUESTIONNAIRES

Two sorts of questionnaires are used in surveys. Some contain a standardized, or fixed-choice, set of questions, to which only a fixed range of responses is possible—for instance, "*Yes/No/ Don't know*" or "*Very likely/Likely/Unlikely/Very unlikely.*" Such surveys have the advantage that responses are easy to compare and count up, since only a small number of categories are involved. On the other hand, because they do not allow for subtleties of opinion or verbal expression, the information they yield is likely to be restricted in scope, if not misleading.

Other questionnaires are open ended: respondents have more opportunity to express their views in their own words; they are not limited to making fixed-choice responses. Open-ended questionnaires typically provide more detailed information than standardized ones. The researcher can follow up answers to probe more deeply into what the respondent thinks. On the other hand, the lack of standardization means that responses may be more difficult to compare statistically.

Questionnaire items are normally listed so that a team of interviewers can ask the questions and record responses in the same predetermined order. All the items must be readily understandable to interviewers and interviewees alike. In the large national surveys undertaken regularly by government agencies and research organizations, interviews are carried out more or less simultaneously across the whole country. Those who conduct the interviews and those who analyze the results could not do their work effectively if they constantly had to be checking with each other about ambiguities in the questions or answers.

Questionnaires should also take into consideration the characteristics of respondents. Will they see the point the researcher has in mind in asking a particular question? Have they enough information to answer usefully? Will they answer at all? The terms of a questionnaire might be unfamiliar to the respondents. For instance, the question "What is your marital status?" might baffle some people. It would be more appropriate to ask, "Are you single, married, separated, or divorced?" Most surveys are preceded by **pilot studies** in order to pick up problems not anticipated by the investigator. A pilot study is a trial run in which a questionnaire is completed by just a few people. Any difficulties can then be ironed out before the main survey is done.

SAMPLING

Often sociologists are interested in the characteristics of large numbers of individuals—for example, the political attitudes of the American population as a whole. It would be impossible to study all these people directly, so in such situations researchers

Studying the Homeless

Since the 1980s, there has been a remarkable growth in the number of homeless people in the United States. But how big is the problem? How can we know whom to count as homeless? These are questions that social scientists have sought to answer, often coming up with dramatically different results.

Until the mid-1980s, the conventional wisdom was that there were over 1 million homeless people, but the statistics were essentially undocumented. Why was it so difficult to know? The reason is that it is difficult to count people living in bus stations, subways, abandoned buildings, doorways, or Dumpsters. In the absence of hard data, politicians relied on estimates provided by "homeless activists." For instance, one prominent activist, Mitch Snyder, told Ted Koppel on ABC's *Nightline* that the number was between 2 and 3 million. When asked where his numbers came from, he responded, "We got on the phone, we made a lot of calls, we talked to a lot of people, and we said, 'Okay, here are some numbers.' "

In his 1994 book *The Homeless,* the sociologist Christopher Jencks stressed how important it is to look at hard data based on documented research instead of political numbers chosen to have the maximum impact on government policy. Jencks's research strategy was to assess carefully data and research collected by other social scientists or government agencies and come up with a more precise definition and count of the homeless. His definition excluded a number of people generally counted as homeless, such a those living in welfare hotels at the expense of social welfare programs, and therefore produced a number far smaller than the rough guesses of journalists and activists.

The sociologist Elliot Liebow studied homelessness entirely differently and wrote about it in his book *Tell Them Who I Am* (1993). Liebow went out on the streets of Washington, D.C., and observed homelessness firsthand. He befriended the homeless women he was studying, volunteered to work in shelters, and helped them get along with their lives. Some would argue that in doing so, Liebow breached the rules of research discussed in this chapter, allowing himself to identify too closely with the group he was studying. But Liebow was able to learn something about homelessness that other research failed to illuminate: What do homeless people do all day? What are their most immediate con-

cerns? What do they do with their limited possessions? Why do they think they are homeless?

The differences between Jencks's and Liebow's studies illustrate the differences between quantitative and qualitative research and between macrosociology and microsociology. By carefully scrutinizing the known data on the homeless, Jencks contributed a better knowledge of the extent of homelessness. By learning more about the day-to-day experiences of being homeless, Liebow contributed a better understanding of the everyday life conditions of the homeless. Both are crucial for coming to grips with the problem and developing more informed welfare policies.

Questions

- What are the benefits of a quantitative method of talking about homelessness or about any social problem? What are the disadvantages of these methods?
- How and why is it advantageous for sociologists to distance themselves from their subjects? How can identifying with one's subject help one's research?

engage in **sampling**—they concentrate on a **sample,** or small proportion of the overall group. One can usually be confident that results from a population sample, as long as it was properly chosen, can be generalized to the total population. Studies of only two to three thousand voters, for instance, can give a very accurate indication of the attitudes and voting intentions of the entire population. But to achieve such accuracy, a sample must be **representative:** The group of individuals studied must be typical of the population as a whole. Sampling is more complex than it might seem, and statisticians have developed rules for working out the correct size and nature of samples.

A particularly important procedure used to ensure that a sample is representative is **random sampling,** in which a sample is chosen so that every member of the population has the same probability of being included. The most sophisticated way of obtaining a random sample is to give each member of the population a number and then use a computer to generate a random list, from which the sample is derived—for instance, by picking every tenth number.

Experiments

An **experiment** can be defined as an attempt to test a hypothesis under highly controlled conditions established by an investigator. Experiments are often used in the natural sciences, as they offer major advantages over other research procedures. In an experimental situation, the researcher directly controls the circumstances being studied. As compared with the natural sciences, the scope for experimentation in sociology is quite restricted. We can bring only small groups of individuals into a laboratory setting, and in such experiments, people know that they are being studied and may behave unnaturally.

Nevertheless, experimental methods can occasionally be applied in a helpful way in sociology. An example is the ingenious experiment carried out by Philip Zimbardo, who set up a make-believe jail, randomly assigning some student volunteers to the role of guards and other volunteers to the role of prisoners (Zimbardo, 1972). His aim was to see how far playing these different parts led to changes in attitude and behavior. The results shocked the investigators. Students who played at being guards quickly assumed an authoritarian manner; they displayed real hostility toward the prisoners, ordering them around and verbally abusing and bullying them. The prisoners, by contrast, showed a mixture of apathy and rebelliousness—a response often noted among inmates in real prisons. These effects were so marked and the level of tension so high that the experiment had to be called off at an early stage. The results, however, were important. Zimbardo concluded that behavior in prisons is more influenced by the nature of the

In Philip Zimbardo's make-believe jail, tension between students playing guards and students playing prisoners became dangerously real. From his experiment Zimbardo concluded that behavior in prisons is influenced more by the nature of the prison itself than the individual characteristics of those involved.

prison situation itself than by the individual characteristics of those involved.

Comparative Research

Each of the research methods described above is often applied in a comparative context. **Comparative research** is of central importance in sociology, because making comparisons allows us to clarify what is going on in a particular area of research. Let's take the American rate of divorce—the number of divorces granted each year—as an example. Divorce rates rose rapidly in the United States after World War II, reaching a peak in the early 1980s. Current trends suggest that as many as 60 percent of couples marrying today will divorce before their tenth wedding anniversary—a statistic that expresses profound changes taking place in the area of sexual relations and family life. Do these changes reflect specific features of American society? We can find out by comparing divorce rates in the United States with those of other countries. Such a comparison reveals that although the U.S. rate is higher than in most other Western societies, the overall trends are similar. Virtually all Western countries have experienced steadily climbing divorce rates over the past half century.

Historical Analysis

As was mentioned earlier, a historical perspective is often essential in sociological research. For we frequently need a *time perspective* to make sense of the material we collect about a particular problem.

Sociologists commonly want to investigate past events directly. Some periods of history can be studied in a direct way, when there are still survivors alive—such as in the case of the Holocaust in Europe during World War II. Research in **oral history** means interviewing people about events they witnessed at some point earlier in their lives. This kind of research work, obviously, can only stretch at the most some sixty or seventy years back in time. For historical research on an earlier period, sociologists are dependent on the use of documents and written records, often contained in the special collections of libraries or the National Archives.

An interesting example of the use of historical documents is sociologist Anthony Ashworth's study of trench warfare during World War I (Ashworth, 1980). Ashworth was concerned with analyzing what life was like for men who had to endure being under constant fire, crammed in close proximity for weeks on end. He drew on a diversity of documentary sources: official histories of the war, including those written about different military divisions and battalions; official publications of the time; the notes and records kept informally by individual soldiers; and personal accounts of war experiences. By drawing on such a variety of sources, Ashworth was able to develop a rich and detailed description of life in the trenches. He discovered that most soldiers formed their own ideas about how often they intended to engage in combat with the enemy and often effectively ignored the commands of their officers. For example, on Christmas Day, German and Allied soldiers suspended hostilities, and in one place the two sides even staged an informal soccer match.

Combining Comparative and Historical Research

Ashworth's research concentrated on a relatively short time period. As an example of a study that investigated a much longer one and that also applied comparative research in a historical context, we can take Theda Skocpol's *States and Social Revolutions* (1979), one of the best-known studies of social change. Skocpol set herself an ambitious task: to produce a theory of the origins and nature of revolution grounded in detailed empirical study. She looked at processes of revolution in three different historical contexts: the 1789 revolution in France, the 1917 revolution in Russia (which brought the communists to power and established the Soviet Union, which was eventually dissolved in 1989), and the revolution of 1949 in China (which created communist China).

By analyzing a variety of documentary sources, Skocpol was able to develop a powerful explanation of revolutionary change, one that emphasized the underlying social structural conditions. She showed that social revolutions are largely the result of unintended consequences. Before the Russian Revolution, for instance, various political groups were trying to overthrow the preexisting regime, but none of these—including the Bolsheviks (communists), who eventually came to power—anticipated the revolution that occurred. A series of clashes and confrontations gave rise to a process of social transformation much more radical than anyone had foreseen.

Research in the Real World: Methods, Problems, and Pitfalls

All research methods, as was stressed earlier, have their advantages and limitations. Hence, it is common to combine several methods in a single piece of research, using each to supplement and check on the others in a process known as **triangulation.** We can see the value of combining methods—and, more generally, the problems and pitfalls of real sociological research—by looking at Laud Humphreys's *Tearoom Trade*.

In a groundbreaking study from 1970, Laud Humphreys, a sociologist, studied the phenomenon within the gay community for some men to pursue impersonal sex in public restrooms. In *Tearoom Trade*, Humphreys went to these public restrooms to be part of these scenes and then conducted surveys of the participants. On the basis of his research, Humphreys was able to cast a new light on the struggles of men who were forced to keep their sexual proclivities secret. His book led to a deeper understanding of the consequences of the social stigma and legal persecution associated with gay lifestyles. One of the questions that Humphreys wanted to answer was: What kinds of men came to the tearooms? But it was very hard for him to find this out, because all he could really do in the bathrooms was

Statistical Terms

Research in sociology often makes use of statistical techniques in the analysis of findings. Some are highly sophisticated and complex, but those most often used are easy to understand. The most common are **measures of central tendency** (ways of calculating averages) and **correlation coefficients** (measures of the degree to which one variable relates consistently to another).

There are three methods of calculating averages, each of which has certain advantages and shortcomings. Take as an example the amount of personal wealth (including all assets such as houses, cars, bank accounts, and investments) owned by thirteen individuals. Suppose the thirteen own the following amounts:

1	$ 000 (zero)	8	$ 80,000
2	$ 5,000	9	$ 100,000
3	$10,000	10	$ 150,000
4	$20,000	11	$ 200,000
5	$40,000	12	$ 400,000
6	$40,000	13	$10,000,000
7	$40,000		

The **mean** corresponds to the average, arrived at by adding together the personal wealth of all thirteen people and dividing the result by 13. The total is $11,085,000; dividing this by 13, we reach a mean of $852,692.31. This mean is often a useful calculation because it is based on the whole range of data provided. However, it can be misleading where one or a small number of cases are very different from the majority. In the above example, the mean is not in fact an appropriate measure of central tendency, because the presence of one very large figure, $10,000,000, skews the picture. One might get the impression when using the mean to summarize this data that most of the people own far more than they actually do.

In such instances, one of two other measures may be used. The **mode** is the figure that occurs most frequently in a given set of data. In our example, it is $40,000. The problem with the mode is that it doesn't take into account the *overall distribution* of the data, i.e., the range of figures covered. The most frequently occurring case in a set of figures is not necessarily representative of their distribution as a whole and thus may not be a useful average. In this case, $40,000 is too close to the lower end of the figures.

The third measure is the **median,** which is the middle of any set of figures; here, this would be the seventh figure, again $40,000. Our example gives an odd number of figures, thirteen. If there had been an even number—for instance, twelve—the median would be calculated by taking the mean of the two middle cases, figures 6 and 7. Like the mode, the median gives no idea of the actual *range* of the data measured.

Sometimes a researcher will use more than one measure of central tendency to avoid giving a deceptive picture of the average. More often, he will calculate the **standard deviation** for the data in question. This is a way of calculating the **degree of dispersal,** or the range, of a set of figures—which in this case goes from zero to $10,000,000.

Correlation coefficients offer a useful way of expressing how closely connected two (or more) variables are. Where two variables correlate completely, we can speak of a perfect positive correlation, expressed as 1.0. Where no relation is found between two variables—they have no consistent connection at all—the coefficient is zero. A perfect negative correlation, expressed as −1.0, exists when two variables are in a completely inverse relation to one another. Perfect correlations are never found in the social sciences. Correlations of the order of 0.6 or more, whether positive or negative, are usually regarded as indicating a strong degree of connection between whatever variables are being analyzed. Positive correlations on this level might be found between, say, social class background and voting behavior.

observe. The norm of silence in the restrooms made it difficult to ask any questions, or even to talk. Plus, it would have been very odd if he had begun to ask personal questions of people who basically wanted to be anonymous.

Humphreys's solution was to try to find out more about the men in the tearooms using survey methods. Standing by the door of the restrooms, he would write down the license plate numbers of people who pulled up to the parking lot and then went into the restrooms for the purpose of engaging in sexual relations. He then gave those license plate numbers to a friend who worked at the Department of Motor Vehicles, securing the addresses of the men.

Months later, Washington University in St. Louis was conducting a door-to-door survey of sexual habits. Humphreys asked the principal investigators in that survey if he could add the names and addresses of his sample of tearoom participants. Humphreys then disguised himself as one of the investigators and went to interview these men at their homes, supposedly just to ask only the survey questions but actually to also learn more about their social backgrounds and lives. He found that most of these men were married and otherwise led very conventional lives. He often interviewed wives and other family members as well.

Human Subjects and Ethical Problems

All research concerned with human beings can pose ethical dilemmas. A key question that sociologists agree must be asked is whether the research poses risks to the subjects that are greater than the risks they face in their everyday lives.

In writing *Tearoom Trade,* Humphreys said he was less than truthful to those whose behavior he was studying. He said he didn't reveal his identity as a sociologist when observing the tearoom. People who came into the tearoom assumed he was there for the same reasons they were and that his presence could be accepted at face value. While he did not tell any direct lies while observing the tearoom, he also did not reveal the real reason for his presence there. Was this particular aspect of his behavior ethical? The answer is that, on balance, this particular aspect of his study did not put any of his subjects at risk. On the basis of what he observed in the tearoom, Humphreys did not collect information about the participants that would have identified them. What he knew about them was similar to what all the other people in the tearoom knew. In this way, his presence did not subject them to any more risk than they already encountered in their everyday lives. At the same time, had Humphreys been completely frank at every stage, the research might not have gotten as far as it did. Indeed, some of the most valuable data that have been collected by sociologists could have never been gathered if the researcher had first explained the project to each person encountered in the research process.

If this were the only dilemma posed by Humphreys's research project, it would not stand out as a notable problem in the ethics of social research. What raised more eyebrows was that Humphreys wrote down the license plate numbers of the people who came into the tearooms, obtained their home addresses from a friend who worked at the Department of Motor Vehicles, and visited their homes in the guise of conducting a neutral survey. Even though Humphreys did not reveal to the men's families anything about their activities in the tearooms, and even though he took great pains to keep the data confidential, the knowledge he gained could have been damaging. Since the activity he was documenting was illegal, police officers might have demanded that he release information about the identities of the subjects. It is also possible that a less skilled investigator could have slipped up when interviewing the subjects' families or that Humphreys could have lost his notes, which could then have been found later by someone else. Considering the number of things that could go wrong in the research process, researchers do not consider projects of this kind to be legitimate.

Humphreys was one of the first sociologists to study the lives of gay men. His account was a humane treatment that went well beyond the existing stock of knowledge on sexual communities. Although none of his research subjects actually suffered as a result of his book, Humphreys himself later agreed with his critics on the key ethical controversy. He said that were he to do the study again, he would not trace license plates or go to people's homes. Instead, after gathering his data in the public tearooms, he might try to get to know a subset of the people well enough to inform them of his goals for the study and then ask them to talk about the significance of these activities in their lives.

In recent years, the federal government has become increasingly strict with universities that make use of government grant money for research purposes. The National Science Foundation and the National Institutes of Health have strict requirements outlining how human subjects must be treated. In response to these requirements, American universities now routinely review all research that involves human subjects. The result of these review procedures has been both positive and negative. On the one hand, researchers are more aware of ethical considerations than ever before. On the other hand, many sociologists are finding it increasingly difficult to get their work done when institutional review boards required them to secure informed consent from their research subjects before they are able to establish a rapport with the subjects. There will likely never be easy solutions to problems of this kind.

Reading a Table

You will often come across tables in reading sociological literature. They sometimes look complex, but are easy to decipher if you follow a few basic steps, listed below; with practice, these will become automatic. (See Table 1.4 as an example.) Do not succumb to the temptation to skip over tables; they contain information in concentrated form, which can be read more quickly than would be possible if the same material were expressed in words. By becoming skilled in the interpretation of tables, you will also be able to check how far the conclusions a writer draws actually seem justified.

1. Read the title in full. Tables frequently have longish titles, which represent an attempt by the researcher to state accurately the nature of the information conveyed. The title of Table 1.4 gives first the *subject* of the data, second the fact that the table provides material for comparison, and third the fact that data are given only for a limited number of countries.

2. Look for explanatory comments, or *notes,* about the data. A note at the foot of Table 1.4 linked to the main column heading indicates that the data cover only licensed cars. This is important, because in some countries the proportion of vehicles properly licensed may be lower than in others. Notes may say how the material was collected, or why it is displayed in a particular way. If the data have not been gathered by the researcher but are based on findings originally reported elsewhere, a **source** will be included. The source sometimes gives you some insight into how reliable the information is likely to be, as well as showing where to find the original data. In our table, the source note makes clear that the data have been taken from more than one source.

3. Read the *headings* along the top and left-hand side of the table. (Sometimes tables are arranged with "headings" at the foot rather than the top.) These tell you what type of information is contained in each row and column. In reading the table, keep in mind each set of headings as you scan the figures. In our example, the headings on the left give the countries involved, while those at the top refer to the levels of car ownership and the years for which they are given.

4. Identify the units used; the figures in the body of the table may represent cases, percentages, averages, or other measures. Sometimes it may be helpful to convert the figures to a form more useful to you: if percentages are not provided, for example, it may be worth calculating them.

5. Consider the conclusions that might be reached from the information in the table. Most tables are discussed by the author, and what he or she has to say should of course be borne in mind. But you should also ask what further issues or questions could be suggested by the data.

TABLE 1.4

Automobile Ownership: Comparisons of Several Selected Countries

Several interesting trends can be seen in the figures in this table. First, the level of car ownership varies considerably between different countries. The number of cars per 1,000 people is more than eight times greater in the United States than in Brazil, for example. Second, there is a clear connection between car ownership ratios as a rough indicator of differences in prosperity. Third, in all the countries represented, the rate of car ownership has increased between 1971 and 2001, but in some the rate of increase is higher than others—probably indicating differences in the degree to which countries have successfully generated economic growth or are catching up.

NUMBER OF CARS PER 1,000 OF THE ADULT POPULATION[a]

	1971	1981	1984	1989	1993[d]	1996[d]	2001[e]
Brazil	12	78	84	98	96	79	95[e]
Chile	19	45	56	67	94	110	NA
Ireland	141	202	226	228	290	307	347[f]
France	261	348	360	475	503	524	585[e]
Greece	30	94	116	150	271	312	NA
Italy	210	322	359	424	586	674	638[e]
Japan	100	209	207	286	506	552	576[e]
Sweden	291	348	445	445	445	450	418[c]
U.K.	224	317	343	366	386	399	554[e]
U.S.	448	536	540	607	747	767	785[e]
West Germany	247	385	312	479	470[b]	528	583[e]

[a] Includes all licensed cars.

[b] Germany as a whole in 1993.

[c] Figure is for the year 1999. Baltic 21 Secretariat, "Passenger Car Density," www.baltic21.org/reports/indicators/tr08.htm.

[d] From World Bank, *World Development Indicators 1999*.

[e] www.toyota.co.jp/IRweb/corp_info/and_the_world/pdf/2003_c07.pdf.

[f] Figure is for the year 2000. For Ireland, see United Nations Economic Commission for Europe, www.unece.org/stats/trend/irl.pdf.

SOURCES: International Road Federation, *United Nations Annual Bulletin of Transport Statistics,* reported in *Social Trends* (London: HMSO, 1987), p. 68; Statistical Office of the European Community, *Basic Statistics of the Community* (Luxembourg: European Union, 1991); data for 1993 from *The Economist, Pocket World in Figures,* 1996; Baltic 21 Secretariat, "Passenger Car Density," www.baltic21.org/reports/indicators/tr08.htm; International Bank for Reconstruction and Development/The World Bank, *World Development Indicators 1999;* Toyota Corporation, "2001 Number and Diffusion Rate for Motor Vehicles in Major Countries," www.toyota.co.jp/IRweb/corp_info/and_the_world/pdf/2003_c07.pdf; United Nations Economic Commission for Europe, "Ireland," www.unece.org/stats/trend/irl.pdf.

Study Outline

www.wwnorton.com/giddens

Developing a Sociological Perspective

- *Sociology* can be identified as the systematic study of human societies giving special emphasis to modern, industrialized systems. The subject came into being as an attempt to understand the far-reaching changes that have occurred in human societies over the past two to three centuries.
- Major social changes have also occurred in the most intimate and personal characteristics of people's lives. The development of romantic love as a basis for marriage is an example of this.
- The practice of sociology involves the ability to think imaginatively and to detach oneself as far as possible from preconceived ideas about social relationships.

Modern Theoretical Approaches

- A diversity of theoretical approaches is found in sociology. The reason for this is not particularly puzzling. Theoretical disputes are difficult to resolve even in the natural sciences, and in sociology we face special difficulties because of the complex problems involved in subjecting our own behavior to study.
- Important figures in the early development of sociological theory include Auguste Comte (1798–1857), Émile Durkheim (1858–1917), Karl Marx (1818–1883), and Max Weber (1864–1920). Many of their ideas remain important in sociology today.
- The main theoretical approaches in sociology are *symbolic interactionism, functionalism, Marxism, feminism, rational choice approach,* and *postmodernism.* To some extent, these approaches complement each other. However, there are also major contrasts between them, which influence the ways in which theoretical issues are handled by authors following different approaches.

Levels of Analysis

- The study of face-to-face interaction is usually called *microsociology*—as contrasted to *macrosociology,* which studies larger groups, institutions, and social systems. Micro and macro analyses are in fact very closely related and each complements the other.

The Research Process

- Sociologists investigate social life by posing distinct questions and trying to find the answers to these by systematic research. These questions may be *factual, comparative, developmental,* or *theoretical.*
- All research begins from a *research problem,* which interests or puzzles the investigator. Research problems may be suggested by gaps in the existing literature, theoretical debates, or practical issues in the social world. There are a number of clear steps in the development of research strategies—although these are rarely followed exactly in actual research.

Research Methods

- In fieldwork, or *participant observation,* the researcher spends lengthy periods of time with a group or community being studied. A second method, *survey research,* involves sending or administering questionnaires to samples of a larger *population.* Documentary research uses printed materials, from archives or other resources, as a source for information. Other research methods include *experiments,* the use of *life histories,* historical analysis, and *comparative research.*
- Each of these various methods of research has its limitations. For this reason, researchers will often combine two or more methods in their work, each being used to check or supplement the material obtained from the others. This process is called *triangulation.*

Key Concepts

anomie (p. 11)
bureaucracy (p. 12)
capitalism (p. 12)
comparative questions (p. 19)
comparative research (p. 26)
developmental questions (p. 19)
empirical investigation (p. 19)
ethnography (p. 22)
experiment (p. 26)
factual questions (p. 19)
feminist theory (p. 16)
functionalism (p. 15)
globalization (p. 7)
hypothesis (p. 21)
ideology (p. 16)
latent functions (p. 15)
macrosociology (p. 18)
manifest functions (p. 15)
Marxism (p. 16)
materialist conception of history (p. 12)
microsociology (p. 18)
oral history (p. 27)
organic solidarity (p. 11)
participant observation (p. 22)
pilot study (p. 23)
population (p. 23)
postmodernism (p. 17)
power (p. 16)
random sample (p. 26)
rational choice approach (p. 16)
representative sample (p. 26)

Review Questions

1. What is the definition of sociology?
   a. Sociology is the study of individuals.
   b. Sociology is the study of group interaction, from the family to the system of nation.
   c. Sociology is the study of human social life, groups, and societies, focusing on the modern world.
   d. Sociology is a branch of the social reform movement. It is dedicated to providing a scientific underpinning for the liberal and social democratic political agendas.

2. What is the sociological imagination?
   a. It is the ability to "think ourselves away" from the familiar routines of our daily lives in order to look at them anew.
   b. It is the study of the way private troubles aggregate into public issues.
   c. It is the world view of Karl Marx.
   d. It is the application of liberal and socialist political values to social scientific inquiry.

3. What is the definition of *functionalism*?
   a. It is the study of the function of a social activity to determine the contribution that the activity makes to society as a whole.
   b. It is the study of the way people function in groups.
   c. It is the study of the way social institutions reproduce social systems.
   d. It was the conservative response to the social reform movement.

4. Structuration is considered to be a double process because
   a. social structure patterns human activity and is created by it.
   b. human societies are complex and often contradictory.
   c. human beings operate in both a personal and a social sphere.
   d. social structures are both biological and social.

5. Sociology can be considered a science because it
   a. uses systematic methods to study a phenomenon.
   b. uses systematic methods of theoretical thinking.
   c. involves the logical assessment of arguments.
   d. All of the above.

6. Who developed the idea of symbolic interactionism in human social life?
   a. Émile Durkheim
   b. Karl Marx
   c. Max Weber
   d. George Herbert Mead

7. According to Karl Marx, the most important changes that occurred in the modern period were tied to the development of
   a. democracy.
   b. socialism.
   c. historical materialism.
   d. capitalism.

8. Why is Émile Durkheim's study of suicide important to sociology?
   a. It introduced Durkheim's concept of social facts.
   b. It showed that suicide, seemingly the most individual of acts, is socially influenced. Suicide rates vary according to the social cohesion of groups.
   c. It showed that the meaning of suicide varies across social groups. It is not the same for Catholics as it is for Protestants.
   d. It started the field known as the sociology of death.

9. Which of the following are the stages in the sociological research process?
   a. Defining the problem / making the problem precise / reviewing the evidence / working out a design / carrying out research / interpreting the results / reporting the findings
   b. Defining the problem / reviewing the evidence / making the problem precise / working out a design / carrying out research / interpreting the results / reporting the findings
   c. Defining the problem / reviewing the evidence / making the problem precise / working out a design / interpreting the results / carrying out research / reporting the findings
   d. Making the problem precise / defining the problem / reviewing the evidence / working out a design / carrying out research / interpreting the results / reporting the findings

10. What is the standard deviation?
    a. A measure of the degree of concentration around the arithmetic mean
    b. A measure of the degree of dispersal, or range, of a set of figures
    c. The median divided by the mode
    d. The degree of variation in respect of group norms

11. What are the main steps that must be taken to administer a social survey?
    a. Making the problem precise enough to study, deciding whether to use fixed-choice or open-ended questions, and generating a representative sample
    b. Doing a pilot study, generating a representative sample of respondents, and calculating correlation coefficients
    c. Deciding whether to use fixed-choice or open-ended questions, doing a pilot study, and generating a representative sample of respondents
    d. Generating a representative sample of respondents, calculating correlation coefficients, and writing up the study

12. What are the main limitations of using documents in sociological research?

    a. They may be partial and difficult to interpret.

    b. They are not as useful as interviews with those who wrote them.

    c. They are quickly outdated by subsequent events.

    d. They do not lend themselves to statistical analysis.

13. All research begins with

    a. a hypothesis.

    b. conclusions.

    c. the research design.

    d. a research problem.

14. How does the text suggest sociologists can conduct good sociological research?

    a. By working in teams, sociologists are less likely to let personal bias influence their research.

    b. By asking subjects numerous questions, including trick questions, sociologists can make sure a subject is telling the truth.

    c. There is no standard for conducting sociological research.

    d. The best results can be obtained by making the questions posed as precise as possible and by gathering factual evidence before making a conclusion.

15. Which of the following research methods tests a hypothesis in a highly controlled environment?

    a. experiment

    b. survey

    c. sampling

    d. participant observation

Thinking Sociologically Exercises

1. Healthy older Americans often encounter exclusionary treatment when younger people assume that they are feeble-minded and thus overlook them for jobs they are fully capable of doing. How would each of the popular theoretical perspectives—functionalism, conflict theory, and symbolic interactionism—explain the dynamics of prejudice against the elderly?

2. Your text discusses the sociology of coffee, suggesting that the consumption of coffee is more than a simple product designed to quench a person's thirst and to help fend off drowsiness. Mention and adequately discuss **five** sociological features of coffee that clearly show its "sociological" nature.

3. Let's suppose the dropout rate in your local high school increased dramatically. Faced with such a serious problem, the board offers you a $500,000 grant to do a study to explain the sudden increase. Following the recommended study procedures outlined in your text, explain how you would go about doing your research. What might be some of the hypotheses to test in your study? How would you prove or disprove them?

4. Explain in some detail the advantages and disadvantages of doing documentary research. What will it yield that will be better than experimentation, surveys, and ethnographic field work? What are its limitations compared with those approaches?

Data Exercises

www.wwnorton.com/giddens
Keyword: Data1

In this chapter you read about some of the early sociological theorists who made important contributions to the development of sociology as a social science, and to our understanding of human behavior. The first data exercise will allow you to become more familiar with the important social theorists in this field, and get some practice using your sociological imagination. After completing this exercise you will understand how broader social forces shape individual experiences.

The Sociological Study of Culture

Know what culture consists of, and recognize how it differs from society.

The Development of Human Culture

Begin to understand how both biological and cultural factors influence our behavior. Learn the ideas of sociobiology and how others have tried to refute them by emphasizing cultural differences.

Disappearing World: Premodern Societies and Their Fate

Learn how societies have changed over time.

Societies in the Modern World

Recognize the factors that changed premodern societies, particularly how industrialization and colonialism influenced global development. Know the differences between the First World, the Second World, and the developing world (Third World) and how they developed.

The Impact of Globalization

Recognize the impact of globalization on your life and the lives of people around the world. Think about the impact of a growing global culture.

CHAPTER TWO

CULTURE AND SOCIETY

just eight years ago, the French president Jacques Chirac was visiting France's new National Library, where he reportedly viewed for the first time a computer mouse. Chirac expressed wonderment at the new technology (Cairncross, 1997). The United States at that time ranked first among major countries in terms of Internet servers; France was not even among the top twenty-five (Starrs, 1997).

France is no less modern than the United States. Why was it so reluctant to come online? Could it be that in 1997, as today, the Internet was dominated by the United States and was thus a powerful source for spreading American culture, along with the English language?

The unofficial language of the Internet is English. Nearly half of all Internet users worldwide are Americans (Nua Online, 2000), and one study (published in French) concluded that 82 percent of all Web sites are in English—even though 94 percent of the world's population speaks some other language (ISOC, 1997; Wallraff, 2000). The French are especially sensitive about the threat of American culture and the English language to their way of life. The French government spends $100 million a year promoting the country's language and culture (Jones, 1998) and has actively sought to curb the "invasion" of English words such as *software* and *computer*. Many French people resent what they call American "cultural imperialism," seen as a form of conquest—one of values and attitudes—and including such unwelcome imports as McDonald's restaurants. McDonald's, their high golden arches a visible symbol of American cultural domination, have even been attacked and burned down in France.

France is not alone in resisting the inroads of American culture. As American culture spreads around the world through film, television, and now the Internet, many people fear the erosion of their own cultures—even as they tune in to *The Simpsons*, sip Coke or Pepsi, and download music from the Web. Is modern technology an irresistible force that will eventually press the world's diverse cultures into a single mold? Or will it permit local cultures to flourish? These are some of the questions we explore in this chapter.

First, however, we look at what culture is and its role in encouraging conformity to shared ways of thinking and acting. We then consider the early development of human culture, emphasizing features that distinguish human behavior from that of other species. After assessing the role of biology in shaping human behavior, we examine the different aspects of culture that make it essential for human society. This leads to a discussion of cultural diversity, examining not only the cultural variations across different societies but also the cultural variations within a society such as the United States.

Cultural variations among human beings are linked to differing types of society, and we will compare and contrast the main forms of society found in history. The point of doing this is to tie together closely the two aspects of human social existence—the different cultural values and products that human beings have developed and the contrasting types of society in which such cultural development has occurred. Too often, culture is discussed separately from society as though the two were disconnected, whereas in fact, as we've already emphasized, they are closely meshed. Throughout the chapter, we will concentrate on how social change has affected cultural development. One instance of this is the impact of technology and globalization on the many cultures of the world, a topic we will explore in the conclusion to this chapter.

The Sociological Study of Culture

The sociological study of culture began with Durkheim in the nineteenth century and soon became the basis of *anthropology*, a social science specifically focused on the study of cultural differences and similarities among the world's many peoples. The work of these early social scientists assumed that "primitive" cultures were inferior, lagging far behind modern European "civilization." However, sociologists and anthropologists now recognize that there are many different cultures, each with its own distinctive characteristics. The task of social science is to understand this cultural diversity, which is best done by avoiding value judgments.

What Is Culture?

Culture consists of the values the members of a given group hold, the languages they speak, the symbols they revere, the norms they follow, and the material goods they create, from tools to clothing. Some elements of culture, especially the beliefs and expectations people have about each other and the world they inhabit, are a component of all social relations. **Values** are abstract ideals. For example, monogamy—being faithful to a single marriage partner—is a prominent value in most Western societies. In other cultures, on the other hand, a person may be permitted to have several wives or husbands simultaneously. **Norms** are definite principles or rules people are expected to observe; they represent the dos and don'ts of social life. Norms of behavior in marriage include, for example, how husbands and wives are supposed to behave toward their in-laws. In some societies, they are expected to develop a close relationship with parents-in-law; in others, they keep a clear distance from each other.

Norms, like the values they reflect, vary widely across cultures. Among most Americans, for example, one norm calls for direct eye contact between persons engaged in conversation; completely averting one's eyes is usually interpreted as a sign of weakness or rudeness. Yet, among the Navajo, a cultural norm calls for averting one's eyes as a sign of respect. Direct eye contact, particularly between strangers, is seen as violating a norm of politeness and consequently as insulting. When a Navajo and a Western tourist encounter one another for the first time, the Navajo's cultural norm calls for averting the eyes, while the tourist's cultural norm calls for direct eye contact. The result is likely to be a misunderstanding: The Navajo may see the tourist as rude and vulgar, while the tourist may see the Navajo as disrespectful or deceptive. Such cultural misunderstandings may lead to unfair generalizations and stereotypes and even promote outright hostility. Values and norms work together to shape how members of a culture behave within their surroundings.

Finally, **material goods** refer to the physical objects that a society creates, which influence the ways in which people live. They include the goods we consume, from the clothes we wear to the cars we drive to the houses we live in; the tools and technologies we use to make those goods, from sewing machines to computerized factories; and the towns and cities that we build as places in which to live and work. A central aspect of a society's material culture is technology.

Today material culture is rapidly becoming globalized, thanks in large part to modern information technology such as the computer and the Internet. As noted at the beginning of this chapter, the United States has been in the forefront of this technological revolution, although most other industrial countries are rapidly catching up. In fact, it no longer makes sense to speak of an exclusively "U.S. technology" any more than it makes sense to speak of a U.S. car. The "world car," with parts manufactured across the planet in a global assembly line, embodies technology developed in Japan, the United States, and Europe. Automobiles have increasingly come to resemble each other, so that it is difficult to distinguish a car made in Japan from one made in Detroit.

When we use the term *culture* in ordinary daily conversation, we often think of the higher things of the mind—art, literature, music, dance. As sociologists employ it, the concept includes these activities but also far more. Culture refers to the ways of life of the individual members or groups within a society: how they dress, their marriage customs and family life, their patterns of work, their religious ceremonies, and their leisure pursuits. The concept also covers the goods they create and the goods that become meaningful for them—bows and arrows, plows, factories and machines, computers, books, dwellings. We should think of culture as a "design for living" or "tool kit" of practices, knowledge, and symbols acquired—as we shall see later—through learning rather than by instinct (Kluckhohn, 1949; Swidler, 1986).

How might we describe American culture? It involves, first, a particular range of values shared by many, if not all, Americans—such as the belief in the merits of individual achievement or in equality of opportunity. Second, these values are connected to specific norms: For example, it is usually expected that people will work hard in order to achieve occupational success (Parsons, 1964; Bellah et al., 1985). Third, it involves the use of material artifacts created mostly through modern industrial technology, such as cars, mass-produced food, clothing, and so forth.

Values and norms vary enormously across cultures. Some cultures value individualism highly, whereas others place great emphasis on shared needs. A simple example makes this clear. Most pupils in the United States would be outraged to find another student cheating on an examination. In the United States, copying from someone else's paper goes against core values of individual achievement, equality of opportunity, hard work, and respect for the rules. Russian students, however, might be puzzled by this sense of outrage among their American peers. Helping each other to pass an examination reflects the value Russians place on equality and on collective problem solving in the face of authority. Think of your own reac-

tion to this example. What does it say about the values of your society?

Even within one society or community, values may conflict: Some groups or individuals might value traditional religious beliefs, whereas others might favor progress and science. Some people might prefer material comfort and success, whereas others might favor simplicity and a quiet life. In our changing age—filled with the global movement of people, ideas, goods, and information—it is not surprising that we encounter instances of cultural values in conflict. Sociological research suggests that such conflicts foster a sense of frustration and isolation in American society (Bellah et al., 1985).

Norms, like the values they reflect, also change over time. Between 1964 and 1999, for example, smoking in the United States declined by over one third (National Center for Health Statistics, 2000). Beginning in 1964, with the U.S. Surgeon General's report "Smoking and Health," which reported definitive medical evidence linking smoking with a large number of serious health problems, the U.S. government waged a highly effective campaign to discourage people from smoking. A strong social norm favoring smoking—once associated with independence, sex appeal, and glamour—has increasingly given way to an equally strong antismoking social norm that depicts smoking as unhealthful, unattractive, and selfish. Today, the percentage of American adults who smoke is only 25 percent, half the rate of 1964, when the

Social norms change over time. When medical evidence linked smoking with serious health problems, a strong social norm in the United States favoring smoking turned toward a strong antismoking social norm.

The uniforms worn by these Tokyo schoolboys reflect the traditional Japanese value of conformity. A government commission proposed that holding on to such traditional values would prevent the Japanese people from aiming for the individual goals they believe will be necessary for success in the twenty-first century.

Surgeon General's Report was issued (U.S. Surgeon General's Office, 2000).

Many of our everyday behaviors and habits are grounded in cultural norms. Movements, gestures, and expressions are strongly influenced by cultural factors. A clear example of this can be seen in the way people smile—particularly in public contexts—across different cultures.

Among the Inuit (Eskimos) of Greenland, for example, one does not find the strong tradition of public smiling that exists in many areas of Western Europe and North America. This does not mean that the Inuit are cold or unfriendly; it is simply not their common practice to smile at or exchange pleasantries with strangers. As the service industry has expanded in Greenland in recent years, however, some employers have made efforts to instill smiling as a cultural value in the belief that smiling and expressing "polite" attitudes toward customers are essential to competitive business practices. Clients who are met with smiles and told to "Have a nice day" are more likely to become repeat customers. In many supermarkets in Greenland, shop assistants are now shown training videos on friendly service techniques; the staff at some have even been sent abroad on training courses. The opening of fast-food restaurants like McDonald's in Greenland has introduced Western-style service approaches for the first time.

McDonald's employees have been taught to greet customers, introduce themselves, and smile frequently. Initially these requirements were met with some discomfort by staff who found the style insincere and artificial. Over time, however, the idea of public smiling—at least in the workplace—has become more accepted.

Culture and Society

"Culture" can be distinguished from "society," but these notions are closely connected. A **society** is a *system of interrelationships* that connects individuals together. No culture could exist without a society; and, equally, no society could exist without culture. Without culture, we would not be human at all, in the sense in which we usually understand that term. We would have no language in which to express ourselves, no sense of self-consciousness, and our ability to think or reason would be severely limited.

Culture also serves as a society's glue, because culture is an important source of conformity, since it provides ready-made ways of thinking and acting for its members. For example, when you say that you subscribe to a particular value, such as formal learning, you are probably voicing the beliefs of your family members, friends, teachers, or others who are significant in your life. When you choose a word to describe some personal experience, that word acquires its meaning in a language you learned from others. When you buy a seemingly unique article of clothing to express your individuality, that garment was very likely created by the design department of a global manufacturer that carefully studied the current tastes of consumers and then ordered the mass production of your "unique" garment.

Cultures differ, however, in how much they value conformity. Research based on surveys of more than one hundred thousand adults in over sixty countries shows that Japanese culture lies at one extreme in terms of valuing conformity (Hofstede, 1997), while at the other extreme lies American culture, one of the least conformist, ranking among the world's highest in cherishing individualism.

American high school and college students often see themselves as especially nonconformist. Like the body piercers of today, the hippies of the 1960s and the punks of the 1980s all sported distinctive clothing styles, haircuts, and other forms of bodily adornment. Yet how individualistic are they? Are young people with dyed hair or nose rings or studs in their tongues or tattoos really acting independently? Or are their styles perhaps as much the "uniforms" of their group as are navy blue suits or basic black among conservative business people? There is an aspect of conformity to their behavior—conformity to their own group.

Since some degree of conformity to norms is necessary for any society to exist, one of the key challenges for all cultures is to instill in people a willingness to conform. This is accomplished in two ways (Parsons, 1964). First, members of all cultures learn the norms of their culture. While this occurs throughout one's life, the most crucial learning occurs during childhood, and parents play a key role. When learning is successful, the norms are so thoroughly ingrained that they become unquestioned ways of thinking and acting; they come to appear "normal." (Note the similarity between the words *norm* and *normal*.)

When the learning of social norms falls short of what is deemed desirable by a society—that is, when a person fails to adequately conform to a culture's norms—a second way of instilling cultural conformity comes into play: *social control*. Social control often involves punishing rule breaking. Punishment includes such informal behavior as rebuking friends for minor breaches of etiquette, gossiping behind their backs, or ostracizing them from the group. Official, formal forms of discipline might range from parking tickets to imprisonment (Foucault, 1979). Émile Durkheim, one of the founders of sociology (introduced in Chapter 1), argued that punishment serves not only to help guarantee conformity among those who would violate a culture's norms and values, but also to vividly remind others what the norms and values are.

The Development of Human Culture

Human culture and human biology are closely intertwined. Understanding how culture is related to the physical evolution of the human species can help us better understand the central role that culture plays in shaping our lives.

Early Human Culture: Adaptation to Physical Environment

Given the archaeological evidence, as well as knowledge of the close similarities in blood chemistry and genetics between chimpanzees and humans, scientists believe that the first humans evolved from apelike creatures on the African continent some 4 million years ago. The first evidence of human-like culture dates back only 2 million years. In these early cultures, early humans fashioned stone tools, derived sustenance by hunting animals and gathering nuts and berries, harnessed the use of fire, and established a highly cooperative way of life. Because early humans planned their hunts, they must also have had some ability for abstract thought.

Members of a 1960s commune pose together for a group portrait (*left*). Punks gather on the street in 1989 (*right*). Though their distinctive styles set them apart from mainstream society, these people are not as nonconformist as they may think they are. Both the hippies and the punks pictured above conform to the norms of their respective social groups.

The Amish and Cell Phones

[***]

Amish settlements have become a cliché for refusing technology. Tens of thousands of people wear identical, plain, homemade clothing, cultivate their rich fields with horse-drawn machinery, and live in houses lacking that basic modern spirit called electricity. But the Amish do use such 20th-century consumer technologies as disposable diapers, in-line skates, and gas barbecue grills. Some might call this combination paradoxical, even contradictory. But it could also be called sophisticated, because the Amish have an elaborate system by which they evaluate the tools they use; their tentative, at times reluctant use of technology is more complex than a simple rejection or a whole-hearted embrace. What if modern Americans could possibly agree upon criteria for acceptance, as the Amish have? Might we find better ways to wield technological power, other than simply unleashing it and seeing what happens? What can we learn from a culture that habitually negotiates the rules for new tools?

Last summer, armed with these questions and in the company of an acquaintance with Amish contacts, I traveled around the countryside of Lancaster County, Pennsylvania. [***] At one farm we passed, a woman was sitting a hundred yards from her house on the edge of a kitchen garden. She wore the traditional garb of the conservative Old Order—a long, unadorned dress sheathed by an apron, her hair covered by a prayer bonnet. She was sitting in the middle of the garden, alone, the very image of technology-free simplicity. But she was holding her hand up to her ear. She appeared to be intent on something, strangely engaged.

"Whenever you see an Amish woman sitting in the field like that," my guide said, "she's probably talking on a cell phone."

"It's a controversy in the making," he continued. A rather large one, it turns out—yet part of the continuum of determining whether a particular technology belongs in Amish life. They've adopted horses, kerosene lamps, and propane refrigerators; should they add cell phones?

Collective negotiations over the use of telephones have ignited intense controversies in the Amish community since the beginning of the 20th century. In fact, a dispute over the role of the phone was the principal issue behind the 1920s division of the Amish church, wherein one-fifth of the membership broke away to form their own church.

Eventually, certain Amish communities accepted the telephone for its aid in summoning doctors and veterinarians, and in calling suppliers. But even these Amish did not allow the telephone into the home. Rather, they required that phones be used communally. Typically, a neighborhood of two or three extended families shares a telephone housed in a wooden shanty, located either at the intersection of several fields or at the end of a common lane. These structures look like small bus shelters or privies; indeed, some phones are in outhouses. Sometimes the telephone shanties have answering machines in them. (After all, who wants to wait in the privy on the off chance someone will call?)

The first Amish person I contacted, I reached by answering machine. He was a woodworker who, unlike some of his brethren, occasionally talked to outsiders. I left a message on his phone, which I later learned was located in a shanty in his neighbor's pasture. The next day the man, whom I'll call Amos, returned my call. We agreed to meet at his farmstead a few days later.

I couldn't help thinking it was awfully complicated to have a phone you used only for calling back—from a booth in a meadow. Why not make life easier and just put one in the house?

"What would that lead to?" another Amish man asked me. "We don't want to be the kind of people who will interrupt a conversation at home to answer a telephone. It's not just how you use the technology that concerns us. We're also concerned about what kind of person you become when you use it."

[***]

I asked another Amish workshop owner whom I'll call Caleb what he thought about technology. He pulled some papers out of a file cabinet, handed them to me, and said, "I share some of this fellow's opinions," pointing to a magazine interview with virtual reality pioneer Jaron Lanier. Asked for an opinion he shared with the dreadlocked-and-dashikied Jaron, he replied, "I agree with his statement that you can't design foolproof machines, because fools are so clever."

Caleb also discussed the Amish resistance to becoming "modern." They're not worried about becoming people without religion or people who use lots of technology, he explained; rather, the Amish fear assimilating the far more dangerous ideas that "progress" and new technologies are usually beneficial, that individuality is a precious value, that the goal of life is to "get ahead." This mind-set, not specific technologies, is what the Amish most object to.

"The thing I noticed about the telephone is the way it invades who you are," Caleb said. "We're all losing who we are because of the telephone and other machines—not just the Amish."

[***]

Donald Kraybill, who is also provost of Messiah College, on the outskirts of Amish country, believes taboos about telephones are "a symbolic way of keeping the technology at a distance and making it your servant, rather than the other way around."

[***]

It's a pretty safe prediction that when the bishops get around to their formal ruling, cell phones will not be deemed appropriate for personal use. In the 1910s, when the telephone was only begin-

ning to change the world at large, the Old Order Amish recognized that the caller at the other end of the line was an interloper, someone who presumed to take precedence over the family's normal, sacred communications. Keeping the telephone in an unheated shanty in a field, or even an outhouse, was keeping the phone in its proper place.

[***] I appreciate the deliberation put into their decision. In fact, similar reflection might highlight conflicts between our own practices and values. How often do we interrupt a conversation with someone who is physically present in order to answer the telephone? Is the family meal enhanced by a beeper? Who exactly is benefiting from call waiting? Is automated voicemail a dark hint about the way our institutions value human time and life? Can pagers and cell phones that vibrate instead of ring solve the problem? Does the enjoyment of virtual communities by growing numbers of people enhance or erode citizen participation in the civic life of geographic communities?

[***]

I never expected the Amish to provide precise philosophical yardsticks that could guide the use of technological power. What drew me in was their long conversation with their tools. We technology-enmeshed "English" don't have much of this sort of discussion. And yet we'll need many such conversations, because a modern heterogeneous society is going to have different values, different trade-offs, and different discourses. It's time we start talking about the most important influence on our lives today.

I came away from my journey with a question to contribute to these conversations: If we decided that community came first, how would we use our tools differently?

SOURCE: Howard Rheingold, "Look Who's Talking," *Wired* 7.01 (Jan. 1999).

Questions

- Do you think cell phones have drastically changed life in Amish communities?
- Why do the Amish believe that telephones change the people that use them?
- How could the use of cellular technology make people more isolated?

Culture enabled early humans to compensate for their physical limitations, such as lack of claws, sharp teeth, and running speed, relative to other animals (Deacon, 1998). In particular, culture freed humans from dependence on the instinctual and genetically determined set of responses to the environment characteristic of other species. The larger, more complex human brain permitted a greater degree of adaptive learning in dealing with major environmental changes such as the Ice Age. For example, humans figured out how to build fires and sew clothing for warmth. Through greater flexibility, humans were able to survive unpredictable challenges in their surroundings and shape the world with their ideas and their tools. In a mere instant of geological time, we became the dominant species on the planet.

Yet early humans were closely tied to their physical environment, since they still lacked the technological ability to modify their immediate surroundings significantly (Harris, 1975, 1978, 1980; Bennett, 1976). Their ability to secure food and make clothing and shelter depended largely on the physical resources that were close at hand. Cultures in different environments varied widely as a result of adaptations by which people fashioned their cultures to be suitable to specific geographic and climatic conditions. For example, the cultures developed by desert dwellers, where water and food were scarce, differed significantly from the cultures that developed in rain forests, where such natural resources abounded. Human inventiveness spawned a rich tapestry of cultures around the world. As you will see at the conclusion of this chapter, however, modern technology and other forces of globalization pose both challenges and opportunities for future global cultural diversity.

Nature or Nurture?

Because humans evolved as a part of the world of nature, it would seem logical to assume that human thinking and behavior are the result of biology and evolution. In fact, one of the oldest controversies in the social sciences is the "nature/nurture" debate: Are we shaped by our biology, or are we products of learning through life's experiences, that is, of "nurture"? Biologists and some psychologists emphasize biological factors in explaining human thinking and behavior. Sociologists, not surprisingly, stress the role of learning and culture. They are also likely to argue that since human beings are capable of making conscious choices, neither biology nor culture wholly determines human behavior.

The "nature/nurture" debate has raged for more than a century, opinion swinging first one way and then the other. For example, in the 1930s and 1940s, many social scientists tended to focus on biological factors, with some researchers seeking (unsuccessfully), for example, to prove that a person's physique determined his or her personality. In the 1960s and 1970s, scholars in different fields emphasized culture. For example, social psychologists argued that even the most severe forms of mental illness were the result of the labels that society attaches to unusual behavior rather than of biochemical processes (Scheff, 1966). Today, partly because of new understandings in genetics and brain neurophysiology, the pendulum is again swinging toward the side of biology.

The resurgence of biological explanations for human behavior began more than twenty-five years ago, when the evolutionary biologist Edward O. Wilson of Harvard University published *Sociobiology: The New Synthesis* (1975). The term **sociobiology** refers to the application of biological principles to explain the social activities of animals, including human beings. Using studies of insects and other social creatures, Wilson argued that genes influence not only physical traits, but behavior as well. For instance, some species of animals engage in elaborate courtship rituals, whereby sexual union and reproduction are achieved. Human courtship and sexual behavior, according to sociobiologists, generally involve similar rituals, based also on inborn characteristics. In most species, to take a second example, males are larger and more aggressive than females and tend to dominate the "weaker sex." Some suggest that genetic factors explain why, in all human societies that we know of, men tend to hold positions of greater authority than women.

One way in which sociobiologists have tried to illuminate the relations between the sexes is by means of the idea of "reproductive strategy." A reproductive strategy is a pattern of behavior, arrived at through evolutionary selection, that favors the chances of survival of offspring. The female body has a larger investment in its reproductive cells than the male—a fertilized egg takes nine months to develop. Thus, according to sociobiologists, women will not squander that investment and are not driven to have sexual relations with many partners; their overriding aim is the care and protection of children. Men, on the other hand, tend toward promiscuity. Their wish to have sex with many partners is sound strategy from the point of view of the species; to carry out their mission, which is to maximize the possibility of impregnation, they move from one partner to the next. In this way, it has been suggested, we can explain differences in sexual behavior and attitudes between men and women.

Sociobiologists do not argue that our genes determine 100 percent of our behavior. For example, they note that depending on the circumstances, men can choose to act in nonaggressive ways. Yet even though this argument would seem to open up the field of sociobiology to culture as an additional explanatory factor in describing human behavior, social scientists have roundly condemned sociobiology for claiming that a propensity for particular behaviors such as violence, is somehow "genetically programmed" into our brains ("Seville Statement on Violence," 1990).

How Nature and Nurture Interact

Most sociologists today would acknowledge a role for nature in determining attitudes and behavior, but with strong qualifications. For example, no one questions that newborn babies come into the world with certain basic human reflexes, such as the automatic ability to "root" for the mother's nipple without being taught to do so. There is also evidence that babies are born with the ability to recognize faces: Babies a few minutes old turn their heads in response to patterns that resemble human faces but not in response to other patterns (Johnson and Morton, 1991; Cosmides and Tooby, 1997). But it is a large leap to conclude that because babies are born with basic reflexes, the behavior of adults is governed by **instincts,** inborn, biologically fixed patterns of action found in all cultures.

Sociologists no longer pose the question as one of nature *or* nurture. Instead they ask how nature and nurture interact to produce human behavior. But their main concern is with how our different ways of thinking and acting are learned in interactions with family, friends, schools, television, and every other facet of the social environment. For example, sociologists argue that it's not some inborn biological disposition that makes American males feel attracted to a *particular* type of woman. Rather, it is the exposure they've had throughout their lives to tens of thousands of magazine ads, TV commercials, and film stars that emphasize specific cultural standards of female beauty.

Early child rearing is especially relevant to this kind of learning. Human babies have a large brain, requiring birth relatively early in their fetal development, before their heads have grown too large to pass through the birth canal. As a result, human babies are totally unequipped for survival on their own, compared with the young of other species, and must spend a number of years in the care of adults. This need, in turn, fosters a lengthy period of learning, during which the child is taught its society's culture.

Because humans think and act in so many different ways, sociologists do not believe that "biology is destiny." If biology were all-important, we would expect all cultures to be highly similar, if not identical. Yet this is hardly the case. For example, pork is forbidden to religious Jews and Muslims, but it is a dietary staple in China. Americans are likely to greet one another with a casual "How are you?" On the other hand, the Yanomamö, a tribe that lives in the rain forests of Venezuela

and Brazil, greet each other with an exchange of gifts and would find the casual American greeting an insult.

This is not to say that human cultures have nothing in common. Surveys of thousands of different cultures have concluded that all known human cultures have such common characteristics as language, forms of emotional expression, rules that tell adults how to raise children or engage in sexual behavior, and even standards of beauty (Brown, 1991). But there is enormous variety in exactly *how* these common characteristics play themselves out.

All cultures provide for childhood socialization, but what and how children are taught vary greatly from culture to culture. An American child learns the multiplication tables from a classroom teacher, while a child born in the forests of Borneo learns to hunt with older members of the tribe. All cultures have standards of beauty and ornamentation, but what is regarded as beautiful in one culture may be seen as ugly in another (Elias, 1987; Elias and Dunning, 1987; Foucault, 1988).

Cultural Diversity

The study of cultural differences highlights the importance of cultural learning as an influence on our behavior. However, not only cultural beliefs vary across cultures; human behavior and practices also vary widely from culture to culture and often contrast radically with what people from Western societies consider "normal." For example, in the modern West, we regard the deliberate killing of infants or young children as one of the worst of all crimes. Yet in traditional Chinese culture, female children were sometimes strangled at birth because a daughter was regarded as a liability rather than an asset to the family. In the West, we eat oysters but we do not eat kittens or puppies, both of which are regarded as delicacies in some parts of the world. Jews and Muslims don't eat pork, whereas Hindus eat pork but avoid beef. Westerners regard kissing as a normal part of sexual behavior, but in other cultures the practice is either unknown or regarded as disgusting. All these different kinds of behavior are aspects of broad cultural differences that distinguish societies from one another.

SUBCULTURES

Small societies tend to be culturally uniform, but industrialized societies are themselves culturally diverse or multicultural, involving numerous different **subcultures.** As you will discover in the discussion of global migration in Chapter 10, processes such as slavery, colonialism, war, migration, and contemporary globalization have led to populations dispersing across borders and settling in new areas. This, in turn,

Decoding the New Cues in Online Society

A sociologist among geeks and a geek among sociologists, Danah Boyd has 278 friends who link her to 1.1 million others.

So says Friendster.com, whose millions of members have transformed it from a dating site into a free-for-all of connectedness where new social rules are born of necessity. A 25-year-old graduate student at the University of California at Berkeley, Ms. Boyd studies Friendster, hovering above the fray with a Web log called Connected Selves (www.zephoria.org/snt) and interviewing Friendster users. Her irrepressible observations have made her a social-network guru for the programmers and venture capitalists who swarm around Friendster and its competitors.

[***]

Ms. Boyd explained Friendster this way: "It allows you to purposely say who the people in your world are and to allow them to see each other, through a connection of you." An individual registered at Friendster has a home page with photos, a brief profile and photos of people to whom they have agreed to link. That person can then browse his or her network or search it for dates or activity partners.

Ms. Boyd says that the real world has a set of properties, which she calls architectures. With its deceptively simple set of features, her thinking goes, Friendster bends or replaces all of the real-world architectures.

For instance, when two people speak to each other, they assume their conversation is fleeting, but e-mail and instant messaging, by making that conversation persistent, offer a new architecture. When two people greet each other on the street, neither can see (nor hope to grasp) the range of the other's social network. For that matter, no individual can see information about his or her own social network: who knows whom, and how.

[***] The basic idea behind Friendster and other social networking sites is not new. Neither is the technology, which is based on a business process patent from a 1997 site called SixDegrees.com that failed because too few people were online at the time.

[***]

Ms. Boyd has found the site populated by a variety of subcultures: a large contingent of gay men from New York City, the Bay Area's Burning Man scene, ravers in Baltimore. Porn queens and venture capitalists share the site with neo-Nazis

and garden-variety hipsters. Most users are in their 20s and 30s. Many are overseas, particularly in Asia.

Bringing all those worlds together is not without its perils. "What social software like Friendster does is collapse our networks in ways we're not used to," Ms. Boyd said.

Devon Lake, 25, a high school teacher, discovered that this fall when she was bombarded with requests from former students to accept them into her Friendster circle, which she uses to keep in touch with her friends from Burning Man, the annual primal gathering in the Nevada desert. The potential costs of putting one part of her network in contact with the other part were too high, so she rebuffed her students and cleaned up her profile by removing anything that could be interpreted as a reference to drugs. "I'm a young teacher, so drawing that line is already a careful balancing act," Ms. Lake said. "It made me feel on my guard about what I posted to the site."

[***]

A lively speaker sometimes inclined to pink hair, Ms. Boyd is part of a cohort of young scholars who are trying to come up with ways to describe these new social behaviors in the online environments in which they have grown up. She and her peers "are talking about this from an inside, embedded perspective," said Genevieve Bell, an anthropologist at Intel Research who was a co-director of Ms. Boyd's master's thesis at M.I.T. "One of the challenges for them is, how do they analyze this thing they have grown up inside of?"

Ms. Boyd grew in up in Lancaster, Pa., and was introduced to far-flung virtual communities in the early 1990s by her younger brother. Soon afterward, their mother wisely signed up for two Compuserve accounts. "It gave me an opportunity to talk to people who were far more like me than anybody I knew in real life," Ms. Boyd said.

She said she comes to her research through experiences as a perpetual outsider. "I didn't grow up in an elite community," she said. "I was the daughter of a single mother. I grew up queer in a rural environment. I grew up as a woman in computer science. I grew up constantly negotiating these spaces where they didn't exactly welcome me with open arms."

After studying computer science as an undergraduate at Brown, she turned to the social side of things at M.I.T., studying at the Media Lab and producing a project that visualized people's e-mail networks.

Taking a year off from school, Ms. Boyd found herself in the Bay Area, hanging out with many of the people who were developing Friendster and other social-network sites. She began a blog to document what she saw; her critiques became useful; people began asking her—and hiring her—to do more.

The chief executive of one social-networking site, tribe.net, Mark Pincus, has sought her advice because she is involved in some of the groups to which his site tries to appeal. "Danah's this researcher, but she also lives the whole thing—the Burning Man scene, the rave scene, the techno music scene," he said.

Her academic supervisors are envious of her advantage. "I look at cyberspace the way a deep-sea diver looks at the sea: through a glass plate," said Ms. Boyd's academic adviser, Peter Lyman, a professor at Berkeley's School of Information Management and Systems. "She is out there swimming in it."

[***]

SOURCE: Michael Erard, "Decoding the New Cues in Online Society," *New York Times,* 27 November, 2003.

Reggae Music

When those knowledgeable about popular music listen to a song, they can often pick out the stylistic influences that helped shape it. Each musical style, after all, represents a unique way of combining rhythm, melody, harmony, and lyrics. And though it doesn't take a genius to notice the differences among grunge, hard rock, techno, and hip-hop, musicians

often combine a number of styles in composing songs. Identifying the components of these combinations can be difficult. But for sociologists of culture, the effort is often rewarding. Different musical styles tend to emerge from different social groups, and studying how styles combine and fuse is a good way to chart the cultural contacts between groups.

Some sociologists of culture have turned their attention to reggae music because it exemplifies the process whereby contacts between social groups result in the creation of new musical forms. Reggae's roots can be traced to West Africa. In the seventeenth century, large numbers of West Africans were enslaved by the British and brought by ship to work in the sugarcane fields of the West Indies. Although the British attempted to prevent slaves from playing traditional African music, for fear it would serve as a rallying cry to revolt, the slaves managed to keep alive the tradition of African drumming, sometimes by integrating it with the European musical styles imposed by the slave owners. In Jamaica, the drumming of one group of slaves, the Burru, was openly tolerated by slaveholders because it helped meter the pace of work.

has led to the emergence of societies that are cultural composites, meaning that the population is made up of a number of groups from diverse cultural and linguistic backgrounds. In modern cities, for example, many subcultural communities live side by side. For example, over ninety different cultural groups can be found in New York City today.

Subcultures do not refer only to people from different cultural backgrounds, or who speak different languages, within a larger society. They concern any segments of the population that are distinguishable from the rest of society by their cultural patterns. Subcultures are very broad in scope and might include Goths, computer hackers, hippies, Rastafarians, and fans of hip-hop. Some people might identify themselves clearly with a particular subculture, whereas others might move fluidly among a number of different ones.

Culture plays an important role in perpetuating the values and norms of a society, yet it also offers important opportunities for creativity and change. Subcultures and countercultures—

groups that largely reject the prevailing values and norms of society—can promote views that represent alternatives to the dominant culture. Social movements or groups of people sharing common lifestyles are powerful forces of change within societies. In this way, subcultures allow freedom for people to express and act on their opinions, hopes, and beliefs.

U.S. schoolchildren are frequently taught that the United States is a vast melting pot, into which various subcultures are assimilated. **Assimilation** is the process by which different cultures are absorbed into a single mainstream culture. Although it is true that virtually all peoples living in the United States take on many common cultural characteristics, many groups strive to retain some subcultural identity. In fact, identification based on race or country of origin in the United States persists and even grows, particularly among African Americans and immigrants from Asia, Mexico, and Latin America (Totti, 1987).

Given the immense cultural diversity and number of subcultures in the United States, a more appropriate metaphor than

called themselves "Rastafarians." The Rastafarian cult soon merged with the Burru, and Rastafarian music came to combine Burru styles of drumming with biblical themes of oppression and liberation. In the 1950s, West Indian musicians began mixing Rastafarian rhythms and lyrics with elements of American jazz and black rhythm and blues. These combinations eventually developed into "ska" music, and then, in the late 1960s, into reggae, with its relatively slow beat, its emphasis on the bass, and its stories of urban deprivation and of the power of collective social consciousness. Many reggae artists, such as Bob Marley, became commercial successes, and by the 1970s, people the world over were listening to reggae music. In the 1980s, reggae was first fused with hip-hop (or rap) to produce new sounds, as can be heard today in the dance hall music of the Jamaican rapper Sean Paul.

The history of reggae is thus the history of contact between different social groups and of the meanings—political, spiritual, and personal—that those groups expressed through their music. Globalization has intensified these contacts. It is now possible for a young musician in Scandinavia, for example, to grow up listening to music produced by men and women in the ghettos of Los Angeles and to be deeply influenced as well by, say, a mariachi performance broadcast live via satellite from Mexico City. If the number of contacts between groups is an important determinant of the pace of musical evolution, we can predict that a veritable profusion of new styles will flourish in the coming years as the process of globalization continues to unfold.

Slavery was finally abolished in Jamaica in 1834, but the tradition of Burru drumming continued, even as many Burru men migrated from rural areas to the slums of Kingston.

It was in these slums that a new religious cult began to emerge—one that would prove crucial for the development of reggae. In 1930, a man who took the title Haile Selassie ("Power of the Trinity") was crowned emperor of the African country of Ethiopia. While opponents of European colonialism throughout the world cheered his accession to the throne, a number of people in the West Indies came to believe that Haile Selassie was a god, sent to earth to lead the oppressed of Africa to freedom. Haile Selassie's original name was Ras Tafari Makonnen, and the West Indians who worshiped him

the assimilationist "melting pot" might be the culturally diverse "salad bowl," in which all the various ingredients, though mixed together, retain some of their original flavor and integrity, contributing to the richness of the salad as a whole. This viewpoint, termed **multiculturalism,** calls for respecting cultural diversity and promoting equality of different cultures. Adherents to multiculturalism acknowledge that certain central cultural values are shared by most people in a society but also that certain important differences deserve to be preserved (Anzaldua, 1990).

CULTURAL IDENTITY AND ETHNOCENTRISM

Every culture displays its own unique patterns of behavior, which seem alien to people from other cultural backgrounds. If you have traveled abroad, you are probably familiar with the sensation that can result when you find yourself in a new culture. Aspects of daily life that you unconsciously take for granted in your own culture may not be part of everyday life in other parts of the world. Even in countries that share the same language, you might find their everyday habits, customs, and behaviors to be quite different. The expression "culture shock" is an apt one! Often people feel disoriented when they become immersed in a new culture. This is because they have lost the familiar reference points that help them understand the world around them and have not yet learned how to navigate in the new culture.

A culture must be studied in terms of its own meanings and values—a key presupposition of sociology. Sociologists endeavor as far as possible to avoid **ethnocentrism,** which is judging other cultures in terms of the standards of one's own. Since human cultures vary so widely, it is not surprising that people belonging to one culture frequently find it difficult to sympathize with the ideas or behavior of those from a different culture. In studying and practicing sociology, we must remove our own cultural blinders in order to see the ways of life of different peoples in an unbiased light. The practice of judging a society by its own standards is called **cultural relativism.**

Applying cultural relativism—that is, suspending your own deeply held cultural beliefs and examining a situation according to the standards of another culture—can be fraught with uncertainty and challenge. Not only can it be hard to see things from a completely different point of view, but sometimes troubling questions are raised. Does cultural relativism mean that all customs and behavior are equally legitimate? Are there any universal standards to which all humans should adhere? Consider, for example, the ritual acts of what opponents have called "genital mutilation" practiced in some societies. Numerous young girls in certain African, Asian, and Middle Eastern cultures undergo clitoridectomies. This is a painful cultural ritual in which the clitoris and sometimes all or part of the vaginal labia of young girls are removed with a knife or a sharpened stone and the two sides of the vulva are partly sewn together as a means of controlling sexual activity and increasing the sexual pleasure of the man.

In cultures where clitoridectomies have been practiced for generations, they are regarded as normal, even expected practice. A study of two thousand men and women in two Nigerian communities found that nine out of ten women interviewed had undergone clitoridectomies in childhood and that the large majority favored the procedure for their own daughters, primarily for cultural reasons. Yet a significant minority believed that the practice should be stopped (Ebomoyi, 1987). Clitoridectomies are regarded with abhorrence by most people from other cultures and by a growing number of women in the cultures where they are practiced (El Dareer, 1982; Lightfoot-Klein, 1989; Johnson-Odim, 1991). These differences in views can result in a clash of cultural values, especially when people from cultures where clitoridectomies are common migrate to countries where the practice is actually illegal.

France is an example. France has a large North African immigrant population, in which many African mothers arrange for traditional clitoridectomies to be performed on their daughters. Some of these women have been tried and convicted under French law for mutilating their daughters. These African mothers have argued that they were only engaging in the same cultural practice that their own mothers had performed on them, that their grandmothers had performed on their mothers, and so on. They complain that the French are ethnocentric, judging traditional African rituals by French customs. Feminists from Africa and the Middle East, while themselves strongly opposed to clitoridectomies, have been critical of Europeans and Americans who sensationalize the practice by calling it "backward" or "primitive," without seeking any understanding of the cultural and economic circumstances that sustain it (Accad, 1991; Johnson-Odim, 1991; Mohanty, 1991). In this instance, globalization has led to a fundamental clash of cultural norms and values

that has forced members of both cultures to confront some of their most deeply held beliefs. The role of the sociologist is to avoid knee-jerk responses and to examine complex questions carefully from as many different angles as possible.

Cultural Universals

Amid the diversity of human behavior, there are some common features. Where these are found in virtually all societies, they are called **cultural universals.** For example, there is no known culture without a grammatically complex **language.** All cultures possess some recognizable form of family system, in which there are values and norms associated with the care of the children. The institution of **marriage** is a cultural universal, as are religious rituals and property rights. All cultures, also, practice some form of incest prohibition—the banning of sexual relations between close relatives, such as father and daughter, mother and son, or brother and sister. A variety of other cultural universals have been identified by anthropologists, including art, dancing, bodily adornment, games, gift giving, joking, and rules of hygiene.

Yet there are variations within each category. Consider, for example, the prohibition against incest. Most often, incest is regarded as sexual relations between members of the immediate family; but among some peoples, it includes cousins, and in some instances all people bearing the same family name. There have also been societies in which a small proportion of the population have been permitted to engage in incestuous practices. This was the case, for instance, within the ruling class of ancient Egypt, when brothers and sisters were permitted to have sex with each other.

Among the cultural characteristics shared by all societies, two stand out in particular. All cultures incorporate ways of expressing meaning and communication, and all depend on material means of production. In all cultures, *language* is the primary vehicle of meaning and communication. It is not the only such vehicle, however. Material culture itself carries meanings, as we shall show in what follows.

LANGUAGE

Language is one of the best examples for demonstrating both the unity and the diversity of human culture, because there are no cultures without language, yet there are thousands of different languages spoken in the world. Anyone who has visited a foreign country armed with only a dictionary knows how difficult it is either to understand anything or to be understood. Although languages that have similar origins have words in common with one another—as do, for example, German with English—most of the world's major language groups have no words in common at all.

Language is involved in virtually all of our activities. In the form of ordinary talk or speech, it is the means by which we organize most of what we do. (We will discuss the importance of talk and conversation in social life at some length in Chapter 4.) However, language is involved not just in mundane, everyday activities, but also in ceremony, religion, poetry, and many other spheres. One of the most distinctive features of human language is that it allows us to extend vastly the scope of our thought and experience. Using language, we can convey information about events remote in time or space and can discuss things we have never seen. We can develop abstract concepts, tell stories, and make jokes.

In the 1930s, the anthropological linguist Edward Sapir and his student Benjamin Lee Whorf advanced the **linguistic relativity hypothesis,** which argues that the language we use influences our perceptions of the world. That is because we are much more likely to be aware of things in the world if we have words for them (Haugen, 1977; Witkowski and Brown, 1982; Malotki, 1983). Expert skiers or snowboarders, for example, uses terms such as *black ice, corn, powder,* and *packed powder* to describe different snow and ice conditions. Such terms enable them to more readily perceive potentially life-threatening situations that would escape the notice of a novice. In a sense, then, experienced winter athletes have a different perception of the world—or at least, a different perception of the alpine slopes—than do novices.

Language also helps give permanence to a culture and an identity to a people. Language outlives any particular speaker or writer, affording a sense of history and cultural continuity, a feeling of "who we are." In the beginning of this chapter, we argued that the English language is becoming increasingly global in its use, as a primary language of both business and the Internet. One of the central paradoxes of our time is that despite this globalization of the English language, local attachments to language persist, often out of cultural pride. For example, the French-speaking residents of the Canadian province of Quebec are so passionate about their linguistic heritage that they often refuse to speak English, the dominant language of Canada, and periodically seek political independence from the rest of Canada.

Languages—indeed, all symbols—are representations of reality. The symbols we use may signify things we imagine, such as mathematical formulas or fictitious creatures, or they may represent (that is, "re-present," or make present again in our minds) things initially experienced through our senses. Human behavior is oriented toward the symbols we use to represent "reality," rather than to the reality itself—and these symbols are determined within a particular culture. Since symbols are representations, their cultural meanings must be interpreted when they are used. When you see a four-footed furry animal, for example, you must determine which cultural

symbol to attach to it. Do you decide to call it a dog, a wolf, or something else? If you determine it is a dog, what cultural meaning does that convey? In American culture, dogs are typically regarded as household pets and lavished with affection. In Guatemalan Indian culture, on the other hand, dogs are more likely to be seen as watchdogs or scavengers and treated with an indifference that might strike many Americans as bordering on cruelty. Among the Akha of northern Thailand, dogs are seen as food and treated accordingly. The diversity of cultural meanings attached to the word *dog* thus requires an act of interpretation. In this way, human beings are freed, in a sense, from being directly tied to the physical world around us.

SPEECH AND WRITING

All societies use speech as a vehicle of language. However, there are other ways of "carrying," or expressing, language—most notably, writing. The invention of writing marked a major transition in human history. Writing first began as the drawing up of lists. Marks would be made on wood, clay, or stone to keep records about significant events, objects, or people. For example, a mark, or sometimes a picture, might be drawn to represent each tract of land possessed by a particular family or set of families (Gelb, 1952). Writing began as a means of storing information and as such was closely linked to the administrative needs of the early civilizations. A society that possesses writing can locate itself in time and space. Documents can be accumulated that record the past, and information can be gathered about present-day events and activities.

Writing is not just the transfer of speech to paper or some other durable material. It is a phenomenon of interest in its own right. Written documents or *texts* have qualities in some ways quite distinct from the spoken word. The impact of speech is always by definition limited to the particular contexts in which words are uttered. Ideas and experiences can be passed down through generations in cultures without writing, but only if they are regularly repeated and passed on by word of mouth. Texts, on the other hand, can endure for thousands of years, and through them those from past ages can in a certain sense address us directly. This is, of course, why documentary research is so important to historians. Through interpreting the texts that are left behind by past generations, historians can reconstruct what their lives were like.

SEMIOTICS AND MATERIAL CULTURE

The symbols expressed in speech and writing are the chief ways in which cultural meanings are formed and expressed. But they are not the only ways. Both material objects and aspects of behavior can be used to generate meanings. A **signifier** is any vehicle of meaning—any set of elements used to

Regensburg Cathedral, built in the Middle Ages, stands at the center of Regensburg, Germany, and towers over the city, symbolizing the central role Christianity played in medieval European life.

Prior to the terrorist attacks of September 11, 2001, the World Trade Center dominated the New York City skyline. Today, the buildings of lower Manhattan's financial district still stand significantly taller than those in other areas of the city. Commerce and business occupy the symbolic center of contemporary American culture.

communicate. The sounds made in speech are signifiers, as are the marks made on paper or other materials in writing. Other signifiers, however, include dress, pictures or visual signs, modes of eating, forms of building or architecture, and many other material features of culture (Hawkes, 1977). Styles of dress, for example, normally help signify differences between the sexes. In our culture, at least until relatively recently, women used to wear skirts and men pants. In other cultures, this is reversed: women wear pants and men skirts (Leach, 1976).

Semiotics—the analysis of nonverbal cultural meanings—opens up a fascinating field for both sociology and anthropology. Semiotic analysis can be very useful in comparing one culture with another. Semiotics allows us to contrast the ways in which different cultures are structured by looking at the cultural meanings of symbols. For example, the buildings in cities are not simply places in which people live and work. They often have a symbolic character. In traditional cities, the main temple or church was usually placed on high ground in or near the city center. It symbolized the all-powerful influence that religion was supposed to have over the lives of the people. In modern societies, by contrast, the skyscrapers of big business often occupy that symbolic position.

Of course, material culture is not simply symbolic; it is also vital for catering to physical needs—in the tools or technology used to acquire food, make weaponry, construct dwellings, and so forth. We have to study both the practical and the symbolic aspects of material culture in order to understand it completely.

Culture and Social Development

Cultural traits are closely related to overall patterns in the development of society. The level of material culture reached in a given society influences, although by no means completely determines, other aspects of cultural development. This is easy to see, for example, in the level of technology. Many aspects of culture characteristic of our lives today—cars, telephones, computers, running water, electric light—depend on technological innovations that have been made only very recently in human history.

The same is true at earlier phases of social development. Prior to the invention of the smelting of metal, for example, goods had to be made of organic or naturally occurring materials like wood or stone—a basic limitation on the artifacts that could be constructed. Variations in material culture provide the main means of distinguishing different forms of human society, but other factors are also influential. Writing is an example. As has been mentioned, not all human cultures have possessed writing—in fact, for most of human history, writing was unknown. The development of writing altered the scope of human cultural potentialities, making different forms of social organization possible from those that had previously existed.

We now turn to analyzing the main types of society that existed in the past and that are still found in the world today. In the present day, we are accustomed to societies that contain many millions of people, many of them living crowded together in urban areas. But for most of human history, the earth was much less densely populated than it is now, and it is only over the past hundred years or so that any societies have existed in which the majority of the population were city dwellers. To understand the forms of society that existed prior to modern industrialism, we have to call on the historical dimension of the sociological imagination.

Disappearing World: Premodern Societies and Their Fate

Premodern societies can actually be grouped into three main categories: hunters and gatherers (Harris's "hunter-collectors"); larger agrarian or pastoral societies (involving agriculture or the tending of domesticated animals); and nonindustrial civilizations or traditional states. We shall look at the main characteristics of these societies in turn (see Table 2.1).

The Earliest Societies: Hunters and Gatherers

For all but a tiny part of our existence on this planet, human beings have lived in **hunting and gathering societies,** small groups or tribes often numbering no more than thirty or forty people. Hunters and gatherers gain their livelihood from hunting, fishing, and gathering edible plants growing in the wild. Hunting and gathering cultures continue to exist in some parts of the world, such as in a few

---

TABLE 2.1

Types of Human Society

TYPE	PERIOD OF EXISTENCE	CHARACTERISTICS
Hunting and gathering societies	50,000 B.C.E. to the present. Now on the verge of complete disappearance.	Consist of small numbers of people gaining their livelihood from hunting, fishing, and the gathering of edible plants. Few inequalities. Differences of rank limited by age and gender.
Agrarian societies	12,000 B.C.E. to the present. Most are now part of larger political entities and are losing their distinct identity.	Based on small rural communities, without towns or cities. Livelihood gained through agriculture, often supplemented by hunting and gathering. Stronger inequalities than among hunters and gatherers. Ruled by chiefs.
Pastoral societies	12,000 B.C.E. to the present. Today mostly part of larger states; their traditional ways of life are being undermined.	Size ranges from a few hundred people to many thousands. Dependent on the tending of domesticated animals for their subsistence. Marked by distinct inequalities. Ruled by chiefs or warrior kings.
Traditional societies or civilizations	6000 B.C.E. to the nineteenth century. All traditional states have disappeared.	Very large in size, some numbering millions of people (though small compared with larger industrialized societies). Some cities exist, in which trade and manufacture are concentrated. Based largely on agriculture. Major inequalities exist among different classes. Distinct apparatus of government headed by a king or emperor.

---

arid parts of Africa and the jungles of Brazil and New Guinea. Most such cultures, however, have been destroyed or absorbed by the spread of Western culture, and those that remain are unlikely to stay intact for much longer. Currently, less than a quarter of a million people in the world support themselves through hunting and gathering—only 0.004 percent of the world's population.

Compared with larger societies—particularly modern societies, such as the United States—little inequality was found in most hunting and gathering groups. The material goods they needed were limited to weapons for hunting, tools for digging and building, traps, and cooking utensils. Thus, there was little difference among members of the society in the number or kinds of material possessions—there were no divisions of rich and poor. Differences of position or rank tended to be limited to age and gender; men were almost always the hunters, while women gathered wild crops, cooked, and brought up the children.

The "elders"—the oldest and most experienced men in the community—usually had an important say in major decisions affecting the group. But just as there was little variation in wealth among members, differences of power were much less than in larger types of society. Hunting and gathering societies were usually participatory rather than competitive: all adult male members tended to assemble together when important decisions were to be made or crises were faced.

Hunters and gatherers moved about a good deal, but not in a completely erratic way. They had fixed territories, around which they migrated regularly from year to year. Since they were without animal or mechanical means of transport, they could take few goods or possessions with them. Many hunting and gathering communities did not have a stable membership; people often moved between different camps, or groups split up and joined others within the same overall territory.

Hunters and gatherers had little interest in developing material wealth beyond what was needed for their basic wants. Their main concerns were with religious values and ritual activities. Members participated regularly in elaborate ceremonials and often spent a great deal of time preparing the dress, masks, paintings, or other sacred objects used in such rituals.

Hunters and gatherers are not merely primitive peoples whose ways of life no longer hold any interest for us. Studying their cultures allows us to see more clearly that some of our institutions are far from being natural features of human life. We shouldn't idealize the circumstances in which hunters and gatherers lived; but the lack of major inequalities of wealth and power and the emphasis on cooperation rather than competition are instructive reminders that the world created by modern industrial civilization is not necessarily to be equated with progress.

Pastoral and Agrarian Societies

About fifteen thousand years ago, some hunting and gathering groups turned to the raising of domesticated animals and the cultivation of fixed plots of land as their means of livelihood. **Pastoral societies** relied mainly on domesticated livestock, while **agrarian societies** grew crops (practiced agriculture). Some societies had mixed pastoral and agrarian economies.

Depending on the environment in which they lived, pastoralists reared animals such as cattle, sheep, goats, camels, or horses. Some pastoral societies still exist in the modern world, concentrated especially in areas of Africa, the Middle East, and Central Asia. They are usually found in regions of dense grasslands or in deserts or mountains. Such regions are not amenable to fruitful agriculture but may support livestock.

At some point, hunting and gathering groups began to sow their own crops rather than simply collect those growing in the wild. This practice first developed as what is usually

---

TABLE 2.2

Some Agrarian Societies Still Remain

COUNTRY	PERCENTAGE OF WORKFORCE IN AGRICULTURE
Nepal	91.1
Rwanda	90.1
Ethiopia	88.3
Uganda	82.1
Bangladesh	64.2
INDUSTRIALIZED SOCIETIES DIFFER	
Japan	6.2
Australia	5.0
Germany	3.8
Canada	3.4
United States	2.8
United Kingdom	2.0

called "horticulture," in which small gardens were cultivated by the use of simple hoes or digging instruments. Like pastoralism, horticulture provided for a more reliable supply of food than was possible from hunting and gathering and therefore could support larger communities. Since they were not on the move, people whose livelihood was horticulture could develop larger stocks of material possessions than people in either hunting and gathering or pastoral communities. Some peoples in the world still rely primarily on horticulture for their livelihood (see Table 2.2).

Traditional Societies or Civilizations

From about 6000 B.C.E. onward, we find evidence of societies larger than any that existed before and that contrast in distinct ways with earlier types. These societies were based on the development of cities, led to pronounced inequalities of wealth and power, and were ruled by kings or emperors. Because writing was used and science and art flourished, they are often called "civilizations."

The earliest civilizations developed in the Middle East, usually in fertile river areas (see Global Map 2.1). The Chinese Empire originated in about 1800 B.C.E., at which time powerful states were also in existence in what are now India and Pakistan. By the fifteenth century, a number of large civilizations also existed in Mexico and Latin America, such as the Aztecs of the Mexican peninsula and the Incas of Peru.

Most traditional (premodern) civilizations were also empires: They achieved their size through the conquest and incorporation of other peoples (Kautsky, 1982). This was true, for instance, of traditional Rome and China. At its height, in the first century C.E., the Roman empire stretched from Britain in northwest Europe to beyond the Middle East. The Chinese empire, which lasted for more than two thousand years, up to the threshold of the twentieth century, covered most of the massive region of eastern Asia now occupied by modern China.

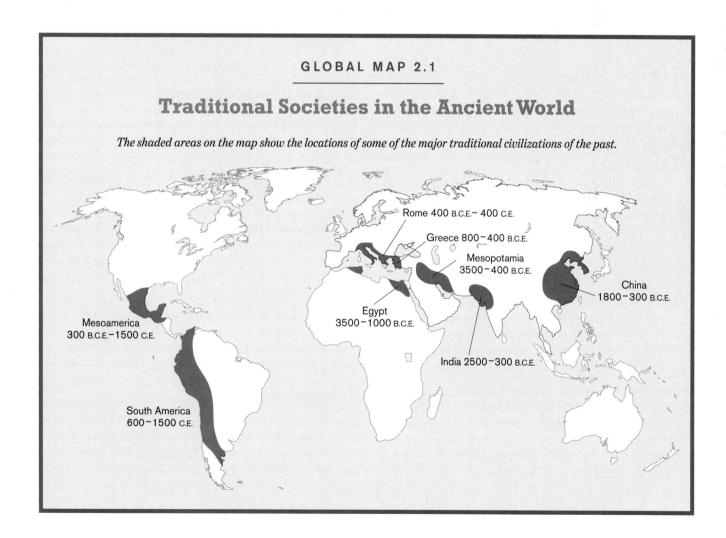

GLOBAL MAP 2.1

Traditional Societies in the Ancient World

The shaded areas on the map show the locations of some of the major traditional civilizations of the past.

Rome 400 B.C.E.– 400 C.E.

Greece 800 – 400 B.C.E.

Mesopotamia 3500 – 400 B.C.E.

China 1800 – 300 B.C.E.

Egypt 3500 – 1000 B.C.E.

Mesoamerica 300 B.C.E.–1500 C.E.

India 2500 – 300 B.C.E.

South America 600 – 1500 C.E.

Societies in the Modern World

What happened to destroy the forms of society that dominated the whole of history up to two centuries ago? The answer, in a word, is **industrialization**—the emergence of machine production, based on the use of inanimate power resources (such as steam or electricity). The industrialized, or modern, societies differ in several key respects from any previous type of social order, and their development has had consequences stretching far beyond their European origins.

The Industrialized Societies

Industrialization originated in eighteenth-century Britain as a result of the industrial revolution, a complex set of technological changes that affected the means by which people gained their livelihood. These changes included the invention of new machines (such as the spinning jenny for weaving yarn), the harnessing of power resources (especially water and steam) for production, and the use of science to improve production methods. Since discoveries and inventions in one field lead to more in others, the pace of technological innovation in **industrialized societies** is extremely rapid compared with that of traditional social systems.

In even the most advanced of traditional civilizations, most people were engaged in working on the land. The relatively low level of technological development did not permit more than a small minority to be freed from the chores of agricultural production. By contrast, a prime feature of industrialized societies today is that the large majority of the employed population work in factories, offices, or shops rather than in agriculture. And over 90 percent of people live in towns and cities, where most jobs are to be found and new job opportunities created. The largest cities are vastly greater in size than the urban settlements found in traditional civilizations. In the cities, social life becomes more impersonal and anonymous than before, and many of our day-to-day encounters are with strangers rather than with individuals known to us. Large-scale organizations, such as business corporations or government agencies, come to influence the lives of virtually everyone.

A further feature of modern societies concerns their political systems, which are more developed and intensive than forms of government in traditional states. In traditional civilizations, the political authorities (monarchs and emperors) had little direct influence on the customs and habits of most of their subjects, who lived in fairly self-contained local villages. With industrialization, transportation and communications became much more rapid, making for a more integrated "national" community.

The industrialized societies were the first nation-states to come into existence. **Nation-states** are political communities with clearly delimited borders dividing them from each other, rather than the vague frontier areas that used to separate traditional states. Nation-state governments have extensive powers over many aspects of citizens' lives, framing laws that apply to all those living within their borders. The United States is a nation-state, as are virtually all other societies in the world today.

The application of industrial technology has been by no means limited to peaceful processes of economic development. From the earliest phases of industrialization, modern production processes have been put to military use, and this has radically altered ways of waging war, creating weaponry and modes of military organization much more advanced than those of nonindustrial cultures. Together, superior economic strength, political cohesion, and military superiority account for the seemingly irresistible spread of Western ways of life across the world over the past two centuries.

Global Development

From the seventeenth to the early twentieth centuries, the Western countries established colonies in numerous areas previously occupied by traditional societies, using their superior military strength where necessary. Although virtually all these colonies have now attained their independence, the process of **colonialism** was central to shaping the social map of the globe as we know it today. In some regions, such as North America, Australia, and New Zealand, which were only thinly populated by hunting and gathering or pastoral communities, Europeans became the majority population. In other areas, including much of Asia, Africa, and South America, the local populations remained in the majority.

Societies of the first of these two types, including the United States, have become industrialized. Those in the second category are mostly at a much lower level of industrial development and are often referred to as less developed societies, or the **developing world.** Such societies include China, India, most of the African countries (such as Nigeria, Ghana, and Algeria), and those in South America (e.g., Brazil, Peru, and Venezuela). Since many of these societies are situated south of the United States and Europe, they are sometimes referred to collectively as the South, and contrasted to the wealthier, industrialized North.

The Developing World

The large majority of less developed societies are in areas that underwent colonial rule in Asia, Africa, and South America. A few colonized areas gained independence early, such as Haiti, which became the first autonomous black republic in January 1804. The Spanish colonies in South America acquired their freedom in 1810, while Brazil broke away from Portuguese rule in 1822.

Some countries that were never ruled from Europe were nonetheless strongly influenced by colonial relationships, the most notable example being China. By force of arms, China was compelled from the seventeenth century on to enter into trading agreements with European powers, by which the Europeans were allocated the government of certain areas, including major seaports. Hong Kong was the last of these. Most nations in the developing world have become independent states only since World War II—often following bloody anticolonial struggles. Examples include India, which shortly after achieving self-rule split into India and Pakistan, a range of other Asian countries (like Myanmar, Malaysia, and Singapore), and countries in Africa (including, e.g., Kenya, Nigeria, the Democratic Republic of Congo, Tanzania, and Algeria).

Although they may include peoples living in traditional fashion, developing countries are very different from earlier forms of traditional society. Their political systems are modeled on systems first established in the societies of the West—that is to say, they are nation-states. Most of the population still live in rural areas, but many of these societies are experiencing a rapid process of city development. Although agriculture remains the main economic activity, crops are now often produced for sale in world markets rather than for local consumption. Developing countries are not merely societies that

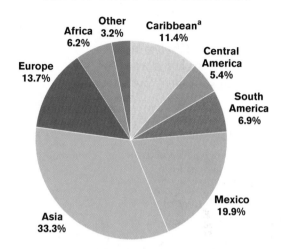

FIGURE 2.1

MOVING TO AMERICA: IMMIGRANTS TO THE UNITED STATES, 1998 (BY AREA FROM WHICH THEY EMIGRATED)

- Other 3.2%
- Caribbean[a] 11.4%
- Central America 5.4%
- South America 6.9%
- Mexico 19.9%
- Asia 33.3%
- Africa 6.2%
- Europe 13.7%

[a]Antigua and Barbuda, the Bahamas, Barbados, Cuba, Dominica, Dominican Republic, Grenada, Haiti, Jamaica, St. Kitts-Nevis, St. Lucia, St. Vincent and the Grenadines, and Trinidad and Tobago.

SOURCE: Immigration and Naturalization Service, *Annual Report: Legal Immigration, Fiscal Year 1998.*

Due to extreme poverty and the lack of land in El Salvador, many Salvadorans are forced to make their homes in public cemeteries.

have "lagged behind" the more industrialized areas. They have been in large part created by contact with Western industrialism, which has undermined the earlier, more traditional systems that were in place there.

Conditions in the more impoverished of these societies have deteriorated rather than improved over the past few years. It has been estimated that in 2000 1.5 billion people were living in poverty in the developing countries, nearly a quarter of the population of the world. Some half of the world's poor live in South Asia, in countries such as India, Myanmar, and Cambodia. About a third are concentrated in Africa. A substantial proportion, however, live on the doorstep of the United States—in Central and South America (see Global Map 2.2).

Once more, the existence of global poverty shouldn't be seen as remote from the concerns of Americans. Whereas in previous generations the bulk of immigrants into the United States came from the European countries, most now come from poor, developing societies (see Figure 2.1). Recent years have seen waves of Hispanic immigrants, nearly all from

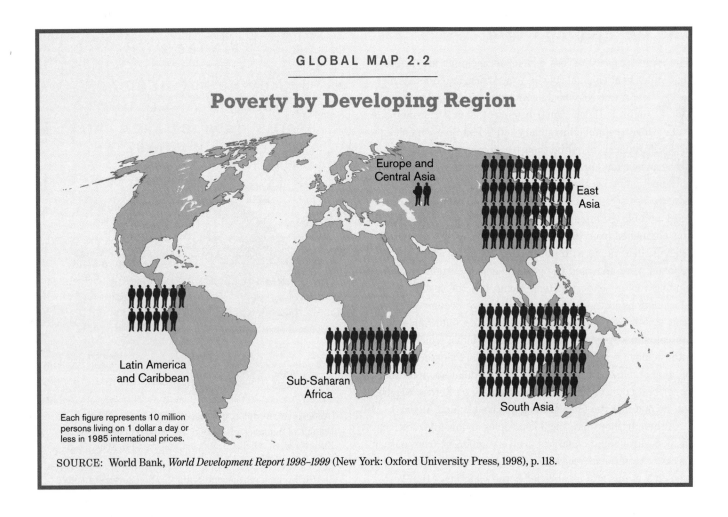

GLOBAL MAP 2.2

Poverty by Developing Region

Europe and
Central Asia

East
Asia

Latin America
and Caribbean

Sub-Saharan
Africa

South Asia

Each figure represents 10 million
persons living on 1 dollar a day or
less in 1985 international prices.

SOURCE: World Bank, *World Development Report 1998–1999* (New York: Oxford University Press, 1998), p. 118.

Latin America. Some U.S. cities near the entry points of much of this immigration, such as Los Angeles and Miami, are bursting with new immigrants and also maintain trading connections with developing countries.

In most developing societies, poverty tends to be at its worst in rural areas. Malnutrition, lack of education, low life expectancy, and substandard housing are generally most severe in the countryside. Many of the poor are to be found in areas where arable land is scarce, agricultural productivity low, and drought or floods common. Women are usually more disadvantaged than men. They encounter cultural, social, and economic problems that even the most underprivileged men do not. For instance, they often work longer hours and, when they are paid at all, earn lower wages. (See also Chapter 8 for a lengthier discussion of gender inequality.)

The poor in developing countries live in conditions almost unimaginable to Americans. Many have no permanent dwellings apart from shelters made of cartons or loose pieces of wood. Most have no running water, sewer systems, or electricity. Nonetheless, millions of poor people also live in the United States, and there are connections between poverty in America and global poverty. Almost half of the people living

in poverty in the United States immigrated from the global South. This is true of the descendants of the black slaves brought over by force centuries ago; and it is true of more recent, and willing, immigrants who have arrived from Latin America, Asia, and elsewhere.

Two African American children play near their home and an open sewer. This poverty-stricken area of Tunica, Mississippi, is sometimes referred to as "Sugarditch."

The Newly Industrializing Economies

Although the majority of developing countries lag well behind societies of the West, some have now successfully embarked on a process of industrialization. These are sometimes referred to as **newly industrializing economies** (NIEs), and they include Brazil, Mexico, Hong Kong, South Korea, Singapore, and Taiwan. The rates of economic growth of the most successful NIEs, such as those in East Asia, are several times those of the Western industrial economies. No developing country figured among the top thirty exporters in the world in 1968, but twenty-five years later South Korea was in the top fifteen.

The East Asian NIEs have shown the most sustained levels of economic prosperity. They are investing abroad as well as promoting growth at home. South Korea's production of steel has doubled in the last decade, and its shipbuilding and electronics industries are among the world's leaders. Singapore is becoming the major financial and commercial center of Southeast Asia. Taiwan is an important presence in the manufacturing and electronics industries. All these changes in the NIEs have directly affected the United States, whose share of global steel production, for example, has dropped significantly over the past thirty years.

The Impact of Globalization

In Chapter 1 it was pointed out that the chief focus of sociology has historically been the study of the industrialized societies. As sociologists, can we thus safely ignore the developing world, leaving this as the domain of anthropology? We certainly cannot. The industrialized and the developing societies have developed in *interconnection* with one another and are today more closely related than ever before. Those of us living in the industrialized societies depend on many raw materials and manufactured products coming from developing countries to sustain our lives. Conversely, the economies of most developing states depend on trading networks that bind them to the industrialized countries. We can only fully understand the industrialized order against the backdrop of societies in the developing world—in which, in fact, by far the greater proportion of the world's population lives.

As the world rapidly moves toward a single, unified economy, businesses and people move about the globe in increasing numbers in search of new markets and economic opportunities. As a result, the cultural map of the world changes: Networks of

Two Masai natives proudly display T-shirts bearing the logos of American football teams. There is almost no place on earth untouched by the globalization of culture.

peoples span national borders and even continents, providing cultural connections between their birthplaces and their adoptive countries (Appadurai, 1986). A handful of languages come to dominate, and in some cases replace, the thousands of different languages that were once spoken on the planet.

It is increasingly impossible for cultures to exist as islands. There are few, if any, places on earth so remote as to escape radio, television, air travel—and the throngs of tourists they bring—or the computer. A generation ago, there were still tribes whose way of life was completely untouched by the rest of the world. Today, these peoples use machetes and other tools made in the United States or Japan, wear T-shirts and shorts manufactured in garment factories in the Dominican Republic or Guatemala, and take medicine manufactured in Germany or Switzerland to combat diseases contracted through contact with outsiders. These people also have their stories broadcast to people around the world through satellite television and the Internet. Within a generation or two at the most, all the world's once-isolated cultures will be touched and transformed by global culture, despite their persistent efforts to preserve their age-old ways of life.

The forces that produce a global culture will be discussed throughout this book. These include:

- television, which brings U.S. culture (through networks and shows such as MTV and *The Simpsons*) into homes throughout the world daily, while also adapting a Swedish cultural product (*Expedition: Robinson*) for a U.S. audience in the form of *Big Brother* and *Survivor*;
- the emergence of a unified global economy, with business whose factories, management structures, and markets often span continents and countries;

- "global citizens," such as managers of large corporations, who may spend as much time crisscrossing the globe as they do at home, identifying with a global, cosmopolitan culture rather than with their own nation's;
- a host of international organizations, including United Nations agencies, regional trade and mutual defense associations, multinational banks and other global financial institutions, international labor and health organizations, and global tariff and trade agreements, that are creating a global political, legal, and military framework; and
- electronic communications (telephone, fax, electronic mail, the Internet and the World Wide Web), which make instantaneous communication with almost any part of the planet an integral part of daily life in the business world.

Does the Internet Promote a Global Culture?

Many believe that the rapid growth of the Internet around the world will hasten the spread of a global culture—one resembling the cultures of Europe and North America, currently home to nearly three-quarters of all Internet users (see Global Map 2.3). Belief in such values as equality between men and women, the right to speak freely, democratic participation in government, and the pursuit of pleasure through consumption are readily diffused throughout the world over the Internet. Moreover, Internet technology itself would seem to foster such values: Global communication, seemingly unlimited (and uncensored) information, and instant gratification are all characteristics of the new technology.

Yet it may be premature to conclude that the Internet will sweep aside traditional cultures, replacing them with radically new cultural values. As the Internet spreads around the world, evidence shows that it is in many ways compatible with traditional cultural values as well, perhaps even a means of strengthening them.

Consider, for example, the Middle Eastern country of Kuwait, a traditional Islamic culture that has recently experienced strong American and European influences. Kuwait, an oil-rich country on the Persian Gulf, has one of the highest average per-person incomes in the world. The government provides free public education through the university level, resulting in high rates of literacy and education for both men and women. Kuwaiti television frequently carries NFL football and other U.S. programming, although broadcasts are regularly interrupted for the traditional Muslim calls to prayer. Half of Kuwait's approximately 2 million people are under twenty-five years old, and, like their youthful counterparts in Europe and North America, many surf the Internet for new ideas, information, and consumer products.

Using the Internet to connect with the world around them is common among young people across cultures. Here, an Iranian girl at a Tehran Internet café reads the latest news on the Iraq crisis.

Although Kuwait is in many respects a modern country, Kuwait law treats men and women differently. Legally, women have equal access to education and employment, yet they are barred from voting or running for political office. Cultural norms treating men and women differently are almost as strong: Women are generally expected to wear traditional clothing that leaves only the face and hands visible and are forbidden to leave home at night or be seen in public at any time with a man who is not a spouse or relative.

Deborah Wheeler (1998) spent a year studying the impact of the Internet on Kuwaiti culture. The Internet is increasingly popular in Kuwait; half of all Internet users in Middle Eastern Arab countries live in this tiny country. The new communications technologies are clearly enabling men and women to talk with each other, in a society where such communications outside of marriage are extremely limited. Wheeler also notes that ironically men and women are segregated in the Internet cafés. Furthermore, she finds that Kuwaitis are extremely reluctant to voice strong opinions or political views online. With the exception of discussing conservative Islamic religious beliefs, which are freely disseminated over the Internet, Kuwaitis are remarkably inhibited online.

Wheeler concludes that Kuwaiti culture, which is hundreds of years old, is not likely to be easily transformed by simple exposure to different beliefs and values on the Internet. The fact that a few young people are participating in global chat rooms does not mean that Kuwaiti culture is adopting the sexual attitudes of the United States or even the form of everyday relations found between men and women in the West. The culture that eventu-

Global Internet Connectivity: Number of Internet Servers, January 1999

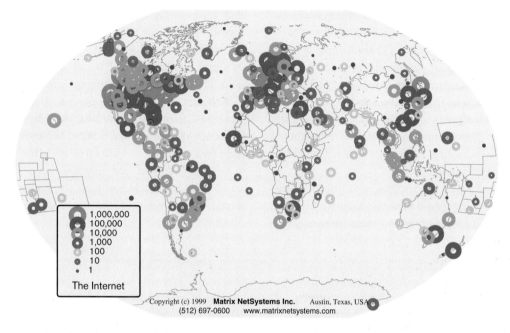

SOURCE: John Quarterman and colleagues at Matrix Information Directory Services (MIDS), www.geog.ucl.ac.uk/casa/martin/atlas/mids_intrworld9901_large.gif.

ally emerges as a result of the new technologies will not be the same as American culture; it will be uniquely Kuwaiti.

Globalization and Local Cultures

The world has become a single *social system* as a result of growing ties of interdependence, both social and economic, that now affect virtually everyone. But it would be a mistake to think of this increasing interdependence, or globalization, of the world's societies simply as the growth of world unity. The globalizing of social relations should be understood primarily as the reordering of *time and distance* in social life. Our lives, in other words, are increasingly and quickly influenced by events happening far removed from our everyday activities.

Globalizing processes have brought many benefits to Americans: a much greater variety of goods and foodstuffs is available than ever before. At the same time, the fact that we are all now caught up in a much wider world has helped cre-

ate some of the most serious problems American society faces, such as the threat of terrorism.

The influence of a growing global culture has provoked numerous reactions at the local level. Many local cultures remain strong or are experiencing a rejuvenation, partly as a response to the diffusion of global culture. Such a response grows out of the concern that a global culture, dominated by North American and European cultural values, will corrupt the local culture. For example, the Taliban, an Islamic movement that controlled most of Afghanistan, sought to impose traditional, tribal values throughout the country. Through its governmental "Ministry for Ordering What Is Right and Forbidding What Is Wrong," the Taliban banned music, closed movie theaters, abolished the use of alcohol, and required men to grow full beards. Women were ordered to cover their entire bodies with *burkas,* tentlike garments with a woven screen over the eyes, out of which to see. They were forbidden to work outside their homes, or even to be seen in public with men who were not their spouses or relations. Violations of these rules were severely punished, sometimes by death. The rise of the Taliban can be understood at least partly as a rejection of the spread of Western culture.

The resurgence of local cultures is sometimes seen throughout the world in the rise of **nationalism,** a sense of identification with one's people that is expressed through a common set of strongly held beliefs. Sometimes these include the belief that the people of a particular nation have historical or God-given rights that supersede those of other people. Nationalism can be strongly political, involving attempts to assert the power of a nation based on a shared ethnic or racial identity over people of a different ethnicity or race. The strife in the former Yugoslavia, as well as parts of Africa and the former Soviet Union, bear tragic witness to the power of nationalism. The world of the twenty-first century may well witness responses to globalization that celebrate ethnocentric nationalist beliefs, promoting intolerance and hatred rather than a celebration of diversity.

New nationalisms, cultural identities, and religious practices are constantly being forged throughout the world. When you socialize with students from the same cultural background or celebrate traditional holidays with your friends and family, you are sustaining your culture. The very technology that helps foster globalization also supports local cultures: The Internet enables you to communicate with others who share your cultural identity, even when they are dispersed around the world. American students who share a passion for a particular type of music can stay up all night in Internet chat rooms with like-minded people: if you are studying abroad you can stay connected with communities back home by logging on to the Web site of your hometown newspaper (Wallraff, 2000). A casual search of the Web reveals thousands of pages devoted to different cultures and subcultures.

Although sociologists do not yet fully understand these processes, they often conclude that despite the powerful forces of globalization operating in the world today, local cultures remain strong and indeed flourish. But is it still too soon to tell whether and how globalization will transform our world, whether it will result in the homogenization of the world's diverse cultures, the flourishing of many individual cultures, or both.

Study Outline

www.wwnorton.com/giddens

The Concepts of Culture

- *Culture* consists of the *values* held by a given group, the *norms* they follow, and the *material goods* they create.

The Development of Human Culture

- Human cultures have evolved over thousands of years and reflect both human biology and the physical environment where the cultures emerged. A defining feature of humankind is its inventiveness in creating new forms of culture.

How Nature and Nurture Interact

- Most sociologists do not deny that biology plays a role in shaping human behavior, especially through the interaction between biology and culture. Sociologists' main concern, however, is with how behavior is learned in the individual's interaction with society.
- Forms of behavior found in all, or virtually all, cultures are called *cultural universals. Language,* the prohibition against incest, institutions of *marriage,* the family, religion, and property are the main types of cultural universals—but within these general categories there are many variations in values and modes of behavior between different societies.
- We live in a world of symbols, or representations, and one of our most important forms of symbolization is language. The *linguistic relativity hypothesis* argues that language influences perception. Language is also an important source of cultural continuity, and the members of a culture are often passionate about their linguistic heritage.
- *Cultural diversity* is a chief aspect of modern culture, and in the United States it is seen in the large number of vibrant *subcultures* as well as in the existence of countercultures. Although some people feel that different subcultures should be *assimilated* into a single mainstream culture, others argue in favor of *multiculturalism.*
- Sociologists try to avoid *ethnocentrism* and instead adopt a stance of *cultural relativism,* attempting to understand a society relative to its own cultural norms and values.

Premodern Societies

- Several types of premodern society can be distinguished. In *hunting and gathering societies,* people do not grow crops or keep livestock but gain their livelihood from gathering plants and hunting animals. *Pastoral societies* are those that raise domesticated animals as their major source of subsistence. *Agrarian societies* depend on the cultivation of fixed plots of land. Larger, more developed, urban societies form traditional states or civilizations.

Societies in the Modern World

- The development of industrialized societies and the expansion of the West led to the conquest of many parts of the world through the process of *colonialism,* which radically changed long-established social systems and cultures.
- In industrialized societies, industrial production (whose techniques are also used in the production of food) is the main basis of the economy. Industrialized countries include the nations of the West, plus Japan, Australia, and New Zealand. They now include those industrialized societies ruled by communist governments. The *developing world,* in which most of the world's population live, is almost all formerly colonized areas. The majority of the population works in agricultural production, some of which is geared to world markets.

The Impact of Globalization

- The increase in global communications and economic interdependence represents more than simply the growth of world unity. Time and distance are being reorganized in ways that bring us all closer together, but even as globalization threatens to make all cultures seem alike, local cultural identifications are resurging around the world. This is seen in the rise of *nationalism,* which can result in ethnic conflict as well as ethnic pride.

Key Concepts

agrarian society (p. 54)
assimilation (p. 48)
colonialism (p. 56)
cultural relativism (p. 50)
cultural universal (p. 50)
culture (p. 38)
developing world (p. 56)
ethnocentrism (p. 49)
hunting and gathering society (p. 53)
industrialization (p. 56)
industrialized society (p. 56)
instinct (p. 45)
language (p. 50)
linguistic relativity hypothesis (p. 51)
marriage (p. 50)
material goods (p. 38)
multiculturalism (p. 49)
nation-state (p. 56)
nationalism (p. 62)
newly industrializing economy (NIE) (p. 58)
norm (p. 38)
pastoral society (p. 54)
semiotics (p. 52)
signifier (p. 51)

society (p. 40)
sociobiology (p. 44)
subculture (p. 45)
values (p. 38)

Review Questions

1. What are values?
   a. Values are those ideas that a culture holds in the highest esteem. They give people a purpose in life.
   b. Values are abstract ideals—for example, in most Western societies, monogamy is considered a virtue. In other cultures, a person may be permitted to have several wives or husbands simultaneously.
   c. Values are lists of "dos" and "don'ts" that regulate everyday behavior.
   d. Values depend on the development of a money economy and systems of credit.
2. What is a signifier?
   a. A signifier is the name given to the meaning of a spoken or written word.
   b. A signifier is any vehicle of meaning, such as speech, writing, dress, and buildings.
   c. A signifier is the meaning of a symbol.
   d. A signifier is an electronic sign.
3. Using one's own cultural values to judge another culture is called
   a. ethnocentrism.
   b. cultural relativism.
   c. multiculturalism.
   d. cultural universals.
4. What is culture?
   a. Culture consists of the values, norms, and material goods of a people. Culture can be described as a "design for living."
   b. Culture is the sum total of a society's artistic expression—all the novels, poems, dance, theater, museums, and so on.
   c. Culture is the material apparatus of everyday life—the chairs, tables, cooking utensils, clothes, shoes, and coats that we use in our daily round.
   d. Culture consists of the values and norms of a society, its founding "myths" and ideals, and its beliefs about the kinds of conduct appropriate in everyday life.
5. What was the basis for the rise of modern societies?
   a. The fall of the Roman Empire
   b. The Renaissance
   c. The Industrial Revolution
   d. The cold war
6. Which of the following is not a cultural universal?
   a. The prohibition against incest
   b. Some form of religion
   c. A concept of property
   d. The idea of adolescence

7. What was colonialism?
   a. The creation by the European powers of a network of colonies in ports of call along their trade routes.
   b. The military conquest of African peoples by Europeans.
   c. The process by which industrial powers incorporated regions rich in natural resources into their economic and political systems.
   d. The impact of trade with the empire on the economies of the European powers.
8. What is the position of sociologists on the debate of nature vs. nurture?
   a. Sociologists believe that "biology is destiny."
   b. Sociologists ask how nature and nurture interact to produce human behavior.
   c. No sociologists today acknowledge a role for nature.
   d. Sociologists do not have a position.
9. Which of the following statements is true about developing countries?
   a. About one quarter of the world's population lives in developing countries.
   b. Very few of them are formerly colonized areas.
   c. The majority of the population works in manufacturing and service sectors.
   d. Some agricultural production in developing countries is geared to world markets.
10. Subcultures are:
   a. abstract ideals, such as American ideals of liberty and justice.
   b. systems of relationships that connect individuals who share the same culture.
   c. smaller segments of society distinguished by unique patterns of behavior.
   d. populations made up of a number of groups from diverse cultural, ethnic, and linguistic backgrounds.

Thinking Sociologically Exercises

1. Mention at least two cultural traits that you would claim are universals; mention two others you would claim are culturally specific traits. Use case study materials from different societies you are familiar with to show the differences between universal and specific cultural traits. Are the cultural universals you have discussed derivatives of human instincts? Explain your answer fully.
2. What does it mean to be ethnocentric? How is ethnocentrism dangerous in conducting social research? How is ethnocentrism problematic among nonresearchers in their everyday lives?

Data Exercises

www.wwnorton.com/giddens
Keyword: Data2

Are you among the millions of Americans whose families have arrived in the United States in the past twenty-five years? Or have you noticed that your community, school, church, or workplace has become more diverse? In the data exercise for Chapter 2 you will learn more about the patterns of immigration to the United States, both historically and currently; how Americans feel about recent immigration; and how your own community has changed as a result of immigration.

Culture, Society, and Child Socialization

Learn about socialization (including gender socialization), and know the most important agencies of socialization.

Socialization Through the Life Course

Learn the various stages of the life course, and see the similarities and differences among different cultures.

CHAPTER THREE

SOCIALIZATION AND THE LIFE CYCLE

t the start of J. K. Rowling's first Harry Potter adventure, *Harry Potter and the Sorcerer's Stone*, the shrewd wizard Albus Dumbledore leaves Harry, a newly orphaned infant, at the doorstep of his nonmagician (or "Muggle") uncle and aunt's house. Harry has already shown himself to have unique powers, but Dumbledore is concerned that if left in the wizarding world, Harry won't mature healthily. "It would be enough to turn any boy's head," he says. "Famous before he can walk and talk! Famous for something he won't even remember. Can't you see how much better off he'll be, growing up away from all that until he's ready to take it?" (Rowling, 1998).

The Harry Potter novels, each of which follows Harry through a single year of his life, are based on the premise that there is no adventure greater than that of growing up. Although Harry attends the Hogwarts School of Witchcraft and Wizardry, it's still a school, because everyone, even a young wizard with limitless power, needs help developing a set of values. We all pass through important life stages: the passage from childhood to adolescence, and then to adulthood. So, for example, as the Harry Potter series progresses, Harry feels the onset of sexual urges, to which he responds with an entirely common awkwardness. Since sports are an important place for many children to learn about camaraderie and ambition, Harry plays the wizard sport Quidditch. Rowling loves to use the paranormal to help us see the enchanting complexities behind the fundamentals of everyday life. In her universe, owls unerringly deliver letters; is this really any stranger than the postal system or e-mail? The function of all classic children's stories is to make the process of growing up more understandable, whether they're set in a fairy-tale universe, our own world, or—as with the innovation of the Harry Potter series—both.

Socialization is the process whereby the helpless infant gradually becomes a self-aware, knowledgeable person, skilled in the ways of the culture into which he or she was born. Socialization among the young allows for the more general phenomenon of **social reproduction**—the process whereby societies have structural continuity over time. During the course of socialization, especially in the early years of life, children learn the ways of their elders, thereby perpetuating their values, norms, and social practices. All societies have characteristics that endure over long stretches of time, even though their members change as individuals are born and die. American society, for example, has many distinctive social and cultural characteristics that have persisted for generations—such as the fact that English is the main language spoken.

Socialization connects the different generations to one another (Turnbull, 1983). The birth of a child alters the lives of those who are responsible for its upbringing—who themselves therefore undergo new learning experiences. Parenting usually ties the activities of adults to children for the remainder of their lives. Older people still remain parents when they become grandparents, of course, thus forging another set of relationships connecting the different generations with each other. Although the process of cultural learning is much more intense in infancy and early childhood than later, learning and adjustment go on through the whole life cycle.

In the sections to follow, we will continue the theme of "nature interacting with nurture," introduced in the previous chapter. We will first analyze the development of the human individual from infancy to early childhood, identifying the main stages of change involved. Different writers have put forward a number of theoretical interpretations about how and why children develop as they do, and we will describe and compare these, including theories that explain how we develop gender identities. Finally, we will move on to discuss the main groups and social contexts that influence socialization during the various phases of individuals' lives.

Culture, Society, and Child Socialization

"Unsocialized" Children

What would children be like if, in some way or another, they were raised without the influence of human adults? Obviously no humane person could bring up a child away from social in-

fluence. There are, however, a number of much-discussed cases of children who have spent their early years away from normal human contact.

THE "WILD BOY OF AVEYRON"

On January 9, 1800, a strange creature emerged from the woods near the village of Saint-Serin in southern France. In spite of walking erect, he looked more animal than human, although he was soon identified as a boy of about eleven or twelve. He spoke only in shrill, strange-sounding cries. The boy apparently had no sense of personal hygiene and relieved himself where and when he chose. He was brought to the attention of the local police and taken to a nearby orphanage. In the beginning he tried constantly to escape and was only recaptured with some difficulty. He refused to tolerate wearing clothes, tearing them off as soon as they were put on him. No parents ever came forward to claim him.

The child was subjected to a thorough medical examination, which turned up no major physical abnormalities. On being shown a mirror, he seemingly saw an image, but did not recognize himself. On one occasion, he tried to reach through the mirror to seize a potato he saw in it. (The potato in fact was being held behind his head.) After several attempts, without turning his head, he took the potato by reaching back over his shoulder. A priest who was observing the boy from day to day and who described this incident, wrote: "All these little details, and many others we could add prove that this child is not totally without intelligence, reflection, and reasoning power. However, we are obliged to say that, in every case not concerned with his natural needs or satisfying his appetite, one can perceive in him only animal behavior. If he has sensations, they give birth to no idea. He cannot even compare them with one another. One would think that there is no connection between his soul or mind and his body" (quoted in Shattuck, 1980; see also Lane, 1976).

Later the boy was moved to Paris and a systematic attempt was made to change him "from beast to human." The endeavor was only partly successful. He was toilet trained, accepted wearing clothes, and learned to dress himself. Yet he was uninterested in toys or games and was never able to learn or speak more than a few words. So far as anyone could tell, on the basis of detailed descriptions of his behavior and reactions, this was not because he was mentally retarded. He seemed either unwilling or unable to master human speech fully. He made little further progress and died in 1828.

What seems to have happened to the wild boy of Aveyron, is that by the time he came into close human contact, he had grown beyond the age at which children readily accomplish the learning of language and other human skills. There is probably a "critical period" for the learning of language and other complex achievements, after which it is too late to master them fully. The wild boy provides some sense of what an "unsocialized" child would be like. He retained many "nonhuman" responses. Yet, in spite of the deprivations he suffered, he displayed no lasting viciousness. He responded quickly to others who treated him sympathetically and was able to acquire a certain minimum level of ordinary human capabilities.

Of course, we have to be cautious about interpreting a case of this sort. In this example it is possible that there was a mental abnormality that remained undiagnosed. Alternatively, the experiences to which the child was subjected may have inflicted psychological damage that prevented him from gaining the skills most children acquire at a much earlier age. Yet there is sufficient similarity between this case history, and others that have been recorded, to suggest how limited our faculties would be in the absence of an extended period of early socialization.

Using their toy wheelbarrows to help their father with the gardening, these boys are, according to Mead, "taking on the role of the other" and achieving an understanding of themselves as separate social agents.

Theories of Child Development

One of the most distinctive features of human beings, compared with other animals, is that humans are *self-aware*. How should we understand the emergence of a sense of self—the awareness that the individual has a distinct identity separate from others? During the first months of life, the infant possesses little or no understanding of differences between human beings and material objects in the environment, and has no awareness of self. Children do not begin to use concepts such as "I," "me," and "you" until the age of two or after. Only gradually do they then come to understand that others have distinct identities, consciousness, and needs separate from their own.

The problem of the emergence of self is much debated and is viewed rather differently in contrasting theoretical perspectives. To some extent, this is because the most prominent theories about child development emphasize different aspects of socialization. The American philosopher and sociologist George Herbert Mead gives attention mainly to how children learn to use the concepts of "I" and "me." Jean Piaget, the Swiss student of child behavior, worked on many aspects of child development, but his best-known writings concern **cognition**—the ways in which children learn to *think* about themselves and their environment.

G. H. MEAD AND THE DEVELOPMENT OF SELF

Since Mead's ideas form the main basis of a general tradition of theoretical thinking, *symbolic interactionism,* they have had a very broad impact in sociology. Symbolic interactionism emphasizes that interaction between human beings takes place through symbols and the interpretation of meanings (see Chapter 1). But in addition, Mead's work provides an account of the main phases of child development, giving particular attention to the emergence of a sense of self.

According to Mead, infants and young children first of all develop as social beings by imitating the actions of those around them. Play is one way in which this takes place, and in their play small children often imitate what adults do. A small child will make mud pies, having seen an adult cooking, or dig with a spoon, having observed someone gardening. Children's play evolves from simple imitation to more complicated games in which a child of four or five years old will act out an adult role. Mead called this "taking the role of the other"—learning what it is like to be in the shoes of another person. It is only at this stage that children acquire a developed sense of self. Children achieve an understanding of themselves as separate agents—as a "me"—by seeing themselves through the eyes of others.

We achieve self-awareness, according to Mead, when we learn to distinguish the "me" from the "I." The "I" is the unsocialized infant, a bundle of spontaneous wants and desires. The "me," as Mead used the term, is the **social self.** Individuals develop **self-consciousness,** Mead argued, by coming to see themselves as others see them. A further stage of child development, according to Mead, occurs when the child is about eight or nine years old. This is the age at which children tend to take part in organized games, rather than unsystematic play. It is at this period that children begin to understand the overall *values* and *morality* according to which social life is conducted. To learn organized games, children must understand the rules of play and notions of fairness and equal participation. Children at this stage learn to grasp what Mead termed the **generalized other**—the general values and moral rules of the culture in which they are developing.

JEAN PIAGET AND THE STAGES OF COGNITIVE DEVELOPMENT

Piaget placed great emphasis on the child's active capability to make sense of the world. Children do not passively soak up information, but instead select and interpret what they see, hear, and feel in the world around them. Piaget described several distinct stages of cognitive development during which children learn to think about themselves and their environment. Each stage involves the acquisition of new skills and depends on the successful completion of the preceding one.

Piaget called the first stage, which lasts from birth up to about age two, the **sensorimotor stage,** because infants learn mainly by touching objects, manipulating them, and physically exploring their environment. Until about age four months or so, infants cannot differentiate themselves from their environment. For example, a child will not realize that her own movements cause the sides of her crib to rattle. Objects are not differentiated from persons, and the infant is unaware that anything exists outside her range of vision. Infants gradually learn to distinguish people from objects, coming to see that both have an existence independent of their immediate perceptions. The main accomplishment of this stage is that by its close children understand their environment to have distinct and stable properties.

The next phase, called the **preoperational stage,** is the one to which Piaget devoted the bulk of his research. This stage lasts from age two to seven. During the course of it, children acquire a mastery of language and become able to use words to represent objects and images in a symbolic fashion. A four-year-old might use a sweeping hand, for example, to represent the concept "airplane." Piaget termed the stage "preoperational" because children are not yet able to use their developing mental capabilities systematically. Children in this stage are **egocentric.** As Piaget used it, this concept does not refer to selfishness, but to the tendency of the child to interpret the world exclusively in terms of his own position. A child during this period does not understand, for instance, that others see objects from a different perspective from his own. Holding a book upright, the child may ask about a picture in it, not realizing that the other person sitting opposite can only see the back of the book.

Children at the preoperational stage are not able to hold connected conversations with another. In egocentric speech, what each child says is more or less unrelated to what the other speaker said. Children talk together, but not *to* one an-

other in the same sense as adults. During this phase of development, children have no general understanding of categories of thought that adults tend to take for granted: concepts such as causality, speed, weight, or number. Even if the child sees water poured from a tall, thin container into a shorter, wider one, she will not understand that the volume of water remains the same—and conclude rather that there is less water because the water level is lower.

A third period, the **concrete operational stage,** lasts from age seven to eleven. During this phase, children master abstract, logical notions. They are able to handle ideas such as causality without much difficulty. A child at this stage of development will recognize the false reasoning involved in the idea that the wide container holds less water than the thin, narrow one, even though the water levels are different. She becomes capable of carrying out the mathematical operations of multiplying, dividing, and subtracting. Children by this stage are much less egocentric. In the preoperational stage, if a girl is asked, "How many sisters do you have?" she may correctly answer "one." But if asked, "How many sisters does your sister have?" she will probably answer "none," because she cannot see herself from the point of view of her sister. The concrete operational child is able to answer such a question with ease.

The years from eleven to fifteen cover what Piaget called the **formal operational stage.** During adolescence, the developing child becomes able to grasp highly abstract and hypothetical ideas. When faced with a problem, children at this stage are able to review all the possible ways of solving it and go through them theoretically in order to reach a solution. The young person at the formal operational stage is able to understand why some questions are trick ones. To the question, "What creatures are both poodles and dogs?" the individual might not be able to give the correct reply but will understand why the answer "poodles" is right and appreciate the humor in it.

According to Piaget, the first three stages of development are universal; but not all adults reach the formal operational stage. The development of formal operational thought depends in part on processes of schooling. Adults of limited educational attainment tend to continue to think in more concrete terms and retain large traces of egocentrism.

Agents of Socialization

Sociologists often speak of socialization as occurring in two broad phases, involving a number of different agents of socialization. **Agents of socialization** are groups or social contexts in which significant processes of socialization occur. Primary socialization occurs in infancy and childhood and is the most intense period of cultural learning. It is the time when children learn language and basic behavioral patterns that form the foundation for later learning. The family is the main agent of socialization during this phase. Secondary socialization takes place later in childhood and into maturity. In this phase, other agents of socialization take over some of the responsibility from the family. Schools, peer groups, organizations, the media, and eventually the workplace become socializing forces for individuals. Social interactions in these contexts help people learn the values, norms, and beliefs that make up the patterns of their culture.

THE FAMILY

Since family systems vary widely, the range of family contacts that the infant experiences is by no means standard across cultures. The mother everywhere is normally the most important individual in the child's early life, but the nature of the relationships established between mothers and their children is influenced by the form and regularity of their contact. This is, in turn, conditioned by the character of family institutions and their relation to other groups in society.

In modern societies, most early socialization occurs within a small-scale family context. The majority of American children spend their early years within a domestic unit containing mother, father, and perhaps one or two other children. In many other cultures, by contrast, aunts, uncles, and grandparents are often part of a single household and serve as caretakers even for very young infants. Yet even within American society there are many variations in the nature of family contexts. Some children are brought up in single-parent households; some are cared for by two mothering and fathering agents (divorced parents and stepparents). A high proportion of women with families are now employed outside the home and return to their paid work relatively soon after the births of their children. In spite of these variations, the family normally remains the major agency of socialization from infancy to adolescence and beyond—in a sequence of development connecting the generations.

Families have varying "locations" within the overall institutions of a society. In most traditional societies, the family into which a person was born largely determined the individual's social position for the rest of his or her life. In modern societies, social position is not inherited at birth in this way, yet the region and social class of the family into which an individual is born affects patterns of socialization quite distinctly. Children pick up ways of behavior characteristic of their parents or others in their neighborhood or community.

Varying patterns of child rearing and discipline, together with contrasting values and expectations, are found in different sectors of large-scale societies. It is easy to understand the influence of different types of family background if we think of what life is like, say, for a child growing up in a poor black family living in a run-down city neighborhood compared to one born into an affluent white family living in an all-white suburb (Kohn, 1977).

Of course, few if any children simply take over unquestioningly the outlook of their parents. This is especially true in the modern world, in which change is so pervasive. Moreover, the very existence of a range of socializing agents in modern societies leads to many divergences between the outlooks of children, adolescents, and the parental generation.

SCHOOLS

Another important socializing agency is the school. Schooling is a formal process: Students pursue a definite curriculum of subjects. Yet schools are agents of socialization in more subtle respects. Children are expected to be quiet in class, be punctual at lessons, and observe rules of school discipline. They are required to accept and respond to the authority of the teaching staff. Reactions of teachers also affect the expectations children have of themselves. These expectations in turn become linked to their job experience when they leave school. Peer groups are often formed at school, and the system of keeping children in classes according to age reinforces their impact.

PEER RELATIONSHIPS

Another socializing agency is the **peer group.** Peer groups consist of children of a similar age. In some cultures, particularly small traditional societies, peer groups are formalized as **age-grades** (normally confined to males). There are often specific ceremonies or rites that mark the transition of men from one age-grade to another. Those within a particular age-grade generally maintain close and friendly connections throughout their lives. A typical set of age-grades consists of childhood, junior warriorhood, senior warriorhood, junior elderhood, and senior elderhood. Men move through these grades not as individuals, but as whole groups.

The family's importance in socialization is obvious, since the experience of the infant and young child is shaped more or less exclusively within it. It is less apparent, especially to those of us living in Western societies, how significant peer groups are. Yet even without formal age-grades, children over four or five usually spend a great deal of time in the company of friends the same age. Given the high proportion of women now in the work force whose young children play together in day-care centers, peer relations are even more important today than before (Corsaro, 1997; Harris, 1998).

Peer relations are likely to have a significant impact beyond childhood and adolescence. Informal groups of people of similar ages, at work and in other situations, are usually of enduring importance in shaping individuals' attitudes and behavior.

THE MASS MEDIA

Newspapers, periodicals, and journals flourished in the West from the early 1800s onward, but they were confined to a fairly small readership. It was not until a century later that such printed materials became part of the daily experience of millions of people, influencing their attitudes and opinions. The spread of **mass media** involving printed documents was soon accompanied by electronic communication—radio, television, records, and videos. American children spend the equivalent of almost a hundred schooldays per year watching television.

Much research has been done to assess the effects of television programs on the audiences they reach, particularly children. Perhaps the most commonly researched topic is the impact of television on propensities to crime and violence.

The most extensive studies are those carried out by George Gerbner and his collaborators, who have analyzed samples of prime-time and weekend daytime TV for all the major American networks each year since 1967. The number and frequency of violent acts and episodes are charted for a range of programs. Violence is defined as physical force directed against the self or others, in which physical harm or death occurs. Television drama emerges as highly violent in character. On average, 80 percent of programs contain violence, with a rate of 7.5 violent episodes per hour. Children's programs show even higher levels of violence, although killing is less commonly portrayed. Cartoons depict the highest number of violent acts and episodes of any type of television program (Gerbner, 1985).

Video games have become a key part of the culture and experience of childhood today. Studies have indicated that playing video games might have a positive effect on children's social and intellectual development.

In general, research on the effects of television on audiences has tended to treat children as passive and undiscriminating in their reactions to what they see. Robert Hodge and David Tripp (1986) emphasized that children's responses to TV involve interpreting, or "reading," what they see, not just registering the content of programs. They suggested that most research has not taken account of the complexity of children's mental processes. TV watching, even of trivial programs, is not an inherently low-level intellectual activity; children read programs by relating them to other systems of meaning in their everyday lives. According to Hodge and Tripp, it is not the violence alone that has effects on behavior, but rather the general framework of attitudes within which it is both presented and read.

In recent years home video games have come into widespread use. In his book *Video Kids* (1991), Eugene Provenzo analyzes the impact of Nintendo. There are currently some 19 million Nintendo, Sony, and Sega games in the United States and many more in other countries. Nearly all are owned and operated by children. Social codes and traditions have developed based on the games and their characters. Of the thirty best-selling toys in the United States in 1990, twenty-five were either video games or video equipment. The games are often directly linked to the characters or stories in films and TV programs; in turn, television programming has been based on Nintendo games. Video games, Provenzo concludes, have become a key part of the culture and experience of childhood today.

But is this impact a negative one? It is doubtful that a child's involvement with Nintendo harms her achievement at school. The effects of video games are likely to be governed by other influences on school performance. In other words, where strong pressures deflect students from an interest in their schoolwork, absorption with TV or video pursuits will tend to reinforce these attitudes. Video games and TV then can become a refuge from a disliked school environment.

But it is also possible that video games can act to develop skills that might be relevant both to formal education and to wider participation in a society that depends increasingly on electronic communication. The sound and look of video games has been a major influence on the development of rave music, rockers like Trent Reznor of Nine Inch Nails, and even films like *The Matrix, Tomb Raider,* and *Final Fantasy.* According to Marsha Kinder, her son Victor's adeptness at Nintendo transferred fruitfully to other spheres. For example, the better he became at video games, the more interested and skillful he was at drawing cartoons. Patricia Greenfield has argued that "video games are the first example of a computer technology that is having a socializing effect on the next generation on a mass scale, and even on a world-wide basis" (Greenfield, 1993).

The mass media are an important influence on socialization, in all forms of society. There are few societies in current times, even among the more traditional cultures, that remain completely untouched by the media. Electronic communication is accessible even to those who are unable to read and write, and in the most impoverished parts of the world it is common to find people owning radios and television sets.

WORK

Work is in all cultures an important setting within which socialization processes operate, although it is only in industrial societies that large numbers of people go "out to work"—that is, go each day to places of work separate from the home. In traditional communities many people farmed the land close to where they lived or had workshops in their dwellings. "Work" in such communities was not so clearly distinct from other activities as it is for most members of the workforce in the modern West. In the industrialized countries, going "out to work" for the first time ordinarily marks a much greater transition in an individual's life than entering work in traditional societies. The work environment often poses unfamiliar demands, perhaps calling for major adjustments in the person's outlook or behavior.

Social Roles

Through the process of socialization, individuals learn about **social roles**—socially defined expectations that a person in a given social position follows. The social role of doctor, for example, encompasses a set of behaviors that should be enacted by all individual doctors, regardless of their personal opinions or outlooks. Because all doctors share this role, it is possible to speak in general terms about the professional role behavior of doctors, irrespective of the specific individuals who occupy that position.

Some sociologists, particularly those associated with the functionalist school, regard social roles as fixed and relatively unchanging parts of a society's culture. They are taken as social facts. According to such a view, individuals learn the expectations that surround social positions in their particular culture and perform those roles largely as they have been defined. Social roles do not involve negotiation or creativity. Rather, they are prescriptive in containing and directing an individual's behavior. Through socialization, individuals internalize social roles and learn how to carry them out.

This view, however, is mistaken. It suggests that individuals simply take on roles, rather than creating or negotiating them. In fact, socialization is a process in which humans can exercise agency; they are not simply passive subjects waiting to be instructed or programmed. Individuals come to understand and assume social roles through an ongoing process of social interaction.

Identity

The cultural settings in which we are born and come to maturity influence our behavior, but that does not mean that humans are robbed of individuality or free will. It might seem as though we are merely stamped into preset molds that society has prepared for us, and some sociologists do tend to write about socialization as though this was the case. But such a view is fundamentally flawed. The fact that from birth to death we are involved in interaction with others certainly conditions our personalities, the values we hold, and the behavior we engage in. Yet socialization is also at the origin of our very individuality and freedom. In the course of socialization each of us develops a sense of identity and the capacity for independent thought and action.

The concept of *identity* in sociology is a multifaceted one and can be approached in a number of ways. Broadly speaking, **identity** relates to the understandings people hold about who they are and what is meaningful to them. These understandings are formed in relation to certain attributes that take priority over other sources of meaning. Some of the main sources of identity include gender, sexual orientation, nationality or ethnicity, and social class. There are two types of identity often spoken of by sociologists: social identity and self-identity (or personal identity). These forms of identity are analytically distinct but are closely related to one another. **Social identity** refers to the characteristics that other people attribute to an individual. These can be seen as markers that indicate who, in a basic sense, that individual is. At the same time, they place that individual in relation to other individuals who share the same attributes. Examples of social identities might include student, mother, lawyer, Catholic, homeless, Asian, dyslexic, married, and so forth. Many individuals have social identities comprising more than one attribute. A person could simultaneously be a mother, an engineer, a Muslim, and a city council member. Multiple social identities reflect the many dimensions of people's lives. Although this plurality of social identities can be a potential source of conflict for people, most individuals organize meaning and experience in their lives around a primary identity that is fairly continuous across time and place.

Social identities therefore involve a collective dimension. They mark ways that individuals are the same as others. Shared identities—predicated on a set of common goals, values, or experiences—can form an important base for social movements. Feminists, environmentalists, labor unionists, and supporters of

"Complete Freedom of Movement": Video Games as Gendered Play Spaces

[In a recent essay, sociologist Henry Jenkins describes how video games are gendered play spaces. He suggests that games like Sega Saturn's *Nights into Dreams* represent a fusion of the boys' and girls' game genre.]

[***] In the frame stories that open [*Nights into Dreams*], we enter the mindscape of the two protagonists as they toss and turn in their sleep. Claris, the female protagonist, hopes to gain recognition on the stage as a singer, but has nightmares of being rejected and ridiculed. Elliot, the male character, has fantasies of scoring big on the basketball court yet fears being bullied by bigger and more aggressive players. They run away from their problems, only to find themselves in Nightopia, where they must save the dream world from the evil schemes of Wileman the Wicked and his monstrous minions. In the dreamworld, both Claris and Elliot may assume the identity of Nights, an androgynous harlequin figure, who can fly through the air, transcending all the problems below. *Nights'* complex mythology has players gathering glowing orbs which represent different forms of energy needed to confront Claris and Elliot's problems—purity (white), wisdom (green), hope (yellow), intelligence (blue) and bravery (red).

The tone of this game is aptly captured by one Internet game critic, Big Mitch (n.d.): "The whole experience of *Nights* is in soaring, tumbling, and freewheeling through colorful landscapes, swooping here and there, and just losing yourself in the moment. This is not a game you set out to win; the fun is in the journey rather than the destination." Big Mitch's response suggests a recognition of the fundamentally different qualities of this game—its focus on psychological issues as much as upon action and conflict, its fascination with aimless exploration rather than goal-driven narrative, its movement between a realistic world of everyday problems and a fantasy realm of great adventure, its mixture of the speed and mobility associated with the boys' platform games with the lush natural landscapes and the sculpted soundtracks associated with the girls' games. Spring Valley is a sparkling world of rainbows and waterfalls and emerald green forests. Other levels allow us to splash through cascading fountains or sail past icy mountains and frozen wonderlands or bounce on pillows and off the walls of the surreal Soft Museum or swim through aquatic tunnels. The game's 3-D design allows an exhilarating freedom of movement, enhanced by design features—such as wind resistance—which give players a stronger than average sense of embodiment. *Nights into Dreams* retains some of the dangerous and risky elements associated with the boys' games. There are spooky places in this game, including nightmare worlds full of day-glo serpents and winged beasties, and there are enemies we must battle, yet there is also a sense of unconstrained adventure, floating through the clouds. Our primary enemy is time, the alarm clock which will awaken us from our dreams. Even when we confront monsters, they don't fire upon us; we must simply avoid flying directly into their sharp teeth if we want to master them. When we lose Nights' magical, gender-bending garb, we turn back into boys and girls and must hoof it as pedestrians across the rugged terrain below, a situation which makes it far less likely we will achieve our goals. To be gendered is to be constrained; to escape gender is to escape gravity and to fly above it all.

Sociologist Barrie Thorne has discussed the forms of "borderwork" which occurs when boys and girls occupy the same play spaces: "The spatial separation of boys and girls [on the same playground] constitutes a kind of boundary, perhaps felt most strongly by individuals who want to join an activity controlled by the other gender."[1] Boys and girls are brought together in the same space, but they repeatedly enact the separation and opposition between the two play cultures. In real world play, this "borderwork" takes the form of chases and contests on the one hand and "cooties" or other pollution taboos on the other. When "borderwork" occurs, gender distinctions become extremely rigid and nothing passes between the two spheres. [***]

As we develop digital playspaces for boys and girls, we need to make sure this same pattern isn't repeated, that we do not create blue and pink ghettos inside the playspace. On the one hand, the opening sequences of *Nights into Dreams*, which frame Elliot and Claris as possessing fundamentally different dreams (sports for boys and musical performance for girls, graffiti-laden inner city basketball courts for boys and pastoral gardens for girls), perform this kind of borderwork, defining the proper place for each gender. On the other

[1]Barrie Thorne, *Gender Play: Girls and Boys in School* (New Brunswick, NJ: Rutgers University, 1993), pp. 64–65.

hand, the androgenous Nights embodies a fantasy of transcending gender and thus achieving the freedom and mobility to fly above it all. To win the game, the player must become both the male and the female protagonists and they must join forces for the final level. The penalty for failure in this world is to be trapped on the ground and to be fixed into a single gender.

Thorne finds that aggressive "borderwork" is more likely to occur when children are forced together by adults than when they find themselves interacting more spontaneously, more likely to occur in prestructured institutional settings like the schoolyard than in the informal settings of the subdivisions and apartment complexes. All of this suggests that our fantasy of designing games which will provide common play spaces for girls and boys may be an illusive one, one as full of complications and challenges on its own terms as creating a "girls only" space or encouraging girls to venture into traditional male turf. We are not yet sure what such a gender neutral space will look like. Creating such a space would mean redesigning not only the nature of computer games but also the nature of society. The danger may be that in such a space, gender differences are going to be more acutely felt, as boys and girls will be repelled from each other rather than drawn together. There are reasons why this is a place where neither the feminist entrepreneurs nor the boys' game companies are ready to go, yet as the girls' market is secured, the challenge must be to find a way to move beyond our existing categories and to once again invent new kinds of virtual play spaces.

SOURCE: Henry Jenkins, *From Barbie to Mortal Kombat: Gender and Computer Games* (Cambridge, Mass.: MIT Press, 1998).

Questions

- Why should both girls and boys play video games?
- How does *Nights into Dreams* challenge real-world gender models?
- What do you think is the best strategy to break down gender distinctions in video games? Why?

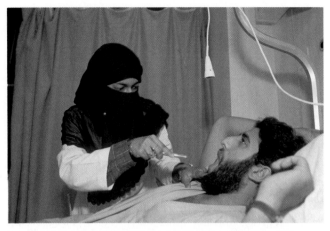

People often exhibit multiple social identities simultaneously, sometimes seemingly conflicting ones. Focusing on her primary identity as a medical professional in this context, a male patient at King Fahd Military Medical Complex in Saudi Arabia allows a doctor who is also a Muslim woman to examine him.

religious fundamentalist and/or nationalist movements are all examples of cases in which a shared social identity is drawn on as a powerful source of personal meaning or self-worth.

If social identities mark ways in which individuals are the same as others, **self-identity** (or personal identity) sets us apart as distinct individuals. Self-identity refers to the process of self-development through which we formulate a unique sense of ourselves and our relationship to the world around us. The notion of self-identity draws heavily on the work of symbolic interactionists. It is the individual's constant negotiation with the outside world that helps to create and shape his or her sense of self. The process of interaction between self and society helps to link an individual's personal and public worlds. Though the cultural and social environment is a factor in shaping self-identity, individual agency and choice are of central importance.

Tracing the changes in self-identity from traditional to modern societies, we can see a shift away from the fixed, inherited factors that previously guided identity formation. If at one time people's identities were largely informed by their membership in broad social groups, bound by class or nationality, they are now more multifaceted and less stable. The processes of urban growth, industrialization, and the breakdown of earlier social formations have weakened the impact of inherited rules and conventions. Individuals have become more socially and geographically mobile. This has freed people from the tightly knit, relatively homogeneous communities of the past in which patterns were passed down in a fixed way across generations. It has created the space for other sources of personal meaning, such as gender and sexual orientation, to play a greater role in people's sense of identity.

In today's world, we have unprecedented opportunities to make ourselves and to create our own identities. We are our own best resources in defining who we are, where we have come from, and where we are going. Now that the traditional signposts of identity have become less essential, the social world confronts us with a dizzying array of choices about who to be, how to live, and what to do, without offering much guidance about which selections to make. The decisions we make in our everyday lives—about what to wear, how to behave, and how to spend our time—help make us who we are. Through our capacity as self-conscious, self-aware human beings, we constantly create and recreate our identities.

Gender Socialization

Agents of socialization play an important role in how children learn **gender roles.** Let's now turn to the study of **gender socialization,** the learning of gender roles through social factors such as the family and the media.

REACTIONS OF PARENTS AND ADULTS

Many studies have been carried out on the degree to which gender differences are the result of social influences. Studies of mother–infant interaction show differences in the treatment of boys and girls even when parents believe their reactions to both are the same. Adults asked to assess the personality of a baby give different answers according to whether or not they believe the child to be a girl or a boy. In one experiment, five young mothers were observed in interaction with a six-month-old called Beth. They tended to smile at her often and offer her dolls to play with. She was seen as "sweet," having a "soft cry." The reaction of a second group of mothers to a child the same age, named Adam, was noticeably different. The baby was likely to be offered a train or other "male toys" to play with. Beth and Adam were actually the same child, dressed in different clothes (Will, Self, and Datan, 1976).

GENDER LEARNING

Gender learning by infants is almost certainly unconscious. Before a child can accurately label itself as either a boy or a girl, it receives a range of pre-verbal cues. For instance, male

Toys play a major role in children's gender learning, as they often emphasize the difference between male and female attributes.

and female adults usually handle infants differently. The cosmetics women use contain scents different from those the baby might learn to associate with males. Systematic differences in dress, hairstyle, and so on provide visual cues for the infant in the learning process. By age two, children have a partial understanding of what gender is. They know whether they are boys or girls, and they can usually categorize others accurately. Not until five or six, however, does a child know that a person's sex does not change, that everyone has gender, and that sex differences between girls and boys are anatomically based.

The toys, picture books, and television programs with which young children come into contact all tend to emphasize differences between male and female attributes. Toy stores and mail-order catalogs usually categorize their products by gender. Even some toys that seem neutral in terms of gender are not so in practice. For example, toy kittens and rabbits are recommended for girls, while lions and tigers are seen as more appropriate for boys.

Vanda Lucia Zammuner studied the toy preferences of children aged between seven and ten in Italy and Holland (Zammuner, 1986). Children's attitudes toward a variety of toys were analyzed; stereotypically masculine and feminine toys as well as toys presumed not to be gender typed were included. Both the children and their parents were asked to assess which toys were suitable for boys and which for girls. There was close agreement between the adults and the children. On average, the Italian children chose gender-differentiated toys to play with more often than the Dutch children—a finding that conformed to expectations, since Italian culture tends to hold a more traditional view of gender divisions than does

Dutch society. As in other studies, girls from both societies chose gender-neutral or boys' toys to play with far more than boys chose girls' toys.

STORYBOOKS AND TELEVISION

Over twenty years ago, Lenore Weitzman and her colleagues carried out an analysis of gender roles in some of the most widely used preschool children's books and found several clear differences in gender roles (Weitzman et al., 1972). Males played a much larger part in the stories and pictures than females, outnumbering females by a ratio of 11 to 1. Including animals with gender identities, the ratio was 95 to 1. The activities of males and females also differed. The males engaged in adventurous pursuits and outdoor activities demanding independence and strength. Where girls did appear, they were portrayed as passive and confined mostly to indoor activities. Girls cooked and cleaned for the males or awaited their return. Much the same was true of the adult men and women represented in the storybooks. Women who were not wives and mothers were imaginary creatures like witches or fairy godmothers. There was not a single woman in all the

Gender-typed toys are ubiquitous, making it difficult to raise children in a truly nonsexist environment. Barbie, one of the most popular and widely recognized "girl" toys, has been influencing children's ideas about what it means to act "female" for fifty years.

books analyzed who held an occupation outside the home. By contrast, the men were depicted as fighters, policemen, judges, kings, and so forth.

More recent research suggests that things have changed somewhat but that the large bulk of children's literature remains much the same (Davies, 1991). Fairy tales, for example, embody traditional attitudes toward gender and toward the sorts of aims and ambitions girls and boys are expected to have. "Some day my prince will come"—in versions of fairy tales from several centuries ago, this usually implied that a girl from a poor family might dream of wealth and fortune. Today, its meaning has become more closely tied to the ideals of romantic love. Some feminists have tried to rewrite some of the most celebrated fairy tales, reversing their usual emphases: "I really didn't notice that he had a funny nose. And he certainly looked better all dressed up in fancy clothes. He's not nearly as attractive as he seemed the other night. So I think I'll just pretend that this glass slipper feels too tight" (Viorst, 1986). Like this version of "Cinderella," however, these rewrites are found mainly in books directed to adult audiences and have hardly affected the tales told in innumerable children's books.

Although there are some notable exceptions, analyses of television programs designed for children conform to the findings about children's books. Studies of the most frequently watched cartoons show that most of the leading figures are male and that males dominate the active pursuits. Similar images are found in the commercials that appear throughout the programs.

There are now some storybooks available with strong, independent girls as the main characters, but few depict boys in nontraditional roles. A mother of a five-year-old boy told of her son's reaction when she reversed the sexes of the characters in a story she read to him:

> In fact he was a bit upset when I went through a book which has a boy and a girl in very traditional roles, and changed all the he's to she's and she's to he's. When I first started doing that, he was inclined to say "you don't like boys, you only like girls." I had to explain that that wasn't true at all, it's just that there's not enough written about girls. (Statham, 1986)

Clearly, gender socialization is very powerful, and challenges to it can be upsetting. Once a gender is "assigned," society expects individuals to act like "females" and "males." It is in the practices of everyday life that these expectations are fulfilled and reproduced (Bourdieu, 1990; Lorber, 1994).

Socialization Through the Life Course

The various transitions through which individuals pass during their lives seem at first sight to be biologically fixed—from childhood to adulthood and eventually to death. But the stages of the human **life course** are social as well as biological in nature. They are influenced by cultural differences and also by the material circumstances of people's lives in given types of society. For example, in the modern West, death is usually thought of in relation to old age, because most people enjoy a life span of seventy years or more. In traditional societies of the past, however, more people died in younger age groups than survived to old age.

Childhood

To people living in modern societies, childhood is a clear and distinct stage of life. Children are distinct from babies or toddlers; childhood intervenes between infancy and the teen

This *Madonna and Child*, painted in the thirteenth century by Duccio da Buoninsegna, depicts the infant Jesus with a mature face. Until recently, children in Western society were viewed as little adults.

years. Yet the concept of childhood, like so many other aspects of social life today, has only come into being over the past two or three centuries. In earlier societies, the young moved directly from a lengthy infancy into working roles within the community. The French historian Philippe Ariès has argued that "childhood," conceived of as a separate phase of development, did not exist in medieval times (Ariès, 1965). In the paintings of medieval Europe, children are portrayed as little adults, with mature faces and the same style of dress as their elders. Children took part in the same work and play activities as adults, rather than in the childhood games we now take for granted.

Right up to the twentieth century, in the United States and most other Western countries, children were put to work at what now seems a very early age. There are countries in the world today, in fact, where young children are engaged in full-time work, sometimes in physically demanding circumstances (for example, in coal mines). The ideas that children have distinctive rights and that the use of child labor is morally repugnant are quite recent developments.

Because of the long period of childhood that we recognize today, societies now are in some respects more child centered than traditional ones. But a child-centered society, it must be emphasized, is not one in which all children experience love and care from parents or other adults. The physical and sexual abuse of children is a commonplace feature of family life in present-day society, although the full extent of such abuse has only recently come to light. Child abuse has clear connections with what seems to us today like the frequent mistreatment of children in premodern Europe.

It seems possible that as a result of changes currently occurring in modern societies, the separate character of childhood is diminishing once more. Some observers have suggested that children now grow up so fast that this is in fact the case. They point out that even small children may watch the same television programs as adults, thereby becoming much more familiar early on with the adult world than did preceding generations.

The Teenager

The idea of the "teenager," so familiar to us today, also didn't exist until recently. The biological changes involved in puberty (the point at which a person becomes capable of adult sexual activity and reproduction) are universal. Yet in many cultures, these do not produce the degree of turmoil and uncertainty often found among young people in modern societies. In cultures that foster age-grades, for example, with distinct ceremonials that signal a person's transition to adulthood, the process of psychosexual development generally seems easier to negotiate. Adolescents in such societies have less to "unlearn" since the pace of change is slower. There is a time when children in Western societies are required to be children no longer: to put away their toys and break with childish pursuits. In traditional cultures, where children are already working alongside adults, this process of unlearning is normally much less jarring.

In Western societies, teenagers are betwixt and between: They often try to follow adult ways, but they are treated in law as children. They may wish to go to work, but they are constrained to stay in school. Teenagers in the West live in between childhood and adulthood, growing up in a society subject to continuous change.

Young Adulthood

Young adulthood seems increasingly to be a specific stage in personal and sexual development in modern societies (Goldscheider and Waite, 1991). Particularly among more affluent groups, people in their early twenties are taking the time to travel and explore sexual, political, and religious affiliations. The importance of this postponement of the responsibilities of full adulthood is likely to grow, given the extended period of education many people now undergo.

Mature Adulthood

Most young adults in the West today can look forward to a life stretching right through to old age. In premodern times, few could anticipate such a future with much confidence. Death through sickness or injury was much more frequent

Before the twentieth century, young children in many Western countries were put to work at an early age. Some, like the coal mining boys above, were made to do dangerous or physically demanding work.

Japanese and American Teenagers

Studies comparing socialization in varying cultural settings show some interesting contrasts. For example, the idea of the teen years as an extended period of transition between childhood and adulthood emerged in America before it did in Japan. In fact, the Japanese term, *cheenayja,* is an adaptation of the American *teenager.* In premodern Japan, the movement from childhood to adulthood occurred in an instant, because it happened as part of an age-grade system (one that included girls). A child would become an adult when he participated in a special rite. Japanese boys became adults at some point between ages eleven and sixteen, depending on their social rank. The parallel ceremony at which girls were recognized as women was the *kami* age, the age at which they began to wear their hair up rather than down.

Just as in most other nonmodern societies, including those of medieval Europe, young people in Japan knew who they would be and what they would be doing when they became adults. The teenage years weren't a time to experiment. Japanese children were schooled to follow closely the ways of their parents, to whom they owed strict obedience; family norms emphasizing the duties of children toward their parents were very strong.

Such norms have endured to the present day, but they have also come under strain with the high pace of industrial

development in contemporary Japan. So are Japanese teenagers now just like American ones? Merry White, a sociologist at Boston University, attempted to answer this question. White interviewed one hundred teens in each culture over a period of three years, trying to gain an in-depth view of their attitudes toward sexuality, school, friendship, and parents (White, 1993). She found big differences between the Japanese and American teenagers, but also came up with unexpected conclusions about both. In neither culture are most teenagers the rebels she expected to find. Instead, she found a

among all age groups than it is today, and women in particular were at great risk because of the high rate of mortality in childbirth.

On the other hand, some of the strains we experience now were less pronounced in previous times. People usually maintained a closer connection with their parents and other kin than in today's more mobile populations, and the routines of work they followed were the same as those of their forebears. In current times, major uncertainties must be resolved in marriage, family life, and other social contexts. We have to "make" our own lives more than people did in the past. The creation of sexual and marital ties, for instance, now depends on individual initiative and selection, rather than being fixed

by parents. This represents greater freedom for the individual, but the responsibility can also impose difficulties.

Keeping a forward-looking outlook in middle age has taken on a particular importance in modern societies. Most people do not expect to be doing the same thing all their lives, as was the case for the majority in traditional cultures. Individuals who have spent their lives in one career may find the level they have reached in middle age unsatisfying and further opportunities blocked. Women who have spent their early adulthood raising a family and whose children have left home may feel themselves to be without any social value. The phenomenon of a "midlife crisis" is very real for many middle-aged people. A person may feel she has thrown away the opportunities that life fairly high degree of conformity to wider cultural ideas and an expressed respect for parents in both countries.

What the adults say of their teenage offspring in Japan and the United States is much the same: "Why don't you listen more to what I say?" "When I was your age . . ." The Japanese and American teens also echo each other in some ways: "Do you like me?" "What should I aim for in my life?" "We're cool, but they aren't." Pop music, films, and videos figure large in the experience of both—as does at least a surface sexual knowledgeability, since from an early age in both cultures sexual information, including warnings about sexual disease, is widespread.

The Japanese teenagers, however, come out well ahead of the Americans in terms of school achievements: 95 percent of Japanese teenagers reach a level in academic tests met by only the top 5 percent of young Americans. And while both express respect for parents, the Japanese teenagers remain much closer to theirs than do most of the American teenagers.

The Japanese teenagers are certainly interested in sex but placed it at the bottom of a list of priorities White presented them with; the Americans put it at the top. Teenagers in Japan are nonetheless sexually very active, probably even more so than their American counterparts. Two thirds of Japanese girls by age fifteen are sexually active. White reports that they are, by Western standards, amazingly forthcoming about their sexual fantasies and practices; nearly 90 percent of the Japanese girls reported that they masturbate twice or more a week.

The Japanese separate clearly three areas of sexuality that are more mixed up for the American teenagers: physical passion, socially approved pairing or marriage, and romantic fantasies. "Love marriages," in which two people establish a

relationship on the basis of emotional and sexual attraction, are now common in Japan. However, they are often the result of an initial introduction of suitable partners arranged by parents, followed by falling in love prior to marriage. Even the most sexually experienced young person in Japan may continue to prefer to have a mature adult arrange an appropriate marriage.

Japanese teenagers often stress that love should grow in marriage, rather than being the basis of choosing a partner in the first place. The sexual activity of young girls tends to involve several older boys and not be bound up with dating. White quotes as typical of young, unmarried Japanese women a respondent who was in her early twenties when interviewed. She first had sexual intercourse at fifteen—like three quarters of her friends—and since had accumulated many "sex friends." These were not *boifurends* (boyfriends), a relationship that implies emotional attachment. She said, "I do it [have sex] because it is fun. However, marriage is a totally different story, you know. Marriage should be more realistic and practical" (White, 1993).

had to offer, or she will never attain goals cherished since childhood. Yet growing older need not lead to resignation or bleak despair; a release from childhood dreams can be liberating.

Old Age

In traditional societies, older people were normally accorded a great deal of respect. Among cultures that included age-grades, the elders usually had a major—often the final—say over matters of importance to the community. Within families, the authority of both men and women mostly increased with age. In industrialized societies, by contrast, older people tend to lack authority within both the

family and the wider social community. Having retired from the labor force, they may be poorer than ever before in their lives. At the same time, there has been a great increase in the proportion of the population over age sixty-five. In 1900, only one in thirty people in the United States was over sixty-five; the proportion today is one in eight and will likely rise to one in five by the year 2030 (U.S. Bureau of the Census, 1996a). The same trend is found in all the industrially advanced countries.

Transition to the age-grade of elder in a traditional culture often marked the pinnacle of the status an individual could achieve. In modern societies, retirement tends to bring the opposite consequences. No longer living with their children and often having retired from paid work, older people may find it difficult to make the final period of their life rewarding. It used to be thought that those who successfully cope with old age do so by turning to their inner resources, becoming less interested in the material rewards that social life has to offer. Although this may often be true, it seems likely that in a society in which many are physically healthy in old age, an outward-looking view will become more and more prevalent. Those in retirement might find renewal in what has been called the "third age," in which a new phase of education begins (see also Chapter 14 on lifelong learning).

Study Outline

www.wwnorton.com/giddens

Culture, Society, and Child Socialization

- *Socialization* is the process whereby, through contact with other human beings, the helpless infant gradually becomes a self-aware, knowledgeable human being, skilled in the ways of the given culture and environment.

Theories of Child Development

- According to G. H. Mead, the child achieves an understanding of being a separate agent by seeing how others behave toward him or her in social contexts. At a later stage, entering into organized games, learning the rules of play, the child comes to understand "the *generalized other*"—general values and cultural rules.
- Jean Piaget distinguishes several main stages in the development of the child's capability to make sense of the world. Each stage involves the acquisition of new cognitive skills and depends on the successful completion of the preceding one. According to Piaget these stages of cognitive development are universal features of socialization.

Agents of Socialization

- *Agents of socialization* are structured groups or contexts within which significant processes of socialization occur. In all cultures, the family is the principal socializing agency of the child during infancy. Other influences include *peer groups,* schools, and the *mass media*.
- Through the process of socialization and interaction with others, individuals learn about *social roles*—socially defined expectations that a person in a given social position will follow. One result of this process is the development of a *social identity,* the characteristics that other people attribute to an individual. If social identities mark ways in which individuals are the same as others, *self-identity* sets us apart as distinct individuals. The concept of self-identity, which draws on symbolic interactionism, refers to the process of self-development through which we formulate a unique sense of ourselves and our relationship to the world around us.

- The development of mass communications has enlarged the range of socializing agencies. The spread of mass printed media was later accompanied by the use of electronic communication. TV exerts a particularly powerful influence, reaching people of all ages at regular intervals every day.
- *Gender socialization* begins virtually as soon as an infant is born. Even parents who believe they treat children equally tend to produce different responses to boys and girls. These differences are reinforced by many other cultural influences.

Socialization Through the Life Cycle

- Socialization continues throughout the life cycle. At each distinct phase of life there are transitions to be made or crises to be overcome. This includes facing death as the termination of physical existence.

Key Concepts

Review Questions

1. What are the main agents of socialization in contemporary society?
   a. Family, schools, the political system, the economic system, and the urban system
   b. Family, schools, peer groups, the mass media, and work
   c. Movies, videos, computers, and the Internet
   d. Newspapers, magazines, radio, and television
2. When does socialization end?
   a. At the beginning of adulthood
   b. During the midlife crisis
   c. On retirement
   d. Socialization never ends because people are in a process of constant interaction.
3. What is the difference between the "I" and the "me"?
   a. The "I" is the unsocialized infant; the "me" is the social self.
   b. The "I" is the id; the "me" is the ego.
   c. The "I" is the private inner self; the "me" is the social self that others see.
   d. The "I" is the inner self who wants, wants, wants; the "me" is the inner self who works out what "I" actually needs.
4. What part do peer groups play in the gender socialization of children?
   a. None.
   b. A significant role. They help children judge the significance of ongoing changes to their bodies—for example, whether the first signs of puberty are treated as a matter of pride or embarrassment.
   c. A marginal role. Peer groups only interpret what parents and media are telling children.
   d. A dominating role. Only peer groups determine how children understand the significance of gender.
5. According to George Herbert Mead's theory of child development, what is the importance of playing organized games at the age of eight or nine?
   a. Children can have fun at an early age and then focus on succeeding at school and work later in life.
   b. Children begin to understand the overall values and morality according to which social life is conducted.
   c. Children learn to be competitive and see others as rivals.
   d. Children learn how to use a computer keyboard, an important skill throughout one's life.
6. In traditional versus modern societies, what is the most important difference regarding how the elderly are generally viewed?
   a. In traditional societies, elders had little authority in the family and community; in modern societies, elders have a great deal of authority.
   b. In traditional societies, elders had a great deal of authority in the family and community; in modern societies, elders have very little authority.
   c. In traditional societies, the concept of "elder" did not exist; in modern societies, people aspire to the age-grade "elder."
   d. In traditional societies, elders were put to death; in modern societies, elders are put in "old-age" homes.
7. The learning of male or female roles takes place through a process called
   a. genderization.
   b. gender socialization.
   c. sexualization.
   d. sex role learning.
8. Groups or social contexts in which significant processes or socialization occur are called:
   a. context operations.
   b. concrete operations.
   c. sensorimotors.
   d. agents of socialization.
9. Jean Piaget's theory of child development is based on:
   a. the stages of cognitive development.
   b. the emergence of a sense of self, of self-awareness.
   c. the importance of sociobiology.
   d. all of the above.
10. Children learn the ways of their elders, thereby perpetuating the values, norms, and social practices of their culture. This process is known as:
    a. evolution.
    b. social interaction.
    c. socialization.
    d. natural selection.

Thinking Sociologically Exercises

1. Concisely review how an individual becomes a social person according to each of the two leading theorists discussed in this chapter: G. H. Mead and Jean Piaget. Which of these two theories seems most appropriate and correct to you? Explain why.
2. Using alcoholic beverages is one of many things we do as a result of socialization. Suggest how the family, peers, schools, and mass media help to establish the desire to consume alcoholic drinks. Of the preceding, which force is the most persuasive? Explain.

Data Exercises

www.wwnorton.com/giddens
Keyword: Data3

In the data exercise for this chapter, you will once again use the General Social Survey data to explore the topic of socialization. Specifically, you will learn more about what behaviors Americans value and believe are important for a child to learn.

The Study of Daily Life

Familiarize yourself with the study of everyday life.

Nonverbal Communication

Know the various forms of nonverbal communication.

Social Rules and Talk

Learn the research process of ethnomethodology, the study of our conversations and how we make sense of each other.

Face, Body, and Speech in Interaction

Recognize the different contexts of our social life and how they are used to convey or hide meaning. Also learn how our social actions are organized in time and space.

Interaction in Time and Space

Understand that interaction is situated, that it occurs in a particular place and for a particular length of time. See that the way we organize our social actions is not unique by learning how other cultures organize their social lives.

Linking Microsociology and Macrosociology

See how face-to-face interactions and broader features of society are closely related.

CHAPTER FOUR

SOCIAL INTERACTION AND EVERYDAY LIFE

ric Schmitz is a personal trainer and fitness director at the Santa Barbara Athletic Club, an upscale health club. He has been employed at the gym since he graduated from the University of Wisconsin–Madison with a degree in Exercise Physiology in 1987.

Schmitz knows hundreds of people who work out at the gym. Some of them he has worked with as fitness director as they were getting to know the machines in their early months there. He has met many others while teaching classes in spinning—a group cycling class. Others he came to know through casual contact, since many of the same people work out at the same time every week.

The personal space is limited within a gym environment, due to the proximity of the exercise equipment. For example, in the weight training circuit at SBAC, one section contains a number of Cybex machines near to one another. Members must work out in close proximity to one another, and their bodies constantly crisscross as they move through their workouts.

It is almost impossible for Schmitz to walk anywhere in this physical space without potentially making eye contact with someone he has at least met. He will greet certain of these patrons the first time he sees them in the day, but afterward it is usually understood that they will go about their own business without acknowledging one another in the way they did earlier.

When passersby quickly glance at each other and then look away again, they demonstrate what Erving Goffman (1967, 1971) calls the **civil inattention** we require of each other in many situations. Civil inattention is not the same as merely ignoring another person. Each individual

Walking along a crowded city street, one engages in civil inattention. Though the people in the photo above can hear the phone conversations these men are having, they make no indication of their awareness.

indicates recognition of the other person's presence but avoids any gesture that might be taken as too intrusive. Can you think of examples of civil inattention in your own life? Perhaps when you are walking down the hall of a dormitory, or trying to decide where to sit in the cafeteria, or simply walking across campus? Civil inattention to others is something we engage in more or less unconsciously, but it is of fundamental importance to the existence of social life, which must proceed efficiently and, sometimes among total strangers, without fear. When civil inattention occurs among passing strangers, an individual implies to another person that she has no reason to suspect his intentions, be hostile to him, or in any other way specifically avoid him.

The best way to see the importance of this is by thinking of examples where it doesn't apply. When a person stares fixedly at another, allowing her face openly to express a particular emotion, it is normally with a lover, family member, or close friend. Strangers or chance acquaintances, whether encountered on the street, at work, or at a party, virtually never hold the gaze of another in this way. To do so may be taken as an indication of hostile intent. It is only where two groups are strongly antagonistic to one another that strangers might indulge in such a practice. Thus, whites in the United States have been known in the past to give a "hate stare" to blacks walking past.

Even friends in close conversation need to be careful about how they look at one another. Each individual demonstrates attention and involvement in the conversation by regularly looking at the eyes of the other, but not staring into them. To look too intently might be taken as a sign of mistrust about, or

at least failure to understand, what the other is saying. Yet if each party does not engage the eyes of the other at all, he is likely to be thought evasive, shifty, or otherwise odd.

The Study of Daily Life

Why should we concern ourselves with such seemingly trivial aspects of social behavior? Passing someone on the street or exchanging a few words with a friend seem minor and uninteresting activities, things we do countless times a day without giving them any thought. In fact, the study of such apparently insignificant forms of **social interaction** is of major importance in sociology—and, far from being uninteresting, is one of the most absorbing of all areas of sociological investigation. There are three reasons for this.

First, our day-to-day routines, with their almost constant interactions with others, give structure and form to what we do; we can learn a great deal about ourselves as social beings, and about social life itself, from studying them. Our lives are organized around the repetition of similar patterns of behavior from day to day, week to week, month to month, and year to year. Think of what you did yesterday, for example, and the day before that. If they were both weekdays, in all probability you got up at about the same time each day (an important routine in itself). You may have gone off to class fairly early in the morning, making a journey from home to school or college that you make virtually every weekday. You perhaps met some friends for lunch, returning to classes or private study in the afternoon. Later, you retraced your steps back home, possibly going out later in the evening with other friends.

Of course, the routines we follow from day to day are not identical, and our patterns of activity on weekends usually contrast with those on weekdays. And if we make a major change in our life, like leaving college to take up a job, alterations in our daily routines are usually necessary; but then we establish a new and fairly regular set of habits again.

Second, the study of everyday life reveals to us how humans can act creatively to shape reality. Although social behavior is guided to some extent by forces such as roles, norms, and shared expectations, individuals perceive reality differently according to their backgrounds, interests, and motivations. Because individuals are capable of creative action, they continuously shape reality through the decisions and actions they take. In other words, reality is not fixed or static—it is created through human interactions. This notion of the social construction of reality lies at the heart of the symbolic interactionist perspective introduced in Chapter 1.

Third, studying social interaction in everyday life sheds light on larger social systems and institutions. All large-scale social systems, in fact, depend on the patterns of social interaction we engage in daily. This is easy to demonstrate. Consider again the case of two strangers passing on the street. Such an event may seem to have little direct relevance to large-scale, more permanent forms of social organization. But when we take into account many such interactions, they are no longer irrelevant. In modern societies, most people live in towns and cities and constantly interact with others whom they do not know personally. Civil inattention is one among other mechanisms that give city life, with its bustling crowds and fleeting, impersonal contacts, the character it has.

In this chapter, we will first learn about the nonverbal cues (facial expressions and bodily gestures) all of us use when interacting with each other. We will then move on to analyze everyday speech—how we use language to communicate to others the meanings we wish to get across. Finally, we will focus on the ways in which our lives are structured by daily routines, paying particular attention to how we coordinate our actions across space and time.

Nonverbal Communication

Social interaction requires numerous forms of **nonverbal communication**—the exchange of information and meaning through facial expressions, gestures, and movements of the body. Nonverbal communication is sometimes referred to as "body language," but this is misleading, because we characteristically use such nonverbal cues to eliminate or expand on what is said with words.

"Face," Gestures, and Emotion

One major aspect of nonverbal communication is the facial expression of emotion. Paul Ekman and his colleagues have developed what they call the Facial Action Coding System (FACS) for describing movements of the facial muscles that give rise to particular expressions (Ekman and Friesen, 1978). By this means, they have tried to inject some precision into an area notoriously open to inconsistent or contradictory interpretations—for there is little agreement about how emotions are to be identified and classified. Charles Darwin, the originator of evolutionary theory, claimed that basic modes of emotional expression are the same in all human beings. Although some have disputed the claim, Ekman's research among people from widely different cultural backgrounds seems to confirm Darwin's view. Ekman and W. V. Friesen carried out a study of an isolated community in New Guinea, whose members had previously had virtually no contact with outsiders. When they were shown pictures of facial expressions convey-

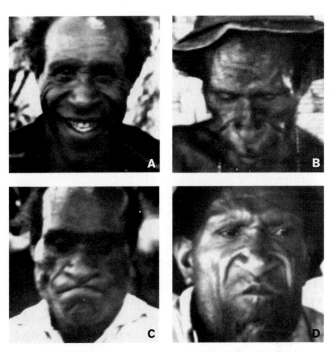

Paul Ekman's photographs of facial expressions from a tribesman in an isolated community in New Guinea helped to test the idea that basic modes of emotional expression are the same among all people. Here the instructions were to show how your face would look if you were a person in a story and (A) your friend had come and you were happy; (B) your child had died; (C) you were angry and about to fight; and (D) you saw a dead pig that had been lying there a long time.

ing six emotions (happiness, sadness, anger, disgust, fear, surprise), the New Guineans were able to identify these emotions.

According to Ekman, the results of his own and similar studies of different peoples support the view that the facial expression of emotion and its interpretation are innate in human beings. He acknowledges that his evidence does not conclusively demonstrate this, and it may be that widely shared cultural learning experiences are involved; however, his conclusions are supported by other types of research. I. Eibl-Eibesfeldt studied six children born deaf and blind to see how far their facial expressions were the same as those of sighted and hearing individuals in particular emotional situations (1972). He found that the children smiled when engaged in obviously pleasurable activities, raised their eyebrows in surprise when sniffing at an object with an unaccustomed smell, and frowned when repeatedly offered a disliked object. Since the children could not have seen other people behaving in these ways, it seems that these responses must be innately determined.

Using the FACS, Ekman and Friesen identified a number of the discrete facial muscle actions in newborn infants that are also found in adult expressions of emotion. Infants seem, for example, to produce facial expressions similar to the adult expression of disgust (pursing the lips and frowning) in response to sour tastes. But although the facial expression of emotion seems to be partly innate, individual and cultural factors influence what exact form facial movements take and the contexts in which they are deemed appropriate. How people smile, for example, the precise movement of the lips and other facial muscles, and how fleeting the smile is all vary among cultures.

There are no gestures or bodily postures that have been shown to characterize all, or even most, cultures. In some societies, for instance, people nod when they mean no, the opposite of Anglo-American practice. Gestures Americans tend to use a great deal, such as pointing, seem not to exist among certain peoples (Bull, 1983). Similarly, a straightened forefinger placed in the center of the cheek and rotated is used in parts of Italy as a gesture of praise but appears to be unknown elsewhere.

Like facial expressions, gestures and bodily posture are continually used to fill out utterances, as well as to convey meanings when nothing is actually said. All three can be used to joke, show irony, or show skepticism. The nonverbal impressions that we convey inadvertently often indicate that what we say is not quite what we really mean. Blushing is perhaps the most obvious example, but innumerable other subtle indicators can be picked up by other people. Genuine facial expressions tend to evaporate after four or five seconds. A smile that lasts longer could indicate deceit. An expression of surprise that lasts too long may indicate deliberate sarcasm—to show that the individual is not in fact surprised after all.

Gender and Nonverbal Communication

Is there a gender dimension to everyday social interaction? There are reasons to believe there is. Because interactions are shaped by the larger social context, it is not surprising that both verbal and nonverbal communication may be perceived and expressed differently by men and women. Understandings of gender and gender roles are greatly influenced by social factors and are related broadly to issues of power and status in society. These dynamics are evident even in standard interactions in daily life. Take as an example one of the most common nonverbal expressions—eye contact. Individuals use eye contact in a wide variety of ways, often to catch someone's attention or to begin a social interaction. In societies where men on the whole dominate women in both public and private life, men may feel freer than women to make eye contact with strangers.

A particular form of eye contact—staring—illustrates the contrasts in meaning between men and women of identical forms of nonverbal communication. A man who stares at a woman can be seen as acting in a "natural" or "innocent" way; if the woman is uncomfortable, she can evade the gaze by looking away or choosing not to sustain the interaction. On the other hand, a woman who stares at a man is often regarded as behaving in a suggestive or sexually leading manner. Taken individually such cases may seem inconsequential; when viewed collectively they help reinforce patterns of gender inequality.

Social Rules and Talk

Although we routinely use nonverbal cues in our own behavior and in making sense of the behavior of others, much of our interaction is done through talk—casual verbal exchange—carried on in informal conversations with others. Sociologists have always accepted that language is fundamental to social life. Recently, however, an approach has been developed that is specifically concerned with how people use language in the ordinary contexts of everyday life.

Ethnomethodology is the study of the "ethnomethods"—the folk, or lay, methods—people use to *make sense* of what others do, and particularly of what they say. We all apply these methods, normally without having to give any conscious attention to them. Often we can only make sense of what is said in conversation if we know the social context, which does not appear in the words themselves. Take the following conversation (Heritage, 1985):

A: *I have a fourteen-year-old son.*

B: *Well, that's all right.*

A: *I also have a dog.*

B: *Oh, I'm sorry.*

What do you think is happening here? What is the relation between the speakers? What if you were told that this is a conversation between a prospective tenant and a landlord? The conversation then becomes sensible: Some landlords accept children but don't permit their tenants to keep pets. Yet if we don't know the social context, the responses of individual B seem to bear no relation to the statements of A. *Part* of the sense is in the words, and *part* is in the way in which the meaning emerges from the social context.

Shared Understandings

The most inconsequential forms of daily talk presume complicated, shared knowledge brought into play by those speaking. In fact, our small talk is so complex that it has so far proved impossible to program even the most sophisticated computers to converse with human beings. The words used in ordinary talk do not always have precise meanings, and we "fix" what we want to say through the unstated assumptions that back it up. If Maria asks Tom: "What did you do yesterday?" the words in the question themselves suggest no obvious answer. A day is a long time, and it would be logical for Tom to answer: "Well, at 7:16, I woke up. At 7:18, I got out of bed, went to the bathroom and started to brush my teeth. At 7:19, I turned on the shower. . . ." We understand the type of response the question calls for by knowing Maria, what sort of activities she and Tom consider relevant, and what Tom usually does on a particular day of the week, among other things.

Garfinkel's Experiments

The "background expectancies" with which we organize ordinary conversations were highlighted by some experiments Harold Garfinkel undertook with student volunteers. The students were asked to engage a friend or relative in conversation and to insist that casual remarks or general comments be actively pursued to make their meaning precise. If someone said, "Have a nice day," the student was to respond, "Nice in what sense, exactly?" "Which part of the day do you mean?" and so forth.

People tend to get upset when apparently minor conventions of talk are not followed, because the stability and meaningfulness of our daily social lives depend on the sharing of unstated cultural assumptions about what is said and why. If we weren't able to take these for granted, meaningful communication would be impossible. Any question or contribution to a conversation would have to be followed by a massive "search procedure" of the sort Garfinkel's subjects were told to initiate, and interaction would simply break down. What seem at first sight to be unimportant conventions of talk, therefore, turn out to be fundamental to the very fabric of social life, which is why their breach is so serious.

"Interactional Vandalism"

We have already seen that conversations are one of the main ways in which our daily lives are maintained in a stable and coherent manner. We feel most comfortable when the tacit conventions of small talk are adhered to; when they are breached, we can feel threatened, confused, and insecure. In most everyday talk, conversants are carefully attuned to the cues they get from others—such as changes in intonation, slight pauses, or gestures—in order to facilitate conversation smoothly. By being mutually aware, conversants "cooperate" in opening and closing interactions, and in taking turns to

speak. Interactions in which one party is conversationally "uncooperative," however, can give rise to tensions.

Garfinkel's students created tense situations by intentionally undermining conversational rules as part of a sociological experiment. But what about situations in the real world in which people "make trouble" through their conversational practices? One study investigated verbal interchanges between pedestrians and street people in New York City to understand why such interactions are often seen as problematic by passersby. The researchers used a technique called **conversation analysis** to compare a selection of street interchanges with samples of everyday talk. Conversation analysis is a methodology that examines all facets of a conversation for meaning—from the smallest filler words (such as "um" and "ah") to the precise timing of interchanges (including pauses, interruptions, and overlaps).

The study looked at interactions between black men—many of whom were homeless, alcoholic, or drug addicted—and white women who passed by them on the street. The men would often try to initiate conversations with passing women by calling out to them, paying them compliments, or asking them questions. But something "goes wrong" in these conversations, because the women rarely respond as they would in a normal interaction. Even though the men's comments are rarely hostile in tone, the women tend to quicken their step and stare fixedly ahead. The following shows attempts by Mudrick, a black man in his late fifties, to engage women in conversation (Duneier and Molotch, 1999):

[Mudrick] begins this interaction as a white woman who looks about 25 approaches at a steady pace:
1. **Mudrick:** *I love you baby.*
She crosses her arms and quickens her walk, ignoring the comment.
2. **Mudrick:** *Marry me.*
Next, it is two white women, also probably in their mid-twenties:
3. **Mudrick:** *Hi girls, you all look very nice today. You have some money? Buy some books.*
They ignore him. Next, it is a young black woman.
4. **Mudrick:** *Hey pretty. Hey pretty.*
She keeps walking without acknowledging him.
5. **Mudrick:** *'Scuse me. 'Scuse me. I know you hear me.*
Then he addresses a white woman in her thirties.
6. **Mudrick:** *I'm watching you. You look nice, you know.*
She ignores him.

Negotiating smooth "openings" and "closings" to conversations is a fundamental requirement for urban civility. These crucial aspects of conversation were highly problematic between the men and women. Where the women resisted the men's attempts at opening conversations, the men ignored

Interactional Vandalism: A Sociologist's Fieldnote

[The author of this selection, Mitchell Duneier, coauthored this textbook. Duneier describes the behavior and lives of poor and sometimes homeless black men who work or beg in New York's Greenwich Village.]

It is well known that streets and sidewalks are places where women are disadvantaged by public harassment. While the things we are witnessing are a case of the larger public harassments that occur between some people working the street and pedestrians of both genders, perhaps for women it is a problem in distinct ways. Keith is attempting to control the woman *as a woman*, knowing that even privileged women occupy vulnerable positions in public space. Like most males (black and white), he has been taught that to be a male is to possess this power, and he feels entitled to control her. I asked after his awareness of the dog's owner as a woman.

"So, you know the dog's name," I said after they left.

"Yeah."

"Do you know the woman's name?"

"No. I'd rather have the dog than her. You know why? Dog don't want nothing but a little attention. Give him some food. Take the fucker out for a walk. Let him watch TV with you, and it's cool. But she wants room and board, clothing, makeup, hairdos, fabulous dinners, and rent, plus they want a salary for giving you some pussy once in a while.". . .

Out on Sixth Avenue one day, I ask Mudrick to tell me a little about his relationship to women on the street. Since most women ignore him, he says, he talks to all of them. That way he might get to have conversations with some of them.

Three white women in their twenties approach, and I am given a demonstration of his method. "Hi, ladies. How you-all feeling, ladies? You-all look very nice, you know. Have a nice day."

I have seen Mudrick engage in such behavior over and over again, but there is no doubt in my mind that this demon-

stration has been for me, a way of responding to the question I had just asked.

"Let me ask you a question, Mudrick. When you do that, explain to me the pleasure you get out of it."

"I get a good kick out of it."

"Explain to me the kick you get out of it."

"It make me feel good and I try to make them happy, the things I say to them, you understand? The things I say, they can't accept. They gotta deal with it."

"What do you mean, 'They gotta deal with it?'"

"They *have* to deal with it. I say sweet things to a woman. Make her feel good. Like, You look nice. You look very nice. I'd like to be with you someday if I can. Try to make you happy. Some womens treated so wrong they scared to talk to the right man. Men treat women *so* wrong. Women don't give a fuck about men. Now they go to women. They gets a woman to be their man. They turn into be a lesbian. Because they scared to mess with a man."

A woman walks by without acknowledging him, and Mudrick tells me that she must be a lesbian. He claims that the women he addresses never feel harassed, because he gives them respect, and he can tell from their smiles that they *like* the attention.

A white woman wearing sunglasses approaches with her friend.

"Hey, you, with the shades on. You look very nice."

"Thank you," she says.

"Your friend look nice, too."

"Thank you."

He tells me that the women never respond by turning away or looking angry.

"What's the worst things that women will do when you say that to them?"

"They can't do anything. Because, the words I say, they don't have any choice."

SOURCE: Reprinted from Mitchell Duneier, *Sidewalk* (New York: Farrar, Straus and Giroux, 1999), pp. 193–95, 210.

Questions

- In what ways do Mudrick and Keith take advantage of social convention and rules of politeness to interact with women?
- Why do you think these homeless men try to talk to women on the street, even though their remarks don't result in dates or even long conversations? What do they get out of it?
- Why are Mudrick's and Keith's questions and compliments to women a form of interactional vandalism?
- Why is the behavior of these men seen as different from the catcalls of construction workers or fraternity brothers?

the women's resistance and persisted. Similarly, if the men succeeded in opening a conversation, they often refused to respond to cues from the women to close the conversation once it had gotten under way (Duneier and Molotch, 1999):

1. **Mudrick:** *Hey pretty.*
2. **Woman:** *Hi how you doin'.*
3. **Mudrick:** *You alright?*
4. **Mudrick:** *You look very nice you know. I like how you have your hair pinned.*
5. **Mudrick:** *You married?*
6. **Woman:** *Yeah.*
7. **Mudrick:** *Huh?*
8. **Woman:** *Yeah.*
9. **Mudrick:** *Where the rings at?*
10. **Woman:** *I have it home.*
11. **Mudrick:** *Y' have it home?*
12. **Woman:** *Yeah.*
13. **Mudrick:** *Can I get your name?*
14. **Mudrick:** *My name is Mudrick, what's yours?*

She does not answer and walks on.

In this instance, Mudrick made nine out of the fourteen utterances in the interaction to initiate the conversation and to elicit further responses from the woman. From the transcript alone, it is quite evident that the woman is not interested in talking, but when conversation analysis is applied to the tape recording, her reluctance becomes even clearer. The woman delays all of her responses—even when she does give them, while Mudrick replies immediately, his comments sometimes overlapping hers. Timing in conversations is a very precise indicator; delaying a response by even a fraction of a second is adequate in most everyday interactions to signal the desire to change the course of a conversation. By betraying these tacit rules of sociability, Mudrick was practicing conversation in a way that was "technically rude." The woman, in return, was also "technically rude" in ignoring Mudrick's repeated attempts to engage her in talk. It is the "technically rude" nature of these street interchanges that make them problematic for passersby to handle. When standard cues for opening and closing conversations are not adhered to, individuals feel a sense of profound and inexplicable insecurity.

The term **interactional vandalism** describes cases like these in which a subordinate person breaks the tacit rules of everyday interaction that are of value to the more powerful. The men on the street often do conform to everyday forms of speech in their interactions with one another, local shopkeepers, the police, relatives, and acquaintances. But when they choose to, they subvert the tacit conventions for everyday talk in a way that leaves passersby disoriented. Even more than physical assaults or vulgar verbal abuse, interactional vandalism leaves victims unable to articulate what has happened.

This study of interactional vandalism provides another example of the two-way links between micro-level interactions and forces that operate on the macro level. To the men on the street, the white women who ignore their attempts at conversation appear distant, cold, and bereft of sympathy—legitimate "targets" for such interactions. The women, meanwhile, may often take the men's behavior as proof that they are indeed dangerous and best avoided. Interactional vandalism is closely tied up with overarching class, gender, and racial structures. The fear and anxiety generated in such mundane interactions help to constitute the outside statuses and forces that, in turn, influence the interactions themselves. Interactional vandalism is part of a self-reinforcing system of mutual suspicion and incivility.

Response Cries

Some kinds of utterances are not talk but consist of muttered exclamations, or what Goffman has called **response cries** (Goffman, 1981). Consider Lucy, who exclaims, "Oops!" after knocking over a glass of water. "Oops!" seems to be merely an uninteresting reflex response to a mishap, rather like blinking your eye when a person moves a hand sharply toward your face. It is not a reflex, however, as shown by the fact that people do not usually make the exclamation when alone. "Oops!" is normally directed toward others present. The exclamation demonstrates to witnesses that the lapse is only minor and momentary, not something that should cast doubt on Lucy's command of her actions.

"Oops!" is used only in situations of minor failure, rather than in major accidents or calamities—which also demonstrates that the exclamation is part of our controlled management of the details of social life. Moreover, the word may be used by someone observing Lucy, rather than by Lucy herself, or it may be used to sound a warning to another. "Oops!" is normally a curt sound, but the "oo" may be prolonged in some situations. Thus, someone might extend the sound to cover a critical moment in performing a task. For instance, a parent may utter an extended "Oops!" or "Oopsadaisy!" when playfully tossing a child in the air. The sound covers the brief phase when the child may feel a loss of control, reassuring him and probably at the same time developing his understanding of response cries.

This may all sound very contrived and exaggerated. Why bother to analyze such an inconsequential utterance in this detail? Surely we don't pay as much attention to what we say as this example suggests? Of course we don't—on a conscious level. The crucial point, however, is that we take for granted an immensely complicated, continuous control of our appearance and actions. In situations of interaction, we are never expected just to be present on the scene. Others expect, as we expect of them, that we will display what Goffman calls "controlled alertness." A fundamental part of being human is continually demonstrating to others our competence in the routines of daily life.

Face, Body, and Speech in Interaction

Let us summarize at this point what we have learned so far. Everyday interaction depends on subtle relationships between what we convey with our faces and bodies and what we express in words. We use the facial expressions and bodily gestures of other people to fill in what they communicate verbally and to check if they are sincere in what they say. Mostly without realizing it, each of us keeps a tight and continuous control over facial expression, bodily posture, and movement in the course of our daily interaction with others.

Face, bodily management, and speech, then, are used to convey certain meanings and to hide others. We also organize our activities in the *contexts* of social life to achieve the same ends, as we shall now see.

Encounters

In many social situations, we engage in what Goffman calls **unfocused interaction** with others. Unfocused interaction takes place whenever individuals exhibit mutual awareness of one another's presence. This is usually the case anywhere large numbers of people are assembled together, as on a busy street, in a theater crowd, or at a party. When people are in the presence of others, even if they do not directly talk to them, they continually communicate nonverbally through their posture and facial and physical gestures.

Focused interaction occurs when individuals directly attend to what others say or do. Except when someone is standing alone, say at a party, all interaction involves both focused and unfocused exchanges. Goffman calls an instance of focused interaction an **encounter**, and much of our day-to-day life consists of encounters with other people—family, friends, colleagues—frequently occurring against the background of unfocused interaction with others present on the scene. Small talk, seminar discussions, games, and routine face-to-face contacts (with ticket clerks, waiters, shop assistants, and so forth) are all examples of encounters.

Encounters always need "openings," which indicate that civil inattention is being discarded. When strangers meet and begin to talk at a party, the moment of ceasing civil inattention is always risky, since misunderstandings can easily occur about the nature of the encounter being established (Goffman, 1971). Hence, the making of eye contact may first be ambiguous and tentative. A person can then act as though he had made no direct move if the overture is not accepted. In focused interaction, each person communicates as much by facial expression and gesture as by the words actually exchanged. Goffman distinguishes between the expressions individuals "give" and those they "give off." The first are the words and facial expressions people use to produce certain impressions on others. The second are the clues that others may spot to check their sincerity or truthfulness. For instance, a restaurant owner listens with a polite smile to the statements of customers about how much they enjoyed their meals. At the same time, he is noting how pleased they seemed to be while eating the food, whether a lot was left over, and the tone of voice they use to express their satisfaction.

Impression Management

Goffman and other writers on social interaction often use notions from the theater in their analyses. The concept of social role, for example, originated in a theatrical setting. **Roles** are socially defined expectations that a person in a given **status** (or **social position**) follows. To be a teacher is to hold a specific position; the teacher's role consists of acting in specified ways toward her pupils. Goffman sees social life as though played out by actors on a stage—or on many stages, because how we act depends on the roles we are playing at a particular time. People are sensitive to how they are seen by others and use many forms of **impression management** to compel others to react to them in the ways they wish. Although we may sometimes do this in a calculated way, usually it is among the things we do without conscious attention. When Philip attends a business meeting, he wears a suit and tie and is on his best behavior; that evening, when relaxing with friends at a football game, he wears jeans and a sweatshirt and tells a lot of jokes. This is impression management.

"Hmmm...what shall I wear today...?"

This glimpse of former Democratic presidential hopeful Howard Dean moments before addressing a crowd provides a metaphorical depiction of front and back regions. Backstage, or in the back region, Dean composes himself with the support of an assistant. When he takes the stage, or begins his front-region performance, he will need to appear confident, knowledgeable, and enthusiastic.

As we just noted above, the social roles that we adopt are highly dependent on our social status. A person's social status can be different depending on the social context. For instance, as a "student" you have a certain status and are expected to act a certain way when you are around your professors. As a "son" or "daughter" you have a different status from a student, and society (especially your parents) has different expectations for you. Likewise, as a "friend" you have an entirely different position in the social order, and the roles you adopt would change accordingly. Obviously, a person has many statuses at the same time. Sociologists refer to the group of statuses that you occupy as a **status set**.

Sociologists also like to distinguish between ascribed status and achieved status. An **ascribed status** is one that you are "assigned" based on biological factors such as race, sex, or age. Thus your ascribed statuses could be "white," "female," and "teenager." An **achieved status** is one that is earned through an individual's own effort. Your achieved statuses could be "high school graduate," "athlete," or "employee." While we may like to believe that it is our achieved statuses that are most important, society may not agree. In any society, some statuses have priority over all other statuses and generally determine a person's overall position in society. Sociologists refer to this as a **master status** (Hughes, 1945; Becker, 1963). The most common master statuses are those based on gender and race. Sociologists have shown that in an encounter, one of the first things that people notice about one another is gender and race (Omi and Winant, 1994). As we shall see shortly, both race and gender strongly shape our social interactions.

FRONT AND BACK REGIONS

Much of social life, Goffman suggested, can be divided into front regions and back regions. **Front regions** are social occasions or encounters in which individuals act out formal roles; they are "onstage performances." Teamwork is often involved in creating front-region performances. Two prominent politicians in the same party may put on an elaborate show of unity and friendship before the television cameras, even though each privately detests the other. A wife and husband may take care to conceal their quarrels from their children, preserving a front of harmony, only to fight bitterly once the children are safely tucked in bed.

The **back regions** are where people assemble the props and prepare themselves for interaction in the more formal settings. Back regions resemble the backstage of a theater or the off-camera activities of filmmaking. When they are safely behind the scenes, people can relax and give vent to feelings and styles of behavior they keep in check when on front stage. Thus, a waitress may be the soul of quiet courtesy when serving a customer but become loud and aggressive once behind the swing doors of the kitchen. Probably few people would continue to patronize restaurants if they could see all that goes on in the kitchens.

Personal Space

There are cultural differences in the definition of **personal space**. In Western culture, people usually maintain a distance of at least three feet when engaged in focused interaction with others; when standing side by side, they may stand closer together. In the Middle East, people often stand closer to each other than is thought acceptable in the West. Westerners visiting that part of the world are likely to find themselves disconcerted by this unexpected physical proximity.

Edward T. Hall, who has worked extensively on nonverbal communication, distinguishes four zones of personal space. Intimate distance, of up to one and a half feet, is reserved for very few social contacts. Only those involved in relationships in which regular bodily touching is permitted, such as lovers or parents and children, operate within this zone of private space. Personal distance, from one and a half to four feet, is the normal spacing for encounters with friends and close acquaintances. Some intimacy of contact is permitted, but this tends to be strictly limited. Social distance, from four to twelve feet, is the zone usually maintained in formal settings such as interviews. The fourth zone is that of public distance, beyond twelve feet, preserved by those who are performing to an audience.

In ordinary interaction, the most fraught zones are those of intimate and personal distance. If these zones are invaded, people try to recapture their space. We may stare at the intruder as if to say, "Move away!" or elbow him aside. When people are forced into proximity closer than they deem desirable, they might create a kind of physical boundary: A reader at a crowded library desk might physically demarcate a private space by stacking books around its edges (Hall, 1969, 1973).

Interaction in Time and Space

Understanding how activities are distributed in time and space is fundamental to analyzing encounters, and also to understanding social life in general. All interaction is situated—it occurs in a particular place and has a specific duration in time. Our actions over the course of a day tend to be "zoned" in time as well as in space. Thus, for example, most people spend a zone—say, from 9:00 A.M. to 5:00 P.M.—of their daily time working. Their weekly time is also zoned: They are likely to work on weekdays and spend weekends at home, altering the pattern of their activities on the weekend days. As we move through the temporal zones of the day, we are also often moving across space as well: To get to work, we may take a bus from one area of a city to another or perhaps commute in from the suburbs. When we analyze the contexts of social interaction, therefore, it is often useful to look at people's movements across **time-space**.

The concept of **regionalization** will help us understand how social life is zoned in time-space. Take the example of a private house. A modern house is regionalized into rooms, hallways, and floors if there is more than one story. These spaces are not just physically separate areas, but are zoned in time as well. The living rooms and kitchen are used most in the daylight hours, the bedrooms at night. The interaction that occurs in these regions is bound by both spatial and temporal divisions. Some areas of the house form back regions, with "performances" taking place in the others. At times, the whole house can become a back region.

Clock Time

In modern societies, the zoning of our activities is strongly influenced by **clock time**. Without clocks and the precise timing of activities, and thereby their coordination across space, industrialized societies could not exist (Mumford, 1973). The measuring of time by clocks is today standardized across the globe, making possible the complex international transport systems and communications we now depend on. World standard time was first introduced in 1884 at a conference of nations held in Washington. The globe was then partitioned into twenty-four time zones, each one hour apart, and an exact beginning of the universal day was fixed.

Fourteenth-century monasteries were the first organizations to try to schedule the activities of their inmates precisely across the day and week. Today, there is virtually no group or organization that does not do so—the greater the number of people and resources involved, the more precise the scheduling must be. Eviatar Zerubavel demonstrated this in his study of the temporal structure of a large modern hospital (1979, 1982). A hospital must operate on a twenty-four-hour basis, and coordinating the staff and resources is a highly complex matter. For instance, the nurses work for one time period in ward A, another time period in ward B, and so on, and are also called on to alternate between day- and night-shift work. Nurses, doctors, and other staff, plus the resources they need, must be integrated together both in time and in space.

Social Life and the Ordering of Space and Time

The Internet is another example of how closely forms of social life are bound up with our control of space and time. The Internet makes it possible for us to interact with people we never see or meet, in any corner of the world. Such technological change "rearranges" space—we can interact with anyone without moving from our chair. It also alters our experience of time, because communication on the electronic highway is almost immediate. Until about fifty years ago, most communication across space required a duration of time. If you sent a letter to someone abroad, there was a time gap while the letter was carried, by ship, train, truck, or plane, to the person to whom it was written.

International Tourism

Have you ever had a face-to-face conversation with someone from another country? Or connected to an overseas Web site? Have you ever traveled to another part of the world? If you answered yes to any of these questions, you have witnessed the effects of globalization on social interaction. Americans, of course, have always interacted with people from foreign lands if for no other reason than America itself is an ethnically and culturally diverse nation. At the same time, globalization—a relatively recent phenomenon—has changed both the frequency and the nature of interactions between people of different nations. The historical sociologist Charles Tilly, in fact, defines globalization in terms of these changes. According to Tilly, "globalization means an increase in the geographic range of locally consequential social interactions" (1995). In other words, with globalization a greater proportion of our interactions come to involve, directly or indirectly, people from other countries.

What are the characteristics of social interactions that take place between individuals of different nations? Important contributions to the study of this problem have been made by those working in the area of the sociology of tourism. Sociologists of tourism note that globalization has greatly expanded the possibilities for international travel, both by encouraging an interest in other countries and by facilitating the movement of tourists across international borders. As a result, more than 45 million foreign tourists visited the United States in 1994—a significant increase from previous decades. These visitors pumped more than $60 billion into the U.S. economy (OECD, 1996). Americans are also traveling the world in record numbers.

People still write letters by hand today, of course, but instantaneous communication has become basic to our social world. Our lives would be almost unimaginable without it. We are so used to being able to switch on the TV and watch the news or make a phone call or send an e-mail message to a friend in another state that it is hard for us to imagine what life would be like otherwise.

Everyday Life in Cultural and Historical Perspective

Some of the mechanisms of social interaction analyzed by Goffman, Garfinkel, and others seem to be universal. But much of Goffman's discussion of civil inattention and other kinds of interaction primarily concerns societies in which contact with strangers is commonplace. What about very small traditional societies, where there are no strangers and few settings in which more than a handful of people are together at any one time?

To see some of the contrasts between social interaction in modern and traditional societies, let's take as an example one of the least developed cultures in terms of technology remaining in the world: the !Kung (sometimes known as the Bushmen), who live in the Kalahari Desert area of Botswana and Namibia, in southern Africa (Lee, 1968, 1969; the exclamation mark refers to a click sound one makes before pronouncing the name). Although their way of life is changing because of outside influences, their traditional patterns of social life are still evident.

The !Kung live in groups of some thirty or forty people, in temporary settlements near water holes. Food is scarce in their environment, and they must walk far and wide to find it. Such roaming takes up most of the average day. Women and children often stay back in the camp, but equally often the whole group spends the day walking. Members of the community will some-

High levels of international tourism, of course, translate into an increase in the number of face-to-face interactions between people of different countries. According to the British sociologist John Urry (1990), many of these interactions are shaped by the "tourist gaze," the expectation on the part of the tourist that he or she will have "exotic" experiences while traveling abroad. "Exotic" experiences are those that violate our everyday expectations about how social interaction and interaction with the physical environment are supposed to proceed. Americans traveling in England, for example, may delight in the fact that the British drive on the left-hand side of the road. Such behavior is disconcerting to American drivers. Our rules of the road are so ingrained that we experience systematic violations of those rules as strange, weird, and exotic. Yet, as tourists, we take pleasure in this strangeness. In a sense, it is what we have paid money to see—along with Big Ben and the Tower of London. Imagine how disappointed you would be if you traveled to a different country only to find that it was almost exactly the same as the city or town in which you grew up.

Yet most tourists do not want their experiences to be *too* exotic. One of the most popular destinations for young Americans in Paris, for example, is a McDonald's restaurant. Some come to see if there is any truth to the line from the movie *Pulp Fiction* that because the French use the metric system, McDonald's "quarter pounder with cheese" hamburgers are called "Royales with cheese" (it is true, by the way). But many others come for the comfort of eating familiar food in a familiar setting. The contradictory demands for the exotic and the familiar are at the heart of the tourist gaze.

The tourist gaze may put strains on face-to-face interactions between tourists and locals. Locals who are part of the tourist industry may appreciate overseas travelers for the economic benefits they bring to the places they visit. Other locals may resent tourists for their demanding attitudes or for the overdevelopment that often occurs in popular tourist destinations. Tourists may interrogate locals about aspects of their everyday lives, such as their food, work, and recreational habits; they may do this either to enhance their understanding of other cultures or to judge negatively those who are different from themselves.

As tourism increases with the march of globalization, sociologists will have to watch carefully to see what dominant patterns of interaction emerge between tourists and locals, and to determine, among other things, whether these interactions tend to be friendly or antagonistic.

times fan out over an area of up to a hundred square miles in the course of a day, returning to the camp at night to eat and sleep. The men may be alone or in groups of two or three for much of the day. There is one period of the year, however, when the routines of their daily activities change: the winter rainy season, when water is abundant and food much easier to come by. The everyday life of the !Kung during this period is centered around ritual and ceremonial activities, the preparation for and enactment of which is very time consuming.

The members of most !Kung groups never see anyone they don't know reasonably well. Until contacts with the outside became more common in recent years, they had no word for "stranger." While the !Kung, particularly the males, may spend long periods of the day out of contact with others, in the community itself there is little opportunity for privacy. Families sleep in flimsy, open dwellings, with virtually all activities open to public view. No one has studied the !Kung with

Goffman's observations on everyday life in mind, but it is easy to see that some aspects of his work have limited application to !Kung social life. There are few opportunities, for example, to create front and back regions. The closing off of different gatherings and encounters by the walls of rooms, separate buildings, and the various neighborhoods of cities common in modern societies are remote from the activities of the !Kung.

The Compulsion of Proximity

In modern societies, in complete contrast to the !Kung—as will be explored in the chapters that follow—we are constantly interacting with others whom we may never see or meet. Almost all of our everyday transactions, such as buying groceries or making a bank deposit, bring us into contact—but *indirect* contact—with people who may live thousands of miles away.

The banking system, for example, is international. Any money you deposit is a small part of the financial investments the bank makes worldwide.

Some people are concerned that the rapid advances in communications technology such as e-mail, the Internet, and e-commerce will only increase this tendency toward indirect interactions. Our society is becoming "devoiced," some claim, as the capabilities of technology grow ever greater. According to this view, as the pace of life accelerates, people are increasingly isolating themselves; we now interact more with our televisions and computers than with our neighbors or members of the community.

Now that e-mail, instant messages, electronic discussion groups, and chat rooms have become facts of life for many people in industrialized countries, what is the nature of these interactions, and what new complexities are emerging from them? In a 1997 study of office workers, almost half of the respondents said that the Internet had replaced the need for face-to-face communication. A third of them admitted to using e-mail deliberately in order to avoid the need for face-to-face communication. Others reported that the use of abusive or offensive e-mails within the workplace had resulted in the complete breakdown of some office relations. Online communication seems to allow more room for misinterpretation, confusion, and abuse than more traditional forms of communication.

Many Internet enthusiasts disagree. They argue that, far from being impersonal, online communication has many inherent advantages that cannot be claimed by more traditional forms of interaction such as the telephone and face-to-face meetings. The human voice, for example, may be far superior in terms of expressing emotion and subtleties of meaning, but it can also convey information about the speaker's age, gender, ethnicity, or social position—information that could be used to the speaker's disadvantage. Electronic communication, it is noted, masks all these identifying markers and ensures that attention focuses strictly on the content of the message. This can be a great advantage for women or other traditionally disadvantaged groups whose opinions are sometimes devalued in other settings (Pascoe, 2000). Electronic interaction is often presented as liberating and empowering, since people can create their own online identities and speak more freely than they would elsewhere.

Who is right in this debate? How far can electronic communication substitute for face-to-face interaction? There is little question that new media forms are revolutionizing the way people communicate, but even at times when it is more expedient to interact indirectly, humans still value direct contact—possibly even more highly than before. People in business, for instance, continue to attend meetings, sometimes flying halfway around the world to do so, when it would seem much simpler and more effective to transact business through a conference call or video link. Family members could arrange "virtual" reunions or holiday gatherings using electronic real-time communications, but we all recognize that they would lack the warmth and intimacy of face-to-face celebrations.

An explanation for this phenomenon comes from Deidre Boden and Harvey Molotch, who have studied what they call the **compulsion of proximity**: the need of individuals to meet with one another in situations of *copresence*, or face-to-face interaction. People put themselves out to attend meetings, Boden and Molotch suggest, because situations of copresence, for reasons documented by Goffman in his studies of interaction, supply much richer information about how other people think and feel, and about their sincerity, than any form of electronic communication. Only by actually being in the presence of people who make decisions affecting us in important ways do we feel able to learn what is going on and confident that we can impress them with our own views and our own sincerity. "Copresence," Boden and Molotch say, "affects access to the body part that 'never lies,' the eyes—the 'windows on the soul.' Eye contact itself signals a degree of intimacy and trust; copresent interactants continuously monitor the subtle movements of this most subtle body part" (1994).

Linking Microsociology and Macrosociology

As we saw in Chapter 1, *microsociology*, the study of everyday behavior in situations of face-to-face interaction, and *macrosociology*, the study of the broader features of society like class or gender hierarchies, are closely connected. We will now turn to examine social encounters on a crowded city sidewalk to illustrate this point.

Women and Men in Public

Take, for example, a situation that may seem "micro" on its face: A woman walking down the street is verbally harassed by a group of men. In her study, *Passing By: Gender and Public Harassment*, Carol Brooks Gardner found that in various settings, most famously, the edges of construction sites, these types of unwanted interaction occur as something women frequently experience as abusive.

Although the harassment of a single woman might be analyzed in microsociological terms by looking at a single interaction, it is not fruitful to view it that simply. Such harassment is typical of street talk involving men and women who are strangers (Gardner, 1995). And these kinds of interactions cannot simply be understood without also looking at the larger background of gender hierarchy in the United States. In this way we can see how micro- and macroanalysis are connected. For example, Gardner linked the harassment of women by men to the larger system of gender inequality, represented by male privilege in public spaces, women's physical vulnerability, and the omnipresent threat of rape.

Without making this link between micro- and macrosociology, we can have only a limited understanding of these interactions. It might seem as though these types of interactions are isolated instances or that they could be eliminated by teaching people good manners. Understanding the link between micro and macro helps us see that in order to attack the problem at its root cause, one would need to focus on eliminating the forms of gender inequality that give rise to such interactions.

Blacks and Whites in Public

Have you ever crossed to the other side of the street when you felt threatened by someone behind you or someone coming toward you? One sociologist who tried to understand simple interactions of this kind is Elijah Anderson.

Anderson began by describing social interaction on the streets of two adjacent urban neighborhoods. His book *Streetwise: Race, Class, and Change in an Urban Community* (1990) found that studying everyday life sheds light on how social order is created by the individual building blocks of infinite micro-level interactions. He was particularly interested in understanding interactions when at least one party was viewed as threatening. Anderson showed that the ways many blacks and whites interact on the streets of a northern city had a great deal to do with the structure of racial stereotypes, which is itself linked to the economic structure of society. In this way, he showed the link between micro interactions and the larger macro structures of society.

Anderson began by recalling Erving Goffman's description of how social roles and statuses come into existence in particular contexts or locations: "When an individual enters the presence of others, they commonly seek to acquire information about him or bring into play information already possessed. . . . Information about the individual helps to define the situation, enabling others to know in advance what he will expect of them and they may expect of him."

Following Goffman's lead, Anderson asked, what types of behavioral cues and signs make up the vocabulary of public interaction? He concluded that

skin color, gender, age, companions, clothing, jewelry, and the objects people carry help identify them, so that assumptions are formed and communication can occur. Movements (quick or slow, false or sincere, comprehensible or incomprehensible) further refine this public

Immediate assumptions based on race, gender, economic status, and style of dress, among other signs and behavioral cues, affect the way strangers behave toward each other. Elijah Anderson's study of social interaction between strangers on urban streets showed a strong connection between such micro-level interactions and the creation of social order.

communication. Factors like time of day or an activity that "explains" a person's presence can also affect in what way and how quickly the image of "stranger" is neutralized. If a stranger cannot pass inspection and be assessed as "safe," the image of predator may arise, and fellow pedestrians may try to maintain a distance consistent with that image. (Anderson, 1990)

Anderson showed that the people most likely to pass inspection are those who do not fall into commonly accepted stereotypes of dangerous persons: "children readily pass inspection, while women and white men do so more slowly, black women, black men, and black male teenagers most slowly of all." In showing that interactional tensions derive from outside statuses such as race, class, and gender, Anderson shows that we cannot develop a full understanding of the situation by looking at the micro interactions themselves. This is how he makes the link between micro interactions and macro processes.

Anderson argues that people are "streetwise" when they develop skills such as "the art of avoidance" to deal with their felt vulnerability toward violence and crime. According to Anderson, whites who are not streetwise do not recognize the difference between different kinds of black men (e.g., middle-class youths vs. gang members). They may also not know how to alter the number of paces to walk behind a "suspicious" person or how to bypass "bad blocks" at various times of day.

Study Outline

www.wwnorton.com/giddens

Social Interaction

- Many apparently trivial aspects of our day-to-day behavior turn out on close examination to be both complex and important aspects of *social interaction*. An example is the gaze—looking at other people. In most interactions, eye contact is fairly fleeting. To stare at another person could be taken as a sign of hostility—or on some occasions, of love. The study of social interaction is a fundamental area in sociology, illuminating many aspects of social life.

Nonverbal Communication

- Many different expressions are conveyed by the human face. It is widely held that basic aspects of the facial expressions of emotion are innate. Cross-cultural studies demonstrate quite close similarities between members of different cultures both in facial expression and in the interpretation of emotions registered on the human face.

Ethnomethodology

- The study of ordinary talk and conversation has come to be called *ethnomethodology*, a term first coined by Harold Garfinkel. Ethnomethodology is the analysis of the ways in which we actively—although usually in a taken-for-granted way—make sense of what others mean by what they say and do.

Face, Body, and Speech in Interaction

- *Unfocused interaction* is the mutual awareness individuals have of one another in large gatherings when not directly in conversation together. *Focused interaction*, which can be divided up into distinct *encounters*, or episodes of interaction, is when two or more individuals are directly attending to what the other or others are saying and doing.
- Social interaction can often be illuminatingly studied by applying the dramaturgical model—studying social interaction as if those involved were actors on a stage, having a set and props. As in the theater, in the various contexts of social life there tend to be clear distinctions between *front regions* (the stage itself) and *back regions*, where the actors prepare themselves for the performance and relax afterward.

Interaction in Time and Space

- All social interaction is situated in time and space. We can analyze how our daily lives are "zoned" in both time and space combined by looking at how activities occur during definite durations and at the same time involve spatial movement.
- Some mechanisms of social interaction may be universal, but many are not. The !Kung of southern Africa, for example, live in small mobile bands, where there is little privacy and thus little opportunity to create front and back regions.

Indirect Interaction

- Modern societies are characterized largely by indirect interpersonal transactions (such as making bank deposits), which lack any copresence. This leads to what has been called the *compulsion of proximity*, the tendency to want to meet in person whenever possible, perhaps because this makes it easier to gather information about how others think and feel, and to accomplish *impression management*.

Key Concepts

achieved status (p. 94)
ascribed status (p. 94)
back region (p. 94)
civil inattention (p. 85)
clock time (p. 95)
compulsion of proximity (p. 98)
conversation analysis (p. 89)
encounter (p. 93)
ethnomethodology (p. 88)
focused interaction (p. 93)
front region (p. 94)
impression management (p. 93)
interactional vandalism (p. 92)
master status (p. 94)
nonverbal communication (p. 87)
personal space (p. 94)
regionalization (p. 95)
response cry (p. 92)
role (p. 93)
social interaction (p. 86)
social position (p. 93)
status (p. 93)
status set (p. 94)
time-space (p. 95)
unfocused interaction (p. 93)

Review Questions

1. What is the difference between achieved status and ascribed status?
   a. There is no difference between achieved and ascribed status.
   b. Achieved status is a social standing that others accord to us on the basis of attributes we can change, whereas ascribed status is a social standing others accord to us on the basis of attributes we cannot change.
   c. Achieved status has to do with gender and ethnicity, whereas ascribed status has to do with social class.
   d. Achieved status is equivalent to economic status, whereas ascribed status is equivalent to cultural and political status.

2. What is the study of nonverbal communication?
   a. The study of the way people use tone of voice and pronunciation to convey the exact meaning of their words.
   b. The study of the use of dress, makeup, and jewelry to convey personal identity.
   c. The study of facial expressions, gestures, and body movements.
   d. The study of human interaction with such regular features of everyday life as pets and computers, which can communicate, but not verbally.

3. Ethnomethodology studies
   a. conversations in a café.
   b. casual greetings.
   c. response cries.
   d. all of the above.

4. Human beings have a "compulsion to proximity," or the need to
   a. use whatever electronic means are available to communicate.
   b. meet up with one another in situations of copresence.
   c. experience sexual intimacy.
   d. perceive themselves as discrete social units.

5. Which of the following is an example of impression management?
   a. A professor relaxes in the office after teaching.
   b. A physician listens to a patient before prescribing medicine.
   c. A candidate dresses appropriately for a job interview.
   d. A mother shops at a local grocery store.

6. If a waiter says, "Enjoy your meal" and you reply, "Enjoy in what sense, exactly?" then you have utilized one of
   a. Ekman's experiments in facial muscle analysis.
   b. Garfinkel's experiments in ethnomethodology.
   c. Goffman's experiments in conversational analysis.
   d. Goffman's experiments in social interactions.

7. According to Erving Goffman, if individuals at a large party exhibit mutual awareness of one another's presence, it is called
   a. mutual attraction.
   b. focused interaction.
   c. unfocused interaction.
   d. an encounter.

8. Men may feel more freedom than women in making eye contact with strangers in societies where
   a. women dominate men in both public and private life.
   b. men dominate women in both public and private life.
   c. women have the same status as men in both public and private life.
   d. there are more men than women.

9. In a study by Ekman and Friesen, when members of an isolated New Guinea community were shown pictures of facial expressions conveying six emotions, they were able to identify
   a. none of the six emotions.
   b. all of the six emotions.
   c. only half of the six emotions.
   d. one emotion, happiness.

10. The social occasions or encounters in which individuals act out formal roles are called
   a. back regions.
   b. middle regions.
   c. front regions.
   d. stage regions.

Thinking Sociologically Exercises

1. Identify the important elements to the dramaturgical perspective. This chapter shows how the theory might be applied in the ministrations of the nurse to his/her patient. Apply the theory similarly to account for a plumber's visit to a client's home. Are there any similarities? Explain.

2. Smoking cigarettes is a pervasive habit found in many parts of the world and a habit that could be explained by both microsociological and macrosociological forces. Give an example of each that would be relevant to explain the proliferation of smoking. How might your suggested micro- and macro-level analyses be linked?

Data Exercises

www.wwnorton.com/giddens
Keyword: Data4

- This chapter highlights the structures and processes of everyday social interactions that have a significant influence on us, but are often overlooked. It is particularly difficult to accept the idea that social factors like class, race, and gender may affect our interactions with and perceptions of the world. The data exercise for this chapter focuses on how race shapes our understanding of reality.

Social Groups

Learn the variety and characteristics of groups, as well as the effect of groups on an individual's behavior.

Networks

Understand the importance of social networks and the advantages they confer on some people.

Organizations

Know how to define an organization and understand how they developed over the last two centuries.

Theories of Organizations

Learn Max Weber's theory of organizations and view of bureaucracy.

Beyond Bureaucracy?

Familiarize yourself with some of the alternatives to bureaucracy that have developed in other societies or in recent times. Think about the influence of technology on how organizations operate.

How Do Groups and Organizations Affect Your Life?

CHAPTER FIVE

GROUPS, NETWORKS, AND ORGANIZATIONS

On March 27, 1997, thirty-nine members of a religious group known as "Heaven's Gate" committed mass suicide in their rented mansion in an upscale suburb of San Diego, California. The twenty-one men and eighteen women ranged in age from twenty-six to seventy-two years old. Most were in their forties and fifties. They were, for the most part, educated and intelligent. They ran a successful Web site design company called, appropriately, "The Higher Source." So passionately were they committed to their group's beliefs that none questioned the decision to die.

Their suicide—committed by ingesting massive overdoses of sleeping pills mixed in applesauce—was intended to free group members of their human bodies, or "vehicles." This was viewed as a necessary step in ascending to the "next level," which they believed was waiting for them in the form of a spacecraft concealed by the Hale-Bopp comet then brightly streaking through the sky. Each purple-shrouded body sported brand-new Nike running shoes and exactly five dollars in quarters to see him or her through the journey.

The group's beliefs would strike most people as a bizarre fusion of Christianity, New Age religion, and science fiction. Members were devotees of such TV series as *Star Trek* and *The X-Files*. The group's leader, Marshall Herff Applewhite (who called himself "Do" for the syllable used to denote the first tone of the musical scale), claimed that extraterrestrials from the "Kingdom of Heaven" were monitoring their "garden Earth" in hopes of offering humanity a chance to move to a "higher evolutionary level." "Do" claimed to be allied with a heavenly partner, "Ti" (Bonnie Lou Nettles, the group's cofounder), who had died twelve years earlier (Heaven's Gate, 1997).

In preparation for their extraterrestrial hereafter, group members followed a strict set of rules. They banned the consumption of drugs and alcohol, terminated all personal attachments outside the group, rejected all material possessions, wore cropped hair and practiced celibacy (many males, following "Do's" lead, were castrated). But the appearance of the Hale-Bopp comet in the spring of 1997 signaled the end of this preparatory stage and the promise of a "boarding pass" to salvation.

Heaven's Gate used the Internet as a recruitment tool as well as a means of earning income for the group. On their Web site, Applewhite called himself the "Present Representative," drawing parallels between himself and Jesus and promising eternal life for those who joined him.

Heaven's Gate may strike you as an extreme case of how groups exercise influence over their members, who are sometimes willing to conform to group expectations even at the cost of their lives. This behavior is distressing in part because obedience to group dictates and the sacrifice of personal freedom go against the grain of our individualistic culture. However, we all conform, at least to some degree, to groups. From small groups of friends to large organizations such as colleges and universities, we are all subject to the constraints and demands of group life. Indeed, through groups, we enjoy human culture, and to different degrees according to our backgrounds, we also benefit from freedoms and opportunities to pursue our chosen goals in life.

In this chapter you will learn about different kinds of groups and their role in shaping your experiences. For example, you will learn how group size affects your behavior in groups and about the nature of leadership. Special attention is given to sociological research into individual conformity to group norms, helping you understand how such ordinary, intelligent persons as those in the Heaven's Gate group could willingly follow their leader to their deaths. We will also examine the role played by organizations in American society, the major theories of modern organizations, and the ways in which organizations are changing in the modern world. The increased impact of technology on organizations and the prominence of the Internet in our group life is also explored. Finally, the chapter concludes with a consideration of the rising role of global organizations in the world today.

Social Groups

Nearly everything of importance in our lives occurs through some type of social group. You and your roommate make up a social group, as do the members of your introductory sociol-

ogy class. A **social group** is a collection of people who share a common identity and regularly interact with one another on the basis of shared expectations concerning behavior. People who belong to the same social group identify with each other, expect each other to conform to certain ways of thinking and acting, and recognize the boundaries that separate them from other groups or people. In our need to congregate and belong, we have created a rich and varied group life that gives us our norms, practices, and values—our whole way of life.

Groups: Variety and Characteristics

We may sometimes feel that we are alone, yet we seldom find ourselves far away from one kind of group or another. Every day nearly all of us move through various social situations, such as one involving an intimate two-person group or one within a large bureaucratic organization. We hang out with groups of friends, study with classmates, play team sports, and go online to find new friends or people who share our interests. Like people nearly everywhere, we are organizational addicts (Aldrich and Marsden, 1988).

However, just because people find themselves in each other's company does not make them a social group. People milling around in crowds, waiting for a bus, or strolling on a beach are said to make up a social aggregate. A **social aggregate** is a simple collection of people who happen to be together in a particular place but do not significantly interact or identify with each other. The people waiting together at a bus station, for example, may be conscious of one another's presence, but they are unlikely to think of themselves as a "we"—the group waiting for the next bus to Poughkeepsie or Des Moines. By the same token, people may comprise a **social category**, people sharing a common characteristic (such as gender or occupation) without necessarily interacting or identifying with one another. The sense of belonging to a common social group is missing.

IN-GROUPS AND OUT-GROUPS

The "sense of belonging" that characterizes social groups is sometimes strengthened by groups' scorning the members of other groups (Sartre, 1965, orig. 1948). Creating a sense of belonging in this way is especially true of racist groups, which promote their identity as "superior" by hating "inferior" groups. Jews, Catholics, African Americans and other people of color, immigrants, and gay people are typically the targets of such hatred. This sense of group identity created through scorn is dramatically illustrated by the rantings on the former Web page of a racist skinhead group that called itself Combat

18: "We are the last of our warrior race, and it is our duty to fight for our people. The Jew will do everything to discredit us, but we hold that burning flame in our hearts that drove our ancestors to conquer whole continents" (Combat 18, 1998).

Such proud, disdainful language illustrates the sociological distinction between in-groups and out-groups. **In-groups** are groups toward which one feels particular loyalty and respect—the groups that "we" belong to. **Out-groups**, on the other hand, are groups toward which one feels antagonism and contempt—"*those* people." Most people occasionally use in-group–out-group imagery to trumpet what they believe to be their group's strengths vis-à-vis some other group's presumed weaknesses. For example, members of a fraternity or a sorority may bolster their feelings of superiority—in academics, sports, or campus image—by ridiculing the members of a different house. Similarly, an ethnic group may prefer its sons and daughters to marry only within the group, a church often holds up its "truths" as the only ones, and immigrants—always outsiders upon arriving in a new country—are sometimes accused of ruining the country for "real Americans."

PRIMARY AND SECONDARY GROUPS

Group life differs greatly in how intensely group members experience it. Beginning with the family—the first group to which most of us belong—many of the groups that shape our personalities and lives are those in which we experience strong emotional ties. This experience is common not only for families, but also for groups of friends, including gangs or other peer groups, all of which are known as **primary groups**. Primary groups are usually small groups characterized by face-to-face interaction, intimacy, and a strong, enduring sense of commitment. In this type of group, there is also often an experience of unity, a merging of the self with the group into one personal "we." Individuals in these groups are also more likely to enjoy relationships for their own sake. Friends may ask you to take advantage of their offer of good theater seats or help writing a paper, but they will be hurt if they feel that that is all you want from them. The sociologist Charles Horton Cooley (1864–1929) termed such groups "primary" because he believed that they were the basic form of association, exerting a long-lasting influence on the development of our social selves (Cooley, 1964, orig. 1902).

In contrast, **secondary groups** are large and impersonal and often involve fleeting relationships. Secondary groups seldom involve intense emotional ties, powerful commitments to the group itself, or an experience of unity. We seldom feel we can "be ourselves" in a secondary group; rather, we are often playing a particular role, such as employee or student. While Cooley argued that people belong to primary groups mainly because such groups are inherently fulfilling, people join secondary groups to achieve some specific goal: to earn a living, get a college degree, or compete in sports. Examples of secondary groups include business organizations, schools, work groups, athletic clubs, and governmental bodies. Secondary groups may of course become primary groups for some of their members. For example, when students taking a course begin to socialize after class, they create bonds of friendship that constitute a primary group.

For most of human history, nearly all interactions took place within primary groups. This pattern began to change with the emergence of larger, agrarian societies, which included such secondary groups as those based on governmental roles or occupation. Today most of our waking hours are spent within secondary groups, although primary groups remain a basic part of our lives.

Some early sociologists, such as Cooley, worried about a loss of intimacy as more and more interactions revolved around large impersonal organizations. However, what Cooley saw as the growing impersonality and anonymity of modern life may also offer an increasing tolerance of individual differences. Primary groups, which often enforce strict conformity to group standards (Simmel, 1955; Durkheim, 1964, orig. 1893), can be suffocating. Impersonal secondary groups are more likely than primary groups to be concerned with accomplishing a task, rather than with enforcing conformity to group standards of behavior.

REFERENCE GROUPS

We often judge ourselves by how we think we appear to others, which Cooley termed the "looking-glass self." Groups as well as individuals provide the standards by which we make self-evaluations. Robert K. Merton elaborated on Cooley's concept by discussing reference groups as measures by which we

Advertising creates a set of imaginary reference groups meant to influence consumers' buying habits by presenting unlikely—often impossible—ideals to which consumers aspire.

evaluate ourselves (Merton, 1968, orig. 1938). A **reference group** is a group that provides a standard for judging one's own attitudes or behaviors (see also Hyman and Singer, 1968). The family is typically one of the more crucial reference groups in our lives, as are peer groups and coworkers. All these groups provide points of reference for standards or comparisons. However, you do not have to belong to a group for it to be your reference group. For example, regardless of his or her station in life, a person may identify with the wealth and power of Fortune 500 corporate executives, admire the contribution of Nobel Prize–winning scientists, or be captivated by the glitter of the lives of Hollywood stars. Although most of us seldom interact socially with such reference groups as these, we may take pride in identifying with them, glorify their accomplishments, and even imitate the ways of those people who do belong to them. This is why it is critical for children—minority children in particular, whose groups are often represented stereotypically in the media—to be exposed to reference groups that will shape their lives for the better.

The Effects of Size

Another significant way in which groups differ has to do with their size. Sociological interest in group size can be traced to the German sociologist Georg Simmel (1858–1918), who studied and theorized about the impact of small groups on people's behavior. Since Simmel's time, small-group researchers have conducted a number of laboratory experiments to examine the effects of size on both the quality of interaction in the group and the effectiveness of the group in accomplishing certain tasks. (Homans, 1950; Bales, 1953, 1970; Hare, Borgatta, and Bales, 1965; Mills, 1967).

DYADS

The simplest group, which Simmel (1955) called a **dyad**, consists of two persons. Simmel reasoned that dyads, which involve both intimacy and conflict, are likely to be simultaneously intense and unstable. To survive, they require the full attention and cooperation of both parties. If one person withdraws from the dyad, it vanishes. Dyads are typically the source of our most elementary social bonds, often constituting the group in which we are most likely to share our deepest secrets. But dyads can be very fragile. That is why, Simmel believed, a variety of cultural and legal supports for marriage are found in societies where marriage is regarded as an important source of social stability.

TRIADS

Adding a third person changes the group relationship. Simmel used the term **triad** to describe a group consisting of three persons. Triads are apt to be more stable than dyads,

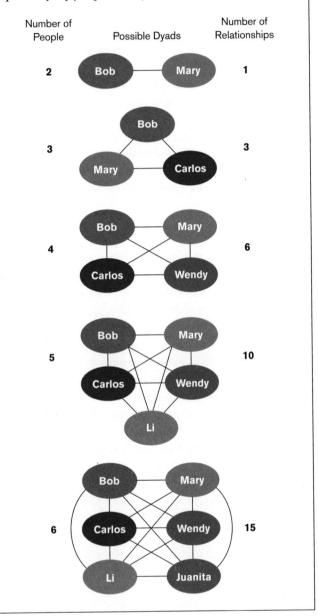

FIGURE 5.1

The larger the number of people, the greater the possible number of relationships. Note that this diagram illustrates only dyads; if triads and more complex coalitions were to be included, the numbers would be still greater (four people yield ten possibilities). Even a small, ten-person group can produce forty-five possible dyads!

Number of People	Possible Dyads	Number of Relationships
2	Bob — Mary	1
3	Bob, Mary, Carlos	3
4	Bob, Mary, Carlos, Wendy	6
5	Bob, Mary, Carlos, Wendy, Li	10
6	Bob, Mary, Carlos, Wendy, Li, Juanita	15

since the presence of a third person relieves some of the pressure on the other two members to always get along and energize the relationship. In a triad, one person can temporarily withdraw attention from the relationship without necessarily threatening it. In addition, if two of the members have a disagreement, the third can play the role of mediator, as when you try to patch up a falling-out between two of your friends.

On the other hand, however, alliances (sometimes termed "coalitions") may form between two members of a triad, enabling them to gang up on the third and thereby destabilize the group. Alliances are most likely to form when no one member is clearly dominant and when all three members are competing for the same thing—for example, when three friends are given a pair of tickets to a concert and have to decide which two will get to go. In forming an alliance, a member is most likely to choose the weaker of the two other members as a partner, if there is one. In what has been termed "revolutionary coalitions," the two weaker members form an alliance to overthrow the stronger one (Caplow, 1956, 1959, 1969).

LARGER GROUPS

Going from a dyad to a triad illustrates an important sociological principle first identified by Simmel: As groups increase in size, their intensity decreases, while their stability increases. There are, of course, exceptions to this principle, but in many cases, it is likely to apply. Increasing the size of a group tends to decrease its intensity of interaction, simply because a larger number of potential smaller group relationships exist as outlets for individuals who are not getting along with other members of the group. In a dyad, only a single relationship, that between two people, is possible; however, in a triad, three different two-person relationships can occur. Adding a fourth person leads to six possible combinations of two-person relationships, and this does not count the subgroups of more than two that could form. In a ten-person group, the number of possible two-person relationships explodes to forty-five! When one relationship doesn't work out to your liking, you can easily move on to another, as you probably often do at large parties.

At the same time, larger groups tend to be more stable than smaller ones because the withdrawal of some members does not threaten the group's survival. A marriage or love relationship falls apart if one person leaves, whereas an athletic team or drama club routinely survives—though it may sometimes temporarily suffer from—the loss of its graduating seniors.

Larger groups also tend to be more exclusive, since it is easier for their members to limit their social relationships to the group itself and avoid relationships with nonmembers. This sense of being part of an in group or clique is sometimes found in fraternities, sororities, and other campus organizations. Cliquishness is especially likely to occur when the group consists of members who are similar to each other in such social characteristics as age, gender, class, race, or ethnicity. A group with a socially diverse membership is likely instead to foster a high degree of interaction with people outside the group (Blau, 1977). For example, if your social group or club is made up of members from different social classes or ethnic groups, it is more likely that you will come to appreciate such social differences from firsthand experience and seek them out in other aspects of your life.

Members of a large, exclusive group such as a fraternity or sorority develop a sense of being part of an in-group or clique. They may choose to limit their social relationships to the group itself.

Beyond a certain size, perhaps a dozen people, groups tend to develop a formal structure. Formal leadership roles may arise, such as president or secretary, and official rules may be developed to govern what the group does. We discuss formal organizations later in this chapter.

Types of Leadership

A **leader** is a person who is able to influence the behavior of other members of a group. All groups tend to have leaders, even if the leader is not formally recognized as such. Some leaders are especially effective in motivating the members of their groups or organizations, inspiring them to achievements that might not ordinarily be accomplished. Such **transformational leaders** go beyond the merely routine, instilling in the members of their group a sense of mission or higher purpose and thereby changing the nature of the group itself (Burns, 1978; Kanter, 1983). These are the leaders who are seen as "leaving their stamp" on their organizations. They can also be a vital inspiration for social change in the world. For example, Nelson Mandela, the South African leader who spent twenty-seven years in prison after having been convicted of treason against the white-dominated South African society, nonetheless managed to build his African National Congress (ANC) political party into a multiracial force for change. Mandela's transformational leadership was so strong that despite his long imprisonment, as soon as he was freed he assumed leadership of the ANC. After Mandela successfully led the ANC in overthrowing South Africa's system of *apartheid*, or racial segregation, he was elected president—leader—of the entire country.

Most leaders are not as visionary as Mandela, however. Leaders who simply "get the job done" are termed **transactional leaders**. These are leaders concerned with accomplishing the group's tasks, getting group members to do their jobs, and making certain that the group achieves its goals. Transactional leadership is routine leadership. For example, the teacher who simply gets through the lesson plan each day—rather than making the classroom a place where students explore new ways of thinking and behaving—is exercising transactional leadership.

Conformity

Not so long ago, the only part of the body that American teenage girls were likely to pierce was the ears—one hole per ear, enough to hold a single pair of earrings. For the vast majority of boys piercing was not an option at all. Today, earrings are common for many males—from teenage boys to male professional athletes, and a growing number of college students now proudly sport multiple earrings, navel rings, and even studs in their tongues. Pressures to conform to the latest styles are especially strong among teenagers and young adults, among whom the need for group acceptance is often acute.

While wearing navel rings or the latest style of jeans may seem relatively harmless, conformity to group pressure can lead to extremely destructive behavior. This might include drug abuse, murder, or, as we saw in the case of Heaven's Gate, even mass suicide. For this reason, sociologists and social psychologists have long sought to understand why most people tend to go along with others and under what circumstances they do not.

GOING ALONG WITH THE GROUP: ASCH'S RESEARCH

Some of the earliest studies of conformity to group pressures were conducted by psychologist Solomon Asch about fifty years ago (1952). In one of his classic experiments, Asch asked individual subjects to decide which of three lines of different length most closely matched the length of a fourth line. The differences were obvious; subjects had no difficulty in making the correct match. Asch then arranged a version of the experiment in which the subjects were asked to make the matches in a group setting, with each person calling out the answer one at a time.

In this version of the experiment, all but one of the subjects were actually Asch's secret accomplices, and these accomplices all practiced a deception on that one subject. Each accomplice picked two lines that were clearly unequal in length as matches. The unwitting subject, one of the last to

FIGURE 5.2

In the Asch task, participants were shown a standard line (left) and then three comparison lines. Their task was simply to say which of the three lines matched the standard. When confederates gave false answers first, three-quarters of participants conformed by giving the wrong answer.

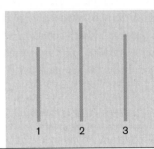

call out an answer, felt enormous group pressure to make the same error. Amazingly, one-third of these subjects gave the same wrong answer as the others in the group at least half of the times the experiment was conducted. They sometimes stammered and fidgeted when doing so, but they nonetheless yielded to the unspoken pressure to conform to the group's decision. Asch's experiments clearly showed that many people are willing to discount their own perceptions rather than buck a group consensus.

OBEDIENCE TO AUTHORITY: MILGRAM'S RESEARCH

Another classic study of conformity was Stanley Milgram's research (1963). Milgram wanted to see how far a person would go when ordered by a scientist to give another person increasingly powerful electric shocks. He did so by setting up an experiment that he told the subjects was about memorizing pairs of words. In reality, it was about obedience to authority.

The male subjects who volunteered for the study were supposedly randomly divided into "teachers" and "learners." In fact, the learners were actually Milgram's employees. The teacher was told to read pairs of words from a list that the learner was to memorize. Whenever the learner made a mistake, the teacher was to give him an electric shock by flipping a switch on a fake but official-looking machine. The control board on the machine indicated shock levels ranging from "15 volts—slight shock" to "450 volts—danger, severe shock." For each mistake, the voltage of the shock was to be increased, until it eventually reached the highest level. In reality, the

(a)

(b)

(c)

(a) The Milgram experiment required participants to "shock" the confederate learner (seated). The research participant (left) helped apply the electrodes that would be used to shock the learner. (b) An obedient participant shocks the learner in the "touch" condition. Fewer than one third obeyed the experimenter in this condition. (c) After the experiment, all of the participants were introduced to the confederate learner so they could see he was not actually harmed.

learner, who was usually carefully concealed from the teacher by a screen, never received any electric shocks. Milgram's study would not be permitted today, since its deception of subjects and potential for doing psychological harm would violate current university ethics standards.

As the experiment progressed, the learner began to scream out in pain for the teacher to stop delivering shocks. (His screams, increasingly louder as the voltage rose, had actually been prerecorded on a tape.) However, Milgram's assistant, who was administering the experiment, exercised his authority as a scientist and ordered the teacher to continue administering shocks if the teacher tried to quit. The assistant would say such things as, "the experiment requires that you continue," even when the learner could be heard protesting—even when he shrieked about his "bad heart."

The teacher was confronted with a major moral decision: Should he obey the scientist and go along with the experiment, even if it meant injuring another human being? Much to Milgram's surprise, over half the subjects in the study kept on administering electric shocks. They continued even until the maximum voltage was reached and the learner's screams had subsided into an eerie silence as he presumably died of a heart attack. How could ordinary people so easily conform to orders that would turn them into possible accomplices to murder?

The answer, Milgram found, was deceptively simple: Ordinary people will conform to orders given by someone in a position of power or authority, even if those orders have horrible consequences. From this, we can learn about groups who perform atrocities, like the Nazi's mass execution of Jews or the Heaven's Gate suicides, on the grounds that they were "just following orders." Milgram's research has sobering implications for anyone who thinks that only "others" will always knuckle under to authority, but "not me" (Zimbardo, Ebbesen, and Maslach, 1977).

GROUPTHINK AND GROUP PRESSURES TO CONFORM: JANIS'S RESEARCH

Common sense tells us that "two minds are better than one." But sociological research has found that pressures to "go along with the crowd" sometime result in worse decisions, rather than creative new solutions to problems. You have probably had the experience of being in a group struggling with a difficult decision and feeling uneasy at voicing your opposition to an emerging consensus. Irving L. Janis (1972, 1989; Janis and Mann, 1977) called this phenomenon **groupthink**, a process by which the members of a group ignore ways of thinking and plans of action that go against the group consensus. Not only does groupthink frequently embarrass potential dissenters into conforming, but it can also produce a shift in perceptions so that alternative possibilities are ruled out without being seriously considered. Groupthink may facilitate reaching a quick consensus, but the consensus may also be ill chosen. It may even be downright stupid.

Janis engaged in historical research to see if groupthink had characterized U.S. foreign policy decisions. He examined several critical decisions, including that behind the infamous Bay of Pigs invasion of Cuba in 1961. John F. Kennedy, then the newly elected president, inherited a plan from the previous administration to help Cuban exiles liberate Cuba from the Communist government of Fidel Castro. The plan called for U.S. supplies and air cover to assist an invasion by an ill-prepared army of exiles at Cuba's Bay of Pigs. Although a number of Kennedy's top advisers were certain that the plan was fatally flawed, they refrained from bucking the emerging consensus to carry it out. As it happened, the invasion was a disaster. The army of exiles, after parachuting into a swamp nowhere near their intended drop zone, was immediately defeated, and Kennedy suffered a great deal of public embarrassment.

Kennedy's advisers were people of strong will and independent judgment who had been educated at elite universities. How could they have failed to adequately voice their concerns about the proposed invasion? Janis identified a number of possible reasons. For one, Kennedy's advisers were hesitant to disagree with the president lest they lose his favor. They also did not want to diminish group harmony in a crisis situation where teamwork was all important. In addition, given the intense time pressure to act, they had little opportunity to consult outside experts who might have offered radically different perspectives. All these circumstances contributed to a single-minded pursuit of the president's initial ideas, rather than an effort to generate effective alternatives.

Although groupthink does not always shape decision making, it sometimes plays a major role. To avoid groupthink, the group must ensure the full and open expression of all opinions, even strong dissent.

Networks

"Who you know is often as important as what you know." This adage expresses the value of having "good connections." Sociologists refer to such connections as **networks**—all the direct and indirect connections that link a person or a group with other people or groups. Your personal networks thus include people you know directly (such as your friends) as well as people you know indirectly (such as your friends' friends). Personal networks often include people of similar race, class, ethnicity, and other types of social background, although there are exceptions. For example, if you subscribe to an online mailing list, you are part of a network that consists of all the people on the list, who may be of different racial or ethnic backgrounds and genders. Because groups and organizations, such as sororities or religious groups, can also be networked—for example, all the chapters of Gamma Phi Beta or Hillel that the national organization comprises—belonging to such groups can greatly extend your reach and influence.

Networks serve us in many ways. Sociologist Mark Granovetter (1973) demonstrated that there can be enormous strength in weak ties, particularly among higher socioeconomic groups. Granovetter showed that upper-level professional and managerial employees are likely to hear about new jobs through connections such as distant relatives or remote acquaintances. Such weak ties can be of great benefit because relatives or acquaintances tend to have very different sets of connections than one's closer friends, whose social contacts are likely to be similar to one's own. Among lower socioeconomic groups, Granovetter argued, weak ties are not neces-

sarily bridges to other networks and so do not really widen one's opportunities (see also Marsden and Lin, 1982; Wellman, Carrington, and Hall, 1988; Knoke, 1990). After graduation from college, you may rely on good grades and a strong résumé to find a job. But it may prove beneficial if it happens that your second cousin went to school with a top person in the organization where you are seeking work.

Most people rely on their personal networks to gain advantages, but not everyone has equal access to powerful networks. Some sociologists argue, for example, that women's business and political networks are weaker than men's, so that women's power in these spheres is reduced (Brass, 1985).

In general, sociologists have found that when women look for work, their job market networks comprise fewer ties than do men's, meaning that women know fewer people in fewer occupations (Marsden, 1987; Moore, 1990). Meager networks tend to channel women into female-typical jobs, which usually offer less pay and fewer opportunities for advancement (Ross and Reskin, 1992; Drentea, 1998). Still, as more and more women move up into higher-level positions, the resulting networks can foster further advancement. One study found that women are more likely to be hired or promoted into job levels that already have a high proportion of women (Cohen, Broschak, and Haveman, 1998).

Networks confer more than economic advantage. You are likely to rely on your networks for a broad range of contacts, from obtaining access to your congressperson or senator to finding a date for Saturday night. Similarly, when you visit another country to study a foreign language or see the Olympics, for example, your friends, school, or religious organization may steer you to their overseas connections, who can then help you find your way around in the unfamiliar environment. When you graduate from school, your alumni group can further extend your network of social support.

The Internet as Social Network

The advantages and potential reach of networks are evident in an increasingly productive means of networking, all but unknown ten years ago: the Internet. Internet use has exploded in recent years. Until the early 1990s, when the World Wide Web was developed, there were few Internet users outside of university and scientific communities. By 2002, however, an estimated 182.13 million Americans used the Internet (Cyberatlas, 2003). With such rapid communication and global reach, it is now possible to radically extend one's personal networks. The Internet is especially useful for networking with like-minded people on specific issues, such as politics, business, hobbies, or romance (Southwick, 1996; Wellman et al., 1996). It also enables people who might otherwise lack contact with others to become part of global networks. For example, shut-ins can join chat rooms to share common interests, and people in small rural communities can now engage in "distance learning" through courses that are offered on the Web.

The Internet fosters the creation of new relationships, often without the emotional and social baggage or constraints that go along with face-to-face encounters. In the absence of the usual physical and social cues, such as skin color or residential address, people can get together electronically on the basis of shared interests rather than similar social characteristics. Such factors as social position, wealth, race, ethnicity, gender, and physical disability are less likely to cloud the social interaction (Coate, 1994; Jones, 1995; Kollock and Smith, 1996). As a consequence, Internet-based social networks may be socially broader based than other networks (Wellman, 1994). Whether this strengthens social diversity—or downgrades its importance—is a matter of debate.

One limitation of Internet-based social networks is that not everyone has equal access to the Internet. Lower-income groups, which disproportionately include minorities, are especially disadvantaged in developing networks online, as are the elderly. Still, within the span of a few years, Internet use has become much more widespread among all groups (Nielsen Media Research, 2001b, 2001c). In the words of one recent study that tracked Internet use among different socioeconomic groups, "The Internet was, at first, an elitist country club reserved only for individuals with select financial abilities and technical skills. . . . Now, nearly every socioeconomic group is aggressively adopting the Web" (Nielsen Media Research, 2001b).

Americans are by far the greatest Internet users in the world, although the rest of the world is rapidly coming on line. Besides in North America, Internet use is highest in Europe and East Asia, where the wealthiest countries are found. Some sociologists think that the Internet will eventually strengthen global ties, perhaps at the expense of local ones. Being able to connect with anyone in the world who shares similar interests may mean that one's own community becomes less important. If this happens, will the ties that have bound people to locality throughout human history slowly disappear?

Organizations

People frequently band together to pursue activities that they could not otherwise readily accomplish by themselves. A principal means for accomplishing such cooperative actions is the **organization**, a group with an identifiable membership that engages in concerted collective actions to achieve a common purpose (Aldrich and Marsden, 1988). An organization can be a small primary group, but it is more likely to be a larger, secondary one: Universities, religious bodies, and business corporations are all examples of organizations. Such organizations are a central feature of all societies, and their study is a core concern of sociology today.

Organizations tend to be highly formal in modern industrial and postindustrial societies. A **formal organization** is rationally designed to achieve its objectives, often by means of explicit rules, regulations, and procedures. The modern bureaucratic organization, discussed later in this chapter, is a prime example of a formal organization. As Max Weber (1979, orig. 1921) first recognized three quarters of a century ago, there has been a long-term trend in Europe and North America toward formal organizations. This rise of formality in organizations is in part the result of the fact that formality is often a requirement for legal standing. For a college or university to be legally accredited, for example, it must satisfy explicit written standards governing everything from grading policy to faculty performance to fire safety. Today, formal organizations are the dominant form of organization throughout the entire world.

Most social systems in the traditional world developed over lengthy periods as a result of custom and habit. Organizations, on the other hand, are mostly designed—established with definite aims in view and housed in buildings or physical

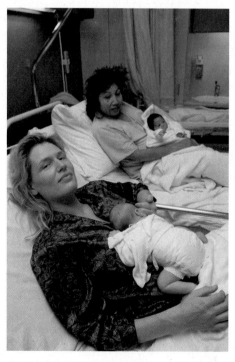

Modern hospitals are complex organizations with impersonal structures and procedures—but they are designed for a very personal outcome.

settings specifically constructed to help realize those aims. The edifices in which hospitals, colleges, or business firms carry on their activities are mostly custom built.

In traditional societies, most people lived in small group settings. In a society such as traditional China, it was rare for members of a local village community ever to meet a national government official. National government edicts barely affected their lives.

In current times, organizations play a much more important part in our everyday lives than was ever true previously. Besides delivering us into this world, they also mark our progress through it and see us out of it when we die. Even before we are born, our parents are involved in birthing classes, pregnancy checkups, and so forth, carried out within hospitals and other medical organizations. Every child born today is registered by government organizations, which collect information on us from birth to death. Most people today die in a hospital—not at home, as was once the case—and each death must be formally registered with the government too.

It is easy to see why organizations are so important to us today. In the premodern world, families, close relatives, and neighbors provided for most needs—food, the instruction of children, work, and leisure-time activities. In modern times, the mass of the population is much more *interdependent* than was ever the case before. Many of our requirements are supplied by people we never meet and who indeed might live many thousands of miles away. A substantial amount of coordination of activities and resources—which organizations provide—is needed in such circumstances.

The tremendous influence organizations have come to exert over our lives cannot be seen as wholly beneficial. Organizations often have the effect of taking things out of our own hands and putting them under the control of officials or experts over whom we have little influence. For instance, we are all *required* to do certain things the government tells us to do—pay taxes, abide by laws, go off to fight wars—or face punishment. As sources of social power, organizations can thus subject the individual to dictates she may be powerless to resist.

Theories of Organizations

Max Weber developed the first systematic interpretation of the rise of modern organizations. Organizations, he argued, are ways of coordinating the activities of human beings, or the goods they produce, in a stable way across space and time. Weber emphasized that the development of organiza-

tions depends on the control of information, and he stressed the central importance of writing in this process: An organization needs written rules for its functioning and files in which its "memory" is stored. Weber saw organizations as strongly hierarchical, with power tending to be concentrated at the top. Was Weber right? If he was, it matters a great deal to us all. For Weber detected a clash as well as a connection between modern organizations and democracy that he believed had far-reaching consequences for social life.

Bureaucracy

All large-scale organizations, according to Weber, tend to be bureaucratic in nature. The word *bureaucracy* was coined by Monsieur de Gournay in 1745, who added the word *bureau*, meaning both an office and a writing table, to *cracy*, a term derived from the Greek verb meaning "to rule." **Bureaucracy** is thus the rule of officials. The term was first applied only to government officials, but it gradually was extended to refer to large organizations in general.

From the beginning the concept was used in a disparaging way. De Gournay spoke of the developing power of officials as "an illness called bureaumania." The French novelist Honoré de Balzac saw bureaucracy as "the giant power wielded by pygmies." This sort of view has persisted into current times: Bureaucracy is frequently associated with red tape, inefficiency, and wastefulness. Other writers, however, have seen bureaucracy in a different light—as a model of carefulness, precision, and effective administration. Bureaucracy, they argue, is in fact the most efficient form of organization human beings have devised, because in bureaucracies all tasks are regulated by strict rules of procedure.

Weber's account of bureaucracy steers a way between these two extremes. A limited number of bureaucratic organizations, he pointed out, existed in the traditional civilizations. For example, a bureaucratic officialdom in imperial China was responsible for the overall affairs of government. But it is only in modern times that bureaucracies have developed fully.

According to Weber, the expansion of bureaucracy is inevitable in modern societies; bureaucratic authority is the only way of coping with the administrative requirements of large-scale social systems. However, Weber also believed bureaucracy exhibits a number of major failings, as we will see, which have important implications for the nature of modern social life.

In order to study the origins and nature of the expansion of bureaucratic organizations, Weber constructed an ideal type of bureaucracy. (*Ideal* here refers not to what is most desirable, but to a pure form of bureaucratic organization. An **ideal type** is an abstract description constructed by accentuating certain features of real cases so as to pinpoint their most essential characteristics.) Weber listed several characteristics of the ideal type of bureaucracy (1979):

1. **There is a clear-cut hierarchy of authority**, such that tasks in the organization are distributed as "official duties." A bureaucracy looks like a pyramid, with the positions of highest authority at the top. There is a chain of command stretching from top to bottom, thus making coordinated decision making possible. Each higher office controls and supervises the one below it in the hierarchy.

2. **Written rules govern the conduct of officials at all levels of the organization.** This does not mean that bureaucratic duties are just a matter of routine. The higher the office, the more the rules tend to encompass a wide variety of cases and demand flexibility in their interpretation.

3. **Officials are full time and salaried.** Each job in the hierarchy has a definite and fixed salary attached to it. Individuals are expected to make a career within the organization. Promotion is possible on the basis of capability, seniority, or a mixture of the two.

4. **There is a separation between the tasks of an official within the organization and his life outside.** The home life of the official is distinct from his activities in the workplace and is also physically separated from it.

5. **No members of the organization own the material resources with which they operate.** The development of bureaucracy, according to Weber, separates workers from the control of their means of production. In traditional communities, farmers and craft workers usually had control over their processes of production and owned the tools they used. In bureaucracies, officials do not own the offices they work in, the desks they sit at, or the office machinery they use.

Weber believed that the more an organization approaches the ideal type of bureaucracy, the more effective it will be in pursuing the objectives for which it was established. He often likened bureaucracies to sophisticated machines operating according to rational principles (see Chapter 1). Yet he recognized that bureaucracy could be inefficient and accepted that many bureaucratic jobs are dull, offering little opportunity for the exercise of creative capabilities. While Weber feared that the rationalization of society could have negative consequences, he concluded that bureaucratic routine and the authority of officialdom over our lives are prices we pay for the technical effectiveness of bureaucratic organizations. Since Weber's time, the rationalization of society has become more widespread. Critics of this development who share Weber's initial concerns have

questioned whether the efficiency of rational organizations comes at a price greater than Weber could have imagined. The most prominent of these critiques is known as "the McDonaldization of society," discussed later in this chapter.

FORMAL AND INFORMAL RELATIONS WITHIN BUREAUCRACIES

Weber's analysis of bureaucracy gave prime place to **formal relations** within organizations, the relations between people as stated in the rules of the organization. Weber had little to say about the informal connections and small-group relations that may exist in all organizations. But in bureaucracies, informal ways of doing things often allow for a flexibility that couldn't otherwise be achieved.

In a classic study, Peter Blau (1963) looked at **informal relations** in a government agency whose task was to investigate possible income-tax violations. Agents who came across problems they were unsure how to deal with were supposed to discuss them with their immediate supervisor; the rules of procedure stated that they should not consult colleagues working at the same level as themselves. Most officials were wary of approaching their supervisors, however, because they felt this might suggest a lack of competence on their part and reduce their promotion chances. Hence, they usually consulted one another, violating the official rules. This not only helped to provide concrete advice; it also reduced the anxieties involved in working alone. A cohesive set of loyalties of a primary group kind developed among those working at the same level. The problems these workers faced, Blau concludes, were probably coped with much more effectively as a result. The group was able to develop informal procedures allowing for more initiative and responsibility than was provided for by the formal rules of the organization.

Informal networks tend to develop at all levels of organizations. At the very top, personal ties and connections may be more important than the formal situations in which decisions are supposed to be made. For example, meetings of boards of directors and shareholders supposedly determine the policies of business corporations. In practice, a few members of the board often really run the corporation, making their decisions informally and expecting the board to approve them. Informal networks of this sort can also stretch across different corporations. Business leaders from different firms frequently consult one another in an informal way and may belong to the same clubs and leisure-time associations.

John Meyer and Brian Rowan (1977) argue that formal rules and procedures in organizations are usually quite distant from the practices actually adopted by the organizations' members. Formal rules, in their view, are often "myths" that people profess to follow but that have little substance in reality. They

The *Columbia* Shuttle Disaster: A Sociological Perspective

The tragic disintegration of the Space Shuttle *Columbia* on February 1, 2003 set me on an unexpected and remarkable eight-month journey in public sociology. In the hours after the accident, I was deluged with calls from the press. I had studied the causes of the 1986 *Challenger* disaster and written the book, *The Challenger Launch Decision: Risky Technology, Culture, and Deviance at NASA* (1996). I was defined as an expert the press could consult to give them bearings on this latest accident. Viewing this as both a teaching opportunity and professional responsibility, I tried to respond to everyone.

What I was teaching were the theoretical explanation and key concepts of the book, linking them to data about *Challenger* and *Columbia* as the changing press questions dictated. Because the investigation went on for months, these conversations became an ongoing exchange where the press brought me new information and I gave a sociological interpretation. I noticed that the concepts of the book—the normalization of deviance, institutional failure, organization culture, structure, missed signals—began appearing in print early in the investigation and continued, whether I was quoted or not.

The book also led to my association with the *Columbia* Accident Investigation Board. Two weeks after the accident, the publicity director at Chicago sent a copy of *The Challenger Launch Decision* to retired Admiral Harold Gehman, who headed the Board's investigation. [***]

The new centrality of sociological ideas and the connection with the *Challenger* accident were not lost on the media. In press conferences, Admiral Gehman stressed the importance of the social causes and used the book's central concepts. When he announced that I would testify before the

Board in Houston, the field's leading journal, *Aviation Week and Space Technology,* headlined "*Columbia* Board Probes the Shuttle Program's Sociology," while the *New York Times* ran "Echoes of *Challenger.*" Unaware of the extent of the book's influence on the Board's thinking, however, I arrived in Houston in late April anxious about the public grilling to come.

But subsequent events showed me the Board was receptive to sociological analysis. I met separately with the Group 2 investigators assigned the decision making and organization chapters to discuss their data and analysis, then gave the Board a pre-testimony briefing, which turned into a three-hour conversation. My testimony covered the social causes of the *Challenger* accident, compared it to the *Columbia* incident, and identified systemic institutional failures common to both. The book's theory and concepts traveled farther as my testimony—like that of other witnesses—was shown live on NASA TV and videostreamed into television, radio, and press centers and the Internet.

[***]

So the Board's report gave equal weight to social causes of the accident—not only because the Admiral believed in the potential of sociology, but also because I, a sociologist, became part of this large team of Board and staff, working under deadline. Information and ideas flew fast and freely between people and chapters. Their extraordinary investigative effort, data, analysis, and insights were integrated into my chapter; sociological connections and concepts became integrated into theirs. [***]

The Admiral kept the press informed of report changes, so prior to report publication, the *New York Times* announced the equal weight the report would give to technical and social causes, identifying me as the source of the Board's approach and author of Chapter 8. Upon the August 26 [2003] release, the language of sociology became commonplace in the press. The theory of the book traveled one more place that week. An [Associated Press] wire story, "NASA Finally Looks to Sociologist," revealed that NASA had invited me to headquarters to talk with top officials, who had shifted from denial to acknowledge that the systemic institutional failures that led to *Challenger* also caused *Columbia.*

Never did I foresee the extent of my involvement or the impact that I ultimately had. [***] The theory and concepts that explained *Challenger* were an analogical fit with the *Columbia* data and made sense of what happened for journalists and the Board. Analogy was the mechanism that enabled the theory and concepts of the book to travel. My book and university affiliation gave me the opportunity to engage in ongoing dialogic teaching—akin to daily grassroots activism—but with two tribunals of power with authoritative voice. Together, the press and the Board were a "polished machinery of dissemination," as Burawoy calls powerful advocacy groups, translating the ideas of the book into grist for critical public dialogue.

SOURCE: Diane Vaughan, "How Theory Travels: A Most Public Public Sociology," *Public Sociology in Action,* ASA Footnotes, Nov/Dec. 2003.

DIANE VAUGHAN *teaches sociology at Boston College. Her other books are* Uncoupling: Turning Points in Intimate Relationships, *and* Controlling Unlawful Organizational Behavior. *Currently, she is writing about the uses of analogy in sociology and doing fieldwork on air traffic control.*

serve to legitimate—to justify—ways in which tasks are carried out, even while these ways may diverge greatly from how things are "supposed to be done" according to the rules.

Formal procedures, Meyer and Rowan point out, often have a ceremonial or ritual character. People will make a show of conforming to them in order to get on with their real work using other, more informal procedures. For example, rules governing ward procedure in a hospital help justify how nurses act toward patients in caring for them. Thus a nurse will faithfully fill in a patient's chart that hangs at the end of the bed but will check the patient's progress by means of other, informal criteria—how well the person is looking and whether he or she seems alert and lively. Rigorously keeping up the charts impresses the patients and keeps the doctors happy, but is not always essential to the nurse's assessments.

Deciding how far informal procedures generally help or hinder the effectiveness of organizations is not a simple matter. Systems that resemble Weber's ideal type tend to give rise to a forest of unofficial ways of doing things. This is partly because the flexibility that is lacking ends up being achieved by unofficial tinkering with formal rules. For those in dull jobs, informal procedures often also help to create a more satisfying work environment. Informal connections between officials in higher positions may be effective in ways that aid the organization as a whole. On the other hand, these officials may be more concerned about advancing or protecting their own interests than furthering those of the overall organization.

THE DYSFUNCTIONS OF BUREAUCRACY

Robert Merton, a functionalist scholar, examined Weber's bureaucratic ideal type and concluded that several elements inherent in bureaucracy could lead to harmful consequences for the smooth functioning of the bureaucracy itself (1957). He referred to these as "dysfunctions of bureaucracy." First, Merton noted that bureaucrats are trained to rely strictly on written rules and procedures. They are not encouraged to be flexible, to use their own judgment in making decisions, or to seek creative solutions; bureaucracy is about managing cases according to a set of objective criteria. Merton feared that this rigidity could lead to *bureaucratic ritualism*, a situation in which the rules are upheld at any cost, even in cases where another solution might be a better one for the organization as a whole.

A second concern of Merton's is that adherence to the bureaucratic rules could eventually take precedence over the underlying organizational goals. Because so much emphasis is placed on the correct procedure, it is possible to lose sight of the big picture. A bureaucrat responsible for processing insurance claims, for example, might refuse to compensate a policyholder for legitimate damages, citing the absence of a form or a form being completed incorrectly. In other words,

processing the claim correctly could come to take precedence over the needs of the client who has suffered a loss.

Merton foresaw the possibility of tension between the public and bureaucracy in such cases. This concern was not entirely misplaced. Most of us interact with large bureaucracies on a regular basis—from insurance companies to local government to the IRS. Not infrequently we encounter situations in which public servants and bureaucrats seem to be unconcerned with our needs. One of the major weaknesses of bureaucracy is the difficulty it has in addressing cases that need special treatment and consideration.

Bureaucracy and Democracy

The diminishing of democracy with the advance of modern forms of organization was another problem that worried Weber a great deal (see also Chapter 13). What especially disturbed him was the prospect of rule by faceless bureaucrats. How can democracy be anything other than a meaningless slogan in the face of the increasing power bureaucratic organizations are wielding over us? After all, Weber reasoned, bureaucracies are necessarily specialized and hierarchical. Those near the bottom of the organization inevitably find themselves reduced to carrying out mundane tasks and have no power over what they do; power passes to those at the top. Weber's student Robert Michels (1967) invented a phrase that has since become famous, to refer to this loss of power: In large-scale organizations, and more generally a society dominated by organizations, he argued, there is an **iron law of oligarchy**. **Oligarchy** means rule by the few. According to Michels, the flow of power toward the top is simply an inevitable part of an increasingly bureaucratized world—hence the term *iron law*.

Was Michels right? It surely is correct to say that large-scale organizations involve the centralizing of power. Yet there is good reason to suppose that the "iron law of oligarchy" is not quite as hard and fast as Michels claimed. The connections between oligarchy and bureaucratic centralization are more ambiguous than he supposed.

We should recognize first of all that unequal power is not just a function of size. In modest-sized groups there can be very marked differences of power. In a small business, for instance, where the activities of employees are directly visible to the directors, much tighter control might be exerted than in offices in larger organizations. As organizations expand in size, power relationships often in fact become looser. Those at the middle and lower levels may have little influence over general policies forged at the top. On the other hand, because of the specialization and expertise involved in bureaucracy, people at the top also lose control over many administrative decisions, which are handled by those lower down.

In many modern organizations power is also quite often openly delegated downward from superiors to subordinates. In many large companies, corporate heads are so busy coordinating different departments, coping with crises, and analyzing budget and forecast figures that they have little time for original thinking. They hand over consideration of policy issues to others below them, whose task is to develop proposals about them. Many corporate leaders frankly admit that for the most part they simply accept the conclusions given to them.

Gender and Organizations

Until some two decades ago, organizational studies did not devote very much attention to the question of gender. Weber's theory of bureaucracy and many of the influential responses to Weber that came in subsequent years were written by men and presumed a model of organizations that placed men squarely at the center. The rise of feminist scholarship in the 1970s, however, led to examinations of gender relations in all the main institutions in society, including organizations and bureaucracy. Feminist sociologists not only focused on the imbalance of gender roles within organizations, they also explored the ways in which modern organizations themselves had developed in a specifically gendered way.

Feminists have argued that the emergence of the modern organization and the bureaucratic career depended on a particular gender configuration. They point to two main ways in which gender is embedded in the very structure of modern organizations. First, bureaucracies are characterized by occupational gender segregation. As women began to enter the labor market in greater numbers, they tended to be segregated into categories of occupations that were low paying and involved routine work. These positions were subordinate to those occupied by men and did not provide opportunities for women to be promoted. Women were used as a source of cheap, reliable labor but were not granted the same opportunities as men to build careers.

Second, the idea of a bureaucratic career was in fact a *male* career in which women played a crucial supporting role. In the workplace, women performed the routine tasks—as clerks, secretaries, and office managers—thereby freeing up men to advance their careers. Men could concentrate on obtaining promotions or landing big accounts because the female support staff handled much of the busywork. In the domestic sphere, women also supported the bureaucratic career by caring for the home, the children, and the man's day-to-day well-being. Women serviced the needs of the male bureaucrat by allowing him to work long hours, travel, and focus solely on his work without concern about personal or domestic issues.

As a result of these two tendencies, early feminist writers argued, modern organizations have developed as male-dominated preserves in which women are excluded from power, denied opportunities to advance their careers, and victimized on the basis of their gender through sexual harassment and discrimination. Although most early feminist analysis focused on a common set of concerns—unequal pay, discrimination, and the male hold on power—there was no consensus about the best approach to take in working for women's equality.

WOMEN IN MANAGEMENT

As women have entered professional occupations in greater numbers in recent decades, the debate over gender and organizations has taken new turns. Many scholars now see an opportunity to assess the impact of women leaders and managers on the organizations in which they work. One of the most hotly contested questions today is whether women managers are making a difference in their organizations by introducing a "female" style of management into contexts that have long been dominated by male culture, values, and behavior.

In recent years, many leadership qualities commonly associated with women have been held up as essential assets for organizations attempting to become more flexible in their operations. Rather than relying on top-down, rigid management styles, organizations are encouraged to adopt policies that ensure employee commitment, collective enthusiasm for organizational goals, shared responsibility, and a focus on people. Communication, consensus, and teamwork are cited by management theorists as key approaches that will distinguish successful organizations in the new global age. These so-called soft management skills are ones traditionally associated with women.

Some writers claim that this shift toward a more "female" management style can already be felt. Women are attaining unprecedented influence at the top levels of power, they argue, and are doing so according to their own rules rather than adopting typically male management techniques (Rosener, 1997). As the success of women's leadership is increasingly felt throughout the organizational world, some predict that a new way of thinking about management will emerge in which men will also adopt many of the techniques long favored by women, such as delegating responsibility, sharing information and resources, and collective goal setting.

Others do not subscribe to the view that women are successfully exercising a distinctly "female" brand of management. In *Managing Like a Man* (1998), Judy Wajcman takes issue with this approach on a number of grounds. First, she argues that the number of women who actually make it to the top levels of power is extremely limited. It is true, she says, that women are making substantial progress within the ranks of middle management, but despite their greater numbers in middle management, women are still largely prevented from accessing power at the highest levels. One out of thirteen senior executives (executive vice president or higher) are women. This is a dramatic increase from one in forty in 1995 (Epstein, 2003). However, many of these positions held by women are "staff" positions or otherwise distanced from direct influence on profit margins. In Fortune 500 companies 90 percent of executive positions with direct influence on profit and loss were held by men (Epstein, 2003). Men continue to receive higher levels of pay for equivalent work and are employed in a broader spectrum of roles than women, who tend to be clustered in fields such as human resources and marketing.

When women do reach top management positions, they tend to manage like men. Although great advances have been made in the past two decades in the areas of equal employment, sexual harassment policies, and overall consciousness about gender issues, Wajcman argues that organizational culture and management style remain overwhelmingly male. In her study of 324 senior-level managers in multinational corporations, she found that management techniques are dominated much more by the overall organizational culture than they are by the gender or personal style of individual managers. In order for women to get access to power and maintain their influence, they must adapt to the prevailing managerial style, which emphasizes aggressive leadership, tough tactics, and top-down decision making.

There is also reason to believe that it is difficult for women to break into traditional mentoring patterns in organizations. The model of mentoring has traditionally been the older man who takes on a young protégé in whom he sees traces of himself at a younger age. The mentor would work behind the scenes to advance the young employee's interests and to facilitate his future career moves. This dynamic is less easy to replicate between older male bosses and younger female employees, and there are not enough women in senior positions

As women climb the corporate ladder, will they change the methods as well as the face of management or will they learn to "manage like men"?

to serve as mentors to younger women. Among Wajcman's respondents, women were more likely than men to cite a lack of career guidance as a major barrier in their advancement.

Wajcman is skeptical about claims that a new age of flexible, decentralized organizations is upon us. Her findings reveal that traditional forms of authoritarian management are still firmly present. In her view, certain surface attributes of organizations may have been transformed, but the gendered nature of organizations—and the overwhelmingly dominant power of men within them—has not been challenged.

Beyond Bureaucracy?

For quite a long while in the development of Western societies, Weber's model held good. In government, hospital administration, universities, and business organizations, bureaucracy seemed to be dominant. Even though, as Peter Blau showed, informal social groups always develop in bureaucratic settings and are in fact effective, it seemed as though the future might be just what Weber had anticipated: constantly increasing bureaucratization.

Bureaucracies still exist aplenty in the West, but Weber's idea that a clear hierarchy of authority, with power and knowledge concentrated at the top, is the only way to run a large organization is starting to look archaic. Numerous organizations are overhauling themselves to become less, rather than more, hierarchical.

Almost four decades ago, Burns and Stalker concluded that traditional bureaucratic structures can stifle innovation and creativity in cutting-edge industries (1994); in today's electronic economy, few would dispute the importance of these findings. Departing from rigid vertical command structures, many organizations are turning to "horizontal," collaborative models in order to become more flexible and responsive to fluctuating markets. In this section we shall examine some of the main forces behind these shifts, including globalization and the growth of information technology, and consider some of the ways in which late modern organizations are reinventing themselves in the light of the changing circumstances.

Organizational Change: The Japanese Model

Many of the changes that can now be witnessed in organizations around the world were first pioneered in Japanese companies some decades ago. Although the Japanese economy has suffered recession in recent years, it was phenomenally successful during the 1980s. This economic success was often attributed to the distinctive characteristics of large Japanese corporations—which differed substantially from most business firms in the West (Vogel, 1979). As we shall see, many of the unique organizational characteristics of Japanese corporations have been adapted and modified in other countries in recent years.

Japanese companies, especially in the 1980s and 1990s, diverged from the characteristics that Weber associated with bureaucracy in several ways:

1. **Bottom-Up Decision Making.** The big Japanese corporations do not form a pyramid of authority as Weber portrayed it, with each level being responsible only to the one above. Rather, workers low down in the organization are consulted about policies being considered by management, and even the top executives regularly meet with them.

2. **Less Specialization.** In Japanese organizations, employees specialize much less than their counterparts in the West. Take the case of Sugao, as described by William Ouchi (1982). Sugao is a university graduate who has just joined the Mitsubeni Bank in Tokyo. He will enter the firm in a management-training position, spending his first year learning generally how the various departments of the bank operate. He will then work in a local branch for a while as a teller and will subsequently be brought back to the bank's headquarters to learn commercial banking. Then he will move out to yet another branch dealing with loans. From there he is likely to return to headquarters to work in the personnel department. Ten years will have elapsed by this time, and Sugao will have reached the position of section chief.

   By the time Sugao reaches the peak of his career, some thirty years after beginning as a trainee, he will have mastered all the important tasks. In contrast, a typical American bank-management trainee of the same age will almost certainly specialize in one area of banking early on and stay in that specialty for the remainder of her working life.

3. **Job Security.** The large corporations in Japan are committed to the long-term employment of those they hire; the employee is guaranteed a job. Pay and responsibility are geared to seniority—how many years a worker has been with the firm—rather than to a competitive struggle for promotion. This still remains a value, although it has weakened in recent years.

4. **Group Orientation.** At all levels of the corporation, people are involved in small cooperative "teams," or work groups. The groups, rather than individual members, are evaluated in terms of their performance. Unlike their Western counterparts, the *organization charts* of Japanese companies—maps of the authority system—show only groups, not individual positions. This is important because it contradicts the supposed *iron law of oligarchy*.

5. **Merging of Work and Private Lives.** In Weber's depiction of bureaucracy, there is a clear division between the work of people within the organization and their activities outside. This is in fact true of most Western corporations, in which the relation between firm and employee is an economic one. Japanese corporations, by contrast, provide for many of their employees' needs, expecting in return a high level of loyalty to the firm. Japanese employees, from workers on the shop floor to top executives, often wear company uniforms. They may assemble to sing the "company song" each morning, and they regularly take part in leisure activities organized by the corporation on weekends. (A few Western corporations, like IBM and Apple, now also have company songs.) Workers receive material benefits from the company over and above their salaries. The electrical firm Hitachi, for example, studied by Ronald Dore (1980), provided housing for all unmarried workers and nearly half of its married male employees. Company loans were available for the education of children and to help with the cost of weddings and funerals.

Studies of Japanese-run plants in the United States and Britain indicate that bottom-up decision making does work outside Japan. Workers seem to respond positively to the greater level of involvement these plants provide (White and Trevor, 1983). It seems reasonable to conclude, therefore, that the Japanese model does carry some lessons relevant to the Weberian conception of bureaucracy. Organizations that closely resemble Weber's ideal type are probably much less effective than they appear on paper, because they do not permit lower-level employees to develop a sense of control over, and involvement in, their work tasks.

Drawing on the example of Japanese corporations, Ouchi (1979, 1982) has argued that there are clear limits to the effectiveness of bureaucratic hierarchy, as emphasized by Weber. Overly bureaucratized organizations lead to internal failures of functioning because of their rigid, inflexible, and uninvolving nature. Forms of authority Ouchi calls *clans*—groups having close personal connections with one another—are more efficient than bureaucratic types of organization. The work groups in Japanese firms are one example, but clan-type systems often develop informally within Western organizations as well.

The Transformation of Management

Most of the components of the Japanese model described above come down to issues of management. While it is impossible to ignore specific production-level practices developed by the Japanese, a large part of the Japanese approach focused on management-worker relations and ensured that employees at all levels felt a personal attachment to the company. The emphasis on teamwork, consensus-building approaches, and broad-based employee participation were in stark contrast to traditional Western forms of management that were more hierarchical and authoritarian.

In the 1980s, many Western organizations began to introduce new management techniques in order to boost productivity and competitiveness. Two popular branches of management theory—*human resource management* and the *corporate culture* approach—indicated that the Japanese model had not gone unnoticed in the West. **Human resource management** is a style of management that regards a company's work-force as vital to its economic competitiveness: If the employees are not completely dedicated to the firm and its product, the firm will never be a leader in its field. In order to generate employee enthusiasm and commitment, the entire organizational culture must be retooled so that workers feel they have an investment in the workplace and in the work process. According to human resource management theory, human resources issues should not be the exclusive domain of designated personnel officers, but should instead be a top priority for all members of company management.

The second management trend—creating a distinctive **corporate culture**—is closely related to human resources management. In order to promote loyalty to the company and pride in its work, the company's management works with employees to build an organizational culture involving rituals, events, or traditions unique to that company alone. These cultural activities are designed to draw all members of the firm—from the most senior managers to the newest employee—together so that they make common cause with each other and strengthen group solidarity. Company picnics, "casual Fridays" (days on which employees can dress down), and company-sponsored community service projects are examples of techniques for building a corporate culture.

In recent years a number of Western companies have been founded according to the management principles described above. Rather than constructing themselves according to a traditional bureaucratic model, companies like the Saturn car company in the United States have organized themselves along these new managerial lines. At Saturn, for example, employees at all levels have the opportunity to spend time at positions in other areas of the company in order to gain a better sense of the operation of the firm as a whole. Shop-floor workers spend time with the marketing team, sharing insights into the way the vehicles are made. Sales staff rotate through the servicing department to become more aware of common maintenance problems that might concern prospective buyers. Representatives from both sales and the shop floor are involved in product design teams in order to discuss shortcomings that the management may not have been aware of in earlier models. A corporate culture focused on friendly and knowledgeable customer service unifies company employees and enhances the sense of company pride.

Technology and Modern Organizations

The development of **information technology**—computers and electronic communication media such as the Internet—is another factor currently influencing organizational structures (Zuboff, 1988; Kanter, 1991). Since data can be processed instantaneously in any part of the world linked to a computer-based communications system, there is no need for physical proximity between those involved. As a result, the introduction of new technology has allowed many companies to "reengineer" their organizational structure. The impact of these changes, while beneficial to organizational efficiency, can have both positive and negative consequences for the individuals within the organization.

Telecommuting is an example of how large organizations have become more decentralized as the more routine tasks disappear, reinforcing the tendency toward smaller, more flexible types of enterprises (Burris, 1998). A good deal of office work, for instance, can be carried out at home by "telecommuters" who use the Internet and other mobile technologies, such as cell phones, to do their work at home or somewhere other than their employer's primary office.

According to the International Telework Association and Council (ITAC), in 2001 28 million Americans telecommuted, which is approximately one fifth of the population of adult workers in the United States (Davis and Polonko, 2001). Of these, 21 percent worked at home, while the rest are about equally divided between working at special telework centers, satellite offices, or working while traveling (ITAC, 2004). Telecommuters in the United States are typically males from the Northeast and West who have college degrees and work in professional or managerial positions (Davis and Polonko, 2001). To reduce costs and increase productivity, several large firms in the United States and elsewhere have set up information networks connecting employees who work from home with the main office.

One rationale for why telecommuting increases productivity is that it eliminates time spent by workers commuting to and from the office, permitting greater concentration of energy on work-related tasks. Hartig et al. (2003) found that telecommuters actually spend more time on paid work when working at home than their counterparts do while working in the office. However, there are repercussions from these new work arrangements. First, the employees lose the human side of work; computer terminals are not an attractive substitute for face-to-face interaction with colleagues and friends at work. In addition, female telecommuters face more stress resulting from greater housework and child-care responsibilities (Olson and Primps, 1984; Olson, 1989). Nearly 59 percent of telecommuters say that they work longer hours because they are working at home, though employers view this increased productivity as a primary benefit of telecommuting (ITAC, 2004). On the other hand, management cannot easily monitor the activities of employees not under direct supervision (Kling, 1996). While this may create problems for employers, it allows employees greater flexibility in managing their non-work roles, thus contributing to increased worker satisfaction (Davis and Polonko, 2001). Telecommuting also creates new possibilities for older and disabled workers to remain independent, productive, and socially connected (Bourma et al., 2004).

The growth of telecommuting is affecting profound changes in many social realms. It is restructuring business management practices and authority hierarchies within businesses (Spinks and Wood, 1996) as well as contributing to new trends in housing and residential development that prioritize spatial and technological requirements for telework in homes, which are built at increasing distances from city centers (Hartig et al., 2003). Finally, some have argued that telecommuting is contributing to a shift in the distribution of income toward the technologically literate while affecting marital and family relationships and altering demands for child care (Raines and Leathers, 2001).

The experiences of telecommuters are reminders that negative consequences can result from the implementation of information technology to reorder organizations. While computerization has resulted in a reduction in hierarchy, it has created a two-tiered occupational structure composed of technical "experts" and less-skilled production or clerical workers. In these restructured organizations, jobs are redefined based more on technical skill than rank or position. For "expert" professionals, traditional bureaucratic constraints are relaxed to allow for creativity and flexibility, but other workers have limited autonomy (Burris, 1993). Although professionals benefit

more from this expanded autonomy, computerization makes production and service workers more visible and vulnerable to supervision (Zuboff, 1988; Wellman et al., 1996). For instance, computerization allows organizations to carefully monitor employees' work patterns to the point that they can count the number of seconds per phone call or keystrokes per minute, which in turn can lead to higher levels of stress for employees.

Granted, the computerization of the workplace does have some positive effects. It has made some mundane tasks associated with clerical jobs more interesting and flexible. It can also promote social networking (Wellman et al., 1996). For example, office computers can be used for recreation; private exchanges with other workers, friends, or family members; and work-related interaction. In some workplaces, computer-mediated communication can promote a more democratic type of workplace interaction. And, as in the case of telecommuting, computerization can contribute to greater flexibility for workers to manage both their personal and professional lives. But in the large majority of workplaces, computerization benefits the professionals who possess the knowledge and expertise about how to gain from it. It has not brought commensurate improvements in the career opportunities or salaries of the average worker (Kling, 1996).

Organizations as Networks

Traditionally, identifying the boundaries of organizations has been fairly straightforward. Organizations were generally located in defined physical spaces, such as an office building, a suite of rooms, or, in the case of a hospital or university, a whole campus. The mission or tasks an organization aimed to fulfill were also usually clear cut. A central feature of bureaucracies, for example, was adherence to a defined set of responsibilities and procedures for carrying them out. Weber's view of bureaucracy was that of a self-contained unit that intersected with outside entities at limited and designated points.

We have already seen how the physical boundaries of organizations are being broken down by the capacity of new information technology to transcend countries and time zones. But the same process is also affecting the work that organizations do and the way in which it is coordinated. Many organizations no longer operate as independent units, as they once did. A growing number are finding that their operations run more effectively when they are linked into a web of complex relationships with other organizations and companies. No longer is there a clear dividing line between the organization and outside groups. Globalization, information technology, and trends in occupational patterns mean that organizational boundaries are more open and fluid than they once were.

The Computerization of the Workplace

For businesses competing in the global economy, investment in information technology—computer and communications equipment—is a necessity. Firms in the financial sector rely heavily on computers to engage in transactions in international financial markets; manufacturing firms depend on communications equipment to coordinate global production processes; and the customers of consumer services firms demand twenty-four-hour-a-day access to their accounts by telephone or the Internet. In short, information technology has become part of the basic infrastructure of business. In the service sector alone, businesses spent approximately $750 billion on information technology hardware between 1980 and 1990 (National Research Council, 1994). This investment was a doubling of the amount spent per worker on technology and enabled firms to process vastly more transactions than they could in the past. Yet the investment in high-tech hardware did not pay off in terms of increased worker productivity until the late 1990s.

Although some of these technologies have made workers' lives easier, there is reason to worry that the new high-tech workplace may erode workers' power and rights. First, business reliance on information technology may undermine coalitions among workers. There is great demand today for employees with high-tech skills, whereas those who finish high school or college with few such skills find themselves eli-gible only for a limited number of positions. Increasingly, there are coming to be two "classes" of employees in firms: a privileged class with high-tech skills and another class relegated to lower-status work. But when employees negotiate with management over such issues as wages, hours, and benefits, employee unity is essential for securing concessions. Will high-tech workers side with lower-skilled employees in workplace disputes, or will they be more likely to side with management? The status of worker rights and benefits in the next century may well hinge on the answer to this question.

An example of organizations as networks can be seen in the powerful strategic alliances formed between top companies. Increasingly the large corporation is less and less a big business and more an "enterprise web"—a central organization that links smaller firms together. IBM, for example, used to be a highly self-sufficient corporation, wary of partnerships with others. Yet in the 1980s and early 1990s, IBM joined with dozens of U.S.-based companies and more than eighty foreign-based firms to share strategic planning and cope with production problems.

Networked organizations offer at least two advantages over more formal, bureaucratic ones: They can foster the flow of information, and they can enhance creativity. As you've already learned, bureaucratic hierarchy can impede the flow of information: One must go through the proper channels, fill out the right forms, and often avoid displeasing people in higher positions. These bureaucratic processes not only impede the sharing of information but also stifle creative problem solving. In networked organizations, by contrast, when a problem arises, instead of writing a memo to your boss and waiting for a reply before you act, you can simply pick up the phone or dash off an e-mail to the person who is responsible for working out a solution. As a result, members of networked organizations learn more easily from one another than do bureaucrats. It is therefore easier to solve routine problems and to foster more innovative solutions to all types of problems (Hamel, 1991; Powell and Brantley, 1992; Powell, Koput, and Smith-Doerr, 1996).

Second, in part because new communications technologies allow the branch offices and production facilities of multinational firms to communicate easily with each other, a higher proportion of manufactured goods is coming to be produced on a transnational basis—a situation that may make individual workers more easily replaceable. The former U.S. Secretary of Labor Robert Reich provides the following example of a global production process: "Precision ice-hockey equipment is designed in Sweden, financed in Canada, and assembled in Cleveland and Denmark for distribution in North America and Europe, respectively, out of alloys whose molecular structure was researched and patented in Delaware and fabricated in Japan. An advertising campaign is conceived in Britain; film footage is shot in Canada, dubbed in Britain, and edited in New York" (Reich, 1991). Although high-tech, high-skilled workers will be needed to carry out many aspects of the production process, these skills may no longer give workers the same bargaining power vis-à-vis management that skilled craftsmanship carried with it in previous eras. Because the manufacturing process has now been broken down into many small components, and because each of these components is carried out at a different production facility, the number of skills that any one worker must have is more limited than was the case in previous eras, making it easier for companies to replace contentious workers. Communications technologies thus arguably further the process that the Marxist scholar Harry Braverman called "the deskilling of labor."

Third, the nature of workplace surveillance is likely to change substantially as information technology becomes even more important for business. Employers have always watched their employees closely, monitoring performance, seeking to improve efficiency, checking to make sure they do not steal.

But as a greater proportion of work comes to be done by computer, the capacity of managers to scrutinize the behavior of their employees increases. Computerized performance evaluations, scrutiny of employee e-mail, and enhanced management access to personal employee information—such an Orwellian scenario becomes more likely as the role of information technology in the workplace expands.

Do you think these dangers are real, or is the impact of information technology on organizations essentially benign for employees? What steps, if any, do you think can be taken to counter these trends?

The "McDonaldization" of Society?

Not everyone agrees that our society and its organizations are moving away from the Weberian view of rigid, orderly bureaucracies. Some critics point out that a number of high-profile cases—such as the Saturn car corporation or Benetton—are seized on by the media and commentators, who in turn pronounce the birth of a trend that does not in fact exist. The idea that we are witnessing a process of debureaucratization, they argue, is overstated.

In a contribution to the debate over debureaucratization, George Ritzer (1993) has developed a vivid metaphor to express his view of the transformations taking place in industri-

alized societies. He argues that although some tendencies toward debureaucratization have indeed emerged, on the whole what we are witnessing is the "McDonaldization" of society. According to Ritzer, McDonaldization is "the process by which the principles of the fast-food restaurants are coming to dominate more and more sectors of American society as well as the rest of the world." Ritzer uses the four guiding principles for McDonald's restaurants—efficiency, calculability, uniformity, and control through automation—to show that our society is becoming ever *more* rationalized with time.

If you have ever visited McDonald's restaurants in two different cities or countries, you will have noticed that there are very few differences between them. The interior decoration may vary slightly and the language spoken will most likely

Workplace Design

In the early nineteen-sixties, Jane Jacobs lived on Hudson Street, in Greenwich Village, near the intersection of Eighth Avenue and Bleecker Street. It was then, as now, a charming district of nineteenth-century tenements and town houses, bars and shops, laid out over an irregular grid, and Jacobs loved the neighborhood. In her 1961 masterpiece, "The Death and Life of Great American Cities," she rhapsodized about [the Village]. . . . It was, she said, an urban ballet.

The miracle of Hudson Street, according to Jacobs, was created by the particular configuration of the streets and buildings of the neighborhood. Jacobs argued that when a neighborhood is oriented toward the street, when sidewalks are used for socializing and play and commerce, the users of that street are transformed by the resulting stimulation: they form relationships and casual contacts they would never have otherwise. The West Village, she pointed out, was blessed with a mixture of houses and apartments and shops and offices and industry, which meant that there were always people "outdoors on different schedules and . . . in the place for different purposes." It had short blocks, and short blocks create the greatest variety in foot traffic. It had lots of old buildings, and old buildings have the low rents that permit individualized and creative uses. And, most of all, it had people, cheek by jowl, from every conceivable walk of life. Sparsely populated suburbs may look appealing, she said, but without an active sidewalk life, without the frequent, serendipitous interactions of many different people, "there is no public acquaintanceship,

no foundation of public trust, no cross-connections with the necessary people—and no practice or ease in applying the most ordinary techniques of city public life at lowly levels." . . .

The parallels between neighborhoods and offices are striking. There was a time, for instance, when companies put their most valued employees in palatial offices, with potted plants in the corner, and secretaries out front, guarding access. Those offices were suburbs—gated communities, in fact—and many companies came to realize that if their best employees were isolated in suburbs they would be deprived of public acquaintanceship, the foundations of public trust, and cross-connections with the necessary people. In the eighties and early nineties, the fashion in corporate America was to follow what designers called "universal planning"—rows of identical cubicles, which resembled nothing so much as a Levittown. Today, universal planning has fallen out of favor, for the same reason that the postwar suburbs like Levittown did: to thrive, an office space must have a diversity of uses—it must have the workplace equivalent of houses and apartments and shops and industry. . . .

The task of the office, then, is to invite a particular kind of social interatction—the casual, nonthreatening encounter that makes it easy for relative strangers to talk to each other. Offices need the sort of social milieu that Jane Jacobs found on the sidewalks of the West Village. "It is possible in a city street neighborhood to know all kinds of people without unwelcome entanglements, without boredom, necessity for excuses, explanations, fears of giving offense, embarrassments respecting impositions or commitments, and all such paraphernalia of obligations which can accompany less limited relationships," Jacobs wrote. If you substitute "office" for "city street neighborhood," that sentence becomes the perfect statement of what the modern employer wants from the workplace. . . .

The point of the new offices is to compel us to behave and socialize in ways that we otherwise would not—to overcome our initial inclination to be office suburbanites. But, in all the studies of the new workplaces, the reservations that employees have about a more social environment tend to diminish once they try it. Human behavior, after all, is shaped by context, but how it is shaped—and whether we'll be happy with the result—we can understand only with experience. Jane Jacobs knew the virtues of the West Village because she lived there. What she couldn't know was that her ideas about com-

munity would ultimately make more sense in the workplace. From time to time, social critics have bemoaned the falling rates of community participation in American life, but they have made the same mistake. The reason Americans are content to bowl alone (or, for that matter, not bowl at all) is that, increasingly, they receive all the social support they need—all the serendipitous interactions that serve to make them happy and productive—from nine to five.

SOURCE: Reprinted from Malcolm Gladwell, "Designs for Working," *New Yorker*, December 11, 2000.

Questions

- Why would it be in a company's interest to direct employees away from individual work and toward group interaction?
- This article describes a model for a white-collar office. Would the same kind of interaction and cooperative work be a productive model for blue-collar or unskilled labor also?
- Gladwell describes the old-fashioned office as a form of suburbia. Does the analogy hold? Why or why not?

differ from country to country, but the layout, the menu, the procedure for ordering, the staff uniforms, the tables, the packaging, and the "service with a smile" are virtually identical. The McDonald's experience is designed to be the same whether you are in Bogota or Beijing. No matter where they are located, visitors to McDonald's know that they can expect quick service with a minimum of fuss and a standardized product that is reassuringly consistent. The McDonald's system is deliberately constructed to maximize efficiency and minimize human responsibility and involvement in the process. Except for certain key tasks such as taking orders and pushing the start and stop buttons on cooking equipment, the restaurants' functions are highly automated and largely run themselves.

Ritzer argues that society as a whole is moving toward this highly standardized and regulated model for getting things done. Many aspects of our daily lives, for example, now involve interactions with automated systems and computers instead of human beings. E-mail and voice mail are replacing letters and phone calls, e-commerce is threatening to overtake trips to the stores, bank machines are outnumbering bank tellers, and prepackaged meals provide a quicker option than cooking. If you have recently tried to call a large organization, such as an airline, you will know that it is almost impossible to speak to a human being. Automated Touch-Tone information services are designed to answer your requests; only in certain cases will you be connected to a live employee of the company. Computerized systems of all sorts are playing an ever greater role in our daily lives. Ritzer, like Weber before him, is fearful of the harmful effects of rationalization on the human spirit and creativity. He argues that McDonaldization is making social life more homogeneous, more rigid, and less personal.

How Do Groups and Organizations Affect Your Life?

Social Capital: The Ties That Bind

One of the principal reasons people join organizations is to gain connections and increase their influence. The time and energy invested in an organization can bring welcome returns. Parents who belong to the PTA, for example, are more likely to be able to influence school policy than those who do not belong. The members know whom to call, what to say, and how to exert pressure on school officials.

Sociologists call these fruits of organizational membership **social capital**, the social knowledge and connections that enable people to accomplish their goals and extend their influence (Loury, 1987; Coleman, 1988, 1990; Putnam, 1993, 1995, 2000). Social capital includes useful social networks, a sense of mutual obligation and trustworthiness, an understanding of the norms that govern effective behavior, and in general, other social resources that enable people to act effectively. For example, college students often become active in the student government or the campus newspaper partly because they hope to learn social skills and make connections that will pay off when they graduate. They may, for example, get to interact with professors and administrators, who then will go to bat for them when they are looking for a job or applying to graduate school.

Differences in social capital mirror larger social inequalities. In general, for example, men have more capital than women, whites more than nonwhites, the wealthy more than the poor. Differences in social capital can also be found among countries. According to the World Bank (2001), countries with high levels of social capital, where businesspeople can effectively develop the "networks of trust" that foster healthy economies, are more likely to experience economic growth. An example is the rapid growth experienced by many East Asian economies in the 1980s, a growth some sociologists have argued was fueled by strong business networks.

Robert Putnam, a political scientist who has completed an extensive study of social capital in the United States, distinguishes two types of social capital: *bridging social capital*, which is outward looking and inclusive, and *bonding social capital*, which is inward looking and exclusive. Bridging social capital unifies people across social cleavages. The capacity to unify people can be seen in such examples as the civil rights movement, which brought blacks and whites together in the struggle for racial equality, and interfaith religious organizations. Bonding social capital reinforces exclusive identities and homogeneous groups; it can be found in ethnic fraternal organizations, church-based women's reading groups, and fashionable country clubs (Putnam, 2000).

People who actively belong to organizations are more likely to feel "connected"; they feel engaged, able to somehow "make a difference." From the standpoint of the larger society, social capital, the bridging form in particular, provides people with a feeling that they are part of a wider community, and one that includes people who are different from themselves. Democracy flourishes when social capital is strong. Indeed, cross-national survey evidence suggests that levels of civic engagement in the United States are among the highest in the world (Putnam, 1993, 2000). But there is equally strong evidence that during the past quarter century, the ties of political involvement, club membership, and other forms of social and civic engagement that bind Americans to one another have significantly eroded. Could it be that democracy is eroding as a result?

Such declines in organizational membership, neighborliness, and trust in general have been paralleled by a decline in democratic participation. Voter turnout has dropped by 25 percent since the 1960s. In recent presidential elections, for example, the winning candidate (George H. W. Bush in 1988, Bill Clinton in 1992 and 1996 and George W. Bush in 2000) received roughly only a quarter of the votes of all those who were eligible to cast a ballot. About half of the eligible voters did not bother to go to the polls. Similarly, attendance at public meetings concerning education or civic affairs has dropped sharply since the 1970s, and three out of four Americans today tell pollsters that they either "never" trust the government or do so only "sometimes" (Putnam, 1995).

Even the recent increase in membership in organizations such as the Sierra Club, the National Organization for Women (NOW), and the American Association of Retired Persons (AARP, with 35 million members) is deceiving: The vast majority of these organizations' members simply pay their annual dues and receive a newsletter. Very few members actively participate, failing to develop the social capital Putnam regards as an important underpinning of democracy. Many of the most popular organizations today, such as twelve-step programs or weight loss groups, emphasize personal growth and health rather than collective goals to benefit society as a whole.

There are undoubtedly many reasons for these declines. For one, women, who were traditionally active in voluntary organizations, are more likely to hold a job than ever before. For another, people are increasingly disillusioned with government and less likely to think that their vote counts. Furthermore, the flight to the suburbs increases commuting time, using up time and energy that might have been available for civic activities. But the principal source of declining civic participation, according to Putnam is simple: television. The many hours Americans spend at home alone watching TV has replaced social engagement in the community.

Conclusion

You know better now how the groups and organizations you belong to exert an enormous influence over your life. They help to determine whom you know, and in many ways who you are. The primary groups of your earliest years were crucial in shaping your sense of self—a sense that changes very slowly thereafter. Throughout your life, groups are a wellspring of the norms and values that enable and enrich social life. At the same time, groups are also a source of nonconformist behavior: The rebel as much as the upright citizen is shaped by group membership.

Although groups remain central in our lives, group affiliation in the United States is rapidly changing. As you have seen in this chapter, conventional groups appear to be losing ground in our daily life. For example, today's college students are less likely to join civic groups and organizations—or even vote—than were their parents, a decline that may well signal a lower commitment to their communities. Some sociologists worry that this signals a weakening of society itself, which could bring about social instability.

As you have also seen, the global economy and information technology are redefining group life in ways that are now beginning to be felt. For instance, your parents are likely to spend much of their careers in a relative handful of long-lasting, bureaucratic organizations; you are much more likely to be part of a larger number of networked, "flexible" ones. Many of your group affiliations will be created through the Internet or through other forms of communication that today can barely be envisioned. It will become increasingly easy to connect with like-minded people anywhere on the planet, creating geographically dispersed groups that span the planet—and whose members may never meet each other face-to-face.

How will these trends affect the quality of your social relationships? For nearly all of human history, most people interacted exclusively with others who were close at hand. The industrial revolution, which facilitated the rise of large, impersonal bureaucracies where people knew one another poorly if at all, changed social interaction. Today, the information revolution is once again changing human interaction. Tomorrow's groups and organizations could provide a renewed sense of communication and social intimacy—or they could spell further isolation and social distance.

Study Outline

www.wwnorton.com/giddens

Social Groups

- *Social groups*, collections of people who share a sense of common identity and regularly interact with one another on the basis of shared expectations, shape nearly every experience in our lives. Among the types of social groups are *in-groups* and *out-groups*, *primary groups* and *secondary groups*.
- *Reference groups* provide standards by which we judge ourselves in terms of how we think we appear to others, what sociologist Charles Horton Cooley termed the "looking-glass self."
- Group size is an important factor in group dynamics. Although their intensity may diminish, larger groups tend to be more stable than smaller groups of two (*dyads*) or three (*triads*). Groups of more than a dozen or so people usually develop a formal structure.
- *Leaders* are able to influence the behavior of the other members of a group. The most common form of leadership is *transactional*, that is, routine leadership concerned with getting the job done. Less common is *transformational leadership*, which is concerned with changing the very nature of the group itself.
- Research indicates that people are highly conformist to group pressure. Many people will do what others tell them to do, even when the consequences could involve injury to others, as demonstrated by Stanley Milgram.
- *Networks* constitute a broad source of relationships, direct and indirect, including connections that may be extremely important in business and politics. Women, people of color, and lower-income people typically have less access to the most influential economic and political networks than do white males in American society.

Organizations

- All modern organizations are in some degree bureaucratic in nature. Bureaucracy is characterized by a clearly defined hierarchy of authority; written rules governing the conduct of officials (who work full time for a salary); and a separation between the tasks of the official within the organization and life outside it. Members of the organization do not own the material resources with which they operate. Max Weber argued that modern bureaucracy is a highly effective means of organizing large numbers of people, ensuring that decisions are made according to general criteria.
- Informal networks tend to develop at all levels both within and between organizations. The study of these informal ties is as important as the more formal characteristics on which Weber concentrated his attention.

Theories of Organizations

- The work of Weber and Michels identifies a tension between bureaucracy and democracy. On the one hand, long-term processes of the centralization of decision making are associated with the development of modern societies. On the other hand, one of the main features of the past two centuries has been expanding pressures toward democracy. The trends conflict, with neither one in a position of dominance.

Gender and Organizations

- Modern organizations have evolved as gendered institutions. Women have traditionally been segregated into certain occupational categories that support the ability of men to advance their careers. In recent years, women have been entering professional and managerial positions in greater numbers, but some believe that women have to adopt a traditionally male management style in order to succeed at top levels.

Alternatives to Bureaucracy

- Large organizations have started to restructure themselves over recent years to become less bureaucratic and more flexible. Many Western firms have adopted aspects of Japanese management systems: more consultation of lower-level workers by managerial executives; pay and responsibility linked to seniority; and groups, rather than individuals, evaluated for their performance.
- New information technology is changing the way in which organizations work. Many tasks can now be completed electronically, a fact that allows organizations to transcend time and space. The physical boundaries of organizations are being eroded by the capabilities of new technology. Many organizations now work as loose networks, rather than as self-contained independent units.

Social Capital

- *Social capital* refers to the knowledge and connections that enable people to cooperate with one another for mutual benefit and extend their influence. Some social scientists have argued that social capital has declined in the United States during the last quarter century, a process they worry indicates a decline in Americans' commitment to civic engagement.

Key Concepts

secondary group (p. 105)
social aggregate (p. 104)
social capital (p. 126)
social category (p. 104)
social group (p. 104)
transactional leader (p. 108)
transformational leader (p. 107)
triad (p. 106)

Review Questions

1. The term for the social knowledge and connections that enable people to accomplish their goals and extend their influence is
   a. cultural capital.
   b. political capital.
   c. social capital.
   d. economic capital.
2. Which kind of group provides standards by which we judge ourselves?
   a. In-group
   b. Primary group
   c. Out-group
   d. Reference group
3. What is the derivation of the word *bureaucracy*?
   a. It was coined in 1910 by Max Weber: "bureau" means "writing table," and "cracy" is derived from the Greek verb "to know."
   b. It was coined in 1745 by Monsieur de Gournay: "bureau" means both office and writing table, and "cracy" is derived from the Greek verb "to rule."
   c. It was coined in 1859 by Karl Marx: "bureau" means house, and "cracy" is derived from the Greek verb "to control."
   d. It was coined in 1810 by Madame de Blancmange: "bureau" means officer, and "cracy" is derived from the Greek verb "to exhibit signs of madness."
4. Which of the following scholars is concerned with the influence of cultural contexts on organizational forms?
   a. Henry Mintzberg
   b. Stuart Clegg
   c. George Ritzer
   d. Peter Blau
5. What is the difference between the way a new employee would be trained in (1) a Western corporation and the way he or she would be trained in (2) a Japanese corporation?
   a. In (1) employees are expected to acquire all relevant training themselves by investing in their own educations, whereas in (2) employees are expected to learn most of the skills relevant to their job through in-house training.
   b. In (1) the employee would spend up to a decade alternating between different branches and divisions and the head office, whereas in (2) the employee would specialize in the affairs of one department in one place from the very beginning.
   c. In (1) employees are expected to learn most of the skills relevant to their job through in-house training, whereas in (2)

employees are expected to acquire all relevant training themselves by investing in their own educations.
   d. In (1) the employee would specialize in the affairs of one department in one place from the very beginning, whereas in (2) the employee would spend up to a decade alternating between different branches and divisions and the head office.
6. Transformational leaders are concerned with
   a. changing the very nature of a group.
   b. getting the job done.
   c. the well-being of group members.
   d. all of the above.
7. What is "bottom-up" decision making?
   a. The American system of letting the stock price and quarterly earnings dictate a firm's business strategy.
   b. A euphemism for paying attention to employees.
   c. The Japanese system of running large organizations with greater levels of participation from rank and file employees.
   d. A euphemism for the point at which the stock price has fallen so far that the directors have—metaphorically—put their heads between their knees.
8. Which of the following is *not* a characteristic of a primary group?
   a. members interacting on a face-to-face basis
   b. intimacy
   c. members interacting to achieve a specific goal
   d. a strong sense of bonding and commitment

Thinking Sociologically Exercises

1. According to George Simmel, what are the primary differences between dyads and triads? Explain, according to his theory, how the addition of a child would alter the relationship between a husband and wife. Does the theory fit this situation?
2. The advent of computers and the computerization of the workplace may change our organizations and relationships with coworkers. Explain how you see modern organizations changing with the adaptation of newer information technologies.

Data Exercises

www.wwnorton.com/giddens
Keyword: Data5

- After reading this chapter you can understand how important group memberships are to personal and social development. However, when individuals get involved in groups society can also benefit, as the discussion of social capital and civic engagement demonstrates. In the data exercise for Chapter 5 you will explore some of the current debate about this important issue.

The Study of Deviant Behavior

Learn how we define deviance and how it is closely related to social power and social class. See the ways in which conformity is encouraged. Familiarize yourself with some traditional explanations for deviance and their limitations as theories.

Society and Crime: Sociological Theories

Know the leading sociological theories of crime and how each is useful in understanding deviance.

Crime and Crime Statistics

Recognize the helpfulness and limitations of crime statistics. Learn some important differences between men and women related to crime. Familiarize yourself with some of the varieties of crime. Think about the best solutions to reduce crime.

Victims and Perpetrators of Crime

Understand that some individuals or groups are more likely to commit or be the victims of crime.

Crime-Reduction Strategies

Consider the ways in which individuals and governments can address crime.

CHAPTER SIX

CONFORMITY, DEVIANCE, AND CRIME

illie was a street vendor who lived and worked on a street in New York City. He earned money by taking magazines out of recycled trash and reselling them to passersby. Willie lived on a corner for about six years, ever since he was released from serving a prison sentence for committing a robbery. During the early 1990s, he was one of approximately 600,000 people released from prison every year—about 1,600 per day (Mauer, 2004).

In 2002, the number of prisoners held in federal, state, and county facilities exceeded 2 million people. One and a half million Americans were detained in prisons and jails for drug offenses, a threefold increase since 1980. This extreme focus on drug offenses has led the United States to become the world leader in this regard, surpassing Russia. The U.S. rate of incarceration is five to eight times higher than Canada and the countries of Western Europe (Garland, 2002).

This dramatic increase in incarceration has had a major impact on the African American and Latino populations in particular. According to Marc Mauer, a leading student of incarceration, "In 1997, the state-wide population of Maryland, Illinois, North Carolina, South Carolina, and Louisiana was two thirds or more white, but prison growth since 1985 was 80% non-white. . . . In New York, where the state's adult minority population is less than 31.7%, nine out of ten new prisoners are from an ethnic or racial minority" (Mauer, 2004).

The impact of the criminal justice system is clear in the lives of people like Willie. While they are in prison, they are not part of the labor force, and thus a large amount of joblessness is not

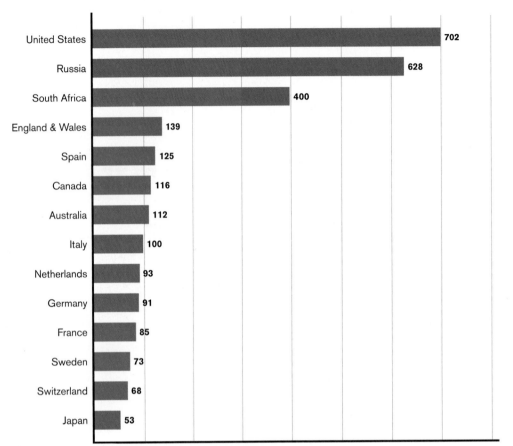

FIGURE 6.1

Incarceration Rates in Selected Industrialized Nations

United States — 702
Russia — 628
South Africa — 400
England & Wales — 139
Spain — 125
Canada — 116
Australia — 112
Italy — 100
Netherlands — 93
Germany — 91
France — 85
Sweden — 73
Switzerland — 68
Japan — 53

Incarceration rate (number of people in prision per 100,000 population)

SOURCE: Marc Mauer, "Comparative Rates of Incarceration: An Examination of Causes and Trends," The Sentencing Project, 2003, www.sentencingproject.org/pdfs/pub9036.pdf.

reflected in the rates of unemployment reported by the government. At the same time, incarceration also increases the long-term chances of unemployment for men like Willie once they are released from prison (Western and Beckett, 1999).

Although the United States has imprisoned over 2 million people at the state and local level over the past few years, it has failed to make adequate preparations for their release (Gonnerman, 2004). From prison, Willie went directly to the streets. He had nowhere to work and nowhere else to go. People he knew from prison were already living on this corner and he heard he could find them there.

Willie is a man who many people would define as a deviant. We all know who deviants are, or so we tend to think. Deviants are those individuals who refuse to live by the rules that the majority of us follow. Sometimes they're violent criminals, drug addicts, or down-and-outs, who don't fit in with what most people would define as normal standards of acceptability. These are the cases that seem easy to identify. Yet things are not quite as they appear—a lesson sociology often teaches us, for it encourages us to look beyond the obvious. The notion of the deviant, as we shall see, is actually not an easy one to define.

We have learned in previous chapters that social life is governed by rules or norms. Our activities would collapse into chaos if we didn't stick to rules that define some kinds of behavior as proper in particular contexts and others as inappropriate. As we learned earlier in talking about the concept of culture, **norms** are definite principles or rules people are expected to observe; they represent the "dos" and "don'ts" of society. Orderly behavior on the highway, for example, would be impossible if drivers didn't observe the rule of driving on the right. No deviants here, you might think, except perhaps for the drunken or reckless driver. If you did think this, you would be incorrect. When we drive, most of us are not merely deviants but criminals. For most drivers regularly drive at well above the legal speed limits—assuming there isn't a police car in sight. In such cases, breaking the law is normal behavior!

We are all rule breakers as well as conformists. We are all also rule creators. Most American drivers may break the law on the freeways, but in fact they've evolved informal rules that are superimposed on the legal rules. When the legal speed limit on the highway is 65 mph, most drivers don't go above 75 or so, and they drive slower when driving through urban areas.

In most European countries, the legal speed limits are higher than in the United States—between 65 and 70 mph, depending on the country. Drivers there break the law most of the time just as they do in the United States, but their informal rules about proper driving produce higher speeds than in America. People regularly drive at 80–90 mph. Conventional rules about what is and isn't reckless driving also vary. Americans who drive in the south of Italy, for example, where drivers break other traffic rules as well, are apt to find the experience a hair-raising one.

When we begin the study of deviant behavior, we must consider which rules people are observing and which they are breaking. Nobody breaks *all* rules, just as no one conforms to all rules. Even an individual who might seem wholly outside the pale of respectable society, such as Willie, is likely to be following many rules of the groups and societies of which he is a member.

For example, when Willie would get enough money for a meal, he would go to a small Chinese restaurant around the corner from where he lived. There he would sit and eat his egg rolls, chow mein, and egg drop soup with the same manners as other diners. In this restaurant, he hardly appears as a deviant. When Willie is out on the street, he follows the rules of the other street vendors who subsisted on the street. In the world of street vendors, he appears as a conformist most of the time. Indeed, some "deviant" groups such as the homeless have strict codes of social behavior for those who live among them. Those who deviate from these informal codes of behavior may be ostracized or expelled from the group and be forced to go elsewhere (Duneier, 1999). Thus, even "deviants" are conformists at times.

Willie's life is an example of what happens to large numbers of people with drug convictions who spend time in the American criminal justice system. Because prisons and jails make little accommodation for people after release, many former prisoners are unable to find homes or jobs in the formal econ-

omy. Working on the street is hardly a long-term solution for men like Willie, and after six years of "staying clean" on Sixth Avenue he was rearrested for another drug offense. This is very common: Almost two thirds of all reentering prisoners are likely to be rearrested within three years (Mauer, 2004).

The Study of Deviant Behavior

The study of deviant behavior is one of the most intriguing yet complex areas of sociology. It teaches us that none of us is quite as normal as we might like to think. It also helps us see that people whose behavior might appear incomprehensible or alien can be seen as rational beings when we understand why they act as they do.

The study of deviance, like other fields of sociology, directs our attention to social *power*, as well as the influence of social class—the divisions between rich and poor. When we look at deviance from or conformity to social rules or norms, we always have to bear in mind the question, *Whose* rules? As we shall see, social norms are strongly influenced by divisions of power and class.

What Is Deviance?

Deviance may be defined as nonconformity to a given set of norms that are accepted by a significant number of people in a community or society. No society, as has already been stressed, can be divided up in a simple way between those who deviate from norms and those who conform to them. Most of us on some occasions transgress generally accepted rules of behavior.

The scope of the concept of deviance is very broad, as some examples will illustrate. Kevin Mitnick has been described as the "world's most celebrated computer hacker." It is probably fair to say that the thirty-six-year-old Californian is revered and despised in equal measure. To the world's estimated 100,000 computer hackers, Mitnick is a pioneering genius whose five-year imprisonment in a U.S. penitentiary was unjust and unwarranted—concrete proof of how misunderstood computer hacking has become with the spread of information technology. To U.S. authorities and high-tech corporations—such as Sun Microsystems, Motorola, and Nokia—Mitnick is one of the world's most dangerous men. He was captured by the FBI in 1995 and later convicted of downloading source codes and stealing software allegedly worth millions of dollars from these and other companies. As a condition of his release

Computer hacker Kevin Mitnick was arrested in 1995 and later convicted of stealing millions of dollars worth of software from a number of technology companies. His release in 2000 was conditioned upon the understanding that he would refrain from using computers or speaking publicly about technology issues.

from prison in January 2000, Mitnick was forbidden to use computers or to speak publicly about technology issues.

Over the past decade or so, hackers have been gradually transformed from a little-noticed population of computer enthusiasts to a much-maligned group of deviants who are believed to threaten the very stability of the information age. Yet, according to Mitnick and others in the hacker community, such depictions could not be further from the truth. "Hacker is a term of honor and respect," claimed Mitnick in an article written shortly after his release from prison. "It is a term that describes a skill, not an activity, in the same way that doctor describes a skill. It was used for decades to describe talented computer enthusiasts, people whose skill at using computers to solve technical problems and puzzles was—and is—respected and admired by others possessing similar technical skills" (Mitnick, 2000). Hackers are quick to point out that most of their activities are not criminal. Rather, they are primarily interested in exploring the edges of computer technology, trying to uncover loopholes and to discover how far it is possible to penetrate into other computer systems. Once flaws have been discovered, the "hacker ethic" demands that the information be shared publicly. Many hackers have even served as consultants for large corporations and government agencies, helping them to defend their systems against outside intrusion.

Deviance does not refer only to individual behavior; it concerns the activities of groups as well. An illustration is the Heaven's Gate cult (discussed earlier, in Chapter 5), a religious group whose beliefs and ways of life were different from those of the majority of Americans. The cult was established in the early 1970s when Marshall Herff Applewhite made his way around the West and Midwest of the United States preaching his beliefs, ultimately advertising on the Internet his belief that civilization was doomed and that the only way people could be saved was to kill themselves so their souls could be rescued by a U.F.O. On March 26, 1997, thirty-nine members of the cult followed his advice in a mass suicide at a wealthy estate in Rancho Santa Fe, California.

The Heaven's Gate cult represents an example of a **deviant subculture**. They were able to survive fairly easily within the wider society, supporting themselves by running a Web site business and recruiting new members by sending e-mail messages to people they thought might be interested in their beliefs. They had plenty of money and lived together in an expensive home in a wealthy California suburb. Their position diverges from that of another deviant subculture that we discussed in the introduction to this chapter: the homeless.

Norms and Sanctions

We most often follow social norms because, as a result of socialization, we are used to doing so. Individuals become committed to social norms through interactions with people who obey the law. Through these interactions, we learn self-control. The more numerous these interactions, the fewer opportunities there are to deviate from conventional norms. And, over time, the longer that we interact in ways that are conventional, the more we have at stake in continuing to act in that way (Gottfredson and Hirschi, 1990).

All social norms are accompanied by sanctions that promote conformity and protect against nonconformity. A **sanction** is any reaction from others to the behavior of an individual or group that is meant to ensure that the person or group complies with a given norm. Sanctions may be positive (the offering of rewards for conformity) or negative (punishment for behavior that does not conform). They can also be formal or informal. Formal sanctions are applied by a specific body of people or an agency to ensure that a particular set of norms is followed. Informal sanctions are less organized and more spontaneous reactions to nonconformity, such as when a student is teasingly accused by friends of working too hard or being a "nerd" if he decides to spend an evening studying rather than going to a party.

The main types of formal sanctions in modern societies are those represented by the courts and prisons. The police, of course, are the agency charged with bringing offenders to trial and possible imprisonment. **Laws** are norms defined by governments as principles that their citizens must follow; sanctions are used against people who do not conform to them. Where there are laws, there are also **crimes**, since crime can most simply be defined as any type of behavior that breaks a law.

It is important to recognize, however, that the law is only a guide to the kind of norms that exist in a society. Oftentimes, subcultures invent their own dos and don'ts. For example, the street people that Willie lives among have created their own norms for determining where each of them can set up the magazines that he sells on the sidewalk. Other homeless vendors don't set up in Willie's spot on the sidewalk because that would show "disrespect." This example further illustrates that even members of so-called deviant groups usually live in accordance with some norms. What makes them deviant subcultures is that these norms are at odds with the norms of the mainstream of society.

We shall now turn to the main sociological theories that have been developed to interpret and analyze deviance. In contrast to some areas of sociology, in which a theoretical perspective has emerged over time as preeminent, many theoretical strands remain relevant to the study of deviance. After a brief look at biological and psychological explanations, we shall turn to the four sociological approaches that have been influential within the sociology of deviance: *functionalist theories*, *interactionist theories*, *conflict theories*, and *control theories*.

The Biological View of Deviance

Some of the first attempts to explain crime were essentially biological in character. The Italian criminologist Cesare Lombroso, working in the 1870s, believed that criminal types could be identified by the shape of the skull. He accepted that social learning could influence the development of criminal behavior, but he regarded most criminals as biologically degenerate or defective. Lombroso's ideas became thoroughly discredited, but similar views have repeatedly been suggested. Another popular method of trying to demonstrate the influence of heredity on criminal tendencies was to study family trees. But this demonstrates virtually nothing about the influence of heredity, because it is impossible to disentangle inherited and environmental influences.

A later theory distinguished three main types of human physique and claimed that one type was directly associated with delinquency. Muscular, active types (mesomorphs), the theory went, are more likely to become delinquent than those of thin physique (ectomorphs) or more fleshy people (endomorphs) (Sheldon et al., 1949; Glueck and Glueck, 1956). This research has also been widely criticized. Even if there were an overall re-

lationship between body type and delinquency, this would show nothing about the influence of heredity. People of the muscular type may be drawn toward criminal activities because these offer opportunities for the physical display of athleticism. Moreover, nearly all studies in this field have been restricted to delinquents in reform schools, and it may be that the tougher, athletic-looking delinquents are more liable to be sent to such schools than fragile-looking, skinny ones. Although older studies on the biological explanations of crime have been dismissed, more recent research has sought to rekindle the argument. In a study of New Zealand children, researchers sought to prove that childrens' propensity to aggression was linked to biological factors present at a child's birth (Moffitt, 1996).

However, studies such as this only show that some individuals might be inclined toward irritability and aggressiveness, and this could be reflected in crimes of physical assault on others. Yet there is no decisive evidence that any traits of personality are inherited in this way, and even if they were, their connection to criminality would at most be only a distant one. In fact, the New Zealand study did not argue that there is a biological cause to crime, but rather that biological factors, when combined with certain social factors such as one's home environment, could lead to social situations involving crime.

The Psychological View of Deviance

Like biological interpretations, psychological theories of crime associate criminality with particular types of personality. Some have suggested that in a minority of individuals, an amoral, or psychopathic, personality develops. **Psychopaths** are withdrawn, emotionless characters who delight in violence for its own sake.

Individuals with psychopathic traits do sometimes commit violent crimes, but there are major problems with the concept of the psychopath. It isn't at all clear that psychopathic traits are inevitably criminal. Nearly all studies of people said to possess these characteristics have been of convicted prisoners, and their personalities inevitably tend to be presented negatively. If we describe the same traits positively, the personality type sounds quite different, and there seems no reason why people of this sort should be inherently criminal. Should we be looking for psychopathic individuals for a research study, we might place the following ad:

ARE YOU ADVENTUROUS?
Researcher wishes to contact adventurous, carefree people who've led exciting, impulsive lives. If you're the kind of person who'd do almost anything for a dare, call 337-XXXX any time. (Widom and Newman, 1985)

Burning Man

Stopped at the gas station for directions to the Burning Man Festival. Grizzled, portly Nevadan local growls: "If ya have to ask, you *don't belong* there!" [***]

Burning Man is an art gig by tradition. Over the longer term it's evolved into something else; maybe something like a physical version of the Internet. The art here is like fan art. It's very throwaway, very appropriative, very cut-and-paste. The camp is like a giant swap meet where no one sells stuff, but people trade postures, clip art, and attitude. People come here in clumps: performance people, drumming enthusiasts, site-specific sculptors, sailplane people, ravers, journalists, cops. [***]

I went to Burning Man. I took my kids. It's not scary, it's not pagan, it's not devilish or satanic. There's no public orgies, nobody gets branded or hit with whips. Hell, it's less pagan than the Shriners. It's just big happy crowds of harmless arty people expressing themselves and breaking a few pointless shibboleths that only serve to ulcerate young people anyway. There ought to be Burning Man festivals held downtown once a year in every major city in America. It would be good for us. We need it. In fact, until we can just relax every once in a while and learn how to do this properly, we're probably never gonna get well.

SOURCE: Bruce Sterling, "Greetings from Burning Man!" *Wired* 4.11 (November 1996). Bruce Sterling's article introduced Burning Man to the wider world, as he described his first trip to the Temporary Autonomous Zone. Since this article was written, attendance has ballooned to over 30,000 people in 2004.

I'm a Burner. I think we should have that straight from the outset.

I wasn't always a Burner. For several years after my first trip to Burning Man, I maintained a more or less objective viewpoint. Even when I went to the playa weeks before the event and helped construct various stages, roads and towers, I was half uncertain whether the event would survive its periodic attacks by the various governments that regulate its existence. There were times when I wasn't even sure it should survive.

Now I'm convinced the event should and will survive, although it may evolve. Actually, my theory is that the event must evolve or it will collapse under the weight of monotony.

This is a theory that won't be tested under any scientific rigor, but my belief is that this is the year that Burning Man grew up. It reached and probably slightly surpassed 30,000 attendees, the number that has often been bandied about by organizers as the end of population increase, the organizational endpoint of this party on the Black Rock Desert. If that's true, then this year was the first true representation of what the Burning Man Festival will be until the fire's put out. But I get ahead of myself. [***]

Burning Man is a counterculture, anticonsumerism art event that happens up near Gerlach every Labor Day weekend. It attracts artists and people who like art. It doesn't generally attract the kind of artists who make paintings you'd hang on a wall in a museum. It attracts the kind of artists who

build fanciful, thought-provoking and inspirational artifacts of steel and gas and light and wood. Especially wood.

Because wood burns.

The festival used to culminate with the burning of a large wood-and-neon man. Hence the name. [***]

The event has been going since 1986, when founder Larry Harvey burned an effigy on Baker Beach in San Francisco. When the event got too large and attracted too much official attention, it moved to the Black Rock Desert playa, about 120 miles north of Reno, in 1990. In years past, local governments castigated event organizers for allowing too much freedom, too much nudity, too many drugs, too few rules. [***]

Back in the day, local businesses accepted the participants' money, but behind their backs they'd often call participants hippies, druggies, weirdoes, freaks, pretty much anything except what they were: artists and tourists. But that was when the participants numbered in the thousands. Now the event is a financial windfall, bringing $10 million, according to some estimates, into the local economy every year. [***]

The question of whether Burning Man will be able to attract 30,000 first- and second-timers will remain moot, as long as Larry Harvey and company can keep the themes and the art fresh. [***]

Back in 1995, Harvey told me that his art, the thing that most interested him about Burning Man, was the movement of people, the art and science of how to motivate and control crowds. At the time, I didn't truly understand what he was talking about, but Saturday I think I did. It was beautiful and frightening and a hint of things to come. [***]

I've seen more children and elderly people this year than I've seen in years past. Other people tell me I'm wrong, but if there are not more children, then the children that are here are being brought to more of the performances and are out riding their bikes and playing in community areas without adult supervision.

I think I understand the reason for this. In reaching maturity, Black Rock City became a safer city. I don't have a feeling for whether drug use has increased or decreased this year. I do feel that users are more discreet. I know drugs are there; I see people on drugs, and I hear people talk about having been on drugs, but nobody offers me cocaine or acid or mushrooms, and the smell of burning herb is infrequent. I've also heard many comments that the police presence has increased this year, but I don't really see evidence of that, either.

Anyway, this is a peaceful city by almost any definition. While bikes are stolen with frequency, apparently often by people who just want to get somewhere fast, who then abandon the bikes, there isn't the kind of violence you'd associate with a rock concert, street festival or classic-car event. [***]

It's difficult to say where Burning Man will go from here. Recent published interviews with Larry Harvey have suggested that he will integrate this Burning Man with the other ones that happen around the world, bringing together a very large community of people who think life should mimic art, instead of the other way round. Maybe he'll be able to institute some political and social change. I wouldn't be surprised.

I don't know; my job won't change, and nearly every year I'll continue to write these essays. It's obvious why I do it—Burning Man is the largest cultural event held in this neck of the woods. More important, though, is why does anybody care to read this stuff? [***]

The reason people want to read about Burning Man is because Burning Man matters.

At least it matters to us Burners. And there are a lot of us.

SOURCE: D. Brian Burghart, "About a Man," *Reno News and Review* (September 4, 2003).

Such people might be explorers, spies, gamblers, or just bored with the routines of day-to-day life. They *might* be prepared to contemplate criminal adventures but could be just as likely to look for challenges in socially respectable ways.

Psychological theories of criminality can at best explain only some aspects of crime. While some criminals may possess personality characteristics distinct from the remainder of the population, it is highly improbable that the majority of criminals do so. There are all kinds of crimes, and it is implausible to suppose that those who commit them share some specific psychological characteristics. Even if we confine ourselves to one category of crime, such as crimes of violence, different circumstances are involved. Some such crimes are carried out by lone individuals, whereas others are the work of organized groups. It is not likely that the psychological makeup of people who are loners will have much in common with the members of a close-knit gang. Even if consistent differences could be linked to forms of criminality, we still couldn't be sure which way the line of causality would run. It might be that becoming involved with criminal groups influences people's outlooks, rather than that the outlooks actually produce criminal behavior in the first place.

Both biological and psychological approaches to criminality presume that deviance is a sign of something "wrong" with the individual, rather than with society. They see crime as caused by factors outside an individual's control, embedded either in the body or the mind. Therefore, if scientific criminology could successfully identify the causes of crime, it would be possible to treat those causes. In this respect, both biological and psychological theories of crime are *positivist* in nature. As we learned in our discussion of Comte in Chapter 1, positivism is the belief that applying scientific methods to the study of the social world can reveal its basic truths. In the case of positivist criminology, this led to the belief that empirical research could pinpoint the causes of crime and in turn make recommendations about how to eradicate it.

Society and Crime: Sociological Theories

Early criminology came under great criticism from later generations of scholars. They argued that any satisfactory account of the nature of crime must be sociological, for what crime is depends on the social institutions of a society. One of the most important emphases of sociological thinking about crime is on the interconnections between conformity and deviance in different social contexts. Modern societies contain many different subcultures, and behavior that conforms to the norms of one particular subculture may be regarded as deviant outside it; for instance, there may be strong pressure on a member of a boys' gang to prove himself by stealing a car. Moreover, there are wide divergences of wealth and power in society that greatly influence opportunities open to different groups. Theft and burglary, not surprisingly, are carried out mainly by people from the poorer segments of the population; embezzling and tax evasion are by definition limited to persons in positions of some affluence.

Functionalist Theories

Functionalist theories see crime and deviance resulting from structural tensions and a lack of moral regulation within society. If the aspirations held by individuals and groups in society do not coincide with available rewards, this disparity between desires and fulfillment will be felt in the deviant motivations of some of its members.

CRIME AND ANOMIE: DURKHEIM AND MERTON

As we saw in Chapter 1, the notion of **anomie** was first introduced by Émile Durkheim, who suggested that in modern societies traditional norms and standards become undermined without being replaced by new ones. Anomie exists when there are no clear standards to guide behavior in a given area of social life. Under such circumstances, Durkheim believed, people feel disoriented and anxious; anomie is therefore one of the social factors influencing dispositions to suicide.

Durkheim saw crime and deviance as social facts; he believed both of them to be inevitable and necessary elements in modern societies. According to Durkheim, people in the modern age are less constrained than they were in traditional societies. Because there is more room for individual choice in the modern world, it is inevitable that there will be some nonconformity. Durkheim recognized that no society would ever be in complete consensus about the norms and values that govern it.

Deviance is also necessary for society, according to Durkheim; it fulfills two important functions. First, deviance has an *adaptive* function. By introducing new ideas and challenges into society, deviance is an innovative force. It brings about change. Second, deviance promotes *boundary maintenance* between "good" and "bad" behaviors in society. A criminal event can provoke a collective response that heightens group solidarity and clarifies social norms. For example, residents of a neighborhood facing a problem with drug dealers might join together in the aftermath of a drug-related shooting and commit themselves to maintaining the area as a drug-free zone.

Durkheim's ideas on crime and deviance were influential in shifting attention from individual explanations to social forces. His notion of anomie was drawn on by the American sociologist Robert K. Merton, who constructed a highly influential theory of deviance that located the source of crime within the very structure of American society (1957).

Merton modified the concept of anomie to refer to the strain put on individuals' behavior when accepted norms conflict with social reality. In American society—and to some degree in other industrial societies—generally held values emphasize material success, and the means of achieving success are supposed to be self-discipline and hard work. Accordingly, it is believed that people who really work hard can succeed no matter what their starting point in life. This idea is not in fact valid, because most of the disadvantaged are given only limited conventional opportunities for advancement, or none at all. Yet those who do not "succeed" find themselves condemned for their apparent inability to make material progress. In this situation, there is great pressure to try to get ahead by any means, legitimate or illegitimate. According to Merton, then, deviance is a by-product of economic inequalities.

Merton identifies five possible reactions to the tensions between socially endorsed values and the limited means of achieving them. *Conformists* accept both generally held values and the conventional means of realizing them, whether or not they meet with success. The majority of the population fall into this category. *Innovators* continue to accept socially approved values but use illegitimate or illegal means to follow them. Criminals who acquire wealth through illegal activities exemplify this type.

Ritualists conform to socially accepted standards although they have lost sight of the values behind these standards. They follow rules for their own sake without a wider end in view, in a compulsive way. A ritualist would be someone who dedicates herself to a boring job, even though it has no career prospects and provides few rewards. *Retreatists* have abandoned the competitive outlook altogether, thus rejecting both the dominant values and the approved means of achieving them. An example would be the members of a self-supporting commune. Finally, *rebels* reject both the existing values and the means but wish actively to substitute new ones and reconstruct the social system. The members of radical political groups fall into this category.

Merton's writings addressed one of the main puzzles in the study of criminology: At a time when society as a whole is becoming more affluent, why do crime rates continue to rise? By emphasizing the contrast between rising aspirations and persistent inequalities, Merton points to a sense of relative deprivation as an important element in deviant behavior.

SUBCULTURAL EXPLANATIONS

Later researchers located deviance in terms of subcultural groups that adopt norms that encourage or reward criminal behavior. Like Merton, Albert Cohen saw the contradictions within American society as the main cause of crime. But while Merton emphasized individual deviant responses to the tension between values and means, Cohen saw the responses occurring collectively through subcultures. In *Delinquent Boys* (1955), Cohen argued that boys in the lower working class who are frustrated with their positions in life often join together in *delinquent subcultures*, such as gangs. These subcultures reject middle-class values and replace them with norms that celebrate defiance, such as delinquency and other acts of nonconformity.

Members of a Los Angeles gang show off scars and tattoos. Are these men, like those in Cohen's *Delinquent Boys*, replacing the values of the middle class with norms that express pride in defiance and nonconformity, in this case bullet and knife wounds?

Richard A. Cloward and Lloyd E. Ohlin (1960) agree with Cohen that most delinquent youths emerge from the lower working class. But they argued that such gangs arise in subcultural communities where the chances of achieving success legitimately are slim, such as among deprived ethnic minorities. Their work rightly emphasized connections between conformity and deviance: Lack of opportunity for success in the terms of the wider society is the main differentiating factor between those who engage in criminal behavior and those who do not.

Recent research by sociologists has examined the validity of claims that immediate material deprivation can lead people to commit crimes. A survey of homeless youth in Canada, for instance, shows a strong correlation between hunger, lack of shelter, and unemployment, on the one hand, and theft, prostitution, and even violent crime on the other (Hagan and McCarthy, 1992).

Functionalist theories rightly emphasize connections between conformity and deviance in different social contexts. We should be cautious, however, about the idea that people in poorer communities, like Willie, aspire to the same level of success as more affluent people. Most tend to adjust their aspirations to what they see as the reality of their situation. Merton, Cohen, and Cloward and Ohlin can all be criticized for presuming that middle-class values have been accepted through society. It would also be wrong to suppose that a mismatch of aspirations and opportunities is confined to the less privileged. There are pressures toward criminal activity among other groups too, as indicated by the so-called white-collar crimes of embezzlement, fraud, and tax evasion, which we will study later.

Interactionist Theories

Sociologists studying crime and deviance in the interactionist tradition focus on deviance as a socially constructed phenomenon. They reject the idea that there are types of conduct that are inherently "deviant." Rather, interactionists ask how behaviors initially come to be defined as deviant and why certain groups and not others are labeled as deviant.

LEARNED DEVIANCE: DIFFERENTIAL ASSOCIATION

One of the earliest writers to suggest that deviance is learned through interaction with others was Edwin H. Sutherland. In 1949, Sutherland advanced a notion that was to influence much of the later interactionist work: He linked crime to what he called **differential association** (Sutherland, 1949). This idea is very simple. In a society that contains a variety of subcultures, some social environments tend to encourage illegal activities, whereas others do not. Individuals become delinquent through associating with people who are the carriers of criminal norms. For the most part, according to Sutherland, criminal behavior is learned within primary groups, particularly peer groups. This theory contrasts with the view that psychological differences separate criminals from other people; it sees criminal activities as learned in much the same way as law-abiding ones and as directed toward the same needs and values. Thieves try to make money just like people in orthodox jobs, but they choose illegal means of doing so.

Differential association can be used to assess Willie's life. Before Willie went to prison, he lived in Pennsylvania Station with a group of homeless men. From this group, he learned how to target and rob restaurant delivery boys, whom he learned were unlikely to report the crime to the police because many of them were illegal immigrants from Mexico and China. Willie would not have known these facts unless he had learned them from associating with others who were already the carriers of criminal norms.

LABELING THEORY

One of the most important interactionist approaches to the understanding of criminality is called **labeling theory**—although this term itself is a label for a cluster of related ideas rather than a unified view. Labeling theory originally came to be associated with Howard S. Becker's studies of marijuana smokers (1963). In the early 1960s, marijuana use was a marginal activity carried on by subcultures rather than the lifestyle choice—that is, an activity accepted by many in the mainstream of society—it is today (Hathaway, 1997). Becker found that becoming a marijuana smoker depended on one's acceptance into the subculture, close association with experienced users, and one's attitudes toward nonusers. Labeling theorists like Becker interpret deviance not as a set of characteristics of individuals or groups, but as a *process* of interaction between deviants and nondeviants. In other words, it is not the act of marijuana smoking that makes one a deviant, but the way others react to marijuana smoking that makes it deviant. In the view of labeling theorists, we must discover why some people become tagged with a "deviant" label in order to understand the nature of deviance itself.

People who represent the forces of law and order or are able to impose definitions of conventional morality on others do most of the labeling. The labels that create categories of deviance thus express the power structure of society. By and large, the rules in terms of which deviance is defined are framed by the wealthy for the poor, by men for women, by older people for younger people, and by ethnic majorities for minority groups. For example, many children wander into other people's gardens, steal fruit, or play truant. In an affluent neighborhood, these might be regarded by parents, teachers, and police alike as relatively innocent pastimes of childhood. In poor areas, they might be seen as evidence of tendencies toward juvenile delinquency.

Once a child is labeled a delinquent, he is stigmatized as a criminal and is likely to be considered untrustworthy by teachers and prospective employers. He then relapses into further criminal behavior, widening the gulf with orthodox social conventions. Edwin Lemert (1972) called the initial act of transgression **primary deviation. Secondary deviation** occurs when the individual comes to accept the label and sees himself as deviant. Other research has shown that how we think of ourselves and how we believe others perceive us influences our propensity for committing crime. One study examining self-appraisals of a random national sample of young men showed that such appraisals are strongly tied to levels of criminality (Matsueda, 1992).

Take, for example, Luke, who smashes a shop window while spending a Saturday night out on the town with his friends. The act may perhaps be called the accidental result of overboisterous behavior, an excusable characteristic of young men. Luke might escape with a reprimand and a small fine. If he is from a "respectable" background, this is a likely result. And the smashing of the window stays at the level of primary deviance if the youth is seen as someone of good character who on this occasion became too rowdy. If, on the other hand, the police and courts hand out a suspended sentence and make Luke report to a social worker, the incident could become the first step on the road to secondary deviance. The process of "learning to be deviant" tends to be reinforced by the very organizations supposedly set up to correct deviant behavior—prisons and social agencies.

Labeling theory is important because it begins from the assumption that no act is intrinsically criminal. Definitions of criminality are established by the powerful through the formulation of laws and their interpretation by police, courts, and correctional institutions. Critics of labeling theory have sometimes argued that certain acts are consistently prohibited across virtually all cultures, such as murder, rape, and robbery. This view is surely incorrect; even within our own culture, killing is not always regarded as murder. In times of war, killing of the enemy is positively approved, and until recently the laws in most U.S. states did not recognize sexual intercourse forced on a woman by her husband as rape.

We can more convincingly criticize labeling theory on other grounds. First, in emphasizing the active process of labeling, labeling theorists neglect the processes that *lead* to acts defined as deviant. For labeling certain activities as deviant is not completely arbitrary; differences in socialization, attitudes, and opportunities influence how far people engage in behavior likely to be labeled deviant. For instance, children from deprived backgrounds are on average more likely to steal from shops than are richer children. It is not the labeling that leads them to steal in the first place so much as the background from which they come.

Second, it is not clear whether labeling actually does have the effect of increasing deviant conduct. Delinquent behavior tends to increase following a conviction, but is this the result of the labeling itself? Other factors, such as increased interaction with other delinquents or learning about new criminal opportunities, may be involved.

Conflict Theory

Conflict theory draws on elements of Marxist thought to argue that deviance is deliberately chosen and often political in nature. Conflict theorists reject the idea that deviance is "determined" by factors such as biology, personality, anomie, social disorganization, or labels. Rather, they argue, individuals actively choose to engage in deviant behavior in response to the inequalities of the capitalist system. Thus, members of countercultural groups regarded as "deviant"—such as supporters of the black power or gay liberation movements—are engaging in distinctly political acts that challenged the social order. Theorists of the **new criminology** framed their analysis of crime and deviance in terms of the structure of society and the preservation of power among the ruling class.

For example, they argued that laws are tools used by the powerful to maintain their own privileged positions. They rejected the idea that laws are neutral and are applied evenly across the population. Instead, they claimed that as inequalities increase between the ruling class and the working class, law becomes an ever more important instrument for the powerful to maintain order. This dynamic can be seen in the workings of the criminal justice system, which had become increasingly oppressive toward working-class "offenders"; or in tax legislation that disproportionately favored the wealthy. This power imbalance is not restricted to the creation of laws, however. The powerful also break laws, scholars argued, but are rarely caught. These crimes on the whole are much more significant than the everyday crime and delinquency that attracts the most attention. But fearful of the implications of pursuing white-collar criminals, law enforcement instead focuses its efforts on less powerful members of society, such as prostitutes, drug users, and petty thieves (Pearce, 1976; Chambliss, 1988).

These studies and others associated with the new criminology were important in widening the debate about crime and deviance to include questions of social justice, power, and politics. They emphasized that crime occurs at all levels of society and must be understood in the context of inequalities and competing interests between social groups.

Control Theory

Control theory posits that crime occurs as a result of an imbalance between impulses toward criminal activity and the social or physical controls that deter it. It is less interested in individuals' motivations for carrying out crimes; rather, it is assumed that people act rationally and that, given the opportunity, everyone would engage in deviant acts. Many types of crime, it is argued, are a result of "situational decisions"—a person sees an opportunity and is motivated to act.

One of the best-known control theorists, Travis Hirschi, has argued that humans are fundamentally selfish beings who make calculated decisions about whether or not to engage in criminal activity by weighing the potential benefits and risks of doing so. In *Causes of Delinquency* (1969), Hirschi claimed that there are four types of bonds that link people to society and law-abiding behavior: attachment, commitment, involvement, and belief. When sufficiently strong, these elements help to maintain social control and conformity by rendering people *unfree* to break rules. If these bonds with society are weak, however, delinquency and deviance may result. Hirschi's approach suggests that delinquents are often individuals whose low levels of self-control are a result of inadequate socialization at home or at school (Gottfredson and Hirschi, 1990).

Some control theorists see the growth of crime as an outcome of the increasing number of opportunities and targets for crime in modern society. As the population grows more affluent and consumerism becomes more central to people's lives, goods such as televisions, video equipment, computers, cars, and designer clothing—favorite targets for thieves—are owned by more and more people. Residential homes are increasingly left empty during the daytime as more and more women take on employment outside the home. Motivated offenders interested in committing crimes can select from a broad range of suitable targets.

Responding to such shifts, many official approaches to crime prevention in recent years have focused on limiting the opportunities for crime to occur. Central to such policies is the idea of *target hardening*—making it more difficult for crimes to take place by intervening directly into potential crime situations. Control theorists argue that rather than changing the criminal, the best policy is to take practical measures to control the criminal's ability to commit crime.

Target hardening techniques and zero tolerance policing have gained favor among politicians in recent years and appear to have been successful in some contexts in curtailing crime. But criticisms of such an approach can also be made. Target hardening and zero tolerance policing do not address the underlying causes of crime but instead are aimed at protecting and defending certain elements of society from its reach. The growing popularity of private security services, car alarms, house alarms, guard dogs, and gated communities has led some people to believe that we are living in an armored society where segments of the population feel compelled to defend themselves against others. This tendency is occurring not only in the United States, as the gap between the wealthiest and the most deprived widens, but is particularly marked in countries such as South Africa, Brazil, and those of the former Soviet Union, where a "fortress mentality" has emerged among the privileged.

There is another unintended consequence of such policies: As popular crime targets are "hardened," patterns of crime may simply shift from one domain to another. Target hardening and zero tolerance approaches run the risk of displacing criminal offenses from better protected areas into more vulnerable ones. Neighborhoods that are poor or lacking in social cohesion may well experience a growth in crime and delinquency as affluent regions increase their defenses.

THE THEORY OF "BROKEN WINDOWS"

Target hardening and zero tolerance policing are based on a theory known as "broken windows" (Wilson and Kelling, 1982). The theory is based on a study by the social psychologist Philip Zimbardo, who abandoned cars without license plates and with their hoods up in two entirely different social settings, the wealthy community of Palo Alto, California, and a poor neighborhood in the Bronx, New York. In both places, both cars were vandalized once passersby, regardless of class or race, sensed that the cars were abandoned and that "no one cared" (Zimbardo, 1969). Extrapolating from this study, the authors of the "broken windows" theory argued that any sign of social disorder in a community, even the appearance of a broken window, encourages more serious crime to flourish. One unrepaired broken window is a sign that no one cares, so breaking more windows—that is, committing more serious crimes—is a rational response by criminals to this situation of social disorder. As a result, minor acts of deviance can lead to a spiral of crime and social decay.

In the late 1980s and 1990s, the "broken windows" theory served as the basis for new policing strategies that aggressively focused on "minor" crimes such as drinking or using drugs in public and traffic violations. Studies have shown that proactive policing directed at maintaining public order can have a positive effect on reducing more serious crimes such as robbery (Sampson and Cohen, 1988). However, one flaw of the "broken windows" theory is that the police are left to identify "social disorder" however they want. Without a systematic definition of disorder, the police are authorized to see almost anything as a sign of disorder and anyone as a threat. In fact, as crime rates fell throughout the 1990s, the number of complaints of police abuse and harassment went up, particularly by young, urban, black men who fit the "profile" of a potential criminal.

Theoretical Conclusions

The contributions of the sociological theories of crime are twofold. First, these theories correctly emphasize the continuities between criminal and "respectable" behavior. The contexts in which particular types of activity are seen as criminal and punishable by law vary widely. Second, all agree that context is important in criminal activities. Whether someone engages in a criminal act or comes to be regarded as a criminal is influenced fundamentally by social learning and social surroundings.

In spite of its deficiencies, labeling theory is perhaps the most widely used approach to understanding crime and deviant behavior. This theory sensitizes us to the ways in which some activities come to be defined as punishable in law and the power relations that form such definitions, as well as to the circumstances in which particular individuals fall foul of the law.

The way in which crime is understood directly affects the policies developed to combat it. For example, if crime is seen as the product of deprivation or social disorganization, policies might be aimed at reducing poverty and strengthening social services. If criminality is seen as voluntaristic, or freely chosen by individuals, attempts to counter it will take a different form. Now let's look directly at the nature of the criminal activities occurring in modern societies, paying particular attention to crime in the United States.

Crime and Crime Statistics

How dangerous *are* our streets compared with yesteryear? Is American society more violent than other societies? You should be able to use the sociological skills you have developed already to answer these questions.

In Chapter 1, for example, we learned something about how to interpret statistics. The statistics of crime are a constant focus of attention on television and in the newspapers. Most TV and newspaper reporting is based on official statistics on crime, collected by the police and published by the government. But many crimes are never reported to the police at all. Some criminologists think that about half of all serious crimes, such as robbery with violence, are not reported. The proportion of less serious crimes, especially small thefts, that don't come to the attention of the police is even higher. Since 1973, the Bureau of the Census has been interviewing households across the country to find out how many members were the victims of particular crimes over the previous six months. This procedure, which is called the National Crime Victimiza-

tion Survey, has confirmed that the overall rate of crime is higher than the reported crime index. For instance, in 1999, only 37 percent of rapes were reported, 61 percent of robberies, 43 percent of assaults, and 49 percent of burglaries.

Public concern in the United States tends to focus on crimes of violence—murder, assault, and rape—even though only about 10 percent of all crimes are violent (see Figure 6.2). In the United States, the most common victims of murder and other violent crimes (with the exception of rape) are young, poor, African American men living in the larger cities (see Figure 6.3). The rate of murder among black male teenagers is particularly high, over seven times the rate for their white counterparts. In general, whether indexed by police statistics or by the National Crime Victimization Survey, violent crime, burglary, and car theft are more common in cities than in the suburbs surrounding them, and they are more common in the suburbs than in smaller towns (see Table 6.1).

In the 1990s, there was a drop in the overall crime rate throughout the United States to its lowest levels since 1973, when the victimization survey was first used. Rates of violent crime in particular dropped substantially, murders by 31 percent and robberies by 32 percent. There is no one prevailing explanation among sociologists for this decline, although many politicians would like to take credit for it. Aggressive new efforts by local police to stop the use of guns certainly contributed to the decrease in homicides, but other social factors were also at work. Foremost among these is related to the declining market for crack cocaine and the stigmatization of crack among young urban dwellers. Another factor was the booming economy of the 1990s, which provided job opportunities for those who may have been enticed to work in the drug trade (Butterfield, 1998).

One reason often given for the relatively high rates of violent crime in the United States is the widespread availability of handguns and other firearms. This is relevant but does not provide a complete answer. Switzerland has very low rates of violent crime, yet firearms are easily accessible. All Swiss males are members of the citizen army and keep weapons in their homes, including rifles, revolvers, and sometimes other automatic weapons, plus ammunition; nor are gun licenses difficult to obtain.

The most likely explanation for the high level of violent crime in the United States is a combination of the availability of firearms, the general influence of the "frontier tradition," and the subcultures of violence in the large cities. Violence by frontiersmen and vigilantes is an honored part of American history. Some of the first established immigrant areas in the cities developed their own informal modes of neighborhood control, backed by violence or the threat of violence. Similarly, young people in African American and Hispanic communities today have developed subcultures of manliness and honor as-

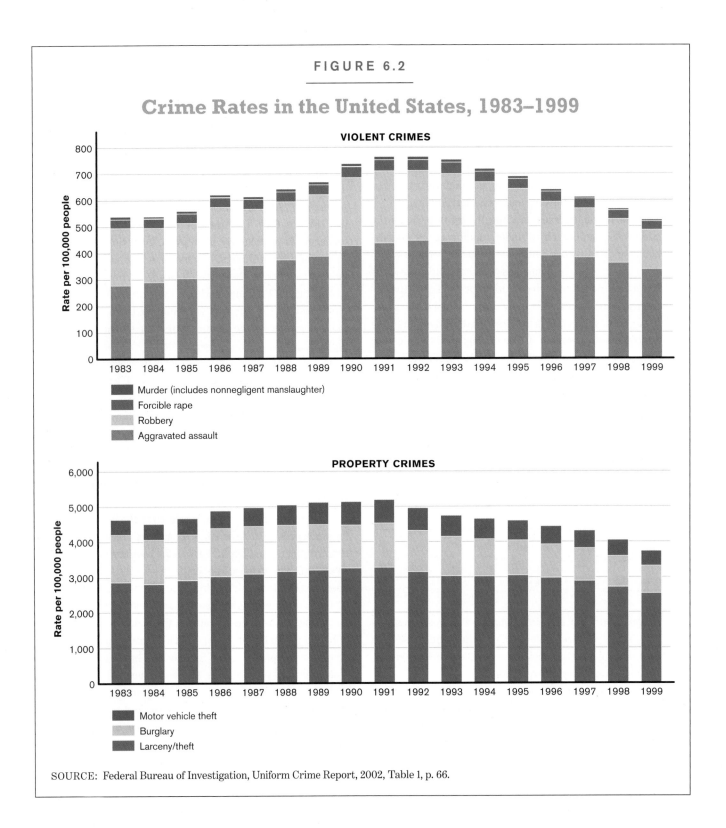

FIGURE 6.2

Crime Rates in the United States, 1983–1999

VIOLENT CRIMES

Rate per 100,000 people

- Murder (includes nonnegligent manslaughter)
- Forcible rape
- Robbery
- Aggravated assault

PROPERTY CRIMES

Rate per 100,000 people

- Motor vehicle theft
- Burglary
- Larceny/theft

SOURCE: Federal Bureau of Investigation, Uniform Crime Report, 2002, Table 1, p. 66.

sociated with rituals of violence, and some belong to gangs whose everyday life is one of drug dealing, territory protection, and violence.

A notable feature of most crimes of violence is their mundane character. Most assaults and homicides bear little re-semblance to the murderous, random acts of gunmen or the carefully planned homicides given most prominence in the media. Murders generally happen in the context of family and other interpersonal relationships; the victim usually knows his or her murderer.

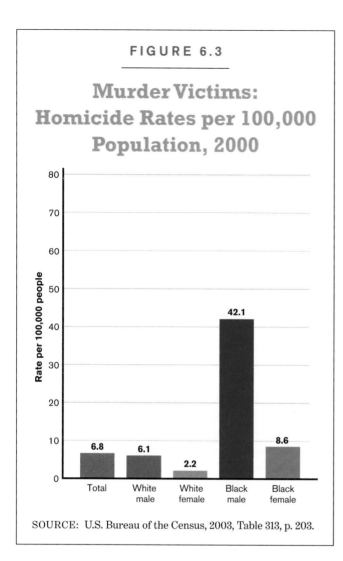

FIGURE 6.3

Murder Victims: Homicide Rates per 100,000 Population, 2000

Rate per 100,000 people

Total	White male	White female	Black male	Black female
6.8	6.1	2.2	42.1	8.6

SOURCE: U.S. Bureau of the Census, 2003, Table 313, p. 203.

Victims and Perpetrators of Crime

Are some individuals or groups more likely to commit crimes or to become the victims of crime? Criminologists say yes—research and crime statistics show that crime and victimization are not randomly distributed among the population. Men are more likely than women, for example, to commit crimes; the young are more often involved in crime than older people.

The likelihood of someone becoming a victim of crime is closely linked to the area where they live. Areas suffering from greater material deprivation generally have higher crime rates. Individuals living in inner-city neighborhoods run a much greater risk of becoming victims of crime than do residents of more affluent suburban areas. That ethnic minorities are concentrated disproportionately in inner-city regions appears to be a significant factor in their higher rates of victimization.

Gender and Crime

Like other areas of sociology, criminological studies have traditionally ignored half the population. Feminists have been correct in criticizing criminology for being a male-dominated discipline in which women are largely invisible in both theoretical considerations and empirical studies. Since the 1970s, many important feminist works have drawn attention to the way in which criminal transgressions by women occur in different contexts from those by men and how women's experiences with the criminal justice system are influenced by certain gendered assumptions about appropriate male and female roles. Feminists have also played a critical role in highlighting the prevalence of violence against women, both at home and in public.

MALE AND FEMALE CRIME RATES

The statistics on gender and crime are startling. For example, of all crimes reported in 2002, an overwhelming 77 percent of arrestees were men (see Table 6.2). There is also an enormous imbalance in the ratio of men to women in prison, not only in the United States but in all the industrialized countries. Women make up only 6 percent of the prison population.

TABLE 6.1

Crime Rates in Metropolitan vs. Rural Areas for 2002

TYPE OF CRIME	METROPOLITAN RATE (PER 100,000 POPULATION)	RURAL RATE
Violent crime	545.6	212.6
Murder	6.2	3.6
Forcible rape	33.8	23.8
Robbery	173.4	16.7
Assault	332.3	168.5
Property crime	3,863.5	1,696.1
Burglary	768.5	558.2
Larceny	2,596.4	1,005.0
Auto theft	498.6	132.8

SOURCE: U.S. Bureau of the Census, 2002, Table 313, p. 203.

TABLE 6.2

Percentage of Crimes Committed by Men, 2002

CRIME	PERCENTAGE MALE
Murder	89.2
Rape	98.6
Robbery	89.7
Assault	79.8
Burglary	86.7
Theft	63.0
Auto theft	83.5
Arson	84.8

Note: Data represent arrests (not charges), estimated by the FBI.

SOURCE: Federal Bureau of Investigation, Uniform Crime Report, 2002, Table 42, p. 251.

There are also contrasts between the types of crimes men and women commit. The offenses of women rarely involve violence and are almost all small scale. Petty thefts like shoplifting and public order offenses such as public drunkenness and prostitution are typical female crimes.

Of course, it may be that the real gender difference in crime rates is less than the official statistics show. In the 1950s, Otto Pollak suggested as much, contending that certain crimes perpetrated by women tend to go unreported. He saw women's predominantly domestic role as providing them with the opportunity to commit crimes at home and in the private sphere. Pollak also argued that female offenders are treated more leniently because male police officers tend to adopt a "chivalrous" attitude toward them (1950).

Pollak's suggestion that women are treated more leniently by the criminal justice system has prompted much debate and examination. The *chivalry thesis* has been applied in two ways. First, it is possible that police and other officials may regard female offenders as less dangerous than men and let pass activities for which males would be arrested. Second, in sentencing for criminal offenses, women tend to be much less likely to be imprisoned than male offenders. A number of empirical studies have been undertaken to test the chivalry thesis, but the results remain inconclusive. One of the main difficulties is assessing the relative influence of gender compared to other factors such as age, class, and race. For example, it appears that older

women offenders tend to be treated less aggressively than their male counterparts. Other studies have shown that black women receive worse treatment than white women at the hands of the police.

In an effort to make female crime more visible, feminists have conducted a number of detailed investigations on female criminals—from girl gangs to female terrorists to women in prison. Such studies have shown that violence is not exclusively a characteristic of male criminality. Women are much less likely than men to participate in violent crime but are not always inhibited from taking part in violent episodes. Why, then, are female rates of criminality so much lower than those of men?

There is some evidence that female lawbreakers are quite often able to escape coming before the courts because they are able to persuade the police or other authorities to see their actions in a particular light. They invoke what has been called the "gender contract"—the implicit contract between men and women whereby to be a woman is to be erratic and impulsive on the one hand and in need of protection on the other (Worrall, 1990).

Yet differential treatment could hardly account for the vast difference between male and female rates of crime. The reasons are almost certainly the same as those that explain gender differences in other spheres. "Male crimes" remain "male" because of differences in socialization and because men's activities and involvements are still more nondomestic than those of most women.

Ever since the late nineteenth century, criminologists have predicted that gender equality would reduce or eliminate the differences in criminality between men and women, but as yet crime remains a gendered phenomenon. Whether the variations between female and male crime rates will one day disappear we still cannot say with any certainty.

Youth and Crime

Popular fear about crime centers on offenses such as theft, burglary, assault, and rape—street crimes that are largely seen as the domain of young working-class males. Media coverage of rising crime rates often focuses on moral breakdown among young people and highlights such issues as vandalism, school truancy, and drug use to illustrate the increasing permissiveness in society. This equation of youth with criminal activity is not a new one, according to some sociologists. Young people are often taken as an indicator of the health and welfare of society itself.

Official statistics about crime rates do reveal high rates of offense among young people. Two fifths of all offenders arrested for criminal offenses in 1999 were under the age of twenty-one.

For both males and females, the peak age of offending was eighteen (U.S. Bureau of Justice Statistics, 2000). Yet we must approach assumptions about youth and crime with some caution. Moral panics about youth criminality may not accurately reflect social reality. An isolated event involving young people and crime can be transformed symbolically into a full-blown crisis of childhood, demanding tough law-and-order responses. The high-profile mass murder at Columbine High School is an example of how moral outrage can deflect attention from larger societal issues. Columbine was a watershed event in media portrayals of youth crime, and some have speculated that it led to "copycat" school killings in high schools in Arkansas, Kentucky, California, and elsewhere. Even though the number of murders committed on school grounds has been declining, attention to these mass murders has led many to think that all young children are potential violent threats. Although the perpetrators of the Columbine killings were labeled "monsters" and "animals," less attention was paid to how easily they were able to obtain the weapons they used to commit these murders.

Similar caution can be expressed about the popular view of drug use by teenagers. A survey of more than seven thousand adolescents aged fifteen and sixteen revealed that more than 94 percent drank alcohol, about one third had smoked a cigarette within the previous thirty days, and 42 percent had tried illegal drugs at least once. Trends in drug use have shifted away from hard drugs such as heroin and toward combinations of substances such as amphetamines, alcohol, and the drug ecstasy. Ecstasy in particular has become a "lifestyle" drug associated with the rave and club subcultures, rather than the basis of an expensive, addictive habit. The war on drugs, some have argued, criminalizes large segments of the youth population who are generally law abiding (Muncie, 1999).

What makes one drug a psychological tool and another a national menace? Ecstasy, the chemical compound MDMA (methylenedioxymethamphetamine), gives users a sustained feeling of pleasure by sending waves of the neurotransmitters serotonin and dopamine into the brain. In this regard, it is not dissimilar to antidepressants such as Prozac, which also influence the amount of serotonin that the brain produces. The use of both ecstasy and antidepressants by college students has risen dramatically in recent years, yet one is illegal and the other is a routinely prescribed medical option. Admittedly, the amphetaminelike and mildly hallucinogenic effects of ecstasy are considerably more dramatic and short lived than the effects of Prozac. Long-term ecstasy use may cause brain damage. Nonetheless, MDMA was legal in the United States until 1985; because it has the effect of overcoming emotional inhibitions, some therapists used it on their patients in therapy sessions. More recently, MDMA has been used to treat rape victims in Spain, sufferers from posttraumatic stress disorder in Switzerland, and end-stage cancer patients in the United States.

The divergent ways in which ecstasy and Prozac have been viewed illustrate how "deviant" behavior is socially defined. From the perspective of lawmakers, MDMA became a dangerous drug as it morphed into ecstasy, now associated with youth culture, parties, and hedonism rather than medicine.

Taking illegal drugs, like other forms of socially deviant behavior, is often defined in racial, class, and cultural terms; different drugs come to be associated with different groups and behaviors. When crack cocaine appeared in the 1980s, it was quickly defined by the media as the drug of choice for black, inner-city kids who listened to hip-hop. Perhaps as a result, jail sentences for crack possession were set at higher levels than sentences for possession of cocaine, which was associated more with white and suburban users. Ecstasy has, until recently, had similar white and middle- or upper-class associations.

Crimes of the Powerful

It is plain enough that there are connections between crime and poverty. But it would be a mistake to suppose that crime is concentrated among the poor. Crimes carried out by people in positions of power and wealth can have farther-reaching consequences than the often petty crimes of the poor.

The term **white-collar crime**, first introduced by Edwin Sutherland (1949), refers to crime typically carried out by people in the more affluent sectors of society. This category of criminal activity includes tax fraud, antitrust violations, illegal sales practices, securities and land fraud, embezzlement, the manufacture or sale of dangerous products, and illegal environmental pollution, as well as straightforward theft. The distribution of white-collar crimes is even harder to measure than that of other types of crime; most do not appear in the official statistics at all.

Efforts made to detect white-collar crime are ordinarily limited, and it is only on rare occasions that those who are caught go to jail. Although the authorities regard white-collar crime in a more tolerant light than crimes of the less privileged, it has been calculated that the amount of money involved in white-collar crime in the United States is forty times greater than the amount involved in crimes against property, such as robberies, burglaries, larceny, forgeries, and car thefts (President's Commission on Organized Crime, 1986). Some forms of white-collar crime, moreover, affect more people than lower-class criminality. An embezzler might rob thousands—or today, via computer fraud, millions—of people.

CORPORATE CRIME

Some criminologists have referred to **corporate crime** to describe the types of offenses that are committed by large corporations in society. Pollution, product mislabeling, and violations of health and safety regulations affect much larger numbers of people than does petty criminality. The increasing power and influence of large corporations and their rapidly growing global reach mean that our lives are touched by them in many ways. Corporations are involved in producing the cars we drive and the food we eat. They also have an enormous impact on the natural environment and financial markets, aspects of life that affect all of us.

Both quantitative and qualitative studies of corporate crime have concluded that a large number of corporations do not adhere to the legal regulations that apply to them (Slapper and Tombs, 1999). Corporate crime is not confined to a few "bad apples" but is instead pervasive and widespread. Studies have revealed six types of violations linked to large corporations: *administrative* (paperwork or noncompliance), *environmental* (pollution, permits violations), *financial* (tax violations, illegal payments), *labor* (working conditions, hiring practices), *manufacturing* (product safety, labeling), and *unfair trade practices* (anticompetition, false advertising).

Sometimes there are obvious victims, as in environmental disasters such as the spill at the Bhopal chemical plant in India and the health dangers posed to women by silicone breast implants. But very often victims of corporate crime do not see themselves as such. This is because in "traditional" crimes the proximity between victim and offender is much closer—it is difficult not to realize that you have been mugged! In the case of corporate crime, greater distances in time and space mean that victims may not realize they have been victimized or may not know how to seek redress for the crime.

The effects of corporate crime are often experienced unevenly within society. Those who are disadvantaged by other types of socioeconomic inequalities tend to suffer disproportionately. For example, safety and health risks in the workplace tend to be concentrated most heavily in low-paying occupations. Many of the risks from health care products and pharmaceuticals have had a greater impact on women than on men, as is the case with contraceptives or fertility treatments with harmful side effects (Slapper and Tombs, 1999).

Organized Crime

Organized crime refers to forms of activity that have some of the characteristics of orthodox business but that are illegal. Organized crime embraces illegal gambling, drug dealing, prostitution, large-scale theft, and protection rackets, among other activities. In *End of Millennium* (1998), Manuel Castells argues that the activities of organized crime groups are becoming increasingly international in scope. He notes that the coordination of criminal activities across borders—with the help of new information technolo-

gies—is becoming a central feature of the new global economy. Involved in activities ranging from the narcotics trade to counterfeiting to smuggling immigrants and human organs, organized crime groups are now operating in flexible international networks rather than within their own territorial realms.

According to Castells, criminal groups set up strategic alliances with each other. The international narcotics trade, weapons trafficking, the sale of nuclear material, and money laundering have all become linked across borders and crime groups. Criminal organizations tend to base their operations in "low-risk" countries where there are fewer threats to their activities. In recent years, the former Soviet Union has been one of the main points of convergence for international organized crime. The flexible nature of this networked crime makes it relatively easy for crime groups to evade the reach of law enforcement initiatives. If one criminal safe haven becomes more risky, the organizational geometry can shift to form a new pattern.

Despite numerous campaigns by the government and the police, the narcotics trade is one of the most rapidly expanding international criminal industries, having an annual growth rate of more than 10 percent in the 1980s and early 1990s and an extremely high level of profit. Heroin networks stretch across the Far East, particularly South Asia, and are also located in North Africa, the Middle East, and Latin America. Supply lines also pass through Vancouver and other parts of Canada, from where drugs are commonly supplied to the United States.

Crime-Reduction Strategies

Despite the misleading picture presented by official statistics, when they are taken together with data from victimization surveys it becomes clear that criminal offenses are assuming a more prominent role in society. Moreover, citizens *perceive* themselves to be at greater risk of falling victim to crime than in times past. Residents of inner-city areas have more reason to be concerned about crime than people living in other settings.

In the face of so many changes and uncertainties in the world around us, we are all engaged in a constant process of risk management. Crime is one of the most obvious risks that confront people in the late modern age. Yet it is not only individuals that have been caught up in risk management: Governments are now faced with societies that seem more dangerous and uncertain than ever before. One of the central tasks of social policy in modern states has been controlling crime and delinquency. But if at one time government sought to guarantee security for its citizens, increasingly policies are aimed at managing insecurity.

Are Prisons the Answer?

Although as measured by police statistics (problematic, as we have seen) rates of violent crime have declined since 1990, many people in the United States have started to view crime as their most serious social concern—more so than unemployment or the state of the economy (Lacayo, 1994). Surveys show that Americans also favor tougher prison sentences for all but relatively minor crimes. The price of imprisonment, however, is enormous: It costs an average of $460,000 to keep a prisoner behind bars for twenty years. Moreover, even if the prison system were expanded, it wouldn't reduce the level of serious crime a great deal. Only about a fifth of all serious crimes result in an arrest—and this is of crimes known to the police, an underestimate of the true rate of crime. And no more than half of arrests for serious crimes result in a conviction. Even so, America's prisons are so overcrowded (see Figure 6.4) that the average convict only serves a third of his sentence. The United States already locks up more people (nearly all men) per capita than any other country.

The United States has by far the most punitive justice system in the world. More than 2 million people are presently incarcerated in American prisons, with another 4.3 million falling under the jurisdiction of the penal system. Although the United States makes up only 5 percent of the world's overall population, it accounts for 25 percent of the world's prisoners.

Support for *capital punishment* (the death penalty) is high in the United States. In 1999, 71 percent of adults surveyed said that they believed in capital punishment; 21 percent opposed it. This represents a significant shift from 1965, when 38 percent of those surveyed supported the death penalty and 47 percent were opposed. The number of individuals awaiting execution has climbed steadily since 1977, when the Supreme Court upheld state capital punishment laws. At the end of 2002, 3,557 prisoners were held on death row. All were convicted of murder. Of these, 98.5 percent were men, 54 percent where white, and 44 percent were black. In 2003, 65 prisoners were executed in 11 states. Sixty-five of these were men, 41 were white and 20 were black (Bureau of Justice Statistics, 2004).

In addition, more than one quarter of African American men are either in prison or under the control of the penal system. Some 57 percent of individuals imprisoned in the United States are serving sentences for nonviolent drug-related crimes.

While we might suppose that imprisoning large numbers of people or stiffening sentences would deter individuals from committing crimes, there is little evidence to support this. In fact,

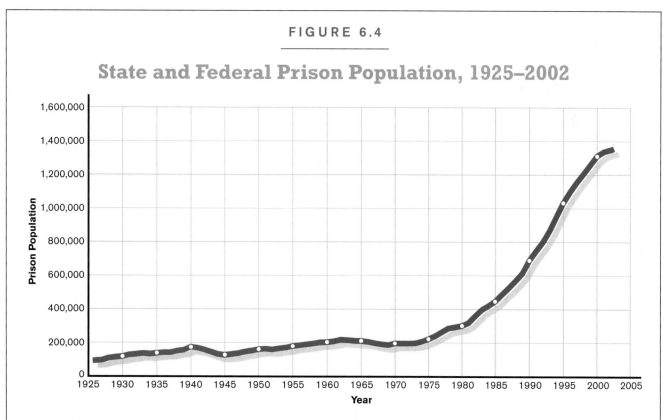

FIGURE 6.4

State and Federal Prison Population, 1925–2002

SOURCE: Marc Mauer, "Comparative Rates of Incarceration: An Examination of Causes and Trends," The Sentencing Project, 2003, www.sentencingproject.org/pdfs/pub9036.pdf.

Drug Trafficking

How easy would it have been for you to purchase marijuana in high school? How easy would it be to do so today? Lamentable as it may seem to some, most young people in the United States have relatively easy access to illegal drugs. According to recent congressional testimony given by the director of the Office of National Drug Control Policy, "nine percent of twelve to seventeen year olds are current drug users . . . 49.6 percent of high school seniors reported having tried marijuana at least once . . . [and] in every grade (eighth, tenth and twelfth) 2.1 percent of students have tried heroin" (McCaffrey, 1998).

What factors determine the availability of illegal drugs in your community? The level of police enforcement is important, of course, as is the extent of local demand. But no less important is the existence of networks of traffickers able to transport the drugs from the countries in which they are grown to your hometown. These networks have been able to flourish in part because of globalization.

While the cultivation of marijuana in the United States represents a major illicit industry, almost all of the world's coca plants and opium poppies are grown in the developing world. The U.S. government spends billions of dollars each year to as-

sociological studies have demonstrated that prisons can easily become schools for crime. Instead of preventing people from committing crimes, prisons often actually make them more hardened criminals. The more harsh and oppressive prison conditions are, the more likely inmates are to be brutalized by the experience. Yet if prisons were made into attractive and pleasant places to live, would they have a deterrent effect?

Although prisons do keep some dangerous men (and a tiny minority of dangerous women) off the streets, evidence suggests that we need to find other means to deter crime. A sociological interpretation of crime makes clear that there are no quick fixes. The causes of crime, especially crimes of violence, are bound up with structural conditions of American society, including widespread poverty, the condition of the inner cities, and the deteriorating life circumstances of many young men.

The Mark of a Criminal Record

A recent experiment by sociologist Devah Pager (2003) showed the long-term consequences of prison on the lives of

felons. Pager had pairs of young black and white men apply for real entry-level job openings throughout the city of Milwaukee. The applicant pairs were matched by appearance, interpersonal style, and, most important, by all job-related characteristics such as education level and prior work experience. In addition to varying the race of the applicant pairs, Pager also had applicants alternate presenting themselves to employers as having criminal records. One member of each of the applicant pairs would check the box "yes" on the applicant form in answer to the question, "Have you ever been convicted of a crime?" The pair alternated each week which young man would play the role of the ex-offender, in order to make sure that it was the criminal record—not the individual —that made a difference in employment outcomes.

The value of this experimental design is that it allows the sociologist to control for all the individual differences that may lead members of one group to be preferred to members of another. If whites, for example, on average have higher levels of education or more steady work experience than blacks, it's hard to determine whether race influences their employment opportunities or whether these other "skill differences" sist developing nations with eradication efforts and also devotes significant resources to stopping the flow of drugs past U.S. borders. In 1995, the federal government spent more than $8.2 billion on the "war on drugs" and between 1981 and 1996 spent a total of $65 billion (Bertram et al., 1996). Despite this massive expenditure, there is little evidence that eradication or interdiction efforts have significantly decreased the supply of illegal drugs in the United States. Why have these efforts failed?

One answer is that the profit is simply too great. Farmers struggling to scratch out a living for themselves in Bolivia or Peru, members of the Colombian drug cartels, and low-level street dealers in the United States all receive substantial monetary rewards for their illegal activities. These rewards create a strong incentive to devise ways around antidrug efforts and to run the risk of getting caught.

Another answer—one discussed at a summit attended by leaders of the eight major industrial powers—is that drug traffickers have been able to take advantage of globalization. First, in their attempts to evade the authorities, traffickers make use of all the communications technologies that are available in a global age. As one commentator put it, drug traffickers "now use sophisticated technology, such as signal interceptors, to plot radar and avoid monitoring . . . [and] they can use faxes, computers and cellular phones to coordinate their activities and make their business run smoothly" (Chepesiuk, 1998). Second, the globalization of the financial sector has helped create

an infrastructure in which large sums of money can be moved around the world electronically in a matter of seconds, making it relatively easy to "launder" drug money (i.e., to make it appear to have come from a legitimate business venture). Third, recent changes in government policy designed to allow the freer flow of persons and legitimate goods across international borders have increased the opportunities for smuggling.

At the same time, globalization may create new opportunities for governments to work together to combat drug trafficking. Indeed, world leaders have called for greater international cooperation in narcotics enforcement, stressing the need for information sharing and coordinated enforcement efforts.

determine the results. The same problem applies to the question of how individuals with criminal records fare in the job market. Some would argue that a criminal record doesn't hold people back; instead, they might argue, it's the fact that people with criminal records don't work as hard as nonoffenders, or aren't as qualified for many jobs. The experiment allowed Pager to make the applicant pairs identical on all job-relevant characteristics so that she could know for sure that any differences she saw were the result of discrimination. It tested whether employers respond differently to otherwise equal candidates on the basis of race or criminal record alone.

Pager's study revealed some striking findings. To begin with, whites were much preferred over blacks, and nonoffenders were much preferred over ex-offenders. Whites with a felony conviction were half as likely to be considered by employers as equally qualified nonoffenders. For blacks the effects were even larger! Black ex-offenders were only one-third as likely to receive a call back compared to nonoffenders. But most surprising was the comparison of these two effects: Blacks with *no criminal history* fared no better than did whites with a felony conviction! Essentially, these results suggest that being a black

male in America today is about the same as being a convicted criminal, at least in the eyes of Milwaukee employers. For those who believe that race no longer represents a major barrier to opportunity, these results represent a powerful challenge. Being a black felon is a particularly tough obstacle to overcome.

Policing

Some sociologists and criminologists have suggested that visible policing techniques, such as patrolling the streets, are reassuring for the public. Such activities are consistent with the perception that the police are actively engaged in controlling crime, investigating offenses, and supporting the criminal justice system. But sociologists also suggest that we need to reassess the role of policing in the late modern age. Although maintaining law and order, interacting with citizens, and providing services are indeed part of a contemporary policing, they represent only a fraction of what the police actually do. Policing, sociologists argue, is now less about controlling crime and more about detecting and managing risks. Most of all, it is

When a Dissertation Makes a Difference

For Devah Pager, a young sociologist from Honolulu, "kulia i ka nu'u"—"to strive for the summit"—means to do research that can influence policy, a realistic quest for her if the last few years are any indication.

As a graduate student at the University of Wisconsin, she studied the difficulties of former prisoners trying to find work and, in the process, came up with a disturbing finding: it is easier for a white person with a felony conviction to get a job than for a black person whose record is clean.

Ms. Pager's study won the American Sociological Association's award for the best dissertation of the year in August [2003], prompting a *Wall Street Journal* columnist to write about it. Howard Dean repeated her main finding in stump speeches and interviews throughout his glory days as the front-runner.

Then, addressing the overall problem convicted felons have re-entering the job market, President Bush announced in the State of the Union message a $300 million program to provide mentoring and help them get work. Jim Towey, the director of the White House Office of Faith-Based and Community Initiatives, said that Ms. Pager's study was one of the many sources of information that helped shape the administration's four-year plan.

Ms. Pager, 32, is thrilled to see the issue receive national attention. More than half a million inmates will leave penal institutions this year, and "the Administration is finally recognizing that the problems created by our incarceration policies can no longer be ignored," she said. Even if the promised amount is trivial, she said, the gesture is important symbolically.

Conversation with Ms. Pager flows easily. Over a plate of pancakes, she brushes aside a crush of thick loose auburn curls to punctuate less serious points with flashes of the wide, arresting smile her colleagues say is emblematic. She is known for her good nature and charismatic style, but it is her research that has made her one of the most promising young sociologists around.

Initially Ms. Pager's interest was race, stirred by her move from Hawaii to Los Angeles to attend the University of California. "I was struck by the level of separation between racial groups on campus, throughout the city," she said. "Race seemed to define space. Hawaii, by contrast, has the highest rate of intermarriage in the country. Growing up, every other person, it seemed, was *hapa*, or half, the term used to describe someone multiracial or mixed." She added, "When you grow up with that being normal, everything else seems strange—and wrong."

She completed a master's degree at Stanford University and a second master's at the University of Cape Town in South Africa, her father's native country. He is a professor of computer science. Her mother, a pediatrician, was born in Australia, making Ms. Pager something of a *hapa* herself, a

Jewish one. A one-year visiting professorship at the University of Hawaii took Ms. Pager's parents to Honolulu from London before she was born. They never left.

"Hawaii is an amazing place to grow up," Ms. Pager said. "It's got a small-town community feeling, despite the fact that Honolulu is a city of about a million people."

Though her family is "solidly upper middle class," she said, her parents obliged her and her two older brothers to work to pay part of their college expenses. "I resented it initially," she said, "but in fact it ended up being a great way for me to get involved in things I wouldn't have been involved with otherwise."

The interest in released prisoners arose while she was studying for her doctorate in Madison, Wisconsin. She organized a karaoke night for the sociology department ("I'm a diva," she wrote in an e-mail message, playing off the pronunciation of her given name. "I love to sing."), and she volunteered for an organization that provides services and shelter to homeless men. There she met many black men with prison records. "It was a nice break to get out and do some direct service," she said. She spent time with the men, distributed their mail and made herself available "as a resource, to allow them to unload." Those who had served jail time often talked about how it complicated the job search. "That was one of the first things that clued me into what an immutable barrier it was standing in their way," she said.

At about this time Human Rights Watch and the Sentencing Project reported that in seven states felony convictions had permanently disenfranchised one in four African American men. An innovative but difficult research plan began to take shape.

Both of her main advisers, Robert M. Hauser and Erik Olin Wright, tried to dissuade her, gently suggesting how hard it is for graduate students to obtain financial support, manage complicated field work and end up with meaningful results.

"She was undaunted," Mr. Wright said. "Her pluckiness is part of what makes her successful. She knew she could do it."

To isolate the effect of a criminal record on the job search, Ms. Pager sent pairs of young, well-groomed, well-spoken college men with identical resumes to apply for 350 advertised entry-level jobs in Milwaukee. The only difference was that one said he had served an 18-month prison sentence for cocaine possession. Two teams were black, two white.

A telephone survey of the same employers followed. For her black testers, the callback rate was 5 percent if they had a criminal record and 14 percent if they did not. For whites, it was 17 percent with a criminal record and 34 percent without.

"I expected there to be an effect of race, but I did not expect it to swamp the results as it did," Ms. Pager said. "It really was a surprise."

Jeff Manza, a colleague at Northwestern University, where she teaches, said, "Devah's work demonstrates in a new and convincing way the extent to which the 'second chance' that Bush talks about runs headlong into the realities of race and the fear of crime and criminals."

Similarly, Reginald Wilkinson, Ohio's top corrections official and the president of the Association of State Correctional Administrators, was impressed by her findings and methodology. "In my estimation, we can't eliminate the race question when we're talking about re-entry," he said. "I think what Professor Pager has done is raise consciousness about this."

More reserved was James J. Heckman of the University of Chicago, a Nobel laureate in economics. In a telephone interview, he said Ms. Pager's findings were important but not surprising. Mr. Heckman, who has written extensive critiques of similarly designed studies, said that she had created "a very clean study" of the impact of a criminal record on job seekers in general, but that he did not buy the race findings.

"I believe there is serious reason for caution here," he said. "The comparison across the black and white pairs is just not strong because it's not an experimental design and the samples are just too small."

Ms. Pager is replicating her research on a grander scale with one of the field's leading experts, Bruce Western of Princeton University, where she will join the sociology faculty this fall.

The new study is another chance to further document the effects of race and imprisonment, another chance at "kulia i ka nu'u."

SOURCE: Brooke Kroeger, "When a Dissertation Makes a Difference," *New York Times*, March 20, 2004.

about communicating knowledge about risk to other institutions in society that demand that information (Ericson and Haggerty, 1997).

According to this view police are first and foremost "knowledge workers." By this sociologists mean that the vast majority of police time is spent on activities aimed at processing information, drafting reports, or communicating data. The "simple" case of an automobile accident in Ontario, Canada, illustrates this point. A police officer is called to the scene of an automobile accident involving two vehicles. No one has been killed, but there are minor injuries and one of the drivers is drunk. The investigation of the incident takes one hour; the drunk driver is criminally charged with the impaired operation of a motor vehicle causing bodily harm and with operating a motor vehicle with excess alcohol. The driver's license is automatically suspended for twelve hours.

Following this routine investigation, the officer spends three hours writing up sixteen separate reports documenting the incident. The officer is required to provide information for the provincial motor registry about the vehicle and people involved; the automobile industry must be informed about the vehicles involved in the accident; the insurance companies need information about the case; the public health system requires details on any injuries; the criminal courts require police information for the prosecution; and the police administration needs reports on the incident for internal records and national databases.

This example reveals how the police are a key node in a complicated information circuit of institutions that are all in the business of risk management. With the help of new forms of technology, police work is increasingly about "mapping" and predicting risk within the population.

This emphasis on information collection and processing can be alienating and frustrating for police. For many police officers, there is a distinction between real police work—such as investigating crimes—and the "donkey work" of reports and paper trails. Bureaucratic reporting procedures such as these are like a one-way mirror for many police officers who do not see the point of the extensive documentation that is required.

Crime and Community

Preventing crime and reducing fear of crime are both closely related to rebuilding strong communities. As we saw in our earlier discussions of the "broken windows" theory, one of the most significant innovations in criminology in recent years has been the discovery that the decay of day-to-day civility relates directly to criminality. For a long while attention was fo-

---

FIGURE 6.5

Justice Employment and Crime Rates

Although the number of police steadily increased between 1982 and 2001, the crime rate dropped, increased, and dropped again during this period. Therefore, no causal link can be made between the number of police and the crime rate.

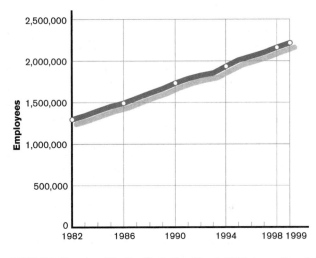
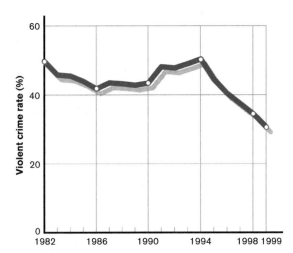

SOURCE: Bureau of Justice Statistics, March 2004, www.ojp.usdoj.gov/bjs/glance/tables/viortrdtab.htm and www.ojp.usdoj.gov/bjs/eande.htm.

cused almost exclusively on serious crime—robbery, assault, and other violent crime. More minor crimes and forms of public disorder, however, tend to have a cumulative effect. When asked to describe their problems, residents of troubled neighborhoods mention abandoned cars, graffiti, prostitution, youth gangs, and similar phenomena.

People act on their anxieties about these issues: They leave the areas in question if they can, or they buy heavy locks for their doors and bars for their windows and abandon public places. Unchecked disorderly behavior signals to citizens that the area is unsafe. Fearful citizens stay off the streets, avoid certain neighborhoods, and curtail their normal activities and associations. As they withdraw physically, they also withdraw from roles of mutual support with fellow citizens, thereby relinquishing the social controls that formerly helped to maintain civility within the community.

COMMUNITY POLICING

What should be done to combat this development? One idea that has grown in popularity in recent years is that the police should work closely with citizens to improve local community standards and civil behavior, using education, persuasion, and counseling instead of incarceration.

Community policing implies not only drawing in citizens themselves, but changing the characteristic outlook of police forces. A renewed emphasis on crime prevention rather than law enforcement can go hand in hand with the reintegration of policing with the community. The isolation of the police from those they are supposed to serve often produces a siege mentality, since the police have little regular contact with ordinary citizens.

In order to work, partnerships among government agencies, the criminal justice system, local associations, and community organizations have to be inclusive—all economic and ethnic groups must be involved (Kelling and Coles, 1997). Government and business can act together to help repair urban decay. One model is the creation of business improvement districts providing tax breaks for corporations that participate in strategic planning and offer investment in designated areas. To be successful, such schemes demand a long-term commitment to social objectives.

Emphasizing these strategies does not mean denying the links between unemployment, poverty, and crime. Rather, the struggle against these social problems should be coordinated with community-based approaches to crime prevention. These approaches can in fact contribute directly and indirectly to furthering social justice. Where social order has decayed along with public services, other opportunities, such as new jobs, decline also. Improving the quality of life in a neighborhood can revive them.

SHAMING AS PUNISHMENT

The current emphasis on imprisonment as a means of deterring crime has a potentially crippling effect on the social ties within certain communities. In recent years, **shaming**, a form of punishing criminal and deviant behavior that attempts to maintain the ties of the offender to the community, has grown in popularity as an alternative to incarceration. According to some criminologists, the fear of being shamed within one's community is an important deterrent to crime. As a result, the public's formal disapproval could achieve the same deterrent effect as incarceration, without the high costs of building and maintaining prisons.

The criminologist John Braithwaite (1996) has suggested that shaming practices can take two forms: reintegrative shaming and stigmatizing shaming. Stigmatizing shaming is related to labeling theory, which we discussed earlier in the chapter, by which a criminal is labeled as a threat to society and is treated as an outcast. As a result, the labeling process and society's efforts to marginalize the individual reinforce that person's criminal conduct, perhaps leading to future criminal behavior and higher crime rates. The much different practice of reintegrative shaming works as follows. People central to the criminal's immediate community—such as family members, employers and coworkers, and friends—are brought into court to state their condemnation of the offender's behavior. At the same time, these people must accept responsibility for reintegrating the offender back into the community. The goal is to rebuild the social bonds of the individual to the community as a means of deterring future criminal conduct.

Japan, with one of the lowest crime rates in the world, has been quite successful in implementing this approach. The process is largely based on a voluntary network of over five hundred thousand local crime prevention associations dedicated to facilitating reintegration into the community and on a criminal justice system that is encouraged to be lenient for this purpose. As a result, in Japan only 5 percent of persons convicted for a crime serve time in prison, as compared to 30 percent in the United States. Though reintegrative shaming is not a standard practice in the American criminal justice system, it is a familiar practice in other social institutions such as the family. Think of a child who misbehaves. The parent may express disapproval of the child's behavior and try to make the child feel ashamed of her conduct, but the parent may also reassure the child that she is a loved member of the family.

Could reintegrative shaming succeed in the United States? In spite of the beliefs that these tactics are "soft" on crime, that Americans are too individualistic to participate in community-based policing, and that high-crime areas are less community oriented, community networks have been successful in working with the police in preventing crime. These social bonds could also be fostered to increase the power of shame and reintegrate offenders into local networks of community involvement.

Study Outline

Deviant Behavior

- Deviant behavior refers to actions that transgress commonly held norms. What is regarded as deviant can shift from time to time and place to place; "normal" behavior in one cultural setting may be labeled "deviant" in another.
- *Sanctions*, formal or informal, are applied by society to reinforce social norms. *Laws* are norms defined and enforced by governments; *crimes* are acts that are not permitted by those laws.

Biological and Psychological Theories of Crime and Deviance

- Biological and psychological theories have been developed claiming that crime and other forms of deviance are genetically determined, but these have been largely discredited. Sociologists argue that conformity and deviance intertwine in different social contexts. Divergencies of wealth and power in society strongly influence opportunities open to different groups of individuals and determine what kinds of activities are regarded as criminal. Criminal activities are learned in much the same way as are law-abiding ones and in general are directed toward the same needs and values.

Society and Crime: Sociological Theories

- Functionalist theories see crime and deviance as produced by structural tensions and a lack of moral regulation within society. Durkheim introduced the term *anomie* to refer to a feeling of anxiety and disorientation that comes with the breakdown of traditional life in modern society. Robert Merton extended the concept to include the strain felt by individuals whenever norms conflict with social reality. Subcultural explanations draw attention to groups, such as gangs, that reject mainstream values and replace them with norms celebrating defiance, delinquency, or nonconformity.
- *Interactionist theories* focus on deviance as a socially constructed phenomenon. Sutherland linked crime to *differential association*, the concept that individuals become delinquent through associating with people who are carriers of criminal norms. *Labeling theory*, a strain of interactionist theory that assumes that labeling someone as deviant will reinforce their deviant behavior, is important because it starts from the assumption that no act is intrinsically criminal (or normal). Labeling theorists are interested in how some behaviors come to be defined as deviant and why certain groups, but not others, are labeled as deviant.
- Conflict theories analyze crime and deviance in terms of the structure of society, competing interests between social groups, and the preservation of power among elites.
- *Control theories* posit that crime occurs when there are inadequate social or physical controls to deter it from happening. The growth of crime is linked to the growing number of opportunities and tar-

gets for crime in modern societies. The theory of broken windows suggests that there is a direct connection between the appearance of disorder and actual crime.

Gender and Crime

- Rates of criminality are much lower for women than for men, probably because of general socialization differences between men and women, and the greater involvement of men in nondomestic spheres. Unemployment and the "crisis of masculinity" have been linked to male crime rates.

Types of Crime

- Popular fear about crime often focuses on street crimes—such as theft, burglary, and assault—that are largely the domain of young, working-class males. Official statistics reveal high rates of offense among young people, yet we should be wary of moral panics about youth crime. Much deviant behavior among youth, such as antisocial behavior and nonconformity, is not in fact criminal.
- *White-collar crime* and *corporate crime* refer to crimes carried out by those in the more affluent sectors of society. The consequences of such crime can be farther-reaching than the petty crimes of the poor, but there is less attention paid to them by law enforcement. *Organized crime* refers to institutionalized forms of criminal activity, in which many of the characteristics of orthodox organizations appear but the activities engaged in are systematically illegal.

Crime, Deviance, and Social Order

- Prisons have developed partly to protect society and partly with the intention of reforming the criminal. Prisons do not seem to deter crime, and the degree to which they rehabilitate prisoners to face the outside world without relapsing into criminality is dubious. Alternatives to prison, such as community-based punishment, have been suggested.

Key Concepts

anomie (p. 138)
community policing (p. 155)
conflict theory (p. 141)
control theory (p. 142)
corporate crime (p. 147)
crime (p. 135)
deviance (p. 133)
deviant subculture (p. 134)
differential association (p. 140)
labeling theory (p. 140)
law (p. 135)
new criminology (p. 141)
norm (p. 133)
organized crime (p. 148)
primary deviation (p. 141)

psychopath (p. 135)
sanction (p. 134)
secondary deviation (p. 141)
shaming (p. 155)
white-collar crime (p. 147)

Review Questions

1. What is deviance?
   a. A transgression of social norms that are accepted by most people in a community
   b. Breaking the law
   c. The kind of behavior engaged in by members of groups that have been marginalized by society
   d. None of the above
2. What is the theory of differential association?
   a. Individuals become delinquents by associating with those who are different from themselves.
   b. Individuals become delinquents by associating with carriers of criminal norms.
   c. Individuals become delinquents by associating with a range of deviant groups.
   d. Individuals become delinquents by associating with such aspects of aggressive male culture as professional wrestling and hunting clubs.
3. Compared with ordinary crimes against property (robberies, burglaries, larceny, etc.), the amount of money stolen in white-collar crime (tax fraud, insurance fraud, etc.) is:
   a. about the same. Crimes against property cost the nation about as much as white-collar crime.
   b. less. White-collar crimes involve only one quarter of the money involved in crimes against property.
   c. more. White-collar crime involves perhaps forty times as much money as crimes against property.
   d. not really comparable. White-collar crimes such as embezzlement affect very few people.
4. Crime is sociological in nature because
   a. anomie is common in modern societies.
   b. the definition of crime depends on the social context.
   c. criminals are socialized into committing crimes.
   d. criminals tend to be psychopaths.
5. Why did Émile Durkheim think a certain amount of crime was functional for society?
   a. Because it gave a healthy release for male aggression.
   b. Because it highlighted the boundaries of social norms.
   c. Because it kept the police and court system active.
   d. Because the existence of crime makes law-abiding citizens more careful about protecting their property.
6. Why is the crime rate so much higher in the United States than in other industrialized countries?
   a. It isn't.
   b. Crime rates in most of America are close to the average for industrialized countries, but the U.S. average is pulled up by very high crime rates in New York City.

c. It is caused by a combination of ready access to firearms, the influence of the "frontier tradition," and the violent subculture of American cities.
d. It comes from the fast pace of American life and our bad diet: the potent concoction of junk food packed with carbohydrates and artificial sweeteners, endless traffic congestion, and violent television shows make Americans more bad tempered and hostile to one another than people in other industrialized countries.

7. Howard S. Becker found a number of reasons to account for a person becoming a marijuana smoker. Which of the following is not a factor mentioned by Becker?
   a. Acceptance into the marijuana subcultures
   b. Close association with experienced users
   c. Peer pressure
   d. Attitudes toward nonusers
8. What is the attitude toward capital punishment in the United States over the past few decades?
   a. More people are in favor of capital punishment.
   b. Fewer people are in favor of capital punishment.
   c. There has been no change in attitude toward capital punishment during the past few decades.
   d. There is no clear trend in people's attitudes toward capital punishment.
9. What is the essence of labeling theory?
   a. Deviance is defined through the process of interaction between deviants and nondeviants.
   b. Deviance is in the eye of the officeholder.
   c. One person's deviance is another's indulgence.
   d. Deviants resist the labels they are given by law enforcement authorities.

Thinking Sociologically Exercises

1. Briefly summarize several leading theories explaining crime and deviance presented in this chapter: differential association, anomie, labeling, conflict, and control theories. Which theory appeals to you more than the others? Explain why.
2. Explain how differences in power and social influence can play a significant role in defining and sanctioning deviant behavior.

Data Exercises

www.wwnorton.com/giddens
Keyword: Data6

- How much do you know about patterns of crime in your community, your state, or in the United States as a whole? What are your sources of information—personal experiences, the experiences of family or friends, or the media? In the data exercise for Chapter 6 you will have a chance to study state-level crime rates and the changes in the rate over time in order to gain a better understanding of what the patterns are like.

Systems of Stratification

Learn about social stratification and the importance of social background in an individual's chances for material success.

Classes in Western Societies Today

Know the class differences that exist in U.S. society, what they are influenced by, and how they are defined and determined.

Inequality in the United States: A Growing Gap Between Rich and Poor

Recognize the many ways in which the gap between rich and poor has grown larger.

Social Mobility

Understand the dynamics of social mobility, and think about your own mobility.

Poverty in the United States

Learn about the conditions of poverty in the United States today, competing explanations for why it exists, and means for combating it.

Social Exclusion

Learn the processes by which people become marginalized in a society and the forms that it takes.

Theories of Stratification in Modern Societies

Become acquainted with the most influential theories of stratification—those of Karl Marx, Max Weber, and Davis and Moore.

Growing Inequality in the United States

CHAPTER SEVEN

STRATIFICATION, CLASS, AND INEQUALITY

cross the street from the campus of New Mexico State University, there is a juice bar and restaurant called Island Juice. The restaurant, which specializes in fruit smoothies and tortilla-wrapped sandwiches ("wraps"), is owned by Richard Rivera, who had the idea for it while attending Chapman University in southern California, where smoothies and wraps became popular in the mid-1990s. As a college student, Rivera never thought he would own a business like Island Juice. Rivera was born in Brooklyn, New York, and grew up in a government-owned housing project. His parents did not attend college and worked most of their lives in a factory. Money was always short in Rivera's family, but his parents saved enough to send him to private Catholic schools, where he excelled in all of his classes and eventually earned a scholarship to Chapman University. He was the first in his family ever to attend college. At Chapman, he studied computer information systems and then later received a master's degree in finance. On receiving his master's degree, he went to work for a number of Fortune 500 companies. Meanwhile, he had the idea for Island Juice and, at the age of twenty-seven, decided to open it in Las Cruces, New Mexico. Between the success of his business and the income from his job, Rivera earns over $200,000 per year. He is living the "American dream."

Is Richard Rivera's story just an isolated incident or does it somehow represent trends in contemporary American society? Will you, like Richard, also make more money than your parents? What about other members of your generation who, unlike you, do not go to college? How much chance does someone from a lowly background have of reaching the top of the economic ladder? For every Richard Rivera in our society, how many people struggle to make ends meet? Why do economic inequalities exist in our society? How unequal are modern societies? What are the reasons for the persistence of poverty in affluent countries like the United States? What social factors will influence your economic position in society? Are your chances any different if you are a woman? How does the globalization of the economy affect your life chances? How about the life chances of others?

These are just a few of the sorts of questions that sociologists ask and try to answer. These questions are the focus of this chapter. The study of social inequalities is one of the most important areas of sociology, because our material resources determine a great deal about our lives.

Sociologists speak of **social stratification** to describe inequalities among individuals and groups within human societies. Often we think of stratification in terms of assets or property, but it can also occur on the basis of other attributes, such as gender, age, religious affiliation, or military rank. The three key aspects of social stratification are class, status, and power (Weber, 1947). Although they frequently overlap, this is not always the case. The "rich and famous" often enjoy high status; their wealth often provides political influence and sometimes direct access to political power. Yet there are exceptions. Drug lords, for example, may be wealthy and powerful, yet they usually enjoy low status. On the other hand, when Mahatma Gandhi died in 1948, his total worldly possessions could be carried in his blanket. Although he chose to live in poverty, he enjoyed the highest status and power in India, having led his country to independence from Britain through nonviolent civil disobedience. In this chapter, we focus on stratification in terms of inequalities based on wealth and income, status, and power. In later chapters, we will look at the ways in which gender (Chapter 9), race and ethnicity (Chapter 10), and age (Chapter 14) all play a role in stratification.

Individuals and groups enjoy unequal access to rewards on the basis of their position within the stratification scheme. Thus, stratification can most simply be defined as **structured inequalities** among different groupings of people. Sociologists believe that these inequalities are built into the system, rather than resulting from individual differences or chance occurrences, such as winning a lottery. It is useful to think of stratification like the geological layering of rock in the earth's surface. Societies can be seen as consisting of "strata" in a hierarchy, with the more favored at the top and the less privileged nearer the bottom.

We can speak of an American system of stratification because individuals' chances for material success are strongly influenced by their social background. We will study stratification and inequality in the United States later in the chapter, but first we need to analyze the different types of stratification that exist and have existed in the past.

Systems of Stratification

All socially stratified systems share three characteristics:

1. **The rankings apply to social categories of people who share a common characteristic without necessarily interacting or identifying with each other.** Women may be ranked differently from men; wealthy people differently from the poor. This does not mean that individuals from a particular category cannot change their rank; however it does mean that the category continues to exist even if individuals move out of it and into another category.

2. **People's life experiences and opportunities depend heavily on how their social category is ranked.** Being male or female, black or white, upper class or working class makes a big difference in terms of your life chances—often as big a difference as personal effort or good fortune (such as winning a lottery).

3. **The ranks of different social categories tend to change very slowly over time.** In U.S. society, for example, only in the last quarter century have women as a whole begun to achieve equality with men (see Chapter 9). Only in the past quarter century have significant numbers of African Americans begun to obtain economic and political equality with whites—even though slavery was abolished nearly a century and a half ago and discrimination outlawed in the 1950s and 1960s (see Chapter 10).

As you saw in Chapter 2, stratified societies have changed throughout human history. The earliest human societies, which were based on hunting and gathering, had very little social stratification—mainly because there was very little by way of wealth or other resources to be divided up. The development of agriculture produced considerably more wealth and, as a result, a great increase in stratification. Social stratification in agricultural societies increasingly came to resemble a pyramid, with a large number of people at the bottom and a successively smaller number of people as you move toward the top. Today, industrial and postindustrial societies are extremely complex; their stratification is more likely to resemble a teardrop, with large number of people in the middle and lower-middle ranks (the so-called middle class), a slightly smaller number of people at the bottom, and very few people as one moves toward the top.

But before turning to stratification in modern societies, let's first review the three basic systems of stratification: slavery, caste, and class.

Slavery

Slavery is an extreme form of inequality, in which certain people are owned as property by others. The legal conditions of slave ownership have varied considerably among different societies. Sometimes slaves were deprived of almost all rights by law, as was the case on Southern plantations in the United States. In other societies, their position was more akin to that of servants. For example, in the ancient Greek city-state of Athens, some slaves occupied positions of great responsibility. They were excluded from political positions and from the military but were accepted in most other types of occupation. Some were literate and worked as government administrators; many were trained in craft skills. Even so, not all slaves could count on such a good fate. For the less fortunate, their days began and ended in hard labor in the mines.

Throughout history, slaves have often fought back against their subjection; the slave rebellions in the American South before the Civil War are one example. Because of such resistance, systems of slave labor have tended to be unstable. High productivity could only be achieved through constant supervision and brutal punishment. Slave-labor systems eventually broke down, partly because of the struggles they provoked and partly because economic or other incentives motivate people to produce more effectively than does direct compulsion. Slavery is simply not economically efficient. Moreover, from about the eighteenth century on, many people in Europe and America came to see slavery as morally wrong. Today, slavery is illegal in every country of the world, but it still exists in some places. Recent research has documented that people are taken by force and held against their will—from enslaved brick makers in Pakistan to sex slaves in Thailand and domestic slaves in France. Slavery remains a significant human rights violation in the world today (Bales, 1999).

Caste Systems

A **caste system** is a social system in which one's social status is given for life. In **caste societies,** therefore, different social levels are closed, so that all individuals must remain at the social level of their birth throughout life. Everyone's social status is based on personal characteristics—such as perceived race or ethnicity (often based on such physical characteristics as skin color), parental religion, or parental caste—that are accidents of birth and are therefore believed to be unchangeable.

A person is born into a caste and remains there for life. In a sense, caste societies can be seen as a special type of class society—in which class position is ascribed at birth, rather than achieved through personal accomplishment. They have typically been found in agricultural societies that have not yet developed industrial capitalist economies, such as rural India or South Africa prior to the end of white rule in 1992.

Prior to modern times, caste systems were found throughout the world. In Europe, for example, Jews were frequently treated as a separate caste, forced to live in restricted neighborhoods and barred from intermarrying (and in some instances even interacting) with non-Jews. The term *ghetto,* for example, is said to derive from the Venetian word for "foundry," the site of one of Europe's first official Jewish ghettos, established by the government of Venice in 1516. The term eventually came to refer to those sections of European towns where Jews were legally compelled to live, long before it was used to describe minority neighborhoods in U.S. cities, with their castelike qualities of racial and ethnic segregation.

In caste systems, intimate contact with members of other castes is strongly discouraged. Such "purity" of a caste is often maintained by rules of **endogamy,** marriage within one's social group as required by custom or law.

CASTE IN INDIA AND SOUTH AFRICA

The few remaining caste systems in the world are being seriously challenged by globalization. The Indian caste system, for example, reflects Hindu religious beliefs and is more than two thousand years old. According to Hindu beliefs, there are four major castes, each roughly associated with broad occupational groupings. The four castes consist of the *Brahmins* (scholars and spiritual leaders) on top, followed by the *Ksyatriyas* (soldiers and rulers), the *Vaisyas* (farmers and merchants), and the *Shudras* (laborers and artisans). Beneath the four castes are those known as the "untouchables" or *Dalits* ("oppressed people"), who—as their name suggests—are to be avoided at all costs. Untouchables are limited to the worst jobs in society such as removing human waste, and they often resort to begging and searching in garbage for their food. In traditional areas of India, some members of higher castes still regard physical contact with untouchables to be so contaminating that mere touching requires cleansing rituals. India made it illegal to discriminate on the basis of caste in 1949, but aspects of the caste system remain in full force today, particularly in rural areas.

As India's modern capitalist economy brings people of different castes together, whether it be in the same workplace, airplane, or restaurant, it is increasingly difficult to maintain the rigid barriers required to sustain the caste system. As more and more of India becomes touched by globalization, it

Women from the Dalit caste (formally known as Untouchables) earn a living as sewage scavengers in the slums of Ranchi. They are paid between 30 and 100 rupees per house per month for retrieving human waste from residential dry latrines and emptying the buckets into nearby gutters and streams.

seems reasonable to assume that its caste system will weaken still further.

Before its abolition in 1992, the South African caste system, termed *apartheid* (pronounced "a-PART-ide"; Afrikaans for "separateness"), rigidly separated black Africans, Indians, "colored" (people of mixed races), and Asians from whites. In this case, caste was based entirely on race. Whites, who made up only 15 percent of the total population, controlled virtually all of the country's wealth, owned most of the usable land, ran the principal businesses and industries, and had a monopoly on political power, since blacks lacked the right to vote. Blacks—who made up three quarters of the population—were segregated into impoverished *bantustans* ("homelands") and were allowed out only to work for the white minority.

Apartheid, widespread discrimination, and oppression created intense conflict between the white minority and the black, mixed-race, and Asian majority. Decades of often violent struggle against apartheid finally proved successful in the 1990s. The most powerful black organization, the African National Congress (ANC), mobilized an economically devastating global boycott of South African businesses, forcing South Africa's white leaders to dismantle apartheid, which was abolished by popular vote among South African whites in 1992. In 1994, in the country's first ever multiracial elections, the black majority won control of the government, and Nelson Mandela—the black leader of the ANC, who had spent twenty-seven years imprisoned by the white government—was elected president.

Class

The concept of **class** is most important for analyzing stratification in industrialized societies like the United States. Everyone has heard of class, but most people in everyday talk use the word in a vague way. As employed in sociology, it has some precision.

A social class is a large group of people who occupy a similar economic position in the wider society. The concept of life chances, introduced by Max Weber, is the best way to understand what class means. Your **life chances** are the opportunities you have for achieving economic prosperity. A person from a humble background, for example, has less chance of ending up wealthy than someone from a more prosperous one. And the best chance an individual has of being wealthy is to start off as wealthy in the first place.

America, it is always said, is the land of opportunity. For some, this is so. There are many examples of people who have risen from lowly circumstances to positions of great wealth and power. There are many more cases, however, of people like Richard Rivera who have done better than their parents but not become superrich. And yet there are more cases of people who have not, including a disproportionate share of women and members of minority groups. The idea of life chances is important because it emphasizes that although class is an important influence on what happens in our lives, it is not completely determining. Class divisions affect which neighborhoods we live in, what lifestyles we follow, and even which sexual or marriage partners we choose (Mare, 1991; Massey, 1996). Yet they don't fix people for life in specific social positions, as the older systems of stratification did. A person born into a caste position has no opportunity of escaping from it; the same isn't true of class.

Class systems differ from slavery and castes in four main respects:

1. **Class systems are fluid.** Unlike the other types of strata, classes are not established by legal or religious provisions. The boundaries between classes are never clear cut. There are no formal restrictions on intermarriage between people from different classes.

2. **Class positions are in some part achieved.** An individual's class is not simply assigned at birth, as is the case in the other types of stratification systems. Social mobility—movement upward and downward in the class structure—is more common than in the other types.

3. **Class is economically based.** Classes depend on economic differences between groups of individuals—inequalities in the possession of material resources. In the other types of stratification systems, noneconomic factors (such as race in the former South African caste system) are generally most important.

4. **Class systems are large scale and impersonal.** In the other types of stratification systems, inequalities are expressed primarily in personal relationships of duty or obligation—between slave and master or lower- and higher-caste individuals. Class systems, by contrast, operate mainly through large-scale, impersonal associations. For instance, one major basis of class differences is in inequalities of pay and working conditions.

WILL CASTE GIVE WAY TO CLASS?

There is some evidence that globalization will hasten the end of legally sanctioned caste systems throughout the world. Most official caste systems have already given way to class-based ones in industrial capitalist societies; South Africa, mentioned earlier, is the most prominent recent example (Berger, 1986). Modern industrial production requires that people move about freely, work at whatever jobs they are suited or able to do, and change jobs frequently according to economic conditions. The rigid restrictions found in caste systems interfere with this necessary freedom. Furthermore, as the world increasingly becomes a single economic unit, caste-like relationships will become more and more vulnerable to economic pressures. Nonetheless, elements of caste persist even in postindustrial societies. For example, some Indian immigrants to the United States seek to arrange traditional marriages for their children along caste lines, while the relatively small number of intermarriages between blacks and whites in the United States suggests the strength of caste barriers.

IS INEQUALITY DECLINING IN CLASS-BASED SOCIETIES?

There is some evidence that at least until recently, the class systems in mature capitalist societies became increasingly open to movement between classes, thereby reducing the level of inequality. In 1955, the Nobel Prize–winning economist Simon Kuznets proposed a hypothesis that has since been called the **Kuznets curve:** a formula showing that inequality increases during the early stages of capitalist development, then declines, and eventually stabilizes at a relatively low level (Kuznets, 1955; see Figure 7.1). Studies of European countries, the United States, and Canada suggested that inequality peaked in these places before World War II, declined through the 1950s, and remained roughly the same through the 1970s (Berger, 1986; Nielsen, 1994).

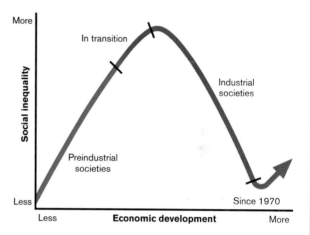

FIGURE 7.1

The Kuznets Curve

The Kuznets Curve, named for the Nobel Prize–winning economist who first advanced the idea in 1955, argues that inequality increases during early industrialization, then decreases during later industrialization, eventually stabilizing at low levels. There is some evidence that inequality may increase once again during the transition to postindustrial society.

SOURCE: Francois Nielsen, "Income Inequality and Industrial Development: Dualism Revisited," *American Sociological Review* 59 (October 1994), pp. 654–77.

Lowered postwar inequality was due in part to economic expansion in industrial societies, which created opportunities for people at the bottom to move up, and because of government health insurance, welfare, and other programs aimed at reducing inequality. However, Kuznets's prediction may well turn out to apply only to industrial societies. As you will see later in this chapter, the emergence of postindustrial society has brought with it an increase in inequality in the United States.

Classes in Western Societies Today

Let us begin our exploration of class differences in modern societies by looking at basic divisions of income, wealth, educational attainment, and occupational status within the population as a whole.

Income

Income refers to wages and salaries earned from paid occupations, plus unearned money from investments. One of the most significant changes occurring in Western countries over the past century has been the rising real income of the majority of the working population. (Real income is income excluding rises owing to inflation, to provide a fixed standard of comparison from year to year.) Blue-collar workers in Western societies now earn three to four times as much in real income as their counterparts at the turn of the century, even if their real income has dropped over the past twenty years. Gains for white-collar, managerial, and professional workers have been higher still. In terms of earnings per person (per capita) and the range of goods and services that can be purchased, the majority of the population today are vastly more affluent than any peoples have previously been in human history. One of the most important reasons for this growth is the increasing productivity—output per worker—that has been secured through technological development in industry. The volume of goods and services produced per worker has risen more or less continually since the 1900s.

Nevertheless, income distribution is quite unequal. In 2001, the top 5 percent of earners in the United States received 21 percent of total income; the highest 20 percent obtained 47.7 percent; and the bottom 20 percent received only 4.2 percent (see Figure 7.2). Between 1977 and 2001, income inequality has increased dramatically. The average pretax earnings of the bottom 80 percent of people in the United States declined by 11.7 percent (U.S. Bureau of the Census, 2002). During the same period, the richest fifth saw their incomes grow by 16.6 percent before taxes, while the richest 5 percent of the population increased their share of all income by over 40 percent—and the tax burden on these people was lower in 2001 than it had been in 1977. For the top 1 percent of earners, incomes approximately doubled during the same period. And despite the growth of the economy and the creation of millions of new jobs, these trends

FIGURE 7.2

Distribution of Income in the United States, 1967–2001

SOURCE: U.S. Bureau of the Census, 2002e.

continued throughout the 1990s, leading some observers to deem the United States a "two-tiered society" (Freeman, 1999).

Wealth

Wealth refers to all assets individuals own: cash, savings and checking accounts, investments in stocks, bonds, real estate properties, and so on. While most people earn their income from their work, the wealthy often derive the bulk of theirs from investments, some of them inherited. Some scholars argue that wealth—not income—is the real indicator of social class.

Wealth is highly concentrated in the United States, with enormous differences according to income, age, and education. The wealthiest 10 percent of families in 2001, for example, had a median net worth of $833,600—105 times as much as the poorest 20 percent of families, whose median net worth was only $7,900 (see Table 7.1). Education also pays off in terms of wealth: The median net worth of college graduates is more than eight times greater than that of high school dropouts. Owning a home makes a great difference, since homes are the principal asset for most families: Homeowners' net worth is $171,700, compared with only $4,800 for renters. Finally, age matters also, at least to some extent: Net worth, like income, increases with age, although it peaks by age seventy-five, after which savings are likely to be used as income and thus depleted.

If one excludes the ownership of cars and homes—which for most people are not really sources of wealth that can be used to pay the bills or used to get richer—the difference in wealth between high-income families and everyone else is even more pronounced. Net financial assets are far lower for minority groups than whites (Oliver and Shapiro, 1995). Between 1983 and 2000, the net financial assets of white Americans nearly tripled, from $19,900 to $58,716 (see Table 7.2). African Americans, on average, began to accumulate net financial assets only in the 1990s; by 2000, the median net worth was $6,166. Households of Hispanic origin have only recently begun to realize this important source of wealth; their median financial net worth has grown dramatically from effectively zero in 1998 to surpass African Americans with a median net worth of $6,766 in 2000.

What are some of the reasons for the racial disparity in wealth? Is it simply that blacks have less money with which to purchase assets? To some degree, the answer is yes. The old adage "It takes money to make money" is a fact of life for those who start with little or no wealth. Since whites historically have enjoyed higher incomes and levels of wealth than blacks, whites are able to accrue even more wealth, which they then are able to pass on to their children (Conley, 1999). In fact, economists estimate that more than half the wealth that one accumulates in a lifetime can be traced to a person's progeni-

tors. But family advantages are not the only factors. Oliver and Shapiro argued that it is easier for whites to obtain assets, even when they have fewer resources than blacks, because discrimination plays a major role in the racial gap in home ownership. Blacks are rejected for mortgages 60 percent more often than whites, even when they have the same qualifications and credit worthiness. When blacks do receive mortgages, the authors found, they pay on average a 0.5 percent higher interest rate, or about $12,000 more over the life of a thirty-year, median fixed-rate mortgage. These issues are particularly important since home ownership is the primary means of the accumulation of wealth for most American families.

Differences in wealth often take the form of differences in privilege, which in turn affects a person's life chances as much as income does. Members of Congress, high-level military officers at the Pentagon, and White House staff members do not have gargantuan salaries like the chief executive officers of corporations. What they do have, however, are privileges that translate into wealth. Members of Congress and White House staff members enjoy access to limousines and military aircraft, not to mention expense accounts that pay for many of their meals and hotel bills when they travel.

Education

Sociologists also believe that education, or the number of years of schooling a person has completed, is an important dimension of social stratification. The value of a college education has increased significantly in the past twenty years as a result of the increased demand for and wages paid to educated workers in the more computer- and information-based economy (Danziger and Gottschalk, 1995). Education is one of the strongest predictors of one's occupation, income, and wealth later in life. As we will see later in this chapter, how much education one receives is often influenced by the social class of one's parents.

Racial differences in levels of education persist, and this explains in part why racial differences in income and wealth also persist. In 2001, roughly 89 percent of whites and Asian Americans had completed high school, whereas only 79.5 percent of African Americans had a high school degree (Infoplease.com, 2003).

Occupation

Status refers to the prestige that goes along with one's social position. In the United States and other industrialized societies, occupation is an important indicator of one's social standing. Occupational status depends heavily on one's level of

TABLE 7.1

Median Family Net Worth, by Percentile of Family Income, Age, and Housing Tenure, 2001

	PERCENTAGE OF ALL U.S. FAMILIES	MEDIAN NET WORTH ($)
All families	100	86,100
Percentile of income		
Less than 20	20	7,900
20–39.9	20	37,200
40–59.9	20	62,500
60–79.9	20	141,500
80–89.9	10	263,100
90–100	10	833,600
Education of head of household		
No high school diploma	16	25,500
High school diploma	31.7	58,100
Some college	18.3	71,600
College degree	34	213,300
Age of head (years)		
Less than 35	22.7	11,600
35–44	22.3	77,600
45–54	20.6	132,000
55–64	13.2	181,500
65–74	10.7	176,300
75 or more	10.4	151,400
Housing status		
Owner	67.7	171,700
Renter or other	32.3	4,800
Percentile of net worth		
Less than 25	25	1,100
25–49.9	25	40,800
50–74.9	25	156,100
75–89.9	15	430,200
90–100	10	1,301,900

SOURCE: U.S. Federal Reserve Board, "Family Net Worth, by Selected Characteristics of Families, 1992, 1995, 1998, and 2001" surveys, December 2003. www.federalreserve.gov/pubs/bulletin/2003/0103lead.pdf.

TABLE 7.2

Median Financial Net Worth ($), 1983–2000: Whites, African Americans, and Latinos

RACE/ETHNICITY	1983	1989	1992	1995	1998	2000
White	19,900	26,900	21,900	19,300	37,600	67,000
African American	0	0	200	200	1,200	6,166
Latino	0	0	0	0	0	6,766

SOURCE: Hartman, 2000; Wolff, 2000; U.S. Census Bureau, 2003.

educational attainment. In fact, in studies where persons are asked to rate jobs in terms of how "prestigious" they are, the occupations that are ranked most highly are those requiring the most education (Treiman, 1977). These studies use what is called the Standard International Occupational Prestige Scale. Research shows that physicians, college professors, lawyers, and dentists are at the top of the scale, while garbage collectors and gas station attendants are at the bottom. About at the middle are jobs such as registered nurse, computer programmer, and insurance sales representative. Interestingly, similar rankings occur regardless of who does the ranking and in what country. Comparisons of status rankings across fifty-five countries show that there is a general agreement as to how high status an occupation is (see Table 7.3).

A Picture of the U.S. Class Structure

Although money clearly cannot buy everything, one's class position can make an enormous difference in terms of lifestyle. Most sociologists identify social classes in terms of wealth and income, noting how social class makes a difference in terms of consumption, education, health, and access to political power. The purpose of the following discussion is to describe broad class differences in the United States. Bear in mind that there are no sharply defined boundaries between the classes.

THE UPPER CLASS

The **upper class** consists of the very wealthiest Americans—those households earning more than $145,099 or approximately 5 percent of all American households (U.S. Bureau of the Cen-

sus, 2002a). Most Americans in the upper class are wealthy but not superrich. They are likely to own a large suburban home as well as a town house or a vacation home, to drive expensive automobiles, to fly first class to vacations abroad, to educate their children in private schools and colleges, and to have their desires attended to by a staff of servants. Their wealth stems in large part from their substantial investments, from stocks and bonds to real estate. They are politically influential at the national, state, and local levels. The upper class does include the superwealthy as well—the heads of major corporations, people who have made large amounts of money through investments or real estate, those fortunate enough to have inherited great wealth from their parents, a few highly successful celebrities and professional athletes, and a handful of others.

At the very top of this group are the superrich, people who have accumulated vast fortunes permitting them to enjoy a lifestyle unimaginable to most Americans. The superrich are highly self-conscious of their unique and privileged social class position; some give generously to such worthy causes as the fine arts, hospitals, and charities. Their homes are often lavish and sometimes filled with collections of fine art. Their common class identity is strengthened by such things as being listed in the social register or having attended the same exclusive private secondary schools (to which they also send their children). They sit on the same corporate boards of directors and belong to the same private clubs. They contribute large sums of money to their favorite politicians and are likely to be on a first-name basis with members of Congress and perhaps even with the president (Domhoff, 1998).

 The turn of this century saw extraordinary opportunities for the accumulation of such wealth. Globalization is one reason. Those entrepreneurs who are able to invest globally often prosper, both by selling products to

Income Inequality in the Global Economy

Although many economists, politicians, and businesspeople have sung the praises of globalization, there is reason to approach such claims cautiously. Globalization may well be increasing economic inequality in the world's advanced industrial societies. Although the U.S. economy has been consistently growing since the end of the recession of 1982–1983, the gap between the wages of high-skilled and low-skilled workers has also been increasing. In 1979, college graduates taking entry-level positions earned on average 37 percent more than those without college degrees. By 1993, the differential had grown to 77 percent (*USA Today* magazine, May 1998). And although this growing "wage premium" has encouraged more Americans to go to college—such that nearly 27 percent of the American work force had college degrees in 2002, compared with 18 percent in 1979 (U. S. Census, 2002c; *Business Week,* December 15, 1997)—it has also helped widen the gap between the wealthiest and the poorest workers. As an analyst for the U.S. Department of Labor put it, "it is by now almost a

foreign consumers, and by making profits cheaply by using low-wage labor in developing countries. The information revolution is another reason for the accumulation of wealth. Before the dot-com bubble finally burst in 2001, young entrepreneurs with startup high-tech companies such as Yahoo! or eBay made legendary fortunes. As a consequence, the number of superrich Americans has exploded in recent years. At the end of World War II, there were only thirteen thousand people worth a million dollars or more in the United States. In 2004, there were nearly 5 *million* millionaires in the United States, along with 277 *billionaires* (*Forbes,* 2004). The four hundred richest Americans are worth more than a *trillion* dollars—equal to almost one tenth the gross domestic product of the United States and only slightly less than the gross domestic product of China (Sklair, 1999).

Unlike "old-money" families such as the Rockefellers or the Vanderbilts, who accumulated their wealth in earlier generations and thus are viewed as a sort of American aristocracy, this "new wealth" often consists of upstart entrepreneurs such as Microsoft's Bill Gates, whose net worth—estimated

by *Forbes* at $46.6 billion in 2004—makes him the wealthiest individual in the world (*Forbes,* 2004).

THE MIDDLE CLASS

When Americans are asked to identify their social class, the large majority claim to be middle class. The reason is partly the American cultural belief that the United States is relatively free of class distinctions. Few people want to be identified as being too rich or too poor. Most Americans seem to think that others are not very different from their immediate family, friends, and coworkers (Vanneman and Cannon, 1987; Simpson, Stark, and Jackson, 1988; Kelley and Evans, 1995). Many blue-collar workers, for example, prefer to think of themselves as middle class rather than working class (although sociologists would classify blue-collar workers as working class). Since people rarely interact with others outside of their social class, they tend to see themselves as like "most other people," who they then regard as being "middle class" (Kelley and Evans, 1995).

platitude . . . that wage inequality has increased quite sharply since the late 1970s, for both men and women" (U.S. Dept. of Labor, 1997).

Although few studies have directly implicated globalization as a cause of this growing inequality, there is reason to view it as an indirect causal factor. It is true that whereas countries such as the United States, Canada, and the United Kingdom have witnessed a growth in earnings inequality since the late 1970s, countries like Germany, Japan, and France—which have, presumably, been equally affected by the forces of globalization—have seen either a decline or little change in inequality. At the same time, many of the factors that sociologists see as causes of inequality are clearly linked to globalization. First, in some cases, U.S. companies that manufacture in the United States lowered wages to compete with other U.S. firms that manufacture their products overseas, especially in the developing world. Second, globalization has encouraged immigration to the United States. Immigrants—many of whom are relegated to low-wage work—increase the competition for jobs among those in the low-wage labor pool, lowering wages somewhat in this segment of the labor market. Third, globalization has undermined the strength of U.S. labor unions. A number of studies have shown that when firms that used to do the bulk of their manufacturing in one region begin to spread their manufac-

turing base out across countries and continents, it becomes increasingly difficult for unions to organize workers and negotiate with management. But strong unions decrease earnings inequality through their commitment to raising wages.

Of course, globalization is not the only cause of inequality. Many researchers, for example, blame increasing inequality on the spectacular growth of high-tech industries, which employ mostly well-paid, white-collar workers and offer little in the way of traditional blue-collar employment. Still, it seems safe to conclude that globalization is not without its role in the growing stratification of American society.

The **middle class** is a catchall for a diverse group of occupations, lifestyles, and people who earn stable and sometimes substantial incomes at primarily white-collar jobs. It grew throughout much of the first three quarters of the twentieth century, then shrank during most of the last quarter century. During the late 1990s, however, economic growth halted this decline. Whether this trend will continue will depend on whether or not the economy expands or contracts during the next several years. Currently, the middle class includes slightly more than half of all American households. While the middle class was once largely white, today it is increasingly diverse, both racially and culturally, including African Americans, Asian Americans, and Latinos.

The American middle class can be subdivided into two groups: the upper middle class and the lower middle class.

The Upper Middle Class The *upper middle class* consists of relatively high-income professionals (doctors and lawyers, engineers and professors), mid-level corporate managers, peo-

ple who own or manage small businesses and retail shops, and even some large-farm owners. Household incomes in this group range from about $83,500 to perhaps $154,498. It includes approximately 15 percent of all American households (U.S. Bureau of the Census, 2002a). Its members are likely to be college educated, and many hold advanced degrees. Their children almost always receive a college education as well. Their jobs have historically been relatively secure, as well as likely to provide them with retirement programs and health benefits. They own comfortable homes, often in the suburbs or in trendy downtown neighborhoods. They drive the more expensive late-model cars or sport utility vehicles. They have some savings and investments. They are likely to be active in local politics and civic organizations.

The Lower Middle Class The *lower middle class* in the United States consists of trained office workers (for example, secretaries and bookkeepers), elementary and high school teachers, nurses, salespeople, police officers, firefighters, and

TABLE 7.3

Occupational Prestige in the United States and Around the World

OCCUPATION	UNITED STATES	AVERAGE OF 55 COUNTRIES	OCCUPATION	UNITED STATES	AVERAGE OF 55 COUNTRIES
Supreme Court judge	85	82	Professional athlete	51	48
College president	82	86	Social worker	50	56
Physician	82	78	Electrician	49	44
College professor	78	78	Secretary	46	53
Lawyer	75	73	Real estate agent	44	49
Dentist	74	70	Farmer	44	47
Architect	71	72	Carpenter	43	37
Psychologist	71	66	Plumber	41	34
Airline pilot	70	66	Mail carrier	40	33
Electrical engineer	69	65	Jazz musician	37	38
Biologist	68	69	Bricklayer	36	34
Clergy	67	60	Barber	36	30
Sociologist	65	67	Truck driver	31	33
Accountant	65	55	Factory worker	29	29
Banker	63	67	Store sales clerk	27	34
High school teacher	63	64	Bartender	25	23
Registered nurse	62	54	Lives on public aid	25	16
Pharmacist	61	64	Cab driver	22	28
Veterinarian	60	61	Gas station attendant	22	25
Classical musician	59	56	Janitor	22	21
Police officer	59	40	Waiter or waitress	20	23
Actor or actress	55	52	Garbage collector	13	13
Athletic coach	53	50	Street sweeper	11	13
Journalist	52	55	Shoe shiner	9	12

SOURCE: Treiman, 1997.

others who provide skilled services. Often members of this group enjoy relatively high status; it is their relatively low income that determines their class position. Household incomes in this group, which includes about 40 percent of American households, range from about $33,314 to $83,499 (U.S. Bureau of the Census, 2002a). They may own a modest house, although many live in rental units. Their automobiles may be late models, but they are not the more expensive varieties. Almost all have a high school education, and some have college degrees. They want their children to have a college education, although this will usually have to be paid for with the help of work-study programs and student loans. They are less likely to be politically active beyond exercising their right to vote.

THE WORKING CLASS

The **working class,** which makes up about 20 percent of all American households, includes primarily blue-collar and pink-collar laborers. Household incomes in this group range from perhaps $17,970 to $33,300 (U.S. Bureau of the Census, 2002a), and at least two people in each household will usually have to work to make ends meet. Family income is just enough to pay the rent or the mortgage, to put food on the table, and perhaps to save for a summer vacation. The working class includes factory workers, mechanics, secretaries, office workers, sales clerks, restaurant and hotel workers, and others who earn a modest weekly paycheck at a job that involves little control over the size of their income or working conditions. As you will see later in this chapter, many blue-collar jobs in the United States are threatened by economic globalization, and so members of the working class today are likely to feel insecure about their own and their family's future.

The working class is racially and ethnically diverse. While older members of the working class may own a home that was bought a number of years ago, younger members are likely to rent. The home or apartment is likely to be in a lower-income suburb or a city neighborhood. The household car, a lower-priced model, is unlikely to be new. Children who graduate from high school are unlikely to go to college and will attempt to get a job immediately instead. Most members of the working class are not likely to be politically active even in their own community, although they may vote in some elections.

THE LOWER CLASS

The **lower class,** which makes up roughly 15 percent of American households, includes those who work part time or not at all; household income is typically lower than $17,000 (U.S. Bureau of the Census, 2002a). Most lower-class individuals are found in cities, although some live in rural areas and earn a little money as farmers or part-time workers. Some manage to find employment in semiskilled or unskilled manufacturing or service jobs, ranging from making clothing in sweatshops to cleaning houses. Their jobs, when they can find them, are dead-end jobs, since years of work are unlikely to lead to promotion or substantially higher income. Their work is probably part time and highly unstable, without benefits such as medical insurance, disability, or social security. Even if they are fortunate enough to find a full-time job, there are no guarantees that it will be around next month or even next week. Many people in the lower class live in poverty. Very few own their own homes. Most of the lower class rent, and some are homeless. If they own a car at all, it is likely to be a used car. A higher percentage of the lower class is nonwhite than is true of other social classes. Its members do not participate in politics, and they seldom vote.

THE "UNDERCLASS"

In the lower class, some sociologists have recently identified a group they call the **underclass** because they are "beneath" the class system in that they lack access to the world of work and mainstream patterns of behavior. Located in the highest-poverty neighborhoods of the inner city, the underclass is sometimes called the "new urban poor."

The underclass includes many African Americans, who have been trapped for more than one generation in a cycle of poverty from which there is little possibility of escape (Wacquant, 1993, 1996; Wacquant and Wilson, 1993; Wilson, 1996).

Jerry Yang, cofounder of Yahoo! was part of the explosion of wealth associated with the dot-com information revolution.

These are the poorest of the poor. Their numbers have grown rapidly over the past quarter century and today include unskilled and unemployed men, young single mothers and their children on welfare, teenagers from welfare-dependent families, and many of the homeless. They live in poor neighborhoods troubled by drugs, teenage gangs, drive-by shootings, and high levels of violence. They are the truly disadvantaged, people with extremely difficult lives who have little realistic hope of ever making it out of poverty.

The emergence of an underclass of the new urban poor has been attributed to social forces that have come together during the past quarter century (Sawhill, 1989; Wacquant, 1993, 1996; Wilson, 1996). First, economic globalization has led to unemployment among workers lacking education and skills, since many unskilled and semiskilled jobs have moved to low-wage countries. The threat of such job loss, in turn, has depressed wages in the remaining unskilled jobs. Since African Americans and recent immigrants from Latin America (and to some extent Asia) provide much of the unskilled labor in the United States, they are particularly disadvantaged in today's labor market. Furthermore, racial discrimination has made it especially difficult for minority groups to compete for the dwindling supply of unskilled jobs.

Second, government programs that once provided assistance for the poor were cut back sharply during the 1980s under the Reagan and elder Bush administrations, so that the poor were left with few resources to use to get ahead. These problems were compounded during the Clinton administration, whose welfare reforms severely restricted the length of time people could remain on welfare. This approach reduced the number of people on welfare, and the growing economy of the 1990s provided low-wage jobs for many welfare recipients. A sustained economic slowdown, however, could swell the ranks of the new urban poor, by leaving a growing number of people both jobless and without welfare benefits.

More recently, some sociologists have argued that members of the underclass perpetuate their own inequality because the difficult conditions they face have made them "ill suited to the requirements of the formally rational sector of the economy" (Wacquant, 2002). Although these scholars see the sources of such behavior in the social structure, they believe the culture of the underclass has taken on a life of its own, serving as both cause and effect. Such claims have generated considerable controversy, inspiring a number of studies that have taken issues with these claims. Those who stand on the other side argue that although urban poverty is an immobile stratum, it is not simply a "defeated" and disconnected class, as theorists of the underclass believe. Thus, studies of fast-food workers and homeless street vendors have argued that the separations between the urban poor and the rest of society are not as great as scholars of the underclass believe (Newman, 2000; Duneier, 1999).

Inequality in the United States: A Growing Gap Between Rich and Poor

The United States prides itself on being a nation of equals. Indeed, except for the Great Depression of the 1930s, inequality declined throughout much of the twentieth century, reaching its lowest levels during the 1960s and early 1970s. But during the past quarter century inequality has started to increase once again. The rich have gotten much, much richer. Middle-class incomes have stagnated. The poor have grown in number and are poorer than they have been since the 1960s. Currently, the gap between rich and poor in the United States is the largest since the Census Bureau started measuring it in 1947 (U.S. Bureau of the Census, 2000b) and the largest in the industrial world (see Figure 7.3). One statistical analysis of income and poverty among industrial nations found that the United States had the most unequal distribution of household income among all twenty-one industrial countries studied (Sweden had the most equal) (Smeeding, 2000).

In 1999, the richest 20 percent of all U.S. households accounted for over half of all income generated in the United States (see Figure 7.2). Moreover, their share has steadily increased. Table 7.4 divides American households into five equal-sized groups, based on household income in 1999. It also looks at the richest 5 percent of all households. The table compares the average after-tax income of each group in 1999 with the income each group would have had if its share of total income had remained the same as it was in 1974—that is, if inequality had not increased during the twenty-five year period. Four out of the five groups were worse off in 1999 than they would have been had inequality not increased; the range was between $2,200 and $6,000 poorer. The top fifth, on the other hand, was roughly $17,300 richer; the top 5 percent, about $61,300 richer.

Corporate Executives versus Their Workers

The earnings gap between top corporate officials and average working Americans has ballooned in recent years. According to *BusinessWeek* magazine's annual Executive Pay Scoreboard, the average pay of the chief executive officers (CEOs) at 362 of the largest U.S. companies rose from $10.6 million in 1998 to $13.1 million in 2000—a 24 percent increase. The top earner was John Reed, CEO of the financial conglomerate Citicorp Group, who took home $293 million, mostly in stocks in his company (*BusinessWeek,* 2001). According to *Forbes* magazine (2001c) the eight hundred CEOs of the largest U.S. firms took home $6 billion that year in total pay.

The average U.S. factory worker averaged $13.74 an hour in 2000, earning $28,574 for the entire year, assuming he or she labored for fifty-two weeks a year, forty hours a week (U.S. Bureau of Labor Statistics, 2001a). In other words, the average CEO earned about 458 times as much as the average factory worker in 2000. Moreover, the gap has grown sharply: Average worker pay (not adjusting for inflation) increased by roughly one third between 1990 and 2000, whereas the average CEO pay increased sixfold.

The difference between executive and worker compensation is even more pronounced if one takes into account that U.S. firms today rely increasingly on workers in low-income countries. To take one example, *Forbes* reported that Millard Drexler earned $173 million in 1999 as CEO of Gap. Inc., America's largest clothing retailer (*Forbes,* 2001c). Virtually all of the thousand or so factories that make Gap clothing are in low-wage countries, where it can be estimated that workers average perhaps $800 a year (roughly $3 a day). The Gap's "wage gap" between Drexler's pay and that of the average Gap worker is 216,250 to 1!

FIGURE 7.3

Income Inequality in Selected Industrialized Countries: Ratio of Richest 20 Percent to Poorest 20 Percent for 1999

In the 1990s, the richest fifth of all Americans were on average nine times richer than the poorest fifth, one of the highest ratios in the industrialized world. In Japan, at the other extreme, the ratio was about 3.4 to 1.

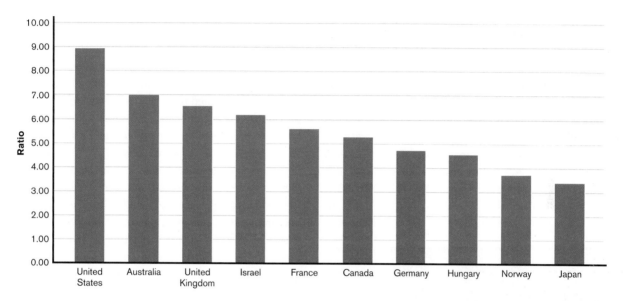

SOURCE: World Bank, *World Development Indicators,* 2000, Table 2.8.

TABLE 7.4

How Has an Increase in Income Inequality Affected American Households?

INCOME CATEGORY	ACTUAL 1999 MEAN INCOME ($)	1999 INCOME IF INEQUALITY HAD NOT CHANGED FROM 1974 ($)	DIFFERENCE: HOW MUCH POORER OR RICHER ($)
Lowest fifth	9,940	12,148	−2,208
Second fifth	24,436	29,103	−4,668
Middle fifth	40,879	46,914	−6,035
Fourth fifth	63,555	67,664	−4,109
Highest fifth	135,401	118,133	+17,268
Top 5 percent	235,392	174,080	+61,311

SOURCE: Calculations based on U.S. Bureau of the Census, 2000j.

Minorities versus White Americans

There are substantial differences in income based on race and ethnicity, since minorities in the United States are more likely to hold the lowest-paying jobs. Black and Latino household income, for example, averages about two thirds that of whites (see Figure 7.4). For blacks, this is a slight improvement over previous years, as a growing number of blacks have gone to college and moved into middle-class occupations. For Latinos, however, the situation has worsened, as recent immigrants from rural areas in Mexico and Central America find themselves working at low-wage jobs (U.S. Bureau of the Census, 2001a).

Oliver and Shapiro (1995) found that the "wealth gap" between blacks and whites is even greater than the income gap. While blacks on average earned two thirds that of whites, their net worth was only a tenth as much. Moreover, these differences increased between 1967 and 1988. More recent data show that the wealth gap has decreased only slightly: In 2000, whites had a median net worth of $58,716, compared with $6,166 for blacks and $6,766 for Hispanics (U.S. Bureau of the Census, 2003). Oliver and Shapiro also found that when blacks attained educational or occupational levels comparable to whites, the wealth gap still did not disappear. For example, the net worth of college-educated blacks was only $17,000 in 1988, compared with nearly $75,000 for whites.

Oliver and Shapiro (1995) argue that blacks have encountered numerous barriers to acquiring wealth throughout American history, beginning with slavery and continuing to the present day. After the Civil War ended slavery in 1865, legal discrimination (such as mandatory segregation in the South or separate schools) tied the vast majority of blacks to the lowest rungs of the economic ladder, until racial discrimination was made illegal by the Civil Rights Act of 1964. Nonetheless, discrimination has remained, and although some blacks have moved into middle-class occupations, many have remained poor or in low-wage jobs where the opportunities for accumulating wealth are nonexistent. Among those who successfully started businesses, many found there were racial barriers to breaking into the more profitable white markets. In effect, many blacks have suffered from a vicious cycle that prevents them from accumulating wealth. Less wealth means less social and cultural capital: fewer dollars to invest in schooling for one's children, a business, or the stock market—investments that in the long run would create greater wealth for future investments.

Demonstrators protest the Gap for exploiting low-wage workers in the Third World.

Social Mobility

In studying stratification and inequality, we must consider not only the differences between economic positions but also what happens to the individuals who occupy them. **Social mobility** refers to the movement of individuals and groups between different class positions as a result of changes in occupation, wealth, or income.

There are two ways of studying social mobility. First, we can look at people's own careers—how far they move up or down the socioeconomic scale in the course of their working lives. This is called **intragenerational mobility**. Alternatively, we can analyze where children are on the scale compared with their parents or grandparents. Mobility across the generations is called **intergenerational mobility**.

Another important distinction sociologists make is between structural mobility and exchange mobility. If there were such a thing as a society with complete equality of opportunity—where each person had the same chance of getting on in life as everyone else—there would be a great deal of downward as well as upward mobility. This is what is meant by **exchange mobility**: There is an exchange of positions,

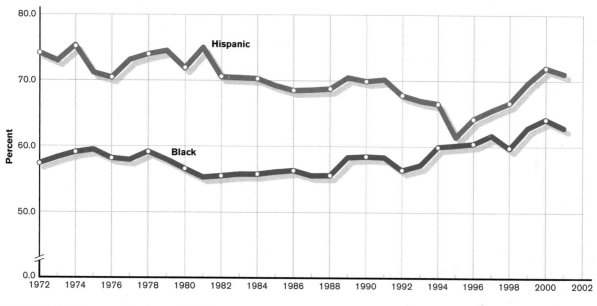

FIGURE 7.4

Black and Hispanic Income Compared to Whites'

During the past decade and a half, blacks have seen their income improve slightly relative to whites. By 2001, blacks were averaging 62.9 percent of whites' income ($39,248 for blacks, versus $62,444 for whites)— up from 57.6 percent of white income in 1972. Latinos, on the other hand, were worse off relative to whites than they had been 24 years earlier. In 2001, Latinos were averaging 71.1 percent of white income, compared with 74.4 percent of white income in 1972. Overall, the relative position of both blacks and Latinos improved slightly during the latter part of the 1990s due to the sustained economic growth of that period.

SOURCE: U.S. Bureau of the Census, 2002b.

such that more talented people in each generation move up the economic hierarchy, while the less talented move down.

In practice, there is no society that even approaches full equality of opportunity, and most mobility, whether intra- or intergenerational, is **structural mobility**, upward mobility made possible by an expansion of better-paid occupations at the expense of more poorly paid ones. Most mobility in the United States since World War II has depended on continually increasing prosperity. Levels of downward mobility, therefore, have been historically low.

Opportunities for Mobility: Who Gets Ahead?

Why is it more difficult for someone from the "new urban poor" to become an upper-class professional? Many people in modern societies believe it is possible for anyone to reach the top

through hard work and persistence. Why should it be difficult to do so? Sociologists have sought to answer these questions by trying to understand which social factors are most influential in determining an individual's status or position in society.

In a classic study of social mobility in the United States, the sociologists Peter Blau and Otis Dudley Duncan surveyed over twenty thousand men in order to assess intergenerational mobility (1967). Blau and Duncan concluded that while there has been a great deal of **vertical mobility,** or movement along the socioeconomic scale, nearly all of it was between occupational positions quite close to one another. Long-range mobility, that is from working class to upper-middle class, was rare. Why? Blau and Duncan sought to answer this question by assessing the impact of social background in determining ultimate social status. They concluded that the key factor behind status was educational attainment. But a child's education is influenced by its family's social status; this, in turn, affects the child's social position later in life. The sociologists William Sewell and Robert

Defending Workers at Berkeley

After four years of steady service as a food service worker at the University of California at Berkeley, Sam makes twelve dollars and seven cents an hour. Approaching his fiftieth birthday, Sam is barely able to make ends meet. He does not own a home. "No, of course not. I stay in a little studio apartment, and I have great grandchildren. It's not easy. By the time I pay my rent and buy my food and put gas in my car, I'm already waiting for the next paycheck two days after maybe I've gotten the [last] paycheck. [***] Every now and then I get to go to a movie or something to just kind of break up the boredom, but it's not very often that I do anything different than go to work and come home. . . . It's not easy. It's not easy at all."

The standard of living that Sam's salary permits him is a far cry from the one he had anticipated when he started working as a young man, thirty years ago. Back then, Sam had what he considered to be a good job at Ford down in Milpitas [California]. That was when "you came to work and did your job. You automatically got put on [steady employment] and had benefits . . . you had medical, dental and all of that. You had a paycheck every week and you didn't have to worry about getting paid all of your money, which is a bad problem here [at Cal]. You got your vacation without any hassle." Sam

worked happily at Ford until 1983 when the plant closed. Before he got laid off, Sam had been making thirteen dollars and thirty-nine cents an hour, not at all an unreasonable salary given the Bay Area cost of living at that time. He never imagined that twenty years later his hourly wage would be lower, even without adjusting for inflation. [***]

Sam's story is not unique. Behind the stately façade of America's most prestigious public university, custodians, food service workers, groundskeepers, and clerical workers toil under conditions that betray the very principles which we want our university to embody. And yet, students, professors, and administrators know surprisingly little about the sacrifices made and injuries suffered by those who clean their classrooms and dormitories, cook their meals, maintain the grounds, and record their grades.

As sociology graduate students at the University of California at Berkeley, we usually focus our scholarly attention on "the world out there," far beyond Sproul Plaza and Sather Gate. In our capacity as graduate student instructors, we encourage our students to explore the causes of poverty, the repercussions of inequality, and the often invisible power dynamics in our society. Rarely do we, as scholars and teachers

in the making, explore the social ills that exist right here in our cherished halls of learning.

[***]

Many workers, like most students and professors, also came to U.C. Berkeley with high expectations about contributing to a world-class educational institution. What we discovered, however, is that their expectations were quickly crushed once they got on the job. Not wanting to complain, they tell cautiously at first, but passionately once they get going about finding themselves on the brink of poverty and routinely facing dangerous and degrading employment practices. [***]

Workers' experiences at U.C. Berkeley can only be understood against the backdrop of the widespread corporatization of American universities. This transformation of the university reflects the rise over the last three decades of a free market fundamentalism which posits that unregulated capitalism is the best system, both morally and practically, for organizing all spheres of society. [***]

As we became aware of the increasing corporatization of the university, we formed a graduate student research collective and worked with the guidance of author and journalist Barbara Ehrenreich. Our collective built on a confluence of movements. We were inspired by the student initiatives for economic justice springing up around the country, especially the movement for a living wage at Harvard Univeristy. We were also emboldened by calls to sociologists, voiced by prominent members of our faculty, to conduct Public Sociology—sociological research that seeks to open up public dialogue about the pressing issues of our time. We thus decided to use the tools available to us as budding social scientists to study and report on the working conditions and everyday experiences of University workers.

[***]

Three troubling themes emerged from these interviews. First, wages have not kept up with the rising costs of living; many workers cannot afford the basic necessities of life— reasonable housing, childcare, and transportation. Second, the conditions of work are unacceptably dangerous. Once injured, workers are treated as if they are disposable and do not receive the physical and emotional care they deserve. Finally, many workers [***] report routinely being treated with disrespect by their supervisors. The lack of standardized procedures leaves workers subject to the luck of the draw: some supervisors are fair; others make unreasonable demands and take advantage of their power.

Organized around these three main themes of wages, health and safety, and dignity and respect, this report tells a story about the university that is seldom told, presented

through the voices of those who are seldom heard. With the publication and dissemination of this report, we hope to accomplish three concrete objectives:

Education: to educate students, faculty, parents and alumni about the wages and working conditions of the U.C. Berkeley workforce.

Mobilization: in coalition with campus unions and other student groups, to mobilize the collective energies of the campus community to send an unequivocal message to university administrators that it is unacceptable for members of our community to work for less than a living wage, to be endangered by their work, or to be accorded less than the dignity and respect any other member of the university community would expect and deserve.

Change: to call on the university administration to take ten steps—outlined in the conclusion of this report—that will improve the wages and working conditions of university employees.

[***]

SOURCE: Gretchen Purser, Amy Schalet, and Ofer Sharone, *Berkeley's Betrayal: Wages and Working Conditions at Cal.* (Berkeley, CA: University Labor Research Project, 2004). To view the entire report, visit www.berkeleysbetrayal.org.

GRETCHEN PURSER is a Ph.D. candidate in sociology at the University of California at Berkeley. Her research focuses on the contingent labor market and urban poverty in the United States. AMY SCHALET is a postdoctoral fellow at the Center for Reproductive Health Research and Policy at the University of California at San Francisco. She has written and taught on the American welfare state in comparative perspective. She is currently preparing her book on adolescent sexuality and parental panic in the United States and the Netherlands for publication with Chicago University Press. OFER SHARONE is a Ph.D. candidate in sociology at the University of California at Berkeley. He specializes in the sociology of work and researches overwork and unemployment in the United States and Israel.

Hauser later confirmed Blau and Duncan's conclusions (1980). They added to the argument by claiming that the connection between family background and educational attainment occurs because parents, teachers, and friends influence the educational and career aspirations of the child and that these aspirations then become an important part of the status attainment process throughout the child's life. Sewell and Hauser sought to prove that social status was influenced by a pattern of related social influences going back to one's birth: Family background affects the child's aspirations, which in turn affect the child's educational attainment, which in turn affects the adult's later occupational prestige, and so on and so on.

The French sociologist Pierre Bourdieu has also been a major figure in examining the importance of family background to social status, but his emphasis is on the cultural advantages that parents can provide to their children (1984, 1988). Bourdieu argues that among the factors responsible for social status the most important is the transmission of cultural capital. Those who own economic capital often manage to pass much of it on to their children. The same is true, Bourdieu argues, of the cultural advantages that coming from a "good home" confers. These advantages stem partly from having greater economic capital, which succeeding generations inherit, thus perpetuating inequalities. As we have seen, wealthier families are able to afford to send their children to better schools, an economic advantage that benefits the children's social status as adults. In addition to this material advantage, parents from the upper and middle classes are mostly highly educated themselves and tend to be more involved in their children's education—reading to them, helping with homework, purchasing books and learning materials, and encouraging their progress. Bourdieu notes that working-class parents are concerned about their children's education, but they lack the economic and cultural capital to make a difference. Bourdieu's study of French society confirmed his theory. He found that a majority of office professionals with high levels of educational attainment and income were from families of the "dominant class" in France. Likewise, office clerical workers often originated from the working classes.

The socioeconomic order in the United States is similar. Those who already hold positions of wealth and power have many chances to perpetuate their advantages and to pass them on to their offspring. They can make sure their children have the best available education, and this will often lead them into the best jobs. Most of those who reach the top had a head start; they came from professional or affluent backgrounds. Studies of people who have become wealthy show that hardly anyone begins with nothing. The large majority of people who have "made money" did so on the basis of inheriting or being given at least a modest amount initially—which they then used to make more. In American society, it's better to start at the top than at the bottom (Jaher, 1973; Rubinstein, 1986; Duncan et al., 1998).

Downward Mobility

Although downward mobility is less common than upward mobility, about 20 percent of men in the United States are downwardly mobile intergenerationally, although most of this movement is short range. A person with **short-range downward mobility** moves from one job to another that is similar—for example, from a routine office job to semiskilled blue-collar work. Downward intragenerational mobility, also a common occurrence, is often associated with psychological problems and anxieties. Some people are simply unable to sustain the lifestyle into which they were born. But another source of downward mobility among individuals arises through no fault of their own. During the late 1980s and early 1990s, corporate America was flooded with instances in which middle-aged men lost their jobs because of company mergers or takeovers. These executives either had difficulty finding new jobs or could only find jobs that paid less than their previous jobs.

Many of the intragenerational downwardly mobile are women. It is still common for women to abandon promising careers on the birth of a child. After spending some years raising children, such women often return to the paid work force at a level lower than when they left—for instance, in poorly paid, part-time work. (This situation is changing, although not as fast as might be hoped.)

Gender and Social Mobility

Although so much research into social mobility has focused on men, in recent years more attention has begun to be paid to patterns of mobility among women. At a time when girls are outperforming boys in school and females are outnumbering males in higher education, it is tempting to conclude that long-standing gender inequalities in society may be relaxing their hold. Has the occupational structure become more open to women, or are their mobility chances still guided largely by family and social background?

One study traced the lives of nine thousand people born during the same week in 1970. In the most recent survey of the respondents, at age twenty-six, it was found that for both men and women family background and class of origin remain powerful influences. The study concluded that the young people who were coping best with the transition to adulthood were those who had obtained a better education, postponed children and marriage, and had fathers in professional occupations. Individuals who had come from disadvantaged backgrounds had a greater tendency to remain there.

The study found that, on the whole, women today are experiencing much greater opportunity than did their counterparts in the previous generation. Middle-class women have benefited the most. They were just as likely as their male peers to go to college and to move into well-paid jobs on graduation. This trend toward greater equality was also reflected in women's heightened confidence and sense of self-esteem, compared with a similar cohort of women born just twelve years earlier.

Poverty in the United States

At the bottom of the class system in the United States are the millions of people who exist in conditions of poverty. Many do not maintain a proper diet and live in miserable conditions; their average life expectancy is lower than that of the majority of the population. In addition, the number of individuals and families who have become homeless has greatly increased over the past twenty years.

In defining poverty, a distinction is usually made between absolute and relative poverty. **Absolute poverty** means that a person or family simply can't get enough to eat. People living in absolute poverty are undernourished and, in situations of famine, may actually starve to death. Absolute poverty is common in the poorer developing countries.

In the industrial countries, **relative poverty** is essentially a measure of inequality. It means being poor as compared with the standards of living of the majority. It is reasonable to call a person poor in the United States if he lacks the basic resources needed to maintain a decent standard of housing and healthy living conditions.

Measuring Poverty

When President Lyndon B. Johnson began his War on Poverty in 1964, around 36 million Americans lived in poverty. Within a decade, the number had dropped sharply, to around 23 million (see Figure 7.5 for changes in poverty rates since 1959). But then, beginning in the early 1970s, poverty again began to climb, peaking in 1993 at 39 million people. Since that time, the number of poor has dropped by 4.4 million people, and in 2002, it stood at 34.6 million people, roughly 12 percent of the population (U.S. Bureau of the Census, 2003a). Yet even this level of poverty greatly exceeds that of most other industrial and postindustrial nations. In the mid-1990s, for example, when the U.S. poverty rate was around 14 percent, France's was 10 percent, Canada's and Germany's 7 percent (Smeeding, Rainwater, and Burtless, 2000).

What does it mean to be poor in the world's richest nation? The U.S. government calculates the **poverty line** as an income equal to three times the cost of a nutritionally adequate diet—a strict no-frills budget that assumes a nutritionally adequate diet could be purchased in 1999 for only $3.86 per day for each member, along with about $7.72 on all other items (including rent and utilities, clothing, medical expenses, and transportation). For a family of four persons in 2002, that works out to an annual cash income of $18,244 (U.S. Bureau of the Census, 2003b).

How realistic is this formula? Some critics believe it *over*estimates the amount of poverty. They point out that the current standard fails to take into account noncash forms of income available to the poor, such as food stamps, Medicare, Medicaid, and public housing subsidies, as well as cash obtained from work at odd jobs that is concealed from the government. For example, one study looked at the poorest tenth of all families with children, comparing government survey data on their reported income with comparable data on their reported expenditures (Mayer and Jencks, 1994). It found that these families actually spent twice as much, on average, as the income they reported to the government.

Other critics argue that the government's formula greatly *under*estimates the amount of poverty. They argue that to label a three-person family as "nonpoor" in 1999 because it earned more than $12,680 (less than $35 a day) is simply unrealistic. Some scholars point out that such figures are based on an assumption from a half century ago that an "average" family spends a third of its income on food, even though more recent studies show that the actual figure is closer to one sixth, and that as much as three quarters of a poor family's income may go to rent alone (Schwarz and Volgy, 1992; Stone, 1993; Joint Center for Housing Studies, 1994; Dolbeare, 1995). By this reasoning, food expenditures should be multiplied by at least 6, rather than 3, to yield the poverty level. Patricia Ruggles (1990, 1992), an adviser to the University of Wisconsin's Institute for Research on Poverty, estimates that this formula would effectively double the official number of Americans living in poverty. That would mean that in 2000, over 62 million people were living in poverty, or 22.6 percent—almost a quarter—of the population, instead of the official Census Bureau estimate for that year of 31.1 million people, or only 11.3 percent of the population.

The official U.S. poverty rate is the highest among the major industrial and postindustrial nations, more than three times that of such European countries as Sweden or Norway (Smeeding, Rainwater, and Burtless, 2000). The largest concentrations of poverty in the United States are found in the South and the Southwest, in central cities, and in rural areas. Among the poor, 12.7 million Americans (or 4.6 percent of the country) live in extreme poverty: Their incomes are only *half* of the official poverty level, meaning that they live at near-starvation levels (U.S. Bureau of the Census, 2000e, 2000f).

The Information Revolution and Inequality

What impact will the information revolution have on social inequality?

The answer in part depends on how well the American educational system responds to the challenge of preparing students for a high-technology world. A good education can pay off in the digital society. Although Bill Gates may be the world's richest college dropout (Gates left Harvard to found Microsoft), he is clearly the exception to the rule.

Recall what has happened to blue-collar factory work—the kinds of jobs that made possible a middle-class lifestyle throughout much of this century. As you have seen in this chapter, thanks to the information revolution, U.S. businesses today can relocate their manufacturing operations around the globe with the click of a mouse, filling out orders on their suppliers' Web pages almost as easily as consumers buy books on Amazon.com. Beginning in the late 1970s, U.S. firms began to take advantage of modern information technology to downsize, moving their production to low-wage countries. The re-

sult: stagnant or declining wages for much of the American working class. Inequality has increased for people whose skills limit them to blue-collar work.

College graduates today earn more than they did a decade ago—the higher the degree, the greater the gains. High school dropouts, on the other hand, earn less (Hout, 1997). One U.S. Census Bureau study (2002e) found that in 2001, men with a professional degree had a median income of $81,602, three times as much as men with only a high school diploma ($28,343). The U.S. Bureau of Labor Statistics (2001b) predicts that between 1998 and 2008 the four fastest-growing occupations will all be directly related to the digital society. Jobs for computer engineers, computer support specialists, and computer systems analysts will more than double, while jobs for database administrators will increase approximately 80 percent. These are all jobs in which education pays a large dividend.

How well are students today being educated for tomorrow's digital world? A recent U.S. Department of Education

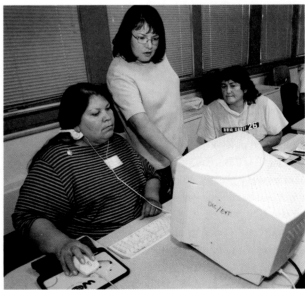

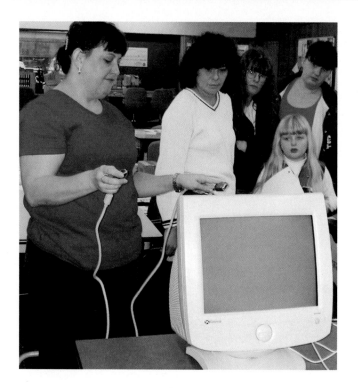

with science and technology training. The program would provide elementary school children and their families with help in buying computers, connecting to the Internet, and learning skills required to use them (Carnevale, 2000). A growing number of American colleges and universities, as well as some private companies, are beginning to provide "virtual high schools" over the Internet, offering college prep and advanced placement courses to students in inner-city schools that traditionally lack such offerings (Carr, 1999; Carr and Young, 1999). The state of Maine recently approved a program to provide every seventh- and eighth-grade student with a laptop computer to be used throughout high school. Maine, which currently ranks thirty-seventh in the nation in per capita income, hopes that a high-tech future will reverse its economic fortunes (*Ellsworth American,* 2001; Goldberg, 2001).

It is still too early to give a final grade to American schools. The digital revolution is fairly recent, and schools and teachers are only beginning to catch up with it. It remains to be seen whether the new information technology ultimately reinforces existing social inequalities—or is used to overcome them.

study (NCES, 2000) gives mixed grades to public schools. The report, *Teachers' Tools for the 21st Century,* surveyed public school teachers in 1999, asking them about the technology that was available in their classrooms and how well prepared they were to use it. The good news was that virtually all of the teachers reported that their schools had computers connected to the Internet. Nearly all had at least one computer in their classroom, and two thirds of the classrooms were hooked up to the Internet as well. The bad news was that only half of the teachers used computers or the Internet to teach their students. Perhaps this was because only a third reported feeling prepared to use computers and the Internet in their classrooms.

Current patterns of computer use in public schools reinforce existing social stratification. For example, teachers in white middle-class schools were much more likely to use computers for Internet research than teachers in schools with large numbers of poor minority students. They were also less likely to report that outdated, unreliable computers were a barrier to their classroom instruction (NCES, 2000). Poor inner-city schools, which often lack basic instructional materials such as textbooks, much less computers, are especially ill equipped to prepare their students.

There are some promising signs that the digital revolution may yet reach a broad cross section of American students. For example, Brown University, in conjunction with MCI World-Com, recently announced a small program to finance twenty college-community partnerships to help provide low-income children in inner-city schools and on Indian tribal reservations

Questions

- Describe how the advent of computers and the information technology industry could affect the kind of jobs available in the United States. How could the American occupational makeup change? How has it changed already?
- Can the use of computers in schools close the digital divide? Why or why not?
- How might the rise in high-tech jobs and the end of blue-collar jobs affect American society and lifestyle? Will society be increasingly stratified? How might it become more egalitarian?

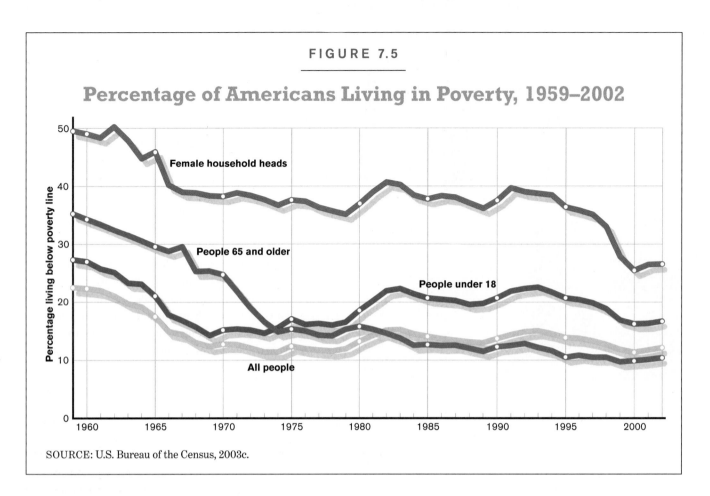

FIGURE 7.5

Percentage of Americans Living in Poverty, 1959–2002

Female household heads

People 65 and older

People under 18

All people

Percentage living below poverty line

SOURCE: U.S. Bureau of the Census, 2003c.

Who Are the Poor?

What do you think about poverty? Most Americans of all social classes think of the poor as people who are unemployed or on welfare. Americans also tend to display more negative attitudes toward welfare provisions and benefits than people in other Western countries. Surveys repeatedly show that the majority of Americans regard the poor as being responsible for their own poverty and are antagonistic to those who live on "government handouts." For example, a Gallup poll found that 55 percent of the public believed that lack of effort by the poor was the principal reason for poverty. Nearly two thirds believed that government assistance programs reduced incentives to work. These views, however, are out of line with the realities of poverty. The poor are as diverse as other groups.

WORKING POOR

Many Americans are the **working poor,** that is, people who work but whose earnings are not high enough to lift them above poverty. The 2003 U.S. minimum wage, $5.15 an hour, results in a yearly income of $10,300, if the person is working full time. This is only about three quarters of the poverty-level income of $14,494 for a single parent supporting two children

(U.S. Bureau of the Census, 2003b). About one third of those officially living in poverty are actually working. In 1999, the working poor included 2.5 million Americans who worked full time and another 9.1 million working part time. Most poor people, contrary to popular belief, don't receive welfare payments, because they earn too much to qualify for welfare.

Katherine Newman spent two years documenting the lives of three hundred low-wage workers and job seekers at fast-food restaurants in Harlem, a predominantly African American section of New York City. Her award-winning book *No Shame in My Game* found that the people interviewed were hard workers who valued their jobs, despite the low status associated with "slinging burgers." Moreover, Newman found that the working poor had to overcome enormous obstacles simply to survive: They typically lacked adequate educations, and some attended school while working; they had no health insurance to cover medical costs; and many were supporting families on poverty-level wages (Newman, 2000).

POVERTY, RACE, AND ETHNICITY

Poverty rates are much higher among most minority groups, even though more than two thirds of the poor are white. As Table 7.5 shows, blacks and Latinos continue to earn around

TABLE 7.5

Median Income and Poverty Rates
for Households in 2002, by Race and Ethnicity

	WHITE	ASIAN AMERICAN	LATINO	BLACK	TOTAL U.S.
Median income ($)*	46,305	53,635	33,565	29,470	42,816
Percentage of median income of whites	100	116	72	64	92
Poverty rate (%)**	8	10.1	21.8	24.1	12.1

*2001 data

**2002 data

SOURCE: U.S. Bureau of the Census, 2002b, 2003a.

two thirds of what whites earn in the United States, while experiencing three times the poverty rate whites experience. This is because they often work at the lowest-paying jobs and because of racial discrimination. Asian Americans have the highest income of any group, but their poverty rate is almost one and a half times that of whites, reflecting the recent influx of relatively poor immigrant groups.

Latinos have somewhat higher incomes than blacks, although their poverty rate is comparable. Nonetheless, the number of blacks living in poverty has declined considerably in recent years. In 1959, 55.1 percent of blacks were living in poverty; by 2002 that figure had dropped to 23.9 percent. The recent high point for black poverty came during the recession of 1992, when 33.4 percent of the black population was poor. Since that time, the number of blacks in poverty has fallen by 2.5 million. This is mainly because the economic expansion of the 1990s created new job opportunities. A similar pattern is seen for Latinos: Poverty grew steadily between 1972 and 1994, peaking at 30.7 percent of the Latino population. By 1999, however, the poverty rate for Latinos had fallen to 22.8 percent (U.S. Bureau of the Census, 2000g).

THE FEMINIZATION OF POVERTY

Much of the growth in poverty is associated with the **feminization of poverty,** an increase in the proportion of the poor who are female. Growing rates of divorce, separation, and single-parent families have placed women at particular disadvantage, since it is extremely difficult for unskilled or semi-

skilled, low-income, poorly educated women to raise children by themselves while they also hold down a job that could raise them out of poverty. As a result, in 2002 over a quarter (26.5 percent) of all single-parent families headed by women were poor, compared to only 5.3 percent of married couples with children (U.S. Bureau of the Census, 2003c).

Households headed by single parents are much more likely to live in poverty than those headed by married couples, and the incidence of poverty is far higher if the single parent is a woman. The feminization of poverty is particularly acute among families headed by Latino women (see Table 7.6). Although the rate declined by nearly 5 percent in four years, 41.4 percent of all female-headed Latino families lived in poverty in 2002. An almost identical percentage (41.3 percent) of female-headed African American families also live in poverty; both considerably higher than that of white female-headed families (26.2 percent) (U.S. Bureau of the Census, 2003d).

A single woman attempting to raise children alone is caught in a vicious cycle of hardship and poverty. If she does succeed in finding a job, she must find someone to take care of her children, since she cannot afford to hire a baby-sitter or pay for day care. From her standpoint, she will take in more money if she accepts welfare payments from the government and tries to find illegal part-time jobs that pay cash not reported to the government rather than find a regular full-time job paying minimum wage. Even though welfare will not get her out of poverty, if she finds a regular job she will lose her welfare altogether. As a result, she and her family may even be worse off economically.

TABLE 7.6

Families with Children: Percentage in Poverty, by Race and Ethnicity, Marital Status, and Sex of Head of Household, 2002

	MARRIED COUPLE	MALE HEAD	FEMALE HEAD
White	4.1	10.4	26.2
Black	8.5	26.5	41.3
Latino	17.7	23.6	41.4
Asian	5.9	19	21.2

SOURCE: U.S. Bureau of the Census, 2003d.

CHILDREN IN POVERTY

Given the high rates of poverty among families headed by single women, it follows that children are the principal victims of poverty in the United States. Child poverty rates (defined as poverty among people under eighteen) in the United States are by far the highest in the industrial world. Nonetheless, the child poverty rate has varied considerably over the last forty years, declining when the economy expands or the government increases spending on antipoverty programs and rising when the economy slows and government antipoverty spending falls. The child poverty rate declined from 27.3 percent of all children in 1959 to 14.4 percent in 1973—a period associated with both economic growth and the War on Poverty declared by the Johnson administration (1963–1969). During the late 1970s and 1980s, as economic growth slowed and cutbacks were made in government antipoverty programs, child poverty grew, exceeding 20 percent during much of the period. The economic expansion of the 1990s saw a drop in child poverty rates, and in 2002 the rate had fallen to 16.3 percent, a twenty-year low (U.S. Bureau of the Census, 2003e).

The statistics are significantly higher for racial minorities and children of single mothers. In 2002, those in poverty included 8.9 percent of white children, 28.2 percent of Latino children, 32.1 percent of black children, and 56.4 percent of children who lived with single mothers (U.S. Bureau of the Census, 2003f).

Child poverty is not due only to the state of the national economy, or government spending on antipoverty programs. As the above statistics show, child poverty is most severe among children who live with single mothers. During the past forty years, the number of single-parent families headed by women more than doubled, contributing to the increase in child poverty.

Explaining Poverty: The Sociological Debate

Explanations of poverty can be grouped under two main headings: theories that see poor individuals as responsible for their own poverty and theories that view poverty as produced and reproduced by structural forces in society. These competing approaches are sometimes described as "blame the victim" and "blame the system" theories, respectively. We shall briefly examine each in turn.

There is a long history of attitudes that hold the poor responsible for their own disadvantaged positions. Early efforts to address the effects of poverty, such as the poorhouses of the nineteenth century, were grounded in a belief that poverty was the result of an inadequacy or pathology of individuals. The poor were seen as those who were unable—due to lack of skills, moral or physical weakness, absence of motivation, or below-average ability—to succeed in society. Social standing was taken as a reflection of a person's talent and effort; those who deserved to succeed did so, while others less capable were doomed to fail. The existence of winners and losers was regarded as a fact of life.

Such outlooks have enjoyed a renaissance, beginning in the 1970s and 1980s, as the political emphasis on entrepreneurship and individual ambition rewarded those who "succeeded" in society and held those who did not responsible for the circumstances in which they found themselves. Often explanations for poverty were sought in the lifestyles of poor people, along with the attitudes and outlooks they supposedly espoused. Oscar Lewis (1968) set forth one of the most influential of such theories, arguing that a **culture of poverty** exists among many poor people. According to Lewis, poverty is not a result of individual inadequacies, but is a result of a larger social and cultural atmosphere into which poor children are socialized. The culture of poverty is transmitted across generations because young people from an early age see little point in aspiring to something more. Instead, they resign themselves fatalistically to a life of impoverishment.

The culture of poverty thesis has been taken further by the American sociologist Charles Murray. According to Murray, individuals who are poor through "no fault of their own"—such as widows or widowers, orphans, or the disabled—fall into a different category from those who are part of the **dependency cul-**

ture. By this term, Murray refers to poor people who rely on government welfare provision rather than entering the labor market. He argues that the growth of the welfare state has created a subculture that undermines personal ambition and the capacity for self-help. Rather than orienting themselves toward the future and striving to achieve a better life, those dependent on welfare are content to accept handouts. Welfare, he argues, has eroded people's incentive to work (Murray, 1984).

Theories such as these seem to resonate among the U.S. population. Surveys have shown that the majority of Americans regard the poor as responsible for their own poverty and are suspicious of those who live "for free" on "government handouts." Many believe that people on welfare could find work if they were determined to do so. Yet, as we have seen, these views are out of line with the realities of poverty.

A second approach to explaining poverty emphasizes larger social processes that produce conditions of poverty that are difficult for individuals to overcome. According to such a view, structural forces within society—factors like class, gender, ethnicity, occupational position, education attainment, and so forth—shape the way in which resources are distributed (Wilson, 1996). Writers who advocate structural explanations for poverty argue that the lack of ambition among the poor that is often taken for the dependency culture is in fact a *consequence* of their constrained situations, not a cause of it. Reducing poverty is not a matter of changing individual outlooks, they claim, but instead requires policy measures aimed at distributing income and resources more equally throughout society. Child-care subsidies, a minimum hourly wage, and guaranteed income levels for families are examples of policy measures that have sought to redress persistent social inequalities.

Both theories have enjoyed broad support, and we consistently encourage variations of each view in public debates about poverty. Critics of the culture of poverty view accuse its advocates of "individualizing" poverty and blaming the poor for circumstances largely beyond their control. They see the poor as victims, not as freeloaders who are abusing the system. Yet we should be cautious about accepting uncritically the arguments of those who see the causes of poverty as lying exclusively in the structure of society itself. Such an approach implies that the poor simply passively accept the difficult situations in which they find themselves.

Combating Poverty: Welfare Systems

Well-developed and systematically administered welfare programs, in conjunction with government policies that actively assist in keeping down unemployment, reduce poverty levels.

But an economic and political price has to be paid for this. Such a society requires high levels of taxation; and the government bureaucracies needed to administer the complex welfare system tend to acquire considerable power, even though they are not democratically elected.

Being poor does not necessarily mean being *mired* in poverty. A substantial proportion of people in poverty at any one time have either enjoyed superior conditions of life previously or can be expected to climb out of poverty at some time in the future.

As we saw in the last section, critics of existing welfare institutions in the United States have argued that these produce "welfare dependency," meaning that people become dependent on the very programs that are supposed to allow them to forge an independent and meaningful life for themselves. They become not just materially dependent, but psychologically dependent on the arrival of the welfare check. Instead of taking an active attitude toward their lives, they tend to adopt a resigned and passive one, looking to the welfare system to support them.

Others deny that such dependency is widespread. "Being on welfare" is commonly regarded as a source of shame, they say, and most people who are in such a position probably strive actively to escape from it as far as possible.

However widespread it may be, tackling welfare dependency has become a main target of attempts at reform of American welfare institutions. Among the most significant of such reforms have been welfare-to-work programs, whose driving force is to move recipients from public assistance into paid jobs. Daniel Friedlander and Gary Burtless (1994) studied four different government-initiated programs designed to encourage welfare recipients to find paid work. The programs were roughly similar. They provided financial benefits for welfare recipients who actively searched for jobs as well as guidance in job hunting techniques and opportunities for education and training. The target populations were mainly single-parent family heads of households who were recipients of Aid to Families with Dependent Children, at the time, the largest cash welfare program in the country. Friedlander and Burtless found that the programs did achieve results. People involved in such programs were able either to enter employment or to start working sooner than others who didn't participate. In all four programs, the earnings produced were several times greater than the net cost of the program. The programs were least effective, however, in helping those who needed them the most—those who had been out of work for a lengthy period, the long-term unemployed (Friedlander and Burtless, 1994).

In 1996, Congress enacted and President Bill Clinton signed a law to "end welfare as we know it." The resulting program, Temporary Assistance for Needy Families (TANF), required that welfare recipients begin work after receiving benefits for

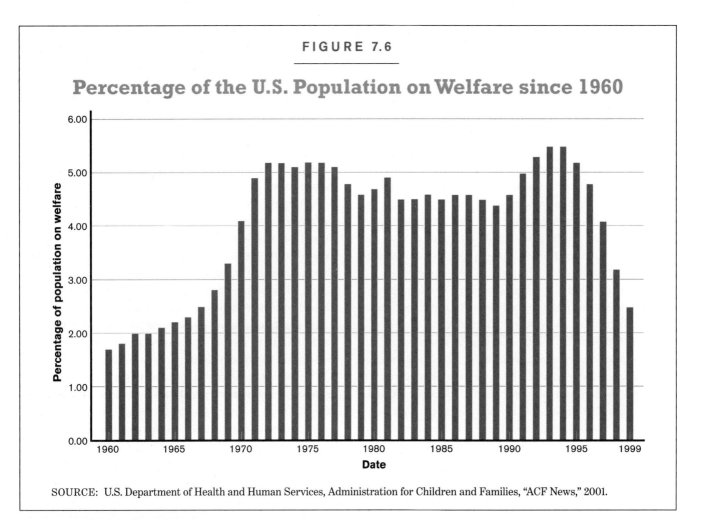

FIGURE 7.6

Percentage of the U.S. Population on Welfare since 1960

SOURCE: U.S. Department of Health and Human Services, Administration for Children and Families, "ACF News," 2001.

two years. Families were cut off entirely after a cumulative five years of assistance. Prior to this reform, there were no time limits or work requirements imposed by the federal government for welfare recipients, many of whom are single mothers.

Although welfare-to-work programs succeeded in reducing welfare claims from 5.1 million families to 2.7 million families in its first three years (see Figure 7.6), some statistics suggest that the outcomes are not entirely positive. Among those who had left welfare for work, only 61 percent had found jobs, 20 percent relied on help from family members or private charities, and about 19 percent had no work or source of independent income. Among those working, the average wage was $6.61 an hour. For about half of this group, this amounted to less than what they had received from the welfare system. Only 23 percent had health insurance through their employer. In Wisconsin, the state that was one of the first to introduce welfare-to-work programs, two thirds of former welfare recipients live below the poverty line. Most have difficulty finding enough money for food and other essentials (Loprest, 1999).

Kathryn Edin and Laura Lein (1997) have shown that for low-income mothers, the costs of leaving welfare for work can outweigh the advantages. These mothers face expenses for food, rent, and other necessities that often exceed their income. Mothers who work must often pay for child care, so that their expenses surpass those of unemployed mothers. In addition, the jobs available to low-income mothers tend to be less stable and to pay less than welfare.

Because their expenses exceed their income, both working and welfare mothers must often find other sources of money. Mothers on welfare tend to rely on aid from charitable agencies or side work, which is likely to be unreported. (Reporting additional income can reduce or end welfare benefits.) Low-income working mothers also rely on support from people in their social networks, such as family members or boyfriends, to help pay the costs of daily life. Pointing to such findings, critics argue that the apparent success of the welfare-to-work initiatives in reducing the number of people on welfare conceals some troublesome patterns in the actual experiences of those who lose their welfare benefits. Moreover, even the most hopeful studies were conducted during a period of economic expansion. When growth slows—or declines—it will be increasingly difficult, if not impossible, for welfare recipients to find any jobs at all.

Social Exclusion

What are the social processes that lead to a large number of people's being marginalized in society? The idea of **social exclusion** refers to new sources of inequality—ways in which individuals may become cut off from involvement in the wider society. It is a broader concept than that of the underclass and has the advantage that it emphasizes *processes*—mechanisms of exclusion. For instance, people who live in a dilapidated housing project, with poor schools and few employment opportunities in the area, may effectively be denied opportunities for self-betterment that most people in society have. It is also different from poverty as such. It focuses attention on a broad range of factors that prevent individuals or groups from having opportunities that are open to the majority of the population.

Social exclusion can take a number of forms, so that it may occur in isolated rural communities cut off from many services and opportunities or in inner-city neighborhoods marked by high crime rates and substandard housing. Exclusion and inclusion may be seen in economic terms, political terms, and social terms.

The concept of social exclusion raises the question of agency. After all, the word *exclusion* implies that someone or something is being shut out by another. Certainly in some instances, individuals are excluded through decisions that lie outside their own control. Banks might refuse to grant a current account or credit cards to individuals living in a certain zip code. Insurance companies might reject an application for a policy on the basis of an applicant's personal history and background. An employee laid off later in life may be refused further jobs on the basis of his or her age.

But social exclusion is not only the result of people's being excluded; it can also result from people excluding themselves from aspects of mainstream society. Individuals can choose to drop out of education, to turn down a job opportunity and become economically inactive, or to abstain from voting in political elections. In considering the phenomenon of social exclusion, we must once again be conscious of the interaction between human agency and responsibility on the one hand and the role of social forces in shaping people's circumstances on the other hand.

Crime and Social Exclusion

Some sociologists have argued that in industrialized societies such as the United States there are strong links between crime and social exclusion. There is a trend among late modern societies, they argue, away from inclusive goals (based on citizenship rights) and toward arrangements that accept and even promote the exclusion of some citizens (Young, 1998,

1999). Crime rates may be reflecting the fact that a growing number of people do not feel valued by—or feel they have an investment in—the societies in which they live.

Elliott Currie is a sociologist who has investigated the connections between social exclusion and crime in the United States, particularly among young people. Currie argues that American society is a "natural laboratory" that is already demonstrating the "ominous underside" of market-driven social policy: rising poverty and homelessness, drug abuse, and violent crime. He notes that young people are increasingly growing up on their own without the guidance and support they need from the adult population. While faced by the seductive lure of the market and consumer goods, young people are also confronted by diminishing opportunities in the labor market to sustain a livelihood. This can result in a profound sense of relative deprivation and a willingness to turn to illegitimate means of sustaining a desired lifestyle.

According to Currie, there are several main links between crime and social exclusion. First, shifts in the labor market and government taxation and minimum wage policies have led to an enormous growth in both relative and absolute poverty within the American population. Second, this rise in social exclusion is felt in local communities, which suffer from a loss of stable livelihoods, transient populations, increasingly expensive housing, and a weakening of social cohesion. Third, economic deprivation and community fragmentation strain family life. Adults in many poor families are forced to take on multiple jobs to survive—a situation that produces perpetual stress, anxiety, and absence from home. The socialization and nurturing of children is, as a result, weakened; the overall "social impoverishment" of the community means that there is little opportunity for parents to turn to other families or relatives for support. Fourth, the state has rolled back many of the programs and public services that could reincorporate the socially excluded, such as early childhood intervention, child care, and mental health care.

Finally, the standards of economic status and consumption that are promoted within society cannot be met through legitimate means by the socially excluded population. According to Currie, one of the most troublesome dimensions to this connection between social exclusion and crime is that legitimate channels are bypassed in favor of illegal ones. Crime is favored over alternative means, such as the political system or community organization (Currie, 1998).

THE HOMELESS

No discussion of social exclusion is complete without reference to the people who are traditionally seen as at the very bottom of the social hierarchy: the **homeless.** The growing problem of homelessness is one of the most distressing signs of changes in the American stratification system. The homeless are a

With a sign for assistance strapped to his back, Rick Cathy, his wife, and their five-year-old daughter make their way to Sacramento. The family, originally from Buffalo, New York, was on the road continuously for more than eighteen months after losing their home.

percent increase in the number of homeless families applying for help over the previous year (Bernstein, 2001).

There are many reasons why people become homeless. One problem is that about a third of the homeless suffer from mental illness, and a third are substance abusers; as many as half have both problems (Blau, 1992; Burt, 1992). One reason for the widespread incidence of such problems among the homeless is that many public mental hospitals have closed their doors. The number of beds in state mental hospitals has declined by as many as half a million since the early 1960s, leaving many mentally ill people with no institutional alternative to a life on the streets or in homeless shelters. Such problems are compounded by the fact that many homeless people lack family, relatives, or other social networks to provide support.

The rising cost of housing is another factor, particularly in light of the increased poverty noted elsewhere in this chapter. Declining incomes at the bottom, along with rising rents, create an affordability gap between the cost of housing and what poor people can pay in rents (Dreier and Appelbaum, 1992). An estimated 5.4 million families spend more than half of their income on housing, leaving them barely a paycheck away from a missed rental payment and eventual eviction (NLIHC, 2000). The housing affordability gap has been worsened by the loss of government programs aimed at providing low-cost housing for the poor during the 1980s, which removed a crucial safety net just as poverty was increasing in the United States.

The sociological imagination enables us to understand how personal characteristics and larger social forces can combine to increase the risk of becoming homeless. Imagine two hard-working people with similar personal problems—for example, both struggle with alcoholism, depression, and family problems. One is an unskilled worker in a low-wage job, whereas the other is a doctor with a substantial income. Which one is more likely to become homeless?

The unskilled worker has little margin for mistakes, misfortunes, or economic changes that could threaten his or her job. During a time when American firms are moving their lowest-paying, least-skilled work overseas, the workers who hold such jobs are especially vulnerable to job loss and homelessness. A bout with too much drinking might be all that it takes to be thrown out of work. On the other hand, the doctor's job is unlikely to be threatened by globalization. Furthermore, he or she most likely has health insurance that covers counseling for personal problems and perhaps even costly treatment for alcoholism. There are likely other resources to fall back on as well: savings, investments, credit and loans, and friends and family who can afford to help out. This is not to say that only poor people run the risk of becoming homeless: If you have ever volunteered at a homeless shelter, you may have been surprised to encounter formerly middle-class families who "ran out of luck." But the people overwhelmingly

common sight in nearly every U.S. city and town and are increasingly found in rural areas as well. Two generations ago, the homeless were mainly elderly, alcoholic men who were found on the skid rows of the largest metropolitan areas. Today they are primarily young single men, often of working age. The fastest-growing group of homeless, however, consists of families with children, who make up as much as 40 percent of those currently homeless (Shinn and Weitzman, 1996). A study by the U.S. Conference of Mayors estimates that about a quarter of the urban homeless population are children under eighteen, while single men make up about half of the population, and single women about one seventh. More than half of the homeless population is African American, and about a third is white. Very few homeless are Latino or Asian American immigrants, possibly because these groups enjoy close-knit family and community ties that provide a measure of security against homelessness (Waxman and Hinderliter, 1996). As many as 40 percent of homeless men are veterans, many of the Vietnam War (Rosenheck et al., 1996).

No one really knows how many homeless people there are, since it is extremely difficult to count people who do not have a stable residence (Appelbaum, 1990). Estimates of the number of homeless vary widely. The most recent estimate is that there are 462,000 homeless people in the United States on any given day, and that 2.3 million adults and children experience a spell of homelessness at least once during a year (Urban Institute, 2000). One survey of twenty-five cities, conducted by the U.S. Conference of Mayors in 2001, found a 17 at risk of becoming homeless are those who face a combination of low-paying jobs, poverty, and high housing costs along with a tangle of personal problems (Burt, 1992).

Theories of Stratification in Modern Societies

So far, we have examined closely types of class division, inequality, social mobility, poverty, and social exclusion. In this section, we step back and look at some broad theories by which thinkers have attempted to *understand* stratification. The most influential theoretical approaches are those developed by Karl Marx and Max Weber. Most subsequent theories of stratification are heavily indebted to their ideas.

Marx: Means of Production and the Analysis of Class

For Marx, the term *class* refers to people who stand in a common relationship to the **means of production**—the means by which they gain a livelihood. In modern societies, the two main classes are those who own the means of production—industrialists, or **capitalists**—and those who earn their living by selling their labor to them, the working class. The relationship between classes, according to Marx, is an exploitative one. In the course of the working day, Marx reasoned, workers produce more than is actually needed by employers to repay the cost of hiring them. This **surplus value** is the source of profit, which capitalists are able to put to their own use. A group of workers in a clothing factory, say, might be able to produce a hundred suits a day. Selling half the suits provides enough income for the manufacturer to pay the workers' wages. Income from the sale of the remainder of the garments is taken as profit.

Marx believed that the maturing of industrial capitalism would bring about an increasing gap between the wealth of the minority and the poverty of the mass of the population. In his view, the wages of the working class could never rise far above subsistence level, while wealth would pile up in the hands of those owning capital. In addition, laborers would daily face work that is physically wearing and mentally tedious, as is the situation in many factories. At the lowest levels of society, particularly among those frequently or permanently unemployed, there would develop an "accumulation of misery, agony of labor, slavery, ignorance, brutality, moral degradation" (1977).

Marx was right about the persistence of poverty in industrialized countries and in anticipating that large inequalities of wealth and income would continue. He was wrong in supposing that the income of most of the population would remain extremely low. Most people in Western countries today are much better off materially than were comparable groups in Marx's day.

Weber: Class and Status

There are two main differences between Weber's theory and that of Marx. First, according to Weber, class divisions derive not only from control or lack of control of the means of production, but from economic differences that have nothing directly to do with property. Such resources include especially people's skills and credentials, or qualifications. Those in managerial or professional occupations earn more and enjoy more favorable conditions at work, for example, than people in blue-collar jobs. The qualifications they possess, such as degrees, diplomas, and the skills they have acquired, make them more "marketable" than others without such qualifications. At a lower level, among blue-collar workers, skilled craft workers are able to secure higher wages than the semiskilled or unskilled.

Second, Weber distinguished another aspect of stratification besides class, which he called "status." *Status* refers to differences between groups in the social honor, or prestige, they are accorded by others. Status distinctions can vary independent of class divisions. Social honor may be either positive or negative. For instance, doctors and lawyers have high prestige in American society. **Pariah groups,** on the other hand, are negatively privileged status groups, subject to discrimination that prevents them from taking advantage of opportunities open to others. The Jews were a pariah group in medieval Europe, banned from participating in certain occupations and from holding official positions.

Possession of wealth normally tends to confer high status, but there are exceptions to this principle. In Britain, for instance, individuals from aristocratic families continue to enjoy considerable social esteem even after their fortunes have been lost. Conversely, "new money" is often looked on with some scorn by the well-established wealthy.

Whereas class is an objective measure, status depends on people's subjective evaluations of social differences. Classes derive from the economic factors associated with property and earnings; status is governed by the varying lifestyles that groups follow.

Weber's writings on stratification are important because they show that other dimensions of stratification besides class strongly influence people's lives. Most sociologists hold that Weber's scheme offers a more flexible and sophisticated basis for analyzing stratification than that provided by Marx.

Davis and Moore: The Functions of Stratification

Kingsley Davis and Wilbert E. Moore (1945) provided a functionalist explanation of stratification, arguing that it has beneficial consequences for society. They claimed that certain positions or roles in society are functionally more important than others, such as brain surgeons, and these positions require special skills for their performance. However, only a limited number of individuals in any society have the talents or experience appropriate to these positions. In order to attract the most qualified people, rewards need to be offered, such as money, power, and prestige. Davis and Moore determined that since the benefits of different positions in any society must be unequal, then all societies must be stratified. They concluded that social stratification and social inequality are functional because they ensure that the most qualified people, attracted by the rewards bestowed by society, fill the roles that are most important to a smoothly functioning society.

Davis and Moore's theory suggests that a person's social position is based solely on his innate talents and efforts. Not surprisingly, their theory has been met with criticism by other sociologists. For example, Melvin Tumin critiqued the theory for several reasons (Tumin, 1953). First, he argued that the functional importance of a particular role is difficult to measure and that the rewards that a society bestows on those in "important" roles do not necessarily reflect their actual importance. For instance, who is more important to society, a lawyer or a schoolteacher? If, on average, a lawyer earns four or five times the amount that a schoolteacher does, does that accurately reflect his or her relative importance to society? Second, Tumin argued that Davis and Moore overlooked the ways in which stratification limits the discovery of talent in a society. As we have seen, the United States is not entirely a meritocratic society. Those at the top tend to have unequal access to economic and cultural resources, such as the highest quality education, which help the upper classes transmit their privileged status from one generation to the next. For those without access to these resources, even those with superior talents, social inequality serves as a barrier to reaching their full potential.

Growing Inequality in the United States

Throughout this chapter, we have touched on the various ways in which changes in the American economy have affected social stratification, emphasizing the importance of both globalization and changes in information technology. We have pointed out that the global spread of an industrial capitalist economy, driven in part by the information revolution, has helped to break down closed caste systems around the world and replace them with more open class systems. The degree to which this process will result in greater equality in countries undergoing capitalist development will be explored in the next chapter.

What do these changes hold in store for you? On the one hand, new jobs are opening up, particularly in high-technology fields that require special training and skills and pay high wages. A flood of new products is flowing into the United States, many made with cheap labor that has lowered their costs. This has enabled consumers such as yourselves to buy everything from computers to automobiles at costs lower than you otherwise would have paid, thereby contributing to a rising standard of living.

But these benefits come with potentially significant costs. As you have read throughout this chapter, you live in a fast-paced world, in which you may find yourselves competing for jobs with workers in other countries who work for lower wages. This has already been the case for the manufacturing jobs that once provided the economic foundation for the working class and segments of the middle class. Companies that once produced in the United States—from automobiles to apparel to electronics—now use factories around the world, taking advantage of labor costs that are a fraction of those in the United States. Will the same hold true for other, more highly skilled jobs—jobs in the information economy itself? Many jobs that require the use of computers—from graphic design to software engineering—can be done by anyone with a high-speed computer connection, anywhere in the world. The global spread of dot-com companies will open up vastly expanded job opportunities for those with the necessary skills and training—but it will also open up equally expanded global competition for those jobs.

Partly as a result of these forces, inequality has increased in the United States since the early 1970s, resulting in a growing gap between rich and poor. The global economy has permitted the accumulation of vast fortunes at the same time that it has contributed to declining wages, economic hardship, and poverty in the United States. Homelessness is at least in part due to these processes, as is the emergence of an underclass of the new urban poor. Although the working class is especially vulnerable to these changes, the middle class is not exempt: A growing number of middle-class households experienced downward mobility from the late 1970s through the mid-1990s, until a decade of economic growth (now over) benefited all segments of American society. Although it is always hazardous to try to predict the future, global economic integration will likely continue to increase for the foreseeable future.

How this will affect your jobs and careers—and stratification in the United States—is much more difficult to foresee.

The world today is undergoing a transformation as profound as the industrial revolution. The impact of that transformation will be felt well into the twenty-first century, touching our lives in every way. In the next chapter, we will further examine the impact of this transformation on stratification and inequality in other countries in the world, especially the poorer countries that have recently begun to industrialize.

Study Outline

www.wwnorton.com/giddens

Social Stratification

- *Social stratification* refers to the division of people socioeconomically into layers, or strata. When we talk of social stratification, we draw attention to the unequal positions occupied by individuals in society. In the larger traditional societies and in industrialized countries today there is stratification in terms of *wealth,* property, and access to material goods and cultural products.
- Three major types of stratification systems can be distinguished: *slavery, caste,* and *class.* Whereas the first two of these depend on legal or religiously sanctioned inequalities, class divisions are not "officially" recognized but stem from economic factors affecting the material circumstances of people's lives.

Class Systems

- Classes derive from inequalities in possession and control of material resources and access to educational and occupational opportunities. An individual's class position is at least in some part achieved, for it is not simply "given" from birth. Some recent authors have suggested that cultural factors such as lifestyle and consumption patterns are important influences on class position. According to such a view, individual identities are now more structured around lifestyle choices than they are around traditional class indicators such as occupation.
- Class is of major importance in industrialized societies, although there are many complexities in the class system within such societies. The main class divisions are between people in the *upper, middle,* and *lower working classes,* and the *underclass.*

Inequality in the United States

- Most people in modern societies are more affluent today than was the case several generations ago. Yet the distribution of *wealth* and *income* remains highly unequal. Between the early 1970s and the late 1990s, partly as a result of economic globalization, the gap between rich and poor grew. Incomes at the top increased sharply, while many ordinary workers and families saw their incomes drop as higher-wage manufacturing jobs moved offshore to low-wage countries.

Social Mobility

- In the study of *social mobility,* a distinction is made between *intragenerational* and *intergenerational mobility.* The first of these refers to movement up or down the social scale within an individual's working life. Intergenerational mobility is movement across the generations, as when the daughter or son from a blue-collar background becomes a professional. Social mobility is mostly of limited range. Most people remain close to the level of the family from which they came, though the expansion of white-collar jobs in the last few decades has provided the opportunity for considerable short-range upward mobility.

Poverty

- Poverty remains widespread in the United States. Two methods of assessing poverty exist. One involves the notion of *absolute poverty,* which is a lack of the basic resources needed to maintain a healthy existence. *Relative poverty* involves assessing the gaps between the living conditions of some groups and those enjoyed by the majority of the population.
- Problems of declining income and poverty are especially pronounced among racial and ethnic minorities, families headed by single women, and persons lacking education. The *feminization of poverty* is especially strong among young, poorly educated women who are raising children on their own.

Social Exclusion

- Social exclusion refers to processes by which individuals may become cut off from full involvement in the wider society. People who are socially excluded, due to poor housing, inferior schools, or limited transportation, may be denied the opportunities for self-betterment that most people in society have. Homelessness is one of the most extreme forms of social exclusion. Homeless people lacking a permanent residence may be shut out of many everyday activities that most people take for granted.

Theories of Stratification

- The most prominent and influential theories of stratification are those developed by Marx and Weber. Marx placed the primary emphasis on class, which he saw as an objectively given characteristic of the economic structure of society. He saw a fundamental split between the owners of capital and the workers who do not own capital. Weber accepted a similar view, but distinguished another aspect of stratification, *status*. Status refers to the esteem, or "social honor," given to individuals or groups.

Key Concepts

absolute poverty (p. 179)
capitalist (p. 189)
caste society (p. 161)
caste system (p. 161)
class (p. 162)
culture of poverty (p. 184)
dependency culture (p. 184)
endogamy (p. 161)
exchange mobility (p. 174)
feminization of poverty (p. 183)
homeless (p. 187)
income (p. 164)
intergenerational mobility (p. 174)
intragenerational mobility (p. 174)
Kuznets curve (p. 163)
life chances (p. 162)
lower class (p. 171)
means of production (p. 189)
middle class (p. 169)
pariah group (p. 189)
poverty line (p. 179)
relative poverty (p. 179)
short-range downward mobility (p. 178)
slavery (p. 161)
social exclusion (p. 187)
social mobility (p. 174)
social stratification (p. 160)
status (p. 165)
structural mobility (p. 175)
structured inequalities (p. 160)
surplus value (p. 189)
underclass (p. 171)
upper class (p. 167)
vertical mobility (p. 175)
wealth (p. 165)
working class (p. 170)
working poor (p. 182)

Review Questions

1. What is the difference between income and wealth?
   a. Income is the wages and salaries that you earn; wealth is what you are worth if you sell everything you own.
   b. Income is salary; wealth is the interest that accrues on investments.
   c. Income is money in the bank; wealth is locked up in physical assets.
   d. Income and wealth are the same thing.
2. What is the basis of Karl Marx's theory of class?
   a. Class is a byproduct of the Industrial Revolution.
   b. Modern societies are divided into those who own the means of production and those who sell their labor.
   c. People with power will always use it to protect their material interests.
   d. Class is a transitory system of stratification between feudal estates and the classlessness of communist society.
3. Which of the following is *not* true about the impact of globalization in the United States?
   a. Some manufacturing jobs have been lost.
   b. You may be competing for jobs with someone from a less-developed country.
   c. Inequality has declined as a result of globalization.
   d. Those with high skill levels are likely to get high compensation.
4. According to William Sewell and Robert Hauser, how does family background influence one's educational attainment?
   a. Family background determines the type of school children attended.
   b. Family background is a good indicator of family income, which had a direct impact on the economic resources parents could provide for their children.
   c. Family background influences one's educational aspiration.
   d. Family background influences educational attainment through its cultural capital.
5. What is the difference between intragenerational mobility and intergenerational mobility?
   a. Intragenerational mobility is about matters of social status, whereas intergenerational mobility is about matters of social class.
   b. Intragenerational mobility is the comparison of parents' class position with those achieved by their children, whereas intergenerational mobility is a person's movement up or down the socioeconomic scale in his or her working life.
   c. Intragenerational mobility is a person's movement up or down the socioeconomic scale in his or her working life, whereas intergenerational mobility is the comparison of parents' class position with those achieved by their children.
   d. Intragenerational mobility is a comparison of the occupational achievement of siblings, whereas intergenerational mobility is a comparison of parents' occupational achievement and with that of their children.
6. The feminization of poverty is highest among:
   a. Latino female-headed families.
   b. Asian American female-headed families.
   c. white female-headed families.
   d. all female-headed families.

7. How does Murray explain the cause of the underclass in the inner cities?
   a. Murray maintains that racist barriers are the key to accounting for the urban underclass.
   b. Murray sees economic factors (class) as most important in accounting for the urban underclass.
   c. Murray argues that welfare dependence explains the existence of the urban underclass.
   d. All of the above.
8. What is the relationship between social exclusion and crime?
   a. Social exclusion reduces the crime rate.
   b. Social exclusion increases the crime rate.
   c. Social exclusion has no effect on the crime rate.
   d. No clear evidence is available.
9. Which of the following systems of stratification permits the least amount of mobility?
   a. Caste
   b. Class
   c. Slavery
   d. Clan
10. As the economy prospers and more better-paying jobs become available, the result will be more
   a. exchange mobility.
   b. structural mobility.
   c. downward mobility.
   d. none of the above.

Thinking Sociologically Exercises

1. If you were doing your own study of status differences in your community, how would you measure people's social class? Base your answer on the textbook's discussion of these matters to explain why you would take the particular measurement approach you've chosen. What would be its value(s) and shortcoming(s) compared with adopting alternative measurement procedures?
2. Using occupation and occupational change as your mobility criteria, view the social mobility within your family for three generations. As you discuss the differences in jobs among your grandfather, father, and yourself, apply all these terms correctly: *vertical* and *horizontal mobility*, *upward* and *downward mobility*, *intragenerational* and *intergenerational mobility*. Explain fully why you think people in your family have moved up, moved down, or remained at the same status level.

Data Exercises

www.wwnorton.com/giddens
Keyword: Data7

- As you learned in Chapter 7, the stratification that exists among different groups of individuals is not only real, but has important consequences. These structured inequalities influence opportunities for achieving economic prosperity, referred to as *life chances* by sociologists. The data exercise for Chapter 7 explores the differences in social class at the community level.

Global Inequality: Differences Among Countries

Understand the systematic differences in wealth and power among countries.

Life in Rich and Poor Countries

Recognize the impact of different economic standards of living on people throughout the world.

Can Poor Countries Become Rich?

Analyze the success of the newly industrializing economies.

Theories of Global Inequality

Consider various theories explaining why some societies are wealthier than others, as well as how global inequality can be overcome.

Why Global Economic Inequality Matters to You

CHAPTER EIGHT

GLOBAL INEQUALITY

the past quarter century has seen the appearance of more global billionaires than ever before in history. In 2004, there were 587 billionaires worldwide—277 in the United States, 164 in Europe, 73 in Asia, 25 in Latin America, 17 in Canada, 24 in the Middle East, 5 in Australia, and 2 in Africa (*Forbes*, 2004). Their combined assets in 2004 were estimated at $1.9 trillion—greater than the total gross national income of 140 countries (calculated from World Bank, 2003). The success of America's high-technology economy, coupled with the financial crisis that struck Asia in the late 1990s, enabled the United States to lay claim to over half the world's billionaires.

As of 2004, the wealthiest person in the world was Microsoft Corporation's founder Bill Gates, with a net worth of $46.6 billion in that year—down from $63 billion in 2000, thanks to the decline in the stock market. Gates, whose fortune is based largely on ownership of his company's stock, would seem the personification of American entrepreneurialism: a computer nerd turned capitalist whose software provides the operating system for nearly all personal computers. During the late 1990s, Gates was the first person in history to have a net worth in excess of $100 billion. Shortly after achieving this mark, the lofty value of Microsoft's stock began to decline, leaving Gates's fortune greatly reduced but still sufficient to rank him number one in wealth in the world.

Gates was followed by the financier Warren Buffett, at $42.9 billion. Buffet is an investor and CEO of Berkshire Hathway, Inc., which owns companies such as Geico Direct Auto Insurance, Dairy Queen, and See's Candies. In 2003, Buffet became an adviser to California's governor,

Arnold Schwarzenegger. Next came Karl Albrecht, with $23 billion. Albrecht is the owner of the German discount supermarket chain Aldi and the American gourmet grocery store Trader Joe's. Fourth on the list is Prince Alwaleed Bin Talal Alsaud of Saudi Arabia, whose investments have established his worth at $21.5 billion. Now this nephew of the king is transforming himself from businessman to activist, calling for a range of reforms in his country: elections, women's rights, and job creation. Among the twenty-five richest people, thirteen were from the United States, five were from Europe, two were from Hong Kong, two were from Russia, one was from Canada, one was from Saudi Arabia, and one was from Mexico (*Forbes,* 2004). If Bill gates typifies the American high-tech entrepreneur, Hong Kong's Li Ka-shing—who was number 19 on the list and Asia's richest man—is the hero in a rags-to-riches story that characterizes the success of many Asian businessmen. Li (his surname) began his career by making plastic flowers; in 2004, his $12.4 billion in personal wealth derived from a wide range of real estate and other investments throughout Asia.

Globalization—the increased economic, political, and social interconnectedness of the world—has produced the opportunities for unthinkable wealth. Yet at the same time it has produced widespread poverty and suffering. Consider, for example, Wirat Tasago, a twenty-four-year-old garment worker in Bangkok, Thailand. Tasago—along with more than a million other Thai garment workers, most of whom are women—labors from 8 A.M. until about 11 P.M. six days a week, earning little more than $3 an hour working days that can last sixteen hours (Dahlburg, 1995). Billions of workers such as Tasago are being drawn into the global labor force, many working in oppressive conditions that would be unacceptable, if not unimaginable, under U.S. labor laws. And these are the fortunate ones: Those who remain outside the global economy are frequently even worse off.

In the previous chapter, we examined the American class structure, noting vast differences among individuals' income, wealth, work, and quality of life. The same is true in the world as a whole: Just as we can speak of rich or poor individuals within a country, so we can talk about rich or poor countries in the world system. A country's position in the global economy affects how its people live, work, and even die. In this chapter, we look closely at the systematic differences in wealth and power between countries in the late twentieth and early twenty-first centuries. We examine what differences in economic standards of living mean for people throughout the world. We then turn to the newly industrializing economies of the world to understand which countries are improving their fortunes and why. This will lead us to a discussion of different theories that attempt to explain why global inequality exists and what can be done about it. We conclude by speculating on the future of economic inequality in a global world.

Global Inequality: Differences Among Countries

Global inequality refers to the systematic differences in wealth and power that exist among countries. These differences between countries exist alongside differences within countries: Even the wealthiest countries today have growing numbers of poor people, while less wealthy nations are producing many of the world's superrich. Sociology's challenge is not merely to identify all such differences, but to explain why they occur—and how they might be overcome.

One simple way to classify countries in terms of global inequality is to compare the wealth produced by each country for its average citizen. This approach measures the value of a country's yearly output of goods and services produced by its total population and then divides that total by the number of people in the country. The resulting measure is termed the *per-capita gross national income (GNI),* a measure of the country's yearly output of goods and services per person. The World Bank (2003), an international lending organization that provides loans for development projects in poorer countries, uses this measure to classify countries as high-income (an annual 2002 per person gross national income of $9,076 or more, in 2002 dollars), upper-middle-income ($2,936–9,075), lower-middle-income ($736–2,935), or low-income (under $735). This system of classification will help us better understand why there are such vast differences in living standards between countries.

Figure 8.1 shows how the World Bank (2003) divides 132 countries, containing nearly 6 billion people, into the three economic classes. (There are 74 other economies in the world, encompassing about 178 million people, for which the World Bank did not provide data, either because the data were lacking or because the economies had fewer than 1.5 million people.) The figure shows that while 40 percent of the world's population live in low-income countries, only 16 percent live in high-income countries. Bear in mind that this classification is based on *average* income for each country; it therefore masks income inequality *within* each country. Such differences can be significant, although we do not focus on them in this chapter. For example, the World Bank classifies India as a low-income country, since its per-person gross national income in

FIGURE 8.1

Population and Per Capita Income in Low-, Middle-, and High-Income Countries, 2002

Like most countries, the world as a whole is highly unequal. Forty percent of the people in the world live in low-income countries, while 16 percent live in high-income countries. The average income of people in high-income countries is 63 times that of people in low-income countries. The remainder of the world's population—about 44 percent—live in middle-income countries. According to the World Bank, the world has become considerably more "middle class" in recent years: In 1999, the World Bank reclassified China from low-income to middle-income, moving its 1.3 billion people (22 percent of the world's population) into the latter category. Although China's average income has risen to global middle-class standards, the large majority of China's people remain distinctly low income.

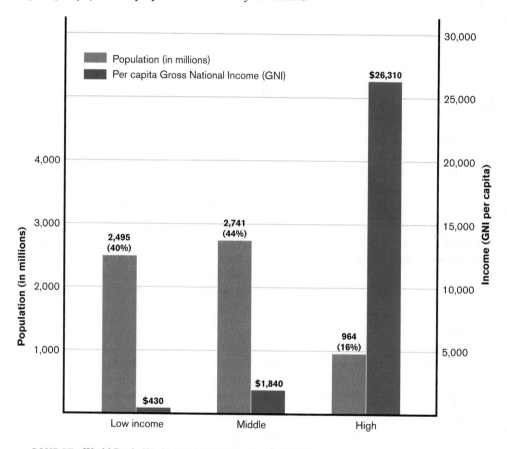

SOURCE: World Bank, World Development Indicators, 2003.

2002 was only $480. Yet despite widespread poverty, India also boasts a large and growing middle class. China, on the other hand, was reclassified in 1999 from low- to middle-income, since its gross national income per capita in that year was $780 (recall the World Bank's lower limit for a middle-income country is $736). Yet even though its average income

now confers middle-class status on China, it nonetheless has hundreds of millions of people living in poverty.

Comparing countries on the basis of economic output alone may be misleading, however, since gross national income includes only goods and services that are produced for cash sale. Many people in low-income countries are farmers or herders who produce for their own families or for barter, involving non-cash transactions. The value of their crops and animals is not taken into account in the statistics. Further, economic output is not a country's whole story: Countries possess unique and widely differing languages and traditions. Poor countries are no less rich in history and culture than their wealthier neighbors, but the lives of their people are much harsher.

High-Income Countries

The *high-income countries* are generally those that were the first to industrialize, a process that began in England some two hundred fifty years ago and then spread to Europe, the United States, and Canada. About thirty years ago, Japan joined the ranks of high-income, industrialized nations, while Singapore, Hong Kong, and Taiwan moved into this category only within the last decade or so. The reasons for the success of these Asian latecomers to industrialization are much debated by sociologists and economists. We will look at these reasons later in the chapter.

High-income countries account for only 16 percent of the world's population (roughly 965 million people)—yet lay claim to almost 81 percent of the world's annual output of wealth (derived from World Bank, 2003b). High-income countries offer decent housing, adequate food, drinkable water, and other comforts unknown in many parts of the world. Although these countries often have large numbers of poor people, most of their inhabitants enjoy a standard of living unimaginable by the majority of the world's people.

Middle-Income Countries

The *middle-income countries* are primarily found in East and Southeast Asia and also include the oil-rich countries of the Middle East and North Africa, the Americas (Mexico, Central America, Cuba and other countries in the Caribbean, and South America), and the once communist republics that formerly made up the Soviet Union and its East European allies (see Global Map 8.1). Most of these countries began to industrialize relatively late in the twentieth century and therefore are not yet as industrially developed (nor as wealthy) as the high-income countries. The countries that the Soviet Union once comprised, on the other hand, are highly industrialized, although their living standards have eroded during the past decade as a result of the collapse of communism and the move to capitalist economies. In Russia, for example, the wages of ordinary people dropped by nearly a third between 1998 and 1999, while retirement pensions dropped by nearly

half: Millions of people, many of them elderly, suddenly found themselves destitute (CIA, 2000).

In 2002, middle-income countries included 44 percent of the world's population (2.7 billion people) but accounted for only 16 percent of the wealth produced in that year. Although many people in these countries are substantially better off than their neighbors in low-income countries, most do not enjoy anything resembling the standard of living common in high-income countries. The ranks of the world's middle-income countries expanded between 1999 and 2000, at least according to the World Bank's system of classification, when China—with 1.3 billion people (22 percent of the world's population)—was reclassified from low- to middle-income because of its economic growth. This reclassification is somewhat misleading, however. China's average per-person income of $940 per year is barely above the cutoff for low-income countries ($736), and a large majority of its population in fact is low income by World Bank standards.

Low-Income Countries

Finally, the *low-income countries* include much of eastern, western, and sub-Saharan Africa; Vietnam, Cambodia, Indonesia, and a few other East Asian countries; India, Nepal, Bangladesh, and Pakistan in South Asia; East and Central European countries such as Georgia and Ukraine; and Haiti and Nicaragua in the Western Hemisphere. These countries have mostly agricultural economies and are only recently beginning to industrialize. Scholars debate the reasons for their late industrialization and widespread poverty, as we will see later in this chapter.

In 2002, the low-income countries included over 40 percent of the world's population (2.5 billion people) yet produced only 3.4 percent of the world's yearly output of wealth. What is more, this inequality is increasing. Fertility is much higher in low-income countries than elsewhere, where large families provide additional farm labor or otherwise contribute to family income. (In wealthy industrial societies, where children are more likely to be in school than on the farm, the economic benefit of large families declines, so people tend to have fewer children.) Because of this, the populations of low-income countries (with the principal exception of India) are growing more than three times as fast as those of high-income countries (see Table 8.1).

In many of these low-income countries, people struggle with poverty, malnutrition, and even starvation. Most people live in rural areas, although this is rapidly changing: Hundreds of millions of people are moving to huge, densely populated cities, where they live either in dilapidated housing or on the open streets (see Chapter 15).

Growing Global Inequality: The Rich Get Richer, the Poor Get Poorer

During the last thirty years, the overall standard of living in the world has slowly risen. The average global citizen is today better off than ever before (see Table 8.2). Illiteracy is down, infant deaths and malnutrition are less common, people are living longer, average income is higher, and poverty is down. Since these figures are averages, however, they hide the substantial differences among countries: Many of these gains have been in the high- and middle-income countries, while living standards in many of the poorest countries have declined. Overall, the gap between rich and poor countries has widened.

From 1988 to 2002, average per-person GDP rose 34 percent in low-income countries and 54 percent in high-income countries, widening the global gap between rich and poor (see Figure 8.2). (Average income in middle-income countries remained largely unchanged.) By 2002, the average person in a typical high-income country earned $26,310, sixty-one times as much as the roughly $310 earned by his or her counterpart in a low-income country. Some 1.5 billion people—about a quarter of the world's population at that time—were estimated to live in poverty (World Bank, 2000–2001).

TABLE 8.1

Differences in Fertility and Population Growth: Low-, Middle-, and High-Income Countries

	INCOME LEVEL		
	LOW	MIDDLE	HIGH
Annual births per woman, 2002	3.5	2.1	1.7
Average yearly percent population growth, 1990–2002	1.6	1.3	.06

NOTE: No data for 1997.

SOURCE: World Bank, World Development Indicators, 2003.

TABLE 8.2

The Global Quality of Life Has Risen During the Past 30 Years

QUALITY OF LIFE INDICATORS	1968	1998
Percentage illiterate	53	30
Average number of children per woman	6	3
Number of children who die in first year	1 in 4	1 in 8
Number of infants who die each year	12 million	7 million
Number of people suffering from malnutrition	4 out of 10	2 out of 10
Life expectancy at birth	50 years	61 years
Annual per person income	roughly $700	roughly $1,100
Percentage living on less than $1/day	roughly 50	roughly 25

SOURCE: Salter, 1998.

Rich and Poor Countries: The World by Income, 2002

Like individuals in a country, the countries of the world as a whole can be seen as economically stratified. In general, those countries that experienced industrialization the earliest are the richest, while those that remain agricultural are the poorest. An enormous—and growing—gulf separates the two groups.

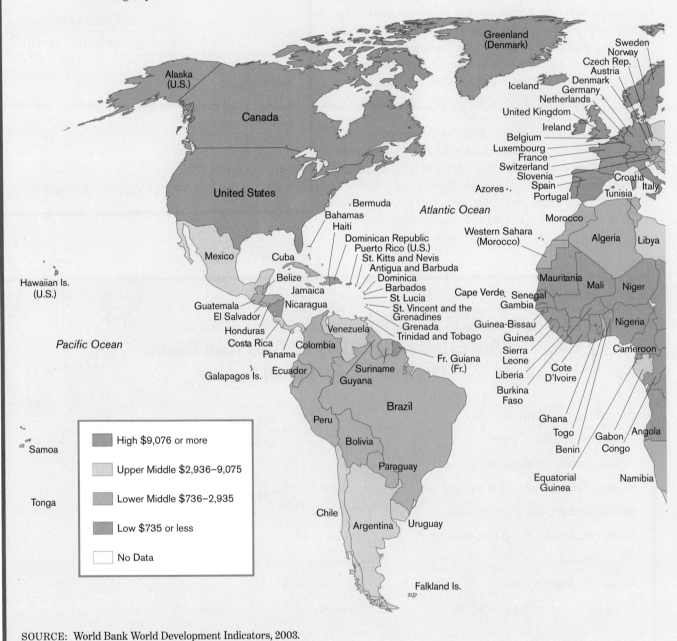

Legend:
- High $9,076 or more
- Upper Middle $2,936–9,075
- Lower Middle $736–2,935
- Low $735 or less
- No Data

SOURCE: World Bank World Development Indicators, 2003.

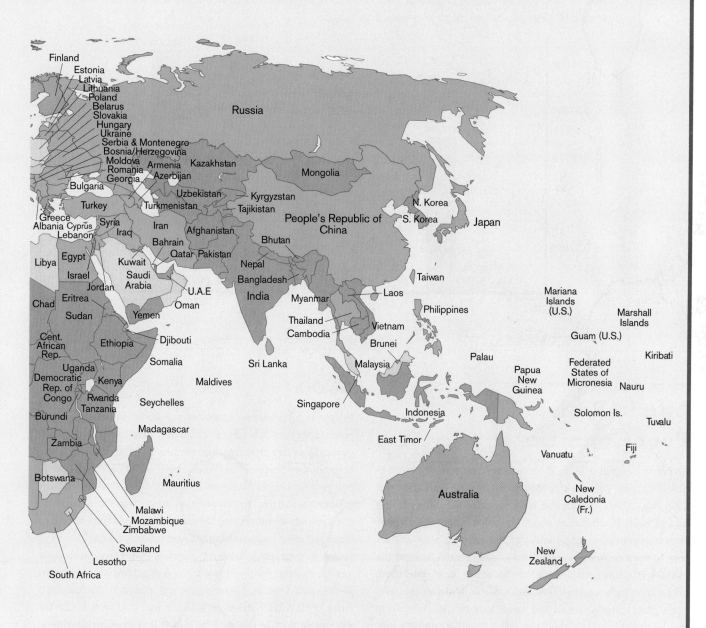

Finland
Estonia
Latvia
Lithuania
Poland
Belarus
Slovakia
Hungary
Ukraine
Serbia & Montenegro
Bosnia/Herzegovina
Moldova
Romania
Georgia
Bulgaria
Turkey
Greece
Albania Cyprus
Lebanon
Libya
Egypt
Israel
Jordan
Chad
Eritrea
Sudan
Cent.
African
Rep.
Uganda
Democratic
Rep. of
Congo
Burundi
Rwanda
Tanzania
Zambia
Botswana
Malawi
Mozambique
Zimbabwe
Swaziland
Lesotho
South Africa

Russia

Armenia
Azerbijan

Kazakhstan

Syria
Iraq

Iran

Uzbekistan

Turkmenistan
Tajikistan

Kyrgyzstan

Mongolia

Afghanistan

Bhutan

Bahrain
Qatar Pakistan
Kuwait
Saudi
Arabia
U.A.E
Oman

Yemen

Djibouti

Ethiopia

Somalia

Kenya

Seychelles

Madagascar

Mauritius

Nepal
Bangladesh
India

Sri Lanka

Maldives

People's Republic of
China

N. Korea
S. Korea

Japan

Taiwan

Myanmar

Laos

Thailand
Cambodia

Vietnam

Brunei

Malaysia

Singapore

Philippines

Indonesia

East Timor

Palau

Papua
New
Guinea

Mariana
Islands
(U.S.)

Guam (U.S.)

Federated
States of
Micronesia

Marshall
Islands

Kiribati

Nauru

Solomon Is.

Vanuatu

New
Caledonia
(Fr.)

Australia

Fiji

Tuvalu

New
Zealand

NOTE: The map presents economies classified according to World Bank estimates of 2003 GNI per capita.
Not shown on the map because of space constraints are French Polynesia (high income); American Samoa
(upper middle income); Kiribati and Tonga (lower middle income); and Tuvalu (no data).

FIGURE 8.2

GDP per Person in Low-, Middle-, and High-Income Countries, 1988, 1993, and 2002

Despite overall growth in the global economy, the gap between rich and poor countries has not declined in recent years. Between 1988 and 2000, per-person GDP in low-income countries increased an average of 1.4 percent a year, far less than in high-income countries (2.2 percent). As a consequence, the average person in a high-income country earned roughly 61 times as much as the average person in a low-income country. Average per-person GDP in middle-income countries remained unchanged.

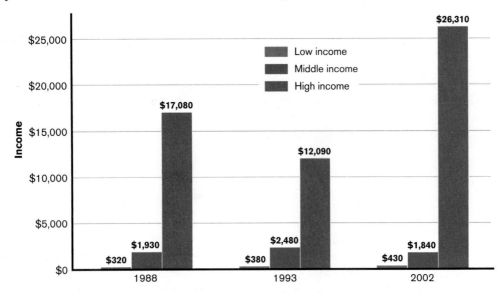

SOURCE: World Bank, 1990, 1995, 2000–2001.

Life in Rich and Poor Countries

An enormous gulf in living standards separates most people in rich countries from their counterparts in poor ones (*Harvard Magazine,* 2000). Wealth and poverty make life different in a host of ways. For instance, about one third of the world's poor are undernourished, and almost all are illiterate and lack access to even primary-school education. Although most of the world is still rural, within a decade there are likely to be more urban than rural poor (World Bank, 1996). Many of the poor come from tribes or racial and ethnic groups that differ from the dominant groups of their countries, and their poverty is at least in part the result of discrimination (Narayan, 1999).

Here we look at differences between high- and low-income countries in terms of health, starvation and famine, and education and literacy.

Health

People in high-income countries are far healthier than their counterparts in low-income countries. Low-income countries generally suffer from inadequate health facilities, and when they do have hospitals or clinics, these seldom serve the poorest people. People living in low-income countries also lack proper sanitation, drink polluted water, and run a much greater risk of contracting infectious diseases. They are more likely to suffer malnourishment, starvation, and famine. All of these factors contribute to physical weakness and poor health, making people in low-income countries susceptible to illness and disease. There is growing evidence that the high rates of HIV/AIDS infection found in many African countries are due in part to the weakened health of impoverished people (Stillwagon, 2001).

Because of poor health conditions, people in low-income countries are more likely to die in infancy and less likely to live to old age than people in high-income countries. Infants are eleven times more likely to die at birth in low-income countries than they are in high-income countries, and—if they survive birth—they are likely to live on average eighteen years fewer (see Table 8.3). Children often die of illnesses that are readily treated in wealthier countries, such as measles or diarrhea. In some parts of the world, such as sub-Saharan Africa, a child is more likely to die before the age of five than to enter secondary school (World Bank, 1996). Still, conditions have improved in low- and middle-income countries: Between 1980 and 2002, for example, the infant mortality rate dropped from 97 (per thousand live births) to 81 in low-income countries and from 60 to 29 in middle-income countries. AIDS, and growing poverty in some regions of the world, have contributed to the increase in infant mortality in the poorest countries in recent years.

During the past three decades, some improvements have occurred in most of the middle-income countries of the world and in some of the low-income countries as well. Throughout the world, infant mortality has been cut in half, and average life expectancy has increased by ten years or more because of the wider availability of modern medical technology, improved sanitation, and rising incomes.

Hunger, Malnutrition, and Famine

Hunger, malnutrition, and famine are major global sources of poor health. These problems are nothing new. What seems to be new is their extent—the fact that so many people in the world today appear to be on the brink of starvation. A recent study by the United Nations World Food Program (2001) estimates that 830 million people go hungry every day, 95 percent of them in developing countries. The program defines "hunger" as a diet of 1,800 or fewer calories a day—an amount insufficient to provide adults with the nutrients required for active, healthy lives.

According to the World Food Program study, 200 million of the world's hungry are children under five, who are underweight because they lack adequate food. Every year hunger kills an estimated 12 million children. Yet more than three quarters of all malnourished children under the age of five in the world's low- and middle-income countries live in countries that actually produce a food surplus (Lappe et al., 1998).

Most famine and hunger today are the result of a combination of natural and social forces. Drought alone affects an estimated 100 million people in the world today. In countries such as Sudan, Ethiopia, Eritrea, Indonesia, Afghanistan, Sierra Leone, Guinea, and Tajikistan, the combination of drought and internal warfare has wrecked food production, resulting in starvation and death for millions of people. In Latin Amer-

TABLE 8.3

Differences in Infant Mortality and Life Expectancy: Low-, Middle-, and High-Income Countries, 2002

	INCOME LEVEL		
	LOW	MIDDLE	HIGH
Annual infant deaths per 1,000 live births	81	29	5
Life expectancy at birth (years)	59	70	78

SOURCE: World Bank, World Development Indicators, 2003.

ica and the Caribbean, 53 million people (11 percent of the population) are malnourished—a number that rises to 180 million (33 percent) in sub-Saharan Africa, and 525 million (17 percent) in Asia (UNWFP, 2001).

The AIDS epidemic has also contributed to the problem of food shortages and hunger, killing many working-age adults. One recent study by the United Nations Food and Agricultural Organization (FAO) predicts that HIV/AIDS–caused deaths in the ten African countries most afflicted by the epidemic will reduce the labor force by 26 percent by the year 2020. Of the estimated 26 million people worldwide infected with HIV, 95 percent live in developing countries. According to the FAO, the epidemic can be devastating to nutrition, food security, and agricultural production, affecting "the entire society's ability to maintain and reproduce itself" (UN FAO, 2001).

The countries affected by famine and starvation are for the most part too poor to pay for new technologies that would increase their food production. Nor can they afford to purchase sufficient food imports from elsewhere in the world. At the same time, paradoxically, as world hunger grows, food production continues to increase. Between 1965 and 1999, for example, world production of grain doubled. Even allowing for the substantial world population increase over this period, the global production of grain per person was 15 percent higher in 1999 than it was thirty-four years earlier. This

An Afghan shepherd leads his herd in search of water in Kabul. Four years of harsh and successive drought in many areas of land-locked Afghanistan has caused the water level to drop drastically. Hundreds of people and tens of thousands of animals have died due to drought-related problems in various parts of the country.

growth, however, is not evenly distributed around the world. In much of Africa, for example, food production per person declined in recent years. Surplus food produced in high-income countries such as the United States is seldom affordable to the countries that need it most.

Can Poor Countries Become Rich?

As we saw in Chapter 2, by the mid-1970s a number of low-income countries in East Asia were undergoing a process of industrialization that appeared to threaten the global economic dominance of the United States and Europe (Amsden, 1989). This process began with Japan in the 1950s but quickly extended to the **newly industrializing economies (NIEs),** that is, the rapidly growing economies of the world, particularly in East Asia but also in Latin America. The East Asian NIEs included Hong Kong in the 1960s and Taiwan, South Korea, and Singapore in the 1970s and 1980s. Other Asian countries began to follow in the 1980s and the early 1990s, most notably China, but also Malaysia, Thailand, and Indonesia. Today, most are middle income, and some—such as Hong Kong, South Korea, Taiwan, and Singapore—have moved up to the high-income category.

Figure 8.3 compares the economic growth of seven East Asian countries (including Japan) with the United States from 1980 to 1999. These are all places that were poor only two generations ago. The low- and middle-income economies of the East Asian region as a whole averaged 7.7 percent growth a year during that period, a rate that is extraordinary by world standards (World Bank, 2000–2001). By 1999, the gross domestic product per person in Singapore was virtually the same as that in the United States. China, the world's most populous country, has one of the most rapidly growing economies on the planet. At an average annual growth rate of 10 percent between 1980 and 1999, the Chinese economy doubled in size.

Economic growth in East Asia has not been without its costs. These have included the sometimes violent repression of labor and civil rights, terrible factory conditions, the exploitation of an increasingly female work force, the exploitation of immigrant workers from impoverished neighboring countries, and widespread environmental degradation. Nonetheless, thanks to the sacrifices of past generations of workers, large numbers of people in these countries are prospering.

The economic success of the East Asian NIEs can be attributed to a combination of factors. Some of these factors are historical, including those stemming from world political and economic shifts. Some are cultural. Still others have to do with the ways these countries pursued economic growth. Following are some of the factors that aided their success:

1. **Historically, Taiwan, South Korea, Hong Kong, and Singapore were once part of colonial situations that, while imposing many hardships, also helped to pave the way for economic growth.** Taiwan and Korea were tied to the Japanese Empire; Hong Kong and Singapore were former British colonies. Japan eliminated large landowners who opposed industrialization, and both Britain and Japan encouraged industrial development, constructed roads and other transportation systems, and built relatively efficient governmental bureaucracies in these particular colonies. Britain also actively developed both Hong Kong and Singapore as trading centers (Gold, 1986; Cumings, 1987). Elsewhere in the world—for example, in Latin America and Africa—countries that are today poor did not fare so well in their dealings with richer, more powerful nations.

2. **The East Asian region benefited from a long period of world economic growth.** Between the 1950s and the mid-1970s, the growing economies of Europe and the United States provided a big market for the clothing,

footwear, and electronics that were increasingly being made in East Asia, creating a "window of opportunity" for economic development. Furthermore, periodic economic slowdowns in the United States and Europe forced businesses to cut their labor costs and spurred the relocation of factories to low-wage East Asian countries (Henderson and Appelbaum, 1992).

3. **Economic growth in this region took off at the high point of the cold war, when the United States and its allies, in erecting a defense against communist China, provided generous economic and military aid.** Direct aid and loans fueled investment in such new technologies as transistors, semiconductors, and other electronics, contributing to the development of local industries. Military assistance frequently favored strong (often military) governments that were willing to use repression to keep labor costs low (Mirza, 1986; Cumings, 1987, 1997; Deyo, 1987; Evans, 1987; Amsden, 1989; Henderson, 1989; Haggard, 1990; Castells, 1992).

4. **Some sociologists argue that the economic success of Japan and the East Asian NIEs is due in part to their cultural traditions, in particular, their shared Confucian philosophy.** Nearly a century ago, Max Weber (1977) argued that the Protestant belief in thrift, frugality, and hard work partly explained the rise of capitalism in Western Europe. Weber's argument has been applied to Asian economic history. Confucianism, it is argued, inculcates respect for one's elders and superiors, education, hard work, and proven accomplishments as the key to advancement as well as a willingness to sacrifice today to earn a greater reward tomorrow. As a result of these values, the Weberian argument goes, Asian workers and managers are highly loyal to their companies, submissive to authority, hard working, and success oriented. Workers and capitalists alike are said to be frugal. Instead of living lavishly, they are likely to reinvest their wealth in further economic growth (Berger, 1986; Wong, 1986; Berger and Hsiao, 1998; Redding, 1990; Helm, 1992).

This explanation has some merit, but it overlooks the fact that businesses are not always revered and respected in Asia. Students and workers throughout the East Asian NIEs have opposed business and governmental policies they felt to be unfair, often at the risk of imprisonment and sometimes even their lives (Deyo, 1989; Ho, 1990). Furthermore, such central Confucian cultural values as thrift appear to be on the decline in Japan and the NIEs, as young people—raised in the booming prosperity of recent years—increasingly value conspicuous consumption over austerity and investment (Helm, 1992).

5. **Many of the East Asian governments followed strong policies that favored economic growth.** Their governments played active roles in keeping labor costs low, encouraged economic development through tax breaks and other economic policies and offered free public education.

Whether the growth of these economies will continue is unclear. In 1997–1998, a combination of poor investment decisions, corruption, and world economic conditions brought these countries' economic expansion to an abrupt halt. Their stock markets collapsed, their currencies fell, and the entire global economy was threatened. The experience of Hong Kong was typical: After thirty-seven years of continuous growth, the economy stalled and its stock market lost more than half its value. It remains to be seen whether the "Asian meltdown," as the newspapers called it in early 1998, will have a long-term effect on the region or is merely a blip in its recent growth. Once their current economic problems are solved, many economists believe, the newly industrializing Asian economies will resume their growth, although perhaps not at the meteoric rates of the past.

Singapore, along with Taiwan, South Korea, and Hong Kong, was transformed from a low-income country to a relatively prosperous, newly industrialized country.

FIGURE 8.3

Percentage Growth in GDP in Selected East Asian Countries, the United States, and the World as a Whole, 1980–1990 and 1990–1999

The East Asian economies grew at historically unprecedented rates during 1980s and 1990s. The economies of the low- and middle-income countries in the region as a whole grew nearly 150 percent over the period, or an average of 7.7 percent a year. By way of comparison, the U.S. economy grew only 61 percent, or 3 percent per year—only slightly more than the economies of Japan, the other high-income industrial countries of the world, and the world as a whole. China, the world's largest economy, was also one of the fastest growing, growing by an average of over 9 percent a year and doubling in size. By 2000, GDP per capita was higher in Japan ($44,830) than in the United States ($31,966), and almost as high in Singapore ($28,229). Economic growth was somewhat slower during the 1990s than the 1980s, in East Asia as well as throughout the rest of the world. The East Asian economic crisis of 1998–1999 briefly halted the rapid economic growth of the region, which since has largely recovered.

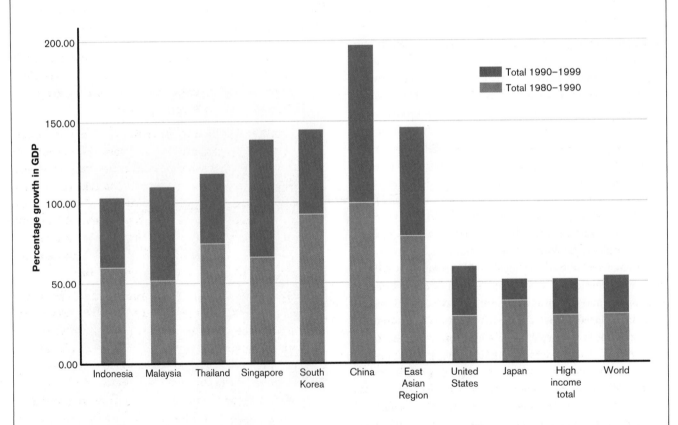

SOURCE: World Bank, 2000–2001; World Development Indicators, 2003.

Theories of Global Inequality

What causes global inequality? How can it be overcome? In this section we shall examine four different kinds of theories that have been advanced over the years to explain global inequality: market-oriented, dependency, world-systems, and state-centered theories. These theories each have strengths and weaknesses. One shortcoming of all of them is that they frequently give short shrift to the role of women in economic development. By putting the theories together, however, we should be able to answer a key question facing the 85 percent of the world's population living outside high-income countries: How can they move up in the world economy?

Market-Oriented Theories

Forty years ago, the most influential theories of global inequality advanced by American economists and sociologists were **market-oriented theories.** These theories assume that the best possible economic consequences will result if individuals are free, uninhibited by any form of governmental constraint, to make their own economic decisions. Unrestricted capitalism, if allowed to develop fully, is said to be the avenue to economic growth. Government bureaucracy should not dictate which goods to produce, what prices to charge, or how much workers should be paid. According to market-oriented theorists, governmental direction of the economies of low-income countries results only in blockages to economic development. In this view, local governments should get out of the way of development (Rostow, 1961; Warren, 1980; Berger, 1986; Ranis and Mahmood, 1992; Ranis, 1996).

Market-oriented theories reflect the belief that "any country can make it if it does it 'our way' "—that is, like the United States and other similar high-income countries. These theories inspired U.S. government foreign-aid programs that attempted to spur economic development in low-income countries by providing money, expert advisers, and technology, paving the way for U.S. corporations to make investments in these countries.

One of the most influential early proponents of such theories was W. W. Rostow, an economic adviser to former U.S. president John F. Kennedy, whose ideas helped shape U.S. foreign policy toward Latin America during the 1960s. Rostow's explanation is one version of a market-oriented approach, termed "modernization theory." **Modernization theory** argues that low-income societies can develop economically only if they give up their traditional ways and adopt modern economic institutions, technologies, and cultural values that emphasize savings and productive investment.

According to Rostow (1961), the traditional cultural values and social institutions of low-income countries impede their economic effectiveness. For example, many people in low-income countries, in Rostow's view, lack a strong work ethic: They would sooner consume today than invest for the future. Large families are also seen as partly responsible for "economic backwardness," since a breadwinner with many mouths to feed can hardly be expected to save money for investment purposes.

But to modernization theorists, the problems in low-income countries run even deeper. The cultures of such countries, according to the theory, tend to support "fatalism"—a value system that views hardship and suffering as the unavoidable plight of life. Acceptance of one's lot in life thus discourages people from working hard and being thrifty to overcome their fate. In this view, then, a country's poverty is due largely to the cultural failings of the people themselves. Such failings are reinforced by government policies that set wages and control prices and generally interfere in the operation of the economy. How can low-income countries break out of their poverty? Rostow viewed economic growth as going through several stages, which he likened to the journey of an airplane:

1. **Traditional stage.** This is the stage just described. It is characterized by low rates of savings, the supposed lack of a work ethic, and the so-called fatalistic value system. The airplane is not yet off the ground.

2. **Takeoff to economic growth.** The traditional stage, Rostow argued, can give way to a second one: economic takeoff. This occurs when poor countries begin to jettison their traditional values and institutions and start to save and invest money for the future. The role of wealthy countries, such as the United States, is to facilitate this growth. They can do this by financing birth-control programs or providing low-cost loans for electrification, road and airport construction, and starting new industries.

3. **Drive to technological maturity.** According to Rostow, with the help of money and advice from high-income countries, the airplane of economic growth would taxi down the runway, pick up speed, and become airborne. The country would then approach technological maturity. In the aeronautical metaphor, the plane would slowly climb to cruising altitude, improving its technology, reinvesting its recently acquired wealth in new industries, and adopting the institutions and values of the high-income countries.

4. **High mass consumption.** Finally, the country would reach the phase of high mass consumption. Now people are able to enjoy the fruits of their labor by achieving a high standard of living. The airplane (country) cruises along on automatic pilot, having entered the ranks of high-income countries.

What Can You Do About Child Labor?

Does child labor still exist in the world today? According to the United Nations International Labor Organization, more than 250 million boys and girls between the ages of five and fourteen are working in developing countries, about one out of every four children in the world. Some 50 to 60 million children between the ages of five and eleven work under hazardous conditions. Child labor is found throughout the developing world—in Asia (61 percent of the children are engaged in labor), Africa (32 percent), and Latin America (7 percent). They are forced to work because of a combination of family poverty, lack of education, and traditional indifference among some people in many countries to the plight of those who are poor or who are ethnic minorities (ILO, 2000; UNICEF, 2000).

Two thirds of working children labor in agriculture, with the rest in manufacturing, wholesale and retail trade, restaurants and hotels, and a variety of services, including working as servants in wealthy households. At best, these children work for long hours with little pay and are therefore unable to go to school and develop the skills that might eventually enable them to escape their lives of poverty. Many, however, work at hazardous and exploitative jobs under slavelike conditions, suffering a variety of illnesses and injuries. The International Labor Organization provides a grisly summary: "wounds, broken or complete loss of body parts, burns and skin diseases, eye and hearing impairment, respiratory and gastro-intestinal illnesses, fever, headaches from excessive heat in the fields or factories" (ILO, 2000).

A United Nations report provides several examples:

In Malaysia, children may work up to 17-hour days on rubber plantations, exposed to insect and snake bites. In the United Republic of Tanzania, they pick coffee, inhaling pesticides. In Portugal, children as young as 12 are subject to the heavy labor and myriad dangers of the construction industry. In Morocco, they hunch at looms for long hours and little pay, knotting the strands of luxury carpets for export. In the United States, chil-

dren are exploited in garment industry sweatshops. In the Philippines, young boys dive in dangerous conditions to help set nets for deep-sea fishing.

Conditions in many factories are horrible:

Dust from the chemical powders and strong vapors in both the storeroom and the boiler room were obvious. . . . We found 250 children, mostly below 10 years of age, working in a long hall filling in a slotted frame with sticks. Row upon row of children, some barely five years old, were involved in the work. (UNICEF, 1997)

One form of child labor that is close to slavery is "bonded labor." In this system children as young as eight or nine are pledged by their parents to factory owners in exchange for small loans. These children are paid so little that they never manage to reduce the debt, condemning them to a lifetime of bondage. One recent case of bonded labor that attracted international attention was that of Iqbal Masih, a Pakistani child who, at age four, was sold into slavery by his father in order to borrow six hundred rupees (roughly $16) for the wedding of his firstborn son. For six years, Iqbal spent most of his time chained to a carpet-weaving loom, tying tiny knots for hours on end. After fleeing the factory at age ten, he began speaking to labor organizations and schools about his experience. Iqbal paid a bitter price for his outspokenness: At age thirteen, while riding his bicycle in his hometown, he was gunned down by agents believed to be working for the carpet industry (Free the Children, 1998; India's Tiny Slaves, 1998).

Abolishing exploitative child labor will require countries around the world to enact strong child-labor laws and be willing to enforce them. International organizations, such as the United Nations' International Labor Organization (ILO), have outlined a set of standards for such laws to follow. In June 1999, the ILO adopted Convention 182, calling for the abolition of the "Worst Forms of Child Labor." These are defined as including:

- all forms of slavery or practices similar to slavery, such as the sale and trafficking of children, debt bondage and serfdom, and forced or compulsory labor, including forced or compulsory recruitment of children for use in armed conflict;
- the use, procuring, or offering of a child for prostitution, for the production of pornography, or for pornographic performances;
- the use, procuring, or offering of a child for illicit activities, in particular for the production and trafficking of drugs as defined in the relevant international treaties; and
- work that, by its nature or the circumstances in which it is carried out, is likely to harm the health, safety, or morals of children. (ILO, 1999)

Countries must also provide free public education and require that children attend school full time (UNICEF, 2000). But at least part of the responsibility for solving the problem lies with the global corporations that manufacture goods using child labor—and, ultimately, with the consumers who buy those goods. Here are two things that you can do right now:

1. **Check the Label.** Mind what you are buying. Begin by looking at the label. When you purchase clothing, rugs, and other textiles, the label will tell you where it was made, if unionized labor was used, and, in a few cases, whether it is certified to be "sweatshop free." Avoid buying garments made in countries with known human rights abuses, such as Myanmar (Burma). If the product has a label indicating it was made with union labor, it is likely to be free from child labor. "Sweatshop free" labels, although still rare, are likely to become more common in coming years, as labor and consumer groups pressure the U.S. government to more closely monitor imported goods. In one well-publicized campaign that grew out of Iqbal's tragic experience, Indian human rights activists developed the "Rugmark" label, which certifies that the carpet is free of child labor. The U.S. Department of Labor is also working toward a way of certifying goods that are sold in the United States to be "sweatshop free," although at this time there is no way to do so reliably: The millions of factories around the world involved in making consumer goods are too vast and dispersed to monitor.

2. **Join Up.** Join (or start) an antisweatshop campaign at your own college or university. There is a national campaign, organized by United Students Against Sweatshops, to require schools to engage in "responsible purchasing" when they buy or sell clothing, athletic equipment, and other goods that carry the school logo. Schools are urged to sign agreements with all their vendors that require full disclosure of the names and locations of the factories where the goods are made, certifying that the goods are free from child labor and other forms of exploitation. School sales are a multibillion-dollar business, and if schools set a high standard, manufacturers will be forced to take notice.

In a global economy, you can choose what you buy, as well as influence others to make informed and ethical choices about the products they consume. Be a smart shopper—it can make a difference.

Rostow's ideas remain influential. Indeed, the prevailing view among economists today, **neoliberalism,** argues that free-market forces, achieved by minimizing governmental restrictions on business, provide the only route to economic growth. Neoliberalism holds that global free trade will enable all countries of the world to prosper; eliminating governmental regulation is seen as necessary for economic growth to occur. Neoliberal economists therefore call for an end to restrictions on trade and often challenge minimum wage and other labor laws, as well as environmental restrictions on business.

Sociologists, on the other hand, focus on the cultural aspects of Rostow's theory: Whether and how certain beliefs and institutions hinder development (Davis, 1987; So, 1990). These include religious values, moral beliefs, belief in magic, and folk traditions and practices. Sociologists also examine other conditions that resist change, particularly the belief local cultures have that moral decay and social unrest accompany business and trade.

Dependency Theories

During the 1960s, a number of theorists questioned market-oriented explanations of global inequality such as modernization theory. Many of these critics were sociologists and economists from the low-income countries of Latin America and Africa who rejected the idea that their countries' economic underdevelopment was due to their own cultural or institutional faults. Instead, they build on the theories of Karl Marx, who argued that world capitalism would create a class of countries manipulated by more powerful countries just as capitalism within countries leads to the exploitation of workers. The **dependency theorists,** as they are called, argue that the poverty of low-income countries stems from their exploitation by wealthy countries and the multinational corporations that are based in wealthy countries. In their view, global capitalism locked their countries into a downward spiral of exploitation and poverty.

According to dependency theories, this exploitation began with **colonialism,** a political-economic system under which powerful countries establish, for their own profit, rule over weaker peoples or countries. Powerful nations have colonized other countries usually to procure the raw materials needed for their factories and to control markets for the products manufactured in those factories. Under colonial rule, for example, the petroleum, copper, iron, and food products required by industrial economies are extracted from low-income countries by businesses based in high-income countries. Although colonialism typically involved European countries establishing colonies in North and South America, Africa, and Asia, some Asian countries (such as Japan) had colonies as well.

Although Nigeria is the world's eighth largest producer of oil, the overwhelming majority of the profits generated in the energy trade go to oil companies and the military government, providing no benefit to the country's poverty-stricken inhabitants. These women are protesting Royal Dutch Shell's exploitation of Nigeria's oil and natural gas resources.

Even though colonialism ended throughout most of the world after World War II, the exploitation did not: Transnational corporations continued to reap enormous profits from their branches in low-income countries. According to dependency theory, these global companies, often with the support of the powerful banks and governments of rich countries, established factories in poor countries, using cheap labor and raw materials to maximize production costs without governmental interference. In turn, the low prices set for labor and raw materials prevented poor countries from accumulating the profit necessary to industrialize themselves. Local businesses that might compete with foreign corporations were prevented from doing so. In this view, poor countries are forced to borrow from rich countries, thus increasing their economic dependency.

Low-income countries are thus seen not as underdeveloped, but rather as misdeveloped (Emmanuel, 1972; Amin, 1974; Frank, 1966, 1969a, 1969b, 1979; Prebisch, 1967, 1971). With the exception of a handful of local politicians and businesspeople who serve the interests of the foreign corporations, people fall into poverty. Peasants are forced to choose between starvation and working at near-starvation wages on foreign-controlled plantations and in foreign-controlled mines and factories. Since dependency theorists believe that such exploitation has kept their countries from achieving economic growth, they typically call for revolutionary changes that would push foreign corporations out of their countries altogether (Frank, 1966, 1969a, 1969b).

Whereas market-oriented theorists usually ignore political and military power, dependency theorists regard the exercise of power as central to enforcing unequal economic relationships. According to this theory, whenever local leaders question such unequal arrangements, their voices are quickly suppressed. Unionization is usually outlawed, and labor organizers are jailed and sometimes killed. When people elect a government opposing these policies, that government is likely to be overthrown by the country's military, often backed by the armed forces of the industrialized countries themselves. Dependency theorists point to many examples: the role of the CIA in overthrowing the Marxist governments of Guatemala in 1954 and Chile in 1973 and in undermining support for the leftist government in Nicaragua in the 1980s. In the view of dependency theory, global economic inequality is thus backed up by force: Economic elites in poor countries, backed by their counterparts in wealthy ones, use police and military power to keep the local population under control.

The Brazilian sociologist Enrique Fernando Cardoso, once a prominent dependency theorist, argued twenty years ago that some degree of **dependent development** was nonetheless possible—that under certain circumstances, poor countries can still develop economically, although only in ways shaped by their reliance on the wealthier countries (Cardoso and Faletto, 1979). In particular, the governments of these countries could play a key role in steering a course between dependency and development (Evans, 1979). Today, as the immediate past president of Brazil, Cardoso has changed his thinking, calling for greater integration of Brazil into the global economy.

World-Systems Theory

During the last quarter century, sociologists have increasingly seen the world as a single (although often conflict-ridden) economic system. Although dependency theories hold that individual countries are economically tied to one another, **world-systems theory** argues that the world capitalist economic system is not merely a collection of independent countries engaged in diplomatic and economic relations with one another but rather must be understood as a single unit. The world-systems approach is most closely identified with the work of Immanuel Wallerstein and his colleagues. Wallerstein showed that capitalism has long existed as a global economic system, beginning with the extension of markets and trade in Europe in the fifteenth and sixteenth centuries (Wallerstein, 1974a, 1974b, 1979, 1990, 1996a, 1996b; Hopkins and Wallerstein,

1996). The world system is seen as comprising four overlapping elements (Chase-Dunn, 1989):

- a world market for goods and labor;
- the division of the population into different economic classes, particularly capitalists and workers;
- an international system of formal and informal political relations among the most powerful countries, whose competition with one another helps shape the world economy; and
- the carving up of the world into three unequal economic zones, with the wealthier zones exploiting the poorer ones.

World-systems theorists term these three economic zones "core," "periphery," and "semiperiphery." All countries in the world system are said to fall into one of the three categories. **Core countries** are the most advanced industrial countries, taking the lion's share of profits in the world economic system. These include Japan, the United States, and the countries of Western Europe. The **peripheral countries** comprise low-income, largely agricultural countries that are often manipulated by core countries for their own economic advantage. Examples of peripheral countries are found throughout Africa and to a lesser extent in Latin America and Asia. Natural resources, such as agricultural products, minerals, and other raw materials, flow from periphery to core—as do the profits. The core, in turn, sells finished goods to the periphery, also at a profit. World-systems theorists argue that core countries have made themselves wealthy with this unequal trade, while at the same time limiting the economic development of peripheral countries. Finally, the **semiperipheral countries** occupy an intermediate position: These are semi-industrialized, middle-income countries that extract profits from the more peripheral countries and in turn yield profits to the core countries. Examples of semiperipheral countries include Mexico in North America; Brazil, Argentina, and Chile in South America; and the newly industrializing economies of East Asia. The semiperiphery, though to some degree controlled by the core, is thus also able to exploit the periphery. Moreover, the greater economic success of the semiperiphery holds out to the periphery the promise of similar development.

Although the world system tends to change very slowly, once-powerful countries eventually lose their economic power and others take their place. For example, some five centuries ago the Italian city-states of Venice and Genoa dominated the world capitalist economy. They were superseded by the Dutch, then the British, and currently the United States. Today, in the view of some world-systems theorists, American dominance is giving way to a more "multipolar" world where economic power will be shared among the United States, Europe, and Asia (Arrighi, 1994).

An important offshoot of the world systems approach is a concept that emphasizes the global nature of economic

Women and Economic Development

Although the theories of economic development reviewed in this chapter largely ignore women, women in fact play a key role in the global economy (Blumberg, 1995; Scott, 1995). Even where women contributed to revolutionary social change—such as in Vietnam, where more than a quarter of a million female soldiers died on behalf of communism during the Vietnam War—their economic role has not been fully acknowledged (Tétreault, 1994).

Today, women make up a major part of the work force in the world's factories. Yet studies that stress cheap factory work in the global economy often fail to examine the central importance of women's labor. In export-processing zones throughout the world, young women assemble clothing, electronics, and other components into finished products for sale in Europe and North America. The jobs in these factories pay little and offer few opportunities for advancement. They are repetitive, monotonous, and frequently hazardous. These factories often employ women as young as fourteen or fifteen years old, who work long hours for low wages.

Women make up a large portion of the world's work force for two very different sorts of reasons (Fernández Kelly, 1987;

Tiano, 1994). First, many are compelled to work in factories by their husbands or parents who need additional income. Second, many women view these jobs—however unsatisfactory—as preferable to unpaid work at home, since wage earning provides them with a measure of economic stability and financial independence.

Women are often the most exploited of workers. Because they are seen as less likely to protest than men, from the standpoint of employers they are "ideal" workers who will take a lot of abuse. The following accounts are from four women who work in giant Mexican denim factories, where they sew stonewashed jeans for major U.S. manufacturers for forty-eight to sixty hours a week. They spoke to a U.S. human rights delegation under conditions of secrecy, fearful that they would lose their jobs for speaking out:

Cristina:

I've worked there for five years. I earn 280 pesos a week [U.S. $35]. I pay 72 pesos a week [U.S. $9] to get a ride

Luz:

Supervisors yelled at us and pressured us. Once a supervisor threw pants at me and yelled at me because the stitches weren't exactly the same on 30 pairs of pants. I had to re-do these pants before I left as punishment. . . . We had to contribute 3 pesos a month to buy soap, Pine Sol and Ajax to clean the bathroom. Then they assign us to take turns cleaning the bathroom after we've finished our work for the day, because there's no one who works there to clean the bathrooms. They don't have toilet paper in the bathrooms, we have to bring it from home. We're only supposed to go to the bathroom once a day. . . . (NICWJ, 1998)

It is important not only to recognize women's contribution to the global economy, but to take steps to avoid their exploitation as well.

Questions

- The text calls women "often the most exploited of workers." At the same time, it mentions that women often choose to work outside the home. How can you reconcile these two seemingly contradictory remarks? What drives women to work in exploitative jobs?
- How can exploited workers get pay raises or increased benefits? What tactics might they use? What role does gender play in salary negotiations?
- Compare the photographs with the quotes from the workers. Do the words and the images create different impressions? How? Why?

to work. I'm never allowed to take a vacation. Monday through Friday, I work from 8:15 in the morning to 8:15 or 8:30 at night. I get one hour for lunch. Saturday I work from 8 A.M. to 4 or 5 P.M., with no break. I am very hungry by the time I leave work. I'm never paid anything extra if I work more hours.

Elena:

If there's something the matter with the stitching, we have to sew them by hand to fix them. So only when we finish with all the repairs can we leave. We can't leave earlier because they won't give us our IDs. If we get to work five minutes late, they deduct 10 pesos from our pay. Sometimes if we arrive late they won't let us into the factory until 9 A.M., and they deduct 30 or more pesos for this.

Carolina:

We don't have any safety equipment besides mouth covers and aprons; nothing for our hands or eyes, and there aren't any machine guards either. If we lose scissors or other equipment, they make us pay for it.

activities. **Global commodity chains** are worldwide networks of labor and production processes yielding a finished product. These networks consist of all pivotal production activities that form a tightly interlocked "chain" extending from the raw materials needed to create the product to its final consumer (Gereffi, 1995; Gereffi, 1996; Hopkins and Wallerstein, 1996; Appelbaum and Christerson, 1997).

The commodity-chain approach argues that manufacturing is becoming increasingly globalized. Manufactures accounted for approximately three quarters of the world's total economic growth during the period 1990–1998. The sharpest growth has been among middle-income countries: Manufactures accounted for only 54 percent of these countries' exports in 1990, compared with 71 percent just eight years later. Yet the high rate of increase of manufactures as a share of world exports has since slowed; in 2002, 75 percent of world exports were manufactures (World Trade Organization, 2003). China, which has moved from the ranks of low- to middle-income countries in part because of its role as an exporter of manufactured goods, partly accounts for this trend. Yet the most profitable activities in the commodity chain—engineering, design, and advertising—are likely to be found in the core countries, while the least profitable activities, such as factory production, usually are found in peripheral countries.

Although manufacturing in the global commodity chain typically takes place in peripheral countries, an exception to this trend has developed. Low-wage, low-profit factories known as sweatshops are today reappearing in core countries, sometimes for the first time in half a century or more. A sweatshop is a small factory that has numerous violations of wage, health, and safety laws. In New York City and Los Angeles, for example, more than 100,000 workers labor in tiny garment factories that make many of the brands of clothing you can buy in major department stores. Many laborers work for less than minimum wage, in buildings described by government officials as firetraps.

The private experience of these workers is shaped by larger social forces. First, garment workers in New York and Los Angeles are in direct competition with workers in the Caribbean and Mexico, where wages are a tenth as much as in the United States. If workers in New York and Los Angeles want to keep their jobs, they are often forced to settle for sweatshop wages and conditions. Otherwise, the work will be moved to another country. Second, most garment workers are immigrants, many lacking proper papers. If they complain about their working conditions, they will lose their jobs and possibly be deported.

The global economy has brought sweatshops back to the United States, a country where they were largely unknown for more than half a century. The global economy has also provided the immigrants to work in them.

State-Centered Theories

Some of the most recent explanations of successful economic development emphasize the role of state policy in promoting growth. Differing sharply from market-oriented theories, **state-centered theories** argue that appropriate government policies do not interfere with economic development but rather can play a key role in bringing it about. A large body of research now suggests that in some regions of the world, such as East Asia, successful economic development has been state led. Even the World Bank, long a strong proponent of free-market theories of development, has changed its thinking about the role of the state. In its 1997 report *The State in a Changing World,* the World Bank concludes that without an effective state, "sustainable development, both economic and social, is impossible" (World Bank, 1997).

Strong governments contributed in various ways to economic growth in the East Asian NIEs during the 1980s and 1990s (Appelbaum and Henderson, 1992; Amsden, Kochanowicz, and Taylor, 1994; Evans, 1995; Cumings, 1997; World Bank, 1997):

1. **East Asian governments have sometimes aggressively acted to ensure political stability, while keeping labor costs low.** They have accomplished this by acts of repression, such as outlawing trade unions, banning strikes, jailing labor leaders, and, in general, silencing the voices of workers. The governments of Taiwan, South Korea, and Singapore in particular have engaged in such practices.

2. **East Asian governments have frequently sought to steer economic development in desired directions.** For example, state agencies have often provided cheap loans and tax breaks to businesses that invest in industries favored by the government. Sometimes this strategy has backfired, resulting in bad loans held by the government (one of the causes of the region's economic problems during the late 1990s). Some governments have prevented businesses from investing their profits in other countries, forcing them to invest in economic growth at home. Sometimes governments have owned and therefore controlled key industries.

3. **East Asian governments have often been heavily involved in social programs such as low-cost housing and universal education.** The world's largest public housing systems (outside of socialist or formerly socialist countries) have been in Hong Kong and Singapore, where government subsidies keep rents extremely low. As a result, workers don't require high wages to pay for their housing, so they can compete better

with American and European workers in the emerging global labor market. In Singapore, which has an extremely strong central government, well-funded public education and training help to provide workers with the skills they need to compete effectively in the emerging global labor market. The Singaporean government also requires businesses and individual citizens alike to save a large percentage of their income for investment in future growth.

Evaluating Global Theories of Inequality

Each of these four sets of theories of global inequality just discussed has its strengths and weaknesses. Together they enable us to better understand the causes and cures for global inequality.

1. **Market-oriented theories** recommend the adoption of modern capitalist institutions to promote economic development, as the recent example of East Asia attests. They further argue that countries can develop economically only if they open their borders to trade, and they can cite evidence in support of this argument. But market-oriented theories also fail to take into account the various economic ties between poor countries and wealthy ones—ties that can impede economic growth under some conditions and enhance it under others. They tend to blame low-income countries themselves for their poverty rather than looking to the influence of outside factors, such as the business operations of more powerful nations. Market-oriented theories also ignore the ways government can work with the private sector to spur economic development. Finally, they fail to explain why some countries manage to take off economically while others remain grounded in poverty and underdevelopment.

2. **Dependency theories** address the market-oriented theories' neglect in considering poor countries' ties with wealthy countries by focusing on how wealthy nations have economically exploited poor ones. However, although dependency theories help to account for much of the economic backwardness in Latin America and Africa, they are unable to explain the occasional success story among such low-income countries as Brazil, Argentina, and Mexico or the rapidly expanding economies of East Asia. In fact, some countries once in the low-income category have risen economically even in the presence of multinational corporations. Even some former colonies, such as Hong Kong and Singapore, both once dependent on Great Britain, count among the success stories.

3. **World-systems theory** seeks to overcome the shortcomings of both market-oriented and dependency theories by analyzing the world economy as a whole. Rather than beginning with individual countries, world-systems theorists look at the complex global web of political and economic relationships that influence development and inequality in poor and rich nations alike. Within the world-systems framework, the concept of *global commodity chains* takes this notion one step further, focusing on global businesses and their activities rather than relationships between countries. World-systems theory is thus well suited to understanding the global economy at a time when businesses are increasingly free to set up operations anywhere, acquiring an economic importance that rivals that of many countries. Yet this is also a weakness of the commodity chains approach: It tends to emphasize the importance of business decisions over other factors, such as the role that both workers and governments play in shaping a country's economy (Amsden, 1989; Deyo, 1989; Evans, 1995; Cumings, 1997).

4. **State-centered theories** stress the governmental role in fostering economic growth. They thus offer a useful alternative to both the prevailing market-oriented theories, with their emphasis on states as economic hindrances, and dependency theories, which view states as allies of global business elites in exploiting poor countries. When combined with the other theories—particularly world-systems theory—state-centered theories can explain the radical changes now transforming the world economy.

Why Global Economic Inequality Matters to You

Today the social and economic forces leading to a single global capitalist economy appear to be irresistible. The principal challenge to this outcome—socialism—came to an end with the collapse of the Soviet Union in 1991. The largest remaining socialist country in the world today, the People's Republic of China, is rapidly adopting many capitalist economic institutions and is the fastest-growing economy in the world. What does rapid globalization mean for the future of global inequality? No sociologist knows for certain, but many possible scenarios exist. In one, our world might be dominated by large, global corporations, with workers everywhere competing with one another at a global wage. Such a scenario might predict falling wages for large numbers of people in today's high-income countries and rising wages for a few in low-income

Sociology in South Africa

[***]

[***] Sociologists can be caught between their commitment to open debate in the university (and pressures to publish their work in professional journals) and the discipline imposed by involvement in outside organizations. The tendency has been to resolve this contradiction by either retreating into the safer haven of professional sociology or by making your primary loyalty to public sociology. In the latter case, professional sociology simply provides the base for the public sociologist to create a different world outside the university, populated by activists and public intellectuals.

This was the path taken by the two leading public sociologists during the apartheid period, Richard Turner and David Webster. Both were to pay the ultimate price for their public roles when they were assassinated by the apartheid police, Turner on the 8th January 1978 and Webster on the 1st May 1989. Although neither was employed in departments of sociology (Turner was in political science and Webster in social anthropology) they are exemplars of social scientists that deliberately and permanently shifted their orientation to public sociology.

The main themes of Turner's ideas are set out in a remarkable book published in 1972, *The Eye of the Needle*, in which he stressed the capacity of people to change the world in which they live while at the same time providing them with a vision of a future South Africa based on participatory democracy. Most importantly, Turner placed heavy emphasis on the significance of black workers in the economy. He believed that it was through collective organization, especially trade unions, that black people could exercise some control over their lives and influence the direction of change in South Africa.

I chose a different path from that of Turner by trying to resolve the contradiction between the professional and public roles by institutionalizing the link between these two types of sociology inside the university. The key institutional innovation was the creation of a research program, the Sociology of Work Programme (SWOP), in 1983, linking high-quality academic research on the world of work with a broad range of actors within the world of work. In 1988 I became head of the Department of Sociology at the University of the Witwatersrand, where I was able to cement the links between the University based research entity and teaching program with movements outside the University.

[***]

[***] Once you engage in participatory research relations with outside organizations where you jointly identify the problem to be studied, share ideas on how best to conduct the study, and report back on the results, a number of problems emerge. In particular it can lead to attempts to suppress uncomfortable research findings. Our research program experienced this when we investigated how the system of migrant labor created a market for prostitution and a potential AIDS pandemic. We needed to negotiate carefully with our research partners before coming to an agreement to publish these unwelcome facts on the devastating social consequences of migrant labor.

[***]

The research we undertook on AIDS in 1989 "percolated" into the consciousness of union officials and, with the support of sympathetic individuals in the union, they overturned accustomed patterns of thought. It helped clarify the union agenda leading this union to become the first to take up AIDS in a systematic way. But this does not mean that the public sociologist wields a lot of power.

[***]

The production of social knowledge is a political process. [***] This was brought home sharply to our researchers quite early on in the development of our research program, when we embarked on research among underground gold miners around issues of health and safety. We were able to show that even so-called "unskilled workers" exercised a range of tacit skills, tricks of the trade essential to production, but received no formal acknowledgment. Workers, we argued, were able to anticipate rock falls underground. We called the project Talking Rocks.

[***] The powerful employers' association, the Chamber of Mines, systematically attempted to discredit the research, arguing that it was their prerogative to decide who worked where, and it was only their university-accredited rock scientists that had the knowledge to predict rock falls. In the event,

one of the first pieces of legislation to be passed by the new democratic government was an amendent to the Mine Health and Safety Act to allow mine workers to refuse to work in dangerous conditions.

The importance of by whom and how scientific knowledge is accredited is a crucial issue for the public sociologist. It is necessary to engage directly with the discipline and attempt to shape the production of knowledge in the arenas where the discipline is shaped, the professional associations, the journals, and the textbooks.

[***]

SOURCE: Edward Webster, "Sociology in South Africa: Its Past, Present and Future," *Society in Transition* 35, no. 1 (2004): 27–41.

EDWARD WEBSTER is a professor of sociology and the Director of the Sociology of Work Unit at the University of the Witwatersrand, Johannesburg, South Africa. He is the author of Trade Unions and Democratisation in South Africa 1985–1996 *with G. Adler,* Cast in a Racial Mould—Labor Process and Trade Unionism in the Foundries, Essays in Southern African Labour History, *and* Change, Reform and Economic Growth in South Africa. *He is a founder of the* South African Labour Bulletin, *and is currently a secretary of the Research Committee on Labor Movements for the International Sociological Association.*

countries. There might be a general leveling out of average income around the world, although at a level much lower than that currently enjoyed in the United States and other industrialized nations. In this scenario, the polarization between the haves and the have-nots within countries would grow, as the whole world would be increasingly divided into those who benefit from the global economy and those who do not. Such polarization could fuel conflict between ethnic groups and even nations, as those suffering from economic globalization would blame others for their plight (Hirst and Thompson, 1992; Wagar, 1992).

On the other hand, a global economy could mean greater opportunity for everyone, as the benefits of modern technology stimulate worldwide economic growth. According to this more optimistic scenario, the more successful East Asian NIEs, such as Hong Kong, Taiwan, South Korea, and Singapore, are only a sign of things to come. Other NIEs such as Malaysia and Thailand will soon follow, along with China, Indonesia, Vietnam, and other Asian countries. India, the world's second most populous country, already boasts a middle class of around 200 million people, about a quarter of its total population (although roughly the same number live in poverty) (Kulkarni, 1993).

A countervailing trend, however, is the technology gap that divides rich and poor countries, which today appears to be widening, making it even more difficult for poor countries to catch up. The global technology gap is a result of the disparity in wealth between nations, but it also reinforces those disparities, widening the gap between rich and poor countries. Poor countries cannot easily afford modern technology—yet, in the absence of modern technology, they face major barriers to overcoming poverty. They are caught in a vicious downward spiral from which it is difficult to escape.

Jeffrey Sachs, director of the Center for International Development and professor of international trade at Harvard University, and a prominent adviser to many East European and developing countries, claims that the world is divided into three classes: technology innovators, technology adopters, and the technologically disconnected (Sachs, 2000).

Technology innovators are those regions that provide nearly all of the world's technological inventions; they account for no more than 15 percent of the world's population. *Technology adopters* are those regions that are able to adopt technologies invented elsewhere, applying them to production and consumption; they account for 50 percent of the world's population. Finally, the *technologically disconnected* are those regions that neither innovate nor adopt technologies developed elsewhere; they account for 35 percent of the world's population.

Note that Sachs speaks of regions rather than countries: In today's increasingly borderless world, technology use (or exclusion) does not always respect national frontiers. Technologically disconnected regions such as tropical sub-Saharan Africa or the Ganges valley states of India lack access to markets or major ocean trading routes. They are caught in what Sachs terms a "poverty trap," plagued by "tropical infectious disease, low agricultural productivity and environmental degradation—all requiring technological solutions beyond their means" (2000).

What can be done to overcome the technological abyss that divides rich and poor countries? Sachs urges the governments of wealthy countries, along with international lending institutions, to provide loans and grants for scientific and technological development. Sachs notes that very little money is available to support research and development in poor countries. The World Bank, a major source of funding for development projects in poor countries, spends only $60 million a year supporting tropical, agricultural, or health research and development. By way of comparison, Merck, the giant pharmaceutical corporation, spends thirty-five times that much ($2.1 billion) for research and development for its own products. From computers and the Internet to biotechnology, the "wealth of nations" increasingly depends on modern information technology. As long as major regions of the world remain technologically disconnected, it seems unlikely that global poverty will be eradicated.

In the most optimistic view, the republics of the former Soviet Union, as well as the formerly socialist countries of Eastern Europe, will eventually advance into the ranks of the high-income countries. Economic growth will spread to Latin America, Africa, and the rest of the world. Because capitalism requires that workers be mobile, the remaining caste societies around the world will be replaced by class-based societies. These societies will experience enhanced opportunities for upward mobility.

What is the future of global inequality? It is difficult to be entirely optimistic for now. Global economic growth has slowed, and many of the once promising economies of Asia now seem to be in trouble. The Russian economy, in its move from socialism to capitalism, has encountered many pitfalls, leaving many Russians much poorer than ever. It remains to be seen whether the countries of the world will learn from one another and work together to create better lives for their peoples. What is certain is that the past quarter century has witnessed a global economic transformation of unprecedented magnitude. The effects of this transformation in the next quarter century will leave few lives on the planet untouched.

Study Outline

Differences Between Countries

- The countries of the world can be stratified according to their per-person gross national product. Forty percent of the world's population live in low-income countries, compared with only 16 percent in high-income countries.
- An estimated 1.3 billion people in the world, or nearly one in four people, live in poverty today, an increase since the early 1980s. Many are the victims of discrimination based on race, ethnicity, or tribal affiliation.
- In general, people in high-income countries enjoy a far higher standard of living than their counterparts in low-income countries. They are likely to have more food to eat, less likely to starve or suffer from malnutrition, and likely to live longer. Additionally, they are less likely to have large families, and their children are much less likely to die in infancy of malnutrition or childhood diseases.

Can Poor Countries Become Rich?

- Such newly industrializing economies as Hong Kong, Singapore, Taiwan, and South Korea have experienced explosive economic growth since the mid-1970s. This growth is due partly to historical circumstances, to a lesser degree to the cultural characteristics of these countries, and most important, to the central role played by their governments. Whether this growth will continue is now in question, given the economic difficulties some of these countries currently face.

Theories of Global Inequality

- *Market-oriented theories of global inequality,* such as *modernization theory,* claim that cultural and institutional barriers to development explain the poverty of low-income societies. In this view, to eliminate poverty, fatalistic attitudes must be overcome, government meddling in economic affairs ended, and a high rate of savings and investment encouraged.
- *Dependency theories* claim that global poverty is the result of the exploitation of poor countries by wealthy ones. *Dependent development theory* argues that even though the economic fate of poor countries is ultimately determined by wealthy ones, some development is possible within dependent capitalistic relations.
- *World-systems theory* argues that the capitalist world system as a whole—not just individual countries—must be understood if we hope to make sense of global inequality. World-systems theory focuses on the relationships of *core, peripheral,* and *semiperipheral countries* in the global economy; long-term trends in the global economy; and *global commodity chains* that erase national borders.

- *State-centered theories* emphasize the role that governments can play in fostering economic development. These theories draw on the experience of the rapidly growing East Asian newly industrializing economies as an example.

The Future of Global Inequality

- No one can say for sure whether global inequality will increase or decrease in the future. It is possible that some leveling out of wages will occur worldwide, as wages decline in wealthy countries and rise in poor countries. It is also possible that all countries will someday prosper as the result of a unified global economy.

Key Concepts

colonialism (p. 210)
core country (p. 211)
dependent development (p. 211)
dependency theory (p. 210)
global commodity chain (p. 214)
global inequality (p. 196)
market-oriented theory (p. 207)
modernization theory (p. 207)
neoliberalism (p. 210)
newly industrializing economies (NIEs) (p. 204)
peripheral country (p. 211)
semiperipheral country (p. 211)
state-centered theory (p. 214)
world-systems theory (p. 211)

Review Questions

1. Which of the following is considered a high-income country?
   a. Singapore
   b. United States
   c. Taiwan
   d. All of the above
2. Most famine and hunger today are the result of:
   a. natural and social forces.
   b. natural force only.
   c. social force only.
   d. wars.
3. Economic growth in East Asia has its costs. These include:
   a. violent repression of labor and civil rights.
   b. terrible factory conditions.
   c. the exploitation of an increasingly female work force.
   d. all of the above.

Study Guide | **219**

4. Which country has the highest rate of economic growth?
   a. United States
   b. Canada
   c. China
   d. Brazil
5. Which theory argues that the world capitalist economic system must be understood as a single unit, not in terms of individual countries?
   a. State-centered development theory
   b. Modernization theory
   c. Dependency theory
   d. World-systems theory
6. Which theory argues that the poverty of low-income countries stems from their exploitation by wealthy countries and the multinational corporations that are based in wealthy countries?
   a. State-centered development theory
   b. Modernization theory
   c. Dependency theory
   d. World-systems theory
7. Of the estimated 26 million people worldwide infected with HIV/AIDS, what percent live in developing countries?
   a. 5 percent
   b. 35 percent
   c. 75 percent
   d. 95 percent
8. What is the relationship between income and fertility at the national level?
   a. Positive
   b. Negative
   c. No relationship
   d. Can be either positive or negative
9. What percent of the world's population lives in poverty?
   a. About 75 percent
   b. About 50 percent
   c. About 25 percent
   d. About 10 percent
10. _____ claims that cultural and institutional barriers to development explain the poverty of low-income societies.
    a. Dependency-development theory
    b. Modernization theory
    c. Dependency theory
    d. World-systems theory

Thinking Sociologically Exercises

1. Concisely review the four theories offered in this chapter that explain why there are gaps between nations' economic developments and resulting global inequality: market-oriented theory, dependency theory, world-systems theory, and state-centered theories. Briefly discuss the distinctive characteristics of each theory and how each differs from the others. Which theory do you feel offers the most explanatory power to addressing economic developmental gaps?
2. This chapter states that global economic inequality has personal relevance and importance to people in advanced, affluent economies. Briefly review this argument. Explain carefully whether you were persuaded by it or not.

Data Exercises

www.wwnorton.com/giddens
Keyword: Data8

- The nations of the world are not all equal when it comes to national wealth, but have you ever stopped to think about why such inequalities exist? Or what consequences these differences have in terms of patterns of consumption and social development? The data exercise for this chapter will give you an opportunity to learn more about global inequalities and to evaluate the different theoretical perspectives on global stratification.

Gender Differences: Nature versus Nurture

Think about whether differences between women and men are the result of biological differences or social and cultural influences.

Forms of Gender Inequality

Recognize that gender differences are a part of our social structure and create inequalities between women and men. Learn the forms these inequalities take, particularly in the workplace, the family, the educational system, the political system, and as violence against women.

Gender Inequality in Global Perspective

Understand the ways in which women around the world experience economic and political inequality.

Analyzing Gender Inequality

Think about various explanations for gender inequality. Learn some feminist theories about how to achieve gender equality.

Why Gender Inequality Matters

CHAPTER NINE

GENDER INEQUALITY

round midnight one cold night in December, a little before the end of the second shift, Andrea Ellington is standing by the Coke machine in the workers' lounge, cleaning out her oversized pocketbook. She empties its contents, which begin with a gold plastic makeup bag, a wallet, and a bunch of monthly bills. "I gotta go wake my five-year-old daughter up at my mother's house," she says as she opens the makeup bag. "Then I go to the other baby-sitter and get my baby twins. Then I take them home and they've gotta go back to sleep, try to go back to sleep. By the time my daughter gets back to sleep, it's time for her to get back up again" (Interview by the authors).

An African American woman of twenty-three, Andrea Ellington has three children to support on a low-rung clerical salary of $20,000 per year. She has been working at a Chicago law firm for four years; she had taken the job believing that with hard work, eventually she could advance enough to move her family out of public housing, her foremost goal.

Most of the five hundred or so employees in the law office where she works are not attorneys but "support staff," who work in one of many departments at the center of the floors, surrounded by plush attorneys' offices on the perimeter. The Network Center where she types is solely a nighttime word-processing department, with shifts from 4 P.M. to midnight and midnight to 8 A.M. The people who work as word processors are all women. They sit at computer terminals in one of four clusters separated by gray partitions. Almost all of these women who work at night are also rearing children during the day. Most live far from the law firm's gleaming downtown building.

Balancing the commitments of work and family is not only a challenge in terms of time but also money. Raising three children on her modest income, Andrea lives from paycheck to paycheck. She seeks out extra work to help her get by with her everyday responsibilities. As she says, "[working] overtime has helped me pay bills on time, buy clothes for my children, and buy food that I normally have had to wait until each paycheck to get." As a result of Andrea's persistence, her supervisor assigned her to work an extra eight hours of overtime per week, on Sundays. Andrea came to work for the first two Sundays and then began missing her weekend assignments when she couldn't find a baby-sitter for her three children. When her supervisor learned of the absences, she canceled the overtime.

Many people who encounter someone like Andrea Ellington might make certain assumptions about her life. They might assume, for example, that a disproportionate number of women become typists and word processors because it is natural for women to have certain kinds of occupations, including secretarial jobs. They might also assume that mothers should be responsible for taking care of children. Finally, they might assume that Andrea's poverty and low position in society are a result of her natural abilities. It is the job of sociology to analyze these assumptions and allow us to take a much wider view of our society and people like Andrea. Sociology allows us to understand why women are likely to work in low-paying clerical jobs, why women are likely to spend more time on child care, and why women on the whole are less powerful in society than men. Explaining the differences and inequalities between women and men in a society is now one of the most central topics in sociology.

In this chapter, we will explore a sociological approach to gender differences and gender inequality. Gender is a way for society to divide people into two categories: "men" and "women." According to this socially created division, men and women have different identities and social roles. In other words, men and women are expected to think and act in certain different ways. Since in almost all societies, men's roles are valued more than are women's roles, gender also serves as a social status. Men and women are not only different, but also unequal in terms of power, prestige, and wealth. Despite the advances that many women have made in the United States and other Western societies, this remains true today. Sociologists are interested in explaining not only how society differentiates between women and men, but also how these differences serve as the basis for social inequalities (Chafetz, 1990). Some sociologists are also concerned about the ways in which women can achieve positions of equality in society.

In this chapter, we will first look at the origins of gender differences, assessing the debate over the role of biological versus social influences on the formation of gender roles. We will also look to other cultures for evidence on this debate. We will then review the various forms of gender inequality that exist in American society. In this section, we will focus on the prominent social institutions of the workplace, the family, the educational system, and the political system. We will also examine how women are so often the targets of sexual violence. Next, we will examine how economic and political inequality affects women all over the world. We will review the various forms of feminism and assess prospects for future change toward a gender equal society. We will then analyze some theories of gender inequality and apply them to the circumstances of Andrea's life. We conclude the chapter by looking at the role of women around the world as we enter the twenty-first century.

Gender Differences: Nature versus Nurture

We begin by inquiring into the origins of the differences between boys and girls, men and women. The nature-nurture debate, noted earlier in Chapter 2, appears again with some force here. Scholars are divided about the degree to which inborn biological characteristics have an enduring impact on our gender identities as "feminine" or "masculine" and the social roles based on those identities. The debate is really about how much learning there is. No one any longer supposes that our behavior is instinctive in the sense in which the sexual activity of many lower animals—like the celebrated birds and bees—is instinctive. Some scholars, however, allow more prominence than others to social influences in analyzing gender differences.

Before we review these competing theories, we need to make an important distinction between sex and gender. While **sex** refers to physical differences of the body, **gender** concerns the psychological, social, and cultural differences between males and females. The distinction between sex and gender is fundamental, since many differences between males and females are not biological in origin.

The Role of Biology

How much are differences in the behavior of women and men the result of sex rather than gender? In other words, how much are they the result of biological differences? The opinions of researchers are divided. Some hold that innate differences of behavior between women and men appear in some form in all cultures and that the findings of sociobiology point strongly in this direction. Such researchers are likely to draw attention to the fact, for example, that in almost all cultures, men rather than women take part in hunting and warfare. Surely, they argue, this indicates that men possess biologically based tendencies toward aggression that women lack. In looking at the case of the word processors, they might point out that typing is a more passive occupation than being a bicycle messenger (an equivalent job category within the firm), which requires more physical strength and aggressiveness in traffic.

Most sociologists are unconvinced by these arguments. The level of aggressiveness of men, they say, varies widely among different cultures, and women are expected to be more passive or gentle in some cultures than in others (Elshtain, 1981). Theories of "natural difference" are often grounded in data on animal behavior, critics point out, rather than in anthropological or historical evidence about human behavior, which reveals variation over time and place. In the majority of cultures, most women spend a significant part of their lives caring for children and therefore cannot readily take part in hunting or war.

Although the hypothesis that biological factors determine behavior patterns in men and women cannot be dismissed out of hand, nearly a century of research to identify the physiological origins of such an influence has been unsuccessful. There is no evidence of the mechanisms that would link such biological forces with the complex social behaviors exhibited by human men and women (Connell, 1987). Theories that see individuals as complying with some kind of innate predisposition neglect the vital role of social interaction in shaping human behavior.

What does the evidence show? One possible source of information is the differences in hormonal makeup between the sexes. Some have claimed that the male sex hormone, testosterone, is associated with the male propensity to violence (Rutter and Giller, 1984). Research has indicated, for instance, that if male monkeys are castrated at birth, they become less aggressive; conversely, female monkeys given testosterone will become more aggressive than normal females. However, it has also been found that providing monkeys with opportunities to dominate others actually increases the testosterone level. Aggressive behavior may thus affect the production of the hormone, rather than the hormone's causing increased aggression.

Another source of information comes from the experience of identical twins. Identical twins derive from a single egg and have *exactly the same* genetic makeup. In one particular case, one of a pair of identical male twins was seriously injured while being circumcised, and the decision was made to reconstruct his genitals as a female. He was thereafter raised as a girl. The twins at six years old demonstrated typical male and female traits as found in Western culture. The little girl en-

Many children's toys may promote gender stereotyping.

joyed playing with other girls, helped with the housework, and wanted to get married when she grew up. The boy preferred the company of other boys, his favorite toys were cars and trucks, and he wanted to become a firefighter or police officer.

For some time, this case was treated as a conclusive demonstration of the overriding influence of social learning on gender differences. However, when the girl was a teenager, she was interviewed during a television program, and the interview showed that she felt some unease about her gender identity, even perhaps that she was "really" a boy after all. She had by then learned of her unusual background, and this knowledge may very well have been responsible for this altered perception of herself (Ryan, 1985).

Gender Socialization

Another route to take in understanding the origins of gender differences is the study of **gender socialization**, the learning of gender roles with the help of social agencies such as the family and the media (see also Chapter 4). Such an approach makes a distinction between biological sex and social gender—an infant is born with the first and develops the second. Through contact with various agencies of socialization, both primary and secondary, children gradually internalize the social norms and expectations that are seen to correspond with their sex. Gender differences are not biologically determined; they are culturally produced. According to this view, gender inequalities result because men and women are socialized into different roles.

People create gender through social interactions with others, such as family members, friends, and colleagues. This process begins at birth when doctors, nurses, and family members—the first to see an infant—assign the person to a gender category on the basis of physical characteristics. Babies are immediately dressed in a way that marks the sex category: "parents don't want to be constantly asked if their child is a boy or a girl" (Lorber, 1994). Once the child is marked as male or female, everyone who interacts with the child will treat it in accordance with its gender. They do so on the basis of the society's assumptions, which lead people to treat women and men differently, even as opposites (Renzetti and Curran, 1995).

Clearly, gender socialization is very powerful, and challenges to it can be upsetting. Once a gender is "assigned," society expects individuals to act like "females" and "males." It is in the practices of everyday life that these expectations are fulfilled and reproduced (Bourdieu, 1990; Lorber, 1994).

The Social Construction of Gender

In recent years, socialization and gender role theories have been criticized by a growing number of sociologists. Rather than seeing sex as biologically determined and gender as culturally learned, they argue that we should view *both* sex and gender as socially constructed products. Not only is gender a purely social creation that lacks a fixed essence, but the human body itself is subject to social forces that shape and alter it in various ways.

According to such a perspective, writers who focus on gender roles and role learning implicitly accept that there *is* a biological basis to gender differences. In the socialization approach, a biological distinction between the sexes provides a framework that becomes culturally elaborated in society itself. In contrast to this, theorists who believe in the **social construction of gender** reject all biological bases for gender differences. Gender identities emerge, they argue, in relation to perceived sex differences in society and in turn help to shape those differences. For example, a society in which ideas of masculinity are characterized by physical strength and tough attitudes will encourage men to cultivate a specific body image and set of mannerisms. In other words, gender identities and sex differences are inextricably linked within individual human bodies (Connell, 1987; Butler, 1989; Scott and Morgan, 1993).

Gender Identity in Everyday Life

Our conceptions of gender identity are formed so early in life that as adults we mainly take them for granted. Yet gender is more than learning to act like a girl or boy. Gender differences are something we live with every day.

In other words, gender as a physical concept does not exist; we all, as some sociologists put it, "do gender" in our daily interactions with others (West and Zimmerman, 1987). For in-

stance, Jan Morris, the celebrated travel writer, used to be a man. As James Morris, she was a member of the British expedition, led by Sir Edmund Hillary, that successfully climbed Mount Everest. She was, in fact, a very "manly" man—a race car driver and an athlete. Yet she had always felt herself to be a woman in a male body. So she underwent a sex-change operation and lived the rest of her life as a woman.

Jan Morris had to learn how to do gender when she discovered how differently she was expected to behave as a woman,

This photo (top), dated November 30, 1952, shows George Jorgensen before his sex change. After he was discharged from the U.S. Army he traveled to Copenhagen, Denmark, where he had a sex-change operation. After the operation he changed his name to Christine. Christine Jorgensen (bottom), returning from a nightclub engagement in Cuba in 1953.

rather than as a man. As she says, there is "no aspect of existence" that is not gendered. But she did not notice this until she changed her sex.

> It amuses me to consider, for instance, when I am taken out to lunch by one of my more urbane men friends, that not so many years ago th[e] waiter would have treated *me* as he is now treating *him*. Then he would have greeted me with respectful seriousness. Now he unfolds my napkin with a playful flourish, as if to humor me. Then he would have taken my order with grave concern, now he expects me to say something frivolous (and I do). (Morris, 1974)

The subtle ways in which we do gender are so much a part of our lives that we don't notice them until they are missing or radically altered.

This differentiation between the roles and identities that society creates for men and women occurs not only in face-to-face interaction, but is also part of society's institutions, such as the economy, political system, educational system, religions, and family forms. Because gender is so pervasive in structuring social life, gender statuses must be clearly differentiated if society is to function in an orderly manner. However, gender differentiation can also be the basis for inequalities between men and women (Lorber, 1994; West and Fenstermaker, 1995).

Findings from Other Cultures

If gender differences were mostly the result of biology, then we could expect that gender roles would not vary much from culture to culture. However, one set of findings that helps show gender roles are in fact socially constructed comes from anthropologists, who have studied gender in other times and cultures.

NEW GUINEA

In her classic New Guinea study, *Sex and Temperament in Three Primitive Societies*, Margaret Mead (1963) observed wide variability among gender role prescriptions—and such marked differences from those in the United States—that any claims to the universality of gender roles had to be rejected. Mead studied three separate tribes in New Guinea, which varied widely in their gender roles. In Arapesh society, both males and females generally had characteristics and behaviors that would typically be associated with the Western female role. Both sexes among the Arapesh were passive, gentle, unaggressive, and emotionally responsive to the needs of others. In contrast, Mead found that in another New Guinea group, the Mundugumor, both the males and females were characteristically aggressive, suspicious, and, from a Western observer's perspective, excessively cruel, especially toward children. In both cultures, however, men and women were expected to behave very similarly.

Mead then studied the Tchambuli tribe of New Guinea. The gender roles of the males and females were almost exactly reversed from the roles traditionally assigned to males and females in Western society. Mead reported in her autobiography that "among the Tchambuli the expected relations between men and women reversed those that are characteristic of our own culture. For it was Tchambuli women who were brisk and hearty, who managed the business affairs of life, and worked comfortably in large cooperative groups" (1972). Mead also reported that while the women managed the affairs of the family, the men were engaged differently: "Down by the lake shore in ceremonial houses the men carved and painted, gossiped and had temper tantrums, and played out their rivalries" (1972).

THE !KUNG

Another example can be found among the !Kung of the Kalahari desert. Although "men hunt and women gather" in this society, a vast majority of its food comes from the gathering activities of women (See Draper, as cited in Renzetti, 2000). Indeed, !Kung women are respected for their specialized knowledge of the bush: "Successful gathering over the years requires the ability to discriminate among hundreds of edible and inedible species of plants at various stages in their life cycle" (Draper, 1975). In addition, women return from their gathering expeditions armed not only with food for the community but also with valuable information for hunters. Draper noted that "women are skilled in reading the signs of the bush, and they take careful note of animal tracks, their age, and the direction of movement. . . . In general, the men take advantage of women's reconnaissance and query them routinely on the evidence of game movements, the location of water and the like" (1975).

Due to the non-confrontational parenting practices of the !Kung, who oppose violent conflict and physical punishment, children learned that aggressive behavior will not be tolerated by either men or women. The !Kung do have specific sex roles, but it is very common for both men and women to engage in child care. Whereas in the United States it is still common for boys and girls to have very distinct upbringings, this is not true in the !Kung society (See Draper, as cited in Renzetti, 2000).

SUDHEST ISLAND

Recent anthropological evidence continues to contradict the idea that gender inequality is universal. The anthropologist Maria Lepowsky of the University of Wisconsin did ethnographic research with the people of Sudhest Island, 200 miles south of Papua, New Guinea in the South Pacific. After living with them for two years, she concluded that the inhabitants of the island, the Vanatinai society, "offers any adult, regardless of sex or kin group, the opportunity of excelling at prestigious activities" (Lepowsky, 1990, as cited in Renzetti, 2000). Men even participate in child care. On the other hand, even here she did not find absolute equality: Women tend to sweep up pig excrement whereas men hunt wild boar.

MULTIPLE GENDERS

The understanding that only two genders (i.e. male and female) exist is not true among all societies. The Spaniards who came to both North and South America in the seventeenth century noticed men in the native tribes who had taken on the mannerisms of women, as well as women who occupied male roles. Indeed, many citizens of the United States who are intolerant of same-sex marriage are surprised to learn that Native Americans have a long tradition in which men enact female roles and women enact male roles, and which allows same-sex marriage. This fact has now

A *we'wha* (or *berdache*) of the Zuni people of New Mexico.

been documented by anthropologists in over 155 Native American tribes.

A person occupying an opposite gender role is called a *berdache*. But many scholars are unhappy with this term because its derivation does not come from the Native American cultures themselves (it derives from Persia), and some believe it has a negative connotation, not unlike "faggot." Others argue that it is more often a substitute for lover or boyfriend (Roscoe, 2000). In any event, some anthropologists have tried to replace *berdache* with "two-spirit." In fact, "two-spirit" has become a contemporary label used by Native Americans who are gay, lesbian, bisexual, and transgendered.

Berdaches are not the counterpart of transsexuals or transvestites in the United States, however. Roscoe (1991) has studied Zuni *berdaches* and noted that although *berdaches* technically do "cross-dress," their cross-dressing is routine, public, and without erotic motives. Moreover, *berdaches* are not necessarily homosexual; rather, some are heterosexual, some homosexual, and others sexually oriented toward other *berdaches*.

In one society, Roscoe found that both males and females have characteristics typically associated with the female role in the West. In another group, both males and females are aggressive. In both cultures, men and women are expected to behave similarly. These findings demonstrate that culture—not biology—is at the root of gender differences. There was a time in the development of feminist approaches when gender roles and gender socialization were the dominant concepts in understanding why women tended to cluster in particular occupations.

In recent years, however, sociologists have noted that while society teaches people to assume certain "masculine" or "feminine" gender roles, such an approach does not tell us where these gender roles come from or how they can be changed. For this, we need to look at the way that gender is built into the institutions of society (Lorber, 1994). For example, we need to know how the schools Andrea attended and the law firm Andrea works in operate to establish "patterns of expectations" that lead people to assume certain roles (Lorber, 1994).

Forms of Gender Inequality

Anthropologists and historians have found that most groups, collectives, and societies throughout history differentiate between women's and men's societal roles. Although there are considerable variations in the respective roles of

FIGURE 9.1

Women's Participation in the Labor Force[a]

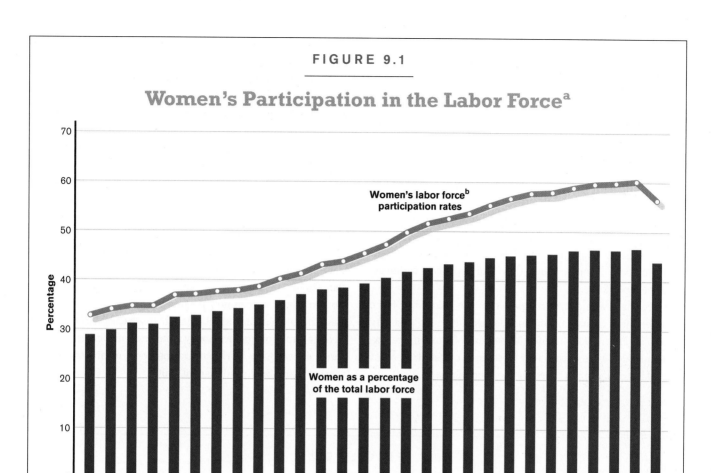

[a]Civilians age 16 and over.

[b]Labor force participants as a percentage of all civilian women age 16 and over.

SOURCE: U.S. Bureau of Labor Statistics, "Household Data, Annual Averages," Tables 1 and 2, www.bls.gov/cps/cpsaat1.pdf and www.bls.gov/cps/cpsaat2.pdf.

women and men in different cultures, there are few instances of a society in which women are more powerful than men. Women everywhere are primarily concerned with child rearing and the maintenance of the home, while political and military activities tend to be resoundingly male. Nowhere in the world do men have primary responsibility for the rearing of children. Conversely, there are few if any cultures in which women are charged with the main responsibility for the herding of large animals, the hunting of large game, deep-sea fishing, or plow agriculture (Brown, 1977). Just because women and men perform different tasks or have different responsibilities in societies does not necessarily mean that women are unequal to men. However, if the work and activities of women and men are valued differently, then the division of labor between them can become the basis for unequal gender relations. In modern societies, the division of labor between the sexes has become less clear cut than it

was in premodern cultures, but men still outnumber women in all spheres of power and influence.

Male dominance in a society is usually referred to as **patriarchy**. Although men are favored in almost all of the world's societies, the degree of patriarchy varies. In the United States, women have made tremendous progress, but several forms of gender inequality still exist.

Sociologists define **gender inequality** as the difference in the status, power, and prestige women and men have in groups, collectives, and societies. In thinking about gender inequality between men and women, we can ask the following questions: Do women and men have equal access to valued societal resources—for example, food, money, power, and time? Second, do women and men have similar life options? Third, are women's and men's roles and activities valued similarly? We will turn to look at the various forms of gender inequality in the workplace, in the home, in education systems, and in politics, as well as in the violence practiced on women. As you read through this section, keep the above questions in mind.

Women and the Workplace

Rates of employment of women outside the home, for all classes, were quite low until well into the twentieth century. Even as late as 1910 in the United States, more than a third of gainfully employed women were maids or house servants. The female labor force consisted mainly of young, single women and children. When women or girls worked in factories or offices, employers often sent their wages straight home to their parents. When they married, they withdrew from the labor force.

Since then, women's participation in the paid labor force has risen more or less continuously, especially in the past fifty years (see Figure 9.1). In 1996, 59 percent of women age sixteen and older were in the labor force. In contrast, 38 percent of working-age women were in the labor force in 1960. An even greater change in the rate of labor-force participation has occurred among married mothers of young children. In 1978, only 14 percent of married women with preschool-age children (under six years old) worked full time year round, yet this figure increased to 35 percent by 1998 (see Figure 9.2) (Cohen and Bianchi, 1999).

How can we explain this increase? One force behind women's increased entry into the labor force was the increase in demand, since 1940, for clerical and service workers like Andrea, as the U.S. economy expanded and changed (Oppenheimer, 1970). From 1940 until the mid- to late 1960s, labor-force activity increased among women who were past their prime child-rearing years. During the 1970s and 1980s, as the marriage age rose, fertility declined, and women's educational attainment increased, the growth in labor force participation spread to younger women. Many women now postpone family formation to complete their education and establish themselves in the labor force. Despite family obligations, today a majority of women of all educational levels now work outside the home during their child-rearing years (Spain and Bianchi, 1996).

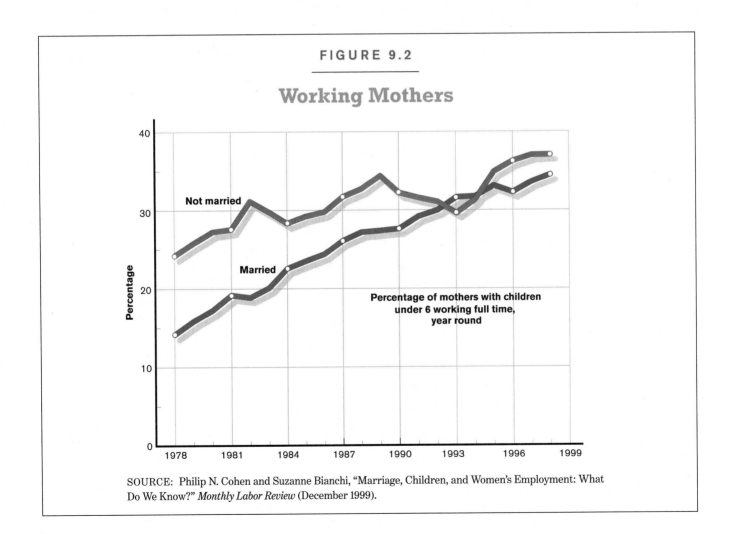

FIGURE 9.2

Working Mothers

Percentage of mothers with children under 6 working full time, year round

SOURCE: Philip N. Cohen and Suzanne Bianchi, "Marriage, Children, and Women's Employment: What Do We Know?" *Monthly Labor Review* (December 1999).

Inequalities at Work

Until recently, women workers were overwhelmingly concentrated in routine, poorly paid occupations. The fate of the occupation of clerk (office worker) provides a good illustration. In 1850 in the United States, clerks held responsible positions, requiring accountancy skills and carrying managerial responsibilities; fewer than 1 percent were women. The twentieth century saw a general mechanization of office work (starting with the introduction of the typewriter in the late nineteenth century), accompanied by a marked downgrading of the status of clerk—together with a related occupation, secretary—into a routine, low-paid occupation. Women filled these occupations as the pay and prestige of such jobs declined. Today, most secretaries and clerks are women.

Studies of particular types of occupations have shown how **gender typing** occurs in the workplace. Expanding areas of work of a lower-level kind, such as secretarial positions or retail sales, draw in a substantial proportion of women. These jobs are poorly paid and hold few career prospects. Men with good educational qualifications aspire to something higher, while others choose blue-collar work. Once an occupation has become gender typed—once it is seen as mainly a "woman's job"—inertia sets in.

These social conditions often tend to reinforce outlooks produced by early gender socialization. Women may grow up believing that they should put their husband's career before their own. (Men also are frequently brought up to believe the same thing.)

Women have recently made some inroads into occupations once defined as "men's jobs" (see Figure 9.3). By the 1990s, women constituted a majority of workers in previously male-dominated professions such as accounting, journalism, psychology, public service, and bartending. In fields such as law, medicine, and engineering, their proportion has risen substantially since 1970. In 2003, a woman was more likely to be in a managerial or professional job than a clerical or service position.

Another important economic trend of the past thirty years was the narrowing of the gender gap in earnings. Between 1970 and 2002, the ratio of women's to men's earnings among full-time, year-round workers increased from 62 to 78 percent (see Table 9.1). Moreover, this ratio increased among all races and ethnic groups. During the 1980s, women's hourly wages

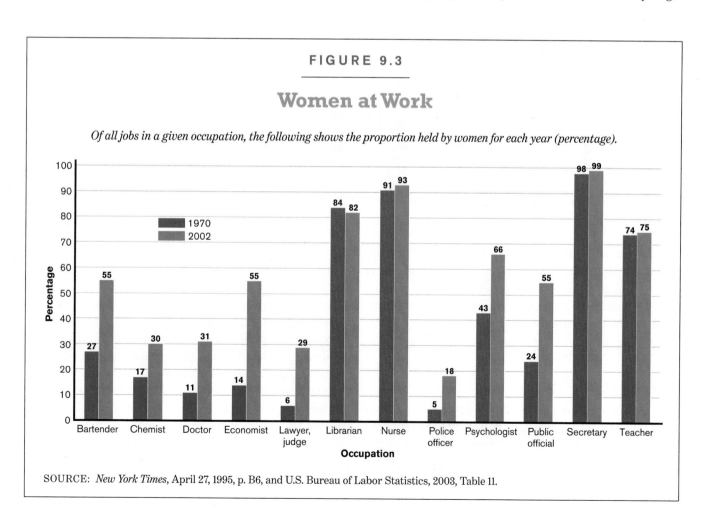

FIGURE 9.3

Women at Work

Of all jobs in a given occupation, the following shows the proportion held by women for each year (percentage).

SOURCE: *New York Times*, April 27, 1995, p. B6, and U.S. Bureau of Labor Statistics, 2003, Table 11.

TABLE 9.1

Women's Earnings Compared with Men's

Although the earnings gap between women and men is narrowing, it remains substantial. It is also significant that since the early 1990s, the gap has remained fairly constant. Analysts wonder whether this is temporary or permanent. The table shows what women earned for each dollar earned by men.

YEAR	EARNINGS RATIO
1970	.62
1980	.64
1990	.71
1991	.74
1992	.75
1993	.76
1994	.76
1995	.75
1996	.75
1997	.74
1998	.76
1999	.76
2000	.76
2001	.76
2002	.78

SOURCE: U.S. Bureau of Labor Statistics, "Women's Earnings Up Relative to Men's in 2002," www.bls.gov/opub/ted/2003/apr/wk3/art03.htm.

ing conditions. After such a ranking, pay is adjusted so that equivalently ranked male- and female-dominated jobs receive equivalent pay (Hartmann et al., 1985).

Although comparable worth policies may help to reduce the gender gap in pay, only a handful of U.S. states have instituted comparable worth policies for public sector employees (Blum, 1991). One reason that comparable worth policies have not been implemented is that they raise multiple technical, political, and economic issues. Perhaps most important is the issue of job evaluation, or the technical process that reduces male- and female-dominated jobs to an underlying common denominator of skill, effort, responsibility, and working conditions so as to compare and rank them independent of the race and gender of job incumbents (Stryker, 1996). Effective implementation requires that job evaluations be free from gender bias. However, substantial research shows that gender-neutral assessments of jobs and required job skills are very difficult. Once men and women know which jobs are predominantly male and which are predominantly female, they tend to attribute to them the job content that best fits with gender stereotypes (Steinberg, 1990).

Opposition to comparable-worth policies has been offered by both economists and feminists. Some economists worry that comparable worth is inflationary and will cause wage losses and unemployment for some (disproportionately women) because of benefits enacted for others. Feminists counter that comparable worth reinforces gender stereotyping rather than breaking down gender barriers at work (Blum, 1991).

Whether or not comparable worth policies are enacted, the surrounding debates show that what jobs society values are determined not by their market or societal worth but by power relations (Blum, 1991).

as a percentage of men's increased from 64 to 79 percent, weekly earnings rose from 63 to 75 percent, and the ratio of annual earnings among all workers (not just those working full time) increased from 46 to 61 percent (Spain and Bianchi, 1996). Despite the lessening of the gender gap in pay, men still earn substantially more than women (see Figure 9.4).

COMPARABLE WORTH

Comparable worth is a policy that compares pay levels of jobs held disproportionately by women with pay levels of jobs held disproportionately by men and tries to adjust pay so that the women and men who work in female-dominated jobs are not penalized. The policy presumes that jobs can be ranked objectively according to skill, effort, responsibility, and work-

THE GLASS CEILING AND THE GLASS ESCALATOR

Although women are increasingly entering "traditionally male" jobs, their entry into such jobs may not necessarily be accompanied by increases in pay—and increases in occupational mobility—due to the "**glass ceiling**." The glass ceiling is a promotion barrier that prevents a woman's upward mobility within an organization. The glass ceiling is particularly problematic for women who work in male-dominated occupations and the professions. Women's progress is blocked not by virtue of innate inability or lack of basic qualifications, but by not having the sponsorship of well-placed, powerful senior colleagues to articulate their value to the organization or profession (Alvarez et al., 1996). As a result, women tend to progress until mid-level management positions, but they do not, in proportionate numbers, move beyond mid-management ranks.

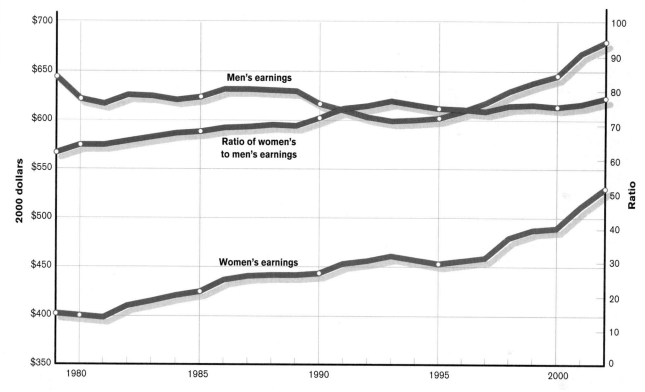

FIGURE 9.4

The Gender Pay Gap

This figure, in which weekly earnings are shown in constant 2000 dollars, illustrates what has been happening to the gender pay gap over time. After narrowing gradually for years, it widened a little after 1993, when men's inflation-adjusted earnings were increasing slightly and women's were not.

SOURCE: U.S. Bureau of Labor Statistics, "Household Data Annual Averages" Table 37, "Median weekly earnings of full-time wage and salary workers by selected characteristics," www.bls.gov/cps/cpsaat37.pdf.

One explanation for women's blocked mobility is based on gender stereotypes. Research shows that college-educated white males in professional jobs tend to identify potential leaders as people who are like themselves. Women are thus assessed negatively because they deviate from this norm or standard (Cleveland, 1996).

What about men who work in female-dominated professions? Do they also face subtle obstacles to promotion? On the contrary, the sociologist Christine Williams (1992) has observed that a **"glass escalator"** pushes these men to the top of their corporate ladders. Williams found that employers singled out male workers in traditionally female jobs, such as nurse, librarian, elementary school teacher, and social worker,

and promoted them to top administrative jobs in disproportionately high numbers. "Often, despite their intentions, they face invisible pressures to move up in their professions. Like being on a moving escalator, they have to work to stay in place," writes Williams (1992). These pressures may take positive forms, such as close mentoring and encouragement from supervisors, or they may be the result of prejudicial attitudes of those outside the profession, such as clients who prefer to work with male rather than female executives. Some of the men in Williams's study faced unwelcome pressure to accept promotions, such as a male children's librarian who received negative evaluations for "not shooting high enough" in his career aspirations.

Sociologist Christine Williams asserts that men in female-dominated professions, such as this elementary school teacher, are routinely promoted to top administrative positions and face constant pressure to advance.

SEXUAL HARASSMENT IN THE WORKPLACE

Sexual harassment is unwanted or repeated sexual advances, remarks, or behavior that are offensive to the recipient and cause discomfort or interference with job performance. Power imbalances facilitate harassment; even though women can and do sexually harass subordinates, because men usually hold positions of authority, it is more common for men to harass women (Reskin and Padavic, 1994).

The U.S. courts have identified two types of sexual harassment. One is the quid pro quo, in which a supervisor demands sexual acts from a worker as a job condition or promises work-related benefits in exchange for sexual acts. The other is the "hostile work environment," in which a pattern of sexual language, lewd posters, or sexual advances makes a worker so uncomfortable that it is difficult for her to do her job (Reskin and Padavic, 1994).

Sociologists have observed that "the great majority of women who are abused by behavior that fits legal definitions of sexual harassment—and who are traumatized by the experience—do not label what has happened to them as sexual harassment" (Paludi and Barickman, 1991).

Women's reluctance to report may be due to the following factors: (1) many still do not recognize that sexual harassment is an actionable offense; (2) victims may be reluctant to come forward with complaints, fearing that they will not be believed, that their charges will not be taken seriously, or that they will be subject to reprisals; (3) it may be difficult to differentiate between harassment and joking on the job (Giuffre and Williams, 1994).

The Family and Gender Issues

BALANCING WORK AND CHILD CARE

One of the major factors affecting women's careers is the male perception that for female employees, work comes second to having children. One study carried out in Britain investigated the views of managers interviewing female applicants for positions as technical staff in the health services. The researchers found that the interviewers always asked the women about whether or not they had, or intended to have, children (this is now illegal in the United States). They virtually never followed this practice with male applicants. When asked why, two themes ran through their answers: Women with children may require extra time off for school holidays or if a child falls sick, and responsibility for child care is a mother's problem rather than a parental one.

Some managers thought their questions indicated an attitude of "caring" toward female employees. But most saw such a line of questioning as part of their task in assessing how far a female applicant would prove a reliable colleague. Although men cannot biologically "have a family" in the sense of bearing children, they can be fully involved in and responsible for child care. Such a possibility was not taken into account by any of the managers studied. The same attitudes were held about the promotion of women. Women were seen as likely to interrupt their careers to care for young children, no matter how senior a position they might have reached. The few women in this study who held senior management positions were all without children, and several of those who planned to have children in the future said they intended to leave their jobs and would perhaps retrain for other positions subsequently.

How should we interpret these findings? Are women's job opportunities hampered mainly by male prejudices? Some managers expressed the view that women with children should *not* work, but should occupy themselves with child care and the home. Most, however, accepted the principle that women should have the same career opportunities as men. The bias in their attitudes had less to do with the workplace itself than with the domestic responsibilities of parenting. So long as most of the population take it for granted that parenting cannot be shared on an equal basis by both women and men, the problems facing women employees will persist.

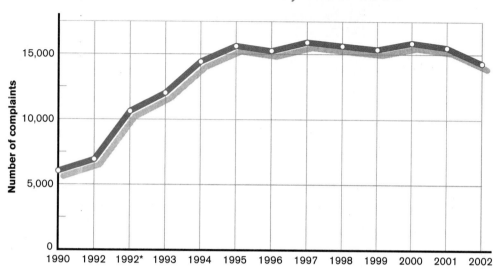

FIGURE 9.5

Increase in Sexual Harassment Complaints in the United States, 1990–2002

*Following Anita Hill's testimony before the Senate.

SOURCE: Equal Employment Opportunity Commission, "Sexual Harassment Charges, EEOC & FEPA combined: FY 1992–FY 2002."

It will remain a fact of life, as one of the managers put it, that women are disadvantaged, compared with men, in their career opportunities.

HOUSEWORK

Although there have been revolutionary changes in women's status in recent decades in the United States, including the entry of women into male-dominated professions, one area of work has lagged far behind: housework. Because of the increase of married women in the workforce and the resulting change in status, it was presumed that men would contribute more to housework. On the whole, this has not been the case. Although men now do more housework than they did three decades ago (about one to two hours more per week) and women do slightly less, the balance is still unequal (Shelton and John, 1993). Sociologists calculate that working women perform fifteen more hours of housework per week than their husbands, in effect a "second shift" of work (Hochschild, 1989; Shelton, 1992). The UN estimates that women in the United States work 6 percent more than men, a majority of which is spent in non-market activities (UN, 2003). These figures do not include time spent on child care, which if factored in would

increase the gap. The UN has estimated that if all of the non-market work of women was accounted for, the official estimate of the size of the world economy would be $11 trillion higher (UN, 1995).

Some sociologists have suggested that this phenomenon is best explained as a result of economic forces: Household work is exchanged for economic support. Because women earn less than men, they are more likely to remain economically dependent on their husbands and thus perform the bulk of the housework. Until the earnings gap is narrowed, women will likely remain in their dependent position. Hochschild has suggested that women are thus doubly oppressed by men: once during the "first shift" and again during the "second shift." But although this dependency model contributes to our understanding of the gendered aspects of housework, it breaks down when applied to situations where the wife earns more than her husband. For instance, of the husbands that Hochschild studied who earned less than their wives, none shared in the housework.

Sociologists argue that underlying this inequitable distribution of tasks is the implicit understanding that men and women are responsible for, and should operate in, different spheres. Men are expected to be providers, while women are

Can men and women truly share equal responsibility for their children or will women always be regarded as the primary caretakers?

expected to tend to their families—even if they are breadwinners as well as mothers. Expectations like this reinforce traditional gender roles learned during childhood socialization. By reproducing these roles in everyday life, men and women "do gender" and reinforce gender as a means for society to differentiate between men and women.

Education and Unequal Treatment in the Classroom

Sociologists have found that schools help foster gender differences in outlook and behavior. Studies document that teachers interact differently—and often inequitably—with their male and female students. These interactions differ in at least two ways: the frequency of teacher-student interactions and the content of those interactions. Both of the patterns are based on—and perpetuate—traditional assumptions about male and female behavior and traits.

One study shows that regardless of the sex of the teacher, male students interact more with their teachers than female students do. Boys receive more teacher attention and instructional time than girls do. This is due in part to the fact that boys are more demanding than girls (AAUW, 1992). Another study reported that boys are eight times more likely to call out answers in class, thus grabbing their teachers' attention. This research also shows that even when boys do not voluntarily participate in class, teachers are more likely to solicit information from them than from girls. However, when girls try to bring attention to themselves by calling out in class without raising their hands, they were reprimanded by comments such as "In this class, we don't shout out answers, we raise our hands" (Sadker and Sadker, 1994).

Sociologists have also found that the content of student-teacher interactions differs depending on the sex of the students. After observing elementary school teachers and students over many years, researchers found that teachers provided boys with assistance in working out the correct answers whereas they simply gave girls the correct answers and did not engage them in the problem-solving process. In addition, teachers posed more academic challenges to boys, encouraging them to think through their answers in order to arrive at the best possible response (Sadker and Sadker, 1994).

Boys were also disadvantaged in several ways, however. Because of their rowdy behavior, they were more often scolded and punished than the girl students. Moreover, boys outnumber girls in special education programs by startling percentages. Sociologists have argued that school personnel may be mislabeling boys' behavioral problems as learning disabilities.

This differential treatment of boys and girls perpetuates stereotypic gender-role behavior. Girls are trained to be quiet, well behaved, and to turn to others for answers, while boys are encouraged to be inquisitive, outspoken, active problem solvers. Female children from ethnic minorities are in some respects doubly disadvantaged. A study of what it was like to be a black female pupil in a white school reported that unlike the boys, the black girls were initially enthusiastic about school but altered their attitudes because of the difficulties they encountered. Even when the girls were quite small, aged seven or eight, teachers would disperse them if they were standing chatting in a group on the playground—in contrast to their treatment of the white children, whose similar behavior was tolerated. Once treated as "troublemakers," they rapidly became so (Bryan, Dadzie, and Scafe, 1987).

Gender Inequality in Politics

Women are playing an increasingly important role in U.S. politics, although they are still far from achieving full equality. Before 1993, there were only two women in the U.S. Senate (out of one hundred Senate members), and twenty-nine in the U.S. House of Representatives (out of 435). Less than a decade later—in 2001—there were a record thirteen women in the Senate and fifty-nine in the House. Currently, there are fourteen women Senators but sixty-eight Representatives (U.S. House of Representatives, 2005). Women in 2003 held a little more than 22 percent of all seats in state legislatures, five times as many as they held in 1969, but only nine governorships (out of fifty) (CAWP, 2001; NGA, 2003). The U.S. Supreme Court had its first woman justice appointed in 1981, and its second twelve years later. It was not until 1984 that a woman was nominated as the vice presidential candidate of either major party, neither of which has ever nominated a woman for the presidency.

Typically, the more local the political office, the more likely it is to be occupied by a woman. Men outnumber women in politics at all levels, but women are often elected members of city and county governing boards and as mayors. In most states, women are less likely to be found as representatives to state government than as representatives at the local level, but even women elected at the state level are more common than women representatives to Congress. The reason is partly that local politics is often part-time work, particularly in smaller cities and towns. Local politics can thus be good "women's work," offering low pay, part-time employment, flexible hours, and the absence of a clear career path. The farther from home the political office, the more likely it is to be regarded as "man's work," providing a living wage, full-time employment, and a lifetime career.

Violence Against Women

Violence directed against women is found in many societies, including the United States. One out of three women has been beaten, coerced into sex, or abused in some other way—most often by someone she knows, including her husband or a male relative (UNFPA, 2003). More women are injured as a result of beatings by spouses than by any other cause, a problem that is ignored by most governments (Human Rights Watch, 1995). In Japan, three out of five women report having been sexually or physically abused by a partner. In India, an estimated twenty thousand brides were killed between 1990 and 1995—usually by being burned alive—for bringing an inadequate dowry to their husbands' families (Wright, 1995). Between 100 and 130 million girls and women worldwide have been subjected to "genital mutilation," while an equal number are "missing," partly as the result of female infanticide in cultures where boys are more highly valued than girls.

In the United States, many scholars argue that the increased depiction of violence in movies, on television, and elsewhere in American popular culture contributes to a climate in which women are often victimized. The most common manifestation of violence against women is rape, although stalking and sexual harassment increasingly are seen as a form of psychological (if not physical) violence as well.

RAPE

Rape can be sociologically defined as the forcing of nonconsensual vaginal, oral, or anal intercourse. As one researcher observed, between consensual sex and rape lies "a continuum of pressure, threat, coercion, and force" (Kelly, 1987). Common to all forms of rape is the lack of consent: At least in principle, "no" means "no" when it comes to sexual relations in most courts of law in the United States. Virtually all rapes are committed by men against women, although men rape other men in prisons and other all-male institutional environments.

Rape is an act of violence, rather than a purely sexual act. It is often carefully planned rather than performed on the spur of the moment to satisfy some uncontrollable sexual desire. Many rapes involve beatings, knifings, and even murder. Even when rape leaves no physical wounds, it is a highly traumatic violation of a woman's person that leaves long-lasting psychological scars.

It is difficult to know with accuracy how many rapes actually occur, since most rapes go unreported. One comprehensive study of American sexual behavior found that 22 percent of the women surveyed reported having been forced into a sexual encounter. Yet the same study found that only 3 percent of the men admitted to having forced a woman into having sex, a discrepancy the study's authors attribute to different perceptions between men and women regarding what constitutes forced sex (Laumann et al., 1994). Based on its semiannual survey of nearly 100,000 Americans, the U.S. Department of Justice estimates that in 2002, there were 148,040 sexual assaults on women, 57,270 attempted rapes, and 116,760 rapes. The total number of sexual assaults, attempted rapes, and rapes (322,060) was nearly 25 percent lower than in 1999—part of an overall decrease in violent crimes since 1994. In fact, criminal victimizations, which include rape and sexual assault, are at their lowest point since 1973 (U.S. Department of Justice, 2003).

Most rapes are committed by relatives (fathers or stepfathers, brothers, uncles), partners, or acquaintances. Among college students, most rapes are likely to be committed by boyfriends, former boyfriends, or classmates. The National College Women Sexual Victimization Study (NCWSV), a national survey of 4,446 women attending two- or four-year colleges or universities, presents a chilling picture of violence against women on campuses across the country (Fisher, Cullen, and Turner, 2000). The study, which was conducted during spring semester 1997, asked college women about their experience with rape, attempted rape, coerced sex, unwanted sexual contact, and stalking during the 1996–1997 school year. Overall, since the beginning of the school year, 1.7 percent had been the victim of a completed rape, and 1.1 percent of an attempted rape. Since students were typically interviewed seven months into the academic year, the authors estimate that over the entire academic year nearly 5 percent of the women in the sample would have fallen victim to a rape or attempted rape. Over the typical five years of a college career, this suggests that between a fifth and a quarter of all women attending college would fall victim to rape or attempted rape—some 2.2 million women.

Masculinity and School Shootings

In a small New York City public school where I worked as a social worker and mediator, I saw gang wars and kids tormenting other kids. When boys harassed and teased others, there was one insult that I heard frequently, the one that was considered the worst of all: "You look gay."

Boys found early that being sensitive, respectful, and kind would earn them no respect. Instead they learned not to back down from a fight or apologize for a mistake, and to defend their honor against any slight, with violence if necessary, no matter how risky the situation nor how minor the offense. The reaction was similar whether or not the targets of this abuse actually identified themselves as gay or straight. This is also what happened in the horrific school shootings that shocked the nation between 1996 and 2003.

After opening fire at his school in 1997, Kentucky student Michael Carneal explained that he was tired of being called a "faggot"; he wanted to kill the "popular preppie students" he blamed for his mistreatment. In 1999, at Columbine High School in Colorado, Eric Harris's manifesto, found after his suicide and shooting with Dylan Klebold, declared their actions a response to being ridiculed and teased. Members of their social group, the Trench Coat Mafia, said Harris and Klebold were harassed initially because they were smart; other boys often attacked them and called them homosexuals. In all, fifteen boys retaliated against such abuse between 1996 and 2003; boys, ages eleven to eighteen, killed thirty-five people and wounded 102 others in thirteen major non-gang-related school shootings (Klein, 2003).

Why did these boys kill? And what do their cases have in common with teenagers who murdered in other major school shootings and the violence I saw in New York City schools? Popular theories include lax gun control laws, media violence, parents, and deviant kids. My firsthand observation of teasing in schools, however, provides sociological insights through a gender lens, and adds an important missing puzzle piece, without which none of these other theories can explain what had happened.

Though the details differ, two common threads run through the horrific school shootings. First, classmates consistently described school shooters as "different": skinny, lanky, chubby, or scrawny (Klein, 2003). Second, all of the teenage killers apparently thought that teasing was enough of a reason to kill.

The pattern is devastating: Boys who appeared less masculine in traditional terms turned to extreme violence. Like the boys I worked with in New York City public schools, the killers had been taught from a young age to defend their "manhood" when teased, to fight to win, and to show the other "who's the man." That's what these killers thought they accomplished: "proving" their masculinity.

How could these students have come to hold such destructive beliefs? Many sociologists have made important contributions toward understanding masculinity and, ultimately, school violence. R. W. Connell (1995) argues that boys feel pressured to achieve *hegemonic masculinity*, which he defines as the form of masculinity that a given society legitimizes most. Men are pressured to embody stereotypical masculine traits such as being unemotional, tough, authoritative, and controlling, if they wish to gain status in a competitive masculinities hierarchy. Thus the boys who killed had been demonized, harassed, and ostracized by "preps and jocks" who accrued status by picking on them. This is consistent with Max Weber's contention that a given status group maintains its cohesion and gains influence through its ability to distance itself from other groups in society and ultimately dominate them (Klein, 2005). Even so, prestige holders must fight to maintain their positions. Popular students often feel compelled to continue to win competitions so they can maintain their social status and differentiate themselves from unpopular kids. Otherwise, they risk a quick loss of power (Klein, 2005).

The sociology of gender can also explain why other students and adults overlooked the killers' threats. In *Slow Motion: Changing Masculinities, Changing Men*, Lynne Segal (1990) argues that homophobia is a means to keep all men in line by oppressing gay men and expressing contempt for men who display emotional qualities associated with femininity. Boys are taught to despise the "feminine enemy within themselves" and to try to destroy any person that draws attention to these rejected aspects of their personality (Klein and Chancer, 2000). Significantly, many of the shooters specifically killed their ex-girlfriends—for instance, in Mississippi, Kentucky, and Arkansas—lashing out against the blow to their manhood suffered as a result of the break-up, and demonstrating another way to differentiate from and express hostility toward femininity. By associating themselves with violent retaliation, they sought to gain greater masculinity status.

These sociological insights suggest ways to prevent future school shootings. If someone had paid attention—perhaps as a result of the insight that sociology offers—warning signs might have been noticed and saved lives. Ending the bullying of "different" boys is not just a matter of punishing bad behavior. It involves providing alternatives to winning social approval through violent demonstrations of power. Parents, counselors, school faculty, and fellow students need sociologists' help to develop new ways to support positive social dynamics, and a clearer understanding of how to avoid condoning destructive behavior, for instance, gay-baiting, bullying, and retaliatory threats that conform to expectations that "boys will be boys." At the same time, male role models among faculty, parents, and student peers should encourage academic success and community participation, not just athletics, competition, and power. These new models of manhood could go far to ameliorate school violence.

This approach has been effective in the New York City public schools where I worked for eleven years as a conflict resolution and mediation coordinator, a teacher, a social worker, and an administrator. I conducted mediation sessions between boys, raised the problem at faculty meetings, and addressed the issue as a community social problem in school assemblies. Students who were picked on talked about what it was like to be teased, and in this setting, other students found

the strength to support them and to shout out their support for a more respectful school environment. Boys and girls alike talked about the importance of being kind, respectful, and sensitive regardless of their gender or sexual identity. In this context, students expressed the importance of apologizing, acknowledging mistakes, and resolving differences peacefully. After these interventions, the school had significantly fewer fights than other schools in the same area.

My experiences show how effectively sociologists can use their recommendations to change the way society thinks about problems like the gay-baiting that makes so many young boys miserable and drives some of them to violence. By analyzing problems that are common in society, identifying previously invisible causes, and helping devise new solutions, sociology provides the tools for creating more peaceful and inclusive communities.

JESSIE KLEIN is a professor at City University of New York/Lehman College in the Department of Sociology and Social Work; her recommendations regarding school violence prevention have appeared in USA Today *and the* New York Times *in addition to many scholarly journals and books. She worked at five New York City public schools: Bayard Rustin High School for the Humanities, Stuyvesant High School, Richard R. Greene High School for Teaching, Norman Thomas High School, and Humanities Preparatory Academy.*

Moreover, fully a tenth of the female students surveyed had been raped prior to the study period (which began in the fall of 1996), and a tenth had been the victims of attempted rape. The study also found that for both completed and attempted rapes, nine out of ten offenders were known to the victim. Fifty-five percent of rape victims used physical force in an effort to thwart the rape, as did 69 percent of attempted rape victims.

The incidence of other forms of victimization reported in the study was substantially higher than that of rape. Nearly one out of six female students reported being the target of attempted or completed sexual coercion or unwanted sexual contact during the current academic year, half involving the use or threat of physical force. More than a third reported that they had experienced a threatened, attempted, or completed unwanted sexual assault at some time during their lives. And about one out of every eight reported having been stalked at some time during the current year, almost always by someone they knew—typically a former boyfriend or classmate. Stalking, it was reported, was emotionally traumatizing and in 15 percent of the incidents involved actual or threatened physical harm.

WHY ARE WOMEN SO OFTEN THE TARGETS OF SEXUAL VIOLENCE?

Some scholars claim that men are socialized to regard women as sex objects and that this at least in part explains the high levels of victimization women reported to the National College Women Sexual Victimization Study (Griffin, 1979; Dworkin, 1981, 1987). Susan Brownmiller (1986), for example, claims that the constant threat of rape contributes to a "rape culture," one that is the result of male socialization that reinforces male domination by fostering a state of continual fear in women. One aspect of a "rape culture" is male socialization to a sense of sexual entitlement, which may encourage sexual conquest and promote insensitivity to the difference between consensual and nonconsensual sex (Scully, 1990).

The fact that "acquaintance rapes" occur suggests that at least some men are likely to feel entitled to sexual access if they already know the woman. A survey of nearly 270,000 first-year college students reported that 55 percent of male students agreed with the statement: "If two people really like each other, it's all right for them to have sex even if they've known each other only for a very short time." Only 31 percent of female students were in agreement, suggesting a rather large gender gap concerning notions of sexual entitlement (ACE, 2001). Another national study of first-year college students found that one out of five males felt they were entitled to have sex if the women "led them on" (Higher Education Research Institute, 1990), while a national survey reported that 43 percent of all men believed that a woman is partly to blame if she is raped after

This sixteenth century sculpture by Giambologna, entitled *The Rape of the Sabines*, depicts the legend in which soldiers following Romulus, the mythical founder of Rome, captured and raped Sabine women in order to populate Rome.

changing her mind about having sex (Yankelovich, 1991). When a man goes out on a date with sexual conquest on his mind, he may force his attentions on an unwilling partner, overcoming her resistance through the use of alcohol, persistence, or both. While such an act may not be legally defined as rape, it would be experienced as such by many women.

Because men are socialized to feel a sense of sexual entitlement to women, rapes are most common when men believe that norms condemning rape somehow do not apply and so they are free to act as they choose. Rapes are thus common in times of war. Japanese soldiers raped as many as twenty thousand women when they conquered the city of Nanking in China in 1937 (Chang and Kirby, 1997). Although this is one of the best-known modern cases of mass rape by conquering troops, war-related rapes are as old as human history. Followers of Rome's legendary founder, Romulus, were reputed to have captured Sabine women in order to populate Rome—an act that was glamorized in the famous sixteenth-century sculpture *The Rape of the Sabines.* American soldiers committed rapes during the Civil War and the Vietnam War.

Gender Inequality in Global Perspective

Women the world over experience economic and political inequality. Although the United States has made major strides during the past quarter century in achieving greater gender inequality, it is by no means the world's leader in this effort.

Economic Inequality

Worldwide, women now make up more than a third of the world's paid workforce in all regions except northern Africa and western Asia (UN, 2000). Women around the world work in the lowest-wage jobs and are likely to make less than men doing similar work—although there is some evidence that the wage gap is slowly decreasing, at least in industrialized countries (ILO, 1995). Because women work a "second shift" the world over, women also work longer hours than men in most countries. A recent United Nations report found that women in the United States worked on average 25 minutes each day more than men—a difference that was considerably smaller than that in Austria (45 minutes) or Italy (103 minutes).

Access to knowledge about birth control enables women to choose to exercise greater control over childbearing, so that many are able to work outside the home. Education also encourages women to seek financial independence from men. More women are getting college degrees and professional jobs than even before. Women make up about half of all college students in the economically developed countries of the industrial world and nearly half in Latin America, although in much of Africa and Asia, they are much less likely to go to college. Women's ability to achieve specialized education in science, engineering, business, and government has been limited, even with increased access to secondary and advanced education in much of the world.

Women remain in the poorest-paying industrial and service-sector jobs in all countries, and in the less industrialized nations, they are concentrated in the declining agricultural sector. The feminization of the global work force has brought with it the increased exploitation of young, uneducated, largely rural women around the world. These women labor under conditions that are often unsafe and unhealthy, at low pay and with nonexistent job security.

Yet at the same time, even poor-paying factory jobs may enable some women to achieve a measure of economic independence and power. In China, for example, as many as 40 to 50 million young women have left their home villages in search of factory jobs in large cities. Such "working sisters" earn and save more than their brothers, a fact that has raised their economic status in Chinese society, where women have traditionally been valued less than men. As one Chinese scholar explains, "A whole generation has learned that women have value and girls have choice. When they have a girl, they will feel differently toward her than their parents and grandparents did" (Farley, 1998). There is some indication that women's changing economic role has changed their self-concept as well. More rural Chinese women are divorcing their husbands now that they can better afford to end unhappy marriages. And in a society where the oppressiveness of life as a woman contributes to one of the highest female suicide rates in the world, fewer women appear to be taking their own lives (Farley, 1998; Rosenthal, 1999).

At the other end of the occupational spectrum, a recent study by the International Labor Organization concludes that women throughout the world still encounter a "glass ceiling" that restricts their movement into the top positions. Even though women have made progress in moving into managerial and professional positions, globally they still hold only 2 to 3 percent of the top corporate jobs, and those who do make it to the top typically earn less than men. In Japan, for example, women are especially likely to face barriers to upper-level positions: When college-educated Japanese women interview for managerial jobs, they are typically assigned to noncareer secretarial work. As many as 40 percent of Japanese companies hire no women college graduates for management-level positions (French, 2001a). On the other hand, in Australia, Canada, Thailand, and the United States women own more than 30 percent of all businesses (ILO, 2003). Female participation in senior management has reached nearly 22 percent in the Netherlands, 21 percent in Canada, and over 36 percent in Hungary. In some developing countries, progress has been even greater: In Chile, for example, 27 percent of senior managers are women; in Singapore, 37 percent (ILO, 1997, 2003a).

Political Inequality

Women play an increasing role in politics throughout the world. In Japan, for example, where women have traditionally faced significant barriers to achieving equality with

TABLE 9.2

United Nations Gender Empowerment Rankings: The Top 10 Countries Plus the United States

RANK	COUNTRY	SEATS IN PARLIAMENT HELD BY WOMEN (%)	FEMALE ADMINISTRATORS AND MANAGERS (%)	FEMALE PROFESSIONAL AND TECHNICAL WORKERS (%)
1	Norway	36.4	25	49
2	Iceland	34.9	27	53
3	Sweden	42.7	29	49
4	Denmark	38	23	50
5	Finland	36.5	27	56
6	Netherlands	32.9	27	46
7	Canada	23.6	35	53
8	Germany	31	27	50
9	New Zealand	30.8	38	54
10	Australia	26.5	26	48
11	United States	13.8	45	54

SOURCE: UNDP, 2002.

men, five women were recently appointed to cabinet-level positions by Junichiro Koizumi, the reform-minded prime minister who took office in spring 2001—one in the key position of foreign minister (French, 2001b). Yet of 188 countries that belong to the United Nations, only nine are presently headed by women. Since World War II, thirty-eight countries have been headed by women; the United States is not among them.

As of mid-2001, women made up only 14 percent of the combined membership of the national legislatures throughout the world. Only in the Scandinavian countries of Sweden, Finland, Norway, and Denmark do women make up a significant part of parliament (39 percent); in the Arab states, it is only 5 percent. The U.S. Congress is 13.8 percent female, placing the United States fifty-third out of 173 countries for which data exist. Women are most likely to hold seats in national legislatures in countries where women's rights are a strong cultural value. These are likely to be countries where women have long had the right to vote and are well represented in the professions. They are also likely to be countries that have strong socialist parties that play a role in government (Kenworthy and Malami, 1999).

The United Nations ranks countries according to a measure of "gender empowerment," which is based on such factors as seats in the national legislature held by women, female administrators and managers (as a percentage of total administrators and managers), female professional and technical workers (as a percentage of total professional and technical workers), and the ratio of women's to men's earned income. By this measure, the United States ranks twelfth—behind the Scandinavian and other northern European countries and Canada and New Zealand (see Table 9.2).

Analyzing Gender Inequality

Investigating and accounting for gender inequality has become a central concern of sociologists. Many theoretical perspectives have been advanced to explain men's enduring dominance over women—in the realm of economics, politics, the family, and elsewhere. In this section, we will review the main theoretical approaches to explaining the nature of gender inequality at the level of society.

Functionalist Approaches

As we saw in Chapter 1, the functional approach sees society as a system of interlinked parts that, when in balance, operate smoothly to produce social solidarity. Thus, functionalist and functionalist-inspired perspectives on gender seek to show that gender differences contribute to social stability and integration. Though such views once commanded great support, they have been heavily criticized for neglecting social tensions at the expense of consensus and for promulgating a conservative view of the social world.

Talcott Parsons, a leading functionalist thinker, concerned himself with the role of the family in industrial societies (Parsons and Bales, 1955). He was particularly interested in the socialization of children and believed that stable, supportive families are the key to successful socialization. In Parsons's view, the family operates most efficiently with a clear-cut sexual division of labor in which females act in *expressive* roles, providing care and security to children and offering them emotional support, and men perform *instrumental* roles—namely, being the breadwinner in the family. Because of the stressful nature of this role, women's expressive and nurturing tendencies should also be used to stabilize and comfort men. This complementary division of labor, springing from a biological distinction between the sexes, would ensure the solidarity of the family according to Parsons.

Feminists have sharply criticized claims of a biological basis to the sexual division of labor, arguing that there is nothing natural or inevitable about the allocation of tasks in society. Women are not prevented from pursuing occupations on the basis of any biological features; rather, humans are socialized into roles that are culturally expected of them. Parsons's view on the "expressive" female has been attacked by feminists and other sociologists who see his views as condoning the subordination of women in the home. There is no basis to the belief that the "expressive" female is necessary for the smooth operation of the family—rather, it is a role that is promoted largely for the convenience of men.

In addition, cross-cultural studies show that even though most societies distinguish between men's and women's roles, the degree to which they differentiate tasks as exclusively male or female and assign different tasks and responsibilities to women and men can vary greatly (Coltrane, 1992). The degree to which certain tasks can be shared between women and men, and even how open groups and societies are to women performing men's activities and roles, differs across cultures and across time. Finally, cultures and societies have assigned different values to women and men and differ in the degree to which men are seen as "naturally" dominant over women. Thus, gender inequalities do not seem to be fixed or static. The division of labor based on gender and the devalua-tion of women relative to men have taken different forms and shapes throughout history.

Biological determinists see differences based on gender and gender inequalities as inevitable and unchangeable because they are consequences of biological necessities—not of social processes. Social constructionists disagree with biological determinists about where to find the sources of gender inequality and whether there is a potential for change: Sociological approaches look at society rather than at nature to explain why gender inequalities exist and how they can change. According to many sociologists, the key to understanding gender inequality is looking at a society's gendered division of labor and the value that society assigns to men's and women's roles (Coltrane, 1992; Collins et al., 1993; Dunn et al., 1993; Baxter and Kane, 1995; Chafetz, 1997). It is also important to recognize that gender inequality is also tied to issues of race and class (Collins, 1990).

Feminist Approaches

The feminist movement has given rise to a large body of theory that attempts to explain gender inequalities and set forth agendas for overcoming those inequalities. **Feminist theories** in relation to gender inequality contrast markedly with one another. Feminist writers are all concerned with women's unequal position in society, but their explanations for it vary substantially. Competing schools of feminism have sought to explain gender inequalities through a variety of deeply embedded social processes, such as sexism, patriarchy, capitalism, and racism. In the following sections, we will look at the arguments behind three main feminist perspectives—liberal, radical, and black feminism.

LIBERAL FEMINISM

Liberal feminism looks for explanations of gender inequalities in social and cultural attitudes. Unlike radical feminists, liberal feminists do not see women's subordination as part of a larger system or structure. Instead, they draw attention to many separate factors that contribute to inequalities between men and women. For example, liberal feminists are concerned with sexism and discrimination against women in the workplace, educational institutions, and the media. They tend to focus their energies on establishing and protecting equal opportunities for women through legislation and other democratic means. Legal advances such as the Equal Pay Act and the Sex Discrimination Act were actively supported by liberal feminists, who argued that enshrining equality in law is important to eliminating discrimination against women. Liberal feminists seek to work through the existing system to bring about reforms in a gradual way. In this respect, they are more

Andrea's Dream

When journalists and sociologists seek to understand race relations, they seldom look closely at highly organized business offices. In trying to account for the disaffection, resistance and rebellious stances of the black poor, they think about the significance of Malcolm X caps, gangsta rap songs and the videotapes of Rodney King's struggles to rise from the pavement. When they want to understand urban poverty, they gravitate toward housing projects and street corners, carryouts and pool halls, and the vast arrays of institutions that comprise ghettos themselves.

Such an exclusive focus overlooks another less sensational story. During the [past few decades], while manufacturing declined, there was a rise in the financial and service sectors. A vast number of Chicago adults like Andrea Ellington participate in the larger society mainly through their work in the labor market that supports law firms, accounting firms and other high-level services.

Though in the past Andrea Ellington had worked overtime at [her law firm] when she needed extra money, recently there hadn't been much extra work in the Network Center, and the supervisor was allocating overtime more carefully. When Andrea could no longer get overtime assignments, she requested a number of cash advances from the personnel director at [the firm] so she could pay her bills on time. Then she wrote a memo to her supervisor, who worked the day shift, asking for more overtime:

"I don't know if the personnel director has brought this to your attention but in the past few weeks I have been requesting cash advances. The reasons are very personal but I did go over a few with him as to why I had been requesting the cash advances. He mentioned to me last Friday that he sympathizes with my situation but he also made very good and valuable sense that the firm is not a bank and should not be responsible for my management of money.

"One of the reasons I started requesting cash advances is because the Center no longer had overtime available because of budget reasons. I understand this, but I also recall you say-

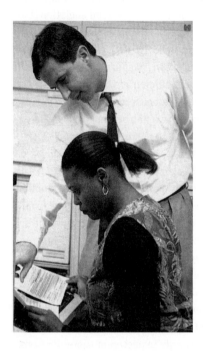

ing that if anyone wants to work overtime he or she should come directly to you. Well, I really depended on the overtime that was available and if there is in any way possible that I can get overtime I would appreciate it greatly. . . . I want to apologize for any inconvenience that I have put upon the firm and especially toward the personnel director. My intent was not to abuse the privilege of cash advances. Please give me a call at home or respond with a memo so that maybe we can discuss this issue further."

The supervisor looked upon Andrea's letter as an act of "incredible conscientiousness." As she put it, "It seemed that she wanted to make sure she didn't overstep her bounds, yet she was coming to us with a problem and trying to solve it in a practical way. I felt that we had to try."

Later that day, the supervisor assigned Andrea to work an extra eight hours of overtime per week, on Sunday. Andrea came to work for the first two Sundays, and then began missing her weekend assignments when she couldn't find a baby-sitter for Lauren, Cubie, and Corey, her three children. When her supervisor learned of her absences, she canceled the overtime.

Andrea wrote again in response to that decision:

"This memo is in regards to the cancellation of overtime hours regarding the litigation project. I really counted on the overtime tremendously and it has been a big help in ways you can't imagine. I know my financial situation is not a priority or a concern of the firm's, but I really need to work the extra hours to get by for an everyday living. . . .

"This overtime has help me pay bills on time, buy cloths for my children, and buy food that I would normally have had to wait until each pay check to get. If the decision was made due to budget reasons by the firm then I have no choice but to try to do the best with what I have, but if you have any information on anyone looking for part-time help or know any agencies that hire for part-time, please inform me as soon as possible on anything you might know of.". . .

[Andrea is again given overtime, and again misses it because she cannot find reliable child care. She goes to see her supervisor.]

"Well, you cut out my overtime. I really need that overtime."

"I'm very sorry, Andrea," the supervisor responded.

"Maybe I can just come in an hour instead of the four hours I was coming in or whatever."

"No."

"Because it was really helping me out there."

The supervisor didn't know what to say. She looked up stonily from her desk.

Andrea says it took everything in her power not to break down and cry. "You know, I just don't make much money for what I do. I know I'm the lowest paid person in the Network Center."

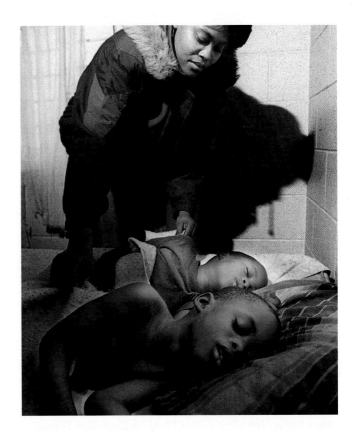

"How do you know?" the supervisor asked.

"That does not matter," Andrea answered. "I just need the money. Because I'm really not making what I should be making in the first place. So at least allow me to have the overtime."

"You're making a decent living," her supervisor said.

There was silence.

Andrea went on. "I might be a paycheck away from being homeless. Thank you."

SOURCE: Mitchell Duneier, "Andrea's Dream: A Single Parent's Fight for Independence," series, *Chicago Tribune*, December 1994, pp. 3–4, 13–15.

Questions

- Andrea belongs to several historically disadvantaged sociological groups: women, single mothers, African Americans, and the poor. In what ways might her problems at work and at home relate to her membership in these groups?

- Andrea is trying to raise a family and to keep her job. How and why do these two goals seem to contradict each other?

The International Women's Movement

Do you have any interest in joining the women's movement? Every year countless American college students are inspired by feminism and enlist in the fight for such causes as reproductive rights, equal pay, or the preservation of welfare benefits for poor women. In today's increasingly globalized world, there is a good chance that those who become active in the U.S. women's movement will come into contact with women pursuing other feminist struggles overseas.

The women's movement, of course, is not simply an American or Western European phenomenon. In China, for example, women are working to secure "equal rights, employment, women's role in production, and women's participation in politics" (Zhang and Xu, 1995). In South Africa, women played a pivotal role in the battle against apartheid and are fighting in the post-apartheid era to improve "the material conditions of the oppressed majority; those who have been denied access to education, decent homes, health facilities, and jobs" (Kemp et al., 1995). In Peru, activists have been working for decades to give women a greater "opportunity to participate in public life" (Blondet, 1995), while "in Russia, women's protest was responsible for blocking the passage of legislation that the Russian parliament considered in 1992 that encouraged women to stay home and perform 'socially necessary labor'" (Basu, 1995).

Although participants in women's movements have, for many years, cultivated ties to activists in other countries, the number and importance of such contacts has increased with

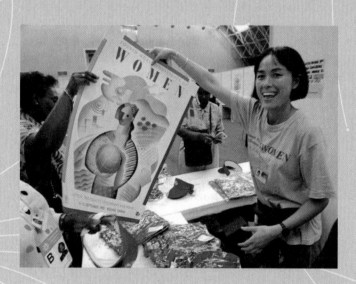

moderate in their aims and methods than radical feminists, who call for an overthrow of the existing system.

While liberal feminists have contributed greatly to the advancement of women over the past century, critics charge that they are unsuccessful in dealing with the root cause of gender inequality and do not acknowledge the systemic nature of women's oppression in society. They say that by focusing on the independent deprivations that women suffer—sexism, discrimination, the "glass ceiling," unequal pay—liberal feminists draw only a partial picture of gender inequality. Radical feminists accuse liberal feminists of encouraging women to accept an unequal society and its competitive character.

RADICAL FEMINISM

At the heart of **radical feminism** is the belief that men are responsible for and benefit from the exploitation of women. The analysis of patriarchy—the systematic domination of females by males—is of central concern to this branch of feminism. Patriarchy is viewed as a universal phenomenon that has existed across time and cultures. Radical feminists often concentrate on the family as one of the primary sources of women's oppression in society. They argue that men exploit women by relying on the free domestic labor that women provide in the home and that as a group, men also deny women access to positions of power and influence in society.

Radical feminists differ in their interpretations of the basis of patriarchy, but most agree that it involves the appropriation of women's bodies and sexuality in some form. Shulamith Firestone (1971), an early radical feminist writer, argues that men control women's roles in reproduction and child rearing. Because women are biologically able to give birth to children, they become dependent materially on men for protection and livelihood. This "biological inequality" is socially organized in the nuclear family. Firestone speaks of a "sex class" to de-globalization. A prime forum for the establishment of cross-national contacts has been the United Nation's Conference on Women, held four times since 1975. Approximately fifty thousand people—of which more than two thirds were women—attended the most recent conference, held in Beijing, China, in 1995. Delegates from 181 nations were in attendance, along with representatives from thousands of nongovernmental organizations (UN Chronicle, 1995). Seeking ways to "ensure women's equal access to economic resources including land, credit, science and technology, vocational training, information, communication and markets," conference participants spent ten days listening to presentations on the state of women worldwide, debating ways to improve their condition, and building professional and personal ties to one another. Mallika Dutt, one of the attendees, recently wrote in the journal *Feminist Studies* that "for most women from the United States, Beijing was an eye-opening, humbling, and transformative experience. U.S. women were startled by the sophisticated analysis and well-organized and powerful voices of women from other parts of the world" (1996). At the same time, according to Dutt, many of the conference participants left Beijing with a "sense of global solidarity, pride, and affirmation" (1996).

The Platform for Action finally agreed to by the conference participants called on the countries of the world to address such issues as:

The persistent and increasing burden of poverty on women;

Violence against women;

The effects of armed or other kinds of conflict on women;

Inequality between men and women in the sharing of power and decision-making;

Stereotyping of women;

Gender inequalities in the management of natural resources;

Persistent discrimination against and violation of the rights of the girl child.

Must women's movements have an international orientation to be effective? Are women's interests essentially the same throughout the world? What might feminism mean to women in the developing world? These and many other questions are being hotly debated as the process of globalization continues apace.

scribe women's social position and argues that women can be emancipated only through the abolition of the family and the power relations that characterize it.

Other radical feminists point to male violence against women as central to male supremacy. According to such a view, domestic violence, rape, and sexual harassment are all part of the systematic oppression of women, rather than isolated cases with their own psychological or criminal roots. Even interactions in daily life—such as nonverbal communication, patterns of listening and interrupting, and women's sense of comfort in public—contribute to gender inequality. Moreover, the argument goes, popular conceptions of beauty and sexuality are imposed by men on women in order to produce a certain type of femininity. For example, social and cultural norms emphasizing a slim body and a caring, nurturing attitude toward men help to perpetuate women's subordination. The objectification of women through the media, fashion, and advertising turns women into sexual objects whose main role is to please and entertain men.

Radical feminists do not believe that women can be liberated from sexual oppression through reforms or gradual change. Because patriarchy is a systemic phenomenon, they argue, gender equality can only be attained by overthrowing the patriarchal order.

The use of patriarchy as a concept for explaining gender inequality has been popular with many feminist theorists. In asserting that "the personal is political," radical feminists have drawn widespread attention to the many linked dimensions of women's oppression. Their emphasis on male violence and the objectification of women has brought these issues into the heart of mainstream debates about women's subordination.

Many objections can be raised, however, to radical feminist views. The main one, perhaps, is that the concept of patriarchy as it has been used is inadequate as a general explanation for women's oppression. Radical feminists have tended to claim that patriarchy has existed throughout history and across cultures—that it is a universal phenomenon. Critics argue, however, that such a conception of patriarchy does not leave room for historical or cultural variations. It also ignores the important influence that race, class, or ethnicity may have on the nature of women's subordination. In other words, it is not possible to see patriarchy as a universal phenomenon; doing so risks *biological reductionism*—attributing all the complexities of gender inequality to a simple distinction between men and women.

BLACK FEMINISM

Do the versions of feminism outlined above apply equally to the experiences of both white and nonwhite women? Many black feminists and feminists from developing countries claim they do not. They argue that ethnic divisions among women are not considered by the main feminist schools of thought, which are oriented to the dilemmas of white, predominantly middle-class women living in industrialized societies. It is not valid, they claim, to generalize theories about women's subordination as a whole from the experience of a specific group of women. Moreover, the very idea that there is a unified form of gender oppression that is experienced equally by all women is problematic.

Dissatisfaction with existing forms of feminism has led to the emergence of a **black feminism** that concentrates on the particular problems facing black women. Black feminist writings tend to emphasize history—aspects of the past that inform the current problems facing black women. The writings of African American feminists emphasize the influence of the powerful legacy of slavery, segregation, and the civil rights movement on gender inequalities in the black community. They point out that early black suffragettes supported the campaign for women's rights but realized that the question of race could not be ignored: Black women were discriminated against on the basis of their race *and* gender. In recent years, black women have not been central to the women's liberation movement in part because "womanhood" dominated their identities much less than concepts of race did.

The African American feminist bell hooks has argued that explanatory frameworks favored by white feminists—for example, the view of the family as a mainstay of patriarchy—may not be applicable in black communities, where the family represents a main point of solidarity against racism. In other words, the oppression of black women may be found in different locations from that of white women.

Black feminists contend, therefore, that any theory of gender equality that does not take racism into account cannot be expected to explain black women's oppression adequately. Class dimensions are another factor that cannot be neglected

Surrounded by minority women at the Houston Civic Center, Coretta Scott King speaks about the resolution on minority women's rights that won the support of the National Women's Conference in 1977. The minority resolution, proposed by representatives of many races, declared that minority women suffered discrimination based on both race and sex.

in the case of many black women. Some black feminists have held that the strength of black feminist theory is its focus on the interplay among race, class, and gender concerns. Black women are multiply disadvantaged, they argue, on the basis of their color, their sex, *and* their class position. When these three factors interact, they reinforce and intensify each other (Brewer, 1993).

Why Gender Inequality Matters

A Chinese saying holds that "women hold up half the sky." In fact, as we have seen in this chapter, women typically hold up far more than half: As the world moves into the twenty-first century, women have become a central part of the world's paid workforce, while at the same time maintaining their traditional responsibilities for home and family.

China was the site of the 1995 United Nations' Fourth World Conference on Women, where some 35,000 people, representing 180 governments and 7,000 women's organizations, discussed the problems of women worldwide. The conference, held in the capital city of Beijing, grappled with a central problem women face the world over: What happens when a country's traditional cultural beliefs conflict with modern notions of women's rights? Globalization has not only brought factories and television to nearly every place on the planet, but has also exposed people throughout the world to ideas about equality and democracy. The modern women's movement has become a global champion of universal rights for women.

The Beijing Women's Conference's final action platform was clear: When cultural traditions conflict with women's rights, women's rights should take precedence. The platform called for women's right to control their own reproduction and sexuality, as well as to inherit wealth and property—two rights that women are denied in many countries. It concluded that no society can truly hope to better the lives if its citizens until it fosters gender equality.

Five years after the Beijing conference, a special session of the United Nations General Assembly reaffirmed these principles, challenging the world's governments to realize the conference's goals. Noting that women occupied only 13 percent of parliament seats worldwide, the UN called for a global increase in women's political power. The Women's Environment and Development Organization, a New York–based women's advocacy group, was more specific in its statement to the

UN: It pushed for equal representation of women in cabinet ministries and legislative bodies by 2005. The goal was set not only to benefit women, but to benefit society as a whole. In the view of the organization's executive director, increased women's representation would help shift a country's policies to "real-life concerns," as is seen in Scandinavia, where women are well represented in all levels of government: "Their commitment to the social safety net, to [an] expansive childcare system, to helping women and men balance work and family needs, I think, reflects women's experiences" (Hogan, 2000).

The feminization of labor has altered the world economy. Will the feminization of politics do the same for global governance? The shift to a greater role for women in economics and politics may well signal a shift to greater equality for all people—not only for women but also for minority people, including sexual minorities—the world over.

Study Outline

www.wwnorton.com/giddens

Gender Differences: Nature versus Nurture

- *Sex* in the sense of physical difference is distinct from *gender* (masculine and feminine), which concerns cultural and psychological differences. It is no simple matter to determine which observable differences are due to biology (sex) and which are socially constructed (gender). Arguments from animal behavior are usually ambiguous. Some researchers claim, for instance, that hormones explain such differences as greater male aggressiveness, but it may just as easily be the case that aggressive behavior causes changes in hormone levels. Studies of gender differences from a variety of human societies have shown no conclusive evidence that gender is biologically determined; rather, biological differences seem to provide a means of marking or differentiating social roles.
- Studies of parent-infant interactions reveal that boys and girls are treated differently right from birth; the same features and behaviors are interpreted as either "masculine" or "feminine" depending on the parents' expectations.

Forms of Gender Inequality

- *Patriarchy* refers to male dominance over women. There are few known societies that are not patriarchal, although the degree and character of inequalities between the sexes varies considerably across cultures. In the United States, women have made considerable progress yet are still unequal in many ways.
- Women's participation in the paid labor force has risen steadily, especially married women's and especially in expanding areas of the economy. Many women, however, are poorly paid and have dim career prospects. Even women who are successful in the corporate world face discrimination in the form of deeply held cultural expectations about the proper role of women in society.
- The increasing number of women in the labor force has had a big impact on family responsibilities like child care and housework. Though men are contributing more to these responsibilities, women still shoulder the bulk of the work. For working women, these household obligations constitute a "second shift."
- The ways schools are organized and how classes are taught have tended to sustain *gender inequalities*. Rules specifying distinct dress for girls and boys encourages sex typing, as do the texts containing established gender images. There is evidence that teachers treat girls and boys differently, and there is a long history of specialized subjects for separate sexes.

Violence Against Women

- Violence perpetrated by men against women is found in many societies—in the form of spousal abuse, rape, and sexual harassment, for example. The most common manifestation of violence against women is *rape*, which is the forcing of nonconsensual intercourse. Some scholars argue that women are often the targets of sexual violence because men are socialized to see women as sex objects and to feel a sense of sexual entitlement to women.

Gender Inequality Throughout the World

- Women throughout the world work in the lowest-wage jobs, and are likely to make less than men doing similar work—although there is some evidence that the wage gap is decreasing slowly, at least in industrialized countries. In developing countries, women are likely to experience exploitative job conditions. Yet at the same time, their enhanced economic role has sometimes resulted in increased economic independence and greater social status.
- Worldwide, women do not share the same political power as men, although thirty-eight countries have been headed by a woman since World War II. The United States is about average among countries in terms of women's representation in the national legislature, but has never had a woman president.
- *Gender* is one of the most important dimensions of inequality, although it was neglected in the study of stratification for a long time. Although there are few societies in which women have more wealth and status than men, there are significant variations in how women's and men's roles are valued within a society. Sociologists have argued that gender inequalities are not fixed. They have also drawn attention to the links between gender inequality and race and class.

Theories of Gender Inequality

- In explaining gender inequality, functionalists have emphasized that gender differences and the sexual division of labor contribute to social stability and integration. Feminist approaches reject the idea that gender inequality is somehow natural. Liberal feminists have explained gender inequality in terms of social and cultural attitudes, such as sexism and discrimination. Radical feminists argue that men are responsible for the exploitation of women through patriarchy—the systematic domination of females by males. Black feminists have seen factors such as class and ethnicity, in addition to gender, as essential for understanding the oppression experienced by nonwhite women.

Key Concepts

black feminism (p. 248)
comparable worth (p. 232)
feminist theories (p. 243)
gender (p. 224)
gender inequality (p. 229)
gender socialization (p. 225)
gender typing (p. 231)
"glass ceiling" (p. 232)
"glass escalator" (p. 233)
liberal feminism (p. 243)

patriarchy (p. 229)
radical feminism (p. 246)
rape (p. 237)
sex (p. 224)
sexual harassment (p. 234)
social construction of gender (p. 226)

Review Questions

1. What's the difference between sex and gender?
   a. Sex refers to the physical differences in the body, whereas gender concerns the psychological, social, and cultural differences between males and females.
   b. Sex is what couples do to conceive, whereas gender is an attribute of their baby.
   c. A culture's understanding of gender determines what types of physical intimacy constitute sex.
   d. There is none. In sociology, as in everyday life, the terms are interchangeable.
2. What is the "glass ceiling"?
   a. It is the "old-boy network" in firms that helps men get ahead by making clear what management expects. Men can see through the "glass ceiling" but women cannot.
   b. It is an invisible barrier that prevents women from achieving the highest positions in a firm, usually because they do not have the sponsorship of a senior manager.
   c. It refers to the earnings gap between white women and women of color.
   d. It is an invisible barrier that prevents women from being hired in the first place because managers expect most women to leave the firm sooner or later to have a family.
3. What is patriarchy?
   a. The name given to societies in which property is passed down by the male lineage.
   b. The name given to societies in which Eastern Orthodoxy is the main religion.
   c. The name given to societies in which women are treated as property.
   d. The name given to male dominance in a society.
4. Which of the following passages best describes women's movement into the labor force?
   a. From 1940 until the mid- to late 1960s, women's participation in the labor force was led by older women, past their childbearing years. From that point on, as women's educational achievements began to catch up with men's, labor force participation spread to younger women.
   b. From 1940 until the mid-1960s, women's participation in the labor force was led by men who wanted their wives to contribute to their household finances. From that point on, as women's educational achievements began to catch up with men's, labor force participation spread to young, unmarried women.

c. From 1940 until the middle to late 1960s, women's participation in the labor force was led by younger women who were more willing to confront traditional conceptions of women's role in the home. From that point on, as the hold of traditional conceptions weakened, older women followed their younger sisters into the labor force.

d. None of the above.

5. What is the "second shift"?

a. The first shift was women's movement into the workforce. The second shift is women's movement into the professions.

b. The first shift was the movement into the workforce of older women with grown-up children. The second shift was the movement into the work force of younger women with small children.

c. The first shift is overcoming traditional male conceptions that a woman's natural role is in the home. The second shift is overcoming male reluctance to treat women as equals in the workplace.

d. The first shift is a woman's day at work. The second shift is the extra responsibility she bears for housework when she gets home.

6. In which country has the women's movement played an important role in improving women's status?

a. China

b. Peru

c. South Africa

d. All of the above.

7. What does it mean for men and women to "do gender"?

a. To "do gender" means to follow traditional conceptions of the responsibilities of men and women in everyday life and to reinforce the idea that gender is a natural means for society to differentiate itself.

b. To "do gender" means to challenge traditional conceptions of the responsibilities of men and women in everyday life and to attack the idea that gender is a natural means for society to differentiate itself.

c. To "do gender" means to take the traditional role of the opposite gender (men acting as women and women as men).

d. To "do gender" refers to the process by which children learn about traditional conceptions of gender roles.

8. Paludi and Barickman found that most women who were abused by behavior that fits legal definitions of sexual harassment

a. filed legal complaints.

b. did not label what had happened to them as sexual harassment.

c. filed legal complaints but withdrew their cases.

d. got compensation from their offenders.

9. Most schoolteachers are women. In classroom discussions,

a. female teachers are more likely to solicit information from boys than from girls.

b. female teachers are more likely to solicit information from girls than from boys.

c. female teachers are no more likely to solicit information from boys than from girls.

d. this has not been studied.

10. According to Firestone and Mitchell, before the development of birth control, why were men dominant over women?

a. Men have superior physical strength.

b. Men controlled women's fertility.

c. Women depended on men for material provision due to constant childbirth and continuous caring for infants.

d. All of the above.

Thinking Sociologically Exercises

1. What does cross-cultural evidence from tribal societies in New Guinea, Africa, and North America suggest about the differences in gender roles? Explain.

2. Why are minority women likely to think very differently about gender inequality than white women? Explain.

Data Exercises

www.wwnorton.com/giddens
Keyword: Data9

- While women in the United States still have a ways to go before they can claim full equality, women in many other nations continue to face extreme disadvantages relative to men. Completing the data exercise for Chapter 9, you will learn more about women's lives in other countries and make global comparisons about women's social status.

Race and Ethnicity: Key Concepts

Learn the cultural bases of race and ethnicity and how racial and ethnic differences create sharp divisions. Learn the leading psychological theories and sociological interpretations of prejudice and discrimination.

Ethnic Relations

Recognize the importance of the historical roots, particularly in the expansion of Western colonialism, of ethnic conflict. Understand the different models for a multiethnic society.

Global Migration

Understand global migration patterns and their impact.

Ethnic Relations in the United States

Familiarize yourself with the history and social dimensions of ethnic relations in America.

Racial and Ethnic Inequality

Learn the forms of inequality experienced by different racial and ethnic groups in the United States. See that the history of prejudice and discrimination against ethnic minorities has created conditions of hardship for many but that some have succeeded despite societal barriers.

CHAPTER TEN

ETHNICITY AND RACE

maureen, a forty-five-year-old black woman who was born in the Caribbean, came to England at the age of twelve with her family. She is the Social Services Manager for Home Care in Leicester, a city located ninety miles north of London in the East Midlands. She has three brothers and ten nieces and nephews. All of her brothers have established families with white English women. She describes six of her nieces and nephews as "dual heritage." Yet she also believes that these children of multiracial heritage will be classified as "black" by those outside the family. Here she sums her view of one of her white sisters-in-law whom she respects: "I feel—she very much wants the child to have a black identity. So, every Sunday she would bring [my niece] up to my mum's house so that she knows her black family. If you say 'Do this for her hair,' she'd be religiously doing it. And she's asked for advice about her hair. And you'd see her plaiting it. And her hair is always so pretty." Maureen and her other black Caribbean family members consider her niece to be "racially" black although she has a white birth mother. They recognize that in spite of having a white mother, this girl will be classified as black because of her physical appearance, and thus she should be trained to identify herself as a black. The labor required of Maureen's white sister-in-law demonstrates how "race," like ethnicity, is learned. They are "socially constructed."

In 1991, according to the UK census 50 percent of UK-born black men had selected a white partner (Modood et al., 1997). The sociologist France Winddance Twine has found in her research among black-white multiracial families in the United States and the United Kingdom (some of her subjects are pictured on p. 252) that some parents train their children to develop what she terms **"racial literacy"** skills in order to help them cope with racial hierarchies and to integrate multiple ethnic identities. Twine defines one dimension of racial literacy as a form of antiracist training which the parents of African-descent children employ to teach their children to recognize the forms of racism that they might encounter (2003). Twine found that there were gaps between how parents viewed their children racially, their children's own racial self-identification, and how they were socially classified outside the home. For example, there were shifts and intense struggles among parents, extended family members, and teachers over a child's racial and ethnic classification (Twine, 1991, 1997, 2004). Twine's research, as well as others, illustrates how difficult it is to easily define the conditions of racial and ethnic group membership for some individuals of multiracial heritage. In recent decades a number of sociologists have turned their attention to this problem of multiracial identity and racial classification schemes. They have argued that a "static measure of race" is not useful for individuals of multiracial heritage who may assert different identities in different social contexts (Harris, 2003; Harris and Sim, 2000; Goldstein and Morning, 2000).

Race and Ethnicity: Key Concepts

In your daily life, you have no doubt used the terms *race* and *ethnicity* many times, but do you know what they mean? In fact, defining these terms is very difficult, but what is most important is that you begin by dispensing with what you think you know. Do not think of race and ethnicity as completely different phenomena.

Ethnicity refers to cultural practices and outlooks of a given community that have emerged historically and tend to set people apart. Members of ethnic groups see themselves as culturally distinct from other groups in a society and are seen by those other groups to be so in return. Different characteristics may serve to distinguish ethnic groups from one another, but the most common are some combination of language, history, religious faith, and ancestry—real or imagined—and styles of dress or adornment. Some examples of ethnic groups in the United States would include Irish Americans, Jewish Americans, Italian Americans, Cuban Americans, and Japanese Americans. Ethnic differences are learned.

The difference between race and ethnicity is not as clear cut as some people think. When you think of it, everything that has been said here about ethnicity would apply very well to Maureen's mixed-race nieces above. Their black relatives and white mother are teaching them many cultural practices that people associate with being black—from how to braid their hair to how to respond to racism. So does this mean that race is really a kind of ethnicity?

In a way it is, but race has certain defining characteristics that make it different from ethnicity. At certain historical moments, ethnic differences take on two additional characteristics. First, some ethnic differences become the basis of stigmas that cannot be removed by conversion or assimilation. Second, these stigmas become the basis of extreme hierarchy.

The mixed-race children with white mothers and black relatives in England look black to many people. Some aspects of their blackness, such as learning to braid their hair from relatives and friends, are cultural practices akin to ethnicity. Yet what makes their blackness into race is the fact that in the United Kingdom, dark skin color has historically been stigmatized, as in the United States. And this stigma has laid the foundation for hierarchy in England, as in the United States.

Race, then, can be understood as a classification system that assigns individuals and groups to categories that are ranked or hierarchical. But there are no clear-cut "races," only a range of physical variations among human beings. Differences in physical type among groups of human beings arise from population inbreeding, which varies according to the degree of contact among different social or cultural groups. Human population groups are a continuum. The genetic diversity *within* populations that share visible physical traits is as great as the diversity *between* them. Racial distinctions are more than ways of describing human differences—they are also important factors in the reproduction of patterns of power and inequality within society.

The process by which understandings of race are used to classify individuals or groups of people is called **racialization**. Historically, racialization meant that certain groups of people came to be labeled as constituting distinct biological groups on the basis of naturally occurring physical features. From the fifteenth century onward, as Europeans came into increased contact with people from different regions of the world, they attempted to "racialize" non-European populations in opposition to the European "white race." In some instances this racialization took on codified institutional forms, as in the case of slavery in the former British, French, and Spanish colonies in the Americas, slavery in the United States, and the establishment of apartheid in South Africa after World War II (1948). More commonly, however, everyday political, educational, legal, and other institutions become racialized through legislation. In the United States after the civil rights movement, de facto racial segregation and racial hierarchies persisted even after state-sanctioned segregation was dismantled. Within a racialized system, an indi-

Celebrating the Chinese New Year with performances and decorations is not just a picturesque event every year in Soho, but an important symbol of cultural continuity for London's Chinese community.

vidual's social life and his or her life chances—including education, employment, incarceration, housing, health care, and legal representation are all shaped and constrained by the racial assignments and racial hierarchies in that system.

In recent years, sociologists who study ethnicity in the United States have come to understand that larger forces that give rise to ethnic-group collective consciousness have declined. For example, people who are Jewish or Irish no longer face the kind of housing discrimination that led them to cluster in particular neighborhoods prior to World War II. In addition, intermarriage between members of different religious groups and European and Asian groups has increased substantially. In the face of such changing conditions, sociologists have noted that ethnic identity, at least in the United States, has less of an impact on the everyday lives of the members of these social groups, unless they choose an ethnic label. As a result, ethnicity is now a choice of whether to be ethnic at all. More and more people must also make a choice about which ethnicity to be (Gans, 1979; Waters, 1990).

Whereas ethnicity is primarily a symbolic option for white Americans, race is not always such a choice for non-whites. And, although it is sometimes a choice for people of "mixed race" whose racial characteristics are ambiguous, for members of many racial groups it is not a choice. One sociologist who has studied how many Americans think about their ancestry and backgrounds has written that "the social and political consequences of being Asian or Hispanic or black are not symbolic for the most part, or voluntary. They are real and often hurtful" (Waters, 1990). Minority group status can have many negative consequences for its members. One such negative consequence is segregation (discussed later in this chapter).

Despite the increase in the number of people in the United States self-identifying as multiracial, many North Americans continue to believe, mistakenly, that race is a natural category and that human beings can be neatly separated into biologically distinct "races." This is a legacy of European colonialization and scientific racism. During the sixteenth century, Europeans began to classify animals, people, and the material culture that they collected as they explored the world. In 1735, Swedish botanist Carolus Linnaeus published what is recognized as the first version of a modern classification scheme of human populations. He grouped human beings into four basic varieties—Europaeus, Americanus, Asiaticus, and Africanus. Linnaeus assumed that each species had qualities of behavior or temperament that were innate and could not be altered. He acquired much of his data from the writings, descriptions, commentaries, and beliefs of plantation owners, missionaries, slave traders, explorers, and travelers. Thus his scientific data were shaped by the prejudices and power that Europeans had over the people whom they conquered (Smedley, 1993).

Racism

Some see **racism** as a system of domination that operates in social processes and social institutions; others see it as operating in the individual consciousness. Racism can refer to explicit beliefs in racial supremacy such as the systems established in Nazi Germany, before the civil rights movement in the United States, and in South Africa under apartheid.

Yet many have argued that racism is more than simply the ideas held by a small number of bigoted individuals. Rather,

Four schoolboys represent the "racial scale" in South Africa; black, Indian, half-caste, and white.

racism is embedded in the very structure and operation of society. The idea of **institutional racism** suggests that racism pervades all of society's structures in a systematic manner. According to this view, institutions such as the police, the health-care industry, and the educational system all promote policies that favor certain groups while discriminating against others.

The idea of institutional racism was developed in the United States in the late 1960s by black power activists (Stokeley Carmichael and Charles Hamilton) and taken up by civil rights campaigners who believed that white supremacy structured all social relations and that racism was the foundation of the very fabric of U.S. society, rather than merely representing the opinions of a small minority. In subsequent years, the existence of institutional racism came to be widely accepted and openly acknowledged in many settings. A 1990s investigation into the practices of the Los Angeles Police Department, in light of the beating of Rodney King, found that institutional racism is pervasive within the police force and the criminal justice system. A similar case occurred more recently in New York City, when police officers shot and killed an unarmed African man from

Guinea, Amadou Diallo. In culture and the arts, institutional racism has been demonstrated to exist in Hollywood films, television broadcasting (negative or limited portrayals of racial and ethnic minorities in programming), and the international modeling industry (industry-wide bias against fashion models who appear to be of non-European ancestry and/or mixed race).

Psychological Interpretations of Prejudice and Discrimination

Psychological theories can help us understand the nature of prejudiced and racist attitudes and also why ethnic differences matter so much to people.

PREJUDICE, DISCRIMINATION, AND RACISM

The concept of race is modern, but prejudice and discrimination have been widespread in human history, and we must first clearly distinguish between them. **Prejudice** refers to opinions or attitudes held by members of one group toward another. A prejudiced person's preconceived views are often based on hearsay rather than on direct evidence, and are resistant to change even in the face of new information. People may harbor favorable prejudices about groups with which they identify and negative prejudices against others. Someone who is prejudiced against a particular group will refuse to give it a fair hearing.

Discrimination refers to *actual behavior* toward another group. It can be seen in activities that distribute rewards and benefits unequally based on membership in the dominant ethnic groups. It involves excluding or restricting members of specific racial or ethnic groups from opportunities that are available to other groups. For example, blacks have been excluded and continue to be underrepresented in entire job categories despite the increase of education among blacks and the emergence of an educated black middle class. Discrimination does not necessarily derive directly from prejudice. For example, white home buyers might steer away from purchasing properties in predominantly black neighborhoods, not because of attitudes of hostility they might feel toward African Americans, but because of worries about declining property values. Prejudiced attitudes in this case influence discrimination, but in an indirect fashion.

STEREOTYPES AND SCAPEGOATS

Prejudice operates mainly through the use of **stereotyping**, which means thinking in terms of fixed and inflexible categories. Stereotyping is often closely linked to the psychological mechanism of **displacement**, in which feelings of hostility or anger are directed against objects that are not the real origin of those feelings. People vent their antagonism against **scapegoats**, others who are blamed for problems that are not their fault. The term *scapegoat* originated with the ancient Hebrews, who each year ritually loaded all their sins onto a goat, which was then chased into the wilderness. Scapegoating is common when two deprived ethnic groups come into competition with one another for economic rewards. People who direct racial attacks against African Americans, for example, are often in a similar economic position to them. They blame blacks for grievances whose real causes lie elsewhere.

Scapegoating is normally directed against groups that are distinctive and relatively powerless, because they make an easy target. Protestants, Catholics, Jews, Italians, racial minorities, and others have played the unwilling role of scapegoat at various times throughout Western history. Scapegoating frequently involves *projection*, the unconscious attribution to others of one's own desires or characteristics. For example, research has consistently demonstrated that when the members of a dominant group practice violence against a minority and exploit it sexually, they are likely to believe that the minority group itself displays these traits of sexual violence. For instance, in the United States before the civil rights movement, some white men's bizarre ideas about the lustful nature of African American men probably originated in their own frustrations, since sexual access to white women was limited by the formal nature of courtship. Similarly, in apartheid South Africa, the belief that black males were exceptionally potent sexually and that black women were promiscuous was widespread among whites. Black males were thought to be sexually dangerous to white women—but in fact, virtually all criminal sexual contact was initiated by white men against black women (Simpson and Yinger, 1986).

MINORITY GROUPS

The term *minority group* as used in everyday life can be quite confusing. This is because the term refers to political power and is not simply a numerical distinction. There are many minorities in a statistical sense, such as people having red hair or weighing more than two hundred fifty pounds, but these are not minorities according to the sociological concept. In sociology, members of a **minority group** are disadvantaged as compared with the dominant group (a group possessing more wealth, power, and prestige) and have some sense of group solidarity, of belonging together. The experience of being subject to prejudice and discrimination usually heightens feelings of common loyalty and interests.

Members of minority groups, such as Spanish-speakers in the United States, often tend to see themselves as a people separated or distinct from the majority. Minority groups are sometimes, but not always, physically and socially isolated from the larger community. Although they tend to be concentrated in certain neighborhoods, cities, or regions of a country, their children may often intermarry with members of the dominant group. People who belong to minority groups sometimes (for example, Jews) actively promote endogamy (marriage within the group) in order to keep alive their cultural distinctiveness.

The idea of a "minority group" is more confusing today than ever before. Some groups that were once clearly identified as minorities, such as Asians and Jews, now have more resources, intermarry at greater rates, and experience less discrimination than they did when they were originally conceived of as minority groups. This highlights the fact that the concept of a minority group is really about disadvantage, rather than a numerical distinction. Perhaps in the future it would be more meaningful for sociologists to use the terms *dominant* and *disadvantaged* to avoid these misunderstandings, but these new terms would be fraught with their own problems! For now, sociologists continue to use the term *minority group*, so it is best for the student to be aware of its definitions and ambiguities as a concept.

Ethnic Relations

In an age of globalization and rapid social change, the rich benefits and complex challenges of ethnic diversity are confronting a growing number of states. International migration is accelerating with the further integration of the global economy; the movement and mixing of human populations seems sure to intensify in years to come. Meanwhile, ethnic tensions and conflicts continue to flare in societies around the world, threatening to lead to the disintegration of some multiethnic states and hinting at protracted violence in others. How can ethnic diversity be accommodated and the outbreak of ethnic conflict averted? Within multiethnic societies what should be the relation between ethnic minority groups and the majority population? There are four primary models of ethnic integration that have been adopted by multiethnic societies in relation to these challenges: assimilation, the "melting pot," pluralism, and multiculturalism. These will be discussed shortly.

To fully analyze ethnic relations in current times, we must first take a historical and comparative perspective. It is impossible to understand ethnic divisions today without giving prime place to the impact of the expansion of Western colonialism on the rest of the world (see Figure 10.1). Global migratory movements resulting from colonialism helped to create ethnic divisions by placing different peoples in close proximity. We will now delve into this history in more detail.

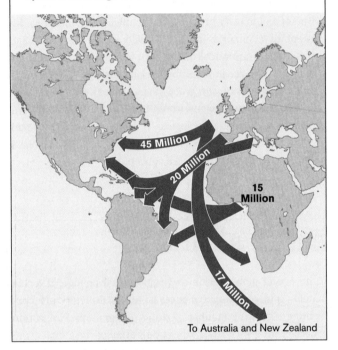

FIGURE 10.1

Colonization and Ethnicity

This map shows the massive movement of peoples from Europe who colonized the Americas, South Africa, Australia, and New Zealand, resulting in the ethnic composition of populations there today. People from Africa were brought to the Americas to be slaves.

45 Million

20 Million

15 Million

17 Million

To Australia and New Zealand

Ethnic Antagonism: A Historical Perspective

From the fifteenth century onward, Europeans began to venture into previously uncharted seas and unexplored land masses, pursuing the aims of exploration and trade but also conquering and subduing native peoples. They poured out by the millions from Europe to settle in these new areas. In the shape of the slave trade, they also occasioned a large-scale movement of people from Africa to the Americas.

These population flows formed the basis of the current ethnic composition of the United States, Canada, the countries of Central and South America, South Africa, Australia, and New Zealand. In all of these societies, the indigenous populations were decimated by disease, war, and genocide and subjected to European rule. They are now impoverished ethnic minorities. Since the Europeans were from diverse na-

tional and ethnic origins, they transplanted various ethnic hierarchies and divisions to their new homelands. At the height of the colonial era, in the nineteenth and early twentieth centuries, Europeans also ruled over native populations in many other regions: South Asia, East Asia, the South Pacific, and the Middle East.

For most of the period of European expansion, ethnocentric attitudes were rife among the colonists, many of whom were convinced that, as Christians, they were on a civilizing mission to the rest of the world. Europeans of all political persuasions believed themselves to be superior to the peoples they colonized and conquered. The early period of colonization coincided with the rise of scientific racism, and ever since then, the legacy of European colonization has generated ethnic divisions that have occupied a central place in regional and global conflicts. In particular, racist views distinguishing the descendants of Europeans from those of Africans became central to European racist attitudes.

The Rise of Racism

Why has racism flourished? There are several reasons. The first reason for the rise of modern racism lies in the exploitative relations that Europeans established with the peoples they encountered and conquered. The slave trade could not have been carried on had Europeans not constructed a belief system that allowed them to justify their actions by convincing themselves that Africans belonged to an inferior, even subhuman race. Racism helped justify colonial rule over nonwhite peoples and denied them the rights of political participation that were being won by whites in their European homelands. The relations between whites and nonwhites varied according to different patterns of colonial settlement—and were influenced as well by cultural differences among Europeans themselves.

Second, an opposition between the colors white and black as cultural symbols was deeply rooted in European culture. White had long been associated with purity, black with evil (there is nothing natural about this symbolism; in some other cultures, it is reversed). The symbol of blackness held negative meanings *before* the West came into extensive contact with black peoples. These symbolic meanings tended to infuse the Europeans' reactions to blacks when they were first encountered on African shores. Although the more extreme expressions of such attitudes have disappeared today, it is difficult not to believe that elements of this black-white cultural symbolism remain widespread.

A third important factor leading to modern racism was simply the invention and diffusion of the concept of race itself. Count Joseph Arthur de Gobineau (1816–1882), who is

A young girl joins members of the Ku Klux Klan at a demonstration against the Martin Luther King Day holiday in Pulaski, Tennessee.

sometimes called the father of modern racism, proposed ideas that became influential in many circles. According to de Gobineau, three races exist: white, black, and yellow. The white race possesses superior intelligence, morality, and will power, and these inherited qualities underlie the spread of Western influence across the world. The blacks are the least capable, marked by an animal nature, a lack of morality, and emotional instability.

The ideas of de Gobineau and others who proposed similar views were presented as supposedly scientific theories. The notion of the superiority of the white race, although completely without value factually, remains a key element of white racism. It is an explicit element, for example, in the ideology of the Ku Klux Klan, and it was the basis of **apartheid** (separate racial development) in South Africa.

Ethnic Conflict

The most extreme and devastating form of group relations in human history involves **genocide**, the systematic, planned destruction of a racial, political, or cultural group. The most horrific recent instance of brutal destructiveness against such a group was the massacre of 6 million Jews in the German concentration camps during World War II. The Holocaust is not the only example of mass genocide in the

twentieth century. Between 1915 and 1923 over a million Armenians were killed by the Ottoman Turkish government. In the late 1970s 2 million Cambodians died in the Khmer Rouge's killing fields. During the 1990s, in the African country of Rwanda, hundreds of thousands of the minority Tutsis were massacred by the dominant Hutu group. And in the former Yugoslavia, Bosnian and Kosovar Muslims were summarily executed by the Serb majority.

The conflicts in the former Yugoslavia have involved attempts at **ethnic cleansing**, the creation of ethnically homogeneous areas through the mass expulsion of other ethnic populations. Croatia, for example, has become an independent "monoethnic" state after a costly war in which thousands of Serbs were expelled from the country. The war—which broke out in Bosnia in 1992 among Serbs, Croats, and Muslims—involved the ethnic cleansing of the Bosnian Muslim population at the hands of the Serbs. Thousands of Muslim men were forced into internment camps and a campaign of systematic rape was carried out against Muslim women. The war in Kosovo in 1999 was prompted by charges that Serbian forces were ethnically cleansing the Kosovar Albanian (Muslim) population from the province.

In both Bosnia and Kosovo, ethnic conflict became internationalized. Hundreds of thousands of refugees spilled over into neighboring areas, further destabilizing the region. Western states intervened both diplomatically and militarily to protect the human rights of ethnic groups who had become targets of ethnic cleansing. In the short term, such interventions succeeded in quelling the systematic violence. Yet they have had unintended consequences as well. The fragile peace in Bosnia has been maintained, but only through the presence of peacekeeping troops and the partitioning of the country into separate ethnic enclaves. In Kosovo a process of reverse ethnic cleansing ensued after the NATO bombing campaign. Ethnic Albanian Kosovars began to drive the local Serb population out of Kosovo; the presence of UN-led "KFOR" troops has been inadequate to prevent ethnic tensions from reigniting.

In other areas of the world, exploitation of minority groups has been an ugly part of many countries' histories. The concept of group closure has been institutionalized in the form of **segregation**, a practice whereby racial and ethnic groups are kept physically separate by law, thereby maintaining the superior position of the dominant group. For instance, in apartheid-era South Africa, laws forced blacks to live separately from whites and forbade sexual relations among races. In the United States, African Americans have also experienced legal forms of segregation. In 1967 the Supreme Court ruled in the case of *Loving v. Virginia* that the prohibition of interracial marriage violated the right to privacy. At that time racial intermarriage was still a crime in most southern states. Interracial marriage had been criminalized for more than two hundred seventy years in every state except Alaska and Hawaii. Economic and social segregation was enforced by law, for instance those requiring blacks and whites to use separate public bathrooms. Even today, segregated residential areas still exist in many cities, leading some to claim that an American system of apartheid has developed (Massey and Denton, 1993).

Models of Ethnic Integration

For many years, the two most common positive models of political ethnic harmony in the United States were those of assimilation and the melting pot (see Figure 10.2). **Assimilation** meant that new immigrant groups would assume the attitudes and language of the dominant white community. The idea of the **melting pot** was different—it meant merging different cultures and outlooks by stirring them all together. A newer model of ethnic relations is **pluralism**, in which ethnic cultures are given full validity to exist separately, yet participate in the larger society's economic and political life. A recent outgrowth of pluralism is **multiculturalism**, in which ethnic groups exist separately and *equally*. It does seem at least possible to create a society in which ethnic groups are separate but equal, as is demonstrated by Switzerland, where French, German, and Italian groups coexist in the same society. But this situation is unusual, and it seems unlikely that the United States could come close to mirroring this achievement in the near future.

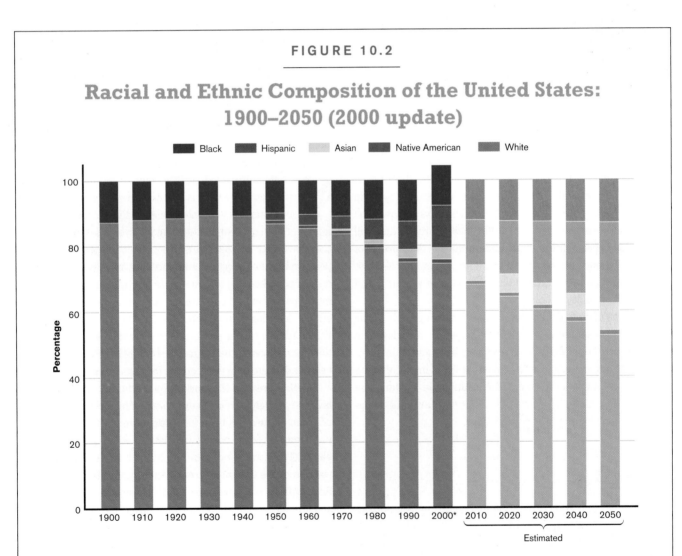

FIGURE 10.2

Racial and Ethnic Composition of the United States: 1900–2050 (2000 update)

Legend: Black, Hispanic, Asian, Native American, White

*Total percentage exceeds 100 percent because starting in 2000, respondents were allowed to identify themselves as belonging to more than one race category.

SOURCE: U.S. Bureau of the Census, Factfinder, 2004, http://factfinder.census.gov/home/saff/main.html?_lang=en.

Global Migration

Today floods of refugees and emigrants move restlessly across different regions of the globe, either trying to escape from such conflicts or fleeing poverty in search of a better life. Often they reach a new country only to find they are resented by people who some generations ago were immigrants themselves. Sometimes there are reversals, as has happened in Southern California and other areas of the United States along the Mexican border. Much of what is now California was once part of Mexico. Today, some Mexican Americans might say, the new waves of Mexican immigrants are reclaiming what used to be their heritage. Except that most of the existing groups in California don't quite see things this way.

MIGRATORY MOVEMENTS

Although migration is not a new phenomenon, it is one that seems to be accelerating as part of the process of global integration. Worldwide migration patterns can be seen as one reflection of the rapidly changing economic, political, and cultural ties among countries. It has been estimated that the world's migrant population in 1990 was more than 80 million people, 20 million of whom were refugees. This number appears likely to continue increasing in the twenty-first century, prompting some scholars to label this the "age of migration" (Castles and Miller, 1993).

Immigration, the movement of people into a country to settle, and **emigration**, the process by which people leave a country to settle in another, combine to produce global migration patterns linking countries of origin and countries of destination. Migratory movements add to ethnic and cultural diversity in many societies and help to shape demographic, economic, and social dynamics. The intensification of global migration since World War II, and particularly over the last two decades, has transformed immigration into an important political issue in many countries. Rising immigration rates in many Western societies have challenged commonly held notions of national identity and have forced a reexamination of concepts of citizenship.

In examining recent trends in global migration, Stephen Castles and Mark Miller (1993) have identified four tendencies that they claim will characterize migration patterns in coming years:

* ACCELERATION. Migration across borders is occurring in greater numbers than ever before.
* DIVERSIFICATION. Most countries now receive immigrants of many different types, in contrast with earlier times when particular forms of immigration, such as labor immigration or refugees, were predominant.
* GLOBALIZATION. Migration has become more global in nature, involving a greater number of countries as both senders and recipients (see Global Map 10.1).
* FEMINIZATION. A growing number of migrants are women, making contemporary migration much less male dominated than in previous times. The increase in female migrants is closely related to changes in the global labor market, including the growing demand for domestic workers, the expansion of sex tourism and "trafficking" in women and the "mail-order brides" phenomenon.

GLOBAL DIASPORAS

Another way to understand global migration patterns is through the study of diasporas. The term **diaspora** refers to the dispersal of an ethnic population from an original homeland into foreign areas, often in a forced manner or under traumatic circumstances. References are often made to the Jewish and African diasporas to describe the way in which these populations have become redistributed across the globe as a result of slavery and genocide. Although members of a diaspora are by definition scattered apart geographically, they are held together by factors such as shared history, a collective memory of the original homeland, or a common ethnic identity that is nurtured and preserved. Robin Cohen has argued that diasporas occur in a number of diverse forms, although the most commonly cited examples are those that occurred involuntarily as a result of persecution and violence.

Aborigines from all over Pitjabjantjaira Country gather to protest and protect their land from mining/mineral development.

Global Migratory Movements since 1973

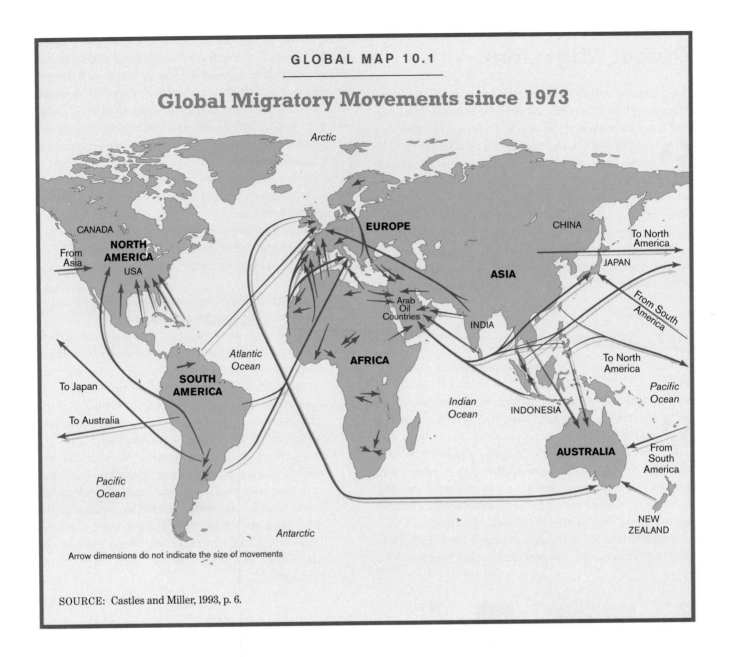

Arrow dimensions do not indicate the size of movements

SOURCE: Castles and Miller, 1993, p. 6.

Despite the diversity of forms, however, all diasporas share certain key features. Cohen suggests that all diasporas meet the following criteria:

- a forced or voluntary movement from an original homeland to a new region or regions;
- a shared memory about the original homeland, a commitment to its preservation, and a belief in the possibility of eventual return;
- a strong ethnic identity sustained over time and distance;
- a sense of solidarity with members of the same ethnic group also living in areas of the diaspora;
- a degree of tension in relation to the host societies; and

- the potential for valuable and creative contributions to pluralistic host societies.

Some scholars have accused Cohen of trying to simplify complex and distinctive migration experiences into a narrow typology, by associating categories of diasporas with particular ethnic groups. Others argue that his conceptualization of diaspora is not sufficiently precise for the analysis he undertakes. Yet despite these critiques, Cohen's study is valuable for demonstrating that diasporas are not static but instead are ongoing processes of maintaining collective identity and preserving ethnic culture in a rapidly globalizing world.

Ethnic Relations in the United States

We concentrate for the rest of the chapter on the origins and nature of ethnic diversity in the United States (see Table 10.1)—and its consequences, which have often been highly contentious. More than most other societies in the world, this country is peopled almost entirely by immigrants. Only a tiny minority, less than 1 percent, of the population today are Native Americans, those whom Christopher Columbus, erroneously supposing he had arrived in India, called Indians.

Before the American Revolution, British, French, and Dutch settlers established colonies in what is now the United States. Some descendants of the French colonists are still to

---

TABLE 10.1

Racial and Ethnic Populations in the United States, 2002

RACE OR ETHNICITY	POPULATION	PERCENTAGE OF TOTAL POPULATION[a]	POPULATION ESTIMATE	SHARE OF TOTAL POPULATION
Total U.S. population			280,540,330	100.00
RACE				
One race	274,595,678	97.6	274,034,883	97.68
White (including Hispanics)	211,460,626	75.1	212,541,793	75.76
White alone (non-Hispanic)			191,238,314	68.17
Black or African American	34,658,190	12.3	33,768,036	12.04
American Indian and Alaska Native	2,475,956	0.9	1,959,347	0.70
Asian	10,242,998	3.6	11,213,133	4.00
Asian Indian	1,678,765	0.6	2,069,584	0.74
Chinese (except Taiwanese)	2,432,585	0.9	2,670,887	0.95
Filipino	1,850,314	0.7	2,013,117	0.72
Japanese	796,700	0.3	802,330	0.29
Korean	1,076,872	0.4	1,147,968	0.41
Vietnamese	1,122,528	0.4	1,169,772	0.42
Other Asian	1,285,234	0.5	1,339,475	0.48
Native Hawaiian and Other Pacific Islander	398,835	0.1	365,474	0.13
Native Hawaiian	140,652	0.0	149,559	0.05
Guamanian or Chamorro	58,240	0.0	61,215	0.02
Samoan	91,029	0.0	63,687	0.02
Other Pacific Islander	108,914	0.0	91,013	0.03
Hispanic or Latino (of any race)	35,305,818	12.5	37,872,475	13.50
Mexican	20,640,711	7.3	23,999,836	8.55
Puerto Rican	3,406,178	1.2	3,608,309	1.29
Cuban	1,241,685	0.4	1,357,744	0.48
Other Hispanic or Latino	10,017,244	3.6	8,906,586	3.17
Some other race	15,359,073	5.5	14,187,100	5.06
Two or more races	6,826,228	2.4	6,505,447	2.32

[a]Percentages do not total 100 percent because Hispanics or Latinos can be of any race.

SOURCE: U.S. Bureau of the Census, "Census 2000 Summary File 1," www.census.gov/Press-Release/www/2001/sumfile1.html.

be found in parts of Louisiana. Millions of slaves were brought over from Africa to North America. Huge waves of European, Russian, Asian, and Latin American immigrants have washed across the country at different periods since then. The United States is one of the most *ethnically diverse* countries on the face of the globe. In this section we will pay particular attention to the divisions that have separated whites and nonwhite minority groups, such as African Americans and Hispanic Americans. The emphasis is on *struggle*. Members of these groups have made repeated efforts to defend the integrity of their cultures and advance their social position in the face of persistent prejudice and discrimination from the wider social environment.

Early Colonization

The first European colonists in what was to become the United States were actually of quite homogeneous background. At the time of the Declaration of Independence, the majority of the colonial population was of British descent, and almost everyone was Protestant. Settlers from outside the British Isles were at first admitted only with reluctance, but the desire for economic expansion meant having to attract immigrants from other areas. Most came from countries in northwest Europe, such as Holland, Germany, and Sweden; such migration into North America dates initially from around 1820. In the century following, about 33 million immigrants entered the United States. No migrant movement on such a scale has ever been documented before or since.

The early waves of immigrants came mostly from the same countries of origin as the groups already established in the United States. They left Europe to escape economic hardship and religious and political oppression, and because of the opportunities to acquire land as the drive westward gained momentum. As a result of successive potato famines that had produced widespread starvation, 1.5 million people migrated from Ireland, settling for the most part in the coastal areas, in contrast to most other immigrants from rural backgrounds. The Irish were primarily from rural areas and accustomed to a life of hardship and despair, and most of them settled in urban industrial areas where they sought work.

A major new influx of immigrants arrived in the 1880s and 1890s, this time mainly from southern and eastern Europe— the Austro-Hungarian empire, Russia, and Italy. Each successive group of immigrants was subject to considerable discrimination on the part of people previously established in the country. Negative views of the Irish, for example, emphasized their supposedly low level of intelligence and drunken behavior. But as they were concentrated within the cities, the Irish Americans were able to organize to protect their inter-

ests and gained a strong influence over political life. The Italians and Polish, when they reached America, were in turn discriminated against by the Irish.

Asian immigrants first arrived in the United States in large numbers in the late nineteenth century, encouraged by employers who needed cheap labor in the developing industries of the West. Some two hundred thousand Chinese emigrated in this period. Most were men, who came with the idea of saving money to send back to their families in China, anticipating that they would also later return there. Bitter conflicts broke out between white workers and the Chinese when employment opportunities diminished. The Chinese Exclusion Act, passed in 1882, cut down further immigration to a trickle until after World War II.

Japanese immigrants began to arrive not long after the ending of Chinese immigration. They were also subject to great hostility from whites. Opposition to Japanese immigration intensified in the early part of the twentieth century, leading to strict limits, or *quotas*, being placed on the numbers allowed to enter the United States.

Most immigrant groups in the early twentieth century settled in urban areas and engaged in the developing industrial economy. They also tended to cluster in ethnic neighborhoods of their own. Chinatowns, Little Italys, and other clearly defined areas became features of most large cities. The very size of the influx provoked backlash from the Anglo-Saxon sections of the

Paddy's Ladder to Wealth is a Free Country An unflattering picture of an Irish immigrant on a ladder holding a brick carrier.

population. During the 1920s, new immigration quotas were set up, which discriminated against new arrivals from southern and eastern Europe. Many immigrants found the conditions of life in their new land little better and sometimes worse than the areas from which they originated.

African Americans in the United States

By 1780, there were nearly 4 million slaves in the American South. Since there was little incentive for them to work, physical punishment was often resorted to. Slaves who ran away were hunted with dogs and on their capture were manacled, sometimes branded with their master's mark, and occasionally even castrated. Slaves had virtually no rights in law whatsoever. But they did not passively accept the conditions their masters imposed on them. The struggles of slaves against their oppressive conditions sometimes took the form of direct opposition or disobedience to orders, and occasionally outright rebellion (although collective slave revolts were more common in the Caribbean than in the United States). On a more subtle level, their response took the form of a cultural creativity—a mixing of aspects of African cultures, Christian ideals, and cultural threads woven from their new environments. Some of the art forms they developed, as in music—for example, the invention of jazz—were genuinely new.

Feelings of hostility toward blacks on the part of the white population were in some respects more strongly developed in states where slavery had never been known than in the South itself. The celebrated French political observer Alexis de Tocqueville noted in 1835, "The prejudice of race appears to be stronger in the states that have abolished slavery than in those where it still exists; and nowhere is it so intolerant as in those states where servitude has never been known" (Tocqueville, 1969). Moral rejection of slavery seems to have been confined to a few more educated groups. The main factors underlying the Civil War were political and economic; most northern leaders were more interested in sustaining the Union than in abolishing slavery, although this was the eventual outcome of the conflict. The formal abolition of slavery changed the real conditions of life for African Americans in the South relatively little. The "black codes"—laws limiting the rights of blacks—placed restrictions on the behavior of the former slaves and punished their transgressions in much the same way as under slavery. Acts were also passed legalizing segregation of blacks from whites in public places. One kind of slavery was thus replaced by another, based on social, political, and economic discrimination.

INTERNAL MIGRATION FROM SOUTH TO NORTH

Industrial development in the North, combined with the mechanization of agriculture in the South, produced a progressive movement of African Americans northward from the turn of the century on. In 1900, more than 90 percent of African Americans lived in the South, mostly in rural areas. Today, less than half of the black population remains in the South; three quarters now live in northern urban areas. African Americans used to be farm laborers and domestic servants, but over a period of little more than two generations, they have become mainly urban, industrial, and service-economy workers. But African Americans have not become assimilated into the wider society in the way in which the successive groups of white immigrants were. They have for the most part been unable to break free from the conditions of neighborhood segregation and poverty that other immigrants faced on arrival. Together with those of Anglo-Saxon origin, African Americans have lived in the United States far longer than most other immigrant groups. What was a transitional experience for most of the later, white immigrants has become a seemingly permanent experience for blacks. In the majority of cities, both South and North, blacks and whites live in separate neighborhoods and are educated in different schools. It has been estimated that 80 percent of either blacks or whites would have to move in order to desegregate housing fully in the average American city.

THE CIVIL RIGHTS MOVEMENT

Struggles by minority groups to achieve equal rights and opportunities have for a long while been a part of the United

Martin Luther King, Jr. addresses a large crowd at a civil rights march on Washington in 1963. Born in 1929, King was a Baptist minister, civil rights leader, and winner of the 1964 Nobel Peace Prize. He was assassinated by James Earl Ray in 1968.

Immigrant America

If globalization is understood as the emergence of new patterns of interconnection among the world's peoples and cultures, then surely one of the most significant aspects of globalization is the changing racial and ethnic composition of Western societies. In the United States, shifting patterns of immigration since the end of World War II have altered the demographic structure of many regions, affecting social and cultural life in ways that can hardly be overstated. Although the United States has always been a nation of immigrants (with the obvious exception of Native Americans), most of those who arrived here prior to the early 1960s were European. Throughout the nineteenth and early twentieth centuries, vast numbers of people from Ireland, Italy, Germany, Russia, and other European and east European countries flocked to America in search of a new life, giving a distinctive European bent to American culture. (Of course, until 1808, another significant group of immigrants—Africans—came not because America was a land of opportunity, but because they had been enslaved.) In part because of changes in immigration policy, however, most of those admitted since 1965 have been Asian or Hispanic. In 1993, for example, of the approximately 900,000 immigrants who were legally admitted to the United States, more than 350,000 came from Asia and more than 300,000 were from Latin America. There are also an estimated 4.5 to 5 million illegal immigrants living in the United States, many of whom are Hispanic. As a result, as

of 1990, 42 percent of U.S. residents who were foreign born were from Latin America, while 25 percent were from Asia. In contrast, in 1900 almost 85 percent of the foreign born were European (Duignan and Gann, 1998).

States. In contrast to other racial and ethnic minorities, blacks and Native Americans have largely been denied opportunities for self-advancement. The National Association for the Advancement of Colored People (NAACP) and the National Urban League, founded in 1909 and 1910 respectively, fought for black civil rights, but began to have some real effect only after World War II, when the NAACP instituted a campaign against segregated public education. This struggle came to a head when the organization sued five school boards, challenging the concept of separate but equal schooling that then prevailed. In 1954, in *Brown v. Board of Education of Topeka, Kansas*, the U.S. Supreme Court unanimously decided that "separate educational facilities are inherently unequal."

This decision became the platform for struggles for civil rights from the 1950s to the 1970s. The strength of the resistance from many whites persuaded black leaders that mass militancy was necessary to give civil rights any real substance. In 1955, a black woman, Rosa Parks, was arrested in Montgomery, Alabama, for declining to give up her seat on a bus to a white man. As a result, almost the entire African American population of the city, led by a Baptist minister, Martin Luther King, Jr., boycotted the transportation system for 381 days. Eventually the city was forced to abolish segregation in public transportation.

Further boycotts and sit-ins followed, with the object of desegregating other public facilities. The marches and demonstrations began to achieve a mass following from blacks and white

Most of these new immigrants have settled in six "port-of-entry" states: California, New York, Texas, Illinois, New Jersey, and Massachusetts. These states are attractive to new immigrants not necessarily because of the job opportunities they afford, but because they house large immigrant communities into which newcomers are welcomed (Frey and Liaw, 1998). As the flow of Asian and Hispanic immigration continues, and as some nonimmigrants respond by moving to regions of the country with smaller immigrant populations, the percentage of residents of port-of-entry states who are white will continue to drop. California was approximately 52 percent white in 1996; by 2010, this number is expected to fall to 40 percent (Maharidge, 1996). "Other states will follow," Dale Maharidge writes in the book *The Coming White Minority* (1996), "Texas sometime around 2015, and in later years Arizona, New York, Nevada, New Jersey, and Maryland. By 2050 the nation will be almost half nonwhite."

The effect of these demographic changes on everyday social life has been profound. Take California as an example. In California's urban centers, residents fully expect street scenes to be multiethnic in character and would be shocked to visit a state like Wisconsin, where the vast majority of public interactions take place between whites. In some California communities, store and street signs are printed in Spanish or Chinese or Vietnamese, as well as in English. Interracial marriages are on the rise, ethnic restaurants have proliferated, and the schools are filled with nonwhite children. In fact, nonwhites make up two thirds of the undergraduate population at the University of California at Berkeley, where Asian students are on the verge of predominating.

Unfortunately, these changes have exacerbated social tensions. Many white Californians have retreated into prosperous suburban enclaves and have grown resentful of immigrants

and nonwhites. Because rates of voter turnout are higher for whites than for other racial groups in the state and because whites control a significant share of the state's wealth, they have managed to pass a number of laws that seek to preserve opportunities for the "coming white minority." Proposition 187, for example, passed in 1994, denied vital public services to illegal immigrants. More recently, the regents of the University of California, in a highly controversial move, decided to abolish affirmative action for the entire nine-campus state university system. Were these decisions based on solid economic and philosophical rationales—the perception that California taxpayers were shouldering too much of the economic burden of illegal immigration or the sense that affirmative action constitutes "reverse discrimination" against whites—or were they motivated principally by xenophobia, the fear of those different from oneself? Whatever the answer, there can be little doubt but that immigration—an important aspect of globalization—is changing the face of American society.

sympathizers. In 1963, a quarter of a million civil rights supporters staged a march on Washington and cheered as King announced, "We will not be satisfied until justice rolls down like the waters and righteousness like a mighty stream." In 1964, the Civil Rights Act was passed by Congress and signed into law by President Lyndon B. Johnson, comprehensively banning discrimination in public facilities, education, employment, and any agency receiving government funds. Further bills in following years were aimed at ensuring that African Americans became fully registered voters and outlawed discrimination in housing.

Attempts to implement the new civil rights legislation continued to meet with ferocious resistance from opponents. Civil rights marchers were insulted and beaten up, and some lost their lives. But in spite of barriers that hampered the full

realization of its provisions, the Civil Rights Act proved to be fundamentally important. Its principles applied not just to African Americans but to anyone subject to discrimination, including other ethnic groups and women. It served as the starting point for a range of movements asserting the rights of oppressed groups.

How successful has the civil rights movement been? On one hand, a substantial black middle class has emerged over the last three to four decades. And many African Americans—such as the writer Toni Morrison, the literary scholar Henry Louis Gates, Secretary of State Condoleezza Rice, media mogul Oprah Winfrey, and basketball player Michael Jordan—have achieved positions of power and influence in the wider society. On the other hand, a large number of African Americans, making up an underclass, live trapped in the ghettos. Scholars have debated whether the existence of the black underclass has resulted primarily from economic disadvantage or dependency on the welfare system. We will examine the forms of inequality that African Americans and other minority groups continue to experience later in this chapter.

Latinos in the United States

The wars of conquest that created the boundaries of the contemporary United States were not only directed against the Native American population but also against Mexico. The territory that later became California, Nevada, Arizona, New Mexico, and Utah, along with a quarter of a million Mexicans—was taken by the United States in 1848 as a result of the American war with Mexico. The terms Mexican American and *Chicano* include the descendants of these people, together with subsequent immigrants from Mexico. The term *Latino* refers to anyone from Spanish-speaking regions living in the United States.

The three main groups of Latinos in the United States are Mexican Americans (around 20.6 million), Puerto Ricans (3.4 million), and Cubans (1.2 million). A further 10 million Spanish-speaking residents are from countries in Central and South America. The Latino population, as mentioned earlier, is increasing at an extraordinary rate—53 percent between 1980 and 1990 and 58 percent between 1990 and 2000—mainly as a result of the large-scale flow of new immigrants from across the Mexican border. Latino residents now slightly outnumber African Americans.

MEXICAN AMERICANS

Mexican Americans continue to reside mainly in California, Texas, and the remaining southwestern states, although there are substantial groups in the midwest and in northern cities. The majority have come to work at low-paying jobs. In the post–World War II period up to the early 1960s, Mexican workers were admitted without much restriction. This was succeeded by a phase in which numbers were limited and efforts made to deport those who had entered illegally. Illegal immigrants today continue to flood across the border. Large numbers are intercepted and sent back each year by immigration officials, but most simply try again, and it is estimated that four times as many escape officials as are stopped.

Since Mexico is a relatively poor country existing alongside the much wealthier United States, it seems unlikely that this flow of people northward will diminish in the near future. Illegal immigrants can be employed more cheaply than indigenous workers, and they are prepared to perform jobs that most of the rest of the population would not accept. Legisla-tion was passed by Congress in 1986 making it possible for illegal immigrants who had lived in the United States for at least five years to claim legal residence.

Many Mexican Americans resist assimilation into the dominant English-speaking culture and, in common with other ethnic groups, have increasingly begun to display pride in their own cultural identity within the United States.

PUERTO RICANS AND CUBANS

Puerto Rico was acquired by the United States through war, and Puerto Ricans have been American citizens since 1917. The island is poor, and many of its inhabitants have migrated to the mainland United States to improve their conditions of life. Puerto Ricans originally settled in New York City, but since the 1960s, they have moved elsewhere. A reverse migration of Puerto Ricans began in the 1970s; more have left the mainland than have arrived since that date. One of the most important issues facing Puerto Rican activists is the political destiny of their homeland. Puerto Rico is at present a commonwealth, not a full state within the United States. For years, Puerto Ricans have been divided about whether the island should retain its present status, opt for independence, or attempt to become the fifty-first state of the Union.

A third Latino group in the United States, the Cubans, differs from the two others in key respects. Half a million Cubans fled communism following the rise of Fidel Castro in 1959, and the majority settled in Florida. Unlike other Latino immigrants, they were mainly educated people from white-collar and professional backgrounds. They have managed to thrive within the United States, many finding positions comparable to those they abandoned in Cuba. As a group, Cubans have the highest family income of all Latinos.

A further wave of Cuban immigrants, from less affluent origins, arrived in 1980. Lacking the qualifications held by the first wave, these people tend to live in circumstances closer to the rest of the Latino communities in the United States. Both sets of Cuban immigrants are mainly political refugees rather than economic migrants. The later immigrants to a large extent have become the "working class" for the earlier immigrants. They are paid low wages, but Cuban employers tend to take them on in preference to other ethnic groups. In Miami, nearly one third of all businesses are owned by Cubans, and 75 percent of the labor force in construction is Cuban.

The Asian Connection

About 3.6 percent of the population of the United States is of Asian origin—10.2 million people. Chinese, Japanese, and Filipinos (immigrants from the Philippines) form the largest groups. But now there are also significant numbers of Asian Indians, Pakistanis, Koreans, and Vietnamese living in America. And as a result of the war in Vietnam, some 350,000 refugees from that country entered the United States in the 1970s.

Most of the early Chinese immigrants settled in California, where they were employed mainly in heavy industries such as mining and railroad construction. The retreat of the Chinese into distinct Chinatowns was not primarily their choice, but was made necessary by the hostility they faced. Since Chinese immigration was ended by law in 1882, the Chinese remained largely isolated from the wider society, at least until recently.

The early Japanese immigrants also settled in California and the other Pacific states. During World War II, following the attack on Pearl Harbor by Japan, all Japanese Americans in the United States were made to report to "relocation centers," which were effectively concentration camps, surrounded by barbed wire and gun turrets. In spite of the fact that most of these people were American citizens, they were compelled to live in the hastily established camps for the duration of the war. Paradoxically, this situation eventually led to their greater integration within the wider society, since, following the war, Japanese Americans did not return to the separate neighborhoods in which they had previously lived. They have become extremely successful in reaching high levels of education and income, marginally outstripping whites. The rate of intermarriage of Japanese Americans with whites is now nearly 50 percent.

Following the passing of a new immigration act in 1965, large-scale immigration of Asians into the United States again took place. Foreign-born Chinese Americans today outnumber those brought up in the United States. The newly arrived Chinese have avoided the Chinatowns in which the long-established Chinese have tended to remain, mostly moving into other neighborhoods.

Racial and Ethnic Inequality

A 1996 *New York Times* headline proclaimed "Quality of Life Is Up for Many Blacks" (Holmes, 1996). The following year, the same paper reported that "New Reports Say Minorities Benefit in Fiscal Recovery" (Holmes, 1997). Since the civil rights movement of the 1960s, has real progress been made? Are improving economic conditions for minority groups part of a long-term process or were they temporary reflections of the booming 1990s economy? Is racial and ethnic inequality primarily the result of a person's racial or ethnic background or does it reflect a person's class position? In other words, is a black American, for example, more likely to live in poverty because of racial discrimination or because of the lower-class status that many blacks hold? In this section, we will first examine the facts: how racial and ethnic inequality is reflected in terms of educational and occupational attainment, income, health, residential segregation, and political power. We will then look at the divergent social statuses found within the largest racial and ethnic groups. We will conclude by looking at how sociologists have sought to explain racial inequality.

Educational Attainment

Differences between blacks and whites in levels of educational attainment have decreased, but these seem more the result of long-established trends rather than the direct outcome of the struggles of the 1960s. After steadily improving their levels of educational attainment for the last fifty years, young African Americans are for the first time close to whites in terms of finishing high school. The number of blacks over the age of twenty-five with high school degrees has increased from about 20 percent in 1960 to 78.5 percent in 2000. By contrast, about 85 percent of whites have completed high school (see Figure 10.3). Some analysts see this development as a hopeful sign and an indicator that young blacks need not live a life of hopelessness and despair. But not all signs have been positive. While more blacks are attending college now than in the 1960s, a much higher proportion of whites than blacks graduate from college today. In today's global economy and job market, which value college degrees, the result is a wide disparity in incomes between whites and blacks (see Figure 10.3).

Another negative trend with potentially far-reaching consequences is the large gap in educational attainment between Hispanics and both whites and blacks. Hispanics have by far the highest high school dropout rate of any group in the United States. While rates of college attendance and success in graduation have gradually improved for other groups, the rate for Hispanics has held relatively steady since the mid-1980s. Only about 10 percent hold a college degree. It is possible that these poor results can be attributed to the large number of poorly educated immigrants from Latin America who have come to the United States in the last two decades. Many of these immigrants have poor English language skills and their children encounter difficulties in schools. One study found, however, that even among Mexican Americans whose families have lived in the United States for three generations or more, there has been a decline in educational attainment (Bean et al., 1994). For these Hispanics with low levels of education and poor language skills, living in the United States has been "the American nightmare, not the American dream" (Holmes, 1997).

Life On the Work Line

Seven days a week—early mornings to mid-afternoons—men from south of the border, mostly from Mexico, hang out in work lines on Queens Boulevard or Roosevelt Avenue. They wait for cars, vans, or trucks belonging to small business owners, contractors, and construction companies who are looking for cheap daylabor. It took six years for Miguel to graduate from being one of the guys on the line to being one of the guys with the boss in the vehicle, picking who works and who doesn't. In between caring for their three kids, Miguel's wife, Marianna, practices aroma and herbal cleansings. They shared their story of [***] migration and survival as undocumented "aliens" from their one-room basement apartment next to the Grand Central Expressway.

[***]

MARIANNA: We went to Tijuana to get away from our mothers—but we ended up with his crazy cousin. A twenty-eight-year-old man married to a sixty-eight-year-old woman. Nothing but a liar and a thief, his cousin. I kept saying "Miguel, let's go north, to New York. We can stay with my father. Make enough to live good and send money home to our families." But Miguel was so macho about the United States.

MIGUEL: I always thought, why would I go to the United States? Just so they could humiliate me for cheap labor. *Never!* [***] The high school I went to was a Socialist school. Always in my mind the United States was an evil place.

Miguel called a cousin who gave him the name of a coyote who could take them across the border.

[***]

MIGUEL: He takes us to a town closer to the border where he has other people waiting to cross. At one o'clock in the morning we leave in a Camaro with California plates. We were three men in a trunk big enough for only one man, [***] I was curled up sideways in the trunk. Another guy was curled up the other way. The third one went across the two of us. [***]

MARIANNA: I was in the backseat with the baby, three other women and two other little girls—all squashed together and a big cloth over everything. I was worried my baby was going to suffocate under the blanket. El Sabrás [the coyote] finally said "Okay, you can uncover the baby, but don't let him look up."

[***]

MIGUEL: The car stops and the trunk door opens. [***] Two hours in the trunk and we could barely stand. Even if your

whole body is numb, you have to make sure not to look suspicious because INS knows the look of people walking out of trunks.

[***]

MIGUEL: We spent whatever money we had left flying from L.A. to New York so Marianna could be near her father and sister. Everyone else in the airplane was white. They were staring at us with our nerves all at an end. Probably they were thinking, look, they are *mojaditos* [slang for Mexicans who cross; literally "the wet ones"]. My father-in-law forgot he was supposed to pick us up at JFK Airport. We're waiting in the cold for a long time, putting quarters in phone booths.

[***]

MIGUEL: Most of the jobs I've had here I got from the work line on Roosevelt Avenue. In the beginning they were day jobs, doing yard work, washing cars, passing out fliers, installing air conditioners. Sometimes the jobs are more steady: busboy, dishwasher, mechanic's assistant, selling carpets.

Work lines are like survival. The one who runs the fastest gets the job. We could be six or seven of us standing around, talking. When a van pulls up, you stop what you're doing and run. If they need two painters, you say you're a painter. If they need a mover, you're a mover. The guy working for the boss looking for people is an instant employment agency. *"You, you, and you come with me."* I'm that guy now. I'm working for a guy who's Turkish and it's easier for him to have me do it, because a lot of Mexican guys don't want to go with an Arab or a Chinese or a Greek.

We ask, "After everything that you've been through, was it worth it, coming to the United States?"

MARIANNA: I pray that my husband will get a job with better pay and that my children have a chance to study and have a good head so they don't become little bums. That's what they learn over here. Children are out by themselves without their parents' permission. Many of them are in gangs. They should be in their homes studying or with their family. Even if they are drawing on the walls, at least they're in their homes. More than anything I want my son, Lalo, to have the opportunity to study. It is better for him here in the U.S., even if it is not better for us.

SOURCE: Warren Lehrer and Judith Sloan, *Crossing the BLVD* (New York: W. W. Norton, 2003).

FIGURE 10.3

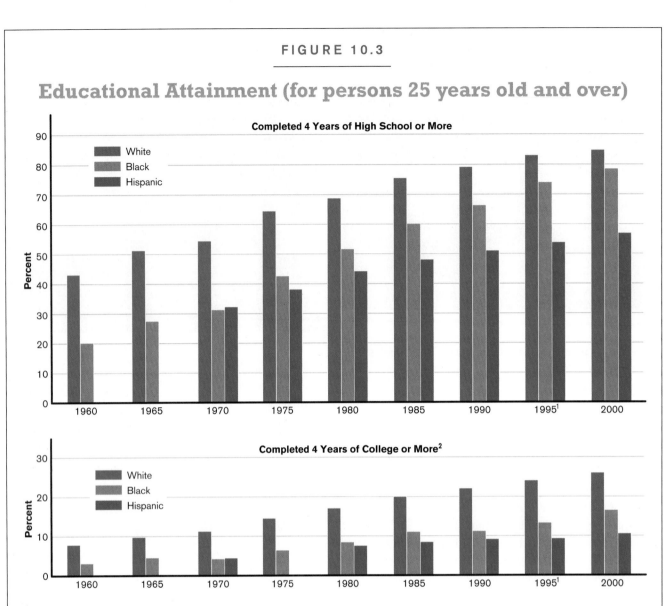

Educational Attainment (for persons 25 years old and over)

Completed 4 Years of High School or More

[Bar chart with legend: White, Black, Hispanic. Y-axis: Percent, 0 to 90. X-axis years: 1960, 1965, 1970, 1975, 1980, 1985, 1990, 1995¹, 2000]

Completed 4 Years of College or More²

[Bar chart with legend: White, Black, Hispanic. Y-axis: Percent, 0 to 30. X-axis years: 1960, 1965, 1970, 1975, 1980, 1985, 1990, 1995¹, 2000]

¹High school graduates or more.

²B.A. degree or more.

SOURCE: U.S. Bureau of the Census, *Statistical Abstract of the United States 2001*, Table 215, p. 139.

Employment and Income

As a result of the increase in educational attainment, blacks now hold a slightly higher proportion of managerial and professional jobs than in 1960, though still not in proportion to their overall numbers. In 1998, out of the approximately 39 million managerial or professional positions in the United States, whites held about 34 million (about 87 percent), African Americans just under 3 million (about 7.5 percent), and Hispanics just under 2 million (about 5 percent). During that same year, black men were about twice as likely as whites to be service workers and about one and one half times as likely to hold a blue-collar job.

The unemployment rate of black and Hispanic men outstrips that of whites by the same degree today as was the case in the early 1960s. Twice as many black and Hispanic men as white men are registered as unemployed (in 1998, 4 percent for whites versus about 8 percent for both blacks and Hispanics). There has also been some debate about whether employment opportunities for minorities have improved or worsened. Statistics on unemployment don't adequately measure economic opportunity, since they measure only those known to be looking for work. A higher proportion of blacks and Hispanics have simply opted out of the occupational system, neither working nor looking for work. They have become disillusioned by the frustration of searching for employment that is not there. Unemployment figures also do not reflect the increasing numbers of young men from minority groups who have been incarcerated (see also Chapter 6). Finally, although many new jobs were created during the economic boom of the 1990s, most of them available to those without a college degree were in lower-paying service occupations. As we just saw, blacks and Hispanics are underrepresented among college graduates.

Nevertheless, the disparities between the earnings of blacks and whites are gradually diminishing. As measured in terms of weekly income, black men now earn 76 percent of the level of pay of whites. In 1959, the proportion was only 49 percent. In terms of household family income (adjusted for inflation), blacks are the only social group to have seen an improvement during the 1990s. By 1995, poverty rates for African Americans had fallen to their lowest rates since the government started tracking the figure in 1955 and continued to improve for the rest of the decade.

Though the economic status of blacks appears to have improved, prospects for Hispanics have stagnated or worsened over the same time period. Between 1989 and 1995, Hispanic household incomes (adjusted for inflation) decreased by about 10 percent. For the first time ever, the poverty rate of Hispanics surpassed that of African Americans. The large influx of immigrants, who tend to be poor, has caused some of the decline in average income, but even among Hispanics born in the United States, income levels declined as well. As one Latino group leader commented, "Most Hispanic residents are caught in jobs like gardener, nanny, and restaurant worker that will never pay well and from which they will never advance" (quoted in Goldberg, 1997).

Health

Jake Najman recently surveyed the evidence linking health to racial and economic inequalities. After studying data for a number of different countries, including the United States, he concluded that for people in the poorest 20 percent, as measured in terms of income, the death rates were 1.5–2.5 times those of the highest 20 percent of income earners. In the United States, the rate of infant mortality for the poorest 20 percent was four times higher than for the wealthiest 20 percent. When differences were measured between whites and African Americans in the United States, rather than only in terms of income, the contrast in infant mortality rates was even higher—five times higher for blacks than for whites. The contrast is also becoming greater rather than less. The same is true of life expectancy—the average age to which individuals at birth can expect to live. In 1984, whites on average could expect to live 5.6 years more than African Americans. By 1996, this had increased to 6.5 years and could increase to 8.2 by 2010.

How might the influence of poverty and race on health be countered? Extensive programs of health education and disease prevention are one possibility. But such programs tend to work better among more prosperous, well-educated groups and in any case usually produce only small changes in behavior. Increased accessibility to health services would help, but probably to a limited degree. The only really effective policy option, it is argued, would be to attack poverty itself, so as to reduce the income gap between rich and poor (Najman, 1993).

Residential Segregation

Neighborhood segregation seems to have declined little over the past quarter century. Studies show that discriminatory practices between black and white clients in the housing market continue (Lake, 1981). Black and white children now attend the same schools in most rural areas of the South and in many of the smaller- and medium-size cities throughout the country. Most black college students now also go to the same colleges and universities as whites, instead of the traditional all-black institutions (Bullock, 1984). Yet in the larger cities a high level of educational segregation persists as a result of the continuing movement of whites to suburbs or rural environs.

In *American Apartheid* (1993), Douglas Massey and Nancy A. Denton argue that the history of racial segregation and its specific urban form, the black ghetto, are responsible for the perpetuation of black poverty and the continued polarization of black and white.

The persistence of segregation, they say, is not a result of impersonal market forces. Even many middle-class blacks still find themselves segregated from the white society. For them, as for poor blacks, this becomes a self-perpetuating cycle. Affluent blacks who could afford to live in comfortable, predominantly white neighborhoods may deliberately choose not to, because of the struggle for acceptance they know they would face. The black ghetto, the authors conclude, was constructed through a series of well-defined institutional practices of racial discrimination—private behavior and public policies by which whites sought to contain growing urban black populations. Until policy makers, social scientists, and private citizens recognize the crucial role of such institutional discrimination in perpetuating urban poverty and racial injustice, the United States will remain a deeply divided and troubled society.

Political Power

Blacks have made some gains in holding local elective offices; the number of black public officials has increased from forty in 1960 to over eight thousand today. The numbers of black

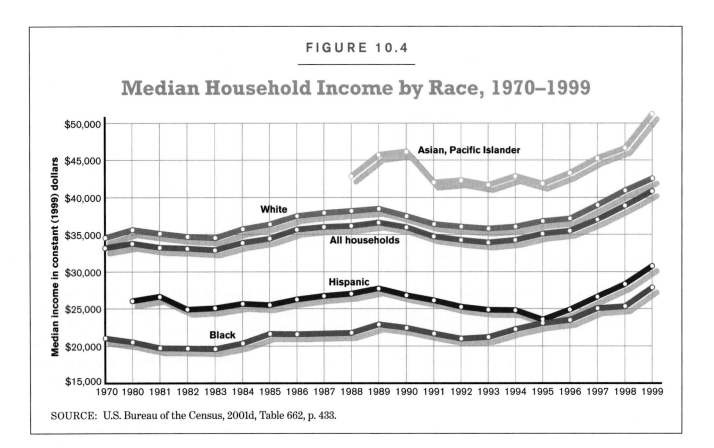

FIGURE 10.4

Median Household Income by Race, 1970–1999

Median income in constant (1999) dollars

Asian, Pacific Islander

White

All households

Hispanic

Black

$50,000
$45,000
$40,000
$35,000
$30,000
$25,000
$20,000
$15,000

1970 1980 1981 1982 1983 1984 1985 1986 1987 1988 1989 1990 1991 1992 1993 1994 1995 1996 1997 1998 1999

SOURCE: U.S. Bureau of the Census, 2001d, Table 662, p. 433.

mayors and judges have increased appreciably. Blacks have been voted into every major political office, except president and vice president, including areas where white voters predominate. In 1992, after congressional districts were reshaped to give minority candidates more opportunity, a record number of African Americans and Latinos were elected to Congress. Yet these changes are still relatively small scale. Black officials still make up only about 2 percent of the elective offices in the United States. Most of these are in relatively minor local positions. The share of representation that Latinos and African Americans have in Congress is not equal to their overall size in American society. Following the defeat of Senator Carol Moseley-Braun in 1998, the U.S. Senate had no black or Latino members.

Gender and Race

The status of minority women in the United States is especially plagued by inequalities (see Figure 10.5). Gender and race discrimination combined make it particularly difficult for these women to escape conditions of poverty. They share the legacy of past discrimination against members of minority groups and women in general. Until about twenty-five years ago, most minority women worked in low-paying occupations such as household work or farmwork or low-wage manufacturing jobs. Changes in the law and gains in education have allowed for more minority women to enter white-collar professions, and their economic and occupational status has improved. By 1987, the average African American female college graduate earned 90 percent of the average for white female college graduates. But in general, female college graduates earn less than men with only high school educations. And white male high school dropouts, on average, earn more than black female college graduates (Rhode, 1990; Higginbotham, 1992).

However unequal the status and pay of minority women, these women play a critical role in their communities. They are often the major or sole wage earners in their families. Yet their incomes are not always sufficient to maintain a family. About half of all families headed by African American or Latino women live at poverty levels.

Divergent Fortunes

When we survey the development and current position of the major ethnic groups in America, one conclusion that emerges is that they have achieved varying levels of success. Whereas successive waves of European immigrants managed to overcome most of the prejudice and discrimination they originally

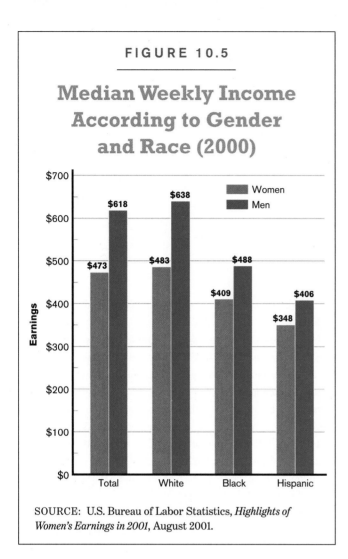

FIGURE 10.5

Median Weekly Income According to Gender and Race (2000)

SOURCE: U.S. Bureau of Labor Statistics, *Highlights of Women's Earnings in 2001*, August 2001.

It seems probable that a division has opened up between the minority of blacks who have obtained white-collar, managerial, or professional jobs—who form a small black middle class—and the majority whose living conditions have not improved. In 1960, most of the nonmanual-labor jobs open to blacks were those serving the black community—a small proportion of blacks could work as teachers, social workers, or less often, lawyers or doctors. No more than some 13 percent of blacks held white-collar jobs, contrasted to 44 percent of whites. Since that date, however, there have been significant changes. Between 1960 and 1970, the percentage of blacks in white-collar occupations doubled—although this level of growth slowed markedly in the 1980s. This increase was greater than that for the half century previous to 1960.

Bart Landry carried out a systematic study of the growing black middle class (1988). He surveyed white-collar blacks and whites in twenty-one metropolitan areas across the country and also analyzed government statistics from the early 1980s. Landry found that middle-class blacks were much better off, and much more numerous, than their predecessors twenty years before (see also Jacoby, 1998). Opportunities have opened up partly through changes in legislation brought into being as a result of the civil rights movement. However, the population of blacks in middle-class jobs remains well below that of whites, and their average incomes are less.

THE ASIAN SUCCESS STORY

Unlike African Americans, other minority groups have outlasted the open prejudice and discrimination they once faced. The changing fate of Asians in the United States is especially remarkable. Until about half a century ago, the level of prejudice and discrimination experienced by the Chinese and Japanese in North America was greater than for any other group of nonblack immigrants. Since that time, Asian Americans have achieved a steadily increasing prosperity and no longer face the same levels of antagonism from the white community. The median income of Asian Americans is now actually higher than that of whites.

This statistic conceals some big discrepancies between and within different Asian groups; there are still many Asian Americans, including those whose families have resided in the United States for generations, who live in poverty. However, the turnaround in the fortunes of Asian Americans, on the whole, is so impressive that some have referred to the Asian American "success story" as a prime example of what minorities can achieve in the United States.

faced and become assimilated into the wider society, other groups have not. These latter groups include two minorities that have lived in North America for centuries, Native Americans and African Americans, as well as Mexicans, Puerto Ricans, and to some extent Chinese.

THE ECONOMIC DIVIDE WITHIN THE AFRICAN AMERICAN COMMUNITY

The situation of blacks is the most conspicuous case of divergent fortunes. After more than two centuries of continuous presence on the North American subcontinent, longer than any other group except for Native Americans and the European settlers, blacks are in the worst situation, with the sole exception of Native Americans, of any ethnic group in the United States. The reasons for this lie in the historical backdrop of slavery and its residue in the long years of struggle that it took to free African Americans from open prejudice and discrimination.

The Cost of Slavery

[Writing columns and opinion pieces for local and national newspapers is one of the traditional ways that sociologists engage a wider public audience. In this *New York Times* article, Dalton Conley weighs in on the debate over reparations for slavery with his own sociological perspective.]

Marching across the South in 1865, Union soldiers seized up to 900,000 acres of "abandoned property." Some radical Northerners hoped to use this land to provide freed slaves with the now-legendary "40 acres and a mule" as restitution for slavery. Their hopes were obviously dashed. But the argument for reparations lives on nearly 140 years later.

While few doubt that slavery was a great wrong, the challenge before us is how to make things right through financial restitution. But just how would we devise a practical formula to determine who gets what?

Most assessments start with the notion of payment for lost wages. One researcher took 1860s prices for slaves as an estimate of their labor value and applied compound interest. The result: $2 trillion to $4 trillion. Six generations after slavery's demise, such approaches present serious difficulties. There are issues of what to do with whites (and blacks) who immigrated here after slavery ended. What about descendants of blacks who lived freely during the antebellum period? Does someone who is born to a white parent and a black parent cancel out? It would take Solomon to solve this.

Perhaps the issue needs to be looked at differently. One way is to recognize slavery as an institution upon which

America's wealth was built. If we take this view, it is not important whether a white family arrived in 1700 or in 1965. If you wear cotton blue jeans, if you take out an insurance policy, if you buy from anyone who has a connection to the industries that were built on chattel labor, then you have benefited from slavery. Likewise, if you are black—regardless of when your ancestors arrived—you live with slavery's stigma.

Extending the reparations argument this broadly frees one to move beyond the issue of lost wages and seek out other factors on which to base a formula. If there were one statistic that captured the persistence of racial inequality, it would be net worth.

The typical white family enjoys a net worth that is more than eight times that of its black counterpart, according to the economist Edward Wolff. Even at equivalent income levels, gaps remain large. Among families earning less than $15,000 a year, the median African American family has a net worth of zero, while the corresponding white family has $10,000 in equity. The typical white family earning $40,000 annually has a nest egg of around $80,000. Its black counterpart has about half that amount.

This equity inequity is partly the result of the head start whites enjoy in accumulating and passing on assets. Some economists estimate that up to 80 percent of lifetime wealth accumulation results from gifts from earlier generations, ranging from the down payment on a home to a bequest by a parent. If the government used such net-worth inequality as a basis, and then factored in measures like population size, it could address reparations by transferring about 13 percent of white household wealth to blacks. A two-adult black family would receive an average reparation of about $35,000.

What would be the effect of wealth redistribution on such a vast scale? My own research—using national data to follow black and white adolescents into adulthood—shows that when we compare families with the same net worth, blacks are more likely to finish high school than whites and are equally likely to complete a bachelor's degree. Racial differences in welfare rates disappear. Thus, one generation after reparations were paid, racial gaps in education should close—eliminating the need for affirmative action.

The unpopularity of this radical plan would no doubt be unprecedented. There are also no guarantees that reparations would be a magic bullet for lingering racial problems. That said, it remains vital, especially during Black History Month, to explore formulas and keep the reparations debate alive. It is important because each resulting dollar amount implies a theory of race, history and equal opportunity. That includes the figure implicit in our current policy—zero—which rests on the most absurd assumption of all: that slavery didn't matter.

SOURCE: Dalton Conley, "The Cost of Slavery," *New York Times*, February 15, 2003.

DALTON CONLEY, associate professor of sociology and director of the Center for Advanced Social Science Research at New York University, is author of Being Black, Living in the Red: Race, Wealth and Social Policy in America *and* Honky.

Miami and Los Angeles both have large Latino populations. In Los Angeles, the large majority of Latinos are well down the ladder of privilege and power. But although both cities experience ethnic tensions, in Miami, Latinos have achieved a position of economic and political prominence not found elsewhere.

In Miami, those of Cuban origin have often moved into positions of considerable influence. Some Cubans have become very successful in business and have become more wealthy than the "old" white families that once ran the city. They haven't been assimilated into the white community but maintain their own customs, institutions, and language. Miami is now a place of "parallel structures" existing alongside one another, each including powerful and wealthy people, not integrated into one unified group. There is much tension, but some Anglo and Cuban politicians now speak of Miami as the capital of the Caribbean—a city not only part of the United States, but looking also to the other societies, mostly developing countries, surrounding it.

Los Angeles has been referred to as "the capital of the Third World" because of its large Latino and Asian populations. The city already contained the largest group of Mexicans in the United States in the 1920s. Then, as now, it was Mexicans who performed most of the menial jobs. Then, as now, most Anglos "were at once aware that this was the case," and "yet they would act as if these people, once they had finished working, went home not to the Old Plaza or, as now, to East L.A., but to another planet" (Rieff, 1991).

Some optimistic observers have suggested that Los Angeles in the twenty-first century will combine Asian family loyalty, Hispanic industriousness, and Anglo-Saxon respect for individual liberty. Is such a vision possible? It would certainly take some profound social changes even to come close. Los Angeles is an ethnic mosaic that symbolizes the increasing diversity of American society as a whole. Will the Hispanic population of the city be able to achieve economic success similar to the Cubans in Miami? Will there exist separate but equal Hispanic communities in Los Angeles as well as in other U.S. cities in the future? How will such successes, if they happen, affect the black urban poor? These are all at the moment open questions, to which no one can give certain answers.

Understanding Racial Inequality

What distinguishes less fortunate groups such as African Americans and Mexican Americans is not just that they are nonwhite, but that they were originally present in America as *colonized peoples* rather than willing immigrants. In a classic analysis, Robert Blauner (1972) suggested that a sharp distinction should be drawn between groups who journeyed voluntarily to settle in the new land and those who were incorporated into the society through force or violence. Native Americans are part of American society as a result of military conquest; African Americans were transported in the slave trade; Puerto Rico was colonized as a result of war; and Mexicans were originally incorporated as a result of the conquest of the Southwest by the United States in the nineteenth century. These groups have consistently been the target of racism, which both reflects and perpetuates their separation from other ethnic communities.

But, given that this has been the case for most of American history, what explains the growth of the black middle class? William Julius Wilson (1978; see also Wilson et al., 1987) has argued that race is of diminishing importance in explaining inequalities between whites and blacks. In his view, these inequalities are now based on class rather than skin color. The old racist barriers are crumbling. What remain are inequalities similar to those affecting all lower-class groups.

Are racial inequalities to be explained primarily in terms of class? It is true that racial divisions provide a means of social closure, whereby economic resources can be monopolized by privileged class groups. But the argument that racial inequality should be explained primarily in terms of class domination, however, has never been a satisfactory one. Ethnic discrimination, particularly of a racial kind, is partly independent of class differences: the one cannot be separated from the other. This still seems to remain true in the United States today.

For instance, opinion surveys show a general decline in hostile attitudes toward blacks over the past thirty years among white Americans (Schuman, Steel, and Bobo, 1985; Bobo and Kluegel, 1991). The overall level of prejudice seems to be diminishing fairly markedly. David Wellman has argued, however, that the concept of prejudice only captures the more open and individual forms of hostile attitudes toward ethnic minorities. Racism can also be expressed in more subtle ways—in terms of beliefs that, regardless of the intentions involved, defend the position of privileged groups. Many sociologists, according to Wellman, have underestimated the true incidence of racism, because they have looked only at its more obvious manifestations. Most studies have investigated prejudice using surveys; but these do not get at the less obvious, complex aspects of people's views about such emotive topics as ethnicity and race.

Wellman sought to illuminate these complex aspects of racism by means of in-depth interviews with 105 white Americans of varying backgrounds. Most of those he interviewed said that they believed that everyone is equal and that they held no hostility toward blacks. Their beliefs and attitudes did not show the rigidities characteristic of prejudice and stereotypical thinking. Yet their views about contexts of social life (such as education, housing, or jobs) in which black rights threatened their own position were effectively antiblack.

These attitudes can still underlie quite rigid institutional patterns of discrimination. Ethnic inequalities are structured into existing social institutions, and patterns of behavior having no immediate connection to ethnicity can serve to reinforce them. Rights and opportunities are not the same thing. Even if it were true that every member of the population accepted that members of all ethnic groups have the same civil rights, major inequalities would persist. There are many examples that demonstrate this. A black person who wishes to obtain a bank loan in order to be able to make home improvements finds it hard to borrow money. The bank might use purely "objective" measures in reaching such decisions, based on the likelihood of the loan repayments being successfully made. Nevertheless, the effect of this institutional racism is the perpetuation of ethnic discrimination (Massey and Denton, 1993).

In sum, although both individual and institutional racism seem to be declining in the United States, the differences between white and nonwhite ethnic groups are long enduring (Ringer, 1985; Conley, 1999). Moreover, the relative success of white ethnics has been to some degree purchased at the expense of nonwhites. A combination of continued white immigration and white racism, up to at least the World War II period, served to keep nonwhites out of the better-paid occupations, forcing them into the least-skilled, most marginal sectors of the economy. With the slowing down of white immigration, this situation is changing, although some newly arrived groups, like the Cubans in Miami, seem to be repeating the process.

Study Outline

www.wwnorton.com/giddens

Race and Ethnicity: Key Concepts

- Ethnic groups have common cultural characteristics that separate them from others within a given population. Ethnic differences are wholly learned, although they are sometimes depicted as "natural."
- *Race* refers to physical characteristics, such as skin color, that are treated by members of a community or society as socially significant—as signaling distinct cultural characteristics. Many popular beliefs about race are mythical. There are no distinct characteristics by means of which human beings can be allocated to different races.
- *Racism* is prejudice based on socially significant physical distinctions. A racist is someone who believes that some individuals are superior, or inferior, to others as a result of racial differences.
- *Displacement* and *scapegoating* are psychological mechanisms associated with *prejudice* and *discrimination*. In displacement, feelings of hostility become directed against objects that are not the real origin of these anxieties. People project their anxieties and insecurities onto scapegoats. Prejudice involves holding preconceived views about an individual or group; discrimination refers to actual behavior that deprives members of a group of opportunities open to others. Prejudice usually involves *stereotypical thinking*—thinking in terms of fixed and inflexible categories.

Ethnic Relations

- Four models of possible future developments in race and ethnic relations can be distinguished—the first stressing Anglo-conformity, or *assimilation*, the second the *melting pot*, the third *pluralism*, and the fourth *multiculturalism*. In recent years there has been a tendency to emphasize the fourth of these avenues, whereby different ethnic identities are accepted as equal and separate within the context of the overall national culture.

Global Migration

- Beginning in the fifteenth century, global migratory movements resulting from exploration, colonialism, and slavery created multiethnic populations in various regions of the world and therefore ethnic and racial antagonism. Today, migration appears to be on the rise as part of the process of globalization.

Ethnic Relations in the United States

- A remarkable diversity of ethnic minorities is found in the United States today, each group having its own distinctive cultural characteristics. Some of the most important minority communities numerically, after blacks, are Native Americans, Mexican Americans, Puerto Ricans, Cubans, Chinese, and Japanese.
- An important distinction must be drawn between those minorities that came to America as willing immigrants and the colonized peoples who either were here already (Native Americans, Mexican Americans) or were brought by force (African Americans) and who were generally incorporated by violence. Racism targeted at these latter groups has been most persistent and most destructive. Gender discrimination compounds the difficulties facing women of color; about half of African American and Latino families that depend primarily on women's incomes live in poverty.

Key Concepts

apartheid (p. 259)

assimilation (p. 260)

diaspora (p. 261)

discrimination (p. 256)

displacement (p. 256)

emigration (p. 261)

ethnic cleansing (p. 259)

ethnicity (p. 254)

genocide (p. 259)

immigration (p. 261)

institutional racism (p. 256)

melting pot (p. 260)

minority group (p. 257)

multiculturalism (p. 260)

pluralism (p. 260)

prejudice (p. 256)

race (p. 254)

"racial literacy" (p. 254)

racialization (p. 254)

racism (p. 255)

scapegoat (p. 257)

segregation (p. 259)

stereotype (p. 256)

Review Questions

1. What is ethnicity?
   a. The physical manifestation of racial difference
   b. Any biologically grounded features of a group of people
   c. Any group outside the white, English-speaking majority
   d. The cultural practices and outlooks of a given community that have emerged historically and tend to set people apart

2. Why has racism flourished in modern societies?
   a. Because there was a symbolic distinction between white and black (denoting good and bad) in European cultures before European explorers went to Africa
   b. Because of the dissemination of the idea of race and the ideologies that developed around it
   c. Because of the relations of exploitation that Europeans established with Africans
   d. All of the above

3. What is the "master status"?
   a. A feature like skin color that dominates our perception, often overriding in our minds a person's other characteristics
   b. Our socioeconomic standing
   c. A feature such as skin color that dominates a person's perception of him- or herself, often overriding all other factors in the way a person sees him- or herself
   d. Our gender and/or sexual orientation

4. By the late 1990s, which of the following groups in U.S. society had the highest rate of poverty?
   a. Whites
   b. African Americans
   c. Hispanics
   d. Asian Americans

5. What is the difference between the assimilation and melting-pot models of integrating new ethnic groups into the dominant society?
   a. The assimilation model refers to the new group adopting the norms and values of the dominant society, whereas the melting-pot model refers to the merging and blending of dominant and ethnic cultures.
   b. The assimilation model refers to members of the new group becoming citizens of the host nation, whereas the melting-pot model refers to members of the new group remaining guest workers and having only the legal rights afforded to those on work visas.
   c. The assimilation model refers to members of the new group learning the language of the host nation and dispersing to the suburbs, whereas the melting-pot model refers to members of the new group sticking to their own language and concentrating in particular urban neighborhoods.
   d. The assimilation model refers to the experience of twentieth-century immigrants to the United States, whereas the melting-pot model refers to the experience of nineteenth-century immigrants.

6. Which of the following groups have *not* been the victim of scapegoating in Western history?
   a. Blacks
   b. Chinese
   c. White Protestants
   d. All have been victims at one time or another.

7. How much difference did the formal abolition of slavery in the United States make to the condition of blacks?
   a. An enormous amount—they were no longer enslaved and were able to move in great numbers to seek manufacturing jobs in the northern cities.
   b. A good deal—their legal situation improved, and the formal rights they won formed the basis of the civil rights movement a century later.
   c. Relatively little—acts were soon passed legalizing the segregation of blacks and whites in public places.
   d. None—all of the conditions of slavery were replicated under sharecropping.

8. What is the difference between prejudice and discrimination?
   a. The terms are synonyms; they can be used interchangeably.
   b. Prejudice refers to opinions or attitudes held by members of one group toward another, while discrimination refers to behavior toward the other group.
   c. Prejudice is a matter of free speech, while discrimination is actionable under the law.
   d. Prejudice refers to behavior toward the other group, while discrimination refers to opinions or attitudes held by members of one group toward another.

9. Which of the following is NOT a characteristic of minority groups?

   a. The members are disadvantaged.

   b. The members have a sense of group solidarity.

   c. The members do not see themselves as set apart from the majority.

   d. The members tend to live and work in certain neighborhoods.

10. The dispersal of an ethnic population from their homeland into foreign areas, often by force, is called:

   a. prejudice.

   b. melting pot.

   c. diaspora.

   d. institutional racism.

Thinking Sociologically Essay Questions

1. Review the discussion of the assimilation of different American minorities, then write a short essay comparing the different assimilation experiences of Asians and Latinos. In your essay identify the criteria for assimilation and discuss which group has assimilated most readily. Then explain the sociological reasons for the difference in assimilation between these two groups.

2. Does affirmative action still have a future in the United States? On the one hand, increasing numbers of African Americans have joined the middle class by earning college degrees, professional jobs, and new homes. Yet blacks are still far more likely than whites to live in poverty, to attend poor schools, and to lack economic opportunity. Given these differences and other contrasts mentioned in the text, do we still need affirmative action?

Data Exercises

www.wwnorton.com/giddens
Keyword: Data10

- The American Indian and Alaska Native populations have often been described as the most disadvantaged racial minorities in the United States, and images of this population are often stereotypical. The data exercise for this chapter provides you with an opportunity to look beyond the stereotypes and learn more about the contemporary status of the American Indian and Alaska Native populations.

Theoretical Perspectives on the Family

Review the development of sociological thinking about the family and family life.

The Family in History

Learn how the family has changed over the last three hundred years.

Changes in Family Patterns Worldwide

See that although a diversity of family forms exist in different societies today, widespread changes are occurring that relate to the spread of globalization.

Marriage and the Family in the United States

Learn about patterns of marriage, childbearing, and divorce. Analyze how different these patterns are today compared with other periods.

The Dark Side of the Family

Learn about sexual abuse and violence within families.

Alternatives to Traditional Forms of Marriage and the Family

Learn some alternatives to traditional marriage and family patterns that are becoming more widespread.

CHAPTER ELEVEN

FAMILIES AND INTIMATE RELATIONSHIPS

the theme of much of this book has been change. We live in a turbulent, difficult, and unfamiliar world today. Whether we like it or not, we all must come to terms with the mixture of opportunity and risk it presents. Nowhere is this observation more true than in the domain of personal and emotional life.

In our personal lives, we now have to deal with "relationships." When someone asks you, "How is your relationship going?" she is usually asking about a sexual involvement. But we are increasingly caught up in relationships with parents, friends, and others. The term *relationship*, as applied to personal life, came into general use only twenty or thirty years ago, as did the idea that there is a need for "commitment" in personal life.

The fact that most of us now think about these changes a great deal, whether we resist them or not, is indicative of the basic transformations that have affected our personal and emotional lives over the past few decades. A relationship is something *active*—you have to work at it. It depends on winning the trust of the other person if it is going to survive over time. Most kinds of sexual relations have become like this now, and so has marriage. Many troubles we see all around us in sexual and family life derive from this necessity to work at relationships, which is in some respects quite new. But opportunities of a positive kind come from it too.

For example, today the couple, married or unmarried, is at the core of what the family is. The couple came to be at the center of family life as the economic role of the family dwindled and love, or love and sexual attraction, became the basis of forming marriage ties. Most people in our society believe that a good relationship is based on emotional communication or intimacy. The idea of intimacy, like so many other familiar notions we've discussed in this book, sounds old but in fact is very new. In the past, marriage was never based on intimacy and emotional communication. No doubt these were important to a good marriage but not the foundation of it. For the modern couple they are. Communication is the means of establishing a good relationship in the first place, and it is the chief rationale for its continuation. A good relationship is a relationship of equals, where each party has equal rights and obligations. In such a relationship, each person has respect and wants the best for the other. Talk, or dialogue, is the basis of making the relationship work. Relationships function best if people don't hide too much from each other—there has to be mutual trust. And trust has to be worked at; it can't just be taken for granted. Finally, a good relationship is one free from arbitrary power, coercion, or violence.

The changes affecting the personal and emotional spheres go far beyond the borders of any particular country, even one as large as the United States. We find the same issues almost everywhere, differing only in degree and according to the cultural context in which they take place. Defenders of the traditional family form argue that the emphasis on relationships comes at the expense of the family as a basic institution of society. Many of these critics now speak of the breakdown of the family. If such a breakdown is occurring, it is extremely significant. The family is the meeting point of a range of trends affecting society as a whole—increasing equality between the sexes, the widespread entry of women into the labor force, changes in sexual behavior and expectations, the changing relationship between home and work. Among all the changes going on today, none is more important than those happening in our personal lives—in sexuality, emotional life, marriage, and the family. There is a global revolution going on in how we think of ourselves and how we form ties and connections with others. It is a revolution advancing unevenly in different parts of the world, with much resistance.

How do we begin to understand the nature of these changes and their impact on our lives? It's only possible to understand what is going on in our personal lives and the family as a social institution today if we know something about how people lived in the past and how people currently live in other societies. So in this chapter, after discussing various theoretical perspectives on the family, we will look at the development of marriage and the family in earlier times, before analyzing the consequences of present-day changes both in the United States and elsewhere.

Basic Concepts

We need first of all to define some basic concepts, particularly those of family, kinship, and marriage. A **family** is a group of persons directly linked by kin connections, the adult members of which assume responsibility for caring for children. **Kinship** ties are connections between individuals, established either through marriage or through the lines of descent that connect blood relatives (mothers, fathers, offspring, grandparents, etc.). **Marriage** can be defined as a socially acknowledged and approved sexual union between two adult individuals. When two people marry, they become kin to one another; the marriage bond also, however, connects together a wider range of kinspeople. Parents, brothers, sisters, and other blood relatives become relatives of the partner through marriage.

Family relationships are always recognized within wider kinship groups. In virtually all societies, we can identify what sociologists and anthropologists call the **nuclear family**, two adults living together in a household with their own or adopted children. In most traditional societies, the nuclear family was part of a larger kinship network of some type. When close relatives in addition to a married couple and children live either in the same household or in a close and continuous relationship with one another, we speak of an **extended family**. An extended family may include grandparents, brothers and their wives, sisters and their husbands, aunts, and nephews.

Whether nuclear or extended, so far as the experience of each individual is concerned, families can be divided into **families of orientation** and **families of procreation**. The first is the family into which a person is born; the second is the family into which one enters as an adult and within which a new generation of children is brought up. A further important distinction concerns place of residence. In the United States, when a couple marry, they are usually expected to set up a separate household. This can be in the same area in which the bride's or groom's parents live, but may be in some different town or city altogether. In some other societies, however, everyone who marries is expected to live close to or within the same dwelling as the parents of the bride or groom. When the couple live near

An extended family gathers for a photograph in Zimbabwe.

or with the bride's parents, the arrangement is called **matrilo-cal**. In a **patrilocal** pattern, the couple live near or with the parents of the groom.

In Western societies, marriage, and therefore the family, is associated with **monogamy**. It is illegal for a man or woman to be married to more than one individual at any one time. But monogamy is not the most common type of marriage in the world as a whole. In a comparison of several hundred present-day societies, George Murdock found that **polygamy**, a marriage that allows a husband or wife to have more than one spouse, was permitted in over 80 percent (Murdock, 1949). There are two types of polygamy: **polygyny**, in which a man may be married to more than one woman at the same time, and **polyandry**, much less common, in which a woman may have two or more husbands simultaneously.

Theoretical Perspectives on the Family

The study of the family and family life has been taken up differently by sociologists with contrasting approaches. Many of the perspectives adopted even a few decades ago now seem much less convincing in the light of recent research and important changes in the social world. Nevertheless it is valuable to trace briefly the evolution of sociological thinking before turning to contemporary approaches to the study of the family.

Functionalism

The functionalist perspective sees society as a set of social institutions that perform specific functions to ensure continuity and consensus. According to this perspective, the family performs important tasks that contribute to society's basic needs and helps to perpetuate social order. Sociologists working in the functionalist tradition have regarded the nuclear family as fulfilling certain specialized roles in modern societies. With the advent of industrialization, the family became less important as a unit of economic production and more focused on reproduction, child rearing, and socialization.

According to the American sociologist Talcott Parsons, the family's two main functions are *primary socialization* and *personality stabilization* (Parsons and Bales, 1955). **Primary socialization** is the process by which children learn the cultural norms of the society into which they are born. Because this happens during the early years of childhood, the family is the most important area for the development of the human personality.

Personality stabilization refers to the role that the family plays in assisting adult family members emotionally. Marriage between adult men and women is the arrangement through which adult personalities are supported and kept healthy. In industrial society, the role of the family in stabilizing adult personalities is said to be critical. This is because the nuclear family is often distanced from its extended kin and is unable to draw on larger kinship ties as families could prior to industrialization.

Parsons regarded the nuclear family as the unit best equipped to handle the demands of industrial society. In the "conventional family," one adult can work outside the home while the second adult cares for the home and children. In practical terms, this specialization of roles within the nuclear family involved the husband adopting the "instrumental" role as breadwinner and the wife assuming the "affective," emotional role in domestic settings.

In our present age, Parsons's view of the family comes across as inadequate and outdated. Functionalist theories of the family have come under heavy criticism for justifying the domestic division of labor between men and women as something natural and unproblematic. Yet viewed in their own historical context, the theories are somewhat more understandable. The immediate post–World War II years saw women returning to their traditional domestic roles and men reassuming positions as sole breadwinners. We can criticize functionalist views of the family on other grounds, however. In emphasizing the importance of the family in performing certain functions, both theorists neglect the role that other social institutions—such as government, media, and schools—play in socializing children. The theories also neglect variations in family forms that do not correspond to the model of the nuclear family. Families that did not conform to the white, suburban, middle-class "ideal" were seen as deviant.

Feminist Approaches

For many people, the family provides a vital source of solace and comfort, love and companionship. Yet it can also be a locus for exploitation, loneliness, and profound inequality. Feminism has had a great impact on sociology by challenging the vision of the family as a harmonious and egalitarian realm. In 1965, one of the first dissenting voices was that of the American feminist Betty Friedan, who wrote of "the problem with no name"—the isolation and boredom that gripped many suburban American housewives who felt relegated to an endless cycle of child care and housework. Others followed, exploring the phenomenon of the "captive wife" (Gavron, 1966) and the damaging effects of "suffocating" family settings on interpersonal relationships (Laing, 1971).

During the 1970s and 1980s, feminist perspectives dominated most debates and research on the family. If previously the sociology of the family had focused on family structures, the historical development of the nuclear and extended family, and the importance of kinship ties, feminism succeeded in directing attention inside families to examine the experiences of women in the domestic sphere. Many feminist writers have questioned the vision of the family as a cooperative unit based on common interests and mutual support. They have sought to show that the presence of unequal power relationships within the family means that certain family members tend to benefit more than others.

Feminist writings have emphasized a broad spectrum of topics, but three main themes are of particular importance. One of the central concerns is the *domestic division of labor*—the way in which tasks are allocated among members of a household. Feminist sociologists have undertaken studies on the way domestic tasks, such as child care and housework, are shared between men and women. Findings have shown that women continue to bear the main responsibility for domestic tasks and enjoy less leisure time than men, despite the fact that more women are working in paid employment outside the home than ever before (Hochschild, 1989; Gershuny et al., 1994; Sullivan, 1997). Pursuing a related theme, some sociologists have examined the contrasting realms of paid and unpaid work, focusing on the contribution that women's unpaid domestic labor makes to the overall economy (Oakley, 1974). Others have investigated the way in which resources are distributed among family members and the patterns of access to and control over household finances (Pahl, 1989).

Second, feminists have drawn attention to the *unequal power relationships* that exist within many families. One topic that has received increased attention as a result of this is the phenomenon of domestic violence. Wife battering, marital rape, incest, and the sexual abuse of children have all received more public attention as a result of feminists' claims that the violent and abusive sides of family life have long been ignored in both academic contexts and legal and policy circles. Feminist sociologists have sought to understand how the family serves as an arena for gender oppression and even physical abuse.

The study of *caring activities* is a third area in which feminists have made important contributions. This is a broad realm that encompasses a variety of processes, from attending to a family member who is ill to looking after an elderly relative over a long period of time. Sometimes caring means simply being attuned to someone else's psychological well-being—several feminist writers have been interested in "emotion work" within relationships. Not only do women tend to shoulder concrete tasks such as cleaning and child care, but they also invest large amounts of emotional labor in maintaining personal relationships (Duncombe and Marsden, 1993). While caring activities are grounded in love and deep emotion, they are also a form of work that demands an ability to listen, perceive, negotiate, and act creatively.

New Perspectives in the Sociology of the Family

Theoretical and empirical studies conducted from a feminist perspective during the last few decades have generated increased interest in the family among both academics and the general population. Terms such as the *second shift*—referring to women's dual roles at work and at home—have entered our everyday vocabulary. But because they often focused on specific issues within the domestic realm, feminist studies of the family did not always reflect larger trends and influences taking place outside the home.

In the past decade, an important body of sociological literature on the family has emerged that draws on feminist perspectives but is not strictly informed by them. Of primary concern are the larger transformations that are taking place in family forms—the formation and dissolution of families and households and the evolving expectations within individuals' personal relationships. The rise in divorce and single parenting, the emergence of "reconstituted families" and gay families, and the popularity of cohabitation are all subjects of concern. Yet these transformations cannot be understood apart from the larger changes occurring in our late modern age. Attention must be paid to the shifts occurring at the societal, and even global, level if we are to grasp the link between personal transformations and larger patterns of change.

The Family in History

Sociologists once thought that prior to the modern period, the predominant form of family in western Europe was of the extended type. Research has shown this view to be mistaken. The nuclear family seems long to have been preeminent. Premodern household size was larger than it is today, but the difference is not especially great. In the United States, for example, throughout the seventeenth, eighteenth, and nineteenth centuries, the average household size was 4.75 persons. The current average is 2.59 (U.S. Bureau of the Census, 2000). Since the earlier figure includes domestic servants, the difference in family size is small.

"The Way We Never Were": Myths of the Traditional Family

Many people in current times feel that family life is being undermined. They contrast what they see as the decline of the family with more traditional forms of family life. Was the family of the past as peaceful and harmonious as many people recall it, or is this a simply idealized fiction? As Stephanie Coontz points out in her book *The Way We Never Were* (1992), as with other visions of a golden age of the past, the rosy light shed on the "traditional family" dissolves when we look back to previous times to see what things really were like.

Many admire the colonial family of early days as a disciplined, stable family. However, colonial families suffered from the same disintegrative forces as their counterparts in Europe. Especially high death rates meant that the average length of marriages was less than twelve years, and more than half of all children saw the death of at least one parent by the time they were twenty-one. The admired discipline of the colonial family was rooted in the strict authority of parents over their children. The way in which this authority was exercised would be considered exceedingly harsh by today's standards.

If we consider the Victorian family of the 1850s, the ideal family still eludes us. In this period, wives were more or less forcibly confined to the home. According to Victorian morality, women were supposed to be strictly virtuous, while men were sexually licentious: Many visited prostitutes and paid regular visits to brothels. In fact, wives and husbands often had little to do with one another, communicating only through their children. Moreover, domesticity wasn't even an option for poorer groups of this period. African American slaves in the South lived and worked frequently in the most appalling conditions. In the factories and workshops of the North, white families worked long hours with little time for home life. Child labor was also rampant in these groups.

Our most recent memory draws us to the 1950s as the time of the ideal American family. This was a period when women worked only in the home, while men were responsible for earning the family wage. Yet large numbers of women didn't actually *want* to retreat to a purely domestic role and felt miserable and trapped in it. Women had held paid jobs during World War II as part of the war effort. They lost these jobs when men returned from the war. Moreover, men were still emotionally removed from their wives and often observed a strong sexual double standard, seeking sexual adventures for themselves but setting strict codes for their spouses.

Betty Friedan's best-selling book *The Feminine Mystique* first appeared in 1963, but its research referred to the 1950s. Friedan struck a chord in the hearts of thousands of women when she spoke of the "problem with no name": the oppressive nature of a domestic life bound up with child care, domestic drudgery, and a husband who only occasionally put in an appearance and with whom little emotional communication was possible. Even more severe than the oppressive home life endured by many women was the alcoholism and violence suffered within many families during a time period when society was not prepared to fully confront these issues.

Let's now look directly at the changes affecting personal life, marriage, and the family in the world today. There is no doubt that some of these changes are profound and far-reaching. But interpreting their likely implications, particularly in the United States, means taking account of just how unrealistic it is to contrast what is happening now with a fictional or mythical view of the traditional family.

Changes in Family Patterns Worldwide

There is a diversity of family forms today in different societies across the world. In some areas, such as more remote regions in Asia, Africa, and the Pacific Rim, traditional family systems are little altered. In most developing countries, however, widespread changes are occurring. The origins of these changes are complex, but several factors can be picked out as especially important. One is the spread of Western culture. Western ideals of romantic love, for example, have spread to societies in which they were previously unknown. Another factor is the development of centralized government in areas previously composed of autonomous smaller societies. People's lives become influenced by their involvement in a national political system; moreover, governments make active attempts to alter traditional ways of behavior. Because of the problem of rapidly expanding population growth, states frequently introduce programs advocating smaller families, the use of contraception, and so forth.

A further influence is the large-scale migration from rural to urban areas. Often men go to work in towns or cities, leaving family members in the home village. Alternatively, a nuclear-family group will move as a unit to the city. In both cases, traditional family forms and kinship systems may become weakened. Finally, and perhaps most important, employment opportunities away from the land and in such organizations as government bureaucracies, mines, plantations, and—where they exist—industrial firms tend to have disruptive consequences for family systems previously centered on landed production in the local community.

In general, these changes are creating a worldwide movement toward the predominance of the nuclear family, breaking down extended-family systems and other types of kinship groups. This was first documented by William J. Goode in his book *World Revolution in Family Patterns* (1963) and has been borne out by subsequent research.

Balancing Family and Work

How many hours each week did your parents spend doing paid work when you were growing up? Did their commitment to work affect the way you or your siblings were raised? One of the ways globalization has affected family life in the United States is by increasing the amount of time that people spend each week at work. While there is some disagreement among researchers as to whether Americans, on average, are putting in more hours at work now than they did in the past, many sociologists give credence to the findings of the economist Juliet Schor, author of the 1992 book *The Overworked American*. Schor argues that workers today spend on average 164 more hours each year at work than they did twenty years ago. Workers are also taking less vacation time than they did previously. Perhaps more significant, the percentage of mothers who are working full time has increased dramatically since the end of World War II. In fact, in a comprehensive study of the multiple roles that modern women occupy, Daphne Spain and Suzanne Bianchi (1996) found that the group of women that saw the most dramatic increase in labor force participation in the United States were married women with young children. Taken together, these facts suggest that parents today have less time available to spend with their children than was the

Directions of Change

The most important changes occurring worldwide are the following:

1. Clans and other kin groups are declining in their influence.
2. There is a general trend toward the free choice of a spouse.
3. The rights of women are becoming more widely recognized, in respect to both the initiation of marriage and decision making within the family.
4. Kin marriages are becoming less common.
5. Higher levels of sexual freedom are developing in societies that were very restrictive.
6. There is a general trend toward the extension of children's rights.

In many countries, especially Western industrial societies, the nuclear family has been the preeminent family form. Given the ethnically diverse character of the United States, there are considerable variations in family and marriage within the country. Some of the most striking include differences between white and African American family patterns, and we need to consider why this is so. We will then move on to examine divorce, remarriage, and stepparenting in relation to contemporary patterns of family life.

case in decades past. As a result, there has been a significant increase in the percentage of children enrolled in day-care programs—and, some would argue, a palpable increase in tension and stress within families as more of the day-to-day parental role is offloaded onto child-care providers.

In her book *The Time Bind* (1997), sociologist Arlie Hochschild suggests that these developments may be related to globalization. Globalization, of course, is not responsible for the gains women have made in securing positions in the paid labor force. Nevertheless, some corporations, according to Hochschild, have responded to the pressures of global competition by encouraging their salaried employees to put in longer hours at work, thus increasing levels of productivity. Why would employees willingly agree to spend so much time at their jobs—often considerably more than forty hours each week—when they are not paid to do so, when they know that such a commitment disrupts their family life, and in an age when computerization has greatly improved workplace efficiency? Shouldn't technological progress allow workers to spend more time with their families rather than less? Hochschild's answer to this question is that some corporations rely on the power of workplace norms to elicit a greater time commitment from their workers. New employees are socialized into a corporate culture in which working long hours is seen as a badge of dedication and professionalism. Employees, seeking status and the approval of their peers and supervisors, become motivated to put as much time into work as possible and to make sure that those around them know precisely how much time they spend working. In some cases, such a corporate culture has arisen unintentionally, as workers respond to the threat of corporate

downsizing by redoubling their commitment to the organization. In other cases—as with the corporation Hochschild studied—executives have consciously sought to shape the culture of the organization, reminding employees through handbooks, speeches, and newsletters that working more than forty hours a week is the mark of a "good" worker.

Although globalization has touched all the nations of the world, its effects on work time seem to vary by country. In France and Germany, for example, workers—sometimes acting through unions, sometimes making their power known at the voting booth—have rejected corporate calls for a longer workweek, and are instead pressuring employers to reduce the workweek and to grant longer vacations. Do Europeans simply value family and leisure time more than Americans? Or would American workers be making the same demands if unions were stronger in this country?

Marriage and the Family in the United States

The United States has long been characterized by high marriage rates. Nearly every American adult eventually marries; almost 95 percent of adults in their early fifties today are or have previously been married. The age at which first marriages are contracted has risen, however, over the past twenty years (it was also high at the turn of the century, declining in the 1922–1950 period). There are several explanations for this trend in the last several decades toward later marriage. Some researchers contend that increases in cohabitation among younger people account for the decreases (or delays) in

marriage among this group. Young people are cohabiting before or instead of marrying. Others argue that increases in postsecondary school enrollment, especially among women, are partially responsible for delays in marriage. Similarly, women's increased participation in the labor force often leads to delays in marriage as women work to establish their careers before marrying and starting a family (Oppenheimer, 1988). Labor force participation also increases economic independence among women. By earning their own income, many women no longer need a male breadwinner in their home. The flip side of the economic independence argument is the idea that the deterioration of men's economic position since the late 1980s has made them less attractive mates and less ready to marry. Some researchers have used this idea—the marriageable men hypothesis—to explain the especially low marriage rates among blacks: Because

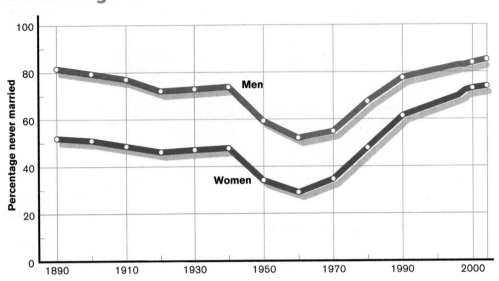

FIGURE 11.1

Percentage of Never-Married 20-to-24-Year-Olds

Men

Women

SOURCE: Cherlin, 1992; U.S. Bureau of the Census, Current Population Reports, "America's Families and Living Arrangements," 2001; U.S. Bureau of the Census, 2002.

black men have suffered the worst economic conditions in the last few decades, they might be viewed by black women as particularly poor marriage candidates. Finally, some researchers believe that modernization and a secular change in attitudes promote individualism and make marriage less important than it once was. The true reason for the decline in marriage is most likely some combination of the above explanations. But we must be careful how we make our comparisons. Although some have argued that the trend since 1970 toward later marriage is a break from tradition, it actually is close to the age of first marriage for the period 1890–1940. To say that people today are postponing marriage is true only if we compare ourselves with the 1950s generation. It might be more accurate to say that the 1950s generation married at an unusually young age.

In 1960, the average age of first marriages was 22.8 for men and 20.3 for women. The comparable ages in 2000 were 26.8 for men and 25.1 for women. Another way of measuring the relations between age and first marriage is to look at the numbers of people who remain unmarried before a certain age (see Figure 11.1). Thus, in 1960, just 28 percent of women aged less than 24 years had never married. In 2002, that proportion was 74 percent. The U.S. census now incorporates a category of "unmarried couples sharing the same household." As this practice of cohabitation is new, it is not easy to make direct comparisons with preceding years. Nonetheless, we can accurately estimate

that the number of couples among younger age groups who live together without being married has risen steeply (see Figure 11.2) from 11 percent around 1970 to 44 percent in the early 1980s and probably about 50 percent today (Cherlin, 1999). By age thirty about 50 percent of women will have cohabited outside marriage (National Center for Health Statistics, 2002).

An extraordinary increase in the proportion of people living alone in the United States has also taken place over recent years—a phenomenon that partly reflects the high levels of marital separation and divorce. More than one in every four households now consists of one person, a rise of 44 percent since 1960. There has been a particularly sharp rise in the proportion of individuals living alone in the twenty-four-to-forty-four age bracket.

Some people still suppose that the average American family is made up of a husband who works in paid employment and a wife who looks after the home, living together with their two children. This is very different from the real situation: Only about 25 percent of children live in households that fit this picture. One reason is the rising rates of divorce: A substantial proportion of the population live either in single-parent households or in stepfamilies, or both. Another is the high proportion of women who work. Dual-career marriages and single-parent families are now the norm (see Figure 11.3). The majority of married women working outside the home also care for a child

FIGURE 11.2

Changes in Cohabitation

Percentage cohabiting before first marriage, for persons marrying in 1965–1974, 1975–1979, and 1980–1984.

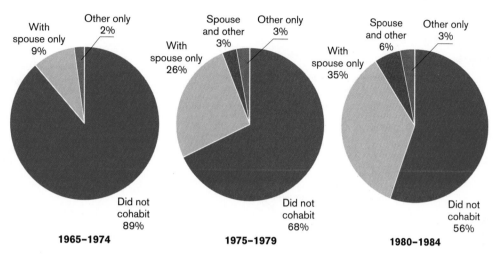

1965–1974

Other only 2%
With spouse only 9%
Did not cohabit 89%

1975–1979

Spouse and other 3%
Other only 3%
With spouse only 26%
Did not cohabit 68%

1980–1984

Spouse and other 6%
Other only 3%
With spouse only 35%
Did not cohabit 56%

SOURCE: Bumpass and Sweet, 1989.

or children. Although many working women are concentrated in jobs with poor or nonexistent promotion prospects, the standard of living of many American couples is dependent on the income contributed by the wife, as well as on the unpaid work she undertakes in the home (see also Chapter 13).

African American Families

As mentioned earlier, there are important differences in white and black family patterns. One of the most striking is that far fewer African American women aged twenty-five to forty-four are married and living with a husband than white women in the same age group. This fact has given rise to heated disputes about the nature of African American families in the United States.

In 2002, 79 percent of white families included a married couple, as compared to 46 percent of black families (U.S. Census, 2000). In 1960, 21 percent of African American families were headed by females; among white families, the proportion was 8 percent. By 2002, the proportion for black families had risen to more than 48 percent, while that for white families was under 18 percent (see Figure 11.4) (U.S. Census, 2002). Female-headed families are more prominently represented among poorer blacks. African Americans in poor urban neighborhoods have experienced little rise in living conditions over the past two

decades: Many are confined to low-wage jobs or are more or less permanently unemployed. In these circumstances, there is little to foster continuity in marital relationships.

But we should not see the situation of African American families purely in a negative light. The director of the National Urban League, a black organization, titled a research report produced in the 1970s "The Strengths of Black Families." These families, the report claimed, show characteristics that promote stability, including strong and adaptable kin ties. Extended kinship networks are important among poor blacks—much more significant, relative to marital ties, than in most white communities. A mother heading a one-parent family is likely to have a close and supportive network of relatives to depend on. This contradicts the idea that black single parents and their children form unstable families. A far higher proportion of female-headed families among African Americans have other relatives living with them than do white families headed by females.

In her book *Lifelines* (1983), Joyce Aschenbrenner provides a comprehensive portrayal of extended kin relationships in African American families. Aschenbrenner gained a new perspective on both white and black family types in the United States as a result of fieldwork she had earlier carried out in Pakistan. From the point of view of the Pakistanis, the white family in the United States seemed weak and "disorganized." They could not understand how a mere couple, let alone a single par-

FIGURE 11.3

The Changing Structure of American Families with Children

Percentage of American children 17 and younger living in each of four types of families, 1790–1990.

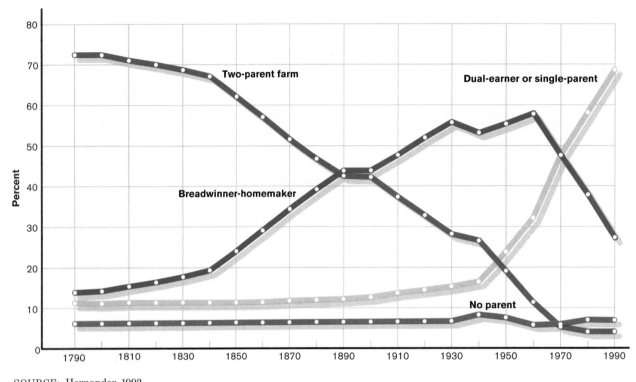

SOURCE: Hernandez, 1993.

ent, could bring up children. The way they thought of the family was closer to the situation of African American families rather than to the usual family structure among whites.

Discussions of the black family, Aschenbrenner suggests, have focused too strongly on the marriage relationship. This emphasis is in line with the overriding importance of marriage in American society, but this relationship does not necessarily form the structure of the African American family. In most societies that include extended families, relationships such as mother-daughter, father-son, or brother-sister may be more socially significant than that between husband and wife (Aschenbrenner, 1983).

Latino Families

As in many other areas, Hispanics are very heterogeneous when it comes to family patterns. Mexicans, Puerto Ricans, and Cubans are three of the largest Hispanic subgroups. In the U.S. census of 1990, Mexicans were the largest Hispanic group—over 58 percent of the whole Hispanic population. Puerto Ricans constituted nearly 10 percent down from 12 percent in 1990, Cubans were just 3.5 percent, and the rest of the Hispanic population was made up of much smaller groups from many Latin American nations (U.S. Census, 2000a).

Mexican American families are characterized by multi-generational households and a high birthrate. Economically, Mexican American families are more well off than Puerto Rican families but less well off than Cuban families. Defying cultural stereotypes of a Mexican American home with a male breadwinner and female homemaker, more than half of all Mexican American women are in the labor force (Ortiz, 1995). Still, ethnographic research indicates that this is due to necessity rather than desire. Many Mexican American families suggest that the breadwinner-homemaker model would be their preference but that they are constrained by finances (Hurtado, 1995).

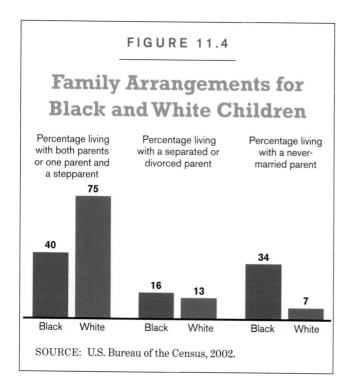

FIGURE 11.4

Family Arrangements for Black and White Children

Percentage living with both parents or one parent and a stepparent

Black 40
White 75

Percentage living with a separated or divorced parent

Black 16
White 13

Percentage living with a never-married parent

Black 34
White 7

SOURCE: U.S. Bureau of the Census, 2002.

Although Puerto Rico is a U.S. commonwealth, Puerto Ricans are still considered part of the umbrella category of Hispanics. However, because of their status as U.S. citizens, Puerto Ricans can and do move about freely between Puerto Rico and the mainland without the difficulties often encountered by immigrants. Because Puerto Ricans do not face as many barriers, even the least able can manage the migration process. The economic upshot of unrestricted migration for Puerto Ricans is that they are the most economically disadvantaged of all the major Hispanic groups.

Puerto Rican families are also characterized by a higher percentage of children born to unmarried mothers than any other Hispanic group—second only to African Americans (Cherlin, 1999). However, consensual unions—cohabiting relationships in which couples consider themselves married but are not legally married—are often the context for births to unmarried mothers.

Cuban American families are the most prosperous of all the Hispanic groups but still less prosperous than whites. Most Cuban Americans have settled in the Miami area and have formed immigrant enclaves in which they rely on other Cubans for their business and social needs (e.g., banking, schools, shopping, etc.). The relative wealth of Cuban Americans is driven largely by family business ownership. In terms of childbearing, Cuban Americans have lower levels of fertility than non-Hispanic whites and equally low levels of nonmarital fertility.

Asian American Families

One of the primary features of the Asian American family is that of dependence on the extended family. In many Asian cultures, family concerns are almost always a priority over individual concerns. Family interdependence also helps Asian Americans prosper financially. Asian American family and friend networks often pool money to help their members start a business or buy a house. This help is reciprocated as the recently endowed family member then contributes to the others. The result is a median family income for Asian Americans that is *higher* than that of the median for non-Hispanic whites.

There is a less detailed body of research on differences among Asian American subgroups than is the case with Hispanic subgroups. However, some fertility differences have been established. Chinese American and Japanese American women have much lower fertility rates than do any other racial/ethnic group. Chinese, Japanese, and Filipino families have lower levels of nonmarital fertility than all other racial/ethnic groups, including non-Hispanic whites. Low levels of nonmarital fertility combined with low levels of divorce for most Asian American groups demonstrate the emphasis on marriage as the appropriate forum for family formation and maintenance.

Native American Families

Kinship ties are also very important in Native American families. As Cherlin (1999) notes, "kinship networks constitute tribal organization; kinship ties confer identity" for Native Americans. However, fewer than half of all Native Americans live on or near tribal lands, so for those who live in cities or away from reservations, kin ties may be less prominent. Furthermore, Native Americans have higher rates of intermarriage than any other racial/ethnic group. In fact, in 1990, less than half of all married Native Americans were married to other Native Americans (Sandefur and Liebler, 1997).

The Native American fertility experience is similar to that of African Americans. Native American women have a high fertility rate and a high percentage of nonmarital fertility. Over half of all Native American women giving birth in 1990 were not married (U.S. National Center for Health Statistics, 1993). Sandefur and Liebler (1997) also report a high divorce rate for Native Americans.

Divorce and Separation

The past thirty years have seen major increases in rates of divorce, together with a relaxation of previously held attitudes of disapproval of divorce.

Marriage and the Family in the United States | **293**

Divorce rates, calculated by looking at the number of divorces per thousand married men or women per year, have fluctuated in the United States in different periods (Figure 11.5). They rose, for example, following World War II, then dropped off before climbing to much higher levels. The divorce rate increased steeply from the 1960s to the late 1970s, reaching a peak in 1980 (thereafter declining somewhat). It used to be common for divorced women to move back to their parents' homes after separation; today, most set up their own households.

Divorce exerts an enormous impact on the lives of children. Since 1970, more than 1 million American children per year have been affected by divorce. In one calculation, about one half of children born in 1980 became members of a one-parent family at some stage in their lives. Since two thirds of women and three fourths of men who are divorced eventually remarry, most of these children nonetheless grew up in a family environment. Only just over 2 percent of children under fourteen in the United States today are not living with either parent. The remarriage figures are substantially lower for African Americans. Only 32 percent of black women and 55 percent of black men who divorce remarry within ten years. Black children are half as likely as white children to be living with both parents or one parent and a stepparent (37 percent versus 76 percent) (Cherlin, 1992).

Lenore Weitzman (1985) has argued that no-fault divorce laws have helped to recast the psychological context of divorce positively (reducing some of the hostility it once generated), but they have had strong negative consequences for the economic position of women. Laws that were designed to be gender-neutral have had the unintended consequence of depriving divorced women of the financial protections that the old laws provided. Women are expected to be as capable as men of supporting themselves after divorce. Yet because most women's careers are still secondary to their work as homemakers, they may lack the qualifications and earning power of men. The living standards of divorced women and their children on average fell by 27 percent in the first year following the divorce settlement. The average standard of living of divorced men, by contrast, *rose* by 10 percent. Most court judgments left the former husband with a high proportion of his income intact; therefore, he had more to spend on his own needs than while he was married (Peterson, 1996).

REASONS FOR DIVORCE

Why has divorce become much more common over recent years? There are several reasons, which involve the wider changes going on in modern societies and in social institu-

FIGURE 11.5

Divorce Rates in the United States

SOURCE: Cherlin, 1999.

tions. As mentioned before, changes in the law have made divorce easier. Additionally, except for a small proportion of wealthy people, marriage today no longer has much connection with the desire to perpetuate property and status from generation to generation. As women become more economically independent, marriage is less of a necessary economic partnership. Greater overall prosperity means that it is easier to establish a separate household in case of marital disaffection (Lee, 1982). The fact that little stigma now attaches to divorce is in some part the result of these developments but adds momentum to them also. A further important factor is the growing tendency to evaluate marriage in terms of the levels of personal satisfaction it offers. Rising rates of divorce do not seem to indicate a deep dissatisfaction with marriage as such, but an increased determination to make it a rewarding and satisfying relationship (Cherlin, 1990).

Other factors that show a positive correlation to the likelihood of divorce are related to an individual's life cycle. They include:

- parental divorce (people whose parents divorce are more likely to divorce);
- premarital cohabitation (people who cohabitate before marriage have a higher divorce rate);
- premarital childbearing (people who marry after having children are more likely to divorce);
- marriage at an early age (people who marry as teenagers have a higher divorce rate);
- a childless marriage (couples without children are more likely to divorce); and
- low incomes (divorce is more likely among couples with low incomes) (White, 1990).

DIVORCE AND CHILDREN

The effects of divorce on children are difficult to gauge. How contentious the relationship is between the parents prior to separation, the ages of the children at the time, whether or not there are brothers or sisters, the availability of grandparents and other relatives, the children's relationship with their individual parents, and how frequently they continue to see both parents can all affect the process of adjustment. Since children whose parents are unhappy with each other but stay together may also be affected, assessing the consequences of divorce for children is doubly problematic.

Research indicates that children often suffer a period of marked emotional anxiety following the separation of their parents. Judith Wallerstein and Joan Kelly studied 131 children of sixty families in Marin County, California, following the separation of the parents. They contacted the children at the time of the divorce, a year and a half after, and five years after. According to the authors, almost all the children experienced intense emotional disturbance at the time of the divorce. Preschool-age children were confused and frightened, tending to blame themselves for the separation. Older children were better able to understand their parents' motives for divorce but frequently worried about its effects on their future and expressed sharp feelings of anger. At the end of the five-year period, however, the researchers found that two thirds were coping reasonably well with their home lives and their commitments outside. A third remained dissatisfied with their lives, were subject to depression, and expressed feelings of loneliness, even in cases where the parent with whom they were living had remarried (Wallerstein and Kelly, 1980).

Wallerstein continued her study of this same group of children, following 116 of the original 131 into young adulthood with interviews at the end of ten-year and fifteen-year periods. The interviews revealed that these children brought memories and feelings of their parents' divorce into their own romantic relationships. Almost all felt that they had suffered in some way from their parents' mistakes. Not surprisingly, most of them shared a hope for something their parents had failed to achieve—a good, committed marriage based on love and faithfulness. Nearly half the group entered adulthood as "worried, underachieving, self-deprecating, and sometimes angry young men and women." Although many of them got married themselves, the legacy of their parents' divorce lived with them. Those who appeared to manage the best were often helped by supportive relationships with one or both parents (Wallerstein and Blakeslee, 1989).

We cannot say, of course, how the children might have fared if their parents had stayed together. The parents and children studied all came from an affluent white area and might or might not be representative of the wider population. Moreover, the families were self-selected: They had approached counselors seeking help. Those who actively seek counseling might be less (or more) able to cope with separation than those who do not.

A more recent study found that the majority of persons whose parents had divorced did not have serious mental health problems. They did find small differences in mental health between those whose parents divorced and those whose parents stayed together (favoring those whose parents stayed together), but much of this difference in mental health had been identified in children at age seven, before any of the families experienced divorce (Cherlin et al., 1998). The most

The American Family

Kansas

As divorce has increased, remarriage and stepparenting have become common family arrangements in both rural and urban America. For children and adults involved in "blended" families, the transition can be both challenging and rewarding. A family in rural Kansas has created friendships and connections that are extended to all of its family members. Six years ago two young girls participated in the wedding of their mother and new stepfather. Since then, the girls have helped to raise their half-brother and to support the family cattle and soybean business. The girls' biological father (a valued parent and friend) is also an active part of the family, visiting frequently, joining celebrations, and involving the girls with their paternal relatives.

"Living here in the Flint Hills country on a farm/ranch, we are involved in 4H, and all school activities. Grandparents, aunts, uncles, and cousins are also a big part of our lives. I feel very fortunate to be a part of this wonderful family. I guess we forget, or just don't think of ourselves as being 'blended,' just a family that enjoys, works, listens, and loves each other to the fullest. The girls are lucky that they have two dads that love and take care of them. I feel this has a great deal to do with our family doing so well together. The two dads do not compete to outdo the other or put the other down. They are both there for the girls and the girls' needs. I think the girls enjoy having a little brother, although being the baby with two older sisters and old parents, he is as spoiled as we can get him, which means he can become a real pain from time to time. But we all love him so much, it's hard to be firm when his smile melts us all."

—Mom, Rural Kansas

South Dakota

Fostering children is a universally understood and commonly practiced Lakota Sioux custom. According to tradition, children in need of help are embraced as family members and foster families are highly regarded within the community. On the Rosebud Sioux Reservation in South Dakota, two sisters and a daughter have taken to heart the Lakota understanding of family and opened their doors to foster children for over twenty years. All of the children (placed by state and private foster agencies) are loved, provided for, celebrated and respected as precious members of the larger community circle.

"Being a 'foster' parent is something that came really naturally to me. Having grown up in a Lakota family, I have a large extended family. I saw so many people come and go through

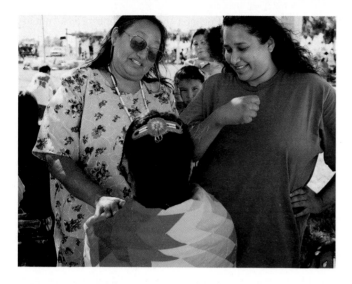

my grandmother's and my mother's house. It didn't matter if they were blood or not, their doors were always open. So I think this is why it was so easy for me to open my home to others. I never really thought about becoming a foster parent. Even before we were officially licensed, we cared for other kids in our home. I married my husband in 1987, when I was nineteen years old, and we got custody of his younger brothers and sisters in the next spring. So, I was nineteen taking care of a sixteen, thirteen, and eleven year old. It was hard, but I had my mom and family to help us. When the kids started to graduate and move on with their lives, the house felt empty, but there is always someone else who needs a family to love and support them. I don't like the word 'foster' because it puts separation between us and the kids. My own kids are happy to have more brothers and sisters. We are a family, and the kids are my kids. You know what they say; the more the merrier. Don't get me wrong; everything isn't always rosy, but you get

past the rough seas, and into calm waters. Even though the older ones are adults and have their own lives, they still come home when they need to or call when they are having a hard time. And we will always be there for all of them."

—Mom, Rosebud Sioux Reservation, South Dakota

Ohio

With the divorce rate estimated to be as high as 50 percent, single parent families are one of the largest and fastest growing family types in America. (In 1997, over one quarter of children lived with only one parent.) Raising the youngest three of his six adopted children, a single parent father in Cleveland cooks, cleans, and cares for his kids between working full-time shifts as an inner city police officer.

"Children are the heart of any family and mine are my heart. Most men think it's a woman's job to raise children, but it's not. I work, clean house, cook and help the kids with homework, and if one of the kids is sick, it's me that takes them to the hospital and sits at their bedside. Whether the times are good or bad, it's dad to the rescue."

—Dad, Cleveland, Ohio

SOURCE: Courteney Coolidge, "American Families: Beyond the White Picket Fence," a photo project, available at http://10families.com.

Questions

- How would you define "family," based on the three examples above?
- In terms of lifestyle and function, what are the differences between these families and the nuclear family?

prominent sociologist of the family in the United States, Andrew Cherlin, has argued that the general effects of divorce on children are:

- Almost all children experience an initial period of intense emotional upset after their parents separate.
- Most resume normal development without serious problems within about two years after the separation.
- A minority of children experience some long-term problems as a result of the breakup that may persist into adulthood (Cherlin, 1999).

Remarriage and Stepparenting

Odd though it might seem, the best way to maximize the chances of marriage, for both sexes, is to have been married previously. People who have been married and divorced are more likely to marry again than single people in similar age groups are to marry for the first time. At all age levels, divorced men are more likely to remarry than divorced women. Two in every three divorced women remarry, but three in every four divorced men eventually marry again. Many divorced individuals also choose to cohabitate instead of remarry. In statistical terms, at least, remarriages are less successful than first marriages: rates of divorce are higher.

This does not mean that second marriages are doomed to fail. People who have been divorced may have higher expectations of marriage than those who remain married to their first spouses. Hence, they may be more ready to dissolve new marriages than those only married once. The second marriages that endure are usually more satisfying, on average, than the first.

A **stepfamily** may be defined as a family in which at least one of the adults is a stepparent. Many who remarry become stepparents of children who regularly visit rather than live in the same household. By this definition, the number of stepfamilies is much greater than shown in available official statistics, since these usually refer only to families with whom stepchildren live. Stepfamilies bring into being kin ties that resemble those of some traditional societies but that are new in Western countries. Children may now have two "mothers" and two "fathers"—their natural parents and their stepparents. Some stepfamilies regard all the children and close relatives from previous marriages as part of the family. If we consider that at least some of the grandparents may be part of the family as well, the result is a situation of some complexity.

Members of stepfamilies are finding their own ways of adjusting to the relatively uncharted circumstances in which they find themselves. Perhaps the most appropriate conclusion to be drawn is that while marriages are broken up by divorce, families on the whole are not. Especially where children are involved, ties persist.

Single-Parent Households

Single-parent households have become increasingly common. As a result of the increase in divorce rates and births before marriage, about one half of all children spend some time in their lives in a single-parent family (Furstenberg and Cherlin, 1991). The vast majority are headed by women, since the mother usually obtains custody of the children following a divorce (in a small proportion of single-parent households, the individual, again almost always a woman, has never been married). There are over 12 million single-parent households in the United States today, and the number may continue to increase (see Figure 11.6). Such households comprise one in five of all families with dependent children. On average, they are among the poorest groups in contemporary society. Many single parents, whether they have ever been married or not, still face social disapproval as well as economic insecurity. Earlier and more judgmental terms such as *deserted wives*, *fatherless families*, and *broken homes* are tending to disappear, however.

Most people do not wish to be single parents, but a growing minority choose to become so—who set out to have a child or children without the support of a spouse or partner. "Single mothers by choice" is an apt description of some parents, normally those who possess sufficient resources to manage satisfactorily as a single-parent household. For the majority of unmarried or never-married mothers, however, the reality is different: There is a high correlation between the rate of births outside marriage and indicators of poverty and social deprivation. As we saw earlier, these influences are very important in explaining the high proportion of single-parent households among families of African American background in the United States.

A debate exists among sociologists about the impact on children of growing up with a single parent. The most exhaustive set of studies carried out to date, by Sara McLanahan and Gary Sandefur, rejects the claim that children raised by only one parent do just as well as children raised by both parents. A large part of the reason is economic—the sudden drop in income associated with divorce. But about half of the disadvantage comes from inadequate parental attention and lack of social ties. Separation or divorce weakens the connection between child and father, as well as the link between the child and the father's network of friends and acquaintances. On the basis of wide empirical research, the authors conclude it is a myth that there are

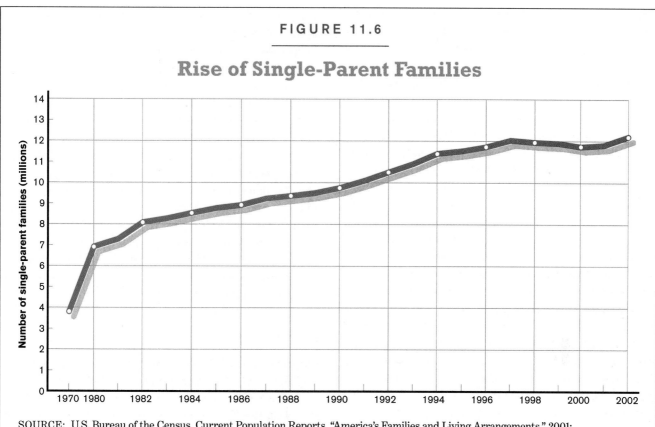

FIGURE 11.6

Rise of Single-Parent Families

Number of single-parent families (millions)

SOURCE: U.S. Bureau of the Census, Current Population Reports, "America's Families and Living Arrangements," 2001; U.S. Bureau of the Census, 2003.

usually strong support networks or extended family ties available to single mothers (McLanahan and Sandefur, 1994).

The Dark Side of the Family

Since family or kin relations are part of almost everyone's experience, family life encompasses virtually the whole range of emotional experience. Family relationships—between wife and husband, parents and children, brothers and sisters, or more distant relatives—can be warm and fulfilling. But they can equally be full of the most extreme tension, driving people to despair or imbuing them with a deep sense of anxiety and guilt. The dark side of family life is extensive and belies the rosy images of family harmony frequently depicted in TV commercials and programs. It can take many forms. Among the most devastating in their consequences, however, are the incestuous abuse of children and domestic violence.

Family Violence

Violence within families is primarily a male domain. The two broad categories of family violence are child abuse and spousal abuse. Because of the sensitive and private nature of violence within families, it is difficult to obtain national data on levels of domestic violence. Data on child abuse is particularly sparse because of the cognitive development and ethical issues involved in studying child subjects.

Child Abuse

Although there are many variations on what constitutes child abuse, the most common definition is serious physical harm (trauma, sexual abuse with injury, or willful malnutrition) with intent to injure. One national study of married or cohabiting adults indicates that about 2 percent of respondent adults abused their children in 1985 (Straus and Gelles, 1986). More recent statistics are based on national surveys of child welfare professionals. These surveys miss children who are not seen by professionals or reported to state agencies. However, they remain the most current source of information on child abuse. In the 1993 National Incidence Study of Child Abuse and Neglect (NIS), almost half of all substantiated cases of child abuse and neglect fell into the neglect category (47 percent). Physical abuse was the next most common violation (25 percent), followed by sexual abuse (15 percent) (Sedlak and Broadhurst, 1996). The most recent statistics based on the National Child Abuse and Neglect Reporting System indicate that in 2001 there were more than 900,000 reported child victims of abuse or neglect. Of these, more than half of all victims (57.2 percent) suffered neglect, 18.6 percent suffered physical abuse, and 9.6 percent were sexually abused (U.S. Department of Health and Human Services, 2003). The number of reported cases of child abuse has stayed the same since 1998. The rate of neglect has increased from 54 percent while the occurrence of physical abuse has dropped from 23 percent and the occurrence of sexual abuse has dropped from 12 percent (U.S. Department of Health and Human Services, 1998; 2003). The highest child victimization rates were for the zero-to-three age group. These studies also show that child abuse is more likely to occur in low-income families and single-parent families.

Spousal Abuse

A 1985 study by Straus and his colleagues found that spousal violence has occurred at least once in the past year in 16 percent of all marriages and at some point in the marriage in 28 percent of all marriages. This does not, however, distinguish between severe acts, such as beating up and threatening with or using a gun or knife, and less severe acts of violence, such as slapping, pushing, grabbing, or shoving one's spouse. When the authors disaggregated this number, they found that approximately 3 percent of all husbands admitted to perpetrating at least one act of severe violence on their spouse in the last year, and this is likely to be an underestimate.

The national survey by Straus and his colleagues also uncovers a finding that is somewhat contrary to most people's beliefs about spousal violence: They find that women reported perpetrating about the same amount of violent acts as men. This lies in stark contrast to much of the literature based on crime statistics, hospital records, and shelter administrative records. These sources all indicate that spousal violence is almost exclusively man-on-woman violence.

Michael Johnson (1995) was able to untangle these inconsistencies. Johnson recognized that the data that were generating such conflicting findings were collected from two very different samples. In the shelter samples, respondents are generally women who were severely beaten by their husbands or partners. The severity of their situation drew them to a shelter. On the other hand, those responding to a national survey are generally living in their homes and have the time, energy, or wherewithal to complete a survey. It is unlikely that individuals who are experiencing extreme violence in the home would respond to a national survey. Furthermore, it is unlikely that those who experience less severe kinds of violence (e.g., slapping) will end up in a domestic violence shelter. Therefore, these are two very different groups of people.

Johnson argued that the spousal abuse in the two samples was also different in character. He referred to the extreme abuse experienced by many in the shelter samples as "patriarchal terrorism." This type of violence is perpetuated by feelings of power and control. The type of violence reported in national surveys is referred to as "common couple violence." This type of violence is generally reactionary to a specific incident and is not rooted in power or control.

SOCIAL CLASS

Although no social class is immune to spousal abuse, several studies indicate that it is more common among low-income couples (Cherlin, 1999). Three decades ago, William Goode suggested that low-income men may be more prone to violence because they have few other means to control their wives, such as through having a higher income or education than their wives (Goode, 1971). In addition, the high levels of stress induced by poverty and unemployment may lead to more violence within families. In support of these assertions, Gelles and Cornell (1990) found that unemployed men are nearly twice as likely as employed men to assault their wives.

Alternatives to Traditional Forms of Marriage and the Family

Cohabitation

Cohabitation—in which a couple lives together in a sexual relationship without being married—has become increasingly widespread in most Western societies. Until a few decades ago, cohabitation was generally regarded as somewhat scandalous. As we saw earlier in the chapter, however, during the 1980s the number of unmarried men and women sharing a household went up sharply. Cohabitation has become widespread among college and university students, although they

FIGURE 11.7

Reasons for Cohabiting

Percentage of cohabiting women and men under thirty-five who agreed that each reason was the most important for "why someone might want to live with a person of the opposite sex without being married."

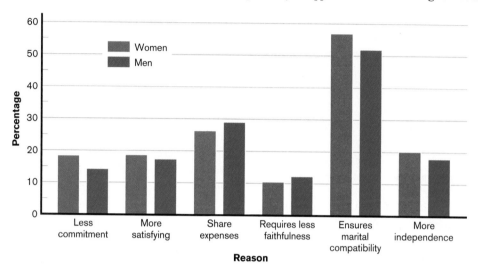

SOURCE: Bumpass, Sweet, and Cherlin, 1991.

were not the initiators of this trend, as many people believe. Bumpass, Sweet, and Cherlin (1991) found that the cohabitation phenomenon started with lower-educated groups in the 1950s. The college-educated population has always had and continues to have lower rates of cohabitation than those who do not go to college. The fact that those who are less educated were initiators in the trend toward cohabitation indicates that for this group, cohabitation may serve as a substitute for marriage, which may involve economic constraints.

While for some cohabitation may be a substitute for marriage, for many it is viewed as a stage in the process of relationship building that precedes marriage. Young people come to live together usually by drifting into it, rather than through calculated planning. A couple who are already having a sexual relationship spend more and more time together, eventually giving up one of their individual homes. The close connection between cohabitation and marriage for many is indicated in Figure 11.7, which shows that the most important reason for cohabitating for both women and men is so that "couples can be sure they are compatible before marriage."

Most cohabiting couples either marry or stop living together, although the chances of a cohabiting union transitioning to a first marriage is related to a number of socioeconomic factors. For instance, the probability that the first

cohabitation will become a marriage within five years is 75 percent for white women, but only 61 percent for Hispanic women and 48 percent for black women. Similarly, the likelihood of a first marriage resulting from cohabitation is positively associated with higher education, the absence of children during cohabitation, higher family income. It is also more likely in communities with low male unemployment rates (Bramlett and Mosher, 2002). Although many view cohabitation as a precursor to marriage, for a large number of people, it does not end in marriage. Only about 35 percent of cohabitors married their partners within three years of starting to live together. Increasingly, we are seeing evidence that cohabitation is not necessarily a "stage in the process" between dating and marriage, but rather it may be an end in itself for an increasing number of cohabitors.

The United States is certainly not alone in the increasing prevalence of cohabitation. Many European countries are experiencing similar, and in some cases much greater, proportions of unions beginning with cohabitation rather than marriage. The Nordic countries of Denmark, Sweden, and Finland, along with France, show particularly high rates of cohabitation. However, unions in the southern European countries of Spain, Greece, and Italy—along with Ireland and Portugal—still largely begin with marriage.

Weighing In on the Gay Marriage Debate

[***]

Virtual Objectivity

Under contemporary conditions of mass communication, the movers, shakers, and makers of public opinion and policy do not merely welcome, but actively seek relevant research data and analysis from sociologists. However, the operative and slippery word here is "relevant." Partisans engaged in public policy controversies deploy social science data selectively on all sides of any issue. [***]

[***]

Since the publication in 2001 of an article I co-authored about research on the effects of lesbian parenthood, I have become one of the social science spin-sters courted by gay marital and parent rights suitors as well as by the mainstream media to perform family sociology in transnational media and court cases. In the process, I have lost some of the innocence I once sustained about the progressive potential of public sociology.

[***]

In July 2001, I naively agreed to a live-broadcast appearance on *The O'Reilly Factor*, a confrontational, reactionary infotainment program on the Fox network. While I sat alone staring into a camera in a Los Angeles studio, a satellite hookup relayed O'Reilly's disembodied voice from across the continent. O'Reilly fired leading questions at me crafted to elicit two desired sound bites—that gay parents produce gay children and that liberal scholars, constrained by "PC" dogma, have suppressed this finding. When I balked at this script and attempted to correct O'Reilly's distorted interpretations of

my published views, he abruptly terminated the interview, and my microphone went dead. In this instance, I was literally "silenced" for refusing to provide the virtual social science data that supported O'Reilly's *a priori* views. [***]

Sound-bite social science cannot accommodate complexity, nuance, ambiguity, or uncertainty—the fundamental features of critical reason and intellectual inquiry. [***]

[***]

[***] News stories need a "hook," and no scholar gets to control the spin by which her work is represented. Unsurprisingly, therefore, most of the print stories reporting about our study featured the controversial issues of gender and sexual differences. Typical and influential in this regard, a Reuters wire service story, published days after our article appeared,

led by overstating our analysis of gender nonconformity and of the defensive way in which prior researchers had reported such findings:

> USC sociologists Judith Stacey and Timothy Biblarz examined 21 studies on the subject [of the effects of parental sexual orientation] dating back to 1980 and found that children of lesbians and gays are more likely to depart from traditional gender roles than children of heterosexual couples. In an interview on Friday, Biblarz said that the study found that information on the subject had previously been stifled and the differences played down. (Tippit 2001)

"Stifled," however, was the reporter's term, not Biblarz's, and our article did not claim that the children ARE more likely to depart from or conform to anything; only that there were good theoretical reasons to expect this and that a few studies reported findings in this direction. It seems likely that Reuters's comparatively sober print formulation of the two sound-bites that O'Reilly failed to elicit from me during my brief appearance on his program actually generated my invitation to appear there in the first place.

To my surprise and satisfaction, the most dramatic departure form the sound-bite treatment of our gay parenting study proved also to be the most influential. "A Rainbow of Differences in Gays' Children," announced a serious and nuanced story in the Science section of the *New York Times* by a reporter endowed with sufficient lead time, resources, responsibility and skills to read and discuss the research with me in some depth. Because of the prestige and influence of the venue, this story initiated a second, even broader round of public notice and courtship by international media, community organizations, social services, and legal rights and advocacy projects. Soon I found myself discussing research regularly with journalists and with social and legal activists pursuing same-sex marriage, gay adoption, and "second-parent" adoption rights in the course of public opinion as well as law.

[***]

Having been too frequently seduced and abandoned, stood up, manipulated, and misunderstood by public suitors, I find myself a more jaded, wary social science spin-ster. I am learning to screen the character and credentials of my companions with greater care, to select reasonably safe public venues in which to meet, to negotiate the terms and limits of our encounters, and to temper my expectations about the prospects for success. Yet, if I have learned to adopt an ambivalent posture toward my public sociology prospects, nonetheless, when courted with sensitivity, I dare to continue to spin.

SOURCE: Judith Stacey, "Marital Suitors Court Social Science Spinsters: The Unwittingly Conservative Effects of Public Sociology." *Social Problems* 51, no. 1: 131–145. © 2004, The Society for the Study of Social Problems, Inc. All rights reserved. Used by permission.

JUDITH STACEY is professor of sociology at New York University. She is the author of In the Name of the Family: Rethinking Family Values in a Postmodern Age, Brave New Families: Stories of Domestic Upheaval in Late Twentieth-Century America, *and* Patriarchy and Socialist Revolution in China *as well as numerous articles. Her areas of research are gender, family, sexuality, feminist and queer theory, and ethnography.*

Gay-Parent Families

Many homosexual men and women now live in stable relationships as couples, and there is a movement afoot to legally recognize these unions as marriages. Four recent decisions, three in the United States and one in Canada, demonstrate the current pulse of this movement.

In November 1998, voters in Hawaii decided to approve a state constitutional amendment to limit legal marriages to one man and one woman. Before the issue was put to the electorate, the Hawaii Supreme Court was closer than ever before to legalizing gay marriage. In fact, in 1993 the state's supreme court ruled that restricting marriage to heterosexual couples was sex discrimination, and the court asked the state of Hawaii to show a compelling reason for the restriction. Many legal observers believe the court would have ruled for gay marriage if not for the vote on the constitutional amendment.

In May 1999, the Supreme Court of Canada ruled that same-sex couples are entitled to equal legal treatment as married couples. That is, same-sex partners are entitled to the same benefits as married partners under Ontario's Family Law Act. The Canada case was initiated when a lesbian filed for spousal support from her ex-partner. Initially, the Family Law Act had permitted only partners of the opposite sex to make a claim for spousal support after a breakup. The court therefore decided to first resolve the constitutional issue of whether same-sex couples have a right to seek spousal support. The Supreme Court's decision was that the Family Law Act's restriction to opposite-sex partners was unconstitutional.

An even more recent decision on the issue of same-sex couples came in July 2000, when the Vermont legislature voted to allow same-sex partners to register their "civil unions" with town clerks. The move allows same-sex couples

Maria Castillo (left) and Georjina Graciano hold their marriage license at City Hall in San Francisco, California, on February 16, 2004. The mayor of San Francisco, Gavin Newsom, ignited a passionate nationwide debate in February 2004 by allowing 4,037 same-sex couples to wed over a four-week period before the California high court annulled the marriages.

Evelyn Rivera's family (her son Mark, nephew Sal, and lesbian partner Debbie Rodriguez) is just one example of the changing idea of the "typical" American family.

access to all the state-granted rights, privileges, and responsibilities of marriage. Though this was a big victory for gay and lesbian marriage advocates, the measure falls short of calling the partnerships "marriage" and instead opts for "civil unions." Also, it is still unclear if a civil union in Vermont will be recognized in other states.

Most recently, in November 2003, the Massachusetts Supreme Court ruled that the state constitution does not forbid gays and lesbians to marry and gave the Massachusetts State Legislature six months to rewrite the state's marriage laws to permit gay marriages. This decision in part encouraged the mayor of San Francisco, Gavin Newsom, to start issuing marriage licenses to gay and lesbian couples. Mayor Newsom has argued that the state referendum, passed in 2000 and which defined marriage as between a man and a woman, violates the state constitution, which prevents discrimination against any social group. This prompted an immediate response from California's governor, Arnold Schwarzenegger, to order the state attorney general to halt the action, and for President George W. Bush to publicly endorse a constitutional amendment "defining and protecting marriage as a union of a man and woman as husband and wife" (CNN, 2004). (The president did not call for a ban on civil unions between homosexuals, which would be left up to the states to determine.)

Although the ultimate outcome—whether these marriages will be respected by state law—is yet to be determined, these events clearly demonstrate the growing social movement toward legalizing gay marriages.

Beyond civil unions or marriages, same-sex couples are forming families with children. Relaxation of previously intolerant attitudes toward homosexuality has been accompanied by a growing tendency for courts to allocate custody of children to mothers living in gay relationships. Techniques of artificial insemination mean that gay women may have children and become gay-parent families without any heterosexual contact. Moreover, only two of the fifty U.S. states—Florida and New Hampshire—have laws preventing lesbians and gay men from adopting children.

Staying Single

Several factors have combined to increase the numbers of people living alone in modern Western societies. One is a trend toward later marriages—people now marry on average about three years later than was the case in 1960; another is the rising rate of divorce. Yet another is the growing number of old people in the population whose partners have died. Being single means different things at different periods of the life cycle. A larger proportion of people in their twenties are unmarried than used to be the case. By their mid-thirties, however, only a small minority of men and women have never been married. The majority of single people aged thirty to fifty are divorced and "in between" marriages. Most single people over fifty are widowed.

More than ever before, young people are leaving home simply to start an independent life rather than to get married (which had been one of the most common paths out of the home in the past). Hence it seems that the trend of "staying single" or living on one's own may be part of the societal trend toward valuing independence at the expense of family life. Still, most people (over 90 percent) ultimately marry, so although independence or "staying single" may be an increasingly common path out of the parental home, a large majority of these people will eventually marry (Goldschneider and Goldschneider, 1999).

Study Outline

www.wwnorton.com/giddens

Kinship, Family, and Marriage: Key Concepts

- *Kinship, family*, and *marriage* are closely related terms of key significance for sociology and anthropology. Kinship comprises either genetic ties or ties initiated by marriage. A family is a group of kin having responsibility for the upbringing of children. Marriage is a union of two persons living together in a socially approved sexual relationship.
- A *nuclear family* refers to a household in which a married couple or single parent lives with their own or adopted children. Where kin in addition to parents and children live in the same household or are involved in close and continuous relationships, we speak of the existence of an *extended family*.
- In Western societies, marriage, and therefore the family, is associated with *monogamy* (a culturally approved sexual relationship between one man and one woman). Many other cultures tolerate or encourage *polygamy*, in which an individual may be married to two or more spouses at the same time. *Polygyny*, in which a man may marry more than one wife, is far more common than *polyandry*, in which a woman may have more than one husband.

The Family in History

- There are many types of families in the world, but there is a trend toward the Western norm of the nuclear family. Some reasons for this trend include: the Western ideal of romantic love, the growth of urbanization and of centralized governments, and employment in organizations outside traditional family influence.

Changes in Family Patterns

- There have been major changes in patterns of family life in the United States during the post–World War II period: A high percentage of women are in the paid labor force, there are rising rates of divorce, and substantial proportions of the population are either in single-parent households or are living with stepfamilies. *Cohabitation* (in which a couple lives together in a sexual relationship outside of marriage) has become increasingly common in many industrial countries.
- Family life is by no means always a picture of harmony and happiness. The "dark side" of the family is found in the patterns of abuse and family violence that often occur within it. Although no social class is immune to spousal abuse, studies do indicate that it is more common among low-income couples.
- Cohabitation and homosexuality have become more common in recent years. It seems certain that alternative forms of social and

sexual relationships to those prevalent in the past will flourish still further. Yet marriage and the family remain firmly established institutions.

Key Concepts

cohabitation (p. 300)
extended family (p. 284)
family (p. 284)
family of orientation (p. 284)
family of procreation (p. 284)
kinship (p. 284)
marriage (p. 284)
matrilocal family (p. 285)
monogamy (p. 285)
nuclear family (p. 284)
patrilocal family (p. 285)
personality stabilization (p. 285)
polyandry (p. 285)
polygamy (p. 285)
polygyny (p. 285)
primary socialization (p. 285)
stepfamily (p. 298)

Review Questions

1. The process by which children learn the cultural norms of the society in which they are born is called
   a. personality stabilization.
   b. primary socialization.
   c. secondary socialization.
   d. personality socialization.
2. Cherlin (1999) and Goode (1971) found that spousal abuse is more common among
   a. high-income couples.
   b. middle-income couples.
   c. low-income couples.
   d. both high- and middle-income couples.
3. What's the difference between families of orientation and families of procreation?
   a. Families of orientation are childless couples and families of procreation are couples with children.
   b. A family of orientation is the family into which a person is born, whereas a family of procreation is the family into which a person enters as an adult and within which their children are raised.
   c. Families of orientation are gay couples and families of procreation are straight couples.

d. A family of orientation is the family into which a person enters as an adult and within which children are raised; whereas a family of procreation is the family into which a person is born.
4. According to Cherlin's research on the effects of divorce on children,
   a. almost all children experience an initial period of calmness.
   b. a majority of children experience some long-term problems as a result of the breakup that may persist into adulthood.
   c. most people whose parents divorced did not experience serious mental problems.
   d. most children resume normal development without serious problems within about six months of separation.
5. What is the "absent father"?
   a. The term refers to the period from the late 1930s through the 1940s when fathers rarely saw their children because of war service.
   b. The term refers to the period from the 1950s through the 1970s when fathers were the family's only breadwinner and would only see their children in the evening and on weekends.
   c. The term refers to the period from the 1970s until today and it refers to fathers who, as a result of separation and divorce, either have infrequent contact with their children or lose touch with them altogether.
   d. All of the above.
6. About half the babies in Sweden are born to unmarried mothers. Nineteen out of twenty of these are born in households with a father, but many will grow up without their own fathers at home, as half of all Swedish marriages end in divorce and unmarried parents split up three times more often than married ones. What kind of social and economic problems are caused by these figures?
   a. Many. Sweden has exactly the same experience as the United States as a result of its high divorce rate.
   b. Some, but fewer than in the United States. There is a greater social taboo against becoming a "deadbeat dad" in the more socialistic climate of Sweden.
   c. Very few. In Sweden, generous welfare benefits mean that single-parent families do not slip into poverty.
   d. None whatsoever.
7. Which one of the following is *not* true regarding the important changes in families occurring worldwide?
   a. There is a general trend toward the free choice of a spouse.
   b. The rights of women are becoming more widely recognized.
   c. Kin marriages are becoming more common.
   d. Higher levels of sexual freedom are developing in societies that were very restrictive.
8. Which theoretical perspective is interested in the experience of women in the domestic sphere?
   a. Functionalism
   b. Symbolic interactionism
   c. Feminism
   d. None of the above

9. What percent of American families is made up of a husband who works in paid employment and a wife who looks after the home, living together with their two children?
    a. 15 percent
    b. 25 percent
    c. 35 percent
    d. 45 percent
10. A(n) _____ is one in which close relatives other than just a married couple and their children live in the same household or in a close and continuous relationship with one another.
    a. nuclear family
    b. extended family
    c. atomic family
    d. distended family

Thinking Sociologically Exercises

1. Using this textbook's presentation, compare the structures and lifestyles between contempory white non-Hispanic, Asian American, Latino, and African American families.

2. Increases in cohabitation and single-parent households suggest that marriage may be beginning to fall by the wayside in our contemporary society. However, this chapter claims that marriage and the family remain firmly established institutions in our society. Explain the rising patterns of cohabitation and single-parent households and show how these seemingly paradoxical trends can be reconciled with the claims offered by this textbook.

Data Exercises

www.wwnorton.com/giddens
Keyword: Data11

• The data exercise for Chapter 11 focuses on recent changes in marriage and family patterns within the United States. It is designed to give you an opportunity to analyze survey data and learn more about what's been happening with these important social institutions.

The Development of Schooling

Know how and why systems of mass education emerged in the United States.

Education and Inequality

Become familiar with the most important research on whether education reduces or perpetuates inequality. Learn the social and cultural influences on educational achievement.

Education and Literacy in the Developing World

Know some basic facts about the education system and literacy rates of developing countries.

The Sociological Study of Religion

Learn the elements that make up religion.

Theories of Religion

Know the sociological approaches to religion developed by Marx, Durkheim, and Weber, as well as the religious economy approach.

Types of Religious Organizations

Learn the various ways religious communities are organized and how they have become institutionalized.

Religion in the United States

Learn about the sociological dimensions of religion in the United States.

Globalization and Religion

Recognize how the globalization of religion is reflected in religious activism in poor countries and the rise of religious nationalist movements.

CHAPTER TWELVE

EDUCATION AND RELIGION

imagine being in the shoes—or the wooden clogs—of Jean-Paul Didion, a peasant boy growing up in a French farming community two centuries ago. In 1750, Jean-Paul is fourteen years old. He cannot read or write, but this is not uncommon; only a few of the adults in his village have the ability to decipher more than the odd word or two of written texts. There are some schools in nearby districts run by monks and nuns, but these are completely removed from Jean-Paul's experience. He has never known anyone well who attended school, save the local priest. For eight or nine years, Jean-Paul has been spending most of his days helping with domestic tasks and working in the fields. The older he gets, the longer each day he is expected to share in the back-breaking chores demanded by the intensive tilling of his father's plot of land.

Jean-Paul is likely never to leave the area in which he was born and may spend virtually the whole of his life within the confines of the village and surrounding fields, only occasionally traveling to other local villages and towns. He may have to wait until he is in his late fifties before inheriting his father's plot of land, sharing control of it with his younger brothers. Jean-Paul is aware that he is "French," that his country is ruled over by Louis XV, and that there is a wider world beyond even France itself. But he only has a vague awareness even of "France" as a distinct political entity. There is no such thing as "news," nor any regular means by which information about events elsewhere reaches him. What he knows of the wider world comes from stories and tales he has heard told by adults and by visiting travelers. Like others in his community, he only learns about major events—such as the death of the king—days, weeks, or sometimes months after they have occurred.

Although in modern terms Jean-Paul is uneducated, he is far from ignorant. He has a sensitive and developed understanding of the family and children, having had to care for those younger than him since he was very young. He is already highly knowledgeable about the land, methods of crop production, and ways of preserving and storing food. His mastery of local customs and traditions is profound, and he can turn his hand to many different tasks over and above agricultural cultivation, such as weaving or basket making.

Jean-Paul is an invented figure, but the above description portrays the typical experience of a boy growing up in preindustrial Europe. Compare this with our situation today. In the industrialized countries, virtually everyone can read and write—that is, people are *literate*. We have all gone through a process of formal schooling. Through education, we become aware of the common characteristics we share with other members of the same society and have at least some sort of knowledge of its geographical and political position in the world and its past history. Religion is another institution that exercises a socializing influence. Under what conditions does religion unite communities, and under what condition does it divide them? The study of religion is a challenging enterprise that places special demands on the sociological imagination. In analyzing religious practices, we must be sensitive to ideals that inspire profound conviction in believers, yet at the same time take a balanced view of them. We must confront ideas that seek the eternal while recognizing that religious groups also promote quite mundane goals, such as acquiring money or followers.

This chapter will focus on the socializing processes of education and religion. To study these issues, we will ask how present-day education developed and analyze its socializing influence. We will also look at education in relation to social inequality and consider how far the educational system serves to encourage or to reduce such inequality. Then we will move to studying religion and the different forms that religious beliefs and practices take. We will also analyze the various types of religious organizations and the impact of social change on the position of religion in the wider world.

The Development of Schooling

The term *school* has its origins in a Greek word meaning "leisure," or "recreation." In premodern societies, schooling existed for the few who had the time and resources available to pursue the cultivation of the arts and philosophy. For some, their engagement with schooling was like taking up a hobby.

For others, like religious leaders or priests, schooling was a way of gaining skills and thus increasing their ability to interpret sacred texts. But for the vast majority of people, growing up meant learning by example the same social habits and work skills as their elders. Learning was a family affair—there were no schools at all for the mass of the population. Since children often started to help with domestic duties and farming work at a very young age, they rapidly became full-fledged members of the community.

Education in its modern form, the instruction of pupils within specially constructed school premises, gradually emerged in the first few years of the nineteenth century, when primary schools began to be constructed in Europe and the United States. One main reason for the rise of large educational systems was the process of industrialization, with its ensuing expansion of cities.

Education and Industrialization

Until the first few decades of the nineteenth century, most of the world's population had no schooling whatsoever. But as the industrial economy rapidly expanded, there was a great demand for specialized schooling that could produce an educated, capable workforce. As occupations became more differentiated and were increasingly located away from the home, it was impossible for work skills to be passed on directly from parents to children.

As educational systems became universal, more and more people were exposed to abstract learning (of subjects like math, science, history, literature, and so on), rather than to the practical transmission of specific skills. In a modern society, people have to be furnished with basic skills—such as reading, writing, and calculating—and a general knowledge of their physical, social, and economic environment, but it is also important that they know how to learn, so that they are able to master new, sometimes very technical, forms of information. An advanced society also needs pure research and insights with no immediate practical value to push out the boundaries of knowledge.

In the modern age, education and qualifications became an important stepping stone into job opportunities and careers. Schools and universities not only broaden people's minds and perspectives, but are expected to prepare new generations of citizens for participation in economic life. The right balance between a generalist education and specific work skills is a difficult one at which to arrive. Specialized forms of technical, vocational, and professional training often supplement pupils' liberal education and facilitate the transition from school to work. Internships and work experience schemes, for example, allow young people to develop specific knowledge applicable to their future careers.

Although many teachers in schools and universities seek above all to provide a well-rounded education, policy makers and employers are concerned to ensure that education and training programs coincide with a country's economic profile and employment demands. Yet in times of rapid economic and technical change, there is not always a smooth match between the priorities of the educational system and the availability of professional opportunities. The rapid expansion of a country's health-care system, for example, would dramatically increase the demand for trained health professionals, laboratory technicians, capable administrators, and computer systems analysts familiar with public-health issues. Industry-wide changes in factory-floor production technology would require a work force with a set of skills that might be in short supply.

Sociological Theories

Sociologists have debated why formal systems of schooling developed in modern societies by studying the social functions that schools provide. For example, some have argued that mass education promotes feelings of nationalism and aided the development of national societies, constituted of citizens from different regions who would know the same history and speak a common language (Ramirez and Boli, 1987). Marxist sociologists have argued that the expansion of education was brought about by employer's need for certain personality characteristics in their workers—self-discipline, dependability, punctuality, obedience, and the like—which are all taught in schools (Bowles and Gintis, 1976). Another influential perspective comes from the sociologist Randall Collins, who has argued that the primary social function of mass education derives from the need for diplomas and degrees to determine one's credentials for a job, even if the work involved has nothing to do with the education one has received. Over time, the practice of credentialism results in demands for higher credentials, which require higher levels of educational attainment. Jobs, such as sales representative, that thirty years ago would have required a high school diploma now require a college degree. Since educational attainment is closely related to class position, credentialism reinforces the class structure within a society (Collins, 1971, 1979).

Education and Inequality

The expansion of education has always been closely linked to the ideals of democracy. Reformers value education for its own sake—for the opportunity it provides for individuals to develop their capabilities. Yet education has also consistently been seen as a means of equalization. Access to universal education, it has been argued, could help reduce disparities of wealth and power. Are educational opportunities equal for everyone? Has education in fact proved to be a great equalizer? Much research has been devoted to answering these questions.

"Savage Inequalities"

Between 1988 and 1990, the journalist Jonathan Kozol studied schools in about thirty neighborhoods around the United States. There was no special logic to the way he chose the schools, except that he went where he happened to know teachers, principals, or ministers. What startled him most was the segregation within these schools and the inequalities among them. Kozol brought these terrible conditions to the attention of the American people in his book *Savage Inequalities*, which became a bestseller (Kozol, 1991).

In his passionate opening chapter, he first took readers to East St. Louis, Illinois, a city that is 98 percent black, had no regular trash collection, and few jobs. Three quarters of its residents were living on welfare at the time. City residents were forced to use their backyards as garbage dumps, which attracted a plague of flies and rats during the hot summer months. East St. Louis also had some of the sickest children in the United States, with extremely high rates of infant death, asthma, and poor nutrition and extremely low rates of immunization. Only 55 percent of the children had been fully immunized for polio, diphtheria, measles, and whooping cough. Among the city's other social problems were crime, dilapidated housing, poor health care, and lack of education.

Kozol showed how the problems of the city affected the school on a daily basis. Teachers often had to hold classes without chalk or paper. One teacher commented on the school's poor conditions by saying, "Our problems are severe. I don't even know where to begin. I have no materials with the exception of a single textbook given to each child. If I bring in anything else—books or tapes or magazines—I bring it in myself. The high school has no VCRs. They are such a crucial tool. So many good things run on public television. I can't make use of anything I see unless I unhook my VCR and bring it into school. The AV equipment in the school is so old that we are pressured not to use it." Comments from students reflected the same concerns. "I don't go to physics class, because my lab has no equipment," said one student. Only 55 percent of the students in this high school ultimately graduate, about one third of whom go on to college.

Kozol also wrote about the other end of the inequality spectrum, taking readers into a wealthy suburban school in Westchester County outside of New York City. This school had 96 computers for the 546 students. Most studied a foreign lan-

The problem of schools falling into disrepair is a chronic one in poverty-stricken areas all over the country. Dilapidated schools like this one in the South Bronx lack funding for even the most basic necessities and, once they have fallen into a state of ruin, there is no money to undertake necessary repairs.

guage for four or five years. Two thirds of the senior class were enrolled in an advanced placement (AP) class. Kozol visited an AP class to ask students about their perceptions of inequalities within the educational system. Students at this school were well aware of the economic advantages that they enjoyed at both home and school. With regard to their views about students less well-off than themselves, the general consensus was that equal spending among schools was a worthy goal but it would probably make little difference since poor students lack motivation and would fail because of other problems. These students also realized that equalizing spending could have adverse affects on their school. As one student said, "If you equalize the money, someone's got to be shortchanged. I don't doubt that [poor] children are getting a bad deal. But do we want everyone to get a mediocre education?"

It is impossible to read these descriptions of life in East St. Louis and Westchester County without believing that the ex-

tremes of wealth and poverty in the public schools are being exposed. Yet, many sociologists have argued that although Kozol's book is a moving portrait, it provides an inaccurate view of educational inequality. Why would Kozol's research not be compelling? There are several reasons, including the unsystematic way that he chose the schools that he studied. But the most important criticism of his work is that sociological research has shown that student achievement varies much more within schools than among schools—the proportions are about 80 percent to 20 percent. This means that differences among schools are not the main sources of inequality in achievement, even though Kozol's study may provoke outrage over these inequalities. This fact does not mean that Kozol was wrong—there are schools at both extremes—but these are not the kinds of extremes that account for most educational inequality in America. Let's now look more closely at the work that sociologists have done to understand this complex relationship between education and inequality.

Sociological research addressing equal educational opportunities falls into two categories: research assessing "between school effects" and research assessing "within school effects." "Between school effects" refer to inequalities among children who go to different schools, asking—for example—whether students who attend schools with more resources end up ahead in the socioeconomic system. "Within school effects" are differences among students in the same school, asking—for example—if dividing students into honors or remedial classes leads to later disparities in educational attainment, occupational prestige, and wealth.

Coleman's Study of "Between School Effects" in American Education

The study of "between school effects" has been the focus of sociological research on the educational system for the past three decades. One of the classic investigations of educational inequality was undertaken in the United States in the 1960s. As part of the Civil Rights Act of 1964, the commissioner of education was required to prepare a report on educational inequalities resulting from differences of ethnic background, religion, and national origin. James Coleman, a sociologist, was appointed director of the research program. The outcome was a study, published in 1966, based on one of the most extensive research projects ever carried out in sociology.

Information was collected on more than half a million pupils who were given a range of achievement tests assessing verbal and nonverbal abilities, reading levels, and mathematical skills. Sixty thousand teachers also completed forms providing data for about four thousand schools. The report found that a large majority of children went to schools that effectively segregated black from white. Almost 80 percent of schools attended by white students contained only 10 percent or less African American students. White and Asian American students scored higher on achievement tests than did blacks and other ethnic minority students. Coleman had supposed his results would also show mainly African American schools to have worse facilities, larger classes, and more inferior buildings than schools that were predominantly white. But surprisingly, the results showed far fewer differences of this type than had been anticipated.

Coleman therefore concluded that the material resources provided in schools made little difference to educational performance; the decisive influence was the children's backgrounds. In Coleman's words, "Inequalities imposed on children by their home, neighborhood, and peer environment are carried along to become the inequalities with which they confront adult life at the end of school" (Coleman et al., 1966). There was, however, some evidence that students from deprived backgrounds who formed close friendships with those from more favorable circumstances were likely to be more successful educationally.

Not long after Coleman's study, Christopher Jencks produced an equally celebrated work that reviewed empirical evidence accumulated on education and inequality up to the end of the 1960s (Jencks et al., 1972). Jencks reaffirmed two of Coleman's conclusions: (1) that educational and occupational attainment are governed mainly by family background and nonschool factors, and (2) that on their own, educational reforms can produce only minor effects on existing inequalities. Jencks's work has been criticized on methodological grounds, but his overall conclusions remain persuasive. Subsequent research has tended to confirm them.

Tracking and "Within School Effects"

The practice of **tracking**—dividing students into groups that receive different instruction on the basis of assumed similarities in ability or attainment—is common in American schools. In some schools, students are tracked only for certain subjects; in others, for all subjects. Sociologists have long believed that tracking is entirely negative in its effects. The conventional wisdom has been that tracking partly explains why schooling seems to have little effect on existing social inequalities, since being placed in a particular track labels a student as either able or otherwise. As we have seen in the case of labeling and deviance, once attached, such labels are hard to break away from. Children from more privileged

backgrounds, in which academic work is encouraged, are likely to find themselves in the higher tracks early on—and by and large stay there (see Figure 12.1).

Jeannie Oakes (1985) studied tracking in twenty-five junior and senior high schools, both large and small and in both urban and rural areas. But she concentrated on differences *within* schools rather than between them. She found that although several schools claimed they did not track students, virtually all of them had mechanisms for sorting students into groups that seemed to be alike in ability and achievement, to make teaching easier. In other words, they employed tracking but did not choose to use the term *tracking* itself. Even where tracking only existed in this informal fashion, she found strong labels developing—high ability, low achieving, slow, average, and so on. Individual students in these groups came to be

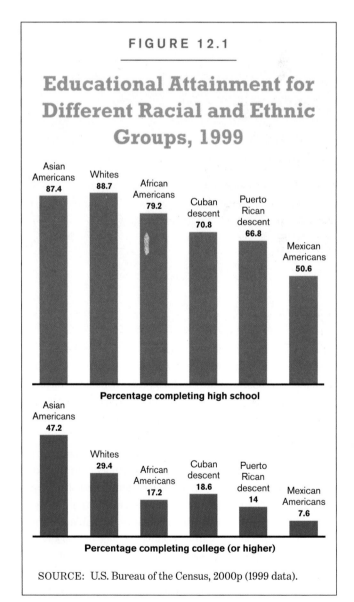

FIGURE 12.1

Educational Attainment for Different Racial and Ethnic Groups, 1999

Asian Americans 87.4
Whites 88.7
African Americans 79.2
Cuban descent 70.8
Puerto Rican descent 66.8
Mexican Americans 50.6

Percentage completing high school

Asian Americans 47.2
Whites 29.4
African Americans 17.2
Cuban descent 18.6
Puerto Rican descent 14
Mexican Americans 7.6

Percentage completing college (or higher)

SOURCE: U.S. Bureau of the Census, 2000p (1999 data).

The Internationalization of Education

How many foreign students are enrolled in your sociology course? How many foreign students are there at your university? In 1943, approximately 8,000 foreign students were enrolled in American colleges and universities. By 2000, this number had skyrocketed to more than 515,000 (U.S. Census, 2002). Although the American university system as a whole grew considerably during this period, such that 515,000 students represented only 3.3 percent of total 2000 student enrollment, it is clear that foreign students are flocking to the United States in record numbers. Most foreign students

today come from Asia—China, Japan, Taiwan, India, and South Korea all send sizeable contingents of students abroad. The United States takes in more foreign students than any other country, and there are six times as many foreign students in the United States as there are American students overseas. What do foreign students in the United States study? At the undergraduate level, more than 20 percent focus on business and management, 16 percent study engineering, and 8 percent concentrate on science (U.S. Census, 2002). More than 20 percent of foreign graduate students study engineering (Lambert, 1995).

Some scholars regard the exchange of international students as a vital component of globalization. Foreign students, in addition to serving as global "carriers" of specialized technical and scientific knowledge, have an important cultural role to play in the globalizing process. Cross-national understandings are enhanced and xenophobic and isolationist attitudes are minimized as native students in host countries develop social ties to their foreign classmates and as foreign students return to their country of origin with an appreciation for the cultural mores of the nation in which they have studied.

Yet there is considerable debate in the United States about what is sometimes called the "internationalization of education." On most college campuses, it is not hard to find disgruntled students who complain that given the competitive nature

defined by teachers, other students, and themselves in terms of such labels. A student in a "high-achieving" group was considered a high-achieving *person*—smart and quick. Pupils in a "low-achieving" group came to be seen as slow, below average —or, in more forthright terms, as dummies, sweathogs, or yahoos. What is the impact of tracking on students in the "low" group? A subsequent study by Oakes found that these students received a poorer education in terms of the quality of courses, teachers, and textbooks made available to them (Oakes, 1990). Moreover, the negative impact of tracking affected mostly African American, Latino, and poor students.

The usual reason given for tracking is that bright children learn more quickly and effectively in a group of others who

are equally able and that clever students are held back if placed in mixed groups. Surveying the evidence, Oakes attempted to show that these assumptions are wrong. The results of later research investigations are not wholly consistent, but a path-breaking study by the sociologist Adam Gamoran and his colleagues concluded that Oakes was partially correct in her arguments. They agreed with Oakes's conclusions that tracking reinforces previously existing inequalities for average or poor students but countered her argument by asserting that tracking does have positive benefits for "advanced" students (Gamoran et al., 1995). The debate about the effects of tracking is sure to continue as scholars continue to analyze more data.

of the U.S. higher education system, the influx of foreign students deprives deserving Americans of educational opportunities. Moreover, although more than two thirds of foreign students receive nothing in the way of scholarships, some top-notch foreign students *are* given financial inducements to attend American schools. The outcry against this practice has been loudest at public universities, which receive support from tax revenue. Critics charge that U.S. taxpayers should not shoulder the financial burden for educating foreign students whose families have not paid U.S. taxes and who are likely to return home after earning their degrees.

Supporters of international education find such arguments unconvincing. Some Americans may lose out to foreign students in the competition for slots at prestigious universities, but this is a small price to pay for the economic, political, and cultural benefits the United States receives from having educated millions of foreign business executives, policy makers, scientists, and professionals over the years—many of whom became sympathetically disposed to the United States as a result of their experiences here. And although some foreign students receive scholarships from American universities, most are supported by their parents. In fact, it is estimated that foreign students pump hundreds of millions of dollars each year into the U.S. economy. Rather than curtail the number of foreign students admitted to American universities, supporters of international education suggest that even more should be done to encourage the exchange of students. On the one hand, greater effort should be made to recruit foreign students, to help them select the university and program that will best meet their needs, and to provide them with a positive social and educational experience while they are in the United States. On the other hand, more Americans should be encouraged to study abroad. American students are notorious for

having poor foreign-language skills and for knowing little about global geography, much less about the cultures of other nations. This ignorance puts the United States at a disadvantage relative to other countries as the world becomes increasingly globalized; encouraging Americans to study overseas may be the best way to inculcate a global worldview.

Should there be a greater focus on international education in American colleges and universities? Should the international exchange of students be expanded? These are among the issues that educational institutions are forced to confront in the context of globalization.

The Social Reproduction of Inequality

The educational system provides more than formal instruction: It socializes children to get along with each other, teaches basic skills, and transmits elements of culture such as language and values. Sociologists have looked at education as a form of social reproduction, a concept discussed in Chapter 1 and elsewhere. In the context of education, social reproduction refers to the ways in which schools help perpetuate social and economic inequalities across the generations. It also directs our attention to the means whereby schools influence the learning of values, attitudes, and habits via the hidden curriculum.

The concept of the **hidden curriculum** addresses the fact that much of what is learned in school has nothing directly to do with the formal content of lessons. Schools, by the nature of the discipline and regimentation they entail, tend to teach students "passive consumption"—an uncritical acceptance of the existing social order. These lessons are not consciously taught; they are implicit in school procedures and organization. The hidden curriculum teaches children that their role in life is "to know their place and to sit still with it" (Illich, 1983). Children spend long hours in school, and as Illich stresses, they learn a great deal more in the school context than is contained in the lessons they are actually taught. Children get an early taste of what the world of work will be like, learning that they are expected to be punctual and apply themselves diligently to the tasks that those in authority set for them.

Another influential theory on the question of how schools reproduce social inequality was introduced by Samuel Bowles and Herbert Gintis. Modern education, they propose, is a response to the economic needs of industrial capitalism. Schools help to provide the technical and social skills required by industrial enterprise, and they instill discipline and respect for authority into the labor force.

Authority relations in school, which are hierarchical and place strong emphasis on obedience, directly parallel those dominating the workplace. The rewards and punishments held out in school also replicate those found in the world of work. Schools help to motivate some individuals toward "achievement" and "success," while discouraging others, who find their way into low-paying jobs.

Schooling has not become the "great equalizer"; rather, schools merely produce for many the feelings of powerlessness that continue throughout their experience in industrial settings. The ideals of personal development central to education can only be achieved if people have the capability to control the conditions of their own life and to develop their talents and abilities of self-expression. Under the current system, schools "are destined to legitimate inequality, limit personal development to forms compatible with submission to arbitrary authority, and aid in the process whereby youth are resigned to their fate" (Bowles and Gintis, 1976). If there were greater democracy in the workplace and more equality in society at large, Bowles and Gintis argue, a system of education could be developed that would provide for greater individual fulfillment.

Intelligence and Inequality

Suppose differences in educational attainment, and in subsequent occupations and incomes, directly reflected differential intelligence. In such circumstances, it might be argued, there is in fact equality of opportunity in the school system, for people find a level equivalent to their innate potential.

WHAT IS INTELLIGENCE?

For years, psychologists, geneticists, statisticians, and others have debated whether there exists a single human capability that can be called **intelligence** and, if so, whether it rests on in-

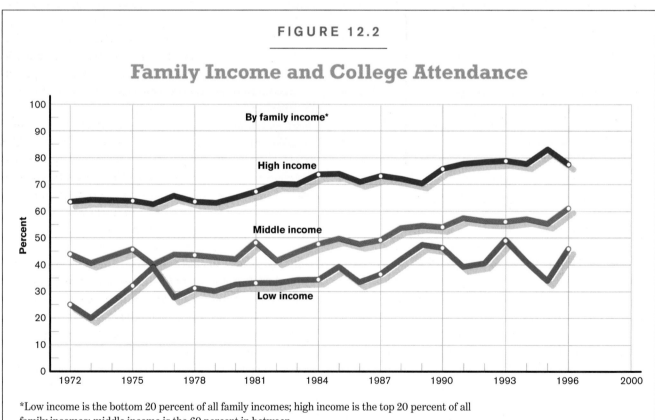

FIGURE 12.2

Family Income and College Attendance

*Low income is the bottom 20 percent of all family incomes; high income is the top 20 percent of all family incomes; middle income is the 60 percent in between.

SOURCE: U.S. Bureau of the Census, 2000d.

nately determined differences. Intelligence is difficult to define because, as the term is usually employed, it covers qualities that may be unrelated to one another. We might suppose, for example, that the "purest" form of intelligence is the ability to solve abstract mathematical puzzles. However, people who are very good at such puzzles sometimes show low capabilities in other areas, such as history or art. Since the concept has proved so resistant to accepted definition, some psychologists have proposed (and many educators have by default accepted) that intelligence should simply be regarded as "what **IQ (intelligence quotient)** tests measure." Most IQ tests consist of a mixture of conceptual and computational problems. The tests are constructed so that the average score is 100 points: Anyone scoring below is thus labeled "below-average intelligence," and anyone scoring above is "above-average intelligence." In spite of the fundamental difficulty in measuring intelligence, IQ tests are widely used in research studies, as well as in schools and businesses.

Scores on IQ tests do in fact correlate highly with academic performance (which is not surprising, since IQ tests were originally developed to predict success at school). They therefore also correlate closely with social, economic, and ethnic differences, since these are associated with variations in levels of educational attainment. White students score better, on average, than African Americans or members of other disadvantaged minorities.

The relationship between race and intelligence is best explained by social rather than biological causes, according to a team of Berkeley sociologists in their 1996 book *Inequality by Design: Cracking the Bell Curve Myth* (Fischer et al., 1996). All societies have oppressed ethnic groups. Low status, often coupled with discrimination and mistreatment, leads to socioeconomic deprivation, group segregation, and a stigma of inferiority. The combination of these forces often prevents racial minorities from obtaining education, and consequently, their scores on standardized intelligence tests are lower.

The average lower IQ score of African Americans in the United States is remarkably similar to that of deprived ethnic minorities in other countries—such as the "untouchables" in India (who are at the very bottom of the caste system), the Maori in New Zealand, and the *burakumin* of Japan. Children in these groups score an average of 10 to 15 IQ points below children belonging to the ethnic majority.

Such observations strongly suggest that the IQ variations between African Americans and whites in the United States result from social and cultural differences. This conclusion receives further support from a comparative study of fourteen nations (including the United States) showing that average IQ scores have risen substantially over the past half century for the population as a whole (Coleman, 1987). IQ tests are regularly updated. When old and new versions of the tests are given to the same group of people, they score significantly higher on the old tests. Present-day children taking IQ tests from the 1930s outscored 1930s groups by an average of 15 points—just the kind of average difference that currently separates blacks and whites. Children today are not innately superior in intelligence to their parents or grandparents; the shift presumably derives from increasing prosperity and social advantages. The average social and economic gap between whites and African Americans is at least as great as that between the different generations and is sufficient to explain the variation in IQ scores. Although there may be genetic variations between individuals that influence scores on IQ tests, these have no overall connection to racial differences.

Educational Reform in the United States

Research done by sociologists has played a big role in reforming the educational system. The object of James Coleman's research, commissioned as part of the 1964 Civil Rights Act, was not solely academic; it was undertaken to influence policy. On the basis of the act, it was decided in the courts that segregated schools violated the rights of minority pupils. But rather than attacking the origins of educational inequalities directly, the courts decided that the schools in each district should achieve a similar racial balance. Thus began the practice of busing students to other schools.

Busing provoked a great deal of opposition, particularly from parents and children in white areas. Busing in fact met with a good deal of success, reducing levels of school segregation quite steeply, particularly in the South. But busing has also produced a number of unintended consequences. Some white parents reacted to busing by either putting their children into private schools or moving to mainly white suburbs where busing wasn't practiced. As a result, in the cities, some schools are virtually as segregated as the old schools were in the past. Busing, however, was only one factor prompting the white flight to the suburbs. Whites also left as a reaction to urban decay: to escape city crowding, housing problems, and rising rates of crime.

While busing is less prominent today as an issue, another problem regarding the American educational system has become an important focus of research: functional illiteracy. Most of the population can read and write at a very basic level, but one in every five adults is functionally illiterate—when they leave school, they can't read or write at the fourth-grade level (U.S. Department of Education, 1993). Of course, the United States is a country of immigrants, who when they

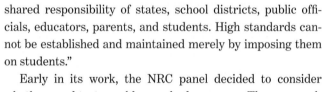

What If We Ended Social Promotion?

[In 1998], I chaired a study of appropriate uses of testing for the National Research Council. The NRC panel was a diverse group of fifteen scholars from all over the country. We wrote our report, "High Stakes: Testing for Tracking, Promotion and Graduation," in response to a congressional mandate. The study was prompted by the Clinton administration's proposal, in 1997, for voluntary national tests of fourth grade reading and eighth grade math. The panel took no position about the value of voluntary national testing for its stated purposes—to tell American students, parents, and teachers how well they are doing relative to high national standards—but we recommended strongly against such tests' use for any high-stakes purpose. The report, published [in 1999], has a lot of useful information about proper test use, and I commend it to readers. One of the strongest recommendations is

that "accountability for educational outcomes should be a shared responsibility of states, school districts, public officials, educators, parents, and students. High standards cannot be established and maintained merely by imposing them on students."

Early in its work, the NRC panel decided to consider whether good tests could serve bad purposes. Thus, we evaluated the consequences of high-stakes educational decisions that may be based, at least in part, on test scores. In particular, we found—as American schools presently operate—that decisions to place students in typical lower-level tracks and decisions to hold students back to repeat the same grade are not educationally sound. Those decisions hurt students, and good tests will not improve them. This is not to say that all forms of tracking are bad for students, or that all grade retention is necessarily bad for students. Our findings were based on the actual and typical, not the ideal. But research evidence based on actual experience should inform new policies.

[***]

We should know that a new policy works before we try it out on a large scale. In its plan to end social promotion, the administration appears to have mixed a number of fine and credible proposals for educational reform with an enforcement provision—flunking kids by the carload lot—about which the great mass of evidence is strongly negative. And this policy [would] hurt poor and minority children most of all.

[***]

Students who have been held back typically do not catch up; in fact, low-performing students learn more if they are promoted—even without remedial help—than if they are held back. One reason for this is that the elementary and secondary school curriculum does not change radically from one grade to the next; there is a lot of review and overlap. Another is that it is simply boring to repeat exactly the same material.

Students who have been held back are much more likely to drop out before completing high school. That effect often occurs many years after a student is held back in grade and thus is invisible—without careful longitudinal study—to those who make the retention decision. The teachers and administrators who make decisions to hold children back do not have to live with the long-term consequences of their decisions.

[***]

There is one more critical point on which the National Research Council report provides strong evidence: We do not practice social promotion in the United States now, and we have not practiced it for many years. Our statistics are not very good; neither the federal government nor most states collect the right data, but we do know a few things.

Age at entry to first grade has increased since 1970. At that time, almost all six-year-olds were in the first grade (about 4 percent of six-year-old boys and 8 percent of six-year-old girls were enrolled below the first grade). In 1996, 18 percent of six-year-olds were enrolled below the first grade. Part of that change is due to holding children back in kindergarten.

Many students are held back during elementary and secondary school. Nationally, among children who entered school in the late 1980s, 21 percent were enrolled below the usual grade at ages six to eight; 28 percent were below the usual grade at ages nine to eleven; 31 percent at ages twelve to fourteen; and this rose to 36 percent at ages fifteen to seventeen. Not counting kindergarten and the later grades of high school, this means that at least 15 percent of children—and probably 20 percent—have been held back at some time in their childhood.

Worse yet, minorities and poor children are the most likely to be held back. Black, Hispanic, and white children enter first grade at just about the same ages, but between entry and adolescence, about 10 percent of white girls fall behind in grade, while 25 percent to 30 percent of minority children fall behind. By ages fifteen to seventeen, 45 percent to 50 percent of black and Hispanic youths are below the expected grade levels for their ages.

Holding students back—flunking them—has a much greater impact on minority and poor youths than on majority, middle-class children. It decreases educational opportunity, and it makes opportunities less equal among groups. For thirty-five years, American education has aimed to reduce social inequality. While much remains to be done, we have made major gains—narrowing differences in test scores in the 1970s and 1980s and reducing the dropout difference between majority and minority children. If we start holding back ever larger numbers of children, we are likely to reverse the progress of the past four decades.

SOURCE: Robert M. Hauser, "What If We Ended Social Promotion?" *Education Week*, April 7, 1999.

ROBERT M. HAUSER is the Vilas research professor of sociology in the Center for Demography at the University of Wisconsin-Madison. He is the editor, with Jay P. Heubert, of the National Research Council's report "High Stakes: Testing for Tracking, Promotion, and Graduation" (National Academy Press, 1999).

In 1970 a U.S. judge in North Carolina ordered that black students be bused to white schools and that white students be bused to black schools. It was hoped that this crosstown "school busing" would end the *de facto* segregation of public schools caused by white students living in predominantly white neighborhoods and black students living in predominantly black neighborhoods.

arrive may not be able to read and write and who may also have trouble with English. But this doesn't explain why America lags behind most other industrial countries in terms of its level of functional illiteracy, because many people affected are not recent immigrants at all.

What is to be done? Some educationists have argued that the most important change that needs to be made is to improve the quality of teaching, either by increasing teachers' pay or by introducing performance-related pay scales, with higher salaries going to the teachers who are most effective in the classroom. Others have proposed giving schools more control over their budgets (a reform that has been carried out in Britain). The idea is that more responsibility for and control over budgeting decisions will create a greater drive to improve the school. Further proposals include the refunding of federal programs such as Head Start to ensure healthy early child development and thus save millions of dollars in later costs. Another proposal that has gained numerous supporters in recent years is that public education should be privatized.

PRIVATIZATION

Widespread concern about the crisis in education has opened the door for *public-private partnerships* aimed at injecting private sector know-how into failing public schools. In 1994, then President Bill Clinton signed into law the Goals 2000: Educate America Act, which authorized states to use federal funds for experiments with school privatization. Local school districts can choose to contract out specific educational services—or the entire school administration—to private companies without losing federal funding. In the past decade, a number of U.S. school districts—including large urban systems such as those in Hartford, Baltimore, and Minneapolis—have invited for-profit educational companies to run their school systems.

Supporters of school privatization argue that state and federal education authorities have shown that they are unable to improve the nation's schools. The educational system, they argue, is wasteful and bureaucratic; it spends a disproportionate amount of its funding on noninstructional administrative costs. Because of their top-heavy nature, it is nearly impossible for school systems to be flexible and innovative. Incompetent teachers are difficult to remove because of the strength of teacher unions.

What backers of school privatization claim can solve these problems is a strong dose of private-sector ideology: competition, experimentation, and incentive. For-profit companies can run school systems more efficiently and produce better outcomes by applying private sector logic. Good teachers would be attracted to teaching—and retained—by performance-based pay schemes, while underperforming teachers could be removed more easily. Competition within and between schools would lead to higher levels of innovation; privatized schools would have more liberty to institutionalize the results of successful experiments.

One of the leading players in the U.S. market for privatized education is the Edison Project, an educational company that manages a chain of eighty public schools in sixteen different states. The verdict on whether the Edison Project is improving educational outcomes in its schools is mixed, and the company itself has been heavily criticized on a number of fronts, including for poor financial management. Critics have been quick to point out that the Edison Project's vision for schools is little more than a slick repackaging of well-known practices from public education, such as cooperative learning and pupil-centered teaching (Molnar, 1996). The company requires that all students in Edison schools have a computer at home—and assists those families that cannot afford them—but it is less clear how this enthusiasm for technology is linked into the curriculum in a meaningful way. Opponents of school privatization argue that companies such as the Edison Project are less serious about reforming education and reducing inequalities than about promoting education reform as a lucrative market for wealthy investors.

The crisis in American schools won't be solved in the short term, and it won't be solved by educational reforms alone, no matter how thoroughgoing. The lesson of sociological research is that inequalities and barriers in educational opportunity reflect wider social divisions and tensions. While the United States remains wracked by racial tensions and the polarization between decaying cities and affluent suburbs persists, the crisis in the school system is likely to prove difficult to turn around.

Education and Literacy in the Developing World

Literacy is the "baseline" of education. Without it, schooling cannot proceed. We take it for granted in the West that the majority of people are literate, but as has been mentioned, this is only a recent development in Western history, and in previous times no more than a tiny proportion of the population had any literacy skills.

Today, over 35 percent of the population of developing countries is still illiterate (see Global Map 12.1). The Indian government has estimated the number of illiterate people in that country alone to be over 285 million, a number that exceeds the total population of the United States. Even if the provision of primary education increased to match the level of population growth, illiteracy would not be markedly reduced for years, because a high proportion of those who cannot read or write are adults. The absolute number of illiterate people is actually rising (Coombs, 1985). According to UNESCO estimates, the total grew from 569 million in 1970 to 625 million in 1980 to 826 million in 2003 (UNESCO, 2003).

Although countries have instituted literacy programs, these have made only a small contribution to a problem of large-scale dimensions. Television, radio, and the other electronic media can be used, where they are available, to skip the stage of learning literacy skills and convey educational programs directly to adults. But educational programs are usually less popular than commercialized entertainment.

During the period of colonialism, colonial governments regarded education with some trepidation. Until the twentieth century, most believed indigenous populations to be too primitive to be worth educating. Later, education was seen as a way of making local elites responsive to European interests and ways of life. But to some extent, the result was to foment discontent and rebellion, since the majority of those who led anticolonial

and nationalist movements were from educated elites who had attended schools or colleges in Europe. They were able to compare first hand the democratic institutions of the European countries with the absence of democracy in their lands of origin.

The education that the colonizers introduced usually pertained to Europe, not the colonial areas themselves. Educated Africans in the British colonies knew about the kings and queens of England, read Shakespeare, Milton, and the English poets, but knew next to nothing about their own countries' histories or past cultural achievements. Policies of educational reform since the end of colonialism have not completely altered the situation even today.

Partly as a result of the legacy of colonial education, which was not directed toward the majority of the population, the educational system in many developing countries is top heavy: Higher education is disproportionately developed, relative to primary and secondary education. The result is a correspondingly overqualified group who, having attended colleges and universities, cannot find white-collar or professional jobs. Given the low level of industrial development, most of the better-paid positions are in government, and there are not enough of those to go around.

In recent years, some developing countries, recognizing the shortcomings of the curricula inherited from colonialism, have tried to redirect their educational programs toward the rural poor. They have had limited success, because usually there is insufficient funding to pay for the scale of the necessary innovations. As a result, countries such as India have begun programs of self-help education. Communities draw on existing resources without creating demands for high levels of finance. Those who can read and write and who perhaps possess job skills are encouraged to take others on as apprentices, whom they coach in their spare time.

The Sociological Study of Religion

While modern education emerged in the nineteenth century, religion is one of the oldest human institutions. Cave drawings suggest that religious beliefs and practices existed more than forty thousand years ago. According to anthropologists, there have probably been about one hundred thousand religions throughout human history (Hadden, 1997a). Sociologists define **religion** as a cultural system of commonly shared beliefs and rituals that provides a sense of ultimate meaning and purpose by creating an idea of reality that is

Adult Literacy Rates Worldwide
(15 years and older)

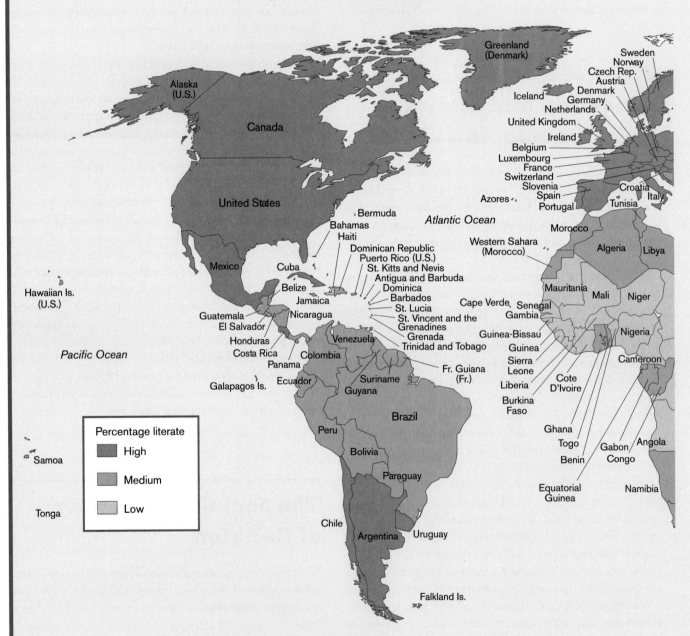

Percentage literate

High

Medium

Low

SOURCE: United Nations, *Human Development Report*, 2003 (2001 data).

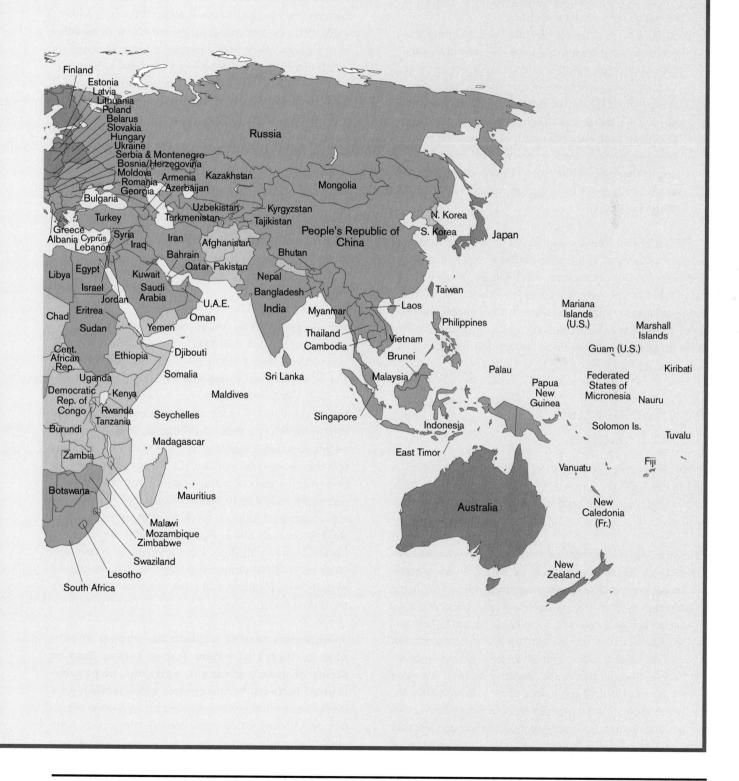

sacred, all-encompassing, and supernatural (Durkheim, 1965, orig. 1912; Berger, 1967; Wuthnow, 1988). There are three key elements in this definition:

1. Religion is a form of culture. You will recall from Chapter 2 that *culture* consists of the shared beliefs, values, norms, and material conditions that create a common identity among a group of people. Religion shares all of these characteristics.

2. Religion involves beliefs that take the form of ritualized practices. All religions thus have a behavioral aspect—special activities in which believers take part and that identify them as members of the religious community.

3. Perhaps most important, religion provides a sense of purpose—a feeling that life is ultimately meaningful. It does so by explaining coherently and compellingly what transcends or overshadows everyday life, in ways that other aspects of culture (such as an educational system or a belief in democracy) typically cannot (Geertz, 1973; Wuthnow, 1988).

What is absent from the sociological definition of religion is as important as what is included: Nowhere is there mention of God. We often think of **theism**—a belief in one or more supernatural deities (the term originates from the Greek word for god)—as basic to religion, but this is not necessarily the case. As we shall see later, some religions, such as Buddhism, believe in the existence of spiritual forces rather than a particular god.

How Sociologists Think About Religion

When sociologists study religion, they do so as sociologists and not as believers (or disbelievers) in any particular faith. This stance has several implications for the sociological study of religion:

1. **Sociologists are not concerned with whether religious beliefs are true or false.** From a sociological perspective, religions are regarded not as being decreed by God but as being socially constructed by human beings. As a result, sociologists put aside their personal beliefs when they study religion. They are concerned with the human rather than the divine aspects of religion. Sociologists ask: How is the religion organized? What are its principal beliefs and values? How is it related to the larger society? What explains its success or failure in recruiting and retaining believers? The question of whether a particular belief is "good" or "true," however important it

may be to the believers of the religion under study, is not something that sociologists are able to address as sociologists. (As individuals, they may have strong opinions on the matter, but one hopes that as sociologists they can keep these opinions from biasing their research.)

2. **Sociologists are especially concerned with the social organization of religion.** Religions are among the most important institutions in society. They are a primary source of the deepest-seated norms and values. At the same time, religions are typically practiced through an enormous variety of social forms. The sociology of religion is concerned with how different religious institutions and organizations actually function. The earliest European religions were often indistinguishable from the larger society, as religious beliefs and practices were incorporated into daily life. This is still true in many parts of the world today. In modern industrial society, however, religions have become established in separate, often bureaucratic, organizations, and so sociologists focus on the organizations through which religions must operate in order to survive (Hammond, 1992). As we will see below, this institutionalization has even led some sociologists to view religions in the United States and Europe as similar to business organizations, competing with each other for members (Warner, 1993).

3. **Sociologists often view religions as a major source of social solidarity.** To the extent that religions provide their believers with a common set of norms and values, they are an important source of social solidarity. Religious beliefs, rituals, and bonds help to create a "moral community" in which all members know how to behave toward one another (Wuthnow, 1988). If a single religion dominates a society, the religion may be an important source of social stability. If a society's members adhere to numerous competing religions, however, religious differences may lead to destabilizing social conflicts. Recent examples of religious conflict within a society include struggles among Sikhs, Hindus, and Muslims in India; clashes between Muslims and Christians in Bosnia and other parts of the former Yugoslavia; and "hate crimes" against Jews, Muslims, and other religious minorities in the United States.

4. **Sociologists tend to explain the appeal of religion in terms of social forces rather than in terms of purely personal, spiritual, or psychological factors.** For many people, religious beliefs are a deeply personal experience, involving a deep sense of connection with forces that transcend everyday reality. Sociologists do not question the depth of such feelings and

experiences, but they are unlikely to limit themselves to a purely spiritual explanation of religious commitment. A person may claim that he or she became religious when God suddenly appeared in a vision, but sociologists are likely to look for more earthly explanations. Some researchers argue that people often "get religion" when their fundamental sense of a social order is threatened by economic hardship, loneliness, loss or grief, physical suffering, or poor health (Berger, 1967; Schwartz, 1970; Glock, 1976; Stark and Bainbridge, 1980). In explaining the appeal of religious movements, sociologists are more likely to focus on the problems of the social order than on the psychological response of the individual.

Theories of Religion

Sociological approaches to religion are still strongly influenced by the ideas of Marx, Durkheim, and Weber. None of the three was religious himself, and all believed that religion would become less and less significant in modern times. Each argued that religion was fundamentally an illusion: The very diversity of religions and their obvious connection to different societies and regions of the world made the claims by their advocates inherently implausible. An individual born into an Australian society of hunters and gatherers would plainly hold different religious beliefs from someone born into the caste system of India or the Catholic Church of medieval Europe.

Marx: Religion and Inequality

In spite of the influence of his views on the subject, Karl Marx never studied religion in any detail. His thinking on religion was mostly derived from the writings of Ludwig Feuerbach, who believed that through a process he called **alienation,** human beings tend to attribute their own culturally created values and norms to alien, or separate, beings (i.e., divine forces or gods), because they do not understand their own history. Thus, the story of the Ten Commandments given to Moses by God is a mythical version of the origins of the moral precepts that govern the lives of Jewish and Christian believers.

Marx accepted the view that religion represents human self-alienation. In a famous phrase, Marx declared that religion was the "opium of the people." Religion defers happiness and rewards to the afterlife, he said, teaching the resigned acceptance of existing conditions in the earthly life. Attention is thus diverted away from inequalities and injustices in this world by the promise of what is to come in the next. Religion

contains a strong ideological element: Religious belief can often provide justifications for those in power. For example, "The meek shall inherit the earth" suggests attitudes of humility and nonresistance to oppression.

Durkheim: Religion and Functionalism

In contrast to Marx, Émile Durkheim spent a good part of his intellectual career studying religion, concentrating particularly on totemism as practiced by Australian aboriginal societies. *The Elementary Forms of the Religious Life,* first published in 1912, is perhaps the most influential single study in the sociology of religion (1965). Durkheim connected religion not with social inequalities or power, but with the overall nature of the institutions of a society. His argument was that totemism represented religion in its most "elementary" form—hence the title of his book.

Durkheim defined religion in terms of a distinction between the sacred and the profane. **Sacred** objects and symbols, he held, are treated as apart from the routine, utilitarian aspects of day-to-day existence—the realm of the **profane.** A totem (an animal or plant believed to have particular symbolic significance), Durkheim argued, is a sacred object, regarded with veneration and surrounded by ritual activities. These ceremonies and rituals, in Durkheim's view, are essential to binding the members of groups together.

Durkheim's theory of religion is a good example of the functionalist tradition of thought in sociology. To analyze the function of a social behavior or social institution like religion is to study the contribution it makes to the continuation of a group, community, or society. According to Durkheim, religion has the function of cohering a society by ensuring that people meet regularly to affirm common beliefs and values.

Weber: The World Religions and Social Change

Durkheim based his arguments on a restricted range of examples, even though he claimed his ideas applied to religion in general. Max Weber, by contrast, embarked on a massive study of religions worldwide. No scholar before or since has undertaken a task of the scope Weber attempted.

Weber's writings on religion differ from those of Durkheim because they concentrate on the connection between religion and social change, something to which Durkheim gave little direct attention. They also contrast with those of Marx, because Weber argued that religion was not necessarily a conservative force; on the contrary, religiously inspired movements have often produced dramatic social transformations. Thus, Protestantism, particularly Puritanism, according to Weber, was the source of the capitalistic outlook found in the modern West. The early entrepreneurs were mostly Calvinists. Their drive to succeed, which helped initiate Western economic development, was originally prompted by a desire to serve God. Material success was a sign of divine favor.

Weber conceived of his research on the world religions as a single project. His discussion of the impact of Protestantism on the development of the West was connected to a comprehensive attempt to understand the influence of religion on social and economic life in various cultures. After analyzing the Eastern religions, Weber concluded that they provided insuperable barriers to the development of industrial capitalism such as took place in the West. This was not because the non-Western civilizations were backward; they were simply oriented toward different values, such as escape from the toils of the material world, from those that came to predominate in Europe.

In traditional China and India, Weber pointed out, there was at certain periods a significant development of commerce, manufacture, and urbanism. But these did not generate the radical patterns of social change involved in the rise of industrial capitalism in the West. Religion was a major influence inhibiting such change. Consider, for example, Hinduism. Hinduism is what Weber called an "other-worldly" religion. That is to say, its highest values stress escape from the toils of the material world to a higher plane of spiritual existence. The religious feelings and motivations produced by Hinduism do not focus on controlling or shaping the material world. On the contrary, Hinduism sees material reality as a veil hiding the true spiritual concerns to which humankind should be oriented. Confucianism also acts to direct activity away from economic "progress," as this came to be understood in the West. Confucianism emphasizes harmony with the world, rather than promoting an active mastery of it. Although China was for a long while the most powerful and culturally most developed civilization in the world, its dominant religious values acted as a brake on a stronger commitment to economic development.

Weber regarded Christianity as a *salvation religion*. According to such religions, human beings can be "saved" if they are converted to the beliefs of the religion and follow its moral tenets. The notions of "sin" and of being rescued from sinfulness by God's grace are important here. They generate a tension and an emotional dynamism essentially absent from the Eastern religions. Salvation religions have a "revolutionary" aspect. Whereas the religions of the East cultivate an attitude of passivity or acceptance within the believer, Christianity demands a constant struggle against sin and so can stimulate

revolt against the existing order. Religious leaders—such as Luther or Calvin—have arisen who reinterpret existing doctrines in such a way as to challenge the extant power structure.

Critical Assessment of the Classical View

Marx, Durkheim, and Weber each identified some important general characteristics of religion, and in some ways their views complement one another. Marx was right to claim that religion often has ideological implications, serving to justify the interests of ruling groups at the expense of others. There are innumerable instances of this in history. For example, the European missionaries who sought to convert "heathen" peoples to Christian beliefs were no doubt sincere in their efforts. Yet their teachings in large part reinforced the destruction of traditional cultures and the imposition of white domination. Almost all Christian denominations tolerated, or endorsed, slavery in the United States and other parts of the world into the nineteenth century. Doctrines were developed proclaiming slavery to be based on divine law, disobedient slaves being guilty of an offense against God as well as their masters (Stampp, 1956).

Yet Weber was certainly correct to emphasize the unsettling and often revolutionary impact of religious ideals on the established social order. In spite of the churches' early support for slavery in the United States, church leaders later played a key role in fighting to abolish the institution. Religious beliefs have prompted social movements seeking to overthrow unjust systems of authority; for instance, religious sentiments played a prominent part in the civil rights movements of the 1960s. Religion has also generated social change through wars fought for religious motives.

These divisive influences of religion, so prominent in history, find little mention in Durkheim's work. Durkheim emphasized above all the role of religion in promoting social cohesion. Yet it is not difficult to redirect his ideas toward explaining religious division, conflict, and change as well as solidarity. After all, much of the strength of feeling that may be generated *against* other religious groups derives from the commitment to religious values generated *within* each community of believers.

Among the most valuable points of Durkheim's writings is his stress on ritual and ceremony. All religions comprise regular assemblies of believers, at which ritual prescriptions are observed. As Durkheim rightly points out, ritual activities also mark the major transitions of life—birth, entry to adulthood (rituals associated with puberty are found in many cultures), marriage, and death (Van Gennep, 1977).

Finally, Marx, Durkheim, and Weber's theories on religion were based on their studies of societies in which a single religion predominated. As a consequence, it seemed reasonable for them to examine the relationship between a predominant religion and the society as a whole. However, in the past fifty years this classical view has been challenged by some U.S. sociologists. Because of their own experience in a society that is highly tolerant of religious diversity, these theorists have focused on religious pluralism rather than on religious domination. Not surprisingly, their conclusions differ substantially from the earlier views as advanced in different ways by Marx, Durkheim, and Weber, each of whom regarded religion as closely bound up with the larger society. Religion was believed to reflect and reinforce society's values, or at least the values of those who were most powerful; to provide an important source of solidarity and social stability; and to be an important engine of social change. According to this view, religion is threatened by the rise of **secular thinking,** that is, worldly thinking, particularly as seen in the rise of science, technology, and rational thought in general.

The classical theories of religion argued that the key problem facing religions in the modern world is **secularization,** or a rise in worldly thinking and a simultaneous decline in the influence of religion. Secularization is typically accompanied by a decrease in religious belief and involvement and results in a weakening of the social and political power of religious organizations. Peter Berger (1967) has described religion in premodern societies as a "sacred canopy" that covers all aspects of life and is therefore seldom questioned. In modern society, however, the sacred canopy is more like a quilt, a patchwork of numerous different religious and secular belief systems. When beliefs are compared and contrasted, it becomes increasingly difficult to sustain the idea that there is any single true faith. According to this view, secularization is the likely result.

Contemporary Approaches: "Religious Economy"

One of the most recent and influential approaches to the sociology of religion is tailored to societies such as the United States, which offer many different faiths from which to pick and choose. Taking their cue from economic theory, sociologists who favor the **religious economy** approach argue that religions can be fruitfully understood as organizations in competition with each other for followers (Stark and Bainbridge, 1987; Finke and Stark, 1988, 1992; Roof and McKinney, 1990; Hammond, 1992; Warner, 1993; Moore, 1994).

Like contemporary economists who study businesses, these sociologists argue that competition is preferable to monopoly when it comes to ensuring religious vitality. This position is exactly opposite to those of the classical theorists. Marx, Durkheim, and Weber assumed that religion weakens when challenged by different religious or secular viewpoints, where-

as the religious economists argue that competition increases the overall level of religious involvement in modern society. Religious economists believe this is true for two reasons. First, competition makes each religious group try that much harder to win followers. Second, the presence of numerous religions means that there is likely to be something for just about everyone. In a culturally diverse society such as the United States, a single religion will probably appeal to only a limited range of followers, whereas the presence of Indian gurus and fundamentalist preachers, in addition to mainline churches, is likely to encourage a high level of religious participation.

The religious-economy approach overestimates the extent to which people rationally pick and choose among different religions, as if they were shopping around for a new car or a pair of shoes. Among deeply committed believers, particularly in societies that lack religious pluralism, it is not obvious that religion is a matter of rational choice. In such societies, even when people are allowed to choose among different religions, most are likely to practice their childhood religion without ever questioning whether or not there are more appealing alternatives. Even in the United States, where the religious-economy approach originated, sociologists may overlook the spiritual aspects of religion if they simply assume that religious buyers are always on spiritual shopping sprees. Wade Clark Roof's study (1993) of fourteen hundred baby boomers found that a third had remained loyal to their childhood faith, while another third had continued to profess their childhood beliefs although they no longer belonged to a religious organization. Thus only a third were actively looking around for a new religion, making the sorts of choices presumed by the religious economy approach.

Types of Religious Organizations

Early theorists such as Max Weber (1963, orig. 1921), Ernst Troeltsch (1931), and Richard Niebuhr (1929) described religious organizations as falling along a continuum, based on the degree to which they are well established and conventional: Churches lie at one end (they are conventional and well established), cults lie at the other (they are neither), and sects fall somewhere in the middle. These distinctions were based on the study of European and U.S. religions. There is much debate over how well they apply to the non-Christian world.

Today, sociologists are aware that the terms *sect* and *cult* have negative connotations, something they wish to avoid. For this reason, contemporary sociologists of religion sometimes use the phrase *new religious movements* to characterize novel

Megachurches as Minitowns

Patty Anderson and her husband, Gary, found faith where they least expected it—he on the free-throw line and she swathed in sweats in an aerobics class.

It happened at the 50,000-square-foot activities center of the Southeast Christian Church [in Louisville, Kentucky,] where pumping iron and praising the Lord go hand and hand. Amenities at the gym include 16 basketball courts and a Cybex health club, free to churchgoers, where the music is Christian and the rules ban cursing even during the crunch.

"I really had no intention of being part of a church," recalled Gary Anderson, a physiology professor at the University of Louisville School of Medicine. But hoops at this 22,000-member megachurch led him to the sanctuary. And after three years, he said, like a slam dunk, "the sermons sunk in."

Southeast Christian is an example of a new breed of megachurch—a full-service "24/7" sprawling village, which offers many of the conveniences and trappings of secular life wrapped around a spiritual core. It is possible to eat, shop, go to school, bank, work out, scale a rock-climbing wall and pray there, all without leaving the grounds.

These churches are becoming civic in a way unimaginable since the thirteenth century and its cathedral towns. No longer simply places to worship, they have become part resort, part mall, part extended family and part town square.

[***]

The churches reflect a desire by congregants for a "universe where everything from the temperature to the theology is safely controlled," [one professor] said. "They don't have to worry about finding schools, social networks or a place to eat. It's all prepackaged."

[***]

"People are looking at churches with a similar cost-benefit analysis they'd give to any other consumer purchase," [a megachurch consultant added]. "There is little brand loyalty. Many are looking for the newest and the greatest."

Dave Stone, the associate minister of Southeast, calls his church, which is open daily from 5:30 A.M. to 11 P.M. , "a refueling station."

"If we can get people to come to our gym," he explained, "it's only a matter of time before we can get them to visit our sanctuary."

The church was deliberately designed like a mall. (The sanctuary is the anchor tenant.) Hallways 20 feet wide with curves enhance "people flow," said Jack Coffee, a church elder and chairman of the building committee. Preschoolers frolic at a Disneyesque play land, with mazes. There is an education wing for Bible classes, a concert-hall-size atrium with glass elevators, crisscrossing escalators and giant monitors that itemize the day's offerings: meetings to help smokers quit, a cross-trainers minimarathon and pat the Bible classes for six-month-olds.

Such amenities are typically paid for by the congregation with three-year capital campaigns, on top of the church's operating budget, which is often financed with tithes, said Malcolm P. Graham, president of Cargill Associates' church division, a fund-raising consultant. A study by the Hartford Institute for Religion Research at the Hartford Seminary finds the average annual income for a megachurch is $4.6 million a year. Annual contributions to Southeast Christian are more than $20 million.

Southeast Christian churchgoers speak of a 22,000-person family, and visitors are regaled with statistics: the coffeepot that serves 5,000 cups an hour, the 403 toilets. Southeast's size has spawned the invention of the Greenlee Communion Dispensing Machine, designed by Wilfred Greenlee, 79, a congregant. It can fill 40 communion cups in 2 seconds.

[***]

Not incidentally, it gives the congregants who flock to church for more than 80 activities each evening—like children's theater and adult computer classes—an excuse to stick around. "If you have to go home for dinner, you don't come back out," [a pastor said].

But some scholars and municipalities are troubled by the civic expansion of 24/7 churches. They are becoming "a parallel universe that's Christianized," in the words of Dr. Scott Thumma, a sociologist of religion at the Hartford Institute.

Dr. Wade Clark Roof, a professor of religion and society at the University of California at Santa Barbara, said he worried that full-service churches are "the religious version of the gated community."

"It's an attempt to create a world where you're dealing with like-minded people," he said. "You lose the dialogue with the larger culture."

[***]

SOURCE: Patricia Leigh Brown, "Megachurches as Minitowns," *New York Times,* May 9, 2002, pp. F1–F6.

Questions

- How might Marx, Durkheim, and Weber each analyze the development of megachurches?
- Are megachurches evidence in favor of the religious economy approach to the sociology of religion?
- In your view, what do megachurches reveal about American society? Are congregants seeking social solidarity or trying to isolate themselves from the rest of society?

religious organizations that lack the respectability that comes with being well established for a long period of time (Hexham and Poewe, 1997; Hadden, 1997b).

Churches and Sects

Churches are large, established religious bodies; one example is the Roman Catholic Church. They normally have a formal, bureaucratic structure, with a hierarchy of religious officials. Churches often represent the conservative face of religion, since they are integrated within the existing institutional order. Most of their adherents are born into and grow up with the church.

Sects are smaller, less highly organized groups of committed believers, usually set up in protest against an established church, as Calvinism and Methodism were initially. Sects aim at discovering and following the "true way" and either try to change the surrounding society or withdraw from it into communities of their own, a process known as *revival*. The members of sects regard established churches as corrupt. Many sects have few or no officials, and all members are regarded as equal participants. For the most part, people are not born into sects, but actively join them in order to further commitments in which they believe.

Denominations and Cults

A **denomination** is a sect that has cooled down and become an institutionalized body rather than an activist protest group. Sects that survive over any period of time inevitably become denominations. Thus, Calvinism and Methodism were sects during their early period of formation, when they generated great fervor among their members; but over the years, they have become more established. (Calvinists today are called Presbyterians.) Denominations are recognized as legitimate by churches and exist alongside them, often cooperating harmoniously with them.

Cults resemble sects, but their emphases are different. Cults are the most loosely knit and transient of all religious organizations. They are composed of individuals who reject what they see as the values of the outside society, unlike sects, which try to revive an established church. They are a form of religious innovation, rather than revival. Their focus is on individual experience, bringing like-minded people together. Like sects, cults often form around the influence of an inspirational leader.

Like sects, cults flourish when there is a breakdown in well-established and widespread societal belief systems. This is happening throughout the world today, in places as diverse as Japan, India, and the United States. When such a breakdown occurs, cults may originate within the society itself, or they may be "imported" from outside. In the United States, examples of homegrown, or indigenous, cults include New Age religions based on such things as spiritualism, astrology, and religious practices adapted from Asian or Native American cultures. Examples of imported cults include the Reverend Sun Myung Moon's Unification Church ("Moonies"), which originated in South Korea, and transcendental meditation.

Religion in the United States

In comparison with the citizens of other industrial nations, Americans are unusually religious. More than half (55 percent) of all Americans surveyed in 1995–1996 claimed to be "strong believers" in God or the sacred (Roof, 1999). About two out of five report having attended religious services in the past week (U.S. Census Bureau, 2003, Table 80), and slightly more than half (54 percent) live in a household where at least one person is a member of a church, mosque, or synagogue (Kosmin, Mayer, and Keysar, 2001). According to public opinion polls, the overwhelming majority of Americans reportedly believe in God and claim they regularly pray, the majority one or more times a day (National Opinion Research Center, 1998). More than eight out of ten Americans report that they believe in an afterlife, and a substantial majority claim to believe in the devil as well (Roof, 1999: Table A-3).

Yet at the same time, one long-term measure of religiosity, based on indicators such as belief in God, religious membership, and attendance at religious services, found that the index reached its highest levels in the 1950s, and has declined ever since—in part because post–World War II "baby boomers" were less religious than their predecessors (Roof, 1999). As Table 12.1 shows, in one national survey overwhelming majorities of Catholics, liberal Protestants, and conservative Protestants reported attending church on a weekly basis while they were children, although their attendance had dropped sharply by the time they had reached their early twenties. Among the three groups, attendance had declined the most among liberal Protestants, and least among conservative Protestants (Roof, 1999).

One survey of more than fifty thousand adults in 2001 and nearly 114,000 adults in 1990 found that religious identification had declined sharply during the eleven-year period. In 1990, 90 percent of all adults identified with some religious group; in 2001, the figure was only 81 percent. The principal

TABLE 12.1

Weekly Attendance at Religious Services

	AGE	
	8–10	EARLY 20s
Roman Catholics	95	28
Liberal Protestants	82	18
Conservative Protestants	91	40

SOURCE: Roof, 1999, Table A–1, p. 319.

decline was among self-identified Christians (from 86 percent to 77 percent). This decline was not because a growing proportion of adults identified with other religions; rather, it was because the number of adults identifying with no religion whatever had grown from 8 percent to 14 percent of the population. Membership in religious institutions showed a parallel decline (Kosmin, Mayer, and Keysar, 2001).

Trends in Religious Affiliation

It is difficult to estimate reliably the number of people belonging to churches, since the U.S. government does not officially collect such data. Nonetheless, based on occasional government surveys, public-opinion polls, and church records, sociologists of religion have concluded that church membership has grown steadily since the United States was founded. About one in six Americans belonged to a religious organization at the time of the Revolutionary War. That number had grown to about one in three at the time of the Civil War, one in two at the turn of the nineteenth century, and two in three in the 1990s (Finke and Stark, 1992).

One reason so many Americans are religiously affiliated is that religious organizations are an important source of social ties and friendship networks. Churches, synagogues, and mosques are communities of people who share the same beliefs and values, and who support one another during times of need. Religious communities thus often play a familylike role, offering help in times of emergency as well as more routine assistance such as child care.

Another reason so many people belong to religious organizations is simply that there are an enormous number of such organizations one can belong to. The United States is the most religiously diverse country in the world, with more than fifteen hundred distinct religions (Melton, 1989). Yet the vast majority of people belong to a relatively small number of religious denominations (see Figure 12.3). Fifty-three percent of Americans identify themselves as Protestants, 25 percent as Catholics, 2 percent as Jews, and 11 percent as "other," a category that includes Eastern Orthodox, Mormons, and Muslims. The remainder (9 percent) say they have no religious affiliation at all (U.S. Census Bureau, 2003, Table 80).

PROTESTANTS: THE GROWING STRENGTH OF CONSERVATIVE DENOMINATIONS

A somewhat clearer picture of recent trends in American religion can be obtained if we break down the large Protestant category into major subgroups. According to the American Religious Identification Survey of more than fifty thousand

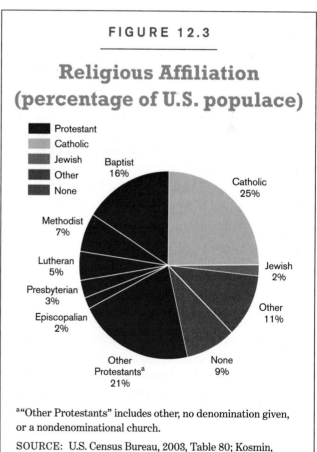

FIGURE 12.3

Religious Affiliation (percentage of U.S. populace)

a"Other Protestants" includes other, no denomination given, or a nondenominational church.

SOURCE: U.S. Census Bureau, 2003, Table 80; Kosmin, Mayer, and Keysar, 2001.

FIGURE 12.4

Loss and Gain in Church Membership, 1965–1989, for Selected Moderate Liberal and Conservative Protestant Churches

During the twenty-four-year period from 1965 to 1989, such mainstream denominations as the United Methodists, the United Church of Christ, the Episcopalians, the Presbyterians, and the Disciples of Christ lost between one fifth and one half of their membership. Conversely, such conservative Protestant churches as the Assemblies of God, the Mormons, and the Church of God more than doubled their membership.

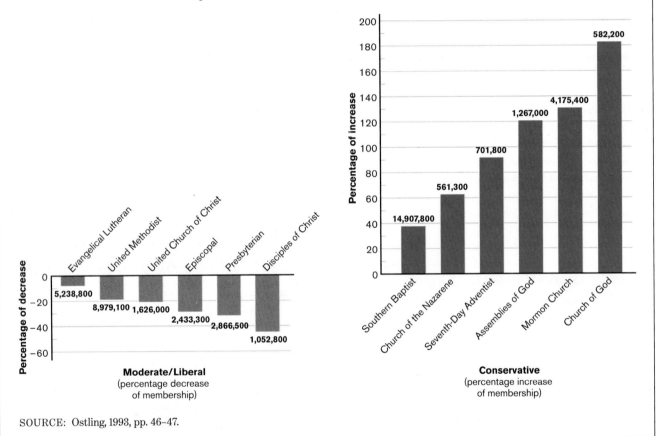

SOURCE: Ostling, 1993, pp. 46–47.

households in 2001, the largest number of households were Baptist, accounting for 31 percent of all Protestants—nearly two and a half times the percentage of the second largest group, Methodists (13 percent). There were far fewer Lutherans (9 percent), Presbyterians (5 percent), and Episcopalians (3 percent) (Kosmin, Mayer, and Keysar, 2001). More than half of all Protestants today describe themselves as "born again" (*The Economist,* 2003).

These figures are important because they indicate the growing strength of conservative Protestants in the United States. Conservative Protestants emphasize a literal interpretation of the Bible, morality in daily life, and conversion through evangelizing. They can be contrasted with the more historically established liberal Protestants, who tend to adopt a more flexible, humanistic approach to religious practice. Somewhere in between are moderate Protestants.

Although all groups of Protestants showed a growth in membership from the 1920s through the 1960s, a major reversal has occurred since that time. Both liberal and moderate churches have experienced a decline in membership, whereas the number of conservative Protestants has exploded. Today twice as many people belong to conservative Protestant groups as liberal ones, and conservative Protestants may soon outnumber moderates as well (Roof and McKinney, 1990). Since the 1960s, the fastest-growing religious group has been self-identified evangelicals. Moreover, although all religious groups lose some converts to other denominations or beliefs, the more conservative religions experienced a net gain in converts during the 1990s, whereas the more liberal religions experienced a net loss (Kosmin, Mayer, and Keysar, 2001; see also Table 12.1).

CATHOLICISM

Although Catholics continue to grow in number, church attendance has shown a sharp decline over the past few decades, beginning in the 1960s and leveling off in the mid-1970s. One of the main reasons was the papal encyclical of 1968 that reaffirmed the ban on the use of contraceptives by Catholics. The encyclical offered no leeway for people whose conscience allowed for the use of contraceptives. They were faced with disobeying the church, and many Catholics did just that. According to one study conducted by the Centers for Disease Control and Prevention, 96 percent of all Catholic women who have had sexual relations report having used contraceptives at one time or another; the General Social Survey found that three out of five Catholics say that contraceptives should be available to teens even without parental approval.

The Catholic Church has shown by far the largest increase in membership, partly because of the immigration of Catholics from Mexico and Central and South America. Yet the growth in Catholic Church membership has also slowed in recent years, as some followers have drifted away, either ceasing to identify themselves as Catholics or shifting to Protestantism.

OTHER RELIGIOUS GROUPS

The number of Jews has declined in recent years as a result of low birthrates, intermarriage, and assimilation. Yet even assimilated Jews often identify themselves as Jewish, and in recent years, there has been a resurgence of interest among some younger American Jews in rediscovering orthodox practices (Eisen, 1983; Goldberg and Rayner, 1987; Danzger, 1989; Blech, 1991; Davidman, 1991; Bamberger, 1992).

TABLE 12.2

Changes in Religious Self-Identification in the United States, 1999–2001

RELIGIOUS SELF-IDENTIFICATION	NET GAIN OR LOSS
Evangelical/Born Again	42%
Nondenominational	37%
No religion	23%
Pentecostal	16%
Buddhist	12%
Jehovah's Witness	11%
Seventh-Day Adventist	11%
Muslim/Islamic	8%
Assemblies of God	7%
Episcopalian/Anglican	5%
Church of God	5%
Mormon	0%
Baptist	−1%
Lutheran	−1%
Presbyterian	−2%
Churches of Christ	−2%
Jewish	−4%
Congregational/UCC	−6%
Methodist	−7%
Catholic	−9%

SOURCE: Kosmin, Mayer, and Keysar, 2001, exhibit 7.

Among other denominations, growing immigration from Asia and Africa may somewhat change the U.S. religious profile. For example, estimates of the number of Muslims in the United States run as high as 3 million; many come from Asia or are African refugees from countries like Somalia and Ethiopia (Haddad, 1979; Roof and McKinney, 1990; Finke and Stark, 1992).

TABLE 12.3

Characteristics of Liberal, Moderate, Conservative, and Black Protestant Denominations

CHARACTERISTICS	LIBERAL	MODERATE	CONSERVATIVE	BLACK
Principal period of appearance	Historic "mainline" churches (pre–Revolutionary War)	Nineteenth century	Twentieth century	Nineteenth and twentieth centuries
Biblical interpretation	Humanistic, flexible	Fairly literal interpretation	Literal interpretation	Fairly literal interpretation, including emphasis on civil rights
Predominant income group	Middle and upper income	Middle income ("middle America")	Lower and middle income	Lower income
Higher education	Many college educated	Some college educated	Few college educated	Few college educated
Predominant region	Northeast, West	Midwest, West	South	South
Examples of denominations	Episcopalian, Presbyterian, United Church of Christ	Methodist, Lutheran, Disciples of Christ, Northern Baptist, Reformed churches	Southern Baptist Convention; Churches of Christ; Church of the Nazarene; Assemblies of God; Seventh-Day Adventist; Fundamentalist, Pentecostal and holiness groups	Black Methodist and Baptist churches

SOURCE: Adapted from Roof and McKinney, 1990.

Religious Affiliation and Socioeconomic Status

Substantial socioeconomic and regional differences exist among the principal religious groupings in the United States (see Table 12.3 for differences among Protestants). *Liberal Protestants* tend to be well educated, somewhat upper income, and middle or upper class. They are concentrated in the northeastern states, and, to a small extent, in the West as well. *Moderate Protestants* fall at a somewhat lower level than liberal Protestants in terms of education, income, and social class. In fact, they are typical of the national average on these measures. They tend to live in the Midwest, and, to some extent, in the West. *Black Protestants* are, on average, the least educated, poorest, and least middle class of any of the religious groups listed in Table 12.3. *Conservative Protestants* have a similar profile, although they fall at a marginally higher level on all these measures.

Catholics strongly resemble moderate Protestants (which is to say, average Americans) in terms of their socioeconomic profile. They are largely concentrated in the Northeast, although many live in the West and the Southwest as well.

Finally, Jews have the most successful socioeconomic profile. Jews tend to be college graduates in middle- or upper-income categories. Whereas the large majority of Jews once lived in the northeastern states, today only half do, since many have moved throughout the United States. One recent study suggests that this high degree of geographical mobility is associated with lowered involvement in Jewish institutions. Jews who move across the country are less likely to belong to synagogues or temples, have Jewish friends, or be married to Jewish spouses (Goldstein and Goldstein, 1996).

In sum, Jews and liberal Protestants are the most heavily middle and upper class; moderate Protestants and Catholics are somewhat in the middle (although the growing number of poor Catholic Latino immigrants may be changing this position); conservative and black Protestants are overwhelmingly lower class. There are political differences across religious groups as well. Jews tend to be the most heavily Democratic of any major religious groups; fundamentalist and evangelical Christians the most Republican. The more moderate Protestant denominations are somewhere in between (Kosmin, Mayer, and Keysar, 2001, exhibit 14).

Globalization and Religion

Religion is one of the most truly global of all social institutions, affecting many aspects of life in the United States. Nearly half of the world's population follow one of two faiths: Christianity or Islam, religions that have long been unconstrained by national borders. The current globalization of religion is reflected in religious activism in poor countries, particularly on the part of Catholic priests and missionaries, and in the rise of religious nationalist movements in opposition to the modern secular state.

Activist Religion and Social Change Throughout the World

Religion has also played a particularly important role in global social changes of the past forty years. In Vietnam in the 1960s, Buddhist priests burned themselves alive to protest the policies of the South Vietnamese government. Their willingness to sacrifice their lives for their beliefs, seen on television sets around the world, contributed to growing U.S. opposition to the war. Buddhist monks in Thailand currently protest deforestation and care for victims of AIDS.

An activist form of Catholicism, termed **liberation theology,** combines Catholic beliefs with a passion for social justice for the poor, particularly in Central and South America and in Africa. Catholic priests and nuns organize farming cooperatives, build health clinics and schools, and challenge government policies that impoverish the peasantry. A similar role is played by Islamic socialists in Pakistan and Buddhist socialists in Sri Lanka (Berryman, 1987; Sigmund, 1990, Juergensmeyer, 1993). Many religious leaders have paid with their lives for their activism, which government and military leaders often regard as subversive.

In some Central and Eastern European countries once dominated by the former Soviet Union, long-suppressed religious organizations provided an important basis for the overturning of socialist regimes during the early 1990s. In Poland, for example, the Catholic Church was closely allied with the Solidarity movement, which toppled the socialist government in 1989. Yet, as the socialist regimes have crumbled, religion has also all too often played a central role in reviving ancient ethnic and tribal hatreds. In Bosnia and elsewhere in the former Yugoslavia, to cite one example, religious differences have helped to justify "ethnic cleansing," with Christian Serbs and to a lesser extent Croatians engaging in the mass murder, rape, and deportation of Muslims from communities and farmlands where they had lived for centuries.

The Global Rise of Religious Nationalism

Perhaps the most important trend in global religion today is the rise of **religious nationalism,** the linking of strongly held religious convictions with beliefs about a people's social and political destiny. In numerous countries around the world, religious nationalist movements reject the notion that religion, government, and politics should be separate and call instead for a revival of traditional religious beliefs that are directly embodied in the nation and its leadership (Beyer, 1994). These nationalist movements represent a strong reaction against the impact of technological and economic modernization on local religious beliefs. In particular, religious nationalists oppose what they see as the destructive aspects of "Western" influence on local culture and religion, ranging from U.S. television to the missionary efforts of foreign evangelicals. As one study notes, in the view of religious nationalists, "God's word is pure—not pluralist" (Marty and Appleby, 1995).

Religious nationalist movements accept many aspects of modern life, including modem technology, politics, and economics. For example, Islamic fundamentalists fighting the Russian army in Chechnya have developed Web sites to help promulgate their views. Osama bin Laden used video and television to reach millions of Muslims around the world. However, at the same time they emphasize a strict interpretation of religious values and completely reject the notion of secularization (Juergensmeyer, 1993, 2001). Nationalist movements do not simply revive ancient religious beliefs. Rather, nationalist movements partly "invent" the past, selectively drawing on different traditions and reinterpreting past events to serve their current beliefs and interests. Violent conflicts between religious groups sometimes result from their differing interpretations of the same historical event (Anderson, 1991; Juergensmeyer, 1993, 2001; Van der Veer, 1994).

Religious nationalism is on the rise throughout the world because in times of rapid social change, unshakable ideas have strong appeal. The collapse of the Soviet Union, the end of the cold war, and today's sweeping global economic and political changes have led many nations to reject the secular solutions offered by the United States and its former socialist enemies, and to look instead to their own past and cultures for answers (Juergensmeyer, 1995c). In the Middle East, many Palestinian Muslims as well as Israeli Orthodox Jews renounce the notion of a secular democratic state, arguing—often violently—for a religious nation purged of nonbelievers. In India, Hindus, Muslims, and Sikhs face off against each other. In India's nationwide elections held in early 1998, the religious nationalist Bharatiya Janata Party (BJP) got more votes than the Congress Party, which had dominated Indian politics since independence half a century earlier. (In 2004, the Congress party regained control of the government.)

RELIGIOUS NATIONALISM AND VIOLENCE

How is it that religious views could give rise to a culture of violence? The sociologist Mark Juergensmeyer (2001), who has studied the relationship between violence and religion, has come to a startling conclusion: Even though virtually all major religious traditions call for compassion and understanding, violence and religion nonetheless go hand in hand. Juergensmeyer, who has studied religious violence among Muslims, Sikhs, Jews, Hindus, Christians, and Buddhists, argues that under the right conditions ordinary conflicts can become recast as religious "cosmic wars" between good and evil that must be won at all costs. Juergensmeyer argues that a violent conflict is most likely to seek religious justification as a "cosmic war" when:

- the conflict is regarded as decisive for defending one's basic identity and dignity—for example, when one's culture is seen as threatened; and
- losing the conflict is unthinkable, although
- winning the conflict is unlikely in any realistic sense. (2001)

If any of these three conditions is present, Juergensmeyer argues, it is more likely that:

> a real-world struggle may be perceived in cosmic terms as a sacred war. The occurrence of all three simultaneously strongly suggests it. A struggle that begins on worldly terms may gradually take on the characteristics of a cosmic war as solutions become unlikely and awareness grows of how devastating it would be to lose. (2001)

In such instances, the proponents of cosmic warfare seek "terror in the mind of God" (the title of his book), justifying the loss of innocent lives as serving God's larger purpose. According to Juergensmeyer, bin Laden and al Qaeda exemplify such "cosmic warfare." They are seeking to defend Islam against an all-engulfing Westernization. He also argues that responding to al Qaeda's violence with still greater violence runs the risk of showing the Islamic world that the conflict is indeed cosmic, particularly if the most powerful nations on earth become embroiled. Based on his interviews with proponents of terrorism around the world, Juergensmeyer concludes that this is just what al Qaeda wants—to be elevated from the status of a minor criminal terrorist organization to a worthy opponent in a global war against the West. This, in the view of some of his interviewees, will increase the appeal of al Qaeda to a wider group of young Islamic men who blame the West for the decline of Islamic influence and the current hardships faced by many Muslims around the world.

Study Outline

www.wwnorton.com/giddens

The Development of Schooling

- Education in its modern form, involving the instruction of pupils within specially designated school premises, began to emerge with the spread of printed materials and higher levels of literacy. Knowledge could be retained, reproduced, and consumed by more people in more places. With industrialization, work became more specialized, and knowledge was increasingly acquired in more abstract rather than practical ways—the skills of reading, writing, and calculating.

Education and Inequality

- The expansion of education in the twentieth century has been closely tied to perceived needs for a literate and disciplined workforce. Although reformers have seen education for all as a means of reducing inequalities, its impact in this respect is fairly limited. Education tends to express and reaffirm existing inequalities more than it acts to change them.

- The formal school curriculum is only one part of a more general process of social reproduction influenced by many informal aspects of learning, education, and school settings. The *hidden curriculum* plays a significant role in such reproduction.
- Because *intelligence* is difficult to define, there has been a great deal of controversy about the subject. Some argue that genes determine one's *IQ;* others believe that social influences determine it. The weight of the evidence appears to be on the side of those arguing for social and cultural influences. A major controversy about IQ has developed as a result of the book *The Bell Curve.* The book claims that races differ in terms of their average level of inherited intelligence. Critics reject this thesis completely.

The Sociological Study of Religion

- There are no known societies that do not have some form of religion, although religious beliefs and practices vary from culture to culture. All religions involve a set of shared beliefs and rituals practiced by a community of believers.
- The sociology of religion is not concerned with whether a particular religion is true or false, but with how it operates as an organization and its relationship to the larger society. Religions are viewed as arising from social relationships and providing a sense of social solidarity to followers.

How Sociologists Think About Religion

- Sociological approaches to religion have been most influenced by the ideas of the three "classical" thinkers: Marx, Durkheim, and Weber. All believed that religion is fundamentally an illusion. They held that the "other" world that religion creates is *our* world, distorted through the lens of religious symbolism.
- To Marx, religion contains a strong ideological element: Religion provides justification for the inequalities of wealth and power found in society. To Durkheim, religion is important because of the cohesive functions it serves, especially in ensuring that people meet regularly to affirm common beliefs and values. To Weber, religion is important because of the role it plays in social change, particularly the development of Western capitalism.
- According to the classical view, religion in modern society is threatened by a long-term process of *secularization* in which the challenge of scientific thinking, as well as the coexistence of numerous competing religions, inevitably leads to the complete demise of religion.
- The more recent *religious economy* approach draws the opposite conclusion: that competition among religious groups and the challenges of secularization force religions to work harder to win followers, thereby strengthening the various groups and countering any trend toward secularization.

Types of Religious Organizations

- Several different types of religious organizations can be distinguished. A *church* is a large, established religious body, having a bureaucratic structure. *Sects* are small and aim at restoring the original purity of doctrines that have become "corrupted" in the hands of official churches. A *denomination* is a sect that has become institutionalized, having a permanent form. A *cult* is a loosely knit group of people who follow the same leader or pursue similar religious ideals.

Religion in the United States

- The United States is one of the most religious among the industrial nations. Although only about one quarter of all Americans report regularly attending church, the large majority claim to believe in God and to engage in regular prayer.
- Mainline liberal and moderate Protestant religious denominations in the United States have experienced declining membership recently, while more conservative or *evangelical* groups have seen an increase. These groups have sought to expand their direct influence in U.S. politics in recent years.

The Global Rise of Religious Nationalism

- Religious nationalism is an important force in the world today, existing in a precarious relationship with modern secular states. They often recast ordinary conflicts as religious "cosmic wars" between good and evil that must be won at all costs. This is especially likely to be the case when the conflict is seen as central to one's beliefs, losing it would be unthinkable, and winning it is unlikely.

Key Concepts

alienation (p. 325)
church (p. 330)
cult (p. 330)
denomination (p. 330)
hidden curriculum (p. 315)
intelligence (p. 316)
IQ (intelligence quotient) (p. 317)
liberation theology (p. 335)
profane (p. 325)
religion (p. 321)
religious economy (p. 327)

religious nationalism (p. 335)
sacred (p. 325)
sect (p. 330)
secular thinking (p. 327)
secularization (p. 327)
theism (p. 324)
tracking (p. 313)

Review Questions

1. What is the "hidden curriculum"?
   a. The "tricks of the trade" that enable teachers to keep discipline in class, sustain student interest, and impart instruction.
   b. The effects of school procedures and organization on students. The hidden curriculum teaches students to know their place and to sit still.
   c. The strategies that students use to make otherwise dull classes interesting.
   d. The political agenda that is seen to animate education: for conservatives it is the liberal obsession with political correctness and multiculturalism; for liberals it is the conservative obsession with standardized testing and the moral character of education.

2. What is "social reproduction"?
   a. The way schools educate each succeeding generation.
   b. The ways schools help perpetuate social and economic inequalities across the generations.
   c. The combined effect of the formal and hidden curricula on student character.
   d. The ways schools handle sex education.

3. What was the main conclusion of the landmark studies of educational inequality carried out in the 1960s by James Coleman and Christopher Jencks?
   a. Educational and occupational attainment are governed mainly by family background and nonschool factors.
   b. Outside the poorest areas, black schools are often as well funded as white schools.
   c. Reform of the educational system is essentially useless without reform of society.
   d. Intelligence is largely a product not of heredity but of the environment and, in particular, the actions of parents.

4. What is shown by sociological research on the impact of tracking in schools?
   a. Tracking does not benefit students, but it does make it easier for teachers to manage classes.
   b. Tracking ameliorates previously existing inequalities for advanced students but has no benefit for average or poor students.
   c. Tracking reinforces previously existing inequalities for average or poor students, but it does have benefits for advanced students.

   d. Tracking works best where there is a proper system of promotion and relegation of good and bad students.

5. One main reason for the rise of large educational systems was the process of
   a. medical innovation.
   b. stock market expansion.
   c. industrialization.
   d. computer innovation.

6. When sociologists study religion, they are concerned with
   a. whether religious beliefs are true or false.
   b. whether religious beliefs are good or bad.
   c. the social organization of religion.
   d. all of the above.

7. The classical theories of religion argued that the key problem facing religions in the modern world is
   a. animism.
   b. the electronic church.
   c. fundamentalism.
   d. secularization.

8. Secularization can be evaluated according to a number of aspects or dimensions. Which of the following is *not* one of them?
   a. Level of industrialization
   b. Social influence of churches
   c. Level of membership
   d. Level of religiosity

9. What is the most important trend in global religion today?
   a. Islamic revivalism
   b. The creation of the Israeli state
   c. Religious nationalism
   d. Secularization

10. According to Max Weber, what was the key factor in hindering the development of capitalism in traditional China and India?
    a. Religion
    b. Science
    c. Technology
    d. Industrialization

Thinking Sociologically Exercises

1. From your reading of this chapter, describe what might be the principal advantages and disadvantages of having children go to private versus public schools in the United States at this time. Assess whether privatization of our public schools would help to improve them.

2. Karl Marx, Émile Durkheim, and Max Weber each had different viewpoints on the nature of religion and its social significance. Briefly explain the viewpoints of each. Which theorist's views have the most to offer in explaining the rise of national and international fundamentalism today? Why?

Data Exercises

www.wwnorton.com/giddens
Keyword: Data12

- The data exercise for this chapter provides you with an opportunity to explore the link between a parent's educational attainment and that of his child. Before you begin, think about your own life.

What are your own educational goals? In what ways did your parents' educational achievements influence your decisions about what kind of education and how much education to pursue?

- In this chapter you have read about the patterns of religious practices in the United States. The data exercise for this chapter will give you a further opportunity to explore not only the differences in religious affiliation and worship among groups within our society, but more importantly, how these patterns are changing.

The Concept of the State

Learn the basic concepts underlying modern nation-states.

Democracy

Learn about different types of democracy, how this form of government has spread around the world, some theories about power in a democracy, and some of the problems associated with modern-day democracy.

Work and the Economy

The Social Significance of Work

Assess the sociological ramifications of paid and unpaid work.

The Social Organization of Work

Understand that modern economies are based on the division of labor and economic interdependence. Learn Marx's theory of alienation. Familiarize yourself with modern systems of economic production.

The Modern Economy

See the importance of the rise of large corporations; consider particularly the global impact of transnational corporations.

The Changing Nature of Work

Learn about the impact of global economic competition on employment. Consider how work will change over the coming years.

CHAPTER THIRTEEN

POLITICS AND ECONOMIC LIFE

S lobodan Milosevic—the "Butcher of the Balkans"—ruled Serbia for thirteen years, increasingly with an iron hand. A fervent Serbian nationalist, Milosevic had sought to restore Serbian control over the warring ethnic groups that had once made up the country of Yugoslavia. After the collapse of the Soviet Union, Yugoslavia—a communist republic—began to break up into a number of independent states, each one dominated by a different ethnic group. Milosevic tried to stop this process, often by brutal means.

Milosevic had risen to power by fanning the fires of nationalism, drawing on centuries-old memories of Serbian power and greatness in hopes of carving a "Greater Serbia" out of Serbia's neighboring republics. He sought to accomplish this by instilling among Serbs fear of their ethnic neighbors, which could then be used to drive other ethnic groups out of their historic homelands.

When Muslim-dominated Bosnia sought to secede from Serbian control in 1992, local Serbian militias, backed by the Serbian military, seized control by launching a reign of terror against Bosnia's Muslim population. Milosevic sought to "purify" Bosnia through "ethnic cleansing," driving Muslims out of the country by mass killings of civilians, widespread rape, and imprisonment of countless men in concentration camps. Televised images of mass graves and hundreds of thousands of Bosnian refugees galvanized world opinion, and the North Atlantic Treaty Organization (NATO) threatened military intervention.

Although peace talks eventually ended the Bosnian conflict and ousted the Serbian military, a similar conflict broke out when Kosovo sought independence in 1998, causing its Serbian minority to fear domination by the ethnic Albanian majority. Once again Milosevic called for ethnic cleansing, and once again the world was horrified by televised images of the mass murder of Bosnian men and teenage boys, with streams of terrified women and children fleeing over mountain passes. This time NATO launched a bombing campaign against Serbia itself, and Milosevic was forced to withdraw his forces from Bosnia.

Serbs were enraged by the Western intervention, and turned their anger against Milosevic. He was forced to call elections in September 2000, but refused to step down when he lost the vote. Hundreds of thousands of people took to the streets, and on October 5 he was toppled from power in a peaceful revolution. Milosevic was turned over to the United Nations and eventually stood trial for crimes against humanity in the UN International War Crimes Tribunal in the Hague, the Netherlands.

The popular uprising that overturned his regime drew on modern technology: although Milosevic controlled the country's television networks and newspapers, he couldn't control satellite TV, the distribution of videotapes, or the use of the Internet. The uprising was also made possible by Western military intervention and economic sanctions, which curbed Milosevic's military power and undermined popular support. And it drew inspiration from the rise of democratic movements throughout the world.

Democratization and the rise of the global economy are two of the major forces in the world. Like so many aspects of contemporary societies, the realms of government, politics, work, and economic life are undergoing major changes. **Government** refers to the regular enactment of policies, decisions, and matters of state on the part of the officials within a political apparatus. **Politics** concerns the means whereby power is used to affect the scope and content of governmental activities. The sphere of the *political* may range well beyond that of government itself. It is frequently intertwined with economics. The **economy** consists of institutions that provide for the production and distribution of goods and services. In this chapter, we will study the main factors affecting political and economic life today. Many people find politics remote and uninteresting. Whether we like it or not, however, all of our lives are touched by what happens in the political and economic spheres. We will begin with a discussion of politics and then turn to work and the economy. Governments influence quite personal activities and, in times of war, can even order us to lay down our lives for aims they deem necessary. The sphere of government is the sphere of political power. All political life is about power: who holds it, how they achieve it, and what they do with it.

Power and Authority

As mentioned in Chapter 1, the study of power is of fundamental importance for sociology. **Power** is the ability of individuals or groups to make their own interests or concerns count, even when others resist. It sometimes involves the direct use of force, such as when Slobodan Milosevic used brutal force in an effort to seize control of Bosnia and Kosovo in an effort to create a "Greater Serbia." Power is an element in almost all social relationships, such as that between employer and employee. This chapter focuses on two aspects of power, governmental and economic power. In the case of governmental power, it is almost always accompanied by ideologies, which are used to justify the actions of the powerful. For example, the Serbian government's use of force in "ethnic cleansing" was justified by an ideology of Serbian nationalism.

Authority is a government's legitimate use of power: Those subject to a government's authority consent to it. Power is thus different from authority. Contrary to what many believe, democracy is not the only type of government people consider legitimate. Dictatorships can have legitimacy as well. But as we shall see later, democracy is presently the most widespread form of government considered legitimate.

The Concept of the State

A **state** exists where there is a political apparatus of government (institutions like a parliament or congress, plus civil service officials) ruling over a given territory, whose authority is backed by a legal system and by the capacity to use military force to implement its policies. All modern states lay claim to specific territories, possess formalized codes of law, and are backed by the control of military force. **Nation-states** have come into existence at various times in different parts of the world (e.g., the United States in 1776 and the Czech Republic in 1993). Their main characteristics, however, contrast rather sharply with those of states in traditional civilizations.

Characteristics of the State

Sovereignty The territories ruled by traditional states were always poorly defined, the level of control wielded by the central government being quite weak. The notion of **sovereignty**— that a government possesses authority over an area with clear-cut borders, within which it is the supreme power—had little relevance. All nation-states, by contrast, are sovereign states.

Citizenship In traditional states, most of the population ruled by the king or emperor showed little awareness of, or interest in, those who governed them. Neither did they have any political rights or influence. Normally only the dominant classes or more affluent groups felt a sense of belonging to an overall political community. In modern societies, by contrast, most people living within the borders of the political system are **citizens**, having common rights and duties and knowing themselves to be members of a national community (Brubaker, 1992). Although some people are political refugees or are "stateless," almost everyone in the world today is a member of a definite national political order.

Nationalism Nation-states are associated with the rise of **nationalism**, which can be defined as a set of symbols and beliefs providing the sense of being part of a single political community. Thus, individuals feel a sense of pride and belonging in being American, Canadian, or Russian. Probably people have always felt some kind of identity with social groups of one form or another—their family, village, or religious community. Nationalism, however, made its appearance only with the development of the modern state. It is the main expression of feelings of identity with a distinct sovereign community.

Nationalistic loyalties do not always fit the physical borders marking the territories of states in the world today. Virtually all nation-states were built from communities of diverse backgrounds. As a result, **local nationalisms** have frequently arisen in opposition to those fostered by the states. Thus, in Canada, for instance, nationalist feelings among the French-speaking population in Quebec present a challenge to the feeling of "Canadianness." Yet while the relation between the nation-state and nationalism is a complicated one, the two have come into being as part of the same process. (We will return to nationalism later in the chapter as we look at its impact on international politics in the modern world.)

We can now offer a comprehensive definition of the nation-state: It is possessed of a government apparatus that is recognized to have sovereign rights within the borders of a territorial area, it is able to back its claims to sovereignty by the control of military power, and many of its citizens have positive feelings of commitment to its national identity.

Citizenship Rights

Most nation-states became centralized and effective political systems through the activities of monarchs who successfully concentrated more and more power in their own hands. Citizenship did not originally carry rights of political participation in these states. Such rights were achieved largely through struggles that limited the power of monarchs, as in Britain, or actively overthrew them—sometimes by a process of revolution, as in the cases of the United States and France, followed by a period of negotiation between the new ruling elites and their subjects (Tilly, 1996).

Three types of rights are associated with the growth of citizenship (Marshall, 1973). **Civil rights** refer to the rights of the individual in law. These include privileges many of us take for granted today but that took a long while to achieve (and are by no means fully recognized in all countries). Examples are the freedom of individuals to live where they choose; freedom of speech and religion; the right to own property; and the right to equal justice before the law. These rights were not fully established in most European countries until the early nineteenth century (see Global Map 13.1). Even where these rights were generally achieved, some groups were not allowed the same privileges. Although the U.S. Constitution granted such rights to Americans well before most European states had them, African Americans were excluded. Even after the Civil War, when blacks were formally given these rights, they were not able to exercise them.

The second type of citizenship rights consists of **political rights**, especially the right to participate in elections and to run for public office. Again, these were not won easily or quickly. Except in the United States, the achievement of full voting rights even for all men is relatively recent and was gained only after a struggle in the face of governments reluctant to admit the principle of the universal vote. In most European countries, the vote was at first limited to male citizens owning a certain amount of property, which effectively limited voting rights to an affluent minority. Universal franchise for men was mostly won by the early years of the twentieth century. Women had to wait longer; in most Western countries, the vote for women was achieved partly as a result of the efforts of women's movements and partly as a consequence of the mobilization of women into the formal economy during World War I.

The third type is **social rights**, the right of every individual to enjoy a certain minimum standard of economic welfare and security. Social rights include such entitlements as sickness benefits, benefits in case of unemployment, and the guarantee of minimum levels of wages. Social rights, in other words, involve welfare provisions. Although in some countries, such as nineteenth-century Germany, welfare benefits were introduced before legal and political rights were fully established, in most societies social rights have been the last to develop. This is because the establishment of civil and particularly political rights has usually been the basis of the fight for social rights. Social rights have been won largely as a result of the political strength poorer groups were able to develop after obtaining the vote.

The broadening of social rights is closely connected with the **welfare state**, which has been firmly established in Western societies only since World War II. A welfare state exists where government organizations provide material benefits for those who are unable to support themselves adequately through paid employment—the unemployed, the sick, the disabled, and the elderly. All Western countries today provide extensive welfare benefits. In many poorer countries, these benefits are virtually nonexistent.

Freedom in Global Perspective

The level of freedom is based on the political rights and civil liberties individuals have in each country. According to Freedom House, the organization that produces the ratings, in 2002 about 41 percent of the world's population lived in free countries, 24 percent lived in partly free countries, and 35 percent lived in not-free countries.

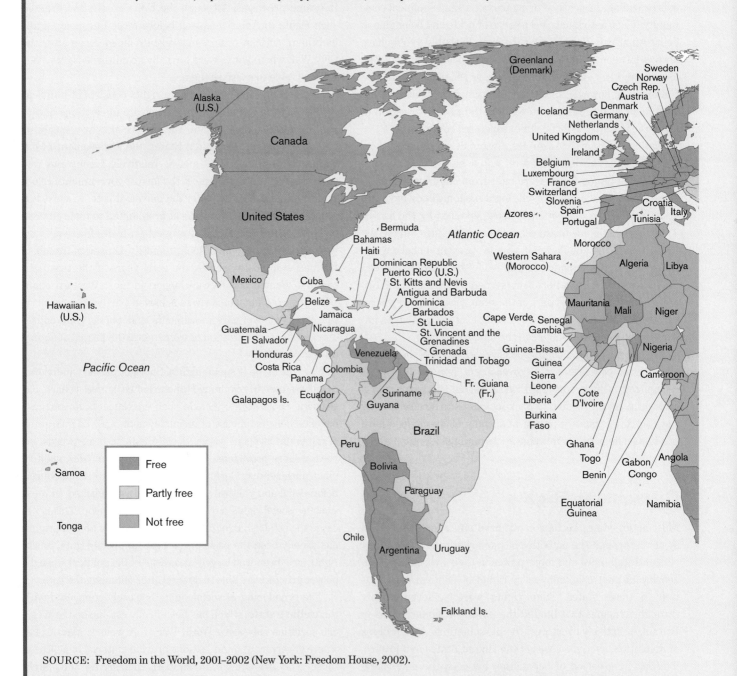

SOURCE: Freedom in the World, 2001–2002 (New York: Freedom House, 2002).

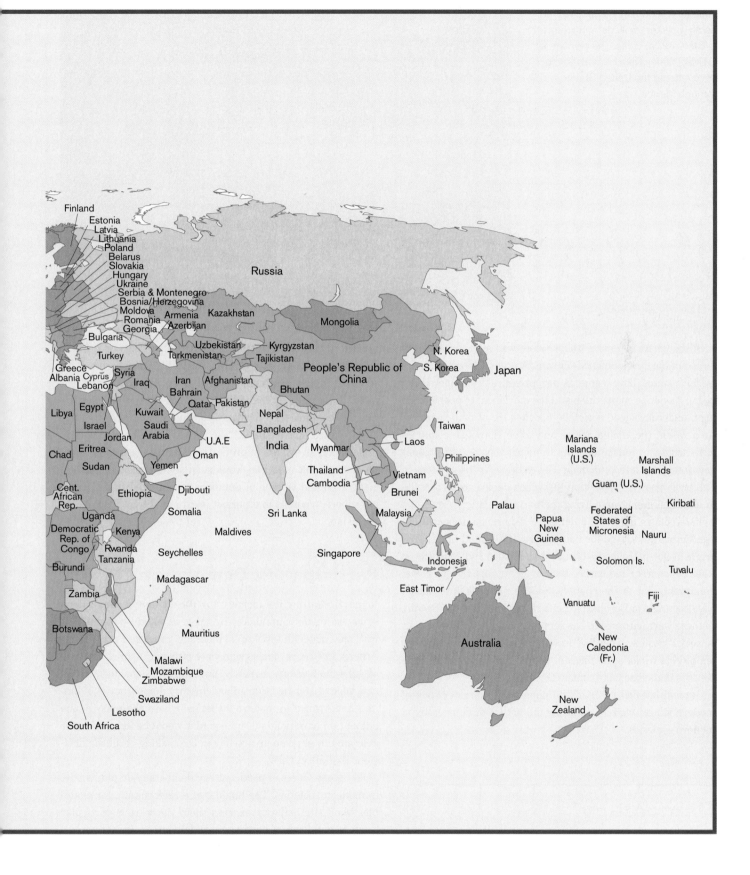

Inmates wear orange jumpsuits in a holding center for illegal immigrants in Brownsville, Texas. The men are all OTMs ("Other Than Mexican") who have entered the United States through Mexico.

Although an extensive welfare state was seen as the culmination of the development of citizenship rights, in recent years welfare states have come under pressure from increasing global economic competition and the movement of people from poor, underdeveloped societies to richer, developed countries. As a result, the United States and some European countries have sought to reduce benefits to noncitizens and to prevent new immigrants from coming. For example, in 1994 voters in California passed Proposition 187, which denied social benefits to all illegal immigrants living there. At the national level, the welfare reform act of 1996 denied a wide range of benefits to *legal* immigrants. And for many years, the United States government has patrolled its border with Mexico and constructed walls of concrete and barbed wire in an attempt to keep illegal immigrants out of the country. Similar patterns of exclusion have occurred in Europe, particularly in Germany and Britain. In these ways, citizenship has served as a powerful instrument of social closure, whereby prosperous nation-states have attempted to exclude the migrant poor from the status and the benefits that citizenship confers (Brubaker, 1992).

Having learned some of the important characteristics of modern states, we now consider the nature of democracy in modern societies.

Democracy

The word *democracy* has its roots in the Greek term *demokratia*, the individual parts of which are *demos* ("people") and *kratos* ("rule"), and its basic meaning is therefore a political system in which the people, not monarchs (kings or queens) or aristocracies (people of noble birth like lords), rule. This sounds simple and straightforward, but it is not. What does it mean to be ruled by the people? The answer to that question has taken contrasting forms, at varying periods and in different societies. For example, "the people" have been variously understood as owners of property, white men, educated men, men, and adult men and women. In some societies, the officially accepted version of **democracy** is limited to the political sphere, whereas in others, it is extended to other areas of social life.

Participatory Democracy

In **participatory democracy** (or **direct democracy**), decisions are made communally by those affected by them. This was the original type of democracy practiced in ancient Athens, in Greece. Those who were citizens, a small minority of Athenian society, regularly assembled to consider policies and make major decisions. Participatory democracy is of limited importance in modern societies, where the mass of the population have political rights and it would be impossible for everyone to participate actively in the making of all the decisions that affect them.

Yet some facets of participatory democracy do play a part in modern societies. The holding of a referendum, for example, when the majority express their views on a particular issue, is one form of participatory democracy. Direct consultation of large numbers of people is made possible by simplifying the issue down to one or two questions to be answered. Referenda are regularly used at the national level in some European countries. They are also employed frequently on a state level in the United States to decide controversial issues. Another element of participatory democracy, a meeting of the whole community, is found at the local level—for example, in some townships in New England.

Monarchies and Liberal Democracies

Some modern states (e.g., Britain and Belgium) still have monarchs, but these are few and far between. Where traditional rulers of this sort are still found, their real power is usually limited or non-existent. In a tiny number of countries, such as Saudi Arabia and Jordan, monarchs continue to hold some degree of control over government, but in most cases they are symbols of national identity rather than personages having any direct power in political life. The queen of England, the king of Sweden, and even the emperor of Japan are all **constitutional monarchs:** Their real power is severely restricted by the constitution, which vests authority in the elected representatives of the people. The vast majority of modern states are republican—there is no king or queen; almost every one, including constitutional monarchies, professes adherence to democracy.

Countries in which voters can choose between two or more parties and in which the mass of the adult population has the right to vote are usually called **liberal democracies**. The United States, the Western European countries, Japan, Aus-

tralia, and New Zealand all fall into this category. Some developing countries, such as India, also have liberal democratic systems.

The Spread of Liberal Democracy

For much of the twentieth century, the political systems of the world were divided primarily between liberal democracy and communism, as found in the former Soviet Union (and which still exists in China, Cuba, and North Korea). **Communism** was essentially a system of one-party rule. Voters were given a choice not between different parties but between different candidates of the same party—the Communist party; sometimes only one candidate ran. There people had no real choice at all. The Communist party was easily the dominant power in Soviet-style societies: It controlled not just the political system but the economy as well.

Since 1989, when the hold of the Soviet Union over Eastern Europe was broken, processes of democratization have swept across the world in a sort of chain-reaction process. The number of democratic nations almost doubled between 1989 and 1999 from 66 to 117. Countries such as Nicaragua in Central America and Zambia and South Africa in Africa have established liberal democratic governments. In China, which holds about a fifth of the world's population, the communist government is facing strong pressures toward democratization. During the 1990s, thousands of people remained in prison in China for the nonviolent expression of

A "smart mob" converges in Central Park, makes bird calls at passing pedestrians, and then disperses after eight minutes. These events are organized entirely through the Internet and e-mail.

The Wave of Democracy

When political sociologists of the future look back on the 1980s and 1990s, one historical development in particular is likely to stand out: the democratization of many of the world's nations. Since the early 1980s, a number of countries in Latin America, such as Chile, Bolivia, and Argentina, have undergone the transition from authoritarian military rule to democracy. Similarly, with the collapse of the Communist bloc in 1989, many East European states—Russia, Poland, and the former Czechoslovakia, for example—have become democratic, adopting written constitutions, working to ensure that disputes will be resolved according to the rule of law, and, most important, holding popular elections. The resignation of the Indonesian dictator Suharto in 1998 following weeks of massive popular protest raised hopes that democratic forces will also come to prevail in that country, perhaps spurring the democratization of other Southeast Asian states. And in Africa, a number of previously undemocratic nations—including Benin, Ghana, Mozambique, and South Africa—have come to embrace democratic ideals. According to one recent estimate, 66 percent of the world's nations now rely on electoral processes to select their leaders (Schwartzman, 1998).

Although a full explanation for these developments would require a detailed analysis of the social and political situations in each country that led up to the transition to democracy, there can be little doubt but that globalizing processes played an important role in this most recent wave of democratization.

First, the growing number of cross-national cultural contacts that globalization has brought with it has invigorated democratic movements in many countries. Globalized media, along with advances in communications technology, have exposed inhabitants of many nondemocratic nations to democratic ideals, in-

their desire for democracy. But some groups, resisted by the Communist government, are still working actively to secure a transition to a democratic system.

Why has democracy become so popular? The reasons have to do with the social and economic changes discussed throughout this book. First, democracy tends to be associated with competitive capitalism in the economic system, and capitalism has shown itself to be superior to communism as a wealth-generating system. Second, the more social activity becomes globalized and people's daily lives become influenced by events happening far away, the more they start to push for information about how they are ruled—and therefore for greater democracy (Huntington, 1991).

Third is the influence of mass communications, particularly television. The chain reaction of the spread of democracy has probably been greatly affected by the visibility of events in the world today. With the coming of new television technologies, particularly satellite and cable, governments can't maintain control over what their citizens see, as noted in the earlier discussion of the former Yugoslavia.

THE INTERNET AND DEMOCRATIZATION

The Internet is another powerful democratizing force. It transcends national and cultural borders, facilitates the spread of ideas around the globe, and allows like-minded people to find creasing internal pressure on political elites to hold elections. Of course, such pressure does not automatically result from the diffusion of the notion of popular sovereignty. More important is that with globalization, news of democratic revolutions and accounts of the mobilizing processes that lead to them are quickly spread on a regional level. News of the revolution in Poland in 1989, for example, took little time to travel to Hungary, providing prodemocracy activists there with a useful, regionally appropriate model around which to orient their work.

Second, international organizations such as the United Nations and the European Union—which, in a globalized world, come to play an increasingly important role—have put external pressure on nondemocratic states to move in democratic directions. In some cases, these organizations have been able to use trade embargoes, the conditional provision of loans for economic development and stabilization, and diplomatic maneuvers of various kinds to encourage the dismantling of authoritarian regimes.

Third, democratization has been facilitated by the expansion of world capitalism. Although transnational corporations are notorious for striking deals with dictators, corporations generally prefer to do business in democratic states—not because of an inherent philosophical preference for political freedom and equality, but because democracies tend to be more stable than other kinds of states, and stability and predictability are essential for maximizing profits. Because political, economic, and military elites, particularly in the developing world and in the former Soviet Union, are often anxious to increase levels of international trade and to encourage transnationals to set up shop in their countries, they have sometimes pursued a democratic agenda of their own, leading to what the political sociologist Barrington Moore, Jr., once called "revolutions from above."

It is true that if globalization were the sole cause of the most recent wave of democratization, all countries today would be democratic. The persistence of authoritarian regimes in such countries as China, Cuba, and Nigeria suggests that globalizing forces are not always sufficient to force a transition to democracy. But democratic moves are afoot even in several of these countries, leading some sociologists to believe that under the influence of globalization, many more nations will become democratic in the years to come.

one another in the realm of cyberspace. More and more people in countries around the world access the Internet regularly and consider it to be important to their lifestyles.

One prominent example of the political role of the Internet is provided by MoveOn.org, a liberal organization that was originally created by the twenty-two-year-old activist Eli Pariser and software entrepreneurs Wes Boyd and Joan Blades to electronically mobilize opposition to the impeachment of former President Bill Clinton. Today MoveOn.org claims 2 million members. It has organized "smart mobs" around other issues, playing a key role in convincing Congress to defeat the proposed Terrorism Awareness Information Program, which would have enabled the government to

collect extensive electronic information on private citizens. In December 2003 it organized some twenty-two hundred simultaneous "house parties" throughout the United States, where a documentary opposed to the Iraq war was viewed by tens of thousands of people. The organization collects millions of dollars through its Web site in support of liberal causes and has attracted some big-money contributors as well: the billionaires George Soros and Peter Lewis together gave the fledgling organization $5 million in late 2003 (Neuman, 2003; Brownstein, 2003; Menn, 2003; Avins, 2003).

Yet as we shall see, political indifference and voter apathy are extremely high in the United States, and winning federal elections requires large sums of money that are unlikely to be raised through small online contributions. How "Internet democracy" plays itself out in the national political arena will depend not only on technology, but on the ability of grassroots efforts to make a real difference in political outcomes.

Democracy in the United States

POLITICAL PARTIES

A political party is an organization of individuals with broadly similar political aims, oriented toward achieving legitimate control of government through an electoral process. Two parties tend to dominate the political system where elections are based on the principle of winner take all, as in the United States. Where elections are based on different principles, as in proportional representation (in which seats in a representative assembly are allocated according to the proportions of the vote attained), five or six different parties, or even more, may be represented in the assembly. When they lack an overall majority, some of the parties have to form a coalition—an alliance with each other to form a government.

In the United States, the system has become effectively a two-party one between the Republicans and Democrats, although no formal restriction is placed on the number of political parties. The nation's founders made no mention of parties in the Constitution because they thought that party conflict might threaten the unity of the new republic.

Two-party systems such as that of the United States tend to lead to a concentration on the "middle ground," where most votes are to be found, excluding more radical views. The parties in these countries often cultivate a moderate image and sometimes come to resemble one another so closely that the choice they offer is relatively slight. A plurality of interests may supposedly be represented by each party but can become blended into a bland program with few distinctive policies. Multiparty systems allow divergent interests and points of view to be expressed more directly and provide scope for the representation of radical alternatives. Green party representatives or representatives of far right parties, found in some European parliaments, are cases in point. On the other hand, no one party is likely to achieve an overall majority, and the government by coalition that results can lead to indecision and stalemate if compromises can't be worked out or to a rapid succession of elections and new governments, none able to stay in power for long.

POLITICS AND VOTING

Building mass support for a party in the United States is difficult, because the country is so large and includes so many different regional, cultural, and ethnic groups. The parties have each tried to develop their electoral strength by forging broad regional bases of support and by campaigning for very general political ideals.

As measured by their levels of membership, party identification, and voting support, each of the major American parties is in decline (Wattenberg, 1996). One study showed that the numbers declaring themselves to be "independent" of either party grew from 22 percent in 1952 to over 39 percent in 2003.

In recent years, Democrats have also lost ground to Republicans: Although Democrats held an edge in party identification during the Clinton years, by the end of 2003 roughly the same number of Americans (30–31 percent) identified with both parties. Moreover, Democrats and Republicans have become increasingly polarized in the past few years. For example, Republicans are much more likely to favor an assertive national security strategy, whereas Democrats are increasingly critical of business and more likely to favor stronger government support for the poor (Wattenberg, 1996; Pew, 2003).

Since the early 1960s the proportion of the population that turns out to vote in the United States has steadily decreased, to the point where today only slightly more than half the electorate votes in presidential elections. The turnout for congressional elections is lower still—around 40 percent (NES, 2003). The presidential election of 2004 bucked this declining trend with voter turnout levels of nearly 59 percent, the highest since the election of 1968. The spike in the number of voters is attributed to campaigns by both parties to mobilize their core constituencies. Furthermore, there are significant differences in turnout by race and ethnicity, age, educational attainment, and income. Turnout is highest among whites and lowest among Hispanics, with blacks and Asian Americans in between. Generally, turnout increases directly with age: Only a little more than a third of all voters in the eighteen-to-twenty-four age group bothered to vote for president in 2000, compared with nearly three-quarters of voters in their sixties. However, in the 2004 presidential election, the number of young voters swelled due to a highly organized voter mobilization campaign. Nearly 52 percent of voters under thirty voted in the election. Education also makes a major difference in voting behavior: Fewer than two in five persons who lack a high school diploma voted in 2000, compared with four out of five with college degrees. Education is, of course, strongly related to income: Turnout was only about a third among persons earning under $5,000, rising to three quarters among those earning over $75,000.

Voter turnout in the United States is among the world's lowest. Sweden's International Institute for Democracy and

Electoral Assistance tracked voter turnout in all countries that held national elections at any time during the period 1945–2002 by comparing the number of voters with the total voting-age population. According to their study, voter turnout in the United States averaged only 48 percent overall, earning it 138th place (out of 169 countries). By way of comparison, voter turnout in Europe over the same period averaged 74 percent; Asia, 70 percent; South America, 62 percent; Mexico, Central America, and the Caribbean, 60 percent; and Africa, 55 percent (Pintor and Gratschew, 2002).

Why is voter turnout so low in the United States? Many studies have found that countries with high rates of literacy, high average incomes, and well-established political freedoms and civil liberties are likely to have high voter turnouts. Yet the United States ranks high on all of these measures, but still fails to motivate people to vote. Compulsory registration is common throughout Europe, and registration is often made easy. In the United States, where voters are required to register well in advance of elections, many fail to do so and are thus disqualified from voting. Not only is registration often compulsory elsewhere, but so too is compulsory voting, now practiced by thirty-three countries. Even though enforcement is often weak or nonexistent, voter turnout tends to be higher where voting is mandated by law (Pintor and Gratschew, 2002).

Another possible reason is that since "winner-take-all"-type elections discourage the formation of third parties, voters may sometimes feel that they lack effective choices when it comes time to vote. A staunch environmentalist may decide there is no point in voting if the Green party candidate has no real chance of winning a seat in Congress; the strong antigovernment voter may draw the same conclusion with regard to the Libertarian party's chances. In many countries (including most European countries), some system of proportional representation is practiced, under which parties receive seats in proportion to the vote they get in electoral districts. Thus, for example, if a district has ten seats in Parliament, and the Conservative party gets 30 percent of the vote, that district would send three representatives to Parliament. Under this system, even small parties can often muster sufficient support to elect one or two representatives. When voters experience a wider range of choices, they are more likely to vote.

Finally, the range of elections is much more extensive in the United States than in other Western societies. In no other country is such a variety of offices at all levels—including sheriffs, judges, city treasurers, and many other posts—open to election. Americans are entitled to do about three or four times as much electing as citizens elsewhere. Low rates of voter turnout thus have to be balanced against the wider extent of voter choice.

INTEREST GROUPS

Interest groups and lobbying play a distinctive part in American politics. An **interest group** is any organization that attempts to influence elected officials to consider their aims when deciding on legislation. The American Medical Association, the National Organization for Women, and the National Rifle Association are but three examples. Interest groups vary in size; some are national; others statewide. Some are permanently organized; others are short lived. *Lobbying* is the act of contacting influential officials to present arguments to convince them to vote in favor of a cause or otherwise lend support to the aims of an interest group. The word *lobby* originated in the British parliamentary system. In days past, members of Parliament did not have offices, so their business was conducted in the lobbies of the Parliament buildings.

To run as a candidate is enormously expensive, and interest groups provide much of the funding at all levels of political office. In the 2000 presidential election, for example, the Republican ticket (Bush-Cheney) raised nearly $200 million; the Democrats (Gore-Lieberman) nearly $135 million (CRP, 2003). Even to run for the House or Senate costs a small fortune. It

Vice President Dick Cheney, center, accepts a rifle from National Rifle Association President Kayne Robinson, right, and NRA Vice President Wayne R. LaPierre, after concluding his keynote address to the annual NRA convention in 2004.

cost about a half million dollars to run for the House of Representatives in 2002, and about $3 million to run for Senate. The most expensive congressional race in history, when Hillary Rodham Clinton (Democrat) beat Rick Lazio (Republican) in the battle to become a senator from New York in 2000, saw a total spending of $70.5 million. By 2002, total spending for all congressional races had reached nearly $1.4 billion (FEC data 6/9/03; CRP, 2003b).

In the 2002 congressional election, 383 out of 390 incumbents running for reelection to the House of Representatives beat out their challengers—a stunning 98 percent success rate. Incumbents have an enormous advantage in soliciting money. In the 2002 race for the House, for example, they raised eight times as much money as their challengers (Common Cause, 2002a). Incumbents are favored as fund-raisers partly because they can curry favor with special interests and other contributors, since they are in a position to assure favorable votes on issues of importance to their funders, as well as obtain spending on pet projects and other "pork" for their districts. Incumbency also provides familiarity—a formidable obstacle for most challengers to overcome. The cost of beating an incumbent has increased significantly in the last quarter century (see Figure 13.1), which is perhaps why 43 percent of all newly elected congressional representatives in 2002

were millionaires—a distinction held by only 1 percent of the American public. (At least 40 percent of all senators are also millionaires.)

About a third of the funding in congressional or senatorial elections comes from political action committees (PACs), which are set up by interest groups to raise and distribute campaign funds. During the 1999–2000 election cycle, PACs made forty-five hundred contributions totaling $579.4 million (Federal Election Commission, 2001). Interest groups and PACs not only help elect candidates—they also influence the outcome of votes in Congress. The Medicare Reform Act of 2003, which creates a $400 billion program to extend prescription drug benefits to the elderly, was heavily pushed by the pharmaceutical industry, which since 1996 has spent more than a half a billion dollars to lobby Congress, the White House, and federal regulators, as well as to launch advertising campaigns aimed at the general public (Common Cause, 2003). Although the long-run benefit to the elderly was hotly debated by members of Congress, there is no question that drug companies will reap considerable benefit.

In 2002 Congress passed the McCain-Feingold campaign finance reform law, which severely restricted the ability to make unlimited campaign contributions. Under federal laws,

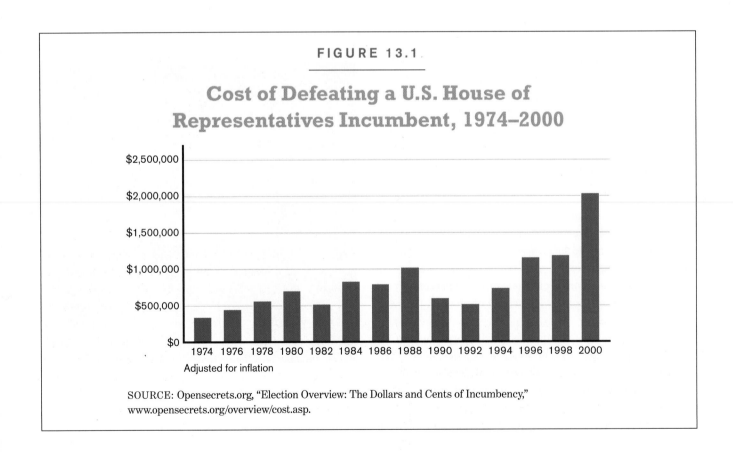

FIGURE 13.1

Cost of Defeating a U.S. House of Representatives Incumbent, 1974–2000

Adjusted for inflation

SOURCE: Opensecrets.org, "Election Overview: The Dollars and Cents of Incumbency," www.opensecrets.org/overview/cost.asp.

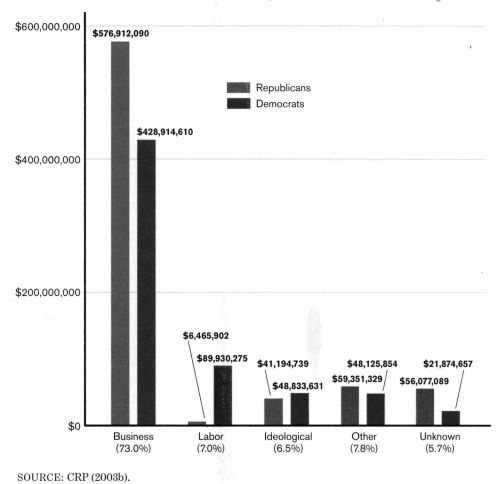

FIGURE 13.2

Business-Labor-Ideology Split in PAC,
Soft, and Individual Donations to
Candidates and Parties, 2002 Election Cycle

Republicans
Democrats

$576,912,090
$428,914,610
$6,465,902
$89,930,275
$41,194,739
$48,833,631
$48,125,854
$59,351,329
$56,077,089
$21,874,657

| Business (73.0%) | Labor (7.0%) | Ideological (6.5%) | Other (7.8%) | Unknown (5.7%) |

SOURCE: CRP (2003b).

some dating back a century, corporations and labor unions are prohibited from contributing to federal campaigns. Legal loopholes, however, permit unlimited "soft-money" contributions to be made to the political parties' "nonfederal accounts," supposedly destined for "party-building" activities unrelated to federal campaigns. In fact, almost all of the money finds its way back into presidential and congressional elections, reaching nearly a half a billion dollars in 2001–2002 (Common Cause, 2002b). The McCain-Feingold law, which was upheld as constitutional in a landmark Supreme Court decision in December 2003, closes the loophole. Candidates for federal elections are once again restricted to raising money from individuals—two thousand dollars per candidate, twenty-five thousand dollars to political parties. However, campaigns have already found a loophole, 527 organizations. These groups are political organizations that typically engage in campaigning and lobbying for candidates and are funded by unlimited soft-money donations. They cannot coordinate their actions with any of the candidates, but they typically support one party or the other. In the 2004 presidential campaign, 527s like MoveOn.org and the Swift Vets and POWs for Truth spent nearly $400 million.

The Political Participation of Women

Voting has a special meaning for women against the background of their long struggle to obtain universal suffrage. The members of the early women's movements saw the vote both as the symbol of political freedom and as the means of achieving greater economic and social equality. In the United States, where the attempts by women to gain voting rights were more active, and often provoked violence, women's leaders underwent considerable hardships to reach this end. Even today, in many countries, women do not have the same voting rights as men.

Women's obtaining the vote has not greatly altered the nature of politics. Women's voting patterns, like those of men, are shaped by party preferences, policy options, and the choice of available candidates. The influence of women on politics cannot be assessed solely through voting patterns, however. Feminist groups have made an impact on political life independently of the franchise, particularly in recent decades. Since the early 1960s, the National Organization for Women (NOW) and other women's groups in the United States have played a significant role in the passing of equal opportunity acts and have pressed for a range of issues directly affecting women to be placed on the political agenda. Such issues include equal rights at work, the availability of abortion, changes in family and divorce laws, and lesbian rights. In 1973, women achieved a legal victory when the Supreme Court ruled in *Roe v. Wade* that women had a legal right to abortion. The 1989 Court ruling in *Webster v. Reproductive Health Services*, which placed restrictions on that right, resulted in a resurgence of involvement in the women's movement.

Yet in general, as in so many other sectors of social life, women are poorly represented among political elites. Following the 2002 midterm elections in the United States, there were fifty-nine female members in the House of Representatives in 2003, making up just under 14 percent of the total membership. This number has almost tripled since the early 1970s, but it is still not representative of the number of female citizens. In 2003 there were only thirteen women in the Senate, representing 13 percent of those sitting in the upper chamber.

What is surprising about the figures on women's involvement at the higher levels of political organizations is not this lack of representation itself, but the slowness with which things seem to be changing. In the business sector, men still monopolize the top positions, but women are now making more inroads into the strongholds of male privilege than previously. As yet at least, this does not seem to be happening in the political sphere—in spite of the fact that nearly all political parties today are nominally committed to securing equal opportunities for women and men. Since 1990, female candidates for political office have been successful *when they have run for office.* The critical factor seems to be that political parties (which are largely run by men) have not recruited as many women to run for office.

From considering the position of women in politics, we now broaden our scope to look at some basic ideas of political power. First, we take up the issue of who actually holds the reins of power, drawing on comparative materials to help illuminate the discussion. We then consider whether democratic governments around the world are "in crisis."

Who Rules? Theories of Democracy

DEMOCRATIC ELITISM

One of the most influential views of the nature and limits of modern democracy was set out by Max Weber and, in rather modified form, by the economist Joseph Schumpeter (1983). The ideas they developed are sometimes referred to as the theory of **democratic elitism**.

Weber began from the assumption that direct democracy is impossible as a means of regular government in large-scale societies. This is not only for the obvious logistical reason that millions of people cannot meet to make political decisions, but because running a complex society demands *expertise*. Participatory democracy, Weber believed, can only succeed in small organizations in which the work to be carried out is fairly simple and straightforward. Where more complicated decisions have to be made, or policies worked out, even in modest-sized groups—such as a small business firm—specialized knowledge and skills are necessary. Experts have to carry out their jobs on a continuous basis; positions that require expertise cannot be subject to the regular election of people who may only have a vague knowledge of the necessary skills and information. While higher officials, responsible for overall policy decisions, are elected, there must be a large substratum of full-time bureaucratic officials who play a large part in running a country (Weber, 1979).

Weber placed a great deal of emphasis on the importance of *leadership* in democracy—which is why his view is referred to as "democratic elitism." He argued that rule by elites is inevitable; the best we can hope for is that those elites effectively represent our interests and that they do so in an innovative and insightful fashion. Parliaments and congresses provide a breeding ground for capable political leaders able to counter the influence of bureaucracy and to command mass support. Weber valued multiparty democracy more for the quality of leadership it generates than for the mass participation in politics it makes possible.

Joseph Schumpeter fully agreed with Weber about the limits of mass political participation. For Schumpeter, as for Weber, democracy is more important as a method of generating effective and responsible government than as a means of providing significant power for the majority. Democracy cannot offer more than the possibility of replacing a given political leader or party by another. Democracy, Schumpeter stated, is the rule of *the politician*, not *the people*. Politicians are "dealers in votes" much as brokers are dealers in shares on the stock exchange. To achieve voting support, however, politicians must be at least minimally responsive to the demands and interests of the electorate. Only if there is some degree of competition to secure votes can arbitrary rule effectively be avoided.

PLURALIST THEORIES

The ideas of Weber and Schumpeter influenced some of the **pluralist theories of modern democracy**, although the pluralists developed their ideas somewhat differently. According to the pluralist view, government policies in a democracy are influenced by continual processes of bargaining among numerous groups representing different interests—business organizations, trade unions, ethnic groups, environmental organizations, religious groups, and so forth. A democratic political order is one in which there is a balance among competing interests, all having some impact on policy but none dominating the actual mechanisms of government. Elections are also influenced by this situation, for to achieve a broad enough base of support to lay claim to government, parties must be responsive to numerous diverse interest groups. The United States, it is held, is the most pluralistic of industrialized societies and, therefore, the most democratic. Competition between diverse interest groups occurs not only at the national level but within the states and in the politics of local communities.

THE POWER ELITE

The view suggested by C. Wright Mills in his celebrated work *The Power Elite* is quite different from pluralist theories (Mills, 1956). Mills argues that during the course of the twentieth century a process of institutional centralization occurred in the political order, the economy, and the sphere of the military. Not only has each of these spheres become more centralized, according to Mills, but they have become increasingly merged with one another to form a unified system of power. Those who are in the highest positions in all three institutional areas come from similar social backgrounds, have parallel interests, and often know one another on a personal basis. They have become a single **power elite** that runs the country—and, given the international position of the United States, also influences a great deal of the rest of the world.

The power elite, in Mills's portrayal, is composed mainly of white Anglo-Saxon Protestants (WASPs). Many are from wealthy families, have been to the same prestigious universities, belong to the same clubs, and sit on government committees with one another. They have closely connected concerns. Business and political leaders work together, and both have close relationships with the military through weapons contracting and the supply of goods for the armed forces. There is a great deal of movement among top positions in the three spheres. Politicians have business interests; business leaders often run for public office; higher military personnel sit on the boards of the large companies.

Since Mills published his study, numerous other research investigations have analyzed the social background and interconnections of leading figures in the various spheres of American society (Dye, 1986). All studies agree on the finding that the social backgrounds of those in leading positions are highly unrepresentative of the population as a whole (Domhoff, 1971, 1979, 1983, 1998).

THE ROLE OF THE MILITARY

Mills's argument that the military plays a central role in the power elite was buttressed by a well-known warning from a former military hero and U.S. president, Dwight David Eisenhower. In his farewell presidential speech in 1961, Eisenhower—who was the supreme commander of the Allied forces in Europe in World War II—warned of the dangers of what he termed the "military-industrial complex." As Eisenhower bluntly put it, "The conjunction of an immense military establishment and a large arms industry is new in the American experience. In the councils of government, we must guard against the acquisition of unwarranted influence, whether sought or unsought, by the military-industrial complex. The potential for the disastrous rise of misplaced power exists and will persist" (Eisenhower Library, 1961).

With the collapse of the Soviet Union in 1991, the United States has emerged as the world's unrivaled military superpower, accounting for nearly half of total military spending—more than the next fifteen countries combined (Table 13.1). In 1989, at the end of the cold war, U.S. defense spending—which had reached $300 billion in that year—began to decline slightly. But the decline was short lived. There turned out to be no "peace dividend" to spend on improving schools, repairing highways, or other domestic needs. By 2001 military spending once again topped $300 billion. It reached $400 billion in 2004, and is projected at $500 billion in 2009, for a total of $2.3 trillion in military spending over the next five years—figures that do not include the cost of military operations in Afghanistan and Iraq (CDI, 2003).

The global "war on terror," discussed below, has instead triggered yet another cycle of military spending. Eisenhower's dire warning seems no less true today than when he uttered it some fifty years ago.

TABLE 13.1

World's Fifteen Largest Military Budgets

RANK	COUNTRY	AMOUNT (BILLIONS)	PERCENT WORLD SHARE
1	United States	$399.1	45.9
2	Russia[a]	$65.0	7.5
3	China[a]	$47.0	5.4
4	Japan	$42.6	4.9
5	United Kingdom	$38.4	4.4
6	France	$29.5	3.4
7	Germany	$24.9	2.9
8	Saudi Arabia	$21.3	2.4
9	Italy	$19.4	2.2
10	India	$15.6	1.8
11	South Korea	$14.1	1.6
12	Brazil[a]	$10.7	1.2
13	Taiwan[a]	$10.7	1.2
14	Israel	$10.6	1.2
15	Spain	$8.4	1.0
Subtotal	(top 15)	$749.7	86.1
World		$870.0	100.0

[a]Figures are for 2001–2003, depending on availability; world total estimated; expenditures used were significantly higher than budget estimates.

SOURCE: Hellman, 2003.

Democracy in Trouble?

As liberal democracy is becoming so widespread, we might expect it to be highly successful. Yet such is not the case. Democracy almost everywhere is in some difficulty. This is not only because it is proving difficult to set up a stable democratic order in Russia and other erstwhile communist societies. Democracy is in trouble in its main countries of origin—the United States is a good example. The numbers of people voting in presidential and other elections have been in decline for some while. In surveys, many people say they don't trust politicians and regard most of them as tricksters.

Forty years ago (in 1964), confidence in government was fairly high: Nearly four out of five people answered "most of the time" or "just about always" when asked, "How much of the time do you trust the government in Washington to do the right thing?" This level of confidence then dropped

steadily for the next twenty years, rising somewhat in the 1980s, then dropping to a low of one in five in 1994. Since that time the level of reported trust has increased steadily. Today—bolstered by an increased confidence in government following the attacks of September 11, 2001—a solid majority of Americans (about three out of every five) report that they trust the government "most of the time" or "just about always."

Of those expressing continuing trust in government, most vote in presidential elections; of those who lack trust, most do not vote. As we have seen, younger people have less interest in electoral politics than older generations have, although the young have a greater interest than their elders in issues like the environment (Nye, 1997). Some have argued that trends like these indicate that people are increasingly skeptical of traditional forms of authority. Connected to this has been a shift in political values in democratic nations from "scarcity values" to "post-materialist values" (Inglehart, 1997). This means that after a certain level of economic prosperity has been reached, voters become concerned less with economic issues than with the quality of their individual (as opposed to collective) lifestyles, such as the desire for meaningful work. As a result, voters are generally less interested in national politics, except for areas involving personal liberty.

The last few decades have also been a period in which, in several Western countries, the welfare state has come under attack. Rights and benefits, fought for over long periods, have been contested and cut back. Rightist parties have attempted to reduce levels of welfare expenditure in their countries. Even in states led by socialist governments, such as Spain, commitment to government provision of public resources has been restricted. One reason for this governmental retrenchment is the declining revenues available to governments as a result of the general world recession that began in the early 1970s. Yet an increasing skepticism also seems to have developed, shared not only by some governments but by many of their citizens, about the effectiveness of relying on the state for the provision of many essential goods and services. This skepticism is based on the belief that the welfare state is bureaucratic, alienating, and inefficient, and that welfare benefits can create perverse consequences that undermine what they were designed to achieve (Giddens, 1998).

Why are so many people dissatisfied with the very political system that seems to be sweeping all before it across the world? The answers, curiously, are bound up with the factors that have helped spread democracy—the impact of capitalism and the globalizing of social life. For instance, while capitalist economies have proved to generate more wealth than any other type of economic system, that wealth is unevenly distributed (see Chapter 7). And economic inequalities influence who votes, joins parties, and gets elected. Wealthy individuals and corporations back interest groups that lobby for elected officials to support their aims when deciding on legislation. Not being subject to election, interest groups are not accountable to the majority of the electorate.

We will also see that globalization makes a great deal of difference to our working lives; the nature of the work we do is being changed by forces of global economic competition.

Work and the Economy

Because politics and government are inextricably linked with economic life, we now turn our attention to the ways that work and the economy have changed, in order to place them in sociological perspective. **Work** may be defined as carrying out tasks that require the expenditure of mental and physical effort, which has as its objective the production of goods and services that cater to human needs. An **occupation**, or job, is work that is done in exchange for a regular wage, or salary. In all cultures, work is the basis of the economic system, or economy.

The study of economic institutions is of major importance in sociology, because the economy influences all segments of society and therefore social reproduction in general. Hunting and gathering, pastoralism, agriculture, industrialism—these different ways of gaining a livelihood have a fundamental influence on the lives people lead. The distribution of goods and variations in the economic position of those who produce them also strongly influence social inequalities of all kinds. Wealth and power do not inevitably go together, but in general the privileged in terms of wealth are also among the more powerful groups in a society.

In the remainder of this chapter, we will analyze the nature of work in modern societies and look at the major changes affecting economic life today. We will investigate the changing nature of industrial production, the ownership structure of large business corporations, and the changing nature of work itself. Modern industry, as has been stressed in other parts of this book, differs in a fundamental way from premodern systems of production, which were based above all on agriculture. Most people worked in the fields or cared for livestock. In modern societies, by contrast, only a tiny proportion of the population works in agriculture, and farming itself has become industrialized—it is carried on largely by means of machines rather than by human hands.

Modern industry is itself always changing—technological change is one of its main features. **Technology** refers to the harnessing of science to machinery to achieve greater productive efficiency. The nature of industrial production also changes in relation to wider social and economic influences. We focus on both technological and economic change, showing how these are transforming industry today.

The Social Significance of Work

To tackle these issues, we need to relate work to the broad contours of our society and to industrial organization as a whole. We often associate the notion of work with drudgery—with a set of tasks that we want to minimize and, if possible, escape from altogether. You may have this very thought in mind as you set out to read this chapter! Is this most people's attitude toward their work, and if so, why? We will try to find out in the following pages.

Work has more going for it than drudgery, or people would not feel so lost and disoriented when they become unemployed. How would you feel if you thought you would never get a job? In modern societies, having a job is important for maintaining self-esteem. Even where work conditions are relatively unpleasant, and the tasks involved dull, work tends to be a structuring element in people's psychological makeup and the cycle of their daily activities.

Unpaid Work

We often tend to think of work, as the notion of being "out of work" implies, as equivalent to having a paid job, but in fact this is an oversimplified view. Nonpaid labor (such as repairing one's own car or doing one's own housework) looms large in many people's lives. Many types of work do not conform to orthodox categories of paid employment. Much of the work done in the informal economy, for example, is not recorded in any direct way in the official employment statistics. The term **informal economy** refers to transactions outside the sphere of regular employment, sometimes involving the exchange of cash for services provided, but also often involving the direct exchange of goods or services.

Someone who comes to fix the television may be paid in cash, "off the books," without any receipt being given or details of the job recorded. People may exchange pilfered or stolen goods with friends or associates in return for other favors. The informal economy includes not only "hidden" cash transactions, but many forms of *self-provisioning* that people carry on inside and outside the home. Do-it-yourself activities and household appliances and tools, for instance, provide goods and services that would otherwise have to be purchased (Gershuny and Miles, 1983).

Housework, which has traditionally mostly been carried out by women, is usually unpaid. But it is work, often very hard and exhausting work, nevertheless. Volunteer work, for charities or other organizations, has an important social role. Having a paid job is important—but the category of "work" stretches more widely.

The Social Organization of Work

One of the most distinctive characteristics of the economic system of modern societies is the existence of a highly complex **division of labor:** Work has become divided into an enormous number of different occupations in which people specialize. In traditional societies, nonagricultural work entailed the mastery of a craft. Craft skills were learned through a lengthy period of apprenticeship, and the worker normally carried out all aspects of the production process from beginning to end. For example, a metalworker making a plow would forge the iron, shape it, and assemble the implement itself. With the rise of modern industrial production, most traditional crafts have disappeared altogether, replaced by skills that form part of more large-scale production processes. An electrician working in an industrial setting today, for instance, may inspect and repair only a few parts of one type of machine; different people will deal with the other parts and other machines.

The contrast in the division of labor between traditional and modern societies is truly extraordinary. Even in the largest traditional societies, there usually existed no more than twenty or thirty major craft trades, together with such specialized pursuits as merchant, soldier, and priest. In a modern industrial system, there are literally thousands of distinct occupations. The U.S. Census Bureau lists some twenty thousand distinct jobs in the American economy. In traditional communities, most of the population worked on farms and were economically self-sufficient. They produced their own food, clothes, and other necessities of life. One of the main features of modern societies, by contrast, is an enormous expansion of **economic interdependence**. We are all dependent on an immense number of other workers—today stretching right across the world—for the products and services that sustain our lives. With few exceptions, the vast majority of people in modern societies do not produce the food they eat, the houses in which they live, or the material goods they consume.

Industrial Work

Writing some two centuries ago, Adam Smith, one of the founders of modern economics, identified advantages that the division of labor provides in terms of increasing productivity. His most famous work, *The Wealth of Nations*, opens with a description of the division of labor in a pin factory. A person working alone could perhaps make 20 pins per day. By breaking down that worker's task into a number of simple operations, however, ten workers carrying out specialized jobs in collaboration with one another could collectively produce 48,000 pins per day. The rate of production per worker, in other words, is increased from 20 to 4,800 pins, each specialist operator producing 240 times more than when working alone.

More than a century later, these ideas reached their most developed expression in the writings of Frederick Winslow Taylor, an American management consultant. Taylor's approach to

One of Henry Ford's most significant innovations was the introduction of the assembly line, which allowed for mass production of the Model T.

what he called "scientific management" involved the detailed study of industrial processes in order to break them down into simple operations that could be precisely timed and organized.

Taylor's principles were appropriated by the industrialist Henry Ford. In 1908, Ford designed his first auto plant at Highland Park, Michigan, to manufacture only one product—the Model T Ford—thereby allowing the introduction of specialized tools and machinery designed for speed, precision, and simplicity of operation. One of Ford's most significant innovations was the introduction of the assembly line, said to have been inspired by Chicago slaughterhouses, in which animals were disassembled section by section on a moving conveyor belt. Each worker on Ford's assembly line was assigned a specialized task, such as fitting the left-side door handles as the car bodies moved along the line. By 1929, when production of the Model T ceased, over 15 million cars had been assembled.

Work and Alienation

Karl Marx was one of the first writers to grasp that the development of modern industry would reduce many people's work to dull, uninteresting tasks. According to Marx, the division of labor alienates human beings from their work. For Marx, **alienation** refers to feelings of indifference or hostility not only to work, but to the overall framework of industrial production within a capitalist setting.

In traditional societies, he pointed out, work was often exhausting—peasant farmers sometimes had to toil from dawn to dusk. Yet peasants held a real measure of control over their work, which required much knowledge and skill. Many industrial workers, by contrast, have little control over their jobs, only contribute a fraction to the creation of the overall product, and have no influence over how or to whom it is eventually sold. Work thus appears as something alien, a task that the worker must carry out in order to earn an income but that is intrinsically unsatisfying.

Industrial Conflict

There have long been conflicts between workers and those in economic and political authority over them. Riots against conscription and high taxes and food riots at periods of harvest failure were common in urban areas of Europe in the eighteenth century. These "premodern" forms of labor conflict continued up to not much more than a century ago in some countries. For example, there were food riots in several large Italian towns in 1868 (Geary, 1981). Such traditional forms of confrontation were not just sporadic, irrational outbursts of violence: The threat or use of violence had the effect of lower-

ing the price of grain and other essential foodstuffs (Rudé, 1964; Thompson, 1971; Booth, 1977).

Industrial conflict between workers and employers at first tended to follow these older patterns. In situations of confrontation, workers would quite often leave their places of employment and form crowds in the streets; they would make their grievances known through their unruly behavior or by engaging in acts of violence against the authorities. Workers in some parts of France in the late nineteenth century would threaten disliked employers with hanging (Holton, 1978). Use of the *strike* as a weapon, today commonly associated with organized bargaining between workers and management, developed only slowly and sporadically.

STRIKES

We can define a **strike** as a temporary stoppage of work by a group of employees in order to express a grievance or enforce a demand (Hyman, 1984).

Workers choose to go out on strike for many specific reasons. They may be seeking to gain higher wages, forestall a proposed reduction in their earnings, protest against technological changes that make their work duller or lead to layoffs, or obtain greater security of employment. However, in all these circumstances the strike is essentially a mechanism of power: a weapon of people who are relatively powerless in the workplace and whose working lives are affected by managerial decisions over which they have little or no control. It is usually a weapon of last resort, to be used when other negotiations have failed, because workers on strike either receive no income or depend on union funds, which might be limited.

This photo shows members of the Service Employees International Union picketing outside city hall in Los Angeles. The county workers, who include nurses and medical staff, library workers, and staff workers at the civic center, beaches, and harbors, are demanding raises, improved job security, and better benefits.

New Strategies for the Labor Movement

[***]

[***] How can labor be a leader in making the local and regional economic development policy that helps shape employer choice on competitive strategy work better for workers and the community? How can labor make that leadership part of and useful to its realization of broader political and organizing ambitions?

Like many local labor movements, Wisconsin labor has been struggling with these questions for years. And for years now, we at the Center on Wisconsin Strategy (COWS) have been working with Wisconsin's labor on a series of projects—among them the Wisconsin Regional Training Partnerships (WRTP) and Milwaukee Jobs Initiative (MJI), both centered in the Milwaukee metro area; and more recently the Jobs With a Future (JWF) project in the Madison metro area, an environment quite different from Milwaukee's—that attempt to answer them.

In different ways, all these projects are aimed simultaneously at upgrading the skills, wages, and career advancement

Joel Rogers

opportunities for workers near the bottom of the labor market; building industry competitiveness through modernization, better work force development practices, and other means; and increasing worker voice and power in firm and industry decision making. And all these projects are framed by a certain broader view of what labor needs to do to advance in today's economy—beginning with a clear definition of its role in the economy. In order to find the popular support and political cachet for its own advancement, labor has always needed to do big things for the broader society. This necessity has commonly meant solving problems that capital cannot solve on its own.

In the past, labor's signal contribution was to ensure "effective demand"—raising wage floors enough to promise investors markets for expanded production. These opportunities in turn increased the productivity of that output, which lowered the real cost of consumption goods, which could then be ever more widely purchased by better-paid workers in an unending upward spiral of living standards. But for a host of reasons, the conditions under which labor made that contribution have been undermined since the early 1970s. In proximate result, wages have stagnated or declined for most of the working population, inequality has soared, and even in that handful of industrial sectors that provided the foundation of postwar private-sector union power, that power has been drastically diminished. More immediately still, perhaps, labor has no clear function, beyond obstruction, in a fully marketized economy subject to increased competitive pressures.

This is the familiar starting point for the strategy considered here: to make labor again "part of the solution" to problems of industrial order. This time, however, we must focus as much on the supply side and framing conditions of that order (that is, the organization of production itself and the rules by which it is socially constrained) as on the demand side and the operation of internal labor markets. More specifically, labor must harness its residual strength and unique position in the economy to support

Laura Dresser

nections between the WRTP and the MJI have helped place more than 1,300 "disadvantaged" central city workers—including many former AFDC/TANF recipients—in jobs that more than doubled their previous year's earnings (from an average of $9,000 to $23,000 annually), while providing health insurance and clear opportunities for further advancement. Upon examination, this MJI/WRTP work may prove the most cost-effective job-training and welfare-to-work program in the country—in large measure because it starts with employer demand and commitment to working with the program rather than with the individual served by it—with among the highest rates of participant job retention.

[***]

New Directions

Looking to the future, the WRTP has several new items on its plate. Most important is replication in other sectors. With an RSA grant of its own from the U.S. Department of Labor, WRTP is creating new partnerships in construction, data networking, health care, hospitality, and transportation. While the specific needs of each industry differ, the basic steps are the same. First, steering committees of business and labor leaders have been formed in each sector, with an emphasis on coalition building and recruiting firms and unions. The next stage is that the committees develop strategic plans to meet the staffing and training needs of their industry, drawing on research and firm surveys. Pilot recruiting and training programs are then put in place and evaluated. Throughout, the fledgling partnerships are benefiting enormously from the groundwork already laid by the mature manufacturing partnership (such as ties to community colleges, public agencies, and community groups, and knowledge of public-funding streams).

[***]

a form of production—the "high road"—that is socially superior to present business practices. Such a high road would provide advantages to labor more or less immediately, but also further the interest of the broader society and even a significant share of capital itself. Specifically, labor helps to organize employers willing to take the high road to the point where they embark on it together to realize the efficiencies that come of their collective organization. In return for labor leadership, employers share some of that gain with labor—a sort of productivity bargaining, or rent-sharing, on a grand scale. This strategy also anticipates high-road employers' allying with labor against the most salient threat to them both: low-road firms and the public policies that support them. This arrangement, then, becomes the shared political program of a new "social partnership" between labor and capital: to close off the low road, to help build the high road, and to enable workers and firms now stuck on the first to be able to travel the second.

[***]

The aggregate results of the WRTP are impressive. Taken together, WRTP members have stabilized manufacturing employment in the Milwaukee metro area, and indeed contributed about 6,000 additional industrial jobs to it over the past five years. Among member firms, productivity is way up—exceeding productivity growth in nonmember firms. Once-stagnant wages are also up, and easily outpace wage growth outside the partnership. Individual firm commitment to training frontline workers is evident in direct training costs of some $20 million annually—an increase of almost that magnitude from prior levels. Direct training reaches some 6,000 workers (one-quarter of whom are people of color) each year. Because entry-level job requirements among member firms are known and broadly shared, moreover, the WRTP has been able to offer employment opportunities to those traditionally neglected in Milwaukee metro's labor market. Con-

SOURCE: Annett Bernhardt, Laura Dresser, and Joel Rogers, "Taking the High Road in Milwaukee: The Wisconsin Regional Training Partnership," *Working USA* 5, no. 3 (January 2002): 109.

ANNETT BERNHARDT, LAURA DRESSER, and JOEL ROGERS all work at the Center on Wisconsin Strategy (COWS), a research and policy center based at the University of Wisconsin that was instrumental in the creation of the Wisconsin Regional Training Partnership (WRTP) and still provides it with technical assistance and staffing. Bernhardt is a senior research associate at COWS; Dresser is the research director; Rogers is the director and also a professor of law, political science, and sociology at the university.

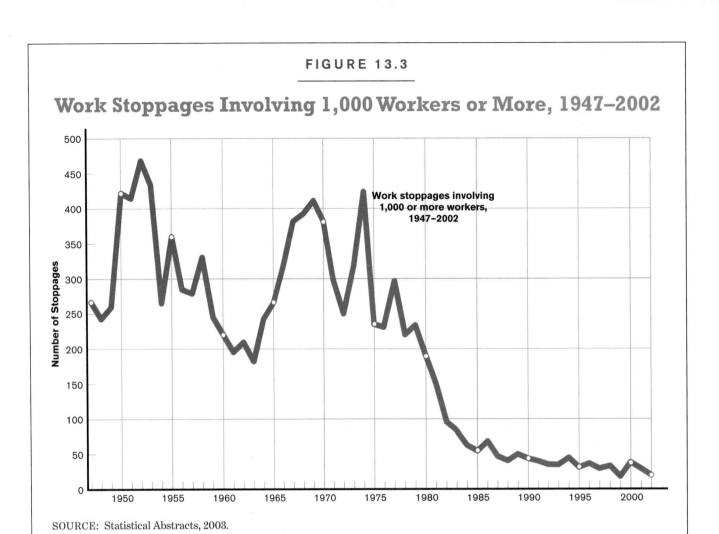

FIGURE 13.3

Work Stoppages Involving 1,000 Workers or More, 1947–2002

Work stoppages involving
1,000 or more workers,
1947–2002

Number of Stoppages

SOURCE: Statistical Abstracts, 2003.

Labor Unions

Although their levels of membership and the extent of their power vary widely, union organizations exist in all Western countries, which also all legally recognize the right of workers to strike in pursuit of economic objectives. In the early development of modern industry, workers in most countries had no political rights and little influence over the conditions of work in which they found themselves. Unions developed as a means of redressing the imbalance of power between workers and employers. Whereas workers had virtually no power as individuals, through collective organization their influence was considerably increased. An employer can do without the labor of any particular worker but not without that of all or most of the workers in a factory or plant. Unions originally were mainly "defensive" organizations, providing the means whereby workers could counter the overwhelming power that employers wielded over their lives.

After 1980, unions suffered declines across the advanced industrial countries. In the United States, the share of the work force belonging to unions declined from 23 percent in 1980 to under 13 percent in 2003 (Hirsch and Macpherson, 2004). There are several prominent explanations for the difficulties confronted by unions since 1980. Perhaps the most common is the decline of the older manufacturing industries and the rise of the service sector. Traditionally, manufacturing has been a stronghold for labor, whereas jobs in services are resistant to unionization. However, this explanation has recently come under scrutiny. The sociologist Bruce Western (1997) argues that such an explanation cannot account for the experience of the 1970s, which was generally (although not in the United States) a good period for unions and yet was also characterized by a structural shift from manufacturing to services. Similarly, a significant share of growth in service-sector employment has occurred in social services—typically public-sector union jobs. Therefore, Western argues that declines in unionization *within* manufacturing may be more significant than declines across sectors. Explanations that are consistent with the fall in union density within as well as among industries include: the recession in world economic activity, associated with high levels of unemployment, which weakens the bargaining position of labor; the increasing intensity of international competition, particularly from Far Eastern countries where wages are often lower than in the West; and the rise to power in many countries of rightist governments that launched an aggressive assault on unions in the 1980s.

Decline in union membership and influence is something of a general phenomenon in the industrialized countries and is not to be explained wholly in terms of political pressure applied by rightist governments against the unions. Unions usually become weakened during periods when unemployment is high, as has been the case for a considerable while in many Western countries. Trends toward more flexible production tend to diminish the force of unionism, which flourishes more extensively where many people are working together in large factories.

The Modern Economy

Modern societies are, in Marx's term, capitalistic. **Capitalism** is a way of organizing economic life that is distinguished by the following important features: private ownership of the means of production; profit as incentive; free competition for markets to sell goods, acquire cheap materials, and utilize cheap labor; and restless expansion and investment to accumulate capital. Capitalism, which began to spread with the growth of the Industrial Revolution in the early nineteenth century, is a vastly more dynamic economic system than any other that preceded it in history. Although the system has had many critics, such as Marx, it is now the most widespread form of economic organization in the world.

So far, we have been looking at industry mostly from the perspective of occupations and employees. We have studied how patterns of work have changed and the factors influencing the development of labor unions. But we have also to concern ourselves with the nature of the business firms in which the work force is employed. (It should be recognized that many people today are employees of government organizations, although we will not consider these here.) What is happening to business corporations today, and how are they run?

Corporations and Corporate Power

Since the turn of the twentieth century, modern capitalist economies have been more and more influenced by the rise of large business **corporations**. The share of total manufactur-ing assets held by the two hundred largest *manufacturing* firms in the United States has increased by 0.5 percent each year from 1900 to the present day; these two hundred corporations now control over half of all manufacturing assets. The two hundred largest *financial* organizations—banks, building societies, and insurance companies—account for more than half of all financial activity. There are numerous connections between large firms. For example, financial institutions hold well over 30 percent of the shares of the largest two hundred manufacturing firms.

Of course, there still exist thousands of smaller firms and enterprises within the American economy. In these companies, the image of the **entrepreneur**—the boss who owns and runs the firm—is by no means obsolete. The large corporations are a different matter. Ever since Adolf Berle and Gardiner Means published their celebrated study *The Modern Corporation and Private Property* seventy years ago, it has been accepted that most of the largest firms are not run by those who own them (Berle and Means, 1982). In theory, the large corporations are the property of their shareholders, who have the right to make all important decisions. But Berle and Means argued that since share ownership is so dispersed, actual control has passed into the hands of the managers who run firms on a day-to-day basis. *Ownership* of the corporations is thus separated from their *control*.

Whether they are run by owners or managers, the power of the major corporations is very extensive. When one or a handful of firms dominate in a given industry, they often cooperate in setting prices rather than freely competing with one another. Thus, the giant oil companies normally follow one another's lead in the price charged for gasoline. When one firm occupies a commanding position in a given industry, it is said to be in a **monopoly** position. More common is a situation of **oligopoly**, in which a small group of giant corporations predominate. In situations of oligopoly, firms are able more or less to dictate the terms on which they buy goods and services from the smaller firms that are their suppliers.

The emergence of the global economy has contributed to a wave of mergers and acquisitions on an unprecedented scale, which have created oligopolies in industries such as communications and media. In 1998, the German auto maker Daimler-Benz purchased Chrysler for $38 billion, and Exxon purchased the oil giant Mobil for $86 billion. In 1999, AT&T acquired the media corporation MediaOne for $5 billion to create the world's largest cable company. Also in 1999, CBS purchased Viacom for $35 billion. In 2000, Britian's Vodafone Airtouch took over Germany's Mannesmann for $130 billion in the world's largest hostile takeover. In that same year, Time Warner and the internet service provider America Online announced the largest merger in history—worth over $166 billion (PBS, 2003). As the global market becomes increasingly integrated, we are likely to see even more mergers and acquisitions on an even larger scale.

Types of Corporate Capitalism

There have been three general stages in the development of business corporations, although each overlaps with the others and all continue to coexist today. The first stage, characteristic of the nineteenth and early twentieth centuries, was dominated by **family capitalism**. Large firms were run either by individual entrepreneurs or by members of the same family and then passed on to their descendants. The famous corporate dynasties, such as the Rockefellers and Fords, belong in this category. These individuals and families did not just own a single large corporation, but held a diversity of economic interests and stood at the apex of economic empires.

Most of the big firms founded by entrepreneurial families have since become public companies—that is, shares of their stock are traded on the open market—and have passed into managerial control. In the large corporate sector, family capitalism was increasingly succeeded by **managerial capitalism**. As managers came to have more and more influence through the growth of very large firms, the entrepreneurial families were displaced. The result has been described as the replacement of the family in the company by the company itself. The corporation emerged as a more defined economic entity. In studying the two hundred largest manufacturing corporations in the United States, Michael Allen found that in cases where profit showed a decline, family-controlled enterprises were unlikely to replace their chief executive, but manager-controlled firms did so rapidly (Allen, 1981).

There is no question that managerial capitalism has left an indelible imprint on modern society. The large corporation drives not only patterns of consumption but also the experience of employment in contemporary society—it is difficult to imagine how the work lives of many Americans would be different in the absence of large factories or corporate bureaucracies. Sociologists have identified another area in which the large corporation has left a mark on modern institutions. **Welfare capitalism** refers to a practice that sought to make the corporation—rather than the state or trade unions—the primary shelter from the uncertainties of the market in modern industrial life. Beginning at the end of the nineteenth century, large firms began to provide certain services to their employees, including child care, recreational facilities, profit-sharing plans, paid vacations, and group life and unemployment insurance. These programs often had a paternalistic bent, such as that sponsoring "home visits" for the "moral education" of employees. Viewed in less benevolent terms, a major objective of welfare capitalism was coercion, as employers deployed all manner of tactics—including violence—to avoid unionization.

Despite the overwhelming importance of managerial capitalism in shaping the modern economy, many scholars now see the contours of a third, different phase in the evolution of the corporation emerging. They argue that managerial capitalism has today partly ceded place to **institutional capitalism**. This term refers to the emergence of a consolidated network of business leadership, concerned not only with decision making within single firms but also with the development of corporate power beyond them. Institutional capitalism is based on the practice of corporations holding shares in other firms. In effect, interlocking boards of directors exercise control over much of the corporate landscape. This reverses the process of increasing managerial control, since the managers' shareholdings are dwarfed by the large blocks of shares owned by other corporations. Rather than investing directly by buying shares in a business, individuals now invest in money market, trust, insurance, and pension funds that are controlled by large financial organizations, which in turn invest these grouped savings in industrial corporations.

The Transnational Corporations

With the intensifying of globalization, most large corporations now operate in an international economic context. When they establish branches in two or several countries, they are referred to as **transnational**, or **multinational corporations**. *Transnational* is the preferred term, indicating that these companies operate across many different national boundaries. The United Nations Committee on Trade and Development (UNCTAD) estimated that in 2002 over 650,000 transnational corporations controlled assets outside their home countries (UNCTAD, 2002).

The largest transnationals are gigantic; their wealth outstrips that of many countries. The scope of these companies' operations is staggering. The combined sales of the world's largest five hundred transnational corporations totaled $13.7 trillion in 2003—nearly half (46 percent) of the value of goods and services produced by the entire world (World Bank, 2003; *Fortune*, 2003).

One hundred ninety-two of the top five hundred transnational corporations in the world are based in the United States, contributing about 40 percent of the total global sales. The share of American companies has, however, fallen significantly since 1960, during which time Japanese companies have grown dramatically; only five Japanese corporations were included in the top two hundred in 1960, as compared with eighty-eight in 2003. Of the fifty largest Asian corporations, forty of them are Japanese (*Fortune*, 2003).

The Changing Nature of Work

The globalizing of economic production, together with the spread of information technology, is altering the nature of the jobs most people do. As discussed earlier, the proportion of people working in blue-collar jobs in industrial countries has progressively fallen. Fewer people work in factories than before. New jobs have been created in offices and in service centers such as supermarkets and airports. Many of these new jobs are filled by women.

Work and Technology

The relationship between technology and work has long been of interest to sociologists. How is our experience of work affected by the type of technology that is involved? As industrialization has progressed, technology has assumed an ever greater role at the workplace—from factory automation to the computerization of office work. The current information technology revolution has attracted renewed interest in this question. Technology can lead to greater efficiency and productivity, but how does it affect the way work is experienced by those who carry it out? For sociologists, one of the main questions is how the move to more complex systems influences the nature of work and the institutions in which it is performed.

AUTOMATION AND THE SKILL DEBATE

The concept of **automation**, or programmable machinery, was introduced in the mid-1800s, when Christopher Spencer, an American, invented the Automat, a programmable lathe that made screws, nuts, and gears. Automation has thus far affected relatively few industries, but with advances in the design of industrial robots, its impact is certain to become greater. A robot is an automatic device that can perform functions ordinarily done by human workers. The term *robot* comes from the Czech word *robota*, or serf, popularized about fifty years ago by the playwright Karel Čapek.

The majority of the robots used in industry worldwide are to be found in automobile manufacture. The usefulness of robots in production thus far is relatively limited, because their capacity to recognize different objects and manipulate awkward shapes is still at a rudimentary level. Yet it is certain that automated production will spread rapidly in coming years; robots are becoming more sophisticated, while their costs are decreasing.

Container ships are cargo ships that carry all of their load in truck-size containers. As this technique greatly accelerates the speed by which goods can be transported to and from ports, these ships now carry the majority of the world's dry cargo.

The reach of the transnationals over the past thirty years would not have been possible without advances in transport and communications. Air travel now allows people to move around the world at a speed that would have seemed inconceivable even sixty years ago. Technological innovations, referred to together as "containerization," have permitted the rapid movement and distribution of bulk goods around the world. The best example of containerization is the development of extremely large ocean-going vessels (superfreighters) that carry tractor trailers full of goods. These trailers can be easily loaded and sealed at the point of manufacture, loaded onto ships and moved across an ocean, than transferred onto a train or truck and delivered to a store, where the trailers are finally opened and unloaded.

Telecommunications technologies now permit more or less instantaneous communication from one part of the world to another. Satellites have been used for commercial telecommunications since 1965, when the first satellite could carry 240 telephone conversations at once. Current satellites can carry 12,000 simultaneous conversations! The larger transnationals now have their own satellite-based communications systems. The Mitsubishi Corporation, for instance, has a massive network across which 5 million words are transmitted to and from its headquarters in Tokyo each day.

FIGURE 13.4

Where Does Your Car Come From?

This schematic shows how automobile parts are produced in several countries and then sent to a central plant for final production of the car.

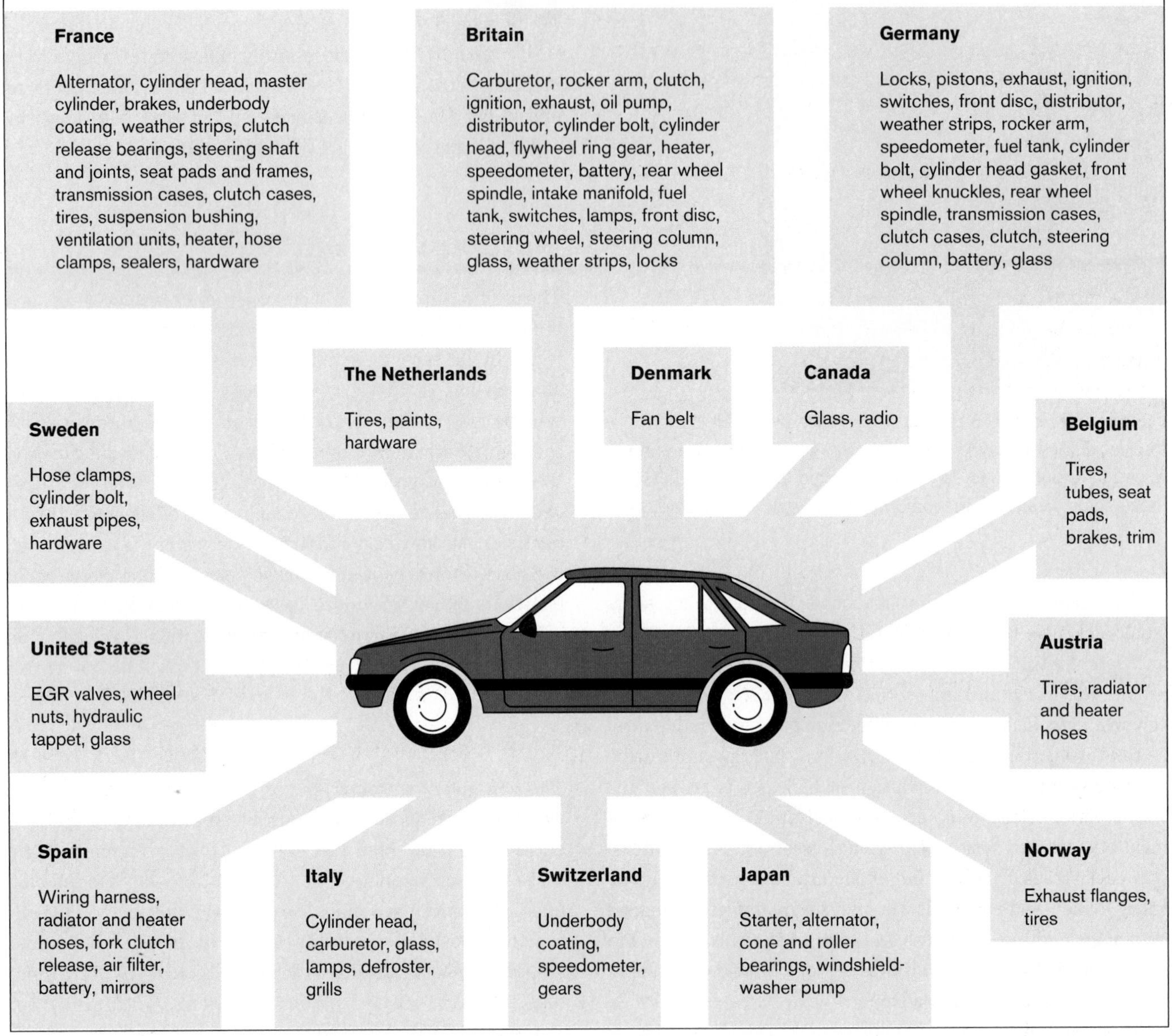

France

Alternator, cylinder head, master cylinder, brakes, underbody coating, weather strips, clutch release bearings, steering shaft and joints, seat pads and frames, transmission cases, clutch cases, tires, suspension bushing, ventilation units, heater, hose clamps, sealers, hardware

Britain

Carburetor, rocker arm, clutch, ignition, exhaust, oil pump, distributor, cylinder bolt, cylinder head, flywheel ring gear, heater, speedometer, battery, rear wheel spindle, intake manifold, fuel tank, switches, lamps, front disc, steering wheel, steering column, glass, weather strips, locks

Germany

Locks, pistons, exhaust, ignition, switches, front disc, distributor, weather strips, rocker arm, speedometer, fuel tank, cylinder bolt, cylinder head gasket, front wheel knuckles, rear wheel spindle, transmission cases, clutch cases, clutch, steering column, battery, glass

The Netherlands

Tires, paints, hardware

Denmark

Fan belt

Canada

Glass, radio

Sweden

Hose clamps, cylinder bolt, exhaust pipes, hardware

Belgium

Tires, tubes, seat pads, brakes, trim

United States

EGR valves, wheel nuts, hydraulic tappet, glass

Austria

Tires, radiator and heater hoses

Spain

Wiring harness, radiator and heater hoses, fork clutch release, air filter, battery, mirrors

Italy

Cylinder head, carburetor, glass, lamps, defroster, grills

Switzerland

Underbody coating, speedometer, gears

Japan

Starter, alternator, cone and roller bearings, windshield-washer pump

Norway

Exhaust flanges, tires

The spread of automation provoked a heated debate among sociologists and experts in industrial relations over the impact of the new technology on workers, their skills, and their level of commitment to their work. In his influential *Alienation and Freedom* (1964), Robert Blauner examined the experience of workers in four different industries with varying levels of technology. Blauner measured the extent to which workers in each industry experienced alienation in the form of powerlessness, meaninglessness, isolation, and self-estrangement. He concluded that workers on assembly lines were the most alienated of all, but that levels of alienation were somewhat lower at workplaces using automation. In other words, Blauner argued that the introduction of automation to factories was responsible for *reversing* the otherwise steady trend toward increased worker alienation.

A very different thesis was set forth by Harry Braverman in the famous *Labor and Monopoly Capital* (1974). In Braverman's eyes, automation was part of the overall "deskilling" of the industrial labor force. In both industrial settings and modern offices, the introduction of technology contributed to this overall degradation of work by limiting the need for creative human input. Instead, all that was required was an unthinking, unreflective body capable of endlessly carrying out the same unskilled task.

A newer study sheds some more light on this debate. The sociologist Richard Sennett studied the people who worked in a bakery that had been bought by a large food conglomerate and automated with the introduction of high-tech machinery. Instead of using their hands to mix the ingredients and knead the dough and their noses and eyes to judge when the bread was done baking, the bakery's workers had no physical contact with the materials or the loaves of bread. In fact, the entire process was controlled and monitored via computer screen. The production process involved little more than pushing buttons on a computer. In fact, one time when the computerized machinery broke down, the entire production process was halted because none of the bakery's "skilled" workers were trained or empowered to repair the problem. The workers that Sennett observed wanted to be helpful, to make things work again, but they could not, because automation had diminished their autonomy (Sennett, 1998). The introduction of computerized technology in the workplace has led to a general increase in all workers' skills, but has also led to a bifurcated work force composed of a small group of highly skilled professionals with high degrees of flexibility and autonomy in their jobs and a larger group of clerical, service, and production workers who lack autonomy in their jobs.

GLOBAL PRODUCTION

For much of the twentieth century, the most important business organizations were large manufacturing firms that controlled both the making of goods and their final sales. Giant automobile companies such as Ford and General Motors typify this approach. Such companies employ tens of thousands of factory workers making everything from components to the final cars, which are then sold in the manufacturers' showrooms. Such manufacture-dominated production processes are organized as large bureaucracies, often controlled by a single firm.

During the past quarter century, however, another form of production has become important—one that is controlled by giant retailers. In retailer-dominated production, firms such as Wal-Mart and Kmart buy products from manufacturers, who in turn arrange to have their products made by independently owned factories. The sociologists Edna Bonacich and Richard Appelbaum, for example, show that in clothing manufacturing, most manufacturers actually employ no garment workers at all. Instead, they rely on

thousands of factories around the world to make their apparel, which they then sell in department stores and other retail outlets. Clothing manufacturers do not own any of these factories and therefore are not responsible for the conditions under which the clothing is made.

Two thirds of all clothing sold in America is made in factories outside the United States, where workers are paid a fraction of U.S. wages. (In China, workers are lucky to make $40 a month.) Bonacich and Appelbaum argue that such competition has resulted in a global "race to the bottom," in which retailers and manufacturers will go anyplace on earth where they can pay the lowest wages possible. One result is that much of the clothing we buy today was likely made in sweatshops by young workers—most likely teenage girls—who get paid pennies for making clothing or athletic shoes that sell for $50, $100, or even more (Bonacich and Appelbaum, 2000).

Trends in the Occupational Structure

The occupational structure in all industrialized countries has changed very substantially since the beginning of the twentieth century (see Figure 13.5). In 1900, about three quarters of the employed population was in manual work, either farming or blue-collar work such as manufacturing. White-collar professional and service jobs were much fewer in number. By 1960, however, more people worked in white-collar professional and service jobs than in manual labor. By 1993, the occupational system had basically reversed its structure from 1900. Almost three quarters of the employed population worked in white-collar professional and service jobs, while the rest worked in blue-collar and farming jobs. In the period 2001–2004, the United States lost 2.6 million manufacturing jobs. By 2010, blue-collar work will have declined even further, with most of the increase in new jobs occurring in the service industries. As we saw in Chapter 9, over the course of the twentieth century, numerous women joined the paid labor force. In 1998, however, 42 percent of working women had service-based or clerical positions, while only 16 percent of men had these types of jobs. Likewise, 38 percent of men held blue-collar manual jobs, while only 10 percent of women were in such positions.

The reasons for the transformation of the occupational structure seem to be several. One is the continuous introduction of labor-saving machinery, culminating in the spread of information technology and computerization in industry in recent decades. Another is the rise of the manufacturing industry in other parts of the world, primarily Asia. The older industries in Western societies have experienced major job cutbacks because of their inability to compete with the more efficient Asian producers, whose labor costs are lower. As we have seen,

FIGURE 13.5

The Changing Occupational Structure

The United States has lost a large number of manufacturing and other blue-collar jobs in the twentieth century. Many new professional/managerial and other white-collar jobs have been created. However, a large proportion entail work in the service industries, and although these can be classified as white-collar, they resemble blue-collar jobs in terms of pay.

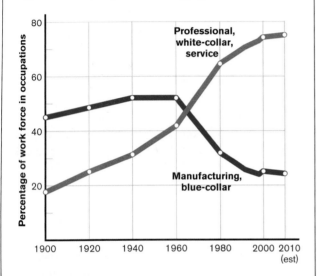

SOURCE: *Historical Statistics of the United States*, vol. 1; U.S. Bureau of Labor Statistics, 2000.

this global economic transformation forced American companies to adopt new forms of production, which in turn forced employees to learn new skills and new occupations as manufacturing-related jobs moved to other countries. A final important trend is the decline of full-time paid employment with the same employer over a long period of time. Not only has the transformation of the global economy affected the nature of day-to-day work, it has also changed the career patterns of many workers.

THE KNOWLEDGE ECONOMY

Taking these trends into account, some observers suggest that what is occurring today is a transition to a new type of society no longer based primarily on industrialism. We are entering, they claim, a phase of development beyond the industrial era altogether. A variety of terms have been coined to describe this new social order, such as the *postindustrial society*, the *information age*, and the *"new" economy*. The term that has come into most common usage, however, is the **knowledge economy**.

A precise definition of the knowledge economy is difficult to formulate, but in general terms, it refers to an economy in which ideas, information, and forms of knowledge underpin innovation and economic growth. In a knowledge economy, much of the work force is involved not in the physical production or distribution of material goods, but in their design, development, technology, marketing, sale, and servicing. These employees can be termed "knowledge workers." The knowledge economy is dominated by the constant flow of information and opinions and by the powerful potentials of science and technology.

How widespread is the knowledge economy at the start of the twenty-first century? A recent study by the Organization for Economic Cooperation and Development has attempted to gauge the extent of the knowledge economy among developed nations by measuring the percentage of each country's overall business output that can be attributed to knowledge-based industries (see Figure 13.6). Knowledge-based industries are understood broadly to include high technology, education and training, research and development, and the financial and investment sector. Among OECD countries as a whole, knowledge-based industries accounted for more than half of all business output in the mid-1990s. Western Germany had a high figure of 58.6 percent, and the United States, Japan, Britain, Sweden, and France were all at or over 50 percent.

Investments into the knowledge economy—in the form of public education, spending on software development, and research and development—now make up significant part of many countries' budgets. Sweden, for example, invested 10.6 percent of its overall gross domestic product in the knowledge economy in 1995. France was a close second because of its extensive spending on public education.

THE CONTINGENT WORK FORCE

Another important employment trend of the past decade has been the replacement of full-time workers by part-time workers who are hired and fired on a contingency basis. Most temporary workers are hired for the least-skilled, lowest-paying jobs. As a general rule, part-time jobs do not include the benefits associated with full-time work, such as medical insurance, paid vacation time, or retirement benefits. Because employers can save on the costs of wages and benefits, the use of part-time workers has become increasingly common. Researchers

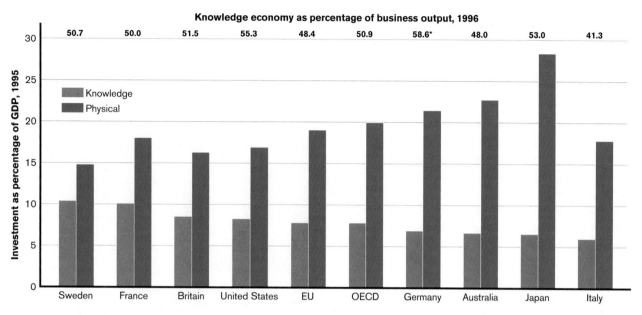

FIGURE 13.6

The Weight of the Knowledge Economy in Investment and Output by Country and Economic Region, 1995–1996

Knowledge economy as percentage of business output, 1996

50.7	50.0	51.5	55.3	48.4	50.9	58.6*	48.0	53.0	41.3

Investment as percentage of GDP, 1995

Knowledge
Physical

Sweden   France   Britain   United States   EU   OECD   Germany   Australia   Japan   Italy

*West Germany

SOURCE: OECD. From *The Economist*, October 16, 1999, p. 145.

estimate that contingency workers make up between 29 and 33 percent of the American work force. This is up from 20 to 23 percent just ten years ago.

The temporary employment agency Manpower, Inc., founded in Milwaukee, Wisconsin, in 1948, has become a global leader in the provision of temporary workers. This company employed 1.9 million temps in 36 countries in 2001 and was the 182nd largest corporation in the world (Manpower, Inc., 2003). Manpower provides labor on a "flexible" basis to 95 percent of Fortune 500 companies. Clearly, temporary labor has become a critical component of the worldwide organization of work and occupations.

There has been some debate over the psychological effects of part-time work on the work force. Many temporary workers fulfill their assignments in a prompt and satisfactory manner, but others rebel against their tenuous positions by shirking their responsibilities or sabotaging their results. Some temporary workers have been observed trying to "look busy" or to work longer than necessary on rather simple tasks. Finally, contingency workers have tried to avoid emotionally intensive work that would require

them to become psychologically committed to their employer.

However, some recent surveys of work indicate that part-time workers register higher levels of job satisfaction than those in full-time employment. This may be because most part-time workers are women, who have lower expectations for their careers than men or who are particularly relieved to escape from the monotony of domestic work. Yet many individuals seem to find reward precisely in the fact that they are able to balance paid work with other activities and enjoy a more varied life. Some people might choose to "peak" their lives, giving full commitment to paid work from their youth to their middle years, then perhaps changing to a second career, which would open up new interests.

Unemployment

The idea of work is actually a complex one. All of us work in many ways besides in paid employment. Cleaning the house, planting a garden, and going shopping are plainly all work.

Layoffs and Downsizing

When the last worker passed through the doors of White Furniture Company in May of 1993, hardly anyone beyond the city limits of Mebane, North Carolina, noticed. In national terms, it made little difference that 203 men and women were out of work or that a venerable, family-owned firm (the "South's oldest maker of fine furniture") had been sold to a conglomerate and now was being shut down. After all, what happened to White's is hardly unique. In the 1990s, in every walk of life and on all social levels, Americans have had to learn a new vocabulary of economic anxiety—layoff, outsourcing, buyout, off-shoring, downsizing, closing. The statistics are mind-numbing: 70,000 people laid off from General Motors in 1991; 50,000 workers from Sears and 63,000 from IBM in 1993; 40,000 from AT&T in 1996. In these times, why should we care about the closing of one furniture factory in a small southern town?

There are many reasons to care, not least that the story of White Furniture Company is a study in miniature of work—what it means when you have it, what it means when you don't. Behind the grim headlines are real men and women who, like the White workers, are devastated not just by the lack of income but by the end of a way of life based on doing a

job and doing it well. The wages at White Furniture may have been low; the equipment was antiquated and the working conditions harsh—incessant noise, fumes pervading the air, the factory building cold in winter and sweltering in summer. Yet, looking back, White's workers mourn the closing of the plant and, mostly, they mourn the loss of their craft and their companions. Factory work—industrialization—had a high price tag. Now we are seeing, everywhere around us and on every social level, the dire cost of post-industrialism. . . .

A closing doesn't happen in the melodramatic way one might expect: a door slamming shut and two hundred people out in the cold. It happens in bits and pieces, one worker at a time. At White's there was a grim logic to the layoffs. They followed production. The last piece of furniture came down the line, was worked on, and then the line closed down behind it, and the workers in that section would be let go. A few workers made one last walk-through of the plant, saying good-bye to their friends, but most just left.

The layoffs started in the kiln area where the lumber was brought in to the yard. After the lumber ran through the saws in the rough mill, those people would be let go. After the wood

was glued together, the workers on the glue machine left. The piece was machined, and the next day the machine room was empty. The last piece of furniture was sanded, assembled, and then finished, with workers from each department leaving in turn. Finally, the piece went to rub and pack, where it was prepared for shipping and then boxed. The last piece on the line was ready to be sent away. And so were the last workers. You finished your job. You were called away from your department an hour or so before closing time. You sat in the personnel room and signed some papers. The personnel officer shook your hand. And then it was over.

There's a reason for laying off people in this way: it is the best way to ensure that a plant shutdown will be orderly, economical, and efficient. Yet, as many industrial psychologists have noted, people who leave their jobs like this typically feel despair, isolation, and shame. They feel oppressed by the enormity of what lies ahead for them, at the mercy of forces beyond their control. There is little sense of solidarity with other workers, either those who have gone before or those who will be laid off in the future. There is no opportunity for collective anger or organized protest. No one knows who is being laid off, when, how many, or who will be next. . . .

Despite the fact that other companies paid better, workers stayed at White's out of some combination of job satisfaction,

friendship, loyalty, desire for security, and personal pride of craft. To use a formulation that is typically reserved for middle-class rather than for blue-collar workers, they chose to stay at White's because it was a career, not just a job. White's wasn't perfect, and none of the workers says it was. Yet metaphors of death run through the comments so many of the workers make about the closing precisely because people felt that something of themselves died when White Furniture closed. . . .

[James Gilland worked at White Furniture Company from 1951 until 1992.] When you ask him about his job at White's, he answers with his philosophy of work: "Changing jobs is one of the worst things that anybody can do today as a young person. The best thing to do is to start looking when you're young and find a job that you're really interested in, one that you like, that you think you can work with. It's just like getting married. Somebody that you think you can live with the rest of your life. A job is the same way."

SOURCE: Bill Bamberger and Cathy N. Davidson, *Closing: The Life and Death of an American Factory* (New York: DoubleTake/W. W. Norton, 1998), pp. 17, 41, 72, 168.

Questions

- How is James Gilland's view of job loyalty outdated? How could it be revised to fit current hiring and firing patterns?
- Judging from the photographs, what do the impending layoffs and closing of the factory mean to the workers?
- Company buyouts and layoffs are more and more prevalent. Under these uncertain conditions, what can boost workers' morale and inspire pride in their work?

But for two centuries or more, Western society has been built around the central importance of paid work. The experience of unemployment—being unable to find a job when one wants it—is still a largely negative one. And unemployment does bring with it unfortunate effects including, sometimes, falling into poverty. Yet as we shall see, some today are arguing that we should think about the relation between being "in work" and "out of work" in a completely different way from the way we did in the recent past.

Rates of unemployment fluctuated considerably over the course of the twentieth century. In Western countries, unemployment reached a peak in the early 1930s, when some 20 percent of the work force were out of work in the United States. The economist John Maynard Keynes, who strongly influenced public policy in Europe and the United States during the post–World War II period, believed that unemployment results from consumers' lacking sufficient resources to buy goods. Governments can intervene to increase the level of demand in an economy, leading to the creation of new jobs; and the newly employed then have the income with which to buy more goods, thus creating yet more jobs for people who produce them. State management of economic life, most people came to believe, meant that high rates of unemployment belonged to the past. Commitment to full employment became part of government policy in virtually all Western societies. Until the 1970s, these policies seemed successful, and economic growth was more or less continuous.

During the 1970s and 1980s, however, Keynesianism was largely abandoned. In the face of economic globalization, governments lost the capability to control economic life as they once did. One consequence was that unemployment rates shot up in many countries.

Several factors probably explain the increase in unemployment levels in Western countries at that time. One was the rise of international competition in industries on which Western prosperity used to be founded. In 1947, 60 percent of steel production in the world was carried out in the United States. Today, the figure is only about 15 percent, whereas steel production has risen by 300 percent in Japan, Singapore, Taiwan, and Hong Kong. A second factor was the worldwide economic recession of the late 1980s, which has still not fully abated. A third reason was the increasing use of microelectronics in industry, the net effect of which has been to reduce the need for labor power. Finally, beginning in the 1970s more women sought paid employment, meaning that more people were chasing a limited number of available jobs.

During this time, rates of unemployment tended to be lower in the United States, for example, than in some European nations. This is perhaps because the sheer economic strength of the country gives it more power in world markets than smaller, more fragile economies. Alternatively, it may be that the exceptionally large service sector in the United States provides a greater source of new jobs than in

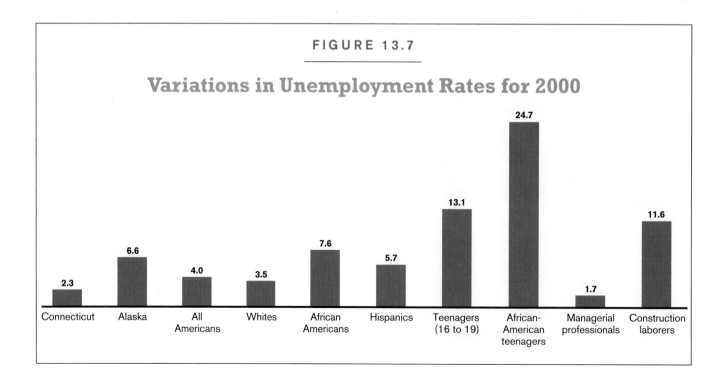

FIGURE 13.7

Variations in Unemployment Rates for 2000

countries where more of the population has traditionally been employed in manufacturing. And within countries, unemployment is not equally distributed. It varies by race or ethnic background, by age, and by industry and geographic region (see Figure 13.7). Ethnic minorities living in central cities in the United States have much higher rates of long-term unemployment than the rest of the population. A substantial proportion of young people are among the long-term unemployed, again especially among minority groups.

The Future of Work

Over the past twenty years, in all the industrialized countries except the United States, the average length of the working week has become shorter. Workers still undertake long stretches of overtime, but some governments are beginning to introduce new limits on permissible working hours. In France, for example, annual overtime is restricted to a maximum of 130 hours a year. In most countries, there is a general tendency toward shortening the average working career. More people would probably quit the labor force at sixty or earlier if they could afford to do so.

If the amount of time given over to paid employment continues to shrink, and the need to have a job becomes less central, the nature of working careers might become substantially reorganized. Job sharing or flexible working hours, which arose primarily as a result of the increasing numbers of working parents trying to balance the commitments of workplace and family, for example, might become more common. Some work analysts have suggested that sabbaticals of the university type should be extended to workers in other spheres: People would be entitled to take a year off in order to study or pursue some form of self-improvement. Perhaps more individuals will engage in "life planning," in which they arrange to work in different ways (paid, unpaid, full or part time, etc.) at different stages in their lives. Thus, some people might choose to enter the labor force in their late thirties, having followed a period of formal education in their early twenties with time devoted to pursuits like travel. People might *opt* to work part time throughout their lives, rather than being forced to because of a lack of full-time employment opportunities.

The nature of the work most people do and the role of work in our lives, like so many other aspects of the societies in which we live, are undergoing major changes. The chief reasons are global economic competition, the widespread introduction of information technology and computerization, and the large-scale entry of women into the work force.

How will work change in the future? It appears very likely that people will take a more active look at their lives than in the past, moving in and out of paid work at different points. These are only positive options, however, when they are deliberately chosen. The reality for most is that regular paid work remains the key to day-to-day survival and that unemployment is experienced as a hardship rather than an opportunity.

Study Outline
www.wwnorton.com/giddens

Government and Power

- The term *government* refers to a political apparatus in which officials enact policies and make decisions. *Politics* refers to the use of power to affect government actions.
- *Power* is the capacity to achieve one's aims even against the resistance of others, and often involves the use of force. A government is said to have *authority* when its use of power is legitimate. Such legitimacy derives from the consent of those being governed. The most common form of legitimate government is democratic, but other legitimate forms are also possible.

The Concept of the State

- A *state* is characterized by a political apparatus (government institutions), including civil service officials, ruling over a geographically defined territory, and whose authority is backed by a legal system and that has the capacity to use force to implement policies.
- All modern states have certain additional features: *sovereignty*, the idea that government has authority over a given area; *citizenship*, the idea that people have common rights and duties and are aware of their part in the state; and *nationalism*, the sense of being part of a broader, unifying political community.
- Most nation-states became centralized through the activities of monarchs who concentrated social power. Citizens initially had few rights of political participation, or none at all; such rights were achieved only through a long process of struggle that continues to this day. *Civil rights* refer to the freedoms and privileges guaran-

teed to individuals by law. *Political rights* ensure that citizens may participate in politics (by voting, for example). *Social rights* guarantee every individual some minimum standard of living. Social rights are the basis for the *welfare state*, which supports citizens who are unable to support themselves.

Democracy

- The term *democracy* literally means rule by the people, but this phrase can be interpreted in various ways. For instance, "the people" has often really meant "adult male property owners," while "rule" might refer to government policies, administrative decisions, or both.
- Several different forms of democracy exist, including: *participatory democracy*, also called *direct democracy*, which occurs when everyone is immediately involved in all decision making, although this can be cumbersome for larger groups; *liberal democracy*, which is a system in which citizens have a choice to vote between at least two political parties for representatives who will be entrusted with decision making; and *constitutional monarchy*, which includes a royal family whose powers are severely restricted by a constitution, which puts authority in the hands of democratically elected representatives.

Democracy in the United States

- A political party is an organization oriented toward achieving legitimate control of government through an electoral process. There is usually some connection between voting patterns and class differences. In many Western countries there has recently been a decline in allegiance to traditional parties and a growing disenchantment with the party system in general.
- Women achieved the right to vote much later than men in all countries and continue to be poorly represented among political elites. They have been influential on social and civil rights issues, and most Western countries have passed equal rights legislation over recent years.

Who Rules?

- According to Weber and Schumpeter, the level of democratic participation that can be achieved in a modern, large-scale society is limited. The rule of *power elites* is inevitable, but multiparty systems provide the possibility of choosing *who* exercises power. The *pluralist theorists* add the claim that the competition of *interest groups* limits the degree to which ruling elites are able to concentrate power in few hands.
- The number of countries with democratic governments has rapidly increased in recent years, due in large part to the effects of globalization and mass communication and to the spread of com-

petitive capitalism. But democracy is not without its problems; people everywhere have begun to lose faith in the capacity of politicians and governments to solve problems and to manage economies, and many no longer vote.

The Social Significance of Work

- *Work* is the carrying out of tasks that involve the expenditure of mental and physical effort and has as its objective the production of goods and services catering to human needs. An *occupation* is work that is done in exchange for a regular wage. In all cultures work is the basis of the *economy*.
- A distinctive characteristic of the economic system of modern societies is the development of a highly complex and diverse *division of labor*. The division of labor means that work is divided into different occupations requiring specialization. One result is *economic interdependence:* We are all dependent on each other to maintain our livelihoods.

Industrial Work

- The principles of scientific management, created by Taylor, divides work into simple tasks that can be timed and organized. Henry Ford extended the principles of scientific management to mass production and tied them to mass markets.

Organizations and Economic Life

- Union organizations, together with recognition of the right to *strike*, are characteristic features of economic life in all Western countries. Unions emerged as defensive organizations, concerned to provide a measure of control for workers over their conditions of labor.
- The modern economy is dominated by the large *corporations*. When one firm has a commanding influence in a given industry, it is in a *monopoly* position. When a cluster of firms wields such influence, a situation of *oligopoly* exists. Through their influence on government policy and on the consumption of goods, the giant corporations have a profound effect on people's lives.

Transnational Corporations

- Corporations have undergone profound transformations in recent years because of increasing world interdependence, or globalization. The modern corporation is increasingly an enterprise web of many smaller firms linked together, rather than a single big business.

- *Multinational* or *transnational corporations* operate across different national boundaries. The largest of them exercise tremendous economic power. Half of the one hundred largest economic units are not countries, but privately owned companies.

Work and Social Change

- Major changes have occurred in the occupational system during the course of the century. Particularly important has been the relative increase in non-manual occupations at the expense of manual ones.
- Unemployment has been a recurrent problem in the industrialized countries in the twentieth century. As work is a structuring element in a person's psychological makeup, the experience of unemployment is often disorienting. The impact of new technology seems likely to further increase unemployment rates.
- Major changes are currently occurring in the nature and organization of work. It seems certain that these will become even more important in the future. Nonetheless, work remains for many people the key basis of generating resources necessary to sustain a varied life.

Key Concepts

alienation (p. 359)
authority (p. 342)
automation (p. 365)
capitalism (p. 363)
citizen (p. 343)
civil rights (p. 343)
communism (p. 347)
constitutional monarchy (p. 347)
corporation (p. 363)
democracy (p. 346)
democratic elitism (p. 354)
direct democracy (p. 346)
division of labor (p. 358)
economic interdependence (p. 358)
economy (p. 342)
entrepreneur (p. 363)
family capitalism (p. 364)
government (p. 342)
informal economy (p. 357)
institutional capitalism (p. 364)
interest group (p. 351)
knowledge economy (p. 368)
liberal democracy (p. 347)
local nationalisms (p. 343)
managerial capitalism (p. 364)

monopoly (p. 363)
nation-state (p. 342)
nationalism (p. 343)
occupation (p. 357)
oligopoly (p. 363)
participatory democracy (p. 346)
pluralist theories of modern democracy (p. 355)
political rights (p. 343)
politics (p. 342)
power (p. 342)
power elite (p. 355)
social rights (p. 343)
sovereignty (p. 342)
state (p. 342)
strike (p. 359)
technology (p. 357)
transnational/multinational corporation (p. 364)
welfare capitalism (p. 364)
welfare state (p. 343)
work (p. 357)

Review Questions

1. What is the difference between politics and government?
   a. There is none.
   b. Politics involves the exercise of power in regard to the actions of government, whereas government is concerned with the enactment of policies, decisions, and matters of state.
   c. Politics involves the government's legitimate use of power, whereas government is concerned with the way power is used to influence the state's activities.
   d. Politics involves the enactment of policies, decisions, and matters of state, whereas government is concerned with the exercise of power in regard to the actions of government.

2. What is the difference between power and authority?
   a. Power is a Marxist concept, whereas authority is a Weberian concept.
   b. Power is the ability of individuals or groups to make their interests count, even in the face of opposition from others, whereas authority is the use of power by government where the exercise of that power is seen as legitimate by those who are subject to it.
   c. Power is the ability to spend money to solve a problem, whereas authority is the respect a person is accorded by others.
   d. Power is the use of power by government where the exercise of that power is seen as legitimate by those who are subject to it, whereas authority is the ability of individuals or groups to make their interests count, even in the face of opposition from others.

3. What was Max Weber's theory of democracy?
   a. Democratic elitism
   b. Pluralism
   c. The power elite
   d. The "iron law of oligarchy"
4. What are the three rights associated with the growth of citizenship?
   a. Civil, political, and social rights
   b. Civil, voting, and welfare rights
   c. Civil, social, and economic rights
   d. Civil, human, and animal rights
5. When and why did women win the vote in most Western countries?
   a. The vote was given to women in the general wave of social reforms that followed World War II.
   b. The vote was won through the efforts of the suffragist movement and as a consequence of women's mobilization in World War I.
   c. Voting rights were accorded to women, as well as to blacks, in the Voting Rights Act of 1965.
   d. Women were allowed to vote as a result of their increased participation in the economy and their increasing economic independence from men.
6. In 1998 women made up 13 percent of the membership of the House of Representatives and 9 percent of the Senate. Why has women's participation in the higher echelons of the American political system remained so modest?
   a. Women are running for office in larger numbers than ever, but voters are not electing them to office because the majority still regard politics as a "man's game."
   b. The political parties (which are largely run by men) have not recruited many women to run for high political office.
   c. Women are being elected to lower offices, but more of them need to work their way up through the seniority system before they are given the chance to run for the House or Senate.
   d. Female candidates find it harder to raise money than male candidates.
7. What is liberal democracy and where can it be found in the modern world?
   a. It is a nation-state where most adults have the right to vote and where two or more parties are involved in competitive elections. Generally, these conditions are found in the developed world, although some Third World countries have liberal democracies.
   b. It is a political system that has a large established and competitive liberal or social democratic party that is in a position to effect the composition of government. Some nations—for example, Mexico and Ireland—have no liberal or social democratic party and are therefore not liberal democracies.
   c. It is a nation-state whose constitution formally commits its government to the preservation of human rights. These conditions are found all over the world but are not always observed.

d. It is a political system in which there has been an alternation of power between parties. This is regarded as a crucial test of the robustness of a democracy and did not occur in some democracies in developed nations—such as Italy and Japan—before the 1980s.
8. From a sociological perspective, women who are housewives
   a. don't have a job.
   b. want a job.
   c. do *work*, although they are not part of the paid labor force.
   d. None of the above.
9. What is the informal economy?
   a. It refers to domestic labor within the home.
   b. It refers to transactions outside the sphere of regular employment, sometimes involving the exchange of cash for services provided, but also often involving the direct exchange of goods and services.
   c. It refers to transactions between small businesses.
   d. It refers to the economy in traditional societies.
10. What is the definition of a strike?
    a. A spontaneous stoppage of work by a group of employees to show their employers how angry they are at the company's actions.
    b. A temporary stoppage of work by a group of employees in order to express a grievance or enforce a demand.
    c. The culmination of a series of industrial actions that usually begin with increased absenteeism, which includes a slowdown and may involve a lockout.
    d. All of the above.
11. The decline in unionization can be attributed to
    a. the recession in world economic activity.
    b. the increasing intensity of international competition.
    c. the rise to power in many countries of rightist governments that launched an aggressive assault on unions in the 1980s.
    d. All of the above.
12. The majority of the robots used in industry worldwide are to be found in
    a. computer production.
    b. electronic production.
    c. automobile production.
    d. furniture production.

Thinking Sociologically Exercises

1. Discuss the differences between the "pluralistic" and the "power elite" theories of democratic political processes. Which theory do you find most appropriate to describe U.S. politics in recent years?

2. Discuss some of the important ways that the nature of work will change for the contemporary worker as companies apply more automation and larger-scale production processes and as oligopolies become more pervasive. Explain each of these trends and how they affect workers, both now and in the future.

Data Exercises

**www.wwnorton.com/giddens
Keyword: Data13**

- In the data exercise for this chapter you will learn more about the patterns of political participation. Did you know that more people are registered to vote today than 30 years ago, but fewer do? As you work through the exercise think about who is opting out of participation and why they are.

- Approximately how many hours do you work each week? In what ways does the kind of job or even a worker's sex affect the number of hours worked? You may think that these social factors have nothing to do with structuring the work week, but after completing the data exercise for this chapter you may be surprised by what you learn.

The Sociology of Health and Illness

Recognize that health and illness are culturally and socially determined. Learn the social and cultural differences in the distribution of disease. Learn more about HIV/AIDS as a sociological phenomenon.

Human Sexuality

Learn about the debate over the importance of biological versus social and cultural influences on human sexual behavior. Explore the cultural differences in sexual behavior and patterns of sexual behavior today.

Aging

The Graying of U.S. Society

Learn some basic facts about the increase in the proportion of the U.S. population that is becoming elderly.

How Do People Age?

Understand that aging is a combination of biological, psychological, and sociological processes.

Growing Old: Competing Sociological Explanations

Consider the various theories of aging, particularly those that focus on how society shapes the social roles of the elderly and emphasize aspects of age stratification.

Aging in the United States

Evaluate the experience of growing old in the United States.

Globalization: The Graying of the World Population

Assess the social issues of graying on a global level.

CHAPTER FOURTEEN

HEALTH, ILLNESS, SEXUALITY, AND AGING

ook at the two photographs on the next page. The images of a sunken face and an emaciated body are almost identical. The young girl on the left is Somalian, dying from a simple lack of food. The young woman on the right is an American teenager, dying because, in a society with a superabundance of food, she chose not to eat or to eat so sparingly that her life was endangered.

The social dynamics involved in each case are utterly different. Starvation from lack of food is caused by factors outside people's control and affects only the very poor. The American teenager, living in the wealthiest country in the world, is suffering from anorexia, an illness with no known physical origin; obsessed with the ideal of achieving a slim body, she has eventually given up eating altogether. Anorexia and other eating disorders are illnesses of the affluent, not of those who have little or no food. It is completely unknown in the developing countries where food is scarce, such as Somalia.

Throughout much of human history, a few people such as saints or mystics have deliberately chosen to starve themselves for religious reasons. They were almost always men. Today, anorexia primarily affects women, and it has no specific connection to religious beliefs. It is an illness of the body, and thus we might think that we would have to look to biological or physical factors to explain it. But health and illness, like other topics we've studied, are also affected by social and cultural influences, such as the pressure to achieve a slim body.

Although it is an illness that expresses itself in physical symptoms, anorexia is closely related to the idea of being on a diet, which in turn is connected with changing views of physical

Take a look at the two women above: The first woman is painfully thin as a result of famine and malnutrition, sadly common problems in an area of the world plagued by frequent drought and crop failure. The second has become painfully thin by her own doing; people suffering from anorexia feel compelled by a variety of personal and social pressures to lose weight, and will often continue to view themselves as overweight even when they have reached a state of emaciation.

attractiveness, particularly of women, in modern society. In most premodern societies, the ideal female shape was a fleshy one. Thinness was not regarded as desirable at all—partly because it was associated with lack of food and therefore with poverty. Even in Europe in the 1600s and 1700s, the ideal female shape was well proportioned. Anyone who has seen paintings of the period, such as those by Rubens, will have noticed how curvaceous (even plump) the women depicted in them are. The notion of slimness as the desirable feminine shape originated among some middle-class groups in the late nineteenth century, but it has become generalized as an ideal for most women only recently.

Anorexia thus has its origins in the changing body image of women in the recent history of modern societies. It was first identified as a disorder in France in 1874, but it remained obscure until the past thirty or forty years (Brown and Jasper, 1993). Since then, it has become increasingly common among young women. So has bulimia—bingeing on food, followed by self-induced vomiting. Anorexia and bulimia are often found together in the same individual. Someone may become extremely thin through a starvation diet and then enter a phase of eating enormous amounts and purging in order to maintain a normal weight, followed by a period of again becoming very thin. Today, somewhere between 2 and 6 percent of the total U.S. population is afflicted with these conditions; over 85 percent of those affected are under the age of twenty (Rader Programs, 2003). Ninety percent of

those who suffer from these disorders are women. Anorexia has the highest mortality rate of any psychological disorder; 20 percent of those who suffer from anorexia will die from it (EDC, 2003).

Anorexia and other eating disorders are no longer obscure forms of illness in modern societies. The occurrence of eating disorders in the U.S. has doubled since 1960 (EDC, 2003). About 95 percent of U.S. college women say that they want to lose weight and up to 85 percent suffer serious problems with eating disorders at some point in their college careers. Around 25 percent experience bulimic episodes or anorexia. In American society, 60 percent of girls age thirteen have already begun to diet; this proportion rises to over 80 percent for young women of eighteen. College men also suffer similar experiences, though not in the same proportions. About 50 percent of American male college students claim that they want to lose weight, while about 30 percent are on diets (Hesse-Biber, 1997). Over 80 percent of ten-year-old children are afraid of being fat (EDC, 2003).

Nor is obsession with slenderness—and the resulting eating disorders—limited to women in the United States and Europe. As Western images of feminine beauty have spread to the rest of the world, so too have their associated illnesses. Eating disorders were first documented in Japan in the 1960s, a consequence of that country's rapid economic growth and incorporation into the global economy. Anorexia is now found among 2 percent of young Japanese women, and is occurring in younger and younger women (Curtin, 2003). During the past several years, eating problems have surfaced among young, primarily affluent women in Hong Kong and Singapore, as well as in urban areas in Taiwan, China, the Philippines, India, and Pakistan (Efron, 1997).

Once again, something that may seem to be a purely personal trouble—difficulties with food and despair over one's appearance—turns out to be a public issue. If we include not just life-threatening forms of anorexia but also obsessive concern with dieting and bodily appearance, eating disorders are now part of the lives of millions of people; they are found not only in the United States today but in all the industrial countries.

The astonishing spread of eating disorders brings home clearly the influence of social factors on our lives. The field known as **sociology of the body** investigates the ways in which our bodies are affected by these social influences. As human beings, we obviously all possess bodies. But the body isn't something we just have, and it isn't only something physical that exists outside of society. Our bodies are deeply affected by our social experiences, as well as by the norms and values of the groups to which we belong. It is only recently that sociologists have begun to recognize the profound nature of the interconnections between social life and the body.

Therefore this field is quite a new area, but it is one of the most exciting.

Sociology of the body draws together a number of basic themes, which we will make use of throughout the chapter. One major theme is the effects of social change on the body. A second theme is the increasing separation of the body from "nature"—from our surrounding environment and our biological rhythms. Our bodies are being invaded by the influence of science and technology, ranging from machines to diets, and this is creating new dilemmas. The invention of a range of reproductive technologies, for example, has introduced new options but has also generated intense social controversies. We will look at two such controversies, over genetic engineering and abortion, later in the chapter.

The term *technology* should not be understood in too narrow a way here. In its most basic sense, it refers to material technologies such as those involved in modern medicine—for example, the scanning machine that allows a doctor to chart a baby's development prior to birth. But we must also take account of what Michel Foucault (1988) has called "social technologies" affecting the body. By this phrase, he means that the body is increasingly something we have to "create" rather than simply accept. A **social technology** is any kind of regular intervention we make into the functioning of our bodies in order to alter them in specific ways. An example is dieting, so central to anorexia.

In this chapter, we will first analyze why eating disorders have become so common. From there, we will study the social dimensions of health and illness. Then we will turn to human sexuality, again by looking at the social and cultural influences on our sexual behavior. We will conclude with aging and the "graying" of the world population.

The Sociology of Health and Illness

To understand why eating disorders have become so commonplace in current times, we should think back to the social changes analyzed earlier in the book. Anorexia actually reflects certain kinds of social change, including the impact of globalization.

The rise of eating disorders in Western societies coincides directly with the globalization of food production, which has increased greatly in the last three or four decades. The invention of new modes of refrigeration and container transportation have allowed food to be stored for long periods and to be delivered from one side of the world to the other. Since the 1950s, supermarket shelves have been abundant with foods from all parts of the world (for those who can afford it—now the majority of the population in Western societies). Most of them are available all the time, not just, as was true previously, when they are in season locally.

For the past decade or so, almost *everyone* in the United States and the other developed countries has been on a diet. This does not mean that everyone is desperately trying to get thin. Rather, when all foods are available more or less all the time, we must *decide* what to eat—in other words, construct a diet, where "diet" means the foods we habitually consume. First, we have to decide what to eat in relation to the many sorts of new medical information with which science now bombards us—for instance, that cholesterol levels are a factor in causing heart disease. Second, we can now worry about the calorie content of different foods. In a society in which food is abundant, we are able for the first time to design our bodies in relation to our lifestyle habits (such as jogging, bicycling, swimming, and yoga) and what we eat. Eating disorders have their origins in the opportunities, but also the profound strains and tensions, this situation produces.

Why do eating disorders affect women in particular and young women most acutely? To begin with, it should be pointed out that not all those suffering from eating disorders are women; about 10 percent are men. But men don't suffer from anorexia or bulimia as often as women, partly because widely held social norms stress the importance of physical attractiveness more for women than for men and partly because desirable body images of men differ from those of women.

Anorexia and other eating disorders reflect a situation in which women play a much larger part in the wider society than they used to but are still judged as much by their appearance as by their attainments. Eating disorders are rooted in feelings of shame about the body. The individual feels herself to be inadequate and imperfect, and her anxieties about how others perceive her become focused through her feelings about her body. Ideals of slimness at that point become obsessive—shedding weight becomes the means of making everything all right in her world.

The spread of eating disorders reflects the influence of science and technology on our ways of life today: Calorie counting has only been possible with the advance of technology. But the impact of technology is always conditioned by social factors. We have much more autonomy over the body than ever before, a situation that creates new possibilities of a positive kind as well as new anxieties and problems. What is happening is part of what sociologists call the **socialization of nature.** This phrase refers to the fact that phenomena that used to be "natural," or given in nature, have now become social— they depend on our own social decisions.

The Body Project

A century ago, American women were lacing themselves into corsets and teaching their adolescent daughters to do the same; today's teens shop for thong bikinis or midriff blouses on their own, and their middle-class mothers are likely to be uninvolved until the credit card bill arrives in the mail. These contrasting images might suggest a great deal of progress, but American girls at the end of the twentieth century actually suffer from body problems more pervasive and more dangerous than the constraints implied by the corset. Historical forces have made coming of age in a female body a different and more complex experience today than it was a century ago. Although sexual development—the onset of menstruation and the appearance of breasts—occurs in every generation, a girl's experience of these inevitable biological events is shaped by

the world in which she lives, so much so, that each generation, at its own point in history, develops its own characteristic body problems and projects. Every girl suffers some kind of adolescent angst about her body; it is the historical moment that defines how she reacts to her changing flesh. From the perspective of history, adolescent self-consciousness is quite persistent, but its level is raised or lowered, like the water level in a pool, by the cultural and social setting. [***]

In a New Year's resolution written in 1982, a girl wrote: "I will try to make myself better in any way I possibly can with the help of my budget and baby-sitting money. I will lose weight, get new lenses, already got new haircut, good makeup, new clothes and accessories." This concise declaration clearly captures how girls feel about themselves in the contemporary

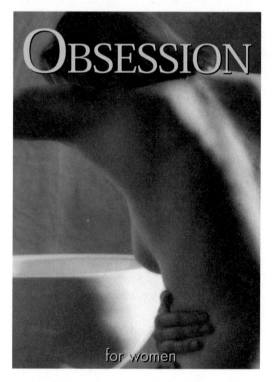

world. Like many adults in American society, girls today are concerned with the shape and appearance of their bodies as a primary expression of their individual identity. [***]

Today, unlike in the Victorian era, commercial interests play directly to the body angst of young girls, a marketing strategy that results in enormous revenues for manufacturers of skin and hair products as well as diet foods. Although elevated body angst is a great boost to corporate profits, it saps the creativity of girls and threatens their mental and physical health. Progress for women is obviously filled with ambiguities. [***]

Adolescent girls today face the issues girls have always faced—Who am I? Who do I want to be?—but their answers, more than ever before, revolve around the body. The increase in anorexia nervosa and bulimia in the past thirty years suggests that in some cases the body becomes an obsession, leading to recalcitrant eating behaviors that can result in death. But even among girls who never develop full-blown eating disorders, the body is so central to definitions of the self that psychologists sometimes use numerical scores of "body esteem" and "body dissatisfaction" to evaluate a girl's mental health. In the 1990s, tests that ask respondents to indicate levels of satisfaction or dissatisfaction with their own thighs or buttocks have become a useful key for unlocking the inner life of many American girls.

Why is the body still a girl's nemesis? Shouldn't today's sexually liberated girls feel better about themselves than their corseted sisters of a century ago? The historical evidence [***],

based on research that includes diaries written by American girls in the years between the 1830s and the 1990s, suggests that although young women today enjoy greater freedom and more options than their counterparts of a century ago, they are also under more pressure, and at greater risk, because of a unique combination of biological and cultural forces that have made the adolescent female body into a template for much of the social change of the twentieth century. I use the body as evidence to show how the mother-daughter connection has loosened, especially with regard to the experience of menstruation and sexuality; how doctors and marketers took over important educational functions that were once the special domain of female relatives and mentors; how scientific medicine, movies, and advertising created a new, more exacting ideal of physical perfection; and how changing standards of intimacy turned virginity into an outmoded ideal. The fact that American girls now make the body their central project is not an accident or a curiosity: it is a symptom of historical changes that are only now beginning to be understood.

SOURCE: Joan Jacobs Brumberg, *The Body Project* (New York: Vintage, 1997).

Questions

- What cultural and social factors may have driven girls to view their bodies as a primary source of their identities?
- How do the insecurities of adolescent girls affect the rest of the population, male and female?
- Can our culture avoid commodifying the body? Why are adolescent girls a primary target for marketers and manufacturers?

Sociological Perspectives on Health and Illness

One of the main concerns of sociologists is to examine the experience of illness—how being sick, chronically ill, or disabled is experienced and interpreted by sick persons and by those with whom they come in contact. If you have ever been ill, even for a short period of time, you know that patterns in everyday life are temporarily modified and your interactions with others become transformed. This is because the normal functioning of the body is a vital, but often unnoticed, part of our lives. We depend on our bodies to operate as they should; our very sense of self is predicated on the expectation that our bodies will facilitate, not impede, our social interactions and daily activities.

Illness has both personal and public dimensions. When we fall ill, not only do *we* experience pain, discomfort, confusion, and other challenges, but others are affected as well. People in close contact with us may extend sympathy, care, and support. They may struggle to make sense of the fact of our illness or to find ways to incorporate it into the patterns of their own lives. Others with whom we come into contact may also react to illness; these reactions in turn help to shape our own interpretations and can pose challenges to our sense of self.

Two ways of understanding the experience of illness have been particularly influential in sociological thought. The first, associated with the functionalist school, sets forth the norms of behavior that individuals are thought to adopt when sick. The second view, favored by symbolic interactionists, is a broader attempt to reveal the interpretations that are ascribed to illness and how these meanings influence people's actions and behavior.

THE SICK ROLE

The prominent functionalist thinker Talcott Parsons advanced the notion of the **sick role** in order to describe the patterns of behavior that the sick person adopts in order to minimize the disruptive impact of illness (Parsons, 1951). Functionalist thought holds that society usually operates in a smooth and consensual manner. Illness is therefore seen as a dysfunction that can disrupt the flow of this normal state of being. A sick individual, for example, might not be able to perform all of his or her standard responsibilities or might be less reliable and efficient than usual. Because sick people are not able to carry out their normal roles, the lives of people around them are disrupted: Assignments at work go unfinished and cause stress for coworkers, responsibilities at home are not fulfilled, and so forth.

According to Parsons, people learn the sick role through socialization and enact it—with the cooperation of others—when they fall ill. There are three pillars of the sick role:

1. **The sick person is not personally responsible for being sick.**

2. **The sick person is entitled to certain rights and privileges, including a withdrawal from normal responsibilities.**

3. **The sick person must work to regain health by consulting a medical expert and agreeing to become a patient.**

EVALUATION

The sick role model has been an influential theory that reveals clearly how the ill person is an integral part of a larger social context. But a number of criticisms can be levied against it. Some writers have argued that the sick-role formula is unable to capture the *experience* of illness. Others point out that it cannot be applied universally. For example, the sick role theory does not account for instances when doctors and patients disagree about a diagnosis or have opposing interests. It also fails to explain those illnesses that do not necessarily lead to a suspension of normal activity, such as alcoholism, certain disabilities, and some chronic diseases. Furthermore, assuming the sick role is not always a straightforward process. Some individuals suffer for years from chronic pain or from symptoms that are repeatedly misdiagnosed. They are denied the sick role until a clear diagnosis of their condition is made. In other cases, social factors such as race, class, and gender can affect whether and how readily the sick role is granted. The sick role cannot be divorced from the social, cultural, and economic influences that surround it.

The realities of life and illness are more complex than the sick role suggests. The increasing emphasis on lifestyle and health in our modern age means that individuals are seen as bearing ever greater responsibility for their own well-being. This contradicts the first premise of the sick role—that the individual is not to blame for his or her illness. Moreover, in modern societies the shift away from acute infectious disease toward chronic illness has made the sick role less applicable. Whereas the sick role might be useful in understanding acute illness, it is less useful in the case of chronic illness: There is no one formula for chronically ill or disabled people to follow. Living with illness is experienced and interpreted in a multiplicity of ways by sick people—and by those who surround them.

We will now turn to some of the ways that sociologists of the symbolic interactionist school have attempted to understand the experience of illness.

ILLNESS AS "LIVED EXPERIENCE"

Symbolic interactionists are interested in the ways people interpret the social world and the meanings they ascribe to it. Many sociologists have applied this approach to the realm of health and illness in order to understand how people experience being ill or perceive the illness of others. How do people react and adjust to news about a serious illness? How does illness shape individuals' daily lives? How does living with a chronic illness affect an individual's self-identity?

One theme that sociologists have explored is how chronically ill individuals learn to cope with the practical and emotional implications of their illness. Certain illnesses demand regular treatments or maintenance that can affect people's daily routines. Undergoing dialysis or insulin injections, or taking large numbers of pills demand that individuals adjust their schedules in response to illness. Other illnesses can have unpredictable effects on the body, such as the sudden loss of bowel or bladder control or violent nausea. Individuals suffering from such conditions often develop strategies for managing their illness in day-to-day life. These include both practical considerations—such as always noting the location of the toilet when in an unfamiliar place—as well as skills for managing interpersonal relations, both intimate and commonplace. Although the symptoms of the illness can be embarrassing and disruptive, people develop coping strategies to live life as normally as possible (Kelly, 1992).

At the same time, the experience of illness can pose challenges for individuals to manage their illnesses within the overall context of their lives (Jobling, 1988; Williams, 1993). Illness can place enormous demands on people's time, energy, strength, and emotional reserves. Corbin and Strauss (1985) studied the *regimes of health* that the chronically ill develop in order to organize their daily lives. They identified three types of "work" contained in people's everyday strategies. *Illness work* refers to those activities involved in managing their condition, such as treating pain, doing diagnostic tests, or undergoing physical therapy. *Everyday work* pertains to the management of daily life—maintaining relationships with others, running household affairs, and pursuing professional or personal interests. *Biographical work* involves those activities that the ill person does as part of building or reconstructing their personal narrative. In other words, it is the process of incorporating the illness into one's life, making sense of it, and developing ways of explaining it to others. Such a process can help people restore meaning and order to their lives after coming to terms with the knowledge of chronic illness.

The work of symbolic interactionists on living with illness is one of the most relevant dimensions of the sociology of the body. We are living in a society in which individuals are living longer and leading more active lives in their later years than ever before, but in some cases this also means living longer with illness and anxiety.

Changing Conceptions of Health and Illness

Cultures differ in what they consider healthy and normal, as the discussion of eating disorders showed. All cultures have known concepts of physical health and illness, but most of what we now recognize as medicine is a consequence of developments in Western society over the past three centuries. In premodern cultures, the family was the main institution coping with sickness or affliction. There have always been individuals who specialized as healers, using a mixture of physical and magical remedies, and many of these traditional systems of treatment survive today in non-Western cultures throughout the world. For instance, Ayurvedic medicine (traditional healing) has been practiced in India for nearly two thousand

Ayurvedic treatment: Ayurvedic physician Kumar Das uses a hot iron rod and fabric soaked in herbs to heal an arthritic hip.

years. It is founded on a theory of the equilibrium of psychological and physical facets of the personality, imbalances of which are treated by nutritional and herbal remedies. Chinese folk medicine is similarly based on a conception of the overall harmony of the personality, involving the use of herbs and acupuncture, a technique in which needles are strategically inserted into a patient's skin.

Modern medicine introduced a view of disease that sees its origins and treatment as physical and explicable in scientific terms. The application of science to medical diagnosis and cure was the major feature of the development of modern health care systems. Other, closely related features were the acceptance of the hospital as the setting within which serious illnesses were to be dealt with and the development of the medical profession as a body with recognized codes of ethics and significant social power. The scientific view of disease was linked to the requirement that medical training be systematic and long term; self-taught healers were excluded. Although professional medical practice is not limited to hospitals, the hospital provided an environment in which doctors for the first time were able to treat and study large numbers of patients, in circumstances permitting the concentration of medical technology.

Alternative Medicine

Industrialized countries have some of the best-developed, best-resourced medical facilities in the world. Why, then, is there a growing interest in alternative medicine? From herbal remedies to acupuncture, from reflexology to chiropractic treatments, modern society is witnessing an explosion of health care alternatives that lie outside, or overlap with, the official medical system. First, it is important to stress that not everyone who uses alternative medicine does so as a substitute for orthodox treatment (although some alternative approaches, such as homeopathy, reject the basis of orthodox medicine entirely). Many people combine elements of both approaches. For this reason, some scholars prefer to call nonorthodox techniques *complementary* medicine, rather than alternative medicine (Saks, 1992).

There are many reasons that individuals might seek the services of an alternative medicine practitioner. Some people perceive orthodox medicine to be deficient or incapable of relieving chronic, nagging pains or symptoms of stress and anxiety. Others are dissatisfied with the way modern health care systems function—long waits, referrals through chains of specialists, financial restrictions, and so forth. Connected to this are concerns about the harmful side effects of medication and the intrusiveness of surgery—both techniques favored by modern health care systems. The asymmetrical power relationship between doctors and patients is at the heart of some people's choice to avail themselves of alternative medicine. They feel that the role of the passive patient does not grant them enough input into their own treatment and healing. Finally, some individuals profess religious or philosophical objections to orthodox medicine, which tends to treat the mind and body separately. They believe that the spiritual and psychological dimensions of health and illness are often not taken into account in the practice of orthodox medicine. All these concerns are implicit or explicit critiques of the **biomedical model of health,** the foundation on which the Western medical establishment operates. The biomedical model of health defines disease in objective terms and believes that the healthy body can be restored through scientifically based medical treatment.

The growth of alternative medicine presents a number of interesting questions for sociologists to consider. First and foremost, it is a fascinating reflection of the transformations occurring within modern societies. We are living in an age where more and more information is available—from a variety of sources—to draw on in making choices about our lives. Health care is no exception in this regard. Individuals are increasingly becoming health consumers—adopting an active stance towards their own health and well-being.

Another issue of interest to sociologists relates to the changing nature of health and illness in the late modern period. Many of the conditions and illnesses for which individuals seek alternative medical treatment seem to be products of the modern age itself. Insomnia, anxiety, stress, depression, fatigue, and chronic pain (caused by arthritis, cancer, and other diseases) are all on the rise in industrialized societies. Although these conditions have long existed, they appear to be causing greater distress and disruption to people's health than ever before. Ironically, it seems that these consequences of modernity are ones that orthodox medicine has great difficulty in addressing. Alternative medicine is unlikely to overtake mainstream health care altogether, but indications are that its role will continue to grow.

The Social Basis of Health

The twentieth century witnessed a significant overall rise in life expectancy for people who live in industrialized countries. Diseases such as polio, scarlet fever, and tuberculosis have virtually been eradicated. Compared with those in other parts of the world, standards of health and well-being are relatively high. Many of these advances in public health have been attributed to the power of modern medicine. It is a commonly held assumption that medical research has been—and will continue to be—successful in uncovering the biological causes of disease and in developing effective treatments to control them. As medical knowledge and expertise grow, the argument runs, we can expect to see sustained and steady improvements in public health.

Although this approach to health and disease has been extremely influential, it is somewhat unsatisfactory for sociologists. This is because it ignores the important role of social and environmental influences on patterns of health and illness. The improvements in overall public health over the past century cannot conceal the fact that health and illness are not distributed evenly throughout the population. Research has shown that certain groups of people tend to enjoy much better health than others. These *health inequalities* appear to be tied to larger socioeconomic patterns.

SOCIAL CLASS–BASED INEQUALITIES IN HEALTH

Think about the way that we have previously defined "social class" in Chapter 7, as a concept that partakes of education, income, and occupation. In American society, people with better educations, higher incomes, and more prestigious occupations have better health. What is fascinating is that each of these dimensions of social class may be related to health and mortality for different reasons.

Income is the most obvious. In countries such as the United States, where medical care is expensive and many persons are not covered by insurance, those with more financial resources have better access to physicians and medicine. But inequalities in health also persist in countries like Great Britain, which have national health insurance. Differences in occupational status may lead to inequalities in health and illness even when medical care is more or less evenly distributed. One study of health inequalities in Great Britain, *The Black Report* (Townsend and Davidson, 1982), found that manual workers had substantially higher mortality rates than professional workers, even though Britain's health service had made great strides in equalizing the distribution of health care. Those who work in offices or in domestic settings are at less risk of injury or exposure to hazardous materials.

Differences in education, a third dimension of social class, also are correlated with inequalities in health and illness. Numerous studies document that education is positively related to preventative health behaviors. One set of researchers found that better-educated people are significantly more likely to engage in aerobic exercise and to know their blood pressure, and are less likely to smoke or be overweight (Shea et al., 1991). Other researchers have found that poorly edu-

cated people tend to engage in more cigarette smoking; they also tend to have more problems associated with cholesterol and body weight (Winkleby et al., 1992).

RACE-BASED INEQUALITIES IN HEALTH

Life expectancy at birth in 2000 was about eighty years for white females but just seventy-five years for black females. Likewise, life expectancy at birth in 2000 was seventy-five years for white males yet just sixty-nine years for black males (U.S. Bureau of the Census, 2001d).

Health differences between blacks and whites are significant. When we note such differences, we are making use of a variable—race—that although different from social class, cannot be completely separated from it. One primary reason for inequalities of health between blacks and whites has to do with the fact that as a group blacks have less money than whites. Sixty-two percent of black households have no financial assets at all, almost twice the rate for white households (U.S. Bureau of the Census, 1998). And the median income of a black man is only 12 percent of that of a white man (U.S. Bureau of the Census, 2002).

Some of the differences in black and white health go beyond economic causes to differences in cultural conditions. Take, for example, racial gaps in mortality. Young black men are more susceptible to murder than any other group. In 2000, a black person was six times more likely to be murdered than a white person (Bureau of Justice Statistics, 2002a). Homicide victimization rates for both whites and blacks peaked between 1993 and 1994. The murder rate for white males between fourteen and seventeen increased from 9.4 per 100,000 in 1984 to a high of 22.4 in 1994. By 2000, the murder rate for young white men had declined to 7.9 per 100,000, lower than in 1984. For young black males, the murder rate increased by over 500 percent between 1984 and 1994 (from 47.6 per 100,000 in 1984 to 244 in 1993). Since then the murder rate for blacks has declined to 62.8 per 100,000, which is nearly 800 percent higher than for whites and still over 30 percent higher than the murder rate for young black men in 1984 (Bureau of Justice Statistics, 2002a). This rise in violent crime has accompanied the rise of widespread crack cocaine addiction, a cultural condition of poor African American neighborhoods plagued by high levels of unemployment (Wilson, 1996).

Besides the life expectancy and homicide rates, other race-based inequalities in health status are stark. There is a higher prevalence of hypertension among blacks—especially black men, a difference that may be biological. There are racial differences in cigarette smoking, with blacks smoking significantly more than whites. This may be due in some measure to cultural differences between blacks and whites, as well as the

FIGURE 14.1

Cultural and Material Influences on Health

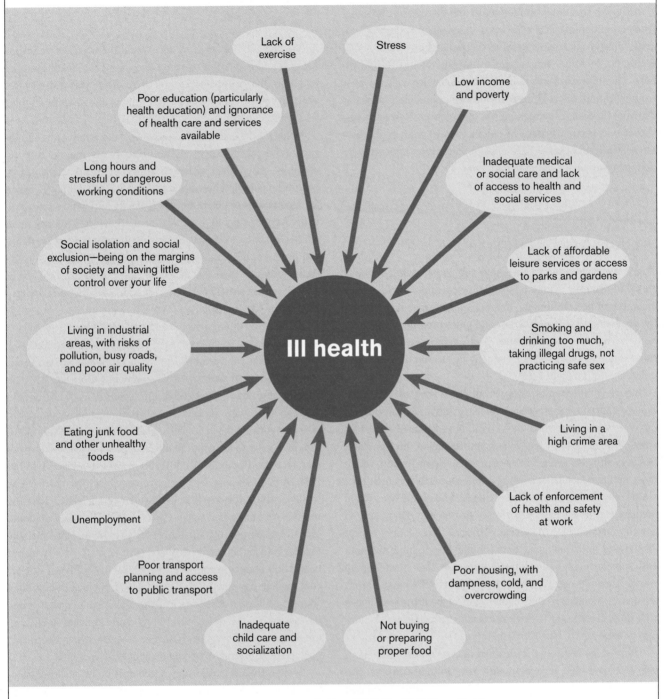

SOURCE: K. Browne, *An Introduction to Sociology,* 2nd ed. (Cambridge, UK: Polity, 1998). From *Sociology Review* 9.2 (November 1999), p. 5. Crown copyright.

way in which the cigarette industry has deliberately targeted African Americans as a market.

But despite these depressing inequalities, it is important to note that some progress has been made in eradicating them. According to the National Center for Health Statistics (2003), racial differences in cigarette smoking have decreased. In 1965, half of white men and 60 percent of black men age eighteen and over smoked cigarettes. By 2001, only 25 percent of white men and 27 percent of black men smoked. In 1965, roughly equal proportions of black and white women age eighteen and older smoked (33–34 percent). In 2001, a smaller proportion of black women (20 percent) smoked than did white women (22 percent).

Prevalence of hypertension among blacks has been greatly reduced. In the early 1970s, half of black adults suffered from hypertension. By 1994, however, roughly 36 percent of black adults suffered from hypertension (National Center for Health Statistics, 2003).

Patterns of physician visitation, hospitalization, and preventive medicine have also changed. In 1987, only 30 percent of white women and 24 percent of black women aged forty and older reported having a mammogram within the past two years. By 2000, the rate for white women more than doubled to 71 percent, and that for black women increased over 2.5 times to 68 percent (National Center for Health Statistics, 2003c). Between 1983 and 2001, the proportion of blacks who had visited the dentist within the past year had increased from 39 percent to 57 percent, while the figure for whites increased from 57 percent to 67 percent (National Center for Health Statistics, 2003d).

How might the influence of poverty on health be countered? Extensive programs of health education and disease prevention are one possibility. But such programs tend to work better among more prosperous, well-educated groups and in any case usually produce only small changes in behavior. Increased accessibility to health services would help, but probably to a limited degree. The only really effective policy option is to attack poverty itself, so as to reduce the income gap between rich and poor (Najman, 1993).

GENDER-BASED INEQUALITIES IN HEALTH

Women in the United States are likely to live longer than men. This gender gap is, interestingly, a relatively recent phenomenon. In the United States, there was only a two-year difference in female and male life expectancies in 1900. By 1940, this gap increased to 4.4 years, and by 1970, the gap had widened to 7.7 years. The gender gap has since been stabilized at about 6 years (Cleary, 1987; National Center for Health Statistics, 2001).

Despite the female advantage in mortality, most large surveys show women more often report poor health. Women have higher rates of illness from acute conditions and nonfatal chronic conditions, including arthritis, osteoporosis, and depressive and anxiety disorders. They are slightly more likely to report their health as fair to poor, they spend about 40 percent more days in bed each year, and their activities are restricted due to health problems about 25 percent more than men. In addition, they make more physician visits each year and have twice the number of surgical procedures performed on them as do men (National Center for Health Statistics, 1996, 2003e, 2003f).

There are two main explanations for women's poorer health, yet longer lives: (1) Greater life expectancy and age brings poorer health; (2) women make greater use of medical services including preventive care (Centers for Disease Control and Prevention, 2003a). In 2000, the average number of visits to physician offices, hospital emergency rooms, and hospital outpatient departments was 25 percent higher for women than for men. Men may experience as many or more health symptoms as women, but men may ignore symptoms, may underestimate the extent of their illness, or may utilize preventive services less often (Waldron, 1986).

The Developing World: Colonialism and the Spread of Disease

There is good evidence that the hunting and gathering communities of the Americas, prior to the arrival of the Europeans, were not as subject to infectious disease as the European societies of the period. Many infectious organisms only thrive when human populations are living above the density characteristic of hunting and gathering life. Permanently settled communities, particularly large cities, risk contamination of water supplies by waste products. Hunters and gatherers were less vulnerable in this respect because they moved continuously across the countryside.

The expansion of the West in the colonial era transmitted certain diseases into other parts of the world where they had not existed previously. Smallpox, measles, and typhus, among other major maladies, were unknown to the indigenous populations of Central and South America prior to the Spanish conquest in the early sixteenth century. The English and French colonists brought the same diseases to North America (Dubos, 1959). Some of these illnesses produced epidemics so severe that they ravaged or completely wiped out native populations, which had little or no resistance to them.

In Africa and subtropical parts of Asia, infectious diseases have almost certainly been rife for a long period of time. Tropical and subtropical conditions are especially conducive to diseases such as malaria, carried by mosquitoes, and sleeping sickness, carried by the tsetse fly. Yet it seems probable that prior to contact with the Europeans, levels of risk from infectious diseases were lower. There was always the threat of epidemics, drought, or natural disaster, but colonialism led to major changes in the relation between populations and their environments, producing harmful effects on health patterns. The Europeans introduced new farming methods, upsetting the ecology of whole regions. For example, wide tracts of East Africa today are completely devoid of cattle as a result of the uncontrolled spread of the tsetse fly, which multiplied as a result of the changes the intruders introduced. (The tsetse fly carries illnesses which are fatal to both humans and livestock.) Before the arrival of the Europeans, Africans successfully maintained large herds in these same areas (Kjekshus, 1977).

The most significant consequence of the colonial system was its effect on nutrition and therefore on levels of resistance to illness as a result of the changed economic conditions involved in producing for world markets. In many parts of Africa in particular, the nutritional quality of native diets became substantially depressed as cash-crop production supplanted the production of native foods.

This was not simply a one-way process, however, as the early development of colonialism also radically changed Western diets, having a paradoxical impact so far as health is concerned. On the one hand, Western diets were improved by the addition of a range of new foods either previously unknown or very rare, such as bananas, pineapples, and grapefruit. On the other hand, the importation of tobacco and coffee, together with raw sugar, which began increasingly to be used in all manner of foods, has had harmful consequences. Smoking tobacco, especially, has been linked to the prevalence of cancer and heart disease.

Infectious Diseases Today in the Developing World

Although major strides have been made in reducing, and in some cases virtually eliminating, infectious diseases in the developing world, they remain far more common there than in the West. The most important example of a disease that has almost completely disappeared from the world is smallpox, which, even as recently as the 1960s, was a scourge of Europe as well as many other parts of the world. Campaigns against malaria have been much less successful. When the insecticide DDT was first produced, it was hoped that the mosquito, the prime carrier of malaria, could be eradicated. At first, considerable progress was made, but this has slowed down because some strains of mosquito have become resistant to DDT.

Human Immunodeficiency Virus (HIV) and Acquired Immune Deficiency Syndrome (AIDS)

One devastating exception to the trend of eliminating infectious diseases in the developing world is HIV/AIDS, which has become a global epidemic. The true number of people infected with HIV is unknown, but estimates put the figure at between 34 and 46 million worldwide, with 40 million being the most frequently cited. In 2003 alone, over 3 million people worldwide died from AIDS-related illnesses (UNAIDS, 2003). Using middle-range estimates, about 550,000 people are living with HIV/AIDS in Western Europe, 995,000 in North America, 2.1 million in Latin America and the Caribbean, and nearly 27 million in sub-Saharan Africa (see Global Map 14.1). The main impact of the epidemic is still to come, because of the time it takes for HIV infection to develop into full-blown AIDS. The majority

Looking AIDS in the Face: Anonymous (covering face) is a university student at Maputo University in Mozambique. Due to the extreme stigma he might face, he chose not to include any of his clothes in the photograph for fear of being identified. "I can't be identified because it may have a bad impact on my position as a university student. . . . Here in Mozambique there is discrimination promoted by the government. In one of his speeches the prime minister said Mozambique should not invest in educating people with AIDS as there is no hope for them. . . . If my faculty discovered my status there is real possibility that they would discriminate against me. Even if they don't expel me straight away, they would try all sorts of devious means to get rid of me."

of people affected in the world today are heterosexuals. As of 2002, more than half are women. In sub-Saharan Africa, young women are more than 2.5 times more likely than men to be infected with HIV/AIDS. Worldwide, at least four HIV infections are contracted heterosexually for every instance of homosexual spread. In high-income countries the rate of new infections has been on the decline, yet the demographics of who is infected with HIV/AIDS are striking. In the United States, there were 40,000 new infections in 2003. Of these, nearly half were in African Americans, who constitute only 12 percent of the total population. HIV/AIDS is now the leading cause of death among African American women aged twenty-five to thirty-four in the United States (UNAIDS, 2003).

Although the overall spread of AIDS in Western societies has slowed as the result of prevention programs, the opposite has been true in the developing world, where health education is limited and the medical establishment is poor.

In countries heavily affected by the HIV/AIDS epidemic, only 1 percent of pregnant women receives health care services aimed at preventing mother-to-child HIV transmission (UN-AIDS, 2003). Besides the devastation caused by HIV/AIDS to individuals who suffer from it, the AIDS epidemic is creating a range of severe social consequences, including the explosion in the number of orphaned children stemming from the deaths of HIV-infected parents. In sub-Saharan Africa, the parents an estimated 13 million children have died as a result of HIV/AIDS

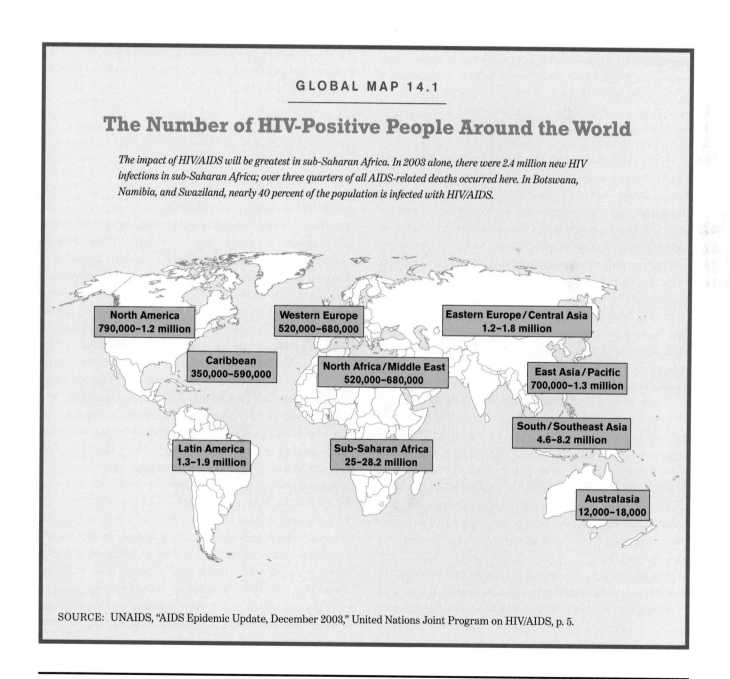

GLOBAL MAP 14.1

The Number of HIV-Positive People Around the World

The impact of HIV/AIDS will be greatest in sub-Saharan Africa. In 2003 alone, there were 2.4 million new HIV infections in sub-Saharan Africa; over three quarters of all AIDS-related deaths occurred here. In Botswana, Namibia, and Swaziland, nearly 40 percent of the population is infected with HIV/AIDS.

North America
790,000–1.2 million

Western Europe
520,000–680,000

Eastern Europe/Central Asia
1.2–1.8 million

Caribbean
350,000–590,000

North Africa/Middle East
520,000–680,000

East Asia/Pacific
700,000–1.3 million

South/Southeast Asia
4.6–8.2 million

Latin America
1.3–1.9 million

Sub-Saharan Africa
25–28.2 million

Australasia
12,000–18,000

SOURCE: UNAIDS, "AIDS Epidemic Update, December 2003," United Nations Joint Program on HIV/AIDS, p. 5.

An eleven-year-old orphan girl sells her grandmother's brooms for $0.03 (U.S.) each in order to buy food in a shanty compound in Kitwe, Zambia. Seventy percent of the world's HIV-infected people live in sub-Saharan Africa and more than a million children in Zambia alone have been orphaned by parents who have succumbed to AIDS.

diseases in developing nations could either be cut by half or eradicated altogether simply by the provision of ready supplies of safe water (Doyal and Pennell, 1981). Only about a quarter of the city residents in developing countries have water-borne sewage facilities; some 30 percent have no sanitation at all. These conditions provide breeding grounds for diseases such as cholera (Dwyer, 1975).

Human Sexuality

The global AIDS epidemic and attempts to halt its spread are further examples of the socialization of nature. As with the study of health and illness, scholars have also differed over the importance of biological versus social and cultural influences on human sexual behavior, another important facet of the sociology of the body.

(see Global Map 14.1). In Uganda alone, 77 percent of the population is under the age of eighteen; 30 percent of those are orphans (AIDS Orphans Educational Trust, 2003). The decimated population of working adults combined with the surging populations of orphans sets the stage for massive social instability, as economies break down and governments are unable to provide for the social needs of orphans who become targets for recruitment into gangs and armies who train them to fight as soldiers.

In fact, basic medical resources are still lacking in the vast majority of developing countries. The hospitals that do exist, together with trained doctors, tend to be heavily concentrated in urban areas, where their services are mostly monopolized by the affluent minority. Most developing countries have introduced some form of national health service, organized by the central government, but the medical services available are usually very limited. The small section of the wealthy utilizes private health care, sometimes traveling to the West when sophisticated medical treatment is needed. Conditions in many developing world cities, particularly in the shantytowns, make the control of infectious diseases very difficult: Many shantytowns almost completely lack basic services such as water, sewage, and garbage disposal.

Studies carried out by the World Health Organization suggest that more than two thirds of people living in urban areas in developing countries draw their water from sources that fail to meet minimal safety standards. It has been estimated that seventeen out of the twenty-five common water-related

Social Influences on Sexual Behavior

Judith Lorber distinguishes as many as ten different sexual identities: straight (heterosexual) woman, straight man, lesbian woman, gay man, bisexual woman, bisexual man, transvestite woman (a woman who regularly dresses as a man), transvestite man (a man who regularly dresses as a woman), transsexual woman (a man who becomes a woman), and transsexual man (a woman who becomes a man). Sexual practices themselves are even more diverse. Freud argued that human beings are born "polymorphously perverse." By this he meant that human beings are born with a wide range of sexual tastes that are ordinarily curbed through socialization—although some adults may follow these even when, in a given society, they are regarded as immoral or illegal. Freud first began his research during the Victorian period, when many people were sexually prudish; yet his patients still revealed to him an amazing diversity of sexual pursuits.

Among possible sexual practices are the following: A man or woman can have sexual relations with women, men, or both. This can happen with one partner at a time or with two or more partners participating. One can have sex with oneself (masturbation) or with no one (celibacy). Someone can have sexual relations with transsexuals or people who erotically cross-dress; use pornography or sexual devices; practice sadomasochism (the erotic use of bondage and the inflicting of pain); have sex with animals; and so on (Lorber, 1994). In most societies, sexual norms encourage some practices and discourage or condemn others. Such norms, however, vary between different cultures. Homosexuality is a case in point. As will be discussed later, some cultures have either tolerated or actively encouraged homosexuality in certain contexts. Among the ancient Greeks, for instance, the love of men for boys was idealized as the highest form of sexual love.

Accepted types of sexual behavior also vary between different cultures, which is one way we know that most sexual responses are learned rather than innate. The most extensive study was carried out five decades ago by Clellan Ford and Frank Beach (1951), who surveyed anthropological evidence from more than two hundred societies. Striking variations were found in what is regarded as "natural" sexual behavior and in norms of sexual attractiveness. For example, in some cultures, extended foreplay, perhaps lasting hours, is thought desirable and even necessary prior to intercourse; in others, foreplay is virtually nonexistent. In some societies, it is believed that overly frequent intercourse leads to physical debilitation or illness. Among the Seniang of the South Pacific, advice on the desirability of spacing out lovemaking is given by the elders of the village—who also believe that a person with white hair may legitimately copulate every night!

In most cultures, norms of sexual attractiveness (held by both females and males) focus more on physical looks for women than for men, a situation that seems to be gradually changing in the West as women increasingly become active in spheres outside the home. The traits seen as most important in female beauty, however, differ greatly. In the modern West, a slim, small body build is admired, while in other cultures a much more generous shape is regarded as most attractive. Sometimes the breasts are not seen as a source of sexual stimulus, whereas in some societies great erotic significance is attached to them. Some societies place great store on the shape of the face, whereas others emphasize the shape and color of the eyes or the size and form of the nose and lips.

Sexuality in Western Culture

Western attitudes toward sexual behavior were for nearly two thousand years molded primarily by Christianity. Although different Christian sects and denominations have held divergent views about the proper place of sexuality in life, the dominant view of the Christian church was that all sexual behavior is suspect, except that needed for reproduction. During some periods, this view produced an extreme prudishness in society at large. But at other times, many people ignored or reacted against the church's teachings, commonly engaging in practices (such as adultery) forbidden by religious authorities. As was mentioned in Chapter 1, the idea that sexual fulfillment can and should be sought through marriage was rare.

In the nineteenth century, religious presumptions about sexuality became partly replaced by medical ones. Most of the early writings by doctors about sexual behavior, however, were as stern as the views of the church. Some argued that any type of sexual activity unconnected with reproduction causes serious physical harm. Masturbation was said to bring on blindness, insanity, heart disease, and other ailments, while oral sex was claimed to cause cancer. In Victorian times, sexual hypocrisy abounded. Many Victorian men, who were on the face of things sober, well-behaved citizens, devoted to their wives, regularly visited prostitutes or kept mistresses. Such behavior was treated leniently, whereas "respectable" women who took lovers were regarded as scandalous and shunned in polite society if their behavior came to light. The differing attitudes toward the sexual activities of men and women formed a double standard, which has long existed and whose residues still linger on today.

In current times, traditional attitudes exist alongside much more liberal attitudes toward sexuality, which developed particularly strongly in the 1960s. Some people, particularly those influenced by Christian teachings, believe that premarital sex is wrong and generally frown on all forms of sexual behavior except heterosexual activity within the confines of marriage—although it is now much more commonly accepted that sexual pleasure is a desirable and important feature of marriage. Others, by contrast, condone or actively approve of premarital sex and hold tolerant attitudes toward different sexual practices. Sexual attitudes have undoubtedly become more permissive over the past thirty years in most Western countries. In movies and plays, scenes are shown that previously would have been completely unacceptable, while pornographic material is readily available to most adults who want it. (Pornography is reportedly the predominant use for the World Wide Web.)

Sexual Behavior: Kinsey's Study

We can speak much more confidently about public values concerning sexuality in the past than we can about private practices, for by their nature such practices mostly go undocumented. When Alfred Kinsey began his research in the United States in the 1940s and 1950s, it was the first time a major investigation of actual sexual behavior had been undertaken. Kinsey and his co-researchers faced condemnation from religious organizations, and his work was denounced as immoral in the newspapers and in Congress. But he persisted, and eventually obtained sexual life histories of 18,000 people, a reasonably representative sample of the white American population (Kinsey et al., 1948, 1953).

Kinsey's results were surprising to most and shocking to many, because they revealed a great difference between the

The Spread of AIDS

There can be no question but that the threat of AIDS has significantly affected American sexual mores. Men and women, straight and gay, have come to realize the dangers posed by unprotected sex, and in many segments of the population, condom use has become the norm. As a result, the rate of transmission of HIV, the virus that causes AIDS, has dropped significantly in the United States. And although there remains no cure for the disease, the use of antiretroviral drugs has greatly increased the longevity of HIV-positive Americans.

The story is very different in the developing world. According to statistics released during the 1998 World AIDS Conference, 90 percent of those with HIV live in developing nations, with the vast majority living in Africa. Because condom availability in the developing world is low, because most governments in the developing world offer little in the way of sex

public expectations of sexual behavior prevailing at that time and actual sexual conduct. The gap between publicly accepted attitudes and actual behavior that Kinsey's findings demonstrated was probably especially great at that particular period, just after World War II. A phase of sexual liberalization had begun rather earlier, in the 1920s, when many younger people felt freed from the strict moral codes that had governed earlier generations. Sexual behavior probably changed a good deal, but issues concerning sexuality were not openly discussed in the way that has become familiar now. People participating in sexual activities that were still strongly disapproved of on a public level concealed them, not realizing the full extent to which others were engaging in similar practices. The more permissive era of the 1960s brought openly declared attitudes more into line with the realities of behavior.

Sexual Behavior since Kinsey

In the 1960s, the social movements that challenged the existing order of things, like those associated with countercultural, or "hippie," lifestyles, also broke with existing sexual norms.

These movements preached sexual freedom, and the invention of the contraceptive pill for women allowed sexual pleasure to be clearly separated from reproduction. Women's groups also started pressing for greater independence from male sexual values, the rejection of the double standard, and the need for women to achieve greater sexual satisfaction in their relationships. Until recently it was difficult to know with accuracy how much sexual behavior had changed since the time of Kinsey's research.

In the late 1980s, Lillian Rubin interviewed a thousand Americans between the ages of thirteen and forty-eight to try to discover what changes have occurred in sexual behavior and attitudes over the past thirty years or so. According to her findings, there have indeed been significant changes. Sexual activity typically begins at a younger age than was true for the previous generation; moreover, the sexual practices of teenagers tend today to be as varied and comprehensive as those of adults. There is still a double standard, but it is not as powerful as it used to be. One of the most important changes is that women now expect, and actively pursue, sexual pleasure in relationships. They expect to receive, not only to provide, sexual satisfaction—a education, and because many mothers with HIV unknowingly pass the disease on to their children, in areas of Africa, one in four adults is infected with the AIDS virus. With rates of transmission showing no signs of decreasing, AIDS threatens to reduce the average life expectancy drastically in many developing nations. One sign of hope is that antiretroviral therapies—which can cost thousands of dollars per patient per year and thus could be out of reach for all but the wealthy few—are now being supplied by American pharmaceutical companies at little or no cost, thanks in part to protests and pressures placed on pharmaceutical companies by African governments and activists.

The specter of AIDS in the developing world also poses a direct threat to the West—because of globalization. Westerners are traveling to the developing world in record numbers, either as tourists or on business. Although HIV cannot be transmitted through casual contact, it is certainly the case that many Americans or Europeans who travel to developing countries will have sexual contacts while they are there, some by using the services of prostitutes. Thailand, for example, has a flourishing sex-tourism business, with some major hotels and tour companies catering to foreigners who wish to take advantage of the country's semilegal prostitution industry (Truong, 1990). Because many of these prostitutes are HIV positive, American tourists, businesspeople, or military personnel who employ

them and who fail to practice safe sex are at risk of contracting the virus and then spreading it on their return to the United States. Diseases, no less than people or goods, cross international borders more easily in a globalized world.

phenomenon that Rubin argues has major consequences for both sexes.

Women are more sexually available than once was the case; but along with this development, which most men applaud, has come a new assertiveness many men find difficult to accept. The men Rubin talked to often said they "felt inadequate," were afraid they could "never do anything right," and found it "impossible to satisfy women these days" (Rubin, 1990).

Men feel inadequate? Doesn't this contradict much of what we have learned in this textbook so far? For in modern society, men continue to dominate in most spheres, and they are in general much more violent toward women than the other way around. Such violence is substantially aimed at the control and continuing subordination of women. Yet a number of authors have begun to argue that masculinity is a burden as much as a source of reward. Much male sexuality, they add, is compulsive rather than satisfying. If men were to stop using sexuality as a means of control, not only women but they themselves would gain.

In 1994, a team of researchers, led by Edward Laumann, published *The Social Organization of Sexuality: Sexual Practices in the United States,* the most comprehensive study of sexual

behavior since Kinsey. To the surprise of many, their findings reflect an essential sexual conservatism among Americans. For instance, 83 percent of their subjects had had only one partner (or no partner at all) in the preceding year, and among married people the figure rises to 96 percent. Fidelity to one's spouse is also quite common: Only 10 percent of women and less than 25 percent of men reported having an extramarital affair during their lifetime. According to the study, Americans average only three partners during their entire lifetime (see Table 14.1). Despite the apparent ordinariness of sexual behavior, some distinct changes emerge from this study, the most significant being a progressive increase in the level of premarital sexual experience, particularly among women. In fact, over 95 percent of Americans getting married today are sexually experienced.

In addition, sexual experience is increasing among high school students. Sexual permissiveness among young people is much greater today than it was thirty years ago. According to the Centers for Disease Control and Prevention, in 2001 nearly half (46 percent) of all high school students reported having had sexual intercourse; 14 percent reported having had four or more partners (CDC, 2003b). U.S. rates are far higher than

TABLE 14.1

Sex in America: Social Influences on Sexual Behavior

TOTAL	SEX PARTNERS IN THE PAST 12 MONTHS				SEX PARTNERS SINCE AGE 18					MEDIAN NUMBER OF SEX PARTNERS SINCE AGE 18
	NONE	1	2–4	5+	NONE	1	2–4	5–10	11–20	21+	
	12%	71%	14%	3%	3%	26%	30%	22%	11%	9%	3
Men	10%	67%	18%	5%	3%	20%	21%	23%	16%	17%	6
Women	14	75	10	2	3	32	36	20	6	3	2
Ages 18–24	11%	57%	24%	9%	8%	32%	34%	15%	8%	3%	2
25–29	6	72	17	6	2	25	31	22	10	9	4
30–34	9	73	16	2	3	21	29	25	11	10	4
35–39	10	77	11	2	2	19	30	25	14	11	4
40–44	11	75	13	1	1	22	28	24	14	12	4
45–49	15	75	9	1	2	26	24	25	10	14	4
50–54	15	79	5	0	2	34	28	18	9	9	2
55–59	32	65	4	0	1	40	28	15	8	7	2
Never married, not living with someone	25%	38%	28%	9%	12%	15%	29%	21%	12%	12%	4
Never married, living with someone	1	75	20	5	0	25	37	16	10	13	3
Married	2	94	4	1	0	37	28	19	9	7	2
Divorced, separated, or widowed, not living with someone	31	41	26	3	0	11	33	29	15	12	5
Divorced, separated, or widowed, living with someone	1	80	16	3	0	0	32	44	12	12	6

those in Japan and China, where only a small percentage of all young people report having had sexual relationships (Toufexis, 1993; Tang and Zuo, 2000). Considering that the General Social Survey in 1998 reported that over 70 percent of respondents believed that teenage sex is "always wrong" and another 16 percent believed it is "almost always wrong" (GSS, 1998), parental beliefs and adolescent behavior are clearly in conflict.

One study of the sexual behavior of tens of thousands of American middle and high school students concluded that early sexual activity was higher among students who were from single-parent families, from a lower socioeconomic status, who demonstrated lower school performance and intelligence, and had lower religiosity—and among students with high levels of "body pride" (Halpern et al., 2000; Lammers et al., 2000).

TOTAL	SEX PARTNERS IN THE PAST 12 MONTHS				SEX PARTNERS SINCE AGE 18						MEDIAN NUMBER OF SEX PARTNERS SINCE AGE 18
	NONE	1	2–4	5+	NONE	1	2–4	5–10	11–20	21 +	
Less than high school degree	16%	67%	15%	3%	4%	27%	36%	19%	9%	6%	3
High school degree or equivalent	11	74	13	3	3	30	29	20	10	7	3
Some college or vocational school	11	71	14	4	2	24	29	23	12	9	4
College graduate	12	69	15	4	2	24	26	24	11	13	4
Advanced degree	13	74	10	3	4	25	26	23	10	13	4
No religion	11%	67%	17%	6%	3%	16%	29%	20%	16%	16%	5
Mainline Protestant	11	74	13	2	2	23	31	23	12	8	4
Conservative Protestant	13	70	14	3	3	30	30	20	10	7	3
Catholic	13	72	13	3	4	27	29	23	8	9	3
Jewish	4	78	15	4	0	24	13	30	17	17	6
Other religion	15	63	15	6	3	42	20	16	8	13	3
White	12%	73%	12%	3%	3%	26%	29%	22%	11%	9%	3
Black	13	60	21	6	2	18	34	24	11	11	4
Hispanic	11	70	17	3	3	36	27	17	8	9	2
Asian	15	77	8	0	6	46	25	14	6	3	1
Native American	12	76	10	2	5	28	35	23	5	5	3

SOURCE: Laumann et al., 1994.

Sexual Orientation

Another important aspect of sexuality concerns *sexual orientation,* the direction of one's sexual or romantic attraction. The term *sexual preference,* which is sometimes incorrectly used instead of *sexual orientation,* is misleading and is to be avoided, since it implies that one's sexual or romantic attraction is entirely a matter of personal choice. As you will see below, sexual orientation results from a complex interplay of biological and social factors not yet fully understood.

The most commonly found sexual orientation in all cultures, including the United States, is *heterosexuality,* a sexual or romantic attraction for persons of the opposite sex (*hetero* comes from the Greek word meaning "other" or "different"). Heterosexuals in the United States are also sometimes referred to as "straight." It is important to bear in mind that although heterosexuality may be the prevailing norm in most cultures, it is not "normal" in the more fundamental sense that it is somehow dictated by some universal moral or religious standard. Like all forms of behavior, heterosexual behavior is socially learned within a particular culture.

Homosexuality involves a sexual or romantic attraction for persons of one's own sex. Today, the term *gay* is used to refer to male homosexuals, *lesbian* for female homosexuals, and *bi* as a shorthand for *bisexuals,* people who experience sexual or

The Political Work of Drag

While many sociologists tend to focus on abstract concepts or faraway places, some scholars write about the issues and places that are part of their everyday lives—their own communities. Verta Taylor and Leila Rupp are two of the United States' leading scholars of gender and social movements. Their book *Drag Queens of the 801 Cabaret* is an example of how sociological research can be used to illuminate the aspects of everyday community life that are usually taken for granted.

Taylor is chair of the Department of Sociology at the University of California, Santa Barbara, and Rupp is chair of the Women's Studies Program, but when they are not occupied in Santa Barbara they live in Key West, Florida, where they have a second home. Key West is a small island city with diverse communities—Cuban, Bahamian, gay, hippy—and is a destination for many gay and lesbian tourists. Taylor and Rupp have been going there for over twenty years and know the town intimately.

One night they walked into the 801 Cabaret to see a new drag show, and they were utterly entranced with what was going on. They had seen men impersonating women in other drag shows, but these performers made no effort to pass as women. They spoke in their male voices, talked about tucking away their male genitals, and mimed sexual acts with various audience members. Through their performance, the drag queens were remolding and simultaneously creating new gender and sexual possibilities. Knowing that drag has a long history building gay communities and educating straight audiences about gay life and alternative gender forms, Taylor and Rupp saw this as a perfect research project.

To depict the social world of the 801 Cabaret, Taylor and Rupp used ethnographic methods. They spent three years attending the shows and hanging out behind the scenes. In the process, they developed a special rapport with the drag queens and got them to open up about all aspects of their lives. They also conducted focus groups with audience members to find out why all sorts of people—gay and straight, men and women, tourists and locals—come to the show and what they take away. The book is naturalistic ethnography because it shows the way people live in their natural setting. It teaches readers about the people behind a stereotype and humanizes them in the best traditions in careful ethnography.

In addition, Taylor and Rupp make an important argument about what the drag queens are doing. Not only are they

the drag queens . . . when I heard they would be doing a special performance for the 800 or so Sociology 1 students. . . . My assumption was wrong. . . . The ladies put on an incredible show filled with entertainment as well as subtle political messages. The packed crowd ate it up. From the moment the three queens came out on the stage doing their rendition of En Vogue's 'Free Your Mind,' guys and girls alike were waving dollar bills in the air."

The UCSB student went on to write: "Here at UCSB, we are used to seeing tan, buff men and gorgeous blondes walking around campus. This time, we got both in one. It takes balls—pun definitely intended—to bare it all in front of a group of 18 to 22 year olds. I expected some people to walk out. No one did. . . . I just wanted to thank the drag queens for coming all the way from Key West and opening our hearts and minds. They are an inspiration to all to be confident in who you are. . . . I also want to thank Verta Taylor for believing we could handle such an event. I myself am thankful that my stereotypical impression of the students here has been challenged. And to the girls at the 801 Cabaret, you made my day."

dancing and entertaining, but something more serious is taking place. The performers are doing political work because their shows solidify community among gay, lesbian, bisexual, and transgender audience members at the same time that they impart messages about the blurred boundaries between masculine and feminine and gay and straight to curious tourists who wander into the show.

How is work like this public sociology? Because it stimulates discussion about what it means to be a man or woman and what it means to be gay or straight in a number of different venues. People in Key West read the book, debating what was going on at the cabaret in the local papers. Across the country, scholars, journalists, and activists respond to the notion that drag performances can serve as an important tactic for gay and lesbian social movements.

After the book appeared, the two professors invited the drag queens to visit their classes at UCSB. Three of the girls performed in Taylor's Introduction to Sociology class, and for the last number, one of them stripped, leaving on only the wig and makeup. Karen Sikola, a student in the class, wrote the next day in the student paper, *The Nexus*: "When I first came to this school, I was under the impression that many of the students here were pretty closed minded. So I was nervous for

The drag queens at the 801 Cabaret dressed Verta Taylor and Leila Rupp in drag so that they would understand how the audience objectifies their bodies.

romantic attraction for persons of either sex. (*Lesbian* derives from the name of the Greek island Lesbos, the birthplace of Sappho, the renowned ancient Greek poet who taught poetry to a devoted following of young women.) Although it is difficult to know for sure because of the stigma attached to homosexuality, which may result in the underreporting of sexuality in demographic surveys, current estimates find that from 2 to 5 percent of all women and 3 to 10 percent of all men in the United States are homosexual or bisexual (Burr, 1993; Laumann et al., 1994; GSS, 1997).

The term *homosexual* was first used by the medical community in 1869 to characterize what was then regarded as a personality disorder. The American Psychiatric Association did not remove homosexuality from its list of mental illnesses until 1973, nor from its highly influential *Diagnostic and Statistical Manual of Mental Disorders* (DSM) until 1980. These long-overdue steps were taken only after prolonged lobbying and pressure by homosexual rights organizations. The medical community was belatedly forced to acknowledge that no scientific research had ever found homosexuals as a group to be psychologically unhealthier than heterosexuals (Burr, 1993).

In some cultures, same-sex relationships are the norm in certain contexts and do not necessarily signify what today is termed "homosexuality." For example, the anthropologist Gilbert Herdt reported that among more than twenty tribes that he studied in Melanesia and New Guinea, ritually prescribed same-sex encounters among young men and boys were regarded as necessary for subsequent masculine virility (Herdt, 1981, 1984, 1986; Herdt and Davidson, 1988). Ritualized male-male sexual encounters also occurred among the Azande of Africa's Sudan and Congo (Evans-Pritchard, 1970), Japanese samurai warriors in the nineteenth century (Leupp, 1995), and highly educated Greek men and boys at the time of Plato (Rouselle, 1999).

IS SEXUAL ORIENTATION INBORN OR LEARNED?

Most sociologists currently believe that sexual orientation—whether homosexual, heterosexual, or something else—results from a complex interplay among biological factors and social learning. Since heterosexuality is the norm for most people in U.S. culture, a great deal of research has focused on why some people become homosexual. Some scholars argue that biological influences are the most important, predisposing certain people to become homosexual from birth (Bell, Weinberg, and Hammersmith, 1981; Green, 1987). Biological explanations for homosexuality have included differences in such things as brain characteristics of homosexuals (Maugh and Zamichow, 1991; LeVay, 1996) and the impact on fetal development of the mother's in utero hormone production during pregnancy (Blanchard and Bogaert, 1996; Manning, Koukourakis, and

Brodie, 1997; McFadden and Champlin, 2000). Such studies, which are based on small numbers of cases, give highly inconclusive (and highly controversial) results (Healy, 2001). It is virtually impossible to separate biological from early social influences in determining a person's sexual orientation.

Studies of twins hold some promise for understanding if there is any genetic basis for homosexuality, since identical twins share identical genes. In two related studies, Bailey and Pillard (1991, 1993) examined 167 pairs of brothers and 143 pairs of sisters, with each pair of siblings raised in the same family, in which at least one sibling defined himself or herself as homosexual. The results of this study seem to show that homosexuality, like heterosexuality, results from a combination of biological and social factors. Among both the men and the women studied, roughly one out of every two identical twins was homosexual, compared with one out of every five fraternal twins, and one out of every ten adoptive brothers and sisters (Bailey and Pillard, 1991, 1993; see also Maugh, 1991, 1993; Burr, 1993). In other words, a woman or man is five times as likely to be lesbian or gay if her or his identical twin is lesbian or gay than if his or her sibling is lesbian or gay but related only through adoption. These results offer some support for the importance of biological factors, since the higher the percentage of shared genes, the greater the percentage of cases in which both siblings were homosexual. However, since approximately half of the identical twin brothers and sisters of homosexuals were not themselves homosexual, a great deal of social learning must also be involved; otherwise one would expect *all* identical twin siblings of homosexuals to be homosexual as well.

HOMOPHOBIA

Homosexuality has long been stigmatized in the United States. **Homophobia,** a term coined in the late 1960s, refers to an aversion or hatred of homosexuals and their lifestyles, along with behavior based on such aversion. It is a form of prejudice that is reflected not only in overt acts of hostility and violence toward lesbians and gays, but also in various forms of verbal abuse that are widespread in American culture: for example, using terms like *fag* or *homo* to insult heterosexual males, or using female-related offensive terms such as *sissy* or *pansy* to put down gay men.

One recent study of homophobia in U.S. schools concluded that the estimated 2 million lesbian, gay, and bisexual middle and high school students are frequently the targets of humiliating harassment and sometimes physical abuse. *Hatred in the Hallways,* which was based on interviews with lesbian, gay, and bisexual students as well as youth service providers, teachers, administrators, counselors, and parents in seven states, found harassment to be a common and painful experience among lesbian, gay, and bisexual students (Bochenek and Brown, 2001). The study cited a CBS poll reporting that a third of eleventh-grade students knew about incidents of sexual harassment of gays and lesbians, while more than a quarter admitted to engaging in harassment.

Such homophobia is widespread in U.S. culture: According to public opinion polls, three out of five Americans report believing that homosexuality is "morally wrong" (Gallup, 1998). Until recently, homosexuality was still legally punishable in some states. Many of the laws were originally written to apply to heterosexuals as well as homosexuals, but they were mainly used to justify taking children away from gay and lesbian parents or to arrest them for engaging in—or even disucssing—homosexual sex. In five states—Arkansas, Kansas, Missouri, Oklahoma, and Texas—sodomy laws explicitly targeted same-sex sexual relationships. In the 2003 case Lawrence v. Texas, however, the Supreme Court struck down the states' anti-sodomy laws and ruled that homosexuals have the same rights to sex and relationships as heterosexuals.

THE MOVEMENT FOR GAY AND LESBIAN CIVIL RIGHTS

Until recently, most gays and lesbians hid their sexual orientation, for fear that "coming out of the closet" would cost them their jobs, families, and friends and leave them open to verbal and physical abuse. Yet, since the late 1960s, many gays and lesbians have acknowledged their homosexuality openly, and in some cities the lives of lesbian and gay Americans has to a large extent been normalized (Seidman, Meeks, and Traschen, 1999). New York City, San Francisco, London, and other large metropolitan areas around the world have thriving gay and lesbian communities. "Coming out" may be important not only for the person who does so, but for others in the larger society: Previously "closeted" lesbians and gays come to realize they are not alone, while heterosexuals are forced to recognize that people whom they have admired and respected are homosexual.

The current global wave of gay and lesbian civil rights movements began partly as an outgrowth of the U.S. social movements of the 1960s, which emphasized pride in racial and ethnic identity. One pivotal event was the Stonewall riots in June 1969, when New York City's gay community—angered by continual police harassment—fought the New York Police Department for two days, a public action that for most people (gay or not) was practically unthinkable (Weeks, 1977; D'Emilio, 1983). The Stonewall riots became a symbol of gay pride, heralding the "coming out" of gays and lesbians, who insisted not only on equal treatment under the law, but also on a complete end to the stigmatization their lifestyle. In 1994, on the twenty-fifth anniversary of the Stonewall riots, one hundred thousand people attended the International March on the United Nations to Affirm the Human Rights of Lesbian and

The Stonewall Inn nightclub raid is regarded as the first shot fired in the battle for gay rights in the United States. The twenty-fifth anniversary of the event was commemorated in New York City with a variety of celebrations as well as discussions on the evolution and future of gay rights.

Gay People. It is clear that significant strides have been made, although discrimination and outright homophobia remain serious problems for many lesbian, gay, and bisexual Americans.

Today there is a growing movement around the world for the civil rights of gays and lesbians. The International Lesbian and Gay Association, which was founded in 1978, today has more than three hundred fifty member organizations in some eighty countries (ILGA, 2001). It holds international conferences, supports lesbian and gay social movement organizations around the world, and lobbies international organizations. For example, it convinced the Council of Europe to require all of its member nations to repeal laws banning homosexuality. In general, active lesbian and gay social movements tend to thrive in countries that emphasize individual rights and liberal state policies (Frank and McEneaney, 1999).

Aging

In addition to health, illness, and sexuality, the social construction of aging is an important component of the sociology of the body. More and more Americans are leading longer, healthier, and more productive lives than ever before. In 2000, there were nearly 4.2 million Americans eighty-five or older, including some 52,000 over one hundred years old (U.S. Census, 2000). Growing old can be a fulfilling and rewarding experience. Or it can be filled with physical distress and social isolation. For most elderly Americans, the experience of aging lies somewhere in between.

In this section, we shall examine the nature of aging in U.S. society, exploring what it means to grow old in a world that is rapidly changing. We begin with a brief snapshot of how the American population is growing older. We then look at the ways in which people adapt to growing old, at least in the eyes of sociologists. This will lead us to a discussion of aging in the United States, focusing on some of the special challenges and problems that the elderly face. We conclude with a discussion of the graying of the world population and what it can mean for you.

The Graying of U.S. Society

The world's population is getting older.

About two thousand years ago, the average newborn Roman baby could expect to live to the ripe old age of twenty-two. In fact, for most of human history the average life expectancy at birth was less than twenty years, with most people failing to survive the first few years of life. The average baby born into the world today can expect to live to be sixty-five, although there is enormous variation depending on where the baby is born—from an average life expectancy of eighty in Japan to one of thirty-eight in Sierra Leone (Weiss, 1997). These changes are due to many factors. Modern agriculture, sanitation systems, epidemic control, and medicine have all contributed to a decline in mortality throughout the world. In most societies today, fewer children die in infancy, and more adults survive to become elderly.

The U.S. population, like other industrial societies, is aging even faster than the preindustrial societies of the world. Thanks to better nutrition and health care, people are living longer. They are also having fewer children. As a result, the median age of the population is rising. In 1850, half the population were younger than nineteen, and half were older. Today, half are over thirty-five; by the middle of the century, half will be over forty (see Figure 14.2).

As a result, the United States and other industrial societies are said to be **graying**, that is, experiencing an increase in the proportion of the population becoming elderly. "Graying" is the result of two long-term trends in industrial societies: the tendency of families to have fewer children (discussed in Chapter 15) and the fact that people are living longer. The average life expectancy at birth for all Americans increased from forty-seven years for someone born in 1900 to seventy-seven years for someone born today (see Figure 14.2). The average U.S. male born today can expect to live to about seventy-four; for females, the figure is nearly eighty. Most of these gains occurred in the first half of the twentieth century and were largely due to the improved chances for survival among the young. Although relatively few people made it to age sixty-five in the year 1900, most of those who did could expect to live to age seventy-seven, almost as long as most of those people who make it to sixty-five today can expect to live—to eighty-two (U.S. Bureau of the Census, 1996a).

Because of the graying of the American population, there are today nearly 35 million Americans older than sixty-five, a figure forecast to reach 80 million people by the year 2030 (U.S. Census, 2000; Treas, 1995). According to U.S. Census estimates, 25 percent of all people reaching age sixty-five today will live to be ninety. By the middle of this century, that figure is expected to rise to 42 percent. According to some projections, by that time there may be as many as a million living Americans who have celebrated their one-hundredth birthday (Weiss, 1997).

These trends have enormous importance for the future of American society. In a culture that often worships eternal youth, what will happen when a quarter of the population is over sixty-five?

How Do People Age?

In examining the nature of aging we will draw on studies of **social gerontology**, a discipline concerned with the study of the social aspects of aging. Studying aging is a bit like examining a moving target: As people grow older, society itself changes at the same time, and so does the very meaning of being "old" (Riley, Foner, and Waring, 1988). For Americans born in the first quarter of the twentieth century, a high school education was regarded as more than sufficient for most available jobs, and most people did not expect to live much past their mid-fifties—and then only at the cost of suffering a variety of disabilities. Today those very same people find themselves in their seventies and eighties; many are relatively healthy, unwilling to disengage from work and social life, and in need of more schooling than they ever dreamed would be necessary.

What does it mean to age? **Aging** can be sociologically defined as the combination of biological, psychological, and social processes that affect people as they grow older (Abeles and Riley, 1987; Riley, Foner, and Waring, 1988; Atchley, 2000). These three processes suggest the metaphor of three different, although interrelated, developmental "clocks": (1) a biological one, which refers to the physical body; (2) a psychological one, which refers to the mind and mental capabilities; and (3) a social one, which refers to cultural norms, values, and role expectations having to do with age. Our notions about the meaning of age are rapidly changing, both because recent research is dispelling many myths about aging and because advances in nutrition and health have enabled many people to live longer, healthier lives than ever before.

FIGURE 14.2

Median Age, U.S. Population, 1850–2050

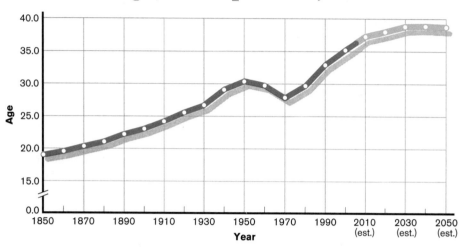

SOURCE: U.S. Bureau of the Census, "National Population Projections," 2002, www.census.gov/population/www/projections/natproj.html.

FIGURE 14.3

Average Life Expectancy at Birth for Males and Females, 1900–2001 in the United States

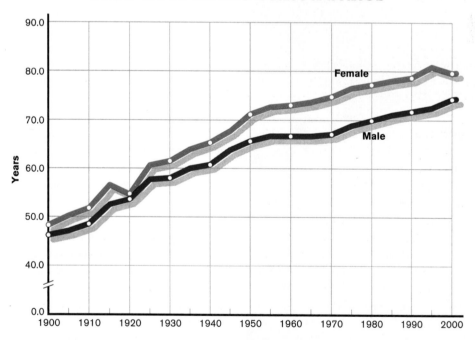

SOURCE: Centers for Disease Control and Prevention, "Life Expectancy at Birth, at 65 years of age, according to race and sex: United States, selected years 1900–2001," Table 27, 2002, www.cdc.gov/nchs/data/hus/tables/2003/03hus0273.pdf.

Growing Old: Competing Sociological Explanations

Social gerontologists have offered a number of theories regarding the nature of aging in U.S. society. Some of the earliest theories emphasized individual adaptation to changing social roles as a person grows older. Later theories focused on how society shapes the social roles of the elderly, often in inequitable ways, and emphasized various aspects of age stratification. The most recent theories have been more multifaceted, focusing on the ways in which the elderly actively create their lives within specific institutional contexts (Hendricks, 1992).

The First Generation of Theories: Functionalism

The earliest theories of aging reflected the functionalist approach that was dominant in sociology during the 1950s and 1960s. They emphasized how individuals adjusted to changing

Some societies have traditionally revered the elderly. Here the young respect the old with an offering of tea, a traditional Chinese custom.

social roles as they aged and how those roles were useful to society. The earliest theories often assumed that aging brings with it physical and psychological decline and that changing social roles have to take this decline into account (Hendricks, 1992).

Talcott Parsons, one of the most influential functionalist theorists of the 1950s, argued that U.S. society needs to find roles for the elderly consistent with advanced age. He expressed concern that the United States, with its emphasis on youth and its avoidance of death, had failed to provide roles that adequately drew on the potential wisdom and maturity of its older citizens. Moreover, given the graying of U.S. society that was evident even in Parsons's time, he argued that this failure could well lead to older people's becoming discouraged and alienated from society. In order to achieve a "healthy maturity," Parsons (1960) argued, the elderly need to adjust psychologically to their changed circumstances, while society needs to redefine the social roles of the elderly. Old roles (such as work) have to be abandoned, while new forms of productive activity (such as volunteer service) need to be identified.

Parsons's ideas anticipated those of **disengagement theory**, the notion that it is functional for society to remove people from their traditional roles when they become elderly, thereby freeing up those roles for others (Cumming and Henry, 1961; Estes, Binney, and Culbertson, 1992). According to this perspective, given the increasing frailty, illness, and dependency of elderly people, it becomes increasingly dysfunctional for them to occupy traditional social roles they are no longer capable of adequately fulfilling. The elderly therefore should retire from their jobs, pull back from civic life, and eventually withdraw from other activities as well. Disengagement is assumed to be functional for the larger society because it opens up roles formerly filled by the elderly for younger people, who presumably will carry them out with fresh energy and new skills. Disengagement is also assumed to be functional for the elderly, because it enables them to take on less taxing roles consistent with their advancing age and declining health. A number of studies of older adults indeed report that the large majority feel good about retiring, which they claim has improved their morale and increased their happiness (Crowley, 1985; Palmore et al., 1985; Howard et al., 1986; Atchley, 2000).

Although there is obviously some truth to disengagement theory, the idea that elderly people should completely disengage from the larger society takes for granted the prevailing stereotype that old age necessarily involves frailty and dependence. As a result, no sooner did the theory appear than these very assumptions were challenged, often by some of the theory's original proponents (Cumming, 1963, 1975; Henry, 1965; Maddox, 1965, 1970; Hochschild, 1975; Hendricks, 1992). These challenges gave rise to another functionalist theory of aging, which drew conclusions quite opposite to those of disengagement theory: *activity theory*.

According to **activity theory**, elderly people who are busy and engaged, leading fulfilling and productive lives, can be functional for society. Activity theory regards aging as a normal part of human development and argues that elderly people can best serve society, as well as themselves, by remaining active as long as possible. Although there may come a time in most peoples' lives when disengagement will best serve their interests as well as society's, activity theory argues that an active individual is much more likely to remain healthy, alert, and socially useful. In this view, people should remain engaged in their work and other social roles as long as they are capable of doing so. If a time comes when a particular role becomes too difficult or taxing, then other roles can be sought—for example, volunteer work in the community.

Activity theory finds support in research showing that continued activity well into old age is associated with enhanced mental and physical health (Schaie, 1983; Rowe and Kahn, 1987; Birren and Bengston, 1988). For example, there is some evidence that continued part- or full-time employment is associated with higher morale and happiness, possibly because of the expanded friendship networks that result from continued work (Soumerai and Avorn, 1983; Conner, Dorfman, and Tompkins, 1985; Riddick, 1985; Bosse et al., 1987; Mor-Barak et al., 1992).

Critics of functionalist theories of aging argue that these theories emphasize the need for the elderly to adapt to existing conditions, either by disengaging from socially useful roles or by actively pursuing them, but that they do not question whether or not the circumstances faced by the elderly are just. In reaction another group of theorists arose—those growing out of the social conflict tradition (Hendricks, 1992).

The Second Generation of Theories: Social Conflict

Unlike their predecessors, whose emphasis was on how well the elderly could be integrated into the larger society, the second generation of theorists focused on sources of social conflict between the elderly and society (Hendricks, 1992). Much like other theorists who were studying social conflict in U.S. society during the 1970s and early 1980s, these theorists stressed the ways in which the larger social structure helped to shape the opportunities available to the elderly; unequal opportunities were seen as creating the potential for conflict.

According to this view, many of the problems of aging—such as poverty, inadequate health care, or lack of decent nursing homes—are systematically produced by the routine operation of social institutions. A capitalist society, the reasoning goes, favors those who are most economically powerful. While there are certainly some elderly people who have "made

it" and are set for life, many have not—and these people must fight to get even a meager share of society's scarce resources.

Conflict theories of aging flourished during the 1980s, when a shrinking job base and cutbacks in federal spending threatened to pit different social groups against each other in the competition for scarce resources. The elderly were seen as competing with the young for increasingly scarce jobs and dwindling federal dollars. Conflict theorists further pointed out that even among the elderly, those who fared worst were women, low-income people, and minorities, in a cumulating spiral of social conflict (McKinlay, 1975; Estes, Swan, and Gerard, 1982; Estes, Zones, and Swan, 1984; Estes, 1986, 1991; Hendricks and Hendricks, 1986; Hendricks, 1992; Atchley, 2000).

The Third Generation of Theories: Self-Concept and Aging

The most recent theories reject what they regard as the one-sided emphases of both functionalism and conflict theory. They view the elderly as playing an active role in determining their own physical and mental well-being, rather than as merely adapting to the larger society (functionalism) or as victims of the stratification system (social conflict). Circumstances such as family, work, and living situation are important sources of one's self-concept, which in turn affects one's life satisfaction. The elderly are seen as playing a significant role in shaping those circumstances (Dannefer, 1989; Hendricks, 1992; Schaie and Hendricks, 2000).

One recent research project, for example, involved a partnership between the Margaret Warner School of Education and Human Development at the University of Rochester (N.Y.) and two local nursing homes. The project was set up to study how changes in the organizational culture of the homes—as seen in such things as architecture, physical layout, and programming—can affect resident satisfaction and well-being. The objective was to increase social interaction among residents, involving them in satisfying and useful activities. In the words of the gerontologist Dale Dannefer, who headed the project, "If we expect people in nursing homes to improve their health and thrive, to remain socially engaged and make contributions to the lives of others, it should show up in measurable gains in their health and functional status" (quoted in Dickman, 1999). These recent theories also emphasize the increasing diversity among the elderly, showing how people age differently depending on their circumstances (Nelson and Dannefer, 1992). Many provide detailed ethnographic accounts of what it means to grow old in U.S. society, with concrete illustrations from elderly peoples' lives (Gubrium, 1986, 1991, 1993; Gubrium and Sankar, 1994).

Older people are informed by experience, and possess knowledge and skills that can be beneficial to young people. In turn, keeping active and maintaining close contact with young people can be vital in shaping a positive self-concept among the elderly.

Aging in the United States

The elderly make up a highly diverse category about whom few broad generalizations can be made. For one thing, the elderly reflect the diversity of U.S. society that we've made note of elsewhere in this textbook: They are rich, poor, and in between; they belong to all racial and ethnic groups; they live alone and in families of various sorts; they vary in their political values and preferences; and they are gay and lesbian as well as heterosexual. Furthermore, like other Americans, they are diverse with respect to health: While some suffer from mental and physical disabilities, most lead active, independent lives.

There are significant racial differences among the elderly. Whites, on average, live six years longer than African Americans, largely because blacks have much higher rates of poverty and therefore are more likely to suffer from inadequate health care. As a result, a much higher percentage of whites are el-

derly than other racial groups (see Table 14.2). The combined effect of race and sex is substantial—white women live, on average, fifteen years longer than black men. Hispanics are graying the least, partly because this category includes many young immigrant workers with large families.

Currently, one tenth of the elderly population in the United States is foreign born. In California, New York, Hawaii, and other states that receive large numbers of immigrants, as much as one fifth of the elderly population was born outside the United States (Treas, 1995). Most elderly immigrants either do not speak English well or do not speak it at all. Integrating elderly immigrants into U.S. society poses special challenges: some are highly educated, but most are not. Many require special education and training programs. Most lack a retirement income, so that they are dependent on their families or public assistance for support. Among those who arrived in the United States after 1980, one quarter were receiving welfare in 1989, nearly four times the rate of elderly people born in this country (Treas, 1995).

Finally, as people live to increasingly older ages, the elderly are becoming diverse in terms of age itself. It is useful to distin-

---

TABLE 14.2

Percentage of Population over 65 and over 85, in Different Racial Groups, 2000

A higher percentage of whites is elderly than any other group. This is the result of lower fertility (whites have fewer children on average) and greater longevity (whites tend to live longer than most other racial and ethnic groups).

RACIAL GROUP	OVER AGE 65	OVER AGE 85
White	12.8	1.2
Black	7.8	0.8
Asian/Pacific Islander	7.3	0.6
American Indian	6.6	0.2
TOTAL	10.4	0.8

SOURCE: U.S. Bureau of the Census, 2001c.

guish between different age categories of the elderly, such as the "**young old**" (ages sixty-five to seventy-four), the "**old old**" (ages seventy-five to eighty-four), and the "**oldest old**" (age eighty-five and older) (see Figure 14.4). The "young old" are most likely to be economically independent, healthy, active, and engaged; the "oldest old"—the fastest-growing segment of the elderly population—are most likely to encounter difficulties such as poor health, financial insecurity, isolation, and loneliness. These differences are not necessarily due only to the effects of aging. The "young old" came of age during the post–World War II period of strong economic growth and benefited as a result: They are more likely to be educated; to have acquired wealth in the form of a home, savings, or investments; and to have had many years of stable employment. These advantages are much less likely to be enjoyed by the "oldest old," partly because their education and careers began at an earlier time, when economic conditions were not so favorable (Treas, 1995).

What is the experience of growing old in the United States? Although the elderly do face some special challenges, most elderly people lead relatively healthy, satisfying lives. Still, one national survey found a substantial discrepancy between what most Americans under sixty-five thought life would be like when they passed that milestone and the actual experiences of those who had (see Figure 14.5). In this section, we examine differences among the elderly in the United States, along with some of the common problems that they confront; in the next section, we will look at their growing political ability to do something about these problems.

Poverty

Relatively few elderly people live in poverty, although some of the very poorest people are elderly, particularly among minorities. Since older people have for the most part retired from work, their income is based primarily on **Social Security** and private retirement programs. Social Security and **Medicare** have been especially important in lifting many elderly people out of poverty. Yet people who depend solely on these two programs for income and health care coverage are likely to live modestly at best. Social Security accounts for only about 40 percent of the income of the typical retiree;

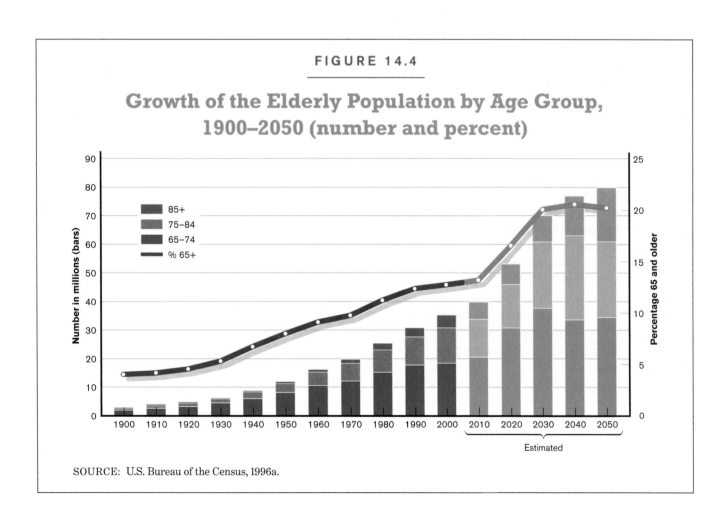

FIGURE 14.4

Growth of the Elderly Population by Age Group, 1900–2050 (number and percent)

SOURCE: U.S. Bureau of the Census, 1996a.

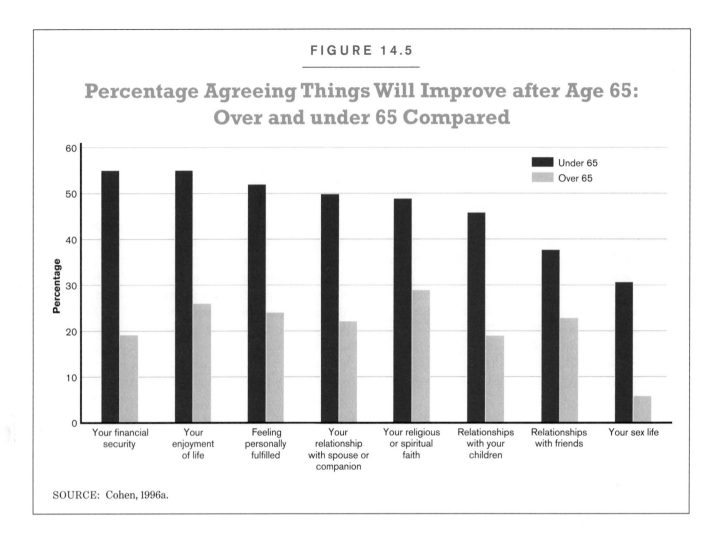

FIGURE 14.5

Percentage Agreeing Things Will Improve after Age 65: Over and under 65 Compared

Legend: ■ Under 65 ▨ Over 65

Categories (x-axis): Your financial security; Your enjoyment of life; Feeling personally fulfilled; Your relationship with spouse or companion; Your religious or spiritual faith; Relationships with your children; Relationships with friends; Your sex life

Y-axis: Percentage (0 to 60)

SOURCE: Cohen, 1996a.

most of the remainder comes from investments and private pension funds, and sometimes earnings. Low-income households in particular are likely to rely heavily on Social Security, which accounts for as much as three quarters of all income for retirees living on less than $10,000 a year (Atchley, 2000). Yet even the combination of Social Security and private pensions results in modest retirement incomes for most people (Krueger, 1995). Although almost all elderly are covered by Medicare, about 75 percent of persons between sixty-five and seventy-four are covered by private health insurance as well (U.S. Bureau of the Census, 1996a).

The economic conditions of the elderly have improved steadily over the past thirty years. As Figure 14.6 shows, in 1959, 35 percent of all people over sixty-five lived in poverty. That figure began to drop during President Lyndon B. Johnson's War on Poverty in the mid-1960s, when Medicare was enacted and Social Security benefits increased. By the early 1970s, poverty rates among the elderly had dropped to below 15 percent, and today they hover around 10 percent. This is two thirds the rate of poverty among children, 26

percent of whom were poor in 2001 (Proctor and Dalaker, 2002). Race appears to be much more important than age in explaining poverty among the elderly (see Figure 14.7). Among whites, only 8.1 percent of the elderly reported poverty-level incomes in 2001, compared with 21.9 percent of blacks and 21.8 percent of Hispanics (Proctor and Dalaker, 2002).

Social Isolation

One of the common stereotypes about the elderly is that they are isolated from human contact. This is not true of the majority of older people, however. Four out of five older people have living children, and the vast majority of them can rely on their children for support if necessary (AARP, 1997). More than nine out of ten adult children report believing that maintaining parental contact is important to them, including the provision of financial support if it is needed (Finley, Roberts, and Banahan, 1988). The reverse is also true: Many studies have

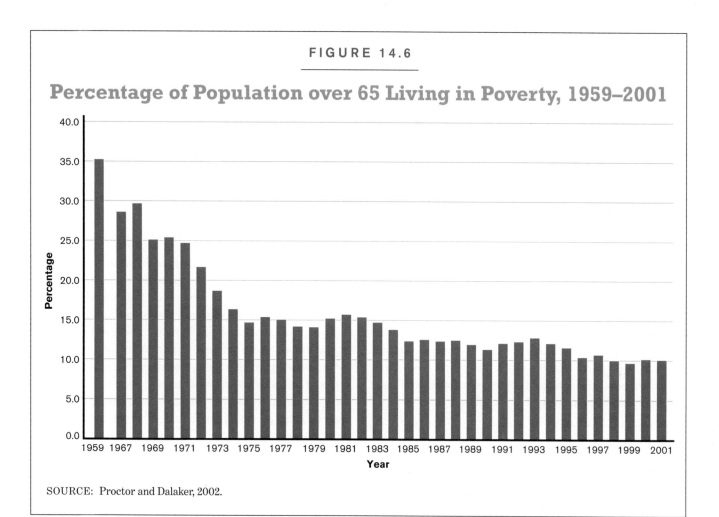

FIGURE 14.6

Percentage of Population over 65 Living in Poverty, 1959–2001

SOURCE: Proctor and Dalaker, 2002.

found that elderly parents continue to provide support for their adult children, particularly during times of difficulty, such as divorce. Most elderly parents and adult children report feeling that the amount of support they receive from the other is fair. Being geographically distant from family members does not seem to be a problem either, since 85 percent of elderly people with children live close to at least one of them (Bankoff, 1983; Moss, Moss, and Moles, 1985; Greenberg and Becker, 1988; Peterson and Peterson, 1988; Bengston, Rosenthal, and Burton, 1990).

Future generations may suffer more from social isolation than do elderly people today. Changing patterns of gender relations, including increases in divorce and a decline in remarriage, may mean that an increasing proportion of elderly people will live alone (Goldscheider, 1990). A majority of such people will likely be women, given the fact that women on average outlive men. Among people over sixty, there are only seventy-one men for every one hundred women; for those seventy or older, the number of men per one hundred women drops to sixty-two. Partly because of the dearth of older men, only about half of all women aged sixty-five to seventy-four

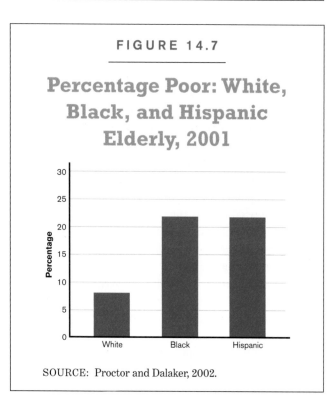

FIGURE 14.7

Percentage Poor: White, Black, and Hispanic Elderly, 2001

SOURCE: Proctor and Dalaker, 2002.

live with a spouse or a mate, compared with nearly four out of five men in that age range. Among those over seventy-five, only a quarter of all women live with a mate; the rate for men is seventy percent (Treas, 1995).

The fact that women outlive men means that elderly women are more likely to experience problems of isolation and loneliness. These problems are compounded by cultural values that make "growing old gracefully" easier for men than for women. In U.S. culture, youth and beauty are viewed as especially desirable qualities for women. Older men, on the other hand, are more likely to be valued for their material success: Graying at the temples is a sign of distinction for a man, rather than a call for a visit to the hairdresser. As a result, elderly divorced or widowed men are much more likely to find a mate than elderly women who are living alone, since the pool of eligible mates for elderly men is more likely to include potential partners who are many years younger. One study of fifty-nine elderly women who had lost their husbands found that some eventually managed to overcome their grief, while others never fully recovered from their husband's death (Hunter, 1990). The widows who overcame their grief tended to be much more satisfied with their social support networks than those who did not.

Prejudice

Discrimination on the basis of age is now against federal law. Nonetheless, prejudices based on false stereotypes are common. **Ageism** is prejudice and/or discrimination based on age and, like all prejudices, is fueled in part by stereotypes. The elderly are frequently seen as perpetually lonely, sad, infirm, forgetful, dependent, senile, old-fashioned, inflexible, and embittered.

There are a number of reasons for such prejudice. The previously mentioned American obsession with youthfulness, reflected in popular entertainment and advertising, leads many younger people to disparage their elders, frequently dismissing them as irrelevant. The new information technology undoubtedly reinforces these prejudices, since youthfulness and computer abilities seem to go hand in hand. In the fast-paced world of MTV, the Web, and dot-com businesses that seem to flourish and perish overnight, young people may come to view the elderly as anachronistic. Associated with the emphasis of youthfulness is a fear-filled avoidance of reminders of death and dying. Such fear carries over into negative attitudes toward the elderly, who serve as a constant reminder of one's mortality (Fry, 1980).

In one study (Levin, 1988), college students were shown a photograph of the same man at ages twenty-five, fifty-two, and seventy-three and were asked to rate him in terms of a variety of personality characteristics. The ratings were significantly more negative for the man depicted at age seventy-three. When he looked old in his photograph, the students were more likely to perceive him negatively, even though they knew absolutely nothing about him. The mere fact of his being elderly was sufficient to trigger a negative cultural stereotype. Widely shared cultural stereotypes of "grumpy old men" can lead to private opinions that are hurtful to older people.

Physical Abuse

Cases of elderly abuse certainly exist, but most research suggests that it is not so widespread as is commonly believed. One random survey among two thousand noninstitutionalized elderly people in the Boston area found that only about 2 percent had experienced physical violence, although these figures may be somewhat low because abuse rates may be higher among those who are unable to respond to surveys. Fewer than 1 percent reported being seriously neglected in terms of their daily needs, while about 1 percent claimed they were subject to chronic verbal aggression. These figures represent a small percentage of the elderly population. Still, they do represent eight thousand to nine thousand cases in the Boston area alone. Although elderly men reported higher rates of abuse than did elderly women, 57 percent of the abused women (compared with 6 percent of the men) reported suffering injuries (Pillemer and Finkelhor, 1988).

It is widely believed that abuse results from the anger and resentment that adult children feel when confronted with the need to care for their infirm parents (Steinmetz, 1983; King, 1984). Most studies, however, have found this to be a false stereotype. More than half of the abuse reported in the abovementioned Boston study was perpetrated by a spouse; only a quarter of the cases occurred at the hands of an adult child (Pillemer and Finkelhor, 1988). Furthermore, in cases when a child abused an elderly parent, it was found that he or she was more likely to be financially dependent on the parent, rather than the reverse. The child may feel resentment about being dependent, while the parent may be unwilling to terminate the abusive relationship because he or she feels obligated to help the child (Pillemer, 1985).

Health Problems

The prevalence of chronic disabilities among the elderly has declined in recent years (Manton, Corder, and Stallard, 1993), and most elderly people rate their health as reasonably good and free of major disabilities. Still, elderly people obviously suffer from more health problems than most younger people, and health difficulties often increase with advancing age. In 1990, the elderly accounted for about a third of all U.S. health care expenditures (Clark, 1993). Nearly half of all noninstitutionalized persons over sixty-five report having at least some problems with arthritis, while about a third report suffering from such ailments as high blood pressure, heart disease, or hearing loss (Treas, 1995). One out of ten people diagnosed for the first time as having HIV/AIDS is over fifty and a quarter of these are over sixty; nearly three times as many people sixty and older died of AIDS in 1992 as did those under twenty (Bennet, 1992; UN AIDS, 2002). Age-related health conditions, such as osteoporosis, create complications for the treatment of the elderly living with AIDS and accelerates the progression from HIV to AIDS (UN AIDS, 2002).

Two out of three noninstitutionalized people over seventy-five consider their health to be "good," "very good," or "excellent" compared with others their age (U.S. Bureau of the Census, 1996a). Not surprisingly, the percentage of people needing help with daily activities increases with age: Whereas only about one in ten people between the ages sixty-five and seventy-five report needing daily assistance, the figure rises to one in five for people between seventy-five and seventy-nine, and to one in three for people between eighty and eighty-four. Half of all people over eighty-five require assistance (U.S. Bureau of the Census, 1996a).

Paradoxically, there is some evidence that the fastest-growing group of elderly, the "oldest old" (those eighty-five and older), tend to enjoy relative robustness, which partially accounts for their having reached their advanced age. This is possibly one of the reasons that health care costs for a person who dies at ninety are about a third of those for a person who dies at seventy (Angier, 1995). Unlike many other Americans, the elderly are fortunate in having access to public health insurance (Medicare) and therefore medical services. The United States, however, stands virtually alone among the industrialized nations in failing to provide adequately for the complete health care of its most senior citizens (Hendricks and Hatch, 1993; Hendricks and Rosenthal, 1993).

Although some 42 million Americans lacked health insurance in 1996 (about 16 percent of the population), only 1 percent of the elderly lacked coverage (Weinberg, 1996). Ninety-six percent of the elderly are covered to some extent by Medicare. But since this program covers less than half of the total health care expenses of the elderly, nearly two out of three supplement Medicare with their own private insurance (Treas, 1995). The rising costs of private insurance, unfortunately, have made this option impossible for a growing number of the elderly. Despite Medicare, the elderly still spend nearly one fifth of their income on health care (Hess, 1990). At present, the rising costs of Medicare have made it a candidate for federal budget cuts.

When the elderly become physically unable to care for themselves, they may wind up in nursing homes. Only about one out of every twenty people over age sixty-five is in a nursing home, a figure that rises to about one out of every five among people over eighty-five (Atchley, 2000). Medicaid, the government program that provides health insurance for the poor, covers long-term supervision and nursing costs, although only when most of one's assets (except for one's home) have been used up. About three out of five elderly people in nursing homes receive assistance from Medicaid (Hudson, 1995). Since the average cost of a nursing home is now over $66,000 a year (Chicago Tribune, 2003), the nonpoor elderly who require such institutionalization may find that their lifetime savings will be quickly depleted. Nursing homes have long had a reputation for austerity and loneliness. In fact, however, the quality of most has improved in recent years, both because federal programs such as Medicaid help to cover the cost of care and because of federal quality regulations.

Still, living for many years in a nursing home was the most widely cited concern about growing old, according to a recent national survey (see Table 14.3). Perhaps that is why the aver-

---

TABLE 14.3

What Is Your Worst Fear about Growing Old?

When it comes to growing old, most Americans fear boredom and death far less than they fear winding up living in a nursing home lonely, isolated, and mentally incapacitated by Alzheimer's disease.

Living for many years in a nursing home	64%
Developing Alzheimer's disease	56%
Becoming a financial burden on others	47%
Being lonely	36%
Loss of physical attractiveness	34%
Death	28%
Having nothing to do	26%

SOURCE: Washington Post National Survey, as reported in Cohen, 1997.

age length of stay in nursing homes dropped from 1,026 days in 1985 to 876 days in 2003, as more elderly people seek home care (Chicago Tribune, 2003; Dey, 1997).

Globalization: The Graying of the World Population

An "elder explosion" is sweeping the world today. The 1998 report of the United Nations Population Fund (UNFPA) notes that the sixty-five-and-older population worldwide grew by about 9 million in 1998. By 2010, the elderly population will grow by 14.5 million; by 2050, 21 million. The most rapid growth of the sixty-five-and-older group will take place in the industrialized nations of the world, where families have fewer children and people live longer than in poorer countries. In the industrialized countries, the percentage of the population that is elderly grew from 8 percent in 1950 to 14 percent in 1998, and it is projected to reach 25 percent by 2050. After the middle of the century, the developing nations will follow suit, as they experience their own elder explosion, though only in the United States and other developed nations will the elderly continue to outnumber the population under fifteen (U.S. Census, 1998).

The populations of most of the world's societies are aging as the result of a decline in both birth and death rates, although the populations of the poorer countries continue to have shorter life spans because of poverty, malnutrition, and disease (see Chapter 15). According to United Nations estimates (UNFPA, 1998), the world's average life expectancy grew from forty-six in 1950 to fifty in 1985 and will reach seventy-one by 2025. At that time, some 800 million people will be over sixty-five, nearly a threefold increase in numbers from 1990. Among the very old (those over eighty-five), whose medical and service needs are the greatest, the number will increase by half in North America, while it will double in China and grow nearly one and a half times in West Africa (Sokolovsky, 1990). This growth will place major demands on the resources of many countries that are already too poor to support their populations adequately.

This explosion has enormous implications for social policy. Over one hundred fifty nations currently provide public assistance for people who are elderly or disabled, or for their survivors when they die. Elderly people are especially likely to require costly health care services. Their rapid growth in numbers threatens to strain the medical systems in many industrial nations, where the cost of providing health care to the elderly threatens to overwhelm government budgets.

Countries vary widely in what they are doing to cope with their growing numbers of older people. As we have seen already, the United States relies primarily on Social Security and Medicare to serve the financial and health needs of the elderly. Other industrial nations provide a much broader array of services. In Japan, for example, men and women remain active well into old age because the Japanese culture encourages this activity and because business policies often support postretirement work with the same company one worked for before retirement. A number of national laws in Japan support the employment and training of older workers, and private businesses also support retraining.

Societies that have large extended families and practice ancestor worship are more likely to treasure their elders, honoring them at public events and seeking their counsel in political matters. In countries such as Thailand, China, and Japan, reverence for ancestors remains strong (Cowgill, 1968; Falk, Falk, and Tomashevich, 1981; Glascock and Feinman, 1981; Seefeldt and Keawkungwal, 1985). Yet globalization has begun to change the treatment of the elderly throughout the world (Fry, 1980; Homes, 1983; Foner, 1984; Cowgill, 1986). As more and more people live to old age, respect for them has tended to decline. The reason is partly that their growing numbers result in a greater economic burden on their families. Additionally, as previously agrarian societies become a part of the emerging global economy, traditional ways of thinking and behaving are likely to change. When extended families are uprooted from farms and move into cities in search of factory work, their ability to support nonworking members is likely to decline. In those societies that are highly family oriented, the responsibility for supporting elderly parents and working for outside income often falls on young women. Research conducted in Taiwan, for example, has found that young girls often work a full day in a nearby factory, returning home during lunch and after work to care for infirm parents or grandparents (Cheng and Hsiung, 1992).

The combination of graying and globalization will shape the lives of elderly people throughout the world well into this century. Traditional patterns of family care will be challenged, as family-based economies continue to give way to labor on the farms and in the offices and factories of global businesses. Like the industrial nations earlier in the twentieth century, all societies will be challenged to find roles for their aging citizens. This challenge will include identifying new means of economic support, often financed by government programs. It will also entail identifying ways to incorporate rather than isolate the elderly, by drawing on their considerable reserves of experience and talents.

Study Outline

www.wwnorton.com/giddens

The Sociology of the Body

- The field of the *sociology of the body* studies how the social world affects our bodies and is particularly concerned with processes of social change. Modern *social technologies* have managed, for instance, to separate the body from nature; an example is the notion of dieting, which involves planned interventions in the functioning of our bodies in order to modify or regulate them in various ways.
- Food production in the modern world has been globalized: Technologies of transportation and of storage (refrigeration) have meant that now everyone in the developed world is on a diet in some sense, having to *decide* what to eat every day. Such decisions are influenced by social relations. Women especially are judged by physical appearance, but feelings of shame about the body can lead anyone to compulsive dieting, exercising, or bodybuilding to make the body conform to social expectations.

The Experience of Health and Illness

- Sociologists are interested in the experience of illness—how being sick, chronically ill, or disabled is experienced by the sick person and by those nearby. The idea of the *sick role,* developed by Talcott Parsons, suggests that a sick person adopts certain forms of behavior in order to minimize the disruptive impact of illness. A sick individual is granted certain privileges, such as the right to withdraw from normal responsibilities, but in return must work actively to regain health by agreeing to follow medical advice.
- Symbolic interactionists have investigated how people cope with disease and chronic illness in their daily lives. The experience of illness can provoke changes in individuals' self-identity and in their daily routines. This dimension of the sociology of the body is becoming increasingly relevant for many societies; people are now living longer than ever before and tend to suffer more from chronic debilitating conditions than from acute illnesses.

Social Factors and Disease

- Health and illness are connected to population issues as well as being strongly affected by social factors such as class, race, and gender. Modern Western medicine, which arose in the past two or three centuries, views illness as having physical origins and hence as being explicable in scientific terms.
- The expansion of the West was accompanied by the spread of infectious diseases in what is now the developing world. Moreover, the colonial system, with its stress on cash crops, negatively affected the nutrition of developing-world people.

Status and Illness

- Susceptibility to the major illnesses is strongly influenced by socioeconomic status. For example, people in the industrialized world tend to live longer than those in the developing world; the richer tend to be healthier, taller, and stronger than those from less privileged backgrounds.

Human Sexuality

- Researchers have examined both biological and cultural influences on human sexual behavior, concluding that sexuality, like gender, is mostly socially constructed. There is an extremely wide range of possible sexual practices, but in any given society only some will be approved and reflected in social norms. Because these norms also vary widely, however, we can be quite certain that most sexual responses are learned rather than innate.

The Graying of U.S. Society

- Because of low mortality and fertility rates, American society is rapidly graying, or aging. There are today some 34 million Americans older than sixty-five, a figure forecast to reach 80 million by the year 2030. The elderly are a large and rapidly growing category that is extremely diverse economically, socially, and politically.

Theories of Aging

- Functionalist theories of aging originally argued that the disengagement of the elderly from society was desirable. *Disengagement theory* held that the elderly should pull back from their traditional social roles as younger people move into them. *Activity theory*, on the other hand, soon came to emphasize the importance of being engaged and busy as a source of vitality.
- Conflict theorists of aging have focused on how the routine operation of social institutions produces various forms of inequality among the elderly.
- The most recent theories regard the elderly as capable of taking control over their own lives and playing an active role in politics and the economy.

Aging and Inequality

- Most of the elderly in U.S. society manage to lead independent lives that they report to be largely satisfying and fulfilling. Still, some suffer from poverty, social isolation, and costly medical problems, as well as from *ageism*, prejudice, and/or discrimination based on age.
- By providing the elderly with retirement income and critical health care insurance, Social Security and Medicare have helped to raise a significant number of elderly people out of poverty. There is some debate over whether these programs are overly generous to the elderly and therefore threaten *generational equity*. In fact, however, the levels of support they offer are modest. Considerable debate nonetheless exists over whether their future funding is likely to be sound.

Globalization and Social Change

• Globalization threatens the traditional roles of the elderly in many societies. The role of the elderly throughout the world is in a rapid state of transition.

Key Concepts

activity theory (p. 404)

ageism (p. 410)

aging (p. 402)

biomedical model of health (p. 386)

conflict theory of aging (p. 405)

disengagement theory (p. 404)

graying (p. 402)

homophobia (p. 400)

Medicare (p. 407)

"oldest old" (p. 407)

"old old" (p. 407)

sick role (p. 384)

social gerontology (p. 402)

Social Security (p. 407)

social technology (p. 381)

socialization of nature (p. 381)

sociology of the body (p. 380)

"young old" (p. 407)

Review Questions

1. Which of the following diseases was transmitted to other parts of the world as a result of the expansion of the West in the colonial era?
   a. Smallpox
   b. Measles
   c. Typhus
   d. All of the above

2. Which of the following statements is true?
   a. About 95 percent of U.S. college women say that they want to lose weight.
   b. About 80 percent of U.S. college men say that they want to lose weight.
   c. About 50 percent of U.S. college women suffer serious problems with an eating disorder at some point in their college careers.
   d. About 50 percent of U.S. college men are on diets.

3. According to Talcott Parsons, which of the following is one of the three pillars of the sick role?
   a. The sick person is personally responsible for being sick.
   b. The sick person is not entitled to withdrawal from normal responsibilities.
   c. The patient should work to regain health by exercising and dieting.
   d. The sick person should consult a medical expert.

4. According to a recent study, how many lesbian, gay, and bisexual middle and high school students are frequently the targets of humiliating harassment, and sometimes physical abuse?
   a. A quarter million
   b. Half a million
   c. One million
   d. Two million

5. Kinsey's findings from the 1940s and 1950s showed Americans to be much more liberal about sexuality than Laumann's findings from the 1990s. What best explains the differences in their results?
   a. Sexually transmitted disease has made Americans much more cautious about whom they have sex with.
   b. In the 1930s and 1940s people were much more prudish when asked about sex than they are today, but much more experimental in private. Today people are much more open when talking about sex, but much more conservative in what they are actually prepared to engage in.
   c. XXX-rated videos; nowadays everyone's seen it all, and figured out that much of it is not for them.
   d. Differences in methodology: Kinsey went looking for people he felt would talk about sexuality, whereas Laumann based his study on survey data from a national study.

6. According to statistics released during the 1998 World AIDS Conference, 90 percent of those with HIV live in developing nations, with the vast majority living in
   a. Africa.
   b. America.
   c. Asia.
   d. Europe.

7. The graying of the population in the United States is the result of a
   a. lower fertility rate.
   b. longer life expectancy.
   c. lower mortality rate.
   d. lower fertility rate and longer life expectancy.

8. Aging can be sociologically defined as the combination of _____ processes that affect people as they grow older.
   a. biological, psychological, and social
   b. cultural, structural, and social
   c. biological, cultural, and social
   d. psychological, cultural, and social

9. What is the central argument of the functional theory in the analysis of aging?
   a. An elderly person should never retreat from active social roles after he/she retires.
   b. Whether to retreat from one's active social roles depends on one's health condition.

c. An elderly person should retreat from active social roles after he/she retires.

d. An elderly person should retreat from active social roles even before he/she retires.

10. The second generation of aging theories emphasizes

a. how well the elderly were integrated into the larger society.

b. how an elderly person can play an active role in determining his or her own physical and mental well-being.

c. how life style and exercise improve one's health.

d. the sources of social conflict between the elderly and society.

11. In the industrialized countries, the percentage of the population that is elderly is projected to reach _____ by 2050.

a. 15 percent

b. 25 percent

c. 35 percent

d. 45 percent

Thinking Sociologically Exercises

1. Statistical studies of our national health persistently show a gap in life expectancies between the rich and the poor. Review all the major factors that would explain why rich people on average live about eight years longer than poor people.

2. Briefly discuss the competing theories about growing old that are presented in this chapter. How do these theories compare with each other? Which theory do you feel is most appropriate to explain aging and why do you feel this way about it?

Data Exercises

www.wwnorton.com/giddens
Keyword: Data14

- This chapter addressed many issues related to health and human sexuality. Without question, these two topics come together in discussing the contemporary HIV/AIDS pandemic. In this chapter you learned that those nations that are most disadvantaged economically are the very nations that have been hardest hit by HIV/AIDS. This exercise will give you a chance to learn more about those countries and how they are coping with the enormous consequences of the disease.

- If you are a traditional age student, you've probably not given much thought to aging, but our society is aging rapidly; we are experiencing *the graying of America*. The data exercise for this chapter provides you with an opportunity to learn more about what is happening in the United States and throughout the world, and what this demographic change means for society.

Living in Cities

Learn how cities have changed as a result of industrialization and urbanization.

Theories of Urbanism

Learn how theories of urbanism have placed increasing emphasis on the influence of socioeconomic factors on city life.

Urbanism in the United States

Learn about the recent key developments affecting American cities in the last several decades: suburbanization, urban decay, and gentrification.

Cities and Globalization

See that global economic competition has a profound impact on urbanization and urban life.

Urbanization in the Developing World

Recognize the challenges of urbanization in the developing world.

World Population Growth

Learn why the world population has increased dramatically and understand the main consequences of this growth.

Population Growth and the Environment

See that the environment is a sociological issue related to urbanization and population growth.

CHAPTER FIFTEEN

URBANIZATION, POPULATION, AND THE ENVIRONMENT

nder the leadership of former Mayor Rudolph Giuliani, New York City became what urban sociologists call a "tourist city," attracting over 30 million visitors a year from all over the globe. As in many urban areas around the world, tourism has had a great effect on both the street life and the economic well-being of the city. For example, whereas the neighborhood around Times Square was once full of porn shops, X-rated theaters, strip joints, drug dealers, and cheap restaurants, it is now home to the Disney Store, theme restaurants, mainstream movie theaters, and other tourist attractions. In addition, the amount of money spent by tourists on theater tickets, hotel rooms, restaurant meals, and the like has pumped billions of dollars into the local economy. Once feared and shunned because of its so-called urban problems, New York is now one of the world's leading tourist destinations, where millions go for the "New York experience." The paradox of a "tourist city" like New York is that while the appeal of tourism is the opportunity to experience something different, cities that are remade to attract tourism seem more and more alike (Judd and Fainstein, 1999).

Nevertheless, cities like New York still offer people opportunities to escape the conformity and provincialism of life elsewhere. People who may have once flocked to Times Square now go to neighborhoods like the East Village, where they hang out on St. Marks Place or Eighth Street and have access to "hip" bars, music shops, and tattoo and piercing parlors. On a weekend night, a scene like Eighth Street is a destination for high school and college students—from both New York and its surrounding suburbs—from all different social and ethnic groups. Here, they move about

New York City's East Village has experienced a remarkable transformation. The neighborhood, which began as a prosperous residential area during colonial times and became a tenement district in the nineteenth century, later attracted artists and bohemians and thrived for many decades as an artists' colony within the city. Today rising rents make it increasingly unviable as an artists' district but it is still regarded as a haven for the city's counterculture.

among older white ethnics who are longtime neighborhood residents, college professors and other urban professionals of all races who have bought apartments in the neighborhood, gays of all classes and races, drug dealers who were forced out of nearby Washington Square Park, and homeless people who make a life for themselves on the sidewalks. Every fifteen minutes or so, double-decker buses drop off tourists who spend time strolling the Village's streets.

Eighth Street is an interesting location to a sociologist because it raises two central questions about urban life: Is social life in cities distinctive from social life outside cities? How much is urban life influenced by larger social forces? One defining characteristic of cities is the frequency of interactions between strangers. Even within the same neighborhood or apartment building, it's highly unlikely that people will know most of their neighbors. This fact alone makes life in cities today different from life elsewhere or during earlier times in history. Although city life is distinctive, cities are closely tied to social processes that cut across the globe. One of the processes that we will explore in this chapter is the movement of people. So while it is easy for one to assume that "urban" problems such as crime and homelessness are unique to cities, sociologists have shown they are neither distinctive to cities nor caused by city life.

The study of cities, and the understanding that a defining feature of urban life is the interaction between strangers, has been a central concern of American sociology since the early 1920s. This was when a group of sociologists at the University of Chicago did field studies of small social worlds within that city.

One such study, *The Taxi-Dance Hall* (Cressey, 1932), focused on the dance halls where immigrant men went for female companionship, buying tickets for dances with women. This early study looked at the dance hall as a place that could only exist in a city because such institutions depended on interaction between strangers. The early sociologists of the Chicago School argued that many people move from small towns to cities to get away from the suffocating atmosphere of "everyone knowing everyone else's business" and the social norms and moralistic codes that enforce conformity. But these same sociologists did not yet understand—as sociologists do today—that the conditions they observed in cities were socially constructed. They thought the patterns they observed were natural and would likely be the same in any city. In this chapter, we will see how urban sociologists ultimately came to a different understanding.

Living in Cities

An inescapable part of modern life, cities provide sociologists with a laboratory for studying the diversity of social life and conflict. Cities are the capitals of civilization: They are culturally lively, commercially dynamic, and alluring. They are efficient in providing for a large number of the population in a small amount of space. However, an entire literature has been devoted to the problems of city life, including poverty, racial and ethnic exclusion and antagonism, and crime.

In all modern societies, in contrast to the premodern era, most of the population live in urban areas, and even those who don't are affected by city life. We will first of all study the origins of cities and the vast growth in the numbers of city dwellers that has occurred over the past century. From there, we will review the most influential theories of urban life. We then move on to consider patterns of urban development in North America, compared with cities in the developing world. Cities in the developing world are growing at an enormous rate. We will consider why this is happening and at the same time look at changes now taking place in world population patterns. We will conclude by assessing the connections among urbanization, world population growth, and environmental problems.

Cities in Traditional Societies

The world's first cities appeared about 3500 B.C.E., in the river valleys of the Nile in Egypt, the Tigris and Euphrates in what is now Iraq, and the Indus in what is today Pakistan. Cities in traditional societies were very small by modern standards. Babylon, for example, one of the largest ancient Near Eastern cities, extended over an area of only 3.2 square miles and at its height, around 2000 B.C.E., probably numbered no more than fifteen to twenty thousand people. Rome under Emperor Augustus in the first century B.C.E. was easily the largest premodern city outside China, with some three hundred thousand inhabitants —the population of Birmingham, Alabama, or Tucson, Arizona, today.

Most cities of the ancient world shared certain features. They were usually surrounded by walls that served as a military defense and emphasized the separation of the urban community from the countryside. The central area of the city was almost always occupied by a religious temple, a royal palace, government and commercial buildings, and a public square. Although it usually contained a market, the center was different from the business districts found at the core of modern cities, because the main buildings were nearly always religious and political (Sjoberg, 1960, 1963; Fox, 1964; Wheatley, 1971).

The dwellings of the ruling class or elite tended to be concentrated in or near the center. The less privileged groups lived toward the perimeter of the city or outside the walls, moving inside if the city came under attack. Different ethnic and religious communities were often allocated to separate neighborhoods, where their members both lived and worked. Sometimes these neighborhoods were also surrounded by walls. "Streets" were usually strips of land on which no one had yet built. A few traditional civilizations boasted sophisticated road systems linking various cities, but these existed mainly for military purposes, and transportation for the most part was slow and limited. Merchants and soldiers were the only people who regularly traveled over long distances.

Although cities were the main centers for science, the arts, and cosmopolitan culture, their influence over the rest of the country was always weak. No more than a tiny proportion of the population lived in the cities, and the division between cities and countryside was pronounced. By far the majority of people lived in small rural communities and rarely came into contact with more than the occasional state official or merchant from the towns.

Industrialization and Urbanization

The contrast in size between the largest modern cities and those of premodern civilizations is extraordinary. The most populous cities in the industrialized countries number over 26 million inhabitants. A **conurbation**—a cluster of cities and towns forming a continuous network—may include even larger numbers of people. The peak of urban life today is represented by what is called the **megalopolis,** the "city of cities." The term

was originally coined in ancient Greece to refer to a city-state that was planned to be the envy of all civilizations. The term was first applied in modern times to refer to the Northeast Corridor of the United States, an area covering some 450 miles from north of Boston to below Washington, D.C. In this region, about 40 million people live at a density of over 700 persons per square mile. An urban population almost as large and dense is concentrated in the lower Great Lakes region.

Britain was the first society to undergo industrialization, beginning in the mid-eighteenth century. The process of industrialization generated increasing **urbanization**—the movement of the population into towns and cities, away from the land. In 1800, fewer than 20 percent of the British population lived in towns or cities with more than ten thousand inhabitants. By 1900, this proportion had risen to 74 percent. London held about 1.1 million people in 1800; by the beginning of the twentieth century, it had increased in size to a population of over 7 million, at that date the largest city ever seen in the world. It was a vast manufacturing, commercial, and financial center at the heart of the still-expanding British empire.

The urbanization of most other European countries and the United States took place somewhat later. In 1800, the United States was more of a rural society than were the leading European countries. Fewer than 10 percent of Americans lived in communities with populations of more than 2,500 people. Today, well over three quarters of Americans are city dwellers. Between 1800 and 1900, as industrialization grew in the United States, the population of New York City leapt from 60,000 people to 4.8 million.

Urbanization in the twenty-first century is a global process, into which the developing world is being drawn more and more (Kasarda and Crenshaw, 1991). From 1900 to 1950, world urbanization increased by 239 percent, compared with a global population growth of 49 percent. The past fifty years have seen a greater acceleration in the proportion of people living in cities. From 1950 to 1986, urban growth worldwide was 320 percent, while the population grew by 54 percent. Most of this growth has occurred in cities in developing world societies. In 1975, 39 percent of the world's population lived in urban areas; the figure was around 50 percent in 2000 and is predicted to be 63 percent in 2025. Eastern and southern Asia will comprise about half of the world's people in 2025. By that date, the urban populations of the developing countries will exceed those of Europe or the United States.

Along with this worldwide urbanization come the effects of globalization. For example, the rise of urban-industrial areas in developing countries has brought intensified economic competition to industries in U.S. cities. South Korea's shoe industry has led to the impoverishment of urban areas in Massachusetts that formerly relied on that industry for their prosperity.

Similarly, Baltimore has had to adjust to losing much of the market for its steel industry to Japan. We will examine later in the chapter how the global economy has influenced forms of city life in recent years.

Theories of Urbanism

The Chicago School

A number of writers associated with the University of Chicago from the 1920s to the 1940s—especially Robert Park, Ernest Burgess, and Louis Wirth—developed ideas that were for many years the chief basis of theory and research in urban sociology. Two concepts developed by the "Chicago School" are worthy of special attention. One is the so-called **ecological approach** to urban analysis; the other, the characterization of urbanism as a *way of life,* developed by Wirth (Park, 1952; Wirth, 1938). It is important to understand these ideas as they were initially conceived by the Chicago School and to see how they have been revised and even supplanted by later sociologists.

URBAN ECOLOGY

Ecology is a term taken from a physical science: the study of the adaptation of plant and animal organisms to their environment. In the natural world, organisms tend to be distributed in systematic ways over the terrain, such that a balance or equilibrium between different species is achieved. The Chicago School believed that the siting of major urban settlements and the distribution of different types of neighborhoods within them can be understood in terms of similar principles. Cities do not grow up at random, but grow in response to advantageous features of the environment. For example, large urban areas in modern societies tend to develop along the shores of rivers, in fertile plains, or at the intersection of trading routes or railways.

According to Park, cities become ordered into "natural areas," through processes of competition, invasion, and succession—all of which occur in biological ecology. If we look at the ecology of a lake in the natural environment, we find that competition among various species of fish, insects, and other organisms operates to reach a fairly stable distribution among them. This balance is disturbed if new species invade—try to make the lake their home. Some of the organisms that used to proliferate in the central area of the lake are driven out to eke out a more precarious existence around its fringes. The invading species are their successors in the central sections.

Patterns of location, movement, and relocation in cities, according to the ecological view, have a similar form. Different neighborhoods develop through the adjustments made by inhabitants as they struggle to gain their livelihoods. A city can be pictured as a map of areas with distinct and contrasting social characteristics. Cities can be seen as formed in concentric rings, broken up into segments. In the center are the **inner-city** areas, a mixture of big business prosperity and decaying private houses. Beyond these are older established neighborhoods, housing workers employed in stable manual occupations. Further out still are the suburbs in which higher-income groups tend to live. Processes of invasion and succession occur within the segments of the concentric rings. Thus as property decays in a central or near-central area, ethnic minority groups might start to move into it. As they do so, more of the preexisting population start to leave, precipitating a wholesale flight to neighborhoods elsewhere in the city or out to the suburbs.

Another aspect of the **urban ecology** approach emphasized the *interdependence* of different city areas. *Differentiation*—the specialization of groups and occupational roles—is the main way in which human beings adapt to their environment. Groups on which many others depend will have a dominant role, often reflected in their central geographical position. Business groups, for example, such as large banks or insurance companies, provide key services for many in a community and hence are usually to be found in the central areas of settlements (Hawley, 1950, 1968).

URBANISM AS A WAY OF LIFE

Wirth's thesis of **urbanism** as a *way of life* is concerned less with whether cities are natural or socially constructed than with what urbanism *is* as a form of social existence. Urbanism is related to the focus, identified earlier in this chapter, with how life in cities is distinctive or different from life elsewhere. In cities, Wirth points out, large numbers of people live in close proximity to each other, without knowing most others personally—a fundamental contrast to small, traditional villages. Most contacts between city dwellers are fleeting and partial and are means to other ends rather than being satisfying relationships in themselves. Interactions with sales clerks in stores, cashiers in banks, passengers or ticket collectors on trains are passing encounters, entered into not for their own sake but as means to other aims.

Wirth was among the first to address the "urban interaction problem" (Duneier and Molotch, 1999), the necessity for city dwellers to respect social boundaries when so many people are in close physical proximity all the time. Wirth elaborates that "the reserve, the indifference, and the blasé outlook that urbanites manifest in their relationships may thus be regarded as devices for immunizing themselves against the personal claims and expectations of others." Many people walk down the street in cities acting unconcerned about the others near them. Through such appearance of apathy they can avoid unwanted transgression of social boundaries.

Wirth's ideas have deservedly enjoyed wide currency. However, in assessing Wirth's ideas, we should consider that neighborhoods involving close kinship and personal ties seem often to be actively *created* by city life; they are not just remnants of a preexisting way of life that survive for a period within the city. Claude Fischer has put forward an interpretation of why large-scale urbanism tends actually to promote diverse subcultures, rather than swamping everyone within an anonymous mass. Those who live in cities, he points out, are able to collaborate with others of like background or interests to develop local connections; and they can join distinctive religious, ethnic, political, and other subcultural groups. A small town or village does not allow the development of such subcultural diversity (Fischer, 1984).

A large city is a world of strangers, yet it supports and creates personal relationships. This is not paradoxical. We have to separate urban experience into the public sphere of encounters with strangers and the more private world of family, friends, and work colleagues. It may be difficult to meet people when one first moves to a large city. But anyone moving to a small, established rural community may find the friendliness of the inhabitants largely a matter of public politeness—it may take years to become accepted. This is not the case in the city. Although one finds a diversity of strangers, each is a potential friend. And once within a group or network, the possibilities for expanding one's personal connections increase considerably.

Wirth's ideas retain some validity, but in the light of subsequent contributions it is clear that they are overgeneralized. Modern cities frequently involve impersonal, anonymous social relationships, but they are also sources of diversity—and, sometimes, intimacy.

JANE JACOBS: "EYES AND EARS UPON THE STREET"

Like most sociologists in the twentieth century, the Chicago School researchers were professors who saw their mission as contributing to a scholarly literature and advancing the field of social science.

At certain moments in the history of sociology, however, advances have also come from thinkers working outside universities without formal training in sociology. One such person was Jane Jacobs, who published *The Death and Life of Great American Cities* in 1961.

Jacobs was an architecture critic with a high school education, but through her own independent reading and research in the 1950s, she transformed herself into one of the most learned figures in the emerging field of urban studies. She is known as a public intellectual, because her main goal was to speak to the educated public, rather than to contribute to a scholarly literature. Nevertheless, her work has had an impact on scholarship in sociology as well.

Like sociologists such as Louis Wirth of the Chicago School before her, Jacobs argued that "cities are, by definition, full of strangers," some of whom are dangerous. She tried to explain what makes it possible for cities to meet the challenge of "assimilating strangers" in such a way that strangers can feel comfortable together. She argued that cities are most habitable when they feature a diversity of uses, thereby ensuring that many people will be coming and going on the streets at any time. When enough people are out and about, Jacobs argued, "respectable" eyes and ears dominate the street and are fixed on strangers, who will thus not get out of hand. Underneath the seeming disorder of a busy street is the very basis for order in "the intricacy of sidewalk use, bringing with it a constant succession of eyes." The more people are out, or looking from their windows at the people who are out, the more their gazes will safeguard the street.

It is very common for people to make the mistake of believing that certain principles are natural to social life, only to discover later on that these principles only hold up under particular social conditions. The world has changed a great deal since Jacobs wrote *The Death and Life of Great American Cities*. Whereas when Jacobs was writing, most of the people on the sidewalks she discussed were similar in many respects, today homeless people, drug users, panhandlers, and others representing economic inequalities, cultural differences, and extremes of behavior can make sidewalk life unpredictable (Duneier, 1999). Under these conditions, strangers do not necessarily feel the kind of solidarity and mutual assurance she described. Sociologists today must ask, What happens to urban life when "the eyes and ears upon the street" represent vast inequalities and cultural differences? Do the assumptions Jacobs made still hold up? In many cases the answer is yes, but in other cases the answer is no. Four decades after her book was published, Jacobs's ideas remain extremely influential.

Urbanism and the Created Environment

Whereas the earlier Chicago School of sociology emphasized that the distribution of people in cities occurs naturally, more recent theories of the city have stressed that urbanism is not a natural process, but has to be analyzed in relation to major patterns of political and economic change.

According to this view, it is not the stranger on the sidewalk who is most threatening to many urban dwellers, especially the poor; instead, it is the stranger far away, working in a bank or real estate development company, who has the power to make decisions that transform whole blocks or neighborhoods (Logan and Molotch, 1987). This focus on the political economy of cities, and on different kinds of strangers, represented a new direction for urban sociology.

HARVEY: THE RESTRUCTURING OF SPACE

Urbanism, David Harvey emphasizes, is one aspect of the **created environment** brought about by the spread of industrial capitalism. In modern urbanism, Harvey points out, space is continually *restructured*. The process is determined by where large firms choose to place their factories, research and development centers, and so forth; the controls that governments operate over both land and industrial production; and the activities of private investors, buying and selling houses and land.

The activities of private home buyers are strongly influenced by how far, and where, business interests buy up land, as well as by rates of loans and taxes fixed by local and central government. After World War II, for instance, there was vast expansion of suburban development outside major cities in the United States. This was partly due to ethnic discrimination and the tendency of whites to move away from inner-city areas. However, it was made possible, Harvey argues, only because of government decisions to provide tax concessions to home buyers and construction firms, and by the setting up of special credit arrangements by financial organizations. These provided the basis for the building and buying of new homes on the peripheries of cities and at the same time promoted demand for industrial products such as the automobile (Harvey, 1973, 1982, 1985).

CASTELLS: URBANISM AND SOCIAL MOVEMENTS

Like Harvey, Manuel Castells stresses that the spatial form of a society is closely linked to the overall mechanisms of its development. However, the nature of the created environment is not just the result of the activities of wealthy and powerful people. Castells stresses the importance of the struggles of underprivileged groups to alter their living conditions. Urban problems stimulate a range of social movements, concerned with improving housing conditions, protesting against air pollution, defending parks, and combating building development that changes the nature of an area. For example, Castells has studied the gay movement in San Francisco, which succeeded in restructuring neighborhoods around its own cultural values— allowing many gay organizations, clubs, and bars to flourish— and gained a prominent position in local politics (Castells, 1977, 1983).

The Castro district in San Francisco is not only open but celebratory about its thriving gay and lesbian population.

Urbanism in the United States

What are the main trends that have affected city development in the United States over the past several decades? How can we explain the decay of central-city areas? These are questions we will take up in the following sections. One of the major changes in urban patterns in the period since World War II is the movement of large parts of city populations to newly constructed suburbs; this movement outward has been a particularly pronounced feature of American cities and is related directly to central-city decay. We therefore begin with a discussion of suburbia before moving on to look at the inner city.

Suburbanization

In the United States, **suburbanization,** the massive development and inhabiting of towns surrounding a city, rapidly increased during the 1950s and 1960s, a time of great economic growth. World War II had previously absorbed most industrial resources, but by the 1950s, war rationing had ended, and the post–war economic boom facilitated moving out of the city. The Federal Housing Administration (FHA) provided assistance in obtaining mortgage loans, making it possible in the early post-

This aerial photograph taken in 1948 shows a portion of Levittown, New York, shortly after the mass-produced suburb was completed. Located on Long Island farmland just 25 miles east of Manhattan, William Levitt's concept to resolve the postwar housing crisis represented the future of suburbia— an entirely new kind of home and non-urban culture.

war period for families to buy housing in the suburbs for less than they would have paid for rent in the cities. The FHA did not offer financial assistance to improve older homes or to build new homes in the central areas of ethnically mixed cities; its large-scale aid went only to the builders and buyers of suburban housing.

Early in the 1950s, lobbies promoting highway construction launched Project Adequate Roads, aimed at inducing the federal government to support the building of highways. In 1956, the Highway Act was passed, authorizing $32 billion to be used for building such highways. The new highway program led to the establishment of industries and services in suburban areas themselves. Consequently, the movement of businesses from the cities to the suburbs took jobs from the manufacturing and service industries with them. Many suburban towns became essentially separate cities, connected by rapid highways to the other suburbs around them. From the 1960s on, the proportion of people commuting between suburbs increased more steadily than the proportion commuting to cities.

Although suburbia in the United States is white dominated, more and more members of racial and ethnic minorities are moving there. From 1980 to 1990, the suburban population of blacks grew by 34.4 percent, of Latinos by 69.3 percent, and of Asians by 125.9 percent. In contrast, the suburban white population grew by only 9.2 percent. In the following decade, from 1990 to 1999, the movement of racial and ethnic minority groups to the suburbs slowed, but remained diverse. The suburban population of blacks grew by 14.2 percent, Latinos by 40 percent, Asians by 45 percent, and whites by 7.6 percent (U.S.

Bureau of the Census, 1999). Members of minority groups move to the suburbs for reasons similar to those who preceded them: better housing, schools, and amenities. Like the people who began the exodus to suburbia in the 1950s, they are mostly middle-class professionals. According to the chairman of the Chicago Housing Authority, "Suburbanization isn't about race now; it's about class. Nobody wants to be around poor people because of all the problems that go along with poor people: poor schools, unsafe streets, gangs" (DeWitt, 1994).

Nevertheless, the suburbs remain mostly white. Minority groups constituted only 18 percent of the total suburban population in 1999 (U.S. Bureau of the Census, 1999). Three out of every four African Americans continue to live in the center cities, compared with one in every four whites. Most black suburban residents live in black-majority neighborhoods in towns bordering the city.

While the last several decades saw a movement from the cities to the suburbs, they also witnessed a shift in the regional distribution of the U.S. population from north to south and east to west. As a percentage of the nation's total population, the Northeast dropped from 25 to 18.9 percent and the Midwest from 29 to 22.6 percent. Meanwhile the population of the South increased from 30.7 to 35.7 percent and that of the West from 15.6 to 22.8 percent (U.S. Bureau of the Census, 2002).

Urban Problems

Inner-city decay is partially a consequence of the social and economic forces involved in the movement of businesses, jobs, and middle-class residents from major cities to the outlying suburbs over the last fifty years. The manufacturing industries that provided employment for the urban blue-collar class largely vanished and were replaced by white-collar service industries. Millions of blue-collar jobs disappeared, and this affected in particular the poorly educated, drawn mostly from minority groups. Although the overall educational levels of minority groups improved over this period, the improvement was not sufficient to keep up with the demands of an information-based economy (Kasarda, 1993). William Julius Wilson has argued that the problems of the urban underclass grew out of this economic transformation (1991, 1996; see Chapter 8).

These economic changes also contributed to increased residential segregation of different racial and ethnic groups and social classes, as we saw in Chapter 10. Discriminatory practices by home sellers, real estate agents, and mortgage lending institutions further added to this pattern of segregation (Massey and Denton, 1993). In the early 1990s, more than 90 percent of African Americans in the United States lived in neighborhoods, both urban and suburban, that were 60 percent or more black (Farley and Frey, 1994). The social isolation of minority groups,

Americans on the Move

How many times did your parents move from one residence to another while you were growing up? America has a high rate of residential mobility. In 1999–2000, 16.1 percent of Americans changed their place of residence at least once. Of these, over half (56 percent) moved to another home within the same county (U.S. Bureau of the Census, 2001). Although this number is no higher than the annual mobility rates of Canada, Australia, and New Zealand, Americans do tend to move more than residents of other industrially developed countries such as France, the United Kingdom, Japan, and Belgium. Yet except for a sharp increase in mobility in the mid-1980s, fueled by recovery from the recession of 1982–1983, mobility rates in the United States are in long-term decline. In the 1950s and 1960s, approximately 20 out of every 100 Americans moved at least once

every year. Mobility rates began to fall in the 1970s and, since the late 1980s, have consistently hovered around 17 percent.

Why do people move? According to a 1991 survey, the most commonly cited reason for moving was to improve one's housing situation: to buy a better home, to make the transition from renting to owning, and so on. Many respondents also cited employment factors as a reason for moving (Gober, 1993).

Because many Americans move for job-related reasons, migration patterns tend to reflect regional patterns of economic development. For example, the Northeast and Midwest, long home to much of the nation's industrial manufacturing, have suffered what demographers call an "out-migration" as a result of the deindustrialization of the American economy. Much of the growth in service-sector work and high-tech production has occurred in the South and West, and millions of Americans have left the Northeast and Midwest in search of jobs in these areas. The Midwest has slowly been able to recover from this situation, shifting its economic base to more viable forms of production and thus attracting enough new residents from other regions to counter the out-migration to the South and West. But the Northeast continues to lose residents at a rapid pace. In 1994, the Northeast lost a total of 61,000 residents, while the West gained 379,000 and the South gained 827,000 (Hansen, 1995). In 2000, the population of the Northeast continued to decline, with another 252,000 residents moving elsewhere. The South lost an additional 227,000, while the West also lost 57,000 residents. The Midwest received the only net gain of residents with 82,000 new people moving in (U.S. Bureau of the Census, 2001).

particularly those in the underclass or "ghetto poor," can escalate urban problems such as crime, lack of economic opportunities, poor health, and family breakdown (Massey, 1996).

Adding to these difficulties is the fact that city governments today operate against a background of almost continual financial crisis. As businesses and middle-class residents moved to the suburbs, the cities lost major sources of tax revenue. High rates of crime and unemployment in the city require it to spend more on welfare services, schools, police, and overall upkeep. Yet because of budget constraints, cities are

forced to cut back many of these services. A cycle of deterioration develops, in which the more suburbia expands, the greater the problems faced by city dwellers become.

Urban Renewal and Gentrification

Urban decay is not wholly a one-way process; it can stimulate countertrends, such as **urban renewal,** or **gentrification.** Dilapidated areas or buildings may become renovated as more

It is all too easy to view these demographic shifts as the result of natural and inevitable long-term processes: High-tech and service sector work comes to account for a greater share of the GNP, these industries naturally spring up in the South and West, making the regions attractive even for traditional manufacturing firms that wish to relocate, and the Northeast is depopulated.

A better explanation begins with—of all things—globalization. As globalization has proceeded, a number of important transformations have taken place in the economic sector. Changes in the financial infrastructure have made it easier for investors to put their money into enterprises anywhere on the globe, and corresponding improvements in communications technology, transportation, and managerial practices have made it more practical for businesses to move their production sites to wherever their costs will be minimized. Capital, economists and sociologists say, has become increasingly mobile under the influence of globalization.

Whereas the mobility of capital sometimes translates into American firms shifting the site of their production to the developing world, in other cases it means that firms will open in or relocate to regions of this country where their production costs will be low. All else being equal, if unions are strong in one region and weak in another, firms are more likely to do business in the region with the weak unions, because they will be able to get away with paying lower wages. Firms also prefer to operate in cities and states that are eager for new development and likely to grant substantial tax breaks. In general, state and local governments in the South and West have been more willing than governments in the Northeast to grant tax breaks to firms, and unions tend to be weaker in these regions than in the Northeast. These factors—in addition to cheaper land and energy—have helped pull some firms out of the Northeast and into the South and West, and have encouraged many startup firms to set up shop in the South and West. Although the dynamics involved are clearly complex, globaliza-

tion and the mobility of capital appear to lay behind recent trends in regional economic development and therefore underlie key patterns in regional migration.

Should attempts be made to halt these changes? What would migration patterns look like if unions were strong in all regions and if cities and states refused to grant generous tax breaks to corporate America? Is the depopulation of the Northeast a good or bad thing?

affluent groups move back into cities. Such a renewal process is called gentrification because those areas or buildings become upgraded and return to the control of the urban "gentry"—high-income dwellers—rather than remaining in the hands of the poor.

In *Streetwise: Race, Class, and Change in an Urban Community* (1990), the sociologist Elijah Anderson analyzed the impact of gentrification on cities. Although the renovation of a neighborhood generally increases its value, it rarely improves the living standards of its current low-income residents, who are usually

forced to move out. The poor residents who continue to live in the neighborhood receive some benefits in the form of improved schools and police protection, but the resulting increase in taxes and rents usually force them to leave for a more affordable neighborhood, most often deeper into the ghetto.

The white newcomers had come to the city in search of cheap "antique" housing, closer access to their city-based jobs, and a trendy urban lifestyle. They professed to be "open minded" about racial and ethnic differences; in reality, however, little fraternizing took place between the new and old

InnerCity Entrepreneurs

In the eight years since Roosevelt St. Louis launched Nouvelle Creation Catering, the Mattapan [Massachusetts] business has expanded from a two-person to a seven-person operation and become a leader in its field—catering of Caribbean and African American style food.

But Nouvelle Creation recently hit a wall. St. Louis, who has no formal business training and few well-connected friends,

was finding it difficult to fully capitalize on the market represented by the local minority community.

"My goal is to be the first professional, on-site catering facility in Boston that specializes in Caribbean and Southern cuisine," says St. Louis. "The biggest challenge I face is that when people hear about us, they assume that the quality of our food must be low, because top-quality catering for ethnic cuisine is uncommon. Expanding my business right now is going to require that I do a lot of social networking to get the word out."

It was to assist business owners like St. Louis that Daniel Monti, a [College of Arts and Science (CAS)] sociology professor, and Andrew Wolk, a [School of Management] research associate, recently launched InnerCity Entrepreneurs (ICE). A collaboration between the CAS sociology department, [Boston University's] Entrepreneurial Management Institute, and Roxbury Community College's Small Business Development Institute, ICE provides educational and networking resources to minority and inner-city business owners, with an eye toward helping them break into the city's larger business networks and at the same time strengthen their communities. It's supported by a $100,000 grant from Citizens Bank Foundation.

"There's a lot of technical assistance available out there for start-ups, but virtually nothing for established businesses that want to grow," says Monti. "We want to find owners of small businesses who have passed the three- to five-year survival

ICE also has developed a group of private industry experts from fields such as law, accounting, banking, equity financing, human resources, and real estate, who serve as guest speakers in the course and are available to answer the business owners' questions and help them network.

[***]

According to Monti, who says the idea for ICE stems from research he completed for his 1999 book *American City*, among the most revealing aspects of the project will be how its participants improve not just their businesses, but their neighborhoods.

"History has taught us that two important ways of building community in America are how businesspeople do it, and how members of ethnic groups do it," he says. "Those two strategies are very different, but I believe they can be complementary, and by combining them, ICE is trying to jump-start that entire community-building process. Business leaders tend to be very engaged in the community, in ways that most people don't observe. And in a city like Boston, which is perceived as being not particularly nurturing to new immigrant groups, the newer populations, such as the blacks, Latinos, and Asians, are going to be more successful economically, and culturally, if they learn to work together."

SOURCE: David J. Craig, "InnerCity Entrepeneurs Gives Small Businesses a Shot at the Big Leagues," *B.U.Bridge* VII, no. 26 (April 2, 2004), www.bu.edu/bridge.

DANIEL MONTI is Associate Professor of Sociology at Boston University. He is the author of The American City: A Social and Cultural History *and* Wannabe: Gangs in Suburbs and Schools. *He is currently involved in an ongoing study of American civic culture in cities across the United States. He is also working with minority and ethnic businesspeople in the Boston area to develop new businesses in minority communities and measure the impact of economic development programs.*

test, train them in how to grow their business, and put them in the same room so that by reaching a hand across the table, they can extend their markets."

So starting in January [2004], St. Louis and thirteen other business owners from around Boston have been attending a three-hour course at BU every two weeks that teaches skills in areas such as financial management, cost analysis, hiring and training, and goal-setting. Participants are required to create a three-year growth plan and during the yearlong course complete assignments that evaluate various aspects of their performance. They also agree to take part in a five-year panel study, headed by Monti, on the factors that enable small businesses in the inner city to grow, and the ways that the growth of businesses contributes to the vitality of inner-city communities, particularly by producing business leaders who become civic leaders.

"The course work gets the participants to step back and analyze their businesses in ways that most small business owners don't usually find the time to do," says Wolk, who directs ICE and teaches the course. "It's very interactive in that the participants use their own businesses as case studies, test out in their business what they learn in the course, and then come back and talk about it. The course has essentially become a part of their job now."

Does gentrification of a run-down inner-city area necessarily result in the dispossession of the existing population, or do renewed interest and an infusion of money in such areas promote a revitalization that works to their advantage? Not long ago, Clinton Street was a grim, graffiti-ridden streetscape (*top*) but it has evolved into a lively restaurant row on New York's Lower East Side (*bottom*).

residents unless they were of the same social class. Over time, the neighborhood was gradually transformed into a white middle-class enclave.

Cities and Globalization

In premodern times, cities were self-contained entities that stood apart from the predominantly rural areas in which they were located. Road systems sometimes linked major urban areas, but travel was a specialized affair for merchants, soldiers, and others who needed to cross distances with any regularity. Communication between cities was limited. The picture at the start of the twenty-first century could hardly be more

different. Globalization has had a profound effect on cities by making them more interdependent and encouraging the proliferation of horizontal links between cities across national borders. Physical and virtual ties between cities now abound and global networks of cities are emerging.

Global Cities

The role of cities in the new global order has been attracting a great deal of attention from sociologists. Globalization is often thought of in terms of a duality between the national level and the global, yet it is the largest *cities* of the world that comprise the main circuits through which globalization occurs (Sassen, 1998). The functioning of the new global economy is dependent on a set of central locations with developed informational infrastructures and a hyperconcentration of facilities. It is in such points that the "work" of globalization is performed and directed. As business, production, advertising, and marketing assume a global scale, there is an enormous amount of organizational activity that must be done in order to maintain and develop these global networks.

Saskia Sassen has been one of the leading contributors to the debate on cities and globalization. She uses the term **global city** to refer to urban centers that are home to the headquarters of large, transnational corporations and a superabundance of financial, technological, and consulting services. In *The Global City* (1991), Sassen bases her work on the study of three such cities: New York, London, and Tokyo. These cities share four traits:

1. They have developed into command posts—centers of direction and policy making—for the global economy.
2. Such cities are the key locations for financial and specialized service firms, which have become more important in influencing economic development than is manufacturing.
3. They are the sites of production and innovation in these newly expanded industries.
4. These cities are markets on which the "products" of financial and service industries are bought, sold, or otherwise disposed of.

Within the highly dispersed world economy of today, cities like these provide for central control of crucial operations. Global cities are much more than simply places of coordination, however; they are also contexts of production. What is important here is not the production of material goods, but the production of the specialized services required by business organizations for administering offices and factories scattered across the world, and the production of financial innovations and markets. Services and financial goods are the "things" the global city makes.

Inequality and the Global City

The new global economy is highly problematic in many ways. Nowhere can this be seen more clearly than in the new dynamics of inequality visible within the global city. The central business district juxtaposed with impoverished inner-city areas in many global cities should be seen as interrelated phenomena, as Sassen and others remind us. The growth sectors of the new economy—financial services, marketing, high technology—are reaping profits far greater than any found within traditional economic sectors. As the salaries and bonuses of the very affluent continue to climb, the wages of those employed to clean and guard their offices are dropping. Sassen argues that we are witnessing the "valorization" of work located at the forefront of the new global economy and the "devalorization" of work that occurs behind the scenes (1998).

Those who work in finances and global services receive high salaries, and the areas where they live become gentrified. At the same time, orthodox manufacturing jobs are lost, and the very process of gentrification creates a vast supply of low-wage jobs—in restaurants, hotels, and boutiques. Affordable housing is scarce in gentrified areas, forcing an expansion of low-income neighborhoods.

Within global cities, a geography of "centrality and marginality" is taking shape—as Mitch Duneier's study in New York's Greenwich Village revealed (Duneier, 1999). Alongside resplendent affluence there is acute poverty. Yet although these two worlds coexist side by side, the actual contact between them can be surprisingly minimal. As Mike Davis has noted in his study of Los Angeles, there has been a "conscious 'hardening' of the city surface against the poor" (1990). Accessible public spaces have been replaced by walled compounds, neighborhoods guarded by electronic surveillance, and "corporate citadels."

According to Davis, life is made as "unliveable" as possible for the poorest and most marginalized residents of Los Angeles. Benches at bus stops are short or barrel-shaped to prevent people from sleeping on them, the number of public toilets is fewer than in any other North American city, and sprinkler systems have been installed in many parks to deter the homeless from living in them. Police and city planners have attempted to contain the homeless population within certain regions of the city, but in periodically sweeping through and confiscating makeshift shelters, they have effectively created a population of "urban bedouins."

The city of Los Angeles has taken steps to dissuade the homeless from sleeping in public places. Notice that the bench pictured here is not long enough for a person to stretch out on and that the shape and placement of the slats would make it quite uncomfortable for any extended period of time.

Urbanization in the Developing World

In 2000, 2.9 billion people, or 47 percent of the world's population, lived in cities. The world's urban population could reach 5 billion people, or over 60 percent of the world's population, by 2030. According to some estimates, 4 million of these urban dwellers will be residents of cities in the developing world. Currently, 40 percent of the populations of developing countries live in cities, but by 2030 urban dwellers are expected to account for 56 percent of the populations of developing countries. As Global Map 15.1 shows, most of the thirty-three cities projected to have more than 8 million residents in 2015 are located in the developing world. Most people in developed countries already live in cities. In 2000, 75 percent of the population of developed countries lived in cities, yet by 2030, 83 percent of people living in developed countries are anticipated to live in cities (UN Population Division, 2002).

Why is the rate of urban growth in the world's lesser developed regions so much higher than elsewhere? Two factors in particular must be taken into account. First, rates of population growth are higher in developing countries than they are in industrialized nations. Urban growth is fueled by *high fertility rates* among people already living in cities.

Second, there is widespread *internal migration* from rural areas to urban ones—as in the case of the developing Hong Kong–Guangdong megacity. People are drawn to cities in the developing world either because their traditional systems of rural production have disintegrated or because the urban areas offer superior job opportunities. Rural poverty prompts many people to try their hand at city life. They may intend to migrate to the city only for a relatively short time, aiming to return to their villages once they have earned enough money. Some actually do return, but most find themselves forced to stay, having for one reason or another lost their position in their previous communities.

GLOBAL MAP 15.1

The Thirty-Three Cities Expected to Have More Than 8 Million Inhabitants in 2015

Los Angeles (United States) 14.4

Mexico City (Mexico) 20.4

New York (United States) 17.9

Paris (France) 9.8

Moscow (Russia) 8.1

Teheran (Iran) 8.1

Beijing (China) 11.6

Istanbul (Turkey) 11.3

Lahore (Pakistan) 8.7

Delhi (India) 20.8

Tianjin (China) 10.3

Seoul (Korea) 9.9

Cairo (Egypt) 11.5

Karachi (Pakistan) 16.1

Dhaka (Bangladesh) 22.7

Tokyo (Japan) 27.1

Bogotá (Colombia) 8.9

Lagos (Nigeria) 15.9

Mumbai (Bombay) (India) 22.5

Shanghai (China) 13.5

Osaka (Japan) 11.0

Lima (Peru) 9.3

Rio de Janeiro (Brazil) 11.5

Kinshasa (Democratic Republic of Congo) 9.8

Bangalore (India) 8.3

Calcutta (India) 16.7

Hong Kong (China) 8.0

Metro Manila (Philippines) 12.5

São Paulo (Brazil) 21.2

Madras (India) 8.0

Bangkok (Thailand) 9.8

Jakarta (Indonesia) 17.2

Buenos Aires (Argentina) 13.1

SOURCE: United Nations, World Urbanization Report, 2001 Revision, Ch. 6.

Challenges of Urbanization in the Developing World

ECONOMIC IMPLICATIONS

As a growing number of unskilled and agricultural workers migrate to urban centers, the formal economy often struggles to absorb the influx into the work force. In most cities in the developing world, it is the *informal economy* that allows those who cannot find formal work to make ends meet. From casual work in manufacturing and construction to small-scale trading ac-tivities, the unregulated informal sector offers earning opportunities to poor or unskilled workers.

The OECD (Organization for Economic Cooperation and Development) estimates that a billion new jobs will be needed by 2025 to sustain the estimated population growth in cities in the developing world. It is unlikely that all of these jobs will be created within the formal economy. Some development analysts argue that attention should be paid to formalizing or regulating the large informal economy, where much of the excess work force is likely to cluster in the years to come.

The overcrowded streets of the Hong Kong–Guangdong megacity.

ENVIRONMENTAL CHALLENGES

The rapidly expanding urban areas in developing countries differ dramatically from cities in the industrialized world. Although cities everywhere are faced with environmental problems, those in developing countries are confronted by particularly severe risks. Pollution, housing shortages, inadequate sanitation, and unsafe water supplies are chronic problems for cities in less developed countries.

Housing is one of the most acute problems in many urban areas. Cities such as Calcutta and São Paulo are massively congested. In São Paulo, it is estimated that there was a 5.4 million shortfall in habitable homes in 1996. Some scholars estimate that the shortage is as high as 20 million, if the definition of "habitable housing" is interpreted more strictly. (Barcelona Field Studies Centre, 2003).

Congestion and overdevelopment in city centers lead to serious environmental problems in many urban areas. Mexico City is a prime example. Ninety-four percent of Mexico City consists of built-up areas, with only 6 percent of land being open space. The level of green spaces—parks and open stretches of green land—is far below that found in even the most densely populated North American or European cities. Pollution is a major problem, coming mostly from the cars, buses, and trucks that pack the inadequate roads of the city, the rest deriving

from industrial pollutants. It has been estimated that living in Mexico City is equivalent to smoking forty cigarettes a day.

SOCIAL EFFECTS

Many urban areas in the developing world are overcrowded and underresourced. Poverty is widespread, and existing social services cannot meet the demands for health care, family planning advice, education, and training. The unbalanced age distribution in developing countries adds to their social and economic difficulties. Compared to industrialized countries, a much larger proportion of the population in the developing world is under the age of fifteen. A youthful population needs support and education, and during that time its members would not be economically productive. But many developing countries lack the resources to provide universal education. When their families are poor, many children must work full time, and others have to eke out a living as street children, begging for whatever they can. When the street children mature, most become unemployed, homeless, or both.

The Future of Urbanization in the Developing World

In considering the scope of the challenges facing urban areas in developing countries, it can be difficult to see prospects for change and development. Conditions of life in many of the world's largest cities seem likely to decline even further in the years to come. But the picture is not entirely negative.

First, although birthrates remain high in many countries, they are likely to drop in the years to come as urbanization

Families sit on the sidewalk with their belongings after being evicted by police from a central São Paulo building. Hundreds of squatters had settled in São Paulo buildings until, facing forced eviction by riot police, they were compelled to leave.

Newspaper salesman Alvarado uses a mask to protect himself from air pollution as he sells papers at a busy crossroad in Mexico City. Behind him a screen indicates the day's pollution levels.

proceeds. This in turn will feed into a gradual decrease in the rate of urbanization itself. In West Africa, for example, the rate of urbanization should drop to 3.4 percent per year by 2020, down from an annual rate of over 4.5 percent growth over the previous three decades (UN Population Division, 2002).

Second, globalization is presenting important opportunities for urban areas in developing countries. With economic integration, cities around the world are able to enter international markets, to promote themselves as locations for investment and development, and to create economic links across the borders of nation-states. Globalization presents one of the most dynamic openings for growing urban centers to become major forces in economic development and innovation. Indeed, many cities in the developing world are already joining the ranks of the world's global cities.

World Population Growth

There are currently over 6 billion people in the world. It was estimated that "baby number 6 billion" was born on October 12, 1999, although of course no one can know when and where this event happened. Paul Ehrlich calculated in the 1960s that if the rate of population growth at that time continued, nine hundred years from now (not a long period in world history as a whole) there would be 60,000,000,000,000,000 (60 quadrillion) people on the face of the earth. There would be one hundred people for every

square yard of the earth's surface, including both land and water. The physicist J. H. Fremlin worked out that housing such a population would require a continuous two-thousand-story building covering the entire planet. Even such a stupendous structure would have only three or four yards of floor space per person (Fremlin, 1964).

Such a picture, of course, is nothing more than nightmarish fiction designed to drive home how cataclysmic the consequences of continued population growth would be. The real issue is what will happen over the next thirty or forty years, by which time, if current trends are not reversed, the world's population will already have grown to intolerable levels. Partly because governments and other agencies heeded the warnings of Ehrlich and others twenty years ago by introducing population-control programs, there are grounds for supposing that world population growth is beginning to trail off. Estimates calculated in the 1960s of the likely world population by the year 2000 turned out to be inaccurate. The World Bank estimated the world population was just over 6 billion in 2000, compared with some earlier estimates of over 8 billion. Nevertheless, considering that a century ago there were only 1.5 billion people in the world, this still represents growth of staggering proportions. Moreover, the factors underlying population growth are by no means completely predictable, and all estimates have to be interpreted with caution.

Population Analysis: Demography

The study of population is referred to as **demography.** The term was invented about a century and a half ago, at a time when nations were beginning to keep official statistics on the nature and distribution of their populations. Demography is concerned with measuring the size of populations and explaining their rise or decline. Population patterns are governed by three factors: births, deaths, and migrations. Demography is customarily treated as a branch of sociology, because the factors that influence the level of births and deaths in a given group or society, as well as migrations of population, are largely social and cultural.

Basic Demographic Concepts

Among the basic concepts used by demographers, the most important are crude birthrates, fertility, fecundity, and crude death rates. **Crude birthrates** are expressed as the number of live births per year per thousand of the population. They are called "crude" rates because of their very general character. Crude birthrates, for example, do not tell us what proportions of a population are male or female, or what the age distribution of a population is (the relative proportions of young and old people in the population). Where statistics are collected that relate birth or death rates to such categories, demographers speak of "specific" rather than "crude" rates. For instance, an age-specific birthrate might specify the number of births per thousand women in different age groups.

If we wish to understand population patterns in any detail, the information provided by specific birthrates is normally necessary. Crude birthrates, however, are useful for making overall comparisons between different groups, societies, and regions. Thus the crude birthrate in the United States is 15 per thousand. Other industrialized countries have lower rates, such as 9 per thousand in Germany, Russia, and Italy. In many other parts of the world, crude birthrates are much higher. In India, for instance, the crude birthrate is 25 per thousand; in Ethiopia it is 48 per thousand (World Bank, 1998).

Birthrates are an expression of the fertility of women. **Fertility** refers to how many live-born children the average woman has. A fertility rate is usually calculated as the average number of births per thousand women of childbearing age.

Fertility is distinguished from **fecundity,** which means the potential number of children women are biologically capable of bearing. It is physically possible for a normal woman to bear a child every year during the period when she is capable of conception. There are variations in fecundity according to the age at which women reach puberty and menopause, both of which differ among countries as well as among individuals. Although there may be families in which a woman bears twenty or more children, fertility rates in practice are always much lower than fecundity rates, because social and cultural factors limit breeding.

Crude death rates (also called "mortality rates") are calculated in the same way as birthrates—the number of deaths per thousand of population per year. Again, there are major variations among countries, but death rates in many societies in the developing world are falling to levels comparable to those of the West. The death rate in the United States in 1996 was 8 per thousand. In India it was 9 per thousand; in Ethiopia it was 17 per thousand. A few countries have much higher death rates. In Sierra Leone, for example, the death rate is 27 per thousand. Like crude birthrates, crude death rates only provide a very general index of **mortality** (the number of deaths in a population). Specific death rates give more precise information. A particularly important specific death rate is the **infant mortality rate:** the number of babies per thousand births in any year who die before reaching age one. One of the key factors underlying the population explosion has been reductions in infant mortality rates.

Declining rates of infant mortality are the most important influence on increasing **life expectancy**—that is, the number of years the average person can expect to live. In 1900, life expectancy at birth in the United States was about forty years. Today it has increased to nearly seventy-four years. This does not mean, however, that most people at the turn of the century died when they were about forty years of age. When there is a high infant mortality rate, as there is in many developing nations, the average life expectancy—which is a statistical average—is brought down. If we look at the life expectancy of only those people who survive the first year of life, we find that in 1900 the average person could expect to live to age fifty-eight. Illness, nutrition, and the influence of natural disasters are the other factors influencing life expectancy. Life expectancy has to be distinguished from **life span,** which is the maximum number of years that an individual could live. Although life expectancy has increased in most societies in the world, life span has remained unaltered. Only a small proportion of people live to be one hundred or more.

Dynamics of Population Change

Rates of population growth or decline are measured by subtracting the number of deaths per thousand over a given period from the number of births per thousand—this is usually calculated annually. Some European countries have negative growth rates—in other words, their populations are declining. Virtually all of the industrialized countries have growth rates of less than 0.5 percent. Rates of population growth were high in the eighteenth and nineteenth centuries in Europe and the United States but have since leveled off. Many developing countries today have rates of between 2 and 3 percent (see Global Map 15.2). These may not seem very different from the rates of the industrialized countries, but in fact, the difference is enormous.

The reason is that growth in population is **exponential.** An ancient Persian myth helps to illustrate this concept. A courtier asked a ruler to reward him for his services by giving him twice as many grains of rice for each service than he had the time before, starting with a single grain on the first square of a chess board. Believing himself to be on to a good thing, the king commanded grain to be brought up from his storehouse. By the twenty-first square, the storehouse was empty; the fortieth square required ten billion grains of rice (Meadows et al., 1972). In other words, starting with one item and doubling it, doubling the result, and so on, rapidly leads to huge figures: 1:2:4:8:16:32:64:128, and so on. In seven operations the figure has risen by 128 percent. Exactly the same principle applies to population growth. We can measure this effect by means of the **doubling time,** the period of time it takes for the population to double. A population growth of 1 percent will produce a doubling

Urbanization and Migration

Population Movements

Notable shifts in population movement today involve rapid urbanization, the movement of refugees and displaced persons, and international migration. Movements of people, which will continue and increase in the future, affect patterns of development. Much of this movement is forced by conditions such as poverty or environmental degradation.

Virtually all population growth in the next decades will be concentrated in the urban areas of the world. Urban growth has outpaced employment and services and is often accompanied by poverty, yet cities offer opportunities for social change and economic development.

Although accounting for only 2 percent of the global population, a growing number—now 125 million people—are living outside the countries of their birth (including refugees and undocumented migrants). International migration is projected to remain high during the twenty-first century. The more developed regions are expected to remain net receivers of international migrants, with an average gain of about 2 million per year over the next 50 years.

Half the World in Cities

- As of 2000, 2.9 billion people were living in urban areas, comprising 47 percent of the world population.
- By 2030, 4.9 billion are expected to live in urban areas, or 60 percent of the world population.

Most of this population increase will be absorbed by the urban areas of less developed regions, while their rural populations will grow very slowly. By 2007, the number of urban dwellers is also expected to exceed the number of rural dwellers for the first time in history.

Rapid urban growth on today's scale strains the capacity of local and national governments to provide even the most

basic of services such as water, electricity and sewerage. The environment, natural resources, social cohesion and individual rights are at risk. Squatter settlements and overcrowded slums are home to tens of millions, like the *favelas* that cling to the hillsides of Rio de Janeiro and the tombs used as homes by tens of thousands in Cairo's "City of the Dead." In some developing countries, notably in Africa, this growth reflects rural crisis rather than urban-based development.

But cities also speed up social transformation, opening new avenues for human development, especially for women. Cities can give women greater access to schooling, to reproductive health services including family planning and sexual health, and to work with fair wages.

Causes That Motivate International Migration

- The search for a better life for oneself and family;
- Income disparities among and within regions;
- The labor and migration policies of sending and receiving countries;
- Political conflict (which drives migration across borders as well as within countries);
- Environmental degradation, including the loss of farmland, forests and pasture (most "environmental refugees" go to cities rather than abroad);

- "Brain drain," or the migration of more educated young people from developing countries to fill gaps in the work forces of industrialized countries.

SOURCE: United Nations Population Fund, "Urbanization and Migration," Population Issues Briefing Kit 2001, www.unfpa.org/modules/briefkit/07.htm.

Questions

- What political or social changes might reduce the pressure to migrate?
- What is the connection between environmental problems and the shift toward urbanization?
- The article mentions certain benefits from living in a city rather than in rural areas. What are they, and why do you think migrants seek them in spite of the many negative aspects of city life?

Population Growth Rate, 1980–2002

Annual percentage increase

	Less than 1.0
	1.0–1.9
	2.0–2.9
	3.0 or more

SOURCE: World Bank, World Development Indicators, 2003.

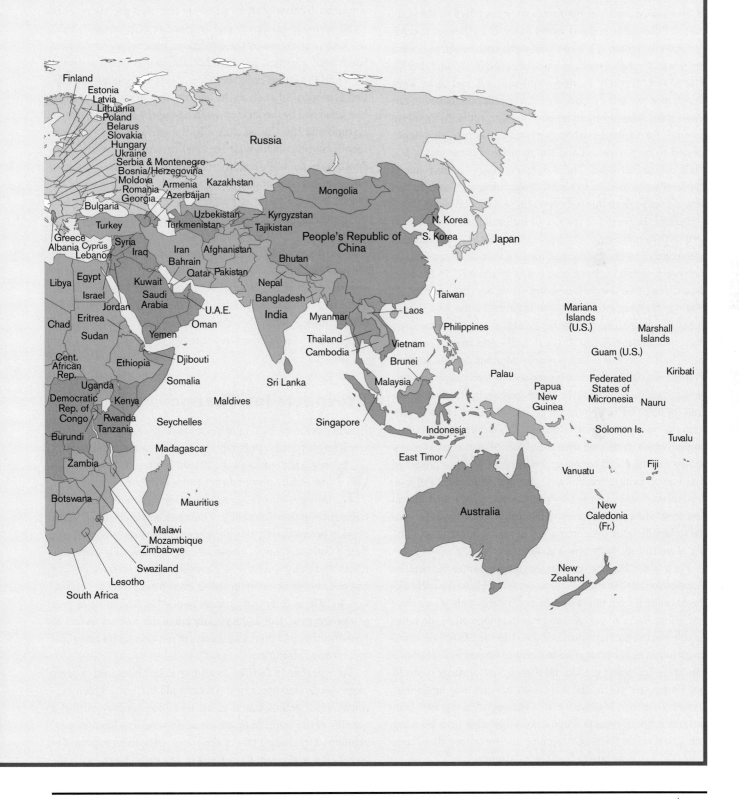

of numbers in seventy years. At 2 percent growth, a population will double in thirty-five years, while at 3 percent it will double in twenty-three years.

Malthusianism

In premodern societies, birthrates were very high by the standards of the industrialized world today. Nonetheless, population growth remained low until the eighteenth century because there was a rough overall balance between births and deaths. The general trend of numbers was upward, and there were sometimes periods of more marked population increase, but these were followed by increases in death rates. In medieval Europe, for example, when harvests were bad, marriages tended to be postponed and the number of conceptions fell, while deaths increased. These complementary trends reduced the number of mouths to be fed. No preindustrial society was able to escape from this self-regulating rhythm (Wrigley, 1968).

During the period of the rise of industrialism, many looked forward to a new age in which scarcity would be a phenomenon of the past. The development of modern industry, it was widely supposed, would create a new era of abundance. In his celebrated work *Essay on the Principle of Population* (1976; orig. 1798), Thomas Malthus criticized these ideas and initiated a debate about the connection between population and food resources that continues to this day. At the time Malthus wrote, the population in Europe was growing rapidly. Malthus pointed out that whereas population increase is exponential, food supply depends on fixed resources that can be expanded only by developing new land for cultivation. Population growth therefore tends to outstrip the means of support available. The inevitable outcome is famine, which, combined with the influence of war and plagues, acts as a natural limit to population increase. Malthus predicted that human beings would always live in circumstances of misery and starvation, unless they practiced what he called "moral restraint." His cure for excessive population growth was for people to strictly limit their frequency of sexual intercourse. (The use of contraception he proclaimed to be a "vice.")

For a while, **Malthusianism** was ignored, since the population development of the Western countries followed a quite different pattern from that which he had anticipated—as we shall see below. Rates of population growth trailed off in the nineteenth and twentieth centuries. Indeed, in the 1930s there were major worries about population decline in many industrialized countries, including the United States. The upsurge in world population growth in the twentieth century has again lent some credence to Malthus's views, although few support them in their original version. Population expansion in developing countries seems to be outstripping the resources that those countries can generate to feed their citizenry.

The Demographic Transition

Demographers often refer to the changes in the ratio of births to deaths in the industrialized countries from the nineteenth century onward as the **demographic transition.** The notion was first worked out by Warren S. Thompson, who described a three-stage process in which one type of population stability would be eventually replaced by another as a society reached an advanced level of economic development (Thompson, 1929).

Stage one refers to the conditions characteristic of most traditional societies, in which both birth and death rates are high and the infant mortality rate is especially large. Population grows little if at all, as the high number of births is more or less balanced by the level of deaths. Stage two, which began in Europe and the United States in the early part of the nineteenth century—with wide regional variations—occurs when death rates fall while fertility remains high. This is therefore a phase of marked population growth. It is subsequently replaced by stage three, in which, with industrial development, birthrates drop to a level such that population is again fairly stable.

The theory of demographic transition directly opposes the ideas of Malthus. Whereas for Malthus, increasing prosperity would automatically bring about population increase, the thesis of demographic transition emphasizes that economic development, generated by industrialism, would actually lead to a new equilibrium of population stability.

Prospects for Change

Fertility remains high in developing-world societies because traditional attitudes to family size have been maintained. Having large numbers of children is often still regarded as desirable, providing a source of labor on family-run farms. Some religions are either opposed to birth control or affirm the desirability of having many children. Contraception is opposed by Islamic leaders in several countries and by the Catholic Church, whose influence is especially marked in South and Central America. The motivation to reduce fertility has not always been forthcoming even from political authorities. In 1974, contraceptives were banned in Argentina as part of a program to double the population of the country as fast as possible; this was seen as a means of developing its economic and military strength.

Yet a decline in fertility levels has at last occurred in some large developing countries. An example is China, which currently has a population of about 1.3 billion people—almost a quarter of the world's population as a whole. The Chinese government established one of the most extensive programs of population control that any country has undertaken, with the object of stabilizing the country's numbers at close to their current level. The government instituted incentives (such as better housing and free health care and education) to promote single-child families, whereas families who have more than one child face special hardships (wages are cut for those who have a third child). As a response to this government program, some families went to the extreme of killing their female infants. There is evidence that China's antinatal policies, however harsh they may appear, have had a substantial impact on its population (Mirsky, 1982). Yet there is also much resistance within the country. People are reluctant to regard parents with one child as a proper family.

China's program demands a degree of centralized government control that is either unacceptable or unavailable in most other developing countries. In India, for instance, many schemes for promoting family planning and the use of contraceptives have been tried but with only relatively small success. India in 1988 had a population of 789 million. In 2000, its population just topped 1 billion. And even if its population-growth rate does diminish, by 2050, India will be the most populous country in the world, with over 1.5 billion people.

Some claim that the demographic changes that will occur over the next century will be greater than any before in all of human history. It is difficult to predict with any precision the rate at which the world population will rise, but the United Nations has several fertility scenarios. The "high" scenario places the world's population at more than 25 billion people by 2150! The "medium" fertility scenario, which the UN deems most likely, assumes that fertility levels will stabilize at just over two children per woman, resulting in a world population of 10.8 billion people in 2150.

This overall population increase conceals two distinct trends. First, most developing countries will undergo the process of demographic transition described above. This will result in a substantial surge in the population, as death rates fall. India and China are each likely to see their populations reach 1.5 billion people. Areas in Asia, Africa, and Latin America will similarly experience rapid growth before the population eventually stabilizes.

The second trend concerns the developed countries that have already undergone the demographic transition. These societies will undergo very slight population growth, if any at all. Instead, a process of aging will occur in which the number of young people will decline in absolute terms and the older segment of the population will increase markedly. This will have widespread economic and social implications for developed countries: As the dependency ratio increases, pressure will mount on health and social services. Yet, as their numbers grow, older people will also have more political weight and may be able to push for higher expenditures on programs and services of importance to them.

What will be the consequences of these demographic changes? Some observers see the makings of widespread social upheaval—particularly in the developing countries undergoing demographic transition. Changes in the economy and labor markets may prompt widespread internal migration as people in rural areas search for work. The rapid growth of cities will be likely to lead to environmental damage, new public-health risks, overloaded infrastructures, rising crime, and impoverished squatter settlements.

Famine and food shortages are another serious concern. There are already 842 million people in the world who suffer from hunger or undernourishment (FAO, 2003). In some parts of the world, more than a third of the population is undernourished (see Figure 15.1). As the population rises, levels of food output will need to rise accordingly to avoid widespread scarcity. Yet this scenario is unlikely; many of the world's poorest areas are particularly affected by water shortages, shrinking farmland, and soil degradation—processes that reduce, rather than enhance, agricultural productivity. It is almost certain that food production will not occur at a level to ensure self-sufficiency. Large amounts of food and grain will need to be imported from areas where there are surpluses. According to the Food and Agricultural Organization (FAO), by 2010 industrialized countries will be producing 1,614 pounds of grain per person, compared to only 507 pounds per head in the developing world.

Technological advances in agriculture and industry are unpredictable, so no one can be sure how large a population the world might eventually be able to support. Yet even at current population levels, global resources may already be well below those required to create living standards in the less developed world comparable to those of the industrialized countries.

Population Growth and the Environment

Today the human onslaught on the environment is so intense that few natural processes are uninfluenced by human activity. Nearly all cultivable land is under agricultural production. What used to be almost inaccessible wildernesses are now often nature reserves, visited routinely by thousands of tourists. Modern industry, still expanding worldwide, has led to steeply climbing demands for sources of energy and raw materials. Yet the world's supply of such energy sources and raw materials is limited, and some key resources are bound to run out if global consumption is not restricted. Even the world's climate, as we shall see, has probably been affected by the global development of industry.

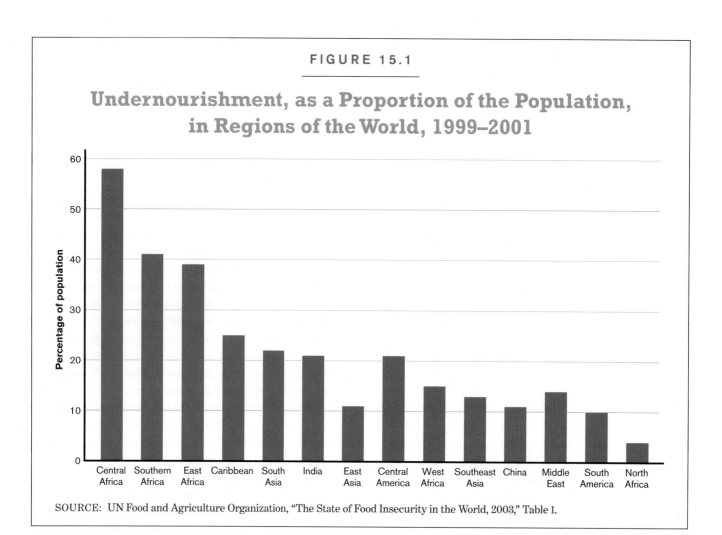

FIGURE 15.1

Undernourishment, as a Proportion of the Population, in Regions of the World, 1999–2001

Y-axis: Percentage of population

X-axis categories: Central Africa, Southern Africa, East Africa, Caribbean, South Asia, India, East Asia, Central America, West Africa, Southeast Asia, China, Middle East, South America, North Africa

SOURCE: UN Food and Agriculture Organization, "The State of Food Insecurity in the World, 2003," Table 1.

Global Environmental Threats

One problem we all face concerns **environmental ecology.** The spread of industrial production may already have done irreparable damage to the environment. Ecological questions concern not only how we can best cope with and contain environmental damage, but also the very ways of life within industrialized societies. If the goal of continuous economic growth must be abandoned, new social institutions will probably be pioneered. Technological progress is unpredictable, and it may be that the earth will in fact yield sufficient resources for processes of industrialization. At the moment, however, this does not seem feasible, and if the developing countries are to achieve living standards comparable to those currently enjoyed in the West, global readjustments will be necessary.

Global environmental threats are of several basic sorts: pollution, the creation of waste that cannot be disposed of in the short term or recycled, and the depletion of resources that cannot be replenished. The amount of domestic waste—what goes into our garbage cans—produced each day in the industrialized societies is staggering; these countries have sometimes been called the "throw-away societies" because the volume of items discarded as a matter of course is so large.

When environmental analysts speak of waste materials, however, they mean not only goods that are thrown away, but also gaseous wastes pumped into the atmosphere. Examples are the carbon dioxide released into the atmosphere by the burning of fuels such as oil and coal in cars and power stations, and gases released into the air by the use of such things as aerosol cans, material for insulation, and air-conditioning units. Carbon dioxide is the main influence on the process of global warming that many scientists believe is occurring, while the other gases attack the ozone layer around the earth.

Global warming is thought to happen in the following way. The buildup of carbon dioxide in the earth's atmosphere functions like the glass of a greenhouse. It allows the sun's rays to pass through but acts as a barrier to prevent them from passing back. The effect is to heat up the earth; global warming is sometimes termed the "greenhouse effect" for this reason. If global warming is indeed taking place, the consequences are likely to be devastating. Among other things, sea levels will rise as the polar ice caps melt and the oceans will warm and expand. Cities that lie near the coasts or in low-lying areas will be flooded and become uninhabitable. Large tracts of fertile land will become desert.

The ozone layer, which is high in the earth's atmosphere, forms a shield that protects against ultraviolet radiation. The gases used in aerosols and refrigerants produce particles that react with the ozone layer in such a way as to weaken it. It is thought that these chemicals have produced detectable holes in the ozone layer at both poles and thinning elsewhere. The radiation that is let into the earth's atmosphere produces a variety of potentially harmful effects, including an increase in cataracts of the eyes (which can cause blindness) and in levels of skin cancer.

Modern industry, still expanding worldwide, has led to steeply climbing demands for sources of energy and raw materials. Yet the world's supply of such energy sources and raw materials is limited. Even at current rates of use, for example, the known oil resources of the world will be completely consumed by the year 2050. New reserves of oil may be discovered, or alternative sources of cheap energy invented, but there plainly is a point at which some key resources will run out if global consumption is not limited.

Sustainable Development

Rather than calling for a reining back of economic growth, more recent developments turn on the notion of **sustainable development.** Sustainable development means that growth should, at least ideally, be carried on in such a way as to recycle physical resources rather than deplete them and to keep levels of pollution to a minimum. Critics see the notion of sustainable development as too vague and as neglecting the specific needs of poorer countries. According to the critics, the idea of sustainable development tends to focus attention only on the needs of richer countries; it does not consider the ways in which the high levels of consumption in the more affluent countries are satisfied at the expense of other people. For instance, demands on Indonesia to conserve its rainforests could be seen as unfair, because Indonesia has a greater need than the industrialized countries for the revenue it must forgo by accepting conservation.

Consumption, Poverty, and the Environment

Much of the debate surrounding the environment and economic development hinges on the issue of consumption patterns. *Consumption* refers to the goods, services, energy, and

resources that are used up by people, institutions and societies. It is a phenomenon with both positive and negative dimensions. On the one hand, rising levels of consumption around the world mean that people are living under better conditions than in times past. Consumption is linked to economic development—as living standards rise, people are able to afford more food, clothing, personal items, leisure time, vacations, cars, and so forth. On the other hand, consumption can have negative impacts as well. Consumption patterns can damage the environmental resource base and exacerbate patterns of inequality.

The inequalities in consumption between rich and poor are significant. The richest 20 percent of the world's population accounts for 86 percent of private consumption expenditures, whereas the poorest 20 percent accounts for only 1.3 percent (see Figure 15.2). The richest 20 percent consumes 58 percent of total energy, 84 percent of all paper, 45 percent of all meat and fish, and owns 87 percent of all the vehicles.

Current consumption patterns are not only highly unequal, but they also are having a severe impact on the environment. For example, the consumption of fresh water has doubled since 1960, the burning of fossil fuels has almost quintupled in the past fifty years, and the consumption of wood is up by 40 percent over twenty-five years ago. Fish stocks are declining, wild species are becoming extinct, water supplies are diminishing, and wooded areas are shrinking in size (UNDP, 1998). Patterns of consumption are not only depleting existing natural elements, but are also contributing to its degradation through waste products and harmful emissions.

Finally, although the rich are the world's main consumers, the environmental damage that is caused by growing consumption has the heaviest impact on the poor. The wealthy are in a better position to enjoy the many benefits of consumption without having to deal with its negative effects. On a local level, affluent groups can usually afford to move away from problem areas, leaving the poor to bear most of the costs. Chemical plants, power stations, major roads, railways, and airports are often sited close to low-income areas. On a global level, we can see a similar process at work: Soil degradation, deforestation, water shortages, lead emissions, and air pollution are all concentrated within the developing world. Poverty also intensifies these environmental threats. People with few resources have little choice but to maximize the resources that are available to them. As a result, more and more pressures are put on a shrinking resource base as the human population increases.

Prospects for Change

There can be no question but that global warming is a global problem. Greenhouse gases released in the atmosphere do not simply affect the climate of the country in which they were

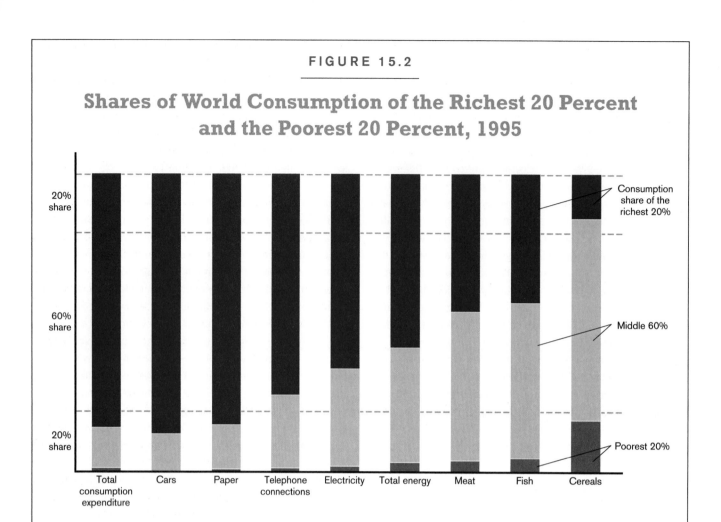

FIGURE 15.2

Shares of World Consumption of the Richest 20 Percent and the Poorest 20 Percent, 1995

Consumption share of the richest 20%

Middle 60%

Poorest 20%

20% share

60% share

20% share

Total consumption expenditure · Cars · Paper · Telephone connections · Electricity · Total energy · Meat · Fish · Cereals

SOURCE: UNDP, 1998, p. 2.

produced, but alter climatic patterns for the entire world. For this reason, many policy makers and scientists believe that any viable solution to the problem must also be global in scale. Yet the political difficulties in negotiating an international treaty to reduce greenhouse gases are enormous and suggest that although globalization has ushered in a new era of international cooperation, the world is still far from being able to speak decisively with a unified political voice about many of the issues that it confronts.

In December 1997, delegates from 166 nations gathered in Kyoto, Japan, in an effort to hammer out an agreement to reduce global warming. The summit was the culmination of two years of informal discussion among the countries. World leaders, faced with mounting scientific evidence that global warming is indeed occurring, and under pressure from voters to adopt environmentally friendly policies, clearly recognized that international action of some kind was needed. But faced as well with intense lobbying by industry, which fears it will bear the brunt of the cost for reducing fossil fuel emissions, world lead-

ers felt compelled to balance safeguarding the environment against the threat of economic disruption.

As a result, the pollution reductions agreed to by the countries are meager. Thirty-eight of the advanced industrial nations represented at the conference agreed to reduce total emission levels by 2010 to approximately 5 percent below what they were in 1990. But different countries agreed to different specific targets: The United States agreed (upon ratification by the U.S. Congress) to reduce emission levels by 7 percent, the fifteen countries of the European Union pledged an 8 percent reduction, and Japan promised a 6 percent cut. The nations also tentatively agreed to establish an emissions "trading" system whereby a country that has reduced emissions levels beyond its target will be able to sell emissions "credits" to countries that have been unable to meet their goals. The agreement also includes commitments on behalf of the industrialized countries to assist developing countries by providing technology and funding to help overcome their limited capacity to respond to climate change.

To become an active and enforceable treaty, the Kyoto Protocol must receive support from countries that emit 55 percent of global greenhouse emissions. This finally happened in November 2004 when Russia ratified the agreement. This brought the total number of ratifying countries to 127, including China, India, Japan, New Zealand, and the European Union. Notably, Australia and the United States have refused to ratify the treaty even though the United States is responsible for the largest single share of global greenhouse gases of any country.

While politicians hailed the accord as an important first step in dealing with global warming, there are three serious problems with the Kyoto agreement. First, while many newly industrialized countries, such as China, India, and Russia, have now ratified the treaty, the terms of the agreement largely exempt them from making emission reductions. Because the reduction of greenhouse gas emissions requires expensive technology upgrades for factories and other industrial infrastructure, opponents of the agreement have argued that the exemption for developing countries gives them an unfair competitive advantage in the global market. Yet this critique fails to take into account that developed countries produce over five times more emissions per person than developing countries (UN, 2004). This holds true even for China, which has the world's largest population and has been industrializing rapidly. The United States alone is responsible for over 25 percent of carbon dioxide emissions (BBC, 2001a). Second, many environmentalists warn that the reduction in greenhouse gases agreed to at Kyoto is not enough to reverse the trend toward global warming—only to slow its onset. Unless much greater emissions reductions are achieved, the world will still experience most of the disastrous consequences of global warming in the next century. Others, including President George W. Bush, have suggested that the science that supports the Kyoto

Protocol is inconclusive and provides insufficient evidence that the measures adopted in the agreement would have their intended effect (White House Press Office, 2001). This is contrary to the United Nations Intergovernmental Panel on Climate Change (IPCC), which reviewed all of the available scientific research on climate change and determined that in fact, global warming is a result of human production of greenhouse gases and must be addressed immediately to avert a climatic disaster. Third, and most problematic, the Kyoto accord, which must be ratified by the legislative bodies of all the signatory countries, faces stiff political opposition. Industry leaders and conservative politicians in the United States, for example, claim that reaching even the 7 percent reduction agreed to by the U.S. delegation would be tremendously expensive and that the environmental regulations required to achieve even this modest goal would hamstring U.S. business and retard economic growth. The former House Speaker Newt Gingrich said the United States "surrendered" to pressure in Kyoto and called the proposed treaty an outrage that would cripple the American economy. In 2001, in an attempt to satisfy American business interests, President Bush proposed an alternative strategy to lower greenhouse gas emissions through a system of government incentives for voluntary emission reductions by private businesses. Countries that ratified the treaty denounced the Bush plan as ineffective and openly criticized the unwillingness of the United States to ratify the Kyoto Protocol or seriously address the global problems created in no small part by American industrialism.

It is clear that modern technology, science, and industry are not exclusively beneficial in their consequences. Sociologists perceive a responsibility to examine closely the social relations and institutions that brought about the current state of affairs, because rescuing the situation will require a profound consciousness of human authorship.

Study Outline

www.wwnorton.com/giddens

Traditional Cities

- Traditional cities differed in many ways from modern urban areas. They were mostly very small by modern standards, were surrounded by walls, and their centers were dominated by religious buildings and palaces.

Living in Cities

- In traditional societies, only a small minority of the population lived in urban areas. In the industrialized countries today, between 60 percent and 90 percent do so. Urbanism is also increasing very rapidly in developing countries.

Theories of Urbanism

- Early approaches to urban sociology were dominated by the work of the Chicago School. The members of this school saw urban processes in terms of ecological models derived from biology. Louis Wirth developed the conception of urbanism as a "way of life." These approaches have more recently been challenged, though without being discarded altogether.
- Later approaches to urban theory have placed more emphasis on the influence of broader socioeconomic factors—particularly those deriving from industrial capitalism—on city life.

Suburbanization

- The expansion of suburbs—*suburbanization*—has contributed to *inner-city* decay. Wealthier groups and businesses tend to move out of the central city in order to take advantage of lower tax rates. This begins a cycle of deterioration, in which the more suburbia expands, the greater the problems faced by those living in the central cities. *Urban renewal* (also called *gentrification*)—the refurbishing of old buildings to put them to new uses—has become common in many large cities.

Urban Development

- Urban analysis today must be prepared to link global and local issues. Factors that influence urban development locally are sometimes part of much more international processes. The structure of local neighborhoods and their patterns of growth and decline often reflect changes in industrial production internationally.
- Massive urban development is occurring in developing countries. Cities in these societies differ in major respects from those characteristic of the West. The majority of the population live in illegal make-shift housing, in conditions of extreme poverty.
- Population growth is one of the most significant global problems currently faced by humanity. About a quarter of the world's population suffers from malnutrition, and over 10 million people die of starvation each year. This misery is concentrated in the developing countries.

Demography

- The study of population growth is called *demography*. Much demographic work is statistical, but demographers are also concerned with trying to explain why population patterns take the form they do. The most important concepts in population analysis are *birthrates, death rates, fertility,* and *mortality*.
- The changes in population patterns that have occurred in the industrialized societies are usually analyzed in terms of a process of *demographic transition*. Prior to industrialization, both birth and death rates were high. During the beginning of industrialization, there was population growth because death rates were reduced while birthrates took longer to decline. Finally a new equilibrium was reached with low birthrates balancing low death rates.
- World resources are finite, even if the limits of what can be produced are continually revised due to technological developments. Energy consumption and the consumption of raw materials and other goods are vastly higher in the Western countries than in other areas of the world. These consumption levels depend, moreover, on resources transferred from developing regions to the industrially developed nations. If resources were shared equally, there would be a significant drop in Western living standards.
- There are few aspects of the natural world that have not been affected by human activity. The industrialization of agriculture, the depletion of natural resources, the pollution of air and water, and the creation of vast mountains of unrecyclable waste are all sources of threat to the future survival of humanity. Addressing these issues will mean, among other things, that richer nations will have to revise their expectations of persistent economic growth.

Key Concepts

conurbation (p. 419)
created environment (p. 422)
crude birthrate (p. 432)
crude death rate (p. 433)
demographic transition (p. 438)
demography (p. 432)
doubling time (p. 433)
ecological approach (p. 420)
environmental ecology (p. 440)
exponential growth (p. 433)
fecundity (p. 433)
fertility (p. 433)
gentrification (p. 424)
global city (p. 428)
infant mortality rate (p. 433)
inner city (p. 420)
life expectancy (p. 433)
life span (p. 433)
Malthusianism (p. 438)
megalopolis (p. 419)
mortality (p. 433)
suburbanization (p. 422)
sustainable development (p. 441)
urban ecology (p. 420)
urban renewal (p. 424)
urbanism (p. 420)
urbanization (p. 419)

Review Questions

1. Most cities of the ancient world shared certain common features. Which one of the following is *not* one of those features?
   a. Cities were surrounded by walls.
   b. The central area of the city was occupied by a religious temple.
   c. The dwellings of the ruling class or elite tended to be concentrated in or near the center.
   d. Cities' influence over the rest of the countries was strong.
2. The inequalities in consumption between rich and poor are significant. The richest 20 percent of the world's population accounts for _____ percent of private consumption expenditures.
   a. 26
   b. 46
   c. 86
   d. 96
3. The Chicago School applied an ecological approach to the study of cities. What were the main concepts of this approach?
   a. Cities became ordered into "natural areas"—concentric rings—through processes of competition, invasion, and succession.

b. The main concepts were differentiation and interdependence.

c. Urbanism is a specific "way of life."

d. Cities processed strangers by policing streets and pooling immigrants from the same backgrounds in their own neighborhoods.

4. According to Wirth, what function do "the reserve, the indifference, and the blasé outlook of urbanites" have in everyday living?

a. They are devices for immunizing urbanites against the personal claims and expectations of others.

b. They are devices for demonstrating the sophistication and critical acumen of the urbanite.

c. They are devices for reminding out-of-towners of their place as visitors.

d. They are devices for getting about town in a hurry.

5. What's the difference between *fertility* and *fecundity*?

a. *Fertility* refers to how many births the average woman has, whereas *fecundity* refers to how many of those births were of children who survived past one year of age.

b. *Fertility* refers to a woman's ability to ovulate, whereas *fecundity* refers to a man's ability to produce healthy sperm.

c. *Fertility* refers to how many live-born children the average woman has, whereas *fecundity* refers to the potential number of children women are biologically capable of having.

d. *Fertility* is the rate of live births of individuals, whereas *fecundity* is the rate of live birth of twins.

6. What is the Malthusian perspective on population?

a. Population growth will inevitably outstrip the food supply.

b. Food supply and population growth will always be in balance.

c. Agricultural technology will ensure enough food supply for the world's population.

d. All of the above.

7. According to Saskia Sassen, an urban center that is home to the headquarters of large, transnational corporations and a superabundance of financial, technological, and consulting service is called a

a. prime city.

b. modern city.

c. global city.

d. developed city.

8. Why is the rate of urban growth in the world's less-developed regions so much higher than elsewhere?

a. Rates of population growth are higher in developing countries than they are in industrialized nations.

b. Rates of population growth are lower in developing countries than they are in industrialized nations.

c. There is widespread internal migration from rural to urban areas.

d. a and c.

9. Who argues that "cities are, by definition, full of strangers"?

a. Louis Wirth

b. Manuel Castells

c. Jane Jacobs

d. Amos Hawley

10. Which of the following statements is true about sustainable development?

a. The use of renewable resources helps to promote economic growth.

b. The protection of animal species and biodiversity helps sustainable development.

c. The commitment to maintaining clean air, water, and land benefits development.

d. All of the above

Thinking Sociologically Exercises

1. Explain what makes the urbanization now occurring in developing countries, such as Brazil and India, different from and more problematic than the urbanization that took place a century ago in New York, London, Tokyo, and Berlin.

2. Following analysis presented in this chapter, concisely explain how the expanded quest for cheap energy and raw materials and present-day dangers of environmental pollution and resource depletion threaten not only the survival of people in developed countries, but also that of people in less developed countries.

Data Exercises

www.wwnorton.com/giddens
Keyword: Data15

- One of the basic concerns of a society is the quality of life of its citizens. The overall quality of life is reflected in a society's measure of life expectancy or how long its citizens can expect to live, given current mortality levels. The data exercise for this chapter explores the association between life expectancy and national income.

Influences on Social Change

Recognize that three main factors influence social change: the physical environment, the political organization, and cultural factors.

Change in the Modern Period

Analyze modern social change, particularly the impact of economic, political, and cultural factors.

Social Movements

Learn some basic theories about social movements, and assess the impact of globalization and technology on social movements today.

Globalization

Recognize the dimensions, causes, and consequences of globalization.

CHAPTER SIXTEEN

GLOBALIZATION IN A CHANGING WORLD

human beings have inhabited the earth for about half a million years. Agriculture, the necessary basis of fixed settlements, is only around twelve thousand years old. Civilizations date back no more than six thousand years or so. If we were to think of the entire span of human existence thus far as a twenty-four-hour day, agriculture would have come into existence at 11:56 P.M. and civilizations at 11:57. The development of modern societies would not get under way until 11:59 and 30 seconds! Yet perhaps as much change has taken place in the last 30 seconds of this human day as in all the time leading up to it.

The pace of change in the modern era is easily demonstrated if we look at rates of technological development. As the economic historian David Landes has observed:

Modern technology produces not only more, faster; it turns out objects that could not have been produced under any circumstances by the craft methods of yesterday. The best Indian hand-spinner could not turn out yarn so fine and regular as that of the [spinning] mule; all the forges in eighteenth century Christendom could not have produced steel sheets so large, smooth and homogeneous as those of a modern strip mill. Most important, modern technology has created things that could scarcely have been conceived in the pre-industrial era: the camera, the motor car, the airplane, the whole array of electronic devices from the radio to the high-speed computer, the nuclear power plant, and so on almost ad infinitum. . . . The result has been an enormous increase in the output and variety of goods and services and this alone has changed man's way of life more than anything since the discovery of fire: The Englishman of 1750 was closer in material things to Caesar's legionnaires than to his own great-grandchildren. (1969)

The modes of life and social institutions characteristic of the modern world are radically different from those of even the recent past. During a period of only two or three centuries—a minute sliver of time in the context of human history—human social life has been wrenched away from the types of social order in which people lived for thousands of years.

Far more than any generation before us, we face an uncertain future. To be sure, conditions of life for previous generations were always insecure: People were at the mercy of natural disasters, plagues, and famines. But though we are largely immune from plague and famine in the industrialized countries today, we must deal now with the social forces we ourselves have unleashed.

Defining Change

There is a sense in which everything changes, all of the time. Every day is a new day; every moment is a new instant in time. The Greek philosopher Heraclitus pointed out that a person cannot step into the same river twice. On the second occasion, the river is different, since the water has been flowing in the meantime, and the person has changed in subtle ways, too. Although this observation is in a sense correct, we do of course normally want to say that it is the same river and the same person stepping into it on two occasions. There is sufficient continuity in the shape of the river and in the physique and personality of the person with wet feet to say that each remains the same.

All accounts of change also involve showing what remains stable, as a baseline against which to measure changes. Even in the rapidly moving world of today, there are continuities with the distant past. Major religious systems, for example, such as Judaism, Christianity, or Islam retain their ties with ideas and practices initiated some two thousand years ago. Yet most institutions in modern societies clearly change much more rapidly than did institutions of the traditional world.

How should we define social change? **Social change** is the transformation over time of the institutions and culture of a society. In this chapter, we will look at attempts to interpret patterns of social change affecting human history as a whole; we will then consider why the modern period should be associated with such especially profound and rapid social change and discuss the methods social movements use to enact change. This will be followed by a discussion of globalization, especially in terms of where the major lines of social change in modern societies and in the global order as a whole seem to be leading.

Influences on Social Change

Social theorists have tried for the past two centuries to develop a single grand theory that explains the nature of social change. But no single-factor theory has a chance of accounting for the diversity of human social development from hunting and gathering and pastoral societies to traditional civilizations and finally to the highly complex social systems of today. In analyzing social change, we can at most accomplish two tasks. We can identify the three main factors that have consistently influenced social change: the physical environment, political organization, and cultural factors. We can also develop theories that account for particular periods of change, such as modern times.

The Physical Environment

The physical environment often has an effect on the development of human social organization (Diamond, 1997). This is clearest in more extreme environmental conditions, where people must organize their ways of life in relation to weather conditions. People in polar regions necessarily develop different habits and practices from those living in subtropical areas. People who live in Alaska, where the winters are long and cold and the days very short, tend to follow different patterns of social life from people who live in the much warmer American South. Most Alaskans spend more of their lives indoors and, except for the summer months, plan outdoor activities carefully, given the frequently inhospitable environment in which they live.

Less extreme physical conditions can also affect society. The native population of Australia has never stopped being hunters and gatherers, since the continent contained hardly any indigenous plants suitable for regular cultivation or animals that could be domesticated to develop pastoral production. The world's early civilizations mostly originated in areas that contained rich agricultural land—for instance, in river deltas. The ease of communications across land and the availability of sea routes are also important: Societies cut off from others by mountain ranges, impassable jungles, or deserts often remain relatively unchanged over long periods of time.

Yet the direct influence of the environment on social change is not very great. People are often able to develop considerable productive wealth in relatively inhospitable areas. This is true, for example, of Alaskans, who have been able to develop oil and mineral resources in spite of the harsh nature of their surrounding environment. Conversely, hunting and gathering cultures have frequently lived in highly fertile regions without becoming involved in pastoral or agricultural production.

There is little direct relation between the environment and the systems of production that develop. The evolutionists' emphasis on adaptation to the environment is thus less illuminating than Marx's ideas in explaining social development. For Marx stressed that human beings rarely just adapt to their surrounding circumstances, as animals do. Humans always seek to master the world around them rather than take it as given. Moreover, there is no doubt that types of production strongly influence the level and nature of social change, although they do not have the overriding impact Marx attributed to them.

Political Organization

A second factor strongly influencing social change is the type of political organization that operates in a society. In hunting and gathering societies, this influence is at a minimum, since there are no political authorities capable of mobilizing the community. In all other types of society, however, the existence of distinct political agencies—chiefs, lords, monarchs, and governments—strongly affects the course of development a society takes. Political systems are not, as Marx argued, direct expressions of underlying economic organization; quite different types of political order may exist in societies that have similar production systems. For instance, some societies based on industrial capitalism have had authoritarian political systems (Nazi Germany and South Africa under apartheid); others are much more democratic (the United States, Britain, and Sweden).

Military strength played a fundamental part in the establishment of most traditional states; it influenced their subsequent survival or expansion in an equally basic way. But the connections between the level of production and military strength are again indirect. A ruler may choose to channel resources into building up the military, for example, even when this impoverishes most of the rest of the population—as happened in Iraq in the 1980s under the rule of Saddam Hussein or in North Korea during the 1990s under Kim Jong-Il.

Cultural Factors

The third main influence on social change consists of cultural factors, which include the effects of religion, communication systems, and leadership. As we have seen, religion may be either a conservative or an innovative force in social life. Some forms of religious belief and practice have acted as a brake on change, emphasizing above all the need to adhere to traditional values and rituals. Yet, as Max Weber emphasized, religious convictions frequently play a mobilizing role in pressures for social change. For instance, American church leaders promote attempts to lessen poverty or diminish inequalities in society.

A particularly important cultural influence that affects the character and pace of change is the nature of communication systems. The invention of writing, for instance, allowed for the keeping of records, making possible increased control of material resources and the development of large-scale organizations. In addition, writing altered people's perception of the relation between past, present, and future. Societies that write keep a record of past events and know themselves to have a history. Understanding history can help in developing a sense of the overall movement or line of evolution a society is following, which people can then actively seek to promote further.

Under the general heading of cultural factors we should also place leadership. Individual leaders have had an enormous influence in world history. We have only to think of great religious figures (such as Jesus), political and military leaders (such as Julius Caesar), or innovators in science and philosophy (such as Isaac Newton) to see that this is the case. A leader capable of pursuing dynamic policies and generating a mass following or radically altering preexisting modes of thought can overturn a previously established order.

Change in the Modern Period

What explains why the last two hundred years, the period of modernity, have seen such a tremendous acceleration in the speed of social change? This is a complex issue, but it is not difficult to pinpoint some of the factors involved. Not surprisingly, we can categorize them along lines similar to factors that have influenced social change throughout history, except that we will subsume the impact of the physical environment within the overall importance of economic factors.

Economic Influences

Of economic influences, the farthest reaching is the impact of industrial capitalism. Capitalism differs in a fundamental way from preexisting production systems, because it involves the constant expansion of production and the ever-increasing accumulation of wealth. In traditional production systems, levels of production were fairly static as they were geared to habitual, customary needs. Capitalism promotes the constant revision of the technology of production, a process into which science is increasingly drawn. The rate of technological innovation fostered in modern industry is vastly greater than in any previous type of economic order.

The impact of science and technology on how we live may be largely driven by economic factors, but it also stretches beyond the economic sphere. Science and technology both influence and are influenced by political and cultural factors. Scientific and technological development, for example, helped create modern forms of communication such as radio and television. As we have seen, such electronic forms of communication have produced changes in politics in recent years. Radio, television, and the other electronic media have also come to shape how we think and feel about the world.

Political Influences

The most important political factor that has helped to speed up patterns of change in the modern era is the emergence of the modern state, which has proved a vastly more efficient mechanism of government than the types that existed in premodern societies. Government plays a much bigger role in our lives, for better or worse, than it did before modern industrial societies came on the scene.

Many changes in the political sphere have been spurred by economic transformations. For instance, the expanded role of government called for in the New Deal in the 1930s was a response to mass unemployment. But the political system affects economic life just as much as the other way around. Thus, the New Deal was a response to economic change, but the political programs it created in turn had a big impact on later economic development, serving to help reduce unemployment and introduce a period of increased prosperity before and after World War II.

Cultural Influences

Among the cultural factors affecting processes of social change in modern times, the development of science and the secularization of thought have each contributed to the *critical* and *innovative* character of the modern outlook. We no longer assume that customs or habits are acceptable merely because they have the age-old authority of tradition. On the contrary, our ways of life increasingly require a "rational" basis. For instance, a design for a hospital would not be based mainly on traditional tastes, but would consider its capability for serving the purpose of a hospital—effectively caring for the sick.

In addition to *how* we think, the *content* of ideas has also changed. Ideals of self-betterment, freedom, equality, and democratic participation are largely creations of the past two or three centuries. Such ideals have served to mobilize processes of social and political change, including revolutions. These ideas cannot be tied to tradition, but rather suggest the constant re-vision of ways of life in the pursuit of human betterment. Although they initially were developed in the West, such ideals have become genuinely universal in their application, promoting change in most regions of the world.

Current Change and Future Prospects

Where is social change leading us today? What are the main trends of development likely to affect our lives as the twenty-first century opens? Social theorists do not agree on the answers to these questions, which obviously involve a great deal of speculation. We will look at several different perspectives: the notion that we are a postindustrial society, the idea that we have reached a postmodern period, and finally and in the most detail, theories that have focused on the dimensions, causes, and consequences of globalization.

TOWARD A POSTINDUSTRIAL SOCIETY?

Some observers have suggested that what is occurring today is a transition to a new society no longer primarily based on industrialism. We are entering, they claim, a phase of development beyond the industrial era altogether. A variety of terms have been coined to describe this new social order, such as **information society, service society,** and **knowledge society.** The term that has come into most common usage, however—first employed by Daniel Bell in the United States and Alain Touraine in France—is **postindustrial society** (Touraine, 1974; Bell, 1976), the *post* (meaning "after") referring to the sense that we are moving beyond the old forms of industrial development.

The diversity of names is one indication of the myriad ideas put forward to interpret current social changes. But one theme that appears consistently is the significance of *information* or *knowledge* in the society of the future. Our way of life, based on the manufacture of material goods, centered on the power machine and the factory, is being displaced by one in which information is the basis of the productive system.

The clearest and most comprehensive classical portrayal of the postindustrial society is provided by Daniel Bell in *The Coming of the Post-Industrial Society* (1976). The postindustrial order, Bell argues, is distinguished by a growth of service occupations at the expense of jobs that produce material goods. The blue-collar worker, employed in a factory or workshop, is no longer the most essential type of employee. White-collar (clerical and professional) workers outnumber blue-collar, with professional and technical occupations growing fastest of all.

People working in higher-level white-collar occupations specialize in the production of information and knowledge. The production and control of what Bell calls "codified knowledge"—systematic, coordinated information—is society's main strategic resource. Those who create and distribute this knowledge—scientists, computer specialists, economists, engineers, and professionals of all kinds—increasingly become the leading social groups, replacing the industrialists and entrepreneurs of the old system. On the level of culture, there is a shift away from the "work ethic" characteristic of industrialism; people are freer to innovate and enjoy themselves in both their work and their domestic lives.

Some of the developments cited by the postindustrial theorists are important features of the current era, but it is not obvious that the concept of the postindustrial society is the best way to come to terms with them. Moreover, the forces behind the changes going on today are political and cultural as well as economic.

POSTMODERNITY

Some authors have recently gone as far as saying that the developments now occurring are even more profound than signaling the end of the era of industrialism. They claim that what is happening is nothing short of a movement beyond modernity—the attitudes and ways of life associated with modern societies, such as our belief in progress, the benefits of science, and our capability to control the modern world. A **postmodern** era is arriving, or has already arrived.

The advocates of postmodernity claim that modern societies took their inspiration from the idea that history has a shape—it "goes somewhere" and leads to progress—and that now this notion has collapsed. There are no longer any "grand narratives"—overall conceptions of history—that make any sense (Lyotard, 1985). Not only is there no general notion of progress that can be defended, there is no such thing as history. The postmodern world is thus a highly pluralistic and diverse one. In countless films, videos, and TV programs, images circulate around the world. We come into contact with many ideas and values, but these have little connection with the history of the areas in which we live, or indeed with our own personal histories. Everything seems constantly in flux. History ends alongside modernity, it is said, because there is no longer any way of describing in general terms the pluralistic universe that has come into being.

Most contemporary social theorists accept that information technology and new communications systems, together with other technological changes, are producing major social transformations for all of us. However, the majority disagree with core ideas of the postmodernists, who argue that our attempts to understand general processes in the social world are doomed, as is

Fredric Jameson describes the Westin Bonaventure Hotel, located in downtown Los Angeles, as an original postmodern space. The architecture distorts viewers' sense of place—the glass exterior mirrors the building's surroundings rather than permitting a view inside—and the symmetrical design of the interior challenges viewers' ability to comprehend the space through which they are walking.

the notion we can change the world for the better. Writers such as Ulrich Beck and one of the authors of this textbook, Anthony Giddens, claim that we need as much as ever to develop general theories of the social world and that such theories can help us intervene to shape it in a positive way. Such theories have focused on how contemporary societies are becoming globalized, while everyday life is breaking free from the hold of tradition and custom. But these changes should not spell the end of attempts at social and political reform. Marx's dreams of a socialist alternative to capitalism are dead. But some of the values that drove the socialist project—those of social community, equality, and caring for the weak and vulnerable—are still very much alive.

Social Movements

In addition to economics, technology, politics, and culture one of the most common causes of social change occurs through **social movements**—collective attempts to further a common interest or secure a common goal through action outside the sphere of established institutions. A wide variety of social movements, some enduring, some transient, have existed in modern societies. They are as evident a feature of the contemporary world as are the formal, bureaucratic organizations they often oppose. Many contemporary social movements are international in scope and rely heavily on the use of information technology in linking local campaigners to global issues.

Why Do Social Movements Occur?

Sociology arose in the late nineteenth century as part of an effort to come to grips with the massive political and economic transformations that Europe underwent on its way from the preindustrial to the modern world (Moore, 1966). Perhaps because sociology was founded in this context, sociologists have never lost their fascination with these transformations.

Since mass social movements have been so important in world history over the past two centuries, it is not surprising that a diversity of theories exists to try to account for them. Some theories were formulated early in the history of the social sciences; the most important was that of Karl Marx. Marx, who lived well before any of the social movements undertaken in the name of his ideas took place, intended his views to be taken not just as an analysis of the conditions of revolutionary change, but as a means of furthering such change. Whatever their intrinsic validity, Marx's ideas had an immense practical impact on twentieth-century social change.

We shall look at four frameworks for the study of social movements, many of which were developed in the context of revolution: economic deprivation, resource mobilization, structural strain, and fields of action.

ECONOMIC DEPRIVATION

Marx's view of social movements is based on his interpretation of human history in general (see Chapter 1). According to Marx, the development of societies is marked by periodic class conflicts that, when they become acute, tend to end in a process of revolutionary change. Class struggles derive from the *contradictions*—unresolvable tensions—in societies. The main sources of contradiction can be traced to economic changes, or changes in the forces of production. In any stable society, there is a balance between the economic structure, social relationships, and the political system. As the forces of production alter, contradiction is intensified, leading to open clashes between classes—and ultimately to revolution.

Contrary to Marx's expectations, revolutions failed to occur in the advanced industrialized societies of the West. Why? The sociologist James Davies, a critic of Marx, pointed to periods of history when people lived in dire poverty but did not rise up in protest. Constant poverty or deprivation does not make people into revolutionaries; rather, they usually endure such conditions with resignation or mute despair. Social protest, and ultimately revolution, is more likely to occur, Davies argued, when there is an *improvement* in people's living conditions. Once standards of living have started to rise, people's levels of expectation also go up. If improvement in actual conditions subsequently slows

Relative deprivation between the peasantry and the elite in France led to the overthrow of the monarchy.

down, propensities to revolt are created because rising expectations are frustrated (Davies, 1962). Thus, it is not absolute deprivation that leads to protest but **relative deprivation**—the discrepancy between the lives people are forced to lead and what they think could realistically be achieved.

As Charles Tilly has pointed out, however, Davies's theory does not show how and why different groups *mobilize* to seek revolutionary change. Protest might well often occur against a backdrop of rising expectations; to understand how it is transformed into a mass social movement, we need to identify how groups become collectively organized to make effective political challenges.

RESOURCE MOBILIZATION

In *From Mobilization to Revolution*, Charles Tilly analyzed processes of revolutionary change in the context of broader forms of protest and violence (Tilly, 1978). He distinguished four main components of **collective action**, action taken to contest or overthrow an existing social order:

1. The *organization* of the group or groups involved. Protest movements are organized in many ways, varying from the spontaneous formation of crowds to tightly disciplined revolutionary groups. The Russian Revolution, for example, began as a small group of activists.
2. *Mobilization*, the ways in which a group acquires sufficient resources to make collective action possible. Such resources may include supplies of material goods, political support, and weaponry. Lenin was able to acquire material and moral support from a sympathetic peasantry, together with many townspeople.

3. The *common interests* of those engaging in collective action, what they see as the gains and losses likely to be achieved by their policies. Some common goals always underlie mobilization to collective action. Lenin managed to weld together a broad coalition of support because many people had a common interest in removing the existing government.

4. *Opportunity*. Chance events may occur that provide opportunities to pursue revolutionary aims. Numerous forms of collective action, including revolution, are greatly influenced by such incidental events. There was no inevitability to Lenin's success, which depended on a number of contingent factors—including success in battle. If Lenin had been killed, would there have been a revolution?

Collective action itself can simply be defined as people acting together in pursuit of interests they share—for example, gathering to demonstrate in support of their cause. Some of these people may be intensely involved, others may lend more passive or irregular support. Effective collective action, such as action that culminates in revolution, usually moves through stages 1 to 4.

Typical modes of collective action and protest vary with historical and cultural circumstances. In the United States today, for example, most people are familiar with forms of demonstration like mass marches, large assemblies, and street riots, whether or not they have participated in such activities. Other types of collective protest, however, have become less common or have disappeared altogether in most modern societies (such as fights between villages, machine breaking, or lynching). Protesters can also build on examples taken from elsewhere; for instance, guerrilla movements proliferated in various parts of the world once disaffected groups learned how successful guerrilla actions can be against regular armies. And, as discussed above, a new form of collective action may be emerging—"smart-mobbing" and other forms of social protest accomplished through the Internet.

STRUCTURAL STRAIN

Neil Smelser (1963) distinguished six conditions underlying the origins of collective action in general, and social movements in particular:

1. *Structural conduciveness* refers to the general social conditions promoting or inhibiting the formation of social movements of different types.

2. Just because the conditions are conducive to the development of a social movement does not mean those conditions will bring them into being. There must be structural strain—tensions (or, in Marx's terminology, contradictions) that produce conflicting interests within societies. Uncertainties, anxieties, ambiguities, or direct clashes of goals, are expressions of such strains.

3. The third condition Smelser outlined is the spread of *generalized beliefs*. Social movements do not develop simply as responses to vaguely felt anxieties or hostilities. They are shaped by the influence of definite ideologies, which crystallize grievances and suggest courses of action that might be pursued to remedy them.

4. *Precipitating factors* are events or incidents that actually trigger direct action by those who become involved in the movement.

5. The first four conditions combined, Smelser argued, might occasionally lead to street disturbances or outbreaks of violence. But such incidents do not lead to the development of social movements unless there is a coordinated group that becomes mobilized for action. *Leadership* and some means of *regular communication* among participants, together with funding and material resources, are necessary for a social movement to exist.

6. Finally, the manner in which a social movement develops is strongly influenced by the *operation of social control*. The governing authorities may respond to initial protests by intervening in the conditions of conduciveness and strain that stimulated the emergence of the movement. A harsh reaction might encourage further protest and help solidify the movement. Also, doubt and divisions within the police and military can be crucial in deciding the outcome of confrontations with revolutionary movements.

Smelser's model is useful for analyzing the sequences in the development of social movements, and collective action in general. Smelser's theory treats social movements as *responses* to situations, rather than allowing that their members might spontaneously organize to achieve desired social changes. In this respect his ideas contrast with the approach developed by Alain Touraine.

FIELDS OF ACTION

Alain Touraine (1977, 1981) developed his analysis of social movements on the basis of four main ideas. The first, which he called **historicity**, explains why there are so many more movements in the modern world than there were in earlier times. In modern societies, individuals and groups know that social activism can be used to achieve social goals and reshape society.

Second, Touraine focused on the *rational objectives* of social movements. Such movements do not just come about as

The Antisweatshop Movement

"We have the university by the balls," said Nati Passow, a University of Pennsylvania junior, in a meeting with his fellow anti-sweatshop protestors. "Whatever way we twist them is going to hurt." Passow was one of thirteen Penn students—the group later grew to include forty—occupying the university president's office around the clock in early February [2000] to protest the sweatshop conditions under which clothing bearing the U-Penn logo is made. The Penn students, along with hundreds of other members of United Students Against Sweatshops nationwide, were demanding that their university withdraw from the Fair Labor Association (FLA), an industry-backed monitoring group, and instead join the Worker Rights Consortium (WRC), an organization independent of industry influence, founded by students in close cooperation with scholars, activists and workers'-rights organizations in the global south.

At first the administration met the students with barely polite condescension. In one meeting, President Judith Rodin was accompanied by U-Penn professor Larry Gross, an earring-wearing baby boomer well known on campus for his left-wing views, who urged the protesters to have more faith in the administration and mocked the sit-in strategy, claiming he'd "been there, done that." President Rodin assured them that a task force would review the problem by February 29, and there was no way she could speed up its decision. She admonished them to "respect the process."

Watching the Penn students negotiate with this university's president, it was clear they didn't believe any of her assurances. They knew there was no reason to trust that the administration would meet one more arbitrary deadline after missing so many others—so they stayed in the office. After eight days of torture by folk-singing, acoustic guitar, recorders, tambourines and ringing cell phones, as well as a flurry of international news coverage, Judith Rodin met the protesters halfway by withdrawing from the FLA. (To students' frustration, the task force decided in early April to postpone a decision about WRC membership until later [that] spring.)

The most remarkable thing about the Penn students' action was that it wasn't an isolated or spontaneous burst of idealism. Penn's was just the first antisweatshop sit-in of the year; by mid-April students at the universities of Michigan, Wisconsin, Oregon, Iowa and Kentucky, as well as SUNY-Albany, Tulane, Purdue and Macalester had followed suit. And the sit-in wasn't the protesters' only tactic: Purdue students held an eleven-day hunger strike. The protests were a coordinated effort; members of United Students Against Sweatshops (USAS), which was founded three years ago and now has chapters at more than 200 schools, work closely with one another, a process made easier by the many listservs and Web sites that the students use to publicize actions, distribute information and help fuel turnout.

Though the largest, most successful—and before Seattle, the most visible—thread of the movement has focused on improving work conditions in the $2.5 billion collegiate apparel industry, university licensing policies have not been the only targets of recent anticorporate agitation on campus. This year, from UC-Davis to the University of Vermont, students have held globalization teach-ins, planned civil disobedience for the April IMF/World Bank meetings, protested labor policies at the Gap and launched vigorous campaigns to drive Starbucks out of university dining services. Students at Johns Hopkins and at Wesleyan held sit-ins demanding better wages for university workers. And at the end of March hundreds of students, many bearing hideously deformed papier-mâché puppets to illustrate the potential horrors of biotechnology, joined Boston's carnivalesque protest against genetic engineering.

With a *joie de vivre* that the American economic left has probably lacked since before WWI, college students are increasingly engaged in well-organized, thoughtful and morally outraged resistance to corporate power. These activists, more than any student radicals in years, passionately denounce the wealth gap, globally and in the United States, as well as the lack of democratic accountability in a world dominated by corporations. While some attend traditionally political schools like Evergreen, Michigan and Wisconsin, this movement does not revolve around usual suspects; some of this winter's most dramatic actions took place at campuses that have always been conservative, like the University of Pennsylvania, Virginia Commonwealth and Johns Hopkins. . . . It is neither too soon, nor too naïvely optimistic, to call it a movement.

SOURCE: Liza Featherstone, "The New Student Movement," *The Nation*, May 15, 2000.

Questions

- Many antisweatshop activists view their protests as a political and moral crusade. Do you agree with them that morals and politics should influence economic behavior? How does this affect your understanding of the study of sociology?
- What techniques did the students use to present their point of view? How did media coverage influence their methods of political protest?
- The students involved in these protests attend prestigious schools, for the most part. How does their membership in an elite group complicate their response to the issue of globalization and its discontents?

irrational responses to social divisions or injustices; rather, they develop from specific views and rational strategies as to how injustices can be overcome.

Third, Touraine saw a process of *interaction* in the shaping of social movements. Movements do not develop in isolation; instead, they develop in deliberate antagonism with established organizations and sometimes with other rival social movements.

Fourth, social movements and change occur in the context of what Touraine called "fields of action." A **field of action** refers to the connections between a social movement and the forces or influences against it. The process of mutual negotiation among antagonists in a field of action may lead to the social changes sought by the movement as well as to changes in the social movement itself and in its antagonists. In either circumstance, the movement may evaporate—or become institutionalized as a permanent organization.

Globalization and Social Movements

Social movements come in all shapes and sizes. Some are very small, numbering no more than a few dozen members; others may include thousands or even millions of people. Although some social movements carry on their activities within the laws of the society in which they exist, others operate as illegal or underground groups. It is characteristic of protest movements, however, that they operate near the margins of what is defined as legally permissible by governments at any particular time or place.

Social movements often arise with the aim of bringing about change on a public issue, such as expanding civil rights for a segment of the population. In response to social movements, countermovements sometimes arise in defense of the status quo. The campaign for women's right to abortion, for example, has been vociferously challenged by antiabortion ("pro-life") activists, who believe that abortion should be illegal.

Often, laws or policies are altered as a result of the action of social movements. These changes in legislation can have far-ranging effects. For example, it used to be illegal for groups of workers to call their members out on strike, and striking was punished with varying degrees of severity in different countries. Eventually, however, the laws were amended, making the strike a permissible tactic of industrial conflict.

NEW SOCIAL MOVEMENTS

The last three decades have seen an explosion of social movements in countries around the globe. These various movements—ranging from the civil rights and feminist movements of the 1960s and 1970s to the antinuclear and ecological movements of the 1980s to the gay rights campaign of the 1990s—are often referred to by commentators as **new social movements**. This description seeks to differentiate contemporary social movements from those that preceded them in earlier decades. They are often concerned with the quality of private life as much as with political and economic issues, calling for large-scale changes in the way people think and act.

In other words, what makes new social movements "new" is that—unlike conventional social movements—they are not based on single-issue objectives that typically involve changes in the distribution of economic resources or power. Rather, they involve the creation of collective identities based around entire lifestyles, often calling for sweeping cultural changes. New social movements have emerged in recent years around issues such as ecology, peace, gender and sexual identity, gay and lesbian rights, women's rights, alternative medicine, and opposition to globalization.

Because new social movements involve new collective identities, they can provide a strong incentive for action. Social movements are always plagued by the "free-rider" problem—how can they motivate people to devote their time and resources, when they will benefit from the movement's success regardless of their personal involvement? With new social movements, however, participation is viewed as a moral obligation (and even a pleasure), rather than a calculated effort to achieve some specific goal. Moreover, the forms of protest chosen by new social movements are a form of "expressive logic" whereby participants make a statement about who they are: Protest is an end in itself, a way of affirming one's identity, as well as a means to achieving concrete objectives (Polletta and Jasper, 2001).

Many observers believe that new social movements are a unique product of late modern society and are profoundly different in their methods, motivations, and orientations from forms of collective action in earlier times.

The rise of new social movements in recent years is a reflection of the changing risks facing human societies. The conditions are ripe for social movements—increasingly traditional political institutions are unable to cope with the challenges before them. They find it impossible to respond creatively to the threats facing the natural environment, the potential dangers of nuclear energy and genetically modified organisms, and the powerful effects of information technology. Existing democratic political institutions cannot hope to fix these new problems. As a result, these unfolding challenges are frequently ignored or avoided until it is too late and a full-blown crisis is at hand.

The cumulative effect of these new challenges and risks is a sense that people are losing control of their lives in the midst of rapid change. Individuals feel less secure and more isolated—a combination that leads to a sense of powerlessness. By contrast, corporations, governments, and the media appear to be dominating more and more aspects of people's lives, heightening the sensation of a runaway world. There is a growing sense that left to its own logic, globalization will present ever-greater risks to citizens' lives.

Although faith in traditional politics seems to be waning, the growth of new social movements is evidence that citizens in late modern societies are not apathetic or uninterested in politics, as is sometimes claimed. Rather, there is a belief that direct action and participation is more useful than reliance on politicians and political systems. More than ever before, people are supporting social movements as a way of highlighting complex moral issues and putting them at the center of social life. In this respect, new social movements are helping to revitalize democracy in many countries. They are at the heart of a strong civic culture or **civil society**—the sphere between the state and the marketplace occupied by family, community associations, and other noneconomic institutions.

Technology and Social Movements

In recent years, two of the most influential forces in late modern societies—information technology and social movements—have come together, with astonishing results. In our current information age, social movements around the globe are able to join together in huge regional and international networks comprising nongovernmental organizations, religious and humanitarian groups, human rights associations, consumer protection advocates, environmental activists, and others who campaign in the public interest. These electronic networks now have the unprecedented ability to respond immediately to events as they occur, to gain access to and share sources of information, and to put pressure on corporations, governments, and international bodies as part of their campaigning strategies. The enormous protests against the World Trade Organization that took place in Seattle, Prague, and Genoa, for example, were organized in large part through Internet-based networks. And, as we saw earlier, Web-based organizations such as MoveOn.org played an influential role in the anti–Iraq war movement.

The Internet has been at the forefront of these changes, although mobile phones, fax machines, and satellite broadcasting have also hastened their evolution. With the press of a button, local stories are disseminated internationally. Grassroots activists from Japan to Bolivia can meet online to share informational resources, exchange experiences, and coordinate joint action.

This last dimension—the ability to coordinate international political campaigns—is the most worrisome for governments and the most inspiring to participants in social movements. In the last decade, the number of international social movements has grown steadily with the spread of the Internet. From global protests in favor of canceling Third World debt to the international campaign to ban land mines (which culminated in a Nobel Peace Prize), the Internet has proved its ability to unite campaigners across national and cultural borders. Some observers argue that the information age is witnessing a migration of power away from nation-states into new nongovernmental alliances and coalitions.

Globalization

The concept of globalization has become widely used in debates in politics, business, and the media over the past few years. A decade ago, the term *globalization* was relatively unknown. Today it seems to be on the tip of everyone's tongue. Globalization refers to the fact that we all increasingly live in one world, so that individuals, groups, and nations become more *interdependent*.

Globalization is often portrayed solely as an economic phenomenon. Some make much of the role of transnational corporations whose massive operations stretch across national borders, influencing global production processes and the international distribution of labor. Others point to the electronic integration of global financial markets and the enormous volume of global capital flows. Still others focus on the unprecedented scope of world trade, involving a much broader range of goods and services than ever before.

Although economic forces are an integral part of globalization, it would be wrong to suggest that they alone produce it. Globalization is created by the coming together of political, social, cultural, and economic factors. It has been driven forward above all by the development of information and communication technologies that have intensified the speed and scope of interaction between people all over the world. As a simple example, think of the 2002 soccer World Cup. Because of global television links, some matches were watched by over 2 billion people across the world.

Factors Contributing to Globalization

The explosion in global communications has been facilitated by some important advances in technology and the world's telecommunications infrastructure. In the post–World War II era, there has been a profound transformation in the scope and intensity of telecommunications flows. Traditional telephonic communication, which depended on analog signals sent through wires and cables with the help of mechanical crossbar switching, has been replaced by integrated systems in which vast amounts of information are compressed and transferred digitally. Cable technology has become more efficient and less expensive; the development of fiber-optic cables has dramatically expanded the number of channels that can be carried. Whereas the earliest transatlantic cables laid in the 1950s were capable of carrying fewer than a hundred voice paths, by 1997 a single transoceanic cable could carry some 600,000 voice paths (Held et al., 1999). The spread of communications satellites, beginning in the 1960s, has also been significant in expanding international communications. Today a network of more than two hundred satellites is in place to facilitate the transfer of information around the globe.

The impact of these communications systems has been staggering. In countries with highly developed telecommunications infrastructures, homes and offices now have multiple links to the outside world, including telephones (both land lines and mobile phones), fax machines, digital and cable television, electronic mail, and the Internet. The Internet has emerged as the fastest-growing communication tool ever developed—some 140 million people worldwide were using the Internet in mid-1998. More than 604 million people were estimated to be online by 2003.

These forms of technology facilitate the compression of time and space: Two individuals located on opposite sides of the planet—in Tokyo and London, for example—not only can hold a conversation in real time, but can also send documents and images to one another with the help of satellite technology. Widespread use of the Internet and mobile phones is deepening and accelerating processes of globalization; more and more people are becoming interconnected through the use of these technologies and are doing so in places that have previously been isolated or poorly served by traditional communications (see Figure 16.1). Although the telecommunications infrastructure is not evenly developed around the world (see Table 16.1), a growing number of countries now have access to international communications networks in a way that was previously impossible.

Globalization is also being driven forward by the integration of the world economy. In contrast to previous eras, the global economy is no longer primarily agricultural or industrial in its basis. Rather, it is increasingly dominated by activity that is weightless and intangible (Quah, 1999). This *weightless economy* is one in which products have their base in information, as is the case with computer software, media and entertainment products, and Internet-based services. This new economic context has been described using a variety of terms that we have already discussed, including *postindustrial society, information society,* and *knowledge society.* The emergence of the knowledge society has been linked to the development of a broad base of consumers who are technologically literate and eagerly integrate new advances in computing, entertainment, and telecommunications into their everyday lives.

The very operation of the global economy reflects the changes that have occurred in the information age. Many aspects of the economy now work through networks that cross national boundaries, rather than stopping at them (Castells, 1996). In order to be competitive in globalizing conditions, businesses and corporations have restructured themselves to be more flexible and less hierarchical in nature. Production practices and organizational patterns have become more flexible, partnering arrangements with other firms have become commonplace, and participation in worldwide distribution networks has become essential for doing business in a rapidly changing global market.

The Causes of Increasing Globalization

POLITICAL CHANGES

A number of influences are driving forces behind contemporary globalization. One of the most significant of these is the collapse of Soviet-style communism, which occurred in a series of dramatic revolutions in Eastern Europe in 1989 and culminated in the dissolution of the Soviet Union itself in 1991. Since the fall of Communism, countries in the former Soviet bloc—including Russia, Ukraine, Poland, Hungary, the Czech Republic, the Baltic states, the states of the Caucasus and Central Asia, and many others—are moving toward Western-style political and economic systems. They are no longer isolated from the global community, but are becoming integrated within it. This development has meant the end to the system that existed during the cold war, when countries of the First World stood apart from those of the Second World. The collapse of communism has hastened processes of globalization but should also be seen as a result of globalization itself. The centrally planned communist economies and the ideological and cultural control of communist political authority were ultimately unable to survive in an era of global media and an electronically integrated world economy.

A second important political factor leading to intensifying globalization is the growth of international and regional mechanisms of government. The United Nations and the European

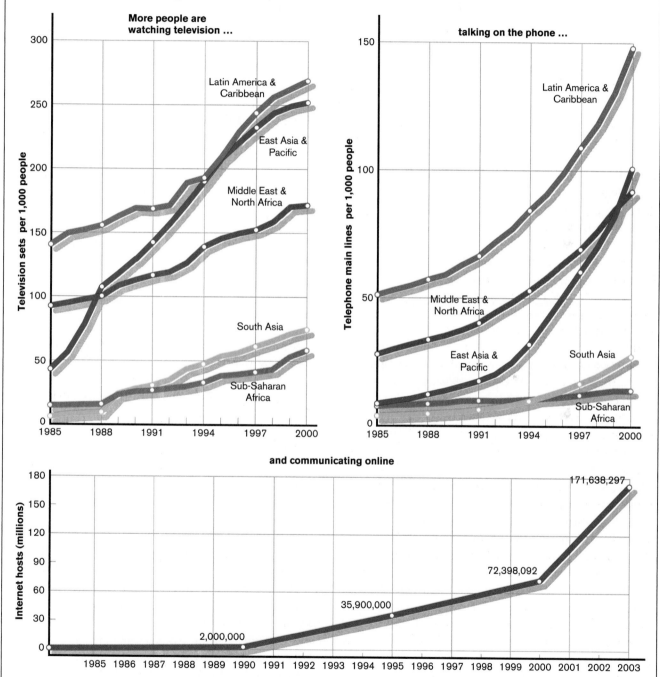

FIGURE 16.1

The Multiplication of Television Sets and Telephones in Regions of the World, 1985–2000, and the Explosion in Online Communication

SOURCES: World Bank data from UNDP, 1999, p. 26; World Bank, World Development Indicators, 2002; United Nations, Human Development Report, 2003.

TABLE 16.1

Global Unevenness of Telecommunications Infrastructure and Use, 2002

	POPULATION (MILLIONS)	TELEPHONE MAINLINES (PER 1,000)*	CELLULAR SUBSCRIBERS (PER 1,000)*	PERSONAL COMPUTERS (PER 1,000)†
China	1,262.5	137	110	16
France	58.9	573	605	304
Germany	82.2	634	682	336
India	1,016.0	38	6	5
Japan	126.8	586	588	315
Sweden	8.9	739	790	507
United Kingdom	59.7	587	770	338
United States	281.6	667	451	585

*Data source: UN Human Development Report, 2003.

†2000 data; source: World Development Indicators, 2002.

Union are the two most prominent examples of international organizations that bring together nation-states into a common political forum. Whereas the UN does this as an association of individual nation-states, the EU is a more pioneering form of transnational governance in which a certain degree of national sovereignty is relinquished by its member states. The governments of individual EU states are bound by directives, regulations, and court judgments from common EU bodies, but they also reap economic, social, and political benefits from their participation in the regional union.

Finally, globalization is being driven by international governmental organizations (IGOs) and international non-governmental organizations (INGOs; see also Chapter 6). An *international governmental organization* is a body that is established by participating governments and given responsibility for regulating or overseeing a particular domain of activity that is transnational in scope. The first such body, the International Telegraph Union, was founded in 1865. Since that time, a great number of similar bodies have been created to regulate issues ranging from civil aviation to broadcasting to the disposal of hazardous waste. In 1909, there were 37 IGOs in existence to regulate transnational affairs; by 1996, there were 260 (Held et al., 1999).

As the name suggests, INGOs differ from international governmental organizations in that they are not affiliated with government institutions. Rather, they are independent organizations that work alongside governmental bodies in making policy decisions and addressing international issues. Some of the best-known INGOs—such as Greenpeace, Médecins San Frontières (Doctors Without Borders), the Red Cross, and Amnesty International—are involved in environmental protection and humanitarian relief efforts. But the activities of thousands of lesser-known groups also link together countries and communities (see Figure 16.2).

INFORMATION FLOWS

We have seen how the spread of information technology has expanded the possibilities for contact among people around the globe. It has also facilitated the flow of information about people and events in distant places. Every day, the global media bring news, images, and information into people's homes, linking them directly and continuously to the outside world. Some of the most gripping events of the past two decades—such as the fall of the Berlin Wall, the violent crackdown on democratic protesters in China's Tiananmen Square, and the terrorist attacks of September 11, 2001—have unfolded through the media before a truly global audience. Such events, along with thousands of less dramatic ones, have re-

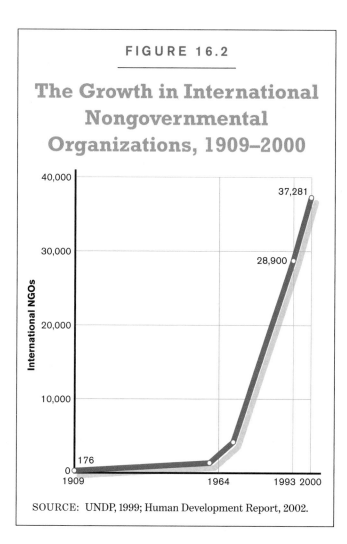

FIGURE 16.2

The Growth in International Nongovernmental Organizations, 1909–2000

SOURCE: UNDP, 1999; Human Development Report, 2002.

sulted in a reorientation in people's thinking from the level of the nation-state to the global stage. Individuals are now more aware of their interconnectedness with others and more likely to identify with global issues and processes than was the case in times past.

This shift to a global outlook has two significant dimensions. First, as members of a global community, people increasingly perceive that social responsibility does not stop at national borders but instead extends beyond them. Disasters and injustices facing people on the other side of the globe are not simply misfortunes that must be endured but are legitimate grounds for action and intervention. There is a growing assumption that the international community has an obligation to act in crisis situations to protect the physical well-being or human rights of people whose lives are under threat. In the case of natural disasters, such interventions take the form of humanitarian relief and technical assistance. In recent years, earthquakes in Armenia and Turkey, floods in Mozambique, famine in Africa, hurricanes in Central America, and the tsunami that hit Asia and Africa have been rallying points for global assistance.

Second, a global outlook means that people are increasingly looking to sources other than the nation-state in formulating their own sense of identity. This is a phenomenon that is both produced by and further accelerates processes of globalization. Local cultural identities in various parts of the world are experiencing powerful revivals at a time when the traditional hold of the nation-state is undergoing profound transformation. In Europe, for example, inhabitants of Scotland and the Basque region of Spain might be more likely to identify themselves as Scottish or Basque—or simply as Europeans—rather than as British or Spanish. The nation-state as a source of identity is waning in many areas as political shifts at the regional and global level loosen people's orientations toward the states in which they live.

TRANSNATIONAL CORPORATIONS

Among the many economic factors driving globalization, the role of **transnational corporations** is particularly important. Transnational corporations are companies that produce goods or market services in more than one country. These may be relatively small firms with one or two factories outside the country in which they are based or gigantic international ventures whose operations crisscross the globe.

Transnational corporations are at the heart of economic globalization: They account for two thirds of all world trade, they are instrumental in the diffusion of new technology around the globe, and they are major actors in international financial markets. As one observer has noted, they are "the linchpins of the contemporary world economy" (Held et al., 1999). Some five hundred transnational corporations had annual sales of more than $10 billion in 2003, while only eighty-two *countries* could boast gross domestic products of at least that amount. In other words, the world's leading transnational corporations are larger economically than most of the world's countries. In fact, the combined sales of the world's largest five hundred transnational corporations totaled $13.7 trillion—nearly half (46 percent) of the value of goods and services produced by the entire world (calculated from World Bank, 2003, and *Fortune,* 2003).

The "electronic economy" is another factor that underpins economic globalization. Banks, corporations, fund managers, and individual investors are able to shift funds internationally with the click of a mouse. This new ability to move "electronic money" instantaneously carries with it great risks, however. Transfers of vast amounts of capital can destabilize economies, triggering international financial crises such as the ones that spread from the Asian "tiger economies" to Russia and beyond in 1998. As the global economy becomes increasingly integrated, a financial collapse in one part of the world can have an enormous effect on distant economies.

The political, economic, social, and technological factors described above are joining together to produce a phenomenon that lacks any earlier parallel in terms of its intensity and scope. The consequences of globalization are many and far reaching, as we will see later in this chapter. But first we will turn our attention to the main views about globalization that have been expressed in recent years.

The Globalization Debate

In recent years, globalization has become a hotly debated topic. Most people accept that important transformations are occurring around us, but the extent to which it is valid to explain these as "globalization" is contested. This is not entirely surprising. As an unpredictable and turbulent

process, globalization is seen and understood very differently by observers. David Held and his colleagues (1999) have surveyed the controversy and divided its participants into three schools of thought: *skeptics, hyperglobalizers,* and *transformationalists.* These three tendencies within the globalization debate are summarized in Table 16.2.

THE SKEPTICS

Some thinkers argue that the idea of globalization is overrated—that the debate over globalization is a lot of talk about something that is not new. The skeptics in the globalization controversy believe that present levels of economic interdependence are not unprecedented. Pointing to nineteenth-century statistics on

---

TABLE 16.2

Conceptualizing Globalization: Three Tendencies

	SKEPTICS	TRANSFORMATIONALISTS	HYPERGLOBALIZERS
WHAT'S NEW?	Trading blocs, weaker geogovernance than in earlier periods	Historically unprecedented levels of global interconnectedness	A global age
DOMINANT FEATURES	World less interdependent than in 1890s	"Thick" (intensive and extensive) globalization	Global capitalism, global governance, global civil society
POWER OF NATIONAL GOVERNMENTS	Reinforced or enhanced	Reconstituted, restructured	Declining or eroding
DRIVING FORCES OF GLOBALIZATION	Governments and markets	Combined forces of modernity	Capitalism and technology
PATTERN OF STRATIFICATION	Increased marginalization of global South	New architecture of world order	Erosion of old hierarchies
DOMINANT MOTIF	National interest	Transformation of political community	McDonald's, Britney Spears, etc.
CONCEPTUALIZATION OF GLOBALIZATION	As internationalization and regionalization	As the reordering of interregional relations and action at a distance	As a reordering of the framework of human action
HISTORICAL TRAJECTORY	Regional blocs/clash of civilizations	Indeterminate: global integration and fragmentation	Global civilization
SUMMARY ARGUMENT	Internationalization depends on government acquiescence and support	Globalization transforming government power and world politics	The end of the nation-state

SOURCE: Adapted from Held et al., 1999, p. 10.

---

world trade and investment, they contend that modern globalization differs from the past only in the intensity of interaction between nations.

The skeptics agree that there may now be more contact among countries than in previous eras, but in their eyes the current world economy is not sufficiently integrated to constitute a truly globalized economy. This is because the bulk of trade occurs within three regional groups—Europe, Asia-Pacific, and North America (Hirst, 1997).

Many skeptics focus on processes of *regionalization* within the world economy—such as the emergence of major financial and trading blocs. To skeptics, the growth of regionalization is evidence that the world economy has become less integrated rather than more (Boyer and Drache, 1996; Hirst and Thompson, 1999). Compared with the patterns of trade that prevailed a century ago, they argue, the world economy is less global in its geographical scope and more concentrated on intense pockets of activity.

According to the skeptics, national governments continue to be key players because of their involvement in regulating and coordinating economic activity. Governments, for example, are the driving force behind many trade agreements and policies of economic liberalization.

THE HYPERGLOBALIZERS

The hyperglobalizers take an opposing position to that of the skeptics. They argue that globalization is a very real phenomenon whose consequences can be felt almost everywhere. They see globalization as a process that is indifferent to national borders. It is producing a new global order, swept along by powerful flows of cross-border trade and production. One of the best-known hyperglobalizers, the Japanese writer Kenichi Ohmae, sees globalization as leading to a "borderless world"—a world in which market forces are more powerful than national governments (Ohmae, 1990, 1995).

Much of the analysis of globalization offered by hyperglobalizers focuses on the changing role of the nation-state. It is argued that individual countries no longer control their economies because of the vast growth in world trade. Some hyperglobalizers believe that the power of national governments is also being challenged from above—by new regional and international institutions, such as the European Union, the World Trade Organization, and others.

Taken together, these shifts signal to the hyperglobalizers the dawning of a global age (Albrow, 1997) in which national governments decline in importance and influence.

THE TRANSFORMATIONALISTS

The transformationalists take more of a middle position. They see globalization as the central force behind a broad spectrum of changes that are currently shaping modern societies. According to them, the global order is being transformed, but many of the old patterns still remain. Governments, for instance, still retain a good deal of power in spite of the advance of global interdependence. These transformations are not restricted to economics alone, but are equally prominent within the realms of politics, culture, and personal life. Transformationalists contend that the current level of globalization is breaking down established boundaries between internal and external, international and domestic. In trying to adjust to this new order, societies, institutions, and individuals are being forced to navigate contexts where previous structures have been shaken up.

Unlike hyperglobalizers, transformationalists see globalization as a dynamic and open process that is subject to influence and change. It is developing in a contradictory fashion, encompassing tendencies that frequently operate in opposition to one another. Globalization is not a one-way process, as some claim, but a two-way flow of images, information, and influences. Global migration, media, and telecommunications are contributing to the diffusion of cultural influences. The world's vibrant "global cities" are thoroughly multicultural, with ethnic groups and cultures intersecting and living side by side. According to transformationalists, globalization is a decentered and reflexive process characterized by links and cultural flows that work in a multidirectional way. Because globalization is the product of numerous intertwined global networks, it cannot be seen as being driven from one particular part of the world.

Rather than losing sovereignty, as the hyperglobalizers argue, countries are seen by transformationalists as restructuring in response to new forms of economic and social organization that are nonterritorial in basis (e.g., corporations, social movements, and international bodies). They argue that we are no longer living in a state-centric world; governments are being forced to adopt a more active, outward-looking stance toward governance under the complex conditions of globalization (Rosenau, 1997).

The Impact of Globalization on Our Lives

Although globalization is often associated with changes within big systems—such as the world financial markets, production and trade, and telecommunications—the effects of globalization are felt equally strongly in the private realm.

Globalization is fundamentally changing the nature of our everyday experiences. As the societies in which we live undergo

Internationalizing Public Sociologies

[***]

The SSF and Kibera Collaboration

Sociologists Without Borders/Sociólogos Sin Fronteras [SSF] is committed to building alliances in Third World countries, and while we encourage members to do this on their own, we are also building our own SSF partnerships to provide such opportunities. We will be seeking such a partnership in Quito,

Ecuador, with a relatively large NGO that is connected to many local communities, but like any new partnership, this will slowly evolve once it is off the ground. We are eager to start moving in that direction because our first partnership with CFK [Carolina for Kibera] in Kibera, Nairobi, has proven to be so successful for SSF.

So far the partnership has involved two steps: first, our becoming familiar with the programs of CFK, which include inter-tribal youth soccer teams, a girls' reproductive health center, health outreach programs, and the health clinic; and, second, setting up the Nairobi Fellowship, which, beginning in 2003, is awarded annually to a student. Our first recipient of the Fellowship was Olivier Crespel, who was selected by members from the Spanish chapter of SSF, and our next recipient will be an American student. When I visited Kibera in September, many people asked me when Olivier ("the nice young man with the guitar") would be coming back. We were truly fortunate with the choice of Olivier. He started an inter-tribal youth band with traditional African instruments, learned quite a bit of Swahili, and having traveled earlier in African countries, felt very comfortable in Kibera.

Kibera is the biggest slum in Africa, with an estimated population of over [750,000] people. It evolved from a Nubian refugee settlement into a multitribal community, without planning or city services. Kiberans are extremely poor and they have high rates of AIDS, malaria, and tuberculosis. There are no streets in Kibera. Instead, there are narrow dirt pathways on which people cook and carry out craft work, and vend things such as used articles of clothing, vegetables, and cassettes. When people can find work it is usually in textile factories located far away in an industrial park outside of Kibera, and the pay is abysmal.

SSF hopes to expand this partnership, anticipating grant proposals that will bring jobs to young people and promote innovative technologies, including recycling programs for plastics and Internet capabilities that use alternative energy sources. There are many opportunities for expanding this partnership to include youth programs, women's enterprises, and, especially, health programs. (Approximately 40 percent of the adult population is HIV positive.) In contrast with the charity model, SSF works hand-in-hand with the residents of Kibera so that they set the priorities in their own terms, and SSF tries to provide resources. It is a variation on service-learning, and it is our intent that the residents and the NGO are steering us. They are the experts.

It is important to stress the SSF-CKF partnership in Kibera is one that we hope will serve as a model for what Michael Burawoy refers to as "de-provincializing" American sociology. I stress three aspects of this. First, Kibera is the living expression of exploitation and oppression, not only in Africa, but on the entire planet. The casualties of colonial imperialism, capitalism, and globalization, Kiberans live lives deprived of all the basic human rights—the rights to food, security, health care, clean water, jobs, etc. They nevertheless live their lives with determination and great dignity. Second, African social science is very different from American social science, and if we are to pluralize our epistemology, we can learn from the residents of Kibera why this is the case. Third, if we are to participate in global political and social movements for justice and human rights, we need to share a language with Africans, Latin Americans, Asians, and Europeans.

Kibera was a good place for SSF to begin our international, collaborative projects. It will allow us to seek alliances with our African colleagues, provide students and ourselves with opportunities to advance human rights and social justice projects arm in arm with the poor residents of Kibera, and begin to work in

local, regional, and even global coalitions that are opposed to oppression and injustices. It is my hope that SSF can form alliances with other Nairobi NGOs that are working on issues related to socioeconomic, health, and environment rights, and that we make good use of our sociological expertise in these alliances. We learn a great deal about the dynamics of the pathologies of globalization and neoliberalism when we see first-hand how the multinationals, property owners, and pharmaceutical companies deny Kiberans of their basic human rights. It is one thing to theorize about the injustices of globalization, but it is quite another to jump in and engage in the politics and practices to battle these injustices. Kibera offers Sociologists Without Borders members opportunities to battle injustices where they are most acute and most chilling.

SOURCE: Judith Blau, "Internationalizing Public Sociologies," *Sociologists Without Borders*, www.sociologistswithoutborders.org.

JUDITH BLAU is Professor of Sociology at the University of North Carolina, Chapel Hill. She is the author of several books, including Race in the Schools: The End of White Dominance?, Social Contracts and Economic Markets, *and* The Shape of Culture: A Study of Contemporary Cultural Patterns in the United States, *as well as numerous articles. She is currently the editor of* Social Forces: An International Journal of Social Research.

Advancements such as laptop computers and the Internet have allowed those in remote areas, such as these Aboriginal children in rural Australia, unprecedented access to technology and the ability to communicate easily with people all around the world.

profound transformations, the established institutions that used to underpin them have become out of place. This is forcing a redefinition of intimate and personal aspects of our lives, such as the family, gender roles, sexuality, personal identity, our interactions with others, and our relationships to work. The way we think of ourselves and our connections with other people is being profoundly altered through globalization.

THE RISE OF INDIVIDUALISM

In our current age, individuals have much more opportunity to shape their own lives than once was the case. At one time, tradition and custom exercised a very strong influence on the path of people's lives. Factors such as social class, gender, ethnicity, and even religious affiliation could close off certain avenues for individuals or open up others. In times past, individuals' personal identities were formed in the context of the community into which they were born. The values, lifestyles, and ethics prevailing in that community provided relatively fixed guidelines according to which people lived their lives.

Under conditions of globalization, however, we are faced with a move toward a new *individualism* in which people have actively to construct their own identities. The weight of tradition and established values is retreating as local communities interact with a new global order. Globalization is forcing people to live in a more open, reflexive way. This means that we are constantly responding and adjusting to the changing environment around us; as individuals, we evolve with and within the larger context in which we live. Even the small choices we make in our daily lives—what we wear, how we spend our leisure time, and how we take care of our health

and our bodies—are part of an ongoing process of creating and recreating our self-identities.

WORK PATTERNS

Globalization has unleashed profound transformations within the world of work. New patterns of international trade and the move to a knowledge economy have had a significant impact on long-standing employment patterns. Many traditional industries have been made obsolete by new technological advances or are losing their share of the market to competitors abroad whose labor costs are lower than in industrialized countries. Global trade and new forms of technology have had a strong effect on traditional manufacturing communities, where industrial workers have been left unemployed and without the types of skills needed to enter the new knowledge-based economy. These communities are facing a new set of social problems, including long-term unemployment and rising crime rates, as a result of economic globalization.

If at one time people's working lives were dominated by employment with one employer over the course of several decades—the so-called job-for-life framework—today many more individuals create their own career paths, pursuing individual goals and exercising choice in attaining them. Often this involves changing jobs several times over the course of a career, building up new skills and abilities, and transferring them to diverse work contexts. Standard patterns of full-time work are being dissolved into more flexible arrangements: working from home with the help of information technology, job sharing, short-term consulting projects, flextime, and so forth (Beck, 1992).

Women have entered the work force in large numbers, a fact that has strongly affected the personal lives of people of both sexes. Expanded professional and educational opportunities have led many women to put off marriage and children until after they have begun a career. These changes have also meant that many working women return to work shortly after having children, instead of remaining at home with young children as was once the case. These shifts have required important adjustments within families, in the nature of the domestic division of labor, in the role of men in child rearing, and with the emergence of more family-friendly working policies to accommodate the needs of dual-earner couples.

POPULAR CULTURE

The cultural impacts of globalization have received much attention. Images, ideas, goods, and styles are now disseminated around the world more rapidly than ever before. Trade, new information technologies, the international media, and global migration have all contributed to the free movement of culture across national borders. Many people believe that we now live in a single information order—a massive global network where information is shared quickly and in great volumes. A simple example should illustrate this point clearly.

Have you seen the film *Titanic*? It is quite likely that you have. It is estimated that hundreds of millions of people in countries around the world have seen *Titanic,* either in theaters, on cable, or on DVD. The 1997 film, which recounts the story of a young couple who fall in love aboard the ill-fated ocean liner, is one of the most popular films ever made. What can account for the enormous popularity of a film like *Titanic*? And what does its success tell us about globalization? At one level, *Titanic* was popular for very straightforward reasons: It combined a relatively simple plotline (a romance against the backdrop of tragedy) with a well-known historical event (the 1912 sinking of the *Titanic,* in which more than 1,600 people perished). The film was also lavishly produced, with great attention to detail, and included state-of-the-art special effects.

But another reason for *Titanic's* popularity is that it reflected a particular set of ideas and values that resonated with audiences worldwide. One of the film's central themes is the possibility of romantic love prevailing over class differences and family traditions. While such ideas are generally accepted in most Western countries, they are still taking hold in many other areas of the world. The success of a film like *Titanic* reflects the changing attitudes toward personal relationships and marriage, for example, in parts of the world where more traditional values have been favored. Yet *Titanic,* along with many other Western films, can also be said to *contribute* to this shift in values. Western-made films and television programs, which dominate the global media, tend to advance a set of political, social, and economic agendas that reflect specifically Western worldview. Some people worry that globalization is leading to the creation of a global culture in which the values of the most powerful and affluent—in this instance, Hollywood filmmakers—overwhelm the strength of local customs and tradition. According to this view, globalization is a form of cultural imperialism in which the values, styles, and outlooks of the Western world are being spread so aggressively that they smother individual national cultures.

Others, by contrast, have linked processes of globalization to a growing *differentiation* in cultural traditions and forms. Rather than cultural homogeneity, they claim that global society is now characterized by an enormous diversity of cultures existing side by side. Local traditions are joined by a host of additional cultural forms from abroad, presenting people with a bewildering array of lifestyle options from which to choose. Rather than a unified global culture, what we are witnessing is the fragmentation of cultural forms (Baudrillard, 1988). Estab-

lished identities and ways of life grounded in local communities and cultures are giving way to new forms of hybrid identity composed of elements from contrasting cultural sources (Hall, 1992).

Globalization and Risk

The consequences of globalization are far reaching, affecting virtually all aspects of the social world. Yet because globalization is an open-ended and internally contradictory process, it produces outcomes that are difficult to predict and control. Another way of thinking of this dynamic is in terms of *risk*. Many of the changes wrought by globalization are presenting us with new forms of risk that differ greatly from those that existed in previous eras. Unlike risks from the past, which had established causes and known effects, today's risks are incalculable in origin and indeterminate in their consequences.

THE SPREAD OF "MANUFACTURED RISK"

Humans have always had to face risks of one kind or another, but today's risks are qualitatively different from those that came in earlier times. Until quite recently, human societies were threatened by **external risk**—dangers such as drought, earthquakes, famines, and storms that spring from the natural world and are unrelated to the actions of humans. Today, however, we are increasingly confronted with various types of **manufactured risk**—risks that are created by the impact of our own knowledge and technology on the natural world. As we shall see, many environmental and health risks facing contemporary societies are instances of manufactured risk—they are the outcomes of our own interventions into nature.

Environmental Risks One of the clearest illustrations of manufactured risk can be found in threats currently posed by the natural environment (see Chapter 15). One of the consequences of accelerating industrial and technological development has been the steady spread of human intervention into nature. There are few aspects of the natural world that remain untouched by humans—urbanization, industrial production and pollution, large-scale agricultural projects, the construction of dams and hydroelectric plants, and nuclear power are just some of the ways in which human beings have had an impact on their natural surroundings. The collective outcome of such processes has been the creation of widespread environmental destruction whose precise cause is indeterminate and whose consequences are similarly difficult to calculate.

In our globalizing world, ecological risk confronts us in many guises. Concern over global warming has been mounting in the scientific community for some years; it is now generally accepted that the earth's temperature has been increasing from the buildup of harmful gases within the atmosphere. The potential consequences of global warming are devastating: If polar ice caps continue to melt as they currently are, sea levels will rise and may threaten low-lying land masses and their human populations. Changes in climate patterns have been cited as possible causes of the severe floods that afflicted parts of China in 1998 and Mozambique in 2000.

Health Risks In the past decade, the dangers posed to human health by manufactured risks have attracted great attention. In the media and public health campaigns, for example, people have been urged to limit their exposure to the harmful ultraviolet rays of the sun and to apply sunscreen to prevent burning. In recent years, sun exposure has been linked to a heightened risk of skin cancer in many parts of the world. This is thought to be related to the depletion of the ozone layer—the layer of the earth's atmosphere that normally filters out ultraviolet light. Due to the high volume of chemical emissions that are produced by human activities and industry, the concentration of ozone in the atmosphere has been diminishing and, in some cases, ozone holes have opened up.

There are many examples of manufactured risk that are linked to food. Modern farming and food production techniques have been heavily influenced by advances in science and technology. For example, chemical pesticides and herbicides are widely used in commercial agriculture, and many animals (such as chickens and pigs) are pumped full of hormones and antibiotics. Some people have suggested that farming techniques such as these compromise food safety and could have an adverse effect on humans.

THE GLOBAL "RISK SOCIETY"

Manufactured risks have presented individuals with new choices and challenges in their everyday lives. Because there is no roadmap to these new dangers, individuals, countries, and transnational organizations must negotiate risks as they make choices about how lives are to be lived. The German sociologist Ulrich Beck, who has written extensively about risk and globalization, sees these risks contributing to the formation of a global *risk society* (1992). As technological change progresses more and more rapidly and produces new forms of risk, we must constantly respond and adjust to these changes. The risk society, he argues, is not limited to environmental and health risks alone; it includes a whole series of interrelated changes within contemporary social life: shifting employment patterns, heightened job insecurity, the declining influence of tradition and custom on self-identity, the erosion of traditional family patterns, and the democratization of personal relationships. Because personal futures are much less fixed than they were in traditional societies, decisions of all kinds present risks for individuals. According to Beck, an important aspect of the risk society is that its hazards are not restricted spatially, temporally, or socially (1995). Today's risks affect all countries and all social classes; they have global, not merely personal, consequences.

Globalization and Inequality

Beck and other scholars have drawn attention to risk as one of the main outcomes of globalization and technological advance. New forms of risk present complex challenges for both individuals and whole societies that are forced to navigate through unknown terrain. Yet globalization is generating other important challenges as well.

Globalization is proceeding in an uneven way. The impact of globalization is experienced differentially, and some of its consequences are far from benign. Next to mounting ecological problems, the expansion of inequalities within and between societies is one of the most serious challenges facing the world at the start of the twenty-first century.

INEQUALITY AND GLOBAL DIVISIONS

As we learned in our discussion of types of society (Chapter 2), the vast majority of the world's wealth is concentrated in the in-

British Ministry of Agriculture officials watch as the carcasses of sheep and cattle are incinerated on a farm near Wigton in Cumbria, England, on March 16, 2001. Britain was compelled to kill tens of thousands of animals in order to prevent the spread of foot-and-mouth disease.

dustrialized or developed countries of the world, whereas the nations of the developing world suffer from widespread poverty, overpopulation, inadequate educational and health care systems, and crippling foreign debt. The disparity between the developed and the developing world widened steadily over the course of the twentieth century and is now the largest it has ever been.

The 1999 *Human Development Report,* published by the United Nations, revealed that the average income of the fifth of the world's population living in the richest countries was 74 times greater than the average income of the fifth living in the poorest. In the late 1990s, more than one fifth of the world's population accounted for 86 percent of the world's overall consumption, 82 percent of export markets, and 74 percent of telephone lines. The two hundred richest people in the world doubled their net worth between 1994 and 1998; the assets of the top three billionaires in the world in 1998 exceeded the combined gross domestic product (GDP) of all the least developed countries and the 600 million people who lived in them (UNDP, 1999).

In much of the developing world, levels of economic growth and output over the past century have not kept up with the rate of population growth, whereas the level of economic development in industrialized countries has far outpaced it. These opposing tendencies have led to a marked divergence between the richest and poorest countries of the world. The distance between the world's richest and poorest country was approximately 3 to 1 in 1820, 11 to 1 in 1913, 35 to 1 in 1950, 72 to 1 in 1992, and 173 to 1 in 2001 (see Figure 16.3). Over the past century, among the richest quarter of the world's population,

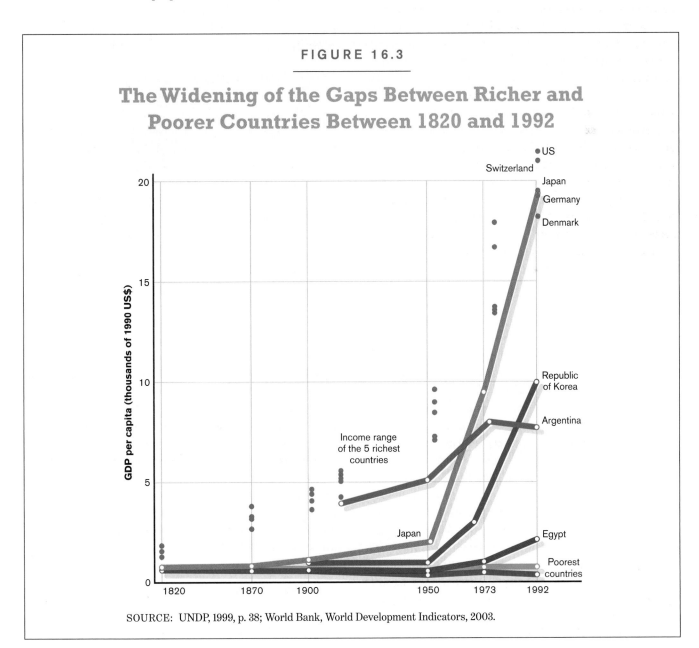

FIGURE 16.3

The Widening of the Gaps Between Richer and Poorer Countries Between 1820 and 1992

SOURCE: UNDP, 1999, p. 38; World Bank, World Development Indicators, 2003.

The Manufactured Risks of Electronic Viruses and World Climate Change

Globalization comes with many unfamiliar, manufactured risks. Among them are two that may have had a direct impact on you. On May 4, 2000, chaos engulfed the electronic world when a virus nicknamed the "love bug" succeeded in overloading computer systems worldwide. Launched from a personal computer in Manila, the capital of the Philippines, the "love bug" spread rapidly across the globe and forced almost a tenth of the world's e-mail servers to shut down. The virus was carried worldwide through an e-mail message with the subject heading "I Love You." When recipients opened the file that was attached to the message, they unknowingly activated the virus in their own computer. The "love bug" would then replicate itself and automatically send itself on to all the e-mail addresses listed in the computerized address book, before attacking information and files stored on the computer's hard drive. The virus spread westward around the globe as employees, first in Asia, then in Europe and North America, arrived to work in the morning and checked their e-mail. By the end of day, the

"love bug" was estimated to have caused more than $1.5 billion of damage worldwide.

The "love bug" was a particularly fast-spreading virus, but it was not the first of its kind. Electronic viruses have become

income per head has increased almost sixfold, while among the poorest quarter, the increase has been less than threefold.

Globalization seems to be exacerbating these trends by further concentrating income, wealth, and resources within a small core of countries (see Figure 16.4). As we have seen in this chapter, the global economy is growing and integrating at an extremely rapid rate. The expansion of global trade has been central to this process—between 1990 and 1997, international trade grew by 6.5 percent. Even though this rate of growth has fallen to 3 percent in 2002 (WTO 2003), only a handful of developing countries had managed to benefit from that rapid growth, and the process of integration into the global economy has been uneven. Some countries—such as the East Asian economies, Chile, India, and Poland—have fared well, with growth in exports of over 5 percent. Other countries—such as Russia, Venezuela, and Algeria—have seen few benefits from expanding trade and globalization (UNDP, 1999). Findings from the World Bank support this picture: Among ninety-three nations in the developing world, only twenty-three can be said

to be "rapid integrators." There is a danger that many of the countries most in need of economic growth will be left even further behind as globalization progresses (World Bank, 2000).

Free trade is seen by many as the key to economic development and poverty relief. Organizations such as the World Trade Organization (WTO) work to liberalize trade regulations and to reduce barriers to trade between the countries of the world. Free trade across borders is viewed as a win-win proposition for both developed and developing countries alike. While the industrialized economies are able to export their products to markets around the world, it is claimed that developing countries will also benefit by gaining access to world markets. This, in turn, is supposed to improve their prospects for integration into the global economy.

THE CAMPAIGN FOR GLOBAL JUSTICE

Not everyone agrees that free trade is the solution to poverty and global inequality. In fact, many critics argue that free trade more common—and more dangerous—as computers and electronic forms of communication have grown in importance and sophistication. Viruses such as the "love bug" demonstrate how interconnected the world has become with the advance of globalization. You might think that in this particular instance global interconnectedness proved to be quite a disadvantage, since a harmful virus was able to spread so rapidly around the globe. Yet many positive aspects of globalization are reflected in this case as well. As soon as the virus was detected, computer and security experts from around the world worked together to prevent its spread, protect national computer systems, and share intelligence about the virus's origins.

Another aspect of manufactured risk and one you likely have noticed—or been directly affected by—is the unusual weather in recent years. Scientists and disaster experts have pointed out that extreme weather events—such as unseasonably hot temperatures, droughts, floods, and cyclones—have been occurring with ever greater frequency. In 1998 alone, for example, eighty separate natural catastrophes were recorded at points around the globe, including devastating floods in China, hurricanes in Latin America, wildfires in Indonesia, and severe ice storms in North America. Since that time, drought has gripped regions as diverse as Ethiopia, southern Afghanistan, and the midwestern United States; floods have ravaged Venezuela and Mozambique; violent windstorms have battered parts of Europe; and a plague of locusts has swarmed through the Australian outback.

Although no one can be certain, many people believe that these natural disasters are caused in part by global warming (the heating up of the earth's atmosphere). If carbon dioxide emissions that contribute to global warming continue unchecked, it seems likely that the earth's climate will be irreversibly harmed. Who is to blame for global warming, and what can be done to slow its progress? As with so many aspects of our changing world, the risks associated with global warming are experienced worldwide, yet its precise causes are nearly impossible to pinpoint. In an age of globalization, we are constantly reminded of our interdependence with others: The actions of individuals or institutions in one part of the world can, and do, have significant consequences for people everywhere.

is a rather one-sided affair that benefits those who are already well off and exacerbates existing patterns of poverty and dependency within the developing world. Recently, much of this criticism has focused around the activities and policies of the World Trade Organization (WTO), which is at the forefront of efforts to increase global trade.

In December 1999, more than fifty thousand people from around the world took to the streets of Seattle to protest during the WTO's so-called Millennium Round of trade talks. Negotiators from the WTO's 134 member states (the number of members has since risen to 146) had come together to discuss and agree on measures to liberalize conditions for global trade and investment in agriculture and forest products, among other issues. Yet the talks broke off early with no agreements reached. The trade unionists, environmentalists, human rights activists, farmers, and representatives from hundreds of NGOs were triumphant—not only had the demonstrations succeeded in disrupting the talks, but internal disputes among delegates had also risen to the surface. The Seattle protests were heralded as

the biggest victory to date for campaigners for "global justice." Since that time, every ministerial meeting of the WTO has been met by massive demonstrations by those excluded from the processes of setting the rules for global trade.

But what is this campaign about, and does it represent the emergence of a powerful antiglobalization movement, as some commentators have suggested? In the months following the Seattle protests, similar demonstrations were held in other cities around the world, such as London and Washington, D.C. These events were much smaller than those that took place in Seattle, but they were organized around similar themes. Protesters argued that free trade and economic globalization succeed in further concentrating wealth in the hands of a few, while increasing poverty for the majority of the world's population. Most of these activists agree that global trade is necessary and potentially beneficial for national economies, but they claim that it needs to be regulated by *different* rules from those favored by the WTO. They argue that trade rules should be oriented, first and foremost, to protecting human rights, the environment,

FIGURE 16.4

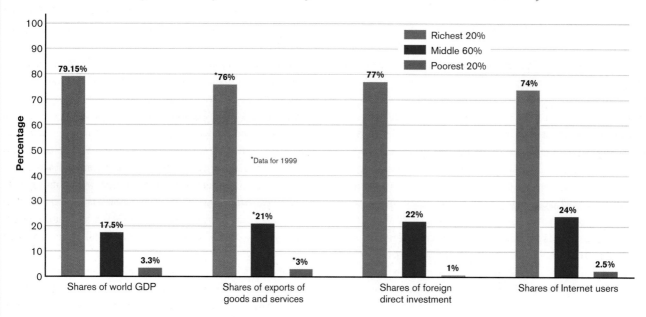

Shares of the Richest and the Poorer Countries in Global Income, Trade, Finance, and Communications, 2000

SOURCE: World Bank, World Development Indicators, 2002.

labor rights, and local economies—not in ensuring larger profits for already rich corporations.

The protesters claim that the WTO is an undemocratic organization that is dominated by the interests of the world's richest nations—particularly the United States. Such imbalances have very real consequences. For example, although the WTO has insisted that developing nations open their markets to imports from industrialized countries, it has allowed developed countries to maintain high barriers to agricultural imports and provide vast subsidies for their domestic agriculture production in order to protect their own agricultural sectors. Between 1995 and 2001, the United States government spent $114 billion to boost the income of crop and livestock farmers (Environmental Working Group, 2003). This has meant that the world's poorest countries, many of which remain predominantly agricultural, do not have access to the large markets for agricultural goods in developed countries.

A similar divide exists over the protection of intellectual property rights—an issue monitored by a WTO multilateral agreement called TRIPS (Trade-Related Aspects of Intellectual Property Rights). Industrial countries own 97 percent of all patents worldwide, but the concept of intellectual property rights is alien to the developing world. There has been a significant increase in the number of patent claims over the past two decades as biotechnology companies and research institutes push to control and "own" more and more forms of knowledge, technology, and biodiversity. Many samples of plant material, for example, have been taken from biodiverse areas such as rain forests and developed by pharmaceutical companies into profitable—and patented—medicines. Local knowledge about the medicinal uses of the plants is often used in developing and marketing the medicines, yet the indigenous people of the area receive no compensation for their contribution. As industrialized countries within the WTO push to strengthen intellectual property laws, many people in developing countries argue that such a move works against the needs of their countries. Research agendas are dictated by profit interests, not human interests, and valuable forms of technology may end up out of the reach of poorer countries that could benefit greatly from their use.

Another criticism of the WTO is that it operates in secret and is not accountable to citizens who are directly affected by its decisions. In many ways, these criticisms are valid. Trade disputes between members of the WTO are decided behind closed doors by an unelected committee of "experts." When a decision is handed down, it is legally binding on all member states and enforceable through a mechanism that authorizes WTO member nations to enact punitive trade policies unless the losing nation complies with the decision. The WTO can also challenge or override laws in individual nations that are seen as barriers to trade. This includes national laws or bilateral agreements designed to protect the environment, conserve scarce resources, safeguard public health, or guarantee labor standards and human rights.

Protesters against the WTO and other international financial institutions such as the World Bank and the International Monetary Fund argue that exuberance over global economic integration and free trade is forcing people to live in an economy rather than a society. Many are convinced that such moves will further weaken the economic position of poor societies by allowing transnational corporations to operate with few or no safety and environmental regulations. Commercial interests, they claim, are increasingly taking precedence over concern for human well-being. Not only within developing nations, but in industrialized ones as well, there needs to be more investment in "human capital"—public health, education, and training—if global divisions are not to deepen even further. The key challenge for the twenty-first century is to ensure that globalization works for people everywhere, not only for those who are already well placed to benefit from it.

Conclusion: The Need for Global Governance

As globalization progresses, existing political structures and models appear unequipped to manage a world full of risks, inequalities, and challenges that transcend national borders. It is not within the capacity of individual governments to control the spread of HIV/AIDS, to counter the effects of global warming, or to regulate volatile financial markets. Many of the processes affecting societies around the world elude the grasp of current governing mechanisms. In light of this governing deficit, some have called for new forms of global governance that could address global issues in a global way. As a growing number of challenges operate above the level of individual countries, it is argued that responses to them must also be transnational in scope.

Although it may seem unrealistic to speak of governance above the level of the nation-state, some steps have already been taken toward the creation of a global democratic structure, such as the formation of the United Nations and the European Union. The EU in particular can be seen as an innovative response to globalization and could well become a model for similar organizations in other parts of the world where regional ties are strong. New forms of global governance could help to promote a cosmopolitan world order in which transparent rules and standards for international behavior, such as the defense of human rights, are established and observed.

The years that have passed since the end of the cold war have been marked by violence, internal conflict, and chaotic transformations in many areas of the world. Some have taken a pessimistic view, seeing globalization as accelerating crisis and chaos. Others see vital opportunities to harness globalizing forces in the pursuit of greater equality, democracy, and prosperity. The move toward global governance and more effective regulatory institutions is certainly not misplaced at a time when global interdependence and the rapid pace of change link all of us together more than ever before. It is not beyond our abilities to reassert our will on the social world. Indeed, such a task appears to be both the greatest necessity and the greatest challenge facing human societies at the start of the twenty-first century.

Study Outline

www.wwnorton.com/giddens

Influences on Social Change

- *Social change* may be defined as the transformation, over time, of the institutions and culture of a society. The modern period, although occupying only a small fraction of human history, has shown rapid and major changes, and the pace of change is accelerating.

- The development of social organization and institutions, from hunting and gathering to agrarian to modern industrial societies, is far too diverse to be accounted for by any single-factor theory of social change. At least three broad categories of influences can be identified: The physical environment includes such factors as climate or the availability of communication routes (rivers, mountain passes); these are important to consider, especially as they affect early economic development, but should not be overemphasized. Political organization (especially military power) affects all societies, traditional and modern, with the possible exception of hunting and gathering societies. Cultural factors include religion (which can act as a brake on change), communication systems (such as the invention of writing), and individual leadership.

Change in the Modern Period

- The most important economic influence on modern social change is industrial capitalism, which depends on and promotes constant innovation and revision of productive technology. Science and technology also affect (and are affected by) political factors, the most important of which is the emergence of the modern state with its relatively efficient forms of government. Cultural influences include another effect of science and technology, the critical and innovative character of modern thinking, which constantly challenges tradition and cultural habits.

Current Changes and Future Prospects

- Social theorists have speculated on where social change will lead us. One influential line of thinking about where modern society is headed holds that the industrial era is being superseded by a *postindustrial society* based on the importance of information and service, rather than on manufacturing and industrialization. Some authors go further and speak not only of the end of industrialism, but of the end of modernity itself. Our beliefs in progress, in the benefits of science, and in our ability to control the modern world are diminishing, say the *postmodernists;* and there is such a diversity and plurality of individual concerns and points of view that it is no longer possible to have any overarching conception of history or of where we are headed.

Social Movements

- *Social movements*, by contrast, involve a collective attempt to further common interests through collaborative action outside the sphere of established institutions. The term *new social movements* is applied to a set of social movements that have arisen in Western countries since the 1960s in response to the changing risks facing human societies. Unlike earlier social movements, new social movements are single-issue campaigns oriented to nonmaterial ends and draw support from across class lines. Information technology has become a powerful organizing tool for many new social movements.

Theories of Revolution and Social Movements

- Theories of social movements and revolutions overlap. Marx argued that class struggles deriving from the *contradictions*, or unresolvable tensions within society, lead to revolutionary changes. James Davies argues that social movements occur from *relative deprivation*, a discrepancy between the lives people actually lead and what people believe to be possible. Charles Tilly analyzes revolutionary change from a broader context of *collective action*, which refers to

action taken to contest or overthrow an existing social order. Collective action culminating in social movements progresses from organization, mobilization, the perception of common interests, and finally the opportunity to act. For Tilly, social movements occur in circumstances of *multiple sovereignty*, a situation in which the government lacks full control.

- Neil Smelser's theory treats social movements as responses to situations, which undergo a series of stages. Alain Touraine argues that social movements rest on *historicity*, which is the idea that people know that social activism can shape history and affect society. Social movements occur in *fields of action*, which refers to the connection between a movement and the forces acting against it.

Globalization

- Globalization is often portrayed as an economic phenomenon, but this view is too simplified. Globalization is produced by the coming together of political, economic, cultural, and social factors. It is driven forward above all by advances in information and communication technologies that have intensified the speed and scope of interaction among people around the world.
- Several factors are contributing to increasing globalization. First, the end of the cold war, the collapse of Soviet-style communism, and the growth of international and regional forms of governance have drawn the countries of the world closer together. Second, the spread of information technology has facilitated the flow of information around the globe and has encouraged people to adopt a global outlook. Third, transnational corporations have grown in size and influence, building networks of production and consumption that span the globe and link economic markets.
- Globalization has become a hotly debated topic. Skeptics believe that the idea of globalization is overrated and that current levels of interconnectedness are not unprecedented. Some skeptics focus instead on processes of regionalization that are intensifying activity within major financial and trade groups. Hyperglobalizers take an opposing position, arguing that globalization is a real and powerful phenomenon that threatens to erode the role of national governments altogether. A third group, the transformationalists, believes that globalization is transforming many aspects of the current global order—including economics, politics, and social relations—but that old patterns still remain. According to this view, globalization is a contradictory process, involving a multidirectional flow of influences that sometimes work in opposition.
- Globalization is not restricted to large, global systems. Its impact is felt in our personal lives, in the way we think of ourselves and our connections with others. Globalizing forces enter our local contexts and our intimate lives both through impersonal sources such as the media and the Internet and through personal contacts with people from other countries and cultures.

Globalization and Risk

- Globalization is an open-ended, contradictory process—it produces outcomes that are difficult to control and predict. Globalization is presenting us with new forms of risk that differ from those that existed previously. *External risk* refers to dangers that spring from the natural world, such as earthquakes. *Manufactured risks* are risks that are created by the impact of human knowledge and technology on the natural world. Some believe that we are living in a global-risk society in which human societies everywhere are faced with risks (e.g., global warming) that have been produced by our own interventions into nature.

- Globalization is proceeding rapidly but unevenly. It has been marked by a growing divergence between the richest and poorest countries of the world. Wealth, income, resources, and consumption are concentrated among the developed societies, whereas much of the developing world struggles with poverty, malnutrition, disease, and foreign debt. Many of the countries most in need of the economic benefits of globalization are in danger of being marginalized.

World Trade Organization

- Barriers to international trade have been steadily reduced in recent decades, and many believe that free trade and open markets will allow developing countries to integrate more fully into the global economy. Opponents to this approach argue that international trade bodies, such as the World Trade Organization, are dominated by the interests of the richest countries and ignore the needs of the developing world. They claim that trade rules must, first and foremost, protect human rights, labor rights, the environment, and national economies, rather than simply ensuring larger profits for corporations.

Global Governance in the Future

- Globalization is producing risks, challenges, and inequalities that cross national borders and elude the reach of existing political structures. Because individual governments are unequipped to handle these transnational issues, there is a need for new forms of global governance that can address global problems in a global way. Reasserting our will on the rapidly changing social world may be the greatest challenge of the twenty-first century.

Key Concepts

civil society (p. 457)
collective action (p. 452)
external risk (p. 467)
field of action (p. 456)
historicity (p. 453)
information society (p. 450)
knowledge society (p. 450)

manufactured risk (p. 467)
new social movements (p. 456)
postindustrial society (p. 450)
postmodernism (p. 451)
relative deprivation (p. 452)
service society (p. 450)
social change (p. 448)
social movement (p. 451)
structural strain (p. 453)
transnational corporation (p. 461)

Review Questions

1. What is the sociology of social change?
   a. The study of revolution
   b. The study of the transformation over time of the institutions and culture of society
   c. The study of social movements
   d. The study of collective behavior
2. According to hyperglobalizers, which one of the following statements is true?
   a. Internationalization depends on government acquiescence and support.
   b. Globalization is making national politics more powerful.
   c. Globalization means the end of the nation-state.
   d. Globalization has no impact on how nation-states or governments operate.
3. What is the argument of the "end of history" thesis?
   a. The "end of history" is the end of the Industrial Revolution and the coming of postindustrial society.
   b. The "end of history" is the end of the great ideological struggles that erupted in the wake of the Industrial Revolution: Capitalism has finally beaten socialism, and liberal democracy is unchallenged.
   c. The "end of history" is the end of the belief that humanity can make progress, through the application of science and the development of technology, toward controlling its own destiny.
   d. The "end of history" is the end of World War II.
4. In 1992, the distance in terms of wealth between the world's richest and poorest countries was approximately
   a. 3 to 1.
   b. 11 to 1.
   c. 35 to 1.
   d. 72 to 1.
5. What is the relationship between science/technology and politics?
   a. Science and technology influence changes in politics.
   b. Politics influences how science and technology develop.
   c. Science and technology both influence and are influenced by political factors.

d. Science and technology have no influence on politics.

6. According to Daniel Bell, what is postindustrial society's main strategic resource?
   a. The production and control of computers
   b. The production and control of nuclear weapons
   c. The production and control of food
   d. The production and control of codified knowledge

7. Which of the following can be controlled by individual governments?
   a. The spread of HIV/AIDS
   b. The effects of global warming
   c. Volatile financial markets
   d. None of the above

8. The "unevenness" of globalization is in part due to the fact that political and economic power is concentrated in the hands of
   a. the United States.
   b. the United Nations.
   c. a few core countries.
   d. oil-rich countries.

9. What is the theory of relative deprivation?
   a. Social movements go through four stages of collective action: organization, mobilization, dissemination of common interests, and seizing on opportunities to further the cause.
   b. It is not absolute deprivation that leads to protest but comparison of present living standards with those of the upper class.
   c. It is not absolute deprivation that leads to protest but relative deprivation—the discrepancy between the lives people are forced to lead and what they think could realistically be achieved.
   d. It is not absolute deprivation that leads to protest but comparison of one's living standards with those of the more fortunate members of one's family.

10. Which two thinkers were responsible for "structural strain" theory and "fields of action" theory?
    a. Neil Smelser and Alain Touraine

b. Mary Hartman and Lois Banner
c. Charles Tilly and Theda Skocpol
d. William Chafe and David Aberle

Thinking Sociologically Exercises

1. Discuss the many influences on social change: environmental, political, and cultural factors. Summarize how each element can contribute to social change.

2. According to this chapter, we now live in a society where we are increasingly confronted by various types of manufactured risks. Briefly explain what these risks consist of. Do you think the last decade has brought us any closer to or further away from confronting the challenges of manufactured risks? Explain.

Data Exercises

www.wwnorton.com/giddens
Keyword: Data16

• What role have transnational corporations played in the development of a global economy? In what ways do they adapt their products and operations to local markets and in what ways do they ignore cultural differences? The data exercise for this chapter will give you an opportunity to investigate the global operations of a selected number of transnational corporations.

HOW TO USE LIBRARIES

Libraries, especially large ones, can seem like daunting places. People can feel somewhat lost when confronted with the apparently innumerable sources of information that libraries contain. They may therefore end up using only a small proportion of what a library has to offer, perhaps with damaging effects on their academic work. It is a good idea to get to know—at the beginning of your course—the range of resources libraries have. If you do this early on, the "lost" feeling will not last long!

All the information available in the library is stored and cataloged systematically, in order to make finding things easy. Most smaller libraries operate with *open stacks*—the books can be visibly inspected on the shelves, and the user can select whichever volume she wants directly. Most larger collections keep only a proportion of their books on open shelves and store others in vaults, where less space is required to keep them. In these libraries, anyone who wishes to use or borrow a book must ask for it or fill in a request slip.

If you are looking for a particular book, you will be able to look it up under author or title in the index or catalog. This may be a computerized list, drawers of index cards, or microfiche—or all three. Once you find the book's catalog number you can then either order it from library staff by quoting that number or find it on the open shelves, which are always arranged by catalog number. All—or most—sociology books will be in one area. Any librarian will be able to explain how the cataloging system works. To find books on a particular topic when you don't know any names or titles, you need to use a subject index (again, this may be computerized or on cards). A subject index lists books by topics—such as "class," "bureaucracy," etc.

Many of the larger libraries today have computer-trace systems, which are very easy to operate and are normally available to all library users. You simply key in the area about which you require bibliographical information, and the computer will display a list of relevant titles.

Most libraries provide similar services, but different libraries have their own ways of doing things, and there are variations in cataloging systems. Never be afraid to ask the librarian or assistants for their help if there is any procedure that puzzles you. You should not be worried about bothering them; librarians are trained professionals, committed to making sure that the library resources are available to everyone who wants to make use of them. They are usually highly knowledgeable about the range of material the library contains and only too willing to provide guidance.

Sources of General Information in Sociology

If you are beginning the study of a particular topic in sociology and want to find some general information about it, there are a number of useful sources. Several dictionaries of sociology are available. These provide brief discussions of major concepts and accounts of the ideas of some of the leading contributors to the discipline. The major encyclopedias—like the *World Book Encyclopedia*—contain many entries relevant to sociological topics, such as "city," "crime," "family," "middle class," "prejudice," "research," and "statistics." The entries in dictionaries and encyclopedias virtually always provide short lists of books or articles as a guide to further reading.

There are other ways in which books and articles relevant to a given issue can be traced. The *International Bibliography of the Social Sciences*, published annually by UNESCO, offers a comprehensive listing of works that have appeared in different social science subjects over the course of any year. Thus, for example, you can look up the heading "Sociology of education" and find a range of up-to-date materials in that field. An equally useful source is *Sociological Abstracts*, which not only lists books and articles in the different areas of sociology, but gives a short description of the contents of each.

Sociological Journals

It is worth familiarizing yourself with the main journals in sociology. Journals usually appear three or four times a year. The information and debates they contain are often more up to date than those in books, which take longer to write and publish. Journal articles are sometimes quite technical, and a person new to sociology may not find them readily understandable. But all the leading journals regularly publish articles of general interest, accessible to those with only limited knowledge of the subject.

The most important sociology journals include the *American Sociological Review* and the *American Journal of Sociology*.

Writing Research Papers

On some occasions, you may wish to use the library to pursue a particular research project, perhaps in the course of writing a thesis. Such a task might involve carrying out a more in-depth search for relevant sources than is required for normal study.

If you need statistical information concerning the United States, a good place to start is *Statistical Abstract of the United States*, which is available from the Government Printing Office in Washington, D.C. This volume contains selected statistical information on many areas of American social life.

Newspaper articles provide a mine of valuable information for the sociological researcher. A few newspapers are what are sometimes called "journals of record." That is to say, they not only carry news stories, but also record sections from congressional speeches, government reports, and other official sources. The *New York Times*, the *Washington Post*, and the *Los Angeles Times* are the most important examples, and each produces an index of topics and names that have appeared in its pages.

Once you start using a library regularly, you are likely to find that it is more common to feel overwhelmed by the number of works available in a particular area than to experience difficulty in tracing relevant literature. One way of dealing with this problem is to base your selection of books or articles on reading lists provided by professors. Where such lists are not available, the best procedure to follow is to define the information you require as precisely as possible. This will allow you to narrow the range of choice to feasible limits. If your library is an open-stack one, it is worth looking through a number of potentially useful books or articles before selecting those you decide to work with. In making the decision, keep in mind *when* the book was written. New developments are constantly taking place in sociology and in the other social sciences, and obviously older books will not cover these.

GLOSSARY

Words in bold type within entries refer to terms found elsewhere in the glossary.

AARP: American Association of Retired Persons.

absolute poverty: The minimal requirements necessary to sustain a healthy existence.

achieved status: Social status based on an individual's effort.

activity theory: A functionalist theory of aging which holds that busy, engaged people are more likely to lead fulfilling and productive lives.

age-grades: The system found in small traditional cultures by which people belonging to a similar age-group are categorized together and hold similar rights and obligations.

ageism: Discrimination or **prejudice** against a person on the grounds of age.

agencies of socialization: Groups or social contexts within which processes of **socialization** take place.

aging: The combination of biological, psychological, and social processes that affect people as they grow older.

agrarian societies: Societies whose means of subsistence are based on agricultural production (crop growing).

alienation: The sense that our own abilities as human beings are taken over by other entities. The term was originally used by Marx to refer to the projection of human powers onto gods. Subsequently he used the term to refer to the loss of workers' control over the nature and products of their labor.

Alzheimer's disease: A degenerative disease of the brain resulting in progressive loss of mental capacity.

andragogy: Term coined by educators to refer to adult learning.

animism: A belief that events in the world are mobilized by the activities of spirits.

anomie: A concept first brought into wide usage in sociology by Durkheim, referring to a situation in which social **norms** lose their hold over individual behavior.

apartheid: The system of racial **segregation** established in South Africa.

ascribed status: Social **status** based on biological factors such as **race, sex,** or age.

assimilation The acceptance of a **minority group** by a majority population, in which the new group takes on the **values** and **norms** of the dominant **culture.**

authoritarian personality: A set of specific personality characteristics, including a rigid and intolerant outlook and an inability to accept ambiguity.

authority: A **government**'s legitimate use of **power.**

automation: Production processes monitored and controlled by machines with only minimal supervision from people.

back region: An area apart from **front region** performances, as specified by Erving Goffman, in which individuals are able to relax and behave informally.

biomedical model of health: The set of principles underpinning Western medical systems and practices. The biomedical model of health defines diseases objectively, in accordance with the presence of recognized symptoms, and believes that the healthy body can be restored through scientifically based medical treatment. The human body is likened to a machine that can be returned to working order with the proper repairs.

black feminism: A strand of **feminist theory** that highlights the multiple disadvantages of **gender, class,** and **race** that shape the experiences of nonwhite women. Black feminists reject the idea of a single, unified gender oppression that is experienced evenly by all women and argue that early feminist analysis reflected the specific concerns of white, middle-class women.

bureaucracy: A type of **organization** marked by a clear hierarchy of authority and the existence of written rules of procedure and staffed by full-time, salaried officials.

capitalism: An economic system based on the private ownership of **wealth,** which is invested and reinvested in order to produce profit.

capitalists: People who own companies, land, or stocks (shares) and use these to generate economic returns.

caste: A form of stratification in which a person's **social position** is fixed at birth and cannot be changed. There is virtually no intermarriage between the members of different castes.

caste society: A society in which different social levels are closed, so that all individuals must remain at the social level of their birth throughout life.

caste system: A social system in which one's social status is given for life.

church: A large body of people belonging to an established religious organization. The term is also used to refer to the place in which religious ceremonies are carried out.

citizen: A member of a political community, having both rights and duties associated with that membership.

citizenship: A people's common rights and duties and consciousness of their relationship to the **state.**

civil inattention: The process whereby individuals in the same physical setting demonstrate to one another that they are aware of each other's presence.

civil rights: Legal rights held by all **citizens** in a given national community.

civil society: The realm of activity that lies between the **state** and the market, including the **family,** schools, community associations, and noneconomic institutions. Civil society, or civic culture, is essential to vibrant democratic societies.

clan (business model): Work groups having close personal connections with one another, which some argue is more efficient and productive than other forms of business organization.

class: Although it is one of the most frequently used concepts in **sociology,** there is no clear agreement about how the notion should be defined. Most sociologists use the term to refer to socioeconomic variations between groups of individuals that create variations in their material prosperity and power.

clock time: Time as measured by the clock, in terms of hours, minutes, and seconds. Before the invention of clocks, time reckoning was based on events in the natural world, such as the rising and setting of the sun.

cognition: Human thought processes involving perception, reasoning, and remembering.

cohabitation: Two people living together in a sexual relationship of some permanence, without being married to one another.

colonialism: The process whereby Western nations established their rule in parts of the world away from their home territories.

community policing: A renewed emphasis on crime prevention rather than law enforcement to reintegrate policing within the community.

comparable worth: Policies that attempt to remedy the gender pay gap by adjusting pay so that those in female-dominated jobs are not paid less for equivalent work.

comparative questions: Questions concerned with drawing comparisons between different human societies for the purposes of sociological **theory** or research.

comparative research: Research that compares one set of findings on one society with the same type of findings on other societies.

compulsion of proximity: People's need to interact with others in their presence.

concrete operational stage: A stage of cognitive development, as formulated by Piaget, in which the child's thinking is based primarily on physical perception of the world. In this phase, the child is not yet capable of dealing with abstract concepts or hypothetical situations.

conflict theory: Argument that deviance is deliberately chosen and often political in nature.

conflict theory of aging: Argument that emphasizes the ways in which the larger social structure helps to shape the opportunities available to the elderly. Unequal opportunities are seen as creating the potential for conflict.

contradiction: A term used by Marx to refer to mutually antagonistic tendencies in a society.

control: A statistical or experimental means of holding some **variables** constant in order to examine the causal influence of others.

control theory: A **theory** that views **crime** as the outcome of an imbalance between impulses toward criminal activity and controls that deter it. Control theorists hold that criminals are rational beings who will act to maximize their own reward unless they are rendered unable to do so through either social or physical controls.

conurbation: An agglomeration of towns or cities into an unbroken urban environment.

conversational analysis: The empirical study of conversations, employing techniques drawn from **ethnomethodology.** Conversation analysis examines details of naturally occurring conversations to reveal the organizational principles of talk and its role in the production and reproduction of social order.

core countries: According to **world-systems theory,** the most advanced industrial countries, which take the lion's share of profits in the world economic system.

corporate crime: Offenses committed by large corporations in society. Examples of corporate crime include pollution, false advertising, and violations of health and safety regulations.

corporate culture: An organizational culture involving rituals, events, or traditions that are unique to a specific company.

corporations: Business firms or companies.

correlation coefficient: A measure of the degree of **correlation** between **variables.**

created environment: Constructions established by human beings to serve their needs, derived from the use of man-made **technology**—including, for example, roads, railways, factories, offices, private homes, and other buildings.

crime: Any action that contravenes the **laws** established by a political authority. Although we may think of criminals as a distinct subsection of the population, there are few people who have not broken the law in one way or another during their lives. While laws are formulated by state authorities, it is not unknown for those authorities to engage in criminal behavior in certain situations.

crude birthrate: A statistical measure representing the number of births within a given population per year, normally calculated in terms of the number of births per thousand members. Although the crude birthrate is a useful index, it is only a general measure, because it does not specify numbers of births in relation to age distribution.

crude death rate: A statistical measure representing the number of deaths that occur annually in a given population per year, normally calculated as the ratio of deaths per thousand members. Crude death rates give a general indication of the **mortality** levels of a community or society, but are limited in their usefulness because they do not take into account the age distribution.

cult: A fragmentary religious grouping to which individuals are loosely affiliated, but which lacks any permanent structure.

cultural relativism: The practice of judging a **society** by its own standards.

cultural universals: **Values** or modes of behavior shared by all human **cultures.**

culture: The **values, norms,** and **material goods** characteristic of a given group. Like the concept of **society,** the notion of culture is widely used in **sociology** and the other social sciences (particularly anthropology). Culture is one of the most distinctive properties of human social association.

culture of poverty: The thesis, popularized by Oscar Lewis, that poverty is not a result of individual inadequacies but is instead the outcome of a larger social and cultural atmosphere into which successive generations of children are socialized. The culture of poverty refers to the **values,** beliefs, lifestyles, habits, and traditions that are common among people living under conditions of material deprivation.

degree of dispersal: The range or distribution of a set of figures.

demographic transition: An interpretation of population change, which holds that a stable ratio of births to deaths is achieved once a certain level of economic prosperity has been reached. According to this notion, in preindustrial societies there is a rough balance between births and deaths, because population increase is kept in check by a lack of available food, by disease, or by war. In modern societies, by contrast, population equilibrium is achieved because **families** are moved by economic incentives to limit the number of children.

demography: The study of populations.

denomination: A religious **sect** that has lost its revivalist dynamism and become an institutionalized body, commanding the adherence of significant numbers of people.

dependency culture: A term popularized by Charles Murray to describe individuals who rely on state welfare provision rather than entering the labor market. The dependency culture is seen as the outcome of the "paternalistic" welfare state that undermines individual ambition and people's capacity for self-help.

dependency ratio: The ratio of people of dependent ages (children and the elderly) to people of economically active ages.

dependency theories: Marxist theories of economic development arguing that the poverty of low-income countries stems directly from their exploitation by wealthy countries and the **multinational corporations** that are based in wealthy countries.

dependent development theory: A Marxist-influenced theory holding that although low-income countries are poor because of their exploitation by high-income countries, under certain circumstances they can still develop economically, but only in ways shaped by their reliance on the wealthier countries.

developing world: The less-developed societies, in which industrial production is either virtually nonexistent or only developed to a limited degree. The majority of the world's population live in less-developed countries.

developmental questions: Questions that sociologists pose when looking at the origins and path of development of **social institutions** from the past to the present.

deviance: Modes of action that do not conform to the **norms** or **values** held by most members of a group or **society.** What is regarded as deviant is as variable as the norms and values that distinguish different **cultures** and **subcultures** from one another. Forms of behavior that are highly esteemed by one group are regarded negatively by others.

deviant subculture: A **subculture** whose members hold values that differ substantially from those of the majority.

diaspora: The dispersal of an ethnic population from an original homeland into foreign areas, often in a forced manner or under traumatic circumstances.

differential association: An interpretation of the development of criminal behavior proposed by Edwin H. Sutherland, according to whom criminal behavior is learned through association with others who regularly engage in **crime.**

direct democracy: A form of **participatory democracy** that allows **citizens** to vote directly on **laws** and policies.

discourse: The framework of thinking in a particular area of social life. For instance, the discourse of criminality refers to the way people in a given **society** think and talk about **crime.**

discrimination: Behavior that denies to the members of a particular group resources or rewards that can be obtained by others. Discrimination must be distinguished from **prejudice:** Individuals who are prejudiced against others may not engage in discriminatory practices against them; conversely, people may act in a discriminatory fashion toward a group even though they are not prejudiced against that group.

disengagement theory: A functionalist theory of **aging** which holds that it is functional for society to remove people from their traditional roles when they become elderly, thereby freeing up those roles for others.

displacement: The transferring of ideas or emotions from their true source to another object.

dominant group: The opposite of a **minority group;** the dominant group possesses more **wealth, power,** and **prestige** in a **society.**

doubling time: The time it takes for a particular level of population to double.

downward mobility: Social mobility in which individuals' **wealth, income,** or **status** is lower than what they or their parents once had.

dyad: A group consisting of two persons.

ecological approach: A perspective on urban analysis emphasizing the "natural" distribution of city neighborhoods into areas having contrasting characteristics.

economic interdependence: The fact that in the **division of labor,** individuals depend on others to produce many or most of the goods they need to sustain their lives.

economy: The system of production and exchange that provides for the material needs of individuals living in a given **society.** Economic institutions are of key importance in all social orders. What goes on in the economy usually influences other areas in social life. Modern economies differ substantially from traditional ones, because the majority of the population is no longer engaged in agricultural production.

egocentric: According to Piaget, the characteristic quality of a child during the early years of her life. Egocentric thinking involves understanding objects and events in the environment solely in terms of the child's own position.

emigration: The movement of people out of one country in order to settle in another.

empirical investigation: Factual inquiry carried out in any area of sociological study.

encounter: A meeting between two or more people in a situation of face-to-face interaction. Our daily lives can be seen as a series of different encounters strung out across the course of the day. In modern societies, many of these encounters are with strangers rather than people we know.

endogamy: The forbidding of marriage or sexual relations outside one's **social group.**

entrepreneur: The owner/founder of a business firm.

environmental ecology: A concern with preserving the integrity of the physical environment in the face of the impact of modern industry and **technology.**

ethnic cleansing: The creation of ethnically homogeneous territories through the mass expulsion of other ethnic populations.

ethnic-group closure: The maintenance of boundaries against others, the prohibition against intermarriage between groups, and restrictions on social contact with other groups.

ethnicity: Cultural **values** and **norms** that distinguish the members of a given group from others. An ethnic group is one whose members share a distinct awareness of a common cultural identity, separating them from other groups. In virtually all **societies,** ethnic differences are associated with variations in **power** and material **wealth.** Where ethnic differences are also racial, such divisions are sometimes especially pronounced.

ethnocentrism: The tendency to look at other **cultures** through the eyes of one's own culture, and thereby misrepresent them.

ethnography: The firsthand study of people using **participant observation** or interviewing.

ethnomethodology: The study of how people make sense of what others say and do in the course of day-to-day social interaction. Ethnomethodology is concerned with the "ethnomethods" by which people sustain meaningful interchanges with one another.

exchange mobility: The exchange of positions on the socioeconomic scale such that talented people move up the economic hierarchy while the less talented move down.

experiment: A **research method** in which **variables** can be analyzed in a controlled and systematic way, either in an artificial situation constructed by the researcher or in naturally occurring settings.

exponential growth: A geometric, rather than linear, rate of progression, producing a fast rise in the numbers of a population experiencing such growth.

extended family: A **family** group consisting of more than two generations of relatives living either within the same household or very close to one another.

external risk: Dangers that spring from the natural world and are unrelated to the actions of humans. Examples of external risk include droughts, earthquakes, famines, and storms.

factual questions: Questions that raise issues concerning matters of fact (rather than theoretical or moral issues).

family: A group of individuals related to one another by blood ties, **marriage,** or adoption, who form an economic unit, the adult members of which are responsible for the upbringing of children. All known **societies** involve some form of family system, although the nature of family relationships varies widely. While in modern societies the main family form is the **nuclear family, extended family** relationships are also found.

family capitalism: Capitalistic enterprise owned and administered by entrepreneurial **families.**

family of orientation: The **family** into which an individual is born.

family of procreation: The **family** an individual initiates through **marriage** or by having children.

fecundity: A measure of the number of children that it is biologically possible for a woman to produce.

feminism: Advocacy of the rights of women to be equal with men in all spheres of life. Feminism dates from the late eighteenth century in Europe, and feminist movements exist in most countries today.

feminist theory: A sociological perspective that emphasizes the centrality of **gender** in analyzing the social world and particularly the uniqueness of the experience of women. There are many strands of feminist theory, but they all share the desire to explain **gender inequalities** in **society** and to work to overcome them.

feminization of poverty: An increase in the proportion of the poor who are female.

fertility: The average number of live-born children produced by women of childbearing age in a particular **society.**

focused interaction: Interaction between individuals engaged in a common activity or in direct conversation with one another.

formal operational stage: According to Piaget's theory, a stage of cognitive development at which the growing child becomes capable of handling abstract concepts and hypothetical situations.

formal organization: Means by which a group is rationally designed to achieve its objectives, often by means of explicit rules, regulations, and procedures.

formal relations: Relations that exist in groups and **organizations,** laid down by the **norms,** or rules, of the official system of authority.

front region: A setting of social activity in which people seek to put on a definite "performance" for others.

functionalism: A theoretical perspective based on the notion that social events can best be explained in terms of the functions they perform—that is, the contributions they make to the continuity of a **society.**

gender: Social expectations about behavior regarded as appropriate for the members of each **sex.** Gender refers not to the physical attributes distinguishing men and women but to socially formed traits of masculinity and femininity. The study of gender relations has become one of the most important areas of **sociology** in recent years.

gender inequality: The inequality between men and women in terms of **wealth, income,** and **status.**

gender roles: Social roles assigned to each **sex** and labeled as masculine or feminine.

gender socialization: The learning of **gender roles** through social factors such as schooling, the media, and **family.**

gender typing: Women holding **occupations** of lower **status** and pay, such as secretarial and retail positions, and men holding **jobs** of higher status and pay, such as managerial and professional positions.

generalized other: A concept in the **theory** of George Herbert Mead, according to which the individual takes over the general **values** of a given group or **society** during the **socialization** process.

generational equity: The striking of a balance between the needs and interests of members of different generations.

genocide: The systematic, planned destruction of a racial, political, or cultural group.

gentrification: A process of **urban renewal** in which older, deteriorated housing is refurbished by affluent people moving into the area.

geragogy: Term coined by educators to refer to older-adult learning.

glass ceiling: A promotion barrier that prevents a woman's upward mobility within an **organization.**

glass escalator: The process by which men in traditionally female professions benefit from an unfair rapid rise within an **organization.**

global city: A city—such as London, New York, or Tokyo—that has become an organizing center of the new global economy.

global commodity chain: A worldwide **network** of labor and production processes yielding a finished product.

global inequality: The systematic differences in **wealth** and **power** between countries.

globalization: The development of social and economic relationships stretching worldwide. In current times, we are all influenced by **organizations** and social **networks** located thousands of miles away. A key part of the study of globalization is the emergence of a **world system**—for some purposes, we need to regard the world as forming a single social order.

graying: A term used to indicate that an increasing proportion of a **society's** population is becoming elderly.

group closure: The maintenance of boundaries against others, the prohibition of intermarriage between groups, and restrictions on social contact with other groups.

groupthink: A process by which the members of a group ignore ways of thinking and plans of action that go against the group consensus.

heterosexism: The process by which nonheterosexual people are categorized and discriminated against on the basis of their sexual orientation.

hidden curriculum: Traits of behavior or attitudes that are learned at school but not included within the formal curriculum—for example, **gender** differences.

higher education: Education in colleges or universities.

homeless: People who have no place to sleep and either stay in free shelters or sleep in public places not meant for habitation.

homophobia: An irrational fear or disdain of homosexuals.

housework (domestic labor): Unpaid work carried on, usually by women, in the home; domestic chores such as cooking, cleaning, and shopping.

human resource management: A style of management that regards a company's work force as vital to its economic competitiveness.

hunting and gathering societies: Societies whose mode of subsistence is gained from hunting animals, fishing, and gathering edible plants.

hypothesis: An idea or a guess about a given state of affairs, put forward as a basis for empirical testing.

I: The pronoun used to refer used to refer to oneself as speaker or writer.

ideal type: A "pure type," constructed by emphasizing certain traits of a social item that do not necessarily exist in reality. An example is Max Weber's ideal type of bureaucratic organization.

identity: The distinctive characteristics of a person's or group's character that relate to who they are and what is meaningful to them. Some of the main sources of identity include **gender,** sexual orientation, nationality or **ethnicity,** and social **class.**

ideology: Shared ideas or beliefs that serve to justify the interests of **dominant groups.** Ideologies are found in all **societies** in which there are systematic and ingrained inequalities between groups. The concept of ideology connects closely with that of **power,** since ideological systems serve to legitimize the power that groups hold.

immigration: The movement of people into one country from another for the purpose of settlement.

impression management: Preparing for the presentation of one's **social role.**

income: Payment, usually derived from wages, salaries, or investments.

industrialization: The process of the machine production of goods. See also **industrialized societies.**

industrialized societies: Strongly developed **nation-states** in which the majority of the population work in factories or offices rather than in agriculture, and most people live in urban areas.

infant mortality rate: The number of infants who die during the first year of life, per thousand live births.

informal economy: Economic transactions carried on outside the sphere of orthodox paid employment.

informal relations: Relations that exist in groups and **organizations** developed on the basis of personal connections; ways of doing things that depart from formally recognized modes of procedure.

information society: A **society** no longer based primarily on the production of **material goods** but on the production of knowledge. The notion of the information society is closely bound up with the rise of **information technology.**

information technology: Forms of **technology** based on information processing and requiring microelectronic circuitry.

in-group: A group toward which one feels particular loyalty and respect—the groups to which "we" belong.

inner city: The areas composing the central neighborhoods of a city, as distinct from the suburbs. In many modern urban settings in the **First World,** inner-city areas are subject to dilapidation and decay, the more affluent residents having moved to outlying areas.

instinct: A fixed pattern of behavior that has genetic origins and that appears in all normal animals within a given species.

institutional capitalism: Capitalistic enterprise organized on the basis of institutional shareholding.

institutional racism: Patterns of **discrimination** based on **ethnicity** that have become structured into existing social institutions.

intelligence: Level of intellectual ability, particularly as measured by **IQ (intelligence quotient)** tests.

interactional vandalism: The deliberate subversion of the tacit rules of conversation.

intergenerational mobility: Movement up or down a social stratification hierarchy from one generation to another.

intragenerational mobility: Movement up or down a **social stratification** hierarchy within the course of a personal career.

IQ (intelligence quotient): A score attained on tests of symbolic or reasoning abilities.

"iron law of oligarchy": A term coined by Weber's student Robert Michels meaning that large **organizations** tend toward centralization of **power,** making **democracy** difficult.

job: See **occupation.**

kinship: A relation that links individuals through blood ties, **marriage,** or adoption. Kinship relations are by definition part of marriage and the **family,** but extend much more broadly. While in most modern societies few social obligations are involved in kinship relations extending beyond the immediate family, in other cultures kinship is of vital importance to social life.

knowledge economy: A **society** no longer based primarily on the production of **material goods** but based instead on the production of knowledge. Its emergence has been linked to the development of a broad base of consumers who are technologically literate and have made new advances in computing, entertainment, and telecommunications part of their lives.

knowledge society: Another common term for **information society**—a **society** based on the production and consumption of knowledge and information.

Kuznets curve: A formula showing that inequality increases during the early stages of capitalist development, then declines, and eventually stabilizes at a relatively low level; advanced by the economist Simon Kuznets.

labeling theory: An approach to the study of **deviance** that suggests that people become "deviant" because certain labels are attached to their behavior by political authorities and others.

language: The primary vehicle of meaning and communication in a society, language is a system of **symbols** that represent objects and abstract thoughts.

latent functions: Functional consequences that are not intended or recognized by the members of a social system in which they occur.

law: A rule of behavior established by a political authority and backed by state **power.**

leader: A person who is able to influence the behavior of other members of a group.

liberal feminism: Form of **feminist theory** that believes that **gender inequality** is produced by unequal access to **civil rights** and certain social resources, such as education and employment, based on **sex.** Liberal feminists tend to seek solutions through changes in legislation that ensure that the rights of individuals are protected.

liberation theology: An activist Catholic religious movement that combines Catholic beliefs with a passion for social justice for the poor.

life chances: A term introduced by Max Weber to signify a person's opportunities for achieving economic prosperity.

life course: The various transitions people experience during their lives.

life span: The maximum length of life that is biologically possible for a member of a given species.

linguistic relativity hypothesis: A **hypothesis,** based on the **theories** of Sapir and Whorf, that perceptions are relative to **language.**

lower class: A social class comprised of those who work part time or not at all and whose household income is typically lower than $17,000 a year.

macrosociology: The study of large-scale groups, **organizations,** or social systems.

Malthusianism: A doctrine about population dynamics developed by Thomas Malthus, according to which population increase comes up against "natural limits," represented by famine and war.

managerial capitalism: Capitalistic enterprises administered by managerial executives rather than by owners.

manifest functions: The functions of a type of social activity that are known to and intended by the individuals involved in the activity.

manufactured risk: Dangers that are created by the impact of human knowledge and **technology** on the natural world. Examples of manufactured risk include global warming and genetically modified foods.

market-oriented theories: Theories about economic development that assume that the best possible economic consequences will result if individuals are free to make their own economic decisions, uninhibited by governmental constraint.

marriage: A socially approved sexual relationship between two individuals. Marriage almost always involves two persons of opposite sexes, but in some cultures, types of homosexual marriage are tolerated. Marriage normally forms the basis of a **family of procreation**— that is, it is expected that the married couple will produce and bring up children. Some societies permit **polygamy,** in which an individual may have several spouses at the same time.

Marxism: A body of thought deriving its main elements from Marx's ideas.

master status: The **status**(es) that generally determine(s) a person's overall position in **society.**

material goods: The physical objects that a **society** creates, which influence the ways in which people live.

materialist conception of history: The view developed by Marx, according to which material, or economic, factors have a prime role in determining historical change.

matrilocal family: A **family** system in which the husband is expected to live near the wife's parents.

mean: A statistical measure of central tendency, or average, based on dividing a total by the number of individual cases.

means of production: The means whereby the production of **material goods** is carried on in a **society,** including not just **technology** but the social relations between producers.

measures of central tendency: The ways of calculating averages.

median: The number that falls halfway in a range of numbers—a way of calculating central tendency that is sometimes more useful than calculating a **mean.**

Medicare: A program under the U.S. Social Security Administration that reimburses hospitals and physicians for medical care provided to qualifying people over sixty-five years old.

megalopolis: The "city of all cities" in ancient Greece—used in modern times to refer to very large **conurbations.**

melting pot: The idea that ethnic differences can be combined to create new patterns of behavior drawing on diverse cultural sources.

microsociology: The study of human behavior in contexts of face-to-face interaction.

middle class: A social **class** composed broadly of those working in white-collar and lower managerial occupations.

millenarian movement: Beliefs held by certain types of **religious movements,** according to which cataclysmic changes will occur in the near future, heralding the arrival of a new epoch.

minority group (or ethnic minority): A group of people in a minority in a given **society** who, because of their distinct physical or cultural characteristics, find themselves in situations of inequality within that society.

mode: The number that appears most often in a given set of data. This can sometimes be a helpful way of portraying central tendency.

modernization theory: A version of market-oriented development theory that argues that low-income societies develop economically only if they give up their traditional ways and adopt modern economic institutions, **technologies,** and cultural **values** that emphasize savings and productive investment.

monogamy: A form of **marriage** in which each married partner is allowed only one spouse at any given time.

monopoly: A situation in which a single firm dominates in a given industry.

mortality: The number of deaths in a population.

multiculturalism: Ethnic groups exist separately and share *equally* in economic and political life.

multimedia: The combination of what used to be different media requiring different **technologies** (e.g., visuals and sound) on a single medium, such as a CD-ROM or Web site.

multinational corporations: Business corporations located in two or more countries.

neoliberalism: The economic belief that free market forces, achieved by minimizing government restrictions on business, provide the only route to economic growth.

network: A set of informal and formal social ties that links people to each other.

new criminology: A branch of criminological thought, prominent in Britain in the 1970s, that regarded **deviance** as deliberately chosen and often political in nature. The new criminologists argued that **crime** and deviance could only be understood in the context of **power** and inequality within **society.**

new left realism: A strain of criminology, popularized in the 1980s by the work of Jock Young, that focused on the victims of **crime** and called for criminology to engage practically with issues of crime control and social policy.

newly industrializing economies (NIEs): Developing countries that over the past two or three decades have begun to develop a strong industrial base, such as Singapore and Hong Kong.

new racism: Racist outlooks, also referred to as "cultural racism," that are predicated on cultural or religious differences rather than biological ones.

new religious movements: The broad range of religious and spiritual groups, **cults,** and **sects** that have emerged alongside mainstream **religions.** New religious movements range from spiritual and self-help groups within the **New Age movement** to exclusive sects such as the Hare Krishnas.

nontheistic religions: Religions based on a belief in the existence of divine spiritual forces rather than a god or gods.

nonverbal communication: Communication between individuals based on facial expression or bodily gesture rather than on **language.**

norms: Rules of conduct that specify appropriate behavior in a given range of social situations. A norm either prescribes a given type of behavior or forbids it. All human groups follow definite norms, which are always backed by **sanctions** of one kind or another—varying from informal disapproval to physical punishment.

nuclear family: A **family** group consisting of a wife, a husband (or one of these), and dependent children.

occupation: Any form of paid employment in which an individual regularly works.

"old old": Sociological term for persons aged seventy-five to eighty-four.

"oldest old": Sociological term for persons aged eighty-five and older.

oligarchy: Rule by a small minority within an **organization** or **society.**

oligopoly: The domination of a small number of firms in a given industry.

oral history: Interviews with people about events they witnessed or experienced at some point earlier in their lives.

organic solidarity: According to Émile Durkheim, the social cohesion that results from the various parts of a **society** functioning as an integrated whole.

organization: A large group of individuals with a definite set of authority relations. Many types of organizations exist in **industrialized societies,** influencing most aspects of our lives. While not all organizations are bureaucratic, there are close links between the development of organizations and bureaucratic tendencies.

organized crime: Criminal activities carried out by **organizations** established as businesses.

out-group: A group toward which one feels antagonism and contempt—"those people."

pariah groups: Groups who suffer from negative **status discrimination**—they are looked down on by most other members of society. The Jews, for example, have been a pariah group throughout much of European history.

participant observation (fieldwork): A method of research widely used in **sociology** and anthropology, in which the researcher takes part in the activities of the group or community being studied.

pastoral societies: Societies whose subsistence derives from the rearing of domesticated animals.

patriarchy: The dominance of men over women. All known **societies** are patriarchal, although there are variations in the degree and nature of the **power** men exercise, as compared with women. One of the prime objectives of women's movements in modern societies is to combat existing patriarchal institutions.

patrilocal family: A **family** system in which the wife is expected to live near the husband's parents.

peer group: A friendship group composed of individuals of similar age and social **status.**

peripheral countries: Countries that have a marginal role in the world **economy** and are thus dependent on the core producing societies for their trading relationships.

personality stabilization: According to the theory of **functionalism,** the **family** plays a crucial role in assisting its adult members emotionally. **Marriage** between adult men and women is the arrangement through which adult personalities are supported and kept healthy.

personal space: The physical space individuals maintain between themselves and others.

pilot study: A trial run in **survey** research.

pluralism: A model for ethnic relations in which all ethnic groups in the United States retain their independent and separate identities, yet share equally in the rights and **powers** of **citizenship.**

polyandry: A form of **marriage** in which a woman may simultaneously have two or more husbands.

polygamy: A form of **marriage** in which a person may have two or more spouses simultaneously.

polygyny: A form of **marriage** in which a man may simultaneously have two or more wives.

population: The people who are the focus of social research.

postindustrial society: A notion advocated by those who believe that processes of social change are taking us beyond the industrialized order. A postindustrial society is based on the production of information rather than **material goods.** According to postindustrialists, we are currently experiencing a series of social changes as profound as those that initiated the industrial era some two hundred years ago.

postmodernism: The belief that **society** is no longer governed by history or progress. Postmodern society is highly pluralistic and diverse, with no "grand narrative" guiding its development.

poverty line: An official **government** measure to define those living in poverty in the United States.

prejudice: The holding of preconceived ideas about an individual or group, ideas that are resistant to change even in the face of new information. Prejudice may be either positive or negative.

preoperational stage: A stage of cognitive development, in Piaget's theory, in which the child has advanced sufficiently to master basic modes of logical thought.

prestige: The respect accorded to an individual or group by virtue of their **status.**

primary deviation: According to Edwin Lemert, the actions that cause others to label one as a deviant.

primary group: A group that is characterized by intense emotional ties, face-to-face interaction, intimacy, and a strong, enduring sense of commitment.

primary socialization: The process by which children learn the cultural **norms** of the **society** into which they are born. Primary socialization occurs largely in the **family.**

profane: That which belongs to the mundane, everyday world.

projection: Attributing to others feelings that a person actually has herself.

psychopath: A specific personality type; such individuals lack the moral sense and concern for others held by most normal people.

race: Differences in human physical characteristics used to categorize large numbers of individuals.

racialization: The process by which understandings of **race** are used to classify individuals or groups of people. Racial distinctions are more than ways of describing human differences; they are also important factors in the reproduction of patterns of **power** and inequality.

"racial literacy": The skills taught to children of multiracial families to help them cope with racial hierarchies and to integrate multiple ethnic identities.

racism: The attribution of characteristics of superiority or inferiority to a population sharing certain physically inherited characteristics. Racism is one specific form of **prejudice,** focusing on physical variations between people. Racist attitudes became entrenched during the period of Western colonial expansion, but seem also to rest on mechanisms of **prejudice** and **discrimination** found in human **societies** today.

radical feminism: Form of **feminist theory** that believes that **gender inequality** is the result of male domination in all aspects of social and economic life.

random sampling: Sampling method in which a sample is chosen so that every member of the **population** has the same probability of being included.

rape: The forcing of nonconsensual vaginal, oral, or anal intercourse.

rational choice approach: More broadly, the **theory** that an individual's behavior is purposive. Within the field of criminology, rational choice analysis argues that deviant behavior is a rational response to a specific social situation.

rationality: See also **rationalization.** The belief that rules and efficiency should guide modern **societies.**

reference group: A group that provides a standard for judging one's attitudes or behaviors.

regionalization: The division of social life into different regional settings or zones.

relative poverty: Poverty defined according to the living standards of the majority in any given society.

religion: A set of beliefs adhered to by the members of a community, incorporating **symbols** regarded with a sense of awe or wonder together with ritual practices. Religions do not universally involve a belief in supernatural entities.

religious economy: A theoretical framework within the sociology of **religion,** which argues that religions can be fruitfully understood as **organizations** in competition with one another for followers.

religious nationalism: The linking of strongly held religious convictions with beliefs about a people's social and political destiny.

representative sample: A sample from a larger **population** that is statistically typical of that population.

research methods: The diverse methods of investigation used to gather empirical (factual) material. Different research methods exist in **sociology,** but the most commonly used are fieldwork (or **participant observation**) and **survey** methods. For many purposes, it is useful to combine two or more methods within a single research project.

research process: The manner by which the study of a given subject proceeds from investigation to published findings.

resource allocation: Inequalities in the distribution of **wealth** and goods resulting from limited resources.

response cries: Seemingly involuntary exclamations individuals make when, for example, being taken by surprise, dropping something inadvertently, or expressing pleasure.

role: The expected behavior of a person occupying a particular **social position.** The idea of **social role** originally comes from the theater, referring to the parts that actors play in a stage production. In every **society,** individuals play a number of social roles.

sacred: Describing something that inspires attitudes of awe or reverence among believers in a given set of religious ideas.

sample: A small proportion of a larger **population.**

sampling: Studying a proportion of individuals or cases from a larger **population** as representative of that population as a whole.

sanction: A mode of reward or punishment that reinforces socially expected forms of behavior.

scapegoat: An individual or group blamed for wrongs that were not of their doing.

science: In the sense of physical science, the systematic study of the physical world. Science involves the disciplined marshaling of empirical data, combined with **theoretical approaches** and **theories** that illuminate or explain those data. Scientific activity combines the creation of boldly new modes of thought with the careful testing of **hypotheses** and ideas. One major feature that helps distinguish science from other idea systems (such as **religion**) is the assumption that *all* scientific ideas are open to criticism and revision.

secondary deviation: According to Edwin Lemert, following the act of **primary deviation,** secondary deviation occurs when an individual accepts the label of deviant and acts accordingly.

secondary group: A group characterized by its large size and by impersonal, fleeting relationships.

sect: A **religious movement** that breaks away from orthodoxy.

secularization: A process of decline in the influence of **religion.** Although modern **societies** have become increasingly secularized, tracing the extent of secularization is a complex matter. Secularization can refer to levels of involvement with religious organizations (such as rates of **church** attendance), the social and material influence wielded by religious organizations, and the degree to which people hold religious beliefs.

secular thinking: Worldly thinking, particularly as seen in the rise of **science, technology,** and rational thought in general.

segregation: The practices of keeping racial and ethnic groups physically separate, thereby maintaining the superior position of the **dominant group.**

self-consciousness: Awareness of one's distinct **social identity** as a person separate from others. Human beings are not born with self-consciousness but acquire an awareness of self as a result of early **socialization.** The learning of **language** is of vital importance to the processes by which the child learns to become a self-conscious being.

self-identity: The ongoing process of self-development and definition of our personal **identity** through which we formulate a unique sense of ourselves and our relationship to the world around us.

semiotics: The study of the ways in which nonlinguistic phenomena can generate meaning—as in the example of a traffic light.

semiperipheral countries: Countries that supply sources of labor and raw materials to the **core** industrial **countries** and the world economy but are not themselves fully **industrialized societies.**

sensorimotor stage: According to Piaget, a stage of human cognitive development in which the child's awareness of its environment is dominated by perception and touch.

service society: A concept related to the one of **postindustrial society,** it refers to a social order distinguished by the growth of service occupations at the expense of industrial jobs that produce **material goods.**

sex: The biological and anatomical differences distinguishing females from males.

sexual harassment: The making of unwanted sexual advances by one individual toward another, in which the first person persists even though it is clear that the other party is resistant.

shaming: A way of punishing criminal and deviant behavior based on rituals of public disapproval rather than incarceration. The goal of shaming is to maintain the ties of the offender to the community.

short-range downward mobility: Social mobility that occurs when an individual moves from one position in the **class** structure to another of nearly equal **status.**

sick role: A term associated with the functionalist Talcott Parsons to describe the patterns of behavior that a sick person adopts in order to minimize the disruptive impact of his or her illness on others.

signifier: Any vehicle of meaning and **communication.**

slavery: A form of **social stratification** in which some people are literally owned by others as their property.

social age: The **norms, values,** and **roles** that are culturally associated with a particular chronological age.

social aggregate: A simple collection of people who happen to be together in a particular place but do not significantly interact or identify with one another.

social capital: The social knowledge and connections that enable people to accomplish their goals and extend their influence.

social category: People who share a common characteristic (such as **gender** or **occupation**) but do not necessarily interact or identify with one another.

social change: Alteration in basic structures of a **social group** or **society.** Social change is an ever-present phenomenon in social life, but has become especially intense in the modern era. The origins of modern **sociology** can be traced to attempts to understand the dramatic changes shattering the traditional world and promoting new forms of social order.

social constraint: The conditioning influence on our behavior of the groups and **societies** of which we are members. Social constraint was regarded by Émile Durkheim as one of the distinctive properties of **social facts.**

social construction of gender: The learning of **gender roles** through **socialization** and interaction with others.

social exclusion: The outcome of multiple deprivations that prevent individuals or groups from participating fully in the economic, social, and political life of the **society** in which they live.

social fact: According to Émile Durkheim, the aspects of social life that shape our actions as individuals. Durkheim believed that social facts could be studied scientifically.

social gerontology: The study of **aging** and the elderly.

social group: A collection of people who regularly interact with one another on the basis of shared expectations concerning behavior and who share a sense of common **identity.**

social identity: The characteristics that are attributed to an individual by others.

social institution: Basic modes of social activity followed by the majority of the members of a given **society.** Institutions involve **norms** and **values** to which large numbers of people conform, and all institutionalized modes of behavior are protected by strong **sanctions.** Institutions form the bedrock of a society, because they represent relatively fixed modes of behavior that endure over time.

social interaction: The process by which we act and react to those around us.

socialization: The social processes through which children develop an awareness of social **norms** and **values** and achieve a distinct sense of self. Although

socialization processes are particularly significant in infancy and childhood, they continue to some degree throughout life. No individuals are immune from the reactions of others around them, which influence and modify their behavior at all phases of the **life course.**

socialization of nature: The process by which we control phenomena regarded as "natural," such as reproduction.

social mobility: Movement of individuals or groups between different **social positions.**

social position: The **social identity** an individual has in a given group or **society.** Social positions may be general in nature (those associated with **gender roles**) or may be more specific (occupational positions).

social roles: Socially defined expectations of an individual in a given **status,** or **social position.**

Social Security: A government program that provides economic assistance to persons faced with unemployment, disability, or agedness.

social self: The basis of **self-consciousness** in human individuals, according to the theory of G. H. Mead. The social self is the **identity** conferred upon an individual by the reactions of others. A person achieves self-consciousness by becoming aware of this **social identity.**

social stratification: The existence of **structured inequalities** between groups in **society,** in terms of their access to material or symbolic rewards. While all societies involve some forms of stratification, only with the development of state-based systems did wide differences in **wealth** and **power** arise. The most distinctive form of stratification in modern societies is **class** divisions.

social structure: The underlying regularities or patterns in how people behave and in their relationships with one another.

social technology: A means by which we try to alter our bodies in specific ways—for example, dieting.

society: A group of people who live in a particular territory, are subject to a common system of political **authority,** and are aware of having a distinct **identity** from other groups. Some societies, like **hunting and gathering societies,** are small, numbering no more than a few dozen people. Others are large, numbering millions—modern Chinese society, for instance, has a population of more than a billion people.

sociobiology: An approach that attempts to explain the behavior of both animals and human beings in terms of biological principles.

sociological imagination: The application of imaginative thought to the asking and answering of sociological questions. Someone using the sociological imagination "thinks himself away" from the familiar routines of daily life.

sociology: The study of human groups and **societies,** giving particular emphasis to analysis of the industrialized world. Sociology is one of a group of social sciences, which include anthropology, economics, political science, and human geography. The divisions between the various social sciences are not clear-cut, and all share a certain range of common interests, concepts, and methods.

sociology of the body: Field that focuses on how our bodies are affected by social influences. Health and illness, for instance, are determined by social and cultural influences.

standard deviation: A way of calculating the spread of a group of figures.

state-centered theories: Development **theories** that argue that appropriate **government** policies do not interfere with economic development, but rather can play a key role in bringing it about.

status: The social honor or **prestige** that a particular group is accorded by other members of a **society.** Status groups normally display distinct styles of life— patterns of behavior that the members of a group follow. Status privilege may be positive or negative. **Pariah** status **groups** are regarded with disdain or treated as outcasts by the majority of the **population.**

status set: An individual's group of social **statuses.**

stepfamily: A **family** in which at least one partner has children from a previous **marriage,** living either in the home or nearby.

stereotype: A fixed and inflexible category.

stereotypical thinking: Thought processes involving rigid and inflexible categories.

strike: A temporary stoppage of **work** by a group of employees in order to express a grievance or enforce a demand.

structural mobility: Mobility resulting from changes in the number and kinds of **jobs** available in a **society.**

structuration: The two-way process by which we shape our social world through our individual actions and by which we are reshaped by **society.**

structured inequality: Social inequalities that result from patterns in the **social structure.**

subculture: Values and **norms** distinct from those of the majority, held by a group within a wider **society.**

suburbanization: The development of suburbia, areas of housing outside **inner cities.**

suffragists: Members of early women's movements who pressed for equal voting rights for women and men.

surplus value: The value of a worker's labor power, in **Marxist** theory, left over when an employer has repaid the cost of hiring the worker.

survey: A method of sociological research in which questionnaires are administered to the **population** being studied.

sustainable development: The notion that economic growth should proceed only insofar as natural resources are recycled rather than depleted; biodiversity is maintained; and clean air, water, and land are protected.

symbol: One item used to stand for or represent another—as in the case of a flag, which symbolizes a nation.

symbolic interactionism: A **theoretical approach** in **sociology** developed by George Herbert Mead, which emphasizes the role of **symbols** and **language** as core elements of all human interaction.

technology: The application of knowledge of the material world to production; the creation of material instruments (such as machines) used in human interaction with nature.

theism: A belief in one or more supernatural deities.

theoretical approach: A perspective on social life derived from a particular theoretical tradition. Some of the major theoretical traditions in **sociology** include **functionalism, symbolic interactionism,** and **Marxism.** Theoretical approaches supply overall perspectives within which sociologists work and influence the areas of their research as well as the modes in which research problems are identified and tackled.

theoretical questions: Questions posed by sociologists when seeking to explain a particular range of observed events. The asking of theoretical questions is crucial to allowing us to generalize about the nature of social life.

theory: An attempt to identify general properties that explain regularly observed events. Theories form an essential element of all sociological works. While theories tend to be linked to broader **theoretical approaches,** they are also strongly influenced by the research results they help generate.

third generation theory of aging: Theory that views the elderly as playing an active role in determining their own physical and mental well-being rather than as merely adapting to the larger society or as victims of the stratification system.

time-space: When and where events occur.

timetable: The means by which **organizations** regularize activities across time and space.

tracking: Dividing students into groups according to ability.

transactional leader: A **leader** who is concerned accomplishing the group's tasks, getting group members to do their **jobs,** and making certain that the group achieves its goals.

transformational leader: A **leader** who is able to instill in the members of a group a sense of mission or higher purpose, thereby changing the nature of the group itself.

transnational corporations: Business **corporations** located in two or more countries.

triad: A group consisting of three persons.

triangulation: The use of multiple **research methods** as a way of producing more reliable empirical data than is available from any single method.

underclass: A **class** of individuals situated at the bottom of the class system, normally composed of people from **ethnic minority** backgrounds.

unfocused interaction: Interaction occurring among people present in a particular setting but not engaged in direct face-to-face **communication.**

upper class: A social **class** broadly composed of the more affluent members of **society,** especially those who have inherited **wealth,** own businesses, or hold large numbers of stocks (shares).

urban ecology: An approach to the study of urban life based on an analogy with the adjustment of plants and organisms to the physical environment. According to ecological theorists, the various neighborhoods and zones within cities are formed as a result of natural processes of adjustment on the part of **populations** as they compete for resources.

urbanism: A term used by Louis Wirth to denote distinctive characteristics of urban social life, such as its impersonality.

urbanization: The development of towns and cities.

urban renewal: The process of renovating deteriorating neighborhoods by encouraging the renewal of old buildings and the construction of new ones.

values: Ideas held by individuals or groups about what is desirable, proper, good, and bad. What individuals value is strongly influenced by the specific **culture** in which they happen to live.

vertical mobility: Movement up or down a hierarchy of positions in a **social stratification** system.

wealth: Money and material possessions held by an individual or group.

welfare capitalism: Practice in which large **corporations** protect their employees from the vicissitudes of the market.

white-collar crime: Criminal activities carried out by those in white-collar, or professional, **jobs**.

work: The activity by which people produce from the natural world and so ensure their survival. Work should not be thought of exclusively as paid employment. In traditional cultures, there was only a rudimentary monetary system, and few people worked for money. In modern **societies**, there remain types of work that do not involve direct payment (e.g., **housework**).

working class: A social **class** broadly composed of people working in blue-collar, or manual, **occupations**.

working poor: People who work, but whose earnings are not enough to lift them above the **poverty line**.

world-systems theory: Pioneered by Immanuel Wallerstein, this **theory** emphasizes the interconnections among countries based on the expansion of a capitalist world **economy**. This economy is made up of **core countries**, **semiperipheral countries**, and **peripheral countries**.

"young old": Sociological term for persons aged sixty-five to seventy-four.

ABC. 1999. "Support for Gun Control Stable," ABC News Poll (May 18). http://more.abcnews.go.com/sections/us/ DailyNews/guns_poll990518.html, accessed 5/18/99.

Abdul-Rauf, Muhammad. 1975. *Islam: Creed and Worship.* Washington, DC: Islamic Center.

Abeles, Ronald P.; and Riley, Matilda White. 1987. "Longevity, social structure, and cognitive aging," in Carmi Schooler and K. Warner Schaie, eds., *Cognitive Functioning and Social Structure over the Life Course.* Norwood, NJ: Ablex.

Aberle, David. 1966. *The Peyote Religion among the Navaho.* Chicago: Aldine Press.

Accad, Evelyne. 1991. "Contradictions for contemporary women in the Middle East," in Chandra Talpade Mohanty, Ann Russo, and Lourdes Torres, eds., *Third World Women and the Politics of Feminism.* Bloomington: Indiana University Press.

Adorno, Theodor W., et al. 1950. *The Authoritarian Personality.* New York: Harper and Row.

Ahmed, Akbar S.; and Donnan, Hastings. 1994. "Islam in the Age of Postmodernity," in Akbar S. Ahmed and Hastings Donnan, eds., *Islam, Globalization, and Postmodernity.* London: Routledge.

AIDS Orphans Educational Trust. 2003. "AIDS Orphans Educational Trust–Uganda." www.orphanseducation. org, accessed 12/28/04.

Akintoye, Stephen. 1976. *Emergent African States: Topics in Twentieth Century African History.* London: Longman.

Al Ahmad, Jalal. 1997; orig. 1962. *Gharbzadegi: Weststruckedness.* Costa Mesa, CA: Mazda Publications.

Albrow, Martin. 1997. *The Global Age: State and Society beyond Modernity.* Stanford, CA: Stanford University Press.

Aldrich, Howard E.; and Marsden, Peter V. 1988. "Environments and organizations," in Neil J. Smelser, ed., *Handbook of Sociology.* Newbury Park, CA: Sage.

Allen, Beverly. 1996. *Rape Warfare: The Hidden Genocide in Bosnia-Herzegovina and Croatia.* Minneapolis, MN: University of Minnesota Press.

Allen, Michael P. 1981. "Managerial power and tenure in the large corporation." *Social Forces,* vol. 60.

Alvarez, Rodolfo, et al. 1996. "Women in the professions: Assessing progress," in Paula J. Dubeck and Kathryn Borman, eds., *Women and Work: A Handbook.* New York: Garland.

Amenta, Edwin. 1998. *Bold Relief: Institutional Politics and the Origins of Modern American Social Policy.* Princeton, NJ: Princeton University Press.

American Association of Retired Persons (AARP) 2003. "Fact Sheet: What is AARP?" www.aarp.org/leadership/ Articles/a2002-12-18-aarpfactsheet.html, accessed 1/10/05.

American Association for the Advancement of Retired People (AARP). 1997. "Report of Social Security Advisory Council." www.aarp.org/focus/ssecure/part 2/advisory.htm, accessed 11/24/03.

American Association of University Women (AAUW). 1992. *How Schools Shortchange Girls.* Washington, DC: American Association of University Women Educational Foundation.

American Civil Liberties Union (ACLU). 2000. "Status of U.S. sodomy laws." www.aclu.org/issues/gay/sodomy.html, accessed 1/10/05.

American Council on Education, (ACE). 2001. *The American Freshman: National Norms for Fall 2000.* Los Angeles, California: UCLA Higher Education Research Institute and ACE. Results also published in "This year's freshmen at 4-year colleges: Their opinions, activities, and goals." *Chronicle of Higher Education,* January 26.

Amin, Samir. 1974. *Accumulation on a World Scale.* New York: Monthly Review Press.

Amsden, Alice H. 1989. *Asia's Next Giant: South Korea and Late Industrialization.* New York: Oxford University Press.

———; Kochanowicz, Jacek; and Taylor, Lance. 1994. *The Market Meets Its Match: Restructuring the Economies of Eastern Europe.* Cambridge, MA: Harvard University Press.

Anderson, Benedict. 1991. *Imagined Communities: Reflections on the Origin and Spread of Nationalism.* Revised ed. New York: Routledge.

Anderson, Elijah. 1990. *Streetwise: Race, Class, and Change in an Urban Community.* Chicago: University of Chicago Press.

Angier, Natalie. 1994. "Feminists and Darwin: Scientists try closing the gap." *New York Times,* June 21.

———. 1995. "If you're really ancient, you may be better off." *New York Times,* June 11.

Annie E. Casey Foundation. 2003. "Kids Count." www.aecf.org/cgi-bin/aeccensus.cgi?action=profileresults& area=39S, accessed 12/28/04.

Anzaldua, Gloria. 1990. *Making Face, Making Soul: Haciendo Caras: Creative and Cultural Perspectives by Feminists of Color.* San Francisco: Aunt Lute Foundation.

Appadurai, Arjun. 1986. "Introduction: commodities and the politics of value," in A. Appadurai, ed., *The Social Life of Things.* Cambridge: Cambridge University Press.

Appelbaum, Richard P. 1990. "Counting the homeless," in J. A. Momeni, ed., *Homeless in the United States,* vol. 2. New York: Praeger.

———; and Christerson, Brad. 1997. "Cheap labor strategies and export-oriented industrialization: Some lessons from the East Asia/Los Angeles apparel connection." *International Journal of Urban and Regional Research,* vol. 21, no. 2.

———; and Henderson, Jeffrey. eds., 1992. *States and Development in the Asian Pacific Rim.* Newbury Park, CA: Sage.

Apter, Terri. 1994. *Working Women Don't Have Wives: Professional Success in the 1990s.* New York: St. Martin's Press.

Ariès, Philippe. 1965. *Centuries of Childhood.* New York: Random House.

Arjomand, Said Amir. 1988. *The Turban for the Crown: The Islamic Revolution in Iran.* New York: Oxford University Press.

Arrighi, Giovanni. 1994. *The Long Twentieth Century: Money, Power, and the Origin of Our Times.* New York: Verso.

Asch, Solomon. 1952. *Social Psychology.* Englewood Cliffs, NJ: Prentice-Hall.

Aschenbrenner, Joyce. 1983. *Lifelines: Black Families in Chicago.* Prospect Heights, IL: Waveland Press.

Ashworth, Anthony E. 1980. *Trench Warfare: 1914–1918.* London: Macmillan.

Atchley, Robert C. 2000. *Social Forces and Aging: An Introduction to Social Gerontology.* 9th ed. Belmont, CA: Wadsworth.

Avins, Mimi. 2003. "MoveOn redefines party politics," *Los Angeles Times* December 9, p. A-1.

Ayres, Robert; and Miller, Steven. 1985. "Industrial robots on the line," in Tom Forester, ed., *The Information Technology Revolution.* Cambridge, MA: MIT Press.

Bahrami, Homa; and Evans, Stuart. 1995. "Flexible recycling and high-technology entrepreneurship." *California Management Review,* vol. 22.

Bailey, J. Michael. 1993. "Heritable factors influence sexual orientation in women." *Archives of General Psychiatry,* vol. 50.

———; and Pillard, Richard C. 1991. "A genetic study of male sexual orientation." *Archives of General Psychiatry,* vol. 48.

Bales, Kevin. 1999. *Disposable People: New Slavery in the Global Economy.* Berkeley, CA: University of California Press.

Bales, Robert F. 1953. "The egalitarian problem in small groups," in Talcott Parsons, ed., *Working Papers in the Theory of Action.* Glencoe, IL: Free Press.

———. 1970. *Personality and Interpersonal Behavior.* New York: Holt, Rinehart, and Winston.

Balmer, Randall. 1989. *Mine Eyes Have Seen the Glory: A Journey into the Evangelical Subculture in America.* New York: Oxford University Press.

Balswick, J. O. 1983. "Male inexpressiveness," in Kenneth Soloman and Norman B. Levy, eds., *Men in Transition: Theory and Therapy.* New York: Plenum Press.

Baltes, Paul B.; and Schaie, K. Warner. 1977. "The myth of the twilight years," in S. Zarit, ed., *Readings in Aging and Death: Contemporary Perspectives.* New York: Harper and Row.

Banfield, Edward. 1970. *The Unheavenly City.* Boston: Little, Brown.

Bankoff, Elizabeth A. 1983. "Aged parents and their widowed daughters: A support relationship." *Gerontologist,* vol. 38.

Barcelona Field Studies Centre. 2003. "Sao Paulo Growth and Management." www.geographyfieldwork.com/SaoPauloManagement.htm, accessed 12/28/04.

Barker, Martin. 1981. *The New Racism: Conservatives and the Ideology of the Tribe.* Frederick, MD: University Press of America.

Barlow, John, et al. 1995. "Harper's forum: what are we doing online?" *Harper's* (August).

Barnet, Richard J.; and Cavanagh, John. 1994. *Global Dreams: Imperial Corporations and the New World Order.* New York: Simon and Schuster.

Bart, Pauline B.; and O'Brien, Patricia H. 1985. *Stopping Rape: Successful Survival Strategies.* New York: Pergamon Press.

Barth, Frederick. 1969. *Ethnic Groups and Boundaries.* London: Allen and Unwin.

Basham, A. L. 1989. *The Origins and Development of Classical Hinduism.* Boston: Beacon Press.

Basu, Amrita, ed. 1995. *The Challenge of Local Feminisms: Women's Movements in Global Perspective.* Boulder, CO: Westview.

Baudrillard, Jean. 1988. *Jean Baudrillard: Selected Writings.* Stanford, CA: Stanford University Press.

Baxter, Jeanine; and Kane, Emily. 1995. "Dependence and independence: A cross national analysis." *Gender and Society,* vol. 9, no. 2.

BBC News. 2001. "Bin Laden's Warning: Full Text." http://news.bbc.co.uk/1/hi/world/south_asia/1585636.stm, accessed 1/10/05.

———. 2001a. "Anger at US Climate Retreat." http://news.bbc.co.uk/1/hi/sci/tech/1248278.stm, accessed 1/10/05.

Beall, C.; and Goldstein, M. C. 1982. "Work, aging, and dependency in a Sherpa population in Nepal." *Social Science and Medicine,* vol. 16, no. 2.

Bean, Frank D., et al. 1994. *Illegal Mexican Migration and the U.S./Mexico Border.* Washington, DC: U.S. Commission on Immigration Reform.

Beck, Ulrich. 1992. *Risk Society.* London: Sage.

———. 1995. *Ecological Politics in an Age of Risk.* Cambridge, UK: Polity Press.

———; and Beck-Gernsheim, Elisabeth. 1995. *The Normal Chaos of Love.* Cambridge, UK: Polity Press.

Becker, Gary. 1964. *Human Capital.* New York: National Bureau of Economic Research.

———. 1991. *A Treatise on the Family.* Cambridge, MA: Harvard University Press.

Becker, Howard S. 1950. *Through Values to Social Interpretation.* Durham, NC: Duke University Press.

———. 1963. *Outsiders: Studies in the Sociology of Deviance.* New York: Macmillan.

Beechey, Veronica; and Perkins, Tessa. 1987. *A Matter of Hours: Women, Part-Time Work, and the Labour Market.* Cambridge, UK: Polity Press.

Beijing Women's Conference. 1995. "Declaration and Platform for Action." Critical Areas of Concern No. 43. Fourth World Conference on Women: Action for Equality, Development, and Peace, Beijing, September 15, 1995.

Belgrave, Linda Liska. 1988. "The effects of race difference in work history, work attitudes, economic resources, and health in women's retirement." *Research on Aging,* vol. 10.

Bell, A.; Weinberg, M.; and Hammersmith, S. 1981. *Sexual Preference: Its Development in Men and Women.* Bloomington: Indiana University Press.

Bell, Daniel. 1976. *The Coming of Post-Industrial Society: A Venture in Social Forecasting.* New York: Basic Books.

Bellah, Robert N. 1968. "Civil Religion in America," in William G. McLoughlin and Robert N. Bellah, eds., *Religion in America.* Boston: Houghton Mifflin.

———. 1975. *The Broken Covenant.* New York: Seabury Press.

———, et al. 1985. *Habits of the Heart: Individualism and Commitment in American Life.* New York: Harper and Row.

Bellman, Beryl. 1984. *The Language of Secrecy: Symbols and Metaphors in Poro Ritual.* New Brunswick, NJ: Rutgers University Press.

Bendick, Marc; Jackson, Charles; and Reinoso, Victor. 1993. "Measuring employment discrimination through controlled experiments," in *The Review of Black Political Economy.* Washington, DC: Fair Employment Council of Greater Washington.

Bengston, Vern L.; Rosenthal, Carolyn; and Burton, Linda. 1990. "Families and aging: Diversity and heterogeneity," in Robert H. Binstock and Linda K. George, eds., *Handbook of Aging and the Social Sciences.* 3rd ed. New York: Academic Press.

Bennet, James. 1992. "The old people sit and talk, about AIDS and secrecy." *New York Times,* September 21.

Bennett, John W. 1976. *The Ecological Transition: Cultural Anthropology and*

Human Adaptation. New York: Pergamon Press.

Berger, Peter L. 1963. *Invitation to Sociology.* Garden City, NY: Anchor Books.

———. 1967. *The Sacred Canopy: Elements of a Sociological Theory of Religion.* Garden City, NY: Anchor Books.

———. 1986. *The Capitalist Revolution: Fifty Propositions about Prosperity, Equality, and Liberty.* New York: Basic Books.

———; and Hsiao, Hsin-Haung Michael. 1988. *In Search of an East Asian Development Model.* New Brunswick, NJ: Transaction.

———; and Luckmann, Thomas. 1966. *The Social Construction of Reality: A Treatise in the Sociology of Knowledge.* Garden City, NY: Doubleday.

Berle, Adolf; and Means, Gardiner C. 1982. *The Modern Corporation and Private Property.* Originally published 1932. Buffalo, NY: Heim.

Bernhardt, Annett; Dresser, Laura; and Rogers, Joel. 2002. "Taking the high road in Milwaukee: The Wisconsin regional training partnership." *WorkingUSA* vol. 5, no. 3: 109.

Bernstein, Nina. 2001. "Homeless shelters in New York fill to highest levels since 80's." *New York Times,* February 7.

Berryman, Phillip. 1987. *Liberation Theology: Essential Facts About the Revolutionary Movement in Central America and Beyond.* Philadelphia: Temple University Press.

Bertelson, David. 1986. *Snowflakes and Snowdrifts: Individualism and Sexuality in America.* Lanham, MD: University Press of America.

Bertram, Eva, et al. 1996. *Drug War Politics.* Berkeley, CA: University of California Press.

Beyer, Peter. 1994. *Religion and Globalization.* Thousand Oaks, CA: Sage.

Birren, J. E.; and Bengston, V. L., eds. 1988. *Emerging Theories of Aging.* New York: Springer.

———; and Cunningham, W. 1985. "Research on the psychology of aging," in J. E. Birren and K. Warner Schaie, eds., *The Handbook of Aging.* 2nd ed. New York: Van Nostrand.

Blanchard, Ray; and Bogaert, A. F. 1996. "Homosexuality in men and number of older brothers." *American Journal of Psychiatry,* vol. 153.

Blankenhorn, David. 1995. *Fatherless America: Confronting Our Most Urgent Social Problem.* New York: Basic Books.

Blau, Joel. 1992. *The Visible Poor: Homelessness in the United States.* New York: Oxford University Press.

Blau, Judith. "Internationalizing public sociologies," *Sociologists Without Borders,*
www.sociologistswithoutborders.org, accessed 12/27/04.

Blau, Peter. 1963. *The Dynamics of Bureaucracy.* Chicago: University of Chicago Press.

———. 1977. *Inequality and Heterogeneity: A Primitive Theory of Social Structure.* New York: Free Press.

———; and Duncan, Otis Dudley. 1967. *The American Occupational Structure.* New York: Wiley.

Blauner, Robert. 1964. *Alienation and Freedom.* Chicago: University of Chicago Press.

———. 1972. *Racial Oppression in America.* New York: Harper and Row.

Block, Fred. 1990. *Postindustrial Possibilities: A Critique of Economic Discourse.* Berkeley: University of California Press.

Blondet, Cecilia. 1995. "Out of the kitchen and onto the streets: Women's activism in Peru," in Amrita Basu, ed., *The Challenge of Local Feminisms.* Boulder, CO: Westview.

Bluestone, Barry. 1988. "Deindustrialization and unemployment in America." *Review of Black Political Economy,* vol. 17.

———; and Harrison, Bennett. 1982. *The Deindustrialization of America.* New York: Basic Books.

Blum, Linda M. 1991. *Between Feminism and Labor: The Significance of the Comparable Worth Movement.* Berkeley, CA: University of California Press.

Blumberg, Rae Lesser, ed. 1995. *Engendering Wealth and Well-Being: Empowerment for Global Change.* Boulder, CO: Westview.

Bobak, Laura. 1996. "India's Tiny Slaves," *Ottawa Sun,* October 23.

Bobo, Lawrence; and Kluegel, James R. 1991. "Modern American prejudice: Stereotypes, social distance, and perceptions of discrimination toward Blacks, Hispanics, and Asians." Paper presented at the 1991 meeting of the American Sociological Association.

Bochenek, Michael A.; and Brown, Widney. 2001. *Hatred in the Hallways: Violence and Discrimination against Lesbian, Gay, Bisexual, and Transgender Students in U.S. Schools.* New York: Human Rights Watch, www.hrw.org/reports/2001/uslgbt/toc.htm, May 30, accessed 12/28/04.

Boden, Deirdre; and Molotch, Harvey. 1994. "The compulsion of proximity," in Deirdre Boden and Roger Friedland, eds., *Nowhere: Space, Time, and Modernity.* Berkeley, CA: University of California Press.

Bohan, Suzanne. 1999. "Bohemian grove and global elite." *Sacramento Bee,* www.mt.net/~watcher/bohemiangrove.html, August 2, accessed 12/28/04.

Bonacich, Edna; and Appelbaum, Richard P. 2000. *Behind the Label: Inequality in the Los Angeles Garment Industry.* Berkeley, CA: University of California Press.

Bonnell, Victoria E.; and Hunt, Lynn, eds. 1999. *Beyond the Cultural Turn.* Berkeley, CA: University of California Press.

Bonney, Norman. 1992. "Theories of social class and gender." *Sociology Review,* vol. 1.

Booth, Alan. 1977. "Food riots in the northwest of England, 1770–1801." *Past and Present,* no. 77.

Borjas, George J. 1994. "The economics of immigration." *Journal of Economic Literature,* vol. 32.

Bosse, R., et al. 1987. "Mental health differences among retirees and workers: Findings from the normative aging study." *Psychology and Aging,* vol. 2.

Boswell, John. 1995. *The Marriage of Likeness: Same-Sex Unions in Pre-Modern Europe.* London: Fontana.

Bourdieu, Pierre. 1984. *Distinction: A Social Critique of Judgement of Taste.* Cambridge, MA: Harvard University Press.

———. 1988. *Language and Symbolic Power.* Cambridge, UK: Polity Press.

———. 1990. *The Logic of Practice.* Stanford, CA: Stanford University Press.

Bowen, Kurt. 1996. *Evangelism and Apostasy: The Evolution and Impact of Evangelicals in Modern Mexico.* Montreal: McGill-Queens University Press.

Bowlby, John. 1953. *Child Care and the Growth of Love.* Baltimore, MD: Penguin.

Bowles, Samuel; and Gintis, Herbert. 1976. *Schooling in Capitalist America.* New York: Basic Books.

Boyer, Robert; and Drache, Daniel. eds. 1996. *States against Markets: The Limits of Globalization.* New York: Routledge.

Braithwaite, John. 1996. "Crime, shame, and reintegration," in P. Cordella and L. Siegal, eds., *Readings in Contemporary Criminological Theory.* Boston: Northeastern University Press.

Bramlett, M.D.; and Mosher W.D. 2002. "Cohabitation, marriage, divorce, and remarriage in the United States." National Center for Health Statistics. *Vital Health Stat* vol. 23, no. 22.

Brass, Daniel J. 1985. "Men's and women's networks: A study of interaction patterns and influence in an organization." *Academy of Management Journal,* vol. 28.

Braverman, Harry. 1974. *Labor and Monopoly Capital.* New York: Monthly Review Press.

Brennan, Teresa. 1988. "Controversial discussions and feminist debate," in Naomi Segal and Edward Timms, eds., *The Origins and Evolution of Psychoanalysis*. New Haven, CT: Yale University Press.

Brewer, Rose M. 1993. "Theorizing race, class and gender: The new scholarship of black feminist intellectuals and black women's labor," in Stanlie M. James and Abena P. A. Busia, eds., *Theorizing Black Feminisms: The Visionary Pragmatism of Black Women*. New York: Routledge.

Brimelow, Peter. 1995. *Alien Nation: Common Sense About America's Immigration Disaster*. New York: Random House.

Britain, Samuel. 1975. "The economic contradictions of democracy." *British Journal of Political Science,* vol. 15.

Brookfield, Stephen. 1986. *Understanding and Facilitating Adult Learning*. San Francisco: Jossey-Bass.

Brown, Catrina; and Jasper, Karin, eds. 1993. *Consuming Passions: Feminist Approaches to Eating Disorders and Weight Preoccupations*. Toronto: Second Story Press.

Brown, Donald E. 1991. *Human Universals*. New York: McGraw-Hill.

Brown, Judith K. 1977. "A note on the division of labor by sex," in Nona Glazer and Helen Y. Waehrer, eds., *Woman in a Man-Made World*. 2nd ed. Chicago: Rand McNally.

Brownmiller, Susan. 1975. *Against Our Will: Men, Women, and Rape*. New York: Simon and Schuster.

———. 1986. *Against Our Will: Men, Women, and Rape*. Rev. ed. New York: Bantam.

Brownstein, Ronald. 2003. "Liberal group flexes online muscle in its very own primary," *Los Angeles Times,* June 23, p. A-9.

Brubaker, Rogers. 1992. *The Politics of Citizenship*. Cambridge, MA: Harvard University Press.

Bruce, Steve. 1990. *Pray TV: Televangelism in America*. New York: Routledge.

———; Kivisto, Peter; and Swatos, William H., eds. 1995. *The Rapture of Politics: The Christian Right as the U.S. Approaches the Year 2000*. New Brunswick, NJ: Transaction Publishers.

Bryan, Beverly; Dadzie, Stella; and Scafe, Suzanne. 1987. "Learning to resist: Black women and education," in Gaby Weiner and Madeleine Arnot, eds., *Gender under Scrutiny: New Inquiries in Education*. London: Hutchinson.

Buechler, Steven M. 2000. *Social Movements in Advanced Capitalism: The Political Economy and Cultural Construction of Social Activism*. New York: Oxford University Press.

Bull, Peter. 1983. *Body Movement and Interpersonal Communication*. New York: Wiley.

Bullock, Charles, III. 1984. "Equal education opportunity," in Charles S. Bullock III and Charles M. Lamb, eds., *Implementation of Civil Rights Policy*. Monterey, CA: Brooks and Cole.

Bumpass, Larry; and Lu, Hsien-Hen. 2000. "Trends in cohabitation and implications for children's family context in the United States." *Population Studies,* vol. 54.

———; and Sweet, James A. 1989. "National estimates of cohabitation: Cohort levels and union stability." *Demography,* vol. 26.

———; Sweet, James A.; and Cherlin, Andrew. 1991. "The role of cohabitation in declining rates of marriage." *Journal of Marriage and the Family,* vol. 53 (November).

Bureau of Justice Statistics. 2002a. "Racial differences exist with blacks disproportionately represented among homicide victims and offenders." www.ojp.usdoj.gov/bjs/homicide/race.htm, accessed 12/28/04.

———. 2002b. "Homicide trends in the U.S.: Age, gender, and race trends." www.ojp.usdoj.gov/bjs/homicide/tables/oarstab.htm, accessed 12/28/04.

Burghart, D. Brian. 2003. "About a Man," *Reno News and Review,* September 4.

Burns, James MacGregor. 1978. *Leadership*. New York: Harper and Row.

Burns, Thomas; and Stalker, G. M. 1994. *The Management of Innovation*. Rev. ed. Oxford, UK: Oxford University Press.

Burr, Chandler. 1993. "Homosexuality and biology." *Atlantic Monthly,* March.

Burris, Beverly H. 1993. *Technocracy at Work*. Albany: State University of New York Press.

———. 1998. "Computerization of the workplace," in *Annual Review of Sociology,* vol. 24. Palo Alto, CA: Annual Reviews.

Burt, Martha R. 1992. *Over the Edge: The Growth of Homelessness in the 1980s*. New York: Russell Sage.

Business Journal. 2000. "Judge tosses insurer's bid to keep redlining data secret." http://sanjose.bizjournals.com/sanjose/stories/2000/09/11/daily42.html, accessed 1/11/05.

BusinessWeek. 2001. "Executive pay." *BusinessWeek Online,* www.businessweek.com/magazine/content/01_16/b3728013.htm, April 16, accessed 12/28/04.

Butler, Judith. 1989. *Gender Trouble: Feminism and the Subversion of Identity*. New York: Routledge.

Butler, Tim; and Savage, Mike. 1995. *Social Change and the Middle Classes*. London: UCL Press.

Butterfield, Fox. 1998. "Decline of violent crimes is linked to crack market." *New York Times,* December 28, p. A18.

Byrd, Max. 1978. *London Transformed: Images of the City in the Eighteenth Century*. New Haven, CT: Yale University Press.

Byrne, David. 1995. "Deindustrialization and dispossession." *Sociology,* vol. 29.

Cairncross, Frances. 1997. *The Death of Distance: How the Communications Revolution Will Change Our Lives*. Boston: Harvard Business School Press.

Campbell, Beatrix. 1993. *Goliath: Britain's Dangerous Places*. London: Methuen.

Caplow, Theodore. 1956. "A theory of coalition in the triad." *American Sociological Review,* vol. 20.

———. 1959. "Further development of a theory of coalitions in triads." *American Journal of Sociology,* vol. 64.

———. 1969. *Two Against One: Coalitions in Triads*. Englewood Cliffs, NJ: Prentice Hall.

Capps, Walter H. 1990. *The New Religious Right: Piety, Patriotism, and Politics*. Columbia: University of South Carolina Press.

Cardoso, Fernando H.; and Faletto, Enzo. 1979. *Dependency and Development in Latin America*. Berkeley, CA: University of California Press.

Carnevale, Dan. 2000. "Brown U. and MCI WorldCom join to help colleges try to close the digital divide," *The Chronicle of Higher Education* (June 9).

Carr, Sarah. 1999. "U. of Nebraska's Class.com hooks up with a Kentucky school," *The Chronicle of Higher Education* (October 22).

———; and Young, Jeffrey R. 1999. "As distance-learning boom spreads, colleges help set up virtual high schools." *The Chronicle of Higher Education* (October 22).

Cashmore, E. Ellis. 1987. *The Logic of Racism*. New York: HarperCollins.

Castells, Manuel. 1977. *The Urban Question: A Marxist Approach*. Cambridge, MA: MIT Press.

———. 1983. *The City and the Grass Roots: A Cross-Cultural Theory of Urban Social Movements*. Berkeley, CA: University of California Press.

———. 1992. "Four Asian tigers with a dragon head: A comparative analysis of the state, economy, and society in the Asian Pacific Rim," in Richard P. Appelbaum and Jeffrey Henderson, eds., *States and Development in the Asian Pacific Rim.* Newbury Park, CA: Sage.

———. 1996. *The Rise of the Network Society.* Malden, MA: Blackwell.

———. 1997. *The Power of Identity.* Malden, MA: Blackwell.

———. 1998. *End of Millennium.* Malden, MA: Blackwell.

Castles, Stephen; and Miller, Mark J. 1993. *The Age of Migration: International Population Movements in the Modern World.* London: Macmillan.

CDI. 2003. "Highlights of the budget request," Washington, D.C.: Center for Defense Information (February 3). www.cdi.org/program/document.cfm? DocumentID=1041&StartRow=11& ListRows=10&appendURL=&Orderby= D.DateLastUpdated&ProgramID= 15&from_page=index.cfm, accessed 1/11/05.

Center for American Women and Politics (CAWP). 2001. "Fact Sheets." Eagleton Institute of Politics, Rutgers University.

Center for Public Integrity. 2003. "How the feds stack up," Washington, D.C. : The Center for Public Integrity (May 15), www.publicintegrity.org/hiredguns/report .aspx?aid=167, accessed 1/10/05.

Centers for Disease Control and Prevention (CDC). 2003a. "National ambulatory care survey, 2001 summary." Advanced Data From Vital and Health Statistics, Number 337 (August 11), www.cdc.gov/nchs/data/ ad/ad337.pdf, accessed 12/29/04.

———. 2003b. "Health topics: Sexual behavior." www.cdc.gov/nccdphp/dash/ sexualbehaviors/index.htm, accessed 12/29/04.

———. 2000. *Youth Risk Behavior Trends from CDC's 1991, 1993, 1995, 1997, and 1999 Youth Risk Behavior Surveys.* www.cdc.gov/ HealthYouth/yrbs/factsheet.htm, accessed 1/10/05.

Central Intelligence Agency (CIA). 2000. *CIA World Factbook.* www.cia.gov/cia/ publications/factbook/geos/rs.html#Econ, accessed 12/29/04.

Chafe, William H. 1974. *The American Woman: Her Changing Social, Economic, and Political Roles, 1920–1970.* New York: Oxford University Press.

———. 1977. *Women and Equality: Changing Patterns in American Culture.* New York: Oxford University Press.

Chafetz, Janet Saltzman. 1990. *Gender Equity: An Integrated Theory of Stability and Change.* Newbury Park, CA: Sage.

———. 1997. "Feminist theory and sociology: Underutilized contributions for mainstream theory." *Annual Review of Sociology,* vol. 23.

Chambliss, William J. 1973. "The saints and the roughnecks." *Society,* November.

———. 1988. *On the Take: From Petty Crooks to Presidents.* Bloomington: Indiana University Press.

Chaney, David. 1994. *The Cultural Turn: Scene-Setting Essays in Contemporary Cultural History.* New York: Routledge.

Chang, Iris; and Kirby, William C. 1997. *The Rape of Nanking: The Forgotten Holocaust of World War II.* New York: Basic Books.

Charleston Business Journal. 2004. "Are 'all-American cars' still made in America?" www.charlestonbusiness.com/pub/6_ 18/news/2930-1.html, accessed 1/11/05.

Chase-Dunn, Christopher. 1989. *Global Formation: Structures of the World Economy.* Cambridge, MA: Basil Blackwell.

Chaves, Mark. 1993. "Intraorganizational power and internal secularization in Protestant denominations." *American Journal of Sociology,* vol. 99 (July): 1–48.

———. 1994. "Secularization as declining religious authority." *Social Forces,* vol. 72.

Cheng, Lucie; and Hsiung, Ping-Chun. 1992. "Women, export-oriented growth, and the state: The case of Taiwan," in Richard P. Appelbaum and Jeffery Henderson, eds., *States and Development in the Asian Pacific Rim.* Newbury Park, CA: Sage.

Chepesiuk, Ron. 1998. *Hard Target: The United States War against International Drug Trafficking, 1982–1997.* Jefferson, NC: McFarland and Company.

Cherlin, Andrew. 1990. "Recent changes in American fertility, marriage, and divorce." *Annals of the American Academy of Political and Social Science,* vol. 510 (July).

———. 1992. *Marriage, Divorce, Re-Marriage.* Rev. ed. Cambridge, MA: Harvard University Press.

———. 1999. *Public and Private Families: An Introduction.* 2nd ed. New York: McGraw Hill.

———, et al. 1998. "Effects of parental divorce on mental health throughout the life course." *American Sociological Review,* vol. 63.

Chicago Tribune. 2003. "Cost of a nursing home room jumps, study finds." www. chicagotribune.com/classified/realestate/ over55/chi-0308300022aug31,0,364422.

story?coll=chi-classifiedover55-hed (August 31, 2003), accessed 12/29/04.

Chodorow, Nancy. 1978. *The Reproduction of Mothering.* Berkeley, CA: University of California Press.

———. 1988. *Psychoanalytic Theory and Feminism.* Cambridge, UK: Polity Press.

Cicourel, Aaron V. 1968. *The Social Organization of Juvenile Justice.* New York: Wiley.

Clark, Philip G. 1993. "Public policy in the United States and Canada: Individualism, familial obligation, and collective responsibility in the care of the elderly," in Jon Hendricks and Carolyn J. Rosenthal, eds., *The Remainder of Their Days: Domestic Policy and Older Families in the United States and Canada.* New York: Garland Press.

Clawson, Dan, et al. 1999. *Dollars and Votes: How Business Campaign Contributions Subvert Democracy.* Philadelphia: Temple University Press.

Cleary, Paul D. 1987. "Gender differences in stress-related disorders," in Rosalind C. Barnett, ed., *Gender and Stress.* New York: Free Press.

Clegg, Stewart. 1990. *Modern Organizations: Organization Studies in the Postmodern World.* London: Sage.

Cleveland, Jeanette N. 1996. "Women in high-status nontraditional occupations," in Paula J. Dubeck and Kathryn Borman, eds., *Women and Work: A Handbook.* New York: Garland.

ClickZ Stats. 2003. "Population explosion!" www.clickz.com/stats/sectors/ geographies/article.php/5911_151151, accessed 12/29/04.

Cloward, Richard A.; and Ohlin, L. 1960. *Delinquency and Opportunity.* New York: Free Press.

CNN. 2004. "Bush calls for ban on same-sex marriages." http://edition.cnn.com/2004/ ALLPOLITICS/02/24/elec04.prez.bush. marriage/index.html (February 25), accessed 12/29/04.

Coate, J. 1994. "Cyberspace innkeeping: Building online community." Online paper, www.well.com:70/0/Community/ innkeeping, accessed 12/29/04.

Cohen, Albert. 1955. *Delinquent Boys: The Culture of the Gang.* Glencoe, IL: Free Press.

Cohen, Lisa E.; Broschak, Joseph P.; and Haveman, Heather A. 1998. "And then there were more? The effect of organizational sex composition on the hiring and promotion of managers." *American Sociological Review,* vol. 63, no. 5.

Cohen, P.; and Bianchi, Suzanne. 1999. "Marriage, children and women's employment: What do we know?" *Monthly Labor Review,* vol. 122 no. 12: 22–30.

Cohen, Robin. 1997. *Global Diasporas: An Introduction.* London: UCL Press.

Cohen, Susan. 1997. "Old glory." *Washington Post Magazine,* June 1.

Cohn, Norman. 1970a. *The Pursuit of the Millennium.* London: Paladin.

———. 1970b. "Medieval millenarianism," in Sylvia L. Thrupp, ed., *Millennial Dreams in Action: Studies in Revolutionary Religious Movements.* New York: Schocken Books.

Coleman, James S. 1987. "Families and schools." *Educational Researcher,* vol. 16, no. 6.

———. 1988. "Social capital in the creation of human capital." *American Journal of Sociology,* supplement, vol. 94.

———. 1990. *The Foundations of Social Theory.* Cambridge, MA: Harvard University Press.

———, et al. 1966. *Equality of Educational Opportunity.* Washington, DC: U.S. Government Printing Office.

Collins, James; and Porras, Jerry. 1994. *Built to Last.* New York: Century.

Collins, Jane. 2000. "Quality by other means." Unpublished manuscript, Department of Sociology, University of Wisconsin–Madison.

Collins, Patricia Hill. 1990. *Black Feminist Thought: Knowledge, Consciousness, and the Politics of Empowerment.* Boston: Unwin Hyman.

Collins, Randall. 1971. "Functional and conflict theories of educational stratification." *American Sociological Review,* vol. 36.

———. 1979. *The Credential Society: An Historical Sociology of Education.* New York: Academic Press.

———, et al. 1993. "Toward an integrated theory of gender stratification." *Sociological Perspectives,* vol. 36.

Coltrane, Scott. 1992. "The micropolitics of gender in non-industrial societies." *Gender and Society,* vol. 6.

Combat 18. 1998. www.combat18.org, accessed 1/10/05.

Common Cause. 2002a. "The soft money laundromat: Top soft money donors 1/1/01 through 12/31/02." www.commoncause. org/laundromat/stat/topdonors01.htm, accessed 7/1/03.

———. 2002b. "Campaign finance reform: Election 2002—incumbent advantage," www.commoncause.org/news/default.cfm ?ArtID=38, accessed 11/6/02.

———. 2003. "Spending more than a half billion on political contributions, lobbying and ad campaigns, Phrma wins big on Medicare," www.commoncause.org/ action/070103_phrma_report.pdf, accessed 7/1/03.

Computer World. 2002. "The Best Places to Work in IT: United States," www.computerworld.com/departments/ surveys/bestplaces/bestplaces_us_region_ sort/0, 10984,,00.html, accessed 1/20/05.

Conley, Dalton. 1999. *Being Black, Living in the Red: Race, Wealth, and Social Policy in America.* Berkeley and Los Angeles: University of California Press.

———. 2003. "The cost of slavery," *New York Times,* February 15.

Connell, R. W. 1987. *Gender and Power: Society, the Person, and Sexual Politics.* Boston: Allen and Unwin.

Conner, K. A.; Dorfman, L. T.; and Tompkins, J. B. 1985. "Life satisfaction of retired professors: The contribution of work, health, income, and length of retirement." *Educational Gerontology,* vol. 11.

Conti, Joseph A. 2003. "Trade, power, and law: Dispute resolution in the World Trade Organization, 1995–2002." Masters Thesis. University of California, Santa Barbara.

Cooley, Charles Horton. 1964. *Human Nature and the Social Order.* Originally published 1902. New York: Schocken Books.

Coombs, Philip H. 1985. *The World Crisis in Education.* New York: Oxford University Press.

Coontz, Stephanie. 1992. *The Way We Never Were: American Families and the Nostalgia Trap.* New York: Basic Books.

Corbin, Juliet; and Strauss, Anselm. 1985. "Managing chronic illness at home: Three lines of work." *Qualitative Sociology,* vol. 8.

Corsaro, William. 1997. *The Sociology of Childhood.* Thousand Oaks, CA: Pine Forge Press.

Cosmides, Leda; and Tooby, John. 1997. "Evolutionary psychology: A primer." University of California at Santa Barbara: Institute for Social, Behavioral, and Economic Research Center for Evolutionary Psychology, available at www.psych.ucsb.edu/research/cep/ primer.htm, accessed 1/11/05.

Coward, Rosalind. 1984. *Female Desire: Women's Sexuality Today.* London: Paladin.

Cowgill, Donald O. 1968. "The social life of the aged in Thailand." *Gerontologist,* vol. 8.

———. 1986. *Aging around the World.* Belmont, CA: Wadsworth.

Cox, Oliver C. 1959. *Class, Caste, and Race: A Study in Social Dynamics.* New York: Monthly Review Press.

Cox, Peter R. 1976. *Demography.* 5th ed. New York: Cambridge University Press.

Cox, W. Michael; and Alm, Richard. 1999. *Myths of Rich and Poor: Why We're Better Off Than We Think.* New York: Basic Books.

Craig, David J. 2004. "InnerCity Entrepeneurs gives small businesses a shot at the big leagues." *B. U. Bridge,* vol. VII, no. 26 (April), www.bu.edu/bridge/archive/2004/04-02/innercity.html, accessed 12/29/04.

Craner, Lorne W. 2002. "Promoting corporate social responsibility abroad: The human rights and democracy perspective," Remarks at the 2002 Surrey Memorial Lecture, National Policy Association (June 18), www.state.gov/g/ drl/rls/rm/11405.htm, accessed 12/29/04.

Cressey, Paul. 1932. *The Taxi-Dance Hall.* Chicago: University of Chicago Press.

Crompton, Rosemary. 1998. *Class and Stratification: An Introduction to Current Debates.* 2nd ed. Cambridge, UK: Polity Press.

Crow, Graham; and Hardey, Michael. 1992. "Diversity and ambiguity among lone-parent households in modern Britain," in Catherine Marsh and Sara Arber, eds., *Families and Households: Divisions and Change.* London: Macmillan.

CRP. 2003a. "2000 Presidential Race: Total Raised and Spent," Center for Responsive Politics. www.opensecrets.org/2000elect/ index/AllCands.htm, accessed 12/29/04.

———. 2003b. "Election overview 2002 cycle: Business-labor-ideology split in PAC, soft & individual donations to candidates and parties" Center for Responsive Politics, based on data released by the FEC on Monday, June 9, 2003. www.opensecrets. org/overview/blio.asp?cycle=2002, accessed 12/29/04.

Cumings, Bruce. 1987. "The origins and development of the northeast Asian political economy: Industrial sectors, product cycles, and political consequences," in F. C. Deyo, ed., *The Political Economy of the New Asian Industrialism.* Ithaca, NY: Cornell University Press.

———. 1997. *Korea's Place in the Sun: A Modern History.* New York: Norton.

Cumming, Elaine. 1963. "Further thoughts on the theory of disengagement." *International Social Science Journal,* vol. 15.

———. 1975. "Engagement with an old theory." *International Journal of Aging and Human Development,* vol. 6.

————; and Henry, William E. 1961. *Growing Old: The Process of Disengagement.* New York: Basic.

Currie, Elliott. 1998. *Crime and Punishment in America.* New York: Henry Holt.

Curtin, J. Sean. 2003. "Youth trends in Japan: Part four—anorexia and other teenage eating disorders on the rise." Japanese Institute of Global Communications. www.glocom.org/special_topics/social_trends/20030701_trends_s46, accessed 12/29/04.

Curtiss, Susan. 1977. *Genie: A Linguistic Study of a Modern Day "Wild Child."* New York: Academic Press.

Cutler, Stephen J.; and Grams, Armin E. 1988. "Correlates of everyday self-reported memory problems." *Journal of Gerontology,* vol. 43.

Dahlburg, John-Thor. 1995. "Sweatshop case dismays few in Thailand." *Los Angeles Times,* August 27, p. A-4.

D'Andrade, Roy. 1995. *The Development of Cognitive Anthropology.* New York: Cambridge University Press.

Dannefer, Dale. 1989. "Human action and its place in theories of aging." *Journal of Aging Studies,* vol. 3.

Danziger, Sheldon H.; and Gottschalk, Peter. 1995. *America Unequal.* Cambridge, MA: Harvard University Press.

————, et al., eds. 1994. *Confronting Poverty: Prescriptions for Change.* Cambridge, MA: Harvard University Press.

Davenport, W. 1965. "Sexual patterns and their regulations in a society of the southwest Pacific," in F. Beech, ed., *Sex and Behavior.* New York: Wiley.

Davies, Bronwyn. 1991. *Frogs and Snails and Feminist Tales.* Sydney: Allen and Unwin.

Davies, James C. 1962. "Towards a theory of revolution." *American Sociological Review,* vol. 27.

Davis, Donald; and Polonko, Karen. 2001. "Telework America 2001 Summary," International Telework Association & Council, www.telecommute.org/telework/twa2001.htm, accessed 1/20/05.

Davis, Kingsley; and Moore, Wilbert E. 1945. "Some principles of stratification." *American Sociological Review,* vol. 10 (April).

Davis, Mike. 1990. *City of Quartz: Excavating the Future in Los Angeles.* New York: Verso.

Davis, Stanley M. 1987. *Future Perfect.* Reading, MA: Addison-Wesley.

————. 1988. *2001 Management: Managing the Future Now.* New York: Simon and Schuster.

Davis, Winston. 1987. "Religion and development: Weber and East Asia experience," in Myron Weiner and Samuel Huntington, eds., *Understanding Political Development.* Boston: Little, Brown.

Deacon, Terrance W. 1998. *The Symbolic Species: The Co-Evolution of Language and the Brain.* New York: Norton.

de Beauvoir, Simone. 1974. *The Second Sex.* Originally published 1949. New York: Random House.

Delany, Samuel R. 1999. *Times Square Red, Times Square Blue.* New York: New York University Press.

D'Emilio, John. 1983. *Sexual Politics, Sexual Communities: The Making of a Homosexual Minority in the United States, 1940–1970.* Chicago: University of Chicago Press.

Dertouzos, Michael L. 1989. *Made in America: Regaining the Productive Edge.* Cambridge, MA: MIT Press.

de Tocqueville, Alexis. 1969. *Democracy in America.* Originally published 1835. New York: Doubleday.

Devault, Marjorie L. 1991. *Feeding the Family: The Social Organization of Caring as Gendered Work.* Chicago: University of Chicago Press.

de Witt, Karen. 1994. "Wave of suburban growth is being fed by minorities." *New York Times,* August 15, pp. A1, B6.

Dey, Achintya N. 1997. "Characteristics of elderly nursing home residents: Data from the 1995 national nursing home survey." *Advance Data,* vol. 289 (July 2).

Deyo, Fred C. 1987. *The Political Economy of the New Asian Industrialism.* Ithaca, NY: Cornell University Press.

————. 1989. *Beneath the Miracle: Labor Subordination in the New Asian Industrialism.* Berkeley, CA: University of California Press.

Diamond, Jared. 1997. *Guns, Germs, and Steel: The Fates of Human Societies.* New York: Norton.

Dicken, Peter. 1992. *Global Shift: The Internationalization of Economic Activity.* 2nd ed. London: Chapman.

Dickman, Sharon. 1999. "Can life in nursing homes by meaningful?" University of Rochester press release, June 23.

Dicum, Gregory; and Luttinger, Nina. 1999. *The Coffee Book: Anatomy of an Industry from Crop to the Last Drop.* New York: New Press.

Diekema, David A. 1991. "Televangelism and the mediated charismatic relationship," *Social Science Journal,* vol. 28, no. 2: 143–62.

DiMaggio, Paul. 1997. "Culture and cognition." *Annual Review of Sociology,* vol. 23.

DiPrete, Thomas A.; and Grusky, David B. 1990. "Structure and trend in the process of stratification for American men and women." *American Journal of Sociology,* vol. 96.

————; and Nonnemaker, K. Lynn. 1997. "Structural change, labor market turbulence, and labor market outcomes." *American Sociological Review,* vol. 62.

————; and Soule, Whitman T. 1988. "Gender and promotion in segmented job ladder systems." *American Sociological Review,* vol. 53.

Dobash, R. Emerson; and Dobash, Russell P. 1992. *Women, Violence, and Social Change.* New York: Routledge.

Dolbeare, Cushing. 1995. *Out of Reach: Why Everyday People Can't Find Affordable Housing.* Washington, DC: Low Income Housing Information.

Domhoff, G. William. 1974. *The Bohemian Grove and Other Retreats.* New York: Harper and Row.

————. 1998 (earlier editions 1971, 1979, 1983). *Who Rules America?: Power and Politics in the Year 2000.* Belmont, CA: Mayfield.

Dore, Ronald. 1980. *British Factory, Japanese Factory: The Origins of National Diversity in Industrial Relations.* Berkeley, CA: University of California Press.

Doyal, Lesley; and Pennell, Imogen. 1981. *The Political Economy of Health.* Boston: South End Press.

Drake, St. Clair; and Cayton, Horace R. 1945. *Black Metropolis: A Study of Negro Life in a Northern City.* New York: Harcourt, Brace.

Draper, P. 1975. "!Kung women: Contrasts in sexual egalitarianism in foraging and sedentary contexts," in R. R. Reiter, ed., *Toward an Anthropology of Women.* New York: Monthly Review Press.

Dreier, Peter; and Appelbaum, Richard P. 1992. "The housing crisis enters the 1990s." *New England Journal of Public Policy,* spring–summer.

Drentea, Patricia. 1998. "Consequences of women's formal and informal job search methods for employment in female-dominated jobs." *Gender and Society,* vol. 12.

Du Bois, W. E. B. 1903. *The Souls of Black Folk.* New York: Dover.

Dubos, René. 1959. *Mirage of Health.* New York: Doubleday/Anchor.

Duignan, Peter; and Gann, L. H., eds. 1998. *The Debate in the United States over Immigration.* Stanford, CA: Hoover Institution Press.

Duncan, Greg J.; Brooks-Gunn, Jeanne; Yeung, W. Jean; Smith, Judith R. 1998. "How much does childhood poverty affect the life chances of children?" *American Sociological Review,* vol. 63, no. 3 (June): 406–23.

Duncan, Otis Dudley. 1971. "Observations on population." *New Physician,* April 20.

Duncombe, Jean; and Marsden, Dennis. 1993. "Love and intimacy: The gender division of emotion and emotion work: A neglected aspect of sociological discussion of heterosexual relationships." *Sociology,* vol. 27.

Duneier, Mitchell. 1999. *Sidewalk.* New York: Farrar, Straus, and Giroux.

———; and Molotch, Harvey. 1999. "Talking city trouble: Interactional vandalism, social inequality, and the urban interaction problem." *American Journal of Sociology,* vol. 104.

Dunn, Dana; Almquist, Elizabeth M.; and Saltzman Chafetz, Janet. 1993. "Macrostructural perspectives on gender inequality," in Paula England, ed., *Theory on Gender, Feminism on Theory.* New York: Aldine DeGrutyer.

Dunn, William. 1993. *The Baby Bust: A Generation Comes of Age.* Ithaca, NY: American Demographics Books.

Duranti, Alessandro. 1994. *From Grammar to Politics: Linguistic Anthropology in a Western Samoan Village.* Berkeley, CA: University of California Press.

Durkheim, Émile. 1964. *The Division of Labor in Society.* Originally published 1893. New York: Free Press.

———. 1965. *The Elementary Forms of the Religious Life.* Originally published 1912. New York: Free Press.

———. 1966. *Suicide.* Originally published 1897. New York: Free Press.

Duster, Troy. 1990. *Backdoor to Eugenics.* New York: Routledge.

Dutt, Mallika. 1996. "Some reflections on U.S. women of color and the United Nations fourth world conference on women and NGO forum in Beijing, China." *Feminist Studies,* vol. 22.

Dworkin, Andrea. 1981. *Pornography: Men Possessing Women.* New York: Pedigree.

———. 1987. *Intercourse.* New York: Free Press.

Dworkin, R. M. 1993. *Life's Dominion: An Argument About Abortion, Euthanasia, and Individual Freedom.* New York: Knopf.

Dwyer, D. J. 1975. *People and Housing in Third World Cities.* London: Longman.

Dychtwald, K. 1990. *Age Wave: How the Most Important Trend of Our Time Will Change Your Future.* New York: Bantam Books.

Dye, Thomas R. 1986. *Who's Running America?* 4th ed. Englewood Cliffs, NJ: Prentice Hall.

Eating Disorder Coalition (EDC). 2003. "Statistics." www.eatingdisorderscoalition. org/reports/statistics.html, accessed 12/29/04.

Ebomoyi, Ehigie. 1987. "The prevalence of female circumcision in two Nigerian communities." *Sex Roles,* vol. 17, nos. 3–4.

The Economist. 1990. *The Economist Book of Vital World Statistics.* New York: Times Books.

———. 2003. "A Nation Apart," May 6, www.economist.com/surveys/showsurvey. cfm?issue=20031108, accessed 12/29/04.

Edin, K.; and Lein, L. 1997. "Work, welfare, and single mothers' economic survival strategies." *American Sociological Review,* vol. 62, no. 2.

Efron, Sonni. 1997. "Eating disorders go global," *Los Angeles Times,* October 18, p. A-1.

Ehrenreich, Barbara; and Ehrenreich, John. 1979. "The professional-managerial class," in Pat Walker, ed., *Between Labor and Capital.* Boston: South End.

Eibl-Eibesfeldt, I. 1972. "Similarities and differences between cultures in expressive movements," in Robert A. Hinde, ed., *Nonverbal Communication.* New York: Cambridge University Press.

Eisenhower Library. 1961. "Farewell Address," Abilene, Kansas: The Dwight D. Eisenhower Presidential Library. www.eisenhower.utexas.edu/farewell.htm, accessed 12/29/04.

Ekman, Paul; and Friesen, W. V. 1978. *Facial Action Coding System.* New York: Consulting Psychologists Press.

el Dareer, Asma. 1982. *Woman, Why Do You Weep? Circumcision and Its Consequences.* Westport, CT: Zed.

Elias, Norbert. 1987. *Involvement and Detachment.* London: Oxford University Press.

———; and Dunning, E. 1987. *Quest for Excitement: Sport and Leisure in the Civilizing Process.* Oxford, UK: Blackwell.

Ell, Kathleen. 1996. "Social networks, social support, and coping with serious illness: The family connection." *Social Science and Medicine,* vol. 42.

Ellsworth American. 2001. "Laptop Computers for Students," editorial, *Ellsworth American,* www.ellsworthamerican. com/archive/edit2001/02_01/ea_edit2-02- 08-01.html, accessed 1/10/05.

Elshtain, Jean Bethke. 1981. *Public Man: Private Woman.* Princeton, NJ: Princeton University Press.

Emmanuel, Arghiri. 1972. *Unequal Exchange: A Study of the Imperialism of Trade.* New York: Monthly Review Press.

England, Paula. 1992. *Comparable Worth: Theories and Evidence.* New York: Aldine de Gruyter.

Environmental Working Group. 2003. "EWG Farm Subsidy Database" www.ewg.org/ farm/findings.php, accessed 12/29/04.

Epstein, Gene. 2003. "More women advance, but sexism persists," *Barron's* www. collegejournal.com/salaryhiring/industries/ seniorexecs/20030605-epstein.html, accessed 1/11/05.

Equal Employment Opportunity Commission (EEOC). 1993. "National database fiscal year 1983 to fiscal year 1992." Washington, DC: Equal Employment Opportunity Commission.

———. 2003. "Sexual harassment charges, EEOC and FEPAs combined: FY1992– FY2002," www.eeoc.gov/stats/ harass.html, accessed 7/5/03.

Erard, Michael. 2003. "Decoding the new cues in online society," *New York Times,* November 27.

Ericson, Richard; and Haggerty, Kevin. 1997. *Policing the Risk Society.* Toronto: University of Toronto Press.

Erikson, Kai. 1966. *Wayward Puritans: A Study in the Sociology of Deviance.* New York: Wiley.

Erikson, R.; and Goldthorpe, J. H. 1992. *The Constant Flux: A Study of Class Mobility in Industrial Societies.* Oxford, UK: Oxford University Press.

Esposito, John L. 1984. *Islam and Politics.* Syracuse, NY: Syracuse University Press.

Estes, Carol L. 1986. "The politics of aging in America." *Aging and Society,* vol. 6.

———. 1991. "The Reagan legacy: Privatization, the welfare state, and aging," in J. Myles and J. Quadagno, eds., *States, Labor Markets, and the Future of Old Age Policy.* Philadelphia: Temple University Press.

———; Binney, Elizabeth A.; and Culbertson, Richard A. 1992. "The gerontological imagination: Social influences on the development of gerontology, 1945–present." *Aging and Human Development,* vol. 35.

———; Swan, J.; and Gerard, L. 1982. "Dominant and competing paradigms in gerontology: Toward a political economy of aging." *Aging and Society,* vol. 2.

———, et al. 1984. *Political Economy, Health, and Aging.* Boston: Little, Brown.

Estrich, Susan. 1987. *Real Rape.* Cambridge, MA: Harvard University Press.

Etzioni-Halévy, Eva. 1985. *Bureaucracy and Democracy: A Political Dilemma.* New York: Routledge, Chapman and Hall.

Europa. 2000. "European enlargement: A historical opportunity." http://europa.eu.

int/comm/enlargement/docs/newsletter/weekly_070700.htm, accessed 1/10/05.

Evans, David J. 1992. "Left realism and the spatial study of crime," in David J. Evans et al., eds., *Crime, Policing, and Place: Essays in Environmental Criminology.* New York: Routledge.

Evans, Peter. 1979. *Dependent Development.* Princeton, NJ: Princeton University Press.

———. 1987. "Class, state, and dependence in East Asia: Some lessons for Latin Americanists," in F. C. Deyo, ed., *The Political Economy of the New Asian Industrialism.* Ithaca, NY: Cornell University Press.

———. 1995. *Embedded Autonomy: States and Industrial Transformation.* Princeton, NJ: Princeton University Press.

Evans, Richard J. 1977. *The Feminists: Women's Emancipation Movements in Europe, America, and Australasia, 1840–1920.* New York: Barnes & Noble.

Evans-Pritchard, E. E. 1956. *Nuer Religion.* New York: Oxford University Press.

———. 1970. "Sexual inversion among the Azande." *American Anthropologist,* vol. 72.

Falk, G.; Falk, U.; and Tomashevich, V. 1981. *Aging in America and Other Cultures.* Saratoga, CA: Century Twenty-One.

Farley, Maggie. 1998. "Women in the new China." *Los Angeles Times,* November 22.

Farley, Reynolds; and Frey, William H. 1994. "Change in the segregation of whites from blacks during the 1980s: Small steps toward a more integrated society." *American Sociological Review,* vol. 59, no. 1.

Featherman, David L.; and Hauser, Robert M. 1978. *Opportunity and Change.* New York: Academic Press.

FEC. 2001. "PAC activity increases in 2000 election cycle," Federal Election Commission, News releases, Media Advisories (May 31), www.fec.gov/press/press2001/053101pacfund/053101pacfund.html, accessed 1/11/05.

Ferguson, Kathy E. 1984. *The Feminist Case against Bureaucracy.* Philadelphia: Temple University Press.

Fernández, Kelly; and Patricia, María. 1987. "Technology and employment along the U.S.-Mexico border," in Cathryn L. Thorup, ed., *The United States and Mexico: Face to Face with the New Technology.* New Brunswick, NJ: Transaction Books.

Filkins, Dexter. 1998. "Afghans pay dearly for peace." *Los Angeles Times,* October 22, p. A-1.

FinanceAsia.com. 2003. "A week in tech," (July 5). www.financeasia.com/articles/

FF609444-A13D-11D7-81FC0090277E174B.cfm, accessed 7/5/03.

Finke, Roger; and Stark, Rodney. 1988. "Religious economies and sacred canopies: Religious mobilization in American cities, 1906." *American Sociological Review,* vol. 53.

———. 1992. *The Churching of America, 1776–1990: Winners and Losers in Our Religious Economy.* New Brunswick, NJ: Rutgers University Press.

Firestone, Shulamith. 1971. *The Dialectic of Sex.* London: Paladin.

Fischer, Claude S. 1984. *The Urban Experience.* 2nd ed. New York: Harcourt Brace Jovanovich.

———, et al. 1996. *Inequality by Design: Cracking the Bell Curve Myth.* Princeton, NJ: Princeton University Press.

Fischer, David H. 1978. *Growing Old in America,* expanded ed. New York: Oxford University Press.

Fisher, Bonnie S.; Cullen, Francis T.; and Turner, Michael G. 2000. *The Sexual Victimization of College Women.* Washington, DC: U.S. Department of Justice, National Institute of Justice, Bureau of Justice Statistics (December), NJJ 182369, www.ncjrs.org/pdffiles1/nij/182369.pdf, accessed 12/29/04.

Foner, Nancy. 1984. *Ages in Conflict: A Cross-Cultural Perspective on Inequality between Old and Young.* New York: Columbia University Press.

Forbes. 2000. "The world's richest people." (June 29).

———. 2001a. "The world's richest people." (June 21), www.forbes.com/2001/06/21/billionairesindex.html, accessed 12/29/04.

———. 2001b. "Forbes top CEO's: Corporate America's most powerful people." http://www.forbes.com/lists/home.jhtml?passListID=12&passYear=2001&passListType=Person, accessed 12/29/04.

———. 2002. (March 4).

———. 2003. "Survival of the richest" www.forbes.com/billionaires/freeforbes/2003/0317/087.html, accessed 12/29/04.

Ford, Clellan S.; and Beach, Frank A. 1951. *Patterns of Sexual Behavior.* New York: Harper and Row.

Forrest, Drew; and Streek, Barry. 2001. "Mbeki in bizarre AIDS outburst" *Daily Mail and Guardian* (Johannesburg) October 26. www.aegis.com/news/dmg/2001/MG011021.html, accessed 12/29/04.

Fortune. 2003. "Global 500" (July 21), www.fortune.com/fortune/global500, accessed 12/14/03.

Foucault, Michel. 1971. *The Order of Things: An Archaeology of the Human Sciences.* New York: Pantheon.

———. 1978. *The History of Sexuality.* New York: Pantheon.

———. 1979. *Discipline and Punish: The Birth of the Prison.* New York: Random House.

———. 1987. *The Use of Pleasure.* Harmondsworth, UK: Penguin.

———. 1988. "Technologies of the self," in Luther H. Martin, Huck Gutman, and Patrick H. Hutton, eds., *Technologies of the Self: A Seminar with Michel Foucault.* Amherst, MA: University of Massachusetts Press.

Fowles, Richard; and Merva, Mary. 1996. "Wage inequality and criminal activity: An extreme bounds analysis for the United States, 1975–1990." *Criminology,* vol. 34, no. 2.

Fox, Oliver C. 1964. "The pre-industrial city reconsidered." *Sociological Quarterly,* vol. 5.

Frank, Andre Gundar. 1966. "The development of underdevelopment." *Monthly Review,* vol. 18.

———. 1969a. *Latin America: Under-development or Revolution.* New York: Monthly Review Press.

———. 1969b. *Capitalism and Under-development in Latin America: Historical Studies of Chile and Brazil.* New York: Monthly Review Press.

———. 1979. *Dependent Accumulation and Underdevelopment.* London: Macmillan.

Frank, David John; and McEneaney, Elizabeth H. 1999. "The individualization of society and the liberalization of state policies on same-sex sexual relations, 1984–1995." *Social Forces,* vol. 7, no. 3.

Fredrickson, George M. 1998. *The Comparative Imagination: On the History of Racism, Nationalism, and Social Movements.* Berkeley and Los Angeles: University of California Press.

———. *Freedom in the World, 1997–1998.* New York: Freedom House.

Freeman, Richard B. 1999. *The New Inequality: Creating Solutions for Poor America.* Boston: Beacon Press.

———; and Rogers, Joel. 1999. *What Workers Want.* Ithaca, NY: ILR Press and Russell Sage Foundation.

Free the Children. 1998. www.freethechildren.org, accessed 12/29/04.

Freidson, Eliot. 1970. *Profession of Medicine: A Study of the Sociology of Applied Knowledge.* New York: Dodd, Mead.

Fremlin, J. H. 1964. "How many people can the world support?" *New Scientist,* (October 19).

French, Howard W. 2001a. "Diploma at hand, Japanese women find glass ceiling reinforced with iron." *New York Times,* January 1, p. A1.

———. 2001b. "Japan's new premier picks precedent-setting cabinet." *New York Times,* April 27, p. A1.

Freud, Sigmund. 1971. *The Psychopathology of Everyday Life.* New York: Norton.

Frey, William; and Liaw, Kao-Lee. 1998. "The impact of recent immigration on population redistribution in the United States," in James Smith and Barry Edmonston, eds., *The Immigration Debate.* Washington, DC: National Academy Press.

Friedan, Betty. 1963. *The Feminine Mystique.* New York: Norton.

Friedlander, Daniel; and Burtless, Gary. 1994. *Five Years After: The Long-Term Effects of Welfare-to-Work Programs.* New York: Russell Sage.

Fries, James F. 1980. "Aging, natural death, and the compression of morbidity." *New England Journal of Medicine,* vol. 303.

Frobel, Folker; Heinrichs, Jurgen; and Kreye, Otto. 1979. *The New International Division of Labor.* New York: Cambridge University Press.

Fry, C. L. 1980. *Aging in Culture and Society.* New York: Bergin.

Fryer, David; and McKenna, Stephen. 1987. "The laying off of hands—unemployment and the experience of time," in Stephen Fineman, ed., *Unemployment: Personal and Social Consequences.* London: Tavistock.

Fukuyama, Francis. 1989. "The end of history?" *National Interest,* vol. 16 (summer).

Furstenberg, Frank F., Jr.; and Cherlin, Andrew J. 1991. *Divided Families.* Cambridge, MA: Harvard University Press.

Gallup Organization. 1998. Gallup/CNN/*USA Today* Poll, July 21.

Gamoran, Adam, et al. 1995. "An organizational analysis of the effects of ability grouping." *American Educational Research Journal,* vol. 32, no. 4.

Gans, Herbert J. 1979. "Symbolic ethnicity: The future of ethnic groups and cultures in America." *Ethnic and Racial Studies,* vol. 2 (January).

Ganzeboom, H. B. G.; Luijkx, R.; and Treiman, D. 1989. "Intergenerational class mobility in comparative perspective." *Research in Social Stratification and Mobility,* vol. 8.

Gardner, Beatrice; and Gardner, Allen. 1969. "Teaching sign language to a chimpanzee." *Science,* no. 165.

———. 1975. "Evidence for sentence constituents in the early utterances of child and chimpanzee." *Journal of Experimental Psychology,* vol. 104.

Gardner, Carol Brooks. 1995. *Passing By: Gender and Public Harassment.* Berkeley and Los Angeles: University of California Press.

Garfinkel, Harold. 1963. "A conception of, and experiments with, 'trust' as a condition of stable concerted actions," in O. J. Harvey, ed., *Motivation and Social Interaction.* New York: Ronald Press.

Gavron, Hannah. 1966. *The Captive Wife: Conflicts of Housebound Mothers.* London: Routledge and Kegan Paul.

Geary, Dick. 1981. *European Labor Protest, 1848–1939.* New York: St. Martin's Press.

Geertz, Clifford. 1973. *The Interpretation of Cultures.* New York: Basic Books.

———. 1983. *Local Knowledge: Further Essays in Interpretative Anthropology.* New York: Basic Books.

Gelb, I. J. 1952. *A Study of Writing.* Chicago: University of Chicago Press.

Gelles, Richard; and Cornell, C. P. 1990. *Intimate Violence in Families.* 2nd ed. Newbury Park, CA: Sage.

Gellner, Ernest. 1983. *Nations and Nationalism.* Ithaca, NY: Cornell University Press.

General Social Survey (GSS). 1997. "General Social Surveys, 1972–1994: [Cumulative File]." Accessed and Analyzed online through the University of Michigan Inter-university Consortium for Political and Social Research (ICPSR), http:webapp. icpsr.umich.edu/cocoon/ICPSR-StUDY/03728.xml, accessed 1/10/05.

Gerbner, George, et al. 1985. "Television's mean world: violence profile no. 14–15." Philadelphia: Annenberg School of Communication, University of Pennsylvania.

Gereffi, Gary. 1995. "Contending paradigms for cross-regional comparison: Development strategies and commodity chains in East Asia and Latin America," in Peter H. Smith, ed., *Latin America in Comparative Perspective: New Approaches to Methods and Analysis.* Boulder, CO: Westview Press.

———. 1996. "Commodity chains and regional divisions of labor in East Asia." *Journal of Asian Business,* vol. 12, no. 1.

Gershuny, Jonathan, et al., 1994. "The domestic labor revolution: A process of lagged adaptation," in Michael Anderson, Frank Bechofer, and Jonathan Gershuny, eds., *The Social and Political Economy of the Household.* Oxford, UK: Oxford University Press.

———; and Miles, I. D. 1983. *The New Service Economy: The Transformation of Employment in Industrial Societies.* London: Francis Pinter.

Gibbons, John H. 1990. *Trading around the Clock: Global Securities Markets and Information Technology.* Washington, DC: Government Printing Office.

Gibson, P. 1989. "Gay male and lesbian youth suicide." Report of the Secretary's Task Force on Youth Suicide. Washington, D.C.: U.S. Department of Health and Human Services.

Giddens, Anthony. 1984. *The Constitution of Society.* Cambridge, UK: Polity Press.

———. 1995. *Beyond Left and Right: The Future of Radical Politics.* Stanford, CA: Stanford University Press.

———. 1998. *The Third Way: The Renewal of Social Democracy.* Cambridge, UK: Polity Press.

Gill, Colin. 1985. *Work, Unemployment, and the New Technology.* New York: Basil Blackwell.

Gilligan, Carol. 1982. *In a Different Voice: Psychological Theory and Women's Development.* Cambridge, MA: Harvard University Press.

Ginzburg, Carlo. 1980. *The Cheese and the Worms.* London: Routledge and Kegan Paul.

Gissing, George. 1983. *Demos: A Story of English Socialism.* Originally published 1892. New York: Routledge, Chapman and Hall.

Giuffre, Patti A.; and Williams, Christine L. 1994. "Boundary lines: Labeling sexual harassment in restaurants." *Gender and Society,* vol. 8.

Gladwell, Malcolm. 2000. "Designs for Working," *New Yorker,* December 11.

Glascock, A.; and Feinman, S. 1981. "Social asset or social burden: An analysis of the treatment for the aged in non-industrial societies," in C. L. Fry, ed., *Dimensions: Aging, Culture, and Health.* New York: Praeger.

———. 1986. "Toward a comparative framework: Propositions concerning the treatment of the aged in non-industrial societies," in C. L. Fry and J. Keith, eds., *New Methods for Old Age Research: Strategies for Studying Diversity.* South Hadley, MA: Bergin and Garvey.

Glassner, Barry. 1999. *The Culture of Fear: Why Americans Are Afraid of the Wrong Things.* New York: Basic Books.

Glenn, Evelyn Nakano. 1994. "Introduction," in Grace Change, Linda Rennie Forcey, and Evelyn Nakano Glenn, eds., *Mothering: Ideology, Experience, and Agency.* New York: Routledge.

Glock, Charles Y. 1976. "On the origin and evolution of religious groups," in Charles Y. Glock and Robert N. Bellah, eds., *The New Religious Consciousness.* Berkeley, CA: University of California Press.

Glueck, Sheldon W.; and Glueck, Eleanor. 1956. *Physique and Delinquency.* New York: Harper and Row.

Gober, Patricia. 1993. *Americans on the Move.* Washington, DC: Population Reference Bureau.

Goe, W. Richard. 1994. "The producer services sector and development within the deindustrializing urban community." *Social Forces,* vol. 72.

Goffman, Erving. 1967. *Interaction Ritual.* New York: Doubleday/Anchor.

——. 1971. *Relations in Public: Microstudies of the Public Order.* New York: Basic Books.

——. 1973. *The Presentation of Self in Everyday Life.* New York: Overlook Press.

——. 1981. *Forms of Talk.* Philadelphia: University of Pennsylvania Press.

Gold, T. 1986. *State and Society in the Taiwan Miracle.* Armonk, NY: M. E. Sharpe.

Goldberg, Carey. 1997. "Hispanic households struggle amid broad decline in income." *New York Times,* January 30, pp. A1, A16.

——. 2001. "School computer money approved," *New York Times,* July 27.

Goldin, Claudia Dale. 1990. *Understanding the Gender Gap: An Economic History of American Women.* New York: Oxford University Press.

Goldscheider, Frances K. 1990. "The aging of the gender revolution: What do we know and what do we need to know?" *Research on Aging,* vol. 12.

——; and Goldscheider, Calvin. 1999. *The Changing Transition to Adulthood: Leaving and Returning Home.* Thousand Oaks, CA: Sage.

——; and Waite, Linda J. 1991. *New Families, No Families? The Transformation of the American Home.* Berkeley, CA: University of California Press.

Goldstein, Sidney; and Goldstein, Alice. 1996. *Jews on the Move: Implications for Jewish Identity.* Albany, NY: SUNY Press.

Goldthorpe, John H. 1983. "Women and class analysis: In defense of the conventional view," *Sociology,* vol. 17.

Goode, William J. 1963. *World Revolution in Family Patterns.* New York: Free Press.

——. 1971. "Force and violence in the family," *Journal of Marriage and the Family,* vol. 33.

——. 1993. *World Changes in Divorce Patterns.* New Haven, CT: Yale University Press.

Goodhardt, G. J.; Ehrenberg, A. S. C.; and Collins, M. A. 1987. *The Television Audience: Patterns of Voting.* 2nd ed. London: Gower.

Gorz, Andre. 1982. *Farewell to the Working Class.* London: Pluto.

Gottfredson, Michael R.; and Hirschi, Travis. 1990. *A General Theory of Crime.* Stanford, CA: Stanford University Press.

Graham, Heather. 1987. "Women's smoking and family health." *Social Science and Medicine,* vol. 25.

——. 1994. "Gender and class as dimensions of smoking behavior: Insights from a survey of mothers." *Social Science and Medicine,* vol. 38.

Graham, Laurie. 1995. *On the Line at Subaru-Isuzu.* Ithaca, NY: Cornell University Press.

Granovetter, Mark. 1973. "The strength of weak ties." *American Journal of Sociology,* vol. 78.

Greeley, Andrew. 1977. *The American Catholic: A Social Portrait.* New York: Basic Books.

——. 1989. *Religious Change in America.* Cambridge, MA: Harvard University Press.

Green, F. 1987. *The "Sissy Boy" Syndrome and the Development of Homosexuality.* New Haven, CT: Yale University Press.

Greenberg, Jan S.; and Becker, Marion. 1988. "Aging parents as family resources." *Gerontologist,* vol. 28.

Greenfield, Patricia Marks. 1993. "Representational competence in shared symbol systems," in R. R. Cocking and K. A. Renninger, eds., *The Development and Meaning of Psychological Distance.* Hillsdale, NJ: Erlbaum.

Griffin, Susan. 1979. *Rape, the Power of Consciousness.* New York: Harper and Row.

Grint, Keith. 1991. *The Sociology of Work.* Cambridge, MA: Polity Press.

Gross, Jane. 1992. "Suffering in silence no more: Fighting sexual harassment." *New York Times,* July 13, p. A1.

Grusky, David B.; and Hauser, Robert M. 1984. "Comparative social mobility revisited: Models of convergence and divergence in 16 countries." *American Sociological Review,* vol. 49.

——; and Sorensen, J. B. 1998. "Can class analysis be salvaged?" *American Journal of Sociology,* vol. 103, no. 5.

The Guardian. 2002. "Top 1% earn as much as the poorest 57%" www.guardian.co.uk/

business/story/0,,635292,00.html, accessed 1/10/05.

Gubrium, Jabber F. 1986. *Oldtimers and Alzheimer's: The Descriptive Organization of Senility.* Greenwich, CT: JAI Press.

——. 1991. *The Mosaic of Care: Frail Elderly and Their Families in the Real World.* New York: Springer.

——. 1993. *Speaking of Life: Horizons of Meaning for Nursing Home Residents.* Hawthorne, NY: Aldine de Gruyter.

——; and Sankar, Andrea, eds. 1994. *Qualitative Methods in Aging Research.* Newbury Park, CA: Sage.

Guibernau, Montserrat. 1999. *Nations without States: Political Communities in a Global Age.* Cambridge, MA: Blackwell.

Habermas, Jürgen. 1975. *Legitimation Crisis.* Trans. Thomas McCarthy. Boston: Beacon Press.

——. 1989. *The Structural Transformation of the Public Sphere: An Inquiry into a Category of Bourgeois Society.* Cambridge, UK: Polity Press.

Hacker, Andrew. 1992. *Two Nations: Black and White, Separate, Hostile, Unequal.* New York: Scribner.

Hadden, Jeffrey. 1990. "Precursors to the globalization of American televangelism," *Social Compass,* vol. 37 (March): 161–67.

——. 1997a. "The concepts 'cult' and 'sect' in scholarly research and public discourse." New Religious Movements Web site, http://religious movements.lib. virginia.edu/cultsect/concult.htm, accessed 1/10/05.

——. 1997b. "New religious movements mission statement." New Religious Movements Web site, http://religous movements.lib.virginia.edu/welcome/ mission.htm, accessed 1/10/05.

——; and Shupe, Anson. 1987. "Televangelism in America," *Social Compass,* vol. 34, no. 1: 61–75.

——. 2004. Religious Broadcasting Web site, "Televangelism." http://religious broadcasting.lib.virginia.edu/televangelis m.html, accessed 1/3/05.

Hagan, John. 1992. "The poverty of a classless criminology." *Criminology,* vol. 30, no. 1.

——; and McCarthy, Bill. 1992. "Mean streets: The theoretical significance of situational delinquency among homeless youth." *American Sociological Review,* vol. 98.

Haggard, Stephan. 1990. *Pathways from the Periphery: The Politics of Growth in Newly Industrializing Countries.* Ithaca, NY: Cornell University Press.

Hall, Edward T. 1969. *The Hidden Dimension.* New York: Doubleday.

———. 1973. *The Silent Language.* New York: Doubleday.

Hall, Stuart. 1992. "The question of cultural identity," in Stuart Hall, David Held, and Tony McGrew, eds., *Modernity and Its Futures.* Cambridge, UK: Polity Press.

———, et al. 1978. *Policing the Crisis: Mugging, the State, and Law and Order.* London: Macmillan.

———, et al. 1982. *The Empire Strikes Back.* London: Hutchinson.

———, et al. 1988. "New times." *Marxism Today,* October.

Halpern, Carolyn Tucker, et al. 2000. "Smart teens don't have sex (or kiss much either)." *Journal of Adolescent Health,* vol. 26, no. 3.

Hamel, G. 1991. "Competition for competence and inter-partner learning within international strategic alliances." *Strategic Management Journal,* summer supplement, vol. 12.

Hamilton, Martha M. 2000. "Web retailer Kozmo accused of redlining; Exclusion of D.C. minority areas cited." *Washington Post,* April 14.

Hammond, Phillip E. 1992. *Religion and Personal Autonomy: The Third Disestablishment in America.* Columbia, SC: University of South Carolina Press.

Handy, Charles. 1994. *The Empty Raincoat: Making Sense of the Future.* London: Hutchinson.

Hansen, Kristin A. 1995. "Geographical mobility: March 1993 to March 1994," in U.S. Bureau of the Census, *Current Population Reports, P20–485.* Washington, DC: U.S. Government Printing Office.

Hare, A. Paul; Borgatta, Edgar F.; and Bales, Robert F. 1965. *Small Groups: Studies in Social Interaction.* New York: Knopf.

Harris, Judith Rich. 1998. *The Nurture Assumption: Why Children Turn Out the Way They Do.* New York: Free Press.

Harris, Marvin. 1975. *Cows, Pigs, Wars, and Riches: The Riddles of Culture.* New York: Random House.

———. 1978. *Cannibals and Kings: The Origins of Cultures.* New York: Random House.

———. 1980. *Cultural Materialism: The Struggle for a Science of Culture.* New York: Vintage Books.

Hartley, Eugene. 1946. *Problems in Prejudice.* New York: Kings Crown Press.

Hartman, Chris. 2000. "Facts and figures on wealth." Inequality.org, www.inequality.org/factsfr.html, accessed 1/3/05.

Hartman, Mary; and Banner, Lois, eds. 1974. *Clio's Consciousness Raised: New Perspectives on the History of Women.* New York: Norton.

Hartman, Moshe; and Hartman, Harriet. 1996. *Gender Equality and American Jews.* Albany: SUNY Press.

———; and Swann, Charles. 1981. *Prime Time Preachers: The Rising Tide of Televangelism.* Reading, MA: Addison-Wesley.

Hartmann, Heidi I., et al. 1985. "An agenda for basic research on comparable worth," in H. I. Hartmann et al., eds., *Comparable Worth: New Directions for Research.* Washington, DC: National Academy Press.

Harvard Magazine. 2000. "The world's poor: A Harvard Magazine roundtable." *Harvard Magazine,* vol. 103, no. 2. www.harvard-magazine.com/on-line/1100134.html, accessed 1/11/03.

Harvey, David. 1973. *Social Justice and the City.* Oxford, UK: Blackwell.

———. 1982. *The Limits to Capital.* Oxford, UK: Blackwell.

———. 1985. *Consciousness and the Urban Experience: Studies in the History and Theory of Capitalist Urbanization.* Oxford, UK: Blackwell.

———. 1989. *The Condition of Postmodernity.* Cambridge, MA: Blackwell.

Hathaway. 1997. "Marijuana and tolerance: Revisiting Becker's sources of control." *Deviant Behavior,* vol. 18, no. 2.

Haugen, Einar. 1977. "Linguistic relativity: Myths and methods," in William C. McCormack and Stephen A. Wurm, eds., *Language and Thought: Anthropological Issues.* The Hague: Mouton.

Hauser, Robert M. 1999. "What if we ended social promotion?" *Education Week* (April 7).

Hawkes, Terence. 1977. *Structuralism and Semiotics.* Berkeley, CA: University of California Press.

Hawley, Amos H. 1950. *Human Ecology: A Theory of Community Structure.* New York: Ronald Press Company.

———. 1968. "Human ecology," in *International Encyclopedia of Social Science,* vol. 4. New York: Free Press.

Hayflick, Leonard. 1994. *How and Why We Age.* New York: Ballantine Books.

Hays, Sharon. 2000. "Constructing the centrality of culture—and deconstructing sociology?" *Contemporary Sociology,* vol. 29, no. 4.

Health Care Financing Administration (HCFA). 1997. Medicare. www.hcfa.gov/stats/hstats96/stathili. htm.

Healy, Melissa. 2001. "Pieces of the puzzle." *Los Angeles Times,* http://pqasb.pqarchiver.com/latimes/results.html?RQT=511&sid=1&firstIndex=460&PQACnt=1, accessed 1/10/05.

Heaven's Gate. 1997. Mirror of original Web site is available at TELAH Services, www.wave.net/upg/gate/, accessed 1/11/05.

Hebdige, Dick. 1987. *Cut 'n' Mix: Culture, Identity, and Caribbean Music.* London: Methuen.

Heelas, Paul. 1996. *The New Age Movement.* Oxford: Blackwell.

Heidensohn, Frances. 1985. *Women and Crime.* London: Macmillan.

Heise, David R. 1987. "Sociocultural determination of mental aging," in Carmi Schooler and K. Warner Schaie, eds., *Cognitive Functioning and Social Structure Over the Life Course.* Norwood, NJ: Ablex.

Held, David. 1987. *Models of Democracy.* Stanford, CA: Stanford University Press.

———, et al. 1999. *Global Transformations: Politics, Economics, and Culture.* Cambridge, UK: Polity Press.

Helm, Leslie. 1992. "Debt puts squeeze on Japanese." *Los Angeles Times,* November 21.

Hellman, Christopher. 2003. "Last of the big spenders: U.S. military budget still the world's largest, and growing," Washington, D.C.: Center for Defense Information (May 19). http://www.cdi.org/program/document.cfm?DocumentID=1040&StartRow=1&ListRows=10&appendURL=&Orderby=D.DateLastUpdated&ProgramID=15&from_page=index.cfm, accessed 1/3/05.

Henderson, Jeffrey. 1989. *The Globalization of High Technology Production: Society, Space, and Semiconductors in the Restructuring of the Modern World.* London: Routledge.

———; and Appelbaum, Richard P. 1992. "Situating the state in the Asian development process," in Richard P. Appelbaum and Jeffrey Henderson, eds., *States and Development in the Asian Pacific Rim.* Newbury Park, CA: Sage.

Hendricks, Jon. 1992. "Generation and the generation of theory in social gerontology." *Aging and Human Development,* vol. 35.

———; and Hendricks, C. Davis. 1986. *Aging in Mass Society: Myths and Realities.* Boston: Little, Brown.

Henry, William E. 1965. *Growing Older: The Process of Disengagement.* New York: Basic Books.

Henslin, James M.; and Biggs, Mae A. 1971. "Dramaturgical desexualization: The sociology of the vaginal examination," in James M. Henslin, ed., *Studies in the Sociology of Sex.* New York: Appleton-Century-Crofts.

———. 1997. "Behavior in public places: The sociology of the vaginal examination," in James M. Henslin, ed., *Down to Earth Sociology: Introductory Readings.* 9th ed. New York: Free Press.

Hentoff, Nat. 2002. "The FBI's magic lantern: Ashcroft can be in your computer," *The Village Voice,* May 24.

Herdt, Gilbert. 1981. *Guardians of the Flutes: Idioms of Masculinity.* New York: McGraw-Hill.

———. 1984. *Ritualized Homosexuality in Melanesia.* Berkeley, CA: University of California Press.

———. 1986. *The Sambia: Ritual and Gender in New Guinea.* New York: Holt, Rinehart and Winston.

———; and Davidson, J. 1988. "The Sambia 'urnim-man': Sociocultural and clinical aspects of gender formation in Papua, New Guinea." *Archives of Sexual Behavior,* vol. 17.

Heritage, John. 1985. *Garfinkel and Ethnomethodology.* New York: Basil Blackwell.

Hernandez, D. J. 1993. *America's Children: Resources from Family, Government, and Economy.* New York: Russell Sage Foundation.

Herrnstein, Richard J.; and Murray, Charles. 1994. *The Bell Curve: Intelligence and Class Structure in American Life.* New York: Free Press.

Hess, John L. 1990. "The catastrophic health care fiasco." *The Nation,* vol. 250.

Hesse-Biber, Sharlene. 1997. *Am I Thin Enough Yet?: The Cult of Thinness and the Commercialization of Identity.* New York: Oxford University Press.

Hexham, Irvine; and Poewe, Karla. 1997. *New Religions as Global Cultures.* Boulder, CO: Westview Press.

Higginbotham, Elizabeth. 1992. "Making up with kin and community: Upward social mobility for black and white women." *Gender and Society,* vol. 6, no. 3.

Higher Education Research Institute (HERI). 1990. "The American freshman." Los Angeles: University of California.

Hirsch, Barry T.; and Macpherson, David A. 2004. "Union membership, coverage, density, and employment among all wage and salary workers, 1973–2003." www.trinity.edu/bhirsch/unionstats/All%20Wage%20and%20Salary%20Workers.xls, accessed 1/3/05.

Hirshci, Travis. 1969. *Causes of Delinquency.* Berkeley, CA: University of California Press.

Hirst, Paul. 1997. "The global economy: Myths and realities." *International Affairs,* vol. 73.

———; and Thompson, Grahame. 1992. "The problem of 'globalization': International economic relations, national economic management, and the formation of trading blocs." *Economy and Society,* vol. 24.

———. 1999. *Globalization in Question: The International Economy and the Possibilities of Governance.* Rev. ed. Cambridge, UK: Polity Press.

Ho, S. Y. 1990. *Taiwan: After a Long Silence.* Hong Kong: Asia Monitor Resource Center.

Hochschild, Arlie Russell. 1975. "Disengagement theory: A critique and proposal." *American Sociological Review,* vol. 40.

———. 1983. *The Managed Heart: Commercialization of Human Feeling.* Berkeley, CA: University of California Press.

———. 1997. *The Time Bind.* New York: Metropolitan Books.

———; with Machung, Anne. 1989. *The Second Shift: Working Parents and the Revolution at Home.* New York: Viking.

Hodge, Robert; and Tripp, David. 1986. *Children and Television: A Semiotic Approach.* Cambridge, MA: Polity Press.

Hofstede, Geert. 1997. *Culture's Consequences: International Differences in Work-Related Values.* Newbury Park: Sage.

Hogan, Beatrice. 2000. "U.N.: Women's conference presses for political parity." Radio Free Europe, June.

Holmes, L. D. 1983. *Other Cultures, Elder Years: An Introduction to Cultural Gerontology.* Minneapolis: Burgess.

Holmes, Steven A. 1996. "Quality of life is up for many blacks, data say." *New York Times,* November 18, p. A1.

———. 1997. "New reports say minorities benefit in fiscal recovery." *New York Times,* September 30, p. A1.

Holton, Robert J. 1978. "The crowds in history: Some problems of theory and method." *Social History,* vol. 3.

Homans, George. 1950. *The Human Group.* New York: Harcourt, Brace.

Homans, Hilary. 1987. "Man-made myth: The reality of being a woman scientist in the NHS," in Anne Spencer and David Podmore, eds., *In a Man's World: Essays on Women in Male-Dominated Professions.* London: Tavistock.

Honda Worldwide. 2002. "Honda Accord best-selling car in 2001 regains title after a decade." http://world.honda.com/news/2002/c020103_2.html, accessed 1/3/05.

Hooks, Bell. 1981. *Ain't I a Woman: Black Women and Feminism.* Boston: South End Press.

———. 1996. *Bone Black: Memories of Girlhood.* New York: Henry Holt.

Hopkins, Terence K.; and Wallerstein, Immanuel. 1996. *The Age of Transition: Trajectory of the World-System, 1945–2025.* London: Zed Books.

Horrigan, John, et al. 2003. *The Ever-Shifting Internet Population: A New Look at Internet Access and the Digital Divide.* Washington, D.C.: The PEW Internet and American Life Project (April 16). www.pewinternet.org/ppt/PIP_Ever_Shifting_Internet_Pop_NCI_NIH%206.25.03nn2.ppt, accessed 1/10/05.

Hotz, Robert Lee. 1998. "Boomers firing magic bullets at signs of aging." *Los Angeles Times,* May 4.

Hout, Michael. 1988. "More universalism, less structural mobility: The American occupational structure in the 1980s." *American Journal of Sociology,* vol. 93.

———. 1997. "Inequality at the margins: The effects of welfare, the minimum wage, and tax credits on low-wage labor markets." *Politics and Society* vol. 25 (December): 513–24.

———; and Lucas, Samuel R. 1996. "Education's role in reducing income disparities." *The Education Digest,* vol. 62, no. 3.

Howard, John H., et al. 1986. "Change in Type A behavior a year after retirement." *Gerontologist,* vol. 26.

Huber, Joan. 1990. "Macro-micro link in gender stratification," *American Sociological Review,* vol. 55.

———, ed. 1992. *Micro-Macro Linkages in Sociology.* Newbury Park, CA: Sage.

Hudson, Terese. 1995. "Medicaid's new crisis: Are we pitting the elderly against the poor?" *Hospitals and Health Networks,* May 20.

Hughes, Everett C. 1945. "Dilemmas and contradictions of status." *American Journal of Sociology,* vol. 50.

Hughes, Gordon. 1991. "Taking crime seriously?: A critical analysis of new left realism." *Sociology Review,* vol. 1.

Human Rights Watch. 1995. "The global report on women's human rights," www.hrw.org/about/projects/womrep/, accessed 1/3/05.

Humphreys, Laud. 1970. *Tearoom Trade: Impersonal Sex in Public Places.* Chicago: Aldine.

Hunter, James Davison. 1987. *Evangelism: The Coming Generation.* Chicago: University of Chicago Press.

Hunter, Lisa. 1990. *After Bereavement: A Study of Change in Attitudes about Life among Older Widows.* Ph.D. diss., The Fielding Institute, Santa Barbara, CA.

Huntington, Samuel P. 1991. *The Third Wave: Democratization in the Late Twentieth Century.* Norman, OK: University of Oklahoma Press.

———. 1996. *The Clash of Civilizations and the Remaking of World Order.* New York: Simon and Schuster.

Hurtado, A. 1995. "Variation, combinations, and evolutions: Latino families in the United States," in R. Zambrana, ed., *Understanding Latino Families.* Thousand Oaks, CA: Sage.

Hyman, Herbert H.; and Singer, Eleanor. 1968. *Readings in Reference Group Theory and Research.* New York: Free Press.

Hyman, Richard. 1984. *Strikes.* 2nd ed. London: Fontana.

Illich, Ivan D. 1983. *Deschooling Society.* New York: Harper and Row.

Infoplease.com. 2003. "Educational Attainment by Race and Hispanic Origin, 1940–2001" www.infoplease.com/ipa/A0774057.html, accessed 1/3/05.

Inglehart, Ronald. 1997. *Modernization and Postmodernization: Cultural, Economic and Political Change in 43 Societies.* Princeton, NJ: Princeton University Press.

Intelligence Report. 2001. "Reevaluating the Net." Summer, no. 102. Montgomery, AL: The Southern Poverty Law Center.

International Campaign to Ban Land Mines (ICBL). 2001. www.icbl.org, accessed 1/3/05.

———. 2003. "Ratifications update" www.icbl.org, accessed 1/3/05.

International Labor Organization (ILO). 1995. "Women work more, but are still paid less." Press release. www.ilo.org/public/english/bureau/pr/1995/22.htm, accessed 1/11/05.

———. 1997. "Women's progress in workforce improving worldwide, but occupational segregation still rife: 'Glass ceiling' separates women from top jobs." Geneva: ILO press release ILO/97/35. www.ilo.org/public/english/bureau/inf/pr/1997/35.htm, accessed 1/11/05.

———. 1999. C182 Worst Forms of Child Labour Convention, www.ilo.org/public/english/standards/ipec/ratification/convention/text.htm, accessed 1/11/05.

———. 2000. "Statistical information and monitoring programme on child labour (SIMPOC): Overview and strategic plan 2000–2002." Prepared by the International Program on the Elimination of Child Labour (IPEC) and Bureau of Statistics (STAT), January.

———. 2003a. "Facts on Women at Work" www.ilo.org/public/english/bureau/inf/download/women/pdf/factssheet.pdf, accessed 1/3/05.

———. 2003b. LABORSTA. http://laborsta.ilo.org/, accessed 1/3/05.

International Lesbian and Gay Association (ILGA). 2001. www.ilga.org, accessed 1/3/05.

International Telework Association & Council (ITAC). 2004. "Telework Facts and Figures," www.telecommute.org/resources/abouttelework.htm, accessed 1/20/05.

Internet Society (ISOC). 1997. "Web Languages Hit Parade," http://alis.isoc.org/palmares.en.html, accessed 1/11/05.

Iyer, Pico. 1989. *Video Nights in Katmandu.* New York: Vintage.

Jacobs, Jane. 1961. *The Death and Life of Great American Cities.* New York: Random House.

Jacoby, Sanford. 1997. *Modern Manors: Welfare Capitalism since the New Deal.* Princeton, NJ: Princeton University Press.

Jaher, Frederic Cople, ed. 1973. *The Rich, the Well Born, and the Powerful.* Urbana, IL: University of Illinois Press.

Jamieson, Amie; Shin, Hyon B.; and Day, Jennifer. 2002. "Voting and registration in the election of November 2000: Population characteristics." U.S. Department of Commerce, U.S. Census Bureau. February 2002. www.census.gov/prod/2002pubs/p20-542.pdf, accessed 1/3/05.

Janis, Irving L. 1972. *Victims of Groupthink.* Boston: Houghton Mifflin.

———. 1989. *Crucial Decisions: Leadership in Policy Making and Crisis Management.* New York: Free Press.

———; and Mann, Leon. 1977. *Decision Making: A Psychological Analysis of Conflict, Choice, and Commitment.* New York: Free Press.

Jencks, Christopher. 1994. *The Homeless.* Cambridge, MA: Harvard University Press.

———, et al. 1972. *Inequality: A Reassessment of the Effects of Family and School in America.* New York: Basic Books.

Jenkins, Henry. 1998. *From Barbie to Mortal Kombat: Gender and Computer Games.* Cambridge, MA: MIT Press.

Jensen, Arthur. 1967. "How much can we boost IQ and scholastic achievement?" *Harvard Educational Review,* vol. 29.

———. 1979. *Bias in Mental Testing.* New York: Free Press.

Jobling, Ray. 1988. "The experience of psoriasis under treatment," in Michael Bury and Robert Anderson, eds., *Living with Chronic Illness: The Experience of Patients and Their Families.* London: Unwin Hyman.

John, M. T. 1988. *Geragogy: A Theory for Teaching the Elderly.* New York: Haworth.

Johnson, Michael P. 1995. "Patriarchal terrorism and common couple violence: Two forms of violence against women in U.S. families." *Journal of Marriage and the Family,* vol. 57.

Johnson, M.; and Morton, J. 1991. *Biology and Cognitive Development: The Case of Face Recognition.* Oxford, UK: Blackwell.

Johnson-Odim, Cheryl. 1991. "Common themes, different contexts: Third World women and feminism," in Chandra Mohanty, et al., eds., *Third World Women and the Politics of Feminism.* Bloomington, IN: Indiana University Press.

———; and Strobel, Margaret, eds. 1992. *Expanding the Boundaries of Women's History: Essays on Women in the Third World.* Bloomington, IN: Indiana University Press.

Johnston, Hank; Larana, Enrique; and Gusfield, Joseph R. 1994. "Identities, grievances, and new social movements," in Enrique Larana, Hank Johnston, and Joseph R. Gusfield (eds.), *New Social Movements: From Ideology to Identity.* Philadelphia, PA: Temple University Press.

Joint Center for Housing Studies. 1994. *The State of the Nation's Housing.* Cambridge, MA: Harvard University Press.

Jones, Eric. 1998. "Globalism and the American tide." *National Interest,* vol. 53 (fall).

Jones, Jacqueline. 1986. *Labor of Love, Labor of Sorrow: Black Women, Work, and the Family from Slavery to the Present.* New York: Random House.

Jones, S. G. 1995. "Understanding community in the information age." in S. G. Jones, ed., *CyberSociety: Computer-Mediated Communication and Community.* Thousand Oaks, CA: Sage.

Jordan, Winthrop. 1968. *White over Black.* Chapel Hill: University of North Carolina Press.

Judd, Dennis R.; and Fainstein, Susan S., eds. 1999. *The Tourist City.* New Haven, CT: Yale University Press.

Judge, Ken. 1995. "Income distribution and life expectancy: A critical appraisal." *British Medical Journal,* vol. 311.

Juergensmeyer, Mark. 1993. *The New Cold War? Religious Nationalism Confronts the Secular State.* Berkeley, CA: University of California Press.

———. 2001. *Terror in the Mind of God: The Global Rise of Religious Violence.* Berkeley, CA: University of California Press.

Kamin, Leon J. 1974. *The Science and Politics of IQ.* Hillsdale, NJ: Erlbaum.

Kanter, Rosabeth Moss. 1977. *Men and Women of the Corporation.* New York: Basic Books.

———. 1983. *The Change Masters: Innovation for Productivity in the American Corporation.* New York: Simon and Schuster.

———. 1991. "The future of bureaucracy and hierarchy in organizational theory," in Pierre Bourdieu and James Coleman, eds., *Social Theory for a Changing Society.* Boulder, CO: Westview.

Kasarda, John. 1993. "Urban industrial transition and the underclass," in William Julius Wilson, ed., *The Ghetto Underclass.* Newbury Park, CA: Sage.

———; and Crenshaw, Edward M. 1991. "Third World urbanization: Dimensions, theories, and determinants," in *Annual Review of Sociology 1991.* Vol. 17. Palo Alto, CA: Annual Reviews.

———; and Janowitz, Morris. 1974. "Community attachment in mass society." *American Sociological Review,* vol. 39.

Katz, Jack. 1999. *How Emotions Work.* Chicago: University of Chicago Press.

Katz, Sidney, et al. 1983. "Active life expectancy." *New England Journal of Medicine,* vol. 309.

Kautsky, John J. 1982. *The Politics of Aristocratic Empires.* Chapel Hill, NC: University of North Carolina Press.

Kearny and *Foreign Policy.* 2001. "Measuring Globalization." A. T. Kearney, Inc. and *Foreign Policy* (January–February).

Kedouri, Elie. 1992. *Politics in the Middle East.* New York: Oxford University Press.

Keister, Lisa A. 2000. *Wealth in America: Trends in Wealth Inequality.* New York: Cambridge University Press.

Kelling, George L.; and Coles, Catherine M. 1997. *Fixing Broken Windows: Restoring Order and Reducing Crime in Our Communities.* New York: The Free Press.

Kelley, Jonathan; and Evans, M. D. R. 1995. "Class and class conflict in six western nations." *American Review of Sociology,* vol. 60, no. 2.

Kelly, Liz. 1987. "The continuum of sexual violence," in Jala Hanmer and Mary Maynard, eds., *Women, Violence, and Social Control.* Atlantic Highlands, NJ: Humanities Press.

Kelly, Michael P. 1992. *Colitis: The Experience of Illness.* London: Routledge.

Kelsey, Tim. 1996. "I want to live forever." *Sunday Times News Review,* January 7.

Kemp, Amanda, et al. 1995. "The dawn of a new day: Redefining South African feminism," in Amrita Basu, ed., *The Challenge of Local Feminisms.* Boulder, CO: Westview.

Kenway, Jane, et al. 1995. "Pulp fictions?: Education, markets, and the information superhighway." *Australian Educational Researcher,* vol. 22.

Kenworthy, Lane; and Malami, Melissa. 1999. "Gender inequality in political representation: A worldwide comparative analysis." *Social Forces,* vol. 78, no. 1.

Kern, Steven. 1983. *The Culture of Time and Space: 1880–1918.* Cambridge, MA: Harvard University Press.

Kerr, Clark, et al. 1960. *Industrialism and Industrial Man: The Problems of Labor and Management in Economic Growth.* Cambridge, MA: Harvard University Press.

Kiecolt, K. Jill; and Nelson, Hart M. 1991. "Evangelicals and party realignment, 1976–1988," *Social Science Quarterly,* vol. 72 (September).

King, Nancy R. 1984. "Exploitation and abuse of older family members: An overview of the problem," in J. J. Cosa, ed., *Abuse of the Elderly.* Lexington, MA: Lexington Books.

Kinsey, Alfred C., et al. 1948. *Sexual Behavior in the Human Male.* Philadelphia: Saunders.

———. 1953. *Sexual Behavior in the Human Female.* Philadelphia: Saunders.

Kinsley, David. 1982. *Hinduism: A Cultural Perspective.* Englewood Cliffs, NJ: Prentice Hall.

Kjekshus, H. 1977. *Ecology, Control, and Economic Development in East African History.* Berkeley, CA: University of California Press.

Kling, Robert. 1996. "Computerization at work," in R. Kling, ed., *Computers and Controversy.* 2nd ed. New York: Academic Press.

Kluckhohn, Clyde. 1949. *Mirror for Man.* Tucson: University of Arizona Press.

Knight, F. H. 1933. *Risk, Uncertainty, and Profit.* London: London School of Economics and Political Science.

Knoke, David. 1990. *Political Networks: The Structural Perspective.* New York: Cambridge University Press.

Knorr-Cetina, Karen; and Cicourel, Aaron V., eds. 1981. *Advances in Social Theory and Methodology: Towards an Integration of Micro- and Macro-Sociologies.* Boston: Routledge and Kegan Paul.

Kohn, Melvin. 1977. *Class and Conformity,* 2nd ed. Homewood, IL: Dorsey Press.

Kollock, P.; and Smith, M. A. 1996. "Managing the virtual commons: Cooperation and conflict in computer communities," in S. Herring, ed., *Computer-Mediated Communication.* Amsterdam: John Benjamins.

Kosmin, Barry A. 1991. *Research Report: The National Survey of Religious Identification.* New York: City University of New York Graduate Center.

———; Mayer, Egon; and Keysar, Ariela. 2001. *American Religious Identification Survey (ARIS).* New York: CUNY Graduate Center (December 19). www.gc.cuny.edu/studies/aris.pdf, accessed 1/3/05.

Kozol, Jonathan. 1991. *Savage Inequalities: Children in America's Schools.* New York: Crown.

Kroeger, Brooke. 2004. "When a dissertation makes a difference," *New York Times,* March 20.

Krueger, Colleen. 1995. "Retirees with company heath plans on decline." *Los Angeles Times,* September 22.

Kulkarni, V. G. 1993. "The productivity paradox: Rising output, stagnant living standards." *BusinessWeek,* February 8.

Kuznets, Simon. 1955. "Economic growth and income inequality." *Economic Review,* vol. XLV, no. 1.

Lacayo, Richard. 1994. "Lock 'em up!" *Time,* February 7.

Laing, R. D. 1971. *Self and Others.* London: Tavistock.

Lake, R. 1981. *The New Suburbanites: Race and Housing in the Suburbs.* New Brunswick, NJ: Center for Urban Policy Research, Rutgers University Press.

Lambert, Richard. 1995. "Foreign student flows and the internationalization of higher education," in Katharine Hanson and Joel Meyerson, eds., *International Challenges to American Colleges and Universities.* Phoenix: Orynx Press.

Lammers, Cristina, et al. 2000. "Influences on adolescents' decision to postpone onset of sexual intercourse: A survival analysis of virginity among youths aged 13 to 18 years." *Journal of Adolescent Health,* vol. 26, no. 1.

Land, Kenneth C.; Deane, Glenn; and Blau, Judith R. 1991. "Religious pluralism and church membership." *American Sociological Review,* vol. 56.

Landale, N., and Fennelly, K. 1992. "Informal unions among mainland Puerto Ricans: Cohabitation or an alternative to legal marriage?" *Journal of Marriage and the Family,* vol. 54.

Landes, David S. 1969. *The Unbound Prometheus.* New York: Cambridge University Press.

Landry, Bart. 1988. *The New Black Middle Class.* Berkeley, CA: University of California Press.

Lane, Harlan. 1976. *The Wild Boy of Aveyron.* Cambridge, MA: Harvard University Press.

Lane, James B. 1974. *Jacob A. Riis: The American City.* New York: Kennikat Press.

Lantenari, Vittorio. 1963. *The Religions of the Oppressed: A Study of Modern Messianic Cults.* New York: Knopf.

Lappe, France Moore, et al. 1998. *World Hunger: 12 Myths.* 2nd ed. New York: Grove Press.

Lash, Scott; and Urry, John. 1987. *The End of Organized Capitalism.* Madison, WI: University of Wisconsin Press.

Lashbrook, Jeff. 1996. "Promotional timetables: An exploratory investigation of age norms for promotional expectations and their association with job well-being." *Gerontologist,* vol. 36, no. 2.

Laslett, P. 1991. *A Fresh Map of Life.* Cambridge, MA: Harvard University Press.

Laumann, Edward O., et al. 1994. *The Social Organization of Sexuality: Sexual Practices in the United States.* Chicago: University of Chicago Press.

Lawrence, Bruce B. 1989. *Defenders of God: The Fundamentalist Revolt Against the Modern Age.* San Francisco: Harper & Row.

Lazarsfeld, Paul F.; Berelson, Bernard; and Gaudet, Hazel. 1948. *The People's Choice.* New York: Columbia University Press.

Lea, John; and Young, Jock. 1984. *What Is to Be Done about Law and Order?* London: Penguin.

Leach, Edmund. 1976. *Culture and Communication: The Logic by Which Symbols Are Connected.* New York: Cambridge University Press.

Leadbeater, Charles. 1999. *Living on Thin Air: The New Economy.* New York: Viking.

Lee, Gary. 1982. *Family Structure and Interaction: A Comparative Analysis.* 2nd ed. Minneapolis: University of Minnesota Press.

Lee, Richard B. 1968. "What hunters do for a living, or how to make out on scarce resources," in Richard B. Lee and Irven DeVore, eds., *Man the Hunter.* Chicago: Aldine.

————. 1969. "!Kung bushman subsistence: An input-output analysis," in A. P. Vayda, ed., *Environment and Cultural Behavior.* New York: Natural History Press.

Lees, Andrew. 1985. *Cities Perceived: Urban Society in European and American Thought, 1820–1940.* New York: Columbia University Press.

Lehrer, Warren; and Sloan, Judith. 2003. *Crossing the BLVD: Strangers, Neighbors, Aliens in a New America.* New York: Norton.

Lemert, Edwin. 1972. *Human Deviance, Social Problems, and Social Control.* Englewood Cliffs, NJ: Prentice-Hall.

Leonhardt, David. 2001. "Belt tightening seen as threat to the economy." *New York Times,* July 15, p. 1.

Lepkowsky, M. 1990. "Gender in an egalitarian society: A case study from the Coral Sea," in P. R. Sandy and R. G. Goodenough, eds., *Beyond the Second Sex.* Philadelphia: University of Pennsylvania Press.

Leupp, Gary P. 1995. *Male Colors, the Construction of Homosexuality in Tokugawa Japan.* Berkeley, CA: University of California Press.

Levay, Simon. 1996. *Queer Science: The Uses and Abuses of Research into Homosexuality.* Cambridge, MA: MIT Press.

Levin, William C. 1988. "Age stereotyping: College student evaluations." *Research on Aging,* vol. 10.

Lewis, Oscar. 1968. "The culture of poverty," in Daniel P. Moyhihan, ed., *On Understanding Poverty: Perspectives from the Social Sciences.* New York: Basic Books.

Liebow, Elliot. 1967. *Tally's Corner: A Study of Negro Streetcorner Men.* Boston: Little, Brown.

————. 1993. *Tell Them Who I Am: The Lives of Homeless Women.* New York: Free Press.

Lightfoot-Klein, Hanny. 1989. *Prisoners of Ritual: An Odyssey into Female Genital Circumcision in Africa.* New York: Haworth.

Lipset, Seymour Martin, ed. 1981. *Party Coalitions in the 1980s.* San Francisco: Institute for Contemporary Affairs.

————. 1991. "Comments on Luckmann," in Pierre Bourdieu and James S. Coleman, eds., *Social Theory in a Changing Society.* Boulder, CO: Westview.

————; and Bendix, Reinhard. 1959. *Social Mobility in Industrial Society.* Berkeley, CA: University of California Press.

Littlefield, Nick. 1992. "Education," in Mark Green, ed., *Changing America: Blueprint for the New Administration.* New York: New Market Press.

Locke, John. 2000. "Can a sense of community flourish in cyberspace?" *The Guardian,* March 11.

Lofland, Lyn H. 1973. *A World of Strangers.* New York: Basic Books.

————. 1998. *The Public Realm: Exploring the City's Quintessential Social Territory.* New York: Aldine de Gruyter.

Logan, John R.; and Molotch, Harvey L. 1987. *Urban Fortunes: The Political Economy of Place.* Berkeley, CA: University of California Press.

Long, Elizabeth, ed. 1997. *From Sociology to Cultural Studies: New Perspectives.* Malden, MA: Blackwell.

Longino, Charles F. 1995. *The Old Age Challenge to the Biomedical Model: Paradigm Strain and Health Policy.* Amityville, NY: Baywood Publications.

Loprest, Pamela. 1999. "Families who left welfare: Who are they and how are they doing?" Washington, DC: Urban Institute, www.urban.org/Template.cfm?NavMenuID=24&template=/TaggedContent/ViewPublication.cfm&PublicationID=7297, accessed 1/3/05.

Lorber, Judith. 1994. *Paradoxes of Gender.* New Haven, CT: Yale University Press.

Loury, Glenn. 1987. "Why should we care about group inequality?" *Social Philosophy and Policy,* vol. 5.

Lowe, Graham S. 1987. *Women in the Administrative Revolution: The Feminization of Clerical Work.* Toronto: University of Toronto Press.

Lull, James. 1991. *China Turned On: Television, Reform, and Resistance.* New York: Routledge.

Lyman, Richard. 1995. "Overview," in Katharine Hanson and Joel Meyerson, eds., *International Challenges to American Colleges and Universities.* Phoenix: Orynx Press.

Lynd, Robert; and Lynd, Helen. 1929. *Middletown: A Study in Contemporary American Culture.* New York: Harcourt, Brace, and Co.

Lyon, David. 1989. *The Information Society: Issues and Illusions.* New York: Basil Blackwell.

———. 1994. *The Electronic Eye: The Rise of Surveillance Society.* Minneapolis: University of Minnesota Press.

Lyotard, Jean-François. 1985. *The Post-Modern Condition: A Report on Knowledge.* Minneapolis: University of Minnesota Press.

Macenoin, Deni; and al-Shahi, Ahmed, eds., 1983. *Islam in the Modern World.* New York: St. Martin's Press.

Maddox, G. L. 1965. "Fact and artifact: Evidence bearing on disengagement from the Duke Geriatrics Project." *Human Development,* vol. 8.

———. 1970. "Themes and issues in sociological theories of human aging." *Human Development,* vol. 13.

Madigan, F. C. 1957. "Are sex mortality differentials biologically caused?" *Millbank Memorial Fund Quarterly,* vol. 25.

Maharidge, Dale. 1996. *The Coming White Minority.* New York: Times Books.

Malinowski, Bronislaw. 1982. *"Magic: Science and Religion" and Other Essays.* London: Souvenir Press.

Malotki, Ekkehart. 1983. *Hopi Time: A Linguistic Analysis of the Temporal Concepts in the Hopi Language.* Berlin: Mouton.

Malthus, Thomas. 2003. *Essay on the Principle of Population: A Norton Critical Edition, Revised Edition.* Ed. Philip Appleman. Originally published 1798. New York: Norton.

Manning, John T.; Koukourakis, K.; and Brodie, D. A. 1997. "Fluctuating asymmetry, metabolic rate and sexual selection in human males." *Evolution and Human Behavior,* vol. 18, no. 1.

Manpower, Inc. 2003. "Facts & Figures." www.manpower.co.uk/about_manpower/main_facts_figures.asp, accessed 1/3/05.

Manton, Kenneth G.; Corder, Larry S.; and Stallard, Eric. 1993. "Estimates of change in chronic disability and institutional incidence and prevalence rates in the U.S. elderly population from the 1982, 1984, and 1989 national long term care survey." *Journal of Gerontology,* vol. 48, no. 466.

Mare, Robert D. 1991. "Five decades of educational assortative mating." *American Sociological Review,* vol. 56, no. 1.

Marsden, Peter. 1987. "Core discussion networks of Americans." *American Sociological Review,* vol. 52.

———; and Lin, Nan. 1982. *Social Structure and Network Analysis.* Beverly Hills, CA: Sage.

Marshall, T. H. 1973. *Class, Citizenship, and Social Development: Essays by T. H. Marshall.* Westport, CT: Greenwood Press.

Martin, David. 1990. *Tongues of Fire: The Explosion of Protestantism in Latin America.* Cambridge, UK: Blackwell.

Martin, Kay; and Voorhies, Barbara. 1975. *Female of the Species.* New York: Columbia University Press.

Martin, Richard C. 1982. *Islam: A Cultural Perspective.* Englewood Cliffs, NJ: Prentice Hall.

Martineau, Harriet. 1962. *Society in America.* Originally published 1837. Garden City, NY: Doubleday.

Marty, Martin E.; and Appleby, R. Scott, eds. 1995. *Fundamentalisms Comprehended.* Chicago, IL: University of Chicago Press.

Marx, Karl. 1977. *Capital: A Critique of Political Economy.* Vol. 1. Originally published 1864. New York: Random House.

Massey, Douglas S. 1996. "The age of extremes: Concentrated affluence and poverty in the twenty-first century." *Demography,* vol. 33, no. 4.

———; and Denton, Nancy A. 1993. *American Apartheid: Segregation and the Making of the Underclass.* Cambridge, MA: Harvard University Press.

Matsueda, Ross L. 1992. "Reflected appraisals, parental labeling, and delinquency: Specifying a symbolic interactionist theory." *American Journal of Sociology,* vol. 97.

Matthews, Roger; and Young, Jock, eds. 1986. *Confronting Crime.* London: Sage.

Maugh, Thomas H., II. 1991. "Survey of identical twins links biological factors with being gay." *Los Angeles Times,* December 15.

———. 1993. "Genetic compound found in lesbianism, study says." *Los Angeles Times,* March 12.

———; and Zamichow, Nora. 1991. "Medicine: San Diego's researcher's findings offer first evidence of a biological cause for homosexuality." *Los Angeles Times,* August 30.

Mayer, Susan; and Jencks, Christopher. 1994. "Trends in the economic well-being of children." Unpublished manuscript, cited in David Whitman, "The poor aren't poorer." *U.S. News and World Report* (July 25).

McCaffrey, Barry. 1998. "Prepared statement before the senate committee on the judiciary, 6/17/98." Federal News Service, n.p.

McFadden, Dennis; and Champlin, C. A. 2000. "Comparison of auditory evoked potentials in heterosexual, homosexual, and bisexual males and females." *Journal of the Association for Research in Otolaryngology,* vol. 1.

McKinlay, J. B. 1975. "A case for refocusing downstream: The political economy of illness," in P. Conrad and R. Kern, eds., *The Sociology of Health and Illness: Critical Perspectives.* New York: St. Martin's Press.

McLanahan, Sara; and Sandefur, Gary. 1994. *Growing Up with a Single Parent: What Hurts, What Helps.* Cambridge, MA: Harvard University Press.

McLuhan, Marshall. 1964. *Understanding Media.* London: Routledge and Kegan Paul.

McMichael, Philip. 1996. *Development and Social Change: A Global Perspective.* Thousand Oaks, CA: Pine Forge.

McNeely, Connie L. 1995. *Constructing the Nation-State: International Organization and Prescriptive Action.* Westport, CT: Greenwood.

Mead, Margaret. 1963. *Sex and Temperament in Three Primitive Societies.* Originally published 1935. New York: William Morrow.

———. 1972. *Blackberry Winter: My Earlier Years.* New York: William Morrow.

Meadows, Donnella H., et al. 1972. *The Limits to Growth.* New York: Universe Books.

Meatto, Keith. 2000. "Real reformers, real results: Our seventh annual roundup of student protest." *Mojo Wire Magazine,* September–October, www.mojones.com/mother_jones/SO00/activist_campuses.html, accessed 1/3/05.

Melton, J. Gordon. 1989. *The Encyclopedia of American Religions,* 3rd ed. Detroit, MI: Gale Research Co.

———. 1996. *The Encyclopedia of American Religions,* 5th ed. Detroit, MI: Gale Research Co.

Menn, Joseph. 2003. "The 'geeks' who once shunned activism amid the digital revolution are using their money and savvy to influence public policy," *Los Angeles Times,* August 11, p. A-1.

Merkyl, Peter H.; and Smart, Ninian, eds. 1983. *Religion and Politics in the Modern World.* New York: New York University Press.

Merton, Robert K. 1957. *Social Theory and Social Structure.* Rev. ed. New York: Free Press.

———. 1968. "Social structure and anomie." Originally published 1938. *American Sociological Review,* vol. 3.

———; and Rossi, Alice Kitt. 1968. "Contributions to the theory of reference group behavior," in Robert K. Merton, ed., *Social Theory and Social Structure.* Originally published 1949. Glencoe, IL: Free Press.

Meserve, Jason. 1999. "Bush takes to the Web." *Network World Fusion News* (December 9).

Meyer, John W.; and Rowan, Brian. 1977. "Institutionalized organizations: Formal structure as myth and ceremony." *American Journal of Sociology*, vol. 83.

Michels, Robert. 1967. *Political Parties*. Originally published 1911. New York: Free Press.

Milgram, Stanley. 1963. "Behavioral studies in obedience." *Journal of Abnormal Psychology*, vol. 67.

Milkman, Ruth. 1997. *Farewell to the Factory: Auto Workers in the Late Twentieth Century*. Berkeley, CA: University of California Press.

Mills, C. Wright. 1956. *The Power Elite*. New York: Oxford University Press.

———. 1959. *The Sociological Imagination*. New York: Oxford University Press.

Mills, Theodore J. 1967. *The Sociology of Small Groups*. Englewood, NJ: Prentice-Hall.

Miner, Horace. 1956. "Body ritual among the Nacirema." *American Anthropologist*, vol. 58.

Miniter, Richard. 1997. "This generation means business." *Reader's Digest*, vol. 151.

Mintzberg, Henry. 1979. *The Structuring of Organizations*. Englewood Cliffs, NJ: Prentice-Hall.

Mirsky, Jonathan. 1982. "China and the one child family." *New Society* (February 18), no. 59.

Mirza, H. 1986. *Multinationals and the Growth of the Singapore Economy*. New York: St. Martin's Press.

Mitchell, Juliet. 1975. *Psychoanalysis and Feminism*. New York: Random House.

Mitchell, W. 1995. *City of Bits: Space, Time and the Infobahn*. Cambridge, MA: MIT Press.

Mitnick, Kevin. 2000. "They call me a criminal." *The Guardian* (February 22).

Modood, Tariq, et al. 1997. *Ethnic Minorities in Britain: Diversity and Disadvantage*. London: Policy Studies Institute.

Moen, Phyllis. 1995. "A life course approach to postretirement roles and well-being," in Lynne A. Bond, Stephen J. Cutler, and Armin Grams, eds., *Promoting Successful and Productive Aging*. Newbury Park: Sage.

———. 1996. "Changing age trends: The pyramid upside down?" in U. Bronfenbrenner, P. McClelland, E. Wethington, P. Moen, and S. J. Ceci, eds., *The State of Americans*. New York: Free Press.

Moffitt, Terrie E. 1996. "The neuropsychology of conduct disorder," in P. Cordella and L. Siegel, eds., *Readings in Contemporary Criminological Theory*. Boston: Northeastern University Press.

Mohanty, Chandra Talpade. 1991. "Under Western eyes: Feminist scholarship and colonial discourse," in Chandra Talpade Mohanty, Ann Russo, and Lourdes Torres, eds., *Third World Women and the Politics of Feminism*. Bloomington, IN: Indiana University Press.

Molnar, Alex. 1996. *Giving Kids the Business: The Commercialization of America's Schools*. Boulder, CO: Westview.

Molowe, Jill. 1994. ". . . and throw away the key." *Time* (February 7).

Money, John; and Ehrhardt, Anke A. 1972. *Man and Woman, Boy and Girl*. Baltimore: Johns Hopkins University Press.

Moore, Barrington, Jr. 1966. *Social Origins of Dictatorship and Democracy: Lord and Peasant in the Making of the Modern World*. Boston: Beacon Press.

Moore, Gwen. 1990. "Structural determinants of men's and women's personal networks." *American Sociological Review*, vol. 55.

Moore, Laurence R. 1994. *Selling God: American Religion in the Marketplace of Culture*. New York: Oxford University Press.

Morawska, Eva. 1986. *For Bread with Butter: Life Worlds of East-Central Europeans in Johnstown, Pennsylvania, 1890–1940*. New York: Cambridge University Press.

Mor-Barak, Michal E., et al. 1992. "Employment, social networks, and health in the retirement years." *International Journal of Aging and Human Development*, vol. 35.

Morgan, S. Philip, et al. 1993. "Racial differences in household and family structure at the turn of the century." *American Journal of Sociology*, vol. 98.

Morris, Jan. 1974. *Conundrum*. New York: Harcourt Brace Jovanovich.

Moss, Miriam S.; Moss, Sidney Z.; and Moles, Elizabeth L. 1985. "The quality of relationships between elderly parents and their out-of-town children." *Gerontologist*, vol. 25.

Moynihan, Daniel Patrick. 1965. *The Negro Family: A Case for National Action*. Washington, DC: U.S. Government Printing Office.

———. 1993. "Defining deviancy down." *American Scholar*, vol. 62, no. 1.

Mumford, Lewis. 1973. *Interpretations and Forecasts*. New York: Harcourt Brace Jovanovich.

Muncie, John. 1999. *Youth and Crime: A Critical Introduction*. London: Sage.

Murdock, George Peter. 1949. *Social Structure*. New York: Macmillan.

Murray, Charles A. 1984. *Losing Ground: American Social Policy, 1950–1980*. New York: Basic Books.

Najman, Jake M. 1993. "Health and poverty: past, present, and prospects for the future." *Social Science and Medicine*, vol. 36, no. 2.

Narayan, Deepa. 1999. *Can Anyone Hear Us? Voices From 47 Countries*. Washington, DC: World Bank Poverty Group, PREM (December).

National Center for Health Statistics. 2001. *Health—United States 2001/2000* Washington, DC: U.S. Government Printing Office.

———. 2000. *Health, United States 2001/2000 with Adolescent Chartbook*. Hyattsville, MD: NCHS.

———. 2002a. "New report sheds light on trends and patterns in marriage, divorce, and cohabitation." www.cdc.gov/nchs/pressroom/02news/div_mar_cohab.htm, accessed 1/10/05.

———. 2002b. "Women are having more children, new report shows teen births continue to decline." www.cdc.gov/nchs/pressroom/02news/womenbirths.htm, accessed 1/10/05.

———. 2003a. "Table 61: Current cigarette smoking by adults according to sex, race, Hispanic origin, age and education: The United States, average annual 1990–92, 1995–98 and 1999–2001." www.cdc.gov/nchs/data/hus/tables/2003/03hus061.pdf, accessed 1/3/05.

———. 2003b. "Table 68: Hypertension among persons 20 years of age and over, according to sex, age, race, and Hispanic origin: United States, 1960–62, 1971–74, 1976–80, 1988–94 and 1999–2000." www.cdc.gov/nchs/data/hus/tables/2003/03husupdated.pdf, accessed 1/10/05.

———. 2003c. "Table 80: Use of mammography for women 40 years of age and over according to selected characteristics: United States, selected years 1987–2000." www.cdc.gov/nchs/data/hus/tables/2003/03hus080.pdf, accessed 1/3/05.

———. 2003d. "Table 78: Dental visits in the past year according to selected characteristics: United States, selected years 1997–2001." www.cdc.gov/nchs/data/hus/tables/2003/03hus078.pdf, accessed 1/3/05.

———. 2003e. "Women's health." www.cdc.gov/nchs/fastats/womens_health.htm, accessed 1/11/05.

———. 2003f. "Men's Health." www.cdc.gov/nchs/fastats/men.htm, accessed 1/3/05.

National Governors Association (NGA). 2003. "Trivia." www.nga.org/governors/1,1169,C_TRIVIA^D_2117,00.html, accessed 1/3/05.

National Interfaith Committee for Worker Justice (NICWJ). 1998. "Cross border blues: A call for justice for Maquiladora workers in Tehuacán." (July) Chicago, IL: NICWJ.

National Low Income Housing Coalition (NLIHC). 2000. *Out of Reach: The Growing Gap between Housing Costs and Income of Poor People in the United States.* (September) Washington, DC: The National Low Income Housing Coalition/Low Income Housing Information Service, www.nlihc.org/oor2000/index.htm, accessed 1/3/05.

National Opinion Research Center. 1994, 1998. *General Social Survey.* Chicago: National Opinion Research Center.

National Research Council. 1994. *Information Technology in the Service Society.* Washington, DC: National Academy Press.

NCES. 2000. *Teachers' Tools for the 21st Century: A Report on Teachers' Use of Technology.* National Center for Education Statistics, Office of Educational Research and Improvement, U.S. Department of Education. NCES 2000-102 (September) http://nces.ed.gov/pubs2000/2000102.pdf, accessed 1/3/05.

Negroponte, Nicholas. 1995. *Being Digital.* London: Hodder and Stoughton.

Nelson, E. Anne; and Dannefer, Dale. 1992. "Aged heterogeneity: Fact or fiction? The fate of diversity in gerontological research." *Gerontologist,* vol. 32.

NES. 2003. "The NES Guide to Public Opinion and Electoral Behavior, The National Election Studies, Graph 5A.1.2," Center for Political Studies, University of Michigan. Ann Arbor, MI: University of Michigan, Center for Political Studies. www.umich.edu/~nes/nesguide/graphs/g5a_1_2.htm, accessed 1/3/05.

———. 2003. *The National Election Studies,* "The NES Guide to Public Opinion and Electoral Behavior—Voter Turnout 1948–2002," Table 6A.2. www.umich.edu/~nes/nesguide/toptable/tab6a_2.htm, accessed 1/3/05.

Neuman, Johanna. 2003. "Liberals take a cue from Republicans and turn to big donors to set up think tanks and media outlets to counter the conservative message," *Los Angeles Times,* November 30, p. A-20.

Newman, Katherine S. 2000. *No Shame in My Game: The Working Poor in the Inner City.* New York: Vintage.

New York City Gay and Lesbian Anti-Violence Project. 1996. *Project Annual Report.* www.avp.org, accessed 1/3/05.

Niebuhr, H. Richard. 1929. *The Social Sources of Denominationalism.* New York: Holt.

Nielsen Media Research. 2001a. Nielsen/NetRatings, Weekly Top 10 Usage Data, May 3, www.nielsen-netratings.com, accessed 1/3/05.

———. 2001b. "Internet access for blue collar workers spikes 52 percent, according to Nielsen/Net-ratings," http://209.249.142.22/press_releases/ PDF/pr_010412.pdf, accessed 5/3/01.

———. 2001c. "Lower income surfers are the fastest growing group on the web, according to Nielsen/Netratings." http://209.249.142.22/press_releases/PDF/pr_010313.pdf, accessed 5/3/01.

Nielson, Francois. 1994. "Income inequality and industrial development: Dualism revisited." *American Sociological Review,* vol. 59 (October).

Nordhaus, W. D. 1975. "The political business cycle." *Review of Economic Studies,* vol. 42.

Nua.com. 2000. www.nua.ie/surveys/how_many_online/ index.html, accessed 1/3/05.

Nye, Joseph. 1997. "In government we don't trust." *Foreign Affairs* (fall).

Oakes, Jeannie. 1985. *Keeping Track: How Schools Structure Inequality.* New Haven, CT: Yale University Press.

———. 1990. *Multiplying Inequalities: The Effects of Race, Social Class, and Tracking on Opportunities to Learn Mathematics and Science.* Santa Monica, CA: Rand.

Oakley, Ann. 1974. *the Sociology of Housework.* New York: Pantheon.

———, et al. 1994. "Life stress, support, and class inequality: Explaining the health of women and children." *European Journal of Public Health,* vol. 4.

Offe, Claus. 1984. *Contradictions of the Welfare State.* Cambridge, MA: MIT Press.

———. 1985. *Disorganized Capitalism.* Cambridge, MA: MIT Press.

Ohmae, Kenichi. 1990. *The Borderless World: Power and Strategy in the Industrial Economy.* New York: HarperCollins.

———. 1995. *The End of the Nation State: The Rise of Regional Economies.* New York: Free Press.

Oliver, Melvin L.; and Shapiro, Thomas M. 1995. *Black Wealth/White Wealth: A New Perspective on Racial Inequality.* New York: Routledge.

Olson, M. H. 1989. "Work at home for computer professionals." *ACM Trans. Inf. Sys.,* vol. 7, no. 4.

———; and Primps, S. B. 1984. "Working at home with computers." *Journal of Social Issues,* vol. 40, no. 3.

Omi, Michael; and Winant, Howard. 1994. *Racial Formation in the United States: From the 1960s to the 1990s.* 2nd ed. New York: Routledge.

Oppenheimer, Valerie K. 1970. *The Female Labor Force in the United States.* Westport, CT: Greenwood Press.

———. 1988. "A theory of marriage timing." *American Journal of Sociology,* vol. 94.

Organization for Economic Cooperation and Development (OECD). 1996. *OECD Tourism Statistics.* Paris: OECD.

———. 2003. "OECD economic outlook, June, no. 73, annex table 26: General government total outlays."

Orloff, Ann Shola. 1993. *The Politics of Pensions: A Comparative Analysis of Britain, Canada, and the United States, 1880–1940.* Madison, WI: University of Wisconsin Press.

Ortiz, V. 1995. "The diversity of Latino families," in R. Zambrana, ed., *Understanding Latino Families.* Thousand Oaks, CA: Sage.

Ouchi, William G. 1979. "A conceptual framework for the design of organizational control mechanisms." *Management Science,* vol. 25.

———. 1982. *Theory Z: How American Business Can Meet the Japanese Challenge.* New York: Avon.

Packer, George. 2003. "Smart-mobbing the war," *New York Times,* May 9.

Pager, Devah. 2003. "The mark of a criminal record," *American Journal of Psychology* vol. 108, no. 5: 937–75.

Pahl, Jan. 1989. *Money and Marriage.* London: Macmillan.

Palley, Marian Lief. 1987. "The women's movement in recent American politics," in Sara E. Rix, *The American Woman, 1987–1988.* New York: Norton.

Palmore, Erdman B., et al. 1985. *Retirement: Causes and Consequences.* New York: Springer.

Paludi, Michele A., and Barickman, Richard B. 1991. *Academic and Workplace Sexual Harassment: A Resource Manual.* Albany, NY: SUNY Press.

Park, Robert E. 1952. *Human Communities: The City and Human Ecology.* New York: Free Press.

Parkin, Frank. 1971. *Class Inequality and Political Order: Social Stratification in*

Capitalist and Communist Societies. New York: Praeger.

———. 1979. *Marxism and Class Theory: A Bourgeois Critique.* London: Tavistock.

Parry, Noel; and Parry, Jose. 1976. *The Rise of the Medical Profession.* London: Croom Helm.

Parsons, Talcott. 1951. *The Social System.* Glencoe, IL: Free Press.

———. 1960. "Towards a healthy maturity." *Journal of Health and Social Behavior,* vol. 1.

———. 1964. *The Social System.* New York: Free Press.

———; and Bales, Robert F. 1955. *Family, Socialization, and Interaction Process.* Glencoe, IL: Free Press.

Pascoe, Eva. 2000. "Can a sense of community flourish in cyberspace?" *The Guardian* (March 11).

Patterson, Orlando. 1999. "When 'they' are 'us.'" *New York Times,* April 30, p. A31.

Paul, Diana Y. 1985. *Women in Buddhism: Images of the Feminine in the Mahayana Tradition.* Berkeley, CA: University of California Press.

Pearce, Frank. 1976. *Crimes of the Powerful: Marxism, Crime, and Deviance.* London: Pluto Press.

Perlmutter, Howard V. 1972. "Towards research on and development of nations, unions, and firms as worldwide institutions," in H. Gunter, ed., *Transnational Industrial Relations.* New York: St. Martin's Press.

Peterson, Candida C.; and Peterson, James L. 1988. "Older men's and women's relationships with adult kin: How equitable are they?" *International Journal of Aging and Human Development,* vol. 27.

Peterson, Richard. 1996. "A re-evaluation of the economic consequences of divorce." *American Sociological Review,* vol. 61.

Pew. 2003a. "The 2004 political landscape: evenly divided and increasingly polarized," The PEW Research Center for the People and the Press (November 5). http://people-press.org/reports/display. php3?ReportID=196, accessed 1/3/05.

———. 2003b. *Views of a Changing World 2003,* Washington, D.C.: The Pew Research Center for the People and the Press (June 3). http://people-press.org/ reports/pdf/185.pdf, accessed 1/3/05 topline survey results http://people-press.org/reports/pdf/185topline.pdf, accessed 1/3/05.

Pilkington, Edward. 1992. "Hapless democratic experiment." *The Guardian* (January 28).

Pillemer, Karl. 1985. "The dangers of dependency: New findings in domestic violence against the elderly." *Social Problems,* vol. 33.

———; and Finkelhor, David. 1988. "The prevalence of elder abuse: A random sample survey." *Gerontologist,* vol. 28.

Pinkney, A. 1984. *The Myth of Black Progress.* New York: Cambridge University Press.

Pintor, Rafael López; and Gratschew, Maria. 2002. *Voter Turnout Since 1945: A Global Report.* Stockholm, Sweden: International Institute for Democracy and Electoral Assistance (International IDEA). www.idea.int/publications/turnout/VT_ screenopt_2002.pdf, accessed 1/3/05.

Piore, Michael J.; and Sabel, Charles F. 1984. *The Second Industrial Divide: Possibilities for Prosperity.* New York: Basic Books.

Plett, P. C. 1990. *Training Report: Training of Older Workers in Industrialized Countries.* Geneva: International Labor Organization.

———; and Lester, B. T. 1991. *Training for Older People: A Handbook.* Geneva: International Labor Organization.

Plummer, Kenneth. 1975. *Sexual Stigma: An Interactive Account.* Boston: Routledge and Kegan Paul.

PoliticalMoneyLine. 2003. "Federal Lobby Directory" (December 14) www.tray.com, accessed 1/3/05.

Pollak, Otto. 1950. *The Criminality of Women.* Philadelphia: University of Pennsylvania Press.

Polletta, Francesca; and Jasper, James M. 2001. "Collective Identity and Social Movements," *Annual Review of Sociology* vol. 27: 283–305.

Popenoe, David. 1993. "American family decline, 1960–1990: A review and appraisal." *Journal of Marriage and Family,* vol. 55.

———. 1996. *Life without Father: Compelling New Evidence That Fatherhood and Marriage Are Indispensable for the Good of Children and Society.* New York: Martin Kessler Books.

Portes, Alejandro; and Stepik, Alex. 1993. *City on the Edge: The Transformation of Miami.* Berkeley, CA: University of California Press.

Potter, Karl H. 1992. "Hinduism," in the *American Academic Encyclopedia* (online edition). Danbury, CT: Grolier Electronic.

Powell, W. W.; and Brantley, P. 1992. "Competitive cooperation in biotechnology: Learning through networks?" in N. Nohria and R. Eccles, eds., *Networks and Organizations: Structure, Form and Action.* Boston: Harvard Business School Press.

———; Koput, K. W.; and Smith-Doerr, L. 1996. "Interorganizational collaboration and the locus of innovation: Networks of learning in biotechnology." *Administration Science Quarterly,* vol. 41.

Pratt, Joanne H. 2003. *Teleworking Comes of Age with Broadband.* International Telework Association & Council, www.telecommute.org/pdf/TWA2003_ Executive_Summary.pdf, accessed 1/20/05.

Prebisch, Raul. 1967. *Hacia una dinamica del desarollo Latinoamericano.* Montevideo, Uruguay: Ediciones de la Banda Oriental.

———. 1971. *Change and Development—Latin America's Great Task: Report Submitted to the Inter-American Bank.* New York: Praeger.

President's Commission on Organized Crime. 1986. *Records of Hearings, June 24–26, 1985.* Washington, DC: U.S. Government Printing Office.

Provenzo, Eugene F., Jr. 1991. *Video Kids: Making Sense of Nintendo.* Cambridge, MA: Harvard University Press.

Public Broadcasting System (PBS). 2003. "AOL/Time-Warner merger." www.pbs. org/newshour/bb/business/aol_time_ index.html, accessed 1/3/05.

Purser, Gretchen; Schalet, Amy; and Sharone, Ofer. 2004. *Berkeley's Betrayal: Wages and Working Conditions at Cal.* Berkeley, CA: University Labor Research Project.

Putnam, Robert. 1993. "The prosperous community: Social capital and public life." *American Prospect,* vol. 13.

———. 1995. "Bowling alone: America's declining social capital." *Journal of Democracy,* vol. 6.

———. 2000. *Bowling Alone: The Collapse and Revival of American Community.* New York: Simon and Schuster.

Quadagno, Jill. 1989. "Generational equity and the politics of the welfare state." *Politics and Society,* vol. 17.

Quah, Danny. 1999. *The Weightless Economy in Economic Development.* London: Centre for Economic Performance.

Quinn, Joseph F.; and Burkhauser, Richard V. 1994. "Retirement and labor force behavior of the elderly," in Linda G. Martin and Samuel H. Preston, eds., *Demography of Aging.* Washington, DC: National Academy Press.

Rader Programs. 2003. "Prevalence and Outcome." www.raderprograms.com/ prevalen.htm, accessed 1/3/05.

Raines, Pat; and Leathers, Charles G. 2001. "Telecommuting: The New Wave of Workplace Technology Will Create a Flood of Change in Social Institutions," *Journal of Economic Issues,* vol. 35.

Rainie, Lee; Fox, Susannah; and Fallows, Deborah. 2003. *The Internet and the Iraq*

War: How Online Americans Have Used the Internet to Learn War News, Understand Events, and Promote Their Views . Washington, D.C.: The PEW Internet and American Life Project. http://www. pewinternet.org/PPF/r/87/report_display. asp, accessed 1/10/05.

Ramirez, Francisco O.; and Boli, John. 1987. "The political construction of mass schooling: European origins and worldwide institutionalism." *Sociology of Education,* vol. 60.

Ranis, Gustav. 1996. "Will Latin America now put a stop to 'stop-and-go?' " New Haven, CT: Yale University, Economic Growth Center.

——; and Mahmood, Syed Akhtar. 1992. *The Political Economy of Development Policy Change.* Cambridge, MA: Blackwell.

Redding, S. G. 1990. *The Spirit of Chinese Capitalism.* Berlin: De Gruyter.

Redman, Peter. 1996. "Empowering men to disempower themselves: Heterosexual masculinities, HIV, and the contradictions of anti-oppressive education," in Mairtin Mac an Ghaill, ed., *Understanding Masculinities.* Buckingham, UK: Open University Press.

Reich, Robert. 1991. *The Work of Nations: Preparing Ourselves for 21st-Century Capitalism.* New York: Knopf.

Renzetti, Claire M.; and Curran, Daniel J. 1995. *Women, Men, and Society.* 3rd ed. Needham Heights, MA: Allyn and Bacon.

——. 2000. *Living Sociology.* 2nd ed. Needham Heights, MA: Allyn and Bacon.

Reskin, Barbara; and Padavic, Irene. 1994. *Women and Men at Work.* Thousand Oaks, CA: Pine Forge Press.

——; and Roos, Patricia A. 1990. *Job Queues, Gender Queues: Explaining Women's Inroads into Male Occupations.* Philadelphia: Temple University Press.

Rhode, Deborah L. 1990. "Gender equality and employment policy," in Sara E. Rix, ed., *The American Woman, 1990–1991: A Status Report.* New York: Norton.

Richardson, Diane; and May, Hazel. 1999. "Deserving victims? Sexual status and the social construction of violence." *Sociological Review,* vol. 47.

Riddick, C. C. 1985. "Life satisfaction for older female homemakers, retirees, and workers." *Research on Aging,* vol. 7.

Rieff, David. 1991. *Los Angeles: Capital of the Third World.* New York: Simon and Schuster.

Riesman, David. 1961. *The Lonely Crowd: A Study of the Changing American Character.* New Haven, CT: Yale University Press.

Riis, Jacob A. 1957. *How the Other Half Lives: Studies among the Tenements of New York.* Originally published 1890. New York: Dover.

Riley, Matilda White; Foner, Anne; and Waring, Joan. 1988. "Sociology of age," in Neil J. Smelser, ed., *Handbook of Sociology.* Newbury Park, CA: Sage.

——; Johnson, Marilyn; and Foner, Anne. 1972. *Aging and Society.* New York: Russell Sage Foundation.

Ringer, Benjamin B. 1985. *"We the People" and Others: Duality and America's Treatment of Its Racial Minorities.* New York: Tavistock.

Ritzer, George. 1993. *The McDonaldization of Society.* Newbury Park, CA: Pine Forge Press.

Robinson, Paul. 1994. "The way we do the things we do." *New York Times Book Review,* October 30.

Roof, Wade Clark. 1993. *A Generation of Seekers: The Spiritual Journeys of the Baby Boom Generation.* San Francisco: Harper San Francisco.

——; Carroll, Jackson W.; and Roozen, David A., eds. 1995. *The Post-War Generation and Establishment Religion: Cross-Cultural Perspectives.* Boulder, CO: Westview Press.

——; and McKinney, William. 1990. *American Mainline Religion: Its Changing Shape and Future Prospects.* New Brunswick, NJ: Rutgers University Press.

Roscoe, W. 1991. *The Zuni Man-Woman.* Albuquerque, NM: University of New Mexico Press.

——. 2000. *Changing Ones.* New York, NY: Palgrave Macmillan.

Rosenau, James N. 1997. *Along the Domestic-Foreign Frontier: Exploring Governance in a Turbulent World.* Cambridge, UK: Cambridge University Press.

Rosenbaum, James E. 1979. "Organizational career mobility: Promotion chances in a corporation during periods of growth and contraction." *American Journal of Sociology,* vol. 85.

Rosener, Judy B. 1997. *America's Competitive Secret: Women Managers.* New York: Oxford University Press.

Rosenheck, Robert, et al. 1996. "Homeless veterans," in J. Baumohl, ed., *Homelessness in America.* Phoenix: Oryx Press.

Rosenthal, A. M. 1999. *Thirty-Eight Witnesses: The Kitty Genovese Case.* Berkeley, CA: University of California Press.

Rosenthal, Elisabeth. 1999. "Suicides reveal bitter roots of China's rural life." *New York Times,* January 24.

Ross, Patricia; and Reskin, Barbara. 1992. "Occupational desegregation in the 1970s—integration and economic equity." *Sociological Perspectives,* vol. 35.

Rossi, Alice. 1973. "The first woman sociologist: Harriett Martineau," in *The Feminist Papers: From Adams to de Beauvoir.* New York: Columbia University Press.

Rostow, W. W. 1961. *The Stages of Economic Growth.* Cambridge, UK: Cambridge University Press.

Rousselle, Robert. 1999. "Defining ancient Greek sexuality." *Digital Archives of Psychohistory,* vol. 26, no. 4, www. geocities.com/kidhistory/ja/defining.htm, accessed 1/11/05.

Rowe, R. H.; and Kahn, R. L. 1987. "Human aging: Usual and successful." *Science* (July 10).

Rowling, J. K. 1998. *Harry Potter and the Sorcerer's Stone.* New York: Scholastic.

Rubin, Lillian B. 1990. *Erotic Wars: What Happened to the Sexual Revolution?* New York: Farrar, Straus, and Giroux.

Rubinstein, W. D. 1986. *Wealth and Inequality in Britain.* Winchester, MA: Faber and Faber.

Rudé, George. 1964. *The Crowd in History: A Study of Popular Disturbances in France and England, 1730–1848.* New York: Wiley.

Ruggles, Patricia. 1990. *Drawing the Line: Alternative Poverty Measures and Their Implications for Public Policy.* Washington, DC: Urban Institute Press.

——. 1992. "Measuring poverty." *Focus,* vol. 14. University of Wisconsin-Madison, Institute for Research on Poverty.

Rusting, Ricki L. 1992. "Why do we age?" *Scientific American,* vol. 267.

Rutherford, Jonathan; and Chapman, Rowena. 1988. "Who's that man," in Rowena Chapman and Jonathan Rutherford, eds., *Male Order: Unwrapping Masculinity.* London: Lawrence and Wishart.

Rutter, M.; and Giller, H. 1984. *Juvenile Delinquency: Trends and Perspectives.* New York: Guilford Press.

RWB. 2003. *The Internet Under Surveillance: 2003 Report.* Paris, France: Reporters Without Borders. www.rsf.org/IMG/ pdf/doc-2236.pdf, accessed 1/3/05.

Ryan, Tom. 1985. "The roots of masculinity," in Andy Metcalf and Martin Humphries, eds., *Sexuality of Men.* London: Pluto.

Sabel, Charles F. 1982. *Work and Politics: The Division of Labor in Industry.* New York: Cambridge University Press.

Sachs, Jeffrey. 2000. "A new map of the world." *The Economist* (June 22).

Sadker, Myra; and Sadker, David. 1994. *Failing at Fairness.* New York: Scribner.

Safe-food.org. 2003. "You are eating genetically engineered food. Is it good for you? Do you have a choice?" www.safe-food.org, accessed 1/3/05.

Sahliyeh, Emile, ed. 1990. *Religious Resurgence and Politics in the Contemporary World.* Albany, NY: SUNY Press.

Saks, Mike, ed. 1992. *Alternative Medicine in Britain.* Oxford, UK: Clarendon.

Salter, Howard. 1998. "Making a world of difference: Celebrating 30 years of development progress." U.S. AID press release, June 25.

Sampson, Robert J.; and Cohen, Jacqueline. 1988. "Deterrent effects of the police on crime: A replication and theoretical extension." *Law and Society Review,* vol. 22, no. 1.

Sandefur, Gary; and Libeler, Carolyn. 1997. "The demography of American Indian families." *Population Research and Policy Review,* vol. 16.

Sartre, Jean-Paul. 1965. *Anti-Semite and Jew.* Originally published 1948. New York: Schocken Books.

Sassen, Saskia. 1991. *The Global City: New York, London, Tokyo.* Princeton, NJ: Princeton University Press.

———. 1998. *Globalization and Its Discontents.* New York: New Press.

Savage, David G. 1998. "Same-sex harassment illegal, says high court." *Los Angeles Times,* March 5.

Savage, Mike, et al. 1992. *Property, Bureaucracy, and Culture: Middle Class Formation in Contemporary Britain.* London: Routledge.

Sawhill, Isabel V. 1989. "The underclass: An overview." *Public Interest,* vol. 96.

Sax, L. J., et al. 1999. "The American freshman: National norms for fall 1999." Los Angeles: Higher Education Research Institute, UCLA, www.gseis.ucla.edu/heri/heri.html, accessed 1/3/05.

Sax, L. J.; Lindholm, J. A.; Astin, A. W.; Korn, W. S.; and Mahoney, K. M. (2001) "The American freshman: National norms for fall 2001." Higher Education Research Institute, UCLA Graduate School of Education & Information Studies. www.gseis.ucla.edu/heri/norms_pr_01.html, accessed 1/3/05.

Sayers, Janet. 1986. *Sexual Contradiction: Psychology, Psychoanalysis, and Feminism.* New York: Methuen.

Schaie, K. Warner. 1979. "The primary mental abilities in adulthood: An exploration in the development of psychometric intelligence," in Paul B. Baltes and O. G. Brim, eds., *Lifespan Development and Behavior.* Vol. 2. New York: Academic Press.

———. 1983. *Longitudinal Studies of Adult Psychological Development.* New York: Guilford Press.

———. 1984. "Midlife influences upon intellectual functioning in old age." *International Journal of Behavioral Development,* vol. 7.

———; and Hendricks, Jon, eds. 2000. *The Evolution of the Aging Self: The Societal Impact on the Aging Process.* New York: Springer.

Scheff, Thomas. 1966. *Being Mentally Ill.* Chicago: Aldine.

Schiller, Herbert I. 1989. *Culture Inc.: The Corporate Takeover of Public Expression.* New York: Oxford University Press.

———. 1991. "Not yet the post-imperialist era." *Critical Studies in Mass Communication,* vol. 8.

Schmidt, Roger. 1980. *Exploring Religion.* Belmont, CA: Wadsworth.

Schooler, Carmi. 1987. "Cognitive effects of complex environments during the life span: A review and theory," in Carmi Schooler and K. Warner Schaie, eds., *Cognitive Functioning and Social Structure over the Life Course.* Norwood, NJ: Ablex.

Schor, Juliet. 1992. *The Overworked American.* New York: Basic Books.

Schuman, Howard; Steel, Charlotte; and Bobo, Lawrence. 1985. *Racial Attitudes in America: Trends and Interpretations.* Cambridge, MA: Harvard University Press.

Schumpeter, Joseph. 1934. *The Theory of Economic Development: An Inquiry into Profits, Capital, and Credit.* Cambridge, MA: Harvard University Press.

———. 1983. *Capitalism, Socialism, and Democracy.* Originally published 1942. Magnolia, MA: Peter Smith.

Schwartz, Gary. 1970. *Sect Ideologies and Social Status.* Chicago: University of Chicago Press.

Schwartz, Pepper. 1998. "Stage fright or death wish: Sociology in the mass media," *Contemporary Sociology,* vol. 27, no. 5 (September): 439–45.

Schwartzman, Kathleen. 1998. "Globalization and democracy." *Annual Review of Sociology,* vol. 24.

Schwarz, John E.; and Volgy, Thomas J. 1992. *The Forgotten Americans.* New York: Norton.

Scott, Catherine V. 1995. *Gender and Development: Rethinking Modernization and Dependency Theory.* London: Lynne Rienner Publishers.

Scott, Sue; and Morgan, David. 1993. "Bodies in a social landscape," in Sue Scott and David Morgan, eds., *Body Matters: Essays on the Sociology of the Body.* Washington, DC: Falmer Press.

Scott, W. Richard; and Meyer, John W. 1994. *Institutional Environments and Organizations: Structural Complexity and Individualism.* Thousand Oaks, CA: Sage.

Scully, Diana. 1990. *Understanding Sexual Violence: A Study of Convicted Rapists.* Boston: Unwin Hyman.

Sedlak, Andrea; and Broadhurst, Diane. 1996. *Third National Incidence Study of Child Abuse and Neglect.* Washington, DC: U.S. Department of Health and Human Services.

Seefeldt, C.; and Keawkungwal, S. 1985. "Children's attitudes toward the elderly in Thailand and the United States." *International Journal of Comparative Sociology,* vol. 26.

Segura, Denise A.; and Pierce, Jennifer L. 1993. "Chicana/o family structure and gender personality: Chodorow, familism, and psychoanalytic sociology revisited." *Signs,* vol. 19.

Seidman, Steven. 1997a. *Difference Troubles: Queering Social Theory and Sexual Politics.* Cambridge, UK: Cambridge University Press.

———. 1997b. "Relativizing sociology: The challenge of cultural studies," in Elizabeth Long, ed., *From Sociology to Cultural Studies: New Perspectives.* Malden, MA: Blackwell.

———; Meeks, Chet; and Traschen, Francie. 1999. "Beyond the closet? The changing social meaning of homosexuality in the United States." *Sexualities,* vol. 2, no. 1.

Seltzer, Judith. 2000. "Families formed outside of marriage." *Journal of Marriage and the Family* (November).

Sennett, Richard. 1998. *The Corrosion of Character: The Personal Consequences of Work in the New Capitalism.* New York: Norton.

"Seville Statement on Violence." 1990. *American Psychologist,* vol. 45, no. 10, www.lrainc.com/swtaboo/taboos/seville1.html, accessed 1/3/05.

Sewell, William H., Jr. 1992. "A theory of structure: Duality, agency, and transformation." *American Journal of Sociology,* vol. 98.

———. 1999. "The concept of culture," in Victoria E. Bonnell and Lynn Hunt, eds., *Beyond the Cultural Turn.* Berkeley, CA: University of California Press.

Sewell, William H.; and Hauser, Robert M. 1980. "The Wisconsin longitudinal study of social and psychological factors in aspirations and achievements." *Research in Sociology of Education and Socialization,* vol. 1.

Sharma, Ursula. 1992. *Complementary Medicine Today: Practitioners and Patients.* London: Routledge.

Sharp, H. 1981. "Old age among the Chipewyan," in Pamela T. Amoss and S. Harrells, eds., *Other Ways of Growing Old: Anthropological Perspectives.* Stanford, CA: Stanford University Press.

Shattuck, Roger. 1980. *The Forbidden Experiment: The Story of the Wild Boy of Aveyron.* New York: Farrar, Straus, and Giroux.

Shea, S.; Stein, A. D.; Basch, C. E.; Lantigua, R.; Maylahn, C.; Strogatz, D.; and Novick, L. 1991. "Independent associations of educational attainment and ethnicity with behavioral risk factors for cardiovascular disease." *American Journal of Epidemiology,* vol. 134, no. 6.

Sheldon, William A., et al. 1949. *Varieties of Delinquent Youth.* New York: Harper and Row.

Shelton, Beth Anne. 1992. *Women, Men, and Time: Gender Differences in Paid Work, Housework, and Leisure.* Westport, CT: Greenwood.

———; and John, Daphne. 1993. "Does marital status make a difference?: Housework among married and cohabiting men and women." *Journal of Family Issues,* vol. 14, no. 3.

Shepherd, Gill. 1987. "Rank, gender, and homo-sexuality: Mombasa as a key to understanding sexual options," in Pat Caplan, *The Social Construction of Sexuality.* New York: Tavistock.

Shinn, Marybeth; and Weitzman, Beth. 1996. "Homeless families are different," in J. Baumohl, ed., *Homelessness in America.* Phoenix: Oryx Press.

Siegel, Jacob. 1993. *A Generation of Change: A Profile of America's Older Population.* New York: Russell Sage Foundation.

Sigmund, Paul E. 1990. *Liberation Theology at the Crossroads: Democracy or Revolution?* New York: Oxford University Press.

Simmel, Georg. 1955. *Conflict and the Web of Group Affiliations.* Trans. Kurt Wolff. Glencoe, IL: Free Press.

Simon, Julian. 1981. *The Ultimate Resource.* Princeton, NJ: Princeton University Press.

———. 1989. *The Economic Consequences of Immigration.* Cambridge, MA: Basil Blackwell.

Simpson, George Eaton; and Yinger, J. Milton. 1986. *Racial and Cultural Minorities: An Analysis of Prejudice and Discrimination.* New York: Plenum Press.

Simpson, Ida H.; Stark, David; and Jackson, Robert A. 1988. "Class identification processes." *American Sociological Review,* vol. 53.

Simpson, John H. 1985. "Socio-moral issues and recent presidential elections," *Review of Religious Research,* vol. 27: 115–23.

Sjoberg, Gideon. 1960. *The Pre-Industrial City: Past and Present.* New York: Free Press.

———. 1963. "The rise and fall of cities: A theoretical perspective." *International Journal of Comparative Sociology,* vol. 4.

Sklar, Holly. 1999. "Brother, can you spare a billion?" *Z Magazine* (December), www.zmag.org/ZNET. htm, accessed 1/3/05.

Skocpol, Theda. 1979. *States and Social Revolutions: A Comparative Analysis of France, Russia, and China.* New York: Cambridge University Press.

———. 1992. *Protecting Soldiers and Mothers: The Political Origins of Social Policy in the United States.* Cambridge, MA: Harvard University Press.

Slapper, Gary; and Tombs, Steve. 1999. *Corporate Crime.* Essex, UK: Longman.

Smart, Ninian. 1989. *The World Religions.* Englewood Cliffs, NJ: Prentice Hall.

Smeeding, Timothy M. 2000. "Changing income inequality in OECD countries: Updated results from the Luxembourg income study (LIS)." Luxembourg Income Study Working Paper #252, March. Syracuse, New York: Maxwell School of Citizenship and Public Affairs, Syracuse University, www.lisproject.org/publications/liswps/252.pdf, accessed 1/11/05.

———; Rainwater, Lee; and Burtless, Gary. 2000. "United States poverty in a cross-national context." Luxembourg Income Study Working Paper #244, September. Syracuse, New York: Maxwell School of Citizenship and Public Affairs, Syracuse University, www.lisproject.org/publications/liswps/244.pdf, accessed 1/11/05.

Smelser, Neil J. 1963. *Theory of Collective Behavior.* New York: Free Press.

Smith, Philip; and West, Brad. 2000. "Cultural studies," in *Encyclopedia of Naturalism.* Vol. 1. San Diego, CA: Academic Press.

Smith, Vicki. 1997. "New forms of work organization." *Annual Review of Sociology,* vol. 23.

So, Alvin. 1990. *Social Change and Development: Modernization, Dependency,* and World-Systems Theories. Newbury Park, CA: Sage.

———; and Chiu, Stephen W. K. 1995. *East Asia and the World Economy.* Thousand Oaks, CA: Sage.

Sokolovsky, J., ed. 1990. *The Cultural Context of Aging: Worldwide Perspectives.* New York: Bergin and Garvey.

Sorokin, Pitirim A. 1927. *Social Mobility.* New York: Harper.

Soumerai, S. B.; and Avorn, J. 1983. "Perceived health, life satisfaction, and activity in urban elderly: A controlled study of the impact of part-time work." *Journal of Gerontology,* vol. 38.

Southwick, S. 1996. Liszt: *Searchable Directory of E-Mail Discussion Groups.* www.liszt.com, accessed 1/3/05.

Spain, Daphne; and Bianchi, Suzanne M. 1996. *Balancing Act: Motherhood, Marriage, and Employment among American Women.* New York: Russell Sage Foundation.

Spenner, Kenneth. 1983. "Deciphering Prometheus: Temporal change in the skill level of work." *American Sociological Review,* vol. 48.

Spielberger, C. D.; Crane, R. S.; Kearns, W. D.; Pellegrin, K. L.; Rickman, R. L.; and Johnson, E. H. 1991. "Anger and anxiety in essential hypertension." In C. D. Spielberger, I. G. Sarason, Z. Kulcs, and G. L. Van Heck, eds., *Stress and Emotion.* Vol. 14. New York: Hemisphere/Taylor & Francis.

Spilerman, Seymour. 1977. "Careers, labor market structure, and socioeconomic achievement." *American Journal of Sociology,* vol. 83.

Spinks, W. A.; and Wood J. 1996. "Office-Based Telecommuting: An International Comparison of Satellite Offices in Japan and North America," in *Proceedings of SIGCPR/SIGMIS '96.* Denver, CO: ACM.

Sreberny-Mohammadi, Annabelle. 1992. "Media integration in the third world," in B. Gronbeck et al., eds., *Media, Consciousness, and Culture.* London: Sage.

Stacey, Judith. 1990. *Brave New Families: Stories of Domestic Upheaval in Late Twentieth Century America.* New York: Basic Books.

———. 1993. "Good riddance to 'the family': A response to David Popenoe." *Journal of Marriage and Family,* vol. 55.

———. 1996. *In the Name of the Family: Rethinking Family Values in a Postmodern Age.* Boston: Beacon Press.

———. 2004. "Marital suitors court social science spin-sters: The unwittingly conservative effects of public sociology," *Social Problems,* vol. 51, no. 1: 131–45. © 2004, The Society for the Study of Social Problems, Inc.

Stampp, Kenneth. 1956. *The Peculiar Institution.* New York: Knopf.

Stark, Rodney; and Bainbridge, William Sims. 1980. "Towards a theory of religious commitment." *Journal for the Scientific Study of Religion,* vol. 19.

———. 1985. *The Future of Religion, Secularization, Revival, and Cult Formation.* Berkeley, CA: University of California Press.

———. 1987. *A Theory of Religion.* New Brunswick, NJ: Rutgers University Press.

Starrs, Paul F. 1997. "The sacred, the regional, and the digital." *Geographical Review,* vol. 87, no. 2.

Statham, June. 1986. *Daughters and Sons: Experiences of Non-Sexist Childraising.* New York: Basil Blackwell.

Steinberg, Ronnie J. 1990. "Social construction of skill: Gender, power, and comparable worth." *Work and Occupations,* vol. 17.

Steinmetz, Suzanne K. 1983. "Family violence toward elders," in Susan Saunders, Ann Anderson, and Cynthia Hart, eds., *Violent Individuals and Families: A Practitioner's Handbook.* Springfield, IL: Charles C. Thomas.

Sterling, Bruce. 1996. "Greetings from Burning Man," *Wired* 4.11, November.

Stetz, Margaret; and Oh, Bonnie, eds. 2001. *Legacies of the Comfort Women of World War II.* Armonk, NY: M. E. Sharpe.

Stillwagon, Ellen. 2001. "AIDS and poverty in Africa." *The Nation* (May 21).

Stone, Lawrence. 1980. *The Family, Sex, and Marriage in England, 1500–1800.* New York: Harper and Row.

Stone, Michael. 1993. *Shelter Poverty: New Ideas on Affordable Housing.* Philadelphia: Temple University Press.

Stouffer, Samuel A., et al. 1949. *The American Soldier: Adjustment during Army Life.* Princeton, NJ: Princeton University Press.

Straus, Murray; and Gelles, Richard. 1986. "Societal change and change in family violence from 1975 to 1985 as revealed by two national surveys." *Journal of Marriage and the Family,* vol. 48.

Strauss, William; and Howe, Neil. 1991. *Generations: The History of America's Future, 1584–2069.* New York: Quill.

Strinner, William F. 1979. "Modernization and the family extension in the Philippines: A social-demographic analysis." *Journal of Marriage and the Family,* vol. 41.

Stryker, Robin. 1996. "Comparable worth and the labor market," in Paula J. Dubeck and Kathryn Borman, eds., *Women and Work: A Handbook.* New York: Garland.

Sullivan, Andrew. 1995. *Virtually Normal: An Argument about Homosexuality.* New York: Knopf.

Sullivan, Oriel. 1997. "Time waits for no (wo)man: An investigation of the gendered experience of domestic time." *Sociology,* vol. 31.

Sutherland, Edwin H. 1949. *Principles of Criminology.* Chicago: Lippincott.

Swidler, Ann. 1986. "Culture in action: Symbols and strategies." *American Sociological Review,* vol. 51.

———. 2001. *Talk of Love: How Culture Matters.* Chicago: University of Chicago Press.

Tabor, James D.; and Gallagher, Eugene V. 1995. *Why Waco? Cults and the Battle for Religious Freedom in America.* Berkeley, CA: University of California Press.

Tang, Shengming; and Zuo, Jiping. 2000. "Dating attitudes and behaviors of American and Chinese college students." *Social Science Journal,* vol. 37, no. 1.

Tannenbaum, Frank. 1964. *The Fine Society: A Philosophy of Labour.* London: Cape.

Taylor, Ian; Walton, Paul; and Young, Jock. 1973. *The New Criminology: For a Social Theory of Deviance.* London: Routledge and Kegan Paul.

Tempest, Rone. 1996. "Barbie and the world economy." *Los Angeles Times,* September 22.

Tétreault, Mary Ann. ed. 1994. *Women and Revolution in Africa, Asia, and the New World.* Columbia, SC: University of South Carolina Press.

Thomas, G. M., et al. 1987. *Institutional Structure: Constituting State, Society and the Individual.* Newbury Park, CA: Sage.

Thomas, W. I.; and Znaniecki, Florian. 1966. *The Polish Peasant in Europe and America: Monograph of Our Immigrant Group.* 5 vols. Originally published 1918–20. New York: Dover.

Thompson, E. P. 1971. "The moral economy of the English crowd in the eighteenth century." *Past and Present,* vol. 50.

Thompson, John B. 1990. *Ideology and Modern Culture.* Cambridge, UK: Polity Press.

———. 1995. *The Media and Modernity: A Social Theory of the Media.* Cambridge, UK: Polity Press.

Thompson, Warren S. 1929. "Population." *American Journal of Sociology,* vol. 34.

Thorne, Barrie. 1993. *Gender Play: Girls and Boys in School.* New Brunswick, NJ: Rutgers University Press.

Tiano, Susan. 1994. *Patriarchy on the Line: Labor, Gender, and Ideology in the Mexican Maquila Industry.* Philadelphia: Temple University Press.

Tilly, Charles. 1978. *From Mobilization to Revolution.* Reading, MA: Addison-Wesley.

———. 1992. "How to detect, describe, and explain repertoires of contention." Working Paper No. 150. Center for the Study of Social Change. New York: New School for Social Research.

———. 1995. "Globalization threatens labor's rights." *International Labor and Working Class History,* vol. 47.

———. 1996. "The emergence of citizenship in France and elsewhere," in Charles Tilly, ed., *Citizenship, Identity, and Social History.* Cambridge, UK: Cambridge University Press.

Tinbergen, Niko. 1974. *The Study of Instinct.* Oxford, UK: Oxford University Press.

Tippet, Sarah. 2001. "Parents' Sexual Orientation Matters, Study Finds," Reuters News Agency, April 27.

Tittle, Charles R.; and Meier, Robert F. 1990. "Specifying the SES/delinquency relationship." *Criminology,* vol. 28, no. 2.

———, et al. 1978. "The myth of social class and criminality: An empirical assessment of the empirical evidence." *American Sociological Review,* vol. 43.

Totti, Xavier F. 1987. "The making of a Latino ethnic identity." *Dissent,* vol. 34 (fall).

Toufexis, Anastasia. 1993. "Sex has many accents." *Time* (May 24).

Touraine, Alain. 1974. *The Post-Industrial Society.* London: Wildwood.

———. 1977. *The Self-Production of Society.* Chicago: University of Chicago Press.

———. 1981. *The Voice and the Eye: An Analysis of Social Movements.* New York: Cambridge University Press.

Townsend, Peter; and Davidson, Nick, eds. 1982. *Inequalities in Health: The Black Report.* Harmondsworth, UK: Penguin.

Toyota.com. 2004. "Toyota by the numbers." www.toyota.com/about/operations/numbers/index.html#, accessed 1/3/05.

Treas, Judy. 1995. "Older Americans in the 1990s and beyond." *Population Bulletin,* vol. 5.

Treiman, Donald. 1977. *Occupational Prestige in Comparative Perspective.* New York: Academic Press.

Troeltsch, Ernst. 1931. *The Social Teaching of the Christian Churches.* 2 vols. New York: Macmillan.

Trow, Martin. 1961. "The second transformation of American secondary education." *Comparative Sociology,* vol. 2.

Truman, David B. 1981. *The Governmental Process.* Westport, CT: Greenwood Press.

Truong, Tranh-Dam. 1990. *Sex, Money, and Morality.* London: Zed Books.

Tumin, Melvin M. 1953. "Some principles of stratification: A critical analysis." *American Sociological Review,* vol. 18 (August).

Turnbull, Colin. 1983. *The Human Cycle.* New York: Simon and Schuster.

Turowski, Jan. 1977. "Inadequacy of the theory of the nuclear family: The Polish experience," in Luis Lenero Otero, ed., *Beyond the Nuclear Family Model: Cross-Cultural Perspectives.* Beverly Hills, CA: Sage.

Tuttle, Lisa. 1986. *Encyclopedia of Feminism.* New York: Facts on File.

UNAIDS. 2002. "Impact of AIDS on older populations." www.unaids.org/html/pub/publications/fact_shhets02/fs_older_en_pdf.htm, accessed 1/10/05.

———. 2003. "AIDS Epidemic Update, December 2003." Joint United Nations Program on HIV/AIDS. www.unaids.org/html/pub/publications/irc_pubOb/jc943-epiupdate2003_en_pdf.htm, accessed 1/10/05.

UN Chronicle. 1995. vol. 32, no. 4: 29.

UNICEF. 1997. *The State of the World's Children, 1997.* New York: Oxford University Press.

———. 2000. *State of the World's Children, 2000.* New York: United Nations Children's Fund.

Union of International Associations. 1996–97. "International organizations by year and by type, 1909–1996, in *Yearbook of International Organizations, 1996/97.* Statistics obtained from UIA Web site, www.uia.org/statistics/organizations-stybv296.php, accessed 1/3/05.

Union of International Organizations. 2003. "International organizations by type" www.uia.org/statistics/organizations/ytb199.php, accessed 1/3/05.

United Nations (UN). 1995. "Human Development Report, Gender and Human Development—Overview" http://hdr.undp.org/reports/global/1995/en/pdf/hdr_1995_overview.pdf, accessed 1/3/05.

———. 2000. *The World's Women, 2000: Trends and Statistics.* New York: United Nations.

———. 2003. Table 26. *United Nations Human Development Report,* 2003. www.undp.org/hdr2003/pdf/hdr03_HDI.pdf, accessed 1/3/05.

United Nations Conference on Trade and Development. 2002. *World Investment Report 2002: Transnational Corporations and Export Competitiveness.* New York: United Nations.

United Nations Department of Economic and Social Affairs. 2004. "Progress towards the millennium development goals, 1990–2004. Goal 7—Ensure environmental sustainability." http://unstats.un.org/unsd/mi/techgroup/goals_2004/goal_7-web_2004_fc3rev.doc, accessed 1/3/05.

United Nations Development Program (UNDP). 1998. *Human Development Report 1998.* New York: Oxford University Press.

———. 1999. *Human Development Report 1999.* New York: Oxford University Press.

———. 2000. *Human Development Report 2000.* New York: Oxford University Press.

———. 2002. *Human Development Report 2002.* http://hdr.undp.org/reports/global/2002/en/default.cfm, accessed 1/3/05.

United Nations Educational, Scientific, and Cultural Organization. 2003. "Institute for statistics." www.uis.unesco.org/ev.php?URL_ID=4926&URL_DO=DO_TOPIC&URL_SECTION=201, accessed 1/3/05.

United Nations Food and Agriculture Organization (UN FAO). 1996. "FAO/UNFPA expert group meeting on food production and population growth." United Nations: Food and Agriculture Organization, July 3–5.

———. 1999. "Food outlook, no. 5." United Nations: Food and Agriculture Organization, November.

———. 2001. "The impact of HIV/AIDS on food security." United Nations Food and Agriculture Organization, Conference on World Food Security, May 28–June 1.

———. 2003. "The state of food insecurity in the world, 2003." www.fao.org/docrep/006/j0083e/j0083e00.htm, accessed 1/3/05.

United Nations, Population Division. 2002. "World urbanization prospects, 2001 revision—Data tables and highlights." www.un.org/esa/population/publications/wup2001/wup2001dh.pdf, accessed 1/3/05.

United Nations Population Fund (UNFPA). 1998. *The State of World Population, 1998.* New York: United Nations.

———. 2003. "Ending widespread violence against women." www.unfpa.org/gender/violence.htm, accessed 1/3/05.

United Nations World Commission on Environment and Development (UNWCED). 1987. *Our Common Future.* New York: Oxford University Press.

United Nations World Food Program (UNWFP). 2001. "News release: WFP head releases world hunger map and warns of hunger 'hot spots' in 2001." (January 8) New York: UNWFP.

United Steel Workers of America. 2004. "Unprecedented manufacturing job losses cause worker mobility." www.uswa.org/uswa/program/content/915.php, accessed 3/3/2004.

Urban Institute. 2000. "America's homeless II: Populations and services." www.urban.org/template.cfm?Template=/TaggedContent/VicesPublication.cfm&PublicationID=6846&NavMenuID=95, accessed 1/10/05.

Urry, John. 1990. *The Tourist Gaze.* London: Sage.

U.S. Bureau of Justice. 2000. *Capital Punishment 1999, Statistics Bulletin.* Washington, DC: U.S. Government Printing Office.

U.S. Bureau of Justice Statistics. 2000. *Sourcebook of Criminal Justice Statistics.* Washington, DC: U.S. Government Printing Office.

U.S. Bureau of Labor Statistics. 1989. *Handbook of Labor Statistics.* Washington, DC: U.S. Government Printing Office.

———. 1991. *Employment and Earnings* (January). Washington, DC: U.S. Government Printing Office.

———. 1999. *Employment and Earnings* (January). Washington, DC: U.S. Government Printing Office.

———. 2001a. "Nonfarm payroll statistics from the current employment statistics (national): Total private average hourly earnings of production workers—seasonally adjusted (computed from series EES00500006)." http://146.142.4.24/cgi-bin/surveymost?ee, accessed 1/3/05.

———. 2001b. "Charts from the 'tomorrow's jobs' section of the 2000–2001 occupational outlook handbook." http://stats.bls.gov/oco/images/ocotjc04.gif, accessed 1/3/05.

———. 2003a. "Household data, annual averages" Tables 1 and 2. www.bls.gov/cps/cpsaat1.pdf and www.bls.gov/cps/cpsaat2.pdf, both accessed 1/3/05.

———. 2003b. "Household data annual averages" Table 11. www.bls.gov/cps/cpsaat11.pdf, accessed 1/3/05.

———. 2003c. "Household data annual averages" Table 37. www.bls.gov/cps/cpsaat37.pdf, accessed 1/3/05.

———. 2003d. "Women's earnings up relative to men's in 2002." www.bls.gov/opub/ted/2003/apr/wk3/art03.htm, accessed 1/3/05.

U.S. Bureau of the Census. 1991. "School enrollment: social and economic characteristics of students, October 1991," in *Current Population Reports,* series P-20, no. 469. Washington, DC: U.S. Government Printing Office.

———. 1992. *Statistical Abstract of the United States.* Washington, DC: U.S. Government Printing Office.

———. 1993. *Statistical Abstract of the United States.* Washington, DC: U.S. Government Printing Office.

———. 1994. *World Population Profile: 1994.* Report WP/94. Washington, DC: U.S. Government Printing Office.

———. 1996a. *P23-190 Current Population Reports: Special Studies—651 in the United States,* by Frank B. Hobbs with Bonnie L. Damon. Washington, DC: U.S. Government Printing Office.

———. 1996b. *Statistical Abstract of the United States.* Washington, DC: U.S. Government Printing Office.

———. 1997. "Historical poverty tables—Persons. Table 3. Poverty status of persons, by age, race, and hispanic origin: 1959 to 1996." www.census.gov/ftp/pub/hhes/poverty/histpov/ hstpov3. html, accessed 1/3/05.

———. 1998a. *Statistical Abstract of the United States.* Washington, DC: U.S. Government Printing Office.

———. 1998b. "Marital status and living arrangements," in *Current Population Reports.* Washington, DC: U.S. Government Printing Office.

———. 1998c. "Household and family characteristics (March)," in *Current Population Reports.* Washington, DC: U.S. Government Printing Office.

———. 1998d. "World population profile, 1998—Highlights." www.census.gov/ipc/www/wp98001.html, accessed 1/3/05.

———. 1998e. "Asset ownership of households, 1998." www.census.gov/hhes/www/wealth/1998_2000/wlth98-2.html, accessed 1/4/05.

———. 1999a. "FINC-03. Presence of related children under 18 years old—All families by total money income in 1999, type of family, work experience in 1999, race and Latino origin of reference person" (Current Population Survey, white families.) http://ferret.bls.census.gov/macro/032000/faminc/new03_000.htm, accessed 1/4/05.

———. 1999b. "Population profile of the United States, chapter 2" www.census.gov/population/pop-profile/1999/ chap02.pdf, accessed 1/4/05.

———. 2000a. "Money income in the United States: Current population surveys, table H-1. Income limits for each fifth and top 5 percent of households (all races): 1967 to 1999." www.census.gov/hhes/income/histinc/h01.html, accessed 1/4/05.

———. 2000b. "The changing shape of the nation's income distribution." www.census.gov/prod/2000pubs/p60-204.pdf, accessed 1/4/05.

———. 2000c. "Current population survey: Table A. People and families in poverty by selected characteristics: 1998 and 1999." www.census.gov/hhes/poverty/poverty99/pv99est1.html, accessed 1/4/05.

———. 2000d. "Current population survey: Poverty thresholds in 1999, by size of family and number of related children under 18 years." www.census.gov/hhes/poverty/threshld/thresh99.html, accessed 1/4/05.

———. 2000e. "Current population survey, table 18. Workers as a proportion of all poor people: 1978 to 1999." www.census.gov/hhes/poverty/histpov/hstpov18.html, accessed 1/4/05.

———. 2000f. "Current population survey, table 22. Number and percent of people below 50 percent of poverty level: 1975 to 1999." www.census.gov/hhes/poverty/histpov/hstpov/ 22.html, accessed 1/4/05.

———. 2000g. "Current population survey: 1959 to 1999, table 2. Poverty status of people by family relationship, race, and Latino origin: 1959 to 1999." www.census.gov/hhes/poverty/histpov/hstpov2.html, accessed 1/4/05.

———. 2000h. "Current population survey, poverty in the United States, figure 5. Poverty rate for people in families by family type and presence of work." www.census.gov/prod/2000pubs/p60-210.pdf, accessed 1/4/05.

———. 2000i. "Current population survey, historical poverty tables, table 3. Poverty status of people, by age, race, and Latino origin: 1959 to 1999." www.census.gov/hhes/poverty/histpov/hstpov3.html, accessed 1/4/05.

———. 2000j. "Money income in the United States: Current populations report, table H-2. Share of aggregate income received by each fifth and top 5 percent of households (all races): 1967 to 1999." www.census.gov/hhes/income/histinc/h02.html, accessed 1/4/05.

———. 2000k. "Money income in the United States: Current populations report, historical income tables: H-9, H-9B, H-9C, H-9D, and H-9E." www.census.gov/hhes/income/ histinc/inchhdet.html, accessed 1/4/05.

———. 2000l. "Current population survey, 1960–2000." www.census.gov/hhes/poverty/poverty99/pov99.html, accessed 1/4/05.

———. 2000m. "Poverty in the United States: Current Population Reports." www.census.gov/prod/2000pubs/p60-210.pdf, accessed 1/4/05.

———. 2000n. "Poverty 1999: Table C. Percent of persons in poverty, by state: 1997, 1998, and 1999." www.census.gov/hhes/poverty/poverty99/pv99state.html, accessed 1/4/05.

———. 2000o. "Poverty in the United States 1999." www.census.gov/prod/2000pubs/p60-210.pdf, accessed 1/4/05.

———. 2000p. *Statistical Abstract of the United States.* Washington, DC: U.S. Government Printing Office.

———. 2000q. "P-12; Sex by age." Census 2000 Summary File 1 (SF-1). http://factfinder.census.gov/servlet/DTTable?geo_id=01000US&ds_name=DEC_2000_SF1_U&mt_name=DEC_2000_SF1_U_PCT012&_lang=en&_sse=on, accessed 1/4/05.

———. 2000r. "QT-P10. Households and Families: 2000." http://factfinder.census.gov/servlet/QTTable?geo_id=01000US&ds_name=DEC_2000_SF1_U&qr_name=DEC_2000_SF1_U_QTP10&_lang=en&_sse=on, accessed 1/4/05.

———. 2000s. "QT-P3. Race and Hispanic or Latino: 2000." http://factfinder.census. gov/servlet/QTTable?geo_id=01000US&ds_name=DEC_2000_SF1_U&qr_name=DEC_2000_SF1_U_QTP3&_lang=en&_sse=on, accessed 1/4/05.

———. 2001a. "Asset ownership of households: 1995." www.census.gov/hhes/www/wealth/ 1995/wlth95-1.html, accessed 1/4/05.

———. 2001b. "Household net worth and asset ownership: 1995." Current Population Reports: The Survey of Income and Program Participation, www.census.gov/prod/2001pubs/p70-71.pdf, accessed 1/4/05.

———. 2001c. "The older population in the United States: March 2000 detailed tables (PPL-147)." www.census.gov/population/www/socdemo/age/ppl-147.html, accessed 1/4/05.

———. 2001d. *Statistical Abstract of the United States*. Washington, DC: U.S. Government Printing Office.

———. 2002a. "Table IE-3. Household shares of aggregate income by fifths of the income distribution: 1967 to 2001" www.census.gov/hhes/income/histinc/ie3.html, accessed 1/4/05.

———. 2002b. "Table H-1. Income limits for each fifth and top 5 percent of households (all races): 1967 to 2001" www.census.gov/hhes/income/histinc/h01.html, accessed 1/4/05.

———. 2002c. "Historical income tables: Households; Tables H-9, H-9b, H-9c, H-9d, H-9e." www.census.gov/hhes/income/histinc/inchhdet.html, accessed 1/4/05.

———. 2002d. "Table 1a. Percent of high school and college graduates of the population 15 years and over, by age, sex, race, and Hispanic origin." www.census.gov/population/socdemo/education/ppl-169/tab01a.xls, accessed 1/4/05.

———. 2002e. "Table P-16. Educational attainment—people 25 years old and over by median income and sex: 1991 to 2001." www.census.gov/hhes/income/histinc/p16.html, accessed 1/4/05.

———. 2002f. "Historical income tables: Families, table F-2, share of aggregate income received by each fifth and the top five percent (all races) www.census.gov/hhes/income/histinc/f02.html, accessed 1/4/05.

———. 2002g. "No. 630. Labor union membership by state: 1983 and 2001." www.census.gov/prod/2003pubs/02statab/labor.pdf, accessed 1/4/05.

———. 2002h. "Children's living arrangements and characteristics, 2002." Table FG7. www.census.gov/population/www/socdemo/hh-fam/cps2002.html, accessed 1/4/05.

———. 2002i. "Statistical abstract of the United States, 2001." www.census.gov/prod/2002pubs/01statab/stat-ab01.html, accessed 1/4/05.

———. 2002j. *Statistical Abstract of the United States, 2002*. www.census.gov/prod/www/statistical-abstract-02.html, accessed 1/4/05.

———. 2002k. "Geographical mobility, population characteristics" Current Population Reports, PS20-538. www.census.gov/prod/2001pubs/p20-538.pdf, accessed 1/4/05.

———. 2002l. "Table 20a—Population by region, sex, race and Hispanic origin with percent distribution by race and Hispanic origin, March 2002." www.census.gov/population/socdemo/race/black/ppl-164/tab20.pdf, accessed 1/4/05.

———. 2003a. "Asset ownership of households: 2000." www.census.gov/hhes/www/wealth/1998_2000/wlth00-1.html, accessed 1/4/05.

———. 2003b. "Number in poverty and poverty rate by race and Hispanic origin: 2001 and 2002" www.census.gov/hhes/poverty/poverty02/table1.pdf, accessed 1/4/05.

———. 2003c. "Poverty 2002." www.census.gov/hhes/poverty/threshld/thresh02.html, accessed 1/4/05.

———. 2003d. "People and families by selected characteristics: 2001 and 2002." www.census.gov/hhes/poverty/poverty02/table2.pdf, accessed 1/4/05.

———. 2003e. "Table 4. Poverty status: Status of families, by type of family, presence of related children, race, and Hispanic origin: 1959 to 2002." www.census.gov/hhes/poverty/histpov/hstpov4.html, accessed 1/4/05.

———. 2003f. "Table 3. Poverty status of people, by age, race, and Hispanic origin: 1959 to 2002." www.census.gov/hhes/poverty/histpov/hstpov3.html, accessed 1/4/05.

———. 2003g. "Table 10. Related children in female householder families as a proportion of all related children, by poverty status: 1959 to 2002." www.census.gov/hhes/poverty/histpov/hstpov10.html, accessed 1/4/05.

———. 2003h. *Statistical Abstract of the United States 2000*. Washington, D.C.: U.S. Government Printing Office. www.census.gov/prod/2004pubs/03statab/pop.pdf, accessed 1/4/05.

———. 2003i. "Poverty in the United States, 2002" Current Population Reports, P60-222. Table 2. www.census.gov/prod/2003pubs/p60-222.pdf, accessed 1/4/05.

———. 2003j. "Table 1a. Percent of high school and college graduates of the population 15 years and over, by age, sex, race, and Hispanic origin: March 2002" www.census.gov/population/socdemo/education/ppl-169/tab01a.xls, accessed 1/4/05.

———. 2003k. "Table 7.2. Educational attainment of the population 25 years and over sex and Hispanic origin type: March 2002" www.census.gov/population/socdemo/hispanic/ppl-165/tab07-2.xls, accessed 1/4/05.

———. 2004. American Community Survey. Poverty Status in 1999 by Sex by Age, PCT49. www.census.gov/acs/www, accessed 1/4/05.

U.S. Bureau of Justice Statistics. 2004. "Capital Punishment Statistics," www.ojp.usdoj.gov/bjs/cp.htm, accessed 1/20/05.

U.S. Department of Education, National Center for Education Statistics. 1993. *Adult Literacy in America: A First Look at the Results of the National Adult Literacy Survey*. Washington, DC: U.S. Government Printing Office.

U.S. Department of Health and Human Services. 2000. *Child Maltreatment 1998: Reports from the States to the National Child Abuse and Neglect Data System*. Washington, DC: U.S. Government Printing Office.

———. 2003a. "Child maltreatment, 2001." www.acf.dhhs.gov/programs/cb/publications/cm01/chapterone.htm#highlight, accessed 1/4/05.

———. 2003b. "Child maltreatment, 1998." www.acf.dhhs.gov/programs/cb/publications/cm98/index.htm, accessed 1/4/05.

U.S. Department of Justice. 2000. "Criminal victimization 1999 changes 1998–99 with trends 1993–99." Washington, DC: U.S. Department of Justice, NCJ 182734 182734, www.ojp.usdoj.gov/bjs/pub/pdf/cv99.pdf, accessed 1/4/05.

———. 2003. "Criminal victimization, 2002." www.ojp.usdoj.gov/bjs/pub/pdf/cv02.pdf, accessed 1/4/05.

U.S. Federal Reserve Board. 2000. "Credit cards: Use and consumer attitudes, 1970 to 1998." *Federal Reserve Bulletin,* www.federalreserve.gov/pubs/bulletin/2000/0900lead.pdf, accessed 1/4/05.

U.S. House of Representatives. 2005. Office of the Clerk, Member FAQs, http://clerk.house.gov/members/memFAQ.html, accessed 1/20/05.

U.S. National Center for Health Statistics. 1993. "Childbearing patterns among selected racial/ethnic minority groups—United States, 1990." *Morbidity and Mortality Weekly Report,* May 28.

U.S. Social Security Administration. 1997a. "Highlights of Social Security data, October 1997," SSA Web site, www.ssa.gov/statistics/highlite.html, accessed 10/28/97.

———.1997b. "Social Security accountability report for fiscal year 1997." SSA Web site, www.ssa.gov/finance/97tblcon.pdf, accessed 1/4/05.

U.S. Surgeon General's Office. 2000. "Treating tobacco use and dependence, fact sheet." www.surgeongeneral.gov/tobacco/smokfact.htm, accessed 1/4/05.

Vallas, S.; and Beck, J. 1996. "The transformation of work revisited: The limits of flexibility in American manufacturing." *Social Problems,* vol. 43, no. 3.

van der Veer, Peter. 1994. *Religious Nationalism: Hindus and Muslims in India.* Berkeley, CA: University of California Press.

van Gennep, Arnold. 1977. *The Rites of Passage.* Originally published 1908. London: Routledge and Kegan Paul.

Vanneman, Reeve D.; and Cannon, Lynn W. 1987. *The American Perception of Class.* Philadelphia: Temple University Press.

Vaughan, Diane. 1986. *Uncoupling: Turning Points in Intimate Relationships.* New York: Oxford University Press.

———. 1996. *The Challenger Launch Decision: Risky Technology, Culture, and Deviance at NASA,* Chicago: University of Chicago Press.

———. 2003. "How theory travels: A most public public sociology," *Public Sociology in Action,* ASA Footnotes (Nov/Dec).

Viorst, Judith. 1986. "And the prince knelt down and tried to put the glass slipper on Cinderella's foot," in Jack Zipes, ed., *Don't Bet on the Prince: Contemporary Feminist Fairy Tales in North America and England.* New York: Methuen.

Vogel, Ezra F. 1979. *Japan as Number One: Lessons for America.* New York: Harper Colophon.

Wacquant, Loic J. D. 1993. "Redrawing the urban color line: The state of the ghetto in the 1980s," in Craig Calhoun and George Ritzer, eds., *Social Problems.* New York: McGraw-Hill.

———. 1996. "The rise of advanced marginality: Notes on its nature and implications." *Acta Sociologica,* vol. 39, no. 2.

———. 2002. "Scrutinizing the street: poverty, morality, and the pitfalls of urban ethnography," *American Journal of Sociology,* vol. 107 (May): 1468–1532.

———; and Wilson, William Julius. 1993. "The cost of racial and class exclusion in the inner city," in William Julius Wilson, ed., *The Ghetto Underclass: Social Science Perspectives.* Newbury Park, CA: Sage.

Wagar, Warren. 1992. *A Short History of the Future.* Chicago: University of Chicago Press.

Wajcman, Judy. 1998. *Managing Like a Man: Women and Men in Corporate Management.* Cambridge, UK: Polity Press.

Waldron, Ingrid. 1986. "Why do women live longer than men?" in Peter Conrad and Rachelle Kern, eds., *The Sociology of Health and Illness.* New York: St. Martin's.

Wallerstein, Immanuel. 1974a. *Capitalist Agriculture and the Origins of the European World-Economy in the Sixteenth Century.* New York: Academic Press.

———. 1974b. *The Modern World-System.* New York: Academic Press.

———. 1979. *The Capitalist World Economy.* Cambridge, UK: Cambridge University Press.

———. 1990. *The Modern World-System II.* New York: Academic Press.

———. 1996a. *Historical Capitalism with Capitalist Civilization.* New York: Norton.

———, ed. 1996b. *World Inequality.* St. Paul, MN: Consortium Books.

Wallerstein, Judith S.; and Blakeslee, Sandra. 1989. *Second Chances: Men, Women, and Children a Decade After Divorce.* New York: Ticknor and Fields.

———; and Kelly, Joan Berlin. 1980. *Surviving the Break-Up: How Children and Parents Cope with Divorce.* New York: Basic Books.

Wallis, Roy. 1977. *The Road to Total Freedom.* New York: Columbia University Press.

———. 1984. *The Elementary Forms of New Religious Life.* London: Routledge and Kegan Paul.

Wallraff, Barbara. 2000. "What global language?" *Atlantic Monthly* (November).

Walum, Laurel Richardson. 1977. *The Dynamics of Sex and Gender: A Sociological Perspective.* Chicago: Rand McNally.

Warner, Stephen. 1993. "Work in progress toward a new paradigm for the sociological study of religion in the United States." *American Journal of Sociology,* vol. 98.

Warren, B. 1980. *Imperialism: Pioneer of Capitalism.* London: Verso.

Waters, Mary C. 1990. *Ethnic Options: Choosing Identities in America.* Berkeley, CA: University of California Press.

Wattenberg, Martin P. 1996. *The Decline of American Political Parties, 1952–1994.* Rev. ed. Cambridge, MA: Harvard University Press.

Waxman, Laura; and Hinderliter, Sharon. 1996. *A Status Report on Hunger and Homelessness in America's Cities.* Washington, DC: U.S. Conference of Mayors.

Weber, Max. 1947. *The Theory of Social and Economic Organization.* New York: Free Press.

———. 1963 (orig. 1921). *The Sociology of Religion.* Boston: Beacon Press.

———. 1977. *The Protestant Ethic and the Spirit of Capitalism.* New York: Macmillan.

———. 1979. *Economy and Society: An Outline of Interpretive Sociology.* 2 vols. Berkeley, CA: University of California Press.

Webster, Edward. 2004. "Sociology in South Africa: its past, present and future," *Society in Transition 2004,* vol. 35, no. 1: 27–41.

Weeks, Jeffrey. 1977. *Coming Out: Homosexual Politics in Britain, from the Nineteenth Century to the Present.* New York: Quartet.

———. 1986. *Sexuality.* New York: Routledge, Chapman and Hall.

Weinberg, Daniel H. 1996. "Press briefing on 1996 income, poverty, and health insurance estimates." U.S. Bureau of the Census: Housing and Household Economic Statistics Division, September 29.

Weismantle, Mai. 2001. *Reasons People Do Not Work: Household Economic Studies 1996.* U.S. Census Bureau, Current Population Reports, Series P70-76. Washington, DC: U.S. Government Printing Office.

Weiss, Rick. 1997. "Aging: New answers to old questions." *National Geographic,* vol. 192, no. 5.

Weitzman, Lenore. 1985. *Divorce Revolution: The Unexpected Social and Economic Consequences for Women and Children in America.* New York: Free Press.

———, et al. 1972. "Sexual socialization in picture books for preschool children." *American Journal of Sociology,* vol. 77.

Wellman, Barry S. 1994. "I was a teenage network analyst: The route from the Bronx to the information highway." *Connections,* vol. 17, no. 2.

———; Carrington, Peter J.; and Hall, Alan. 1988. "Networks as personal communities," in Barry Wellman and S. D. Berkowitz, eds., *Social Structures: A Network Approach.* New York: Cambridge University Press.

Wellman, Barry, et al. 1996. "Computer networks as social networks: Collaborative work, telework, and virtual community." *Annual Review of Sociology,* vol. 22.

Wellman, David T., ed. 1977. *Portraits of White Racism.* New York: Cambridge University Press.

———. 1987. *Portraits of White Racism.* New York: Cambridge University Press.

West, Candace; and Fenstermaker, Sarah. 1995. "Doing difference." *Gender and Society,* vol. 9, no. 1.

———; and Zimmerman, Don. 1987. "Doing gender." *Gender and Society,* vol. 1 (June).

Western, Bruce. 1997. *Between Class and Market: Postwar Unionization in the*

Capitalist Democracies. Princeton, NJ: Princeton University Press.

———; and Beckett, Katherine. 1999. "How unregulated is the U.S. labor market?: The penal system as a labor market institution." *American Journal of Sociology,* vol. 104, no. 4.

Wheatley, Paul. 1971. *The Pivot of the Four Quarters.* Edinburgh: Edinburgh University Press.

Wheeler, Deborah L. 1998. "Global culture or culture clash: New information technologies in the Islamic world—a view from Kuwait." *Communication Research,* vol. 25, no. 4.

White, Caroline. 2003. "China is top of the gaggers," *Dot Journalism* (June 27). www.journalism.co.uk/news/story673.html, accessed 1/4/05.

White House Press Office. 2001. "President Bush discusses global climate change," press release, June 11.

White, Lynn K. 1990. "Determinants of divorce: A review of research in the eighties." *Journal of Marriage and the Family,* vol. 52 (November).

White, Merry I. 1993. *The Material Child: Coming of Age in Japan and America.* New York: Free Press.

White, Michael; and Trevor, Malcolm. 1983. *Under Japanese Management: The Experience of British Workers.* New York: Gower.

Widom, Cathy Spatz; and Newman, Joseph P. 1985. "Characteristics of non-institutionalized psychopaths," in David P. Farrington and John Gunn, eds., *Aggression and Dangerousness.* Chichester, UK: Wiley.

Wiener, J. M.; Illston, J.; and Hanley, F. J. 1994. *Sharing the Burden: Strategies for Public and Private Long-Term Care Insurance.* Washington, DC: Brookings Institution.

Wilkinson, Richard. 1996. *Unhealthy Societies: The Afflictions of Inequality.* New York: Routledge.

Will, J.; Self, P.; and Datan, N. 1976. "Maternal behavior and perceived sex of infant." *American Journal of Orthopsychiatry,* vol. 46.

Williams, Christine L. 1992. "The glass escalator: Hidden advantages for men in the 'female' professions." *Social Problems,* vol. 39.

Williams, Simon J. 1993. *Chronic Respiratory Illness.* London: Routledge.

Willis, Paul. 1981. *Learning to Labor: How Working Class Kids Get Working Class Jobs.* New York: Columbia University Press.

Wilson, Bryan. 1982. *Religion in Sociological Perspective.* New York: Oxford University Press.

Wilson, Edward O. 1975. *Sociobiology: The New Synthesis.* Cambridge, MA: Harvard University Press.

———. 1978. *On Human Nature.* Cambridge, MA: Harvard University Press.

Wilson, James Q.; and Kelling, George. 1982. "Broken windows," *Atlantic* (March).

Wilson, William Julius. 1978. *The Declining Significance of Race: Blacks and Changing American Institutions.* Chicago: University of Chicago Press.

———. 1987. *The Truly Disadvantaged: The Inner City, the Underclass, and Public Policy.* Chicago: University of Chicago Press.

———. 1991. "Studying inner-city social dislocations: The challenge of public agenda research." *American Sociological Review,* vol. 56 (February).

———. 1996. *When Work Disappears: The World of the New Urban Poor.* New York: Knopf.

———, et al. 1987. "The changing structure of urban poverty." Paper presented at the annual meeting of the American Sociological Association.

Winkleby, Marilynn A., et al. 1992. "Socioeconomic status and health: How education, income, and occupation contribute to risk factors for cardiovascular disease." *American Journal of Public Health,* vol. 82.

Wirth, Louis. 1938. "Urbanism as a way of life." *American Sociological Review,* vol. 44 (July).

Witkowski, Stanley R.; and Brown, Cecil H. 1982. "Whorf and universals of number nomenclature." *Journal of Anthropological Research,* vol. 38.

Wolf, Naomi. 1992. *The Beauty Myth: How Images of Beauty Have Been Used against Women.* New York: Anchor Books.

Wolff, Edward N. 2000. "Recent trends in wealth ownership, 1983–1998." Tables 8 and 9. Jerome Levy Economic Institute, www.levy.org/default.asp?view=publications_view&pubIDf73a204517, accessed 1/4/05.

Wong, Siu-Lun. 1986. "Modernization and Chinese culture in Hong Kong." *Chinese Quarterly,* vol. 106.

Woodrum, Eric. 1988. "Moral conservatism and the 1984 presidential election," *Journal for the Scientific Study of Religion,* vol. 27: 192–210.

Woolgar, Steve; and Pawluch, Dorothy. 1985. "Ontological gerrymandering: The

anatomy of social problems explanations." *Social Problems,* vol. 32, no. 3.

World Bank. 1994. *World Development Report, 1994.* New York: Oxford University Press.

———. 1995. "World development indicators," in *World Development Report 1995: Workers in an Integrating World.* New York: Oxford University Press.

———. 1996. "Poverty reduction: The most urgent task," Washington, DC: World Bank Brief, www.worldbank.org/html/extdr/offrep/eca/pov.htm, accessed 8/14/96.

———. 1997. *World Development Report 1997: The State in a Changing World.* New York: Oxford University Press.

———. 1998. *World development indicators.* Washington, DC: World Bank.

———. 2000. *World Development Report.* New York: Oxford University Press.

———. 2000–2001. "World development indicators," in *World Development Report 2000–2001: Attacking Poverty.* http://poverty.worldbank.org/library/topic/3389/ accessed 1/4/05.

———. 2001. "PovertyNet: Topics relevant to social capital."

———. 2003a. "Country classifications" www.worldbank.org/data/countryclass/countryclass.html, accessed 1/4/05.

———. 2003b. "GNI per capita 2002, Atlas method" www.worldbank.org/data/databytopic/GNIPC.pdf, accessed 1/4/05.

———. 2003c. "World development indicators 2003" www.worldbank.org/data/onlinedatabases/onlinedatabases.html, accessed 1/4/05.

———. 2003d. *World Development Indicators.* www.worldbank.org/poverty/scapital/topic/index.htm, accessed 1/4/05.

World Commission on Environment and Development (Brundtland Commission), 1987. *Our Common Future.* Oxford, UK: Oxford University Press.

World Trade Organization. 2003a. "International Trade Statistics, 2003—Table IV.20" www.wto.org/english/res_e/statis_e/its2003_e/section4_e/iv20.xls, accessed 1/4/05.

———. 2003b. "International trade statistics, 2003." www.wto.org/english/res_e/statis_e/its2003_e/its03_general_overview_e.htm, accessed 1/4/05.

Worrall, Anne. 1990. *Offending Women: Female Lawbreakers and the Criminal Justice System.* London: Routledge.

Worsley, Peter. 1968. *The Trumpet Shall Sound: A Study of Cargo Cults in Melanesia.* New York: Schocken.

Wright, Erik Olin. 1978. *Class, Crisis, and the State.* London: New Left Books.

——. 1985. *Classes.* New York: Shocken.

——. 1997. *Class Counts: Comparative Studies in Class Analysis.* New York: Cambridge University Press.

——. 2000. *Class Counts: Student Edition.* New York: Cambridge University Press.

Wright, Robin. 1995. "For women around the world, survival is problem no. 1." *Los Angeles Times,* September 3.

Wrigley, E. A. 1968. *Population and History.* New York: McGraw-Hill.

Wuthnow, Robert. 1976. *The Consciousness Reformation.* Berkeley, CA: University of California Press.

——. 1978. *Experimentation in American Religion.* Berkeley, CA: University of California Press.

——. 1988. "Sociology of religion," in Neil J. Smelser, ed., *Handbook of Sociology.* Newbury Park, CA: Sage.

Wyatt, Edward. 1999. "Investors are seeing profits in nation's demands for education." *New York Times,* November 4.

Yankelovich, Claney Shulman. 1991. "What's OK on a date." Survey for *Time* and CNN, May 8.

Young, Jock. 1998. "Breaking windows: Situating the new criminology," in Paul Walton and Jock Young, eds., *The New Criminology Revisited.* London: Macmillan.

——. 1999. *The Exclusive Society: Social Exclusion, Crime, and Difference in Late Modernity.* London: Sage.

Young, Michael; and Schuller, Tom. 1991. *Life after Work: The Arrival of the Ageless Society.* London: HarperCollins London.

——; and Willmott, Peter. 1973. *The Symmetrical Family: A Study of Work and Leisure in the London Region.* London: Routledge and Kegan Paul.

Zammuner, Vanda Lucia. 1986. "Children's sex-role stereotypes: A cross-cultural analysis," in Phillip Shaver and Clyde Hendrick, eds., *Sex and Gender.* Beverly Hills, CA: Sage.

Zeitlin, Irving. 1985. *Ancient Judaism: Biblical Criticism from Max Weber to the Present.* New York: Basil Blackwell.

——. 1988. *The Historical Jesus.* Cambridge, UK: Polity Press.

Zerubavel, Eviatar. 1979. *Patterns of Time in Hospital Life.* Chicago: University of Chicago Press.

——. 1982. "The standardization of time: A sociohistorical perspective." *American Journal of Sociology,* vol. 88.

Zhang, Naihu; and Xu, Wu. 1995. "Discovering the positive within the negative: The women's movement in a changing China," in Amrita Basu, ed., *The Challenge of Local Feminisms.* Boulder, CO: Westview.

Zimbardo, Philip G. 1969. "The human choice: Individuation, reason, and order versus deindividuation, impulse, and chaos," in W. J. Arnold and D. Levine, eds., *Nebraska Symposium on Motivation.* Vol. 17. Lincoln, NE: University of Nebraska Press.

——. 1972. "Pathology of imprisonment." *Society,* vol. 9.

——; Ebbesen, Ebbe B.; and Maslach, Christina. 1977. *Influencing Attitudes and Changing Behavior.* Reading, MA: Addison-Wesley.

Zubaida, Sami. 1996. "How successful is the Islamic Republic in Islamizing Iran?" in J. Beinen and J. Stork, eds., *Political Islam: Essays from the Middle East Report.* Berkeley, CA: University of California Press.

Zuboff, Shoshana. 1988. *In the Age of the Smart Machine: The Future of Work and Power.* New York: Basic Books.

Answers to Review Questions

Chapter 1
1. C
2. A
3. A
4. A
5. C
6. D
7. D
8. D
9. B
10. B
11. B
12. C
13. A
14. D
15. A

Chapter 2
1. B
2. B
3. A
4. A
5. C
6. D
7. C
8. B
9. D
10. C

Chapter 3
1. B
2. D
3. A
4. B
5. B
6. B
7. B
8. D
9. A
10. C

Chapter 4
1. B
2. C
3. D
4. B
5. C
6. B
7. C
8. B
9. B
10. C

Chapter 5
1. C
2. D
3. B
4. B
5. D
6. A
7. C
8. C

Chapter 6
1. A
2. B
3. C
4. B
5. B
6. B
7. C
8. C
9. A
10. A

Chapter 7
1. A
2. B
3. C
4. C

5. C
6. A
7. C
8. B
9. A
10. A

Chapter 8
1. D
2. A
3. D
4. C
5. D
6. C
7. D
8. B
9. C
10. B

Chapter 9
1. A
2. B
3. D
4. D
5. D
6. D
7. C
8. B
9. A
10. C

Chapter 10
1. D
2. D
3. A
4. D
5. C
6. A
7. A

8. B
9. C
10. C

Chapter 11
1. B
2. C
3. B
4. C
5. D
6. C
7. C
8. C
9. B
10. B

Chapter 12
1. B
2. B
3. A
4. C
5. C
6. C
7. D
8. A
9. C
10. A

Chapter 13
1. B
2. B
3. A
4. A
5. B
6. B
7. A
8. C
9. B
10. B

11. D
12. C

Chapter 14
1. D
2. A
3. D
4. D
5. D
6. A
7. D
8. A
9. C
10. D
11. B

Chapter 15
1. D
2. C
3. A
4. A
5. C
6. A
7. C
8. D
9. C
10. D

Chapter 16
1. B
2. C
3. B
4. D
5. C
6. D
7. D
8. C
9. C
10. A

PHOTO CREDITS

Chapter 1: p. 2: Reuters/Corbis; p. 5: Reuters/Corbis; p. 6 (top left): Bo Zaunders/Corbis; p. 6 (top right): Bettmann/Corbis; p. 7: © The New Yorker Collection, 1969 Dana Fradon from www.cartoonbank.com. All rights reserved.; p. 8: Pablo Corral V/Corbis; p. 9: Thomas Hoepker/Magnum/PNI; p. 10: Corbis; p. 11: Bettmann/Corbis; p. 12: (top left): Bettmann/Corbis; p. 12 (bottom right): Granger Collection; p. 13: Bettmann/Corbis; p. 14: The Warder Collection; p. 17: Steve Prezant/Corbis; p. 20: Staatliche Museen zu Berlin/Gemaldegalerie, Berlin; p. 24 (bottom left): Bettmann/Corbis; p. 24 (top right): A. Holbrooke/Corbis; p. 25 (top left): Joseph Rodriguez/Black Star; p. 25 (top right): © Benedict J. Fernandez; p. 26: Philip G. Zimbardo/Stanford Prison Experiment.

Chapter 2: p. 36: AP/Wide World Photos; p. 39: Courtesy The BADvertising Institute; p. 40: Anna Clopet/Corbis; p. 41 (bottom left): Peter Simon/IPN Stock; p. 41 (bottom right): Peter Turnley/Corbis; p. 42 (bottom left): AP/Wide World Photos; p. 42 (top right): Clay Perry/Corbis; p. 43 (bottom left): Kevin Fleming/Corbis; p. 43 (top right): Kelly-Mooney Photography/Corbis; p. 46: Courtesy of Danah Boyd; p. 47: Stephen Welstead/Corbis; p. 48: Bob Krist/Corbis; p. 49: Phil Schermeister/Corbis; p. 52 (top left): Michael Yamashita/Corbis; p. 52 (top right): L. Clarke/Corbis; p. 57: AP/Wide World Photos; p. 58: Jacques Chenet/Corbis; p. 59: Stephen Frink/Corbis; p. 60: Reuters/Corbis.

Chapter 3: p. 66: Photofest; p. 69: Courtesy of Dan Bartell; p. 72: Reed Kaestner/Corbis; p. 75: Steven Rubin/The Image Works; p. 76: Jacques Langevin/Corbis; p. 77 (top left): Hulton-Deutsch/Corbis; p. 77 (bottom right): Lynn Goldsmith/Corbis; p. 78: Alinari Archives/Corbis; p. 79: Corbis; p. 80: © Dick Hemingway; p. 81: AP/Wide World Photos.

Chapter 4: p. 84: AP/Wide World Photos; p. 86: Richard Perry/*The New York Times*;

p. 87: © Ekman 1972–2004; pp. 90–92 (all): © Simon Bond; p. 93: © 1991 Mike Marland; p. 94: Dan Habib/Concord Monitor/Corbis; p. 96: David Samuel Robbins/Corbis; p. 97: AP/Wide World Photos; p. 99: © David Hoffman.

Chapter 5: p. 102: Picture Net/Corbis; p. 105: Dung Vo Trung/Coup D'Etat Productions/Corbis; p. 107: Philip Gould/Corbis; p. 109 (all): Courtesy of Alexandra Milgram; p. 111: Owen Franken/Corbis; p. 114: AP/Wide World Photos; p. 115: Courtesy of Diane Vaughan; p. 118: Howard Grey/Getty Images; p. 122: Jon Feingersh/Masterfile; p. 123: Owen Franken/Corbis; p. 124: AP/Wide World Photos; p. 125: Masterfile.

Chapter 6: p. 130: Henry Diltz/Corbis; p. 134: J. Bounds/RNO/Corbis Sygma; p. 136 (bottom left): Chris Stanford/*Washington Post*; p. 136 (bottom right): Craig Lovell/Corbis; p. 137 (top left): © Gropp/Sipa; p. 137 (top right): AP/Wide World Photos, p. 139: Mark Peterson/Corbis; p. 150: Owen Franken/Corbis; p. 151: Ted Nebia/Corbis; p. 152: Courtesy of Devah Pager.

Chapter 7: 158: Catherine Karnow/Corbis; p. 162: © Johnston/Sipa; p. 168: AP/Wide World Photos; p. 169: Vince Streano/Corbis; p. 171: Vernier Jean Bernar/Corbis Sygma; p. 174: Robert Sorbo/Corbis; p. 176: Courtesy of Ofer Sharone; p. 177: AP/Wide World Photos; p. 180 (both): AP/Wide World Photos; p. 181: (both): AP/Wide World Photos; p. 188: AP/Wide World Photos.

Chapter 8: p. 194: AP/Wide World Photos; p. 204: Reuters/Corbis; p. 205: Corbis; p. 208: Dean Conger/Corbis; p. 209: Danny Lehman/Corbis; p. 210: George Esiri/Reuters/Corbis; p. 212 (bottom left): AP/Wide World Photos; p. 212 (top right): Jack Kurtz/The Image Works; p. 213 (both): AP/Wide World Photos; p. 216: Courtesy of Edward Webster; p. 217: Gideon Mendel/Corbis.

Chapter 9: p. 222: AP/Wide World Photos; p. 225: Corbis Sygma; p. 226 (both): Bettmann/Corbis; p. 228: National Anthropological Archives/Smithsonian Institution; p. 234: Gabe Palmer/Corbis; p. 236: Michael Keller/Corbis; p. 239: Courtesy of Jessie Klein; p. 240: Timothy McCarthy/Art Resource, NY; p. 244: *Chicago Tribune* Photos by Ovie Carter; p. 245 (both): *Chicago Tribune* Photos by Ovie Carter; p. 247: AP/Wide World Photos; p. 248: Bettmann/Corbis.

Chapter 10: p. 252: Michael Smyth; p. 255: Peter Marshall; p. 256: Alain Nogues/Corbis Sygma; p. 259: Mark Peterson/Corbis; p. 261: Penny Tweedle/Panos Pictures; p. 264: Corbis; p. 265: Hulton-Deutsch/Corbis; p. 266: AP/Wide World Photos; p. 267: Adam Woofitt/Corbis; p. 270: © Warren Lehrer 2003 from the book *Crossing the BLVD: Strangers, Neighbors, Aliens in a New America* by Warren Lehrer and Judith Sloan; p. 271: (both): Erik Freeland/Corbis Saba; p. 276 (bottom left): Photo Collection Alexander Alland/Corbis; p. 276 (bottom right): Jeff Greenberg/The Image Works; p. 277: Courtesy of Dalton Conley.

Chapter 11: p. 282: Paul Barton/Corbis; p. 284: Paul Harrison/Panos Pictures; p. 288: Ariel Skelly/Corbis; p. 289: Philip Rostron/Masterfile; pp. 296–297: All photos by Courteney Coolidge from *American Families: Beyond the White Picket Fence*, www.10families.com; p. 302: Courtesy of Dr. Judith Stacey; p. 303: Koopman/Corbis; p. 304 (bottom left): Najlah Feanny/Corbis; p. 304 (top right): Kimberly White/Reuters/Corbis.

Chapter 12: p. 308: Ed Kashi/Corbis; p. 312: J. A. Giordano/Corbis; p. 314: Gary Conner/PhotoEdit/PNI; p. 315: Greg Meadors/Stock Boston/PNI; p. 318: Courtesy of Robert Hauser; p. 319: Will & Deni McIntyre/Corbis; p. 320: Ted Streshinsky/Corbis; p. 328 (both): Rob Carr/*The New York Times*.

INDEX

Automat, 365
automation and skill debate, 365–67
automobiles and automobile industry, 39
  global production, 366, 367
  highway construction and, 423
  mass production, 358, 359
  robots used in manufacture of, 365
Aviation Week and Space Technology, 114
ayurvedic medicine, 385–86
Azande of Africa, 400

Babylon, 418
back regions, 94
Bailey, J. Michael, 400
Balzac, Honoré de, 112
Bamberger, Bill, 371*n*
Baptists, 331
Baudrillard, Jean, 17
Bay of Pigs invasion, 109
Beach, Frank, 393
Beck, Ulrich, 451, 468
Becker, Howard S., 140
Bell, Daniel, 450–51
Bell, Genevieve, 47
Benetton, 123
Benin, 348
berdaches, 228
Berger, Peter, 327
Berle, Adolf, 363
Bernhardt, Annett, 361
Bhopal chemical plant, India, 148
Bianchi, Suzanne, 288
Biblarz, Timothy, 303
bin Laden, Osama, 4, 335
biological aging, 402
biological reductionism, 248
biological view of deviance, 135, 138
biomedical model of health, 386
birth control, *see* contraception
birthrates, crude, 432–33
bisexuality, 397–400
black feminism, 248
black power, 256
Black Report, 387
blacks, *see* African Americans
Blades, Joan, 349
Blau, Judith, 465*n*
Blau, Peter, 113, 118, 175
Blauner, Robert, 278, 366
blended families, 296
blue-collar jobs, 367–68, 423, 450
blushing, 88
Boden, Deirdre, 98
bodily posture, 88
body image, 380, 381–83
body language, *see* nonverbal communication

body, sociology of the, 378–80
  basic themes of, 381
  health and illness, *see* health and illness
  as new field, 381
Bohemian Grove, 126
Bolivia, 348
Bonacich, Edna, 367
bonding social capital, 126
"born again" Christians, 333
Bosnia, 259, 335, 341–42
Boston University, Entrepreneurial Management Institute, 426
Bourdieu, Pierre, 178
Boyd, Danah, 46–47
Boyd, Wes, 349
Braithwaite, John, 155
Branch Davidians, 330
Braverman, Harry, 123, 367
Brazil, 57, 211
bridging social capital, 126
Britain
  citizenship rights in, 343
  health inequalities in, 387
  industrialization in, 419
  introduction of sociology to, 13
  knowledge-based industries, 368
  race and, 253–54
  social status in, 189
"broken windows" theory, 142
Brown, K., 388*n*
Brown, Patricia Leigh, 329*n*
Brownmiller, Susan, 240
Brown University, 181
Brown v. Board of Education, 266
Brumberg, Joan Jacobs, 383*n*
Buddhism, 335
Buffett, Warren, 195–96
bulimia, 380, 381, 383
Bumpass, Larry, 301
Burawoy, Michael, 465
bureaucracy
  alternatives to, 118–26
  coining of term, 112
  Columbia Space Shuttle disaster and, 114–15
  defined, 112
  democracy and, 116–17
  dysfunctions of, 116
  in educational system, 320
  formal relations within, 113
  gender and, 117–18
  global production and, 367
  ideal type of, 112–13
  informal relations within, 113
  political parties and, 354
  ritualism within, 116
  Weber's study of, 12–13, 111, 112–13, 116
  welfare state and, 356
Burgess, Ernest, 420

Burma (Myanmar), 57
Burning Man Festival, 47, 136–37
Burns, Tom, 118
Burtless, Gary, 185
Bush, George H. W., 127
  welfare reforms under, 171
Bush, George W., and Bush administration, 127, 350
  incarceration policies, 152
  same-sex marriage and, 304
Business Week, Executive Pay Scoreboard, 172
busing, school segregation and, 317

cable technology, 458
Cairo, Egypt, 435
Calcutta, India, 431
California
  immigration's effects in, 267, 269, 278
  Proposition 187, 267, 346
Calvin, John, 326
Calvinism, 326, 330
Cambodia, 57
  genocide in, 259
campaign finance, 351–53
Canada
  Quebec separatism, 51, 343
  same-sex couples in, 304
  women in the workforce in, 241
cancer, 390, 468
Çapek, Karel, 365
capitalism
  conflict theory of deviant behavior and, 142
  democracy and, 348, 349
  features of, 363
  Marx's views on, 12, 13
  social change and, 449
  types of corporate, 364
  Weber's beliefs about, 12, 326
  see also industrialization
capitalists, 189
capital punishment, 149
Cardoso, Enrique Fernando, 211
Caribbean, hunger, malnutrition, and famine in, 203
caring activities, feminist view of, 286
Carmichael, Stokeley, 256
Carneal, Michael, 238
Carolina for Kibera (CFK), 464–65
Castells, Manuel, 148, 422
caste societies, 161–62
caste systems, 161–62, 163
Castles, Stephen, 261
Castro, Fidel, 109
cause and effect, 70

Causes of Delinquency (Hirschi), 142
CBS, 363
cell phones, 42–43
Center for Wisconsin Strategy (COWS), 360
Centers for Disease Control and Prevention, 333, 395
Challenger Launch Decision: Risky Technology, Culture, and Deviance at NASA (Vaughan), 114–15
Chechnya, 335
Cheney, Dick, 351
Cherlin, Andrew, 293, 298, 301
Chicago School of sociologists, urbanism theories of, 418, 420–21
Chicanos, 268
childhood stage of human life course, 78–79
children, 402
  abuse of, 79, 299–300
  childcare responsibilities, 223, 224, 234–36, 285, 286, 288–89
  child labor, 208–9
  divorce's impact on, 294, 295–98
  fostering, 296–97
  HIV/AIDS and, 390–91
  hunger, malnutrition, and famine among, 203
  poverty in the U.S. among, 184
  socialization of, *see* socialization
  theories of child development, 70
  "unsocialized," 68–69
  women in the workplace and childcare, 223, 224, 234–35, 288–89
Chile
  democracy in, 348
  women in the workforce in, 241
China, 56, 349
  capitalism in, 205
  communist revolution of 1949, 27
  eating disorders in, 380
  elderly in, reverence of, 412
  European trade forced on, 57
  folk medicine in, 386
  infanticide in, 45
  as middle-income country, 197, 198
  as newly industrializing economy (NIE), 204, 218
  population control policies, 438–39

social exclusion, 187–88
  agency and, 187
  crime and, 187
  the homeless and, 187–88
social facts, 11, 13
social gerontology, 402
  explanation of aging, 404–5
social groups, 104–11
  characteristics of, 104–6
  conformity within, 108–10
  defined, 104
  deviance and, 134
  in-groups, 104–5, 107
  leadership in, 107–8
  out-groups, 104–5
  primary, 105
  reference groups, 105–6
  secondary, 105
  size of, effects of, 106–7
  variety of, 104–6
social identity, 73–76
social interaction and everyday
    life, 85–99, 93
  encounters, 93
  front and back regions, 94
  impression management,
    93–94
  Internet's influence on,
    46–47
  linking macrosociology and
    microsociology,
    98–99
  nonverbal communication,
    see nonverbal
    communication
  personal space, 94–95
  reasons for studying, 86–87
  response cries, 92
  social rules and talk, 88–92
  in time and space, see time-
    space social
    interaction
socialism, 17, 215
social isolation and aging,
    408–10
socialization, 41, 45
  agents of, 70–73
    the family, 71
    mass media, 72–73
    peer relationships, 71
    schools, 71
    work, 73
  defined, 68
  gender, see gender
    socialization
  identity, 73–76
  life course stages, 78–82
    childhood, 78–79
    mature adulthood, 79–80
    teenagers, 79
  old age, 81–82
  primary, 70–71, 285
  secondary, 71
  social roles, 73, 93
  "unsocialized" children,
    68–69

socialization of nature, 381
social mobility, 174–79
  defined, 174
  downward, 178, 189
  education and, 178
  exchange, 174
  gender and, 178–79
  intergenerational, 174, 178
  intragenerational, 174, 178
  opportunities for, 175–78
  structural, 175
social movements
  antisweatshop movement,
    454–55
  feminism, see feminism and
    feminist theory
  frameworks for studying
    economic deprivation,
    452
    fields of action, 453–56
    resource mobilization,
    452–53
    structural strain, 453
  globalization and, 456
  new, 456–57
  technology and, 457
  urbanism and, 422
social networks, 110–11, 118, 122
  Internet as, 110–11
social order, 5
*Social Organization of Sexuality:
  Sexual Practices in the
  United States, The*
  (Laumann), 395
social position, 71, 94
social promotion, 318–19
social reproduction, 68
social rights, 343
social roles, 73, 93
Social Security, 407–8
social self, 69
social status, 94
  education and, 175
  occupation and, 165–67,
    170
  Weber's theory of, 189
social stratification, 159–90
  class and, see class
  defined, 160
  poverty, see poverty
  social exclusion and, see
    social exclusion
  social mobility and, see
    social mobility
  structured inequalities, 160
  systems of, 160–63
    caste systems, 161–62,
    163
    characteristics of, 160
    class, see class
    slavery, 161
  theories of, in modern
    societies, 189–90
    of Davis and Moore, 190
    of Marx, 189
    of Weber, 189

  in the U.S., gap between rich
    and poor, 164, 165,
    172–74, 190
social structure, 7
social technologies, 381
society
  culture and, 40–41
  defined, 40
Society in America (Martineau),
    13–14
sociobiology, 44
Sociobiology: The New Synthesis
  (Wilson), 44
sociological imagination, 5–6
  of college students, 7–8
sociological perspective,
    developing a, 4–10
sociological questions, 18–19
sociological thinking,
    development of, 10–14
Sociólogos sin Fronteras (SSF),
    464–65
sociology
  defined, 3
  as a science, 11, 13, 18
  the word, Comte's invention
    of, 10–11
sociology of the body, see body,
    sociology of the
sodomy laws, 401
"soft-money" contributions, 353
Soros, George, 349
South Africa
  African National Congress,
    107, 162
  apartheid in, 107, 162, 254,
    255, 257, 259
  end of, 163
  democracy in, 347
  sociology in, 216–17
  women's movement in, 246
South America
  colonialism in, 57
  developing societies of, 56
Southeast Christian Church,
    328–29
South Korea, as newly
    industrializing
    economy (NIE), 57,
    59, 204, 205, 218
sovereignty, 342
Soviet Union, former, 347
  collapse of, 355, 458
  economic future of, 218
  middle-income countries, 198
  nationalism and conflict in, 62
  Russian mafia, 148
space-time social interaction,
    see time-space social
    interaction
Spain, 356
  as colonial power, 57
  marriage in, 301
Spain, Daphne, 288
speech, 51
Spencer, Christopher, 365

spousal abuse, 300
Stacey, Judith, 302–303
Stalker, G. M., 118
stalking of women, 237
standard deviation, defined, 28
Standard International
    Occupational
    Prestige Scale, 167
standard of living, global, 199
Starbucks, 455
Stark, Rodney, 327
state
  defined, 342
  nation-states, see nation-
    states
state-centered theories of
    global inequality,
    214–15
State in a Changing World, The
  (World Bank), 214
States and Social Revolution
  (Skocpol), 27
statistics
  crime, interpreting, 143–44,
    145
  statistical terms, definitions
    of, 28
status, social, see social status
status set, 94
steel production, 372
stepfamilies, 290, 298
stereotyping, 256–57
  of the elderly, 410
  gender, glass ceiling and, 233
Sterling, Bruce, 136n
stigmatizing shaming, 155
Stone, Dave, 328–29
Stonewall riots, 401
storybooks, gender learning
    and, 77–78
strategic alliances, 122
stratification, social, see social
    stratification
Straus, Murray, 300
Strauss, Anselm, 385
*Streetwise: Race, Class, and
  Change in an Urban
  Community*
  (Anderson), 99, 425
"Strengths of Black Families,
  The," 291
stress, 386
strikes, 359
structural social mobility, 175
structural strain, 453
structuration of human
    societies, process of,
    7
structured inequalities, 160
subcultures, 45–49
  deviant, 134
  functionalist theories of
    deviance and, 139–40
  norms of, 135
  online, 46–47
  of violence, 143–44